OUTBOARD MOTOR

service manual

volume 2 · 11th edition

INTERTEC PUBLISHING

P.O. Box 12901, Overland Park, KS 66282-2901

Cover photo courtesy of: OMC Outboard Marine Corp.

OUTBOARD MOTOR

service manual
volume 2 · 11th edition

Chrysler	Mercury
Evinrude	Sea King
Force	Suzuki
Johnson	Tohatsu
Mariner	Yamaha

Covers Motors of 30 Horsepower and Above

CONTENTS

FUNDAMENTALS SECTION

DESIGN FUNDAMENTALS
Operating Principles:
Engine Types 4
Fuel System 6
Ignition System 8
Cooling System 13
Drive Unit Fundamentals:
Propeller 14
Gearcase and Lower Housing 15

SERVICE FUNDAMENTALS
Periodic Servicing:
Mid-Season...................................17
Off-Season 17
Pre-Season 17
Salt Water Care...............................18

Troubleshooting:
Chart 18
Special Notes on Troubleshooting..............21
General Maintenance:
Lubrication 21
Spark Plugs 21
Carburetor 22
Speed Control Linkage........................23
Reed Valves 23
Fuel Pump....................................24
Ignition System 24
Cooling System 25
Generating System 25
General Repairs:
Repairing Damaged Threads 26
Disassembly and Assembly 27
Piston, Rings and Cylinder 27
Connecting Rod, Crankshaft and Bearings 29
Submerged Motor 29

SERVICE SECTION

CHRYSLER
30 & 35 HP 30
35, 45, 50 & 55 HP............................39
55, 60 & 65 HP 50
Three- & Four-Cylinder Models.................60

EVINRUDE
28 (1987-1989), 30 & 35 HP (1976-1989) 349
33 & 40 HP (1969-1976) 363
40 (1985-1989), 48 (1987-1989), 50 (1971-1975 &
   1978-1989), 55 (1976-1981) & 60 HP
   (1980-1985) 377
Three-Cylinder 55, 60, 65, 70 & 75 HP 403
Four-Cylinder 85, 90, 100, 110, 115, 120,
   125, 135 & 140 HP (Prior to 1987)............429
Four-Cylinder 88, 90, 100, 110, 120
   & 140 HP (After 1986) 461
Six-Cylinder Models 485
Eight-Cylinder Models 509

FORCE
35 HP 80
50 HP 87
85 & 125 HP 94
150 HP 103

JOHNSON
28 (1987-1989), 30 & 35 HP (1976-1989) 349
33 & 40 HP (1969-1976) 363
40 (1985-1989), 48 (1987-1989), 50 (1971-1975 &
   1978-1989), 55 (1976-1981) & 60 HP
   (1980-1985) 377
Three-Cylinder 55, 60, 65, 70 & 75 HP 403
Four-Cylinder 85, 90, 100, 110, 115, 120,
   125, 135 & 140 HP (Prior to 1987)............429
Four-Cylinder 88, 90, 100, 110, 120
   & 140 HP (After 1986) 461
Six-Cylinder Models 485
Eight-Cylinder Models 509

SERVICE SECTION (CONT.)

MARINER
30 HP 116
40 HP 124
Two-Cylinder 48 & 60 HP 134
Three-Cylinder 50, 60 & 70 HP 142
Four-Cylinder 45, 50, 75, 80 & 85 HP 153
Three-Cylinder 75 & 90 HP (After 1986) 166
90, 115 & 140 (Prior to 1986) 180
Four-Cylinder 100 (After 1987) &
   115 HP (After 1988) 192
135, 150, 150 MAGNUM, 150 MAGNUM II,
   175 & 200 HP 206

MERCURY
Two-Cylinder Models 225
Three-Cylinder Models 238
Three-Cylinder Models
   (After Serial Number A719280) 253
Four-Cylinder Models
   (Except 100 & 115 HP) .267
Four-Cylinder 100 (After 1987) &
   115 HP (After 1988) 290
In-Line Six-Cylinder Models 304
V-6 Models (Except 300 & 3.4L) 320
300 & 3.4L 340

SEA KING
35, 45 & 55 HP 521

SUZUKI
DT30 (Prior to 1988) 531
DT30C (After 1987) 538
DT40 (Prior to 1984) 549
DT35 (After 1986) & DT40 (After 1983) 556
DT50, DT60 & DT65 (Prior to 1985) 567
DT55 & DT65 (After 1984) 577
DT75 & DT85 587
DT115 & DT140 (Prior to 1986) 598
DT90 & DT100 610
DT150, DT150SS, DT175 & DT200 622

TOHATSU
30 HP 632
35 & 40 HP 638
50, 55, 60 & 70 HP 646
90 HP 652

YAMAHA
Two-Cylinder 30 HP (Prior to 1987) 660
Three-Cylinder 30, 40 & 50 HP 668
70 & 90 HP 681
V-4 & V-6 695

DUAL DIMENSIONS

This service manual provides specifications in both the Metric (SI) and U.S. Customary systems of measurement on some models. The first specification is given in the measuring system used during manufacture, while the second specification (given in parenthesis) is the converted measurement. For instance, a specification of "0.28 mm (0.011 inch)" would indicate that the equipment was manufactured using the metric system of measurement and the U.S. equivalent of 0.28 mm is 0.011 inch.

DESIGN FUNDAMENTALS
OPERATING PRINCIPLES

ENGINE TYPES

The power source for the outboard motor does not differ basically from that used to power automobiles, farm or garden tractors, lawn mowers, or many other items of power equipment in use today. All are technically known as "Internal Combustion, Reciprocating Engines."

The source of power is heat formed by the burning of a combustible mixture of petroleum products and air. In a reciprocating engine, this burning takes place in a closed cylinder containing a piston. Expansion resulting from the heat of combustion applies pressure on the piston to turn a shaft by means of a crank and connecting rod.

The fuel mixture may be ignited by means of an electric spark (Otto Cycle Engine) or by the heat of compression (Diesel Cycle). The complete series of events which must take place in order for the engine to run may occur in one revolution of the crankshaft (referred to as Two-Stroke Cycle), or in two revolutions of the crankshaft (Four-Stroke Cycle).

OTTO CYCLE, In a spark ignited engine, a series of five events are required in order to provide power. This series of events are called the **Cycle** (or Work Cycle) and is repeated in each cylinder as long as work is done. The series of events which comprise the work cycle are as follows:

1. The mixture of fuel and air is pushed or drawn into the cylinder, by reducing cylinder pressure to less than the outside pressure, or by applying an initial, higher pressure to the fuel charge.

2. The mixture is compressed, or reduced in volume.

3. The mixture is ignited by a timed electric spark.

4. The burning fuel:air mixture expands, forcing the piston down, thus converting the generated chemical energy into mechanical power.

5. The burned gases are exhausted from the cylinder so that a new cycle can begin.

The series of events comprising the work cycle are commonly referred to as INTAKE, COMPRESSION, IGNITION, EXPANSION (POWER) and EXHAUST.

DIESEL CYCLE. The Diesel Cycle differs from the Otto Cycle in that air alone is drawn into the cylinder during the intake period, then compressed to a much greater degree. The air is heated by compression. Instead of an electric spark, a finely atomized charge of fuel is injected into the combustion chamber where it combines with the heated air and ignites spontaneously. The power and exhaust strokes are almost identical to those of the Otto Cycle.

FOUR-STROKE CYCLE. In a reciprocating engine, each movement of the piston (in or out) in the cylinder is referred to as a Stroke. Thus, one complete revolution of the engine crankshaft accompanies two strokes of the piston.

The most simple and efficient engine design from the standpoint of fuel and exhaust gas mixture movement is the Four-Stroke Cycle shown schematically in fig. 1-1. The first event of the work cycle coincides with the first stroke of the piston as shown at "A". Downward movement of the piston draws a fresh charge of the fuel:air mixture into the cylinder. View "B" shows the compression of the fuel mixture which occurs during the second stroke of the cycle. Ignition occurs at about the time the piston reaches the top of the cylinder on the compression stroke, resulting in the expansion of the burning fuel:air mixture, and in the power stroke as shown at "C". The fourth stroke of the cycle empties the cylinder of the burned gases as shown at "D", and the cylinder is ready for the beginning of another work cycle.

The fact that a full stroke of the piston is available for each major mechanical event of the cycle is ideal, from the standpoint of efficiency, and four-stroke engines are generally most economical where fuel costs alone are considered.

The four-stroke cycle requires a more complicated system of valving, which adds materially to the weight and original cost of the engine. This fact, coupled with the fact that two revolutions of the crankshaft are required for each power stroke, causes the two-stroke engine to compare more favorably when horsepower to weight ratio is considered; and because of the weight advantage, the two-stroke engine has probably reached its highest degree of development for outboard motor use.

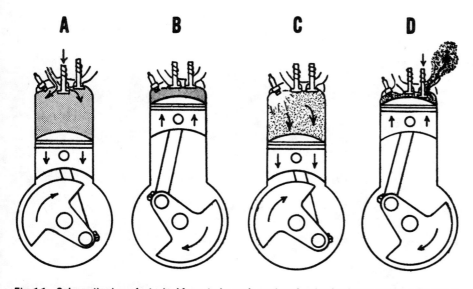

Fig. 1-1—Schematic view of a typical four-stroke cycle engine showing basic principles of operation. Two revolutions of the crankshaft are required to complete the cycle. The first, or INTAKE stroke is shown at "A". As the piston moves downward in cylinder the intake valve is opened allowing a combustible mixture of fuel and air to enter cylinder. The intake valve closes as the piston moves upward in the second, or COMPRESSION stroke as shown in "B." The compressed charge is ignited, and expansion of the burning mixture forces the piston down in the POWER stroke "C". The exhaust valve opens as the piston moves upward in the fourth, or EXHAUST stroke "D", and the cylinder is cleared of burned gases for the beginning of another cycle.

TWO-STROKE CYCLE. In a two-stroke cycle engine, the five events of intake, compression, ignition, power and exhaust must take place in two strokes of the piston; or one revolution of the crankshaft. Thus, a compressed fuel charge is fired each time the piston reaches the top of the cylinder, and each downward stroke is a power stroke. In order to accomplish this, the initial pressure of the incoming fuel-air mixture must be raised to a point somewhat higher than the lowest pressure existing in the cylinder, or a fresh charge of fuel could not be admitted and the engine would not run. This elevation of pressure requires the use of an air pump, or compressor, of approximately the same volume as the cylinder itself. Coincidentally, such an air pump is available with a minimum of additional parts, cost, or friction losses by utilizing the opposite side of the piston and cylinder as the pump. Such engines are called "Crankcase Scavenged," and are almost universally used in the outboard motor industry.

Individual cylinders are often combined and connected in series to the shaft to increase power output. Engine operation is also smoothed by increasing the number of power impulses per crankshaft revolution. A single cylinder, four-stroke cycle engine (with only one power impulse for two shaft revolutions) must have a heavy flywheel to store and deliver the developed energy between power strokes. Increasing the number of cylinders to two, three or four enables the design engineer to increase engine power without a corresponding increase in engine weight.

Figure 1-2 shows a schematic view of the crankcase scavenged, reed valve type, two-stroke cycle engine commonly used. The general sequence of events required for operation is as follows: As the piston moves outward from the crankshaft as shown in view "B", the volume of the closed crankcase is enlarged and the pressure lowered, causing air to be drawn through the carburetor (C), where it is mixed with fuel. This mixture is then drawn through the reed valve (R) and into the crankcase. At the same time, a previous charge of fuel is being compressed between head of piston and closed end of cylinder as shown by the darkened area. As the piston approaches top center, a timed spark ignites the compressed fuel charge and the resultant expansion moves the piston downward on the power stroke. The reed valve (R) closes, and downward movement of piston compresses the next fuel charge in the crankcase as shown in view "A". When the piston nears the bottom of its stroke, the crown of piston uncovers the exhaust port (EX)

in cylinder wall, allowing the combustion products and remaining pressure to escape as shown by the wavy arrow. Further downward movement of piston opens the transfer port (TP) leading from the crankcase to cylinder; and the then higher crankcase pressure forces the compressed fuel:air mixture through

transfer port into the cylinder. The baffle which is built into crown of piston deflects the incoming charge upward, and most of the remaining exhaust gases are driven from the combustion chamber by this fresh charge. Two-stroke cycle, crankcase scavenged engines are sometimes produced with a

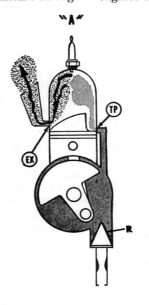

Fig. 1-2—Schematic view of two-stroke cycle, crankcase scavenged engine used in most outboard motors. The same series of events shown in Fig. 1-1 takes place in one revolution of the crankshaft by using the crankcase as a scavenging pump.

C. Carburetor
R. Reed valve
TP. Transfer port
EX. Exhaust port

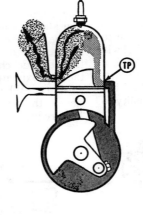

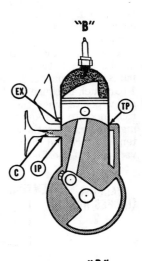

Fig. 1-3—Two-stroke cycle, three port engine. Principles are similar to reed valve or rotary valve types except that a third, intake port is located in cylinder wall and opened and closed by the piston skirt.

C. Carburetor
EX. Exhaust port
IP. Intake port
TP. Transfer port

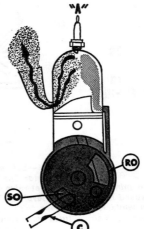

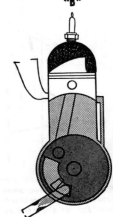

Fig. 1-4—Two-stroke cycle rotary valve engine. The incoming fuel charge is controlled by a rotary valve attached to the crankshaft. The opening in valve (RO) and crankcase (SO) align at the proper time to admit a fresh charge, then close to allow intial crankcase compression.

C. Carburetor
RO. Opening in rotating member
SO. Opening in crankcase wall

fuel induction system other than the inlet reed valve. Although they are not extensively used in outboard motor manufacture, they are mentioned in passing and illustrated schematically in Fig. 1-3 and Fig. 1-4.

In the crankcase scavenged engine, most of the friction parts requiring lubrication are located in the fuel intake system. Lubrication is accomplished by mixing the required amount of oil with the fuel, so that a small amount of oil in the form of a fine mist is drawn into the crankcase with each fuel charge. It should be pointed out that the new oil brought into the crankcase can little more than supplement the losses, therefore it is necessary that the friction parts be well lubricated at the time the engine is started. The use of too much oil in the fuel mixture results in plug fouling, excessive carbon, and poor performance, as well as being wasteful.

FUEL SYSTEM

CARBURETOR. The function of the carburetor is to atomize the fuel and mix it with the air flowing into the engine. The carburetor must also meter the fuel to provide the proper fuel:air ratio for the different engine operating conditions, and the proper density of total charge to satisfy the power and speed requirements.

A gasoline-air mixture is normally combustible between the limits of 25 parts air to 1 part fuel, and 8 parts air to 1 part fuel. Because much of the fuel will not vaporize when the engine is cold, a rich mixture is required for cold starting. The exact ratio will depend on the temperature and the volatility (ability to vaporize) of the fuel.

Carburetor operation is based on the venturi principle, in which a gas or liquid flowing through a restriction (venturi) will increase in speed and decrease in pressure, acting in much the same way as water passing through the nozzle of a garden hose. Refer to Fig. 1-5.

An extension tube (nozzle) from the fuel reservoir is inserted into the air passage with the opening at approximately the narrowest part of the venturi, and the fuel level in the reservoir is maintained at just below the opening of the nozzle. When air passes through the venturi, fuel spills over into the air stream in amounts relative to the pressure drop. If the level in fuel bowl is too high, fuel will spill over into carburetor when engine is not operating. If fuel level is too low, a sufficient amount may not be pulled into the the air stream during certain periods of operation, and a lean mixture could result. The fuel level is usually maintained by means of a float as shown in Fig. 1-6.

A simple carburetor which relies only on the venturi principle will supply a progressively richer mixture as engine speed is increased, and will not run at all at idle speeds. The carburetor must therefore be modified if the engine is to perform at varying speeds. The first step in modification is usually the addition of a separate fuel mixing and metering system designed to operate only at slow engine speeds. A fairly representative idle system is shown schematically in Fig. 1-7. An idle passage is drilled in the carburetor body as shown, leading from the fuel chamber to the air horn at the approximate location of the throttle valve (1). When the throttle valve is closed, the air flow is almost shut off. This reduces the pressure in the inlet

manifold, and therefore the density of the charge in the combustion chamber. The pressure drop at the venturi which is shown in Fig. 1-5 ceases to exist, and fuel cannot be drawn from the main fuel nozzle. The high manifold vacuum above the throttle valve (1–Fig. 1-7) draws fuel up the idle passage through idle jet (5) then through primary idle orifice (2) into the intake manifold. At the same time, air is being drawn through the secondary idle orifice (3) and air metering orifice (4) to mix with the fuel in the idle passage. The sizes of the two orifices (2 and 3) and the idle jet (5) are carefully calculated and controlled. The amount of air passing through metering orifice (4) can be adjusted by the idle mixture adjusting needle (6) to obtain the desired fuel:air mixture for smooth idle.

When throttle valve (1) is opened slightly to a fast idle position (as indicated by the broken lines) both the primary and secondary idle orifices (2 and 3) are subjected to high manifold vacuum. The incoming flow of air through secondary orifice (3) is cut off, which increases the speed of fuel flow through idle jet (5). This supplies the additional fuel needed to properly mix with the greater volume of air passing around the throttle butterfly valve. As the throttle valve is further opened and edge of valve moves away from the idle orifices, the idle fuel system ceases to operate and fuel mixture is again controlled by the venturi of the main fuel system.

In many applications, the main fuel system and idle system will supply the fuel requirements for all operating conditions. In other cases, an additional economizer system is incorporated,

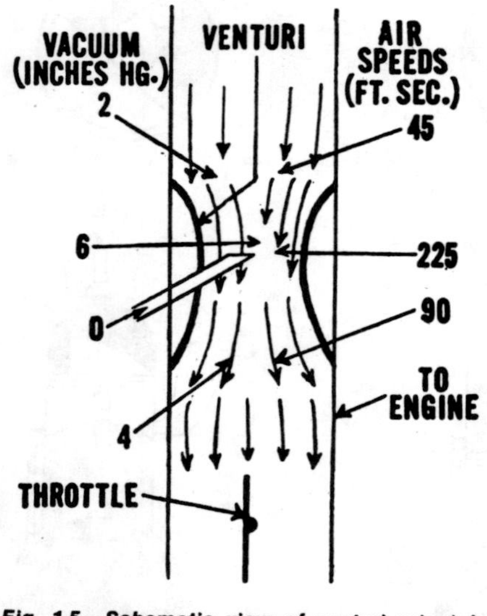

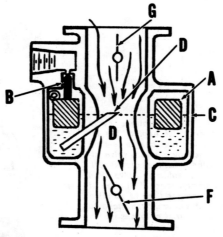

Fig. 1-5—Schematic view of venturi principle. Right hand figures show how air speed is increased by the restriction (venturi) while left hand figures show the accompaning drop in air pressure.

Fig. 1-6—Schematic view of a simple float-type carburetor. The buoyancy of float (A) closes the fuel inlet valve (B) to maintain the fuel at a constant level (C). The pressure drop in the venturi causes fuel to flow out nozzle (D) which protrudes just above the fuel level. Throttle valve is at (F) and choke valve at (G)

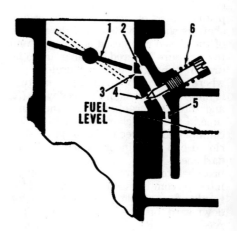

Fig. 1-7—The addition of a separate idle fuel system permits delivery of a correct fuel mixture over a wider range of engine speeds.

1. Throttle valve
2. Upper idle orifice
3. Lower idle orifice
4. Air metering orifice
5. Idle fuel jet
6. Idle mixture level

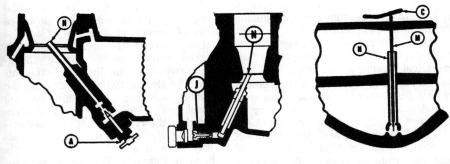

Fig. 1-8—The main fuel metering system may be of many types. Three typical systems are shown. In the left-hand view, the maximum fuel flow through nozzle (N) may be adjusted by the mixture needle (A). In the center view, maximum fuel flow is controlled by the carefully calibrated fixed jet (J). In the right-hand view, the stepped metering needle (M) is moved vertically by a cam (C) on throttle shaft, thus limiting maximum flow to predetermined amounts which vary with throttle setting.

which provides a leaner fuel-air mixture for part throttle operation. Accelerator pumps or an accelerating well which are usually needed for automotive operation are not normally used on outboard motors.

An accelerator pump can be used, however. The accelerator pump can be lever operated or spring operated and vacuum controlled. The purpose of an accelerator pump is to provide an additional charge of fuel at the moment of throttle opening, before balance is restored to the high speed fuel system.

High speed mixture adjustment is controlled by a fixed jet, a fuel adjustment needle, or by a stepped metering rod which is synchronized with the throttle valve. Refer to Fig. 1-8 for a schematic view of the systems.

The basic design of diaphragm type carburetors is shown in Fig. 1-9. Fuel is delivered to inlet (1) by gravity with fuel tank above carburetor, or under pres-

sure from a fuel pump. Atmospheric pressure is maintained on lower side of diaphragm (D) through vent hole (V). When choke plate (C) is closed and engine is cranked, or when engine is running, pressure at orifice (O) is less than atmospheric pressure; this low pressure, or vacuum, is transmitted to fuel chamber (F) above diaphragm through nozzle channel (N). The higher (atmospheric) pressure at lower side of diaphragm will then push the diaphragm upward compressing spring (S) and allowing inlet valve (IV) to open and fuel will flow into the fuel chamber. Some diaphragm type carburetors are equipped with an internal fuel pump.

REED VALVES. The inlet reed (or leaf) valve is essentially a check valve which permits the air-fuel mixture to move in only one direction through the engine. It traps the fuel charge in the crankcase, permitting the inlet pressure to be raised high enough to allow a full charge to enter the cylinder against the remaining exhaust pressure during the short period of time the transfer ports are open. The ideal design for the valve is one which offers the least possible resistance to the flow of gases entering

the crankcase, but completely seals off any flow back through the carburetor during the downward stroke of the piston.

FUEL PUMP. All but the smallest motors normally use a remote fuel tank from which fuel is pumped to the carburetor. Most two-stroke motors use the pulsating, pressure and vacuum impulses in one crankcase to operate the fuel pump. Refer to Fig. 1-10. Operation is as follows:

When the piston moves upward in the cylinder as shown in view "A", a vacuum is created on the back side of diaphragm "D". As the diaphragm moves away from the fuel chamber, inlet check valve (5) opens against the pressure of spring (6) to admit fuel from tank as shown by arrow. When the piston moves downward as shown in view "B", the diaphragm moves into the fuel chamber, causing the inlet check valve to close. The outlet check valve (4) opens and fuel flows to the carburetor. When the carburetor float chamber becomes full and carburetor inlet valve closes, the fuel pump diaphragm will remain in approximately the position shown in "A", but will maintain pressure on carburetor fuel line until additional fuel is required.

On some of the larger motors, a two stage fuel pump of similar construction is connected to two separate crankcases of the motor.

On four-stroke cycle engines, the pump diaphragm is spring loaded in one direction and lever operated in the other. The lever may be actuated by any means, the most common being an eccentric cam on the engine camshaft. As the cam turns, the diaphragm pulsates in much the same way as that described for the pressure-vacuum unit. The strength of the diaphragm return spring determines the standby fuel pressure which will be maintained at the carburetor.

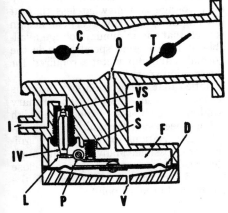

Fig. 1-9—Cross-section drawing of basic design diaphragm type carburetor. Atmospheric pressure actuates diaphragm (D).

C. Choke	N. Nozzle
D. Diaphragm	O. Orifice
F. Fuel chamber	P. Pivot pin
I. Fuel inlet	S. Spring
IV. Inlet valve needle	T. Throttle
L. Lever	V. Vent
	VS. Valve seat

Fig. 1-10—Schematic view of a typical, crankcase operated, diaphragm type fuel pump. Pressure and vacuum pulsations from crankcase pass through connection (C) to rear of diaphragm (D) which induces a pumping action on fuel line as shown.

3. Valve spring	5. Inlet check valve
4. Outlet check valve	6. Valve spring

IGNITION SYSTEM

The timed spark which ignites the fuel charge in the cylinder may be supplied by either a magneto or battery ignition system. To better understand the operation of the components and the differences and similarities of the two systems, they will be combined in this section and the functions of the various units explained and compared.

IGNITION SYSTEM THEORY. In the modern ignition system, a relatively weak electric current of 6 to 12 volts and 2 to 5 amperes is transformed into a momentary charge of minute amperage and extremely high (10,000-25,000) voltage, capable of jumping the spark plug gap in the cylinder and igniting the fuel charge.

To understand the ignition system theory, electricity can be thought of as a stream of electrons flowing through a conductor. The pressure of the stream can be increased by restricting volume, or the volume increased by reducing the resistance to movement, but the total amount of power cannot be increased except by employing additional outside force. The current has an inertia of motion and resists being stopped once it has started flowing. If the circuit is broken suddenly, the force will tend to pile up temporarily, attempting to convert the speed of flow into energy.

A short list of useful electrical terms and a brief explanation of their meanings is as follows:

AMPERE. The unit of measurement used to designate the amount, or quantity of flow of an electrical current.

OHM. The unit measurement used to designate the resistance of a conductor to the flow of current.

VOLT. The unit of measurement used to designate the force, or pressure of an electrical current

WATT. The unit of measurement which designates the ability of an electrical current to perform work; or to measure the amount of work performed.

The four terms are directly interrelated, one ampere equaling the flow of current produced by one volt against a resistance of one ohm. One watt designates the work potential of one ampere at one volt in one second.

BATTERY IGNITION

Fig. 1–11 shows a very simple battery ignition circuit for a single cylinder engine. The system uses breaker points to control the time of ignition. The system may be called a "total loss ignition" if there is no provision for recharging the battery while the engine is running and the intensity of the spark will diminish as the battery's electromotive Force (emF) is reduced.

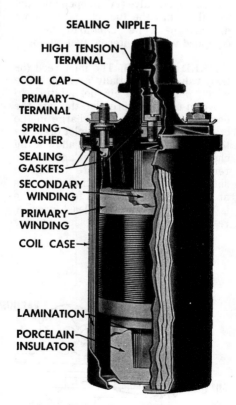

SEALING NIPPLE

HIGH TENSION TERMINAL

COIL CAP

PRIMARY TERMINAL

SPRING WASHER

SEALING GASKETS

SECONDARY WINDING

PRIMARY WINDING

COIL CASE

LAMINATION

PORCELAIN INSULATOR

Fig. 1-12—Cut-away view of typical battery ignition system coil. Primary winding consists of approximately 200-250 turns (loops) of heavier wire; secondary winding consists of several thousand turns of fine wire. Laminations concentrate the magnetic lines of force and increase efficiency of the coil.

When the timer cam is turned so the breaker (contact) points are closed, a complete circuit is completed from the battery through the breaker points, to the coil primary winding, through the ignition switch and finally back to the battery. The electricity flowing through the primary winding of the ignition coil establishes a magnetic field concentrated in the core laminations and surrounding the windings of wire. A cutaway view of a typical ignition coil is shown in Fig. 1-12. The cam is mechanically connected to rotate a specific amount in relation to the crankshaft. At the proper time, the cam will push the breaker points apart, opening the circuit and preventing current from flowing through the primary windings. The interruption stops the flow of current quickly which causes the magnetic field surrounding the primary windings to collapse. Stopping the magnetic field does not cause the field to fade away, but results in a very fast movement from around the coil windings and through the metal lamination, back to the center of the coil primary windings. As the magnetic field collapses, it quickly passes (cuts) through the primary and secondary windings creating an emf as high as 250 volts in the primary and up to 25,000 volts in the secondary windings. The condenser, which is wired parallel with the breaker points absorbs the self-induced current in the primary circuit, then discharges this current when the breaker points close.

Due to resistance of the primary winding, a certain period of time is required for maximum primary current flow after the breaker contact points are closed. At high engine speeds, the points remain closed for a smaller interval of time, hence the primary current does not build up to the maximum and secondary voltage is somewhat less than at low engine speed. However, coil design is such that the minimum voltage available at high engine speed exceeds the normal maximum voltage required for the ignition spark.

Notice that the ignition switch opens to stop current flow to the primary winding which also stops the high voltage necessary for ignition.

Other variations for this battery ignition are possible. Many use solid state electrical components to open and close the primary circuit in place of the mechanical breaker points.

MAGNETO IGNITION

Two of the principal reasons for utilizing a magneto ignition in place of a battery ignition are: Reduced weight and minimum dependence on other systems for ignition.

Fig. 1-11—Diagram of a typical battery ignition system. Refer to text for principles of operation.

1. Battery	5. Condenser
2. Ignition switch	6. Contact points
3. Primary circuit	7. Secondary circuit
4. Ignition coil	8. Spark plug

G1 through G4. Ground connections

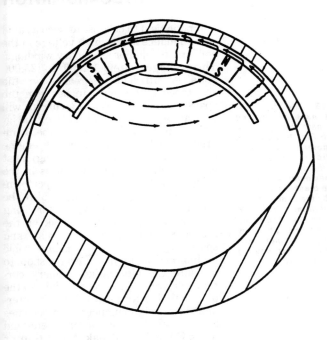

Fig. 1-13—Cut-away view of typical engine flywheel used with flywheel magneto type ignition system. The permanent magnets are usually cast into the flywheel. For flywheel type magnetos having the ignition coil and core mounted to outside of flywheel, magnets would be flush with outer diameter of flywheel.

coil windings and the breaker points which have now been closed by action of the cam.

At the instant the movement of the lines of force cutting through the coil winding sections is at the maximum rate, the maximum flow of current is obtained in the primary circuit. At this time, the cam opens the breaker points interrupting the primary circuit and, for an instant, the flow of current is absorbed by the condenser as illustrated in Fig. 1-16. An emf is also induced in the secondary coil windings, but the voltage is not sufficient to cause current to flow across the spark plug gap.

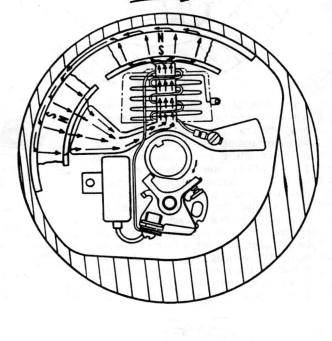

Fig. 1-14—View showing flywheel turned to a position so lines of force of the permanent magnets are concentrated in the left and center core legs and are interlocking the coil windings.

Flywheel Magneto With Breaker Points

Refer to Fig. 1-13 for a cut-away view of a typical flywheel. The arrows indicate lines of force (flux) of the permanent magnets which are carried by the flywheel. As indicated by the arrows, direction of force of the magnetic field is from the north pole (N) of the left magnet to the south pole (S) of the right magnet.

Figs. 1-14, 1-15, 1-16 and 1-17 illustrate the operational cycle of the flywheel type magneto. In Fig. 1-14 the flywheel magnets are located over the left and center legs of the armature (ignition coil) core. As the magnets moved into this position, their magnetic field was attracted by the armature core and a potential voltage (emf) was induced in the coil windings. However, this emf was not sufficient to cause current to flow across the spark plug electrode gap in the high tension circuit and the points were open in the primary circuit.

In Fig. 1-15, the flywheel magnets have moved to a new position to where there magnetic field is being attracted by the center and right legs of the armature core, and is being withdrawn from the left and center legs. As indicated by the heavy black arrows, the lines of force are cutting up through the section of coil windings between the left and center legs of the armature and are cutting down through the coil windings section between the center and right legs. If the left hand rule is applied to the lines of force cutting through the coil sections, it is seen that the resulting emf induced in the primary circuit will cause a current to flow through the primary

Fig. 1-15—View showing flywheel turned to a position so that lines of force of the permanent magnets are being withdrawn from the left and center core legs and are being attracted by the center and right core legs. While this event is happening, the lines of force are cutting up through the coil windings section between the left and center legs and are cutting down through the section between the right and center legs as indicated by the heavy black arrows. As the breaker points are now closed by the cam, a current is induced in the primary ignition circuit as the lines of force cut through the coil windings.

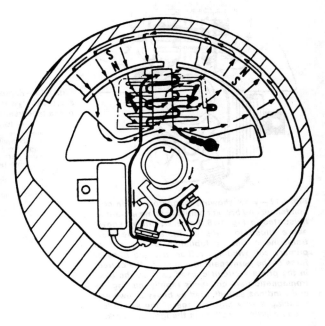

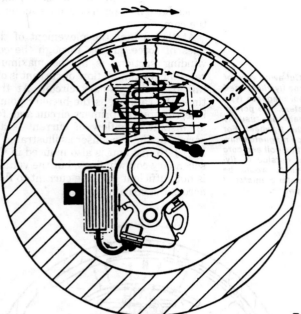

Fig. 1-16—The flywheel magnets have now turned slightly past the position shown in Fig. 1-15 and the rate of movement of lines of magnetic force cutting through the coil windings is at the maximum. At this instant, the breaker points are opened by the cam and flow of current in the primary circuit is being absorbed by the condenser, bringing the flow of current to a quick, controlled stop. Refer now to Fig. 1-17.

magnetic field to collapse at such a rapid rate to induce a very high voltage in the coil high tension or secondary windings. This voltage, often 10,000 to 25,000 volts, is sufficient to break down the resistance of the air gap between the spark plug electrodes and a current will flow across the gap. This creates the ignition spark which ignites the compressed fuel-air mixture in the engine cylinder. Point opening (or timing) must occur when the engine piston is in the proper position for the best performance. Point opening must also be timed to occur when the alternating primary voltage is at its peak or the secondary voltage will be weak and spark plug may not fire. It is impossible or impractical in the average shop to measure the alternating primary current relative to flywheel position, so the proper timing for peak voltage is determined by design engineers and becomes a service specification variously referrmd to as **Edge Gap**, **Break Away Gap** or **Pole Shoe Break.**

The flow of current in the primary windings created a strong electromagnetic field surrounding the coil windings and up through the center leg of the armature core as shown in Fig. 1-17. As the breaker points were opened by the cam, interrupting the primary circuit, this magnetic field starts to collapse cutting the coil windings as indicated by the heavy black arrows. The emf induced in the primary circuit would be sufficient to cause a flow of current across the opening breaker points were it not for the condenser absorbing the flow of current and bringing it to a controlled stop. This allows the electro-

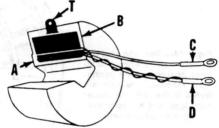

Fig. 1-18—Drawing showing construction of a typical flywheel magneto ignition coil. Primary winding (A) consists of about 200 turns of wire. Secondary winding (B) consists of several thousand turns of fine wire. Coil primary and secondary ground connection is (D); primary connection to breaker point and condenser terminal is (C); and coil secondary (high tension) terminal is (T).

Flywheel Magnetos Without Breaker Points

BREAKERLESS SYSTEM. The solid state (breakerless) magneto ignition system may operate on the same basic principles as the conventional type flywheel magneto previously described. The main difference is that the breaker contact points are replaced by a solid state electronic Gate Controlled Switch (GCS) which has no moving parts. Since, in a conventional system breaker points are closed for a longer period of crank-

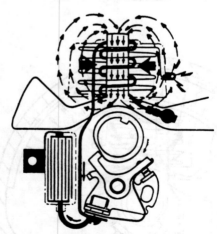

Fig. 1-17—View showing magneto ignition coil, condenser and breaker points at same instant as illustrated in Fig. 1-16, however, arrows shown above illustrate lines of force of the electromagnetic field established by current in primary coil windings rather than lines of force of the permanent magnets. As the current in the primary circuit ceases to flow, the electromagnetic field collapses rapidly, cutting the coil windings as indicated by heavy arrows and inducing a very high voltage in the secondary coil winding resulting in the ignition spark.

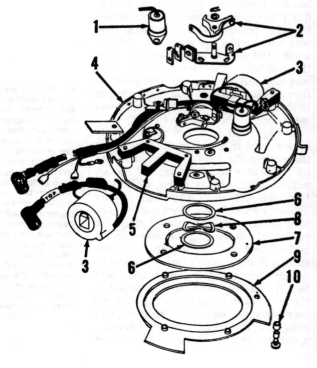

Fig. 1-19—Exploded view of a typical flywheel magneto of the type used on outboard motors.

1. Condenser
2. Contact points
3. Magneto coil
4. Stator plate
5. Coil laminations
6. Washers
7. Mounting adapter
8. Friction washer
9. Throttle control cam
10. Spacer

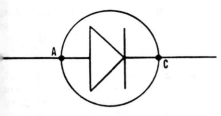

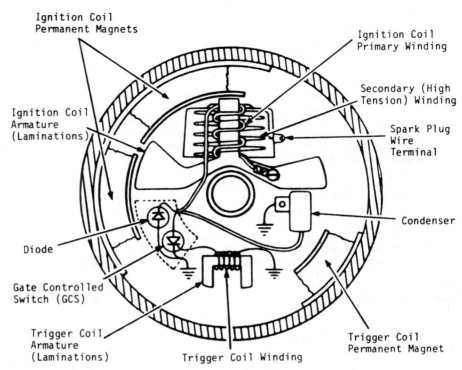

Fig. 1-20—In a diagram of an electrical circuit, the diode is represented by the symbol shown above. The diode will allow current to flow in one direction only, from cathode (C) to anode (A).

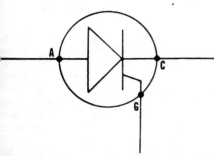

Fig. 1-21—The symbol used for a Gate controlled Switch (GCS) in an electrical diagram is shown above. The GCS will permit current to flow from cathode (C) to anode (A) when "turned on" by a positive electrical charge at gate (G) terminal.

Fig. 1-22—Schematic diagram of typical breakerless magneto igniton system. Refer to Figs. 1-23, 1-24 and 1-25 for schemtic views of operating cycle.

shaft rotation than is the "GCS", a diode has been added to the circuit to provide the same characteristics as closed breaker points.

The same basic principles for electromagnetic induction of electricity and formation of magnetic fields by electrical current as outlined for the coventional flywheel type magneto also apply to the solid state magneto. Therefore the principles of the different components (diode and GCS) will complete the operating principles of the solid state magneto.

The diode is represented in wiring diagrams by the symbol shown in Fig. 1-20. The diode is an electronic device that will permit passage of electrical current (electrons) in one direction only. In electrical schematic diagrams, electron flow is sometimes opposite to direction arrow part of symbol is pointing.

The symbol shown in Fig. 1-21 is used to represent the gate controlled switch (GCS) in wiring diagrams. The GCS acts as a switch to permit passage of current from cathode (C) terminal to anode (A) terminal when in "ON" state and will not permit electric current to flow when in "OFF" state. The GCS can be turned "ON" by a positive surge of electricity at the gate (G) terminal and will remain "ON" as long as current remains positive at the gate terminal or as long as current is flowing through the GCS from cathode (C) to anode (A) terminal.

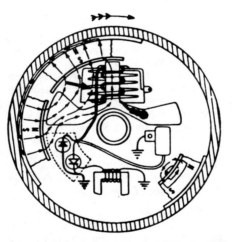

Fig. 1-23—View showing flywheel of breakerless magneto system at instant of rotation where lines of force of ignition coil magnets are being drawn into left and center legs of magneto armature. The diode (see Fig. 1-20) acts as a closed set of breaker points in completing the primary ignition circuit at this time.

The basic components and wiring diagram for the solid state breakerless magneto are shown schematically in Fig. 1-22. In Fig. 1-23, the magneto rotor (flywheel) is turning and the ignition coil magnets have just moved into position so that their lines of force are cutting the ignition coil windings and producing a negative surge of current in the primary windings. The diode allows current to flow and action is same as conventional magneto with breaker

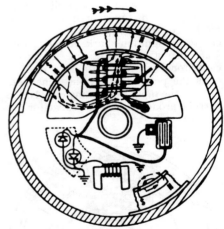

Fig. 1-24—Flywheel is turning to point where magnetic flux lines through armature center leg will reverse direction and current through primary coil circuit will reverse. As current reverses, diode which was previously conducting will shut off and there will be no current. When magnetic flux lines have reversed in armature center leg, voltage potential will again build up, but since GCS is in "OFF" state, no current will flow. To prevent excessive voltage build up, the condenser acts as a buffer.

points closed. As rotor (flywheel) continues to turn as shown in Fig. 1-24, direction of magnetic flux lines will reverse in the armature leg. Direction of current will change in the primary coil circuit and the previously conducting diode will be shut off. At this point, neither diode is conducting. Voltage begins to build up as rotor continues to turn the condenser and acts as a buffer to prevent excessive voltage build up at the GCS before it is triggered.

When the rotor reaches the approximate position shown in Fig. 1-25, maximum flux density has been achieved in the center leg of the armature. At this time the GCS is triggered. Triggering is accomplished by the triggering coil armature moving into the field of a permanent magnet which induces a positive voltage on the gate of the GCS. Primary coil current flow results in the formation of an electro-magnetic field around the primary coil which inducts a voltage of sufficient potential in the secondary coil windings to "fire" the spark plug.

When the rotor (flywheel) has moved the magnets past the armature, the GCS will cease to conduct and revert to the "OFF" state until it is triggered. The condenser will discharge during the time that the GCS was conducting.

CAPACITOR DISCHARGE SYSTEM. The capacitor discharge (CD) ignition system may use a permanent magnet rotor (flywheel) to induce a current in a coil, but unlike the conventional flywheel magneto and solid state breakerless magneto described previously, the current is stored in a capacitor (condenser). Then the stored current is discharged through a transformer coil to create the ignition spark. Refer to Fig. 1-26 for a schematic of a typical capacitor discharge ignition system.

As the permanent flywheel magnets pass by the input generating coil (1), the current produced charges capacitor (6).

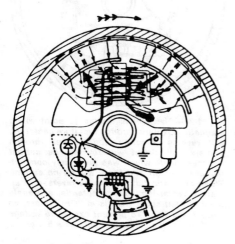

Fig. 1-25—With flywheel in the approximate position shown, maximum voltage potential is present in windings of primary coil. At this time the triggering coil armature has moved into the field of a permanent magnet and a positive voltage is induced on the gate of the GCS. The GCS is triggered and primary coil current flows resulting in the formation of an electromagnetic field around the primary coil which inducts a voltage of sufficient potential in the secondary windings to "fire" the spark plug.

Only half of the generated current passes through diode (3) to charge the capacitor. Reverse current is blocked by diode (3) but passes through Zener diode (2) to complete the reverse circuit. Zener diode (2) also limits maximum voltage of the forward current. As the flywheel continues to turn and magnets pass the trigger coil (4), a small amount of electrical current is generated. This current opens the gate controlled switch (5) allowing the capacitor to discharge through the pulse transformer (7). The rapid voltage rise in the transformer primary coil induces a high voltage secondary current which forms the ignition spark when it jumps the spark plug gap.

SPARK PLUG

In any spark ignition engine, the spark plug provides the means for igniting the compressed fuel-air mixture in the cylinder. Before an electric charge can move across an air gap, the intervening air must be charged with electricity, or ionized. The spark plug gap becomes more easily ionized if the spark plug ground (G4 – Fig. 1-11) is of negative polarity. If the spark plug is properly gapped and the system is not shorted, not more than 7,000 volts may be required to initiate a spark. Higher voltage is required as the spark plug warms up, or if compression pressures or the distance of the air gap is increased. Compression pressures are highest at full throttle and relatively slow engine speeds, therefore, high voltage requirements or a lack of available secondary voltage most often shows up as a miss during maximum acceleration from a slow engine speed. There are many different types and sizes of spark plugs which are designed for a number of specific requirements.

THREAD SIZE. The threaded, shell portion of the spark plug and the attaching holes in the cylinder are manufactured to meet certain industry established standards. The diameter is referred to as "Thread Size." Those com-

monly used are: 10 mm, 14 mm, 18 mm, 7/8 inch and 1/2 inch pipe. The 14 mm plug is almost universal for outboard motor use.

REACH. The length of the thread, and the thread depth in cylinder head or wall are also standardized throughout the industry. This dimension is measured from gasket seat of head to cylinder end of thread. Four different reach plugs commonly used are: 3/8 inch, 7/16 inch, 1/2 inch and 3/4 inch. The first two mentioned are the only ones commonly used in outboard motors.

HEAT RANGE. During engine operation, part of the heat generated during combustion is transferred to the spark plug, and from the plug to the coolant water through the shell threads and gasket. The operating temperature of the spark plug plays an important part in the engine operation. If too much heat is retained by the plug, the fuel-air mixture may be ignited by contact with the heated surface before the ignition spark occurs. If not enough heat is retained, partially burned combustion products (soot, carbon and oil) may build up on the plug tip resulting in "fouling" or shorting out of the plug. If this happens, the secondary current is dissipated uselessly as it is generated instead of bridging the plug gap as a useful spark, and the engine will misfire.

The operating temperature of the plug tip can be controlled, within limits, by altering the length of the path the heat must follow to reach the threads and gasket of the plug. Thus, a plug with a short, stubby insulator around the center electrode will run cooler than one with a long, slim insulator. Most plugs in the more popular sizes are available in a number of heat ranges which are interchangeable within the group. The proper heat range is determined by engine design and the type of service. Like most other elements of design, the plug type installed as original equipment is usually a compromise and is either the most suitable plug for average condi-

Fig. 1-26—Schematic diagram of a typical capacitor discharge ignition system.

1. Generating coil
2. Zener diode
3. Diode
4. Trigger coil
5. Gate controlled switch
6. Capacitor
7. Pulse transformer (coil)
8. Spark plug

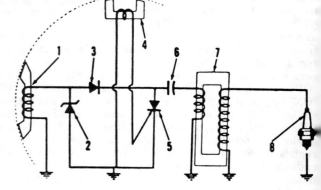

Fig. 1-27—Spark plug tip temperature is controlled by the length of the path heat must travel to reach the coolant medium.

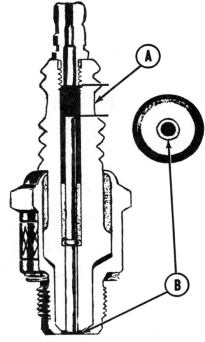

Fig. 1-29—A specially designed surface gap plug offers exceptional freedom from carbon fouling. Features include an air gap (A) in the center element and a circular gap (B) which burns clean. Special voltages are required, and the plug is not interchangeable with other types.

tions; or the best plug to meet the two extremes of service expected. No one spark plug, however, can be ideally suited for long periods of slow-speed operation such as trolling, and still be the best possible type for high-speed operation. Refer to SPARK PLUG SERVICING, in SERVICE FUNDAMENTALS section, for additional information on spark plug selection.

SPECIAL TYPES. Sometimes, engine design features or operating conditions call for special plug types designed for a particular purpose. Special types include SHIELDED PLUGS which are extensively used for inboard marine applications and RESISTOR PLUGS, with built-in resitance. Of special interest when dealing with outboard motors is the two-stroke spark plug shown in the left hand view, Fig. 1-28. In the design of this plug, the ground electrode is shortened so its end aligns with center of insulated electrode rather than completely overlapping as with the conventional plug. This feature reduces the possibility of the gap bridging over by carbon formations. A second special type designed for outboard motor use is the SURFACE GAP plug shown in Fig. 1-29. This spark plug was engineered by Champion Spark Plug Company for use in high-output motors. This plug is capable of efficient operation over a wide range of conditions. It cannot however, be interchanged with a conventional spark plug.

COOLING SYSTEM

The cooling system on most motors consists of a water intake located on the lower motor leg, a coolant pump, and in many cases, a thermostat to control the coolant temperature. As with all internal combustion engines, the cooling system must be designed to maintain a satisfactory operating temperature, rather than the coolest possible temperature. This is made additionally

difficult in the case of the outboard motor because the coolant liquid is not contained in a separate reservoir where coolant temperature can be controlled. Because the temperature of the incoming liquid cannot be controlled, the only possible means of regulating the operating temperature is by the control of the amount of coolant flowing in the system.

On most outboard motors, the flow is held at a relatively constant level regardless of engine speed, by the design of the coolant pump. Refer to Fig. 1-30. At slow engine speeds the rubber impeller blades follow the contour of the offset housing as shown by the solid line. The pump functions as a positive displacement pump, drawing water in (IN) as area between impeller blades increases. Water is forced into outlet passage (OUT) and up into power head as area decreases. As engine speed increases, pump rotative speed and water pressure forces impeller blade away from outside of housing as shown by the

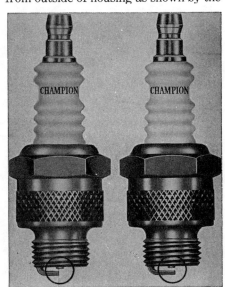

Fig. 1-28—The two stroke plug shown at left, is one of the more important special types in the outboard motor industry.

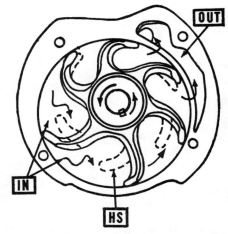

Fig. 1-30—Schematic view of the rubber impeller type water pump which maintains an approximately equal volume of coolant flow at most operating speeds. Water is drawn into pump (IN) as area between vanes increases and is forced into power head (OUT) as area decreases. At high speeds (HS) the blades remain curved and pump operates mostly by centrifugal action.

broken lines (HS). At full speed, the pump operates almost entirely as a centrifugal pump.

Later production motors often use a thermostat to assist in maintaining an efficient operating temperature. The thermostat may recirculate the coolant

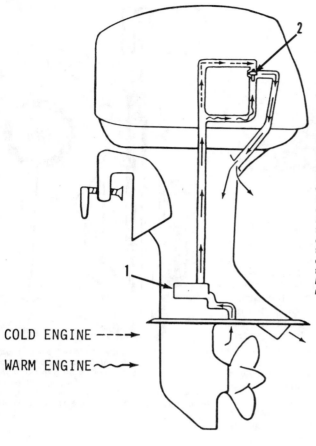

COLD ENGINE ---→

WARM ENGINE ∼∼∼→

Fig. 1-31—Bypass type of thermostat operation used in some motors. When power head temperature is below normal the thermostat (2) closes coolant outlet through power head and opens the bypass outlet. Coolant flow then follows course shown by broken arrows. As operating temperature is reached, thermostat opens coolant passages through power head and closes bypass. The coolant then flows through power head as shown by wavy arrow. The coolant pump is in lower unit as shown by (1).

water in the power head until operating temperature is reached, then open to allow the heated liquid to be exhausted; or, may bypass the power head with the circulated liquid until operating temperature is reached, then circulate coolant through block. Refer to Fig. 1-31.

In almost all liquid-cooled motors, the coolant liquid passes from the power head into the engine exhaust system. The entrance of the water cools the exhaust stream and the exhaust housing which is usually part of the lower motor leg.

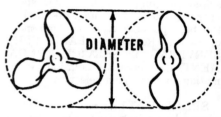

Fig. 1-32—The proper method of measuring the diameter of a two-blade and three-blade propeller is as shown.

DRIVE UNIT FUNDAMENTALS

PROPELLER

An outboard motor propeller moves a boat through the water in somewhat the same manner that a wood screw passes through a piece of wood. Propellers are rated by diameter, pitch and the number of blades; diameter being the distance across a circle described by blade tips as shown in Fig. 1-32, and pitch the forward thrust imparted in one revolution of the propeller as shown by Fig. 1-33. The correct propeller diameter is determined by motor design, especially the items of horsepower and propeller shaft gear ratio, and should usually not be changed from that recommended by the manufacturer. Propeller pitch is more nearly comparable to the transmission gear ratio of an automobile and should be individually selected to suit the conditions of boat design and usage.

Efficiency is greatest when the propeller operates with only moderate slippage, the actual amount depending to a

certain degree upon the application. Normal slippage on a racing hull may be as low as 10 percent, while a slow speed hull may normally be allowed 50-60 percent.

NOTE: Slippage is the difference between the distance a boat actually moves forward with each turn of the propeller, and the theoretical distance indicated by the pitch. For example, a boat equipped with a 12-inch (30.5 cm) pitch propeller which moves forward 9 inches (22.9 cm) with each revolution of the propeller shaft has 25 percent slippage.

The potential speed of a boat depends as much on the design of the boat as upon the power of the motor. Although there are many individual types, most boats will fall into one of two broad categories: (A) the displacement hull; and (B) the planing hull. Refer to Fig. 1-34. When not moving, any boat will displace its own weight in water. A displacement

hull will run at nearly the standing depth when under way. A planing hull will ride up on the water as shown at (2) as it approaches cruising speed, offering much less resistance to the forward movement.

A displacement hull is the only logical design for slow moving boats which cannot attain planing speed. They are also more stable in rough water and ride somewhat easier than a planing hull. A displacement hull requires a minimum pitch propeller as shown at (A–Fig. 1-33). A three-blade propeller offering maximum thrust area is usually used.

Speed is as important as power in the efficient operation of a planing hull. Maximum resistance is encountered as the boat moves into planing position, and peak slippage occurs at that time. Once planing position has been attained, forward speed will increase to the limits imposed by propeller speed and pitch. A two-blade propeller is capable of attaining a somewhat faster forward speed

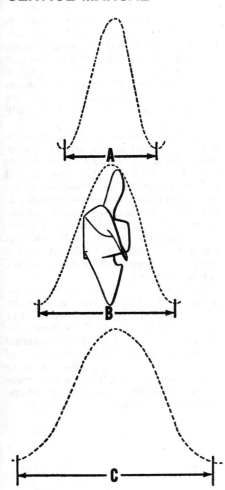

Fig. 1-33—Propeller pitch indicates the theoretical forward movement in one revolution of propeller if there were no slippage. Flat pitch propellers (A) can be likened to low gear in an automobile; while extreme pitch (C) is similar to high gear or overdrive.

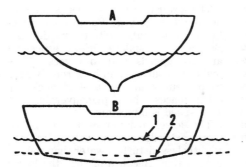

Fig. 1-34—Outboard hulls fall into two general classes; the displacement hull shown at (A) and the planing hull shown at (B). In the displacement hull, the waterline is about the same height on hull when boat is at anchor or under way. The planing hull (B) rises in the water as speed increases, and in extreme conditions barely touches the water surface.

A. Displacement hull
B. Planing hull
1. Standing waterline
2. Planing waterline

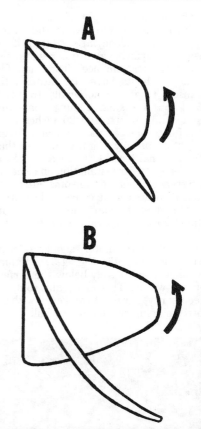

Fig. 1-35—The propeller pitch may be at a constant angle as shown at (A); or of a varying angle (cupped) as shown at (B).

than a three-blade propeller of the same pitch. Planing hulls require a longer pitch propeller, falling somewhere between that shown at (B) and (C), Fig. 1-33.

A propeller is not ideally suited to the same boat and motor under all operating conditions. If a light runabout with a small motor is used to pull a water skier, a lower pitch propeller may be required. The same holds true of a moderate horsepower motor when pulling two or more skiers. A three-blade propeller is usually preferable for water skiing. Top speed may be somewhat reduced over that of a comparable two-blade unit, but performance will usually be improved.

There is no set rule for matching a propeller, boat and motor. The general practice is to select a propeller which will allow the properly tuned and adjusted motor to run in the recommended operating speed range at wide-open throttle. Too little propeller pitch will

cause motor to over-speed, while too much pitch will not allow the motor to reach the proper speed.

Outboard motor propellers are usually made of aluminum or bronze, although some plastic propellers have been made. Stainless steel is sometimes used for racing propellers.

Propellers may be designed with a constant, flat pitch throughout the entire length of the blade as shown at "A"–Fig. 1-35, or with a cupped blade which increases in pitch toward the trailing edge as shown at "B". The flat blade propellers operate efficiently only at relatively slow rotative speeds. Above a certain critical speed, water is moved from the blade area faster than additional water can flow into the area behind the blades, causing "cavitation" and erratic behavior. The extreme turbulence and shock waves caused by cavitation rapidly reduces operating efficiency. The critical speed varies with propeller diameter, the traveling speed of the blade tips being the determining factor. Propeller shape also affects the critical speed, as does any obstruction ahead of the propeller which diverts the water flow. A propeller with curved blades is usually designed for higher speed operation than one with flat blades.

GEARCASE AND LOWER HOUSING

The power head delivers power to a drive shaft which is geared to turn a propeller shaft, thus delivering thrust to propel the boat. The gears, shafts and supporting bearings are contained in a lightweight housing or gearcase. In early motors and in some of today's trolling motors, the power transmitted was small. In today's larger motors, how-

ever, speed and pressure is considerable, requiring precision construction and close attention to bearing and gear clearances.

In spite of the necessity for strength and rigidity, the gearcase must interfere as little as possible with the smooth flow of water to the propeller. This is especially important at the higher speeds where propeller cavitation is a problem. To perform efficiently, the gearcase must be kept as small as possible and well streamlined, as shown in Fig. 1-36 and Fig. 1-37.

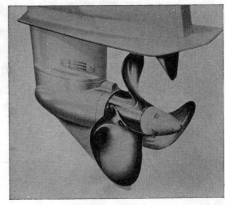

Fig. 1-36—High power, high performance lower unit showing streamlined configuration to eliminate drag and improve the performance.

The operating height of the propeller is important. If too low in the water, speed and efficiency are reduced; if too near the surface, cavitation results, also affecting performance. The manufacturers of boats have standardized the transom height to nominally 15 inches (38.1 cm) for small fishing boats and light utility boats; and 20 inches (50.8 cm) for the larger, faster boats. Actual height is usually slightly greater than the nominal height. Outboard motors are designed for installation on either of the standard height transoms. Most outboard motors can be converted to either a long or short shaft motor by the installation (or removal) of an extension kit.

An outboard motor should operate with the plate (5 – Fig. 1-37) running parallel to and barely below the surface of the water. This is usually (but not necessarily) parallel to and even with the lower planing surface of the hull.

The lower unit also serves as the rudder to steer the boat. Because the direction of thrust turns with the rudder, the system is unusually efficient, especially at slow speeds and in reverse. This makes the outboard unit extremely easy to maneuver in and around docks or other places where maneuverablity at slow speed is important.

The lower portion of the outboard motor propeller continuously operates in slightly less disturbed water than the upper portion. Because of this, the lower portion of the propeller has a tendency to walk the stern of the boat in a direction opposite to its movement. Thus, if a motor is equipped with a propeller which rotates counterclockwise (A – Fig. 1-38), the stern of the boat will move to port as shown by arrow "C"; and boat will pull to starboard when set on a dead ahead course. The opposite will occur if motor is equipped with a propeller rotating clockwise as shown at (B). To compen-

sate for this tendency, some motors are equipped with an adjustable trim tab. Other motors have the lower unit slightly offset with relation to the true centerline for the same reason. When two motors are used, the two propellers are often designed to rotate in opposite directions, and the effect is self-cancelling.

On most outboards, the engine exhaust is vented to the outside underneath the water level to silence engine noise (See 6 – Fig. 1-27). The exhaust usually enters in the disturbed water area immediately behind the propeller to minimize back pressure in the exhaust system. The coolant water as it leaves the power head enters the hot exhaust gases, thus cooling the exhaust and the lower motor housing that serves as the exhaust housing.

Because of variation in the planing angle and built-in transom angle in different types of boats, provision must be made for adjustment of the thrust, or tilt angle (3 – Fig. 1-37). Force of thrust should be parallel to the direction of travel when in planing position. A minor adjustment in the tilt angle can make considerable difference in the speed and performance of the unit.

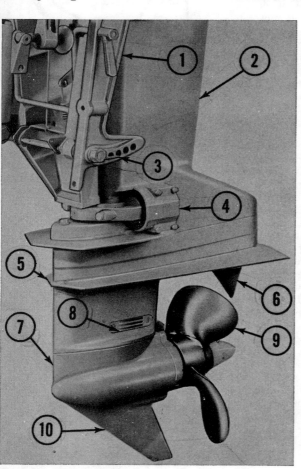

Fig. 1-37—Lower unit, attaching brackets and associated parts showing nomenclature.

1. Stern brackets
2. Lower motor leg
3. Tilt pin
4. Shock mount
5. Antiventilation plate
6. Exhaust outlet
7. Gearcase
8. Water inlet
9. Propeller
10. Skeg

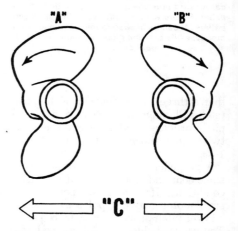

Fig. 1-38—Propellers may be of counterclockwise rotation as shown at "A" or clockwise rotation as shown at "B". The rotation of the propeller has a tendency to pull the stern of the boat off-course in the direction shown by arrow "C".

SERVICE FUNDAMENTALS
PERIODIC SERVICING

Many of the troubles related to outboard motors will be much easier to repair if noticed before they result in extensive damage and sometimes the lack of proper servicing is the primary cause of failure. The following service and inspection schedule can be used as a guide. If the motor is operated under severe conditions, the intervals should be shortened.

NOTE: This schedule of mid-season service, off-season storage and pre-season preparations is taken from the Marine Service Manual of Recommended Practices which is copyrighted by the Boating Industry Association.

MID-SEASON (OR EVERY 50 HOURS)

1. Drain and flush gearcase. Refill to correct level using manufacturer's recommended lubricant.
2. Remove and clean fuel filter bowl. Replace fuel bowl element. Always use new filter bowl gasket.
3. Clean and regap spark plugs to recommended gap. Replace worn or burnt spark plugs. (Use new gaskets and torque plugs to manufacturer's recommendations).
4. Check propeller for correct pitch. Replace if propeller is worn, chipped or badly bent.
5. Lubricate all grease fittings, using manufacturer's recommended lubricant.
6. Check remote control box, cables and wiring harness.
7. Check steering controls; lubricate mechanical steering.
8. Lubricate all carburetor and magneto linkages with manufacturer's recommended lubricant.
9. Adjust tension on magneto and/or generator drive belts.
10. Clean and coat battery terminals with grease.
11. Check water pump and thermostat operation.
12. Check breaker points' condition and timing.
13. Check carburetor and ignition synchronization.
14. Check carburetor adjustment.

OFF-SEASON STORAGE

Operate motor in test tank, or on boat, at part throttle with shift lever in neutral. Rapidly inject rust preventative oil (with pump type oil can) into carburetor air intake, or intakes, until motor is smoking profusely. Stop motor immediately to prevent burning oil out of cylinders. This will lubricate and protect internal parts of powerhead while motor is in storage. If motor was last operated in salt water, run it in fresh water before preparing it for storage.

1. Place motor on a stand in normal upright position. Remove motor cover.
2. Retard throttle all the way and disconnect spark plug leads. Manually rotate motor flywheel several times to draing the water from water pump.
3. Drain carburetor float chamber. Remove fuel filter bowl–drain, clean and replace filter element and gasket.
4. Clean and lubricate electric starter drive mechanism.
5. Completely drain and clean fuel tank.
6. Remove propeller and check for condition and pitch. Clean and liberally lubricate propeller shaft. Replace propeller drive pin if bent or worn. Replace propeller using new cotter pin or tab lockwasher.
7. Drain and refill gearcase, using the manufacturers recommended lubricant.

8. Wipe over entire external motor surface with a clean cloth soaked in light oil.
9. Store in an upright position in a dry, well-ventilated room. To prevent accidental starting, leave spark plug leads disconnected.
10. Remove battery from boat and keep it charged while in storage.

PRE-SEASON PREPARATION

1. Remove, clean, inspect and properly gap spark plugs. Replace defective plugs. (Use new gaskets and torque plugs to manufacturer's recommendations.)
2. Remove oil level plug from gearcase and check for proper oil level.
3. Thoroughly clean and refinish surfaces as required.
4. Check battery for full charge and clean terminals. Clean and inspect battery cable connections. Check polarity before installing battery cables. Cover cable connections with grease to prevent corrosion.
5. If possible, run motor in test tank prior to installing on boat. Check water pump and thermostat operation.

Proper maintenance is important.

SALT WATER CARE

Motors that are operated in salt water require some special care to combat the possibility of corrosion resulting from such use. If possible, tilt motor out of water and flush cooling system and outside of lower unit with fresh water immediately after each use.

Special care is needed if motor is used in salt water.

The aluminum-silicon alloys used for outboard motor castings are relatively resistant to corrosion from oxidation but are very susceptible to galvanic action and the resultant corrosion if unprotected.

Oxidation is the destruction of a useful form of metal resulting from a chemical combination of the element with oxygen. Although oxidation can occur under water, the most favorable environment is the atmosphere under extreme conditions of warmth and humidity. Rust is an iron oxide and the best known example of oxidation. The oxidation of aluminum leaves a white, powdery coating on the surface of the metal which protects it from further oxidation, and aluminum can withstand years of exposure to the atmosphere without harmful effect.

Briefly described, galvanic action is an electrical process where atoms of one metal are carried in a solution and deposited on the surface of a dissimilar metal. Chrome or nickel plating are controlled forms of galvanic action. Each metallic element has a particular degree of susceptibility to galvanic corrosion, and pure aluminum is second only to magnesium in this scale. The aluminum alloys are somewhat less susceptible than pure metal, and galvanic action can be effectively stopped by painting or other surface protection. Aluminum parts are protected by a process known as anodizing, which deposits a hard, protective coating of aluminum oxide over the surface. The anodized surface is impervious to corrosion from any source, but is only effective if unbroken. Scratches or abrasion can expose the unprotected metal.

Galvanic action is more prevalent in salt water because of the presence of minerals in the water which makes it more effective as a conductor. The action can be hastened by the presence of stray electric currents, and batteries or other sources of electricity should be disconnected when not in use. Some protection is offered by attaching a small block of more susceptible metal in the water near the part to be protected. This small block then becomes the target of galvanic action and is consumed, but the valuable part is spared.

All motors, but especially those used in salt water, should have an adequate coverage of approved paint. Paint bonds well to an anodized aluminum surface, but is difficult to apply to uncoated aluminum. Use only an approved paint, applied according to instructions.

WARNING: Most manufacturers do not recommend the use of antifouling paint on any part of the motor. Antifouling paints contain mercury or copper which can cause galvanic corrosion in the presence of aluminum.

TROUBLE-SHOOTING

Intelligent service is normally divided into two basic functions; that of determining the cause of trouble, and correcting the trouble after cause has been determined. The cause may be obvious in many cases, where broken, worn or damaged parts are apparent. Repair in these cases becomes merely a matter of renewal and adjustment. Many of the performance problems, however, are not so apparent and the first task of the experienced service technician is that of determining the cause.

The experienced serviceman generally develops and follows a logical sequence in trouble-shooting which will most likely lead him quickly to the source of trouble. Some of the points to check may not be applicable to certain outboard motors.

NOTE: This sequence (items 1 through 27) is taken from the Marine Service Manual or Recommended Practices which is copyrighted by the Boating Industry Association.

1. Manual starter rope pulls out, but pawls do not engage.
   A. Friction spring bent or burred.
   B. Excess grease on pawls or spring.
   C. Pawls bent or burred.

Develop an orderly procedure when trouble-shooting.

2. Starter rope does not return.
   A. Recoil spring broken or binding.
   B. Starter housing bent.
   C. Loose or missing parts.

3. Clattering manual starter.
   A. Friction spring bent or burred.
   B. Starter housing bent.
   C. Excess grease on pawls or spring.
   D. Dry starter spindle.

4. Electric starter inoperative.
   A. Loose or corroded connections or ground.
   B. Starting circuit safety switch open, or out of adjustment.
   C. Under capacity or weak battery or corroded battery terminals.
   D. Faulty starter solenoid.
   E. Moisture in electric starter motor.
   F. Broken or worn brushes in starter motor.
   G. Faulty fields.
   H. Faulty armature.
   I. Broken wire in harness or connector.
   J. Faulty starter key or push button switch.
   K. Worn or frayed insulation.

5. Electric starter does not engage but solenoid clicks.
   A. Loose or corroded connections or ground.
   B. Weak battery.
   C. Faulty starter solenoid.
   D. Broken wire in electric harness.
   E. Loose or stripped post on starter motor.
   F. See steps in number 4.

6. Hard to start or won't start.
   A. Empty gas tank.
   B. Gas tank air vent not open.
   C. Fuel lines kinked or severely pinched.
   D. Water or dirt in fuel system.
   E. Clogged fuel filter or screens.
   F. Motor not being choked to start.
   G. Engine not primed—pump primer system.
   H. Carburetor adjustments too lean (not allowing enough fuel to start engine).
   I. Timing and sychronizing out of adjustment.
   J. Manual choke linkage bent—auto choke out of adjustment.
   K. Spark plugs improperly gapped, dirty or broken.
   L. Fuel tank primer inoperative (pressurized system).
   M. Ignition points improperly gapped, burned or dirty.

N. Loose, broken wire or frayed insulation in electrical system.
O. Reed valves not seating or stuck shut.
P. Weak coil or condenser.
Q. Faulty gaskets.
R. Cracked distributor cap or rotor.
S. Loose fuel connector.
T. Electronic ignition component malfunction.

7. Low speed miss or motor won't idle smoothly and slowly enough.
   A. Too much oil—too little oil.
   B. Timing and sychronizing out of adjustment.
   C. Carburetor idle adjustment (mixture lean or rich).
   D. Ignition points improper (gap, worn or fouled).
   E. Weak coil or condenser.
   F. Loose or broken ignition wires.
   G. Loose or worn magneto plate.
   H. Spark plugs (improper gap or dirty).
   I. Head gasket, reed plate gasket (blown or leaking).
   J. Reed valve standing open or stuck shut.
   K. Plugged crankcase bleeder, check valves, or lines.
   L. Leaking crankcase halves.
   M. Leaking crankcase seals (top or bottom.)
   N. Exhaust gases returning through intake manifold.
   O. Electronic ignition component malfunction.

8. High speed miss or intermittent spark.
   A. Spark plugs improperly gapped or dirty.
   B. Loose, leaking or broken ignition wires.
   C. Breaker points (improper gap or dirty; worn cam or cam follower).
   D. Weak coil or condenser.
   E. Water in fuel.
   F. Leaking head gasket or exhaust cover gasket.
   G. Spark plug heat range incorrect.
   H. Engine improperly timed.
   I. Carbon or fouled combustion chambers.
   J. Magneto or distributor poorly grounded.
   K. Distributor oiler wick bad.
   L. Electronic ignition component malfunction.

9. Coughs, spits, slows.
   A. Idle or high speed needles set too lean.
   B. Carburetor not synchronized.

C. Leaking gaskets in induction system.
D. Obstructed fuel passages.
E. Float level set too low.
F. Improperly seated or broken reeds.
G. Fuel pump pressure line ruptured.
H. Fuel pump (punctured diaphragm), check valves stuck open or closed, fuel lines leak.
I. Poor fuel tank pressure (pressurized system).
J. Worn or leaking fuel connector.

10. Vibrates excessively or runs rough and smokes.
    A. Idle or high speed needles set too rich.
    B. Too much oil mixed with gas.
    C. Carburetor not synchronized with ignition properly.
    D. Choke not opening properly.
    E. Float level too high.
    F. Air passage to carburetor obstructed.
    G. Bleeder valves or passages plugged.
    H. Transom bracket clamps loose on transom.
    I. Prop out of balance.
    J. Broken motor mount.
    K. Exhaust gases getting inside motor cover.
    L. Poor ignition—see number 8.

11. Runs well, idles well for a short period, then slows down and stops.
    A. Weeds or other debris on lower unit or propeller.
    B. Insufficient cooling water.
    C. Carburetor, fuel pump, filter or screens dirty.
    D. Bleeder valves or passages plugged.
    E. Lower unit bind (lack of lubrication or bent.)
    F. Gas tank air vent not open.
    G. Not enough oil in gas.
    H. Combustion chambers and spark plugs fouled, causing preignition.
    I. Spark plug heat range too high or too low.
    J. Wrong propeller (preignition).
    K. Slow speed adjustment too rich or too lean.

12. Won't start, kicks back, backfires into lower unit.
    A. Spark plug wires reversed.
    B. Flywheel key sheared.
    C. Distributor belt timing off (magneto or battery ignition.)
    D. Timing and synchronizing out of adjustment.
    E. Reed valves not seating or broken.

13. No acceleration, low top Rpm.
    A. Improper carburetor adjustments.
    B. Improper timing and synchronization.
    C. Spark plugs (improper gap or dirty).
    D. Ignition system malfunction.
    E. Faulty coil or condenser.
    F. Loose, leaking or broken ignition wires.
    G. Reed valves not properly seated or broken.
    H. Blown head or exhaust cover gasket.
    I. Weeds on lower unit or propeller.
    J. Incorrect propeller.
    K. Insufficient oil in gas.
    L. Insufficient oil in lower unit.
    M. Fuel restrictions.
    N. Scored cylinder – stuck rings.
    O. Marine growth, hooks, rockers or change in load of boat.
    P. Sticky magneto plate.
    Q. Carbon build-up on piston head at deflector.

14. No acceleration, idles well but when put to full power dies down.
    A. High or low speed needle set too lean.
    B. Dirt or packing behind needles and seats.
    C. High speed nozzle obstructed.
    D. Float level too low.
    E. Choke partly closed.
    F. Improper timing and synchronization.
    G. Fuel lines or passages obstructed.
    H. Fuel filter obstructed. Fuel pump not supplying enough fuel.
    I. Not enough oil in gas.
    J. Breaker points improperly gapped or dirty.
    K. Bent gearcase or exhaust tube.

15. Engine runs at high speed only by using hand primer.
    A. Carburetor adjustments.
    B. Dirt or packing behind needles and seat.
    C. Fuel lines or passages obstructed.
    D. Fuel line leaks.
    E. Fuel pump not supplying enough fuel.
    F. Float level too low.
    G. Fuel filter obstructed.
    H. Fuel tank or connector at fault.

16. No power under heavy load.
    A. Wrong propeller.
    B. Weeds or other debris on lower unit or propeller.
    C. Breaker points improperly gapped or dirty.
    D. Stator plate loose.

    E. Ignition timing over advanced or late.
    F. Faulty carburetion and/or faulty ignition.
    G. Prop hub slips.
    H. Scored cylinders or rings stuck.
    I. Carbon build up on piston head at deflector.

17. Cranks over extremely easy on one or more cylinders.
    A. Low compression.
       1. Worn or broken rings.
       2. Scored cylinder or pistons.
       3. Blown head gasket.
       4. Loose spark plugs.
       5. Loose head bolts.
       6. Crankcase halves improperly sealed.
       7. Burned piston.

18. Engine won't crank over.
    A. Manual start lock improperly adjusted.
    B. Pistons rusted to cylinder wall.
    C. Lower unit gears, prop shaft rusted or broken.
    D. Broken connecting rod, crankshaft or driveshaft.
    E. Coil heels binding on flywheel.
    F. Engine improperly assembled.

19. Motor overheats.
    A. Motor not deep enough in water.
    B. Not enough oil in gas or improperly mixed.
    C. Bad thermostat.
    D. Seals or gaskets (burned, cracked or broken).
    E. Impeller key not in place or broken.
    F. Plugged water inlet, outlet or cavity.
    G. Obstruction in water passages.
    H. Broken, pinched or leaking water lines.
    I. Improper ignition timing.
    J. Motor not assembled properly.
    K. Shorted heat light wiring.
    L. Bad water pump impeller, plate, housing or seal.

20. Motor stops suddenly, freezes up.
    A. No oil in gas, or no gas.
    B. Insufficient cooling water.
    C. No lubricant in gearcase.
    D. Rusted cylinder or crankshaft.
    E. Bent or broken rod, crankshaft, drive shaft, prop shaft, stuck piston.
    F. Bad water pump or plugged water passages.

21. Motor knocks excessively.
    A. Too much or not enough oil in gas.
    B. Worn or loose bearings, pistons, rods or wrists pins.
    C. Over advanced ignition timing.
    D. Carbon in combustion chambers and exhaust ports.

    E. Manual starter not centered.
    F. Flywheel nut loose.
    G. Flywheel hitting coil heels.
    H. Bent shift rod (vibrating against exhaust tube).
    I. Loose assemblies, bolts or screws.

22. Generator will not charge.
    A. Battery condition.
    B. Connections loose or dirty.
    C. Drive belt loose or broken.
    D. Faulty regulator or cutout relay.
    E. Field fuse or fusible wire in regulator blown.
    F. Generator not polarized (dc generators).
    G. Open generator windings.
    H. Worn or sticking brushes and/or slip rings.
    I. Faulty rectifier diodes (ac generators).
    J. Faulty ammeter.

23. Low generator output and a low battery.
    A. High resistance at battery terminals.
    B. High resistance in charging circuit.
    C. Faulty ammeter.
    D. Low regulator setting.
    E. Faulty rectifier diodes (ac generators).
    F. Faulty generator.

24. Excessive battery charging.
    A. Regulator set too high.
    B. Regulator contacts stuck.
    C. Regulator voltage winding open.
    D. Regulator improperly grounded.
    E. High resistance in field coil.
    F. Regulator improperly mounted.

25. Excessive fuel consumption.
    A. Hole in fuel pump diaphragm.
    B. Deteriorated carburetor gaskets.
    C. Altered or wrong fixed jets.
    D. Jets improperly adjusted.
    E. Carburetor casting porous.
    F. Float level too high.
    G. Loose distributor pulley.

26. Shifter dog jumps.
    A. Worn shifter dog or worn gear dogs.
    B. Worn linkage.
    C. Remote control adjustment.
    D. Gearcase loose or sprung.
    E. Exhaust housing bent.
    F. Linkage out of adjustment.

27. Electric shift inoperative or slips.
    A. Improper remote control installation.
    B. Faulty coils.
    C. Faulty springs.
    D. Faulty clutch and gear.
    E. Faulty bearings.
    F. Wrong lubricant.
    G. Loose or sprung gearcase.
    H. Shorted wiring.

SPECIAL NOTES ON TROUBLE-SHOOTING

AIR-COOLED MOTORS. Overheating, low power and several other problems on air-cooled motors can sometimes be traced to improper cooling. Make certain that all shrouds are in place before starting motor. Check for dirt or debris accumulated on or between cooling fins. Broken cooling fins can sometimes cause a localized "hot spot."

SPARK PLUG APPEARANCE DIAGNOSIS. The appearance of a spark plug will be altered by use, and an examination of the plug tip can contribute useful information which may assist in obtaining better spark plug life. It must be remembered that the contributing factors differ in two-stroke and four-stroke engine operation and, although the appearance of two spark plugs may be similar, the corrective measures may depend on whether the engine is of two-stroke or four-stroke design. Fig. 2-1 through Fig. 2-6 are provided by Champion Spark Plug Company to illustrate typical observed conditions in two-stroke engines. Listed also are the probable causes and suggested corrective measures.

GENERAL MAINTENANCE

LUBRICATION

Refer to each motor's individual section for recommended type and amount of lubricant used for power head (engine) and gearcase.

FUEL: OIL RATIO. Most two-stroke cycle engines are lubricated by oil that is mixed with the fuel. It is important that the manufacturer's recommended type of oil and fuel:oil ratio be closely followed. Excessive oil or improper fuel type oil will cause low power, plug fouling and excessive carbon build-up. Insufficient amount of oil will result in inadequate lubrication and rapid internal damage. The recommended ratios and type of oil are listed in LUBRICATION paragraph for each motor. Oil should be mixed with gasoline in a separate container before it is poured into the fuel tank. Unleaded gasoline such as marine white should be used when possible. The following table may be useful in mixing the correct ratio.

RATIO	Gasoline	Oil
10:1	.63 Gallon	½ Pint
14:1	.88 Gallon	½ Pint
15:1	.94 Gallon	½ Pint
16:1	1.00 Gallon	½ Pint
20:1	1.25 Gallons	½ Pint
22:1	1.38 Gallons	½ Pint
24:1	1.50 Gallons	½ Pint
25:1	1.56 Gallons	½ Pint
50:1	3.13 Gallons	½ Pint
100:1	6.25 Gallons	½ Pint
10:1	5 U.S. Gallons	4 Pints 64 Fl. Oz.
14:1	5 U.S. Gallons	3 Pints 45¾ Fl. Oz.
15:1	5 U.S. Gallons	2¾ Pints 42½ Fl. Oz.
16:1	5 U.S. Gallons	2½ Pints 40 Fl. Oz.
20:1	5 U.S. Gallons	2 Pints 32 Fl. Oz.
22:1	5 U.S. Gallons	1¾ Pints 29 Fl. Oz.
24:1	3 U.S. Gallons	1 Pint 16 Fl. Oz.
25:1	4 U.S. Gallons	1¼ Pints 20½ Fl. Oz.
50:1	3 U.S. Gallons	½ Pint 7¾ Fl. Oz.
100:1	3 U.S. Gallons	¼ Pint 4 Fl. Oz.

SPARK PLUGS

The recommended type of spark plug, heat range and electrode gap is listed in the CONDENSER SERVICE DATA table for the individual motor. Under light loads or low speed (trolling), a spark plug of the same size with a higher (hotter) heat range may be installed. If subjected to heavy loads or high speed, a colder plug may be necessary.

The spark plug electrode gap should be adjusted on most plugs by bending the ground electrode. Refer to Fig. 2-7. Some spark plugs have an electrode gap which is not adjustable.

Before a plug is cleaned with abrasive, it should be thoroughly degreased with a nonoily solvent and air-dried to prevent a build up of abrasive in recess of plug.

After plug is cleaned by abrasive, and before gap is set, the electrode surfaces between the grounded and insulated electrodes should be cleaned and returned as nearly as possible to original shape by filing with a point file. Failure to properly dress the points can result in high secondary voltage requirements, and misfire of the plugs.

Spark plugs are usually cleaned by abrasive action commonly referred to as "sand blasting." Actually, ordinary sand is not used, but a special abrasive which is nonconductive to electricity even when melted, thus the abrasive cannot short out the plug current. Extreme care should be used in cleaning the plugs after sand blasting, because any particles of abrasive left on the plug may cause damage to piston rings, piston or cylinder walls.

Fig. 2-1—Two-stroke cycle engine plug of correct heat range. Insulators light tan to gray with few deposits. Electrodes not burned.

Fig. 2-2—Damp or wet black carbon coating over entire firing end of plug. Could be caused by prolonged trolling, rich carburetor mixture, too much oil in fuel, crankcase bleed passage plugged, or low ignition voltage. Could also be caused by incorrect heat range (too cold) for operating conditions. Correct the defects or install a hotter plug

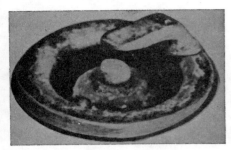

Fig. 2-3—Electrodes badly eroded, deposits white or light gray and gritty, insulator has "blistered" appearance. Could be caused by lean carburetor mixture, fast timing, overloading, or improperly operating cooling system. Could also be caused by incorrect heat range (too hot) for operating conditions. Check timing, carburetor adjustment and cooling system. If recommended operating speed cannot be obtained after tune-up, install flatter pitch propeller. If timing, carburetor adjustment, cooling system and engine speed are correct, install a colder plug.

Fig. 2-4—Gray, metallic aluminum deposits on plug. This condition is caused by internal engine damage. Engine should be overhauled and cause of damage corrected.

Fig. 2-5—Core bridging from center electrode to shell. Fused deposits sometimes have the appearance of tiny beads or glasslike bubbles. Caused by excessive combustion chamber deposits which in turn could be the result of; excessive carbon from prolonged usage; use of improper oil or incorrect fuel:oil ratio; high speed operation immediately following prolonged trolling.

CARBURETOR

The bulk of carburetor service consists of cleaning, inspection and adjustment. After considerable service it may become necessary to overhaul the carburetor and renew worn parts to restore original operating efficiency. Although carburetor condition affects engine operating economy and power, the ignition system and engine compression must also be considered to determine and correct causes. Also, make certain that the fuel:oil ratio is correct and that fuel is fresh (not last year's).

CLEANING AND INSPECTION. Before dismantling carburetor for cleaning and inspection, clean all external surfaces and remove accumulated dirt and grease. If fuel starvation is suspected, all filters in carburetor, fuel pump and/or tank should be inspected. Because of inadequate fuel handling methods, rust and other foreign matter may sometimes block or partially block these filters. Under no circumstances

Fig. 2-6—Gap bridging. Usually results from the same causes outlined in Fig. 2-5.

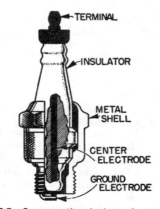

Fig. 2-7—Cross-sectional view of spark plug showing construction and nomenclature.

should these filters be removed from the fuel system. If filters are removed, the blockage will most likely occur within the carburetor and cleaning will be frequent and more difficult.

Refer to appropriate motor repair section for carburetor exploded or cross sectional views. Disassemble the carburetor and note any discrepancies which may cause a malfunction.

Wear of the fuel inlet needle, needle seat, or the float linkage can cause a change in carburetor fuel level and possible flooding. Fuel inlet needle and seat are usually furnished as a matched set, and should be renewed if a groove is noticeable in the valve; or if neoprene seat is damaged on models so equipped. On models with brass seat and tapered steel valve needle, install seat, drop needle into position; then tap outer end of needle with a small hammer to even the seat.

Carburetor flooding can sometimes be caused by a loose fuel valve seat, loose nozzle, cracked carburetor body or binding float. Consider all of these possibilities when service is indicated.

When reassembling, be sure float level (or fuel level) is properly adjusted as listed in the CARBURETOR paragraph of the appropriate motor repair section.

Except for improper fuel, the most common cause of carburetor malfunction is the formation of gum and varnish which plugs or partially plugs the small drillings or calibrated orifices within the

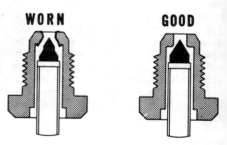

WORN   GOOD

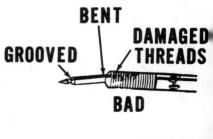

GROOVED   BENT   DAMAGED THREADS

BAD

GOOD

Fig. 2-9—Mixture adjustment needles should be renewed if damaged as shown at top. Never attempt to straighten a bent needle.

carburetor which control fuel flow. This build-up can be of two types, the most common being the gradual accumulation of hard varnish, sometimes mixed with dirt, which slowly builds up on all fuel system surfaces after long use. Over a period of time these deposits change the balance (calibration) of the carburetor or assist in completely blocking some small passsages making carburetor removal necessary. To do a thorough job of cleaning, the carburetor must be completely disassembled, the parts cleaned as recommended by the manufacturer, then the passages blown out with compressed air. It is impractical in most instances to attempt to clean the small passages with needles or wires, although this method is recommended by some. Exercise extreme caution to prevent enlarging passages and be sure that no hidden cross passages are plugged.

A second type of gum is formed by the decomposition of gasoline which is allowed to stand for long periods of time without being used. This form of gum can completely plug the carburetor passages, often causing the fuel inlet valve to stick. Preservative additives have been developed for gasoline which lessens the danger from this type of damage, but the fuel system including the carburetor should be drained when not is use to prevent such damage. This gum can only be loosened by prolonged soaking in a carbon dissolving solvent. Sometimes gum or varnish builds up around the throttle shaft causing the throttle to stick.

Wear damage is slight on the outboard motor carburetor. The throttle valve is not subject to frequent movement or dust abrasion, so wear of throttle valve, shaft and seals is usually negligible. If the throttle shaft does not move freely, check for gum or varnish buildup around shaft. The orifice of metering jets is subject to wear from prolonged use, but such wear cannot be detected by ordinary means. Because the jets are relatively inexpensive, it is common practice to renew them whenever carburetor is disassembled rather than to take a chance on the amount of wear.

Allied to wear damage, but usually from a different cause, is the groove around the tapered point of the mixture adjustment needle valves on carburetors so equipped. Refer to Fig. 2-9. This groove is usuallly caused by carelessness or ignorance, and is the result of bottoming the needle too tightly in the adjustment orifice. A groove on needle prevents the fine gradation of adjustment usually required of a metering needle, making it impossible to make and hold the correct mixture adjustment. When a damaged needle is found, it should be discarded and a new part installed. It should be noted, however, the seat for the needle valve may also be damaged and accurate adjustment may not be possible even with a new needle. When adjusting the valve, always screw the needle down only lightly with the fingers until it bottoms, then back the needle out the number of turns suggested in the individual motor service sections.

ADJUSTMENT. Before attempting to adjust the carburetor, make certain that fuel used is fresh and contains the proper amount and recommended type of oil. Also, make certain that engine compression or ignition system is not the real problem. Check fuel system for air or fuel leaks and clean all of the fuel system filters. When adjusting the carburetor, make certain that exhaust fumes are properly vented and not allowed to be drawn into engine. Also, use the correct test wheel (or propeller) and do not allow motor to overheat.

Carburetor should be adjusted at the altitude that motor is to be operated. At high elevations, because the air is less dense, the main fuel adjustment on some carburetors should be set leaner than at sea level. Some carburetors have a high speed (main) adjustment needle and have a fixed main jet. On models with adjustment needle, the initial setting is listed in the individual motor section. On carburetors with fixed jets available in various sizes, the standard size is listed. At higher altitudes it may be necessary to install a main jet with smaller metering hole (orifice). In some cases, a propeller with less pitch should be installed to permit the recommended high rpm.

To adjust, first obtain the initial setting recommended in the individual motor section.

NOTE: Be careful when turning needles in and do not force, or damage to needle and/or seat may result.

Generally the initial setting for adjusting needles is too rich but should allow motor to start. Run the motor until it reaches normal operating temperature, then adjust needles until fuel mixture is correct throughout entire range of rpm. It is preferable to set mixtures slightly rich. If mixture is too lean, motor may overheat and result in serious damage. If a "flat spot" or "4-cycling" condition cannot be corrected by adjusting carburetor, check synchronization between ignition timing advance and carburetor throttle opening as outlined in SPEED CONTROL LINKAGE section for individual motors.

SPEED CONTROL LINKAGE

The speed control on most outboard motors advances the ignition timing and opens the carburetor throttle valve as the handle is moved to the fast position. To provide correct operation, the throttle valve must be opened exactly the right amount as the ignition timing is changed. Refer to the motor repair section for models which have adjustments to synchronize "throttle" opening with the ignition timing.

A "flat spot" or "4-cycling" condition that cannot be corrected by adjusting carburetor (fuel mixture) is usually caused by incorrect throttle to ignition synchronization and/or ignition system malfunction.

REED VALVES

On two-stroke cycle motors, the incoming fuel-air mixture must be compressed in order for the mixture to properly reach the engine cylinder. On engines utilizing reed type carburetor to crankcase intake valve, a bent or broken reed may not allow compression build up in the crankcase. This condition is usually most noticeable at low speed. Thus, if such an engine seems otherwise OK, remove and inspect the reed valve unit. Refer to appropriate repair section in this manual for information on individual models.

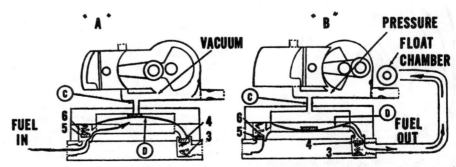

Fig. 2-10—Schematic view of a typical, crankcase operated, diaphragm type fuel pump. Pressure and vacuum pulsations from crankcase pass through connection (C) to rear of diaphragm (D) which induces a pumping action on fuel line as shown.

FUEL PUMP

Diaphragm type fuel pumps can be operated mechanically, electrically or by the vacuum and pressure pulsations in the two-stroke cycle engine crankcase. Refer to Fig. 2-10. Vacuum in the crankcase draws the diaphragm (D) in, pulling fuel past the inlet check valve (5) as shown in view "A". As the piston moves down in the cylinder, pressure is created in the crankcase. The pressure is directed to the back of diaphragm via passage (C) and diaphragm is forced out and trapped fuel is directed to the carburetor past the outlet check valve (4) as shown in view "B".

Passage (C) must be properly sealed. On some motors, the fuel pump is attached directly to the crankcase and passage (C) is sealed with a gasket. Other motors use a hose between the crankcase and fuel pump. Fuel lines (hoses) must not leak air or fuel and fuel filters should be clean. The check valves (4 & 5) should be correctly installed and not leak.

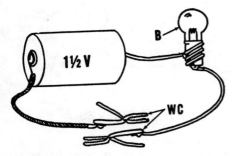

Fig. 2-11—A light can be easily constructed as shown for checking continuity. Bulb (B) should light when wire clamps (WC) are touching.

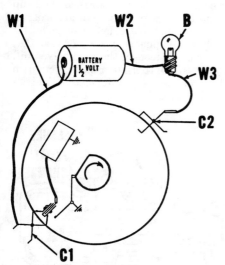

Fig. 2-12—Drawing of typical installation for checking breaker points. Coil wire should be disconnected from terminal before clamp (C1) is connected.

IGNITION SYSTEM

For a quick test of the ignition system, remove the spark plug and hold the spark plug wire with an insulated tool about 1/8-1/4 inch (3.17-6.35 mm) away from cylinder head. Have someone spin the motor and note the condition of spark. Although spark may not be visible in bright daylight, a distinct snap will be noted as the spark jumps gap. On breaker point models, If spark is weak or erratic, adjust breaker point gap and be sure to note point condition. If spark is weak although points are in good condition and properly adjusted, examine the condition of point, condenser and coil wiring, and the insulation on the magneto coils. On all models, look for broken or worn insulation or broken wires. Also check for loose or corroded connections. On models with electronic ignition control, if no external damage is noted, then refer to appropriate model section for electronic ignition control component testing. On motors equipped with a stop switch, check condition of switch and associated wiring. Renew any parts which are damaged or in poor condition.

IGNITION TIMING. On most motors, the ignition timing is advanced as the speed control handle is moved to the fast position. Refer to the SPEED CONTROL LINKAGE section for synchronizing throttle opening to the ignition timing.

Some motors have fixed ignition timing and engine speed is changed only by changing the carburetor throttle valve opening. Fixed ignition timing is usually adjustable but does not change with engine running. Refer to the appropriate motor section for method of adjusting the fixed ignition timing.

On two cylinder motors, ignition timing should be synchronized to fire the cylinders evenly. Refer to the individual motor section for method of checking and adjusting. A timing light constructed as shown in Fig. 2-11 or a continuity (ohm) meter can be used to indicate exact position that ignition breaker points open (ignition occurs). The coil wire must be disconnected from ignition breaker points before using continuity meter (or light).

On breaker point motors, a change in the breaker point (maximum) gap will change the ignition timing. Recommended breaker point gap listed in individual repair sections should be followed closely. Loss of power, loss of speed, "flat spot" and/or overheating may be caused by incorrect breaker point gap.

BREAKER POINTS. Breaker points are usually located under the flywheel. Holes are sometimes provided in the flywheel for checking and adjusting however, flywheel usually must be removed for renewal of ignition points.

Using a small screwdriver, separate and inspect condition of contacts. If burned or deeply pitted, points should be renewed. If contacts are clean to grayish in color, disconnect coil lead wire from breaker point terminal. Connect one lead (C1–Fig. 2-12) to the insulated breaker point terminal and the other (C2) to engine (ground). Light should burn with points closed and go out with points open. If light does not burn, little or no contact is indicated and points should be cleaned or renewed and contact maximum gap should be reset.

NOTE: IN some cases, new breaker point contact surfaces may be coated with oil or wax.

If light does not go out when points are opened, timing light is not connected properly or breaker point insulation is defective. Adjust breaker point gap as follows unless manufacturer specifies adjusting breaker gap to obtain correct ignition timing. First, turn engine so that points are closed to be sure that the contact surfaces are in alignment and seat squarely. Then turn engine so that breaker point opening is maximum and adjust breaker gap to manufacturer's specification. Be sure to recheck gap after tightening breaker point base retaining screws.

CONDENSER. To check condition of the condenser without special test equipment, proceed as follows: The condenser case and wire should be visually checked for any obvious damage. Remove condenser, then connect one end of test lamp (Fig. 2-11) to terminal at end of condenser wire and other end to condenser case. If light goes on, condenser is shorted and should be renewed. It is usually a good practice to renew condenser when new breaker points are installed. If breaker points become pitted rapidly, condenser is usually faulty.

IGNITION COIL. If a coil tester is available, condition of coil can be checked. Sometimes, an ignition coil may perform satisfactorily when cold but fail after engine has run for some time and coil is hot. Check coil when hot if this condition is indicated.

MAGNETO AIR GAP. To fully concentrate the magnetic field of the flywheel, magnets pass as closely to the armature core as possible without danger of metal-to-metal contact. The clearance between the flywheel magnets and the legs of the armature core is called the armature air gap.

On magnetos where the armature and high tension coil are located outside of the flywheel rim, adjustment of the armature air gap is made as follows: Turn the engine so the flywheel magnets are located directly under the legs of the armature core and check the clearance between the armature core and flywheel magnets. If the measured clearance is not within manufacturer's specifications, loosen the armature mounting screws and place shims at thickness equal to minumum air gap specification between the magnets and armature core. The magnets will pull the armature core against the shim stock. Tighten the armature core mounting screws, remove the shim stock and turn the engine through several revolutions to be sure the flywheel does not contact the armature core.

Where the armature core is located under or behind the flywheel, the following methods may be used to check and adjust armature air gap: On some engines, slots or openings are provided in the flywheel through which the armature air gap can be checked. Some engine manufacturers provide a cutaway flywheel or a positioning ring that can be used to correctly set the armature air gap.

Another method of checking the armature air gap is to remove the flywheel and place a layer of plastic tape equal to the minimum specified air gap over the legs of the armature core. Reinstall flywheel and turn engine through several revolutions and remove flywheel; no evidence of contact between the flywheel magnets and plastic tape should be noticed. Then cover the legs of the armature core with a layer of tape of thickness equal to the maximum specified air gap, then reinstall flywheel and turn engine through several revolutions. Indication of the flywheel magnets contacting the plastic tape should be noticed after the flywheel is again removed. If the magnets contact the first thin layer of tape applied to the armature core legs, or if they do not contact the second thicker layer of tape, armature air gap is not within specifications and should be adjusted.

NOTE: Before loosening armature core mounting screws, inscribe a mark on mounting plate against edge of armature core so adjustment of air gap can be gauged.

MAGNETO EDGE GAP. The point of maximum acceleration of the movement of the flywheel magnetic field through the high tension coil (and therefore, the point of maximum current induced in the primary coil windings) occurs when the trailing edge of the flywheel magnet is slightly past the left hand leg of the armature core. The exact point of maximum primary current is determined by using electrical measuring devices, the distance between the trailing edge of the flywheel magnet and the leg of the armature core at this point is measured and becomes a service specification. This distance, which is stated either in thousandths of an inch or in degrees of flywheel rotation, is called the Edge Gap or "E" Gap.

For maximum strength of the ignition spark, the breaker points should just start to open when the flywheel magnets are at the specified edge gap position. Usually, edge gap is nonadjustable and will be maintained at the proper dimension if the contact breaker points are adjusted to the recommended gap and the correct breaker cam is installed. However, magneto edge gap can change (and spark intensity thereby reduced) due to the following:

a. Flywheel drive key sheared.
b. Flywheel drive key worn (loose).
c. Keyway in flywheel or crankshaft worn (oversized).
d. Loose flywheel retaining nut which can also cause any above listed difficulty.
e. Excessive wear on breaker cam.
f. Breaker cam loose or improperly installed on crankshaft.
g. Excessive wear on breaker point rubbing block so points cannot be properly adjusted.

COOLING SYSTEM

When cooling system problems are suspected, first check the water inlet for partial or complete stoppage. If water inlet is clear, refer to the appropriate section and check condition of pump, water passages, gaskets, sealing surfaces and thermostat (if so equipped).

The following conditions can cause motor to overheat with cooling system operating properly.

1. Incorrect type of oil or incorrect fuel-oil ratio.
2. Fuel mixture too lean.
3. Clogged exhaust or exhaust leaking into cooling system.
4. Incorrect ignition timing.
5. Throttle not correctly synchronized to ignition advance.

6. Motor overloaded.
7. Incorrect propeller.
8. Missing or bent shields, fins or blower housing. (On air cooled models, never attempt to run engine without all shields in place).

Various types of temperature indicating devices (including heat sensitive sticks or crayons) are available for checking the operating temperature.

WATER PUMP. Most motors use a rubber impeller type water pump. Refer to Fig. 2-13. At slow engine speed, the impeller blades follow the contour of the offset housing as shown by the solid lines. With this type pump, the impeller blades may be damaged (or completely broken off) if turned in opposite direction of normal rotation. If impeller is damaged, all water passages should be cleaned. Some water passages may be blocked and result in overheating of the blocked area.

GENERATING SYSTEMS

Refer to the individual motor section for explanation of generating system used. Some motors use a combined starter-generator unit, others use combined flywheel alternator – flywheel magneto and others use a belt driven, automotive type generator.

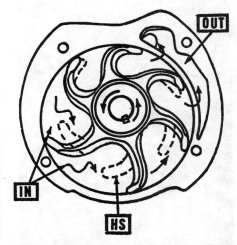

Fig. 2-13—Drawing of impeller type pump. Water is drawn into pump (IN) as area between vanes increases and is forced into power head (OUT) as area decreases. At high speeds the blades remain curved as shown by the broken lines (HS) and pump operates mostly by centrifugal action. Blades may be broken or damaged if turned in reverse of normal direction of rotation.

GENERAL REPAIRS

Because of the close tolerance of the interior parts, cleanliness is of utmost importance. It is suggested that the exterior of the motor and all nearby areas be absolutely clean before any repair is started. Manufacturer's recommended torque values for tightening screw fasteners should be followed closely. The soft threads in aluminum castings are often damaged by carelessness in overtightening fasteners or in attempting to loosen or remove seized fasteners.

Commonly recommended tightening torques, for common screw sizes, are listed below. These recommendations should be followed if specific recommendations are not given in the individual service sections.

SCREW SIZE	TORQUE
#4	4-6 in.-lbs.
	(0.5-0.7 N·m)
#6	8-11 in.-lbs.
	(0.9-1.2 N·m)
#8	15-20 in.-lbs.
	(1.7-2.3 N·m)
#10	25-35 in.-lbs.
	(2.8-3.9 N·m)
#12	35-40 in.-lbs.
	(3.9-4.5 N·m)
¼ inch	60-80 in.-lbs.
	(6.8-9 N·m)
5/16 inch	120-140 in.-lbs.
	(13.5-15.8 N·m)
3/8 inch	220-240 in.-lbs.
	(24.8-27.1 N·m)
7/16, ½ inch	340-360 in.-lbs.
	(38.4-40.7 N·m)

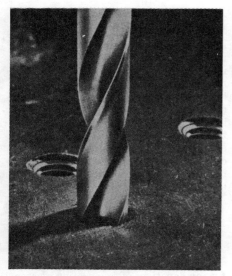

Fig. 2-14—First step in repairing damaged threads is to drill out old threads using exact size drill recommended in instructions provided with thread repair kit. Drill all the way through an open hole or all the way to bottom of blind hole, making sure hole is straight and that centerline of hole is not moved in drilling process. (Series of photos provided by Heli-Coil Corp., Danbury, Conn.)

Aluminum offers unusual resistance to oxidation. This factor combined with the necessary lightness, makes it an ideal construction material for outboard motors. Aluminum is a relatively soft material, however, and cannot be used for all applications. Shafts, gears, bearings and fasteners (such as bolts, nuts, etc.) must be made of steel or other more rugged material. The presence of dissimilar metals brings the additional danger of destruction or seizure of parts due to galvanic action. The dangers are not insurmountable, but must be recognized and kept constantly in mind when performing service on any motor. Remain doubly alert when servicing motors used in salt water. This problem is carefully considered by the manufacturer when selecting materials for construction. Substitution of bolts, nuts or small components other than those recommended by manufacturer is to be avoided whenever possible. Protective or insulating coatings of sealants, paint, and waterproof grease should be used in assembly wherever possible to prevent corrosion or seizure, and to facilitate future disassembly. If the entrance of air and water can be completely eliminated, dangers are much lessened. Outer surfaces of the aluminum castings are probably anodized, which offers excellent protection against deterioration or damage. This thin coating is easily damaged, however, and cannot be renewed at shop level. Avoid scratches, abrasion and rough handling as much as possible, and protect with an approved touch-up paint when assembly is completed.

REPAIRING DAMAGED THREADS

Damaged threads in castings can be repaired by use of thread repair kits which are recommended by a number of manufacturers. Use of thread repair kits is not difficult, but instructions must be carefully followed. Refer to Figs. 2-14 through 2-16 which illustrate the use of thread repair kits manufactured by the Heli-Coil Corporation, Danbury, Connecticut.

Heli-Coil thread repair kits are available through the parts departments of most engine and equipment manufacturers. The thread inserts are available in all National Coarse (USS) sizes from number 4 to 1½ inch. National Fine (SAE) sizes from number 6 to 1½ inch and metric sizes 5 MM X 0.9 MM, 6 MM X 1.0 MM, 8 MM X 1.25 MM, 10 MM X 1.50 MM and 12 MM X 1.25 MM. Also, sizes for repairing 14MM and 18MM spark plug ports are available.

Fig. 2-15—Special drill taps are provided which are the correct size for OUTSIDE of the insert. A standard size tap cannot be substituted.

Fig. 2-16—Shown is the insert and a completed repair. Special tools are provided in kit for installation, together with the necessary instructions.

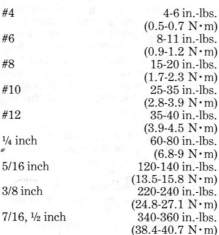

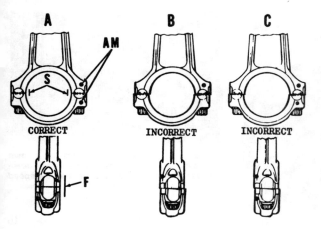

Fig. 2-17—Most connecting rods are provided with marks (AM) which should be aligned as shown in view "A". Bearing surface (S) and sides (F) should be smooth and all machine marks on rod and cap should be perfectly aligned. If cap is reversed as shown in view "B", bearing surface will not be smooth and marks will not be aligned. If incorrect rod cap is installed, machined surfaces will not be smooth even if marks on rod and cap are aligned as shown in view "C".

DISASSEMBLY AND ASSEMBLY

Outboard motors, especially the smaller types, are relatively simple in construction. The larger, more powerful units remain simple in design for the most part, but sometimes offer additional problems in disassembly and assembly.

Two or more identical pistons, rings, connecting rods and bearings may be used in a motor, but parts should never be interchanged when reassembling. As parts are removed, they should all be marked to identify the correct position. All wearing parts seat to the mating parts during operation. If parts are mixed during reassembly, a new wear pattern is established and early failure may result. Connecting rods are made with the cap and only this one cap will fit the rod perfectly. Refer to Fig. 2-17. If the original cap is incorrectly installed (as shown in view "B"–Fig. 2-17) or if another rod cap is installed (View "C"–Fig. 2-17), the bearing surface will not be smooth and true. Most connecting rods have raised marks (AM) on rod and cap to facilitate reassembly. Some manufacturers machine the rod as one piece and fracture (break) the cap away. The broken joint will fit together perfectly only when correctly installed.

A given amount of heat applied to aluminum will cause it to expand a greater amount than will steel under similar conditions. Because of the different expansion characteristics, heat is usually recommended for easy installation of bearings, pins, etc., in aluminum or magnesium castings. Sometimes, heat can be used to free parts that are seized or where an interference fit is used. Heat, therefore, becomes a service tool and the application of heat, one of the required service techniques. An open flame is not usually advised because it destroys the paint and other protective coatings and because a uniform and controlled temperature with open flame is difficult to obtain. Methods commonly

used for heating are: 1. In oil or water, 2. With a heat lamp, 3. Electric hot plate, 4. In an oven or kiln. See Fig. 2-18. The use of hot water or oil gives a fairly accurate temperature control but is somewhat limited as to the size and type of part that can be handled. Thermal crayons are available which can be used to determine the temperature of a heated part. These crayons melt when the part reaches specified temperature, and a number of crayons for different temperatures are available. Temperature indicating crayons are usually available at welding equipment supply houses.

The crankcase and inlet manifold must be completely sealed against both vacuum and pressure. Exhaust manifold and cylinder head must be sealed against water leakage and pressure. Mating surfaces of water inlet, and exhaust areas between power head and lower unit must form a tight seal.

When disassembled, it is recommended that all gasket surfaces, and mating surfaces without gaskets, be carefully checked for nicks, burrs and warped surfaces which might interfere with a tight seal. The cylinder head, cylinder head cover, head end of

cylinder block, and some mating surfaces of manifolds and crankcase may be checked, and lapped if necessary, to provide a smooth surface. Flat surfaces can be lapped by using a surface plate or a smooth piece of plate glass, and a sheet of fine sandpaper or lapping compound. Use a figure-eight motion with minimum pressure, and remove only enough metal to eliminate the imperfection. Finish lap using lapping compound or worn emery cloth. Thoroughly clean the parts with new oil on a clean, soft rag, then wash with soapsuds and clean rags.

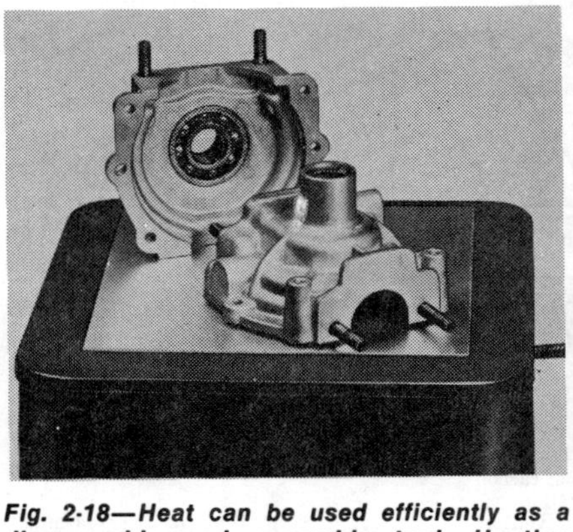

Mating surfaces of crankcase halves may be checked on the lapping block, and high spots or nicks removed, but surface must not be lowered. Bearing clearances must not be lessened by removing metal from the joint. If extreme care is used, a slightly damaged crankcase may be salvaged in this manner.

Gaskets and sealing surfaces should be lighly and carefully coated with an approved gasket cement or sealing compound unless the contrary is stated. Make sure entire surface is coated, but avoid letting excesss cement squeeze out into crankcase, bearings or other passages.

PISTON, RINGS, PIN AND CYLINDER

When servicing pistons, rings and cylinders, it is important that all recommended tolerances be closely observed. Parts that are damaged should be carefully examined to determine the cause. A scored piston as shown in Fig. 2-19 is obviously not a result of normal wear and if the cause is not corrected, new parts may be similarly damaged in a short time. Piston scoring can be caused by overheating, improper fuel:oil mixture, carburetor out of adjustment, in-

Fig. 2-18—Heat can be used efficiently as a disassembly and assembly tool. Heating crankcase halves on electric hot plate (above) will allow bearings to be easily removed.

Fig. 2-19—If parts are excessively damaged, cause should be determined and corrected before returning motor to service.

Fig. 2-20—Gap between ends of ring should be within recommended limits.

Fig. 2-22—Ring side clearance in groove should be measured with gage as shown. Clearance should be within recommended limits and the same all the way around piston.

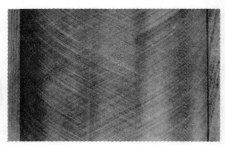

Fig. 2-23—A cross-hatch pattern as shown should be obtained by moving hone up and down cylinder bore as it is being turned by slow speed electric drill.

correct ignition timing and/or speed control linkage not correctly adjusted.

Before installing new piston rings, check ring end gap as follows: Position the ring near the top of cylinder bore. The bottom of piston (skirt) should be used to slide the ring in cylinder to locate ring squarely in bore. Measure the gap between end of ring using a feeler gage as shown in Fig. 2-20. Slide the ring down in the cylinder to the area of transfer and exhaust ports and again measure gap. Rings may break if end gap is too tight at any point; but, will not seal properly if gap is too wide. Variation in gap indicates cylinder wear (usually near the ports).

Ring grooves in the piston should be carefully cleaned and examined. Use caution when cleaning to prevent damage to piston. Carelessness can result in poor motor performance and possibly extensive internal engine damage. Refer to Fig. 2-21. When installing rings on piston, expand only far enough to slip over the piston and **do not twist rings.** After installing rings on piston, use feeler gage to measure ring side clearance in groove as shown in Fig. 2-22. Excessive side clearance will prevent an effective seal and may cause rings to break.

Cylinder bore should be honed to remove glaze from cylinder walls before installing new piston rings. Ridge at top and bottom of ring travel should be removed by honing. If ridge is not removed, new rings may catch enough to bend the ring lands as shown at (G–Fig. 2-21). The finished cylinder should have light cross-hatched pattern as shown in Fig. 2-23. After honing, wash cylinder assembly with soap and water to remove all traces of abrasive. After cylinder is dry, swab cylinder bore with oil making sure that it is absolutely clean.

Some manufacturers have oversize piston and ring sets available for use in repairing engines in which the cylinder bore is excessively worn and standard size piston and rings cannnot be used. If care and approved procedures are used in oversizing the cylinder bore, installation of an oversize piston and ring set should result in a highly satisfactory overhaul.

The cylinder bore may be oversized by using either a boring bar or a hone; however, if a boring bar is used it is usually recommended the cylinder bore be finished with a hone. Refer to Fig. 2-23. Before attempting to rebore or

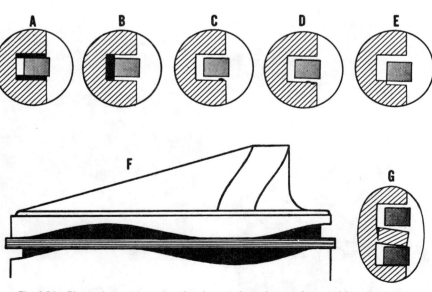

Fig. 2-21—Piston ring grooves must be clean and not damaged to provide a good seal.

A. Carbon on sides of groove may cause ring to stick in groove.
B. Carbon on bottom (back) of groove may prevent rings from compressing.
C. Small pieces of carbon & (C) or nicks (D) in
D. groove will prevent a good seal.
E. If groove is worn as shown, renew the piston.
F. If groove is not straight, renew piston.
G. Renew piston if ring land is bent.

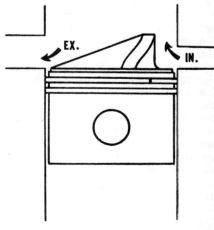

Fig. 2-24—Deflector type piston must be installed with long sloping side toward exhaust port and inlet deflector on transfer port side.

hone the cylinder to oversize, carefully measure the cylinder bore to be sure that new, standard size piston and rings will not fit within tolerance. Also, it may be possible that the cylinder is excessively worn or damaged and that reboring or honing to largest oversize will not clean up the worn or scored surface.

When assembling piston to connecting rod, observe special precautions outlined in the individual motor sections. Deflector type pistons must be installed with long sloping side toward exhaust port and the inlet deflector toward the transfer ports as shown in Fig. 2-24. If connecting rod has an oil hole at piston pin or crankpin end, hole should be toward top of motor. If piston pin has one closed end, it is normally installed toward exhaust port side of piston.

CONNECTING ROD, CRANKSHAFT AND BEARINGS

Before detaching connecting rods from crankshaft, mark rods and caps for correct assembly to each other and to proper cylinder. Most damage to ball and roller bearings is evident after visual inspection and turning the assembled bearing by hand. If bearing shows evidence of overheating, renew the complete assembly. On models with plain (bushing) bearings, check the crankpin and main bearing journals for wear with a micrometer. Crankshaft journals will usually wear out-of-round with most wear on side that takes the force of power stroke (strokes). If main bearing clearances are excessive, new crankcase seals may not be able to prevent pressure from blowing fuel and oil around crankshaft. All crankcase seals should be renewed when crankshaft, connecting rods and bearings are serviced.

SUBMERGED MOTOR

Almost all motors except small fishing motors are equipped for bolting to the transom. If motor is securely fastened by bolting, water damage cannot occur unless boat is swamped, overturned, or sunk. A safety chain will assist in the recovery of a small motor which vibrates loose and falls overboard. The same arrangement on a large motor could be dangerous, as the transom could be knocked out of boat by a wild motor.

There is a danger from two types of damage when a motor has been submerged. If motor was running when dropped, mechanical damage can result from the inability of water to compress. If mechanical damage is avoided, corrosive action can start almost immediately, especially in salt water.

Problems may develop if motor is dropped overboard.

Corrosion damage is most apt to occur after the motor has been removed from the water as corrosive action is greatest in the presence of heat and oxygen. In case of mechanical damage or for salt water submersion even where no actual damage exists, complete disassembly of the power head is indicated. In addition to the necessary hand tools, fresh water under pressure, and alcohol and oil should be available. Proper care of a submerged motor, therefore, usually indicates that the motor be brought in to a suitable shop for service. If considerable time must elapse before service can be performed, it is best to keep motor submerged in fresh water, adding ice, if available, to keep the water cool. If fresh water is not available, motor is better off submerged in salt water than brought out to air dry.

If an attempt is to be made to run the motor without disassembly, remove the cowling and rinse off any silt or sand. Remove the spark plugs, carburetor and reed valve, if possible; then turn motor over slowly with starter to pump any water out of power head. Blow water from the magneto, spark plugs and wiring. Pour or spray alcohol into the crankcase and cylinders, trying to cover

as many of the metal surfaces as possible. the alcohol will combine with the water remaining in the engine, allowing it to be removed by flushing out, and later by evaporation. Disassemble and clean the carburetor, fuel pump, fuel lines and tank and refill with a fresh fuel:oil mixture. If a spray gun is available, spray a new coating of oil in the crankcases and spark plug holes. After motor is reassembled, it should start if magneto coils are not shorted out by moisture. Do not dry magneto parts in an oven. Excess heat will damage insulation. Check for silt in cooling system inlet before attempting to start the motor. If motor is started, it should be run for at least thirty minutes after it is warm, to give the remaining drops of water an opportunity to evaporate and disappear. The most likely points of corrosion damage are the main bearings and crankshaft journals, especially the lower one, as water drains into these parts and cannot be drained out or thrown out by centrifugal force. Even one drop of water can cause etching of the crankshaft or needle roller which will cause noise and early failure if bearings are of this type.

If silt or sand is present, in cases of salt water submersion, or where mechanical damage exists, the motor should be disassembled and cleaned. The corrosion factors of salt water or the presence of silt will cause early failure and are almost impossible to remove by flushing.

If the motor is to be disassembled, speed is essential, and the motor should be protected as much as possible from corrosion until disassembly is begun. Submersion in some type of liquid will inhibit corrosion temporarily. If several hours must elapse before disassembly can be started, keeping the parts submerged may limit the damage. In the case of large motors where complete submersion would be difficult, remove power head from lower unit and submerge the power head only. Remove the electrical units if tools are available. Alcohol offers the best protection if available. There is no special advantage of oil over fresh water if disassembly is to take place within 24 hours, and it most certainly should.

When motor is disassembled, scrub the parts thoroughly in hot, soapy water and air dry, then immerse in oil or spray with an oil mist until parts are completely coated. Ball or roller bearings which cannot be disassembled for cleaning should be renewed if their condition is at all questionable. It is very difficult to be sure that all traces of silt are removed from such bearings, and renewal at this time is usually cheaper than risking early failure.

CHRYSLER

US MARINE CORP.
105 Marine Drive
Hartford, Wisconsin 53027

CHRYSLER 30 AND 35 HP

30 HP Models

Year Produced	Model
1973, 1974	302HA, 302BA, 303HA, 303BA, 304HA, 304BA, 305HA, 305BA
1975	302HB, 302BB, 303HB, 303BB, 304HB, 304BB, 305HB, 305BB, 306HA, 306BA, 307HA, 307BA
1979	302H9C, 302B9C, 303H9C, 303B9C, 306H9B, 306B9B, 307H9B, 307B9B
1980	306H0C, 305B0C, 307H0C, 307B0C
1981	307H1D, 307B1D
1982	307H2E, 307B2E

35 HP Models

Year Produced	Mode
1976, 1977	350HK, 350BK, 351HK, 351BK 356HK, 356BK, 357HK, 357BK
1978	350H8L, 350B8L, 351H8L, 351B8L 356H8M, 356B8M, 357H8M, 357B8M
1983	357H3N, 357B3N, 357R3N
1984	357H4, 357B4

CONDENSED SERVICE DATA

TUNE-UP	30 HP (Prior to 1976)	30 HP (After 1978)	35 HP
Hp/rpm	30/5000	30/4750	35/5000
Bore – Inches	2.8125	3.00	3.00
Stroke – Inches	2.414	2.414	2.414
Number of Cylinders	2	2	2
Displacement – Cu. In.	29.99	34.10	34.10
Compression at Cranking Speed (Average)	125-135 psi	125-135 psi	120-130 psi
Spark Plug:			
Champion	L4J	L4J	L4J
Electrode Gap – Inches	0.030	0.030	0.030
Magneto:			
Point Gap – Inches	†0.020	See text	†0.020
Timing	See text	See text	See text
Carburetor:			
Make	Tillotson	Tillotson	Tillotson
Model	WB	WB	WB
Fuel:Oil Ratio	**50:1	**50:1	**50:1

†Breaker point gap is 0.015 inch for models 306HA, 306BA, 307HA, 307BA, 356HK, 356BK, 357HK and 357BK. Models 356H8M, 356B8M, 357H8M and 357B8M are equipped with a breakerless ignition system.
**Fuel:oil ratio should be 25:1 for break-in period.

SIZES – CLEARANCES	30 HP (Prior to 1976)	30 HP (After 1978)	35 HP
Piston Ring End Gap:			
Top Ring		0.006-0.016 in.	
Bottom Ring		0.004-0.014 in.	
Piston to Cylinder Clearance		0.0060-0.0095 in.	
Piston Pin Diameter		0.50000-0.50015 in.	
Crankshaft Journal Diameters:			
Upper Main		1.3774-1.3780 in.	
Center Main		1.3446-1.3451 in.	
Lower Main		0.9849-0.9853 in.	
Crankpin		1.1391-1.1395 in.	

TIGHTENING TORQUES (All Values in Inch-Pounds)	30 HP (Prior to 1976)	30 HP (After 1978)	35 HP
Cylinder Head	225	190	225
Flywheel Nut	540	720	540
Spark Plug	120-180	120-180	120-180
Connecting Rod Screws	165-175	180-190	165-175
No. 10-24	30	30	30
No. 10-32	35	35	35
No. 12-24	45	45	45
¼-20	70	70	70
5/16-18	160	160	160
⅜-16	270	270	270

LUBRICATION

The power head is lubricated by oil mixed with the fuel. For normal service after break-in, mix 1/6 pint of two-stroke engine oil with each gallon of gasoline. The recommended ratio is one third (⅓) pint of oil per gallon of gasoline for severe service and during break-in. Manufacturer recommends no-lead automotive gasoline although regular or premium gasoline may be used if octane rating is 85 or higher. Gasoline and oil should be thoroughly mixed.

The lower unit gears and bearings are lubricated by oil contained in the gearcase. Only non-corrosive, leaded, EP90, outboard gear oil such as "Chrysler Outboard Gear Lube" should be used. The gearcase should be drained and refilled every 30 hours. Maintain fluid at level of upper (vent) plug.

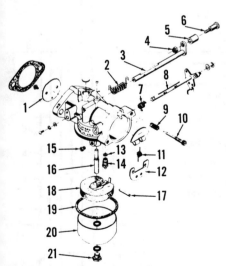

Fig. C7-1—Exploded view of typical Tillotson model WB carburetor.

1. Throttle plate	12. Choke plate
2. Spring	13. Gasket
3. Throttle shaft	14. Fuel inlet valve
4. Nut	15. High speed jet
5. Roller	16. Main nozzle
6. Eccentric screw	17. Float pin
7. Spring	18. Float
8. Choke shaft	19. Gasket
9. Spring	20. Float bowl
10. Idle mixture screw	21. Bowl retaining screw
11. Spring	

To fill gearcase, have motor in upright position and fill through lower hole in side of gearcase until fluid reaches level of upper vent plug hole. Reinstall and tighten both plugs securely, using new gaskets if necessary, to assure a water tight seal.

FUEL SYSTEM

CARBURETOR. A Tillotson WB type carburetor is used on all models. Refer to Fig. C7-1 for an exploded view of the carburetor.

Initial setting of idle mixture screw (10 – Fig. C7-1) is 1¼ turns out from a lightly seated position. Final adjustment of carburetor should be made with engine at normal operating temperature and with outboard in forward gear. Standard main jet size is 0.068 inch on 30 hp motors prior to 1979 and 0.064 inch on 30 hp motors after 1978. Standard main jet on 35 hp motors is 0.066 inch. Standard main jet sizes should be correct for operation below 1250 ft. altitude.

To check float level, remove float bowl and invert carburetor. Side of float nearest main jet should be parallel with gasket surface of carburetor. Adjust float level by bending float tang.

Install throttle plate (1 – Fig. C7-1) so that notch is up and chamfer is towards flange end of carburetor.

SPEED CONTROL LINKAGE. Ignition timing and throttle opening on all models must be synchronized so that throttle is opened as timing is advanced.

To synchronize linkage, first check ignition timing to be sure it is set correctly as outlined in IGNITION TIMING section. Disconnect link (L – Fig. C7-2) from magneto control lever and with throttle closed, turn eccentric screw (S) until roller (R) is exactly centered over mark (M) on throttle cam (C). Reconnect link (L) to magneto contol lever and rotate magneto stator ring until it is against full advance stop. Upper mark (AM) on throttle cam should now be aligned with

roller (R). Disconnect link (L) and turn link ends to adjust length of link so that mark (AM) and roller are aligned when stator is at full advance. Turn throttle stop screw in steering handle shaft on models with manual starter so that screw provides a positive stop just as stator plate reaches full advance stop.

Idle speed in forward gear should be 550-650 rpm on manual start models. Adjust idle of manual start models by turning idle speed screw on side of steering handle. Idle speed in forward gear should be 650-750 rpm on electric start models. Adjust idle speed of electric start models by turning idle speed screw (I – Fig. C7-3) adjacent to exhaust port covers.

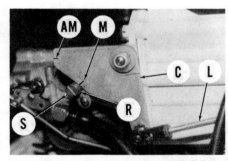

Fig. C7-2—View of throttle cam and linkage. Refer to text for adjustment.

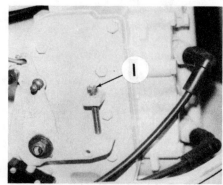

Fig. C7-3—View of idle speed screw (I) used on models with electric starter. Idle speed should be 650-750 rpm with unit in forward gear.

REED VALVES. All models are equipped with a "V" type reed valve. The reed plate is located between the intake manifold and crankcase. Remove carburetor and intake manifold for access to reed valve.

Renew reeds if petals are broken, cracked, warped or bent. Never attempt to bend a reed petal in an effort to improve performance, nor attempt to straighten a damaged reed. Never install a bent or damaged reed. Seating surface of reed plate should be smooth and flat. Install reeds so that petals are centered over openings. Assembled reeds may stand open to a maximum of 0.010 inch at tip end. Reed stop setting should be 9/32 inch when measured from tip of reed stop to reed plate.

PUDDLE DRAIN VALVE. Models prior to 1981 are equipped with a puddle drain valve located in the hose from the bottom of the crankcase cover to the bottom of the transfer port cover. The puddle valve is designed to remove puddled fuel from the crankcase, thus providing smooth operation at all speeds and lessening the possibility of spark plug fouling.

To check operation of puddle valve, disconnect hose ends and blow through each end of hose. Puddle valve should pass air when blowing through crank-

case cover end of hose but not when blowing through transfer port end of hose. Remove puddle valve from hose if it does not operate correctly. Install new puddle valve in hose approximately one inch from end of hose with small hole in puddle valve towards short end of hose. Attach hose to engine with puddle valve end of hose connected to crankcase cover.

FUEL PUMP. All models are equipped with a two-stage diaphragm type fuel pump which is actuated by pressure and vacuum pulsations from the engine crankcases.

NOTE: Either stage of the fuel pump operating independently may permit the motor to run, but not at peak performance.

To remove fuel pump, disconnedt fuel hoses to pump and unscrew six cap screws which retain fuel pump body. Check valves are renewable but be sure a new check valve is needed before removing old check valve as it will be damaged during removal. Unscrew the two retaining screws to remove center check valve. The two outer check valves must be driven out from below. Refer to Fig. C7-5 for view of correct check valve installation. Install check valves care-

Fig. C7-4—Exploded view of reed valve assembly.

1. Inlet manifold
2. Gasket
3. Adapter plate
4. Gasket
5. Reed body
6. Reed petals
7. Reed stop

Fig. C7-5—Fuel pump check valves must be installed as shown for proper operation of fuel pump.

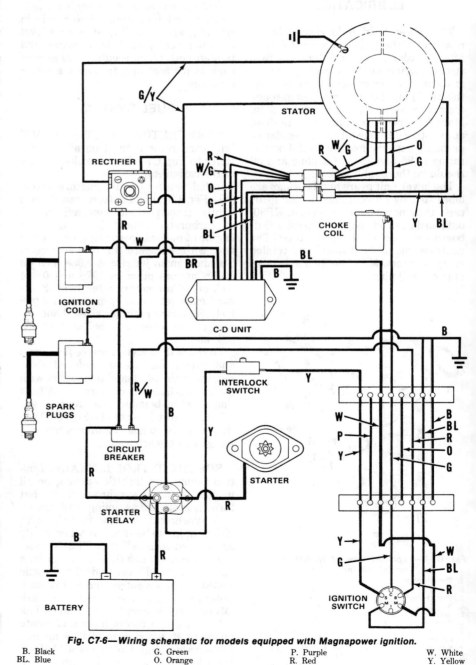

Fig. C7-6—Wiring schematic for models equipped with Magnapower ignition.

B. Black	G. Green	P. Purple	W. White
BL. Blue	O. Orange	R. Red	Y. Yellow

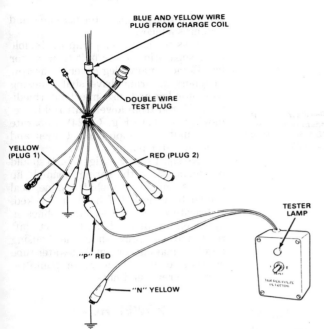

BLUE AND YELLOW WIRE
PLUG FROM CHARGE COIL

DOUBLE WIRE
TEST PLUG

YELLOW
(PLUG 1)

RED (PLUG 2)

"P" RED

"N" YELLOW

TESTER
LAMP

Fig. C7-7—Tester connections for checking low voltage output of charge coils.

ground and attaching it to red (P) lead of T8953 tester as shown in Fig. C7-8. Attach yellow (N) lead of T8953 tester to engine ground. Turn tester switch to position 10 and crank engine. If tester lamp does not light, high voltage windings of charge coil are defective and stator should be renewed. If lamp lights, charge coil operation is satisfactory and trigger coil and CD ignition module circuits for each cylinder must be checked. Remove tester and plug adapter set, then reconnect blue and yellow wire plugs.

Separate the four-wire connection between CD ignition module and trigger coil and attach four wire plug adapter to wire plug from trigger coil as shown in Fig. C7-9. Attach red (P) lead from tester number 22 to red sleeved adapter wire marked "Trigger 1 Pos." and yellow (N) lead to yellow sleeved adapter wire marked "Trigger 1 Neg." Place switch of tester in number 1 position and crank engine. Trigger coil operation is satisfactory if tester lamp lights. Renew trigger housing if tester lamp does not light.

To check operation of number 2 cylinder trigger coil, repeat test procedure for number 1 cylinder trigger coil

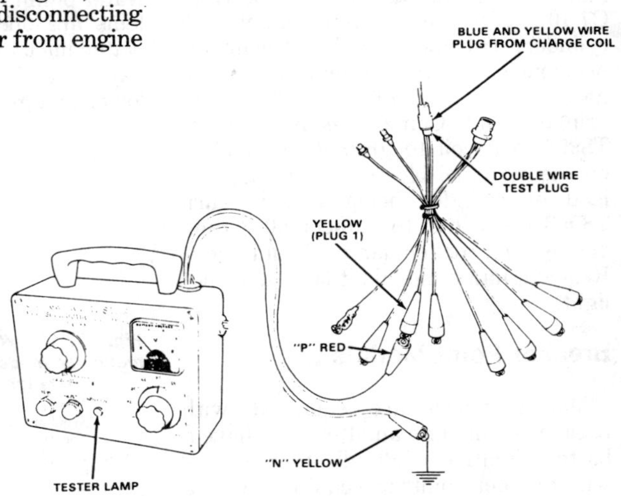

IGNITION

Magnapower Models

These models are equipped with a breakerless, capacitor discharge ignition system. Note wiring diagram in Fig.C7-6. Tapered bore of flywheel and crankshaft end must be clean, dry and smooth before installing flywheel. Renew a chipped or cracked flywheel. Flywheel and crankshaft tapers may be cleaned by using fine valve grinding compound. Apply grinding compound to tapers and rotate flywheel back and forth approximately one quarter turn. Do not spin flywheel on crankshaft. Clean flywheel and crankshaft tapers throughly. Tighten flywheel nut to 45 ft.-lbs. torque.

If ignition malfunction occurs, use Chrysler tool T8953, plug adapter set T11201 and number 22 tester with load coil from tool T8996 and refer to following troubleshooting procedure:

Check and make sure ignition malfunction is not due to spark plug or ignition coil failure. If spark is absent at both cylinders, check condition of charge coil as follows: Separate the blue and yellow wire connection between charge coil and CD ignition module and attach double wire plug adapter to wire plug from charge coil as shown in Fig. C7-7. Attach red (P) lead from tester number 22 to red sleeved adapter wire marked "Plug 2." Attach yellow (N) lead of number 22 tester and yellow sleeved adapter wire marked "Plug 1" to engine

fully to prevent damage. Inspect diaphragm and renew diaphragm if cracked, torn or badly distorted.

ground. Place tester switch in number 2 position and crank engine. If tester lamp does not light, low voltage windings of charge coil are defective and stator should be renewed. If lamp lights, continue charge coil test by disconnecting yellow sleeved wire adapter from engine

Fig. C7-8—Tester connections for checking high voltage output of charge coils.

TESTER LAMP

BLUE AND YELLOW WIRE
PLUG FROM CHARGE COIL

DOUBLE WIRE
TEST PLUG

YELLOW
(PLUG 1)

"P" RED

"N" YELLOW

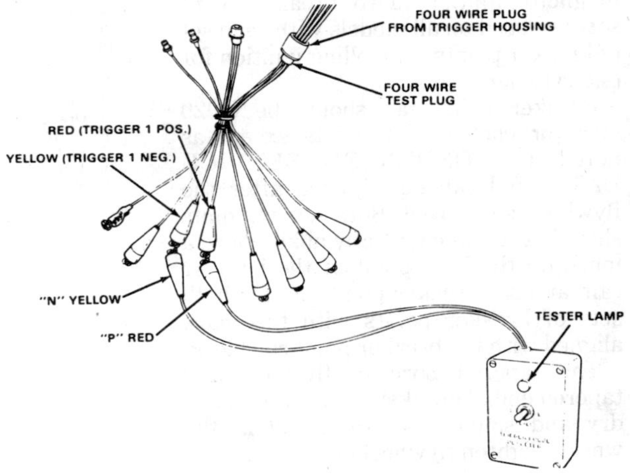

Fig. C7-9—Tester connections for checking operation of trigger coil.

FOUR WIRE PLUG
FROM TRIGGER HOUSING

FOUR WIRE
TEST PLUG

RED (TRIGGER 1 POS.)

YELLOW (TRIGGER 1 NEG.)

"N" YELLOW

"P" RED

TESTER LAMP

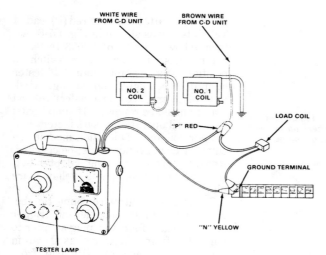

WHITE WIRE FROM C-D UNIT

BROWN WIRE FROM C-D UNIT

NO. 2 COIL

NO. 1 COIL

LOAD COIL

"P" RED

GROUND TERMINAL

"N" YELLOW

TESTER LAMP

Fig. C7-10—View showing tester connections needed to check CD ignition module output.

tion of water pump, water passages and sealing surfaces.

Access to the water pump is possible after separating lower unit from motor leg. Remove motor leg covers. Unscrew fasteners securing drive shaft housing to motor leg and disconnect intermediate shift rod from lower shift rod by removing pin (11 – Fig. C7-24). Separate lower unit from motor leg. Unbolt and remove water pump.

Drive shaft seal (3 – Fig. C7-24) should be installed with spring loaded lip towards top. Drive shaft spline seal should be renewed if hard or cracked. Lubricate water tube seal and splines on upper end of drive shaft. Connect shift rods and carefully slide the housing together making certain that water tube enters seal. Install the water pump retaining screws and nuts.

but connect red (P) lead of tester to red sleeved adapter wire marked "Trigger 2 Pos." and yellow (N) lead to yellow sleeved adapter wire marked "Trigger 2 Neg."

To check ignition module performance for each cylinder, connect yellow (N) lead from tester T8953 to ground terminal of engine terminal block (Fig. C7-10). Disconnect white (number 2 cylinder) or brown (number 1 cylinder) primary lead from ignition coil and connect red (P) lead of tester T8953 to primary lead. Connect leads of tester T8996 load coil to ground terminal of engine terminal block and primary coil lead of cylinder being tested. Turn T8953 tester dial to number 50. Crank engine and tester lamp should light. Renew ignition module if lamp does not light.

Breaker Point Models

Motors which are equipped with breaker points and an alternator have a battery ignition while all other motors with breaker points are equipped with a magneto ignition. Two breaker point sets are used on all models with each set of breaker points controlling ignition for one cylinder.

Breaker point gap should be 0.020 inch for each set of points except as noted in CONDENSED SERVICE DATA, and can be adjusted after the flywheel is removed. Both sets of points should be adjusted exactly alike. Place a mark on the high point of the breaker cam and set breaker point gap for both sets of breaker points with the mark aligned with the breaker point rub block.

The tapered bore in flywheel and tapered end of crankshaft must be clean, dry and smooth before installing flywheel. Tighten flywheel nut to 45 ft.-lbs.

Spark plug electrode gap on all models should be 0.030 inch. Recommended spark plug is Champion L4J.

COOLING SYSTEM

WATER PUMP. All motors are equipped with a rubber impeller type water pump. When cooling system problems are encountered, first check the water inlet for plugging or partial stoppage, then if not corrected, remove the lower unit gearcase and check the condi-

POWER HEAD

R&R AND OVERHAUL. To remove the power head, mount the outboard motor on a stand and remove the engine cove. Disconnect choke rod from carburetor. Detach magneto control shaft gear (13 – Fig. C7-13) from magneto control shaft (13 – Fig. C7-14) on manual start models. Remove bushing (12) and detach magneto control shaft from control shaft link (31 – Fig. C7-17). Loosen set screw in collar (3 – Fig. C7-14) and

Fig. C7-11—Wiring schematic for models with battery ignition.

1. Alternator
2. Breaker plate
3. Neutral interlock switch
4. Top ignition coil
5. Bottom ignition coil
6. Starter relay
7. Choke solenoid
8. Circuit breaker
9. Electric starter motor
10. Rectifier
B. Black
BL. Blue
G. Green
O. Orange
P. Purple
R. Red
W. White
Y. Yellow

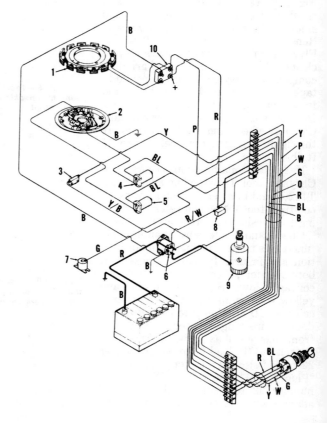

Illustrations courtesy Chrysler

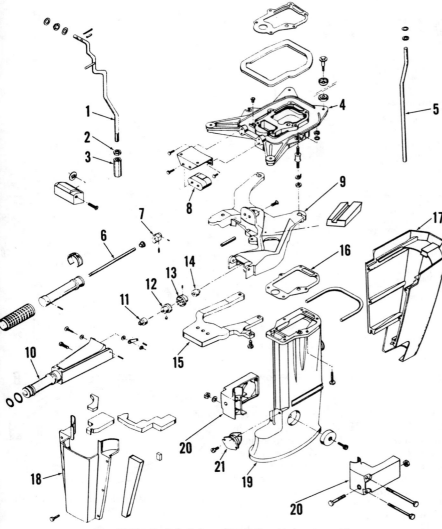

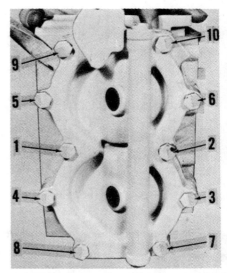

Fig. C7-15—Cylinder head cap screws should be tightened in the sequence shown above.

Fig. C7-13—Exploded view of typical motor leg assembly.

1. Uppper shift rod	9. Kingpin plate	16. Exhaust gasket
2. Locknut	10. Steering handle	17. Rear motor leg cover
3. Coupler	11. Bushing	18. Front motor leg cover
4. Spacer plate	12. Steering handle gear	19. Motor leg
5. Water tube	13. Magneto control shaft	20. Lower shock mount
6. Steering handle shaft	gear	cover
7. Throttle stop	14. Bushing	21. Lower thrust pad
8. Upper thrust mount	15. Carrying handle	

and remove starter and ignition assemblies from upper end of crankshaft. Unbolt and remove upper bearing cage and cylinder head. Remove reed valve assembly and transfer port cover. Unscrew cylinder to crankcase screws (two screws are in reed cavity) and using a suitable pry point separate cylinder and crankcase. Do not pry at machined mating surfaces between cylinder and crankcase.

Crankshaft, pistons and bearings are now accessible for removal and overhaul as outlined in the appropriate following paragraphs. Assemble as outlined in the ASSEMBLY paragraph.

ASSEMBLY. When reassembling, make sure all joint and gasket surfaces are clean, free from nicks and burrs,

remove gear shift knob and shaft (1) on manual start models. On electric start models, disconnect battery leads, red lead from upper terminal of starter relay and black lead from crankcase. On all models, unscrew nut retaining shift lever (20–Fig. C7-17) and detach gear shift linkage from lever. Remove lower shock mount covers, lower thrust pad (21–Fig. C7-13) at front of motor leg and shock and lower nuts of the two studs between the kingpin plate (9) and spacer plate (4). Unscrew motor leg cover bolts and remove rear motor leg cover. Engage reverse lock and pull motor back enough to allow removal of front motor leg cover. Unscrew power head bolts and remove power head.

To disassemble power head, remove seal in bore of bottom end of crankshaft

Fig. C7-14—Exploded view of manual start model support plate assembly.

1. Gear shift knob & shaft
2. Grommet
3. Collar
4. Set screw
5. Gear shift lever
6. Spacer
7. Bushing
8. Grommet
9. Retainer
10. Set screw
11. Spring
12. Bushing
13. Magneto control shaft
14. Latch pin
15. Choke rod
16. Support plate

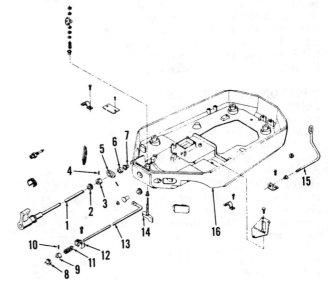

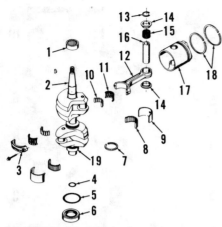

Fig. C7-16—Exploded view of crankshaft assembly.

1. Roller bearing
2. Crankshaft
3. Rod cap
4. Seal
5. "O" ring
6. Seal
7. Seal ring
8. Bearing rollers
9. Bearing liner
10. Bearing rollers
11. Bearing cage
12. Connecting rod
13. Snap ring
14. Spacer
15. Needle bearing
16. Piston pin
17. Piston
18. Piston rings
19. Ball bearing

Fig. C7-17—Exploded view of cylinder block assembly.

1. Seal
2. Bearing cage
3. Gasket
4. Stator ring
5. Crankcase seal
6. Exhaust cover
7. Gasket
8. Exhaust plate
9. Gasket
10. Cylinder block
11. Lower crankcase
12. Dowel pin
13. Thermostat cover
14. Plug
15. Cylinder head
16. Gasket
17. Drain hose
18. Gasket
19. Transfer port cover
20. Gear shift lever
21. Starter interlock rod
22. Bushing retainer
23. Interlock lever pin
24. Bushing
25. Shift interlock lever
26. Shift interlock rod
27. Throttle cam
28. Throttle link
29. Magneto stator link
30. Magneto control lever
31. Magneto control link

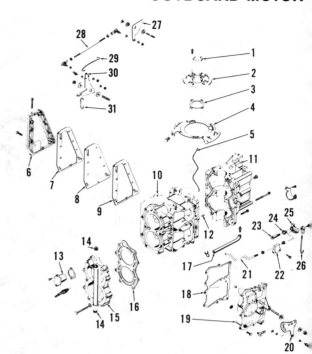

warped surfaces or hardened cement or carbon. The crankcase and inlet manifold must be completely sealed against both vacuum and pressure. Exhaust manifold and cylinder head must be sealed against both vacuum and pressure. Exhaust manifold and cylinder head must be sealed against water leakage and pressure. Mating surfaces of exhaust areas between power head and motor leg must form a tight seal.

Sparingly apply a coating of sealant to mating surfaces of cylinder and crankcase. Tighten crankcase screws in a spiral pattern starting with center screws. Tighten cylinder head screws in sequence shown in Fig. C7-15. Install seal (6—Fig. C7-16) with "O" ring end inserted first until seal is flush with edge of bore. Install a new seal in bore of bottom end of crankshaft. Install long screw for transfer port cover in upper left hand hole as shown in Fig. C7-18. Complete remainder of assembly.

PISTONS, PINS, RINGS & CYLINDERS. Pistons are fitted with two piston rings which should be installed with the beveled inner edge (B—Fig. C7-19) toward closed end of piston. Rings are pinned in place to prevent rotation in ring grooves. Heat piston to approximately 200°F to remove or install piston pin. Do not interchange pistons between cylinders. Pistons and rings are available in standard size and 0.010 and 0.030 inch oversizes.

When assembling piston, pin and connecting rod, match marks on connecting rod and cap must be aligned and long,

tapering side of piston must be towards exhaust port.

CONNECTING RODS, BEARINGS AND CRANKSHAFT. Before detaching connecting rods from crankshaft, mark connecting rod and cap for correct reassembly to each other and in the correct cylinder. The needle rollers and cages at crankpin end of connecting rod should be kept with the assembly and not interchanged.

The bearing rollers and cages used in the connecting rods and the rollers and liners in the center main bearing are available only as a set for each bearing. The complete assembly should be installed whenever renewal is indicated. Connecting rod bearing cages have beveled notches which must be installed together and toward top (flywheel) end of crankshaft. Match marks on connect-

Fig. C7-18—Install long cap screw (L) in upper left hole of transfer port cover.

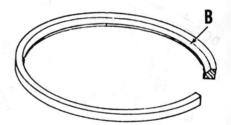

Fig. C7-19—Install piston rings with bevel (B) to top.

ing rod and cap must be on same side as shown in Fig. C7-20. Connecting rod is fractured to provide an uneven surface between rod and cap. Be sure rod and cap are properly meshed before tightening rod screws.

Inspect condition of seal ring (7—Fig. C7-16) and carefully install ring in crankshaft groove. Seal ring (7) must prevent leakage between cylinders and a defective seal will result in poor engine performance.

Fig. C7-20—Match marks on connecting rod and rod cap must be on same side and towards flywheel end of crankshaft.

Illustrations courtesy Chrysler

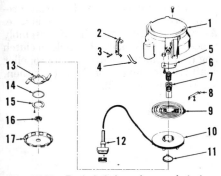

Fig. C7-21—Exploded view of manual starter.

1. Starter housing
2. Interlock lever
3. Pin
4. Spring
5. Plate
6. Spring
7. Rope guide
8. Housing liner
9. Rewind spring
10. Rope & pulley
11. Spring
12. Handle
13. Pawl plate
14. Shims
15. Retainer
16. Flywheel nut
17. Starter cup

Fig. C7-22—Exploded view of electric starter motor.

1. Nut
2. Stop cup
3. Spring
4. Pinion cup
5. Sleeve
6. Pinion
7. Screw shaft
8. Washer
9. Cushion cup
10. Cushion
11. Thrust cup
12. End plate
13. Thrust washer
14. Shim
15. Armature
16. Thrust washer
17. Housing
18. Thrust washer
19. Spring
20. Brushes
21. Brush plate

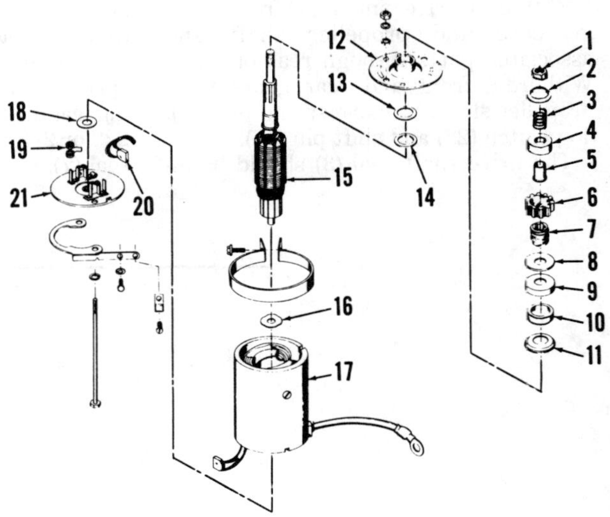

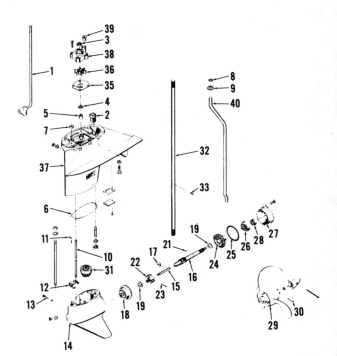

Fig. C7-24—Exploded view of lower unit.

1. Shift rod
2. Water screen
3. Drive shaft seal
4. Seal
5. Bushing
6. Gasket
7. Seal
8. Seal
9. Washer
10. Shift rod
11. Pin
12. Shift arm
13. Pivot pin
14. Gearcase
15. Shift pin
16. Propeller shaft
17. Yoke
18. Front gear & bushing
19. Thrust washer
20. Ball
21. Ball
22. Dog clutch
23. Spring pin
24. Rear gear
25. Cage seal
26. Bearing
27. Bearing cage
28. Seal
29. Propeller
30. Propeller pin
31. Drive pinion & bearing
32. Drive shaft
33. Water pump drive pin
35. Back plate
36. Impeller
37. Drive shaft housing
38. Pump body
39. Grommet
40. Water tube

Before installing crankshaft in crankcase, install bearing liner (9) over dowel pin and place fourteen bearing rollers (8) in liner with a suitable grease to hold rollers in place. Install crankshaft and position remaining sixteen bearing rollers around crank journal. Place remaining bearing liner over rollers so that liner ends dovetail. Upper main bearing (1) should stand 1/8 inch higher than surface of crankcase.

MANUAL STARTER

Refer to Fig. C7-21 for an exploded view of manual starter. To disassemble starter, remove starter from engine, unscrew retainer (15) screws and remove retainer, shims (14), pawl plate (13) and spring (11). Remove rope handle, press interlock lever and allow rope to rewind into starter housing. Press interlock lever and remove rope and pulley (10). If necessary, remove rewind spring.

Install rewind spring in housing with spring wound in counterclockwise direction from outer end of spring. Wind rope on pulley in counterclockwise direction as viewed with pulley in housing. Insert rope through slot of pulley with about nine inches of rope extending from slot. Install rope pulley in housing and place pawl spring (11) on rope pulley with ends pointing up. Install pawl plate (13) with pawl side toward pulley and engage slots with pawl spring (11) ends. Install three shims (0.006, 0.007 and 0.010 inch) and retainer (15). Turn rope pulley approximately two turns counterclockwise to preload rewind spring and pass end of rope through rope guide of starter housing. Attach rope handle and pull rope until it is fully extended. It should still be possible to rotate rope pulley a slight amount after rope is extended to prevent damage to rewind spring.

PROPELLER

Propellers for normal use have three blades and are equipped with a thrust pin to prevent damage. Various pitch propellers are available and should be selected to provide full throttle operation within the recommended limits of 4500-5500 rpm on models prior to 1979 and 4250-5250 rpm on 1979 and later models. Propellers other than those designed for the motor should not be used.

LOWER UNIT

R&R AND OVERHAUL. To remove the lower unit, refer to WATER PUMP section. Drain the gearcase and secure gearcase skeg in a vise. Disassemble and remove the drive shaft and water pump assembly. Remove propeller nut, pin (30 – Fig. C7-24) and propeller (29). Carefully clean exposed end of propeller shaft and remove the two screws securing propeller shaft bearing cage (27) to gearcase. Rotate the bearing cage approximately 1/2-turn until tabs are accessible from the sides; then using a soft hammer, gently tap the bearing cage rearward out of gearcase. Remove the gearcase rear retaining stud nut by working through propeller shaft opening. Unscrew gearcase front retaining stud nut, then lift off drive shaft housing (37).

Withdraw drive pinion (31) from top of gearcase and propeller shaft and associated parts through rear opening. Withdraw front and rear gears from propeller shaft. Remove spring pin (23), dog clutch (22) and shift pin (15).

The drive shaft seal (3) should be installed with spring loaded lip toward top (power head). Rubber coated side of shaft seal (28) should be installed with spring loaded lip toward outside of bearing cage (27). Sparingly apply Loctite 222 or 262 to outer diameter of shift rod seal (7).

Drive gear backlash and bearing preload are fixed and not adjustable. Assemble by reversing the disassembly procedure. Make sure that hole in clutch dog (22) is aligned with slot in propeller shaft (16) and hole in shift pin (15); then, insert spring pin (23).

CHRYSLER
35, 45, 50 AND 55 HP

Year Produced	35 HP	45 HP	50 HP	55 HP
1969	35*†	45*†	.....	55*†
1970	35*§	45*§	.....	55*§
1971	35*§	45*§	.....	55*§
1972	35*§	45*§	.....	55*§
1973	35*§	45*§	.....	55*§
1974	35*§	45*§	.....	55*§
1975	35*§	45*§	.....	55*§
1976	.....	45*§	.....	55*§
1977	.....	45*§	.....	.....
1978	.....	45*§	.....	.....
1979	35*§	45*§	.....	.....
1980	35*§	45*§	.....	.....
1981	35*§	45*§	50*§	.....
1982	.....	45*§	50*§	.....
1983	.....	45*§	50*§	.....
1984	.....	45*§	50*§	.....

*Variation Code:
0 – Standard shaft, manual starter.
1 – Long shaft, manual starter.
2 – Standard shaft, manual starter, with tiller.
3 – Long shaft, manual starter, with tiller.
4 – Standard shaft, electric starter.
5 – Long shaft, electric starter.

6 – Standard shaft, electric starter, with alternator.
7 – Long shaft, electric starter, with alternator.
8 – Same as number 6 except with "Magnapower" ignition.
9 – Same as number 7 except with "Magnapower" ignition.

†Production Code Before 1970:
1, 3 & 5 – USA models.
2, 4 & 6 – Canada models.

§Production Code Beginning in 1970: HA, HB, HC, HD, HE, HF, HG, HH, HJ, HK, HL, HM & HN – USA models. BA, BB, BC, BD, BE, BF, BG, BH, BJ, BK, BL & BN – Canada models.

CONDENSED SERVICE DATA

TUNE-UP	35 HP	45 HP	50 HP	55 HP
Hp/rpm	35/4750	45/5000	50/5000	55/5250
Bore – Inches	3	3⅛	3-3/16	3-3/16
Stroke – Inches	2.54	2.75	2.80	2.80
Number of Cylinders	2	2	2	2
Displacement – Cu. In.	35.9	42.18	44.7	44.7
Compression at Cranking Speed (Average)	95-105 psi	115-125 psi	135-150 psi	145-155 psi
Spark Plug:				
Champion (1969-1977)	L4J	L4J*	.....	L4J*
(1978-1981)	L4J	UL4J	UL4J	.....
(1982-1984)	.....	UL81J	UL4J	.....
Electrode Gap – In.	0.030	0.030	.....	0.030
Ignition:				
Point Gap – In.	0.020§	0.020§	0.015	0.020§
Timing	See Text	See Text	See Text	See Text
Carburetor:				
Make	Tillotson	Tillotson	Tillotson	Tillotson
Model	WB	WB	WB	WB
Fuel:Oil Ratio	**50:1	**50:1	**50:1	**50:1

*A UL-18V Champion spark plug is used on models with "Magnapower" capacitor discharge ignition.
**Use 25:1 fuel:oil ratio for first 10 hours and for severe service.
§Breaker point gap should be 0.015 inch on models with battery ignition or "Magnapower" ignition.

SIZES—CLEARANCES

Piston Ring End Gap		0.006-0.016 in.		0.008-0.015 in.
Piston Ring Groove Width		0.0645-0.0655 in.		.....
Piston to Cylinder Clearance	0.005 in.	0.0038-0.007 in.	0.005-0.007 in.	0.005 in.
Piston Pin:				
Diameter		0.6875-0.68765 in.		
Clearance (Rod)		Needle Bearing		
Clearance (Piston)		0.00025 in. tight to 0.0002 in. loose		
Crankshaft Journal Diameters:				
Upper Main Bearing		1.1815-1.1820 in.		.....
Center Main Bearing		1.1388-1.1392 in.		.....
Lower Main Bearing		1.1245-1.1250 in.		.....
Crankpin		1.1391-1.1395 in.		.....

TIGHTENING TORQUES
(All Values in Inch-Pounds Unless Noted)

	35 HP	45 HP	50 HP	55 HP
Connecting Rod (1969-1979)	165-175	165-175	.....	165-175
(1980-1984)	180-190	180-190	180-190	.....
Cylinder Head	270***	270***	270***	270***
Flywheel Nut	80 Ft.-Lbs.	80 Ft.-Lbs.	80 Ft.-Lbs.	80 Ft.-Lbs.
Main Bearing Bolts	270	270	270	270
Standard Screws:				
6-32	9	9	9	9
10-24	30	30	30	30
10-32	35	35	35	35
12-24	45	45	45	45
1/4-20	70	70	70	70
5/16-18	160	160	160	160
3/8-16	270	270	270	270

***Refer to text for tightening cylinder head screws.

LUBRICATION

The power head is lubricated by oil mixed with the fuel. One-third (1/3) pint of two-cycle or Outboard Motor Oil should be mixed with each gallon of gasoline. The amount of oil in the fuel may be reduced after the first 10 hours of operation (motor is broken in), provided the highest quality SAE 30 Outboard Motor Oil is used and motor is subjected to normal service only. The minimum recommended fuel-oil ratio is 50:1, or half the normally recommended amount of oil. If the amount of oil is reduced, fuel and oil must be thoroughly mixed and idle mixture carefully adjusted to make sure any error is on the "Rich" side.

Manufacturer recommends using no-lead automotive gasoline in motors with less than 55 hp although regular or premium gasoline with octane rating of 85 or greater may also be used. Regular or premium automotive gasoline with octane rating of 85 or greater must be used in motors with more than 54 hp.

The lower unit gears and bearings are lubricated by oil contained in the gearcase. A non-corrosive, leaded, Extreme Pressure SAE 90 Gear Oil, such as "Chrysler Special Purpose Gear Lube" should be used. DO NOT use a hypoid type lubricant. The gearcase should be drained and refilled every 100 hours or once each year, and fluid maintained at the level of upper (vent) plug opening.

To fill the gearcase, position motor in an upright position and fill through lower plug hole on starboard side of gearcase until lubricant reaches level of upper vent plug opening. Reinstall and tighten both plugs, using new gaskets if necessary, to assure a water tight seal.

FUEL SYSTEM

CARBURETOR. Tillotson type WB carburetors are used. Refer to Fig. C8-1. Normal initial setting is one turn open for idle mixture adjustment needle (12). Fixed jet (3) controls high speed mixture. The carburetor model number is stamped on the mounting flange. Float level is 13/32 inch from float to gasket surface (Fig. C8-2). Care must be used in selecting the high speed fixed jet (3). A fixed jet which is too small will result in a lean mixture and possible damage to power head. Jet may be identified by the diameter (in thousandths of an inch) stamped on the visible end of an installed jet. Optional jets are available which will improve performance when

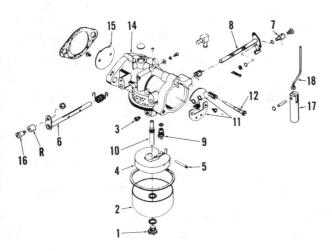

Fig. C8-1 — Exploded view of Tillotson WB type carburetor.

R. Roller
1. Bowl retaining screw
2. Fuel bowl
3. High speed jet
4. Float
5. Float pivot shaft
6. Throttle shaft
7. Connector
8. Choke shaft
9. Inlet needle and seat
10. Main nozzle
11. Choke plate
12. Idle mixture needle
14. Throttle body
15. Throttle plate
16. Eccentric screw
17. Choke solenoid plunger
18. Rod

motor is used in high-altitude locations; optional jet sizes and recommended altitudes are as follows:

35 HP (WB-3A)

Altitude	Jet Size	Part Number
Standard	0.084	014302

35 HP (WB-3C)

Altitude	Jet Size	Part Number
Sea Level-1250 ft.	0.0785	014306
1250-3750 ft.	0.070	013430
3750-6250 ft.	0.068	013967
6250-8250 ft.	0.062	014187

35 HP (WB-12A)

Altitude	Jet Size	Part Number
Sea Level-1250 ft.	0.074	014303
1250-3750 ft.	0.072	015026
3750-6250 ft.	0.070	013430
6250-8250 ft.	0.068	013967

35 HP (WB-12B)

Altitude	Jet Size	Part Number
Sea Level-1250 ft.	0.074	014303
1250-3750 ft.	0.072	015026
3750-6250 ft.	0.070	013430
6250-8250 ft.	0.068	013967

35 HP (WB-17A)

Altitude	Jet Size	Part Number
Sea Level-1250 ft.	0.090	015406
1250-3750 ft.	0.088	013193
3750-6250 ft.	0.086	013949
6250-8250 ft.	0.084	014302

35 HP (WB-17A with "X" stamped on mount flange)

Altitude	Jet Size	Part Number
Standard	0.098	014152

35 HP (WB-17C)

Altitude	Jet Size	Part Number
Sea Level-1250 ft.	0.090	015406
1250-3750 ft.	0.088	013193
3750-6250 ft.	0.086	013949
6250-8250 ft.	0.084	014302

45 HP (WB-4A)

Altitude	Jet Size	Part Number
Standard	0.096	012947

45 HP (WB-4C)

Altitude	Jet Size	Part Number
Sea Level-1250 ft.	0.086	013949
1250-3750 ft.	0.0785	014306
3750-6250 ft.	0.074	014303
6250-8250 ft.	0.068	013967

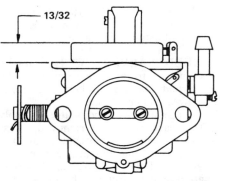

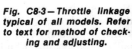

Fig. C8-2 — Correct float level is 13/32 inch when measured as shown between float and gasket surface.

45 HP (WB-11A & WB-11B)

Altitude	Jet Size	Part Number
Sea Level-1250 ft.	0.082	014109
1250-3750 ft.	0.080	013194
3750-6250 ft.	0.0785	014306
6250-8250 ft.	0.076	013191

45 HP (WB-16A)

Altitude	Jet Size	Part Number
Sea Level-1250 ft.	0.086	013949
1250-3750 ft.	0.084	014302
3750-6250 ft.	0.082	014109
6250-8250 ft.	0.080	013194

45 HP (WB-16A with "X" stamped on mount flange)

Altitude	Jet Size	Part Number
Standard	0.088	013193

45 HP (WB-16C)

Altitude	Jet Size	Part Number
Sea Level-1250 ft.	0.090	015406
1250-3750 ft.	0.088	013193
3750-6250 ft.	0.086	013949
6250-8250 ft.	0.084	014302

45 & 50 HP (WB-16D)

Altitude	Jet Size	Part Number
Sea Level-1250 ft.	0.084	014302
1250-3750 ft.	0.082	014109
3750-6250 ft.	0.080	013194
6250-8250 ft.	0.078	014306

55 HP (WB-5A)

Altitude	Jet Size	Part Number
Standard	0.089	013367

55 HP (WB-5B)

Altitude	Jet Size	Part Number
Sea Level-1250 ft.	0.092	014152
1250-3750 ft.	0.084	014302
3750-6250 ft.	0.076	013191
6250-8250 ft.	0.074	014303

55 HP (WB-7A & WB-7B)

Altitude	Jet Size	Part Number
Sea Level-1250 ft.	0.086	013949
1250-3750 ft.	0.084	014302
3750-6250 ft.	0.082	014109
6250-8250 ft.	0.080	013194

55 HP (WB-15A)

Altitude	Jet Size	Part Number
Sea Level-1250 ft.	0.088	013193
1250-3750 ft.	0.086	013949
3750-6250 ft.	0.084	014302
6250-8250 ft.	0.082	014109

55 HP (WB-15A with "X" stamped on mount flange)

Altitude	Jet Size	Part Number
Standard	0.090	015406

55 HP (WB-15C)

Altitude	Jet Size	Part Number
Sea Level-1250 ft.	0.0937	014191
1250-3750 ft.	0.092	014109
3750-6250 ft.	0.090	015406
6250-8250 ft.	0.088	013193

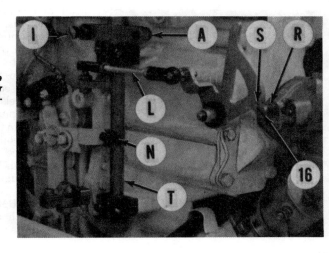

Fig. C8-3 — Throttle linkage typical of all models. Refer to text for method of checking and adjusting.

A. High speed stop
I. Idle stop
L. Throttle link
N. Neutral stop screw
R. Roller
S. Scribed line
T. Tower shaft
16. Eccentric screw

55 HP (WB-27A)

Altitude	Jet Size	Part Number
Sea Level-1250 ft.	0.066	014188
1250-3750 ft.	0.064	014108
3750-6250 ft.	0.062	014187
6250-8250 ft.	0.060	014186

NOTE: Be sure that proper jet is installed before motor is used at a lower altitude.

Choke is properly adjusted when choke plate (11 – Fig. C8-1) is 0.010-0.040 inch open when choke is engaged. On electric choke models, bottom plunger (17) in solenoid and adjust choke plunger rod (18) in connector (7) as required. On manual choke models, pull choke knob and adjust cable in connector at carburetor as required. On all models, make certain choke plate is free and returns to full open position.

SPEED CONTROL LINKAGE. On all models, ignition timing advance and throttle opening must be synchronized so that throttle is opened as timing is advanced.

To synchronize the linkage, first make certain that ignition timing is correctly set as outlined in IGNITION TIMING paragraph. Shift to forward gear and disconnect link (L – Fig. C8-3) from tower shaft (T). With carburetor throttle closed, turn the eccentric screw (16) until roller (R) is exactly centered over the scribed line (S). Move the tower shaft (T) to full advance position and move the throttle cam until carburetor throttle is completely open. Vary the length of link (L) until the ball joint connector will just attach. Snap the ball joint connector onto ball stud and check maximum speed in neutral. Maximum rpm in neutral is approximately 1800 rpm and on late models, is adjusted at neutral stop screw (N). Early models have a non-adjustable neutral stop linkage.

Fig. C8-4 — Reed stop setting should be 9/32 inch when measured as shown. Holes in stops and petals are elongated and should be positioned as shown by arrows for maximum overlap.

Idle speed should be 700-800 rpm in forward gear (800-900 rpm in neutral) and is adjusted at idle screw (I).

REED VALVES. "V" type intake reed valves are used on all models. The reed plate is located between intake manifold and crankcase.

To remove the reed plate assembly after carburetor is removed, first remove the starter assembly and the screws retaining the intake manifold; then lift off the manifold and the reed plate assembly. Refer to Fig. C8-4.

Reed valve must be smooth and even with no sharp bends or broken reeds. Assembled reeds may stand open a maximum of 0.010 inch at tip end. Check seating visually.

Reed stop setting should be 9/32-inch when measured as shown in Fig. C8-4. Renew reeds if petals are broken, cracked, warped or bent. Never attempt to bend a reed petal in an effort to improve performance; nor attempt to straighten a damaged reed. Never install a bent or damaged reed. Seating surface of reed plate should be smooth and flat. When installing reed petals and stops, proceed as follows: Install reed petals, stop, and the four retaining screws leaving screws loose. Slide the reed petals as far as possible toward mounting flange of reed plate and reed stops out toward tip of "Vee" as far as possible as indicated by arrows in Fig. C8-4. Position reed petals and reed stops as outlined to provide maximum overlap; then, tighten the retaining screws.

PUDDLE DRAIN VALVES. All models are equipped with a puddle drain system designed to remove any liquid fuel or oil which might build up in the crankcase; thus providing smoother operation at all speeds and lessening the possibility of spark plug fouling during slow speed operation.

The puddle drain valve housing is located on the starboard side of power head, and can be removed as shown in Fig. C8-5. The reed-type puddle drain valve petals must seat lightly and evenly against valve plate. Reed stops should be adjusted to 0.017-0.023 inch clearance at the tip. Blow out drain passages with compressed air while housing is off.

Later models are equipped with a recirculating puddle drain system. Fluid accumulated in puddle drain during slow speed operation is reintroduced to the cylinders once engine is returned to cruising speed. Inspect hoses and check valves when unit is disassembled.

FUEL PUMP. All models are equipped with a diaphragm type fuel pump which is actuated by pressure and

Fig. C8-5 — View of puddle drain housing removed.

vacuum pulsations from both crankcases as shown in Fig. C8-6. The two stages operate alternately as shown.

NOTE: Either stage operating independently may permit the motor to run, but not at peak performance.

Most fuel pump service can be performed without removing the assembly from power head. Disconnect the pulse hoses and remove the retaining cap screws; then lift off the pump cover and diaphragm. Remove the sediment bowl and strainer. First stage inlet check valve can be driven out from below, using a ½-inch diameter drift. First stage outlet check valve can be lifted out after removing the retaining screws. The check valves must be installed to permit fuel to flow in the proper direction as shown. To renew the second stage outlet check valve, it is first necessary to remove pump body from power head, remove outlet fuel elbow and drive the check valve out from below. Check valve will be damaged, and a new unit must be

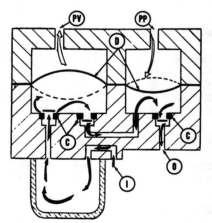

Fig. C8-6 — Cross sectional view of the two stage fuel pump. Broken lines indicate position of diaphragm when pulse pressure and vacuum are reversed.

C. Check valves
D. Diaphragm
I. Fuel inlet
O. Fuel outlet
PP. Pulse pressure
PV. Pulse vacuum

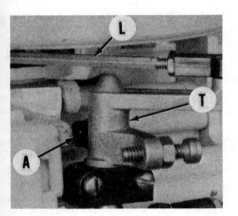

Fig. C8-7 — Special tool is available for positioning piston at correct timing position. Refer to text for proper tool usage.

Fig. C8-8 — Full advance stop (A) on tower shaft (T) should contact housing before adjusting link (L) when setting ignition timing.

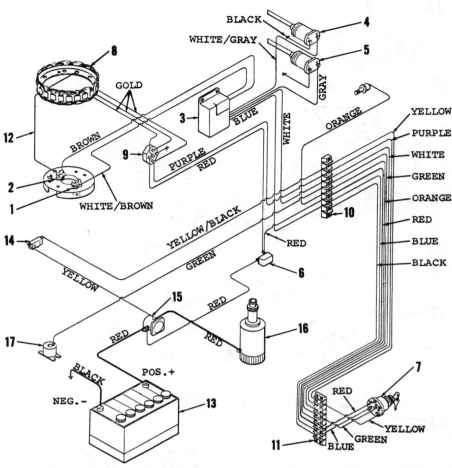

Fig. C8-9 — Wiring diagram for 45 and 55 hp motors with "Magnapower" ignition system. Yellow wires are for starting system, purple for charging, white for tachometer, green for choke, orange for heat indicator, red for battery positive, blue for ignition and black for ground. Note wiring diagram for later model rectifier in Fig. C8-12.

1. Breaker points for top cylinder
2. Breaker points for bottom cylinder
3. Ignition capacitor discharge module
4. Coil for top cylinder
5. Coil for bottom cylinder
6. Circuit breaker
7. Ignition and start switch
8. Alternator stator
9. Rectifier
10. Terminal block at motor
11. Terminal block at dashboard
12. Alternator ground
13. Battery
14. Neutral interlock switch
15. Starter solenoid
16. Starter motor
17. Choke solenoid

installed. DO NOT remove the valve unless renewal is indicated. Install new valve carefully, using an 11/16-inch diameter punch.

Renew the diaphragm if cracked, torn, or badly distorted. Install check valves carefully to prevent damage, and reassemble by reversing the disassembly procedure.

IGNITION SYSTEM

Thirty-five horsepower motors may be equipped with a magneto ignition or a battery ignition with a flywheel mounted alternator. Forty-five and fifty-five horsepower models may be equipped with magneto ignition, battery ignition with a flywheel mounted alternator or "Magnapower" capacitor discharge ignition. Fifty horsepower models are equipped with battery ignition and flywheel mounted alternator only. Refer to the appropriate following paragraphs after determining type of ignition used.

All Models

R&R FLYWHEEL. A special puller (Chrysler Part Number T-8948-1) is used to remove the flywheel on late model units. Pulling bosses are provided on the flywheel for puller installation.

NOTE: Models with alternators must have the three screws that secure the emergency starter collar removed, as well as the emergency starter collar. Make certain that aligning marks on flywheel and emergency starter collar are matched when reassembling.

Flywheels may be removed from models without puller bosses by using a special knockout nut (Chrysler Part Number T-2910). Install the tool and apply upward pressure to rim of flywheel, then bump the tool sharply with a hammer to loosen flywheel from tapered portion of crankshaft.

The manufacturer recommends that mating surfaces of flywheel and crankshaft be lapped before flywheel is reinstalled. If evidence of working exists proceed as follows:

Remove the flywheel key and apply a light coating of valve grinding or lapping compound to tapered portion of crankshaft. Install the flywheel without the key or crankshaft nut and rotate flywheel gently back and forth about ¼-turn. Move flywheel 90° and repeat the operation. Lift off the flywheel, wipe off excess lapping compound and carefully examine crankshaft. A minimum of 90% surface contact should be indicated by the polished surface; continue lapping only if insufficient contact is evident. Thoroughly clean the crankshaft and flywheel bore to remove all traces of lapping compound, then clean both surfaces with a non-oily solvent.

Reinstall crankshaft key and flywheel, then tighten flywheel nut to torque indicated in CONDENSED SERVICE DATA table.

POINT ADJUSTMENT. Breaker point gap should be 0.020 inch for models with magneto ignition and 0.015

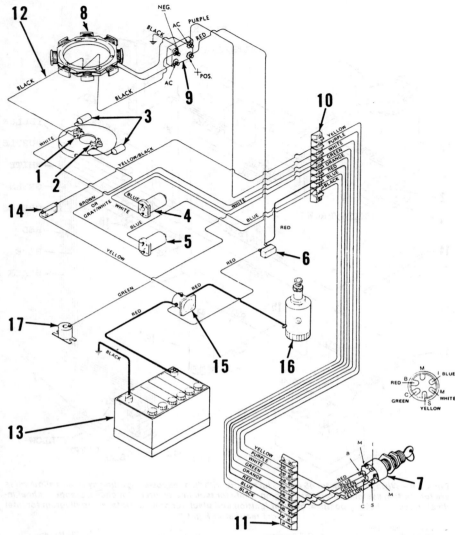

Fig. C8-10 — Wiring diagram for models equipped with battery ignition and flywheel mounted alternator.

1. Breaker points for top cylinder
2. Breaker points for bottom cylinder
3. Condensers
4. Coil for top cylinder
5. Coil for bottom cylinder
6. Circuit breaker
7. Ignition and start switch
8. Alternator stator
9. Rectifier
10. Terminal block at motor
11. Terminal block at dashboard
12. Alternator ground
13. Battery
14. Neutral interlock switch
15. Starter solenoid
16. Starter motor
17. Choke solenoid

magneto ignition models when setting piston position with Chrysler special tool T-8938 or 32° BTDC on all other models when setting piston position with Chrysler special tool T-2937-1. When setting piston position with a dial indicator, the equivalent reading should be 0.210 in. BTDC on 35 and 45 hp magneto ignition models or 0.281 in. BTDC on all other models. To adjust ignition timing, breaker point gap must first be carefully adjusted as previously outlined, then piston position must be accurately determined using a Chrysler special tool or a dial indicator as follows:

To determine piston position using Chrysler special tool (Fig. C8-7), thread the tool body into top spark plug opening. Insert the gage rod into tool body, rotate the crankshaft and carefully position top piston at exactly TDC.

NOTE: Gage rod should be installed with the double scribed line end or the 25-55 HP marked end out.

With the top piston at TDC, thread timing tool body in or out as necessary until the inner scribed line on gage rod is aligned with end of tool body. After gage body is correctly positioned, turn the crankshaft clockwise almost one complete revolution while applying pressure to end of gage rod. Stop the crankshaft just as the first (outer) scribed line on rod aligns with tool body. The crankshaft should be at correct position BTDC for maximum ignition advance timing.

To determine piston position using a dial indicator, insert dial indicator into top spark plug opening, then rotate crankshaft and carefully position piston at exactly TDC. Zero the dial indicator, then turn crankshaft clockwise almost one complete revolution stopping crankshaft just as dial indicator reads desired specification. The crankshaft should be at correct position BTDC for maximum ignition advance timing.

With the crankshaft correctly positioned and breaker point gap properly adjusted, connect one lead from timing test light (with battery) or ohmmeter to the breaker point terminal of number one cylinder and ground other test lead to motor. On magneto models, it may be necessary to disconnect coil ground and condenser and prevent them from contacting engine ground. Move the speed control from slow toward fast (maximum advance) speed position and observe the test light or ohmmeter. The breaker points should just open (test light goes off or ohmmeter registers infinite resistance) when the speed control reaches maximum ignition advance. If the breaker points do not open, shorten rod (L–Fig. C8-8) or if breaker points open too soon, lengthen rod (L).

inch for all other models. Both sets of points must be adjusted as nearly alike as possible.

NOTE: Point gap variation of 0.0015 inch will change ignition timing one degree.

To adjust the points, first remove the flywheel as previously outlined. Turn crankshaft clockwise until the rub block on one set of points is resting on high point of breaker cam approximately 10° from first point of maximum opening. Mark the exact location of rub block contact for use in adjusting the other set of points. Loosen breaker point mounting screws and adjust point gap until a slight drag exists using a 0.020 inch feeler gage for models with magneto ignition and 0.015 inch feeler gage for all other models.

Turn crankshaft until the previously installed mark on breaker cam is aligned with the rub block on the other set of points and adjust the other set of points in the same manner.

NOTE: If mid-range of breaker plate movement is used, final positioning can be made by moving the speed control handle to correctly position the rub block at the same point of breaker cam.

IGNITION TIMING. Crankshaft timing should be 28° BTDC on 35 and 45 hp

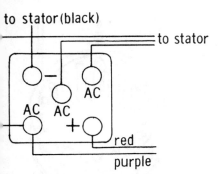

Fig. C8-11—Wiring diagram for rectifier used with three-phase alternator.

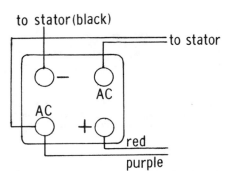

Fig. C8-12—Wiring diagram for rectifier used on later models.

Magnapower Models

TROUBLESHOOTING. Use only approved procedures when testing to prevent damage to components. The fuel system should be checked to make certain that faulty running is not caused by incorrect fuel mixture or contaminated fuel.

CHECKING FOR SPARK. Remove the spark plugs and attach spark plug leads to a spark gap tester. With all wiring attached, attempt to start motor using the electric starter.

NOTE: Two conventional spark plugs (such as Champion L4J) with ground electrodes removed can be used to check for spark. Make certain that test plug shell is grounded against power head when checking.

If good regular spark occurs at tester (or test plugs), check fuel system and spark plugs. Also, make certain that wires from breaker points (1 & 2—Fig. C8-9) to CD ignition module (3), from CD ignition module to ignition coils (4 and 5) and from coils to spark plugs are correct to provide spark to the proper cylinder.

If spark does not occur at tester (or test plugs), make certain that the small black wires on ignition coils (4 and 5) are attached to the negative (−) terminals and are securely grounded to the coil clamp screws. Also check continuity of the spark plug wires. If test plugs still do not spark, proceed with following checks.

WIRING. Engine missing, surging or failure to start can be caused by loose connections, corroded connections or short circuits. Electrical system components may also be damaged by faulty connections or short circuits.

Attach one lead of voltmeter or 12 volt test light (such as Chrysler part T-2951) to the terminal (10—Fig. C8-9) where the blue wires are attached. Ground the other test lead to the metal case (housing) of the CD ignition module unit (3). Turn the ignition switch ON and observe the test light or voltmeter. If the test light glows, current is available to the

CD ignition module. If checking with a voltmeter, voltage should be the same as available at the battery.

If test light does not glow or voltmeter indicates zero or low voltage, check the circuit breaker (6). If the circuit breaker is not faulty, check for broken wires, loose connections, faulty ignition switch or improper ground. Make certain that the CD ignition module (3) is properly grounded. Mounting surfaces on bracket and CD ignition module must be free of all paint and the mounting bracket to motor ground wire must provide a good ground connection. Check the ground strap between power head and support plate. Before proceeding with remaining tests, make certain current is available to the CD ignition module.

BREAKER POINTS. The breaker points are used to trigger the ignition system. Failure of breaker points to make contact (open circuit) or failure to break contact (short circuit) will prevent ignition just as in conventional magneto or battery ignition systems.

Remove the flywheel and check condition and gap of the breaker points as outlined in the preceding POINT ADJUSTMENT paragraphs. Check condition of all wires, making certain that ground wire from breaker plate to the alternator stator has good contact,

Fig. C8-13—Removing thermostat from cylinder head. "Vee" slot should point up when thermostat is installed.

especially at the stator end. Varnish should be scraped from stator before attaching ground wire. Check the BROWN and the WHITE/BROWN wires for short circuit to ground, for loose connections and for broken wire. Refer to IGNITION TIMING paragraphs and Fig. C8-9. Make certain that breaker point wires and coil wires are properly connected to provide spark to the correct cylinder.

IGNITION COILS AND CD IGNITION MODULE. If the preceding checks do not indicate any malfunctions, the ignition coils can be tested using an ignition tester available from Chrysler or several other sources, including the following:

Graham-Lee Electronics, Inc.
4220 Central Ave. N.E.
Minneapolis, Minn. 55421

Merc-O-Tronic Instruments Corp.
215 Branch St.
Almont, Mich. 48003

An alternate method of checking is possible as follows:

Connect one lead of a 12-volt test light (such as Chrysler part number T-2951) to each of the two primary terminals of one ignition coil. Turn ignition switch to the ON position, attempt to start motor with the electric starter and observe test light.

NOTE: After checking one of the ignition coils, connect the 12-volt test light to the primary terminals of the other coil and check the coil.

If the 12-volt test light flashes but spark did not occur at the test plug as tested in the CHECKING FOR SPARK paragraphs, the coil or attaching wires are faulty.

NOTE: The test plug connected to the tension spark plug wire will not fire with test light connected across the primary terminals. Inspect the black ground wire from negative (−) terminal of coil to the coil clamp screw and the high tension spark plug wire.

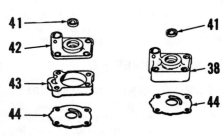

Fig. C8-14—Variations of water pump bodies used on some models. Refer also to Fig. C8-23.

38. Water pump body
41. Seal
42. Cover
43. Pump housing
44. Back plate

Fig. C8-15 — Rear exhaust cover must be removed from motor leg for access to power head rear attaching screw.

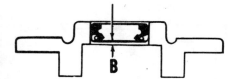

Fig. C8-16 — Cross sectional view of crankshaft upper bearing cage showing correct seal location. Clearance (B) should be 0.150 inch.

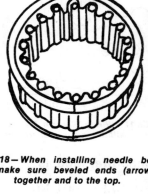

Fig. C8-18 — When installing needle bearin cages, make sure beveled ends (arrow) ar together and to the top.

If the 12-volt test light does not flash, when connected to the coil primary terminals, make certain that current is available to the CD ignition module as outlined in WIRING paragraphs. Make certain that breaker points and associated wires are not faulty as outlined in the BREAKER POINTS paragraphs in the TROUBLESHOOTING section. If current is still not available to the coil primary terminals, the CD ignition module should be renewed.

COOLING SYSTEM

THERMOSTAT. The thermostat is located beneath a separate housing on top, rear face of cylinder head as shown in Fig. C8-13. When installing the thermostat, position with "Vee" slot in visible end up as shown. Power head will overheat if run without thermostat installed.

WATER PUMP. All motors are equipped with a rubber impeller type water pump. Refer to Figs. C8-14 and C8-23. The water pump is mounted in the lower unit drive shaft housing (upper gearcase).

When cooling system problems are encountered, first check the thermostat to see that it is operating properly. Check the water inlet for plugging or partial stoppage, then if trouble is not corrected, remove the lower unit gearcase as outlined in LOWER UNIT section, and check the condition of water pump, water passages and sealing surfaces.

POWER HEAD

REMOVE AND DISASSEMBLE. To overhaul the power head, clamp the motor on a stand or support and remove the engine cover (shroud) and motor leg covers. Remove the starter, flywheel and magneto or alternator; fuel pump, carburetor and intake manifold. Disconnect all interfering wiring and linkage.

Remove the cylinder head, and transfer port and exhaust covers if major repairs are required. Remove the power head attaching screws and lift off the cylinder block, crankshaft and associated parts as a unit.

NOTE: One of the power head attaching screws is located underneath the rear exhaust cover as shown in Fig. C8-15. Cover must be removed for access to the screw.

To disassemble the power head, unbolt and remove the upper bearing cage; then unbolt and remove the crankcase front half. Pry slots are provided adjacent to retaining dowels for separating the crankcase; DO NOT pry on machined mating surfaces of cylinder block and crankcase front half.

Crankshaft, pistons and bearings are now accessible for removal and overhaul as outlined in the appropriate following paragraphs. Assemble as outlined in the ASSEMBLY paragraph.

ASSEMBLY. When reassembling, make sure all joint and gasket surfaces are clean, free from nicks and burrs, warped surfaces or hardened cement or carbon. The crankcase and inlet manifolds must be completely sealed against both vacuum and pressure. Exhaust manifold and cylinder head must be sealed against water leakage and pressure. Mating surfaces of exhaust areas between power head and motor leg must form a tight seal.

Install crankshaft making certain upper, center and lower main bearings are properly positioned over main bearing locating pins in cylinder block. The crankshaft upper seal should be installed with LOWER edge 0.150 inch from bearing counterbore as shown at (B – Fig. C8-16).

Apply 3M-EC750 Sealer to matin surfaces of crankcase in areas adjacen to upper and center main bearings and lower crankshaft seal. Do not apply sealer to areas outside of crankcase sea groove. Immediately install crankcase half and tighten main bearing bolts to 270 in.-lbs. torque. Make sure crank shaft turns freely before proceeding with assembly.

When installing cylinder head, coa the first ¾-inch of screw threads with anti-seize lubricant or equivalent. Tighten the retaining cap screws progressively from the center outward first to 7 in.-lbs. torque, then in 50 in.-lb. incre ments until final torque of 270 in.-lbs. is achieved. After motor has been test ru and cooled, retorque screws to 27 in.-lbs.

PISTONS, PINS, RINGS & CYLIN DERS. Pistons on 35, 45 and early 55 h models are fitted with three rings, whil 50 and late 55 hp model pistons have tw piston rings. Piston rings should be in stalled with the beveled inner edg toward closed end of piston. Rings ar pinned in place to prevent rotation i ring grooves.

The piston pin is a tight fit in pisto bores and rides in a roller bearing in con necting rod. Special tool, part numbe T-2990, should be used when removing or installing piston pin. When assem bling piston, pin and connecting rod make sure long, tapering side of pisto

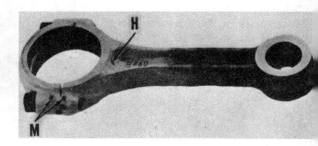

Fig. C8-17 — Correlation marks (M) and oil hole (H) should be toward the top when connecting rod is installed.

...s toward exhaust side of cylinder and ...orrelation marks (M – Fig. C8-17) or ...evel cut on rod are toward top (flywheel) end of crankshaft. Install ...iston pin retaining clips with sharp

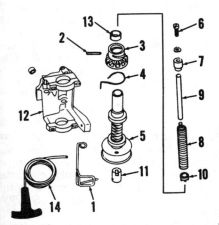

Fig. C8-19 — Exploded view of early model recoil starter assembly. Pinion (3) meshes with teeth on flywheel.

.. Rope guide	8.	Recoil spring
.. Drive pin	9.	Guide post
.. Pinion	10.	Retainer
.. Pinion spring	11.	Retainer extension
.. Starter spool	12.	Mounting bracket
.. Lock screw	13.	Interlock guide
.. Spring drive	14.	Rope

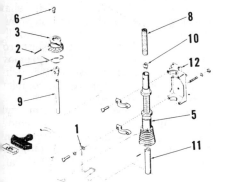

Fig. C8-20 — Exploded view of recoil starter used on late models. Refer to Fig. C8-19 for parts identification.

Fig. C8-21 — View showing tool (T3139) used to preload the recoil spring.

edge out or if bowed retaining rings are used, install with convex side toward piston pin. All friction surfaces should be lubricated with new engine oil when assembling.

Pistons are available in standard sizes on all models and in oversizes on some models.

CONNECTING RODS, BEARINGS AND CRANKSHAFT. Before detaching connecting rods from crankshaft, make certain that rod and cap are properly marked for correct assembly to

Fig. C8-22 — Disconnect the shift rod coupler before attempting to remove gearcase.

each other and in the correct cylinder. The needle rollers and cages at crankpin end of connecting rod should be kept with the assembly and not interchanged.

The bearing rollers and cages used in the two connecting rods and center main bearings are available only as a set which contains the rollers and cage halves for one bearing. The complete assembly should be installed whenever renewal is indicated. Bearing cages have beveled match marks as shown by arrow, Fig. C8-18. Match marks must be installed together and toward top (flywheel) end of crankshaft.

A non-fibrous grease can be used to hold loose needle bearing in position during assembly. All friction surfaces should be lubricated with new engine oil. Check frequently as power head is being assembled, for binding or locking of the moving parts. If binding occurs, remove the cause before proceeding with the assembly. When assembling, follow the procedures outlined in the ASSEMBLY paragraphs. Tightening torques are given in the CONDENSED SERVICE DATA tables.

MANUAL STARTER

Refer to Fig. C8-19 or Fig. C8-20 for exploded views of the recoil starter assembly. Starter pinion (3) engages a starter ring gear on the flywheel.

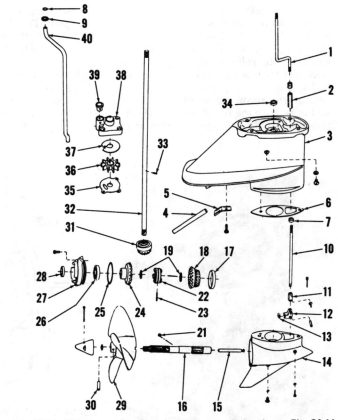

1.	Shift rod	
2.	Nut	
3.	Drive shaft housing	
4.	Inlet water tube	
5.	Inlet plate	
6.	Gasket	
7.	Seal	
8.	Seal	
9.	Washer	
10.	Shift rod	
11.	Link	
12.	Shift arm	
13.	Yoke	
14.	Gearcase	
15.	Shift pin	
16.	Propeller shaft	
17.	Bearing cup	
18.	Front gear	
19.	Thrust washer	
21.	Ball	
22.	Dog clutch	
23.	Spring pin	
24.	Rear gear	
25.	Cage seal	
26.	Bearing	
27.	Bearing cage	
28.	Seal	
29.	Propeller	
30.	Propeller pin	
31.	Drive pinion	
32.	Drive shaft	
33.	Drive pin	
34.	Shaft seal	
35.	Back plate	
36.	Impeller	
37.	Top plate	
38.	Pump body	
39.	Grommet	
40.	Water tube	

Fig. C8-23 — Exploded view of typical early lower unit and associated parts. Refer also to Fig. C8-14 for other types of water pumps. Refer to Fig. C8-24 for later type lower unit.

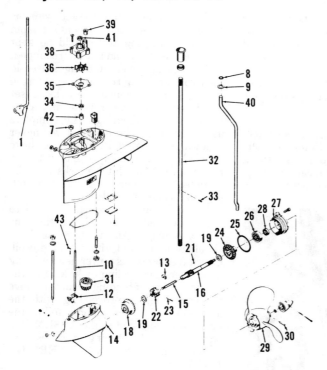

Fig. C8-24—Exploded view of lower unit used on later models. Refer to Fig. C8-23 for parts identification except for: 41. Drive shaft seal; 42. Upper drive shaft bearing; 43. Pin.

Secure rope guide with remaining clam screw. Thread rope through suppo plate and install starter handle. Wi recoil spring and drive pinion (3) stalled, use the special tool to wind th recoil spring counterclockwise 8½ turns Align the holes in pinion (3), spool (and spring drive (7); then install th drive pin (2). Remove the tool and secur the pin with the locking screw (6). Reco spring cavity should be partially fille with Lubriplate or similar grease whe reassembling.

PROPELLER

The propellers for normal use hav three blades and are protected by cushioning-slip clutch. Various prope lers are available and should be selecte to provide full throttle operation withi the recommended limits of 4500-500 rpm for 1969 55 hp motors; 5000-550 rpm for 1970 and later 55 hp motor 4400-5100 rpm for 35 hp motors 4500-5500 rpm for 45 and 50 hp motor Propellers other than those designed fo the motor should not be used.

LOWER UNIT

R&R AND OVERHAUL. To remov the lower unit gearcase and drive shai housing on early style lower unit shov in Fig. C8-23, first remove the motor le covers and disconnect the shift ro coupler as shown in Fig. C8-22, remov the screws securing drive shaft housin to motor leg and remove the complet lower unit drive assembly.

To remove lower unit on later styl lower unit shown in Fig. C8-24, remov motor leg covers and unbolt lower un from motor leg. Remove pin (43) cor necting intermediate shift rod (1) an

To disassemble the starter, first remove the engine cover, then remove screw (6) in top of starter shaft.

NOTE: This screw locks pin (2) in place.

Thread special tool T3139-1 in threaded hole from which screw (6) was removed. Tighten the tool until it bottoms; then turn tool handle slightly counterclockwise to relieve recoil spring tension, and push out pin (2). Allow the tool and spring drive (7) to turn clockwise to unwind the recoil spring (8). Pull up on tool to remove the recoil spring and components. Guide post (9) and spring re-

tainer (10) can be lifted out after recoil spring is removed.

Recoil spring, pinion (3) or associated parts can be renewed at this time. To renew the starter rope, remove clamps on mounting bracket (12) then remove the spool. Tie one end of starter rope in a knot, then thread the free end through hole in spool (5). Wind rope around spool counterclockwise as viewed from the top and reinstall assembly leaving the inside clamp retaining screw out at this time. Insert end of rope guide (1) in hole on retainer extension (11), then insert assembly into bottom of spool (5).

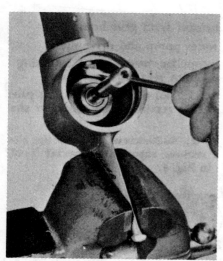

Fig. C8-25—Gearcase rear nut is accessible through propeller shaft opening as shown.

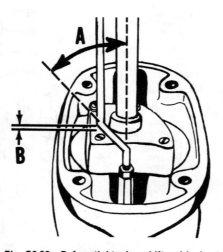

Fig. C8-26—Before tightening shift rod locknut on early units, angle (A) should be 28° with a minimum clearance (B) of 1/16-inch. Refer to text.

Fig. C8-27—Check the shift linkage adjustmen by marking detent positions as shown. Refer t text.

Illustrations courtesy Chrysle

lower shift rod (10). Separate lower unit from motor leg.

Drain the gearcase and secure gearcase skeg in a vise. Disassemble and remove the drive shaft and water pump assembly (32 through 38 – Fig. C8-23 or C8-24). Remove propeller nut, pin (30) and propeller (29). Carefully clean exposed end of propeller shaft and remove the two screws securing propeller shaft bearing cage (27) to gearcase. Rotate the bearing cage approximately ½-turn until tabs are accessible from the sides; then using a soft hammer, gently tap the bearing cage rearward out of gearcase. Remove the gearcase rear retaining stud nut working through propeller shaft opening as shown in Fig. C8-25. Remove shift rod (1 – Fig. C8-23 or C8-24), nut (2 – Fig. C8-23) and the gearcase front retaining stud nut, then lift off drive shaft housing.

Withdraw drive pinion (31) from top of gearcase and propeller shaft and associated parts through rear opening. Withdraw front and rear gears from propeller shaft. Remove spring pin (23), clutch dog (22) and shift pin (15).

The drive shaft seal (34) should be installed with spring loaded lip toward top (power head). Propeller shaft seal (28) should be installed with spring loaded lip toward outside of bearing cage (27).

Drive gear backlash and bearing preload are fixed and not adjustable. Assemble by reversing the disassembly procedure. Make sure that hole in dog clutch (22) is aligned with slot in propeller shaft (16) and hole in shift pin (15); then, insert spring pin (23).

When reinstalling shift rod (1 – Fig. C8-23) refer to Fig. C8-26. Upper end of shift rod must point to rear, starboard, so that angle (A) from housing centerline is approximately 28 degrees; and bend of rod must clear pump housing (B) approximately 1/16-inch, when shifted to lowermost (forward detent) position.

After early stage lower unit is installed, refer to Fig. C8-27 and adjust the shift linkage coupling as follows: Using the shift lever, move the linkage through Forward, Neutral and Reverse detent positions and mark the intermediate shift link where it emerges from motor leg as shown at (F, N & R). If marks are not equally spaced (caused by interference in linkage), adjust by means of the turnbuckle connector (C) until interference is removed.

CHRYSLER 55, 60 AND 65 HP

55 HP Models

Year Produced	Models
1977	558HH, 558BH, 559HH, 559BH, 558HJ, 558BJ, 559HJ, 559BJ
1978	558HK, 558BK, 559HK, 559BK
1979	558H9L, 558B9L, 559H9L, 559B9L
1980	559H0M, 559B0M, 559H0N
1981	559H1N, 559B1N
1982	559H2P, 559B2P
1983	559H3R, 559B3R, 559V3S

60 HP Models

Year Produced	Models
1974, 1975, 1976	608HA, 608BA, 609HA, 609BA
1984	608H4, 608B4

65 HP Models

Year Produced	Models
1977	659HA, 659BA
1978	659H8B, 659B8B

CONDENSED SERVICE DATA

TUNE-UP

Hp/rpm	55/5000
	60 & 65/5250
Bore-Inches	3.375
Stroke-Inches	2.80
Number of Cylinders	2
Displacement-Cu. In.	49.9
Compression at Cranking Speed (Average)	150-165 psi
Spark Plug:	
Champion (1974-1980)	UL18V
(1981-1984)	L20V
Ignition:	
Point Gap	Breakerless
Timing	See Text
Carburetor:	
Make	Tillotson
Model	WB
Fuel:Oil Ratio	50:1

*Use 25:1 fuel:oil ratio for first 10 hours and for severe service.
**Publication not authorized by manufacturer.
***Refer to text for tightening cylinder head screws.

SIZES-CLEARANCES

Piston rings:	
End Gap	**
Side Clearance	**
Piston to Cylinder:	
Clearance	**
Piston Pin:	
Diameter	*
Clearance (Rod)	**
Crankshaft Bearing	
Clearance	Roller Bearing

TIGHTENING TORQUES
(All Values in Inch-Pounds Unless Noted)

Connecting Rod	270-280
Cylinder Head	225***
Flywheel Nut	90 Ft.-Lbs.
Main Bearing Bolts	270
Standard Screws:	
10-24	30
10-32	25
12-24	45
1/4-20	70
5/16-18	160
3/8-16	270

LUBRICATION

The power head is lubricated by oil mixed with the fuel. One-third (1/3) pint of two-stroke or Outboard Motor Oil should be mixed with each gallon of gasoline. The amount of oil in the fuel may be reduced after the first 10 hours of operation (motor is broken in), provided BIA certified TC-W or TC-2 oil is used and motor is subjected to normal service only. The minimum recommended fuel:oil ratio is 50:1, or half the normally recommended amount of oil. If the amount of oil is reduced, fuel and oil must be thoroughly mixed and idle mixture carefully adjusted to make sure any error is on the "Rich" side.

Regular grade automotive gasoline is recommended if octane rating is 85 or higher. Premium grade gasoline may be used if regular is not available.

Extreme Pressure SAE 90 Gear Oil, such as "Chrysler Special Purpose Gear Lube" should be used. DO NOT use a hypoid type lubricant. The gearcase should be drained and refilled every 100 hours or once each year, and fluid maintained at the level of upper (vent) plug opening.

To fill the gearcase, have motor in an upright position and fill through lower plug hole on starboard side of gearcase until lubricant reaches level of upper vent plug opening. Reinstall and tighten both plugs, using new gaskets if necessary, to assure a water tight seal.

FUEL SYSTEM

CARBURETOR. Tillotson carburetors are used on all models. Tillotson

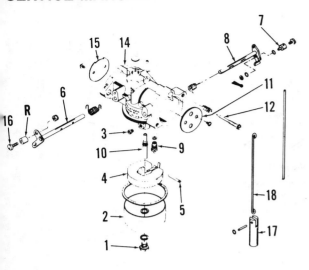

Fig. C9-1 — Exploded view of typical Tillotson WB model carburetor.

1. Bowl retaining screw
2. Fuel bowl
3. High speed jet
4. Float
5. Float pivot shaft
6. Throttle shaft
7. Choke link connector
8. Choke shaft
9. Inlet needle and seat
10. Main nozzle
11. Choke plate
12. Idle mixture needle
14. Throttle body
15. Throttle plate
16. Eccentric screw

Fig. C9-4 — Exploded view of inlet manifold and reed valve assembly.

1. Reed stop
2. Reed petals
3. Reed body
4. Gasket
5. Adapter plate
6. Gasket
7. Inlet manifold
8. By-pass check valve

WB29A carburetors are used on 65 hp models while WB23A carburetors are used on early 60 hp models and WB27A carburetors are used on later 60 hp models. Tillotson WB27A or WB27B carburetors are used on 55 hp models. Normal initial setting is one turn open for idle mixture adjustment needle (12–Fig. C9-1). Standard high speed jet (3) sizes for sea level operation are: WB23A-0.070; WB27A, WB27B-0.066; WB29A-0.068.

Care must be used in selecting the high speed fixed jet (3–Fig. C9-1). A fixed jet which is too small will result in a lean mixture and possible damage to power head. Jet may be identified by the diameter (in thousandths of an inch) stamped on visible end of installed jet. Optional jets are available which will improve performance when motor is used in high-altitude locations.

Float level (L–Fig. C9-2) should be 13/32 inch.

Throttle plates in carburetors must be synchronized to obtain maximum performance. Detach throttle link from tower shaft and rotate cam plate away from throttle roller on carburetor. Remove "E" ring from throttle arm of upper carburetor and detach end of throttle tie bar from upper carburetor

arm. Loosen tie bar screw (S–Fig. C9-3). Throttle plates should be closed in both carburetors. Attach upper end of tie bar to upper carburetor arm and tighten tie bar screw. Check to be sure throttle plates are closed. Attach throttle link to tower shaft.

SPEED CONTROL LINKAGE. On all models, ignition timing advance and throttle opening must be synchronized so that throttle is opened as timing is advanced.

To synchronize the linkage, first make certain that ignition timing is correctly set as outlined in IGNITION TIMING paragraph. Shift to forward gear and disconnect throttle link (L–Fig. C9-3) from tower shaft (T). With carburetor throttle closed, turn the eccentric screw (16) until roller (R) is exactly centered

over the scribed mark (M). Move the tower shaft (T) to full advance position and move the throttle cam until carburetor throttle is completely open. Vary the length of link (L) until the ball joint connector will just attach. Snap the ball joint connector onto ball stud and check maximum speed in neutral. If maximum rpm in neutral is not 1800-2500 rpm, it may be necessary to readjust speed control linkage.

Idle speed should be 700-800 rpm in forward gear (800-900 rpm in neutral) and is adjusted at idle screw (I–Fig. C9-3).

REED VALVES. "Vee" type intake reed valves are used on all models. The reed plate is located between intake manifold and crankcase and may be removed after removing carburetors.

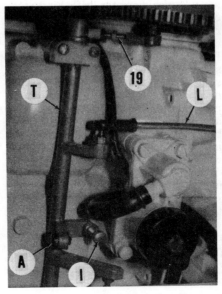

Fig. C9-2 — Float level (L) should be 13/32 inch.

Fig. C9-3 — View of tower shaft and carburetor linkage.

A. High speed stop	M. Cam mark	S. Screw	16. Eccentric screw
I. Idle speed screw	R. Roller	T. Tower shaft	19. Ignition timing rod
L. Throttle link			

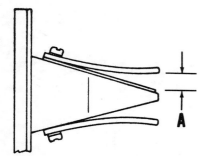

Fig. C9-5 — Reed stops should be 0.27-0.29 inch (A) from seating surface of reed block.

Fig. C9-7 — Exploded view of fuel pump.

1. Seal
2. Base
3. Gasket
4. Diaphragm
5. Check valve
6. Gasket
7. Pump housing
8. Gasket
9. Filter
10. Fuel filter inlet

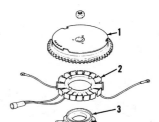

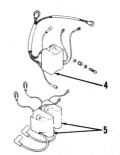

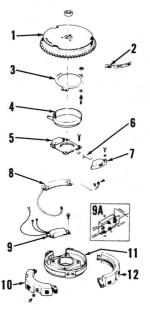

Fig. C9-9 — Exploded view of Magnapower II ignition system. Inset (9A) shows regulator/rectifier used on models after 1976.

1. Flywheel
2. Timing decal
3. Timing ring retainer
4. Timing ring
5. Trigger module bracket
6. Trigger module clip
7. Trigger module
8. Capacitors
9. Regulator/rectifier
10. Alternator
11. Bearing cage & seal
12. CD ignition module

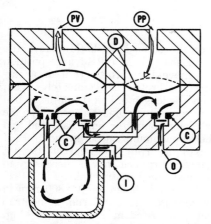

Fig. C9-6 — Cross sectional view of the two stage fuel pump used on all models. Broken lines indicate position of diaphragm when pulse pressure and vacuum are reversed.

C. Check valve
D. Diaphragm
I. Fuel inlet
O. Fuel outlet
PP. Pulse pressure
PV. Pulse vacuum

Reed valve must be smooth and even, with no sharp bends or broken reeds. Assembled reeds may stand open a maximum of 0.010 inch at tip end. Check seating visually.

Reed stop setting should be 0.27-0.29 inch (A – Fig. C9-5). Renew reeds if petals are broken, cracked, warped or bent. Never attempt to bend a reed petal in an effort to improve performance; nor attempt to straighten a damaged reed. Never install a bent or damaged reed. Seating surface of reed plate should be smooth and flat.

BY-PASS VALVES. All models are equipped with a by-pass drain system designed to remove any liquid fuel or oil which might build up in the crankcase; thus providing smoother operation at all speeds and lessening the possibility of spark plug fouling during slow speed operation.

The by-pass system is a recirculating type. Fluid accumulated in the crankcase during slow speed operation is rein-troduced to the cylinders once the engine is returned to cruising speed. Inspect hoses and check valves (8 – Fig. C9-4 and 8 – Fig. C9-23).

FUEL PUMP. All models are equipped with a diaphragm type fuel pump which is actuated by pressure and vacuum pulsations from both crankcases. The two stages operate alternately as shown.

NOTE: Either stage operating independently may permit the motor to run, but not at peak performance.

Most fuel pump service can be performed without removing the assembly from power head. Disconnect the pulse hoses and remove the retaining cap screws; then lift off the pump cover and diaphragm. Remove the sediment bowl and strainer. First stage inlet check valve can be driven out from below, using a ½-inch diameter drift. First stage outlet check valve can be lifted out after removing the retaining screws. The check valves must be installed to permit fuel to flow in the proper direction as shown in Fig. C9-6. To renew the second stage outlet check valve, it is first necessary to remove pump body from power head, remove outlet fuel elbow and drive the check valve out from below. Check valve will be damaged, and a new unit must be installed. DO NOT remove the valve unless renewal is indicated. Install new valve carefully, using an 11/16-inch diameter punch.

Renew the diaphragm if cracked or torn, or badly distorted. Install check valves carefully to prevent damage, and reassemble by reversing the disassembly procedure.

IGNITION SYSTEM

All models are equipped with a breakerless, capacitor discharge ignition system. Two types of ignition systems

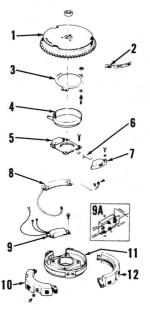

Fig. C9-10 — Exploded view of Prestolite ignition system.

1. Flywheel
2. Stator
3. Trigger coil
4. CD ignition module
5. Ignition coils

are used, "Magnapower" (Fig. C9-9) and Prestolite (Fig. C9-10). Refer to the appropriate following paragraphs after determining type of ignition used.

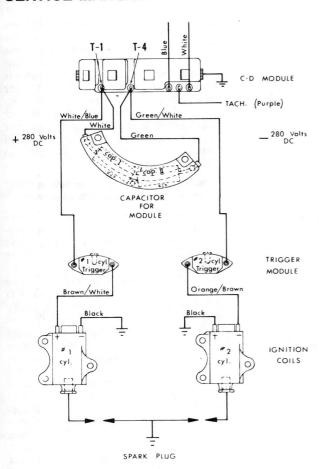

Fig. C9-11 — Schematic of Magnapower II ignition system.

Place lower unit in water and connect a suitable power timing light or Chrysler timing light number T8978 to upper spark plug. With engine in fully retarded position, crank engine with starter and note timing marks. If timing marks are not within three degrees of TDC, repeat static timing procedure. To check advanced ignition timing, run engine at 5000 to 5500 rpm with timing light connected to upper spark plug and note timing marks. Turn timing rod (19 – Fig. C9-3) between tower shaft and timing ring arm to adjust advanced ignition timing.

NOTE: Engine should be stopped when turning ignition timing rod.

Magnapower Models

TROUBLESHOOTING. If ignition malfunction is suspected, install test plugs in place of the spark plugs and observe spark while engine is being cranked with starter. If ignition spark is satisfactory, install plugs known to be good and run engine to check performance. If engine miss or failure to start is due to ignition malfunction and not faulty spark plugs, proceed as follows: Detach spark plug wires from spark plugs. Crank engine with ignition switch in "ON" position to charge capacitors. Using a suitable insulated tool such as a plastic handled screwdriver, ground flywheel to terminal (T-1 – Fig. C9-12) and then ground flywheel to terminal (T-4). If a good spark is present at both terminals, then the CD ignition module and capacitors are good. To check upper cylinder trigger module, connect "Coil N" lead from Chrysler CD ignition tester number T8953 (Electro-Specialties, Milwaukee, Wis.) to a good ground and

All Models

R&R FLYWHEEL. A special puller (Chrysler part number T-8948-1) is used to remove the flywheel. Pulling bosses are provided on the flywheel for puller installation. Flywheel should be renewed if flywheel is chipped or cracked as an unbalanced condition may be produced.

The manufacturer recommends that mating surfaces of flywheel and crankshaft be lapped before flywheel is reinstalled. If evidence of working exists proceed as follows:

Remove the flywheel key and apply a light coating of valve grinding or lapping compound to tapered portion of crankshaft. Install the flywheel without the key or crankshaft nut and rotate flywheel gently back and forth about ¼-turn. Move flywheel 90° and repeat the operation. Lift off the flywheel, wipe off excess lapping compound and carefully examine crankshaft. A minimum of 90% surface contact should be indicated by the polished surface; continue lapping only if insufficient contact is evident. Thoroughly clean the crankshaft and flywheel bore to remove all traces of lapping compound, then clean both surfaces with a non-oily solvent.

Reinstall crankshaft key and flywheel, then tighten flywheel nut to torque indicated in CONDENSED SERVICE DATA table.

IGNITION TIMING. Remove both spark plugs and thread body of special timing gage (Chrysler part number TA-2937-1) into top spark plug opening. Insert the gage rod into tool body, rotate the crankshaft and carefully position top piston at exactly TDC.

NOTE: Gage rod should be installed with "25 through 55" end out.

With the top piston at TDC, thread timing tool body in or out as necessary until the inner scribed line on gage rod is aligned with end of tool body. After gage body is correctly positioned, turn the crankshaft clockwise almost one complete revolution while applying pressure to end of gage rod. Stop the crankshaft just as the first (outer) scribed line on rod aligns with tool body. Piston should be positioned at 32 degrees BTDC and timing mark on carburetor adapter flange should be aligned with 32 degree mark on flywheel timing decal. If marks do not align, install a new decal or make new marks on flywheel.

Fig. C9-12 — View of CD module showing location of (T-1) and (T-4) terminals.

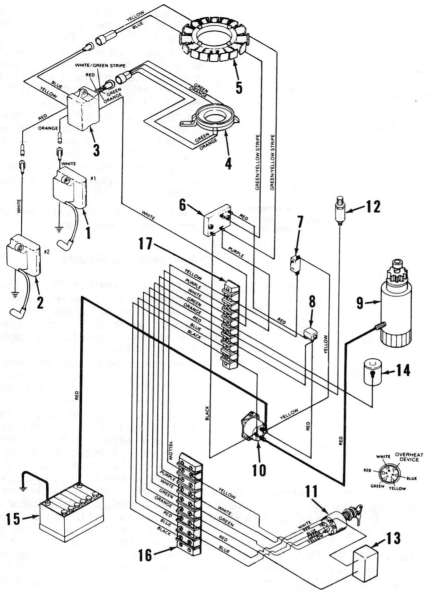

Fig. C9-13 — Wiring diagram for motors with Prestolite ignition system.

1. Ignition coil for top cylinder
2. Ignition coil for bottom cylinder
3. CD ignition module
4. Trigger coil
5. Stator
6. Regulator/rectifier
7. Neutral interlock switch
8. Circuit breaker
9. Starter
10. Starter solenoid
11. Ignition switch
12. Heat indicator
13. Overheat warning device
14. Choke solenoid
15. Battery
16. Terminal block at dashboard
17. Terminal block at motor

proceed as follows: Remove flywheel and disconnect trigger module leads. Unbolt trigger module plate and rotate plate so that trigger module positions are reversed. Connect trigger module leads and former upper cylinder trigger module is now the bottom cylinder trigger module and former bottom cylinder trigger module is now the upper cylinder trigger module. Install flywheel and crank engine with ignition switch in "ON" position.

NOTE: Leave ignition switch in "ON" position to retain charge in capacitors.

Repeat spark test at T-1 and T-4 terminals. If little or no spark is now present at opposite terminal, i.e. no spark at terminal T-1 in first test and no spark at terminal T-4 in next test, trigger module is faulty and should be renewed. If same terminal still has little or no spark, CD ignition module or capacitor is faulty and may be checked as follows: Disconnect capacitor and trigger leads from terminal (T-1 or T-4) that has little or no spark. Connect a spade terminal or terminal (T-1 or T-4) and connect Chrysler CD ignition tester number T8953 (Electro-Specialties, Milwaukee, Wis.) to spade terminal. To check T-1 terminal, connect "Coil P" lead from tester to T-1 terminal and "Coil N" lead to a good ground. To check T-4 terminal, connect "Coil N" lead from tester to T-4 terminal and "Coil P" lead to a good ground. Set dial of tester to "50" and crank engine. If tester lights, CD ignition module is good and capacitor module should be renewed. If tester does not light, CD ignition module is faulty and should be renewed.

Prestolite Models

TROUBLESHOOTING. Use only approved procedures when testing to prevent damage to components. The fuel system should be checked to make cer-

connect "Coil P" lead from CD tester to positive (+) terminal of upper cylinder ignition coil. Set dial of tester to "65" and crank engine. If lamp lights on tester, trigger module is operating correctly. If lamp does not light, renew trigger module. To check operation of bottom cylinder trigger module, connect "Coil P" lead of CD ignition tester to a good ground and connect "Coil N" lead to negative (−) terminal of bottom cylinder ignition coil. Repeat test procedure used for upper cylinder trigger module.

If little or no spark was present when T-1 and T-4 terminals were tested, note which terminal had little or no spark and

Fig. C9-14 — Tester connections for checking voltage output of charge coil.

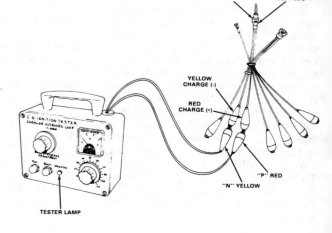

Illustrations courtesy Chrysler

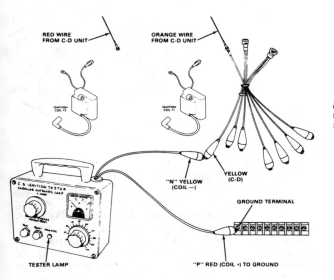

Fig. C9-15 — Tester connections for checking trigger coil operation.

Fig. C9-16 — View showing tester connections needed to check CD ignition module output.

wire plug from trigger coil as shown in Fig. C9-15. Attach red (P) lead from number 22 tester to red sleeved adapter wire marked Trigger 1 Pos. and yellow (N) lead to yellow sleeved adapter wire marked Trigger 1 Neg. Place switch of tester in number 1 position and crank engine. Trigger coil operation is satisfactory if tester lamp lights. Renew trigger housing if tester lamp does not light.

To check operation of number 2 cylinder trigger coil, repeat test procedure for number 1 cylinder trigger coil but connect red (P) lead of tester to red sleeved adapter wire marked Trigger 2 Pos. and yellow (N) tester lead to yellow sleeved adapter wire marked Trigger 2 Neg.

To check CD ignition module performance for each cylinder, separate primary lead connections between CD ignition module and ignition coils. Connect single wire adapter to orange (number 1 cylinder) or red (number 2 cylinder) wire from CD ignition module (Fig. C9-16), then attach yellow (N) lead of T8953 tester to yellow sleeved adapter wire marked C-D. Attach red (P) tester lead to ground terminal of engine terminal block. Turn tester switch to position 60 and crank engine. Renew CD module if tester lamp does not light.

COOLING SYSTEM

The thermostat is located in the cylinder head and is accessible after removing engine covers surrounding engine. All models are equipped with a rubber impeller type water pump. Water pump is mounted in lower unit drive shaft housing.

tain that faulty running is not caused by incorrect fuel mixture or contaminated fuel. If ignition malfunction is suspected, use Chrysler tool T8953, plug adapter set T11237 and number 22 tester. Check and make sure ignition malfunction is not due to spark plug or ignition coil failure. Install test plugs in place of the spark plugs and observe spark while engine is being cranked with starter. If spark is absent at both cylinders, check condition of charge coil as follows:

Separate the blue and yellow wire connection between charge coil (stator) and CD ignition module and attach double wire plug adapter to wire plug from charge coil as shown in Fig. C9-14. Attach red (P) lead from T8953 tester to red sleeved adapter wire marked Charge (+). Attach yellow (N) lead of tester to yellow sleeved adapter wire marked Charge (−). Turn tester switch to position 60 and crank engine. If tester lamp does not light, charge coil is defective and stator should be renewed. If lamp lights, charge coil operation is satisfactory and trigger coil and CD ignition module circuits for each cylinder

must be checked. Remove tester and plug adapter set, then reconnect blue and yellow wire plugs.

Separate the four-wire connection between CD ignition module and trigger coil and attach four-wire plug adapter to

Fig. C9-17 — Exploded view of electric starter.

1. Brush plate
2. Brush spring
3. Thrust washers
5. End housing
6. Armature
7. Housing
8. Brush terminal
9. Nut
10. Stop
11. Spring
12. Pinion
13. End plate
14. Thrust washers

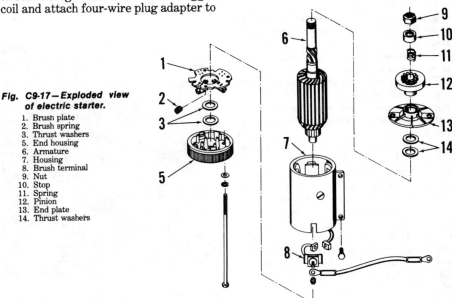

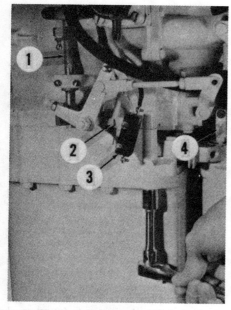

Fig. C9-18 — View of right side of power head showing location of tower shaft (1), interlock switch bracket (2), interlock switch (3) and upper shift rod (4).

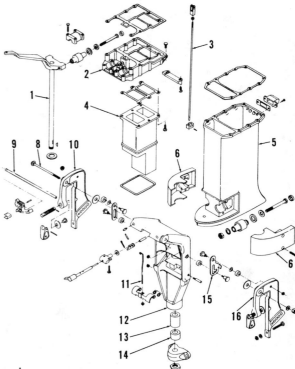

Fig. C9-19 — Exploded view of motor leg assembly.

1. King pin
2. Spacer plate
3. Upper shift rod
4. Exhaust tube
5. Motor leg
6. Lower shock mount cover
8. Pivot bolt
9. Lock bar
10. Stern bracket
11. Link
12. Swivel bracket
13. Bearing
14. Spacer
15. Tilt stop
16. Stern bracket

When cooling system problems are encountered, first check the thermostat to see that it is operating properly. Check the water inlet for plugging or partial stoppage, then if trouble is not corrected, remove the lower unit gearcase as outlined in LOWER UNIT section, and check the condition of water pump, water passages and sealing surfaces.

POWER HEAD

REMOVE AND DISASSEMBLE. Cylinder head may be removed without removing power head. Refer to CYLINDER HEAD section for cylinder head removal.

To remove power head, remove engine covers and disconnect fuel line from fuel pump. Disconnect upper shift rod (4 – Fig. C9-18) from shift arm. Unscrew power head retaining nuts and lift power head off spacer plate.

To gain access to short block assembly, remove flywheel and ignition, carburetors, carburetor adapter and reed valve. Remove starter motor, starter relay, circuit breaker, exhaust port cover and fuel pump. Remove tower-shaft (1 – Fig. C9-18), gear shift linkage and interlock switch bracket (2). Remove remote cable bracket and stabilizer bar at front of engine.

To disassemble the power head, unbolt and remove the upper and lower bearing cages; then unbolt and remove the crankcase front half. Pry slots are provided for separating the crankcase; DO NOT pry on machined mating surfaces of cylinder block and crankcase front half.

Crankshaft, pistons and bearings are now accessible for removal and overhaul as outlined in the appropriate following paragraphs. Assemble as outlined in the ASSEMBLY paragraph.

ASSEMBLY. When reassembling, make sure all joint and gasket surfaces are clean and free from nicks, burrs, warped surfaces, hardened cement or carbon. The crankcase and inlet manifolds must be completely sealed against both vacuum and pressure. Exhaust manifold and cylinder head must be sealed against water leakage and pressure. Mating surfaces of exhaust areas between power head and spacer plate must form a tight seal.

Install crankshaft making certain upper and center main bearings are properly positioned over main bearing locating pins in cylinder block. With new crankcase seal installed in seal groove, apply a suitable sealer to mating surfaces of crankcase in areas adjacent to upper, center and lower main bearings and around main bearing bolt holes. Immediately install crankcase front half and tighten main bearing bolts to 270 in.-lbs. torque. Make sure crankshaft turns freely before proceeding with assembly.

Renew outer "O" ring (21 – Fig. C9-22) and seals (20 and 23) in lower bearing cage (22) as required. Press small diameter seal (23), with spring loaded lip away from crankshaft, into bearing cage until it bottoms. Press large diameter

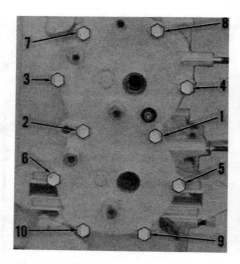

Fig. C9-20 — View showing cylinder head bolt tightening sequence.

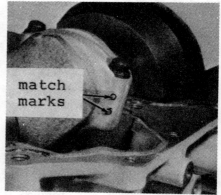

Fig. C9-21 — Match marks on rod and cap should be aligned and toward top of engine.

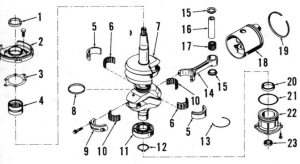

Fig. C9-22 — Exploded view of piston and crankshaft assemblies.

1. Seal
2. Upper bearing cage
3. Gasket
4. Roller bearing
5. Bearing outer race
6. Bearing and cage
7. Crankshaft
8. Crankcase seal
9. Rod cap
10. Bearing and cage
11. Ball bearing
12. Snap ring
13. Snap ring
14. Connecting rod
15. Spacer
16. Piston pin
17. Needle bearing
18. Piston
19. Piston ring
20. Seal
21. Seal
22. Lower bearing cage
23. Seal

signed for right-hand rotation. Diameter of propeller for 55 and 60 hp models is 11½ inches with a 12-inch pitch while 65 hp propeller has 10-inch diameter and 13-inch pitch.

LOWER UNIT

60 Hp And Early 55 Hp Models

R&R AND OVERHAUL. To remove lower unit from motor leg, unscrew six bolts securing lower unit to motor leg, remove pin (14 – Fig. C9-24) connecting intermediate shift rod and lower shift rod (15) and separate lower unit from motor leg.

Drain gearcase and secure gearcase skeg in a vise. Disassemble and remove water pump assembly (1 through 6). Remove propeller nut, pin and propeller. Carefully clean exposed end of propeller shaft and remove the two screws securing propeller shaft bearing cage (34) to gearcase. Remove bearing cage with Chrysler tool number T8948 or a suitable puller. Unscrew stud nuts and separate gearcase and drive shaft housing. Drive shaft and drive pinion (19) will remain with drive shaft housing. Thread a 5/16-inch lag screw into top of shift rod seal (10) and press against bottom of screw to remove seal from housing. Unscrew drive pinion (19) retaining screw and separate pinion from drive shaft. Press drive shaft out of drive shaft housing then press upper drive shaft bearing cup out of housing.

seal (20), with spring loaded lip toward crankshaft, into bearing cage until seal is 0.009-0.012 inch below cage surface.

CYLINDER HEAD. To remove cylinder head, remove covers surrounding engine. Remove ignition coils, spark plugs and thermostat. Unscrew cylinder head screws and separate cylinder head from engine. Unscrew cylinder head cover screws and water temperature switch and separate cylinder head cover and cylinder head.

Apply an anti-seize liquid to cylinder head screws and tighten in sequence shown in Fig. C9-20. Tighten screws to an initial torque reading of 70 in.-lbs. and then tighten in increments of 50 in.-lbs. until a final torque reading of 225 in.-lbs. is attained.

PISTONS, PINS, RINGS & CYLINDERS. Pistons are equipped with two piston rings which are pinned in place to prevent rotation. Piston pin rides in roller bearing in small end of connecting rod.

On early models, assemble piston, pin and connecting rod with long tapering side of piston crown toward exhaust side of cylinder and alignment marks (Fig. C9-21) toward the top end of crankshaft. On late models, disassembly of piston, pin and rod for repair is not required as components are renewable only as a complete unit.

CONNECTING RODS, BEARINGS AND CRANKSHAFT. Before detaching connecting rods from crankshaft, make certain that rod and cap are properly marked for correct assembly to each other and in the correct cylinder. The needle rollers and cages at crankpin end of connecting rod should be kept with the assembly and not interchanged. The bearing rollers and cages used in the two connecting rods and center main bearing are available only as a set which contains the cages and rollers for one bearing. Center main bearing outer

races are held together by snap ring (13 – Fig. C9-22).

To install connecting rod on crankshaft, apply a light coating of a suitable grease to connecting rod and install bearing cage half and seven bearing rollers in rod. Position rod and bearing against crankpin and install remaining bearing cage and nine bearing rollers on crankpin. Install rod cap being sure match marks are aligned and rod and cap are properly meshed before tightening screws. Connecting rod and cap will be flush when rod and cap are meshed correctly.

PROPELLER

Standard propeller for 55, 60 and 65 hp models has three blades and is de-

Fig. C9-23 — Exploded view of cylinder block assembly.

1. Exhaust port cover
2. Gasket
3. Exhaust port plate
4. Gasket
5. Cylinder block
6. Seal
7. Front crankcase half
8. By-pass check valve
9. Dowel pin
10. Ignition timing rod
11. Tower shaft
12. Throttle link
13. Shift link
14. Gasket
15. Cylinder head
16. Gasket
17. Thermostat cover
18. Gasket
19. Thermostat
20. Grommet
21. Thermoswitch
22. Cylinder head cover

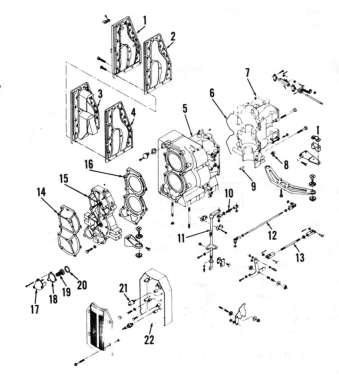

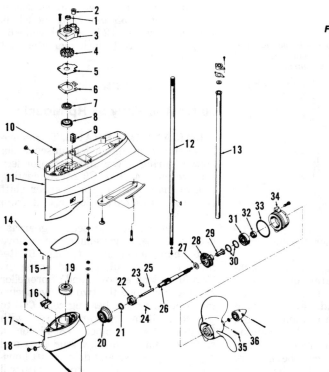

Fig. C9-24 — Exploded view of lower unit.

1. Drive shaft seal
2. Water tube seal
3. Water pump housing
4. Impeller
5. Back plate
6. Gasket
7. Drive shaft seal
8. Bearing
9. Water inlet screen
10. Shift rod seal
11. Drive shaft housing
12. Drive shaft
13. Water tube
14. Shift rod pin
15. Lower shift rod
16. Pivot coupling
17. Pivot pin
18. Gearcase
19. Drive pinion & bearing
20. Forward gear & bearing
21. Thrust washer
22. Shift coupling
23. Shift yoke
24. Shift pin
25. Shift shaft
26. Propeller shaft
27. Thrust washer
28. Reverse gear
29. Bushing
30. Shims
31. Bearing
32. Seal
33. "O" ring
34. Bearing cage
35. Shear pin
36. Nut

Drive gear backlash is controlled by means of shim pack (30) installed between bushing (29) flange and bearing (31) cone. Backlash adjustment requires the use of the special test jig and dial indicator as shown in Fig. C9-25. Shaft end play in the special test fixture should be zero, plus or minus 0.001 inch. Shims are available in thicknesses of 0.005, 0.006 and 0.008 inch.

After backlash has been adjusted, the propeller shaft bearings must be adjusted by varying the thickness of front thrust washer (21 – Fig. C9-24). The bearings should be adjusted to 0.004-0.006 inch end play. Thrust washers are available in thicknesses from 0.056 inch to 0.086 inch in 0.003 inch increments. To measure the bearing adjustment, assemble propeller shaft components (20 through 34) except yoke (23) and "O" ring (33) in gearcase. Install a 0.056 inch thrust washer (21). Measure propeller shaft end play.

To assemble the propeller shaft, refer to Fig. C9-24. Slide the shift coupling (22) onto propeller shaft with hole in coupling aligned with slot in shaft. Position shift shaft (25) inside propeller shaft and align hole with hole in coupling. Drive pin (24) through holes in coupling, propeller shaft and shift shaft. Install pivot coupling (16), pivot pin (17) and lower shift rod (15). Slide the forward gear (20) and bearing cone on front end

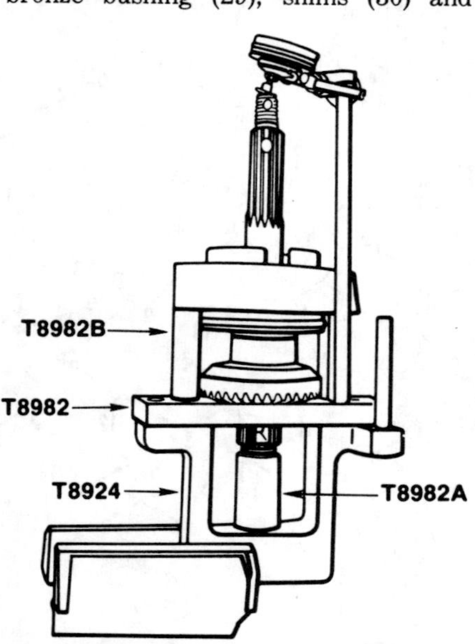

Withdraw propeller shaft and associated parts.

NOTE: Shift yoke (23) will be free to drop when propeller shaft is removed. Do not lose the yoke.

Slip the forward gear and bearing assembly (20) from the propeller shaft. Shift coupling (22) and shift shaft (25) can be removed after driving pin (24) out. Bearing (31) must be pressed off shaft to remove reverse gear (28), bronze bushing (29), shims (30) and

thrust washer (27). Keep the thrust washers (21 & 27) with their respective gears. The washers are similar but NOT interchangeable.

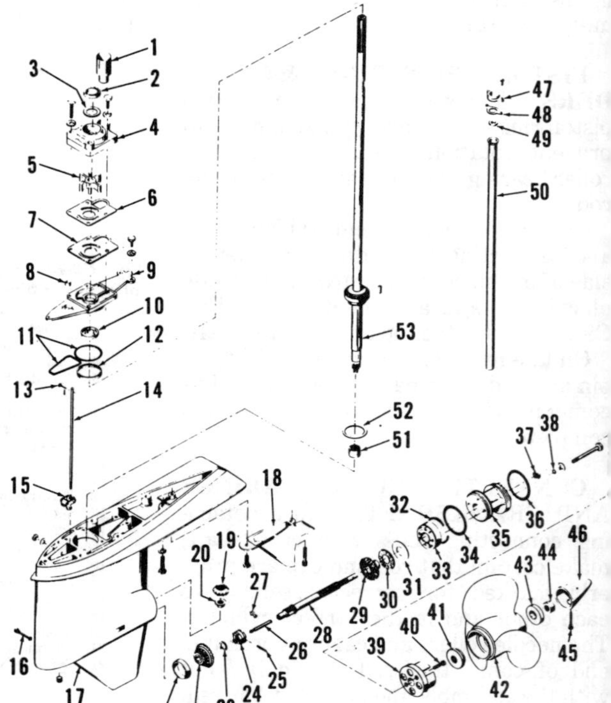

Fig. C9-26 — Exploded view of lower drive unit used on 65 hp and late 55 hp models.

1. Water tube seal
2. Drive shaft seal
3. Spacer
4. Water pump housing
5. Impeller
6. Lower plate
7. Gasket
8. Shift rod seal
9. Gearcase cover
10. Drive shaft seal
11. Cover seals
12. Crush ring
13. Pin
14. Lower shift rod
15. Pivot coupling
16. Pivot pin
17. Gearcase
18. Exhaust snout
19. Drive pinion
20. Nut
21. Bearing cup
22. Forward gear & bearing
23. Shim
24. Shift coupling
25. Shift pin
26. Shift shaft
27. Shift yoke
28. Propeller shaft
29. Reverse gear
30. Thrust bearing
31. Thrust washer
32. Retainer clips
33. Bearing & cage
34. "O" ring
35. Spool
36. "O" ring
37. Seal
38. "O" ring
39. Anode
40. Screw
41. Spacer
42. Propeller
43. Washer
44. Nut
45. Pin
46. Prop extension
47. Bracket
48. Seal
49. Grommet
50. Water tube
51. Bearing
52. Shim
53. Drive shaft

Fig. C9-25 — View of special tools used to determine thickness of shims for correct gear backlash.

T8982B
T8982
T8924
T8982A

of propeller shaft and position the yoke (23) in front slot of shift shaft (25). Carefully slide the assembled propeller shaft into gearcase housing making sure that tabs of shift yoke (23) engage both forked slots in pivot coupling (16). Carefully install bearing cage using new seal (32) and "O" ring (33). Assemble drive shaft, drive pinion and bearings in drive shaft housing (11). Apply Loctite 271 or 290 to drive pinion retaining screw threads. Tighten pinion retaining screw so drive shaft just turns freely without binding. Tap on screw to be sure bearings are seated and retighten screw.

Be sure to install shift rod pin (14) after mating drive shaft housing with motor leg.

65 Hp And Late 55 Hp Models

R&R AND OVERHAUL. Remove lower front shock mount cover and remove shift rod pin (13 – Fig. C9-26). Unscrew six screws and separate gearcase from motor leg. Drain lubricant and remove propeller and exhaust snout (18).

Disassemble and remove water pump components (1 through 7). Turn shift rod (14) counterclockwise until disengaged from pivot coupling (15) and remove rod. Remove cover (9) and anode (39). Remove screws securing bearing spool (35) and using a suitable puller withdraw spool from gearcase. Remove retaining clips (32), bearing and cage (33), thrust washer (31), thrust bearing (30) and reverse gear (29). Withdraw propeller shaft (28) with components (22 through 27). Unscrew pinion nut (20), withdraw drive shaft (53) and remove pinion gear (19). Unscrew pivot pin (16) and remove pivot coupling (15).

Use the following procedure to check reverse gear backlash: Install a 0.050 inch spacer (Chrysler T8997) in place of shims (52). Install forward gear and bearing (22), drive shaft (53), pinion gear (19) and nut (20). Tighten nut (20) to 600 in.-lbs. Insert Chrysler shim tool number T8997B in forward gear (22) so flat portion of tool is towards pinion gear (19). Pull up on drive shaft and using a feeler gage measure gap between large OD of tool and pinion gear. Subtract measured

gap from 0.055 inch (0.050 inch spacer plus 0.005 inch desired backlash) to obtain thickness of shim pack (52). Remove 0.050 inch shim, install shim pack (52) and repeat above procedure. Gap between pinion gear (19) and large OD of shim tool should be 0.004-0.006 inch.

To check propeller shaft end play, install components (21 through 32) and bearing spool (35). Shim (23) should be thinnest available (0.054 inch). Do not install "O" rings on spool. Tighten spool retaining screws to 150 in.-lbs. Measure end play of propeller shaft and install shims (23) necessary to obtain 0.009-0.011 inch end play.

To reassemble lower unit, reverse disassembly procedure. Tighten pinion nut (20) to 600 in.-lbs. Install seal (37) with lip towards propeller. "O" rings (34 & 36) have different diameters and must be installed correctly on bearing spool (35). Chamfered end of spool is installed first. Tighten bearing spool (35) retaining screws to 150 in.-lbs. Install seals (8 & 10) with lip towards gearcase. Tighten cover (9) to 70 in.-lbs. Install seal (2) with lip towards power head.

CHRYSLER

3 AND 4 CYLINDER MODELS

Year Produced	70 hp	75 hp	85 hp	90 hp	100 hp	105 hp
1969	70*†	.....	85*†	.....	.....	105*†
1970	70*§	.....	85*§	.....	.....	105*§
1971	70*§	.....	85*§	.....	.....	105*§
1972	70*§	.....	85*§	.....	.....	105*§
1973	70*§	.....	85*§	.....	.....	105*§
1974	.....	75*§	.....	90*§	.....	105*§
1975	.....	75*§	.....	90*§	.....	105*§
1976	.....	75*§	.....	90*§	.....	105*§
1977	.....	75*§	.....	90*§	.....	105*§
1978	.....	75*§	85*§	.....	.....	105*§
1979	70*§	75*§	85*§	.....	.....	.....
1980	70*§	75*§	85*§	.....	100*§	.....
1981	.....	75*§	85*§	.....	100*§	.....
1982	.....	75*§	85*§	.....	.....	105*§
1983	.....	75*§	85*§	90*§	100*§	.....
1984	.....	75*§	85*§	90*§	100*§	.....

Year Produced	115 hp	120 hp	125 hp	130 hp	135 hp	140 hp	150 hp
1969	.....	.....	.....	.....	.....	.....	.....
1970	.....	120*§	.....	.....	135*§	.....	.....
1971	.....	120*§	.....	.....	135*§	.....	.....
1972	.....	120*§	.....	130*§	.....	.....	150*§
1973	.....	120*§	.....	130*§	.....	.....	150*§
1974	.....	120*§	.....	.....	135*§	.....	150*§
1975	.....	120*§	.....	.....	135*§	.....	150*§
1976	.....	120*§	.....	.....	135*§	.....	150*§
1977	.....	120*§	.....	.....	135*§	.....	.....
1978	115*§	.....	.....	.....	.....	140*§	.....
1979	115*§	.....	.....	.....	.....	140*§	.....
1980	115*§	.....	.....	.....	.....	140*§	.....
1981	115*§	.....	125*§	.....	.....	140*§	.....
1982	115*§	.....	125*§	.....	.....	140*§	.....
1983	115*§	.....	.....	.....	.....	140*§	.....
1984	115*§	.....	.....	.....	.....	140*§	.....

*Variation Code:
0 – Standard shaft, manual starter.
1 – Long shaft, manual starter.
2 – Standard shaft, manual starter, with tiller.
3 – Long shaft, manual starter, with tiller.
4 – Standard shift, electric starter.
5 – Long shaft, electric starter.

6 – Standard shaft, electric starter, with alternator.
7 – Long shaft, electric starter, with alternator.
8 – Same as number 6 except with "Magnapower" ignition.
9 – Same as number 7 except with "Magnapower" ignition.

†Production Code Before 1970:
1, 3 & 5 – USA Models.
2, 4 & 6 – Canada Models

§Production Code for 1970 and Later:
HA, HB, HC, HD, HE, HF, HG, HJ & HN – USA Models; BA, BB, BC, BD, BE, BF, BG, BJ, & BN – Canada Models

CONDENSED SERVICE DATA

	70, 75, 85, 90 HP	100, 105, 120, 130 HP 135 HP (1970-1971) 150 HP (1972-1975)	125 HP	115 HP 135 HP (1974-1977) 150 HP (1976)	140 HP
TUNE-UP					
Hp/rpm	70/4750 75/4750 85/5000 90/5000	100 & 105/5000 120 & 130/5250 135 & 150/5400	125/5000	115 & 135/5000 150/5400	140/5250
Bore–Inches	3.3125	3.3125	3.3125	3.375	3.375
Stroke–Inches	*2.80	2.80	2.875	2.80	2.875
Number of Cylinders	3	4	4	4	4
Displacement–Cu. In.	*72.39	96.55	99.23	99.8	103
Spark Plug:					
Champion	L20V	L20V	L20V	L20V	L20V
Electrode Gap	Surface Gap	Surface Gap	Surface Gap	Surface Gap	Surface Gap
Ignition:					
Point Gap	See Text	See Text	See Text	See Text	See Text
Firing Order	1-2-3	1-3-2-4	1-3-2-4	1-3-2-4	1-3-2-4
Carburetor:					
Make	Tillotson	Tillotson	Tillotson	Tillotson	Tillotson
Model	WB	WB	WB	WB	WB
Fuel:Oil Ratio	50:1	50:1	50:1	50:1	50:1

*Performance 85 hp models have a 2.70 in. stroke and a 69.81 cu. in. displacement.

SIZES – CLEARANCES
Piston Ring End Gap	†0.006-0.016 in.
Piston Ring Groove Width	†0.0645-0.0655 in.
Piston to Cylinder Clearance	0.0075-0.0103 in. — 0.006.0.008 in.
Piston Pin:	
Diameter	0.68750-0.68765 in.
Clearance (Rod)	Needle Bearing
Clearance (Piston)	0.00005 in. tight to 0.00040 in. loose
Crankshaft Journal Diameters:	
Upper Main Bearing	1.3789-1.3793 in.
Center Main Bearing	1.3748-1.3752 in.
Lower Main Bearing	1.2495-1.2500 in.
Crankpin	1.1391-1.1395 in.

†A semi-keystone top piston ring is used on 140 hp models and has an end gap of 0.004-0.014 in. Refer to text to check top ring groove wear.

TIGHTENING TORQUES
(All Values in Inch-Pounds Unless Otherwise Noted)
Connecting Rod (1969-1978)	170
(1979-1984)	185
Cylinder Head	225
Flywheel Nut	90 Ft.-Lbs.
Crankcase	270
Standard Screws:	
10-24	30
10-32	35
12-24	45
¼-20	70
5/16-28	160
⅜-16	270

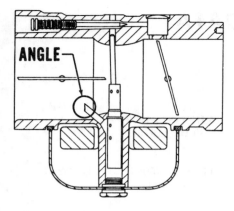

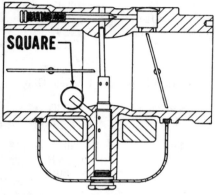

Fig. C10-1—Cross section of WB-2A carburetors showing two different types of air bleed tubes. Angle cut type requires a larger main jet and can be viewed through choke bore. Square cut type is shown at bottom.

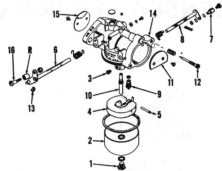

Fig. C10-2—Exploded view of typical Tillotson WB model carburetor. Type TC carburetors are similar.

1. Bowl retaining screw	9. Inlet needle and seat
2. Fuel bowl	10. Main nozzle
3. High speed jet	11. Choke plate
4. Float	12. Idle mixture needle
5. Float pivot shaft	13. Snap ring
6. Throttle shaft	14. Throttle body
7. Choke link connector	15. Throttle plate
8. Choke shaft	16. Eccentric screw

LUBRICATION

The power head is lubricated by oil mixed with the fuel. One-third (1/3) pint of two-stroke engine oil should be mixed with each gallon of gasoline. The amount of oil in the fuel may be reduced after motor is well broken in (at least 10 hours of operation, provided BIA certified TC-W or TC-2 oil is used. The minimum, recommended fuel:oil ratio is 50:1, or one (1) pint of oil for each six (6) gallons of fuel. If the oil amount is reduced, it is extremely important that fuel and oil be thoroughly mixed, that idle mixture adjusting screws be carefully checked to make sure any error of adjustment is on the "Rich" side, and that the recommended high speed jets are used. Regular grade leaded automotive gasoline is recommended. If regular is not available, use a good grade of premium gasoline.

The lower unit gears and bearings are lubricated by oil contained in the gearcase. Only a non-corrosive, leaded outboard, gear oil, EP90 such as "Chrysler Marine Gear Lube" or equivalent should be used. The gearcase should be drained

and refilled every 100 hours or once each year, and fluid maintained at the level of the upper (vent) plug hole.

To fill the gearcase, have the motor in upright position and fill through the lower plug hole in starboard side of gearcase until fluid reaches level of upper vent plug. Reinstall and tighten both plugs securely, using new gaskets if necessary, to assure a water tight seal.

FUEL SYSTEM

CARBURETOR. Tillotson type WB and TC carburetors are used. Refer to Fig. C10-2. The carburetor model number is stamped on the mounting flange. Three carburetors are used on 3-cylinder models. Two carburetors are used on 4-cylinder models.

NOTE: On 3-cylinder motors, make certain that all three carburetors used are the same model number. On 4-cylinder models, both carburetors must be the same model. If WB-2A carburetors are used, both idle bleed tubes should be the same. Refer to Fig. C10-1. On early 3-cylinder models, the choke return spring on choke shaft should be removed from the lower carburetor.

Normal initial setting is one turn open for idle mixture adjustment needle (12 – Fig. C10-2). Fixed jet (3) controls high speed mixture. Idle mixture must be readjusted under load, after motor is warm, for best slow speed performance. Idle mixture needle for all carburetors must be adjusted as nearly as possible for equal performance and all main jets (3) must be the same size.

Care must be used in selecting the high speed fixed jet (3 – Fig. C10-2). A fixed jet which is too small will result in

a lean mixture and possible damage to power head. Jet may be identified by the diameter (in thousandths of an inch) stamped on visible end of installed jet. Optional jets are available which will improve performance when motor is used in high-altitude locations; optional jet and recommended altitudes are as follows:

70 HP (WB-1C)

Altitude	Jet Size	Part Number
Sea Level-1500 ft.	0.070	013430
1500-3000 ft.	0.066	014188
3000-4500 ft.	0.064	014108
4500-6000 ft.	0.062	014187
Above 6000 ft.	0.060	014186

70 HP (WB-8A, WB-8B, WB-8C, WB-26B & WB-31A) Except Models 709H9A & 709B9A

Altitude	Jet Size	Part Number
Sea Level-1500 ft.	0.062	014187
1500-3000 ft.	0.060	014186
3000-4500 ft.	0.058	015337
4500-6000 ft.	0.056	015338
Above 6000 ft.	0.054	015339

70 HP (WB-26B) Models 709H9A & 709B9A

Altitude	Jet Size	Part Number
Sea Level-1500 ft.	0.066	014188
1500-3000 ft.	0.064	014108
3000-4500 ft.	0.062	014187
4500-6000 ft.	0.060	014186
Above 6000 ft.	0.058	015337

75 HP (WB-22A)

Altitude	Jet Size	Part Number
Sea Level-1500 ft.	0.064	014108
1500-3000 ft.	0.062	014187
3000-4500 ft.	0.060	014186
4500-6000 ft.	0.058	015337
Above 6000 ft.	0.056	015338

75 HP (WB-26B)

Altitude	Jet Size	Part Number
Sea Level-1500 ft.	0.066	014188
1500-3000 ft.	0.064	014108
3000-4500 ft.	0.062	014187
4500-6000 ft.	0.060	014186
Above 6000 ft.	0.058	015337

85 HP (WB-6A)

Altitude	Jet Size	Part Number
Sea Level-1500 ft.	0.074	014303
1500-3000 ft.	0.072	015026
3000-4500 ft.	0.070	013430
4500-6000 ft.	0.068	013967
Above 6000 ft.	0.066	014188

85 HP (WB-9A, WB-9B & WB-9D)

Altitude	Jet Size	Part Number
Sea Level-1500 ft.	0.064	014108
1500-3000 ft.	0.062	014187
3000-4500 ft.	0.060	014186
4500-6000 ft.	0.058	015337
Above 6000 ft.	0.056	015338

85 HP (WB-21C)

Altitude	Jet Size	Part Number
Sea Level-1500 ft.	0.072	015026
1500-3000 ft.	0.070	013430
3000-4500 ft.	0.068	013967
4500-6000 ft.	0.066	014188
Above 6000 ft.	0.064	014108

90 HP (WB-21A)

Altitude	Jet Size	Part Number
Sea Level-1500 ft.	0.074	014303
1500-3000 ft.	0.072	015026
3000-4500 ft.	0.070	013430
4500-6000 ft.	0.068	013967
Above 6000 ft.	0.066	014188

100 HP (WB-24B)

Altitude	Jet Size	Part Number
Sea Level-1500 ft.	0.080	013194
1500-3000 ft.	0.078	014306
3000-4500 ft.	0.076	013191
4500-6000 ft.	0.074	014303
Above 6000 ft.	0.072	015026

105 HP (WB-2C and WB-10B)

Altitude	Jet Size	Part Number
Sea Level-1500 ft.	0.088	013193
1500-3000 ft.	0.084	014302
3000-4500 ft.	0.082	014109
4500-6000 ft.	0.080	013194
Above 6000 ft.	0.0785	014306

105 HP (WB-10D & WB-10E)

Altitude	Jet Size	Part Number
Sea Level-1500 ft.	0.084	014302
1500-3000 ft.	0.082	014109
3000-4500 ft.	0.080	013194
4500-6000 ft.	0.0785	014306
Above 6000 ft.	0.076	013191

105 HP (WB-24A)

Altitude	Jet Size	Part Number
Sea Level-1500 ft.	0.078	014306
1500-3000 ft.	0.076	013191
3000-4500 ft.	0.074	014303
4500-6000 ft.	0.072	015026
Above 6000 ft.	0.070	013430

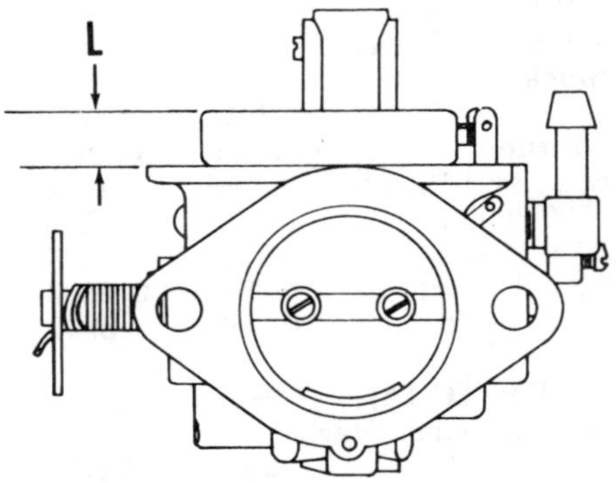

Fig. C10-3—Float level (L) should be 13/32 inch for WB and TC carburetors.

105 HP (WB-24B)

Altitude	Jet Size	Part Number
Sea Level-1500 ft.	0.080	013194
1500-3000 ft.	0.078	014306
3000-4500 ft.	0.076	013191
4500-6000 ft.	0.074	014303
Above 6000 ft.	0.072	015026

115 HP (WB-25B)

Altitude	Jet Size	Part Number
Sea Level-1500 ft.	0.086	013949
1500-3000 ft.	0.084	014302
3000-4500 ft.	0.082	014109
4500-6000 ft.	0.080	013194
Above 6000 ft.	0.078	014306

115 HP (TC-6B)

Altitude	Jet Size	Part Number
Sea Level-1500 ft.	0.0937	014191
1500-3000 ft.	0.092	014190
3000-4500 ft.	0.090	015406
4500-6000 ft.	0.088	013193
Above 6000 ft.	0.086	013949

115 HP (TC-7A)

Altitude	Jet Size	Part Number
Sea Level-1250 ft.	0.090	015406
1250-3750 ft.	0.088	013193
3750-6250 ft.	0.086	013949
6250-8250 ft.	0.084	014302
Above 6000 ft.	0.082	014109

120 HP (WB-13A)

Altitude	Jet Size	Part Number
Sea Level-1500 ft.	0.088	013193
1500-3000 ft.	0.086	013949
3000-4500 ft.	0.084	014302
4500-6000 ft.	0.082	014109
Above 6000 ft.	0.080	013194

120 HP (WB-13C & WB-13D)

Altitude	Jet Size	Part Number
Sea Level-1500 ft.	0.088	013193
1500-3000 ft.	0.086	013949
3000-4500 ft.	0.084	014302
4500-6000 ft.	0.082	014109
Above 6000 ft.	0.080	013194

120 HP (WB-25A)

Altitude	Jet Size	Part Number
Sea Level-1500 ft.	0.080	014302
1500-3000 ft.	0.082	014109
3000-4500 ft.	0.080	013194
4500-6000 ft.	0.078	014306
Above 6000 ft.	0.076	013191

120 HP (WB-25B)

Altitude	Jet Size	Part Number
Sea Level-1500 ft.	0.086	013949
1500-3000 ft.	0.084	014302
3000-4500 ft.	0.082	014109
4500-6000 ft.	0.080	013194
Above 6000 ft.	0.078	014306

125 HP (TC-6B)

Altitude	Jet Size	Number Number
Sea Level-1500 ft.	0.0937	014191
1500-3000 ft.	0.092	014190
3000-4500 ft.	0.090	015406
4500-6000 ft.	0.088	013193
Above 6000 ft.	0.086	013949

130 HP (TC-1A & TC-1B)

Altitude	Jet Size	Number Number
Sea Level-1500 ft.	0.0937	014191
1500-3000 ft.	0.092	014190
3000-4500 ft.	0.090	015406
4500-6000 ft.	0.088	013193
Above 6000 ft.	0.086	013949

135 HP (WB-14B)— Without Exhaust Stacks

Altitude	Jet Size	Part Number
Sea Level-1500 ft.	0.092	014190
1500-3000 ft.	0.090	015406
3000-4500 ft.	0.088	013193
4500-6000 ft.	0.086	013949
Above 6000 ft.	0.084	014302

135 HP (WB-14B)— With Exhaust Stacks

Altitude	Jet Size	Part Number
Sea Level-1500 ft.	0.0937	014191
1500-3000 ft.	0.092	014190
3000-4500 ft.	0.090	015406
4500-6000 ft.	0.088	013193
Above 6000 ft.	0.086	013949

135 HP (TC-5A)

Altitude	Jet Size	Part Number
Sea Level-1500 ft.	0.0937	014191
1500-3000 ft.	0.092	014190
3000-4500 ft.	0.090	015406
4500-6000 ft.	0.088	013193
Above 6000 ft.	0.086	013949

135 HP (TC-5C)

Altitude	Jet Size	Part Number
Sea Level-1500 ft.	0.096	012947
1500-3000 ft.	0.0937	014191
3000-4500 ft.	0.092	014190
4500-6000 ft.	0.090	015406
Above 6000 ft.	0.088	013193

140 HP (TC-5E)

Altitude	Jet Size	Part Number
Sea Level-1500 ft.	0.096	012947
1500-3000 ft.	0.0937	014191
3000-4500 ft.	0.092	014190
4500-6000 ft.	0.090	015406
Above 6000 ft.	0.088	013193

150 HP (TC-1A)— Without Exhaust Stacks

Altitude	Jet Size	Part Number
Sea Level-1500 ft.	0.0937	014191
1500-3000 ft.	0.092	014190
3000-4500 ft.	0.090	015406
4500-6000 ft.	0.088	013193
Above 6000 ft.	0.086	013949

150 HP (TC-1A)— With Exhaust Stacks

Altitude	Jet Size	Part Number
Standard	0.106	016246

Float level (L–Fig. C10-3) should be 13/32-inch for WB and TC carburetors.

Throttle plates in carburetors must be synchronized to obtain maximum performance. The throttle cam (C–Fig. C10-4) actuates only one carburetor. The rod connecting the other carburetor (or carburetors on 3-cylinder models) must be adjusted to open the other carburtor exactly the same amount. On 3-cylinder models, the adjusting clamp screws (A) are on the connecting link near the top and bottom carburetors. On 4-cylinder models, the adjuster is located near the top carburetor.

SPEED CONTROL LINKAGE. On all models, ignition timing advance and throttle opening must be synchronized so that throttle is opened as timing is advanced. If incorrect, the power head may overheat, lack power and will usually not accelerate smoothly.

To synchronize the linkage, first make certain that ignition timing is correctly set as outlined in IGNITION TIMING paragraph.

Disconnect the throttle rod (TR–Fig. C10-5) and move the throttle cam (C–Fig. 4) until mark on cam is aligned with center of roller as shown. Loosen

locknut on roller and turn the eccentric screw until the cam just contacts the roller when index mark is aligned with center of roller. Tighten the locknut. Move the speed control to the maximum speed position and adjust the length of throttle rod (TR–Fig. C10-5) so that it can be connected when carburetor throttles are at maximum opening. Recheck adjustments after connecting throttle rod to make certain that the vertical control shaft contacts the maximum speed stop at the same time carburetor throttles are completely opened.

REED VALVES. "Vee" type intake reed valves are located between the inlet manifold and the crankcase for each cylinder. To remove the reed valve, it is necessary to remove the carburetors and inlet manifold (7–Fig. C10-7 or C10-8). On 3-cylinder models, all three reed valve assemblies (1, 2 & 3) are attached to plate (5). On 4-cylinder models, two reed valve assemblies (1, 2 & 3) are attached to each plate (5). Spacer plate (S) is used on 3-cylinder 85 hp models and late 4-cylinder models.

Seating surface of reed valve body (3) must be smooth and reed petals (2) must not be bent, broken or cracked. Assembled reed petals may stand open a maximum of 0.010 inch at tip end. Check seating visually. Reed stop setting should be measured as shown in Fig. C10-9. Stop should be 0.281 inch on all models without spacer plate (S) and 0.310 inch on models with spacer plate.

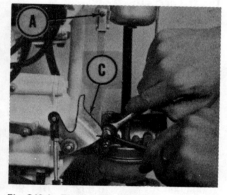

Fig. C10-4—The throttle cam (C) should just contact throttle roller when the index line is aligned with center of roller. Throttle plates should all open and close exactly alike by adjusting at screws (A).

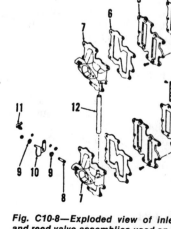

Fig. C10-8—Exploded view of inlet manifolds and reed valve assemblies used on four cylinder models.

S. Spacer plate
1. Reed stop
2. Reed petals
3. Reed body
4. Gasket
5. Adapter plate
6. Gasket
7. Inlet manifold
8. Stud
9. Bushing halves
10. Throttle cam
11. Rod end (ball joint)
12. Balance tube (105 hp)

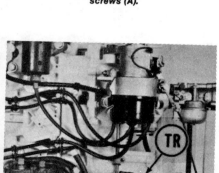

Fig. C10-5 – Refer to text for adjusting speed control linkage. High speed stop screw (HS) is used on early models.

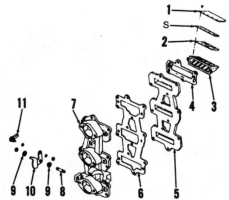

Fig. C10-7—Exploded view of inlet manifold and reed valve assembly used on three cylinder models. Refer to Fig. C10-8 for legend.

PUDDLE DRAIN VALVES. The puddle drain valves are designed to remove any liquid fuel or oil which might build up in the crankcase; thus providing smoother operation.

The puddle drain valve is located on the starboard side of power head as shown in Fig. C10-10 or C10-11. The reed type valve petals (4) must seat lightly and evenly against valve plate (5). Reed stops (3) should be adjusted to 0.017-0.023 clearance at tip. Make certain that screens (6) are in place in valve plate.

On four-cylinder models, one-way check valves are located in drain hoses (8–Fig. C10-11). Check to make certain that air will pass freely through both hoses toward "T" fitting (9), but will not pass from fitting to either of the hoses (8).

FUEL PUMP. A two-stage diaphragm type fuel pump is used which is actuated by pressure and vacuum pulsations picked up from the two lower cylinder crankcases. Refer to Fig. C10-12. The two stages operate alternately as shown.

Fig. C10-9—Reed stops should be 9/32-inch from seating surface of reed block.

NOTE: Either stage operating independently may permit the motor to run, but not at peak performance.

Most fuel pump service can be performed without removing the assembly from power head. Disconnect the pulse hoses and remove the retaining cap screws; then lift off the pump cover and diaphragm. Remove the sediment bowl and strainer. First stage inlet check valve can be driven out from below, using a ½-inch diameter drift. First stage outlet check valve can be lifted out after removing the retaining screws. The check valves must be installed to permit fuel to flow in the proper direction as shown. To renew the second stage outlet check valve, it is first necessary to remove pump body from power head, remove outlet fuel elbow and drive the check valve out from below. Check valve will be damaged, and a new unit must be installed. DO NOT remove the valve unless renewal is indicated. Install new valve carefully, using an 11/16-inch diameter punch.

Renew the diaphragm if cracked, torn or badly distorted. Install check valves carefully to prevent damage, and reassemble by reversing the disassembly procedure.

IGNITION SYSTEM

All models are equipped with a Magnapower capacitor discharge ignition system except the 125 hp models which are equipped with a Prestolite ignition system. Three different Magnapower ignition systems have been used; Delta, Magnapower II and Motorola and may be identified by the location and type of regulator/rectifier on the engine. Models equipped with a Magnapower (Delta) ignition system have a flat plate type of rectifier (A or B–Fig. C10-13) located adjacent to the distributor. Models equipped with a Magnapower II

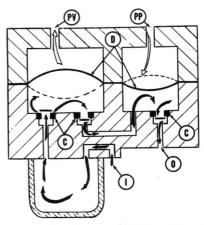

Fig. C10-12—Cross sectional view of the two stage fuel pump used. Broken lines indicate position of diaphragm when pulse pressure and vacuum are reversed.

C. Check valves
D. Diaphragm
I. Fuel inlet
O. Fuel outlet
PP. Pulse pressure
PV. Pulse vacuum

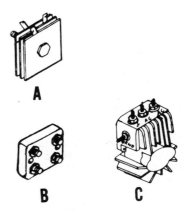

Fig. C10-13—Magnapower ignition systems may be identified by type of rectifier. Flat rectifiers (A and B) are used on Magnapower (Delta) ignition systems while finned aluminum regulator/rectifiers (C) are used on Magnapower (Motorola) systems. Magnapower II regulator/rectifier is located under the flywheel.

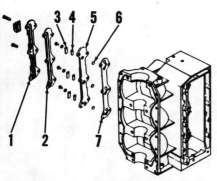

Fig. C10-10 — View of puddle drain valve assembly used on 3-cylinder models. Refer to Fig. C10-11.

1. Cover
2. Gasket
3. Valve stop
4. Valve reed
5. Valve plate
6. Screen
7. Gasket
8. Hoses
9. "Tee" fitting

Fig. C10-11 — Exploded view of puddle drain system used on 4-cylinder models. Hoses (8) contain one way check valves and must be installed so that fluid will pass only in direction of arrows.

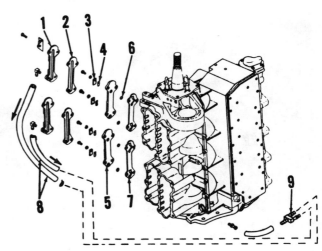

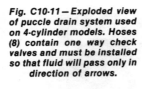

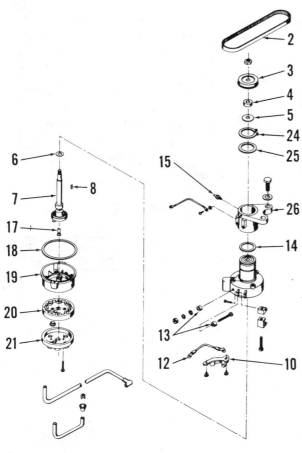

Fig. C10-14 — Exploded view of distributor and bracket assembly. Breakerless ignition distributor is similar but has a trigger in place of breaker points (10).

2. Drive belt
3. Pulley
4. Spacer
5. Thrust washer
6. Spacer
7. Shaft and rotor
8. Key
10. Breaker points
12. Wire
13. Insulators
14. Shims
15. Grease fitting
17. Brush
18. Gasket
19. Distributor cap
20. Seal
21. Cover
24. Snap ring
25. Thrust washer
26. Bracket

fully examine crankshaft. A minimum of 80% surface contact should be indicated by the polished surface; continue lapping only if insufficient contact is evident. Thoroughly clean the crankshaft and flywheel bore to remove all traces of lapping compound, then clean both surfaces with a non-oily solvent.

On models equipped with distributor, slip timing belt off distributor and position belt away from crankshaft so flywheel may be installed without binding timing belt. After installing flywheel, set distributor timing and adjust timing belt tension as outlined in ignition timing section.

On all models, reinstall crankshaft key and flywheel, then tighten flywheel nut to 90 ft.-lbs. torque.

Models With Distributor

DISTRIBUTOR DRIVE BELT. To renew distributor drive belt (2 – Fig. C10-14), first loosen distributor retaining cap screws and slip belt off drive pulley (3). Refer to R&R FLYWHEEL section, then remove flywheel, install new drive belt and reinstall flywheel.

Set top cylinder at TDC by aligning "0°" or "TDC" mark on flywheel with "I" or index mark on pointer. Turn distributor pulley until the match mark (Fig. C10-15) on pulley is toward flywheel and install the drive pulley. Belt should be tightened until slight (one pound) force will deflect belt ¼-inch. If belt is too tight, the speed control linkage may bind. After installation is complete, adjust timing as outlined in IGNITION TIMING section.

DISTRIBUTOR. On breaker point models, point gap should be 0.013-0.015 inch for 3-cylinder motors; 0.009-0.011 inch for 4-cylinder motors. Distributor should be removed for breaker point renewal.

ignition system have the regulator/rectifier encased in a molded housing located under the flywheel. Models equipped with a Magnapower (Motorola) ignition system have a regulator/rectifier in a finned aluminum housing (C) located adjacent to the distributor. Refer to the appropriate following paragraphs after determining type of ignition used.

All Models

R&R FLYWHEEL. A special puller (Chrysler part number T-8948-1) is used to remove the flywheel. Pulling bosses are provided on the flywheel for puller installation. Flywheel should be renewed if flywheel is chipped or cracked as an unbalanced condition may be produced.

The manufacturer recommends that mating surfaces of flywheel and crankshaft be lapped before flywheel is reinstalled. If evidence of working exists proceed as follows:

Remove the flywheel key and apply a light coating of valve grinding or lapping compound to tapered portion of crankshaft. Install the flywheel without the key or crankshaft nut and rotate flywheel gently back and forth about ¼-turn. Move flywheel 90° and repeat the operation. Lift off the flywheel, wipe off excess lapping compound and care-

Fig. C10-15 — View of distributor timing match marks. Refer to text for procedure.

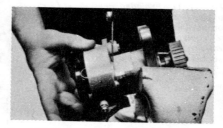

Fig. C10-16 — Distributor body end play in bracket should be 0.001-0.005 inch.

Fig. C10-17 — Refer to text for speed control linkage adjustment.

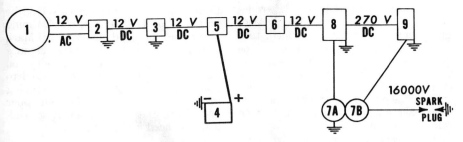

Fig. C10-18—Basic drawing showing flow of current for the Magnapower (Delta) ignition system. Checking for current between the various components should indicate where current flow stops, if a malfunction exists.

1. Alternator
2. Rectifier
3. Trip regulator
4. Battery
5. Circuit breaker
6. Ignition switch
7A. Distributor breaker points
7B. Distributor rotor and cap
8. CD ignition module
9. Ignition coil

Check distributor operation as follows: Position top cylinder at TDC by aligning appropriate mark on flywheel with index mark on timing pointer. Loosen distributor mounting cap screws and slip drive belt off pulley. Install test plugs in place of spark plugs, then switch ignition on. Observe spark while rotating distributor drive pulley. If spark is satisfactory at all cylinders, then no further testing is required. If spark is available to some but not all cylinders, check condition of distributor cap and spark plug wires. If spark is absent at all cylinders, check for spark from coil by inserting a test wire in coil tower and hold the other end of test wire ½-inch from engine ground. Rotate distributor pulley and observe spark. If spark is evident, check for defective coil wire, distributor cap and/or rotor. If spark is absent, check condition of breaker points on models so equipped, and preamplifier on breakerless models.

A general inspection of components may be accomplished by removing the distributor cap without removing the distributor from motor. Check condition and gap of breaker points on models so equipped and for loose carbon from brush (17–Fig. C10-14) that may collect around points causing misfiring. Distributor should be cleaned of carbon after every 50 hours of operation. Inspect rotor and distributor cap for cracks or other damage. Check condition of distributor ground wires. All paint must be removed from areas where ground wires are attached. Check distributor lead wires for short circuits to ground, loose connections and for broken wire.

On breakerless models, check preamplifier operation using a suitable voltmeter. Remove the white/black stripe wire from distributor terminal and connect voltmeter negative lead to terminal. Connect voltmeter positive lead to remaining distributor terminal that has the blue wire attached. Turn ignition switch on, then slowly rotate distributor drive pulley. Preamplifier operation should be considered satisfactory if voltmeter reads battery voltage every time the closed portion of rotor passes preamplifier and no voltage every time open portion of rotor passes preamplifier.

When overhauling, end play of distributor in bracket should be measured with feeler gage as shown in Fig. C10-16. End play should be within limits of 0.001-0.005 inch. Rotor is available only as a unit with the distributor shaft (7–Fig. C10-14). Distributor shaft bearings are included in housing. After installing distributor assembly, refer to DISTRIBUTOR DRIVE BELT section for distributor timing and belt adjustment procedure.

IGNITION TIMING. Crankshaft timing should be 32° BTDC on 135 hp models manufactured after 1971, all 100, 105 and 115 hp models and all 3-cylinder models. When setting piston position with a dial indicator, the equivalent reading should be 0.278 in. BTDC except on performance 85 hp models with 2.70 in. stroke which should have a 0.266 in. dial indicator equivalent.

Crankshaft timing should be 30° BTDC on 135 hp models manufactured prior to 1972 and all 140 and 150 hp models. When setting piston position with a dial indicator, the equivalent reading should be 0.254 in. BTDC on 140 hp models and 0.246 in. BTDC on all other models.

Crankshaft timing should be 34° BTDC on all 120 and 130 hp models. When setting piston position with a dial indicator, the equivalent reading should be 0.312 in. BTDC.

Adjust Ignition Timing. To adjust ignition timing on breaker point models, first refer to preceding timing specification paragraphs, then make certain breaker points are correctly gapped and are in good (or new) condition. Turn the flywheel until the 36° mark on flywheel is aligned with the "–2" mark on timing pointer of 120 and 130 hp models, "–6" mark on 135 and 150 hp models, and "–4" mark on all other models. Connect one lead of a continuity (test) light to the white primary lead wire on distributor and ground other lead to power head. Move speed control lever to the maximum speed position and observe the test light. Loosen locknut (L–Fig. C10-17) and turn the control rod (R)

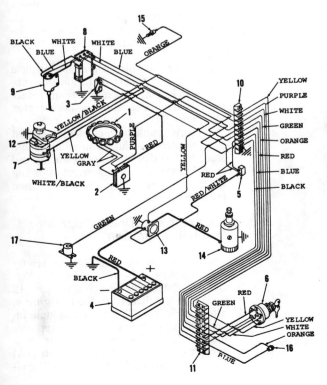

Fig. C10-19—Wiring diagram for Magnapower (Delta) ignition models showing location and color of wires.

1. Alternator stator
2. Bridge rectifier
3. Trip regulator
4. Battery
5. Circuit breaker
6. Ignition-start switch
7. Distributor
8. CD ignition module
9. Coil
10. Terminal block on motor
11. Terminal block at dashboard
12. Starting safety switch
13. Starter solenoid
14. Starter motor
15. Heat indicator sending unit
16. Overheat indicator light
17. Choke solenoid

counterclockwise until breaker points just open as indicated by light going out and tighten locknut (L). Check carburetor synchronization and speed control linkage adjustment as outlined in FUEL SYSTEM section.

To adjust ignition timing on breakerless models, first refer to preceding timing specification paragraphs. Two methods of adjusting breakerless models may be used. One method is to immerse outboard in water and connect a suitable power timing light or Chrysler timing light number T8978 to upper spark plug. With engine throttle in full retard position, crank engine with starter and note timing marks. Timing marks should be within 3° of TDC. If not, check timing marks as outlined in Timing Mark Verification section. To check advance ignition timing, run engine at wide open throttle with timing light connected to upper spark plug and note timing marks. Turn timing link between upper end of tower shaft and distributor to adjust advance ignition timing.

The other method is to static time the engine using a voltmeter. Disconnect the battery, then remove the white/black stripe wire from distributor terminal and connect voltmeter negative lead to terminal. Connect voltmeter positive lead to remaining distributor terminal that has the blue wire attached. Position flywheel so required degree mark on flywheel timing decal (see preceding timing specification paragraphs) is aligned with index mark on timing pointer. Reconnect the battery and turn ignition switch on. With engine throttle at full advance position, turn timing link until voltmeter reads battery voltage. Check adjustment by deflecting play in distributor drive belt. Voltmeter reading should fluctuate from no voltage to battery voltage.

Timing Mark Verification. If the validity of engine timing marks is questioned, verify marks after accurately determining piston position using special timing gage (Chrysler part number TA-2937-1) or a dial indicator as follows:

Disconnect the battery and remove all spark plugs. To determine piston position using special timing gage, thread the tool body into top spark plug opening. Insert the gage rod into tool body, rotate the crankshaft and carefully position piston at exactly TDC.

NOTE: On breaker point models, gage rod should be installed with "70 & up" end out. On breakerless models, gage rod should be installed with "25 through 55" end out.

With the top piston at TDC, thread timing tool body in or out as necessary

until the inner scribed line on gage rod is aligned with end of tool body. After gage body is correctly positioned, turn the crankshaft clockwise almost one complete revolution while applying pressure to end of gage rod. Stop the crankshaft just as the first (outer) scribed line on rod aligns with tool body. Check alignment of timing marks, then remove the timing tool.

On breaker point models, the "36°" mark in flywheel should align with the "I" mark on timing pointer. If incorrect, relocate the pointer.

On breakerless models, the "32°" mark on flywheel timing decal should align with index mark on timing pointer. If incorrect, relocate the pointer or install a new flywheel timing decal.

To determine piston position using a dial indicator, insert dial indicator into top spark plug opening, then rotate crankshaft and carefully position piston at exactly TDC. Zero the dial indicator, then turn crankshaft clockwise almost one complete revolution stopping crankshaft just as dial indicator reads desired specification. Check alignment of timing marks as previously described, then remove the dial indicator.

Models Without Distributor

IGNITION TIMING. Crankshaft timing should be 32° BTDC on all models. When setting piston position with a dial indicator, the equivalent reading should be 0.287 in. BTDC on 125 hp models and 0.278 in. BTDC on all other models.

Adjust Ignition Timing. To adjust ignition timing, first immerse outboard in water and connect a suitable power timing light or Chrysler timing light number T8978 to upper spark plug. With engine throttle in full retard position, crank engine with starter and note

Fig. C10-20 — Current flow through the circuit breaker (5) can be checked using a Chrysler test light (T-2951) or voltmeter. Be sure to check both terminals.

timing marks. Timing marks should be within 2° of TDC. If not, check timing marks as outlined in Timing Mark Verification section. To check advance ignition timing, run engine at wide open throttle with timing light connected to upper spark plug and note timing marks. Turn timing link between upper end of tower shaft and timing ring to adjust advanced ignition timing.

NOTE: Engine throttle should be returned to retarded position and engine stopped before turning ignition timing link.

Timing Mark Verification. If the validity of engine timing marks is questioned, verify marks after accurately determining piston position using special timing gage, (Chrysler part number TA-2937-1) or a dial indicator as follows: Disconnect the battery and remove all spark plugs. To determine piston position using special timing gage, thread the tool body into top spark plug opening. Insert the gage rod with "25 through 55" end out, into tool body. Rotate the crankshaft and carefully position piston at exactly TDC. With the top piston at TDC, thread timing tool body in or out as necessary until the inner scribed line on gage rod is aligned with end of tool body. After gage body is correctly positioned, turn the crankshaft clockwise almost one complete revolution while applying pressure to end of gage rod. Stop the crankshaft just as the first (outer) scribed line on rod aligns with tool body. Check alignment of timing marks. The "32°" mark on flywheel timing decal should align with index mark on timing pointer. If incorrect, relocate the pointer or install a new flywheel timing decal. Remove the timing tool.

To determine piston position using a dial indicator, insert dial indicator into top spark plug opening, then rotate crankshaft and carefully position piston at exactly TDC. Zero the dial indicator, then turn crankshaft clockwise almost one complete revolution stopping crankshaft just as dial indicator reads desired specification. Check alignment of timing marks as previously described, then remove the dial indicator.

Magnapower (Delta) Capacitor Discharge Ignition

The ignition system can be briefly described as follows: Refer to Fig. C10-18. Battery or charging voltage (12 volts DC) is delivered to the CD ignition module (8). The CD ignition module increases this voltage (12 volts) to approximately 270 volts and stores it in a capacitor. When the breaker points (7A) open, a signal is delivered to the CD igni-

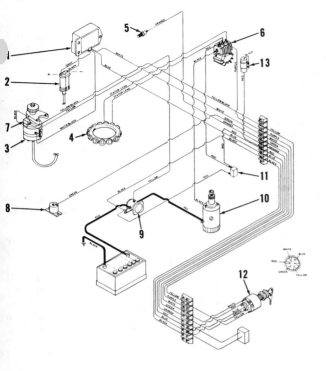

Fig. C10-22—Wiring diagram of early type Magnapower (Motorola) breaker point ignition system. Refer to Fig. C10-23 for parts identification.

tion module to release the 270 volts from the capacitor into the primary winding of coil (9). The coil again increases the voltage to approximately 16000 volts (or whatever is required to fire the spark plug). A wire from the coil to distributor cap and rotor (7B) delivers the secondary voltage (16000 volts) and as the rotor turns, it directs the voltage to the various spark plug wires.

Refer to the following paragraphs for locating trouble and servicing the "Magnapower" ignition system.

TROUBLESHOOTING. Use only approved procedures when testing to prevent damage to components. The fuel system should be checked to make certain that faulty running or failure to start is not caused by incorrect fuel mixture or contaminated fuel.

CHECKING FOR SPARK. A spark gap tester can be used to determine whether the ignition system is delivering current to the spark plugs. The tester is attached to the spark plug leads and grounded to the power head the same as for testing conventional magneto or battery ignition systems. Attempt to start motor with electric starter.

NOTE: Conventional spark plugs (such as Champion J4J) with ground electrodes removed can be used to check for spark. Make certain that shells of test plugs are properly grounded to power head when checking.

If spark occurs regularly at one or more of the tester points (or test plugs), but does not occur regularly or at all at

certain test points, check tester ground and the spark plug wires.

If spark occurs regularly and evenly at all test points, check condition of spark plugs, condition of fuel (and mixture), installation of spark plug leads for correct firing order and ignition timing.

If spark does not occur at any of the test points, proceed with the following checks.

WIRING. Engine missing, surging or failure to start or run can be caused by loose connections, corroded connections or short circuits. Electrical system components may also be damaged by faulty connections or short circuits.

Attach one lead of voltmeter or 12 volt test light (such as Chrysler part number T-2951) to the blue wire terminal at top of CD ignition module (8–Fig. C10-19) and ground other test lead to the metal case (housing) of the CD ignition module. Turn the ignition switch on and observe the test light or voltmeter. If the test light glows, current is available to the CD ignition module. If checking with a voltmeter, voltage should be the same as available at the battery.

If test light does not glow or voltmeter indicates zero or low voltage, check the circuit breaker (5) and trip regulator (3). If the circuit breaker and trip regulator are not faulty, check for broken wires, loose connections, faulty ignition switch or improper ground. A ground wire is used between housing of CD ignition module (8) and power head. Before checking the remaining ignition system components, make certain that current is available to the CD ignition module.

CIRCUIT BREAKER. A 12-volt test light (such as Chrysler part number T-2951) or voltmeter is required for checking. Attach one test lead (Neg. lead of voltmeter) to a suitable ground on the motor. Touch other test lead to each of the two terminals of circuit breaker as shown in Fig. C10-20. If current is available at one of the terminals but not at the other terminal, the circuit breaker is faulty. If the circuit breaker clicks OFF and ON, there is a short circuit in the wiring. Battery voltage should be available at both terminals of circuit breaker.

TRIP REGULATOR. A test light with battery (such as Chrysler part number T-2938) or ohmmeter is required for testing the trip regulator (3–Fig. C10-19). Attach one lead of test light or ohmmeter to each of the two terminals on trip regulator; then, reverse the test leads. Current should pass through the trip regulator with one connection and not when test leads are reversed. Also, make certain that the red wire from the rectifier (2) is attached to terminal of trip regulator which is identified by a yellow washer. The red wire from circuit breaker (5) should be attached to the top terminal of trip regulator, identified by a red washer.

DISTRIBUTOR AND BREAKER POINTS. The breaker points are used to trigger the ignition system. Failure of breaker points to make contact (open circuit) or failure to break contact (short circuit) will prevent ignition just as in conventional magneto or battery ignition systems. Refer to preceding DISTRIBUTOR section for service information.

IGNITION COIL AND C-D UNIT. Check the installation of the coil. The black wire from terminal stud on side of CD ignition module should be connected to "G" terminal of coil. The blue wire from CD ignition module should be connected to "+" terminal of coil. The white wire from CD ignition module should be attached to the "–" terminal of coil. Also, make certain that white/black (breaker point wire), white and blue wires are correctly attached to terminals at top of CD ignition module as shown in Fig. C10-19.

The ignition coils can be tested using an ignition tester available from Chrysler or several other sources, including the following:

GRAHAM-LEE ELECTRONICS, INC.
4220 Central Ave. N.E.
Minneapolis, Minn. 55421

MERC-O-TRONIC INSTRUMENTS CORP.
215 Branch St.
Almont, Mich. 48003

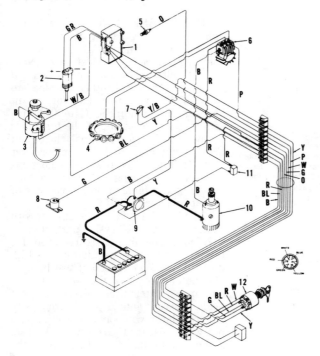

Fig. C10-23—Schematic of Magnapower (Motorola) breakerless ignition system. Schematic for Magnapower (Motorola) ignition system with breaker points is similar but blue (BL) lead to distributor is not used.

1. CD module
2. Ignition coil
3. Distributor
4. Alternator
5. Thermoswitch
6. Regulator/rectifier
7. Interlock switch
8. Choke solenoid
9. Starter relay
10. Starter
11. Circuit breaker
12. Ignition switch
B. Black
BL. Blue
G. Green
GR. Gray
O. Orange
P. Purple
R. Red
W. White
Y. Yellow

If spark occurs regularly at one or more of the tester points (or test plugs), but does not occur regularly or at all at certain test points, check tester ground and the spark plug wires.

If spark occurs regularly and evenly at all test points, check condition of spark plugs, condition of fuel (and mixture), installation of spark plug leads for correct firing order and ignition timing.

If spark does not occur at any of the test points, proceed with the following checks.

WIRING. Engine missing, surging or failure to start or run can be caused by loose connections, corroded connections or short circuits. Electrical system components may also be damaged by faulty connections or short circuits.

Attach one lead of voltmeter or 12 volt test light (such as Chrysler part number T-2951) to ground and check for continuity in ignition wiring. Turn ignition switch on and observe the test light or voltmeter when contacting the other test lead with the input terminal of starter relay (9 – Fig. C10-23), input and output terminals on circuit breaker (11), "B" and "I" terminals on ignition switch (12), red wire connections between ignition switch and CD ignition module and blue wire connections between ignition switch and distributor. Voltmeter should read battery voltage or test light should glow at each test point. Broken wires, loose connections, faulty ignition switch or circuit breaker may be isolated and repaired if test is conducted in sequence.

If the coil is not faulty and all other tests do not indicate a malfunction, renew the CD ignition module. It is important that all other tests are satisfactory before renewing the CD ignition module.

Magnapower (Motorola) Capacitor Discharge Ignition System

Some models are equipped with a Magnapower (Motorola) capacitor discharge ignition system. Three variations of the Motorola ignition system have been used. The first ignition system (Fig. C10-22) has breaker points and an external capacitor. the second and third ignition systems (Fig. C10-23) are similar with the third ignition system using a preamplifier in place of breaker points for a breakerless ignition system.

Troubleshooting and servicing procedures will be for breakerless ignition models but will also apply to breaker point models.

TROUBLESHOOTING. Use only approved procedures when testing to prevent damage to components. The fuel system should be checked to make certain that faulty running or failure to start is not caused by incorrect fuel mixture or contaminated fuel.

CHECKING FOR SPARK. A spark gap tester can be used to determine whether the ignition system is delivering current to the spark plugs. The tester is attached to the spark plug leads and grounded to the power head the same as for testing conventional magneto or battery ignition systems. Attempt to start motor with electric starter.

NOTE: Conventional spark plugs (such as Champion J4J) with ground electrodes removed can be used to check for spark. Make certain that shells of test plugs are properly grounded to power head when checking.

Fig. C10-24—Tester lead connections for testing CD ignition module performance on power head.

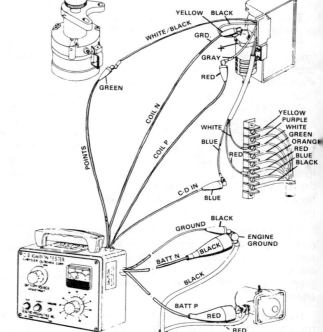

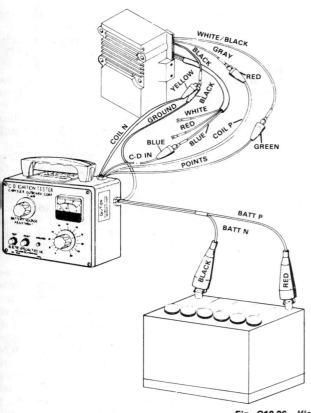

Fig. C10-25—Tester lead connections for testing CD module performance if CD module has been removed from power head.

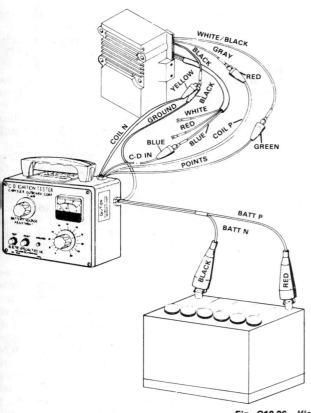

Fig. C10-26—View showing location of Magnapower II CD module (B), regulator/rectifier (C) and alternator (A). Trigger modules (1, 2, 3, & 4) are numbered according to their respective engine cylinders. Location of terminals. (T-1 and T-4) is also shown.

STARTING SYSTEM. Ignition malfunction may also be due to low voltage when starting. Check cranking voltage by attaching voltmeter test leads to engine ground and input side of starter relay. Disconnect spark plug wires to prevent starting and engage electric starter. A minimum reading of 9 volts is required for proper operation of ignition system during starting. If voltage is less than minimum, check and repair starting system as required.

CD IGNITION MODULE. Perform CD ignition module test using Chrysler CD ignition tester number T8953 (Electro-Specialties, Milwaukee, Wis.). Attach tester leads to CD ignition module and ignition wiring as shown in Fig. C10-24 connecting 12-volt power lead (BATT P) last. If CD ignition module has been removed from power head, make tester lead connections as shown in Fig. C10-25. Turn battery voltage adjustment switch as required to obtain a 12-volt reading on voltmeter. Turn indicator switch to position 100, then slowly turn indicator switch counterclockwise while working test button 2-3 times per second until tester lamp lights. Note indicator switch position, if test lamp does not light on or before position 80 and CD ignition module is properly grounded, then CD module is defective and should be renewed. Depress reset button to shut off tester lamp. If lamp

fails to shut off, CD ignition module is defective and should be renewed. If lamp shuts off, alternately depress test and reset buttons at least 5 times to check for intermittent CD ignition module operation. If lamp fails to turn on then off each time, renew CD ignition module. Repeat test procedure and compare indicator switch position reading when test lamp lights with first test. If indicator switch position varies more than 2 points between tests, CD ignition module is defective and should be renewed.

After conducting CD ignition module tests at 12 volts, set battery voltage adjustment switch to obtain a 9-volt reading on voltmeter and repeat entire test sequence using 65 instead of 80 as minimum indicator switch position when test lamp lights.

DISTRIBUTOR AND COIL. All models are equipped with a distributor which contains breaker points on early models and is breakerless on later models. Refer to preceding DISTRIB-

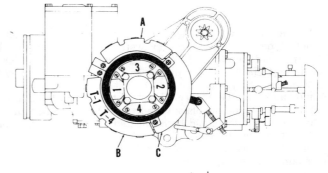

Fig. C10-27—Schematic of Magnapower II ignition system.

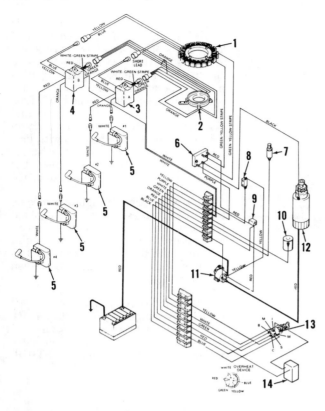

UTOR section for service information on both types of ignition breaker systems.

If a malfunction in the coil is suspected, first check coil for proper installation. The gray wire from CD ignition module should be connected to "+" terminal of coil and the black wire from CD ignition module should be connected to "−" terminal of coil. On breakerless models, a black wire from distributor ground is also connected to "−" terminal of coil.

On all models, ignition coil can be tested using an ignition tester available from Chrysler or several other sources, including the following:

GRAHAM-LEE ELECTRONICS, INC.
4220 Central Ave. N.E.
Minneapolis, Minn. 55421

MERC-O-TRONIC INSTRUMENTS CORP.
215 Branch St.
Almont, Mich. 48003

Magnapower II Capacitor Discharge Ignition System

Later four-cylinder models are equipped with a Magnapower II capacitor discharge ignition system. The CD ignition module, capacitor unit and trigger modules are located under the flywheel as shown in Fig. C10-26. Flywheel may be removed using a suitable puller or Chrysler tool number T8948. Taper of

crankshaft end and flywheel bore must be clean. Flywheel should be renewed if chipped or cracked as an unbalanced condition may be produced.

OPERATION. Voltage necessary for operation of the ignition system is induced in the coil windings of the CD ignition module (Fig. C10-27) by a magnet in the flywheel. The alternating current from the coil windings is rectified and stored in capacitors in the capacitor module. Positive 280 volts is stored by the capacitor connected to terminal T-1 while negative 280 volts is stored by the capacitor connected to terminal T-4. Voltage from the capacitor is applied to the spark plug through the ignition coil and trigger module when the trigger module is activated by the flywheel.

TROUBLESHOOTING. If ignition malfunction is suspected, install a test plug in place of number 1 (top) spark plug and note spark at plug. Repeat procedure with other cylinders to locate faulty spark plug. If engine miss or failure to start is due to ignition malfunction and not faulty spark plugs, proceed as follows: Detach spark plug wires from spark plugs. Crank engine with ignition switch in "ON" position to charge capacitors. Using a suitably insulated tool such as a plastic handled screwdriver, ground flywheel to terminal (T-1 – Fig. C10-27) and then ground flywheel to terminal (T-4). If a good spark is present at both terminals,

then the CD ignition module and capacitors are good. To check number or number 2 cylinder trigger module connect "Coil N" lead from Chrysler CD ignition tester number T8953 (Electro Specialties, Milwaukee, Wis.) to a good ground and connect "Coil I" lead from CD tester to positive (+) terminal of number 1 or number 2 cylinder ignition coil. Set dial of tester to "65" and crank engine. If lamp lights on tester, trigger module is operating correctly. If lamp does not light, renew trigger module. To check operation of number 3 or number 4 cylinder trigger module, connect "Coil P" lead of CD ignition tester to a good ground and connect "Coil N" lead to negative (−) terminal of bottom cylinder ignition coil. Repeat test procedure used for upper cylinder trigger module.

If little or no spark was present when T-1 and T-4 terminals were tested, note which terminal had little or no spark and proceed as follows: Disconnect trigger module lead from terminal (T-1 or T-4) which had little or no arc. Crank engine with ignition switch in "ON" position to charge capacitors and recheck arc. If arc is now good to terminal, inspect wiring to trigger module and if satisfactory, renew trigger module on cylinder which was misfiring. If arc to terminal was still weak or absent, CD ignition module or capacitor is faulty and may be checked as follows: Disconnect capacitor and trigger leads from terminal (T-1 or T-4) that has little or no spark. Connect spade terminal to terminal (T-1 or T-4) and connect Chrysler CD ignition tester number T8953 (Electro-Specialties, Milwaukee, Wis.) to spade terminal. To check T-1 terminal, connect "Coil P" lead from tester to T-1 terminal and "Coil N" lead to a good ground. To check T-4 terminal, connect "Coil N" lead from tester to T-4 terminal and "Coil P" lead to a good ground. Set dial of tester to "50" and crank engine. If tester lights, CD ignition module is good and capacitor module should be renewed. If tester does not light, CD ignition module is faulty and should be renewed.

Prestolite Models

All 125 hp models are equipped with a Prestolite capacitor discharge ignition system. Voltage necessary for ignition system operation is induced in the windings of the stator (1 – Fig. C10-28) by a magnet in the flywheel which develops 225 volts AC. The alternating current from the stator windings is fed to the CD ignition modules (3 and 4) and rectified, then the 225 volts DC is stored in capacitors. Voltage from the capacitors is released to the ignition coils (5) when timing magnets in the flywheel cause the trigger module to close the circuit.

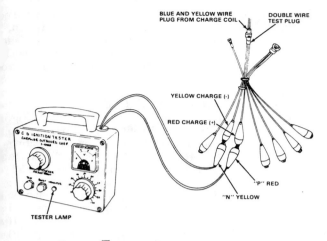

Fig. C10-29—Tester lead connections for checking voltage output of charge coil.

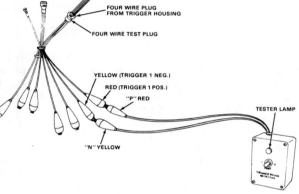

Fig. C10-30—Tester lead connections for checking trigger coil operation.

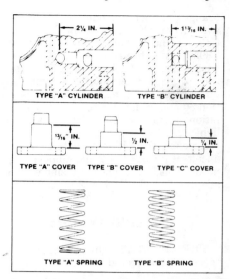

Fig. C10-32—Water by-pass valve components must be matched to hole in cylinder block. Refer to text.

The voltage is then stepped up to 25,000-32,000 volts in the ignition coils and applied to the spark plugs.

TROUBLESHOOTING. Use only approved procedures when testing to prevent damage to components. The fuel system should be checked to make certain that faulty running is not caused by incorrect fuel mixture or contaminated fuel. If ignition malfunction is suspected, use Chrysler tool T8953, plug adapter set T11237, number 22 tester from ignition tester set T8996 and suitable timing light such as Chrysler timing light T8978. Check and make sure ignition malfunction is not due to spark plug or ignition coil failure. Install test plugs in place of the spark plugs and observe spark while engine is being cranked with starter. If spark is absent at both cylinders, check condition of charge coil as follows:

Separate the blue and yellow wire connection between charge coil (stator) and CD ignition module and attach double wire plug adapter to wire plug from charge coil as shown in Fig. C10-29. Attach red (P) lead from T8953 tester to red sleeved adapter wire marked "Charge (+)." Attach yellow (N) lead of tester to yellow sleeved adapter wire marked "Charge (−)." Turn tester

switch to position 50 and crank engine. If tester lamp does not light, charge coil is defective and stator should be renewed. If lamp lights, charge coil operation is satisfactory and trigger coil and CD ignition module circuits for each cylinder must be checked. Remove tester and plug adapter set, then reconnect blue and yellow wire plugs.

To check operation of number 1 and number 2 cylinder trigger coil, separate the four-wire connection between CD ignition module and trigger coil and attach

four-wire plug adapter to wire plug from trigger coil as shown in Fig. C10-30. Attach red (P) lead from number 22 tester to red sleeved adapter wire marked "Trigger 1 Pos." and yellow (N) tester lead to yellow sleeved adapter wire marked "Trigger 1 Neg." Place switch of tester in number 1 position and crank engine. Trigger coil operation is satisfactory if tester lamp lights. Renew trigger housing if tester lamp does not light.

To check operation of number 3 and number 4 cylinder trigger coil, repeat test procedure for number 1 and number 2 cylinder trigger coil but connect red (P) tester lead to red sleeved adapter wire marked "Trigger 2 Pos." and yellow (N) tester lead to yellow sleeved adapter wire marked "Trigger 2 Neg."

To check CD ignition module performance for number 1 and number 3 ignition coils, separate primary lead connectors between CD ignition modules and ignition coils. Connect single wire adapter to

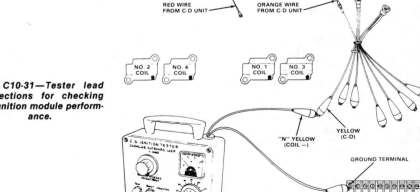

Fig. C10-31—Tester lead connections for checking CD ignition module performance.

orange (number 1 or number 3 cylinder) wire from CD ignition module (Fig. C10-31), then attach yellow (N) lead of T8953 tester to yellow sleeved adapter wire marked C-D. Attach red (P) tester lead to ground terminal of engine terminal block. Turn tester switch to position 60 and crank engine. Renew CD ignition module if tester lamp does not light.

Repeat CD ignition module performance test for number 2 and number 4 ignition coils, by connecting single wire adapter to red (number 2 or number 4 cylinder) wire from CD ignition module.

COOLING SYSTEM

THERMOSTAT. The cooling system thermostat is located beneath a cover on top of the cylinder head. Engine should not be run without a thermostat as engine may overheat.

WATER PUMP. The rubber impeller type water pump is located in the upper gearcase and is driven by the drive shaft. When cooling system problems are encountered, first check the thermostat to see that it is working properly and the water inlet for plugging or partial stoppage. If trouble is not corrected, remove the gearcase as outlined in LOWER UNIT section and check condition of water pump, water passages and sealing surfaces.

BY-PASS VALVE. Water by-pass valve components (7, 8 and 9 – Fig. C10-35 or C10-36) must be matched to hole in cylinder block or overheating may result. Measure depth of hole in cylinder block as shown in Fig. C10-32. If cylinder block is type (A), then type (A) spring and type (A) cover may be used together, or type (B) spring and type (B) cover may be used together. If cylinder block is type (B), then type (B) spring must be used with cover type (C).

POWER HEAD

REMOVE AND DISASSEMBLE. Depending upon the type of maintenance, it is usually easier to remove the distributor, starter, flywheel, alternator and carburetors before removing the power head from the motor leg. To remove the power head, remove all screws (1 – Fig. C10-34) from support plate (8) and nut (2) from upper end of shift rod (9). Disconnect shift rod from lever (10). Remove screws (3) and lift off rear cover (11). Remove screws (4) and nuts (5), then carefully lift power head from the lower unit. Remove screws (6) and stud nuts (7) and remove the exhaust tube (12) and spacer plate (13) from the power head.

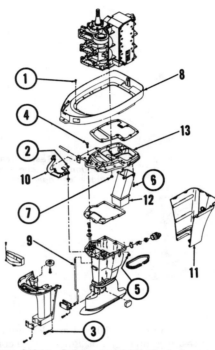

Fig. C10-34—Refer to text for method of removing the power head.

1. Exhaust cover
2. Baffle
3. Thermostat cover
4. Seal
5. Thermostat
6. Cylinder head
7. By-pass valve
8. Spring
9. By-pass valve cover
10. Cylinder head gasket
11. Hoisting plate
12. Cylinder block
13. Crankcase
14. Seal
15. Seal
16. Bearing cage (end cap)
17. "O" ring
18. Crankshaft
19. Top main bearing
20. Bearing & cage
21. Connecting rod
22. Piston pin
23. Piston
24. Piston rings
25. Dowels
26. Snap ring
27. Bearing outer race
28. Bearing & cage
29. Seal strips
30. Lower main bearing
31. Seal
32. Rod cap
36. Stop screw
37. Tower shaft assy.
38. Throttle cam link
39. Distributor link
40. Timing plate
41. Transfer port cover

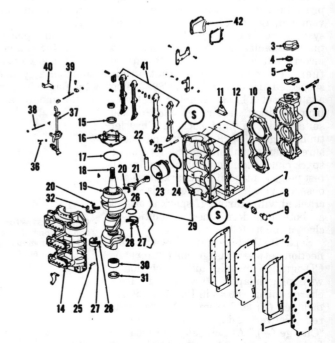

Fig. C10-35— Exploded view of typical three cylinder power head. Refer to Fig. C10-10 for puddle drain system (41).

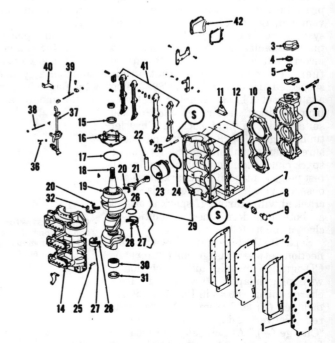

Fig. C10-33—Exploded view of the water pump used on late models. Early type shown in Fig. C10-36 is similar.

1. Drive shaft
2. Impeller drive key
3. Pump housing
4.
5. Impeller
6. Back plate
7. Gasket
8. Drive shaft seal (lower)
9. Snap ring
10. Bearing cone
11. Bearing cup
53. Water line seal
54. Drive shaft seal (upper)

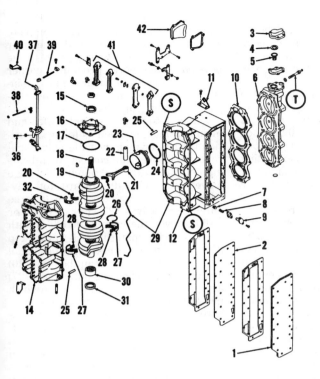

Fig. C10-36—Exploded view of typical four-cylinder power head assembly. Refer to Fig. C10-11 for puddle drain system (41).

1. Exhaust cover
2. Baffle
3. Thermostat cover
4. Seal
5. Thermostat
6. Cylinder head
7. By-pass valve
8. Spring
9. By-pass valve cover
10. Cylinder head gasket
11. Hoisting plate
12. Cylinder block
14. Crankcase half
15. Seal
16. Bearing cage (end cap)
17. "O" ring
18. Crankshaft
19. Top main bearing
20. Bearing & cage
21. Connecting rod
22. Piston pin
23. Piston
24. Piston rings
25. Dowels
26. Snap ring
27. Bearing outer race
28. Bearing & cage
29. Seal strips
30. Lower main bearing
31. Seal
32. Rod cap
36. Stop screw
37. Tower shaft assy.
38. Throttle cam link
39. Distributor link
40. Timing plate
41. Transfer port cover

Clean oil, grease and fingerprints from outer race of upper main bearing (19) and its bore in crankcase.

NOTE: If alcohol or other flammable solvent is used for cleaning, make certain that area is well ventilated and free from sparks, open flames and electrical equipment.

Apply a light coat of "Loctite" to upper bearing bore in cylinder with all main bearings installed. Outer races of center main bearings (27) and lower main bearings (30) should be turned until the bearing locating pins engage holes in the outer races. Position end gaps of crankshaft sealing rings toward crankcase (14). Install the upper bearing cage (16) without seal (15) or "O" ring (17) and tighten the two screws attaching cage to the cylinder. The lower end of crankshaft can be temporarily attached using two screws and a wood block as shown in Fig. C10-37. The upper bearing cage (16—Fig. C10-35 or C10-36) and the wood block will hold the crankshaft in position while connecting rods and pistons are being installed.

Install piston and connecting rod assemblies making certain that long sloping side of piston is toward exhaust side of cylinder and match marks (M—Fig. C10-38) on connecting rod are up toward top of motor (flywheel end). Install the connecting rod bearing cage halves in connecting rod with the ground matching marks on corners together and up toward top of motor (flywheel end of crankshaft). Position bearing rollers in the cages and install rod cap with match marks (M—Fig. C10-38) together. Connecting rod screws should be tightened to 180 in.-lbs. torque.

Remove the upper bearing cage (16—Fig. C10-35 and Fig. C10-36) and the wood block (WB—Fig. C10-37). Install the crankcase seal strips (29—Fig. C10-35 or C10-36) in grooves, then apply 3M-EC750 sealer to mating surfaces of crankcase in areas adjacent to upper and

Refer to Fig. C10-35 or C10-36 and remove the cylinder head (6). Remove the exhaust cover (1), plate (2), transfer port covers (42), by-pass valve (7, 8 and 9) and puddle drain assembly (41) for cleaning. The crankcase front half (14) can be removed after removing all of the retaining stud nuts and screws including those attaching the bearing cage (16). The crankcase halves are positioned with dowel pins (25) and can be separated by prying at the two slots (S). Use extreme care to prevent damage to the crankshaft and do not pry anywhere except the slots provided.

Before removing connecting rods, piston or crankshaft, mark the parts (32, 20, 21, 22 and 23) for correct assembly to each other and in the correct cylinder. Parts (27 and 28) of the center main bearings must be marked for correct assembly to the main bearing journal from which they were removed. Separation of these parts can be easily accomplished with seven containers marked to indicate the correct position.

Refer to the appropriate following paragraphs for service and assembly instructions for crankshaft, connecting rods, pistons, and bearings.

ASSEMBLY. Before assembling, make certain that all joint and gasket surfaces are clean, free from nicks, burrs, warped surfaces or hardened sealer or carbon. The crankcase must be completely sealed against both pressure and vacuum. Exhaust cover and cylinder

head must be sealed against water leakage pressure. Mating surfaces between power head, lower unit and the spacer plate (13—Fig. C10-34) must form a tight seal.

Refer to the appropriate paragraphs for assembling the piston rings to pistons, pistons to connecting rods and main bearings to the crankshaft.

NOTE: It is extremely important that parts (20, 21, 22, 23, 24, 26, 27, 28 and 32—Fig. C10-35 or C10-36) are installed in the same location from which they were removed if the old parts are reinstalled. If parts are intermixed or installed in wrong location, early failure may result.

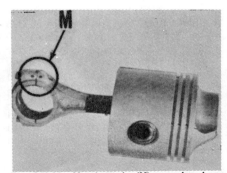

Fig. C10-37 — The crankshaft can be held in position while installing the connecting rods and pistons using a wood block (WB) at lower end and bearing cage at upper end.

Fig. C10-38 — Match marks (M) on rod and cap should be aligned and toward top of motor. The long, tapering side of piston should be toward exhaust ports in cylinder.

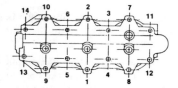

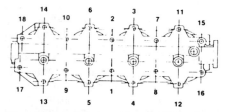

Fig. C10-39—To prevent damage, tighten cylinder head retaining screws in sequence shown to the torque values recommended in text.

center main bearings and lower crankshaft seal. Do not apply sealer to areas outside of crankshaft seal groove. Coat the upper main bearing bore in front crankcase half (14) with "Loctite" and position the crankcase over the cylinder and crankshaft.

NOTE: Make certain that holes in center and lower main bearing races correctly engage the locating dowels in cylinder.

A suitable sealant should be used on threads of screws and studs that attach crankcase halves together and screws and nuts should be tightened to 270 inch-pounds torque. Install new seal (15) in bearing cage (16) with lip down (toward lower unit). Install upper bearing cage and seal assembly using new "O" ring (17) and tighten the four retaining screws to 70 inch-pounds torque.

When installing the cylinder head, coat the first ¾-inch of screw threads with "Permatex #2" or equivalent. Tighten the retaining screws in sequence shoqn in Fig. C10-39 first evenly to 75 in.-lbs., then evenly in 50 in.-lbs. increments until final torque setting is reached. Final torque setting is 225 in.-lbs. for 5/16-18 cap screws and 270 in.-lbs. for 3/8-16 cap screws. After motor has been test run and cooled, re-torque screws to final setting. On models so equipped, the thermoswitch is installed at (T – Fig. C10-35 or C10-36). On later models with cylinder head cover, apply a silicone rubber sealant to mating milled surfaces of head and cover.

PISTONS, PINS, RINGS AND CYLINDERS. On 115, 125 and 140 hp models, pistons are fitted with two rings

while all other models are fitted with three rings. Piston rings should be installed with the beveled inner edge toward closed end of piston. Rings are pinned in place to prevent rotation in ring grooves.

On 140 hp models, a semi-keystone top piston ring is used. Top ring groove in piston for semi-keystone ring is measured for wear using two 0.060 inch diameter pins inserted in ring groove directly opposite each other. Ring groove should be within the limits of 3.347-3.351 inch when measured over pins.

The piston pin is a tight press fit in piston bores and rides in a roller bearing in connecting rod. The special tool, part number T-2990, should be used when removing or installing piston pin. When assembling piston, pin and connecting rod, make sure long, tapering side of piston is assembled for installation toward exhaust side of cylinder and correlation marks (M – Fig. C10-38) on rod are toward top (flywheel) end of crankshaft. Piston pin must be centered in connecting rod bore so that neither end of pin will extend through piston boss as rod is moved from side to side. All friction surfaces should be lubricated with new engine oil when assembling.

CONNECTING RODS, BEARINGS, AND CRANKSHAFT. Before detaching connecting rods from crankshaft, make certain that rod and cap are properly marked for correct assembly to each other and in the correct cylinder. It is important that parts (20, 21, 22, 23, 24, 26, 27, 28 and 32 – Fig. C10-35 or C10-36) are installed in the same location from which they were removed if the old parts are reinstalled. If parts are intermixed or if assembled in wrong location, early failure may result.

The crankshaft upper main bearing is renewable. Place upper main bearing on crankshaft with lettered side towards flywheel, then using a suitable press, install bearing flush to within 0.001 inch of bearing seat.

The bearing roller and cages used in the connecting rods and center main bearings are available only as a set

Fig. C10-40—The center main bearing cage halves are provided with match marks which should be toward flywheel end of crankshaft.

which contains the rollers and cage halves for one bearing. The complete assembly should be installed whenever renewal is required. Bearing cages have beveled match marks ground on corner of cage halves. Match marks must be installed together and toward top (flywheel) end of crankshaft.

When assembling crankshaft and main bearings, proceed as follows: Position the center main bearing halves and rollers (28) over the correct main bearing journal with the notches in cage halves (Fig. C10-40) toward top (flywheel) end of crankshaft. Install the outer race halves (27 – Fig. C10-35 or C10-36) over the cage and rollers with the groove for snap ring (26) toward top (flywheel) end of crankshaft and install snap ring. The lower main bearing (30) and center main bearing outer races (27) are provided with locating holes which must properly engage dowels in bearing bores. Lower seal (31) should be installed with lip down toward lower unit.

A non-fibrous grease can be used to hold loose needle bearings in position during assembly. All friction surfaces should be lubricated with new engine oil. Check frequently as power head is being assembled, for binding or locking of the moving parts. If binding occurs, remove the cause before proceeding with the assembly. When assembling, follow the procedures outlined in the ASSEMBLY paragraphs.

PROPELLER

Propellers for normal use are protected by a cushioning-slip clutch. Both two- and three-blade propellers are used. Solid-hub, high-speed propellers are available, but are not intended for general use. Various pitch propellers are available and should be selected to provide full throttle operation within the recommended limits of 4500-5100 rpm on 70 and 75 hp motors; 4500-5500 rpm on 85, 90, 100, 105, 115 and 125 hp motors; 5000-5500 rpm for 120, 130 and 140 hp motors; 5200-5600 rpm for 135

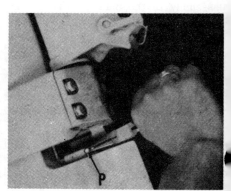

Fig. C10-41—The lower shift rod is attached to the upper rod with a pin shown at (P).

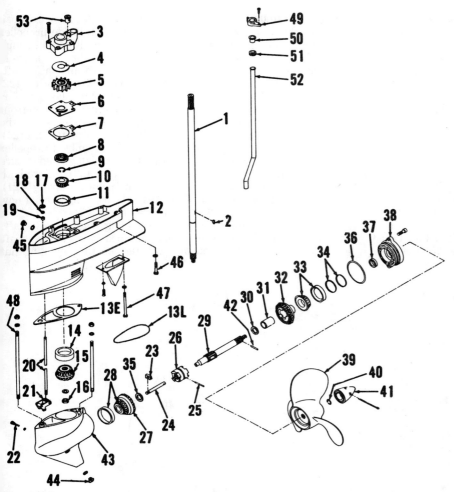

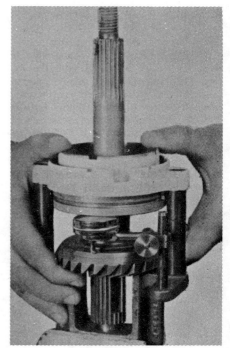

Fig. C10-43 — Special test fixture and dial indicator are used to adjust reverse gear position (backlash).

Fig. C10-42 — Exploded view of drive shaft housing, gearcase and associated parts. Late motors use three studs (48) and seal ring (13L). Earlier motors use two studs (48) and gasket (13E). Refer to Fig. C10-33 for exploded view of water pump used on late models.

1. Drive shaft	15. Bearing cone & drive pinion	28. Bearing cup & cone	41. Nut
2. Water pump key	16. Nut	29. Propeller shaft	42. Shear pin
3. Water pump housing	17. Seal retainer	30. Thrust washer	43. Gearcase housing
4. Top plate	18. Spacer	31. Bearing	44. Filler plug
5. Impeller	19. Shift rod seal	32. Reverse gear	45. Vent plug
6. Back plate	20. Shift rod	33. Bearing cup & cone	46. Screws (6 used)
7. Gasket	21. Pivot coupling	34. Shims	47. Screw
8. Drive shaft seal	22. Pivot pin	35. Thrust washer	48. Stud
9. Snap ring	23. Shift yoke	36. "O" ring	49. Water tube bracket
10. Bearing cone	24. Shift shaft	37. Seal	50. Seal
11. Bearing cup	25. Shift pin	38. Bearing cage	51. Grommet
12. Drive shaft housing	26. Shift coupling	39. Propeller	52. Water tube
14. Bearing cup	27. Forward gear	40. Nut seal	53. Water tube seal

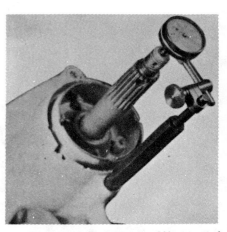

Fig. C10-44 — A dial indicator should be mounted for measuring propeller shaft end play.

and 150 hp motors. Propellers other than those designed for the motor should not be used.

LOWER UNIT

All 90 Hp Models, All 75 Hp Models Prior to 1980 and All Other Models Prior to 1977

R&R AND OVERHAUL. To remove the lower unit gearcase and drive shaft housing from the lower motor leg, remove the pin connecting the upper and lower shift rod (Fig. C10-41). Remove screws (46 and 47 – Fig. C10-42) which attach the drive shaft

housing to lower motor leg and withdraw the complete lower unit drive assembly from the motor leg.

Disassemble and remove the water pump (3 through 7). Remove the propeller and shear pin, and remove any rust or burrs from exposed end of propeller shaft. Remove the stud nuts retaining gearcase housing to driveshaft (upper gearcase) housing.

NOTE: Early motors use two studs (48); late motors use three studs.

Remove shift rod (20); then remove the lower unit gearcase (43). Drive shaft (1), drive pinion (15) and bearings will remain in the drive shaft housing.

Remove the two screws retaining the propeller shaft bearing cage (38) to gearcase, rotate the cage slightly, then tap on ears of cage with a soft hammer to remove the cage. Propeller shaft and associated parts may now be withdrawn.

NOTE: Shift yoke (23) will be free to drop when propeller shaft is removed. Do not lose the yoke.

Slip the forward gear and bearing assembly (27) from the propeller shaft. Shift coupling (26) and shift shaft (24) can be removed after driving pin (25) out. Reverse gear (32) and bearings (31 and 33) can be removed from propeller shaft at the same time using a press.

Keep the thrust washers (30 and 35) with their respective gears. The washers are similar but NOT interchangeable.

Drive gear backlash is controlled by means of shim pack (34) installed between bearing cup (33) and bearing cage (38). Backlash adjustment requires the use of the special test jig (part number J9362) and dial indicator as shown in Fig. C10-43. Shaft end play in the special test fixture should be zero, plus or minus 0.001 inch. Shims are available in thicknesses of 0.006, 0.007 and 0.008 inch.

After backlash has been adjusted, the propeller shaft bearings must be adjusted by varying the thickness of front thrust washer (35–Fig. C10-42). The bearings should be adjusted to approx-

imately zero end play, and must be within the limits of 0.004-0.006 inch end play. Thrust washers are available in thicknesses of 0.059, 0.062, 0.065, 0.068, 0.071, 0.074 and 0.077 inch. To measure the bearing adjustment, assemble the propeller shaft, reverse gear and bearing assembly (29, 30, 31, 32 and 33). Install bearing cage (38) with previously selected shims (34) and cup for bearing (33), omitting the "O" ring (36). Install the propeller shaft assembly, thrust washer (35) and gear assembly (27 and 28) in gearcase (43) and measure end play with a dial indicator as shown in Fig. C10-44.

To assemble the propeller shaft, refer to Fig. C10-42. Slide the shift coupling (26) onto propeller shaft with hole in

coupling aligned with slot in shaft. Position the shift shaft (24) inside propeller shaft and align hole with hole in coupling. Drive the pin (25) through holes in coupling, propeller shaft and shift shaft. Install pivot coupling (21), pivot pin (22) and lower shift rod (20). Slide the forward gear (27) and bearing cone on front end of propeller shaft and position the yoke (23) in front slot of shift shaft (24). Carefully slide the assembled propeller shaft into gearcase housing making sure that tabs of shift yoke (23) engage both forked slots in pivot coupling (21). Carefully install bearing cage using new "O" ring (36) and seal (37).

When assembling the drive shaft, drive pinion and bearings in drive shaft housing (12), tighten the adjusting nut

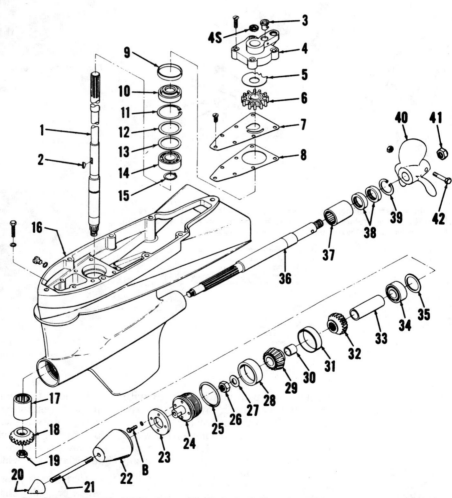

Fig. C10-45 — Exploded view of the racing lower unit. Top plate (5) is not used on all models.

1. Drive shaft	12. Washer	22. Nose cone	34. Ball bearing
2. Impeller drive key	13. Shims (0.006-steel; 0.007-brass; 0.010-black)	23. Retainer	35. Shims (0.006-steel; 0.007-brass; 0.010-black)
3. Water tube seal		24. Bearing cup	
4. Water pump housing		25. "O" ring	
4S. Drive shaft seal	14. Ball bearing	26. Nut	36. Propeller shaft
5. Top plate	15. Snap ring	27. Washer	37. Needle bearing
6. Impeller	16. Gear housing	28. Bearing cup	38. Seals
7. Lower plate	17. Needle bearing	29. Bearing cone	39. Snap ring
8. Gasket	18. Drive pinion	30. Sleeve	40. Propeller
9. Sleeve	19. Nut	31. Sleeve	41. Nut
10. Seal	20. Nose cone nut	32. Driven gear	42. Shear bolt
11. Snap ring	21. Stud	33. Spacer	

(16) finger tight and back off to the first castellation; then install the cotter pin.

After completing the assembly of gearcase to the drive shaft housing (12) and drive shaft housing to the lower motor leg, install the shift rod pin (P – Fig. C10-41).

All Other Models

R&R AND OVERHAUL. Remove lower front shock mount cover and remove shift rod pin (13 – Fig. C10-46). Unscrew six screws and separate gearcase from motor leg. Drain lubricant and remove propeller and exhaust snout (18).

Remove spline seal (55) and retainer (54). Disassemble and remove water pump components (1 through 7). Turn shift rod (14) counterclockwise until disengaged from pivot coupling (15) and remove rod. Remove cover (9) and anode (39). Remove screws securing bearing spool (35) and using a suitable puller withdraw spool from gearcase. Remove retaining clips (32), bearing and cage (33), thrust washer (31), thrust bearing (30) and reverse gear (29). Withdraw propeller shaft (28) with components (22 through 27). Unscrew pinion nut (20), withdraw drive shaft (53) and remove pinion gear (19). Unscrew pivot pin (16) and remove pivot coupling (15).

Use the following procedure to check reverse gear backlash: Install a 0.050 inch spacer (Chrysler T8997) in place of shims (52). Install forward gear and bearing (22), drive shaft (53), pinion gear (19) and nut (20). Tighten nut (20) to 85 ft.-lbs. Insert Chrysler shim tool number T8997B in forward gear (22) so flat portion of tool is towards pinion gear (19). Pull up on drive shaft and using a feeler gage measure gap between large OD of tool and pinion gear. Subtract measured gap from 0.055 inch (0.050 inch spacer plus 0.005 inch desired backlash) to ob-

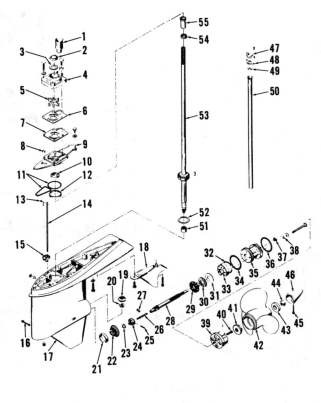

Fig. C10-46 — Exploded view of lower drive unit used on models after 1976.

1. Water tube seal
2. Drive shaft seal
3. Spacer
4. Water pump housing
5. Impeller
6. Lower plate
7. Gasket
8. Shift rod seal
9. Gearcase cover
10. Drive shaft seal
11. Cover seals
12. Crush ring
13. Pin
14. Lower shift rod
15. Pivot coupling
16. Pivot pin
17. Gearcase
18. Exhaust snout
19. Drive pinion
20. Nut
21. Bearing cup
22. Forward gear & bearing
23. Shim
24. Shift coupling
25. Shift pin
26. Shift shaft
27. Shift yoke
28. Propeller shaft
29. Reverse gear
30. Thrust bearing
31. Thrust washer
32. Retainer
33. Bearing & cage
34. "O" ring
35. Spool
36. "O" ring
37. Seal
38. "O" ring
39. Anode
40. Screw
41. Spacer
42. Propeller
43. Washer
44. Nut
45. Pin
46. Prop extension
47. Bracket
48. Seal
49. Grommet
50. Water tube
51. Bearing
52. Shim
53. Drive shaft
54. Seal retainer
55. Seal

tain thickness of shim pack (52). Remove 0.050 inch shim, install shim pack (52) and repeat above procedure. Gap between pinion gear (19) and large OD of shim tool should be 0.004-0.006 inch.

To check propeller shaft end play, install components (21 through 32) and bearing spool (35). Shim (23) should be thinnest available (0.054 inch). Do not install "O" rings on spool. Tighten spool retaining screws to 150 in.-lbs. Measure end play of propeller shaft and install shims (23) necessary to obtain 0.009-0.011 inch end play.

To reassemble lower unit, reverse disassembly procedure. Tighten pinion nut (20) to 85 ft.-lbs. Install seal (37) with lip towards propeller. "O" rings (34 and 36) have different diameters and must be installed correctly on bearing spool (35). Chamfered end of spool is installed first. Tighten bearing spool (35) retaining screws to 150 in.-lbs. Install seals (8 and 10) with lip towards gearcase. Tighten cover (9) to 70 in.-lbs. Install seal (2) with lip towards power head. Install seal (55) with ridged end towards power head.

FORCE

BRUNSWICK MARINE POWER
1939 Pioneer Road
Fond du Lac, WI 54935

35 HP

CONDENSED SERVICE DATA

TUNE-UP
Hp/rpm..................................35/5000
Bore...3 in.
(76.2 mm)
Stroke....................................2.414 in.
(61.3 mm)
Number of Cylinders............................2
Displacement......................34.1 cu. in.
(559 cc)
Compression at Cranking Speed
(Average)..........................125-135 psi
(862.5-931.5 kPa)
Spark Plug:
Champion................................L4J
Electrode Gap.....................0.030 in.
(0.76 mm)
Ignition Type...................................CDI
Carburetor:
Make................................Tillotson
Model.......................................WB
Fuel:Oil Ratio..............................50:1

SIZES—CLEARANCES—CAPACITIES
Piston Ring End Gap:
Top Ring.....................0.006-0.016 in.
(0.15-0.41 mm)
Bottom Ring...............0.004-0.014 in.
(0.10-0.36 mm)
Piston to Cylinder Clearance...........0.0060-0.0095 in.
(0.152-0.241 mm)
Piston Pin Diameter..............0.50000-0.50015 in.
(12.7000-12.7038 mm)

SIZES—CLEARANCES—CAPACITIES CONT.
Crankshaft Journal Diameters:
Upper Main........................1.3774-1.3780 i
(34.986-35.001 mr
Center Main.......................1.3446-1.3451 i
(34.153-34.165 mr
Lower Main........................0.9849-0.9853 mr
(25.016-25.027 mr
Crankpin..........................1.1391-1.1395 i
(28.933-28.943 mr
Gearcase Oil Capacity...........................12 c
(355 m

TIGHTENING TORQUES
Cylinder Head.............................190 in.-lb
(21.5 N·r
Flywheel Nut...........................55-65 ft.-lb
(74.8-88.4 N·r
Standard Screws:
10-24...................................30 in.-lb
(3.4 N·r
10-32...................................35 in.-lb
(4 N·r
12-24...................................45 in.-lb
(5.1 N·r
¼-20....................................70 in.-lb
(7.9 N·r
5/16-18................................160 in.-lb
(18.1 N·r
⅜-16...................................270 in.-lb
(30.5 N·r

LUBRICATION
The power head is lubricated by oil mixed with the fuel. For normal service after break-in, mix ⅙ pint of Quicksilver Premium Blend 2-Cycle Outboard Oil or a NMMA TC-WII certified oil with each gallon of gasoline. The recommended ratio is ⅓ pint of oil per gallon of gasoline for severe service and during break-in. Manufacturer recommends no-lead automotive gasoline although regular or premium gasoline may be used if octane rating is 85 or higher. Gasoline and oil should be thoroughly mixed.

The lower unit gears and bearings are lubricated by oil contained in the gearcase. Recommended gearcase oil is Quicksilver Premium Blend Gear Lube or a suitable noncorrosive EP 90 outboard gear oil. The gearcase should be drained and refilled every 100 hours or at least once per season prior to storage. Maintain fluid at level of upper (vent) plug.

To fill gearcase, have motor in an upright position and fill through lowe hole in side of gearcase until flui reaches level of upper (vent) plug hole Reinstall and tighten both plugs secure ly, using new gaskets if necessary, to assure a water tight seal.

FUEL SYSTEM

CARBURETOR. A Tillotson WB type carburetor is used. Refer to Fig. F5-1 for an exploded view of the carburetor.

Initial setting of idle mixture screw (10) is 1¼ turns out from a lightly seated position. Final adjustment of carburetor should be made with engine at normal operating temperature and with outboard motor in forward gear. Standard main jet size is 0.066 inch.

To check float level, remove float bowl and invert carburetor. Bottom side of float should be parallel with gasket surface of carburetor. Adjust float level by bending float tang.

Intall throttle plate (1) so notch is up and marked side is toward flange end of carburetor.

SPEED CONTROL LINKAGE. Ignition timing and throttle opening on all models must be synchronized so throttle is opened as timing is advanced.

To synchronize linkage, first check ignition timing to be sure it is set correctly as outlined in IGNITION TIMING section. Disconnect link (L – Fig. F5-2) from magneto control lever (T – Fig. F5-3) and with throttle closed, turn eccentric screw (S – Fig. F5-2) until roller (R) is exactly centered over mark (M) on throttle cam (C). Reconnect link (L) to magneto control lever and rotate magneto stator ring until it is against full advance stop. Upper mark (AM) on throttle cam should now be aligned with roller (R). Disconnect link (L) and turn link ends to adjust length of link so mark (AM) and roller are aligned when stator is at full advance.

Adjust idle speed to a maximum 750 rpm in forward gear by turning idle speed screw (I – Fig. F5-3) adjacent to exhasut port covers.

REED VALVES. A "V" type reed valve is used. The reed plate is located between the intake manifold and crankcase. Remove carburetor and intake manifold for access to reed valve.

Renew reeds if petals are broken, cracked, warped or bent. Never attempt to bend a reed petal in an effort to improve performance, nor attempt to straighten a damaged reed. Never install a bent or damaged reed. Seating surface of reed plate should be smooth and flat. Install reeds so petals are centered over openings. Assembled reeds may stand open to a maximum of 0.010 inch (0.25 mm) at tip end. Reed stop setting should be 9/32 inch (7.14 mm) when measured from tip of reed stop to reed plate.

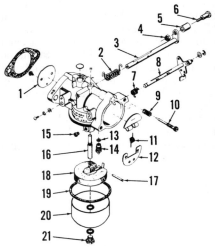

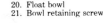

Fig. F5-1—Exoploded view of Tillotson WB carburetor.

1. Throttle plate	12. Choke plate
2. Spring	13. Gasket
3. Throttle shaft	14. Fuel inlet valve assy.
4. Nut	15. High speed jet
5. Roller	16. Main nozzle
6. Eccentric screw	17. Float pin
7. Spring	18. Float
8. Choke shaft	19. Gasket
9. Spring	20. Float bowl
10. Idle mixture screw	21. Bowl retaining screw
11. Spring	

Fig. F5-2 – View of throttle cam and linkage. Refer to text for identification of components and adjustment procedures.

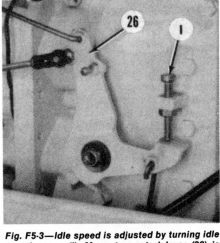

Fig. F5-3—Idle speed is adjusted by turning idle speed screw (I). Magneto control lever (26) is identified.

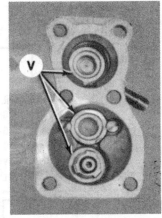

Fig. F5-4—Fuel pump check valves (V) must be installed as shown for proper operation of fuel pump.

FUEL PUMP. All models are equipped with a two-stage diaphragm type fuel pump which is actuated by pressure and vacuum pulsations from the engine crankcases.

NOTE: Either stage of the fuel pump operating independently may permit the motor to run, but not at peak performance.

To remove fuel pump, disconnect fuel hoses to pump and unscrew six cap screws which retain fuel pump body. Check valves are renewable, but be sure a new check valve is needed before removing old check valve as it will be damaged during removal. Unscrew the two retaining screws to remove center check valve. The two outer check valves must be driven out from below. Check valves (V – Fig. F5-4) must be correctly installed as shown. Install check valves carefully to prevent damage. Inspect

diaphragm and renew diaphragm if cracked, torn or badly distorted.

IGNITION

A breakerless, capacitor discharge ignition system is used. Note wiring diagram in Fig. F5-5. Tapered bore of flywheel and crankshaft end must be clean, dry and smooth before installing flywheel. Renew a chipped or cracked flywheel. Flywheel and crankshaft tapers may be cleaned by using fine valve grinding compound. Apply grinding compound to tapers and rotate flywheel back and forth approximately one-quarter turn. Do not spin flywheel on crankshaft. Clean flywheel and crankshaft tapers thoroughly. Tighten flywheel nut to 55-65 ft.-lbs. (74.8-88.4 N·m).

If ignition malfunction occurs, use tester tool T8953, plug adapter set

T11201 and number 22 tester with load coil from tool T8996 and refer to following trouble-shooting procedures:

Check and make sure ignition malfunction is not due to spark plug or ignition coil failure. If spark is absent at both cylinders, check condition of charge coil as follows: Separate the blue and yellow wire connection between charge coil and CD ignition module and attach double wire plug adapter to wire plug from charge coil as shown in Fig. F5-6.

Attach red (P) lead from tester number 22 to red sleeved adapter wire marked "Plug 2." Attach yellow (N) lead of number 22 tester and yellow sleeved adapter wire marked "Plug 1" to engine ground. Place tester switch in number 2 position and crank engine. If tester lamp does not light, low voltage windings of charge coil are defective and stator should be renewed. If lamp lights, continue charge coil test by disconnecting yellow sleeved wire adapter from engine

ground and attaching it to red (P) lead of T8953 tester as shown in Fig. F5-7. Attach yellow (N) lead of T8953 tester to engine ground. Turn tester switch to position 10 and crank engine. If tester lamp does not light, high voltage windings of charge coil are defective and stator should be renewed. If lamp lights, charge coil operation is satisfactory and trigger coil and CD ignition module circuits for each cylinder must be checked. Remove tester and plug adapter set, then reconnect blue and yellow wire plugs.

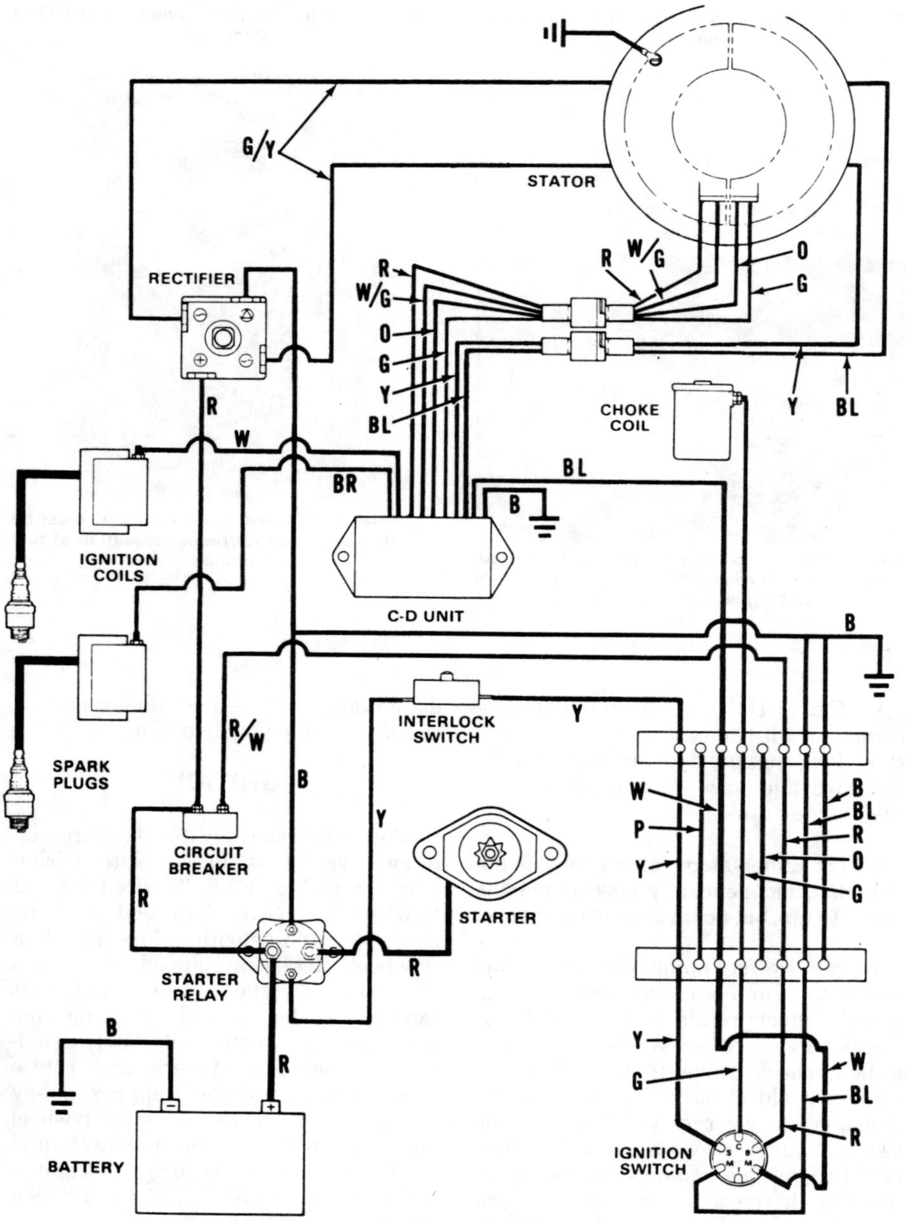

Separate the four wire connection between CD ignition module and trigger coil and attach four-wire plug adapter to wire plug from trigger coil as shown in Fig. F5-8. Attach red (P) lead from tester number 22 to red sleeved adapter wire marked "Trigger 1 Pos." and yellow (N) lead to yellow sleeved adapter wire marked "Trigger 1 Neg." Place switch of tester in number 1 position and crank engine. Trigger coil operation is satisfactory if tester lamp lights. Renew trigger housing if tester lamp does not light.

To check operation of number 2 cylinder trigger coil, repeat test procedure for number 1 cylinder trigger coil but connect red (P) lead of tester to red sleeved adapter wire marked "Trigger 2 Pos." and yellow (N) lead to yellow sleeve adapter wire marked "Trigger 2 Neg."

To check ignition module performance for each cylinder, connect yellow (N) lead from tester T8953 to ground terminal of engine terminal block (Fig. F5-9). Disconnect white (number 2 cylinder) or brown (number 1 cylinder) primary lead from ignition coil and connect red (P) lead of tester T8953 to primary lead. Connect leads of tester T8996 load coil to ground terminal of engine terminal block and primary coil lead of cylinder being tested. Turn T8953 tester dial to number 50. Crank engine and tester lamp should light. Renew ignition module if lamp does not light.

COOLING SYSTEM

WATER PUMP. All motors are equipped with a rubber impeller type water pump. When cooling system problems are encountered, first check the water inlet for plugging or partial stoppage. Then if not corrected, remove the lower unit gearcase and check the condition of water pump, water passages and sealing surfaces.

Access to the water pump is possible after separating lower unit from motor leg. Remove motor leg covers. Unscrew fasteners securing drive shaft housing to motor leg and disconnect intermediate shift rod from lower shift rod.

Fig. F5-5—Wiring schematic of Magnapower ignition system.

B. Black	O. Orange	R. Red	Y. Yellow
G. Green	P. Purple	W. White	BL. Blue

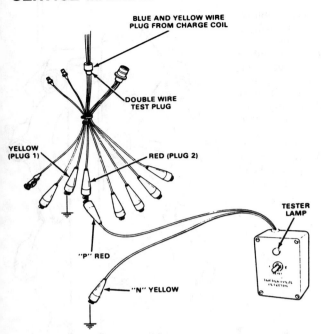

Fig. F5-6—Tester connections for checking low voltage output of charge coils.

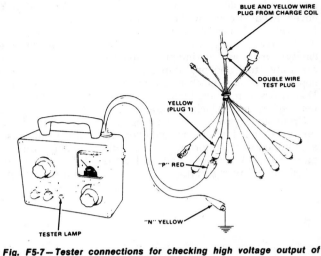

Fig. F5-7—Tester connections for checking high voltage output of charge coils.

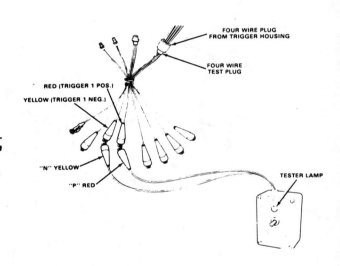

Fig. F5-8—Tester connections for checking operation of trigger coil.

Fig. F5-9—View showing tester connections needed to check CD ignition module output.

by removing pin (13—Fig. F5-16). Separate lower unit from motor leg. Unbolt and remove water pump.

Drive shaft seal (3) should be installed with spring loaded lip towards top. Drive shaft spline seal should be renewed if hard or cracked. Lubricate water tube seal and splines on upper end of drive shaft. Connect shift rods and carefully slide motor leg and drive shaft housing together making certain that water tube enters seal. Complete reassembly in reverse order of disassembly.

POWER HEAD

R&R AND OVERHAUL. To remove the power head, mount the outboard motor on a suitable stand and remove the engine cover. Disconnect the red battery lead from upper terminal of starter relay. Disconnect choke solenoid lead. Remove emergency hand starter assembly. Remove electric starter bracket, interlock switch and any other electrical wiring or component that will interfere with power head removal. Label all wires for correct reassembly. Remove flywheel and stator with ignition and alternator components. Remove fuel pump, carburetor and reed valve assembly. Detach shift linkage and throttle control linkage as needed. Remove lower shock mount covers, lower thrust pad (21—Fig. F5-10) at front of motor leg and shock and lower nuts of the two studs between the kingpin and plate (9) and spacer plate (4).

Unscrew motor leg cover bolts and remove rear motor leg cover. Engage reverse lock and pull outboard motor back enough to allow removal of front motor leg cover. Unscrew power head

retaining screws and withdraw power head.

To disassemble power head, remove seal in bore of bottom end of crankshaft. Unbolt and remove upper bearing cage and cylinder head. Remove transfer port cover, exhaust cover and exhaust plate. Unscrew cylinder block to crankcase screws (two screws are in reed valve cavity). Drive out locating pins, then use a suitable tool and pry at pry point to separate cylinder block and crankcase. Do not pry at machined mating surfaces between cylinder block and crankcase.

Crankshaft, pistons and bearings are now accessible for removal and overhaul as outlined in the appropriate following paragraphs. Assemble as outlined in the ASSEMBLY paragraph.

ASSEMBLY. When reassembling, make sure all joint and gasket surfaces are clean, free from nicks and burrs, warped surfaces or hardened cement or carbon. The crankcase and inlet manifolds must be completely sealed against both vacuum and pressure. Exhaust manifold and cylinder head must be sealed against both vacuum and pressure. Exhaust manifold and cylinder head must be sealed against water leakage and pressure. Mating surfaces of exhaust areas between power head and motor leg must form a tight seal.

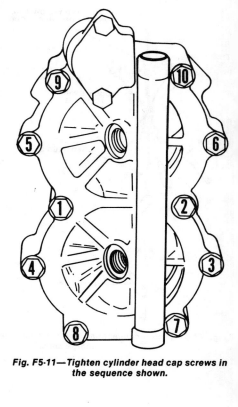

Fig. F5-11—Tighten cylinder head cap screws in the sequence shown.

Sparingly apply a coating of sealant to mating surfaces of cylinder block and crankcase. Tighten crankcase screws in a spiral pattern starting with center screws. Tighten cylinder head screws in sequence shown in Fig. F5-11. Install seal (6–Fig. F2-12) with "O" ring end inserted first until seal is 0.030 inch (0.76 mm) above edge of bore. Install a new seal in bore of bottom end of crankshaft. Install long screw for transfer port cover in upper left-hand hole as identified by (H) in Fig. F5-13. Complete remainder of assembly.

PISTONS, PINS, RINGS & CYLINDERS. Pistons are fitted with two piston rings which should be installed with the beveled inner edge (B–Fig. F5-14) toward top of piston. Piston ring end gap for top ring should be 0.006-0.016 inch (0.15-0.41 mm) and 0.004-0.014 inch (0.10-0.36 mm) for bottom ring. Rings are pinned in place to prevent rotation in ring grooves. Piston must be heated to install piston pin. Do not interchange pistons between cylinders. Piston to cylinder clearance should be 0.0060-0.0095 inch (0.152-0.241 mm).

When assembling piston, pin and connecting rod, match marks on connecting rod and cap must be aligned and long, tapering side of piston must be towards exhaust port.

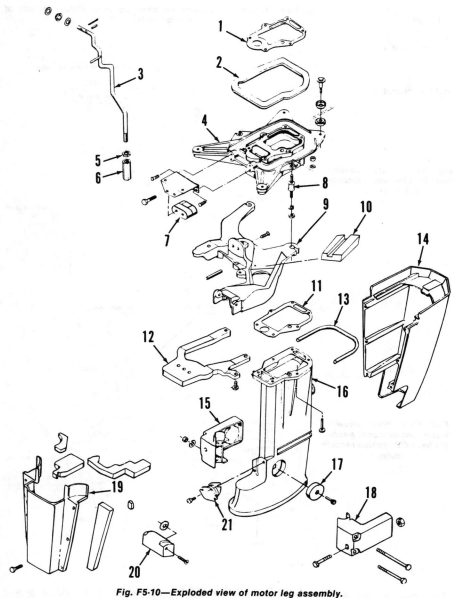

Fig. F5-10—Exploded view of motor leg assembly.

1. Gasket	7. Upper thrust mount	17. Shock mount
2. Seal	8. Stud	18. Shock mount cover (Port)
3. Upper shift rod	9. Kingpin plate	13. Seal
4. Spacer plate	10. Pad	19. Front motor leg cover
5. Locknut	11. Gasket	14. Rear motor leg cover
6. Coupler	12. Carrying handle	15. Shock mount cover (Starboard)
		16. Motor leg
		20. Cover
		21. Thrust pad

CONNECTING RODS, BEARINGS AND CRANKSHAFT. Before detaching connecting rods from crankshaft, mark connecting rod and cap for correct reassembly to each other and in the correct cylinder. The needle rollers and cages at crankpin end of connecting rod should be kept with the assembly and not interchanged.

The bearing rollers and cages used in the connecting rods and the rollers and liners in the center main bearing are available only as a set for each bearing. The complete assembly should be installed whenever renewal is indicated. Connecting rod bearing cages have beveled notches which must be installed together and toward top (flywheel) end of crankshaft. Match marks stamped on connecting rod and cap must be on the same side. Connecting rod is fractured to provide an uneven surface between rod and cap. Be sure rod and cap are properly meshed before tightening rod screws.

Inspect condition of seal ring (7 – Fig. F5-12) and carefully install ring in crankshaft groove. Seal ring (7) must prevent leakage between cylinders and a defective seal will result in poor engine performance.

Before installing crankshaft in crankcase, install bearing liner (9) over dowel

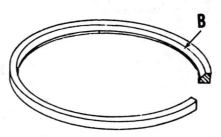

Fig. F5-14—Install piston rings with bevel (B) toward top of piston crown.

pin and place fourteen bearing rollers (8) in liner with a suitable grease to hold rollers in place. Install crankshaft and position remaining sixteen bearing rollers around crankshaft journal. Place remaining bearing liner over rollers so liner ends dovetail. Upper main bearing (1) should stand ⅛ inch (3.17 mm) higher than surface of crankcase.

ELECTRIC STARTER

Electric starter motor shown in Fig. F5-17 is used. Renew any components which are damaged or excessively worn.

A neutral interlock switch is used so engine will start in neutral but not in forward or reverse position. Make sure neutral interlock switch is properly adjusted.

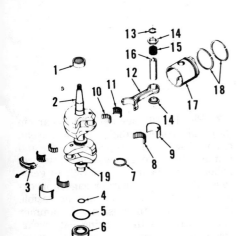

Fig. F5-12—Exploded view of crankshaft assembly.

1. Roller bearing
2. Crankshaft
3. Rod cap
4. Seal
5. "O" ring
6. Seal
7. Seal ring
8. Bearing rollers
9. Bearing liner
10. Bearing rollers
11. Bearing cage
12. Connecting rod
13. Snap ring
14. Spacer
15. Needle bearing
16. Piston pin
17. Piston
18. Piston rings
19. Ball bearing

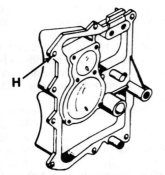

Fig. F5-13—Install long cap screw in upper left-hand hole (H) of transfer port cover.

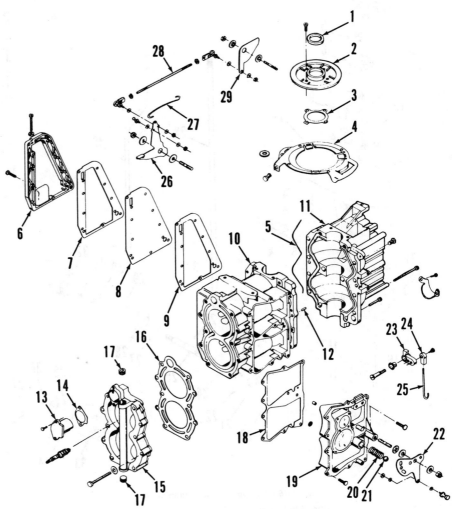

Fig. F5-15—Exploded view of cylinder block assembly.

1. Seal
2. Bearing cage
3. Gasket
4. Stator ring
5. Crankcase seal
6. Exhaust cover
7. Gasket
8. Exhaust plate
9. Gasket
10. Cylinder block
11. Crankcase
12. Dowel pin
13. Thermostat cover
14. Gasket
15. Cylinder head
16. Gasket
17. Plug
18. Gasket
19. Transfer port cover
20. Spring
21. Detent ball
22. Gear shift lever
23. Shift interlock lever
24. Pivot fitting
25. Shift interlock rod
26. Magneto control lever
27. Magneto stator link
28. Throttle link
29. Throttle cam

PROPELLER

Propellers for normal use have three blades and are equipped with a shear pin to prevent damage. Various pitch propellers are available and should be selected to provide full throttle operation within the recommended limits of 4250-5250 rpm. Propellers other than those designed for the motor should not be used.

LOWER UNIT

R&R AND OVERHAUL. To remove the lower unit, refer to WATER PUMP section. Drain the gearcase and secure gearcase skeg in a vise. Disassemble and remove the drive shaft and water pump assembly. Remove the cotter pin

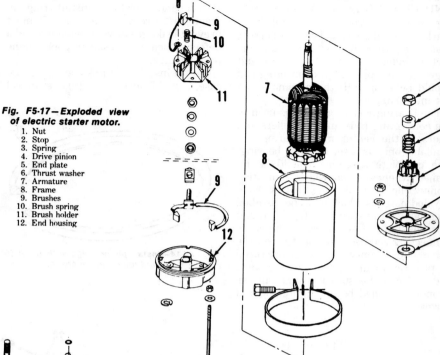

Fig. F5-17 — Exploded view of electric starter motor.
 1. Nut
 2. Stop
 3. Spring
 4. Drive pinion
 5. End plate
 6. Thrust washer
 7. Armature
 8. Frame
 9. Brushes
10. Brush spring
11. Brush holder
12. End housing

(37 – Fig. F5-16), spinner (36), shear pin (34) and propeller (33). Carefully clean exposed end of propeller shaft and remove the two screws securing propeller shaft bearing cage (32) to gearcase. Rotate the bearing cage approximately ½ turn until tabs are accessible from the sides, then use a soft hammer and gently tap the bearing cage rearward out of gearcase. Remove the gearcase rear retaining stud nut by working through propeller shaft opening. Unscrew gearcase front retaining stud nut, then lift off drive shaft housing (11).

Withdraw drive pinion (15) from top of gearcase and propeller shaft and associated parts through rear opening. Withdraw front and rear gears from propeller shaft. Remove spring pin (22), dog clutch (21) and shift pin (24).

The drive shaft seal (3) should be installed with spring loaded lip toward top (power head). Rubber coated side of shaft seal (31) should be installed with spring loaded lip toward outside of bearing cage (32). Sparingly apply Loctite 222 or 262 to outer diameter of shift rod seal (10).

Drive gear backlash and bearing preload are fixed and not adjustable. Assemble by reversing the disassembly procedure. Make sure that hole in dog clutch (21) is aligned with slot in propeller shaft (25) and hole in shift pin (24), then insert spring pin (22).

Fig. F5-16 — Exploded view of lower unit.

1. Shift rod	11. Drive shaft housing	21. Dog clutch	31. Seal
2. Grommet	12. Seal	22. Spring pin	32. Bearing cage
3. Drive shaft seal	13. Pin	23. Yoke	33. Propeller
4. Pump body	14. Shift rod	24. Shift pin	34. Shear pin
5. Impeller	15. Pinion gear & bearing	25. Propeller shaft	35. Seal
6. Back plate	16. Shift arm	26. Ball	36. Spinner
7. Seal	17. Pivot pin	27. Thrust washer	37. Cotter pin
8. Bushing	18. Gearcase	28. Rear gear	38. Drive shaft
9. Water screen	19. Front gear & bearing	29. "O" ring	39. Impeller drive pin
10. Seal	20. Thrust washer	30. Bearing	40. Water tube

FORCE 50 HP

CONDENSED SERVICE DATA

TUNE-UP

Hp/rpm	50/5000
Bore	3-3/16 in.
	(82.6 mm)
Stroke	2.8 in.
	(71.1 mm)
Number of Cylinders	2
Displacement	44.7 cu. in.
	(733 cc)
Compression at Cranking Speed	
(Average)	135-150 psi
	(931.5-1035 kPa)
Spark Plug:	
Champion	L4J
Electrode Gap	0.030 in.
	(0.76 mm)
Breaker Point Gap	0.015 in.
	(0.38 mm)
Carburetor:	
Make	Tillotson
Model	WB
Fuel:Oil Ratio	50:1

SIZES—CLEARANCES—CAPACITIES

Piston Ring End Gap	0.006-0.016 in.
	(0.15-0.41 mm)
Piston Ring Groove Width	0.0645-0.0655 in.
	(1.638-1.664 mm)
Piston to Cylinder Clearance	0.004-0.007 in.
	(0.102-0.178 mm)
Piston Pin Diameter	0.50000-0.50015 in.
	(12.7000-12.7038 mm)
Crankshaft Journal Diameters:	
Upper Main	1.1815-1.1820 in.
	(30.010-30.023 mm)

SIZES—CLEARANCES—CAPACITIES CONT.

Center Main	1.1388-1.1392 in.
	(28.926-28.936 mm)
Lower Main	1.1245-1.1250 in.
	(28.562-28.575 mm)
Crankpin	1.1391-1.1395 in.
	(28.933-28.943 mm)
Gearcase Oil Capacity	12 oz.
	(355 mL)

TIGHTENING TORQUES

Cylinder Head	270 in.-lbs.
	(30.5 N·m)
Flywheel Nut	80 ft.-lbs.
	(108.8 N·m)
Connecting Rod	180-190 in.-lbs.
	(20.3-21.5 N·m)
Main Bearing Screws	270 in.-lbs.
	(30.5 N·m)
Standard Screws:	
10-24	30 in.-lbs.
	(3.4 N·m)
10-32	35 in.-lbs.
	(4 N·m)
12-24	45 in.-lbs.
	(5.1 N·m)
1/4-20	70 in.-lbs.
	(7.9 N·m)
5/16-18	160 in.-lbs.
	(18.1 N·m)
3/8-16	270 in.-lbs.
	(30.5 N·m)

LUBRICATION

The power head is lubricated by oil mixed with the fuel. For normal service after break-in, mix 1/6 pint of Quicksilver Premium Blend 2-Cycle Outboard Oil or a NMMA TC-WII certified oil with each gallon of gasoline. The recommended ratio is 1/3 pint of oil per gallon of gasoline for severe service and during break-in. Manufacturer recommends no-lead automotive gasoline although regular or premium gasoline may be used if octane rating is 85 or higher. Gasoline and oil should be thoroughly mixed.

The lower unit gears and bearings are lubricated by oil contained in the gearcase. Recommended gearcase oil is Quicksilver Premium Blend Gear Lube or a suitable noncorrosive EP 90 outboard gear oil. The gearcase should be drained and refilled every 100 hours or at least once per season prior to storage. Maintain fluid at level of upper (vent) plug.

To fill gearcase, have motor in an upright position and fill through hole in side of gearcase until fluid reaches level of upper (vent) plug hole. Reinstall and tighten both plugs securely, using new gaskets if necessary, to assure a water tight seal.

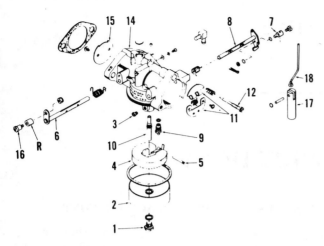

Fig. F6-1 – Exploded view of Tillotson WB type carburetor.

R. Roller
1. Bowl retaining screw
2. Fuel bowl
3. High speed jet
4. Float
5. Float pivot shaft
6. Throttle shaft
7. Connector
8. Choke shaft
9. Inlet needle & seat
10. Main nozzle
11. Choke plate
12. Idle mixture needle
14. Body
15. Throttle plate
16. Eccentric screw
17. Choke solenoid plunger
18. Rod

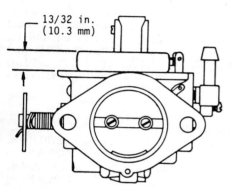

Fig. F6-2 — Correct float level is 13/32 inch (10.3 mm) when measured as shown between float and gasket surface.

FUEL SYSTEM

CARBURETOR. A Tillotson WB type carburetor is used. Refer to Fig. F6-1 for an exploded view of the carburetor.

Initial setting of idle mixture screw (10) is 1 turn out from a lightly seated position. Final adjustment of carburetor should be made with engine at normal operating temperature and with outboard motor in forward gear. Standard main jet size is 0.084 inch.

To check float level, remove float bowl and invert carburetor. Refer to Fig. F6-2. Bottom side of float should be a distance of 13/32 inch (10.3 mm) from float bowl gasket surface. Adjust float level by bending float tang.

SPEED CONTROL LINKAGE. Ignition timing advance and throttle opening must be synchronized so throttle is opened as timing is advanced.

To synchronize the linkage, first make sure that ignition timing is correctly set as outlined in IGNITION TIMING section. Shift to forward gear position and disconnect link (L – Fig. F6-3) from tower shaft (T). With carburetor throttle closed, turn eccentric screw (16) until roller (R) is exactly centered over scrib-

ed line (S). Move tower shaft (T) to full advance position and move the throttle cam until carburetor throttle is completely open. Vary the length of link (L) until the ball joint connector will just attach. Snap the ball joint connector onto ball stud and check maximum speed in neutral. Maximum rpm in neutral should be approximately 1800 rpm and is adjusted at neutral stop screw (N).

Idle speed screw should be 700-800 rpm in forward gear (800-900 rpm in neutral) and is adjusted at idle screw (I).

REED VALVES. "V" type intake reed valves are used. The reed plate is located between intake manifold and crankcase.

To remove the reed plate assembly after carburetor is removed, first remove the electric starter assembly and the screws retaining the intake manifold. Then lift off the intake manifold and the reed plate assembly.

Reed valve must be smooth and even with no sharp bends or broken reeds. Assembled reeds may stand open a maximum of 0.010 inch (0.255 mm) at tip end. Check seating visually.

Reed stop setting should be 9/32 inch (7.1 mm) when measured as shown in

Fig. F6-3 — View of speed control linkage. Refer to text for adjustment procedures.

A. High speed stop
I. Idle stop
L. Throttle link
N. Neutral stop screw
R. Roller
S. Scribed line
T. Tower shaft
16. Eccentric screw

Fig. F6-4. Renew reeds if petals are broken, cracked, warped or bent. Never attempt to bend a reed petal in an effort to improve performance, nor attempt to straighten a damaged reed. Never install a bent of damaged reed. Seating surface of reed plate should be smooth and flat. When installing reed petals and stops, proceed as follows: Install reed petals, stop and the four retaining screws leaving screws loose. Slide the reed petals as far as possible toward mounting flange of reed plate and reed stops out as far as possible toward tip of "V." Position reed petals and reed stops as outlined to provide maximum overlap. A minimum overlap of 0.040 inch (1.01 mm) is required. Tighten the retaining screws to secure position.

PUDDLE DRAIN VALVES. The puddle drain system is designed to remove any liquid fuel or oil which might collect in the crankcase, thus providing smoother operation at all speeds and lessening the possibility of spark plug fouling during slow speed operation.

The puddle drain valve housing is located on the starboard side of the power head and the puddle drain valve components can be disassembled as shown in Fig. F6-5. The reed-type puddle drain valve petals must seat lightly and evenly against valve plate. Reed stops should be adjusted to 0.017-0.023 inch (0.43-0.58 mm) clearance at the tip. Blow out drain passages with compressed air while housing is off.

FUEL PUMP. All models are equipped with a two-stage diaphragm type fuel pump which is actuated by pressure and vacuum pulsations from the engine crankcases.

NOTE: Either stage of the fuel pump operating independently may permit the motor to run, but not at peak performance.

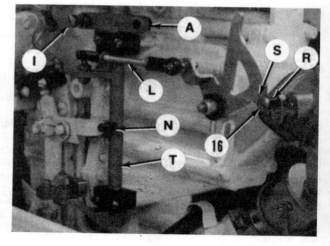

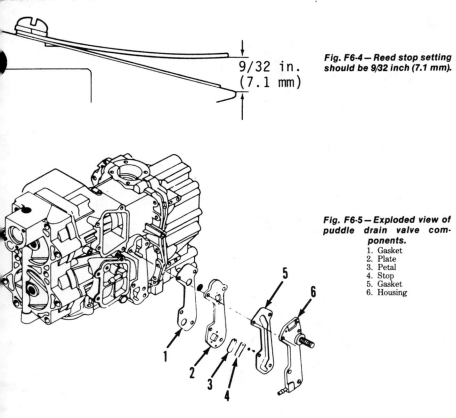

Fig. F6-4 — Reed stop setting should be 9/32 inch (7.1 mm).

Fig. F6-5 — Exploded view of puddle drain valve components.

1. Gasket
2. Plate
3. Petal
4. Stop
5. Gasket
6. Housing

To remove fuel pump, disconnect fuel hoses to pump and unscrew six cap screws which retain fuel pump body. Check valves are renewable, but be sure a new check valve is needed before removing old check valve as it will be damaged during removal. Unscrew the two retaining screws to remove center check valve. The two outer check valves must be driven out from below. Check valves (V – Fig. F6-6) must be correctly installed as shown. Install check valves carefully to prevent damage. Inspect diaphragm and renew diaphragm if cracked, torn or badly distorted.

IGNITION

A battery ignition with a flywheel mounted alternator is used.

R&R FLYWHEEL. A special puller (Part T-8948-1) should be used to remove the flywheel. Threaded holes are provided in the flywheel for installation of three puller screws.

NOTE: The three screws that secure the emergency starter collar must be removed, as well as the emergency starter collar. Make certain that aligning marks on flywheel and emergency starter collar are matched when reassembling.

Correctly position a large screwdriver or pry bar and apply upward pressure (Do Not apply excessive pressure) to rim of flywheel. Then bump jackscrew of puller sharply with a hammer to loosen flywheel from tapered portion of crankshaft.

The manufacturer recommends that mating surfaces of flywheel and crankshaft be lapped before flywheel is reinstalled. If evidence of working exists, proceed as follows:

Remove the flywheel key and apply a light coating of valve grinding or lapping compound to tapered portion of crankshaft. Install the flywheel without the key or crankshaft nut and rotate flywheel gently back and forth about ¼ turn. Move flywheel 90° and repeat the procedure. Lift off the flywheel, wipe off excess lapping compound and carefully examine crankshaft. A minimum of 90 percent surface contact should be indicated by the polished surface. Continue lapping only if insufficient contact is evident. Thoroughly clean the crankshaft and flywheel bore to remove all traces of lapping compound, then clean both surfaces with a non-oily solvent.

Reinstall crankshaft key and flywheel, then tighten flywheel nut to 80 ft.-lbs. (108.8 N·m).

POINT ADJUSTMENT. Breaker point gap should be 0.015 inch (0.38

mm). Both sets of points must be adjusted as nearly alike as possible.

NOTE: Point gap variation of 0.0015 inch (0.038 mm) will change ignition timing one degree.

To adjust the points, first remove the flywheel as previously outlined. Turn crankshaft clockwise until the rub block on one set of points is aligned with mark on breaker cam. Loosen breaker point mounting screws and adjust point gap until a slight drag exists using a 0.015 inch (0.38 mm) feeler gage.

Turn crankshaft until mark on breaker cam is aligned with the rub block on the other set of points and adjust the other set of points in the same manner.

IGNITION TIMING. Crankshaft timing should be 32° BTDC when setting piston position with special tool T-2937-1. When setting piston position with a dial indicator, the equivalent reading should be 0.281 inch (7.14 mm) BTDC. To adjust ignition timing, breaker point gap must first be carefully adjusted as previously outlined, then piston position must be accurately determined using special tool or a dial indicator as follows:

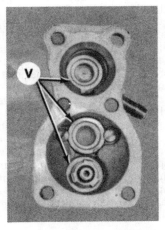

Fig. F6-6 — Fuel pump check valves (V) must be installed as shown for proper operation of fuel pump.

Fig. F6-7 — Special tool is available for positioning piston at correct timing position. Refer to text for proper tool usage.

To determine piston position using special tool T-2937-1 (Fig. F6-7), thread the tool body into top spark plug opening. Insert the gage rod into tool body, rotate the crankshaft and carefully position piston at exactly TDC.

NOTE: Gage rod should be installed with the double scribed line end on the 25-55 HP marked end out.

With the top piston at TDC, thread timing tool body in or out as necessary until the inner scribed line on gage rod is aligned with end of tool body. After gage body is correctly positioned, turn the crankshaft clockwise almost one complete revolution while applying pressure to end of gage rod. Stop the crankshaft just as the first (outer) scribed line on rod aligns with tool body. The crankshaft should be at correct position BTDC for maximum ignition advance timing.

To determine piston position using a dial indicator, insert dial indicator needle into top spark plug opening, then rotate crankshaft and carefully position piston at exactly TDC. Zero the dial indicator, then turn crankshaft clockwise almost one complete revolution stopping crankshaft just as a dial indicator reads 0.281 inch (7.14 mm). The crankshaft should be at correct position BTDC for maximum ignition advance timing.

With the crankshaft correctly positioned and breaker point gaps properly adjusted, connect one lead from timing test light (with battery) or an ohmmeter to the breaker point terminal of number one cylinder and ground other test lead to motor. Move the speed control from slow toward fast (maximum advance) speed position and observe the test light or ohmmeter. The breaker points should just open (test light goes off or ohmmeter registers infinite resistance) when the speed control reaches maximum ignition advance. If the breaker points do not open, shorten rod (L–Fig. F6-8) or if breaker points open too soon, length rod (L).

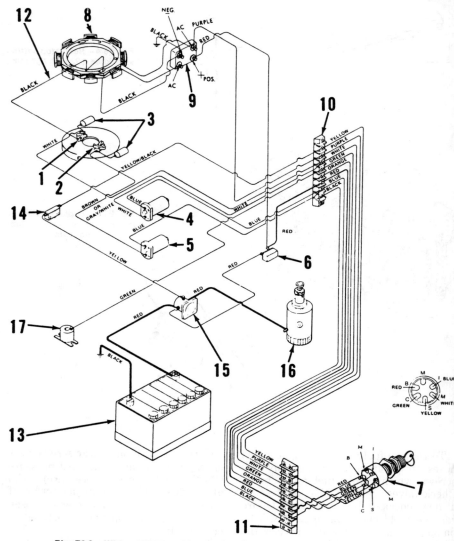

Fig. F6-9 – Wiring diagram of battery ignition and flywheel mounted alternator.

1. Breaker points for top cylinder
2. Breaker points for bottom cylinder
3. Condensers
4. Coil for top cylinder
5. Coil for bottom cylinder
6. Circuit breaker
7. Ignition & start switch
8. Alternator stator
9. Rectifier
10. Terminal block at motor
11. Terminal block at dashboard
12. Alternator ground
13. Battery
14. Neutral interlock switch

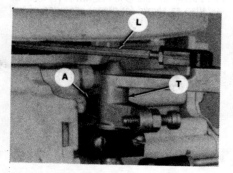

Fig. F6-8 – Full advance stop (A) on tower shaft (T) should contact housing before adjusting link (L) when setting ignition timing.

COOLING SYSTEM

THERMOSTAT. The thermostat is located beneath a separate housing on top, rear face of cylinder head. Remove cover (14 – Fig. F6-10) to gain access to thermostat (16). Install new thermostat as shown in figure.

WATER PUMP. All motors are equipped with a rubber impeller type water pump. Refer to Fig. F6-16. The water pump is mounted on top the lower unit drive shaft housing.

When cooling system problems are encountered, first check the water inlet for plugging or partial stoppage. Then if

trouble is not corrected, remove the lower unit gearcase as outlined in LOWER UNIT section, and check the condition of water pump, water passages and sealing surfaces.

POWER HEAD

REMOVE AND DISASSEMBLE. To overhaul the power head, clamp the outboard motor on a stand or support and remove the engine cover and motor leg covers. Remove the starter collar, flywheel, alternator, fuel pump, carburetor and intake manifold. Disconnect all interfering wiring and linkage. Remove the cylinder head, and transfer port and exhaust covers if major repairs are required. Remove the power head attaching screws and lift off the cylinder block, crankshaft and associated parts a unit.

NOTE: One of the power head attaching screws is located underneath the rear exhaust cover as shown in Fig. F6-11. Cover must be removed for access to the screw.

Fig. F6-11 — Rear exhaust cover must be removed from motor leg for access to power head rear attaching screw.

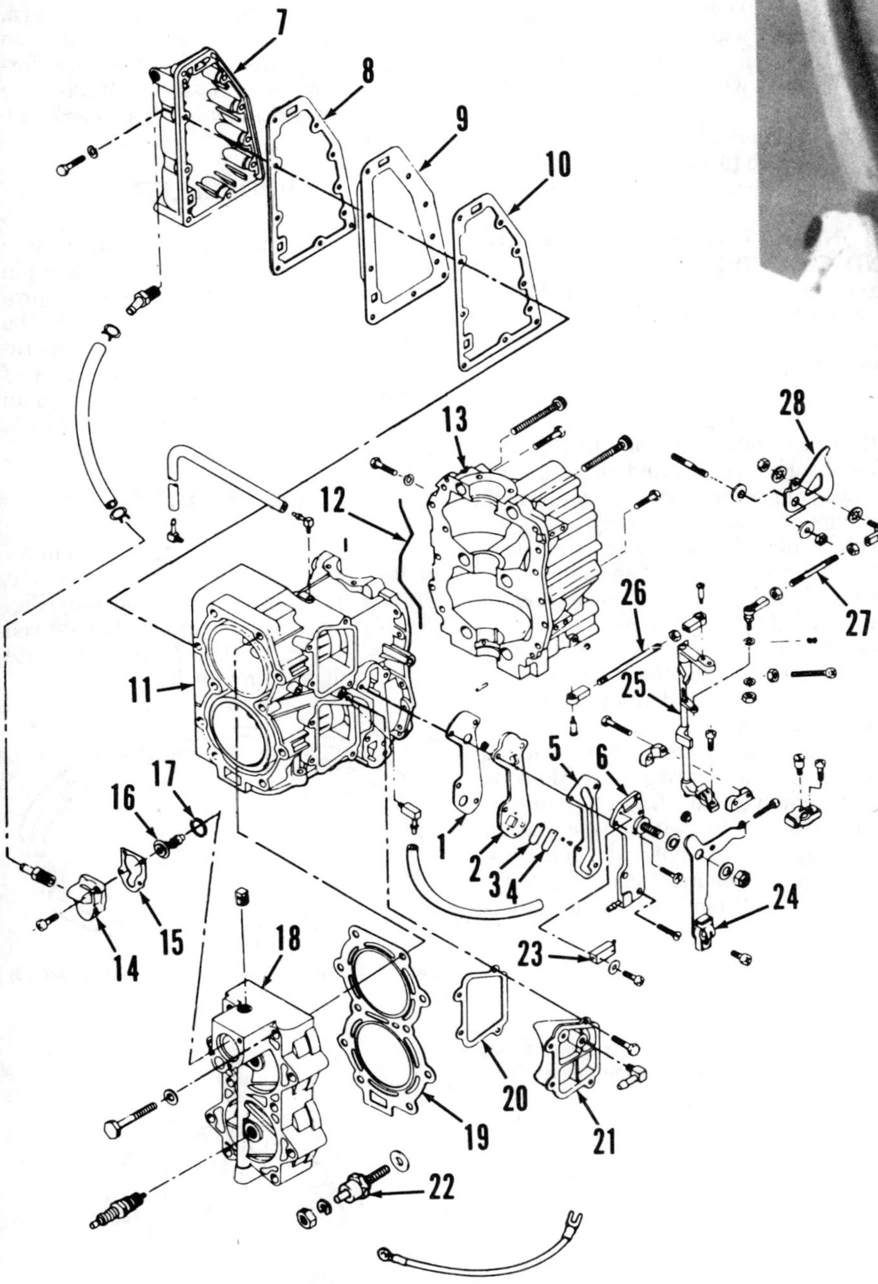

Fig. F6-10 — Exploded view of cylinder block assembly.

1. Gasket	11. Cylinder block	20. Gasket
2. Plate	12. Seal	21. Transfer port
3. Petal	13. Crankcase	22. Thermoswitch
4. Stop	14. Thermostat housing	23. Neutral interlock
5. Gasket	15. Gasket	switch
6. Housing	16. Thermostat	24. Shift arm
7. Exhaust cover	17. Seal	25. Tower shaft
8. Gasket	18. Cylinder head	26. Spark control link
9. Exhaust plate	19. Gasket	27. Throttle link
10. Gasket		28. Throttle cam

To disassemble the power head, unbolt and remove the upper bearing cage; then unbolt and remove the crankcase front half. Pry slots are provided adjacent to retaining dowels for separating the crankcase. DO NOT pry on machined mating surfaces of cylinder block and crankcase front half.

Crankshaft, pistons and bearings are now accessible for removal and overhaul as outlined in the appropriate following paragraphs. Assemble as outlined in the ASSEMBLY paragraph.

ASSEMBLY. When reassembling, make sure all joint and gasket surfaces are clean, free from nicks and burrs, warped surfaces or hardened cement or carbon. The crankcase and inlet manifolds must be completely sealed against both vacuum and pressure. Exhaust manifold and cylinder head must be sealed against water leakage and pressure. Mating surfaces of exhaust areas between power head and motor leg must form a tight seal.

Install crankshaft making certain upper, center and lower main bearings are properly positioned over main bearing locating pins in cylinder block.

Install new crankcase to cylinder block seals (12 – Fig. F6-10). Apply a suitable sealant to mating surfaces of crankcase in areas adjacent to upper and center main bearings and lower crankshaft seal. Do not apply sealant to areas outside of crankcase seal groove. Immediately install crankcase half and tighten main bearing screws to 270 in.-lbs. (30.5 N·m). Make sure crankshaft turns freely before proceeding with assembly.

When installing cylinder head, coat the first ¾ inch (19.05 mm) of screw threads with antiseize lubricant. Follow tightening sequence shown in Fig. F6-12 and torque the cylinder head cap screws first to 75 in.-lbs. (8.5 N·m), then in 50 in.-lbs. (5.6 N·m) increments until final torque of 270 in.-lbs. (30.5 N·m) is obtained. After outboard motor has been test run and cooled, retorque screws to 270 in.-lbs. (30.5 N·m).

PISTONS, PINS, RINGS & CYLINDERS. Pistons are fitted with two piston rings which should be installed with the beveled inner edge (B – Fig. F6-14) toward top of piston. Piston ring end gap for both rings should be 0.006-0.016 inch (0.15-0.41 mm). Rings are pinned in place to prevent rotation in ring grooves. Do not interchange pistons between cylinders. Piston to cylinder clearance should be 0.004-0.007 inch (0.102-0.178 mm).

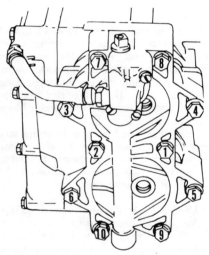

Fig. F6-12—Tighten cylinder head cap screws in the sequence shown.

The piston pin is a tight fit in piston bores and rides in a roller bearing in connecting rod. Special tool T-2990 should be used when removing or installing piston pin. When assembling piston, pin and connecting rod, make sure long, tapering side of piston is toward exhaust side of cylinder and match marks or bevel cut on rod are toward top (flywheel) end of crankshaft. Install piston pin retaining clips with sharp edge out or if bowed retaining rings are used, install with convex side toward piston pin. All friction surfaces should be lubricated with new engine oil when assembling.

Pistons are available in standard sizes and 0.010 inch (0.25 mm) and 0.030 inch (0.76 mm) oversizes.

CONNECTING RODS, BEARINGS AND CRANKSHAFT. Before detaching connecting rods from crankshaft, make certain that rod and cap are properly marked for correct assembly to each other and in the correct cylinder. The needle rollers and cages at crankpin end of connecting rod should be kept with the assembly and not interchanged.

The bearing rollers and cages used in the two connecting rods and center main bearings are available only as a set which contains the rollers and cage halves for one bearing. The complete assembly should be installed whenever renewal is indicated. Bearing cages have beveled match marks as shown by arrow, Fig. F6-15. Match marks must be installed together and toward top (flywheel) end of crankshaft.

A nonfibrous grease can be used to hold loose needle bearing in position during assembly. All friction surfaces should be lubricated with new engine oil. Check frequently as power head is being assembled, for binding or locking of the moving parts. If binding occurs, remove

the cause before proceeding with the assembly. When assembling, follow the procedures outlined in the ASSEMBLY paragraphs. Tightening torques are given in the CONDENSED SERVICE DATA tables.

ELECTRIC STARTER

Electric starter motor shown in Fig. F6-17 is used. Renew any components which are damaged or excessively worn.

A neutral interlock switch is used so engine will start in neutral but not forward or reverse position. Make sure neutral interlock switch is properly adjusted.

PROPELLER

Propellers for normal use have three blades and are equipped with a shear pin to prevent damage. Various pitch propellers are available and should be selected to provide full throttle operation within the recommended limits of 4500-5500 rpm. Propellers other than those designed for the motor should not be used.

LOWER UNIT

To remove lower unit, first remove motor leg covers and unbolt lower unit from motor leg. Remove pin (13 – Fig. F6-16) connecting intermediate shift rod (1) and lower shift rod (14). Separate lower unit from motor leg.

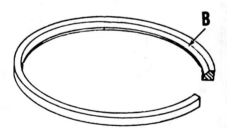

Fig. F6-14 — Install piston rings with bevel (B) toward top of piston crown.

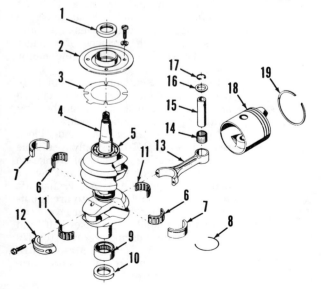

Fig. F6-13—Exploded view of crankshaft assembly.

1. Seal
2. Bearing cage
3. Gasket
4. Crankshaft assy.
5. Ball bearing
6. Bearing rollers & cage half
7. Bearing liner
8. Seal ring
9. Lower main bearing
10. Seal
11. Bearing rollers & cage half
12. Rod cap
13. Connecting rod
14. Needle bearing
15. Piston pin
16. Spacer
17. Snap ring
18. Piston
19. Piston ring (2)

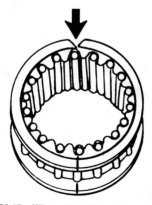

Fig. F6-15—When installing bearing cages, make sure beveled ends (arrow) are together and toward top (flywheel) end of crankshaft.

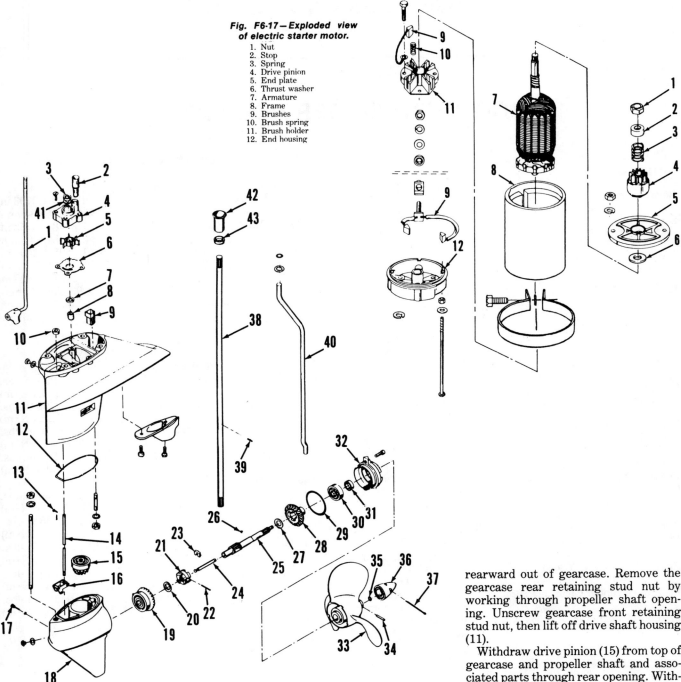

Fig. F6-17 — Exploded view of electric starter motor.

1. Nut
2. Stop
3. Spring
4. Drive pinion
5. End plate
6. Thrust washer
7. Armature
8. Frame
9. Brushes
10. Brush spring
11. Brush holder
12. End housing

Fig. F6-16 — Exploded view of lower unit.

1. Shift rod
2. Grommet
3. Drive shaft seal
4. Pump body
5. Impeller
6. Back plate
7. Seal
8. Bushing
9. Water screen
10. Seal
11. Drive shaft housing
12. Seal
13. Pin
14. Shift rod
15. Pinion gear & bearing
16. Shift arm
17. Pivot pin
18. Gearcase
19. Front gear & bearing
20. Thrust washer
21. Dog clutch
22. Spring pin
23. Yoke
24. Shift pin
25. Propeller shaft
26. Ball
27. Thrust washer
28. Rear gear
29. "O" ring
30. Bearing
31. Seal
32. Bearing cage
33. Propeller
34. Shear pin
35. Seal
36. Spinner
37. Cotter pin
38. Drive shaft
39. Impeller drive pin
40. Water tube
41. Disc
42. Seal
43. Retainer

Drain the gearcase and secure gearcase skeg in a vise. Disassemble and remove the drive shaft and water pump assembly. Remove cotter pin (37), spinner (36), shear pin (34) and propeller (33). Carefully clean exposed end of propeller shaft and remove the two screws securing propeller shaft bearing cage (32) to gearcase. Rotate the bearing cage approximately ½ turn until tabs are accessible from the sides, then use a soft hammer and gently tap the bearing cage

rearward out of gearcase. Remove the gearcase rear retaining stud nut by working through propeller shaft opening. Unscrew gearcase front retaining stud nut, then lift off drive shaft housing (11).

Withdraw drive pinion (15) from top of gearcase and propeller shaft and associated parts through rear opening. Withdraw front and rear gears from propeller shaft. Remove spring pin (22), dog clutch (21) and shift pin (24).

The drive shaft seal (3) should be installed with spring loaded lip toward top (power head). Rubber coated side of shaft seal (31) should be installed with spring loaded lip toward outside of bearing cage (32).

Drive gear backlash and bearing preload are fixed and not adjustable. Assemble by reversing the disassembly procedure. Make sure that hole in dog clutch (21) is aligned with slot in propeller shaft (25) and hole in shift pin (24), then insert spring pin (22).

FORCE 85 AND 125 HP

CONDENSED SERVICE DATA

TUNE-UP

Hp/rpm	85/5000
	125/5000
Bore	3.3125 in.
	(84.1 mm)

Stroke:

85 HP	2.80 in.
	(71.1 mm)
125 HP	2.875 in.
	(73.02 mm)

Number of Cylinders:

85 HP	3
125 HP	4

Displacement:

85 HP	72.39 cu. in.
	(1186 cc)
125 HP	99.23 cu. in.
	(1626 cc)
Compression at Cranking Speed (Average)	145-165 psi
	(931.5-1035 kPa)

Spark Plug—Champion:

85 HP	L20V
125 HP	UL18V
Electrode Gap	Surface Gap
Ignition Type	Breakerless
Carburetor Make	See Text
Fuel:Oil Ratio	50:1

SIZES—CLEARANCES—CAPACITIES

Piston Ring End Gap	0.006-0.016 in.
	(0.15-0.41 mm)
Piston Ring Groove Width	0.0645-0.0655 in.
	(1.638-1.664 mm)
Piston to Cylinder Clearance	0.0075-0.0103 in.
	(0.190-0.262 mm)
Piston Pin Diameter	0.68750-0.68765 in.
	(17.4625-17.4663 mm)

SIZES—CLEARANCES—CAPACITIES CONT.

Crankshaft Journal Diameters:

Upper Main	1.3789-1.3793 in.
	(35.024-35.034 mm)
Center Mains	1.3748-1.3752 in.
	(34.920-34.930 mm)
Lower Main	1.2495-1.2500 in.
	(31.737-31.750 mm)
Crankpin	1.1391-1.1395 in.
	(28.933-28.943 mm)
Gearcase Oil Capacity	26 oz.
	(769 mL)

TIGHTENING TORQUES

Cylinder Head	225 in.-lbs.
	(25.4 N·m)
Flywheel Nut	90 ft.-lbs.
	(122.4 N·m)
Connecting Rod	180-190 in.-lbs.
	(20.3-21.5 N·m)
Crankcase	270 in.-lbs.
	(30.5 N·m)

Standard Screws:

10-24	30 in.-lbs.
	(3.4 N·m)
10-32	35 in.-lbs.
	(4 N·m)
12-24	45 in.-lbs.
	(5.1 N·m)
1/4-20	70 in.-lbs.
	(7.9 N·m)
5/16-18	160 in.-lbs.
	(18.1 N·m)
3/8-16	270 in.-lbs.
	(30.5 N·m)

LUBRICATION

The power head is lubricated by oil mixed with the fuel. For normal service after break-in, mix 1/6 pint of Quicksilver Premium Blend 2-Cycle Outboard Oil or a NMMA TC-WII certified oil with each gallon of gasoline. The recommended ratio is 1/3 pint of oil per gallon of gasoline for severe service and during break-in. Manufacturer recommends regular leaded automotive gasoline. If regular is not available, use a good grade of premium gasoline. No-lead gasoline may be used if octane rating is 85 or higher. Gasoline and oil should be thoroughly mixed.

The lower unit gears and bearings are lubricated by oil contained in the gearcase. Recommended gearcase oil is Quicksilver Premium Blend Gear Lube or a suitable noncorrosive EP 90 outboard gear oil. The gearcase should be drained and refilled every 100 hours or at least once per season prior to storage. Maintain fluid level of "VENT" plug hole.

To fill gearcase, have motor in an upright position and add oil through "FILL" plug hole located on starboard side of gearcase until fluid reaches level of "VENT" plug hole. Reinstall and tighten both plugs securely, using new gaskets if necessary, to assure a water tight seal.

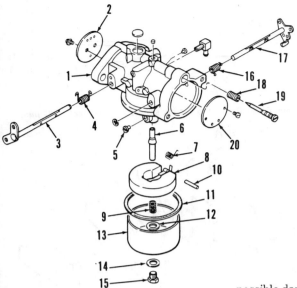

Fig. F7-1 — Exploded view of typical Tillotson type carburetor. Walbro type carburetor is similar.

1. Body
2. Throttle plate
3. Throttle shaft
4. Spring
5. Main jet
6. Main nozzle
7. Spring
8. Float
9. Spring
10. Float pin
11. Gasket
12. Gasket
13. Float bowl
14. Gasket
15. Bowl retaining screw
16. Spring
17. Choke shaft
18. Spring
19. Idle mixture needle
20. Choke plate

on the connecting link near the bottom carburetor.

SPEED CONTROL LINKAGE. Ignition timing advance and throttle opening must be synchronized so throttle is opened as timing is advanced. If incorrect, the power head may overheat, lack power and will usually not accelerate smoothly.

To synchronize the linkage, first make certain that ignition timing is correctly set as outlined in IGNITION TIMING section.

Disconnect the throttle rod (TR – Fig. F7-3) and move throttle cam (C) until mark (M) on cam is aligned with center of roller (R).

NOTE: If throttle cam (C) has two marks (M), roller (R) should be centered between marks.

Loosen locknut on roller (R) and turn the eccentric screw (S) until the cam just contacts the roller when mark (M) or marks are positioned as previously outlined. Tighten the locknut. Move the speed control to the maximum speed position and adjust the length of throttle rod (TR) so rod can be connected when carburetor throttles are at maximum opening. Recheck adjustments after connecting throttle rod to make certain that the vertical control shaft contacts the maximum speed stop at the same time carburetor throttles are completely opened.

REED VALVES. "V" type intake reed valves are located between the inlet manifold and the crankcase for each cylinder. To remove the reed valve, it is necessary to remove the carburetors and inlet manifold (1 – Fig. F7-4 or Fig. F7-5). On 85 hp models, all three reed valve assemblies are attached to adapter plate (3). On 125 hp models, two reed valve assemblies are attached to each adapter plate (3).

FUEL SYSTEM

CARBURETOR. A Tillotson or Walbro type carburetor is used. Refer to Fig. F7-1 for an exploded view of a Tillotson type carburetor. Walbro type carburetor is similar. Three carburetors are used on 85 hp models and two carburetors are used on 125 hp models.

NOTE: The carburetor model number is stamped on the mounting flange. Make sure that all carburetors used are the same type and model number.

Initial setting of idle mixture adjustment needle (19) is 1 turn out from a lightly seated position. Main jet (5) controls high speed mixture. Idle mixture must be readjusted under load, after motor is warm, for best slow speed performance. Idle mixture needle for all carburetors must be adjusted as nearly alike as possible for equal performance and all main jets (5) must be the same size.

Care must be used in selecting the main jet (5). A main jet which is too small will result in a lean mixture and

possible damage to power head. Jet may be identified by the diameter (in thousandths of an inch) stamped on visible end of installed jet. The standard main jet size is 0.72 inch on 85 hp models and 0.937 inch on 125 hp models. Optional jets are available which will improve performance when motor is used high-altitude locations.

To check float level, remove float bowl and invert carburetor. Refer to Fig. F7-2. Bottom side of float should be a distance of 13/32 inch (10.3 mm) from float bowl gasket surface. Adjust float level by bending float tang.

Throttle plates in carburetors must be synchronized to obtain maximum performance. The tie bar connecting the three carburetors on 85 hp models must be adjusted so all three carburetors open the same amount at exactly the same time. The adjusting clamp screws are on the connecting link near the top and bottom carburetors. The tie bar connecting the two carburetors on 125 hp models must be adjusted so both carburetors open the same amount at exactly the same time. The adjusting clamp screw is

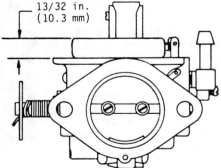

Fig. F7-2 — Correct float level is 13/32 inch (10.3 mm) when measured as shown between float and gasket surface.

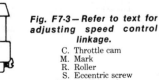

Fig. F7-3 — Refer to text for adjusting speed control linkage.
C. Throttle cam
M. Mark
R. Roller
S. Eccentric screw
TR. Throttle rod

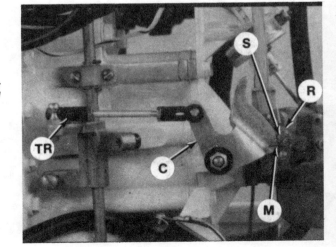

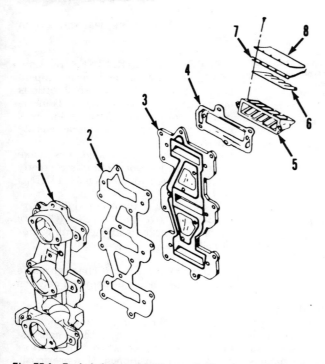

Fig. F7-4 — Exploded view of intake manifold and reed valve assembly used on 85 hp models.

1. Intake manifold
2. Gasket
3. Adapter plate
4. Gasket
5. Reed body
6. Reed petals
7. Spacer
8. Reed stop

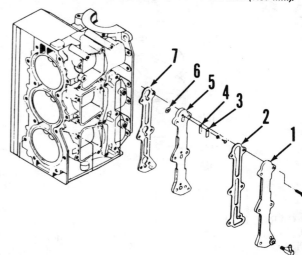

Fig. F7-6 — Reed stop setting should be 0.310 inch (7.87 mm).

0.310 in.
(7.87 mm)

Fig. F7-7 — Exploded view of puddle drain valve components on 85 hp models.

1. Housing
2. Gasket
3. Stop
4. Petal
5. Plate
6. Screen
7. Gasket

Seating surface of reed valve body (5) must be smooth and reed petals (6) must not be bent, broken or cracked. Assembled reed petals may stand open a maximum of 0.010 inch (0.255 mm) at tip end. Check seating visually. Reed stop setting should be 0.310 inch (7.87 mm) when measured as shown in Fig. F7-6. When installing reed petals, a minimum overlap of 0.040 inch (1.01 mm) is required.

PUDDLE DRAIN VALVES. The puddle drain valves are designed to remove any liquid fuel or oil which might build up in the crankcase, thus providing smoother operation at all speeds and lessening the possibility of spark plug fouling during slow speed operation.

The puddle drain valve is located on the starboard side of power head as shown in Fig. F7-7 or F7-8. The reed type valve petals (4) must seat lightly and evenly against valve plate (5). Make sure that screens (6) are in place in valve plate.

FUEL PUMP. All models are equipped with a two-stage diaphragm type fuel pump which is actuated by pressure and vacuum pulsations from the engine crankcases.

NOTE: Either stage of the fuel pump operating independently may permit the motor to run, but not at peak performance.

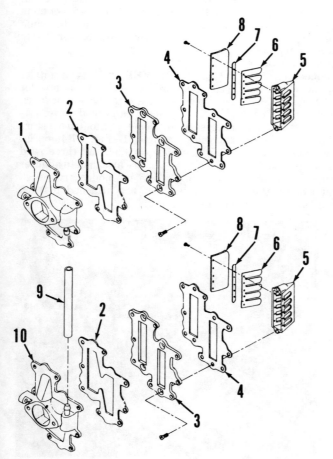

Fig. F7-5 — Exploded view of intake manifolds and reed valve assembly used on 125 hp models.

1. Upper intake manifold
2. Gasket
3. Adapter plate
4. Gasket
5. Reed body
6. Reed petals
7. Spacer
8. Reed stop
9. Balance tube
10. Lower intake manifold

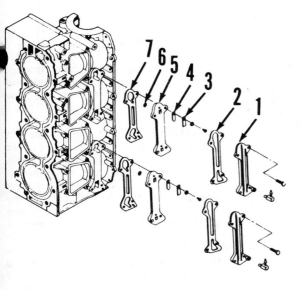

To adjust ignition timing, first immerse lower unit of outboard motor in water and connect timing light T8978 or a suitable power timing light to upper spark plug. With engine throttle in full retard position, crank engine with starter and note timing. Index mark on carburetor adapter flange should be within 2° of TDC mark on flywheel. If not, adjust timing link (L–Fig. F7-10). To check advance ignition timing, run engine at wide-open throttle with timing light connected to upper spark plug and note timing. Timing pointer should align with 32° BTDC mark on flywheel. Turn timing link (L) to adjust advanced ignition timing.

NOTE: Engine throttle should be returned to retarded position and engine stopped before turning ignition timing link.

To remove fuel pump, disconnect fuel hoses to pump and unscrew six cap screws which retain fuel pump body. Check valves are renewable, but be sure a new check valve is needed before removing old check valve as it will be damaged during removal. Unscrew the two retaining screws to remove center check valve. The two outer check valves must be driven out from below. Check valves (V – Fig. F7-9) must be correctly installed as shown. Install check valves carefully to prevent damage. Inspect diaphragm and renew diaphragm if cracked, torn or badly distorted.

IGNITION

A Prestolite ignition system is used on 85 and 125 hp models.

R&R FLYWHEEL. A special puller (Part T-8948-1) should be used to remove the flywheel. Threaded holes are provided in the flywheel for installation of three puller screws.

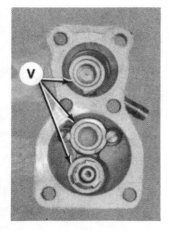

Fig. F7-9 — Fuel pump check valves (V) must be installed as shown for proper operation of fuel pump.

Remove nut securing flywheel to crankshaft and install puller assembly. Rotate puller jackscrew to apply pulling pressure. Then bump jackscrew sharply with a hammer to loosen flywheel from tapered portion of crankshaft.

The manufacturer recommends that mating surfaces of flywheel and crankshaft be lapped before flywheel is reinstalled. If evidence of working exists, proceed as follows:

Remove the flywheel key and apply a light coating of valve grinding or lapping compound to tapered portion of crankshaft. Install the flywheel without the key or crankshaft nut and rotate flywheel gently back and forth about ¼ turn. Move flywheel 90° and repeat the procedure. Lift off the flywheel, wipe off excess lapping compound and carefully examine crankshaft. A minimum of 80 percent surface contact should be indicated by the polished surface. Continue lapping only if insufficient contact is evident. Thoroughly clean the crankshaft and flywheel bore to remove all traces of lapping compound, then clean both surfaces with a non-oily solvent.

Reinstall crankshaft key and flywheel, then tighten flywheel nut to 90 ft.-lbs. (122.4 N·m).

IGNITION TIMING. Crankshaft timing should be 32° BTDC with engine running at wide-open throttle.

Fig. F7-10 — Adjust timing link (L) to alter ignition timing.

TROUBLESHOOTING. Use only approved procedures when testing ignition system to prevent damage to components. The fuel system should be checked to make certain that faulty running is not caused by incorrect fuel mixture or contaminated fuel. If ignition malfunction is suspected, use tool T8953, plug adapter set T11237, number 22 tester from ignition tester set T8996 and timing light T8978 or a suitable power timing light. Check and make sure ignition malfunction is not due to spark plug or ignition coil failure. Install test plugs in place of the spark plugs and observe spark while engine is being cranked with starter. If spark is absent at one or more plugs, check condition of charge coil as follows:

Separate the blue and yellow wire connection between charge coil (stator) and CD ignition module and attach double wire plug adapter to wire from charge coil as shown in Fig. F7-11. Attach red (P) lead from T8953 tester to red sleeved adapter wire marked "Charge (+)." Attach yellow (N) lead of tester to yellow sleeved adapter wire marked "Charge (−)." Turn tester switch to position 50 and crank engine. If tester lamp does not light, charge coil is defective and stator should be renewed. If lamp lights, charge coil operation is satisfactory and trigger coil and CD ignition module circuits for each cylinder must be checked.

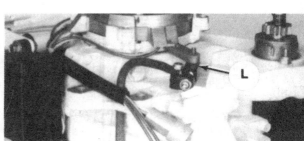

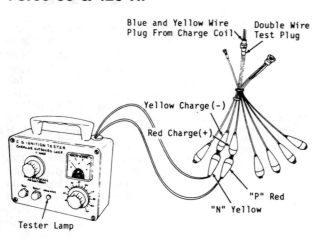

Blue and Yellow Wire Plug From Charge Coil

Double Wire Test Plug

Yellow Charge(-)

Red Charge(+)

"P" Red

"N" Yellow

Tester Lamp

Fig. F7-11 — Tester lead connections for checking voltage output of charge coil.

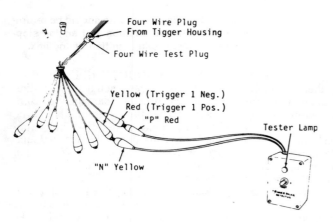

Four Wire Plug From Tigger Housing

Four Wire Test Plug

Yellow (Trigger 1 Neg.)
Red (Trigger 1 Pos.)
"P" Red

Tester Lamp

"N" Yellow

Fig. F7-12 — Tester lead connections for checking trigger coil operation.

COOLING SYSTEM

THERMOSTAT. The cooling system thermostat (21 – Fig. F7-14 or F7-15) is located behind cover (19) on top, front of cylinder head cover. Engine should not be run without a thermostat as engine may overheat.

WATER PUMP. The rubber impeller type water pump is located in the upper gearcase and is driven by the drive shaft. When cooling system problems are encountered, first check the thermostat to see that is working properly and the water inlet for plugging or partial stoppage. If trouble is not corrected, remove the gearcase as outlined in LOWER UNIT section and check condition of water pump, water passages and sealing surfaces. Refer to Fig. F7-20 for an exploded view of water pump assembly.

POWER HEAD

REMOVE AND DISASSEMBLE. Depending upon the type of maintenance, removal of the ignition components, starter, flywheel, alternator, carburetors and linkage and fuel pump prior to power head removal will ease operation. To remove power head, remove support plate retaining screws and withdraw. Remove screws and lift off rear motor leg cover. Detach any components or wiring that will interfere with power head removal. Remove screws and nuts securing power head, then carefully lift power head from lower unit. Remove screws and stud nuts to remove exhaust tube and spacer plate from power head.

Refer to Fig. F7-14 or F7-15 and remove cylinder head cover (23) and cylin-

Remove tester and plug adapter set, then reconnect blue and yellow wire plugs.

To check operation of trigger coil, separate the four-wire connection between CD ignition module and trigger coil and attach four-wire plug adapter to wire plug from trigger coil as shown in Fig. F7-12. Attach red (P) lead from number 22 tester to red sleeved adapter wire marked "Trigger 1 Pos." and yellow (N) tester lead to yellow sleeved adapter wire marked "Trigger 1 Neg." Place switch of tester in number 1 position and crank engine. Trigger coil operation is satisfactory if tester lamp lights. Renew trigger housing if tester lamp does not light. Repeat the previous test procedure but connect red (P) tester lead to red sleeved adapter wire marked "Trigger 2 Pos." and yellow (N) tester lead to yellow sleeved adapter wire marked "Trigger 2 Neg."

To check CD ignition module performance, proceed as follows: Separate primary lead connectors between CD ignition modules and ignition coils. Connect single wire adapter to orange or red wire from CD ignition module (Fig. F7-13).

NOTE: Model 85 hp does not use orange lead from rear CD unit.

Then attach yellow (N) lead of T8953 tester to yellow sleeved adapter wire marked "C-D." Attach red (P) tester lead to ground terminal of engine terminal block. Turn tester switch to position 60 and crank engine. Renew CD ignition module if tester lamp does not light. Repeat CD ignition module performance test for remaining cylinders.

Fig. F7-13 — Tester lead connections for checking CD ignition module performance.

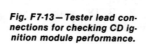

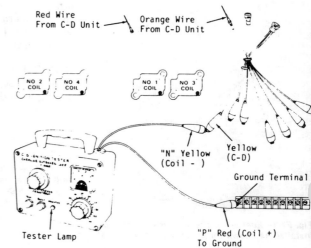

Red Wire From C-D Unit

Orange Wire From C-D Unit

NO 2 COIL   NO 4 COIL

NO 1 COIL   NO 3 COIL

"N" Yellow (Coil -)

Yellow (C-D)

Ground Terminal

"P" Red (Coil +) To Ground

Tester Lamp

the correct cylinder. Center main bearings must be marked for correct assembly to the main bearing journal from which they were removed.

Refer to the appropriate following paragraphs for service and assembly instructions for crankshaft, connecting rods, pistons and bearings.

ASSEMBLY. Before assembling, make certain that all joint and gasket surfaces are clean, free from nicks, burrs, warped surfaces or hardened sealer or carbon. The crankcase must be completely sealed against both pressure and vacuum. Exhaust cover and cylinder head must be sealed against water leakage pressure. Mating surfaces between power head, lower unit and spacer plate must form a tight seal.

Refer to the appropriate paragraphs for assembling the piston rings to pistons, pistons to connecting rods and main bearings to the crankshaft.

NOTE: It is extremely important that each cylinders parts are installed in the same location from which they were removed if the old parts are reinstalled. If parts are intermixed or installed in wrong location, early failure may result.

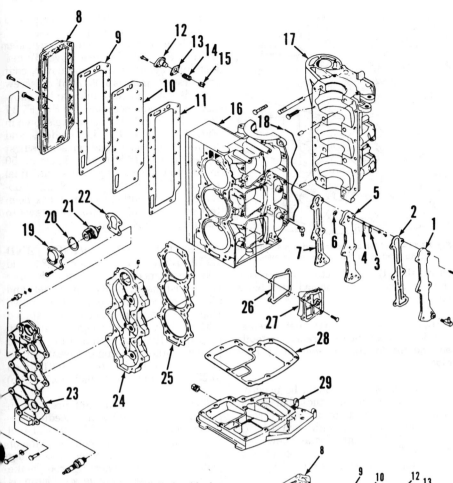

Fig. F7-14 — Exploded view of cylinder block assembly on 85 hp models.

1. Puddle valve housing	16. Cylinder block
2. Gasket	17. Crankcase half
3. Stop	18. Seal strip
4. Petal	19. Thermostat cover
5. Plate	20. Seal
6. Screen	21. Thermostat
7. Gasket	22. Gasket
8. Exhaust cover	23. Cylinder head cover
9. Gasket	24. Cylinder head
10. Baffle	25. Cylinder head gasket
11. Gasket	26. Gasket
12. Bypass valve cover	27. Transfer port cover
13. Gasket	28. Gasket
14. Spring	29. Spacer plate
15. Bypass valve	

der head (24). Remove exhaust cover (8), plate (10), transfer port covers (27), bypass valve (12, 14 and 15) and puddle drain assembly for cleaning. The crankcase front half (17) can be removed after removing all of the retaining stud nuts and screws including those attaching the crankshaft bearing cage. The crankcase halves are positioned with dowel pins and can be separated by prying at the two mating surface pry points. Use extreme care to prevent damage to the crankshaft and do not pry anywhere except the pry points provided.

Before removing connecting rods, piston or crankshaft, mark components for correct assembly to each other and in

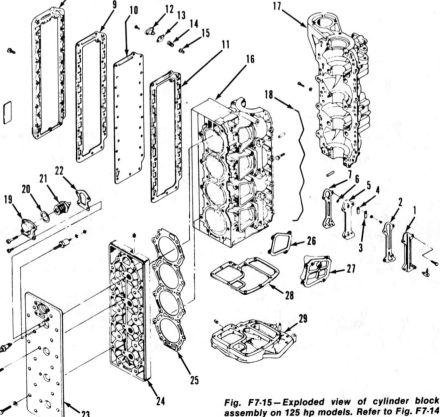

Fig. F7-15 — Exploded view of cylinder block assembly on 125 hp models. Refer to Fig. F7-14 for identification of components.

Install piston and connecting rod assemblies in the correct cylinder making certain that long sloping side of piston is toward exhaust side of cylinder.

Clean oil, grease and fingerprints from outer race of upper main bearing (7–Fig. F7-16) and bearing bore in crankcase.

NOTE: If alchohol or other flammable solvent is used for cleaning, make certain that area is well ventilated and free from sparks, open flames and electrical equipment.

Apply a light coating of Loctite to upper bearing bore in cylinder and position crankshaft in cylinder with all main bearings installed. Outer bearing races (17) and lower main bearing (20) should be turned until the bearing locating pins engage holes in the outer races. Position end gaps of crankshaft sealing rings (19) toward crankcase half.

Install the connecting rod bearing cage halves and rollers. Install rod cap with match marks together. Connecting rod screws should be tightened to 180-190 in.-lbs. (20.3-21.5 N·m).

Install crankcase seal strips (18–Fig. F7-14 or F7-15) in grooves, then apply a suitable sealer inside seal groove and on both sides of seal groove in areas of upper and lower main bearings. Coat the upper main bearing bore in front crank-

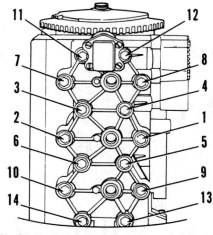

Fig. F7-17 — Tighten cylinder head cap screws on 85 hp models in the sequence shown.

case half (14) with Loctite and position the crankcase over the cylinder block and crankshaft.

NOTE: Make certain that holes in center and lower main bearing races correctly engage the locating dowels in cylinder block.

A suitable sealant should be used on threads of screws and studs that attach crankcase halves together and screws and nuts should be tightened to 270 in.-lbs. (30.5 N·m). Install new seal (3–Fig. F7-16) in bearing cage (4). Install upper bearing cage and seal

assembly with a new "O" ring and tighten the four retaining screws.

Apply a suitable sealant to cylinder head side of cylinder head cover. When installing cylinder head and cover, coat the first ¾ inch (19.05 mm) of screw threads with antiseize lubricant. Follow tightening sequence shown in Fig. F7-17 for 85 hp models and sequence shown in Fig. F7-18 for 125 hp models, and torque the cylinder head cap screws first to 75 in.-lbs. (8.5 N·m). Then in 50 in.-lbs. (5.6 N·m) increments until final torque of 225 in.-lbs. (25.4 N·m) is obtained. After outboard motor has been test run and cooled, retorque screws to 225 in.-lbs. (25.4 N·m).

PISTONS, PINS, RINGS AND CYLINDERS. Pistons on 1984 and 1985 85 hp models are fitted with three rings. Pistons on 1986 85 hp models and all 125 hp models are fitted with two rings. Piston rings should be installed with the beveled inner edge towards top of piston. Rings are pinned in place to prevent rotation in ring grooves. Pistons and rings are available in 0.010 inch (0.25 mm) and 0.030 inch (0.76 mm) oversizes.

The piston pin is a tight press fit in piston bores and rides in a needle bearing in connecting rod. The special tool T-2990 should be used when removing or installing piston pin. When assembling piston, pin and connecting rod, make sure long, tapering side of piston is assembled for installation toward exhaust side of cylinder and connecting rod bevel cut faces towards top (flywheel) end of crankshaft.

All friction surfaces should be lubricated with new engine oil during assembly.

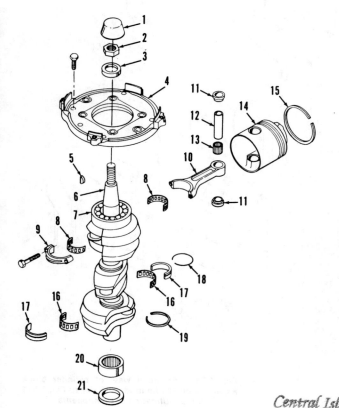

Fig. F7-16 – Exploded view of typical crankshaft assembly.

1. Cover
2. Nut
3. Seal
4. Bearing cage
5. Key
6. Crankshaft assy.
7. Bearing
8. Bearing rollers & cage half
9. Rod cap
10. Connecting rod
11. Spacer
12. Piston pin
13. Needle bearing
14. Piston
15. Piston ring
16. Bearing rollers & cage half
17. Bearing outer race
18. Snap ring
19. Seal ring
20. Lower main bearing
21. Seal

Fig. F7-18 – Tighten cylinder head cap screws on 125 hp models in the sequence shown.

A neutral interlock switch is used so engine will start in neutral but not in forward or reverse position. Make sure neutral interlock switch is properly adjusted.

PROPELLER

Propellers for normal use have three blades and are protected by a cushioning slip clutch. Various pitch propellers are available and should be selected to provide full throttle operation within the recommended limits of 4500-5500 rpm. Propellers other than those designed for the motor should not be used.

Fig. F7-19 — Exploded view of electric starter motor.

1. Nut
2. Stop
3. Spring
4. Drive pinion
5. End plate
6. Armature
7. Frame
8. Brushes
9. Brush holder
10. End housing

CONNECTING RODS, BEARINGS AND CRANKSHAFT.

CONNECTING RODS, BEARINGS AND CRANKSHAFT. Before detaching connecting rods from crankshaft, make certain that rod and cap are properly marked for correct assembly to each other and in the correct cylinder. It is important that each cylinders parts are installed in the same location from which they were removed if the old parts are reinstalled. If parts are intermixed or installed in wrong location, early failure may result.

The crankshaft upper main bearing is renewable. Place upper main bearing on crankshaft with lettered side towards flywheel, then using a suitable press, install bearing flush to within 0.001 inch (0.02 mm) of bearing seat.

The bearing roller and cages used in the connecting rods and center main bearings are available only as a set which contains the rollers and cage halves for one bearing. The complete assembly should be installed whenever renewal is required.

A nonfibrous grease can be used to hold loose needle bearings in position during assembly. All friction surfaces should be lubricated with new engine oil. Check frequently as power head is being assembled, for binding or locking of the moving parts. If binding occurs, remove the cause before proceeding with the assembly. When assembling, follow the procedures outlined in the ASSEMBLY paragraphs.

ELECTRIC STARTER

Electric starter motor shown in Fig. F7-19 is used. Renew any components which are damaged or excessively worn.

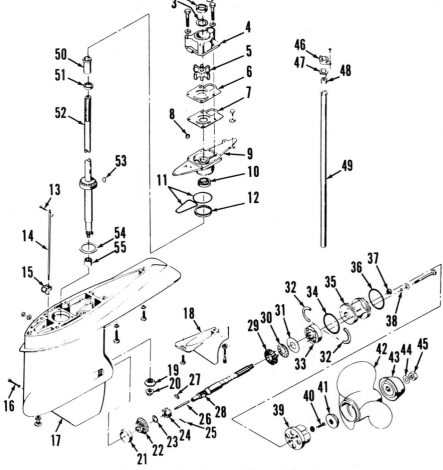

Fig. F7-20 — Exploded view of lower drive unit.

1. Water tube seal	15. Pivot coupling	28. Propeller shaft	42. Propeller
2. Drive shaft seal	16. Pivot pin	29. Reverse gear	43. Washer
3. Spacer	17. Gearcase	30. Thrust bearing	44. Washer
4. Water pump housing	18. Exhaust snout	31. Thrust washer	45. Nut
5. Impeller	19. Drive pinion	32. Retainer clips	46. Bracket
6. Lower plate	20. Nut	33. Bearing & cage	47. Seal
7. Gasket	21. Bearing cup	34. "O" ring	48. Grommet
8. Shift rod seal	22. Forward gear &	35. Spool	49. Water tube
9. Gearcase cover	bearing	36. "O" ring	50. Seal
10. Drive shaft seal	23. Shim	37. Seal	51. Retainer
11. Cover seals	24. Shift coupling	38. "O" ring	52. Drive shaft
12. Crush ring	25. Shift pin	39. Anode	53. Impeller drive key
13. Pin	26. Shift shaft	40. Screw	54. Shim
14. Lower shift rod	27. Shift yoke	41. Spacer	55. Bearing

LOWER UNIT

R&R AND OVERHAUL. Remove shift rod pin (13 – Fig. F7-20). Remove exhaust snout (18) and unscrew seven screws to separate gearcase from motor leg. Drain lubricant and remove propeller.

Disassemble and remove water pump components (1 through 7). Turn shift rod (14) counterclockwise until disengaged from pivot coupling (15) and remove rod. Remove cover (9) and anode (39). Remove screws securing bearing spool (35) and using a suitable puller withdraw spool from gearcase. Remove retaining clips (32), bearing and cage (33), thrust washer (31), thrust bearing (30) and reverse gear (29). Withdraw propeller shaft (28) with components (22 through 27). Unscrew pinion nut (20), withdraw drive shaft (52) and remove pinion gear (19). Unscrew pivot pin (16) and remove pivot coupling (15).

Use the following procedure to check reverse gear backlash: Install a 0.050 inch spacer (tool T8997) in place of shims (54). Install forward gear and bearing (22), drive shaft (52), pinion gear (19) and nut (20). Tighten nut (20) to 85 ft.-lbs. (115.6 N·m). Insert shim tool T8997A in forward gear (22) so flat portion of tool is towards pinion gear (19). Pull up on drive shaft and using a feeler gage measure gap between large OD of tool and pinion gear. Subtract measured gap from 0.055 inch (0.050-spacer plus 0.005 inch desired backlash) to obtain thickness of shim pack (54). Remove 0.050 inch shim, install shim pack (54) and repeat above procedure. Gap between pinion gear (19) and large OD of shim tool should be 0.004-0.006 inch (0.10-0.15 mm).

To check propeller shaft end play, install components (21 through 32) and bearing spool (35). Shim (23) should be thinnest available (0.054 inch). Do not install "O" rings on spool. Tighten spool retaining screws to 160 in.-lbs. (18.1 N·m). Measure end play of propeller shaft and install shims (23) necessary to obtain 0.009-0.011 inch (0.23-0.28 mm) end play.

To reassemble lower unit, reverse disassembly procedure. Tighten pinion nut (20) to 85 ft.-lbs. (115.6 N·m). Install seal (37) with lip towards propeller. "O" rings (34 & 36) have different diameters and must be installed correctly on bearing spool (35). Chamfered end of spool is installed first. Tighten bearing spool (35) retaining screws to 160 in.-lbs. (18.1 N·m). Install seals (8 & 10) with lip towards gearcase. Tighten cover (9) to 70 in.-lbs. (7.9 N·m). Install seal (2) with lip towards power head.

FORCE 150 HP

CONDENSED SERVICE DATA

TUNE-UP

Hp/rpm	150/5250
Recommended Speed Range	5000-5500 rpm
Bore	3.3125 in.
	(84.137 mm)
Stroke	2.870 in.
	(72.90 mm)
Number of Cylinders	5
Displacement	124 cu. in.
	(2032 cc)
Compression at Cranking Speed	145-165 psi
	(999.8-1137.7 kPa)
Spark Plug	Champion UL-18V
Electrode Gap	Surface Gap
Ignition Type	CDI
Fuel:Oil Ratio	50:1
Idle Speed (in gear)	750 rpm
Firing Order	1-5-2-3-4

SIZES—CLEARANCES—CAPACITIES

Piston Ring End Gap:

Top Ring	0.010-0.020 in.
	(0.25-0.51 mm)
Bottom Ring	0.006-0.016 in.
	(0.15-0.41 mm)
Piston Pin Diameter	0.68750-0.68765 in.
	(17.4625-17.4663 mm)
Piston Pin Bore Diameter	0.6876-0.6879 in.
	(17.465-17.473 mm)

Standard Piston Diameter:

Major Diameter	3.308-3.309 in.*
	(84.02-84.03 mm)
Minor Diameter	3.304-3.305 in.*
	(83.92-83.95 mm)
Standard Cylinder Bore Diameter	3.3130-3.3148 in.
	(84.150-84.196 mm)

Max. Allowable Cylinder Bore

Wear	0.002 in.
	(0.05 mm)

Crankshaft Journal Diameters:

Upper Main	1.3789-1.3793 in.
	(35.024-35.034 mm)
Center Mains	1.3748-1.3752 in.
	(34.920-34.930 mm)
Lower Main	1.2495-1.2500 in.
	(31.737-31.750 mm)
Crankpin	1.1391-1.1395 in.
	(28.933-28.943 mm)
Gearcase Oil Capacity	26 oz.
	(0.78 L)

*Piston major diameter is measured at a right angle to piston pin bore; piston minor diameter is measured parallel to piston pin bore.

TIGHTENING TORQUES

Connecting Rod	170 in.-lbs.
	(19.2 N·m)
Cylinder Head	225 in.-lbs.
	(25.4 N·m)
Exhaust Cover	70 in.-lbs.
	(8 N·m)
Flywheel Nut	90 ft.-lbs.
	(122 N·m)
Main Bearing Bolts	270 in.-lbs.
	(30.5 N·m)
Transfer Port Cover	70 in.-lbs.
	(8 N·m)

Standard Screws:

6-32	9 in.-lbs.
	(1.0 N·m)
8-32	20 in.-lbs.
	(2.3 N·m)
10-24	30 in.-lbs.
	(3.4 N·m)
10-32	35 in.-lbs.
	(4.0 N·m)
12-24	45 in.-lbs.
	(5.1 N·m)
1/4-20	70 in.-lbs.
	(8.0 N·m)
5/16-18	160 in.-lbs.
	(18.1 N·m)
3/8-16	270 in.-lbs.
	(30.5 N·m)

LUBRICATION

The power head is lubricated by oil mixed with the fuel. The recommended oil is Quicksilver Premium Blend 2-Cycle Outboard Oil or a suitable NMMA certified TC-WII engine oil. The recommended fuel is unleaded automotive gasoline with minimum octane rating of 85. Fuel:oil ratio for normal service is 50:1. Fuel:oil ratio for severe service and during break-in of a new or rebuilt engine is 25:1.

The lower unit gears and bearings are lubricated by oil contained in the gearcase. Recommended gearcase oil is Quicksilver Premium Blend Gear Lube or a suitable SAE 90 EP outboard gear oil. Lower unit gearcase oil capacity is 26 ounces (0.78 L).

Fill and vent screws are located on starboard side of gearcase. To fill gearcase remove plugs and add the specified lubricant to fill plug hole (front) until lubricant reaches level of vent plug hole. Allow motor to stand in an upright position with vent and fill plugs removed for 1/2 hour minimum, then recheck lubricant level and add as necessary.

FUEL SYSTEM

CARBURETOR. Refer to Fig. F8-1 for exploded view of carburetor. Three carburetors are used and must remain in original locations. Note that bottom carburetor is equipped with pickup roller (25) and top carburetor is equipped with fitting (18) for primer system.

Note that each carburetor uses different size main jet (20). Be sure correct main jet is installed. When disassembling carburetors, note depth of idle tube (5) so tube can be reinstalled in the same position. Position idle tube (5) in carburetor so tube contacts main nozzle toward front of carburetor as shown in Fig. F8-2. Inlet valve seat (11—Fig. F8-1) can be removed by threading a suitable screw into seat (11) and prying out. Install seat (11) by carefully pressing into body (1). Be sure seat (11) is bottomed in body (1).

Initial setting of idle mixture screw (21) is one turn out from a lightly seated position. To adjust float level (L—Fig. F8-3), bend inlet needle tab so float (10) is parallel with float bowl mating surface of carburetor body (1) with carburetor inverted as shown in Fig. F8-3. To adjust float drop, bend tab (T—Fig. F8-4) so float (10) hangs just short of contacting carburetor body casting (1).

Final idle mixture should be adjusted with outboard motor in the water or a suitable test tank. Adjust idle mixture with motor running at normal operating temperature and engaged in forward gear. Adjust top carburetor first. Adjust idle speed to 750 rpm with outboard motor in forward gear and running at normal operating temperature.

SPEED CONTROL LINKAGE. Throttle valves in carburetors must be synchronized to open simultaneously to obtain optimum performance. The tie bar connecting the carburetors must be adjusted so all three carburetors open the same amount at exactly the same time. Ignition timing advance and throttle opening must be synchronized to occur simultaneously.

To synchronize speed control linkage, first make certain that ignition timing is correctly adjusted as outlined in IGNITION TIMING section.

Disconnect throttle rod (TR—Fig. F8-5) from vertical control shaft (V). Loosen tie bar screws (S—Fig. F8-6) and remove play in tie bar (1) by pressing ends (2) toward each other (direction of arrows). Make sure all throttle valves will fully close simultaneously. Securely retighten screws (S). With throttle rod (TR—Fig. F8-5) disconnected from vertical control shaft (V), move throttle cam (C) until roller (R) is centered between marks (M) on cam (C). Roller (R) should just contact cam (C) when marks (M) are aligned with roller (R). If not, loosen locknut on roller (R) and turn eccentric screw (S) so roller (R) just contacts cam (C) with roller centered between marks (M). Reconnect throttle rod (TR) to vertical control shaft (V). Advance throttle to wide open and note position of carburetor throttle valves. Valves should be in horizontal position. If not, loosen jam nuts on throttle rod and adjust throttle rod to position throttle valves horizontal at wide open throttle.

NOTE: Throttle valves can be adjusted past horizontal position resulting in decreased performance. Make sure throttle valves are exactly horizontal at full throttle.

REED VALVES. "V" type reed valves are located between intake manifolds and crankcase. To remove reed valves first remove carburetors, primer valve and intake manifolds (1, 9 and 14—Fig. F8-7). Note that reed valve assemblies can be serviced individually.

Seating surface of reed valve body (5) must be smooth and flat. Reed petals (6) must not be bent, broken or cracked. Assembled reed petals (6) may stand open a maximum of 0.010 inch (0.25 mm) at tip of petal. Reed petals should not be preloaded against seat. Reed stop opening should be 0.300-0.320 inch (7.62-8.13 mm) measured as shown in Fig. F8-8. Renew reed stop (8) if opening is not as specified. When installing reed petals to reed body, reed petal

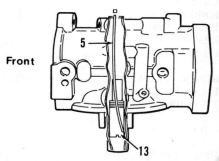

Fig. F8-2—Idle tube (5) must be installed at original depth in carburetor body and must contact main nozzle (13) toward front of carburetor as shown to prevent excessively lean fuel mixture.

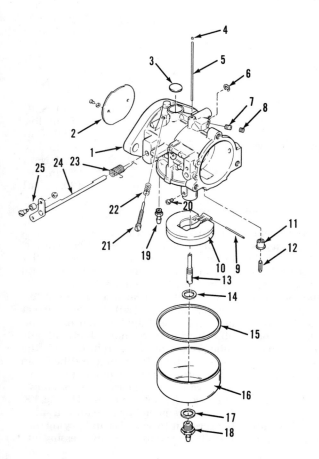

Fig. F8-1—Exploded view of carburetor used.

1. Body
2. Throttle valve
3. Plug
4. Plug
5. Idle tube
6. "E" ring
7. Intermediate jet
8. Plug
9. Pin
10. Float
11. Inlet valve seat
12. Inlet valve needle
13. Main nozzle
14. Gasket
15. Gasket
16. Float bowl
17. Gasket
18. Primer fitting (top carburetor)
19. Fitting (top carburetor)
20. Main jet
21. Idle mixture screw
22. Spring
23. Spring
24. Throttle shaft
25. Pickup roller (bottom carburetor)

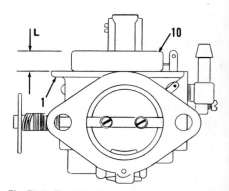

Fig. F8-3—To adjust float level (L), bend inlet needle tab so float (10) is parallel with float bowl mating surface.

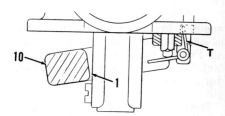

Fig. F8-4—Adjust float drop so float hangs just short of contacting carburetor body (1). Bend tab (T) to adjust.

should overlap seat by a minimum of 0.040 inch (1.02 mm) around entire outer periphery of reed petal.

FUEL RECIRCULATION VALVES. Fuel recirculation valve assemblies are designed to prevent fuel or oil puddling in the crankcase. Recirculation valve assemblies are located on the starboard side of crankcase. Refer to Fig. F8-9 for exploded view of valves.

CDI unit bracket must be unbolted and moved aside to gain assess to recirculation valves. When removing valve and cover assembly (1, 2, or 3), use caution not to damage cover-to-crankcase mating surfaces. Inspect and clean screen covering check valves and renew screen if excessive blockage is noted. To test check valves, attach a suitable hose to valve and alternately blow and suck through valve. Air should flow freely when blowing through valve. Valve should close when attempting to suck through valve. Renew check valve and cover assembly if valve operation is not as specified.

FUEL PUMP. Two separate dual-stage fuel pump assemblies are used. Fuel pumps are actuated by crankcase pulsations.

To remove pumps, disconnect fuel lines and remove six screws securing each pump body to transfer port covers. Be sure to mark fuel lines to ensure proper reassembly. Remove screws (10—Fig. F8-10) to remove center check valve from body (7). Remove second stage valve (top) by tapping out through hole on back side of body (7). Do not remove second stage valve (top) unless renewal is required as valve will be damaged during removal. Remove first stage valve (bottom) by extracting with a suitable hooked tool. Inspect diaphragm (13) and renew if cracked, torn or distorted.

Check valves must be installed as shown in Fig. F8-11. Make sure valves are seated in pump body. Apply sealant US Marine part T-8955 or equivalent to threads of fittings (5—F8-10). Install screen into body with edges of screen facing power head. Install sediment bowls (2) with hose fittings pointing toward four o'clock position.

IGNITION

Prestolite capacitor discharge ignition (CDI) system is used. Note wiring diagram in Fig. F8-14. Individual ignition coils are used for each cylinder. Three CDI modules are used; front module controls ignition coils for cylinders 1 and 2, rear module controls ignition coil for cylinder number 3 and bottom module controls ignition coils for cylinders 4 and 5.

Stator and trigger coil assemblies are located under the flywheel. The manufacturer recommends using special puller (US Marine part T-8948-1) to remove flywheel. Tighten puller jackscrew to apply pulling pressure. Then strike jackscrew sharply with a hammer while prying up on flywheel with a suitable tool to loosen flywheel from crankshaft taper. When installing flywheel, be sure crankshaft taper and flywheel bore are perfectly clean. Install flywheel key into crankshaft slot with outer edge of key positioned parallel with crankshaft centerline. Tighten flywheel nut to 90 ft.-lbs. (122 N·m).

IGNITION TIMING. Make sure flywheel is properly positioned on crankshaft by inserting Timing Tool TA-2937-1 or a suitable dial indicator into spark plug hole of number 1 (top) cylinder. Rotate engine clockwise and locate number 1 piston at TDC. If TDC mark (Fig. F8-12) on flywheel does not align with timing pointer with number 1 piston at

TDC, remove flywheel and inspect for sheared flywheel key, damaged flywheel or crankshaft.

To check ignition timing at cranking speed, proceed as follows: Remove spark plug leads from spark plugs, connect special tool part T-11260-1 or a suitable equivalent spark tester to spark plug leads and ground spark tester. Connect a jumper wire across neutral interlock switch terminals and place motor in forward gear. Rotate vertical control shaft to wide-open throttle. Connect a suitable timing light to number one spark plug lead, crank engine and note timing marks (Fig. F8-12).

NOTE: To obtain the required 32 degrees BTDC timing advance with engine running at full throttle, cranking speed timing must be set at 30 degrees BTDC. Refer to Fig. F8-12 for view of timing marks on flywheel.

To adjust timing, loosen jam nut and turn timing link (L—Fig. F8-13) as necessary. Tighten jam nut and recheck timing.

To check dynamic (engine running) ignition timing, proceed as follows: Immerse lower unit in water and connect a timing light to number 1 spark plug lead.

Note: The manufacturer recommends not performing timing adjustment in a moving boat. Remove propeller and install special tool part TA-8999 or a suitable equivalent test wheel and immerse lower unit in a suitable test tank. If test tank is not available, place boat in water and secure to a dock or other fixture.

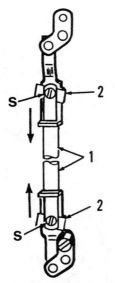

Fig. F8-6—To synchronize carburetor throttle valve movement, loosen screws (S) and remove any play in tie bar (1) by pressing tie bar ends (2) in direction of arrows, then retighten screws (S).

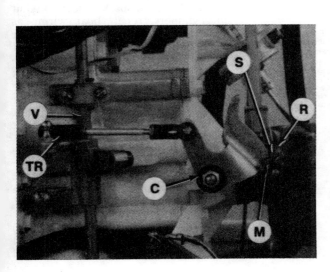

Fig. F8-5—Refer to text for adjusting speed control linkage.

C. Throttle cam
M. Marks
R. Roller
S. Eccentric screw
V. Vertical control shaft
TR. Tower shaft

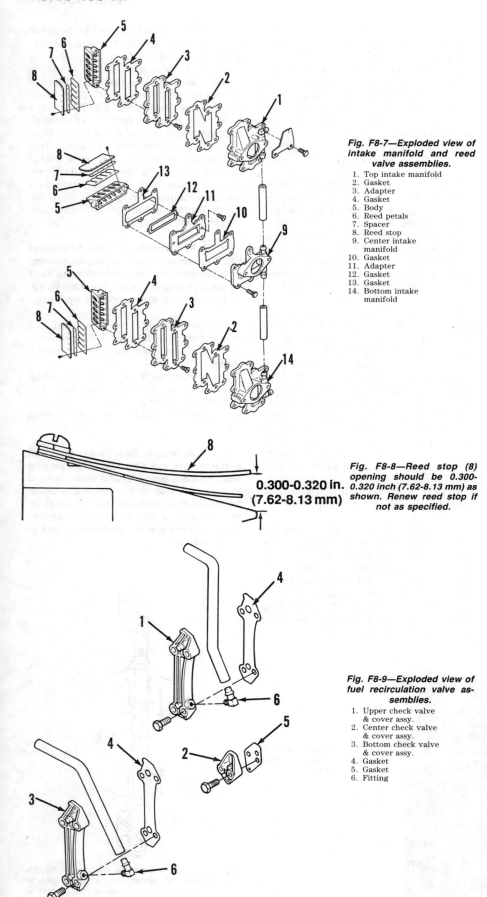

Fig. F8-7—Exploded view of intake manifold and reed valve assemblies.

1. Top intake manifold
2. Gasket
3. Adapter
4. Gasket
5. Body
6. Reed petals
7. Spacer
8. Reed stop
9. Center intake manifold
10. Gasket
11. Adapter
12. Gasket
13. Gasket
14. Bottom intake manifold

**0.300-0.320 in.
(7.62-8.13 mm)**

Fig. F8-8—Reed stop (8) opening should be 0.300-0.320 inch (7.62-8.13 mm) as shown. Renew reed stop if not as specified.

Fig. F8-9—Exploded view of fuel recirculation valve assemblies.

1. Upper check valve & cover assy.
2. Center check valve & cover assy.
3. Bottom check valve & cover assy.
4. Gasket
5. Gasket
6. Fitting

Start engine and allow to warm to normal operating temperature. While observing timing marks (Fig. F8-12) with timing light, move throttle to wide open. Ignition timing at wide-open throttle should be 32 degrees BTDC. Adjust timing link (L—Fig. F8-13) to adjust timing.

TROUBLE-SHOOTING. Use only approved procedures when testing ignition system to prevent damage to ignition components. The fuel system should be checked to make certain that faulty operation is not the result of incorrect fuel mixture, contaminated fuel or other fuel system malfunction.

The required equipment for testing ignition system is as follows: US Marine Multimeter TA-11259 or a suitable equivalent DVA meter capable of reading peak voltage up to 400 volts, and US Marine Spark Tester T-11260-1 or equivalent spark tester.

Begin trouble-shooting process by making sure all connections and grounds are clean and tight. Connect spark tester to spark plug leads, adjust tester spark gap to $7/16$ inch (11 mm) and ground tester to engine. Note that engine cranking speed must be minimum of 600 rpm for accurate test results. Crank engine while noting spark gap. If acceptable spark is noted at all cylinders, proceed as follows: Start engine and allow to warm to normal operating temperature. Using an inductive tachometer, check rpm at spark plug lead of each cylinder while varying engine speed between idle and full throttle. Renew CDI module connected to any cylinder that shows different rpm than other cylinders.

If no spark is noted at one or more cylinders, isolate ignition system by removing black/yellow lead from terminal block (A—Fig. F8-14). Make sure black/yellow lead is not shorted to ground. Crank engine and recheck spark. If normal spark is now noted at all cylinders, repair boat wiring as necessary. If no spark is noted at one or more cylinders, remove CDI bracket from power head and remove black/yellow leads from terminal block (C) located behind bracket. Make sure black/yellow leads are not grounded or contacting each other. If normal spark is now noted at all cylinders, repair boat wiring as necessary.

If no spark is noted at one or more cylinders, test stator output.

NOTE: Stator leads are fragile. Use care when handling leads to prevent damage.

Remove cover from terminal block (D) and disconnect brown/blue stator lead marked 1 and brown/yellow lead marked 2. Set DVA meter selector switch to 400 DVA scale and connect meter between disconnected leads. Crank engine and note meter reading. Meter reading should be 210 volts or more. Reconnect stator leads and repeat test on stator leads marked 3 (brown/black/blue) and 4 (brown/black/yellow). Reconnect leads then repeat test on stator leads marked 5 (brown/green/blue) and 6 (brown/green/yellow). Reading on all stator tests should be 210 volts or more. If reading is intermittent or less than 210 volts on any test, stator should be renewed.

To test number 1 trigger, remove cover from terminal block (B) and connect a jumper wire across neutral safety switch terminals. Disconnect white/brown/yellow and white/brown/orange leads (marked 1). Set DVA meter to 2.0 DVA scale. Connect red meter lead to white/brown/orange trigger lead and black meter lead to white/brown/yellow trigger lead. Crank engine and, while noting meter reading, advance throttle from idle to full throttle position and back to idle. Meter reading should be 0.3 volt or higher. Reconnect number 1 trigger leads to terminal block (B).

Disconnect and repeat test on remaining trigger coils. Be sure to reconnect trigger leads after each test. Meter connections are as follows: Number 2 trigger—connect red meter lead to white/brown/red trigger lead (marked 2) and black meter lead to white/brown/green (marked 2) trigger lead; Number 3 trigger—connect red meter lead to white/black/orange trigger lead (marked 3) and black meter lead to white/black/yellow (marked 3) trigger lead; Number 4 trigger—Connect red meter lead to white/purple/yellow (marked 4) trigger lead and black meter lead to white/purple/orange (marked 4) trigger lead; Number 5 trigger—connect red meter lead to white/purple/red (marked 5) trigger lead and black meter lead to white/purple/green (marked 5) trigger lead. Meter reading should be 0.3 volt or higher on all trigger tests. If reading is intermittent or under 0.3 volt, renew trigger coil assembly.

CDI module output lead connectors are located behind module mounting bracket. Unbolt bracket from power head to gain access to connectors.

To test CDI module output, set DVA meter selector switch to 400 DVA. Connect red meter lead to engine ground. Refer to Fig. F8-14 and disconnect module output lead to number 1 ignition coil and connect black meter lead to blue/orange lead from module. Crank engine and note meter. Reading should be 210 volts or more. Repeat tests on remaining module output-to-ignition coil leads. Be sure red meter lead is connected to engine ground on all tests. CDI module output should be 210 volts or more on all tests. If not, renew defective module.

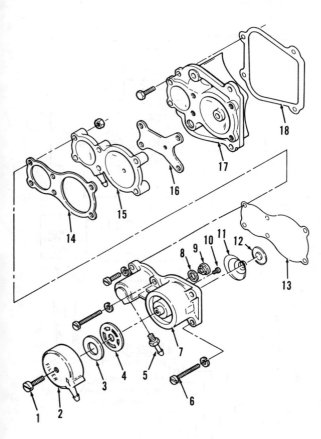

Fig. F8-10—Exploded view of fuel pump. Note that two pumps are used. Refer also to Fig. F8-11.

1. Screw
2. Sediment bowl
3. Gasket
4. Screen
5. Fitting
6. Screw
7. Pump body
8. Gasket
9. Check valve (three used)
10. Screw
11. Booster spring
12. Retainer
13. Diaphragm
14. Gasket
15. Spacer
16. Gasket
17. Transfer port cover
18. Gasket

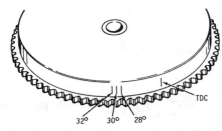

Fig. F8-12—View of timing marks on flywheel.

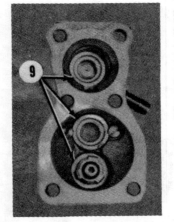

Fig. F8-11—Fuel pump check valves (9) must be installed as shown for proper pump operation.

Fig. F8-13—To adjust ignition timing, loosen jam nut and turn timing link (L).

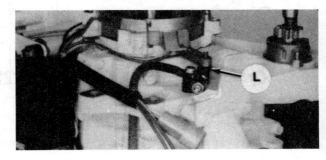

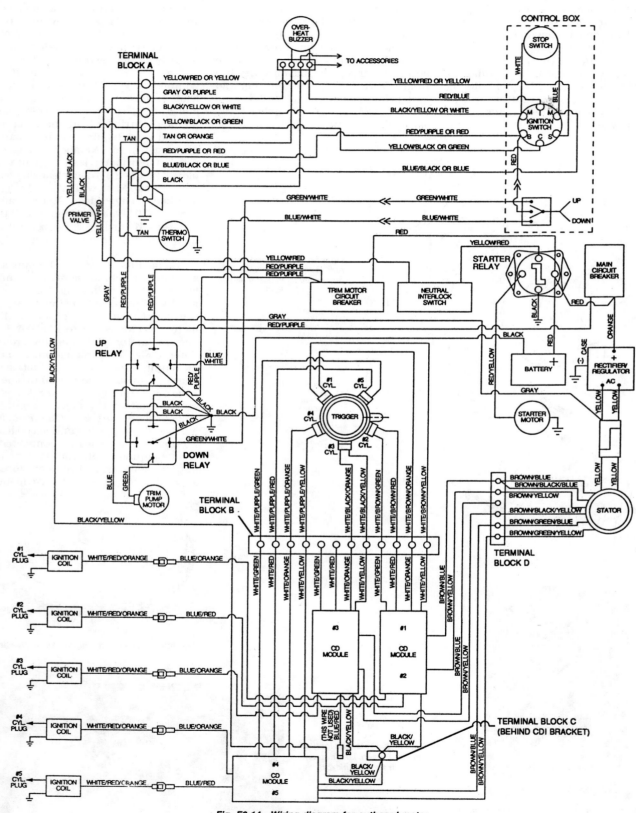

Fig. F8-14—Wiring diagram for outboard motor.

Test ignition coils by connecting coil to output lead of a known good CDI module, crank engine and note spark tester. Be sure stator and triggers are operating properly. If no spark is noted, renew ignition coil.

COOLING SYSTEM

THERMOSTAT. Thermostat is located behind cover at top of cylinder head cover. Test thermostat by immersing in heated water. Renew thermostat if it fails to open at temperature stamped on thermostat.

WATER PUMP. The rubber impeller type water pump is located between lower unit gearcase and drive shaft housing. If cooling system malfunction is noted, first inspect water inlet for plugging or partial restriction and check thermostat for proper operation.

Remove lower unit gearcase as outlined in LOWER UNIT section to check condition of water pump, water passages and sealing surfaces. Inspect impeller (3—Fig. F8-15), plate (6) and housing liner for excessive wear or other damage.

Apply a suitable RTV sealer to housing studs. Rotate impeller in direction of normal rotation when installing into housing liner. Note that upper and lower gaskets (5 and 7) are different design and must be installed in proper location. Tighten four nuts around drive shaft to 70 in.-lbs. (8.0 N·m) and nut adjacent to water tube seal (1) to 40 in.-lbs. (4.5 N·m).

POWER HEAD

REMOVE AND REINSTALL. Depending upon the type of service, removal of ignition components, starter, flywheel, alternator, carburetors and linkage and fuel pumps prior to power head removal will ease operation. To remove power head, remove rear motor leg cover. Remove front motor leg cover and swivel bracket. Slide support plate down on motor leg. Detach any components or wiring that will interfere with power head removal. Remove screws and nuts securing power head, secure a suitable lifting fixture to engine and carefully lift power head from lower unit. When lifting power head, carefully guide exhaust tube flange past water tube mount to prevent damage to exhaust flange. Mount power head on a suitable holding fixture.

Reinstall power head by reversing removal procedure. Apply a suitable antiseize compound to drive shaft splines. Apply a suitable RTV sealant to mating surface of motor leg. Shift gearcase into

forward gear and rotate propeller shaft when lowering power head on motor leg to align crankshaft and drive shaft splines. Tighten power head mounting screws to 270 in.-lbs. (30.5 N·m). Check shift linkage adjustment as outlined in LOWER UNIT section.

DISASSEMBLY. Remove exhaust tube and spacer plate. Remove transfer port covers, intake manifolds, reed valve assemblies, exhaust cover, upper bearing housing, cylinder head cover and cylinder head. Remove crankcase screws and drive out two locating pins toward cylinder head side of engine. Pry points are provided to separate crankcase from cylinder block. Do not damage crankcase and cylinder block mating surfaces.

NOTE: It is imperative that each cylinder's parts are installed in the same location and in the same direction as removed if original parts are reused. If parts are intermixed or installed in the wrong location, early power head failure may result.

Mark all wearing components prior to removal from engine. Use special 12-point socket T-2953 or equivalent to remove connecting rod cap screws. Be sure to retrieve 16 bearing rollers at each crankpin.

NOTE: Do not use a magnet to retrieve loose bearing rollers.

After connecting rod caps are removed, crankshaft can be lifted from cylinder block. Use special piston tool kit T-2990 to remove piston pin. Refer to Fig. F8-17. Place end of shim tool T-2990-C marked "295" between spacer (4—Fig. F8-16) and connecting rod as shown in Fig. F8-17. Other end of shim tool marked "310" is used for reassembly. Be sure to retrieve 26 loose bearing rollers (5) at each piston pin.

Refer to the appropriate service sections for service and assembly instructions for crankshaft, connecting rods, pistons and bearings.

REASSEMBLY. Prior to reassembly, make certain that all joint and gasket surfaces are clean, free from nicks, burrs, warped surfaces or hardened sealer or carbon. The crankcase must be completely sealed against both pressure and vacuum. Exhaust cover and cylinder head must be sealed against water leakage pressure. Mating surfaces between power head, lower unit and spacer plate must form a tight seal. Crankcase and cylinder block are a matched pair and must be renewed as an assembly if mating surfaces are warped or damaged. Renew cylinder

head if warped in excess of 0.012 inch (0.30 mm).

Thoroughly lubricate all friction surfaces with engine oil during reassembly. Renew all seals and gaskets. Apply sealant US Marine Part T-8983 or a suitable equivalent RTV sealant to cylinder block mating surface and threads of crankcase cover attaching screws. Install crankcase locating pins prior to installing crankcase screws. Working from center out, tighten crankcase and main bearing screws to 270 in.-lbs. (30.5 N·m). Check crankshaft rotation as power head is reassembled for binding or unusual noise. If binding or noise is noted, determine and repair cause before proceeding with reassembly.

Tighten cylinder head screws in sequence shown in Fig. F8-18 to 75 in.-lbs. (8.5 N·m), then increase tightness by 50 in.-lbs. (5.6 N·m) increments to final value of 220-230 in.-lbs. (25-26 N·m). Install lower crankshaft seal (18—Fig. F8-16) into bearing (17) with seal lip facing away from engine. Install upper crankshaft seal into upper bearing housing with seal lip facing toward engine. Coat mating surface of upper bearing housing-to-crankcase assembly and threads of bearing housing screws with a suitable RTV sealant. Apply a suitable RTV sealant to cylinder head cover mating surface and tighten securely.

PISTONS, PINS, RINGS AND CYLINDERS. Refer to CONDENSED

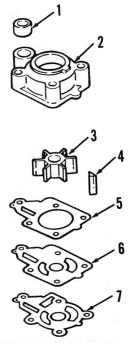

Fig. F8-15—Exploded view of water pump.
1. Seal
2. Housing
3. Impeller
4. Key
5. Gasket
6. Plate
7. Gasket

SERVICE DATA for service specifications. Pistons are equipped with two piston rings. Ring grooves in piston are equipped with locating pins to prevent ring rotation. Install lower piston ring with beveled inner edge facing toward top of piston. Piston ring end gaps may be filed if end gap clearance is insufficient. Pistons and rings are available in 0.010 inch (0.25 mm) and 0.030 inch (0.76 mm) oversize. Piston pin rides on 26 loose bearing rollers.

Pistons are cam ground design. Measure piston major diameter at 90 degrees to piston pin bore centerline. Measure piston minor diameter parallel to pin bore centerline. Piston pin diameter should be 0.68750-0.68765 inch (17.4625-17.4663 mm). Inside diameter of piston pin bore should be 0.6876-0.6879 inch (17.465-17.473 mm).

Measure cylinder bore diameter at points 1/4 inch (6.3 mm) down from top of bore, 1/4 inch (6.3 mm) up from exhaust port and 3/16 inch (4.8 mm) down from intake port, then repeat measurements at 90 degrees to first measurements. Cylinder should be rebored to next oversize if cylinder is tapered or out-of-round in excess of 0.002 inch (0.05 mm). Renew cylinder block and crankcase assembly if cylinder bore wear exceeds 0.030 inch (0.76 mm).

Special piston tool kit T-2990 should be used when installing piston pin. Refer to Fig. F8-17. Position end of shim tool T-2990-C marked "310" between connecting rod and spacer (4—Fig. F8-16) when pressing pin into piston. If end of tool marked "310" will not fit properly it may be necessary to use end of tool marked "295." Install spacers (4) with small diameter facing inward. Piston pin should be a snug fit in pin bore. Assemble piston, pin and connecting rod so long sloping side of piston crown will face exhaust ports when installed. Piston pin must be centered in piston after installation. If pin is pressed beyond center, press pin out of piston and reinstall.

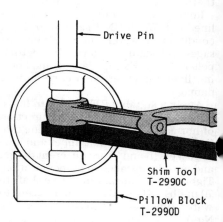

Fig. F8-17—Remove and reinstall piston pin using special piston tool kit T-2990. End of shim tool T-2990C marked "295" is for pin removal and end marked "310" is used for reinstalling pin. Refer to text.

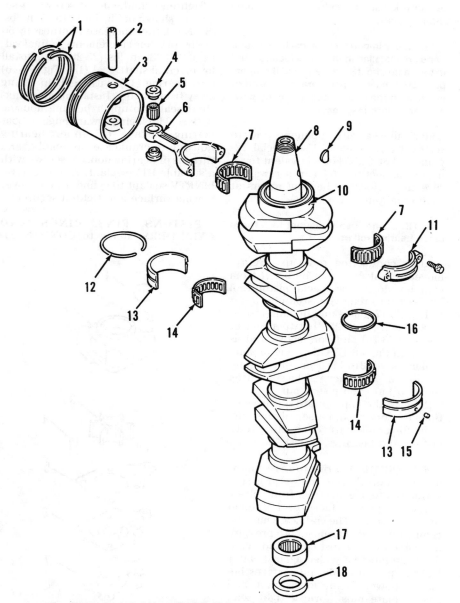

Fig. F8-16—Exploded view of crankshaft, connecting rod and piston assembly.

1. Piston rings
2. Piston pin
3. Piston
4. Spacer
5. Bearing
6. Connecting rod
7. Bearing & cage assy.
8. Crankshaft
9. Woodruff key
10. Bearing
11. Connecting rod cap
12. Retaining ring
13. Bearing race
14. Bearing & cage assy.
15. Pin
16. Seal ring
17. Bearing
18. Seal

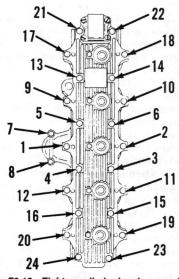

Fig. F8-18—Tighten cylinder head screws in sequence shown. Refer to text.

CRANKSHAFT, CONNECTING RODS AND BEARINGS.
Mark location and direction of all wearing components prior to disassembly. Refer to CONDENSED SERVICE DATA for standard crankshaft journal diameters. Connecting rods ride on 16 loose bearing rollers and cage assembly at each crankpin. Connecting rod small end inside diameter should be 0.8762-0.8767 inch (22.255-22.268 mm) and big end inside diameter should be 1.4528-1.4533 inch (36.901-36.914 mm). To measure big end diameter, install and properly align rod cap and tighten cap screws to 170 in.-lbs. (19.2 N·m).

Press seal (18—Fig. F8-16) into bearing (17) with seal lip facing down until lower edge of seal is flush with lower surface of bearing (17). Lubricate seal lip with a suitable bearing assembly grease. Clean old locking compound from outer surface of top bearing (10) with Locquic Primer T.

Renew crankcase seal rings (16) upon reassembly. Install center main bearings with alignment hole of outer race (13) facing down. Install retaining rings (12) so end gap does not align with parting surface of bearing race (13). Apply a bead of Loctite (US Marine Part T-2963-2) or a suitable locking compound to upper main bearing bore in cylinder block, and outer diameter of upper bearing after crankshaft installation. Position end gaps of crankshaft seal rings (16) facing crankcase cover when installing crankshaft into cylinder block. When crankshaft is fully seated in block, ends of seal rings (16) must touch. After installing crankshaft, carefully rotate seal rings (16) so end gaps face cylinder head side of engine. Make sure alignment holes in bearing races (13) are aligned with locating pins in cylinder block.

NOTE: Alignment pins in cylinder block should be renewed if damaged. Carefully drill into pin, thread an appropriate size screw into pin and pry out of block.

Install rod caps (11) and apply Loctite (US Marine Part T-8936-1) or a suitable thread locking compound to threads of rod cap screws (11). Make sure connecting rod and cap are properly aligned by running a pencil point or similar tool across fracture line. If proper alignment cannot be obtained, renew connecting rod assembly. Tighten rod cap screws in 50 in.-lbs. (5.6 N·m) increments to a final value of 170 in.-lbs. (19.2 N·m). Frequently check crankshaft rotation for binding or unusual noise during reassembly. If binding or noise is noted, determine and repair cause before proceeding with reassembly.

ELECTRIC STARTER

Refer to Fig. F8-19 for exploded view of starter motor used. Disassembly and reassembly is evident after inspection of unit and referral to exploded view.

Make sure battery is fully charged when performing starter tests. Minimum cranking speed is 300 rpm. Normal starter current draw is 80-165 amperes. Minimum battery voltage during cranking is 10.0 volts.

BATTERY CHARGING SYSTEM

Stator output should be approximately 11 amperes at 3500 rpm. To check stator resistance, disconnect two-pin connector between stator and rectifier/regulator. Refer to Fig. F8-14. Connect ohmmeter between yellow leads at connector leading from stator. Renew stator if resistance exceeds 2.0 ohms. Connect ohmmeter between engine ground and each stator lead to check for shorted stator coil. Renew stator or repair shorted stator lead if continuity is noted between engine ground and either stator lead.

To test rectifier/regulator, disconnect all rectifier leads. Connect a suitable ohmmeter between rectifier orange lead and either yellow lead. Note reading and reverse ohmmeter leads. Meter should show continuity in one direction and no continuity in the other. Repeat test with ohmmeter connected between orange lead and the other yellow lead, between yellow leads and between rectifier/regulator case and each yellow lead. Renew rectifier/regulator if ohmmeter shows continuity in both test connections or no continuity in both test connections.

LOWER UNIT

PROPELLER. Standard propeller for normal service has three blades, 12⅝ inch (320.7 mm) diameter and 21 inch 533.4 mm) pitch. Various propellers are available and should be selected to allow a properly tuned and adjusted engine to operate within the recommended speed range of 5,000-5,500 rpm at full throttle.

R&R AND OVERHAUL. To remove gearcase from motor leg, proceed as follows: Disconnect shift rod (13—Fig. F8-20) by removing cotter pin (12) and pin (11). Remove exhaust snout (36) and screw under snout. Remove remaining gearcase mounting screws and separate gearcase from motor leg. Mount lower unit in a suitable holding fixture. Remove drain and vent plugs (21) and drain gearcase lubricant while inspecting for water or other contamination. Do not remove shift coupling pin (19) at this time unless complete gearcase disassembly is required.

During disassembly, note location and thickness of all shims, spacers and thrust washers for reference during reassembly. Referring to Fig. F8-15, remove water pump housing (2), impeller (3), key (4) and plate (6). Remove and discard gaskets (5 and 7). Remove gearcase cover (3—Fig. F8-20) by carefully prying in center of cover. Do not pry on ends of cover (3). Remove "O" rings (6 and 8) and pry seals (4 and 5) from cover (3). Two holes are provided in bottom side of cover (3) to remove shift rod boot (2) using a punch. Some models are equipped with a seal in place of boot (2). Remove seal on models so equipped by threading a suitable screw into seal and

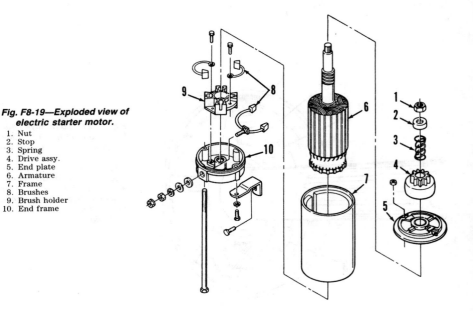

Fig. F8-19—Exploded view of electric starter motor.

1. Nut
2. Stop
3. Spring
4. Drive assy.
5. End plate
6. Armature
7. Frame
8. Brushes
9. Brush holder
10. End frame

driving out from bottom side of cover
(3). Special tool US Marine part T-11293
is required to remove drive shaft bearing race retainer (7). Place retainer tool
T-11293 over drive shaft and rotate tool
to remove retainer ring (7). Remove propeller (53), spacer (50) and anode (49).
Remove four screws (47) with washers
(46) and "O" rings (45). Using a suitable bolt-type puller and two $^1/_4$-inch
screws of appropriate length, extract
bearing spool (43) from gearcase. Thread
puller screws into anode screw holes.

**NOTE: Bearing spool (43) differs slightly
on models equipped with dual port exhaust
system. Referring to Fig. F8-21, bend back
tab washer (58), unscrew retaining ring (57)
using US Marine special tool T-11275 and pull
spool (43) from gearcase using a suitable
puller. Do not lose locating pin (L).**

Remove "O" rings (42 and 44) from
spool (43). Reaching into gearcase with
a screwdriver, remove retaining rings
(41) from groove in gearcase by pushing
on beveled ends of rings (41). Reinstall
spool (43) into gearcase (without "O"
rings) and secure to reverse gear bearing carrier (40) with two screws (47).
Pull spool (43) and bearing carrier (40)
from gearcase as an assembly using bolt-
type puller. Remove screws (47), separate spool (43) and carrier (40) and driv
seal (48) from spool (43). Withdraw propeller shaft assembly (38, 37, 35, 34, 33
and 27) from gearcase. Slide bearing (38)
and reverse gear (37) off shaft (35).
Drive out pin (28) and slide dog clutch
(27) off shaft (35) and remove shift pin
(33). To remove drive shaft (9), secure
pinion nut (29) from turning using a $^7/_8$-
inch socket and handle. Place spline
adapter, US Marine tool TA-6536, on
drive shaft spline and rotate drive shaft
while holding pinion nut until pinion
nut is unscrewed. To remove drive shaft
from gearcase, the manufacturer recommends using special drive shaft puller
US Marine part T-11292. Puller T-11292
engages flat section used for water
pump drive key. Drive shaft is disengaged from pinion gear by tightening
two screws on puller. Lift drive shaft
from gearcase noting location of shims
(16). Note that gearcase may be
equipped with one or more shims (16)
or no shims at all. Reach into gearcase
and remove nut (29), washer (30) and
pinion gear (31). Noting location of
spacer (26), remove forward gear (25).
If drive shaft bearing (32) requires
renewal, drive down into gear cavity using a suitable driver. If not removing
bearing (32), apply a suitable grease to
bearing rollers to prevent rollers from
falling out. Rotate lower shift rod (13)
counterclockwise until shift rod disengages arm (14), then remove rod (13).

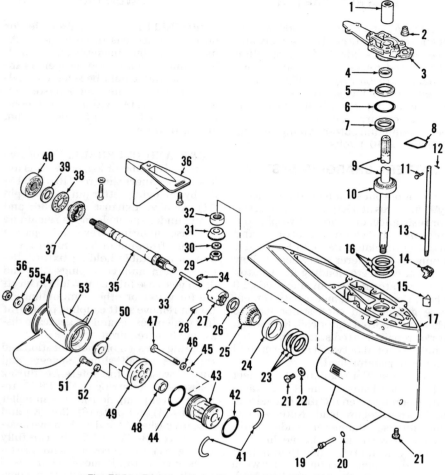

Fig. F8-20—Exploded view of lower unit gearcase assembly.

1. Coupler	13. Lower shift rod	25. Forward gear &	35. Propeller shaft	46. Washer
2. Boot	14. Arm	bearing assy.	36. Exhaust snout	47. Screw
3. Cover	15. Plug	26. Thrust washer	37. Reverse gear	48. Seal
4. Seal	16. Shims	27. Dog clutch	38. Thrust bearing	49. Anode
5. Seal	17. Gearcase	28. Pin	39. Thrust washer	50. Spacer
6. "O" ring	19. Pin	29. Nut	40. Bearing carrier	51. Screw
7. Retainer	20. Seal	30. Washer	41. Retaining rings	52. Washer
8. "O" ring	21. Plug	31. Pinion gear	42. "O" ring	53. Propeller
9. Drive shaft	22. Gasket	32. Bearing	43. Bearing spool	54. Splined washer
10. Bearing & race assy.	23. Shims	33. Shift pin	44. "O" ring	55. Washer
11. Pin	24. Bearing race	34. Shift yoke	45. "O" ring	56. Nut
12. Cotter pin				

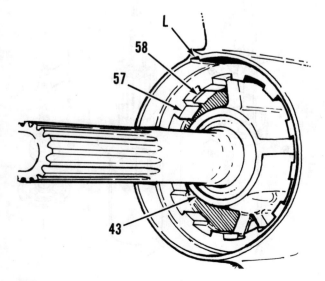

*Fig. F8-21—To remove bear-
ing spool (43) on models
equipped with dual port exhaust, bend back tab washer
(58) and unscrew retaining
ring (57) using US Marine
special tool T-11275. When
installing bearing spool (43),
make sure locating notch (L)
and pin are positioned as
shown.*

Unscrew and remove pin (19), reach into gear cavity and withdraw arm (14). Noting location of shims (23), remove forward gear bearing race (24) from gearcase using a suitable puller to complete gearcase disassembly.

Inspect all components for excessive wear or other damage. Renew all seals, gaskets and "O" rings during reassembly. Note that forward gear (25), forward gear bearing and bearing race (24) are a matched set and not available separately.

If abnormal gear wear is noted, or if any component affecting gear alignment was renewed, shim selection procedure must be performed.

If installing a new forward gear (25) into original or new gearcase housing (17), proceed as follows: Note forward gear code stamped into top of gearcase. Locate and note forward gear code on tag affixed to new forward gear. Referring to shim selection chart in Fig. F8-22, determine shim thickness required by locating where code numbers intersect. For example, if forward gear code stamped in top of gearcase housing is "F" and forward gear code on tag affixed to new forward gear is 8, shim pack (23—Fig. F8-20) thickness should be 0.002 inch.

If installing original forward gear (25)

Stamped-In Gearcase Housing Code	_	_	_	_	Driveshaft/Forward Gear Code															
	3	4	5	6	7	8	9	10	11	12	13	14	15	16	17	18	19	20	21	22
0	.003	.004	.005	.006	.007	.008	.009	.010	.011	.012	.013	.014	.015	.016	.017	.018	.019	.020	.021	.022
1	.004	.005	.006	.007	.008	.009	.010	.011	.012	.013	.014	.015	.016	.017	.018	.019	.020	.021	.022	.023
2	.005	.006	.007	.008	.009	.010	.011	.012	.013	.014	.015	.016	.017	.018	.019	.020	.021	.022	.023	.024
3	.006	.007	.008	.009	.010	.011	.012	.013	.014	.015	.016	.017	.018	.019	.020	.021	.022	.023	.024	.025
4	.007	.008	.009	.010	.011	.012	.013	.014	.015	.016	.017	.018	.019	.020	.021	.022	.023	.024	.025	.026
5	.008	.009	.010	.011	.012	.013	.014	.015	.016	.017	.018	.019	.020	.021	.022	.023	.024	.025	.026	.027
6	.009	.010	.011	.012	.013	.014	.015	.016	.017	.018	.019	.020	.021	.022	.023	.024	.025	.026	.027	.028
7	.010	.011	.012	.013	.014	.015	.016	.017	.018	.019	.020	.021	.022	.023	.024	.025	.026	.027	.028	.029
8	.011	.012	.013	.014	.015	.016	.017	.018	.019	.020	.021	.022	.023	.024	.025	.026	.027	.028	.029	.030
9	.012	.013	.014	.015	.016	.017	.018	.019	.020	.021	.022	.023	.024	.025	.026	.027	.028	.029	.030	.031
	23	24	25	26	27	28	29	30	31	32	33	34	35	36	37	38	39	40	41	42
0	.023	.024	.025	.026	.027	.028	.029	.030	.031	.032	.033	.034	.035	.036	.037	.038	.039	.040	.041	.042
1	.024	.025	.026	.027	.028	.029	.030	.031	.032	.033	.034	.035	.036	.037	.038	.039	.040	.041	.042	.043
2	.025	.026	.027	.028	.029	.030	.031	.032	.033	.034	.035	.036	.037	.038	.039	.040	.041	.042	.043	.044
3	.026	.027	.028	.029	.030	.031	.032	.033	.034	.035	.036	.037	.038	.039	.040	.041	.042	.043	.044	.045
4	.027	.028	.029	.030	.031	.032	.033	.034	.035	.036	.037	.038	.039	.040	.041	.042	.043	.044	.045	.046
5	.028	.029	.030	.031	.032	.033	.034	.035	.036	.037	.038	.039	.040	.041	.042	.043	.044	.045	.046	.047
6	.029	.030	.031	.032	.033	.034	.035	.036	.037	.038	.039	.040	.041	.042	.043	.044	.045	.046	.047	.048
7	.030	.031	.032	.033	.034	.035	.036	.037	.038	.039	.040	.041	.042	.043	.044	.045	.046	.047	.048	.049
8	.031	.032	.033	.034	.035	.036	.037	.038	.039	.040	.041	.042	.043	.044	.045	.046	.047	.048	.049	.050
9	.032	.033	.034	.035	.036	.037	.038	.039	.040	.041	.042	.043	.044	.045	.046	.047	.048	.049	.050	.051

Stamped-In Gearcase Housing Code					Driveshaft/Forward Gear Code															
	3	4	5	6	7	8	9	10	11	12	13	14	15	16	17	18	19	20	21	22
A	.002	.003	.004	.005	.006	.007	.008	.009	.010	.011	.012	.013	.014	.015	.016	.017	.018	.019	.020	.021
B	.001	.002	.003	.004	.005	.006	.007	.008	.009	.010	.011	.012	.013	.014	.015	.016	.017	.018	.019	.020
C	.000	.001	.002	.003	.004	.005	.006	.007	.008	.009	.010	.011	.012	.013	.014	.015	.016	.017	.018	.019
D		.000	.001	.002	.003	.004	.005	.006	.007	.008	.009	.010	.011	.012	.013	.014	.015	.016	.017	.018
E			.000	.001	.002	.003	.004	.005	.006	.007	.008	.009	.010	.011	.012	.013	.014	.015	.016	.017
F				.000	.001	.002	.003	.004	.005	.006	.007	.008	.009	.010	.011	.012	.013	.014	.015	.016
G					.000	.001	.002	.003	.004	.005	.006	.007	.008	.009	.010	.011	.012	.013	.014	.015
H						.000	.001	.002	.003	.004	.005	.006	.007	.008	.009	.010	.011	.012	.013	.014
I							.000	.001	.002	.003	.004	.005	.006	.007	.008	.009	.010	.011	.012	.013
J								.000	.001	.002	.003	.004	.005	.006	.007	.008	.009	.010	.011	.012
K									.000	.001	.002	.003	.004	.005	.006	.007	.008	.009	.010	.011
	23	24	25	26	27	28	29	30	31	32	33	34	35	36	37	38	39	40	41	42
A	.022	.023	.024	.025	.026	.027	.028	.029	.030	.031	.032	.033	.034	.035	.036	.037	.038	.039	.040	.041
B	.021	.022	.023	.024	.025	.026	.027	.028	.029	.030	.031	.032	.033	.034	.035	.036	.037	.038	.039	.040
C	.020	.021	.022	.023	.024	.025	.026	.027	.028	.029	.030	.031	.032	.033	.034	.035	.036	.037	.038	.039
D	.019	.020	.021	.022	.023	.024	.025	.026	.027	.028	.029	.030	.031	.032	.033	.034	.035	.036	.037	.038
E	.018	.019	.020	.021	.022	.023	.024	.025	.026	.027	.028	.029	.030	.031	.032	.033	.034	.035	.036	.037
F	.017	.018	.019	.020	.021	.022	.023	.024	.025	.026	.027	.028	.029	.030	.031	.032	.033	.034	.035	.036
G	.016	.017	.018	.019	.020	.021	.022	.023	.024	.025	.026	.027	.028	.029	.030	.031	.032	.033	.034	.035
H	.015	.016	.017	.018	.019	.020	.021	.022	.023	.024	.025	.026	.027	.028	.029	.030	.031	.032	.033	.034
I	.014	.015	.016	.017	.018	.019	.020	.021	.022	.023	.024	.025	.026	.027	.028	.029	.030	.031	.032	.033
J	.013	.014	.015	.016	.017	.018	.019	.020	.021	.022	.023	.024	.025	.026	.027	.028	.029	.030	.031	.032
K	.012	.013	.014	.015	.016	.017	.018	.019	.020	.021	.022	.023	.024	.025	.026	.027	.028	.029	.030	.031

Fig. F8-22—View showing shim selection chart. Refer to text.

into a new gearcase housing (17), original forward gear code must be established in order to determine shim pack (23) thickness. Locate and note forward gear code stamped in top of ORIGINAL gearcase housing. Using a suitable micrometer, measure total thickness of ORIGINAL shim pack (23) removed from gearcase. Referring to shim chart in Fig. F8-22, follow column adjacent to gearcase housing code of ORIGINAL housing (17) across to thickness of ORIGINAL shims (23). For example, if forward gear code stamped in original gearcase housing is "5" and original shim pack (23) thickness is 0.012 inch, original forward gear (25) code is "7." Then determine new shim pack thickness by noting forward gear code stamped in NEW gearcase housing and referring to shim selection chart. For example, if it was established that "7" is the original forward gear code and the new gearcase housing code is "C," new shim pack thickness should be 0.004 inch.

NOTE: If installing original forward gear assembly (25) into a new gearcase housing, original bearing race (24) must be used as forward gear (25) and bearing assembly and race (24) are a matched set and not available separately.

If installing a new drive shaft assembly (9) into the original or into a new gearcase housing (17), proceed as follows: Locate and note drive shaft code stamped into top of gearcase housing (17). Locate and note drive shaft code on tag affixed to new drive shaft assembly.

NOTE: Drive shaft (9) and pinion gear (31) are a matched assembly and not available separately.

Referring to shim selection chart in Fig. F8-22, determine thickness of shim pack (16—Fig. F8-22) by noting where

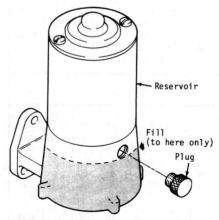

Fig. F8-23—With trim/tilt cylinders fully retracted, fill pump reservoir to bottom of fill plug hole with a good quality SAE 10W-40 engine oil. Do not overfill.

drive shaft code on housing (17) and code on tag affixed to new drive shaft assembly intersect on chart. For example, if drive shaft code "A" is stamped in top of housing (17) and code "15" is on tag affixed to new drive shaft assembly, shim pack (16) thickness should be 0.014 inch.

If installing original drive shaft assembly (9 and 31) into a new gearcase housing, original drive shaft code must be established in order to determine shim pack (16) thickness required. Proceed as follows: Note drive shaft code stamped in top of ORIGINAL housing (17). Using a micrometer, measure thickness of ORIGINAL shim pack (16) removed from housing (17). Referring to shim selection chart, follow column adjacent to gearcase housing code of ORIGINAL housing (17) across to thickness of ORIGINAL shims (16) and note code at top of column. For example, if drive shaft code stamped in top of original housing (17) is "7" and thickness of original shims (16) is 0.019 inch, original drive shaft code is "12." Then determine new shim pack thickness by referring to shim selection chart. For example, if it was established that original drive shaft code is "12" and drive shaft code stamped in new housing is "H," required shim pack (16) thickness is 0.004 inch.

NOTE: Shims (16) and (23) are available in thicknesses of 0.002, 0.003, 0.005 and 0.010 inch.

Reassemble gearcase by reversing disassembly procedure noting the following: Draw bearing (32) into gearcase, with lettered side facing up, until seated against shoulder in bore. Using a suitable needle bearing assembly grease, install 18 bearing rollers into bearing (32). Apply a suitable thread locking compound to threads of a NEW pinion nut (29). Do not reuse old nut (29). Install nut on drive shaft finger tight with groove in inner diameter facing gear (31). Install retainer (7) and tighten to 90 ft.-lbs. (122 N·m) then tighten pinion nut to 85 ft.-lbs. (115.2 N·m). Tighten screws (47) on single port exhaust models to 160 in.-lbs. (18.1 N·m). On dual port exhaust models, install spool (43—Fig. F8-21) as shown with locating notch (L) facing up. Be sure to install locating pin. Install retaining ring (57) with "OFF" cast into ring facing out. Tighten retaining ring (57) to 130 ft.-lbs. (176.2 N·m) and bend over tab washer (58) to secure retaining ring.

After reassembly, pressurize gearcase to 10 psi (69 kPa) and rotate drive shaft, propeller shaft and push/pull on lower shift shaft while observing pressure gage. If gearcase does not hold 10 psi (69

kPa) for five minutes, leakage is evident and must be repaired.

Install gearcase on motor leg and fill with lubricant as outlined in LUBRICATION section. To adjust shift linkage, adjust locknuts on upper shift rod as necessary to provide equal travel between neutral and forward gear position and neutral and reverse gear position. Make sure neutral interlock switch button is depressed when motor is in neutral.

Propeller shaft (35) end play should be within 0.005-0.020 inch (0.13-0.51 mm). Vary thickness of thrust washer (26) to adjust end play. Thrust washer (26) is available in thicknesses of 0.054 inch through 0.089 inch in 0.003 inch increments.

Propeller shaft backlash should be 0.009-0.018 inch (0.23-0.46 mm). To check backlash, install special drive shaft puller US Marine tool T-11292 on drive shaft and tighten tool screws to 70 in.-lbs. (8.0 N·m) to exert upward pressure on drive shaft. Install a suitable dial indicator on gearcase and rock propeller shaft back and forth to check lash. If lash is not within the specified amount, recheck forward gear and drive shaft shimming procedure.

NOTE: If gearcase reassembly and shimming procedures were properly performed and the specified propeller shaft backlash of 0.009-0.018 inch (0.23-0.46 mm) cannot be obtained, contact the service department of Brunswick Marine Power for recommendation.

POWER TRIM/TILT

Hydraulically actuated power tilt and trim system is used. An oil pump driven by a reversible electric motor provides oil pressure. Trim/tilt control switch determines motor and pump rotation thereby retracting or extending tilt and trim cylinders.

Recommended oil is a good quality SAE 10W-40 engine oil. Fill pump reservoir with trim/tilt cylinders fully retracted to bottom of fill plug hole as shown in Fig. F8-23. Do not overfill or motor failure may result from oil being forced into motor. To bleed air from system, extend and retract cylinders through several cycles.

If a malfunction occurs, determine if malfunction is due to wiring or wiring connections, electric motor failure or hydraulic system failure. Refer to schematic drawing in Fig. F8-14 to trouble-shoot electrical system. Note that trim/tilt motor and wiring is protected by a circuit breaker. With the exception of brush renewal, pump, valve body and motor are serviced as a unit assembly.

Perform tilt cylinder leak-down test as follows: Tilt outboard motor to full up position and support with a suitable block placed under gearcase. Remove lower tilt cylinder line (4—Fig. F8-24) from valve body. Plug end of line (4) using a $^3/_{16}$-inch inverted flare fitting and $^1/_8$-inch plug. Make a reference mark on swivel and stern brackets and remove block from under gearcase, allowing motor to be supported by tilt cylinder. Observe reference marks for evidence of leak-down. Note that several hours may be necessary for leak-down to be evident. Inspect condition of tilt cylinder piston check valves, threaded connection between rod and piston, piston "O" ring and cylinder bore if leak-down is evident.

NOTE: The manufacturer recommends servicing tilt cylinder as a unit assembly due to difficult disassembly and reassembly procedure.

Perform valve body leak-down test as follows: Lower outboard motor to full down position and remove lower trim cylinder line (6) from valve body. Cap end of line (6) using $^3/_{16}$-inch inverted flare fitting and $^1/_8$-inch plug. Plug valve body using $^3/_{16}$-inch inverted flare plug. Tilt outboard motor to full up position and allow motor to be supported by tilt cylinder and valve body. Make reference marks on swivel and stern brackets. Observe reference marks for leak-down. Note that several hours may be necessary for leak-down to be evident. If leak-down is evident, renew pump and valve body assembly. If trim system malfunction is noted and leak-down tests prove tilt cylinder and valve body to be in acceptable condition, trim cylinder may be defective.

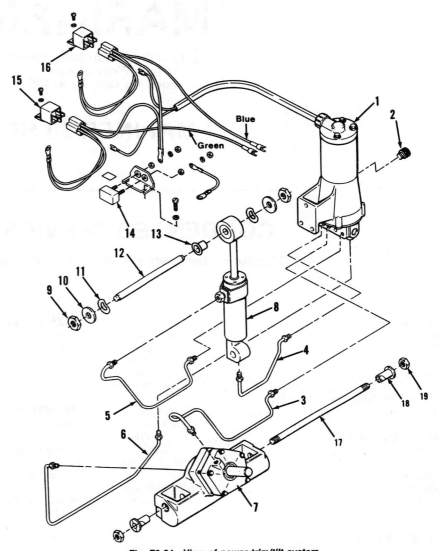

Fig. F8-24—View of power trim/tilt system.

1. Motor, pump & valve body assy.	5. Upper tilt cylinder line	9. Nut
2. Fill plug	6. Lower trim cylinder line	10. Washer
3. Upper trim cylinder line	7. Trim cylinder	11. Wave washer
4. Lower tilt cylinder line	8. Tilt cylinder	12. Shaft
		13. Bushing
		14. Circuit breaker

15. Down solenoid
16. Up solenoid
17. Shaft
18. Bushing
19. Nut

MARINER

BRUNSWICK MARINE POWER
1939 Pioneer Road
Fond du Lac, WI 54935

MARINER 30 HP

CONDENSED SERVICE DATA

NOTE: Metric fasteners are used throughout outboard motor.

TUNE-UP
Hp/rpm 30/4500-5500
Bore . . . . .72 mm
(2.84 in.)
Stroke . . . . .61 mm
(2.40 in.)
Number of Cylinders 2
Displacement . . . . .496 cc
(30.3 cu. in.)
Spark Plug—NGK B7HS
Electrode Gap . . . . .0.5-0.6 mm
(0.020-0.024 in.)
Ignition . . . . .CDI
Idle Speed (in gear) . . . . .600-700 rpm
Fuel:Oil Ratio 50:1

SIZES—CLEARANCES
Piston Ring End Gap . . . . .0.2-0.4 mm
(0.008-0.016 in.)
Lower Piston Ring Side Clearance . . . . .0.04-0.08 mm
(0.0016-0.0032 in.)
Piston Skirt Clearance . . . . .0.060-0.065 mm
(0.0024-0.0026 in.)
Crankshaft Runout—Max. . . . . .0.03 mm
(0.0012 in.)

SIZES—CLEARANCES CONT.
Connecting Rod Small End Shake:
Standard . . . . .0.8 mm
(0.03 in.)
Limit . . . . .2.0 mm
(0.08 in.)

TIGHTENING TORQUES
Crankcase . . . . .24.5-34 N·m
(18-25 ft.-lbs.)
Cylinder Head . . . . .24.5-34 N·m
(18-25 ft.-lbs.)
Flywheel . . . . .149.6-170 N·m
(110-125 ft.-lbs.)
Standard Screws:
4 mm . . . . .2.3 N·m
(20 in.-lbs.)
5 mm . . . . .4.3-6.6 N·m
(38-58 in.-lbs.)
6 mm . . . . .6.6-10.8 N·m
(58-96 in.-lbs.)
8 mm . . . . .13.6-21.8 N·m
(10-16 ft.-lbs.)
10 mm . . . . .27.2-44.9 N·m
(20-33 ft.-lbs.)
12 mm . . . . .35.4-50.3 N·m
(26-37 ft.-lbs.)

LUBRICATION

The power head is lubricated by oil mixed with the fuel. Fuel should be regular leaded, low lead or unleaded gasoline with a minimum pump octane rating of 86. Recommended oil is Quicksilver Formula 50-D Outboard Lubricant. Normal fuel:oil ratio is 50:1;

during engine break-in fuel:oil ratio should be 25:1.

Lower unit gears and bearings are lubricated by oil contained in the gearcase. Recommended oil is Mariner Super Duty Gear Lube. Lubricant is drained by removing vent and drain plugs in the gearcase. Refill through drain plug hole until oil has reached level of vent plug hole.

FUEL SYSTEM

CARBURETOR. Refer to Fig. MR16-1 for an exploded view of carburetor. Use the standard carburetor jet sizes as recommended by the manufacturer for normal operation when used at altitudes of 2500 feet (750 m) and less. Main jet (15—Fig. MR16-1) size should be reduced from standard recommenda-

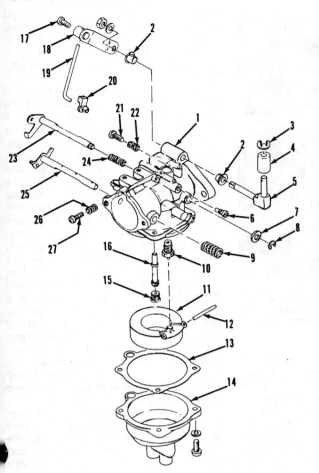

Fig. MR16-1 — Exploded view of carburetor.

1. Body
2. Bushing
3. Clip
4. Cam follower roller
5. Cam follower
6. Pilot jet
7. Washer
8. Clip
9. Spring
10. Fuel inlet valve
11. Float
12. Pin
13. Gasket
14. Float bowl
15. Main jet
16. Main nozzle
17. Screw
18. Throttle arm
19. Link
20. Link keeper
21. Idle mixture screw
22. Spring
23. Throttle shaft
24. Spring
25. Choke shaft
26. Spring
27. Idle speed screw

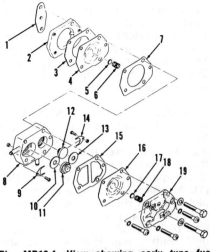

Fig. MR16-4 — View showing early type fuel pump assembly. Late type fuel pump assembly can be identified by ribs on the inlet and outlet nozzle. Late type fuel pump uses reed type check valves instead of umbrella type check valves (11 and 12) as used on early type fuel pump.

1. Gasket
2. Base
3. Gasket
4. Diaphragm
5. Spring plate
6. Spring
7. Gasket
8. Body
9. Retainer
10. Gasket
11. Outlet check valve
12. Inlet check valve
13. Gasket
14. Retainer
15. Gasket
16. Diaphragm
17. Spring plate
18. Spring
19. Cover

tion by one size for altitudes of 2500 to 5000 feet (750 to 1500 m), two sizes for altitudes of 5000 to 7500 feet (1500 to 2250 m) and three sizes for altitudes of 7500 feet (2250 m) and up. Initial adjustment of idle mixture screw (21) is 1-3/8 to 2 turns out from a lightly seated position. Recommended idle speed is 600-700 rpm (in gear) with the engine at normal operating temperature.

To determine the float level, remove the carburetor and float bowl (14). Invert carburetor body (1) and slowly raise float (11). Note whether float (11) is parallel with surface of carburetor body when needle of fuel valve (10) just breaks contact with float (11) tang. If not, adjust float (11) tang until proper float level is obtained.

FUEL FILTER. A fuel filter assembly (1–Fig. MR16-3) is connected between fuel supply line (2) and fuel pump inlet line (3). With the engine stopped, periodically unscrew fuel filter cup (7) from filter base (4) and withdraw filter element (6), "O" ring (5) and gasket (8). Clean cup (7) and filter element (6) in a suitable solvent and blow dry with clean compressed air. Inspect filter element (6). If excessive blockage or damage is noted, renew element.

Reassembly is reverse order of disassembly. Renew "O" ring (5) and gasket (8) during reassembly.

FUEL PUMP. The diaphragm type fuel pump is located on the port side of the engine. Refer to Fig. MR16-4 for an exploded view of fuel pump. Alternating pressure and vacuum pulsations in the crankcase actuates the diaphragm and check valves in the pump.

NOTE: Early type fuel pump assembly uses umbrella type check valves and late type fuel pump assembly uses reed valve type check valves.

Make certain that all gaskets, diaphragms and check valves are in good condition when reassembling unit. Coat gasket (1) with a nonhardening type gasket sealer making certain that passage in center is not blocked with gasket sealer.

REED VALVE. The reed valve assembly is located between the intake manifold and crankcase. Refer to Fig. MR16-6 for a view of reed valve assembly.

Cracked, warped, chipped or bent reed petals will impair operation and should be renewed. Do not attempt to straighten or repair bent or damaged reed petals. Reed petals should seat smoothly against reed plate along their entire length. Reassemble reed stops and reed petals on chamfered side of reed plate (3). Position reed petals so index marks (B–Fig. MR16-7) are show-

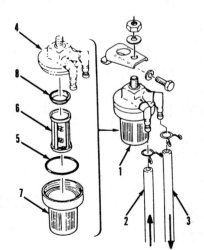

Fig. MR16-3 — Exploded view of fuel filter assembly, fuel hoses and mounting bracket.

1. Fuel filter assy.
2. Fuel supply line
3. Fuel pump inlet line
4. Filter base
5. "O" ring
6. Filter element
7. Cup
8. Gasket

ing between petals. Note that index mark consists of two dots on later models. Height (A) of reed stop should be 5.4 mm (0.21 in.). On later models, the manufacturer does not recommend the adjustment of reed stop height (A). Renew reed stop if height adjustment is incorrect or damage is noted.

SPEED CONTROL LINKAGE. To synchronize ignition and throttle control linkage, first make sure the ignition timing has been correctly adjusted. Detach magneto base plate control rod (3 – Fig. MR16-9) and blockout lever control rod (1). Measure length of magneto base plate control rod from joint center to joint center and adjust to a length of 69.2-70.0 mm (2.58-2.90 in.), then reconnect control rod. Position gear shift lever in "NEUTRAL."

Turn twist grip to full throttle position. Loosen locknuts (N) and turn control cable adjustment (A) until cable slack is 1-2 mm (0.039-0.079 in.), then tighten locknuts.

Fig. MR16-9 — View of blockout lever control rod (1), blockout lever (2) and stator base plate control rod (3). Locknuts (N) and adjuster (A) are used to adjust cable slack. Refer to text.

With the twist grip held in the full throttle position, push magneto base plate to full advance position. Measure length of blockout lever control rod (1) from joint center to joint center and adjust to a length of 91.5 mm (3.6 in.), then reconnect control rod. Blockout lever (2) should contact bottom cowling stopper when twist grip is turned to the full throttle position with the magneto base plate fully advanced and the gear shift lever is in "NEUTRAL" position. If not, readjust blockout lever control rod (1) until the proper adjustment is obtained.

IGNITION

All models are equipped with a capacitor discharge ignition (CDI)

system. If engine malfunction is noted and the ignition system is suspected, make sure the spark plugs and all electrical connections are tight before proceeding to troubleshooting the CD ignition system.

Proceed as follows to test CDI system components: Refer to Fig. MR16-11. To test ignition coil, disconnect black wire (B) and orange wire (O) at connectors and spark plug boots from spark plugs. Use a suitable ohmmeter and connect red tester lead to orange wire (O) and black tester lead to black wire (B). The primary winding resistance reading should be 0.08-0.10 ohms. Connect rod tester lead to terminal end in one spark plug boot and black tester lead to terminal end in remaining spark plug boot. The secondary winding resistance reading should be 3,475-4,025 ohms. Use a suitable coil tester or tester Model 9800 Magneto Analyzer to perform a power test. Connect tester leads as outlined in tester's handbook. A steady spark should jump a 5 mm (13/64 in.) gap when a current value of 1.7-2.1 amperes is applied. A surface insulation test can be performed using a suitable coil tester or tester Model 9800 Magneto Analyzer and following tester's handbook.

To check source (charge) coil, disconnect black wire (B) and brown wire (Br) at connectors leading from magneto base plate. Use a suitable ohmmeter and connect red tester lead to brown wire (Br) and black tester lead to black wire (B). DO NOT rotate flywheel while making test. The ohmmeter should read 121-147 ohms. Reconnect wires after completing test.

To check pulser (trigger) coil, disconnect white wire with red tracer (W/R) at connector leading from magneto base plate and black wire (B) at back of CDI unit. Use a suitable ohmmeter and con-

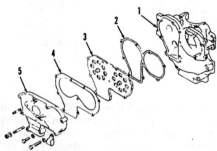

Fig. MR16-6 — Exploded view of reed valve and intake manifold assembly.
1. Crankcase half
2. Gasket
3. Reed valve assy.
4. Gasket
5. Intake manifold

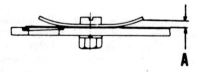

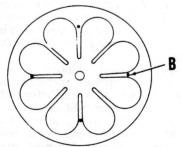

Fig. MR16-7 — Height (A) of reed stop should be 5.4 mm (0.21 in.). Make sure marks (B) are aligned between reed petals when reassembling unit.

Fig. MR16 — 11 — View identifying CDI system components.
1. CDI module
2. Charge coil
3. Pulser coil
4. Lighting coil
5. Stop switch
6. Ignition coil
7. Spark plugs

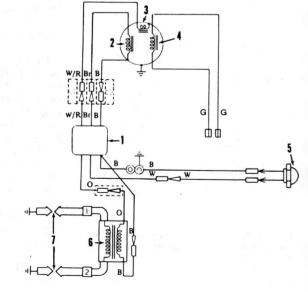

Red Test Lead \ Black Test Lead	CDI UNIT LEADS				
CDI UNIT LEADS	White	Black	Brown	White w/Red	Orange
White	A	B	B	B	B
Black	C	A	D	B	J
Brown	E	F	A	B	J
White w/Red	G	H	I	A	J
Orange	B	B	B	B	A

Fig. MR16-12—Use chart and values listed below to test condition of CD ignition module. Before making test (J), connect CDI module's orange wire and black wire together. Then disconnect wires and perform desired test.

A. Zero
B. Infinity
C. 9,000-19,000 ohms
D. 2,000-6,000 ohms
E. 80,000-160,000 ohms
F. 70,000-150,000 ohms
G. 33,000-63,000 ohms
H. 7,000-17,000 ohms
I. 15,000-35,000 ohms
J. Tester needle should show deflection then return toward infinite resistance

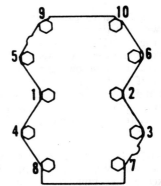

Fig. MR16-17—Tighten crankcase screws in sequence shown above.

nect red tester lead to white wire with red tracer (W/R) and black tester lead to black wire (B). DO NOT rotate flywheel while making test. The ohmmeter should read 12.6-15.4 ohms.

To test CDI module, first disconnect all wires at connectors and remove CDI module from outboard motor. Use a suitable ohmmeter and refer to Fig. MF16-12. With reference to chart, perform CDI module resistance tests.

Renew any components that are not within the manufacturer's recommended limits.

To check ignition timing, rotate flywheel so the timing pointer (TP – Fig. MR 16-13) is aligned with 25° BTDC mark on flywheel. Rotate stator plate so stop bracket tab (T) is against timing pointer. The stamped mark on the stator plate should be aligned with 0° (TDC) mark (5° BTDC mark on Work 30 model) on flywheel. Adjust timing by loosening stop bracket retaining screws and relocating bracket.

COOLING SYSTEM

WATER PUMP. A rubber impeller type water pump is mounted between the drive shaft housing and gearcase. The water pump impeller (6 – Fig. MR 16-15) is driven by a key in the drive shaft.

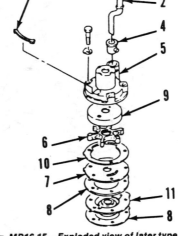

Fig. MR16-15—Exploded view of later type water pump assembly.

1. Seal	8. Gasket
2. Water tube	9. Liner
4. Seal	10. Gasket
5. Pump housing	11. Base
6. Impeller	12. Spacer
7. Plate	

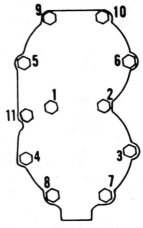

Fig. MR16-18—Tighten cylinder head screws in sequence shown above.

When cooling system problems are encountered, first check water inlet for plugging or partial stoppage. Be sure thermostat located in cylinder head operates properly. If the water pump is suspected defective, separate gearcase from drive shaft housing and inspect

pump. Make sure all seals and mating surfaces are in good condition and water passages are unobstructed. Check impeller (6) and plate (7) for excessive wear. When reassembling, coat gasket surfaces with a thin coating of Perfect Seal.

POWER HEAD

R&R AND OVERHAUL. The power head can be removed for disassembly and overhaul as follows: Clamp outboard motor to a suitable stand and remove engine cowl and starter assembly. Disconnect speed control cables, fuel line and any wiring that will interfere with power head removal. Remove or disconnect any component that will interfere with power head removal. Remove six screws securing power head to drive shaft housing and lift power head free. Remove flywheel, ignition components, carburetor, intake manifold

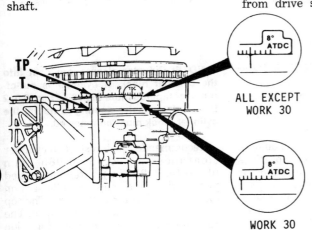

ALL EXCEPT WORK 30

WORK 30

Fig. MR16-13—Full advance occurs when stop bracket tab (T) contacts timing pointer (TP). Refer to text for ignition timing adjustment.

and reed valve assembly. Remove screws retaining exhaust cover (18 – Fig. MR16-20) and withdraw. Crankcase halves can be separated after removal of ten screws securing crankcase half (1) to cylinder block. Crankshaft and pistons are now accessible for removal and overhaul as outlined in the appropriate following paragraphs.

ASSEMBLY. Two-stroke engine design dictates that intake manifold and crankcase are completely sealed against both vacuum and pressure. Exhaust manifold and cylinder head must be sealed against water leakage and pressure. Mating surfaces of water intake and exhaust areas between power head and drive shaft housing must form a tight seal.

Whenever the power head is disassembled, it is recommended that all gasket surfaces of crankcase halves be carefully checked for nicks, burrs or warped surfaces which might interfere with a tight seal. The cylinder head, head end of cylinder block, and the mating surfaces of manifolds and crankcase may be checked and lapped, if necessary, to provide a smooth surface. Do not remove any more metal than is necessary to obtain a smooth finish. Thoroughly clean the parts with new oil on a clean, soft rag, then wash with soapsuds and clean rags.

Mating surface of crankcase halves may be checked on the lapping block, and high spots or nicks removed, but surfaces must not be lowered. If extreme care is used, a slightly damaged crankcase can be salvaged in this manner. In case of doubt, renew the crankcase assembly.

The crankcase halves are positively located during assembly by the use of two dowel pins. Check to make sure that dowel pins are not bent, nicked or distorted and that dowel holes are clean and true. When installing pins, make certain they are fully seated, but do not use excessive force.

The mating surfaces of the crankcase halves must be sealed during reassembly using a nonhardening type of gasket sealer. Make certain that surfaces are thoroughly cleaned of oil and old sealer before making a fresh application. Apply sealer evenly and use sparingly, so excess does not squeeze into crankcase cavity. Cylinder head, gasket (8 – Fig. MR16-20) and exhaust manifold gaskets (15 and 17) should be coated with a good grade of heat resistant gasket sealer.

Tighten the crankcase screws to 24.5-34 N·m (18-25 ft.-lbs.) following the sequence shown in Fig. MR16-17. Tighten the cylinder head screws to 24.5-34 N·m (18-25 ft.-lbs.) following the

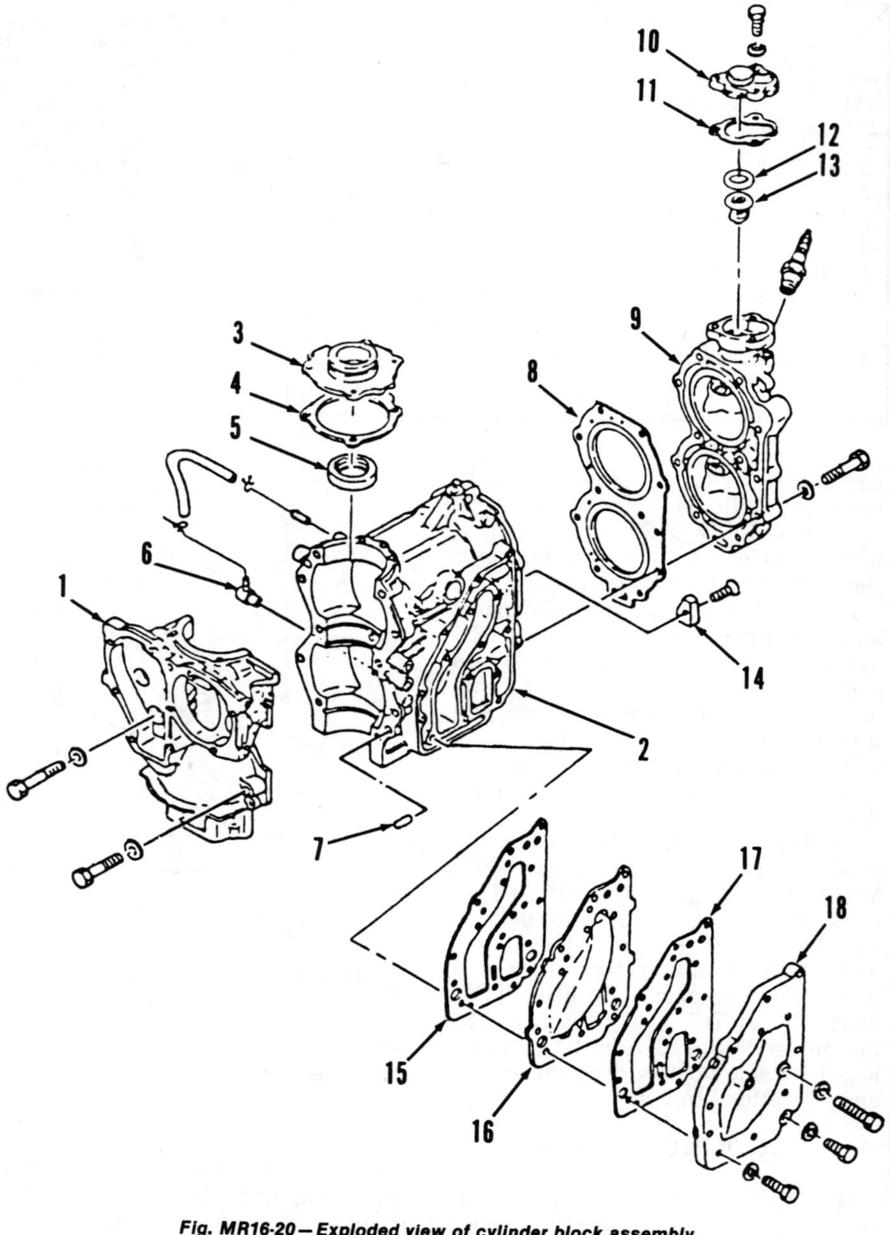

Fig. MR16-20 — Exploded view of cylinder block assembly.

1. Crankcase	6. Check valve	10. Thermostat cover
2. Cylinder block	7. Dowel pin	11. Gasket
3. Oil seal housing	8. Gasket	12. Spacer
4. Gasket	9. Cylinder head	13. Thermostat
5. Oil seal		

14. Anode
15. Gasket
16. Inner exhaust plate
17. Gasket
18. Exhaust cover

sequence shown in Fig. MR16-18. Refer to CONDENSED SERVICE DATA section for general torquing specifications.

PISTONS, PINS, RINGS AND CYLINDERS. Cylinder bore should be measured in several different locations to determine if an out-of-round or tapered condition exists. Inspect cylinder wall for scoring. If minor scoring is noted, cylinders should be honed to smooth out cylinder wall.

NOTE: Cylinder sleeves are cast into the cylinder block. If cylinder is out-of-round or tapered more than 0.54 mm (0.012 in.), or if excessive scoring is noted, the cylinder block must be renewed.

Recommended piston skirt to cylinder clearance is 0.060-0.065 mm (0.0024-0.0026 in.). Recommended piston ring end gap is 0.2-0.4 mm (0.008-0.016 in.) for both rings. The top piston ring is semi-keystone shaped. The recommended lower piston ring side clearance is 0.04-0.08 mm (0.0016-0.0032 in.). Make sure piston rings properly align with locating pins in ring grooves.

When reassembling, install new piston pin retaining clips (4 – Fig. MR16-22) and make sure that "UP" on dome of piston is towards flywheel end of engine. Coat bearings, pistons, rings and cylinder bores with engine oil during assembly.

CONNECTING RODS, CRANK-SHAFT AND BEARINGS. The crankshaft assembly should only be disassembled if the necesary tools and experience are available to service this type of crankshaft.

Maximum crankshaft runout measured at bearing outer races with crankshaft ends supported in lathe centers is 0.03 mm (0.0012 in.). Maximum connecting rod big end side clearance should be less than 0.8 mm (0.032 in.). Standard side-to-side shake of connecting rod small end measured as shown in Fig. MR16-23 should be 0.8 mm (0.03 in.) with a maximum of 2.0 mm (0.08 in.).

Crankshaft, connecting rods and center section components are available only as a unit assembly. Outer main bearings (17 and 24 – Fig. MR16-22) are available individually.

Thirty-four needle bearings (7) are used in each connecting rod small end. Rollers can be held in place with petroleum jelly while installing piston.

Lubricate bearings, pistons, rings and cylinders with engine oil prior to installation. Tighten crankcase and cylinder head screws as outlined in ASSEMBLY section.

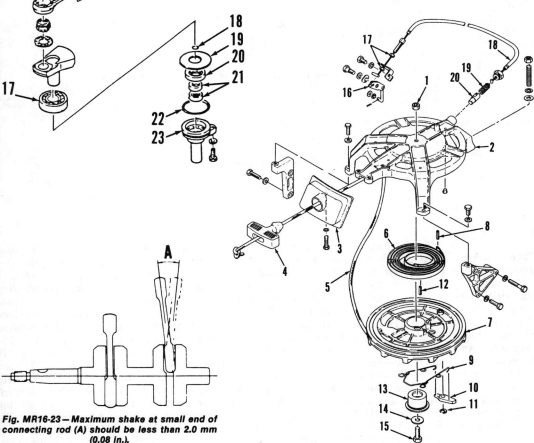

Fig. MR16-22 – Exploded view of crankshaft assembly.
1. Crank half
2. Crankpin
3. Key
4. Clip
5. Piston pin
6. Washer
7. Needle bearings
8. Piston
9. Piston rings
10. Thrust washers
11. Connecting rod
12. Roller bearing
13. Crank half
14. Bearing & snap ring
15. Labyrinth seal
16. Snap ring
17. Bearing
18. "O" ring
19. Washer
20. Oil seal
21. Oil seals
22. "O" ring
23. Lower oil seal housing

Fig. MR16-25 – Exploded view of manual starter assembly.
1. Nut
2. Housing
3. Rope guide
4. Handle
5. Starter rope
6. Rewind spring
7. Pulley
8. Pin
9. Pawl spring
10. Pawl
11. Clip
12. Pin
13. Shaft
14. Washer
15. Bolt
16. Lever & link
17. Adjusting nuts
18. Starter lockout cable
19. Spring
20. Plunger

Fig. MR16-23 – Maximum shake at small end of connecting rod (A) should be less than 2.0 mm (0.08 in.).

Fig. MR16-26 — View showing proper installation of pawl spring (9), pawl (10) and clip (11). Pulley hole (H) is used during pulley withdrawal. Refer to text.

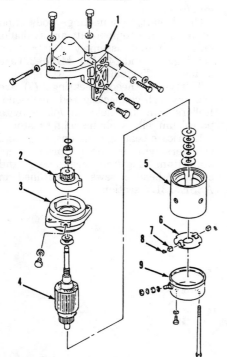

Fig. MR16-28 — Exploded view of electric starter assembly.

1. End frame
2. Drive assy.
3. Frame cover
4. Armature
5. Frame
6. Brush plate
7. Brush
8. Brush spring
9. End cover

Fig. MR16-30 — Exploded view of gearcase assembly.

1. Boot	13. Bearing	25. Pin	37. Key
2. Retainer	14. Shim	26. Spring clip	38. Bearing housing
3. "O" ring	15. Drive shaft tube	27. Shift plunger	39. Needle bearing
4. Lower shift rod	16. Needle bearing	28. Spring guide	40. Oil seals
5. Vent plug	17. Thrust washer	29. Spring	41. Tab washer
6. Water inlet cover	18. Pinion gear	30. Propeller shaft	42. Nut
7. Dowel	19. Nut	31. Thrust washer	43. Spacer
8. Oil level plug	20. Trim tab	32. Reverse gear	44. Spacer
9. Drain plug	21. Shim	33. Shim	45. Washer
10. Key	22. Taper roller bearing	34. Thrust washer	46. Nut
11. Drive shaft	23. Forward gear	35. "O" ring	47. Cotter pin
12. Oil seals	24. Clutch	36. Ball bearing	48. "O" ring

STARTER

MANUAL STARTER. When starter rope (5 – Fig. MR16-25) is pulled, pulley (7) will rotate. As pulley (7) rotates, drive pawl (10) moves to engage with the flywheel thus cranking the engine.

When starter rope (5) is released, pulley (7) is rotated in the reverse direction by force from rewind spring (6). As pulley (7) rotates, the starter rope is rewound and drive pawl (10) is disengaged from the flywheel.

Safety plunger (20) engages lugs on pulley (7) to prevent starter engagement when the gear shift lever is in the forward or reverse position.

To overhaul the manual starter, proceed as follows: Remove the engine top cover. Remove the screws retaining the manual starter to the engine. Remove starter lockout cable (18) at starter housing (2). Note plunger (20) and spring (19) located at cable end; care should be used not to lose components should they fall free. Withdraw the starter assembly.

Check pawl (10) for freedom of movement and excessive wear of engagement area or any other damage. Renew or lubricate pawl (10) with a suitable water-resistant grease and return starter to service if no other damage is noted.

To disassemble, remove clip (11) and withdraw pawl (10) and pawl spring (9). Untie starter rope (5) at handle (4) and allow the rope to wind into the starter. Remove bolt (15), washer (14) and shaft (13), then place a suitable screwdriver blade through hole (H – Fig. MR16-26) to hold rewind spring (6 – Fig. MR16-25) securely in housing (2). Carefully lift pulley (7) with starter rope (5) from housing (2). BE CAREFUL when removing pulley (7) to prevent possible injury from rewind spring. Untie starter rope (5) and remove rope from pulley (7) if renewal is required. To remove rewind spring (6) from housing (2), invert hous-

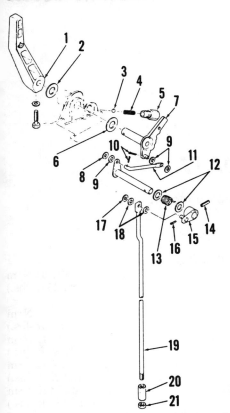

Fig. MR16-31 — Exploded view of shift control linkage.

1. Shift control handle
2. Washer
3. Detent ball
4. Spring
5. Guide
6. Washer
7. Cam
8. Washer
9. Washer
10. Pins
11. Link
12. Washers
13. Spring
14. Pin
15. Arm
16. Cotter pin
17. Washer
18. Washers
19. Upper shift rod
20. Coupler nut
21. Locknut

ing so it sits upright on a flat surface, then tap the housing top until rewind spring (6) falls free and uncoils.

Inspect all components for damage and excessive wear and renew if needed.

To reassemble, first apply a coating of a suitable water-resistant grease to rewind spring area of housing (2). Install rewind spring (6) in housing (2) so spring coils wind in a counterclockwise direction from the outer end. Make sure the spring outer hook is properly secured around starter housing pin (8). Wind starter rope (5) on to pulley (7) approximately 2½ turn counterclockwise when viewed from the flywheel side. Direct remaining starter rope (5) length through notch in pulley (7).

NOTE: Lubricate all friction surfaces with a suitable water-resistant grease during reassembly.

Assemble pulley (7) to starter housing making sure that pin (12) engages hook end in rewind spring (6). Install shaft (13), washer (14) and bolt (15). Apply Loctite 271 or 290, or an equivalent

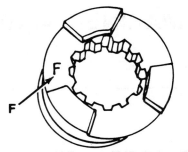

Fig. 16-32 — Install clutch so (F) mark is towards forward gear.

thread fastening solution, on bolt (15) threads, then install nut (1) and securely tighten.

Thread starter rope (5) through starter housing (2), rope guide (3) and handle (4) and secure with a knot. Turn pulley (7) 2 to 3 turns counterclockwise when viewed from the flywheel side, then release starter rope (5) from pulley notch and allow rope to slowly wind onto pulley.

NOTE: Do not apply any more tension on rewind spring (6) than is required to draw starter handle (4) back into the proper released position.

Install spring (9), pawl (10) and clip (11) as shown in Fig. MR16-26. Remount manual starter assembly.

Adjust starter lockout assembly by turning adjusting nuts (17 – Fig. MR16-25) at cable (18) end so starter will engage when gear shift lever is in neutral position, but will not engage when gear shift lever is in forward or reverse position. Plunger (20) end should recess in starter housing (2) 1 mm (0.04 in.) when gear shift lever is in neutral position.

ELECTRIC STARTER. Some models are equipped with an electric starter motor. Refer to Fig. MR16-28 for an exploded view of the starter motor. Commutator undercut should be 0.5-0.8 mm (0.02-0.03 in.) with a minimum limit of 0.2 mm (0.008 in.). Minimum brush length is 10 mm (0.394 in.).

During reassembly, adjust shims so armature end play is 1.5-2.0 mm (0.06-0.08 in.).

LOWER UNIT

PROPELLER AND DRIVE HUB. Lower unit protection is provided by a cushion type hub in the propeller. Standard propeller rotates clockwise, has three blades and measures 251 mm (9-⅞ in.) in diameter and 286 mm (11¼ in.) in pitch.

R&R AND OVERHAUL. Most serv-

ice on lower unit can be performed after detaching gearcase from drive shaft housing. To remove gearcase, attach outboard motor to a suitable stand and remove vent and drain plugs in gearcase to allow lubricant to drain. Loosen locknut (21 – Fig. MR16-31) and remove coupler nut (20). Remove four bolts securing gearcase to drive shaft housing and carefully separate gearcase from drive shaft housing. Remove water pump being careful not to lose impeller key (10 – Fig. MR16-30). Remove propeller.

Disassemble gearcase by bending back locking tab of lockwasher (41), then remove nut (42) and lockwasher (41). Using a suitable puller attached to propeller shaft, extract components (24 through 40) from gearcase. Disassemble propeller shaft assembly as required being careful not to lose shims (33). Detach spring clip (26) and pin (25) to remove dog clutch (24), spring guide (28) and spring (29). Use a suitable puller to separate ball bearing (36) from reverse gear (32).

To remove drive shaft, unscrew pinion gear nut (19) and withdraw drive shaft (11). Forward gear (23) and bearing (22) cone may now be removed. Use a suitable puller to extract bearing cup; do not lose shims (21). Pull oil seals (12) and bearing (13) out of gearcase being careful not to lose shims (14). Remove drive shaft tube (15) then drive bearing (16) down into gear cavity. Lower shift rod (4) may be removed after unscrewing retainer (2).

Inspect gears for wear on teeth and in engagement dogs. Inspect dog clutch (24) for wear on engagement surfaces. Inspect shafts for wear on splines and on friction surfaces of gears and oil seals. Check shift cam for excessive wear on shift ramps. All seals and "O" rings should be renewed on each reassembly.

Assemble gearcase by reversing disassembly procedure. Install oil seals (12) with lips away from bearing (13). Install thrust washer (17) with grooved side facing pinion gear (18). Tighten pinion gear nut (19) to 34-38 N·m (25-28 ft.-lbs.). Forward gear backlash should be 0.2-0.5 mm (0.008-0.020 in.) and reverse gear backlash should be 0.7-1.0 mm (0.028-0.039 in.).

Install dog clutch (24) so "F" marked side (see Fig. MR16-32) is towards forward gear (23 – Fig. MR16-30). Shift plunger (27) is installed with round end towards cam on lower shift rod (4). Apply water resistant grease to drive shaft upper splines.

With gearcase assembled and installed, synchronize gear engagement with gear selector handle by turning shift rod adjusting coupler nut (20 – Fig. MR16-31), then tighten locknut (21).

MARINER 40 HP

CONDENSED SERVICE DATA

NOTE: Metric fasteners are used throughout outboard motor.

TUNE-UP

Hp/rpm 40/4500-5500
Bore . . . . .75 mm
(2.95 in.)
Stroke . . . . .67 mm
(2.64 in.)
Number of Cylinders 2
Displacement . . . . .592 cc
(36.1 cu. in.)
Spark Plug–NGK B8HS
Electrode Gap . . . . .0.6 mm
(0.024 in.)
Ignition . . . . .See Text
Idle Speed (in gear) . . . . .850-950 rpm
Fuel:Oil Ratio 50:1

SIZES – CLEARANCES

Piston Ring End Gap . . . . .0.3-0.5 mm
(0.012-0.020 in.)
Piston Skirt Clearance . . . . .0.050-0.055 mm
(0.0020-0.0022 in.)

TIGHTENING TORQUES

Connecting Rod . . . . .31-34 N·m
(23-25 ft.-lbs.)
Crankcase:
6 mm . . . . .11-12 N·m
(8-9 ft.-lbs.)
10 mm . . . . .37-41 N·m
(27-30 ft.-lbs.)
Cylinder Head . . . . .27-31 N·m
(20-23 ft.-lbs.)
Flywheel . . . . .149.6-170 N·m
(110-125 ft.-lbs.)
Standard Screws:
5 mm . . . . .3.4-5.3 N·m
(30-47 in.-lbs.)
6 mm . . . . .5.9-9.3 N·m
(52-82 in.-lbs.)
8 mm . . . . .13.6-21.8 N·m
(10-16 ft.-lbs.)
10 mm . . . . .27.2-44.9 N·m
(20-33 ft.-lbs.)
12 mm . . . . .35.4-50.3 N·m
(26-37 ft.-lbs.)

LUBRICATION

The power head is lubricated by oil mixed with the fuel. Fuel should be regular leaded, low lead or unleaded gasoline with a minimum pump octane rating of 86. Recommended oil is Quicksilver Formula 50-D Outboard Lubricant. Normal fuel:oil ratio is 50:1, during engine break-in fuel:oil ratio should be 25:1.

Lower unit gears and bearings are lubricated by oil contained in the gearcase. Recommended oil is Mariner Super Duty Gear Lube. Lubricant is drained by removing vent and drain plugs in the gearcase. Refill through drain plug hole until oil has reached level of vent plug hole.

FUEL SYSTEM

SINGLE CARBURETOR MODELS. Use the standard carburetor jet sizes as recommended by the manufacturer for normal operation when used at altitudes of 2500 feet (762 m) or less. Main jet (13 – Fig. MR18-1) should be reduced from standard recommendation when the outboard motor is operated at higher altitudes.

Preliminary adjustment of idle mixture screw (6) is 1⅞ to 2⅜ turns out from a lightly seated position. Recommended idle speed is 850-950 rpm in gear with the engine at normal operating temperature.

To determine the float level, first note the numbers stamped on the top side of the carburetor mounting flange. Invert carburetor body (1–Fig. MR18-2). On models with the numbers "67900" stamped on the flange, float (17) should be parallel (P) with carburetor base. On models with the numbers "67602" stamped on the flange, distance (D) from float (17) base to carburetor base should be 16.5-22.5 mm (21/32-7/8 in.). If correct setting is not obtained, renew inlet needle (15–Fig. MR18-1) and seat (14) and/or float (17) as needed. Renew float bowl "O" ring (19).

FUEL FILTER. A fuel filter assembly (1–Fig. MR18-5) is connected between fuel supply line (2) and fuel pump inlet line (3). With the engine stopped, periodically unscrew fuel filter

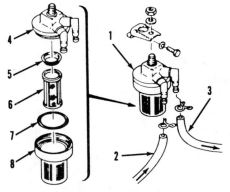

cup (8) from filter base (4) and withdraw filter element (6), "O" ring (7) and gasket (5). Clean cup (8) and filter element (6) in a suitable solvent and blow dry with clean compressed air. Inspect filter element (6). If excessive blockage or damage is noted, renew filter element (6).

Reassembly is reverse order of disassembly. Renew "O" ring (7) and gasket (5) during reassembly.

FUEL PUMP. The diaphragm type fuel pump is located on the port side of the engine. Alternating pressure and vacuum pulsations in the crankcase actuates the diaphragm and check valves in the pump.

NOTE: Three different types of fuel pump assemblies have been used. Shown in Fig. MR18-7 and Fig. MR18-8 are fuel pump assemblies using umbrella type check valves. A third type fuel pump assembly is similar to the fuel pump assembly shown in Fig. MR18-8, except reed type check valves are used instead of the umbrella type check valves (10). The reed valve type fuel pump assembly is identified by ribs on the inlet and outlet nozzles.

Make certain that all gaskets, diaphragms and check valves are in good condtion when reassembling unit. Coat the mounting gasket with a non-hardening type gasket sealer making certain that passage in center is not blocked with gasket sealer.

Fig. MR18-5 – Exploded view of cup type of fuel filter assembly (1).

1. Cup type fuel filter assy.	5. Gasket
2. Inlet fuel line	6. Filter element
3. Discharge fuel line	7. "O" ring
4. Filter base	8. Cup

Fig. MR18-1 – Exploded view of carburetor used on single carburetor models.

1. Carburetor body		12. Main nozzle
2. Plug		13. Main jet
3. Washer		14. Inlet seat
4. Idle speed screw		15. Inlet needle
5. Spring		16. Clip
6. Idle mixture screw		17. Float
7. Spring		18. Pin
8. Plug		19. "O" ring
9. Roller		20. Float bowl
10. Idle jet		21. Drain plug
11. Plug		

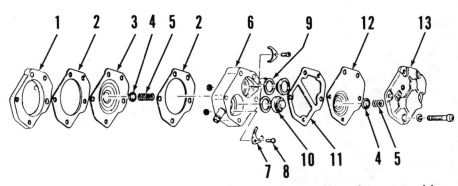

Fig. MR18-7 – Exploded view of diaphragm type fuel pump assembly used on some models.

1. Base	5. Spring	8. Screw	11. Gasket
2. Gasket	6. Body	9. Gasket	12. Diaphragm
3. Diaphragm	7. Retainer	10. Check valve	13. Cover
4. Spring plate			

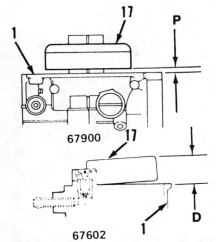

Fig. MR18-2 – Note the numbers on the carburetor mounting flange. Refer to the appropriate illustration and invert carburetor body (1) and note float (17) position. On carburetors with numbers "67900", float (17) should be parallel (P) with carburetor base. On carburetors with numbers "67602", base of float (17) should be a distance (D) of 16.5-22.5 mm (21/32-7/8 in.) from carburetor base.

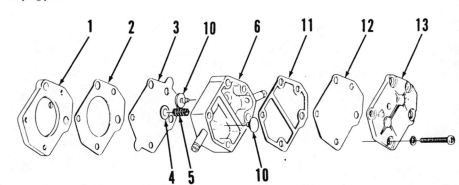

Fig. MR18-8 – Exploded view of diaphragm type fuel pump assembly used on some models. Some models are equipped with reed type check valves in place of umbrella type check valves (10). The reed valve type fuel pump assembly is identified by ribs on the inlet and outlet nozzles.

1. Base	4. Spring plate	6. Body	11. Gasket
2. Gasket	5. Spring	10. Check valves	12. Diaphragm
3. Diaphragm			13. Cover

REED VALVES. Two "V" type reed valve assemblies mounted on a reed plate and located between the intake manifold and crankcase are used on all engines. Reed valves are accessible after removing the intake manifold and reed plate.

Reed valve seats must be smooth and flat. Renew reed valve if petals are bent, broken or otherwise damaged. Do not attempt to straighten bent petals.

Reed valve petals may stand open a maximum of 0.3 mm (0.011 in.) at the tip. Reed valve stop setting (T–Fig. MR18-11) should be 4.8-5.2 mm (0.189-0.205 in.).

Individual components are not available. The reed valve must be serviced as a unit assembly.

CRANKCASE BREATHER. All models are equipped with a crankcase breather system to transfer puddled fuel

and oil from lower crankcase to upper cylinder intake port for burning. A check valve assembly (5–Fig. MR18-29) is installed in the crankcase area of the lower cylinder. Inspect breather hose (6) and renew if required.

SPEED CONTROL LINKAGE. Models With Breaker Point Type Ignition. To synchronize ignition and throttle control linkage, first make sure the ignition timing has been correctly adjusted. When the twist grip is moved completely against the high speed stop, the carburetor throttle should be fully opened. MAKE SURE that the carburetor throttle does not reach the full open position before the ignition timing is fully advanced.

To adjust the speed control linkage, proceed as follows: Move the magneto base plate to the full retard position. Detach magneto control rod (3–Fig. MR18-13) from vertical control shaft (1). Rotate vertical control shaft (1) until pulley (8–Fig. MR18-14) is positioned so bar (9) and pointer (10) are aligned as shown. Loosen locknut (4–Fig. MR18-13) and adjust rod end (5) so it fits over the connecting ball joint without altering the position of the magneto base plate or pulley (8–Fig. MR18-14). Tighten locknut to secure adjustment.

Bar (11) should align with pointer (10) when the throttle control is rotated to the full throttle position. If not, adjust the control cables length by rotating adjustment collars (6–Fig. MR18-13) until pointer (10–Fig. MR18-14) and bar (11) are properly aligned. Recheck the full retard position setting. If not properly aligned, repeat adjustment procedures.

Models With CDI Type Ignition. To synchronize ignition and throttle control linkage, first make sure the ignition timing is correctly adjusted as outlined in IGNITION section. When twist grip is moved completely against the high

speed stop, the carburetor throttle should be fully opened. MAKE SURE that the carburetor throttle does not reach the full open position before the timing is fully advanced.

To adjust the speed control linkage, proceed as follows: Move the stator plate to the full retard position. Detach stator control rod (3–Fig. MR18-15) from vertical control shaft (1). Rotate vertical control shaft (1) until pulley (9) is positioned so raised triangle (8) and pointer (10) are aligned. Loosen locknut (4) and adjust rod end (5) so it fits over the connecting ball joint without altering the position of the stator plate or pulley. Tighten locknut (4) to secure adjustment.

Triangle (11) should align with pointer (10) when the throttle control is rotated to the full throttle position. If not, adjust the control cables length by rotating ad-

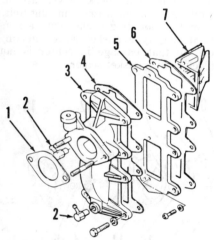

Fig. MR18-10 — Exploded view of intake manifold and reed plate assembly.

1. Gasket
2. Check valve
3. Intake manifold
4. Gasket
5. Reed plate
6. Gasket
7. Reed valve

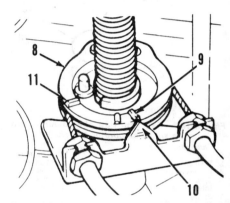

Fig. MR18-14 — View of control shaft pulley (8), bars (9 and 11) and pointer (10). Later models use arrows in place of bars (9 and 11). Refer to text for adjustment procedures.

Fig. MR18-13 — View of speed control linkage used on models with breaker point type ignition system and equipped with a steering handle.

1. Vertical control shaft
2. Throttle control rod
3. Magneto control rod
4. Locknut
5. Rod end
6. Adjustment collars
7. Magneto/throttle control rod

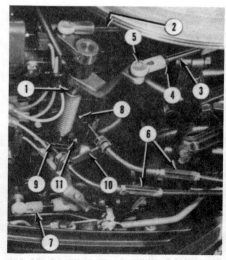

Fig. MR18-15 — View of speed control linkage used on models with CDI type ignition. Refer to text.

1. Vertical control shaft
2. Throttle control rod
3. Stator control rod
4. Locknut
5. Rod end
6. Adjustment collars
7. Throttle/stator control rod
8. Raised triangle
9. Pulley
10. Pointer
11. Triangle

Fig. MR18-11 — Reed valve stop setting (T) should be 4.8-5.2 mm (0.189-0.205 in.).

justment collars (6) until pointer (10) and triangle (11) are properly aligned. Recheck the full retard position setting. If not properly aligned, repeat adjustment procedures.

IGNITION

Breaker Point Models

On early models a flywheel magneto ignition system is used with separate breaker points, condenser and secondary coil for each cylinder. A common primary coil is used.

The breaker point gap should be 0.30-0.40 mm (0.012-0.016 in.) and can be inspected and adjusted through the flywheel openings. Two breaker point assemblies (1–Fig. MR18-17) and two condensers (2) are used. To inspect and, if needed, adjust the breaker point gap, first remove the engine top cover. Remove the screws retaining the manual rewind starter to the engine. Remove the starter lockout cable at the starter housing. Note plunger and spring located at cable end; care should be used not to lose components should they fall free. Withdraw the starter assembly. Remove the screws and lockwashers securing the flywheel cover to the flywheel, then withdraw cover.

Inspect the breaker point surfaces for excessive wear, pitting and damage. If needed, renew breaker point assemblies (1) and condensers (2) as outlined later in this section.

To clean the breaker point contact surfaces, rotate the flywheel until the breaker point contact surfaces are accessible through the opening in the flywheel. Use a point file or sandpaper with a grit rating of 400 to 600. After polishing, wipe the contact surfaces clean with a dry cloth and lightly grease the breaker point arm and lubricator with a suitable lubricant.

Turn the flywheel until the breaker point contact surfaces are at their widest position. Reach through the flywheel opening with a feeler gage of the appropriate size and check the

distance between the point surfaces. If the distance is not within the recommended limits, loosen the point set securing screw and adjust the point set until the correct gap is obtained. Tighten the point set securing screw and recheck the breaker point gap. Repeat the adjustment procedure, if needed, until the correct breaker point gap is obtained. Repeat the adjustment procedure on the other breaker point assembly.

To renew breaker point assemblies, remove flywheel from crankshaft using a suitable puller assembly. Renew breaker point assemblies (1) and condensers (2). Adjust the breaker point gap to the recommended setting as previously outlined. Make sure the securing screws are properly tightened. Be sure the flywheel key is properly positioned in the crankshaft keyway. Reinstall the flywheel and tighten flywheel securing nut to 150-170 N·m (110-125 ft.-lbs.).

To obtain the correct ignition timing, first adjust both breaker point assemblies (1) to the proper point gap as previously outlined. Remove the top spark plug and install a suitable dial indicator assembly into the spark plug hole. Properly synchronize the indicator

Fig. MR18-18 – View shows magneto base plate (5) in the full advance position. Refer to text for timing adjustment procedures.

1. Maximum advance stop bracket
2. Maximum advance stop
3. Bolt
4. Bolt
5. Magneto base plate

with the piston position at TDC. Use a point checker and attach the red tester lead to the grey wire coming from the magneto base plate (top cylinder low voltage coil lead). Connect the black tester lead to engine.

NOTE: A suitable continuity tester can be used.

Place the throttle control in the full throttle position. The magneto base plate (5 – Fig. MR18-18) is in the full advance position when stop (2) is against bracket (1). Slowly turn the flywheel counterclockwise until the tester pointer moves from "CLOSE" to "OPEN", then note dial indicator reading. Dial indicator should read 4.18-4.48 mm (0.165-0.177 in.) BTDC. If not, loosen bolts (3 and 4) and reposition maximum advance stop (2) until proper setting is obtained. Move stop (2) towards bracket (1) if dial indicator reads more than specified BTDC and away from bracket (1) if indicator reads less than specified BTDC. Continue the adjustment procedure until the correct dial indicator reading is obtained when the tester pointer moves from "CLOSE" to "OPEN", then tighten bolts (3 and 4) securing maximum advance stop (1). Repeat procedure for the bottom cylinder. Attach point checker red tester lead to the orange wire coming from magneto base plate (5). Make sure the black tester lead remains attached at the engine ground. Adjust the bottom cylinder full advance timing by varying the breaker point gap.

Remove the dial indicator assembly. Reconnect point checker red tester lead to top cylinder grey wire. Place the magneto base plate in its full retard position as shown in Fig. MR18-19. Slowly turn the flywheel counterclockwise until tester pointer moves from "CLOSE" to "OPEN", then note if pointer on maximum advance stop bracket (1 – Fig. MR18-18) is aligned with the 4° BTDC mark on the flywheel mounted timing decal. If not, loosen locknut (6 – Fig. MR18-19) and adjust screw (7) until the proper setting is obtained.

Fig. MR18-17 – View of breaker point assemblies (1) and condensers (2) used on breaker point type ignition systems.

Fig. MR18-19 – View shows the magneto base plate in the full retard position. Refer to text for timing adjustment procedures.

2. Stop
6. Locknut
7. Adjustment screw

When the ignition timing adjustment is completed, check the speed control linkage adjustment as outlined in the previous SPEED CONTROL LINKAGE section.

CDI Models

Later models are equipped with a capacitor discharge ignition (CDI) system. If engine malfunction is noted and the ignition system is suspected, make sure the spark plugs and all electrical connections are tight before proceeding to troubleshooting the CD ignition system.

Proceed as follows to test CDI system components: Refer to Fig. 18-21. To test ignition coil, disconnect black wire (B) and orange wire (O) at connectors and spark plug boots from spark plugs. Use a suitable ohmmeter and connect red tester lead to orange wire (O) and black tester lead to black wire (B). The primary winding resistance reading should be 0.08-0.10 ohms. Connect red tester lead to terminal end in one spark plug boot and black tester lead to terminal end in remaining spark plug boot. The secondary winding resistance reading should be 3,475-4.025 ohms. Use a suitable coil tester or tester Model 9800 Magneto Analyzer to perform a power test. Connect tester leads as outlined in tester's handbook. A steady spark should jump a 5 mm (13/64 in.) gap when a current value of 1.7-2.1 amperes is applied. A surface insulation test can be performed using a suitable coil tester or tester Model 9800 Magneto Analyzer and following tester's handbook.

To check source (charge) coil, disconnect black wire (B) and brown wire (Br) at connectors leading from magneto base plate. Use a suitable ohmmeter and connect red tester lead to brown wire (Br) and black tester lead to black wire

Fig. MR18-22—Use chart and values listed below to test condition of CD ignition module. Before making test (J), connect CDI module's orange wire and black wire together. Then disconnect wires and perform desired test.

A. Zero
B. Infinity
C. 9,000-19,000 ohms
D. 2,000-6,000 ohms
E. 80,000-160,000 ohms
F. 70,000-150,000 ohms
G. 33,000-63,000 ohms
H. 7,000-17,000 ohms
I. 15,000-35,000 ohms
J. Tester needle should show deflection the return toward infinite resistance

Red Test Lead \ Black Test Lead	CDI UNIT LEADS				
CDI UNIT LEADS	White	Black	Brown	White w/Red	Orange
White	A	B	B	B	B
Black	C	A	D	B	J
Brown	E	F	A	B	J
White w/Red	G	H	I	A	J
Orange	B	B	B	B	A

(B). DO NOT rotate flywheel while making test. The ohmmeter should read 121-147 ohms. Reconnect wires after completing test.

To check pulser (trigger) coil, disconnect white wire with red tracer (W/R) at connector leading from magneto base plate and black wire (B) at back of CDI unit. Use a suitable ohmmeter and connect red tester lead to white wire with red tracer (W/R) and black tester lead to black wire (B). DO NOT rotate flywheel while making test. The ohmmeter should read 12.6-15.4 ohms.

To test CDI module, first disconnect all wires at connectors and remove CDI module from outboard motor. Use a suitable ohmmeter and refer to Fig. MR18-22. With reference to chart, perform CDI module resistance tests.

Renew any components that are not within the manufacturer's recommended limits.

To check ignition timing, proceed as follows:

NOTE: If position of flywheel timing decal is suspect, install a dial indicator in the number 1 (top) cylinder spark plug hole and check top dead center piston position. If dial indicator and timing decal do not agree, reposition decal.

Rotate flywheel (1–Fig. MR18-23) clockwise until 26° mark on timing decal aligns with timing pointer (2). Rotate stator plate (6) until stamped mark (7) on plate aligns with TDC mark on timing decal (3). Maximum advance stop (not shown) on stop plate (5) should contact timing pointer bracket (2). Loosen the two stop plate retaining cap screws (4) and reposition stop plate if required. Cap screw retaining maximum advance side of stop plate is not shown. With maximum advance timing adjusted, hold flywheel (1) at 26° BTDC and rotate stator plate until maximum retard stop on stop plate (5) contacts idle timing adjustment screw (8). At idle, stamped mark (7) on stator plate (6) should align with 22° BTDC mark on timing decal (3). Rotate idle timing adjustment screw as required to obtain desired setting.

When the ignition timing adjustment is completed, check the speed control linkage adjustment as outlined in the previous SPEED CONTROL LINKAGE section.

COOLING SYSTEM

WATER PUMP. A rubber impeller type water pump is mounted between the drive shaft housing and gearcase.

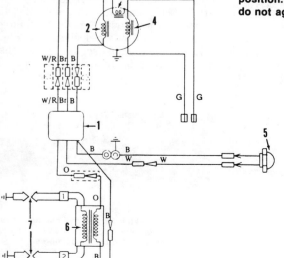

Fig. MR18-21 — View identifying CDI system components.

1. CDI module
2. Charge coil
3. Pulser coil
4. Lighting coil
5. Stop switch
6. Ignition coil
7. Spark plugs

Fig. MR18-23 — View showing ignition timing components on models with CDI type ignition. Refer to text.

1. Flywheel
2. Timing pointer
3. Timing decal
4. Cap screw
5. Stop plate
6. Stator plate
7. Stamped mark
8. Screw

Water pump impeller (6 – Fig. MR18-25) is driven by a key in the drive shaft.

When cooling system problems are encountered, first check water inlet for plugging or partial stoppage. Be sure thermostat located at top, front of cylinder head cover, operates properly. If the water pump is suspected defective, separate gearcase from drive shaft housing and inspect pump. Make sure all seals and mating surfaces are in good condition and water passages are unobstructed. Check impeller (6) and plate (8) for excessive wear. When reassembling, coat gasket surfaces with a thin coating of Perfect Seal.

POWER HEAD

R&R AND OVERHEAD. The power head can be removed for disassembly and overhaul as follows: Clamp outboard motor to a suitable stand and remove engine cowl and starter assembly. Disconnect speed control cables, fuel line and any wiring that will interfere with power head removal. Remove or disconnect any component that will interfere with power head removal.

Remove eight screws securing power head to drive shaft housing and lift power head free. Remove flywheel, ignition components, carburetor, intake manifold and reed valve assembly. Remove screws retaining exhaust cover (9 – Fig. MR18-30) and withdraw. Crankcase halves can be separated after removal of 15 screws securing crankcase half (1) to cylinder block. Crankshaft and pistons are now accessible for removal and overhaul as outlined in the appropriate and following paragraphs.

ASSEMBLY. When reassembling, make sure all joint and gasket surfaces are clean and free from nicks, burrs, warped surfaces, hardened cement or carbon. The crankcase and intake manifolds must be completely sealed against both vacuum and pressure. Exhaust manifold and cylinder head must be sealed against water leakage and pressure.

The crankcase halves are positively located during assembly by the use of two dowel pins. Check to make sure that dowel pins are not bent, nicked or distorted and that dowel holes are clean and true. When installing pins, make certain they are fully seated, but do not use excessive force.

The mating surfaces of the crankcase halves must be sealed during reassembly using a nonhardening type of gasket sealer. Make certain that surfaces are thoroughly cleaned of oil and old sealer before making a fresh application. Apply sealer evenly and use sparingly, so excess does not squeeze into crankcase cavity.

Tighten the crankcase screws to torque specified in the CONDENSED SERVICE DATA following the sequence shown in Fig. MR18-27. Tighten the cylinder head screws to 27-31 N·m (20-23 ft.-lbs.) following the sequence shown in Fig. MR18-28. Refer to CONDENSED SERVICE DATA section for general torquing specifications.

PISTONS, PINS, RINGS AND CYLINDERS. Cylinder bore should be measured in several different locations to determine if an out-of-round or tapered condition exists. Inspect cylinder wall for scoring. If minor scoring is noted, cylinders should be honed to smooth out cylinder wall.

NOTE: Cylinder sleeves are cast into the cylinder block. If cylinder is out-of-round or tapered more than 0.54 mm (0.021 in.), or if excessive scoring is noted, the cylinder block must be renewed.

Recommended piston skirt to cylinder clearance is 0.050-0.055 mm (0.0020-0.0022 in.) Recommended piston ring end gap is 0.3-0.5 mm (0.012-0.020 in.) for both rings. Make sure piston rings properly align with locating pins in ring grooves.

When reassembling, install new piston pin retaining clips (18 – Fig. MR18-29) and make sure that "UP" on dome of piston is towards flywheel end of engine. Coat bearings, pistons, rings and cylinder bores with engine oil during assembly.

Fig. MR18-25 — Exploded view of water pump assembly.

1. Seal	7. Gasket
2. Housing	8. Plate
3. Seal	9. Gasket
4. Liner	10. Base
5. Key	11. Gasket
6. Impeller	

Fig. MR18-27 — Tighten crankcase screws to specified torque following sequence shown.

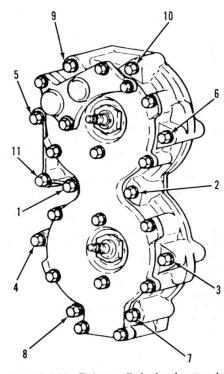

Fig. MR18-28 — Tighten cylinder head screws to 27-31 N·m (20-23 ft.-lbs.) following sequence shown.

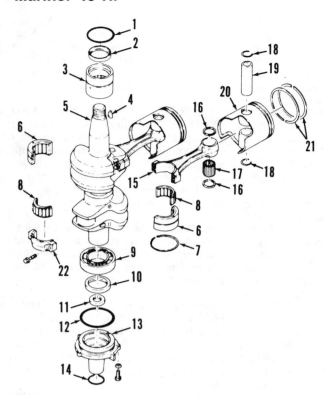

Fig. MR18-29 — Exploded view of crankshaft assembly.

1. "O" ring
2. Seal
3. Bearing
4. Key
5. Crankshaft
6. Bearing assy.
7. Snap ring
8. Cage & roller bearing assy.
9. Ball bearing
10. Seal
11. Seal
12. "O" ring
13. Oil seal housing
14. "O" ring
15. Connecting rod
16. Washers
17. Needle bearings
18. Clips
19. Piston pin
20. Piston
21. Piston rings
22. Rod cap

(7) will rotate. As pulley (7) rotates drive pawl (10) moves to engage with the flywheel thus cranking the engine.

When starter rope (5) is released pulley (7) is rotated in the reverse direction by force from rewind spring (6). As pulley (7) rotates, the starter rope is rewound and drive pawl (10) is disengaged from the flywheel.

Safety plunger (17) engages lugs on pulley (7) to prevent starter engagement when the gear shift lever is in the forward or reverse position.

To overhaul the manual starter, proceed as follows: Remove the engine top cover. Remove the screws retaining the manual starter to the engine. Remove starter lockout cable (19) at starter housing (2). Note plunger (17) and spring (18) located at cable end; care should be used not to lose components should they fall free. Withdraw the starter assembly.

CONNECTING RODS, CRANKSHAFT AND BEARINGS. Before detaching connecting rods from crankshaft, make certain that rod and cap are properly marked for correct assembly to each other and in the correct cylinder. The needle rollers and cages at crankpin end of connecting rod should be kept with the assembly and not interchanged.

Bearing rollers and cages used in connecting rods and center main bearing are available only as a set which contains the cages and rollers for one bearing. Center main bearing outer races are held together by snap ring (7–Fig. MR18-29). Be sure locating holes in upper and center main bearing outer races mate properly with locating dowels (4–Fig. MR18-30) in cylinder block when installing crankshaft assembly.

Connecting rod and cap match marks must be on same side. Be sure cap is properly meshed with connecting rod. Twenty-eight needle bearings (17–Fig. MR18-29) are used in each connecting rod small end. Rollers can be held in place with petroleum jelly while installing piston on connecting rod.

Lubricate bearings, pistons, rings and cylinders with engine oil prior to installation. Tighten crankcase and cylinder head screws as outlined in ASSEMBLY section.

STARTER

MANUAL STARTER. When starter rope (5–Fig. MR18-32) is pulled, pulley

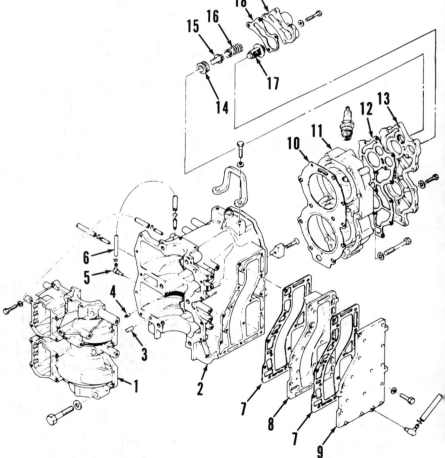

Fig. MR18-30 — Exploded view of cylinder block assembly.

1. Crankcase
2. Cylinder block
3. Dowel pin
4. Dowel pin
5. Check valve assy.
6. Breather hose
7. Gasket
8. Inner exhaust plate
9. Exhaust cover
10. Gasket
11. Cylinder head
12. Gasket
13. Cylinder head cover
14. Grommet
15. Pressure control valve
16. Spring
17. Thermostat
18. Gasket
19. Housing

Check pawl (10) for freedom of movement, excessive wear of engagement area and any other damage. Renew or lubricate pawl (10) with a suitable water-resistant grease and return starter to service if no other damage is noted.

To disassemble, remove clip (11) and withdraw pawl (10) and pawl spring (9). Untie starter rope (5) at handle (4) and allow the rope to wind into the starter. Remove bolt (16), washer (15) and shaft (14), then place a suitable screwdriver blade through hole (H – Fig. MR18-33) to hold rewind spring (6 – Fig. MR18-32) securely in housing (2). Carefully lift pulley (7) with starter rope (5) from housing (2). BE CAREFUL when removing pulley (7) to prevent possible injury from rewind spring. Untie starter rope (5) and remove rope from pulley (7) if renewal is required. To remove rewind spring (6) from housing (2), invert housing so its sits upright on a flat surface, then tap the housing top until rewind spring (6) falls free and uncoils.

Inspect all components for damage and excessive wear and renew if needed.

To reassemble, first apply a coating of a suitable water-resistant grease to re-wind spring area of housing (2). Install rewind spring (6) in housing (2) so spring coils wind in a counterclockwise direction from the outer end. Make sure spring outer hook is properly secured over starter housing pin (8). Wind starter rope (5) onto pulley (7) approximately 2½ turns counterclockwise when viewed from the flywheel side. Direct remaining starter rope (5) length through notch in pulley (7).

NOTE: Lubricate all friction surfaces with a suitable water-resistant grease during reassembly.

Assemble pulley (7) to starter housing making sure that pin (12) engages hook end in rewind spring (6). Install shaft (14), washer (15) and bolt (16). Apply Loctite 271 or 290 or an equivalent thread fastening solution on bolt (16) threads, then install nut (1) and securely tighten.

Thread starter rope (5) through starter housing (2), rope guide (3) and handle (4) and secure with a knot. Turn pulley (7) 2 to 3 turns counterclockwise when viewed from the flywheel side, then release starter rope (5) from pulley notch and allow rope to slowly wind onto pulley.

NOTE: Do not apply any more tension on rewind spring (6) than is required to draw starter handle (4) back into proper released position.

Install spring (9), pawl (10) and clip (11) as shown in Fig. MR18-33. Remount manual starter assembly.

Adjust starter lockout assembly by turning adjusting nuts (N – Fig. MR18-34) at cable (19) end so starter will engage when gear shift lever is in neutral position, but will not engage when gear shift lever is in forward or reverse position.

ELECTRIC STARTER. Some models are equipped with an electric starter motor. Refer to Fig. MR18-36 for an exploded view of the starter motor. Commutator undercut should be 0.5-0.8 mm (0.02-0.03 in.) with a minimum limit of 0.2 mm (0.008 in.). Minimum brush length is 9.5 mm (0.374 in.).

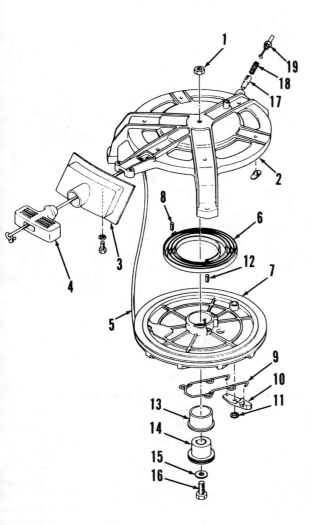

Fig. MR18-32 – Exploded view of manual rewind starter assembly.

1. Nut
2. Housing
3. Rope guide
4. Handle
5. Starter rope
6. Rewind spring
7. Pulley
8. Pin
9. Pawl spring
10. Pawl
11. Clip
12. Pin
13. Bushing
14. Shaft
15. Washer
16. Bolt
17. Plunger
18. Spring
19. Starter lockout cable

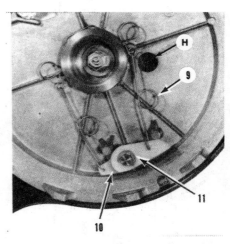

Fig. MR18-33 – View showing proper installation of pawl spring (9), pawl (10) and clip (11). Pulley hole (H) is used during pulley withdrawal. Refer to text.

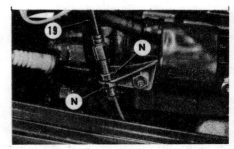

Fig. MR18-34 – View showing starter lockout cable (19) and cable adjustment nuts (N). Refer to text.

LOWER UNIT

Two types of gearcase assemblies have been used—an above prop exhaust type (Fig. MR18-38) and a through prop exhaust type (Fig. MR18-40). Refer to the appropriate following section for service procedures.

Above Prop Exhaust Type Gearcase

PROPELLER AND SHEAR PIN. Lower unit protection is provided by a shear pin. Select a propeller that will allow the engine at full throttle to reach maximum operating range of 4500-5500 rpm.

R&R AND OVERHAUL. Most lower unit service may be performed after separating the gearcase from the drive shaft housing. The gearcase may be removed and disassembled as follows: Attach outboard motor to a suitable stand a remove both vent and drain plugs in gearcase to allow lubricant to

drain. Loosen jam nut (46—Fig. MR18-38) and remove adjustment nut (47). Remove six screws securing gearcase to drive shaft housing and carefully separate gearcase from drive shaft housing. Remove water pump using caution to prevent loss of key (5—Fig.

MR18-25). Remove propeller and unscrew the nine screws securing lower gearcase housing (23—Fig. MR18-38). Propeller shaft (33), complete with gears and bearings, can now be removed. Use caution to prevent loss of cam follower (24). Spring clip (28) retains drive pin (30) in propeller shaft. Drive shaft may be removed from gearcase after removal of snap ring (20). Lower shift rod (50) can be removed after removal of retainer (48).

Inspect gears for wear on teeth and in engagement dogs. Inspect dog clutch (29) for wear on engagement surfaces. Inspect shafts for wear on splines and on friction surfaces of gears and oil seals. Check shift cam for excessive wear on shift ramps. All seals and "O" rings should be renewed on each reassembly.

Backlash between pinion gear (19) and drive gears (27 and 36) should be 0.05-0.15 mm (0.002-0.006 in.) and is adjusted by varying thickness of shims (26 and 37). Adjust gear mesh position by varying thickness of shim (17).

Install dog clutch (29) on propeller shaft (33) so "F" marked side faces forward gear (27).

Fig. MR18-36—Exploded view of electric starter motor.

1. Retainer		9. Positive brush	
2. Stop		10. Spring	
3. Spring		11. Negative brush	
4. Pinion		12. Brush plate	
5. End plate		13. End cover	
6. Armature		14. Washers	
7. Frame		15. Snap ring	
8. Solenoid		16. Dust cover	

Fig. MR18-38—Exploded view of above prop exhaust type gearcase assembly.

1. Seals		13. Dowel pin		25. Bearing		38. Bearing
2. Drive shaft		14. Sleeve		26. Shim		39. Seals
3. Thrust washer		15. Bearing		27. Forward gear		40. Bearing carrier
4. Bearing		16. Thrust bearing		28. Spring clip		41. "O" ring
5. Upper gearcase housing		17. Shim		29. Dog clutch		42. Propeller
6. Wash plug		18. Bearing		30. Pin		43. Washer
7. Vent plug		19. Pinion gear		31. Spring guide		44. Spinner
8. Shift limit screw		20. Snap ring		32. Spring		45. Cotter pin
9. Screen		21. Seal		33. Propeller shaft		46. Jam nut
10. Plug		22. Drain plug		34. Shear pin		47. Adjustment nut
11. Water inlet cover		23. Lower gearcase housing		35. Thrust washer		48. Retainer
12. Anode		24. Cam follower		36. Reverse gear		49. Boot
				37. Shim		50. Lower shift rod

When reassembling gearcase, make sure all case mating surfaces are clean and free of nicks or burrs.

Shift linkage is set by pressing lower shift rod (50) down until cam is against stopper pin (8), then adjusting adjustment nut (47) until shift control lever is in "REVERSE" position. Secure adjustment with jam nut (46).

Through Prop Exhaust Type Gearcase

PROPELLER AND DRIVE HUB. Lower unit protection is provided by a cushion type hub in the propeller. Select a propeller that will allow the engine at full throttle to reach maximum operating range of 4500-5500 rpm.

R&R AND OVERHAUL. Most service on lower unit can be performed after detaching gearcase from drive shaft housing. To remove gearcase, attach outboard motor to a suitable stand and remove vent and drain plugs in gearcase to allow lubricant to drain. Loosen jam nut (48–Fig. MR18-40) and remove adjustment nut (49). Remove six screws securing gearcase to drive shaft housing and carefully separate from drive shaft housing. Remove water pump being careful not to lose impeller key (5–Fig. MR18-25). Remove propeller.

Disassemble gearcase by bending back locking tab of lockwasher (40–Fig. MR18-40), then remove nut (41) and lockwasher (40). Using a suitable puller attached to propeller shaft, extract components (26 through 43) from gearcase. Disassemble propeller shaft assembly as required being careful not to lose shims (34). Detach spring clip (26) and pin (27) to remove dog clutch (28), spring guide (29) and spring (30). Use a suitable puller to separate ball bearing (37) from reverse gear (33).

To remove drive shaft, unscrew pinion gear nut (18) and withdraw drive shaft (4). Forward gear (25) and bearing (24) cone many now be removed. Use a suitable puller to extract bearing cup; do not lose shims (23). Pull race of bearing (5) out of gearcase being careful not to lose shims (6). Remove drive shaft sleeve (7) then drive bearing (8) down into gear cavity. Lower shift rod (52) may be removed after unscrewing retainer (50).

NOTE: Manufacturer recommends renewing tapered roller bearing assembly (5) if removed from drive shaft.

Inspect gears for wear on teeth and in engagement dogs. Inspect dog clutch (28) for wear on engagement surfaces. Inspect shafts for wear on splines and on friction surfaces of gears and oil

seals. Check shift cam for excessive wear on shift ramps. All seals and "O" rings should be renewed on each reassembly.

Assemble gearcase by reversing disassembly procedure. Install oil seals (2) in water pump base with lips facing away from bearing (5). Tighten pinion gear nut (18) to 68-78 N·m (50-58 ft.-lbs.). Forward gear backlash should be 0.10-0.24 mm (0.004-0.009 in.) and

reverse gear backlash should be 0.40-0.54 mm (0.016-0.021 in.).

Install dog clutch (28) so "F" marked side is towards forward gear (25). Apply water-resistant grease to drive shaft upper splines.

With gearcase assembled and installed, synchronize gear engagement with gear selector handle by turning shift rod adjustment nut (49), then tighten jam nut (48).

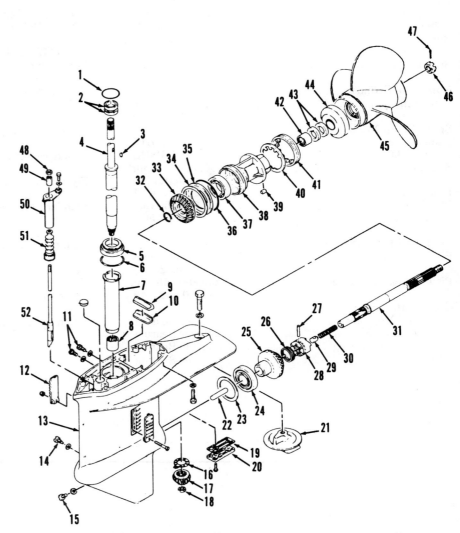

Fig. MR18-40 – Exploded view of through prop exhaust type gearcase assembly.

1. "O" ring	14. Shift limit screw	27. Pin	40. Lockwasher
2. Seals	15. Drain plug	28. Dog clutch	41. Cover nut
3. Key	16. Thrust washer	29. Spring guide	42. Bearing
4. Drive shaft	17. Pinion gear	30. Spring	43. Seals
5. Tapered roller bearing assy.	18. Nut	31. Propeller shaft	44. Thrust hub
6. Shim	19. Gasket	32. Thrust washer	45. Propeller
7. Sleeve	20. Plate	33. Reverse gear	46. Nut
8. Bearing	21. Trim tab	34. Shim	47. Cotter pin
9. Rubber seal	22. Cam follower	35. Thrust washer	48. Jam nut
10. Seal guide	23. Shim	36. "O" ring	49. Adjustment nut
11. Plugs	24. Bearing	37. Bearing	50. Retainer
12. Water inlet covers	25. Forward gear	38. Bearing carrier	51. Boot
13. Gearcase housing	26. Spring clip	39. Key	52. Lower shift shaft

MARINER 48 AND 60 HP (2 cyl.)

CONDENSED SERVICE DATA

NOTE: Metric fasteners are used throughout outboard motor.

TUNE-UP
Hp/rpm:
  Model 48 . . . . .48/5500
  Model 60 . . . . .60/5500
Bore . . . . .82 mm
  (3.23 in.)
Stroke . . . . .72 mm
  (2.83 in.)
Number of Cylinders 2
Displacement . . . . .760 cc
  (46.4 cu. in.)
Spark Plug – NGK:
  Model 48 . . . . .B7HS
  Model 60 . . . . .B8HS
Spark Plug Electrode Gap . . . . .0.7 mm
  (0.027 in.)
Ignition Type . . . . .CDI
Idle Speed (in gear) . . . . .750-850 rpm
Fuel:Oil Ratio 50:1

SIZES – CLEARANCES
Piston Ring End Gap . . . . .0.3-0.5 mm
  (0.012-0.020 in.)
Piston Skirt Clearance . . . . .0.050-0.055 mm
  (0.0019-0.0022 in.)
Crankshaft Bearings:
  Top Main Bearing . . . . .Roller Bearing
  Center Main Bearing . . . . .Roller Bearing
  Lower Main Bearing . . . . .Ball Bearing
  Crankpin . . . . .Roller Bearing

SIZES – CLEARANCES CONT.
Piston Pin Bearing In Rod . . . . .Loose Rollers
  No. of Rollers (each rod) 28

TIGHTENING TORQUES
Connecting rod . . . . .31.4 N·m
  (23 ft.-lbs.)
Crankcase:
  M6 . . . . .5.9-9.3 N·m
  (52-82 in.-lbs.)
  M10 . . . . .39.2 N·m
  (29 ft.-lbs.)
Cylinder head . . . . .27.4-31.4 N·m
  (20-23 ft.-lbs.)
Flywheel . . . . .147 N·m
  (108 ft.-lbs.)
Standard screws:
  5 mm . . . . .4.9-5.4 N·m
  (43-48 in.-lbs.)
  6 mm . . . . .7.9-9.3 N·m
  (70-82 in.-lbs.)
  8 mm . . . . .14.7-19.6 N·m
  (130-173 in.-lbs.)
  10 mm . . . . .29.4-44.1 N·m
  (22-32 ft.-lbs.)
  12 mm . . . . .34.3-49.0 N·m
  (25-36 ft.-lbs.)

LUBRICATION

The power head is lubricated by oil mixed with the fuel. Fuel should be regular leaded, low lead or unleaded gasoline with a minimum pump octane rating of 86. Recommended oil is Quicksilver Formula 50-D Outboard Lubricant. Normal fuel:oil ratio is 50:1; during engine break-in, fuel:oil ratio should be 25:1.

Lower unit gears and bearings are lubricated by oil contained in the gearcase. Recommended oil is Mariner Super Duty Gear Lube. Lubricant is drained by removing vent and drain plugs in the gearcase. Refill through drain plug hole until oil has reached level of vent hole. Lower unit oil capacity is 500 mL (16.9 oz.).

FUEL SYSTEM

CARBURETOR. Two carburetors are used. Refer to Fig. MR20-1 for an exploded view of carburetor. Main jet (13) size is 185 for 48 hp models and 180 for 60 hp models. Idle jet (2) size is 92 for 48 hp models and 100 for 60 hp models. Idle air jet (11) size is 105 for 48 hp models and 100 for 60 hp models. Main air jet (10) size is 160 for all models. Initial setting for idle mixture screw (5) is 1⅛ to 1⅜ turns out.

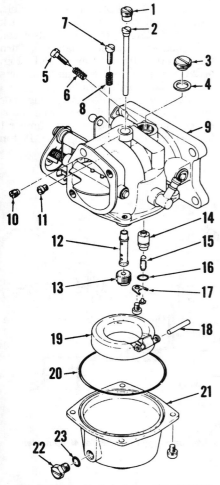

Fig. MR20-1—Exploded view of carburetor.

1. Plug	13. Main jet
2. Pilot jet	14. Fuel inlet seat
3. Plug	15. Fuel inlet valve
4. Washer	16. "O" ring
5. Idle mixture screw	17. Retainer
6. Spring	18. Float pin
7. Idle speed screw	19. Float
8. Spring	20. "O" ring
9. Body	21. Float bowl
10. Main air jet	22. Drain screw
11. Idle air jet	23. "O" ring
12. Nozzle	

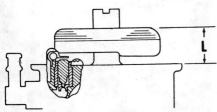

Fig. MR20-2—Float level (L) should be 18 mm (0.7 in.). Adjust float level by bending float arm tang.

Float level is measured with float bowl removed and carburetor inverted as shown in Fig. MR20-2. Float level (L) should be 18 mm (0.7 in.) and is adjusted by bending float arm tang.

To synchronize upper and lower carburetors, detach one end of throttle connector rod (T–Fig. MR20-3) and back out idle speed screw on each carburetor so throttle valve is closed. Adjust length of throttle connector rod by turning rod ends and reattach. Adjust engine idle speed using idle speed screw of lower carburetor. Adjust choke rod clamp (C) so choke valves in carburetors operate uniformly.

SPEED CONTROL LINKAGE. Ignition timing advance and throttle opening must be synchronized so that throttle is opened as ignition timing is advanced.

To synchronize speed control linkage, first make certain that ignition timing is correctly set as outlined in IGNITION TIMING section. Rotate speed control handle so ignition timing is set at 3°-7° before top dead center (BTDC). Detach end of throttle rod (R–Fig. MR20-5) and adjust length of rod by turning rod

Fig. MR20-3—View of carburetors. Synchronize carburetors using throttle connector rod (T) and choke rod clamp (C) as outlined in text.

Fig. MR20-5—View of power head. Refer to text for synchronization of speed control linkage.

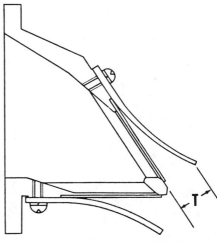

Fig. MR20-6—Reed valve stop setting (T) should be 2.8-3.2 mm (0.11-0.12 in.) for 48 hp models and 9.7-10.1 mm (0.38-0.40 in.) for 60 hp models.

end so when rod end is reattached, cam follower roller (R) just contacts cam (C). Rotate speed control handle to closed position, then recheck adjustment. When rotating speed control handle, roller (R) should contact cam when ignition timing advances to 3°-7° BTDC.

Adjust throttle stop screw (S) so screw contacts boss just as throttle valves reach wide open position.

REED VALVES. A "V" type reed valve assembly located between the intake manifold and crankcase is used on all engines. Reed valves are accessible after removing the carburetors.

Reed valve seats must be smooth and flat. Renew reed valve if petals are bent, broken or otherwise damaged. Do not attempt to straighten bent petals.

Reed valve petals may stand open a maximum of 0.2 mm (0.008 in.) at the tip. Reed valve stop setting (T–Fig. MR20-6) should be 2.8-3.2 mm (0.11-0.12 in.) for 48 hp models and 9.7-10.1 mm (0.38-0.40 in.) for 60 hp models.

Individual components are not available. The reed valve must be serviced as a unit assembly.

CRANKCASE BREATHER. All models are equipped with a crankcase breather system to transfer puddled fuel and oil from lower crankcase to upper cylinder intake port for burning. A check valve (4–Fig. MR20-7) is located in fitting (3). Some models are equipped with check valve (5) in the cylinder block. Inspect breather hose (1) and renew if required.

FUEL PUMP. All models are equipped with a diaphragm type fuel pump as shown in Fig. MR20-8. Inspect diaphragms (4) and renew if deformed,

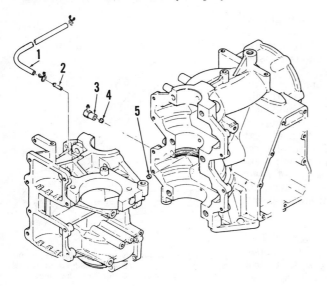

To adjust idle ignition timing, position flywheel at 4° ATDC on 48 hp models or 2° ATDC on 60 hp models. Move magneto base plate so mark (P – Fig. MR20-12) on top of pulser coil is aligned with flywheel mark (F). Turn idle timing screw (IT – Fig. MR20-13) so screw end just contacts magneto base plate boss.

To adjust full throttle ignition timing, position flywheel at 20° BTDC on 48 hp models or 26° BTDC on 60 hp models. Move magneto base plate so mark (P – Fig. MR20-12) on top of pulser coil is aligned with flywheel mark (F). Turn full throttle timing screw (FT – Fig. MR20-14) so screw end just contacts magneto base plate boss.

If flywheel timing decal is damaged or missing, flywheel position may be determined using a dial indicator in number 1 (upper) cylinder spark plug hole. Piston

torn or holed. Determine if check valves (10) operate properly. Renew springs (6 and 13) if damaged or distorted.

IGNITION SYSTEM

All models are equipped with a capacitor discharge ignition system. Ignition system components are accessible after removing flywheel. Refer to Fig. MR20-10 for a practical drawing of ignition system.

IGNITION TIMING. Ignition timing may be adjusted for idle and fuel throttle. If questioned, verify position of timing pointer and flywheel timing decal by installing a dial indicator in number 1 (upper) cylinder spark plug hole and determining piston top dead center. Before checking ignition timing, check length of magneto control rod which should be 52 mm (2-3/64 in.) as shown in Fig. MR20-11.

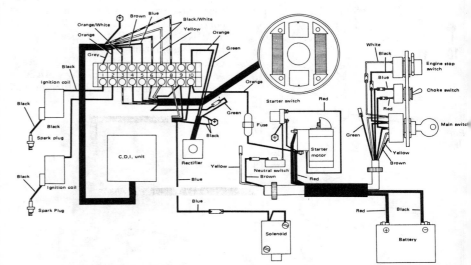

Fig. MR20-10 — Wiring diagram for 60 hp models. Ignition wiring is similar for 48 hp models.

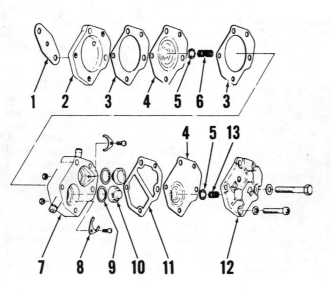

Fig. MR20-8 — Exploded view of fuel pump.
1. Gasket
2. Base
3. Gasket
4. Pump diaphragm
5. Spring plate
6. Spring
7. Body
8. Retainer
9. Gasket
10. Check valve
11. Gasket
12. Cover
13. Spring

Fig. MR20-11 — Magneto control and length should be 52 mm (2-3/64 in.) as shown. Adjust length by detaching and turning rod end.

position at idle should be 0.07-0.17 mm (0.003-0.007 in.) ATDC on 48 hp models or 0.001-0.005′ mm (0.0004-0.002 in.) ATDC on 60 hp models. Piston position at full throttle should be 2.55-3.11 mm (0.099-0.121 in.) BTDC on 48 hp models or 4.39-4.99 mm (0.171-0.195 in.) BTDC on 60 hp models. Adjust timing screws as previously outlined.

After adjusting ignition timing, recheck speed control linkage adjustment.

TROUBLESHOOTING. If ignition system malfunction is suspected, check for spark at spark plugs. Check wiring and be sure all connections are clean and tight. Note the following specifications when inspecting electrical units.

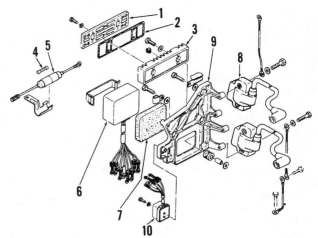

Fig. MR20-15 — View of electrical components used on 60 hp models. Ignition system components used on 48 hp models are similar.

1. Cover
2. Gasket
3. Terminal plate
4. Fuse
5. Fuse holder
6. Ignition module (CDI)
7. Vibration damper
8. Ignition coil
9. Bracket
10. Rectifier
11. Cover
12. Nut
13. Washer
14. Flywheel
15. Timing pointer
16. Timing decal
17. Retainer
18. Lighting coil
19. Charge coil
20. Trigger coil
21. Magneto base plate
22. Pulser coils

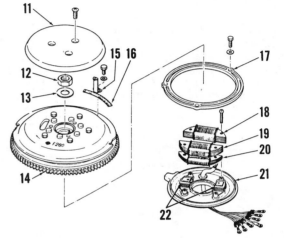

Fig. MR20-12 — View showing location of flywheel timing mark (F) and pulser coil mark (P).

Fig. MR20-13 — Adjust idle speed ignition timing by turning screw (IT). Refer to text.

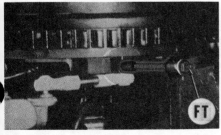

Fig. MR20-14 — Adjust full throttle ignition timing by turning screw (FT). Refer to text.

Disconnect white/red lead and black lead for each pulser coil (22 – Fig. MR20-15) and measure resistance between leads. Resistance should be 8.5 ohms for each pulser coil. Pulser coils are not available individually but must be obtained as a unit assembly with magneto base plate (21).

Disconnect brown lead and blue lead of charge coil (19). Resistance should be 23.5 ohms between charge coil leads.

Disconnect yellow trigger coil lead and measure resistance between yellow lead and ground. Resistance should be 2.2 ohms.

Ignition coil primary resistance should be approximately 0.25 ohms. Ignition coil secondary resistance should be 2000-3000 ohms.

COOLING SYSTEM

A thermostat is located in the cylinder head on 60 hp models while 48 hp models are not so equipped. All models are equipped with a rubber impeller type water pump mounted on top side of lower unit gearcase.

When cooling system problems are encountered, first check the thermostat, if so equipped, to see that it is operating

properly. Check the water inlet for plugging or partial stoppage, then if trouble is not corrected, remove the lower unit gearcase as outlined in LOWER UNIT section, and check the condition of water pump, water passages and sealing surfaces.

POWER HEAD

REMOVE AND DISASSEMBLE. To remove power head, proceed as follows: Remove flywheel. Disconnect manual choke linkage. Disconnect battery leads from starter then disconnect wires from starter solenoid. Disconnect

Fig. MR20-17 — Disconnect shift rod (R) and detach bracket (B) before removing power head.

interfering wires from terminal plate (3 – Fig. MR20-15) and remove electrical unit bracket (9). Disconnect fuel line and exhaust cover hose. Disconnect throttle and shift cables. Disconnect shift rod (R – Fig. MR20-17) and detach bracket (B). Remove bottom cowl covers by unscrewing four screws inside bottom cowl. Unscrew eight nuts securing power head to drive shaft housing and lift off power head.

For access to short block assembly, remove the fuel pump and fuel filter. Remove starter motor on 60 hp models. Remove magneto base plate assembly. Remove air cleaner, carburetors and reed valve assemblies. Remove tower shaft assembly shown in Fig. MR20-18. Remove any other components which interfere with intended service operation.

To disassemble power head, unscrew and remove cylinder head. Remove lower oil seal housing. Unscrew retaining nuts and screws and separate crankcase half from cylinder block. Crankshaft, pistons and bearings are now accessible for removal and overhaul as

outlined in the appropriate following paragraphs. Assemble as outlined in the ASSEMBLY paragraph.

ASSEMBLY. When reassembling, make sure all joint and gasket surfaces are clean and free from nicks, burrs, warped surfaces, hardened cement or carbon. The crankcase and intake mani-

folds must be completely sealed against both vacuum and pressure. Exhaust manifold and cylinder head must be sealed against water leakage and pressure.

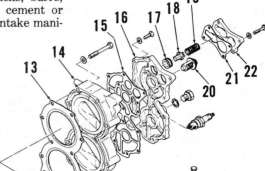

Fig. MR20-19 – Exploded view of cylinder block assembly. Breather valve (5) is not used on all models. Components (17 through 20) are used on 60 hp models.

1. Breather hose
2. Fitting
3. Elbow
4. Breather valve
5. Breather valve
6. Dowel
7. Bearing locator pin
8. Crankcase half
9. Cylinder block
10. Gasket
11. Exhaust cover
12. Anode
13. Gasket
14. Cylinder head
15. Gasket
16. Cover
17. Grommet
18. Water pressure relief valve
19. Spring
20. Thermostat
21. Gasket
22. Cover

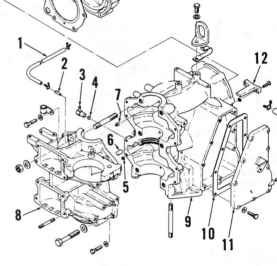

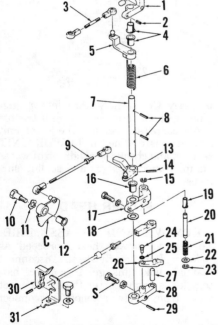

Fig. MR20-18 – Exploded view of tower shaft assembly.

1. Bracket
2. Roll pin
3. Magneto control rod
4. Bushings
5. Magneto control arm
6. Spring
7. Tower shaft
8. Pin
9. Throttle rod
10. Shoulder bolt
11. Wave washer
12. Bushing
13. Lever
14. Pin
15. "E" ring
16. Bushing
17. Bracket
18. Washer
19. Bushing
20. Pin
21. Spring
22. Washer
23. "E" ring
24. Pin
25. Wave washer
26. Retainer
27. Pin
28. Arm
29. Pin
30. Cable clamp
31. Cable bracket
C. Throttle cam
IT. Idle ignition timing screw
S. Throttle stop screw

Fig. MR20-20 – Exploded view of crankshaft assembly.

1. "O" ring
2. Seal
3. Bearing
4. Thrust washer
5. Key
6. Center main bearing
7. Crankshaft
8. Rod bearing
9. Rod cap
10. Ball bearing
11. Seal
12. Seal
13. "O" ring
14. Seal housing
15. Clip
16. Connecting rod
17. Bearing rollers (28)
18. Thrust washer
19. Pin retainer clip
20. Piston pin
21. Piston
22. Lower piston ring
23. Upper piston ring

Reverse disassembly procedure for assembly. Apply engine oil to moving parts prior to assembly. Apply a non-hardening sealer to contact surfaces of crankcase half and cylinder block. Refer to Fig. MR20-21 for tightening sequence of crankcase nuts and screws. Tighten crankcase fasteners initially to 3.9 N·m (34 in.-lbs.) for M6 fasteners and 19.6 N·m (173 in.-lbs.) for M10 fasteners. Tighten crankcase fasteners to a final torque of 7.8 N·m (69 in.-lbs.) for M6 fasteners and 39.2 N·m (28 ft.-lbs.) for M10 fasteners. Do not apply sealant to cylinder head gasket. Refer to Fig.

MR20-22 for tightening sequence of cylinder head screws. Tighten cylinder head screws to 14.7 N·m (130 in.-lbs.) initially, then to a final torque of 29.4 N·m (22 ft.-lbs.).

PISTONS, PINS, RINGS AND CYLINDERS. Each piston is equipped with two piston rings with the top ring a headland type piston ring. Both piston ring grooves have a pin to prevent piston ring rotation. Piston ring end gap should be 0.3-0.5 mm (0.012-0.020 in.) for both rings.

The piston pin rides in 28 loose needle bearing rollers (17–Fig. MR20-20). When assembling piston, pin and connecting rod be sure oil hole (H–Fig. MR20-23) in rod is on same side as "UP" mark in piston crown. Install piston so "UP" mark is towards flywheel end of power head.

CONNECTING RODS, BEARINGS AND CRANKSHAFT. Before detaching connecting rods from crankshaft, make certain that rod and cap are properly marked for correct assembly to each other and in the correct cylinder. The needle rollers and cages at crankpin end of connecting rod should be kept with the assembly and not interchanged.

Bearing rollers and cages used in con-

necting rods and center main bearing are available only as a set which contains the cages and rollers for one bearing. Center main bearing outer races are held together by snap ring (15–Fig. MR20-20). Be sure locating holes in main bearing outer races mate properly with locating dowels (7–Fig. MR20-19) in cylinder block when installing crankshaft assembly.

When installing connecting rod on crankshaft, be sure loose bearing rollers (R–Fig. MR20-24) are installed between bearing cages. Connecting rod and cap match marks (M–Fig. MR20-23) must be on same side. Be sure cap is properly meshed with connecting rod.

STARTER

MANUAL STARTER. The rewind starter used on 48 hp models is shown in Fig. MR20-26. A starter interlock prevents operating manual starter when outboard is in forward or reverse gears. Cable (25) is connected to shift shaft (24) and actuates interlock pawl (3) which engages dogs on rope pulley (11). To adjust starter interlock, position shift lever in neutral position. Position cable (25) in clamps (7) so marks on pawl (3) and cam plate (6) are aligned.

To disassemble starter, detach shift interlock cable (25) from starter housing and remove starter from power head. Remove rope handle from rope and allow rope to wind into starter. Unscrew cap screw (22) and remove components (15 through 21) as well as pawl (13). Carefully remove rope pulley (11) while being careful not to allow rewind spring to uncoil uncontrolled as personal injury may result. Inspect components for damage and excessive wear.

Reverse disassembly procedure to assemble starter. Install rewind spring (10) with coils wound in counterclockwise direction from outer spring end. Apply a suitable grease to bushing (14). Wind rope in counterclockwise direction around pulley as viewed with pulley installed.

ELECTRIC STARTER. An electric starter is used on 60 hp models. Refer to Fig. MR20-27 for an exploded view of starter. Early models were equipped with a solenoid mounted on starter as shown while later models are equipped with a separate starter switch. A safety switch (N–Fig. MR20-28) prevents starter actuation when outboard is in forward or reverse gear.

Maximum no-load current draw should be 60 amperes at 12 volts with starter speed of 7000 rpm minimum. Minimum brush length is 11.5 mm (0.45 in.). Brush spring pressure should be 13.7-17.6 newtons (49-63 oz.). Starter

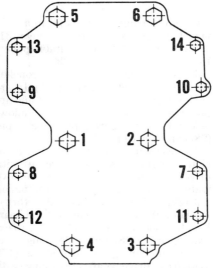

Fig. MR20-21—Use the tightening sequence shown above when tightening crankcase fasteners.

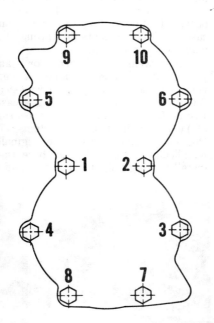

Fig. MR20-22—Use the tightening sequence shown above when tightening cylinder head screws.

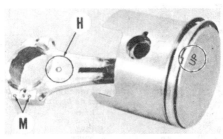

Fig. MR20-23—Assemble rod and piston so oil hole (H) is on same side as "UP" on piston crown. Be sure match marks (M) are on same side when installing cap on rod.

Fig. MR20-24—Be sure to install bearing rollers (R) when installing center main bearing.

motor pinion clearance in engaged position should be 0.3-1.5 mm (0.012-0.059 in.). Pinion to flywheel ring gear backlash should be 3-5 mm (0.118-0.197 in.)

PROPELLER

All models are equipped with a three-bladed, right-hand propeller. The propeller has an integral cushion hub to protect outboard driveline components. Optional propellers are available and should be selected to provide full throttle operation at 5000-5500 rpm.

LOWER UNIT

R&R AND OVERHAUL. Most service on lower unit can be performed by detaching gearcase from the drive shaft housing. To remove gearcase, drain lubricant, unscrew trim tab retaining screw (S – Fig. MR20-30), remove trim tab (50) and unscrew gearcase retaining screw (W) in gearcase trim tab cavity. Unscrew four nuts securing gearcase and separate gearcase from drive shaft housing.

Disassemble the gearcase after re-

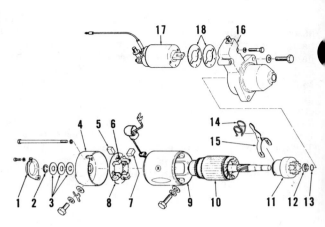

Fig. MR20-27 – Exploded view of electric starter used on 60 hp models. Later models are equipped with a separate starter switch instead of solenoid (17).

1. Dust cover
2. "E" ring
3. Washers
4. End cover
5. Neg. brush
6. Brush spring
7. Pos. brush
8. Brush plate
9. Frame
10. Armature
11. Drive assy.
12. Collar
13. Clip
14. Spring
15. Yoke
16. End frame
17. Solenoid
18. Washer

moving the propeller. Bend back locking tab of lockwasher, unscrew bearing housing nut (41) and remove lockwasher (40). Clamp the outer end of propeller shaft in a soft-jawed vise and remove the gearcase by tapping with a rubber mallet. Be careful not to lose key (37) or shims (32). Forward gear (49) will remain in gearcase. Withdraw the propeller shaft from bearing housing (36) and reverse gear (31).

Clamp bearing housing (36) in a soft-jawed vise and remove reverse gear (31) and bearing (34) using a suitable puller. Remove and discard seals (39).

To remove clutch (26) from propeller shaft, remove retaining ring (27). Insert cam follower (23) in hole in shaft and apply only enough pressure to cam follower end to relieve spring pressure so pin (28) can be driven out.

To disassemble drive shaft and associated parts, position gearcase with drive shaft pointing upwards. Remove water pump assembly. Unscrew pinion nut (22) and remove pinion (21), thrust washer (20), forward gear (49) and bearing (48) cone. Use a suitable puller to extract bearing (48) cup while being careful not to damage or lose shims (47). Withdraw drive shaft (14) along with bearing (16) cone. Using a suitable puller, remove bearing (16) cup while being careful not to damage or lose shims (17). Extract sleeve (18) then remove bearing (19) by driving down into gearcase. Shift components (53 through 60) may now be removed.

If gear wear was abnormal or if any parts that affect gear alignment were renewed, check and adjust gear mesh as follows: Install bearing (19) in gearcase. Install forward gear (49) and bearing (48) using originally installed shims (47). Position shims (17) that were originally installed at bottom of bearing bore, then install bearing (16) cup. Position pinion

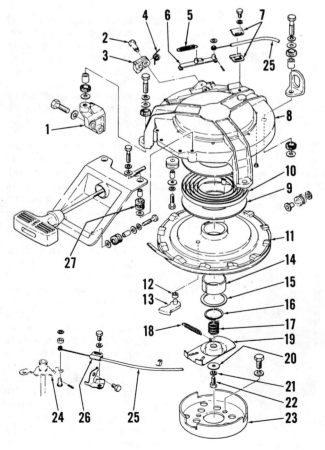

Fig. MR20-26 – Exploded view of manual starter used on 48 hp models.

1. Bracket
2. Pivot screw
3. Pawl
4. Spring
5. Spring
6. Cam plate
7. Cable clamp
8. Starter housing
9. Plate
10. Rewind spring
11. Rope pulley
12. Bushing
13. Pawl
14. Bushing
15. Washer
16. Clip
17. Spring
18. Spring
19. Drive plate
20. Washer
21. Lockwasher
22. Cap screw
23. Starter cap
24. Shift lever
25. Starter lockout cable
26. Cable clamp
27. Rope roller

Fig. MR20-28 – View showing location of neutral start switch (N) on 60 hp models.

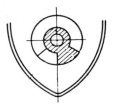

Fig. MR20-31 — With lower unit gears in neutral, install reverse cam (54—Fig. MR20-30) as shown.

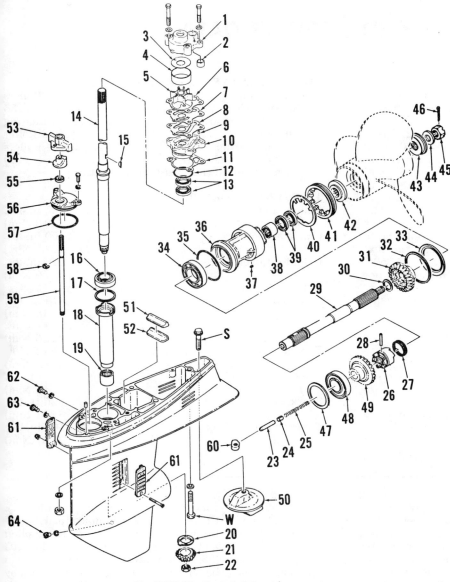

Fig. MR20-30 — Exploded view of gearcase.

1. Water pump housing	19. Needle bearing	35. "O" ring	51. Seal
2. Water tube seal	20. Thrust washer	36. Bearing housing	52. Seal plate
3. Plate	21. Pinion gear	37. Key	53. Reverse rod guide
4. Liner	22. Nut	38. Needle bearing	54. Reverse cam
5. Impeller	23. Cam follower	39. Seals	55. Seal
6. Gasket	24. Slide	40. Lockwasher	56. Shift rod guide
7. Plate	25. Spring	41. Nut	57. "O" ring
8. Gasket	26. Clutch	42. Thrust hub	58. "E" ring
9. Pin	27. Clip	43. Splined spacer	59. Shift rod
10. Base	28. Pin	44. Washer	60. Shift cam
11. Gasket	29. Propeller shaft	45. Nut	61. Water inlet cover
12. "O" ring	30. Thrust washer	46. Cotter pin	62. Vent plug
13. Seals	31. Reverse gear	47. Shim	63. Oil level plug
14. Drive shaft	32. Shim	48. Taper roller bearing	64. Fill plug
15. Key	33. Thrust washer	49. Forward gear	S. Cap screw
16. Taper roller bearing	34. Ball bearing	50. Trim tab	W. Cap screw
17. Shim			
18. Sleeve			

gear (21) and thrust washer (20) in gearcase—thrust washer grooves must be towards gear. Insert drive shaft (14) with bearing (16) cone, install nut (22) and tighten to 69-78 N·m (51-57 ft.-lbs.). Coat gears with gear paint or compound and check mesh position. It will be necessary to push down on end of drive shaft while checking mesh position. If gears do not mesh in center of teeth, add or remove shims (17) as necessary. After setting mesh position, check backlash between teeth of gears (21 and 49). Backlash should be 0.075-0.125 mm (0.003-0.005 in.). To increase backlash, delete shims (47); add shims (47) to decrease backlash. After adjusting backlash, recheck gear mesh position. Install bearings (34 and 38) in bearing housing (36) then install reverse gear (31), shims (32), thrust washer (33) and bearing housing (36) in gearcase and check backlash between gears (21 and 31). If backlash is not 0.15-0.25 mm (0.006-0.010 in.), add or delete shims (32) as required. Adding shims will increase backlash.

When reassembling, long splines of shift rod (59) should be toward top. Install shift cam (60) with "UP" marked side towards top. Assemble shift parts (23 through 28) in propeller shaft. Pin (28) should pass through hole in slide (24). Install a new "O" ring (35) and seals (39) in bearing housing with seal lips facing out towards propeller. Tighten nut (41) to 118-137 N·m (87-100 ft.-lbs.).

Install oil seals (13) in water pump base (10) with seal lips facing up towards impeller. With gears shifted to neutral, install reverse cam (54) as shown in Fig. MR20-31, then install shaft guide (53). Before attaching gearcase to drive shaft housing, apply water resistant grease to upper drive shaft splines and water tube seals. Place water tube into position and be sure gearcase is in neutral gear and shift control lever on engine is in neutral. Complete remainder of assembly by reversing disassembly procedure. Tighten propeller nut to 29.4-39.2 N·m (22-28 ft.-lbs.).

MARINER 50, 60 AND 70 HP (3 cyl.)

CONDENSED SERVICE DATA

TUNE-UP

Hp/rpm 50/5300-5800
                                  60/5000-5500
                                  70/5000-5500
Bore . . . . .2.875 in.
                                  (73.02 mm)
Stroke . . . . .2.559 in.
                                  (65 mm)
Displacement . . . . .49.8 cu.in.
                                  (816 cc)
Firing Order 1-3-2*
Compression at Cranking Speed . . . .†
Ignition . . . . .Solid State
Spark Plugs . . . . .See Text
Fuel:Oil Ratio 50:1
    *On models prior to serial number 5579017, firing order is 1-2-3.
    †Not more than 15 psi (103.5 kPa) variation between cylinders.

SIZES—CLEARANCES

Piston Rings:
  End Gap . . . .*
  Side Clearance . . . .*
Piston Skirt Clearance . . . .*
Crankshaft Bearing Type:
  Top Main . . . . .Ball Bearing
  Main Bearing (2) . . . . .Loose Rollers
    No. of Rollers 56

SIZES—CLEARANCES CONT.

  Main Bearing (3) . . . . .Loose Rollers
    No. of Rollers 56
  Bottom Main Bearing . . . . .Ball Bearing
  Crankpin . . . . .Caged Roller
Piston Pin Bearing . . . . .Loose Rollers
No. of Rollers (each rod) 29
*Publication not authorized by manufacturer.

TIGHTENING TORQUES

Connecting Rods . . . . .180 in.-lbs.
                                (20.3 N·m)
Crankcase Screws . . . . .200 in.-lbs.
                                (22.6 N·m)
Cylinder Cover . . . . .70 in.-lbs.
                                (7.9 N·m)
Exhaust Cover
   1/4 inch . . . . .115 in.-lbs.
                               (13 N·m)
   5/16 inch . . . . .200 in.-lbs.
                               (22.6 N·m)
Flywheel Nut . . . . .85 ft.-lbs.
                              (115.2 N·m)
Reed Screws . . . . .30 in.-lbs.
                                (3.4 N·m)
Spark Plugs . . . . .20 ft.-lbs.
                                (27.1 N·m)
Transfer Port Covers . . . . .160 in.-lbs.
                                (18.1 N·m)

LUBRICATION

The power head is lubricated by oil mixed with the fuel. Fuel should be regular leaded, low lead or unleaded gasoline with a minimum pump octane rating of 86. Recommended oil is Quicksilver Formula 50-D Outboard Lubricant. Normal fuel:oil ratio is 50:1; during engine break-in, fuel:oil ratio should be 25:1.

AutoBlend fuel and oil mixing system is used on Models 50 and 60 after 1985. The AutoBlend system is designed to deliver a constant 50:1 fuel:oil mixture to power head at all engine speeds. To provide sufficient lubrication during break-in of a new or rebuilt engine, a 50:1 fuel and oil mixture should be used in fuel tank in combination with AutoBlend fuel and oil mixing system.

Translucent filter (1—Fig. MR22-1) behind cover (2) should be inspected once per month and renewed each boating season or if sediment inside filter is evident. AutoBlend diaphragm plate should be inspected for cracking, swelling or deterioration once per year. To inspect diaphragm plate, remove eight screws securing main body cover (6) to main body (7), then remove clip securing diaphragm plate to pump shaft.

NOTE: Remove inner ring of screws to remove cover from main body. Outer ring of screws secures main body to reservoir.

Renew diaphragm plate as necessary. Reverse disassembly procedure to reassemble unit. Tighten eight main body cover screws in a crossing pattern to 30 in.-lbs. (3.4 N·m).

To check for proper operation of pump check valves, remove fuel hose and plug outlet (O). Remove fuel hose from inlet (I) and connect a suitable hand-held vacuum pump with gage to inlet (I). Check valves should hold steady vacuum with 8 inches HG (27 kPa) applied and allow leakage with 10 inches HG (33.8 kPa) is applied. Check valves can be removed for inspection or renewal by removing main body (7) from reservoir (5). Check valves are located under cover secured to top of pump by two screws. When reassembling, tighten main body screws in a crossing pattern to 30 in.-lbs. (3.4 N·m).

Lower unit gears and bearings are lubricated by oil contained in the gearcase. Recommended oil is Mariner Super Duty Gear Lube. Lubricant is drained by removing vent and drain plugs in the gearcase. Refill through drain plug hole until oil has reached level of vent plug opening, then allow 1 ounce (30 mL) of oil to drain from gearcase. Lower unit oil capacity is 12.5 fl.oz. (370 mL).

         Illustrations courtesy Mariner

FUEL SYSTEM

CARBURETOR. Standard make of carburetor is a center bowl type Mer-Carb. Two carburetors are used. Note that these carburetors are equipped with an enrichment valve (24—Fig. MR22-2) in place of a choke plate. Preliminary adjustment of idle mixture screw (19) is one turn out from a lightly seated position on all models. Recommended idle speed is 650-750 rpm with engine at normal operating temperature and in forward gear.

Standard main jet (10) size for elevations up to 2500 feet (762 m) are as follows: Model 50 hp—0.058 inch (1.47 mm); 70 hp models and 60 hp prior to serial number 4576237—0.086 inch (2.18 mm); 60 hp models after serial number 4576236—top carburetor 0.0785 inch (1.99 mm), bottom carburetor 0.072 inch (1.83 mm).

Standard vent jet (4) size for elevations up to 2500 feet (762 m) are as follows: Model 50 hp—0.096 inch (2.44 mm); 70 hp models and 60 hp models prior to serial number 4576237—0.066 inch (1.68 mm); 60 hp models after serial number 4576236—0.096 inch (2.44 mm).

When overhauling carburetor, drive float pins (16) and fuel inlet lever pin (18) out toward knurled end of pin. Insert plain end of pin first during assembly. Note that strong (0.034 in. dia. wire) throttle return spring must be used on top carburetor throttle shaft. Numbers on throttle plate (29) must face outward at closed throttle. Be sure rubber insert in fuel inlet valve seat (6) is installed so flat end of insert is toward inlet valve.

To determine the fuel level, invert carburetor body and measure distance (D—Fig. MR22-3) from the carburetor body to base of float (15). Distance (D) should be ¹¹/₁₆ inch (17.5 mm) on solid type float and ¹⁹/₃₂ inch (15.1 mm) on hollow type float. Adjust distance (D) by bending fuel inlet lever (17—Fig. MR22-4) within area (A).

SPEED CONTROL LINKAGE. To synchronize ignition and carburetor opening, proceed as follows: On models with an adjustable timing pointer, a dial indicator must be installed in the top cylinder and the indicator synchronized with the piston position (dial indicator reads zero when piston is at top dead center.)

NOTE: To prevent accidental starting from flywheel rotation, remove all spark plugs and properly ground plug wires.

Rotate the flywheel counterclockwise approximately ¼ turn past the 0.464 inch (12 mm) BTDC reading, then rotate flywheel clockwise until indicator face reads 0.464 inch (12 mm) BTDC. Note position of the timing pointer and reposition if timing pointer (P—Fig. MR22-5) is not aligned with dot (D) on timing decal. Loosen screw (S) to reposition. Remove the dial indicator assembly from the top cylinder after adjustment is completed and reassemble.

Connect a power timing light to the number 1 (top) spark plug wire. With the lower unit properly immersed, start the engine and shift the outboard motor into the "Forward" gear. Run the engine at 5000-5500 rpm. Adjust maximum ignition advance screw (M—Fig. MR22-6) until the timing pointer is aligned with the 23° BTDC mark on the timing decal. Secure ignition advance screw position with the locknut. Stop the engine and remove the timing light.

Move the spark lever until maximum advance screw (M) just contacts the stop boss and adjust secondary pickup screw (W) so carburetor cluster pin (R—Fig. MR22-7) is located on throttle actuator cam (C) as shown.

To prevent damage to the carburetor throttle plate at full throttle, adjust full throttle stop screw (F—Fig. MR22-6) so a clearance of 0.010-0.015 inch (0.25-0.38 mm) is between throttle actuator cam (C—Fig. MR22-8) and cluster

pin (R) when throttle lever is moved to the wide open position.

Adjust idle speed screw (I—Fig. MR22-6) as outlined in the previous CARBURETOR section.

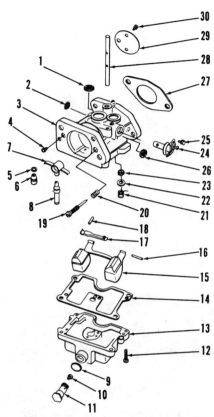

Fig. MR22-2—Exploded view of center bowl type MerCarb carburetor.

1. Welch plug (⁹/₁₆ inch)	16. Pin
2. Fuel inlet strainer	17. Fuel inlet lever
3. Body	18. Pin
4. Vent jet	19. Idle mixture screw
5. Gasket	20. Spring
6. Inlet needle & seat assy.	21. Spring
7. Venturi	22. Flat washer
8. Nozzle	23. Rubber seal
9. Gasket	24. Enrichment valve assy.
10. Main jet	25. Screw & lockwasher
11. Main jet plug	26. Welch plug (⁷/₁₆ inch)
12. Screw	27. Gasket
13. Float bowl	28. Throttle shaft
14. Gasket	29. Throttle plate
15. Float	30. Screw

Fig. MR22-1—View of AutoBlend fuel and oil mixing unit with cover (2) removed.

1. Filter
2. Cover
3. Drain plug
4. Warning horn
5. Reservoir
6. Main body cover
7. Main body
I. Inlet (gasoline)
O. Outlet (fuel & oil mixture)

Fig. MR22-3—To determine float level, invert the carburetor body and measure distance (D) from carburetor body to base of float (15). Distance (D) should be ¹¹/₁₆ inch (17.5 mm).

REED VALVES. The inlet reed valves are located on the intermediate main bearing assemblies. Two reed valve assemblies are used, one for each carburetor. The center cylinder receives a partial fuel:air charge from each reed valve and carburetor.

Reed petals (2–Fig. MR22-10) should be perfectly flat with no more than 0.007 inch (0.18 mm) clearance between free

Fig. MR22-4—Adjust float level by bending fuel inlet lever (17) within area (A).

end of reed petal and seating surface of center main bearing. Reed stop height (A) should be 0.180 inch (4.57 mm). Bend reed stop (1) to adjust. Reed petal seating surface on bearing housing must be smooth and may be refinished on a lapping plate after removing reed stops, reed valves and dowels. Do not attempt to bend or straighten a reed petal to modify performance or to salvage a damaged reed. Never install a bent reed. Lubricate the reed valve units with "Quicksilver" Multipurpose Lubricant or a light distributor cam grease when reassembling.

Each valve unit has four reeds which are available only as a matched set. Crankshaft must be removed before reed valve units can be serviced.

FUEL PUMP. All models are equipped with a diaphragm type fuel pump mounted on power head. Fuel pump is actuated by crankcase pulsations. Early models are equipped with first, second or third design "triangle" shaped pump and later 50- and 60-hp

models are equipped with a "square" shaped pump.

First, second and third design "triangle" shaped fuel pumps are similar. Third design pump is equipped with a filler block to retain check valves in pump housing in place of retainer (R–Fig. MR22-12).

Fuel pressure on "triangle" shaped pump should be minimum of 2 psi (13.8 kPa) at idle and 4 to 4½ psi (27.6-31.0 kPa) at wide-open throttle. Fuel pressure on "square" style pump should be minimum of 3 psi (20.7 kPa) at idle and 6-8 psi (41.4-55.2 kPa) at wide-open throttle.

When assembling first and second design "triangle" shaped pump, make sure tips of retainer (R—Fig. MR22-12) are facing away from check valves. On all "triangle" shaped pumps, install red colored check valve on inlet side of pump.

After installing check valve retainer (4—Fig. MR22-13) on "square" shaped fuel pump, trim off excess end of retainer (4) at ridge to prevent retainer from contacting pump diaphragm.

IGNITION SYSTEM

All models are equipped with a "Thunderbolt" solid state capacitor discharge ignition system consisting of trigger coils, stator, switch box and ignition coils. The trigger coils are contained in a trigger ring module under the flywheel. Diodes, SCR's and capacitors are contained in the switch box. Switch box, trigger ring module and stator must be serviced as unit assemblies.

Check all wires and connections before trouble-shooting ignition circuit. The following test specifications will aid trouble-shooting. Resistance between red and blue stator lead should be 5400-6200 ohms. Resistance between red stator lead and engine ground should be 125-175 ohms. Resistance between white, violet or brown trigger coil lead and white/black trigger coil lead should be 1100-1400 ohms.

Recommended spark plugs are AC V40FFM or Champion L76V.

COOLING SYSTEM

WATER PUMP. The rubber impeller type water pump is housed in the gear

Fig. MR22-5—Timing pointer (P) must align with dot (D) on flywheel timing decal when the piston of the top cylinder is 0.464 inch (12 mm) BTDC. Loosen screw (S) to reposition pointer (P).

Fig. MR22-7—Adjust secondary pickup screw (W—Fig. MR22-6) so carburetor cluster pin (R) locates on throttle actuator cam (C) as shown when maximum ignition advance screw (M—Fig. MR22-6) just contacts the stop boss.

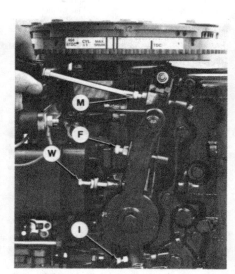

Fig. MR22-6—View showing location of maximum ignition advance screw (M), full throttle stop screw (F), secondary pickup screw (W) and idle speed screw (I). Refer to text.

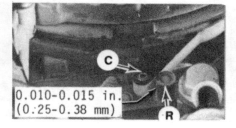

0.010-0.015 in. (0.25-0.38 mm)

Fig. MR22-8—Adjust full throttle stop screw (F—Fig. MR22-6) so there is 0.010-0.015 inch (0.25-0.38 mm) clearance between throttle actuator cam (C) and cluster pin (R) at full throttle.

case housing. The impeller is mounted on and driven by the lower unit drive shaft.

When cooling system problems are encountered, first check the water inlet for plugging or partial stoppage, then if not corrected, remove the gearcase housing as outlined in LOWER UNIT section and examine the water pump, water tubes and seals.

Water pump housing is plastic. Refer to assembly notes, cautions and tightening torques listed in the LOWER UNIT section when assembling.

POWER HEAD

R&R AND DISASSEMBLE. To remove the power head assembly, first disconnect the battery and remove the top side cowling. Remove electric starter, then disconnect all interfering wires and linkage. Remove the stud nuts which secure the power head to lower unit, then jar power head on exhaust side to loosen gasket. Lift power head from lower unit and install on a suitable stand. Remove the flywheel, stator assembly, trigger plate assembly and the carburetors. Exhaust manifold cover, cylinder block cover and transfer port covers should be removed for cleaning and inspection.

Remove the upper and lower crankcase end caps by using a suitable puller attached to threaded holes in caps. Remove the main bearing locking bolts from front crankcase half, remove the flange bolts; then remove crankcase front half by inserting screwdriver in the recesses provided on side flanges. Use extra care not to spring the parts or to mar the machined, mating surfaces. The crankcase half (1–Fig. MR22-14 and cylinder block assembly (2) are matched and align bored, and are available only as an assembly.

Crankshaft, pistons, bearings and connecting rods may now be removed for service as outlined in the appropriate following paragraphs. When assembling, follow the procedures outlined in the ASSEMBLY paragraph.

ASSEMBLY. When assembling, the crankcase must be completely sealed against both vacuum and pressure. Exhaust manifold and water passages must be sealed against pressure leakage. Whenever power head is disassembled, it is recommended that all gasket surfaces and machined joints without gaskets be carefully checked for nicks and burrs which might interfere with a tight seal.

Lubricate all bearing and friction surfaces with engine oil. Loose needle bearings may be held in place during

assembly using a light, nonfibrous grease.

After the crankshaft, connecting rods, pistons and main bearings are positioned in the cylinder, check the crankshaft end play. Temporarily install the crankshaft end caps (4 and 14–Fig. MR22-14) omitting "O" rings (5 and 12), but using shims (6 and 11) that were originally installed. Tighten the end cap to cylinder retaining screws. Use a soft hammer to bump the crankshaft each way to seat bearings, then measure end play.

Bump the crankshaft toward top and measure clearance between the top crankshaft counterweight and the end cap as shown in Fig. MR22-18. Bump the crankshaft toward bottom and again measure clearance between counterweight and top end cap. Subtract the first (minimum) clearance from the second clearance which will indicate the amount of end play. If end play is not within limits of 0.004-0.012 inch (0.102-0.305 mm), add or remove shims (6 and 11–Fig. MR22-14) as necessary, then recheck. The crankshaft should be centered by varying the amount of shims between upper (6) and lower (11) shim stacks. When centering the crankshaft, make certain that end play is correct.

Shims (6 and 11) are available in thicknesses of 0.002, 0.003, 0.005, 0.006, 0.008 and 0.010 inch.

All gaskets and sealing surfaces should be lightly and carefully coated with an impervious liquid sealer. Surface must be completely coated, using care that excess sealer does not squeeze out into bearings, crankcase or other passages.

Check the assembly by turning the crankshaft after each step to check for binding or locking which might indicate improper assembly. Remove the cause before proceeding. Rotate the crankshaft until each piston ring in turn appears in one of the exhaust or transfer ports, then check by pressing on ring with a blunt tool. Ring should spring back when released; if it does not, a broken or binding ring is indicated, and the trouble should be corrected.

Tighten the crankcase exhaust cover and cylinder cover cap screws by first tightening center screws, then tightening screws evenly working outward, away from center of crankcase. Tightening torques are given in the CONDENSED SERVICE DATA table.

PISTONS, PINS, RINGS AND CYLINDERS. Before detaching connecting rods from crankshaft, make sure that rod and cap are properly identified for correct assembly to each other and in the correct cylinder.

Piston rings are interchangeable in

the ring grooves and are pinned in place.

Maximum allowable cylinder bore wear or out-of-round is 0.004 inch (0.102 mm). Excessively worn or slightly

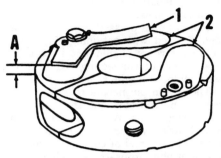

Fig. MR22-10—View of intermediate main bearing housing and reed valve assembly. Height (A) of reed stop should be 0.180 inch (4.57 mm).

Fig. MR22-12—View of early "triangle" shape fuel pump showing inlet (8) and discharge (9) check valves installed. Retainer (R) is secured by screws (10) and retainer tips must point away from check valves. Later design "Triangle" shape fuel pump is similar except a filler block is used to retain check valves (8 and 9) in place of retainer (R).

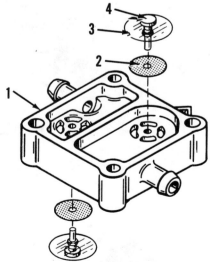

Fig. MR22-13—Exploded view of "square" style fuel pump body and check valves.

1. Body	3. Check valve (clear
2. Check valve (black	plastic)
rubber)	4. Retainer

damaged, standard size cylinders may be repaired by boring and honing to fit an oversize piston. Pistons and rings are available in 0.015 inch (0.38 mm) oversize on early models and 0.015 inch (0.38 mm) and 0.030 inch (0.76 mm) oversizes on later models.

Piston pin is pressed in piston bosses and secured with retaining rings. The retaining rings should not be reused. Piston end of connecting rod is fitted with 29 loose needle rollers.

The piston pin needle rollers use the connecting rod bore and the piston pin as bearing races. When assembling, install bearing washers and needle bearings in piston end of connecting rod using light nonfibrous grease to hold them in place. A Mariner special tool may be used to hold needles in position while positioning piston for installation. Piston must be installed so sharp, vertical side of deflector will be to starboard (intake) side of cylinder bore. Heat piston to approximately 135°F (57°C)

and press piston pin into place. Pin should be centered in piston. Use new piston pin retaining rings on each assembly.

CONNECTING RODS, BEARINGS AND CRANKSHAFT. Upper and lower ends of crankshaft are carried by ball bearings. The two center main bearings (18–Fig. MR22-16) also contain the inlet reed valve assemblies. Two split type outer races (21) each contain 56 loose bearing rollers in two rows. The outer race is held together by a retaining ring (23). The reed valve assembly (18) fits around outer race (21).

The connecting rod uses 29 loose rollers at the piston end and a caged roller bearing at the crankpin end.

Check rod for alignment by placing rod on a surface plate and checking with a light. Rod is bent or distorted if a 0.002 inch (0.051 mm) feeler gage can be inserted between rod and surface plate.

If bearing surface of rod and cap is rough, scored, worn or shows evidence of overheating, renew the connecting rod. Inspect crankpin and main bearing journals. If scored, out-of-round or worn, renew the crankshaft. Check the crankshaft for straightness using a dial indicator and "V" blocks.

Inspect and adjust the reed valves as outlined in REED VALVE paragraph, and reassemble as outlined in ASSEMBLY paragraph.

ELECTRICAL SYSTEM

Refer to Fig. MR22-20 for wiring diagram of electrical system.

The rectifier assembly is designed to protect the ignition switch box if battery terminals or harness plug becomes loose with motor running. However, the rectifier assembly (Fig. MR22-21) will be damaged. If battery terminals are reversed, the rectifier and the ignition switch box will be damaged. The motor

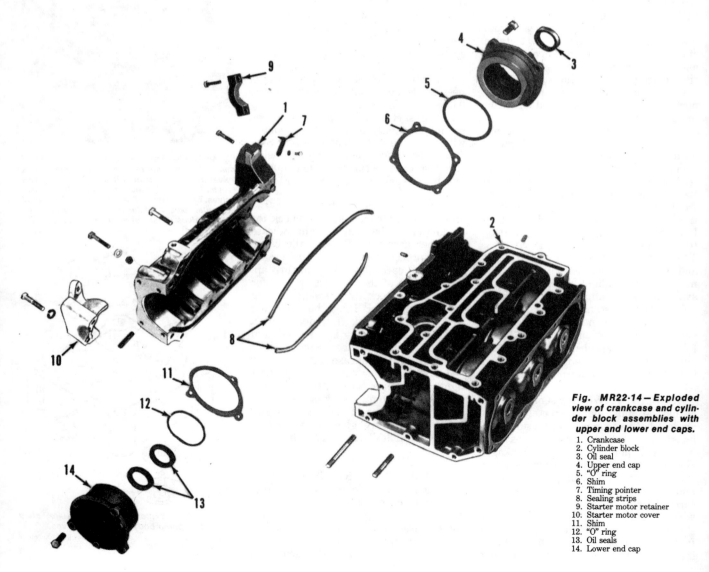

Fig. MR22-14 — Exploded view of crankcase and cylinder block assemblies with upper and lower end caps.

1. Crankcase
2. Cylinder block
3. Oil seal
4. Upper end cap
5. "O" ring
6. Shim
7. Timing pointer
8. Sealing strips
9. Starter motor retainer
10. Starter motor cover
11. Shim
12. "O" ring
13. Oil seals
14. Lower end cap

can be operated without rectifier if the two yellow/red wires (from the alternator) are disconnected from the rectifier and taped separately.

Refer to Fig MR22-21 for correct rectifier connections.

LOWER UNIT

PROPELLER AND DRIVE CLUTCH. Protection for the motor is built into a special cushioning clutch in the propeller hub. No adjustment is possible on the propeller or clutch. Various pitch propellers are available and propeller should be selected for best performance under applicable conditions. Propellers other than those designed for the motor must not be used.

R&R AND OVERHAUL. Most service on lower unit can be performed by detaching the gearcase housing from drive shaft housing. To remove the housing, remove the plastic plug and Allen screw from location (1 – Fig. MR22-23). Remove trim tab (2) and stud nut from under trim tab. Remove stud nut from location (3), two stud nuts (4) from each side and stud nut (5) if so equipped, then withdraw the lower unit gearcase assembly.

NOTE: Use caution to prevent loss of spring (68 – Fig. MR22-24) or plunger (67).

Remove the housing plugs and drain the housing, then secure gearcase in a vise between two blocks of soft wood, with propeller up. Wedge a piece of wood between propeller and antiventilation plate, remove the propeller nut, then remove propeller.

Disassemble the gearcase by removing the gearcase housing cover nut (61 – Fig. MR22-24). Clamp the outer end of propeller shaft in a soft jawed vise and remove the gearcase by tapping with a rubber mallet. Be careful not to lose key (56). Forward gear (43) will remain in housing. Withdraw the propeller shaft from bearing carrier (55) and reverse gear (51).

Clamp the bearing carrier (55) in a soft-jawed vise and remove reverse gear (51) and bearing (53) with an internal expanding puller and slide hammer. Remove and discard the propeller shaft rear seals (58 and 59).

To remove dog clutch (48) from propeller shaft, remove retaining ring (47). Insert cam follower (44) in hole in shaft and apply only enough pressure on end of cam follower to remove the spring pressure, then push out pin (49) with a small punch. The pin passes through

drilled holes in dog clutch and operates in slotted holes in propeller shaft.

To disassemble the drive shaft and associated parts, reposition gearcase in vise with drive shaft projecting upward.

Remove seal (16), splined seal (17), water pump body (23), impeller (25) and impeller drive key (26). Remove the flushing screw and withdraw the remainder of the water pump parts.

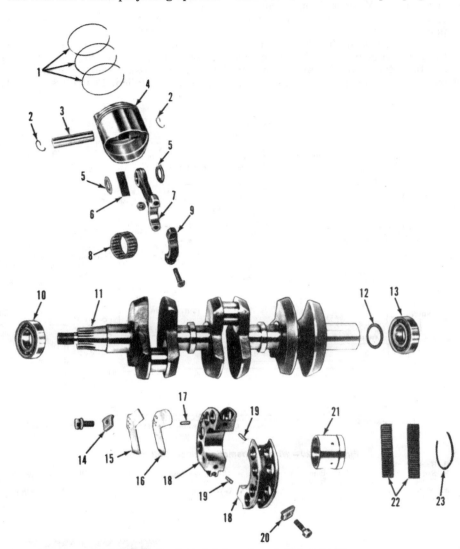

Fig. MR22-16 – Exploded view of crankshaft assembly.

1. Piston rings	12. Shim
2. Clips	13. Ball bearing
3. Piston pin	14. Clamp nut
4. Piston	15. Reed stop
5. Thrust washers	16. Reed petal
6. Needle bearings	17. Locating dowel
7. Connecting rod	18. Reed plate & main bearing housing
8. Caged roller bearing	19. Pin
9. Rod cap	20. Nut
10. Ball bearing	21. Outer race
11. Crankshaft	22. Needle bearings
	23. Retaining ring

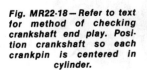

Fig. MR22-18 – Refer to text for method of checking crankshaft end play. Position crankshaft so each crankpin is centered in cylinder.

Clamp upper end of drive shaft in a soft-jawed vise, remove pinion retaining nut (15); then tap gearcase off drive shaft and bearing. Note the position and thickness of shims (11) on drive shaft upper bearing. Mesh position of pinion is controlled by shims (11) placed underneath the bearing.

After drive shaft has been removed, the forward gear (43) and bearing cone can be withdrawn. Use an internal expanding type puller to withdraw bearing cup if removal is required. Remove and save the shim pack (40).

Shift shaft (7) and cam (39) can be removed after removing forward gear and unscrewing bushing (5) from gearcase housing.

If gear wear was abnormal or if any parts that affect gear alignment were renewed, check and adjust gear mesh as follows: Install forward gear (43) and bearing (41) using shims (40) that were originally installed. Position shims (11) that were originally installed at bottom of bearing bore. Install bearing assembly (10) in housing bore against shims (11). Position the drive pinion (14) in housing and insert drive shaft (9), with bearing assembly (10) installed, into housing, bearing (13) and gear (14). Install retaining nut (15). Coat gears (14 and 43) with bearing blue and check mesh position. Due to the spiral cut gears, it will be necessary to press down on end of drive shaft while checking position. If gears do not mesh in center of teeth, add or remove shims (11) under bearing as necessary. After setting mesh position, check backlash between teeth of gears (14 and 43). Backlash should be within limits of 0.003-0.005 inch (0.076-0.127 mm). To increase clearance (backlash), remove part of shim stack (40) behind bearing cup. If gears are too loose, add shims. After changing thickness of shims (40), gears should be recoated with bearing blue and mesh position should be rechecked.

When reassembling, long splines on shift rod (7) should be toward top. Shift cam (39) is installed with notches up and toward rear. Assemble shifting parts (45, 46, 47, 48 and 49) into propeller shaft (50). Pin (49) should be through hole in slide (45). Position follower (44) in end of propeller shaft and insert shaft into bearing (42) and forward gear. Install the reverse gear and bearing carrier assembly using a new "O" ring (54) and seals (58 and 59). Install inner seal (58) with lip toward reverse gear and outer seal (59) with lip toward propeller. Upper oil seal (32) should be installed with lips facing up (toward engine) and lower oil seal (33) should be pressed into water pump base with lips facing down toward propeller shaft. Install remainder of water pump assembly and tighten the screws or nuts to the following recommended torque. Torque 1/4-28 nuts to 30 in.-lbs. (3.4 N·m). Torque 5/16-24 nuts to 40 in.-lbs. (4.5 N·m).

Place shaft (7) in neutral position. Install nylon spacer (2) with grooved side down and position reverse lock cam (1 – Fig. MR22-25) with high point (H) of cam positioned as shown in Fig. MR22-25.

Install splined seal (17 – Fig. MR22-24) on drive shaft splines with splined seal end toward top of drive shaft, then install seal (16) with small end towards top of drive shaft.

Before attaching gearcase housing to the driveshaft housing, make certain that shift cam (39) and the shift lever (on motor) are in neutral gear position. Complete assembly by reversing disassembly procedure. Make certain that spring (19) and plunger (18) are positioned before attaching gearcase to drive shaft housing.

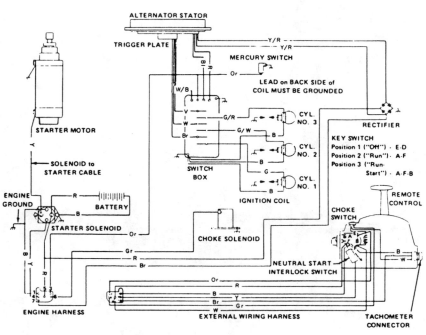

Fig. MR22-20 — Wiring schematic typical of all models.

B. Black			
R. Red	Bl. Blue	G/R. Green with red tracer	W/B. White with black tracer
V. Violet	Br. Brown		
W. White	Gr. Gray	G/W. Green with white tracer	Y/R. Yellow with red tracer
Y. Yellow	Or. Orange		

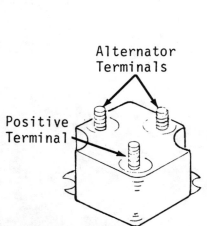

Fig. MR22-21 — Rectifier must be connected as shown or damage to the electrical system will result.

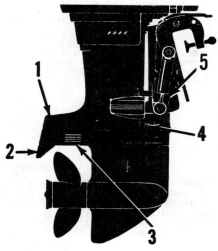

Fig. MR22-23 — To remove the lower unit gearcase assembly, remove the attaching screws and stud nuts from positions indicated.

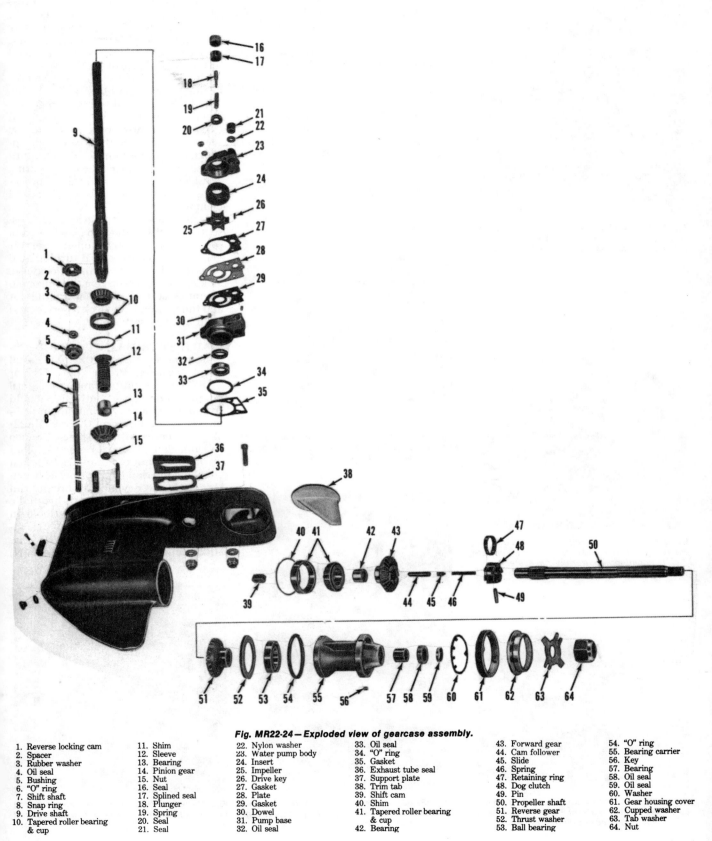

Fig. MR22-24 — Exploded view of gearcase assembly.

1. Reverse locking cam
2. Spacer
3. Rubber washer
4. Oil seal
5. Bushing
6. "O" ring
7. Shift shaft
8. Snap ring
9. Drive shaft
10. Tapered roller bearing
   & cup
11. Shim
12. Sleeve
13. Bearing
14. Pinion gear
15. Nut
16. Seal
17. Splined seal
18. Plunger
19. Spring
20. Seal
21. Seal
22. Nylon washer
23. Water pump body
24. Insert
25. Impeller
26. Drive key
27. Gasket
28. Plate
29. Gasket
30. Dowel
31. Pump base
32. Oil seal
33. Oil seal
34. "O" ring
35. Gasket
36. Exhaust tube seal
37. Support plate
38. Trim tab
39. Shift cam
40. Shim
41. Tapered roller bearing
   & cup
42. Bearing
43. Forward gear
44. Cam follower
45. Slide
46. Spring
47. Retaining ring
48. Dog clutch
49. Pin
50. Propeller shaft
51. Reverse gear
52. Thrust washer
53. Ball bearing
54. "O" ring
55. Bearing carrier
56. Key
57. Bearing
58. Oil seal
59. Oil seal
60. Washer
61. Gear housing cover
62. Cupped washer
63. Tab washer
64. Nut

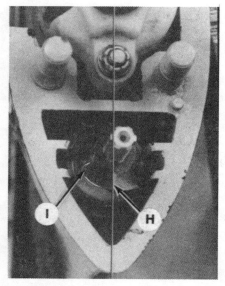

Fig. MR22-25 — The reverse lock cam (1) must be installed on shift shaft splines with high point (H) of cam positioned as shown when in neutral position.

POWER TILT/TRIM

Nonintegral Type (First and Second Design)

FLUID. Recommended fluid is SAE 10W-30 or 10W-40 automotive oil. With outboard in full up position, oil level should reach bottom of fill plug hole threads. Do not overfill. Be sure vent screw remains open to vent pump reservoir.

BLEEDING. To bleed air from hydraulic system on first design tilt/trim unit, position outboard at full tilt and engage tilt lock lever. Without discon-

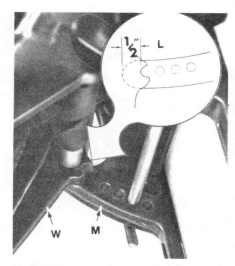

Fig. MR22-32 — Overlap (L) between swivel bracket flange (W) and clamp bracket flange (M) should be ½ inch (12.7 mm).

necting hoses, remove hydraulic trim cylinders. Be sure fluid reservoir is full and remains so during bleeding operation. Remove down circuit bleed screw (D—Fig. MR22-30) and "O" ring. Press "IN" control button for a few seconds, release button and wait approximately one minute. Repeat until expelled oil is air-free. Install "O" ring and bleed screw (D) and repeat procedure on opposite cylinder. Place cylinder in a horizontal position so bleed port (P—Fig. MR22-31) is up and remove up circuit bleed screw (U). Press "UP" and "UP/OUT" control buttons for a few seconds, release buttons and wait approximately one minute. Repeat until expelled oil is air-free. Install "O" ring and bleed screw (U) and repeat procedure on opposite cylinder. Reinstall cylinders.

Second design tilt/trim system is essentially self-bleeding. To bleed air from second design system, open reservoir vent screw two turns and turn manual release valve fully counterclockwise. Making sure reservoir remains full of oil, operate system through several full-out and full-in cycles. Recheck reservoir and refill as necessary.

ADJUST TRIM LIMIT SWITCH. Operate trim control so outboard is in full down position. Press "UP/OUT" or "UP" control button and hold until pump motor stops. Outboard should trim out and stop so a minimum of ½ inch (12.7 mm) overlap (L—Fig. MR22-32) exists between swivel bracket flange (W) and clamp bracket flange (M). Pull up on lower unit to remove slack when checking overlap (L). Note that if cylinder rods enter cylinders more than an additional ⅛ inch (3.2 mm), hydraulic system should be bled as outlined in BLEEDING section. If overlap (L) is incorrect, loosen retainer screw (R—Fig. MR22-33) then turn adjusting nut (N)

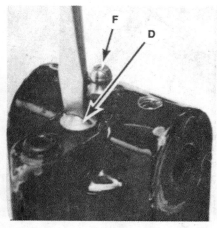

Fig. MR22-30 — View showing location of down circuit bleed screw (D) and grease fitting (F) on early nonintegral power tilt/trim system.

Fig. MR22-31 — View showing location of up circuit bleed screw (U) and bleed port (P) on early nonintegral power tilt/trim system.

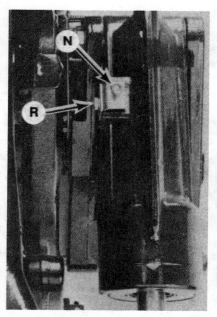

Fig. MR22-33 — Loosen retainer screw (R) and turn trim limit adjusting nut (N) to adjust trim limit switch.

Fig. MR22-34 — View of control valve showing location of up circuit hoses (U) and down circuit hoses (D).

Illustrations courtesy Mariner

counterclockwise to increase overlap or clockwise to decrease overlap. Retighten retainer screw (R) and recheck trim limit adjustment.

PRESSURE TEST. To check hydraulic system pressure, disconnect four hoses attached to control valve as shown in Fig. MR22-34; small hoses are up circuit and large hoses are down circuit.

NOTE: Test gages may be connected at control valve or trim cylinder depending upon which location is more accessible.

Connect a suitable hydraulic pressure gage to one up circuit port (small) and another gage to down circuit port (large). Screw plugs into remaining ports. Check fluid reservoir and fill if necessary. Operate trim control in up direction and note pressure gage reading. Minimum pressure on first design system should be 3500 psi (24.1 MPa) on new pump with a red sleeve on wires or 3200-3500 psi (22.0-24.1 MPa) minimum on used pump with red sleeve on wires. Minimum pressure on all other new pumps (first design) is 3000 psi (20.7 MPa) and minimum pressure on all other used pumps (first design) is 2700-3000 psi (18.6-20.7 MPa). Minimum up pressure on all second design pumps is 2700 psi (18.6 MPa).

Release trim control button. Pressure will drop slightly after stabilizing but should not drop faster than 100 psi (690 kPa) every 15 seconds. Operate trim control in down direction and note pressure gage. Minimum pressure is 500-1000 psi (3.4-6.9 MPa). Release trim control button. Pressure will drop slightly after stabilizing but should not drop more than 100 psi (690 kPa) every 15 seconds. If pressure is normal, inspect trim cylinders and hoses for leakage. If pressure is abnormal, install a known good control valve and recheck pressure. If pressure remains abnormal, install a new pump body.

Integral Type

FLUID AND BLEEDING. Recommended fluid is Quicksilver Power Trim & Steering Fluid or a suitable Type F, FA or Dextron II automatic transmission fluid.

NOTE: Hydraulic system is under pressure. Fill plug (Fig. MR22-35) must not be removed unless outboard is in full up position and tilt lock lever is engaged. Be sure to securely tighten fill plug prior to lowering outboard motor.

To check fluid level, tilt motor to full up position, engage tilt lock lever and slowly remove fill plug (Fig. MR22-35).

Fluid should be visible in fill tube. Fill as necessary and securely tighten fill plug.

To determine if air is present in hydraulic system, trim motor out until both trim rods are slightly extended. Apply downward pressure on lower unit. If trim rods retract into cylinders more than 1/8 inch (3.2 mm), air is present and bleeding is required.

The hydraulic circuit is self-bleeding as the tilt/trim system is operated through several cycles. After servicing system, be sure to check reservoir level after filling and operating system.

Trim limit adjustment is not required. Port trim rod and piston assembly (15—Fig. MR22-36) is equipped with a check

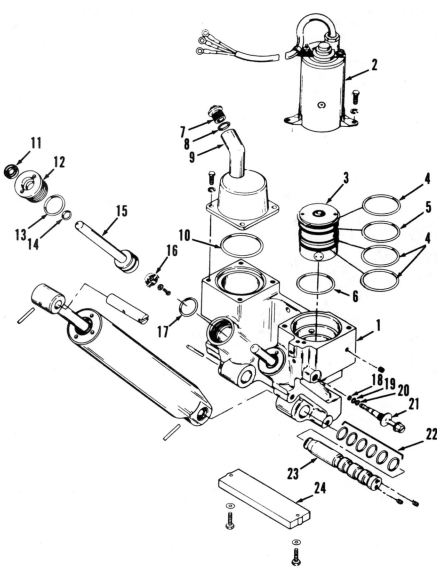

Fig. MR22-36—Exploded view of integral type power tilt/trim system.

1. Manifold	8. "O" ring	14. "O" ring	20. "O" ring
2. Motor	9. Reservoir cover	15. Trim piston & rod	21. Manual release
3. Pump assy.	10. Seal ring	16. Strainer	valve
4. "O" rings	11. Seal	17. "O" ring	22. "O" ring
5. "O" ring	12. Cap	18. "O" ring	23. Shaft
6. "O" ring	13. "O" ring	19. "O" ring	24. Anode plate
7. Fill plug			

Fill plug

Fig. MR22-35—View showing location of fill plug on integral type tilt/trim system.

valve designed to open at a specific pressure, limiting trim range to 20 degrees when engine speed exceeds 2,000 rpm. If engine speed falls below 2,000 rpm, trim angle may exceed 20 degrees; however, once engine speed exceeds 2,000 rpm, propeller thrust will increase pressure in trim cylinders causing check valve in port side trim rod to unseat, bypassing hydraulic fluid to the reservoir and lowering trim angle to 20 degrees maximum. Except for cleaning valve and strainer (16), check valve in port trim rod is not serviceable and should not be removed. If check valve malfunction is evident, renew port trim rod.

HYDRAULIC TESTING. The system can be checked by connecting a 5000 psi (34.5 MPa) test gage to the UP (U—Fig. MR22-38) and DOWN (D—Fig. MR22-39) ports. Prior to connecting test gage, place outboard motor in the full up position and engage tilt lock lever. Unscrew reservoir fill plug and rotate manual release valve (21—Fig. MR22-36) three to four turns counterclockwise to release pressure on system. Remove UP or DOWN Allen head test port plug and connect test gage with suitable adapter and hose. Install fill plug and rotate manual release valve clockwise until seated. System pressure when testing at UP (U—Fig. MR22-38) port should be a minimum of 1300 psi (8.9 MPa). System pressure when testing at DOWN (D—Fig. MR22-39) port should be a minimum of 500 psi (3.5 MPa). Release pressure on system as previously outlined prior to removing test gage. Reinstall Allen head plug.

OVERHAUL. Refer to Fig. MR22-36 for exploded view of manifold and trim cylinder components, and Fig. MR22-37 for exploded view if tilt cylinder components. Special socket 91-44487A1 and a spanner wrench is required to service trim and tilt cylinders. Keep all components clean and away from contamination. Keep components separated and label if necessary for correct reassembly. Lubricate all "O" rings or seal lips with Quicksilver Power Trim & Steering Fluid, Dexron II, Type F or Type FA automatic transmission fluid during reassembly.

Fig. MR22-38—Release pressure on system, then remove Allen head plug (U) and install a 5000 psi (34.5 MPa) test gage with a suitable adapter and hose to test system pressure when operated in the "UP" direction. View identifies location of manual release valve (21).

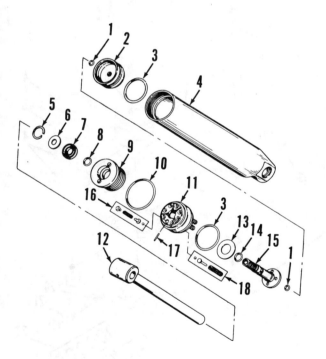

Fig. MR22-37—Exploded view of tilt cylinder assembly.

1. "O" ring
2. Cup
3. "O" ring
4. Cylinder
5. Circlip
6. Washer
7. Scraper
8. "O" ring
9. Cap
10. "O" ring
11. Piston
12. Rod
13. Washer
14. "O" ring
15. Rod end
16. Check valve assy.
17. Pin
18. Check valve assy.

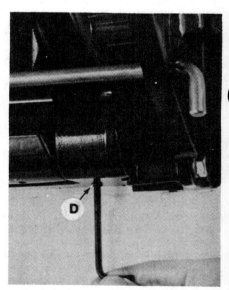

Fig. MR22-39—Release pressure on system, then remove Allen head plug (D) and install a 5000 psi (34.5 MPa) test gage with a suitable adapter and hose to test system pressure when operated in the "DOWN" direction.

MARINER 45, 50, 75, 80 AND 85 HP
(Inline 4-Cylinder)

CONDENSED SERVICE DATA

TUNE-UP

Hp/rpm:

Model 45 . . . . .45/5000-5500
(33.6 kW)

Model 50 .50/5000-5500*
(37.3 kW)

Model 75 . . . . .75/5000-5500
(56 kW)

Model 80 . . . . .80/4800-5500
(59.7 kW)

Model 85 . . . . .85/4800-5500
(63.4 kW)

Bore:

Models 45 & 50 . . . . .2.562 in.
(65.07 mm)

Models 75, 80 & 85 . . . . .2.875 in.
(73.02 mm)

Stroke:

Models 45 & 50 . . . . .2.125 in.
(54 mm)

Models 75, 80 & 85 . . . . .2.562 in.
(65.07 mm)

Displacement:

Models 45 & 50. . . . . .44 cu. in.
(721 cc)

Models 75, 80 & 85 . . . . .66.6 cu. in.
(1091.4 cc)

Firing Order 1-3-2-4
Compression at Cranking Speed . . . .†

Spark Plug:

AC V40FFK
Champion L78V

Ignition . . . . .Thunderbolt Breakerless

Idle Speed in Forward Gear:

Models 45 & 50 . . . . .600-700 rpm
Models 75, 80 & 85 . . . . .550-650 rpm

Fuel:Oil Ratio . . . . .50:1‡

*Full throttle engine speed on Model 50 prior to 1986 is 4800-5500 rpm.
†Compression variation between cylinders should not exceed 15 psi (103.4 kPa).
‡Models after 1985 may be equipped with AutoBlend fuel and oil mixing system.

SIZES—CLEARANCES

Piston Rings:

End Gap . . . . *

SIZES—CLEARANCES CONT.

Side Clearance . . . . *
Piston Skirt Clearance . . . . *

Crankshaft Bearing Type:

Top Main Bearing . . . . .Ball Bearing
Main Bearing (2) . . . . .Bushing with Reed Valve
Center Main Bearing . . . . .Roller†
Main Bearing (4) . . . . .Bushing with Reed Valve
Bottom Main Bearing . . . . .Ball Bearing
Crankpin . . . . .Roller†
Piston Pin Bearing . . . . .Roller†

*Publication not authorized by manufacturer.
†Refer to text for number of rollers at center main bearing, crankpin and piston pin.

TIGHTENING TORQUES

Connecting Rod. . . . . .180 in.-lbs.
(20.3 N·m)

Crankcase Screws . . . . .200 in.-lbs.
(22.6 N·m)

Cylinder Cover:

Models 45 & 50 . . . . .70 in.-lbs.
(7.9 N·m)

Models 75, 80 & 85 . . . . .85 in.-lbs.
(9.6 N·m)

Exhaust Cover:

Models 45 & 50 . . . . .200 in.-lbs.
(22.6 N·m)

Models 75, 80 & 85 . . . . .250 in.-lbs.
(28.2 N·m)

Flywheel:

Models 45 & 50 . . . . .65 ft.-lbs.
(88.1 N·m)

Models 75, 80 & 85 . . . . .100 ft.-lbs.
(135.6 N·m)

Reed Screws:

Models 45 & 50 . . . . .30 in.-lbs.
(3.4 N·m)

Models 75, 80 & 85 . . . . .25 in.-lbs.
(2.8 N·m)

Spark Plugs . . . . .240 in.-lbs.
(27.1 N·m)

Transfer Port Covers:

Models 45 & 50 . . . . .60 in.-lbs.
(6.8 N·m)

Models 75, 80 & 85 . . . . .85 in.-lbs.
(9.6 N·m)

LUBRICATION

The power head is lubricated by oil mixed with the fuel. Fuel should be regular leaded, low lead or unleaded gasoline with a minimum pump octane rating of 86. Recommended oil is Quicksilver Formula 50-D Outboard Lubricant. Normal fuel:oil ratio is 50:1; during engine break-in, fuel:oil ratio should be 25:1.

Models after 1985 may be equipped with AutoBlend fuel and oil mixing system. The AutoBlend system is designed to deliver a constant 50:1 fuel:oil mixture to power head at all engine speeds.

To provide sufficient lubrication during break-in of a new or rebuilt engine, a 50:1 fuel and oil mixture should used in fuel tank in combination with the AutoBlend system.

Translucent filter (1—Fig. MR24-1) behind cover (2) should be inspected once per month and renewed each boating season or if sediment inside filter is evident. AutoBlend diaphragm plate should be inspected for cracking, swelling or deterioration once per year. To inspect diaphragm plate, remove eight screws securing main body cover (6) to main body (7), then remove clip securing diaphragm plate to pump shaft.

NOTE: Remove inner ring of screws to remove cover from main body. Outer ring of screws secures main body to reservoir.

Renew diaphragm plate as necessary. Reverse disassembly procedure to reassemble unit. Tighten eight main body cover screws in a crossing pattern to 30 in.-lbs. (3.4 N·m).

To check for proper operation of pump check valves, remove fuel hose and plug outlet (O). Remove fuel hose from inlet (I) and connect a suitable vacuum pump with gage to inlet (I). Check valves should hold steady vacuum with 8 inches HG (27 kPa) vacuum applied and allow leakage with 10 inches HG (33.8 kPa) vacuum applied. Check valves can be removed for inspection or renewal by removing main body (7) from reservoir (5). Check valves are located under cover secured to top of pump by two screws. When reassembling, tighten main body screws in a crossing pattern to 30 in.-lbs. (3.4 N·m).

Lower unit gears and bearings are lubricated by oil contained in the gear-

case. Recommended oil is Quicksilver Super Duty Gear Lube. Lubricant is drained by removing vent and drain plugs in the gearcase. Refill through drain plug hole until oil has reached level of vent plug opening, then allow 1 ounce (30 mL) of oil to drain from gearcase. Lower unit oil capacity is 12.5 fl. oz. (370 mL) on Models 45 and 50 and 21 fl. oz. (621 mL) on Models 75, 80 and 85.

FUEL SYSTEM

45 And 50 HP Models

CARBURETOR. Refer to Fig. MR24-2 for exploded view of carburetor with integral fuel pump used on 45 and 50 hp models. Some models may be equipped with a similar carburetor without integral fuel pump.

Standard main jet (25) size for operation below 2500 feet (762 M) elevation is 0.055 inch (1.40 mm) on early 50 hp models and 0.057 inch (1.45 mm) on 45 hp and later 50 hp models. Initial setting of idle mixture screw (21) is $1\frac{1}{2}$ turns open on carburetors with integral fuel pump and $1\frac{1}{4}$ to $1\frac{3}{4}$ turns open on carburetors without integral fuel pump. Turning idle mixture screw clockwise will lean mixture. Make final mixture adjustment with engine running at normal operating temperature in forward gear.

To adjust float level, remove float bowl and invert carburetor. Measure distance from float to gasket surface as shown in Fig. MR24-3. Float level should be $\frac{15}{64}$ to $\frac{17}{64}$ inch (6-6.7 mm). Bend float tang (T) to adjust float level. Turn carburetor right side up and check float drop. Float drop should be $\frac{1}{32}$ to $\frac{1}{16}$ inch (0.8-1.6 mm) measured from float to highest point on main jet (25).

SPEED CONTROL LINKAGE. To synchronize ignition and carburetor opening, connect a power timing light to number 1 (top) spark plug wire. Run engine with outboard in forward gear. Open throttle until ignition timing is 7-9 degrees BTDC on models prior to serial number 5531630 or 2 degrees BTDC to 2 degrees ATDC on models after serial number 5531629. Then loosen actuator plate screws (S—Fig. MR24-4) and rotate actuator plate (P) so primary pickup arm (A—Fig. MR24-5) just contacts primary cam (C). Retighten actuator plate screws. Open throttle and adjust maximum ignition advance screw (A—Fig. MR24-6) so ignition timing is 32 degrees BTDC, then stop engine.

NOTE: Due to electronic characteristics of ignition system, maximum advance must

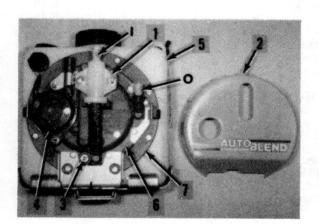

season or if sediment...

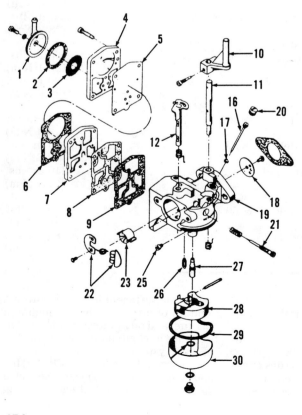

Fig. MR24-1—View of AutoBlend fuel and oil mixing unit with cover (2) removed.

1. Filter
2. Cover
3. Drain plug
4. Warning horn
5. Reservoir
6. Main body cover
7. Main body
I. Inlet (gasoline)
O. Outlet (fuel & oil mixture)

Fig. MR24-2—Exploded view of MerCarb type carburetor with integral fuel pump used on some 45 and 50 hp models. Some 45 and 50 hp models are equipped with a similar carburetor without integral carburetor.

1. Inlet fitting
2. Gasket
3. Screen
4. Cover
5. Diaphragm
6. Gasket
7. Pump body
8. Check valve diaphragm
9. Gasket
10. Throttle lever
11. Throttle shaft
12. Choke shaft
16. Idle tube
17. Gasket
18. Throttle plate
19. Carburetor body
20. Plug
21. Idle mixture screw
22. Choke shutter plates
23. Boost venturi
25. Main jet
26. Inlet needle
27. Main nozzle
28. Float
29. Gasket
30. Float bowl

be set at 32 degrees BTDC to obtain the desired 30 degrees BTDC at 5000 rpm.

Open throttle so maximum advance screw (A) just touches boss and adjust actuator plate secondary pickup screw (W—Fig. MR24-4) so screw just touches secondary pickup arm (R—Fig. MR24-7).

To prevent damage in carburetor throttle plate at full throttle, lightly hold carburetor throttle plate in full open position by turning secondary pickup arm (R). Adjust full throttle stop screw (B—Fig. MR24-6) so there is 0.010-0.015 inch (0.25–0.38 mm) clearance between secondary pickup screw (W—Fig. MR24-7) and pickup arm (R) when full throttle stop screw (B—Fig. MR24-6) just contacts boss.

Turn idle speed screw (I) to obtain idle speed of 550-650 rpm in forward gear on models prior to serial number 5531630 and 600-700 rpm on models after serial number 5531629.

REED VALVES. The inlet reed valves are located on the crankshaft second and fourth main bearing assemblies. Each reed valve passes fuel mixture from one of the carburetors to the two adjoining cylinders. The crankshaft must be removed before reed valve service can be performed.

Reed petals (2—Fig. MR24-8) should be perfectly flat with no more that 0.007 inch (0.18 mm) clearance between free end of reed petal and seating surface of center main bearing. Reed stop height (A) should be ⁵⁄₆₄ inch (3.97 mm). Reed petal seating surface on bearing housing must be smooth and may be refinished on a lapping plate after

removing reed stops, reed valves and dowels. Do not attempt to bend or straighten reed petals. Reed petals should be renewed in complete sets. Renew petal locating pin if damaged.

When installing reed petals, place the reed petal with the cut-out notch (N) to the left as shown.

FUEL PUMP. Some 45 and 50 hp models are equipped with diaphragm type fuel pump mounted on carburetor as shown in Fig. MR24-2. The manufacturer recommends renewing fuel pump gaskets and diaphragms if pump is disassembled.

Some 45 and 50 hp models are equipped with a "square" style fuel pump mounted on power head. Fuel pressure on "square" fuel pump should be a minimum of 2 psi (13.8 kPa) at idle speed and 5.5-6.5 psi (37.9-44.8 kPa) at full throttle.

Renew pump gaskets and diaphragms if pump is disassembled. After installing check valve retainers (4—Fig. MR24-9), trim off excess end of retainer (4) at ridge to prevent retainer from contacting pump diaphragm. Tighten pump assembly mounting screws to 60 in.-lbs. (6.8 N·m).

75, 80 And 85 HP Models

CARBURETOR. Two Mercarb carburetors are used on 75, 80 and 85 hp models. Refer to Fig. MR24-10 for an exploded view of carburetor. Note that these carburetors are equipped with an enrichment valve (24) in place of a choke plate. Initial adjustment of idle mixture screw (19) is one turn open. Standard main jet (10) size for operation below 2500 feet (762 m) altitude is 0.090 inch (2.29 mm). Vent jet (4) size for operation below 2500 feet (762 m) altitude is 0.072 inch (1.83 mm).

When overhauling carburetor, drive float pins (16) and fuel inlet lever pin (18) out toward knurled end of pin. Insert plain end of pin first during assembly. Note that strong (0.034 in. dia. wire) throttle return spring must be used on top carburetor throttle shaft. Numbers on throttle plate (29) must face outwards at closed throttle. Be sure rubber insert

Fig. MR24-4—View of actuator plate (P) and secondary pickup adjusting screw (W) on 45 and 50 hp models. Refer to text for adjustment.

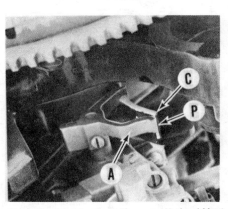

Fig. MR24-5—Primary pickup arm (A) should just contact primary cam (C) at point (P) with ignition timing at 7-9 degrees BTDC on models prior to serial number 5531630, or, 2 degrees BTDC to 2 degrees ATDC on models after serial number 5531629.

Fig. MR24-6—View showing location of ignition timing adjustment screws (A & B) and idle speed screw (I) on 45 and 50 hp models.

Fig. MR24-3—Float level should be ¹⁵⁄₆₄ to ¹⁷⁄₆₄ inch (6-6.7 mm) from float to gasket surface. Float drop is measured with carburetor upright from top of main jet (25) to float. Refer to text.

in fuel inlet valve seat (6) is installed so flat end of insert is towards inlet valve.

To determine the float level, invert the carburetor body and measure distance (D–Fig. MR24-11) from the carburetor body to base of float (15). Distance (D) should be 11/16 inch (17.5 mm) and is adjusted by bending fuel inlet lever (17–Fig. MR24-12) within area (A).

SPEED CONTROL LINKAGE. Check ignition timing pointer alignment as follows: Install a dial indicator gage in number 1 (top) spark plug hole and turn flywheel clockwise until piston is 0.464 inch BTDC. Loosen retaining screw and position timing pointer so that it is aligned with ".464 BTDC" mark on flywheel.

Connect a power timing light to number 1 (top) spark plug wire. Run engine with outboard in forward gear and open throttle until primary cam (B–Fig. MR24-14) just touches throttle lever primary pin (A). Primary cam should contact primary pin at 2°-4°

Fig. MR24-11—To determine float level, invert the carburetor body and measure distance (D) from the carburetor body to base of float (15). Distance (D) should be 11/16 inch (17.5 mm).

Fig. MR24-12—Adjust float level by bending fuel inlet lever (17) within area (A).

Fig. MR24-7—Adjust full throttle stop screw (B—Fig. MR24-6) so 0.010-0.015 inch (0.25-0.38 mm) clearance exists between secondary pickup arm (R) and screw (W) at full throttle.

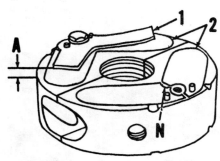

Fig. MR24-8—Intermediate main bearing and reed valve for 50 hp models. Reed petals (2) are right and left hand units. When installing reed petals, place the reed with the cut-out notch (N) on the left as shown.

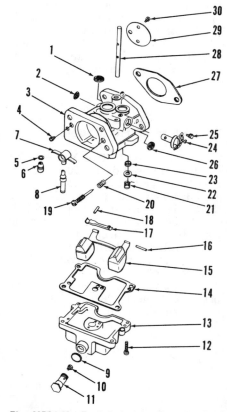

Fig. MR24-10—Exploded view of center bowl type Mercarb carburetor.

1. Welch plug (9/16 inch)
2. Fuel inlet strainer
3. Body
4. Vent jet
5. Gasket
6. Inlet needle & seat assy.
7. Venturi
8. Nozzle
9. Gasket
10. Main jet
11. Main jet plug
12. Screw
13. Float bowl
14. Gasket
15. Float
16. Pin
17. Fuel inlet lever
18. Pin
19. Idle mixture screw
20. Spring
21. Spring
22. Flat washer
23. Rubber seal
24. Enrichment valve assy.
25. Screw & lockwasher
26. Welch plug (7/16 inch)
27. Gasket
28. Throttle shaft
29. Throttle plate
30. Screw

Fig. MR24-14—View of throttle pickup pins (A & C) and cams (B & D) used on 75, 80 and 85 hp models.

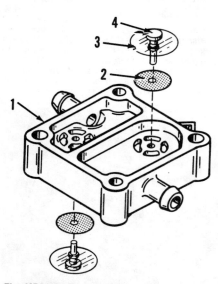

Fig. MR24-9—Exploded view of "square" style fuel pump body and check valves used on some 45 and 50 hp models.

1. Body
2. Check valve (black rubber)
3. Check valve (clear plastic)
4. Retainer

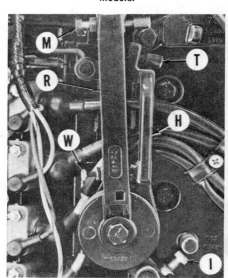

Fig. MR24-15—View of throttle (H) and spark (R) control arms on 75, 80 and 85 hp models.

BTDC on models below serial number 4423112 or 2° BTDC to 2° ATDC on models after serial number 4423111. Turn pickup adjustment screw (W – Fig. MR24-15) to obtain desired pickup point. Open throttle and turn maximum advance adjustment screw (M) so spark arm (R) movement will stop at 27° BTDC. Stop engine.

Carburetor throttle plate must not act as stop for wide open throttle. To prevent damage to carburetor, lightly hold carburetor throttle plate in full open position by turning upper carburetor throttle lever. Adjust full throttle stop screw (T) so there is 0.010-0.015 inch (0.25-0.38 mm) between throttle lever secondary pin (C – Fig. MR24-14) and secondary cam (D) when throttle arm (H – Fig. MR24-15) is in wide open position.

Idle speed should be 550-650 rpm with outboard in forward gear. Turn idle speed screw (1) to adjust idle speed.

REED VALVES. The inlet reed valves are located on the crankshaft second and fourth main bearing assemblies. Each reed valve unit passes fuel mixture from one of the carburetors to the two adjoining cylinders.

Reed petals (2 – Fig. MR24-17) should be perfectly flat with no more than 0.007 inch (0.178 mm) clearance between free end of reed petal and seating surface of center main bearing. Reed stop height should be 0.162 inch (4.11 mm). If reed petals have indented reed block, then reed block should be renewed. Do not attempt to bend or straighten reed petals.

FUEL PUMP. All models are equipped with a diaphragm type fuel pump mounted on the starboard side of power head. Fuel pressure at idle speed should be 2½-3½ psi (17-24 kPa) while fuel pressure at full throttle should be 4¼-5½ psi (29-36 kPa).

When assembling fuel pump install check valves as shown in Fig. MR24-19 with tips of retainer (3) pointing away from check valves.

IGNITION SYSTEM

These models are equipped with a solid state capacitor discharge ignition system consisting of trigger coils, stator, switch box and ignition coils. The trigger coils are contained in a trigger ring module under the flywheel. Diodes, SCR's and capacitors are contained in the switch box. Switch box, trigger ring module and stator must be serviced as unit assemblies. A wiring diagram is shown in Fig. MR24-21.

Check all wires and connections prior to trouble-shooting ignition system. The following test specifications will aid trouble-shooting: Resistance between blue/white stator leads should be 5700-8000 ohms or 5900-6900 ohms on models equipped with stator part 398-5454A21. Resistance between red and red/white stator leads should be 56-75 ohms or 125-175 ohms on models equipped with stator part 398-5454A21. Resistance between trigger coil brown and white/black leads or trigger coil white and violet leads should be 700-1000 ohms.

Ignition coil primary winding resistance should be 0.02-0.04 ohm. Secondary winding resistance should be 800-1100 ohms. No continuity should exist between ignition coil high tension terminal and coil positive (+) or negative (−) terminals on "orange" colored coil. On "blue" or "black" colored coil, 800-1100 ohms resistance should be present between coil high tension terminal and positive (+) or negative (−) terminal.

NOTE: On "orange" colored ignition coils, ground wire leading from back side of coils must be positioned so coils are grounded to engine when installed.

Recommended spark plugs are AC V40FFK or Champion L78V. Surface gap spark plugs should be renewed when center electrode is more than 1/32 inch (0.8 mm) below flat surface of plug.

COOLING SYSTEM

WATER PUMP. The rubber impeller type water pump is housed in the gearcase housing. The impeller is mounted on and driven by the lower unit drive shaft.

When cooling system problems are encountered, first check the water inlet for plugging or partial stoppage, then if not corrected, remove the gearcase as outlined in LOWER UNIT section and examine the water pump, water tubes and seals.

When assembling, observe the assembly notes, cautions and tightening torques listed in the LOWER UNIT section.

POWER HEAD

REMOVE AND DISASSEMBLE. To remove the power head assembly, first disconnect the battery and remove the top and side cowling. Remove electric starter, then disconnect fuel line, all interfering wires and linkage. Remove the stud nuts which secure the power head to lower unit then jar power head on exhaust side to loosen gasket. Lift power head from lower unit and install on a suitable stand. Remove flywheel, ignition components, alternator and carburetors. Exhaust manifold cover, cylin-

Fig. MR24-17—View of intermediate main bearing and reed valve assembly used on 75, 80 and 85 hp models.

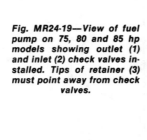

Fig. MR24-19—View of fuel pump on 75, 80 and 85 hp models showing outlet (1) and inlet (2) check valves installed. Tips of retainer (3) must point away from check valves.

der block cover and transfer port covers should be removed for cleaning and inspection.

Remove the main bearing locking bolts from front crankcase half, remove the flange bolts; then remove crankcase front half by inserting screwdriver in the recesses provided on side flanges. Use extra care not to spring the parts or to mar the machined, mating surfaces. Gently tap end caps off crankshaft. The crankcase half (6–Fig. MR24-23 or MR24-24) and cylinder assembly (15) are matched and align bored, and are available only as an assembly.

Crankshaft, pistons, bearings and connecting rods may now be removed for service as outlined in the appropriate following paragraphs. When assembling, follow the procedures outlined in the ASSEMBLY paragraph.

ASSEMBLY. When assembling, the crankcase must be completely sealed against both vacuum and pressure. Exhaust manifold and water passages must be sealed against pressure leakage.

Whenever power head is disassembled, it is recommended that all gasket surfaces and machined joints without gaskets be carefully checked for nicks and burrs that might interfere with a tight seal. On 75, 80 and 85 hp models, make certain that threaded holes in cylinder for attaching water jacket cover (20—Fig. MR24-24) are cleaned.

Lubricate all bearing and friction surfaces with engine oil. Loose needle bearings may be held in place during assembly using a light, nonfibrous grease.

After the crankshaft, connecting rods, pistons and main bearings are positioned in the cylinder, check crankshaft end play. Temporarily install crankshaft end caps (2 and 13—Fig. MR24-23 or MR24-24) omitting sealing rings (4 and 9), but using shims (3 and 10) that were originally installed. Tighten end cap to cylinder retaining screws. Use a soft hammer to bump crankshaft each way to seat bearings, then measure end play.

To measure end play, bump the crankshaft toward top, and measure

clearance between top crankshaft counterweight and end cap as shown in Fig. MR24-26. Bump crankshaft toward bottom and again measure clearance between counterweight and end cap. Subtract first (minimum) clearance from second clearance, which will indicate the amount of end play. If end play is not within limits of 0.004-0.012 inch (0.102-0.305 mm) on 75 hp models or 0.008-0.012 inch (0.203-0.305 mm) on all other models, add or remove shims (3 or 10—Fig. MR24-23 or MR24-24) as necessary, then recheck. The crankshaft should be centered by varying the amount of shims between upper (3) and lower (10) shim stacks. When centering crankshaft, make certain that end play is correct.

On 45 and 50 hp models, apply a continuous $1/16$ inch (1.6 mm) bead of Loctite Master Gasket Sealer (part 92-12564-1) to mating surface of crankcase half (6—Fig. MR24-23). Place bead to the inside of screw holes. Make sure bead is continuous, but avoid excess application.

On all other models (models equipped with seal strips (23—Fig. MR24-24), apply a thin even coat of Permatex #2 Form-a-Gasket Sealer (part 92-72592-1) to mating surface of crankcase half (6). Make sure sealer covers entire mating surface, but avoid excess application.

On 75, 80 and 85 hp models, clean the gasket surfaces and threaded holes of the water jacket cover (20—Fig. MR24-24) and cylinder (15). Coat the first four threads of all screws (22) with Resiweld and allow to set for 10 minutes. Coat gasket surface of water jacket cover and mating surface of cylinder with gasket sealer, then install gasket (21) and water jacket cover (20). Tighten screws (22) evenly from the center outward to a torque of 200 in.-lbs. (22.6 N·m) on early models and 150 in.-lbs. (16.9 N·m) on later models.

On all models, check the assembly by turning the crankshaft after each step to check for binding or locking, which might indicate improper assembly. Remove the cause before proceeding. Rotate the crankshaft until each piston ring in turn appears in one of the exhaust or transfer ports, then check by pressing on ring with a blunt tool. Ring should spring back when released; if it does not, a broken or binding ring is indicated, and the trouble should be corrected.

Tighten the crankcase, exhaust cover and cylinder cover cap screws beginning with screws in center of crankcase and working outward. Tightening torques are given in the CONDENSED SERVICE DATA table.

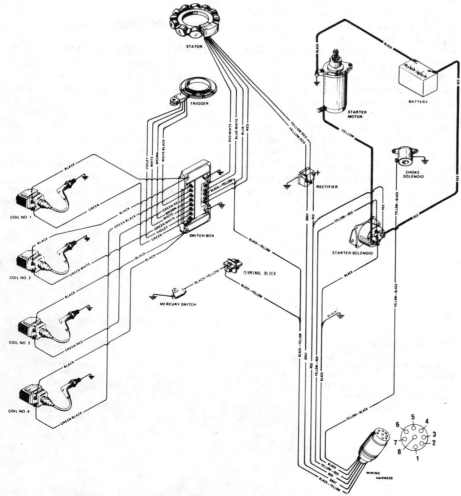

Fig. MR24-21—Wiring diagram for 75 hp and later 80 hp models. Other models are similar.

PISTONS, PINS, RINGS AND CYLINDERS. Before detaching connecting rods from crankshaft, make sure that rod and cap are properly identified for correct assembly to each other and in the correct cylinder.

Maximum allowable cylinder bore wear or out-of-round is 0.004 inch (0.102 mm). Worn or slightly damaged, standard size, cylinders may be repaired by boring and honing to fit an oversize piston. Pistons and rings are available in 0.015 inch (0.38 mm) oversize on early models and 0.015 inch (0.38 mm) and 0.030 inch (0.76 mm) oversizes on later models.

Piston rings are interchangeable in the ring grooves and are pinned in place.

Piston pin is pressed in piston bosses and secured with retaining rings. The retaining rings should not be reused. Two types of retaining rings have been used and must NOT be interchanged. The 45 and 50 hp models use "G" rings; the 75, 80 and 85 hp models use "C" type retaining rings. Piston end of connecting rod is fitted with loose needle rollers. Refer to the CONNECTING RODS, BEARINGS AND CRANKSHAFT section for number of rollers used.

The piston pin needle rollers use the connecting rod bore and the piston pin as bearing races. When assembling, install bearing washers and needle bearings in piston end of connecting rod using suitable needle bearing assembly grease to hold bearing rollers in place. On 75, 80 and 85 hp models, use a torch lamp or suitable equivalent to heat piston to approximately 190°F (88°C), then install and center the piston pin. Special tools are available from the manufacturer for installing and centering the piston pin. Piston must be installed so that sharp, vertical side of deflector will be to starboard (intake) side of cylinder block.

Assemble the connecting rod and piston assemblies, together with the main bearing units to the crankshaft; then install the complete assembly in cylinder half of block. Number 2 and number 3 piston should be started into cylinders first. If available, use the special ring compressor kit (part C-91-31461A2 for 45 and 50 hp models, or part C-91-47844A2 for 75, 80 and 85 hp models). If special ring compressor kit is not available, carefully compress each ring with the fingers. Thoroughly lubricate pistons and rings during reassembly.

CONNECTING RODS, BEARINGS AND CRANKSHAFT. Upper and lower ends of crankshaft are carried by ball bearings. The second and fourth main bearings (10—Fig. MR24-25) also contain the inlet reed valves. The third main

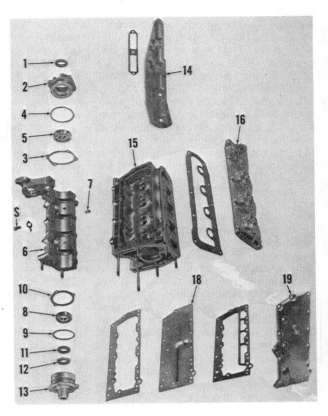

Fig. MR24-23—Exploded view of crankcase and related components used on 45 and 50 hp models.

S. Main bearing screw
1. Oil seal
2. End cap
3. Shim
4. "O" ring
5. Ball bearing
6. Crankcase half
7. Dowel pins
8. Ball bearing
9. "O" ring
10. Shim
11. Oil seal
12. Oil seal
13. End cap
14. Transfer port cover
15. Cylinder half
16. Cylinder cover
18. Exhaust plate
19. Exhaust cover

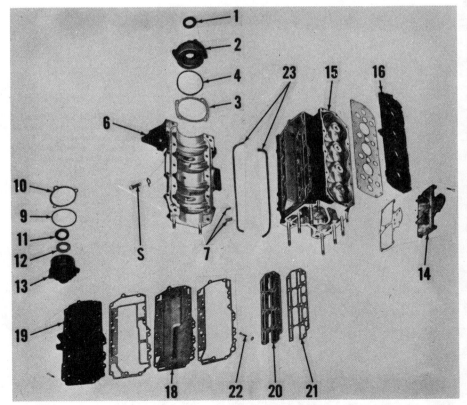

Fig. MR24-24—Exploded view of crankcase and associated parts used on 75, 80 and 85 hp models. Refer to Fig. MR24-23 for parts identification except for: 20. Water jacket cover; 21. Gasket; 22. Screw; 23. Seal strips.

bearing (13) contains loose needle rollers (15) that ride in a split-type outer race (14), held together by a retaining ring (16).

The 45 and 50 hp models use 27 loose needle rollers while 75, 80 and 85 hp models use 28 loose needle rollers in connecting rod small end. The crankpin end of connecting rod contains 25 loose needle rollers on 45 and 50 hp models. A caged roller bearing assembly is used at crankpin end of connecting rod on 75, 80 and 85 hp models. Some 45 and 50 hp models use 28 loose needle rollers (single row bearing) in main bearings and other 45 and 50 hp models use 56 loose rollers (double row bearing) in main bearings. The 75, 80 and 85 hp models use 56 loose needle rollers in main bearings. The manufacturer recommends renewing connecting rod bearings during reassembly.

Check connecting rod for alignment by placing rod on a surface plate and checking with a light and feeler gage. Rod is bent or distorted if 0.002 inch (0.05 mm) feeler gage can be inserted between rod and surface plate.

If bearing surface of rod and cap is rough, scored, worn or shows evidence of overheating, renew the connecting rod. The manufacturer recommends always renewing rod cap screws and nuts.

Apply a suitable thread locking compound to threads of rod cap screws during assembly.

Inspect crankpin and main bearing journals. If scored, out-of-round or worn, renew the crankshaft. Check the crankshaft for straightness using a dial indicator and ''V'' blocks.

Inspect and adjust the reed valves as outlined in REED VALVE section. Complete reassembly as outlined in ASSEMBLY section.

MANUAL STARTER

Refer to Fig. MR24-28 for exploded view of rewind starter used on early 45 and 50 hp models. Rewind starter used on later models is similar except later model starter is equipped with one pawl (12) instead of three as on early models.

Remove the top cowl and the rewind starter assembly from power head. Insert a suitable screwdriver in slot in top of sheave shaft (19) and loosen nut (3). Note that nut (3) has left-hand threads. Allow the screw driver and shaft (19) to turn clockwise until rewind spring unwinds. Pry anchor (22) out of starter handle and remove anchor and handle from rope. Remove nut (3), invert the assembly and remove remaining starter components from housing (5) making

sure rewind spring (7) remains in housing recess as pulley (10) is removed. Remove spring (7) and allow spring to unwind slowly. Care must be taken during spring removal to prevent personal injury.

Lubricate the components with Quicksilver Multipurpose Lubricant, and reassemble by reversing the disas-

Fig. MR24-26—Refer to text for method of checking crankshaft end play. The crankshaft should be centered in the cylinder block.

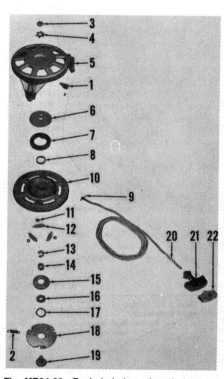

Fig. MR24-28—Exploded view of rewind starter assembly typical of the type used on early 45 and 50 hp models. Starter used on later models is similar.

1. Rope guide	12. Pawls
2. Spring	13. Bushing
3. Nut	14. Spacer
4. Lockwasher	15. Retainer
5. Starter housing	16. Washer
6. Retainer	17. Wave washer
7. Rewind spring	18. Plate
8. Bushing	19. Sheave shaft
9. Rope retaining pin	20. Rope
10. Pulley	21. Handle
11. Wave washers	22. Anchor

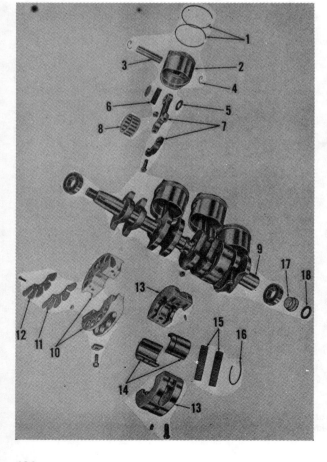

Fig. MR24-25—Exploded view of crankshaft and related components on 75, 80 and 85 hp models. Models 45 and 50 hp are similar.

1. Piston rings
2. Piston
3. Piston pin
4. Retainers
5. Bearing washers
6. Needle rollers
7. Connecting rod
8. Caged needle bearing
9. Crankshaft
10. Intermediate main bearing
11. Reed petals
12. Reed stop
13. Main bearing
14. Outer race
15. Needle rollers
16. Retaining ring
17. Seal retainer
18. Seal

sembly procedure. Install spring guide bushing (8) with chamfered end toward pulley (10). Make sure that pawls (12) are installed with radius to outside and identification dot facing away from pulley (10). Install retainer (15) with cup end facing out and position washer (16) and wave washer (17) in cup. Make certain that tang on spring retainer (6) engages slot in sheave shaft (19). Position starter with end of shaft (19) through housing (5) and install lockwasher (4) and nut (3). Pull free end of rope through starter housing and install handle (21) and anchor (22). Turn pulley shaft (19) counterclockwise until handle is pulled against starter housing, plus an additional 1¼ turns on early model starter and an additional 2 turns on later models, then tighten nut (3). Pull rope to check for proper starter operation.

Loosen neutral start interlock cable attaching screw and position cable so starter operates properly when outboard shifted into the NEUTRAL position only.

ELECTRICAL SYSTEM

Refer to Fig. MR24-21 for a typical wiring diagram. Note the following cautions when servicing electrical components:

DO NOT reverse battery connections. Battery negative (-) terminal is grounded.

DO NOT ''spark'' battery connections to check polarity.

DO NOT disconnect battery cables while engine is running.

DO NOT crank engine if ignition switch boxes are not grounded to engine.

LOWER UNIT

PROPELLER AND DRIVE CLUTCH. Protection for the motor is built into a special cushioning clutch in the propeller hub. No adjustment is possible on the propeller or clutch. Various pitch propellers are available and propeller should be selected to provide full throttle engine operation within rpm range listed in CONDENSED SERVICE DATA table at the beginning of section. Propellers other than those designed for the motor must not be used.

R&R AND OVERHAUL. Most service on lower unit can be performed by detaching gearcase housing from driveshaft housing. To remove housing, remove plastic plug and Allen screw from location (1—Fig. MR24-30). Remove trim tab (2) and screw from under trim tab. Remove stud nut from location (3), and stud nut (5) if so equipped, then withdraw the lower unit gearcase assembly.

NOTE: Do not lose plunger (67—Fig. MR24-32) or spring (68) on 45 and 50 hp models.

Remove plugs and drain oil from housing, then secure gearcase in a soft-jawed vise, with propeller up. Wedge a piece of wood between propeller and antiventilation plate, remove propeller nut, then remove propeller.

Disassemble gearcase by removing gearcase housing cover nut (61—Fig. MR24-32 or MR24-34). Clamp outer end of propeller shaft in a soft-jawed vise

and remove the gearcase by tapping with a rubber mallet. Be careful not to lose key (59) or shims (47). Forward gear (40) will remain in housing. Withdraw propeller shaft from bearing carrier (56) and reverse gear (46).

Clamp bearing carrier (56) in a soft-jawed vise and remove reverse gear (46) and bearing (49) with an internal expanding puller and slide hammer. Remove and discard propeller shaft rear seals (58).

To remove dog clutch (43) from propeller shaft, remove retaining ring (44). Insert cam follower (8) in hole in shaft and apply only enough pressure on end of cam follower to remove spring pressure, then push out pin (42) with a small punch. The pin passes through drilled holes in dog clutch and operates in slotted holes in propeller shaft.

To disassemble the drive shaft and associated parts, reposition gearcase in vise with drive shaft projecting upward. Remove rubber slinger (11), water pump body (16), impeller (19) and impeller drive key (20). Remove flushing screw and withdraw remainder of water pump parts. Clamp upper end of drive shaft in a soft-jawed vise, remove pinion retaining nut or screw (37); then tap gearcase off drive shaft and bearing. Note position and thickness of shims (30 and 30A) on drive shaft upper bearing. On all models, mesh position of pinion is controlled by shims (30) placed underneath the bearing. On models with ball-type upper bearing, shims (30A) control shaft end play. The shims are identical, but should not be interchanged or mixed, except to adjust mesh position of drive pinion.

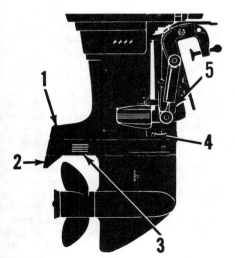

Fig. MR24-30—To remove the lower unit gearcase assembly, remove the attaching screws and stud nuts for position indicated.

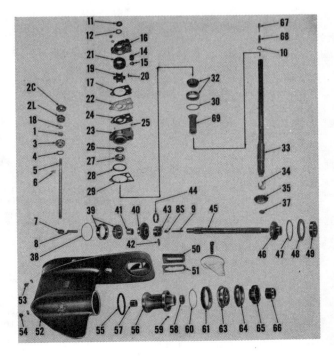

Fig. MR24-32—Exploded view of gearcase assembly used on 45 and 50 hp models. Components (63 and 65) are not used on later models. Two seals (58) are used on later models. Shim (47) is not used on later models. Refer to Fig. MR24-34 for component identification.

After drive shaft has been removed, forward gear (40) and bearing cone can be withdrawn. Use an internal expanding-type puller to withdraw bearing cup if removal is required. Remove and save shim pack (38).

Shift shaft (5) and cam (7) can be removed after removing forward gear and unscrewing bushing (3) from gearcase housing.

If abnormal gear wear is noted, or if any components that affect gear alignment were renewed, check and adjust gear mesh as follows: Install forward gear (40—Fig. MR24-32 or MR24-34) and bearing (39) using shims (38) that were originally installed. Position shims (30) that were originally installed at bottom of bearing bore. On 45 and 50 hp models, install bearing cup (32—Fig. MR24-32) in housing bore against shims (30). On all models, position drive pinion (35—Fig. MR24-32 or MR24-34) in housing and insert drive shaft (33), with bearings (32 and 34) installed, into housing.

On 75, 80 and 85 hp models, the ball bearing (32) must be firmly seated in housing bore. On all models, install retaining screw or nut (37). Coat gears (35 and 40) with bearing blue and check mesh position. On 45 and 50 hp models, it will be necessary to push down on upper end of drive shaft while checking mesh position. On all models, if gears do not mesh in center of teeth, add or remove shims (30) under bearing as necessary. After setting mesh position, check backlash between teeth of gears (35 and 40). Backlash should be 0.003-0.005 inch (0.08-0.13 mm) for 45 and 50 hp models, 0.014-0.016 inch (0.36-0.41 mm) for 85 hp models and 0.008-0.012 inch (0.20-0.30 mm) for 75 and 80 hp models. To increase backlash, decrease thickness of shim pack (38) behind bearing cup. To decrease backlash, add to thickness of shim pack (38). After changing thickness of shims (38), gear mesh pattern should be rechecked.

Install bearing (49), thrust washer (48)

and reverse gear (46) in bearing carrier (56). To check reverse gear (46) backlash on early models equipped with shims (47), install bearing carrier and gear assembly using shims (47) that were originally installed. If backlash is not within limits of 0.003-0.005 inch (0.08-0.13 mm) on 45 and 50 hp models or 0.006-0.008 inch (0.15-0.20 mm) on 75, 80 and 85 hp models, vary thickness of shim pack (47) as necessary to obtain the proper reverse gear backlash.

When reassembling, long splines on shift rod (5—Fig. MR24-32 or MR24-34) should be toward top. Shift cam (7) is installed with notches up and toward rear. Assemble shifting parts (9, 8S, 43, 42 and 44) into propeller shaft (45). Pin (42) should be through hole in slide (8S). Position follower (8) in end of propeller shaft and insert shaft into bearing (41) and forward gear. Install the reverse gear and bearing carrier assembly using new seals (55 and 58). Lip of inner seal (58) should face in and lip of outer seal (58) should face propeller (out).

On 75, 80 and 85 hp models, install shims (30A) above bearing and position new gasket (29) and water pump base (23) on housing. Add shims (30A) until the water pump base stands out slightly from gasket, then measure clearance between gasket and water pump base with a feeler gage. Remove shims (30A) equal to 0.002-0.003 inch (0.051-0.076 mm) less than clearance measured. When water pump is tightened down, compression of a new gasket (29) will be sufficient to hold bearing (32) in position with zero clearance.

Upper oil seal (26) should be installed with lips facing up (toward power head) and lower oil seal (27) should be pressed into water pump base with lips facing down. Install remainder of water pump assembly and tighten the screws or nuts to the following recommended values: Tighten 1/4-28 nuts to 24-30 in.-lbs. (2.7-3.4 N·m). Tighten 5/16-24 nuts to 35-40 in.-lbs. (3.9-4.5 N·m). Tighten 1/4-20 screws to 15-20 in.-lbs. (1.7-2.2 N·m).

Lower spacer (2L—Fig. MR24-32 or MR24-34) is installed with groove down. Install reverse locking cam shown in Fig. MR24-35 with high part of cam aligned as shown with unit in neutral. Push rod guide (2G—Fig. MR24-34) is located in drive shaft housing of all models.

Before attaching gearcase housing to the drive shaft housing, make certain that shaft cam (7—Fig. MR24-32 or MR24-34) and the shift lever (on motor) are in forward gear position on early models and neutral position on late models. In forward gear position, shift shaft (5) should be in clockwise position (viewed from top end of shaft). Complete assembly by reversing disassembly procedure.

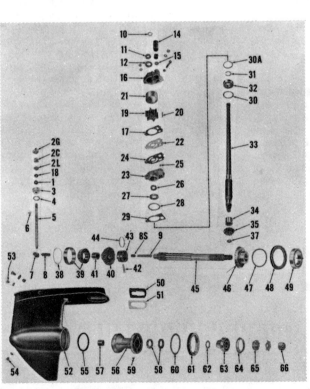

Fig. MR24-34 — Exploded view of gearcase assembly used on 75, 80 and 85 hp models. Shim (47) is not used on later models.

1. Oil seal	16. Water pump body	33. Drive shaft	50. Exhaust tube seal
2C. Reverse locking cam	17. Gasket	34. Roller bearing	51. Support plate
2G. Push rod guide	18. Rubber washer	35. Drive pinion	52. Gear housing
2L. Lower spacer	19. Impeller	37. Nut	53. Vent screw
3. Bushing	20. Drive key	38. Shim	54. Filler screw
4. "O" ring	21. Insert	39. Tapered roller	55. "O" ring
5. Shift shaft	22. Plate	bearing	56. Bearing carrier
6. Snap ring	23. Pump base	40. Forward gear	57. Roller bearing
7. Shift cam	24. Gasket	41. Roller bearing	58. Oil seals
8. Cam follower	25. Dowel	42. Cross pin	59. Key
8S. Slide	26. Oil seal	43. Dog clutch	60. Washer
9. Spring	27. Spring loaded oil seal	44. Retaining ring	61. Gear housing cover
10. "O" ring	28. "O" ring	45. Propeller shaft	62. Thrust washer
11. Rubber ring (slinger)	29. Gasket	46. Reverse gear	63. Thrust hub
12. Oil seal	30 & 30A. Shims	47. Shim	64. Cupped washer
14. Seal	31. Snap ring	48. Thrust washer	65. Splined washer
15. Nylon washer	32. Ball bearing	49. Ball bearing	66. Propeller nut

On 45 and 50 hp models, make certain that spring (68—Fig. MR24-32) and plunger (67) are properly positioned prior to attaching gearcase to drive shaft housing.

POWER TILT/TRIM

Non-Integral Type

FLUID. Recommended fluid is SAE 10W-30 or 10W-40 automotive oil. With outboard in full up position, oil level should reach bottom of fill plug hole threads. Do not overfill.

BLEEDING. To bleed air from hydraulic system, position outboard at full tilt and engage tilt rock lever. Without disconnecting hoses, remove hydraulic trim cylinders. Be sure fluid reservoir is full and remains so during bleeding op-

eration. Remove down circuit bleed screw (D—Fig. MR24-40) and "O" ring. Press "IN" control button for a few seconds, release button and wait approximately one minute. Repeat until expelled oil is air-free. Install "O" ring and bleed screw (D) and repeat procedure on opposite cylinder. Place cylinder in a horizontal position so bleed port (P—Fig. MR24-41) is up and remove up circuit bleed screw (U). Press "UP" and "UP/OUT" control buttons for a few seconds, release buttons and wait approximately one minute. Repeat until expelled oil is air-free. Install "O" ring and bleed screw (U) and repeat procedure on opposite cylinder. Reinstall cylinders.

ADJUST TRIM LIMIT SWITCH. Operate trim control so outboard is in full down position. Press "UP/OUT" or "UP" control button and hold until pump motor stops. Outboard should tilt up and stop so there is ½ inch (12.7 mm) overlap (L–Fig. MR24-42) between swivel

bracket flange (W) and clamp bracket flange (M). Pull up on lower unit to remove slack when checking overlap (L). Note that if cylinder rods enter cylinders more than an additional ⅛ inch (3.17 mm), that hydraulic system should be bled of air as outlined in BLEEDING section. If overlap (L) is incorrect, loosen retainer screw (R – Fig. MR24-43) then turn adjusting nut (N) counterclockwise to increase overlap or clockwise to decrease overlap. Retighten retainer screw (R) and recheck adjustment.

PRESSURE TEST. To check hydraulic system pressure, disconnect four hoses attached to control valve as shown in Fig. MR24-44; small hoses are for up

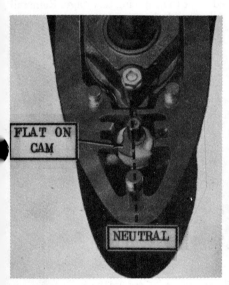

Fig. MR24-35—View of reverse lock cam with a single cam. Cam must be in position shown when lower unit (and shift shaft) is in neutral.

Fig. MR24-41—View showing location of up circuit bleed screw (U) and bleed port (P).

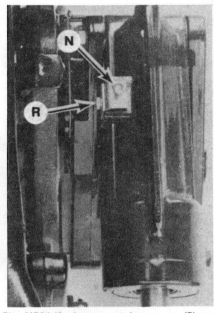

Fig. MR24-43—Loosen retainer screw (R) and turn trim limit adjusting nut (N) to adjust trim limit switch.

Fig. MR24-40—View showing location of down circuit bleed screw (D) and grease fitting (F).

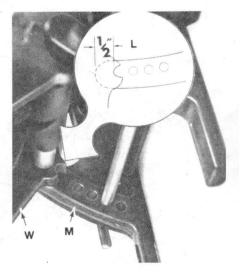

Fig. MR24-42—Overlap (L) between swivel bracket flange (W) and clamp bracket flange (M) should be ½ inch (12.7 mm).

Fig. MR24-44—View of control valve showing location of up circuit hoses (U) and down circuit hoses (D).

circuit while large hoses are for down circuit. Connect a pressure gage to one up circuit port (small) of control valve and another pressure gage to one down circuit port (large). Screw plugs into remaining ports. Check fluid reservoir and fill if necessary. Operate trim control in up direction and note pressure gage reading. Minimum pressure should be 3500 psi (24.1 MPa) on new pumps with a red sleeve on wires or 3200-3500 psi (22.0-24.1 MPa) minimum on used pumps with red sleeve on wires. Minimum pressure on all other new pumps is 3000 psi (20.7 MPa) while minimum pressure on all other used pumps is 2700-3000 psi (18.6-20.7 MPa). Release trim control button. Pressure will drop slightly after stabilizing but should not drop faster than 100 psi (690 kPa) every 15 seconds. Operate trim control in down direction and note pressure gage reading. Minimum pressure is 500-1000 psi (3.4-6.9 MPa). Release trim control

button. Pressure will drop slightly after stabilizing but should not drop faster than 100 psi (690 kPa) every 15 seconds. If pressure is normal, inspect trim cylinders and hoses for leakage. If pressure is abnormal, install a good control valve and recheck pressure. If pressure remains abnormal, install a new pump body.

Integral Type

FLUID AND BLEEDING. Recommended fluid is Dexron II or Type AF automatic transmission fluid. Remove fill plug (7 – Fig. MR24-50) and fill reservoir until fluid is visible in fill tube with the outboard motor in the full-up position.

The hydraulic circuit is self-bleeding as the tilt/trim system is operated through several cycles. After servicing system, be sure to check reservoir level after filling and operating.

HYDRAULIC TESTING. The system can be checked by connecting a 5000 psi (34.5 MPa) test gage to the UP (U – Fig. MR24-52) and DOWN (D – Fig MR24-53) ports. Prior to connecting test gage, place outboard motor in the full-up position and engage tilt lock lever. Unscrew reservoir fill plug and rotate manual release valve (21 – Fig. MR24-52) three to four turns counterclockwise to release pressure on system. Remove UP or DOWN Allen head test port plug and connect test gage with suitable adapter and hose. Install fill plug and rotate manual release valve clockwise until seated. System pressure when testing at UP (U) port should be a minimum of 1300 psi (8.9 MPa). System pressure when testing at DOWN (D – Fig. MR24-53) port should be a minimum of 500 psi (3.5 MPa). Release pressure on system as previously outlined prior to removing test gage. Reinstall Allen head plug.

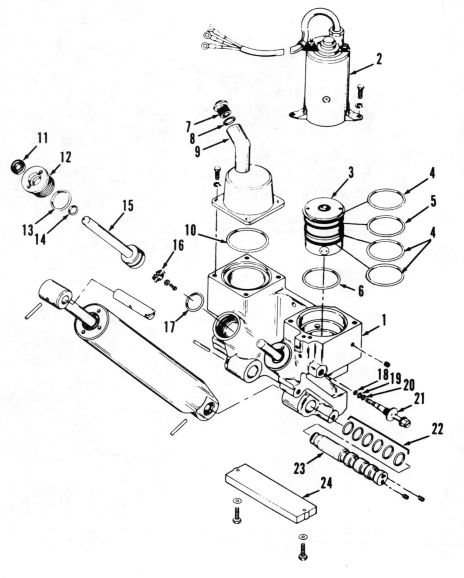

Fig. MR24-50—Exploded view of integral type power tilt/trim system

1. Manifold
2. Electric motor
3. Pump assy.
4. "O" rings (2.614 in. [66.40 mm] ID)
5. "O" rings (2.739 in. [69.57 mm] ID)
6. "O" rings (2.739 in. [69.57 mm] ID)
7. Fill plug
8. "O" ring (0.583 in. [14.81 mm] ID)
9. Reservoir cover
10. Seal ring
11. Seal
12. Cap
13. "O" ring (1.475 in. [37.47 mm] ID)
14. "O" ring (0.612 in. [15.54 mm] ID)
15. Trim piston & rod
16. Strainer
17. "O" ring (1.248 in. [31.70 mm] ID)
18. "O" ring (0.114 in. [2.90 mm] ID)
19. "O" ring (0.208 in. [5.28 mm] ID)
20. "O" ring (0.239 in. [6.07 mm] ID)
21. Manual release valve
22. "O" rings (0.989 in. [25.12 mm] ID)
23. Shaft
24. Anode plate

OVERHAUL. Refer to Fig. MR24-50 for an exploded view of manifold and trim cylinder components, and Fig. MR24-51 for an exploded view of tilt cylinder components. Special Mercury socket 91-44487A1 and a spanner wrench is required to service trim and tilt cylinders. Keep all components clean and away from contamination. Keep components separated and label if needed for correct reassembly. Note "O" ring sizes as stated in legends of Figs. MR24-50 and MR24-51. Lubricate all "O" rings or seal lips with Dexron II or Type AF automatic transmission fluid during assembly.

Fig. MR24-52—Release pressure on system, then remove Allen head plug (U) and install a 5000 psi (34.5 MPa) test gage with a suitable adapter and hose to test system pressure when operated in the "UP" direction. View identifies location of manual release valve (21).

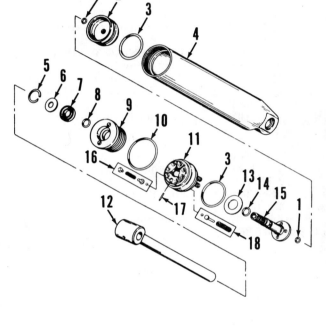

Fig. MR24-51—Exploded view of tilt cylinder components.

1. "O" ring (0.307 in. [7.79 mm] ID)
2. Cup
3. "O" ring (1.957 in. [49.71 mm] ID)
4. Cylinder
5. Circlip
6. Washer
7. Scraper
8. "O" ring (0.854 in. [21.69 mm] ID)
9. Cap
10. "O" ring (2.067 in. [52.5 mm] ID)
11. Piston
12. Rod
13. Washer
14. "O" ring (0.661 in. [16.79 mm] ID)
15. Rod end
16. Check valve assy.
17. Pin
18. Check valve assy.

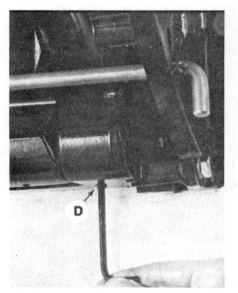

Fig. MR24-53—Release pressure on system, then remove Allen head plug (D) and install a 5000 psi (34.5 MPa) test gage with a suitable adapter and hose to test system pressure when operated in the "DOWN" direction.

MARINER 75 AND 90 HP 3-CYLINDER (AFTER 1986)

CONDENSED SERVICE DATA

TUNE-UP

Hp/rpm:

Model 75 . . . . 75/4750-5250
(56 kW)

Model 90 . . . . 90/5000-5500
(67.1 kW)

Bore . . . . 3.375 in.
(85.72 mm)

Stroke . . . . 2.650 in.
(67.31 mm)

Displacement . . . . 71.12 cu. in.
(1165.4 cc)

Compression at Cranking Speed . . . . *

Firing Order 1-3-2

Ignition Type . . . . CDI

Spark Plug:

   NGK BUHW-2

   AC V40FFK

   Champion L78V

Idle Speed (in gear) . . . . 650-700 rpm

Fuel:Oil Ratio . . . . See Text

Gearcase Oil Capacity . . . . 22.5 fl. oz.
(665.3 mL)

*Compression should not vary more than 15 psi (103.5 kPa) between cylinders.

SIZES-CLEARANCES

Piston Rings:

   End Gap . . . . *

   Side Clearance . . . . *

Piston Skirt Clearance . . . . 0.005 in.
(0.13 mm)

Crankshaft Bearing Type:

   Top Main Bearing . . . . Caged Roller

   Center Main Bearings . . . . Loose Roller

      Number of Rollers . . . . 32 Each

   Bottom Main Bearing . . . . Ball Bearing

Crankpin . . . . Caged Roller

Piston Pin Bearing:

   Type . . . . Loose Roller

   Number of Rollers . . . . 29 Each

*Publication not authorized by manufacturer.

TIGHTENING TORQUES

Connecting Rod . . . . *

Crankcase Cover . . . . †

Crankcase End Cap (Lower) . . . . 150 in.-lbs.
(17 N·m)

Cylinder Block Cover . . . . 165 in.-lbs.
(18.6 N·m)

Exhaust Cover . . . . 165 in.-lbs.
(18.6 N·m)

Flywheel Nut . . . . 120 ft.-lbs.
(162.7 N·m)

Fuel Pump Screws . . . . 40 in.-lbs.
(4.5 N·m)

Intake Manifolds . . . . 150 in.-lbs.
(17 N·m)

Power Head-to-Drive Shaft Housing . . . . 165 in.-lbs.
(18.6 N·m)

Reed Block . . . . 60 in.-lbs.
(6.8 N·m)

Spark Plugs . . . . 20 ft.-lbs.
(27.1 N·m)

*Tighten connecting rod screws to 15 in.-lbs. (1.7 N·m), check rod-to-cap alignment then tighten to 30 ft.-lbs. (40.7 N·m). After tightening to 30 ft.-lbs. (40.7 N·m), tighten screws an additional 90 degrees.

†Tighten large inner crankcase cover screws to 25 ft.-lbs. (33.9 N·m) and small screws to 165 in.-lbs. (18.6 N·m).

LUBRICATION

The power head is lubricated by oil mixed with the fuel. All models are equipped with oil injection. The oil injection pump delivers oil relative to crankshaft speed and throttle position. The recommended fuel is regular leaded, premium low-lead or unleaded gasoline with minimum octane rating of 86. The recommended oil is Quicksilver 2-Cycle Outboard Oil.

During break-in of a new or rebuilt engine (initial 30 gallons [113.6 L] of fuel), use a 50:1 fuel and oil mixture in the fuel tank in combination with the oil injection system to ensure sufficient power head lubrication. After using the first 30 gallons (113.6 L) of fuel, switch to straight gasoline in the fuel tank.

The lower unit gears and bearings are lubricated by oil contained in the gearcase. The recommended gearcase oil is Quicksilver Super Duty Gear Lubricant. Gearcase capacity is 22.5 fl. oz. (665.3 mL). The lower unit gearcase should be drained and refilled after initial 25 hours of operation, then after every 100 hours or seasonally thereafter. Fill gearcase through drain/fill plug hole until oil reaches the first vent plug hole. Refer to Fig. MR25-1. Install first vent plug and continue filling until oil reaches second vent plug hole. When oil reaches second vent plug hole, drain approximately one ounce (30 mL) to allow for oil expansion.

Make sure vent and fill plugs are securely tightened with new gaskets if necessary.

FUEL SYSTEM

CARBURETOR. Refer to Fig. MR25-2 for exploded view of typical WME carburetor. Three WME-8 carburetors are used on 75 hp models and three WME-10 carburetors are used on 90 hp models. Carburetor model number may be stamped on face of air box mounting flange on early models or is stamped on top of mounting flange on all other models.

Initial setting of slow speed mixture screw (5) is 1¼ turns open from a light-

SERVICE MANUAL

Mariner 75 & 90 HP 3 cyl. (After 1986)

ly seated position on each carburetor. Final slow speed mixture adjustment should be performed with engine running at normal operating temperature, in forward gear, with the correct propeller installed and boat in the water, or with the correct test wheel installed and lower unit submersed in a suitable test tank.

Air calibration screw (20) is preset and sealed by the manufacturer, and should not require further adjustment. Conventional carburetor cleaning solutions should not affect the sealant used to secure the factory adjustment.

To check float level, remove float bowl (19) and gasket (13), invert carburetor and measure from float bowl mating surface to float as shown in Fig. MR25-3. Float level should be $^7/_{16}$ inch (11.1 mm) measured as shown. Carefully bend metal tab (T) to adjust.

Standard main jet (16) size for normal operation at elevations up to 2500 feet (762 m) is 0.068 (1.73 mm) on 75 hp models and 0.072 (1.83 mm) on 90 hp models. Standard vent jet (7) size for normal operation at elevations up to 2500 feet (762 m) is 0.094 on all models. Main jet (16) size should be reduced from standard size by 0.002 inch (0.05 mm) for operation at elevations of 2500-5000 feet (762-1524 m), 0.004 inch (0.10 mm) at elevations of 5000-7500 feet (1524-2286 m) and 0.006 inch (0.15 mm) at elevations of 7500 feet (2286 m) and up.

All models are equipped with an electrically operated enrichment valve to provide additional fuel to aid cold starting. Enrichment valve is activated by pushing in on ignition key or by choke button if so equipped. Fuel is gravity fed to the enrichment valve from the float bowl of the top carburetor and is supplied to the power head through fittings in the intake manifold at each carburetor. Enrichment valve can be operated manually by depressing button located on the bottom of the valve.

If enrichment system malfunction is noted, make sure battery voltage is present at valve (yellow/black wire) when key (or choke button) is depressed and that sufficient fuel is being delivered to top fitting of valve.

FUEL PUMP. The diaphragm type fuel pump is activated by crankcase pulsations. Test pump by installing a clear fuel hose between pump and carburetors. Start engine and check for air bubbles in fuel line and fuel output.

Remove fuel pump from power head by unscrewing two Phillips-head screws. Disassemble pump by unscrewing two hex head screws. Inspect all components for wear or damage and renew as necessary. Make sure check valve (17—Fig. MR25-5) is functioning properly. When reassembling pump, lubricate check

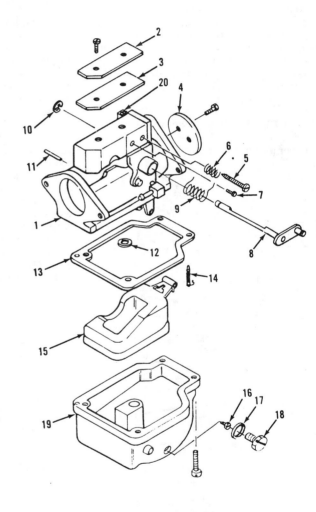

Fig. MR25-2—Exploded view of WME carburetor used on all models.

1. Body
2. Cover
3. Gasket
4. Throttle valve
5. Low speed mixture screw
6. Spring
7. Vent jet (back drag jet)
8. Throttle shaft
9. Spring
10. "E" ring
11. Pin
12. Gasket
13. Gasket
14. Inlet needle
15. Float
16. Main jet
17. Gasket
18. Plug
19. Float bowl
20. Air calibration screw

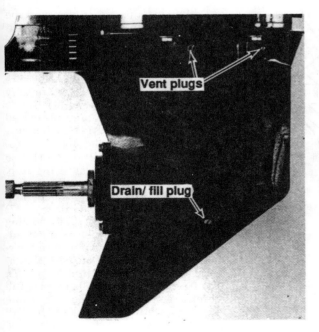

Fig. MR25-1—View of drain/fill and vent plugs. Refer to text when refilling gearcase.

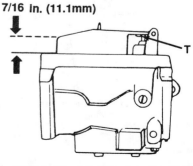

7/16 in. (11.1mm)

Fig. MR25-3—Check float level as shown. Bend metal tab (T) to adjust.

Mariner 75 & 90 HP 3 cyl. (After 1986)

OUTBOARD MOTOR

valve retainers (7) with engine oil or soapy water to ease installation. Trim end of retainer (7) at ridge to prevent retainer from contacting pump diaphragm.

NOTE: Fuel pump components have a "V" tab on one side for directional reference during assembly. Be CERTAIN "V" tabs on all components are aligned.

The manufacturer recommends assembling fuel pump using ¼-inch bolts or dowels as guides to ensure that all components are properly aligned. Be especially careful with gasket (12) and diaphragm (11). The two large holes in diaphragm (11) are provided for oil from injection pump to enter the gasoline flow. Failure to properly align gasket (12) and diaphragm (11) may result in power head damage.

REED VALVES. Reed valve assemblies are located between crankcase cover and intake manifolds. Reed valves

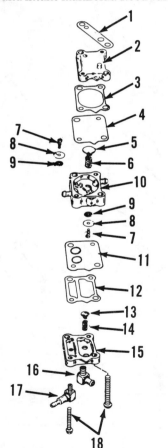

Fig. MR25-5—Exploded view of fuel pump assembly.

1. Gasket	10. Pump body
2. Pump base	11. Boost diaphragm
3. Gasket	12. Gasket
4. Diaphragm	13. End cap
5. End cap	14. Spring
6. Spring	15. Chamber plate
7. Retainer	16. Fitting
8. Check valve	17. Check valve
9. Rubber disc	18. Screws

may be removed for inspection after removing carburetors and intake manifolds.

Do not disassemble reed valve assembly unless necessary. Screw (4—Fig. MR25-6) is installed at the factory using Loctite. Reed petals (2) should be flat and smooth along entire seating surface. Renew reed petals if cracked, chipped or damaged, or if petals stand open in excess of 0.020 inch (0.51 mm). Never attempt to bend or straighten a damaged reed petal.

Make sure reed petals are properly positioned over pins (6) when assembling reed valves. Renew locking tab washer (5) and tighten screw (4) to 60 in.-lbs. (6.8 N·m). It may be necessary to continue tightening screw (4) to align locking tab with flat area of screw but, do not exceed 100 in.-lbs. (11.3 N·m). Be sure to bend locking tab to secure screw (4).

SPEED CONTROL LINKAGE. To verify timing pointer alignment, install a suitable dial indicator into number 1 (top) spark plug hole. Rotate flywheel clockwise until number 1 piston is at TDC. Zero dial indicator and rotate flywheel counterclockwise until dial indicator indicates 0.550 inch (13.97 mm) BTDC, then rotate flywheel clockwise until dial indicator indicates exactly 0.491 (12.47 mm) BTDC. With flywheel in this position, timing pointer should

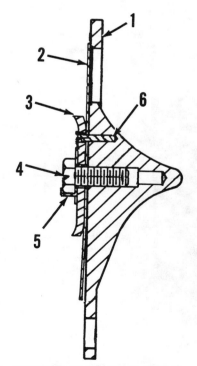

Fig. MR25-6—Sectional view of reed valve assembly.

1. Reed block	4. Screw
2. Reed petal	5. Locking tab washer
3. Retainer	6. Pin

be aligned with .491 timing mark on flywheel. If not, loosen pointer screws and move pointer as necessary to align pointer with .491 timing mark. Tighten timing pointer screws to 20 in.-lbs. (2.3 N·m).

Ignition timing may be adjusted at cranking speed if desired. To adjust ignition timing at cranking speed, proceed as follows: Remove all spark plugs to prevent engine from starting and install a suitable spark gap tool to spark plug leads. Disconnect throttle cable from power head and connect a suitable timing light to number 1 (top) spark plug lead. Shift outboard into neutral gear. While holding throttle arm (10—Fig. MR25-8) in idle position, crank engine while noting timing marks. Adjust idle timing screw (1) to obtain 2 degrees BTDC timing at cranking speed. Next, hold arm (10) so maximum advance screw (2) is against stop. Crank engine while observing timing marks and adjust screw (2) so maximum spark advance is 24 degrees BTDC on models prior to serial number B239242 and 28 degrees BTDC on models after serial number B239241.

NOTE: Maximum spark advance with engine running 5000 rpm should be 22 degrees BTDC on models prior to serial number B239242 and 26 degrees BTDC on models after serial number B239241. Due to the electronic spark advance characteristics of the ignition system, timing adjustment at cranking speed should be set as previously described to obtain the specified spark advance with engine running at 5000 rpm. Timing adjustments performed at cranking speed should be verified, and readjusted if necessary, with engine running at 5000 rpm.

Carburetor throttle valves must be synchronized to open and close at exactly the same time. Proceed as follows to synchronize carburetors: Loosen cam follower screw (3—Fig. MR25-8). Loosen synchronizing screws (4). Make sure all carburetor throttle valves are fully closed and tighten screws (4). Verify that all throttle valves are fully closed after tightening screws (4) and readjust if necessary. Loosen idle stop screw (6) locknut and hold throttle arm (10) so idle stop screw (6) is against the stop. Hold cam follower roller (8) against throttle cam (9) and adjust idle stop screw (6) to align throttle cam mark (7) with center of roller (8). While holding throttle arm (10) in the idle position, adjust cam follower (11) to provide a clearance of 0.025-0.050 inch (0.64-1.27 mm) between roller (8) and throttle cam (7), then retighten screw (3). Loosen full throttle stop screw (5) locknut. While holding throttle arm (10) in the full throttle position, adjust full throttle stop

SERVICE MANUAL

Mariner 75 & 90 HP 3 cyl. (After 1986)

screw (5) so carburetor throttle valves are fully open while allowing approximately 0.015 inch (0.38 mm) free play in throttle linkage to prevent throttle valves from bottoming out. Retighten full throttle stop screw locknut. Make sure stamped mark on oil injection pump body aligns with stamped mark on oil pump control lever with throttle arm in the idle position.

NOTE: Some models may have two stamped marks on oil injection pump body. On models so equipped, disregard the mark on the right side (looking straight at pump) and reference mark on left.

If marks do not align, disconnect and adjust length of oil pump control rod so marks align.

OIL INJECTION SYSTEM

BLEEDING OIL PUMP. Make sure carburetors and oil pump are properly synchronized as outlined in SPEED CONTROL LINKAGE section. To bleed air from oil injection system, loosen bleed screw (B—Fig. MR25-9) three or four turns and allow oil to flow from bleed hole (with engine NOT running) until air bubbles are no longer present in oil pump inlet hose. Retighten bleed screw (B) to 25 in.-lbs. (2.8 N·m). Start engine and run at idle speed until no air bubbles are noted in pump outlet hose.

CHECKING OIL PUMP OUTPUT. A 50:1 (25:1 if during break-in period) fuel and oil mixture must be used in fuel tank while checking pump output.

Remove oil pump output hose from fuel pump and plug fuel pump fitting. Place disconnected end of oil pump outlet hose into a graduated container. Remove oil pump control rod (6—Fig. MR25-9) from pump lever and rotate pump lever to full throttle position (counterclockwise). Connect an accurate tachometer to engine, start engine and allow to run at 700 rpm for 15 minutes. Oil pump output in 15 minutes should be a minimum of 18.7 mL (0.63 oz.). Note that pump output specification is based on test performed at 70° F (21.1° C) room temperature. Actual output may vary depending upon ambient temperature.

IGNITION

An alternator driven capacitor discharge ignition (CDI) system is used. Ignition system consists of the flywheel, stator, trigger assembly, switch box and ignition coils. The stator is mounted below the flywheel and includes two capacitor charging coils. The trigger assembly consists of three trigger coils and

is mounted below the flywheel. Ignition timing is advanced and retarded by rotating trigger assembly in relation to the inner flywheel magnets. Diodes, capacitors and SCR's are contained in the switch box. Switch box, trigger assembly and stator must be serviced as unit assemblies. Refer to Fig. MR25-11 for wiring diagram.

If engine malfunction is noted, and the ignition system is suspected, make sure the spark plugs and all electrical wiring are in acceptable condition and all electrical connections are clean and

tight prior to trouble-shooting CDI system.

To properly test, the switch box and ignition coils require the use of Quicksilver Multi-Meter DVA Tester part 91-99750 or a suitable voltmeter capable of measuring a minimum of 400 DC volts used with Quicksilver Direct Voltage Adaptor (DVA) part 91-89045. Follow instructions provided by tester manufacturer when performing tests. If these testers are not available, a process of elimination must be used when testing the ignition system. Stator and trigger

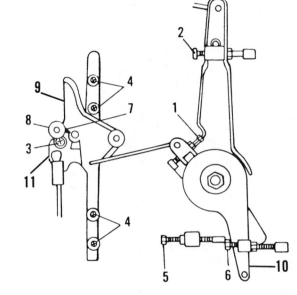

Fig. MR25-8—View of speed control linkage.
1. Idle timing screw
2. Maximum spark advance screw
3. Cam follower screw
4. Carburetor synchronizing screws
5. Full throttle stop screw
6. Idle stop screw
7. Throttle cam mark
8. Cam follower roller
9. Throttle cam
10. Throttle arm
11. Cam follower

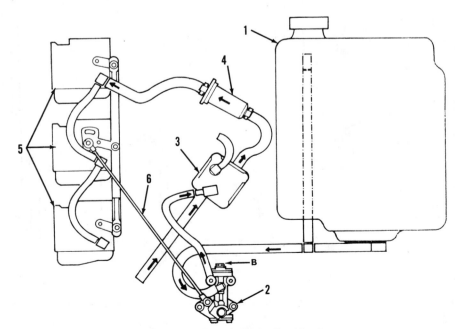

Fig. MR25-9—View of oil injection system.

B. Pump bleed screw
1. Oil tank
2. Oil pump
3. Fuel pump

4. Filter
5. Carburetors
6. Oil pump control rod

Mariner 75 & 90 HP 3 cyl. (After 1986)

OUTBOARD MOTOR

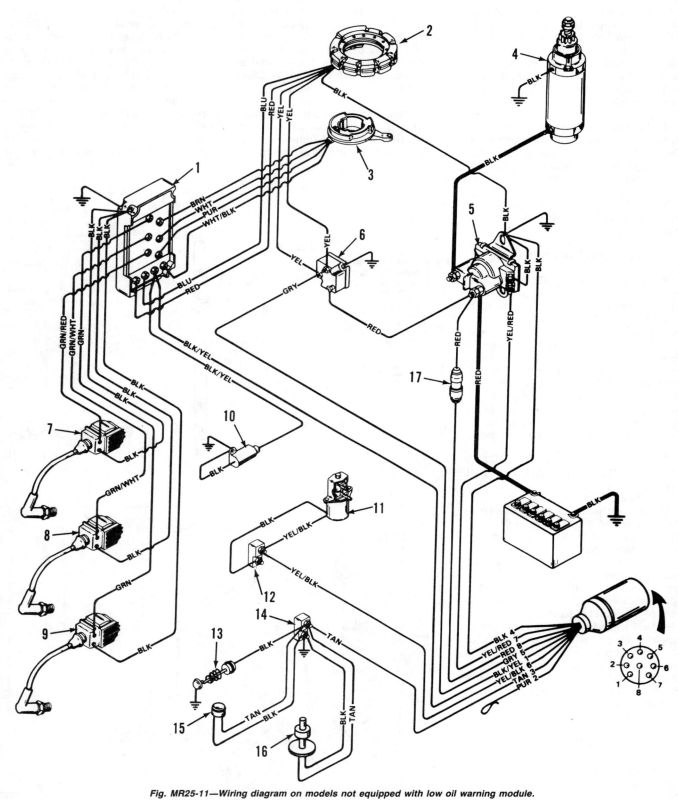

Fig. MR25-11—Wiring diagram on models not equipped with low oil warning module.

1. Switch box
2. Stator
3. Trigger assy.
4. Starter motor
5. Starter solenoid
6. Rectifier
7. Ignition coil (no. 1 cyl)

8. Ignition coil (no. 2 cyl)
9. Ignition coil (no. 3 cyl)
10. Mercury switch
11. Enrichment valve
12. Terminal block

13. Temperature switch
14. Terminal block
15. Test button
16. Low oil sensor
17. Fuse (20 ampere)

G. Green
R. Red
T. Tan
W. White
Y. Yellow
Bl. Blue
Br. Brown

Gr. Gray
Pr. Purple
B/Y. Black with yellow tracer
G/R. Green with red tracer
G/W. Green with white tracer

W/B. White with black tracer
Y/B. Yellow with black tracer
Y/R. Yellow with red tracer

SERVICE MANUAL

Mariner 75 & 90 HP 3 cyl. (After 1986)

assemblies can be effectively tested using a suitable ohmmeter.

NOTE: All tests that involve cranking or running the engine must be preformed with lead wires connected. Switch box case MUST be grounded to engine for all tests or switch box may be damaged.

To test ignition system, proceed as follows:

IGNITION COILS PRIMARY TEST. Connect DVA red test lead to ignition coil positive (+) terminal and black test lead to coil negative (−) terminal. Position tester selector switch to DVA/400. Tester should read 150-250 volts at cranking or idle speed (300-1000 rpm) and 180-280 volts at 1000-4000 rpm. If voltage readings are below specified reading, refer to SWITCH BOX STOP CIRCUIT test. If readings are within specifications, connect a suitable spark tester to ignition coil high tension leads, crank engine and note spark. If weak or no spark is noted, renew ignition coil(s). If normal spark is noted, renew spark plugs. If malfunction is still evident after renewing spark plugs, check ignition timing. If ignition timing is erratic, inspect trigger advance linkage for excessive wear or damage and inner flywheel magnets (shifted position or other damage). If timing is within specifications, problem is not in ignition system.

SWITCH BOX STOP CIRCUIT. Connect DVA black test lead to engine ground and red test lead to black/yellow switch box terminal (orange terminal on early models). Refer to Fig. MR25-11. Set DVA selector switch to DVA/400. Voltage reading at cranking and all running speeds should be 200-360 volts. If reading is within specifications, refer to STATOR tests. If reading is above specified voltages, connect a suitable ohmmeter between trigger brown and white/black leads, white and white/black leads and purple and white/black leads. Trigger resistance should be 1100-1400 ohms at all three connections. If not, renew trigger assembly. If trigger resistance is acceptable, renew switch box and repeat SWITCH BOX STOP CIRCUIT test. If SWITCH BOX STOP CIRCUIT test reading is below specified voltage, disconnect ignition switch, stop switch and mercury switch from black/yellow switch box terminal (orange switch box terminal on early models). With stop switch, ignition switch and mercury switch isolated, repeat SWITCH BOX STOP CIRCUIT test. If reading is now within specification, ignition switch, stop switch or mercury switch is defective. If reading remains below specification refer to STATOR test.

STATOR. Connect DVA black lead to engine ground and red lead to blue switch box terminal. Set DVA selector switch to DVA/400. Voltage reading should be 200-300 volts at cranking and idle speeds and 200-330 volts at 1000-4000 rpm. Switch DVA red test lead to red switch box terminal. Leave black test lead connected to engine ground. Voltage reading should be 20-90 volts at cranking or idle speeds and 130-300 volts at 1000-4000 rpm.

NOTE: A shorted or open capacitor inside switch box will result in faulty stator voltage readings during cranking and running tests. Stator resistance should be check as follows before failing stator.

If either STATOR test is not to specification, proceed as follows: Connect a suitable ohmmeter between blue and red stator leads. Resistance between blue and red stator leads should be 3600-4200 ohms. Next, connect ohmmeter between red stator lead and engine ground, or stator black lead (ground). Resistance should be 90-140 ohms. Renew stator if resistance is not as specified. If stator resistance is as specified, renew switch box and repeat STATOR tests.

IGNITION COILS RESISTANCE TEST. Disconnect wires and high tension lead from coil. Connect a suitable ohmmeter between coil positive (+) and negative (−) terminals. Resistance should be 0.02-0.04 ohm. Connect ohmmeter between coil high tension terminal and negative (−) terminal. Resistance should be 800-1,100 ohms. Renew ignition coil(s) if resistance is not as specified.

NOTE: Ignition coil resistance tests can only detect open or shorted windings. If coil resistance is within specification and still suspected as defective, coil must be tested using DVA meter as previously outlined in IGNITION COIL test. If DVA meter is not available, substitute a known good ignition coil and run engine to test.

COOLING SYSTEM

THERMOSTAT. All models are equipped with a thermostat (4—Fig. MR25-12) and pressure relief valve (7) located under cover (1) in cylinder block cover (12). Thermostat should begin to open at 140°-145° F (60°-63° C). Temperature sensor (11) is provided to activate a warning horn should power head overheat. Be sure the correct sensor (11) in used. Identify sensor (11) by the length of sensor lead; the lead on 190° F (87.8° C) sensor is 18.5 inches (470 mm) long and 15.5 inches (394 mm) long on 240° F (115.6° C) sensor.

WATER PUMP. The rubber impeller type water pump is housed in the gearcase housing. The impeller is mounted on and driven by the lower unit drive shaft.

If cooling system malfunction occurs, first check the water inlet for plugging or partial restriction. If necessary, remove the gearcase as outlined in LOWER UNIT section and inspect water pump, water tubes and seals. Renew cover (5—Fig. MR25-13) if thickness at discharge ports is 0.060 inch (1.5 mm) or less, or if grooves in excess of 0.030 inch (0.76 mm) are noted in top of cover (5). Renew plate (9) if grooves are noted in excess of 0.030 inch (0.76 mm).

NOTE: Sealing bead surrounding center hub of impeller (6) will wear circular grooves in cover (5) and plate (9). Circular grooves caused by impeller sealing bead will not affect water pump operation and should be disregarded when inspecting cover (5) and plate (9).

Rotate drive shaft in clockwise direction when installing cover (5) over impeller (6). Coat outer diameter of seals (14 and 15) with Loctite 271 or a suitable locking compound. Install seals into base (13) back-to-back. Apply Loctite 271 or suitable thread locking compound to threads of screws (11 and 2). Tighten screws (11 and 2) to 60 in.-lbs. (6.8 N·m).

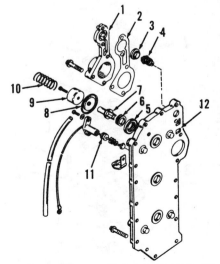

Fig. MR25-12—Exploded view of thermostat (4), pressure relief valve (7) and related components.

1. Cover	8. Diaphragm
2. Gasket	9. Cup
3. Seal	10. Spring
4. Thermostat	11. Temperature sensor
5. Grommet	assy.
6. Gasket	12. Cylinder block
7. Pressure relief valve	cover

Mariner 75 & 90 HP 3 cyl. (After 1986)

OUTBOARD MOTOR

POWER HEAD

REMOVE AND DISASSEMBLE. To remove power head, proceed as follows: Remove front cowl bracket and air box cover. Remove air box, disconnect oil lines and remove oil reservoir. Disconnect throttle linkage and remove carburetors as an assembly. Remove intake manifolds and reed valves. Remove flywheel nut and place a suitable protector cap over crankshaft. Remove flywheel using flywheel puller part 91-73687A1 or a suitable equivalent puller.

NOTE: Do not strike puller bolt to dislodge flywheel from crankshaft or crankshaft or main bearing damage may result.

Remove ignition system components. Remove wiring harness and related components as an assembly. Remove shift linkage. Remove eight screws securing power head to drive shaft housing, install a suitable lifting fixture to power head and lift power head off drive shaft housing.

Remove fuel pump, oil injection pump and related hoses. Remove oil pump driven gear and housing. Refer to Fig. MR25-12 and remove thermostat cover, thermostat, pressure relief valve and related components. Remove cylinder block cover (12—Fig. MR25-14) screws and carefully pry off cover (12). Pry points are provided in cover (12) to prevent damage to mating surfaces. Remove exhaust cover (1) and divider plate (3). Remove lower end cap (8) screws, crankcase cover (5) screws and carefully pry crankcase cover (5) from cylinder block (10). Remove lower end cap (8). Crankshaft, pistons, bearings and connecting rods may now be removed for service as outlined in the appropriate following sections. Refer to ASSEMBLY section for reassembly procedures.

ASSEMBLY. When reassembling the power head, the crankcase must be completely sealed against both vacuum and pressure. All gasket surfaces and machined joints without gaskets should be carefully checked for nicks and burrs which might interfere with a tight seal. Cylinder block and crankcase cover are matched and align bored assembly and not available separately.

Lubricate all bearing and friction surfaces with engine oil. Loose needle bearings should be held in place during reassembly using Quicksilver Needle Bearing Assembly Grease (part C-92-42649A-1) or a suitable equivalent gasoline soluble grease. Lubricate all seal lips using needle bearing assembly grease or suitable gasoline soluble grease.

Prior to assembling crankcase, inspect check valves (13—Fig. MR25-14) by looking through valve. If light is noted while looking through valve, check ball has failed (melted) or is missing. If check ball is present in valve, make sure ball is free to move slightly inside valve. Remove check valves by carefully driving out using a suitable punch. Install check valves with single hole facing crankshaft.

Apply Loctite 271 or a suitable equivalent thread locking compound to outer diameter of all metal cased seals and

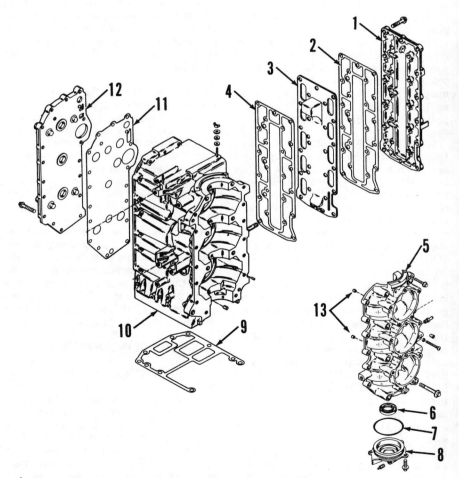

Fig. MR25-13—Exploded view of water pump assembly.

1. Water tube seal	
2. Screw	9. Plate
3. Washer	10. Gasket
4. Insulator	11. Screw
5. Cover	12. Washer
6. Impeller	13. Base
7. Key	14. Seal
8. Gasket	15. Seal

Fig. MR25-14—Exploded view of crankcase assembly.

1. Exhaust cover	8. Lower end cap
2. Gasket	9. Gasket
3. Divider plate	10. Cylinder block
4. Gasket	11. Gasket
5. Crankcase cover	12. Cylinder block
6. Seal	cover
7. "O" ring	13. Check valves

SERVICE MANUAL

Mariner 75 & 90 HP 3 cyl. (After 1986)

any fastener used on moving or rotating components.

Apply a continuous bead, ¹/₁₆-inch (1.6 mm) diameter, of Loctite Master Gasket Sealer (part 92-12564-1) to mating surface of crankcase cover (5—Fig. MR25-14) to seal crankcase assembly. Run bead to the inside of all screw holes. Make sure bead is continuous but avoid excess application.

Tighten large inner crankcase cover screws, in three steps, in sequence shown in Fig. MR25-18 to final tightness of 25 ft.-lbs. (33.9 N·m). After tightening inner cover screws, tighten small outer screws to final tightness of 165 in.-lbs. (18.6 N·m) in sequence shown. While tightening cover screws, check rotation of crankshaft for binding or unusual noise. If binding or noise is noted, repair cause before proceeding. Coat mating surface of lower end cap (8—Fig. MR25-14) with Quicksilver Perfect Seal or equivalent. Rotate crankshaft so each piston ring in turn is visible in exhaust or transfer ports, then check by pressing on rings with a blunt tool. Ring should spring back when released. If not, a broken or binding ring is indicated and must be repaired before proceeding. Tighten exhaust and cylinder block cover screws to 165 in.-lbs. (18.6 N·m) in sequence shown in Figs. MR25-19 and MR25-20 respectively.

Renew gasket (9—Fig. MR25-14) when installing power head on drive shaft housing. Lubricate drive shaft splines with a small amount of Quicksilver 2-4-C or equivalent. Apply Loctite 271 or equivalent to threads of power head mounting screws and tighten to 165 in.-lbs. (18.6 N·m). Remainder of assembly and reinstallation is the reverse of removal procedure. Note the following tightening torques: Trigger and stator assemblies, 60 in.-lbs. (6.8 N·m); Electrical component mounting plate, 165 in.-lbs. (18.6 N·m); Starter motor, 165 in.-lbs. (18.6 N·m); Air box screws, 100 in.-lbs. (11.3 N·m).

PISTONS, PINS, RINGS AND CYLINDERS. Prior to detaching connecting rods from crankshaft, make sure that rod, rod cap and pistons are properly marked for correct reassembly to each other, in the correct cylinder and in the correct direction.

Piston skirt-to-cylinder bore clearance should be 0.005 inch (0.13 mm). Measure piston skirt diameter at right angle to piston pin bore 0.50 inch (12.7 mm) up from bottom of skirt. Maximum allowable cylinder bore wear, taper or out-of-round is 0.003 inch (0.08 mm). Pistons and rings are available in 0.015 inch (0.38 mm) and 0.030 inch (0.76 mm) oversize. Note that oversize pistons weigh approximately the same as standard size pistons. All cylinders do not require oversize boring if one cylinder is excessively worn or damaged.

Piston rings are semikeystone shaped and are pinned to prevent rotation. Install rings with "T" mark facing up.

Always renew piston pin retaining rings (2—Fig. MR25-16) if removed. Piston pin rides in 29 loose needle bearing rollers (5). The manufacturer recommends renewing piston pin bearing rollers (5) when reassembling power head. Piston pin is a snug fit in piston and can be tapped out using a suitable driver and soft-face mallet. When reassembling, hold needle bearing rollers in place with a suitable gasoline soluble grease. Install locating washers (4) with large diameter facing away from pin (7).

Cylinder block is designed to allow piston installation without the use of a piston ring compressor. Install pistons into cylinders with "UP" mark on piston crown facing flywheel end of power head.

CONNECTING RODS, BEARINGS AND CRANKSHAFT. Refer to Fig. MR25-16 for exploded view of crankshaft, connecting rods and bearings. Be sure connecting rods (6), rod caps (9), pistons (3) and all wearing components are marked for reference during reassembly. Top main bearing (13) is a caged needle bearing and bottom main bearing (19) is a ball bearing. Each center main bearing consist of 32 loose bearing rollers (24) and race (25).

Do not remove bearing (19) from crankshaft unless bearing (19) or oil pump drive gear (18) require renewal. Note location of key (17).

Some models are equipped with a wear sleeve and "O" ring in place of carrier (21) and seal (22). Carefully heat wear sleeve to remove, on models so equipped. To install wear sleeve, apply Loctite 271 or equivalent to inner diameter of sleeve and drive sleeve squarely on crankshaft until bottomed using a suitable wooden block and hammer.

Inspect crankshaft splines for excessive wear and crankshaft for straightness using a dial indicator and "V" blocks. Inspect crankshaft bearing surfaces and renew crankshaft if scored,

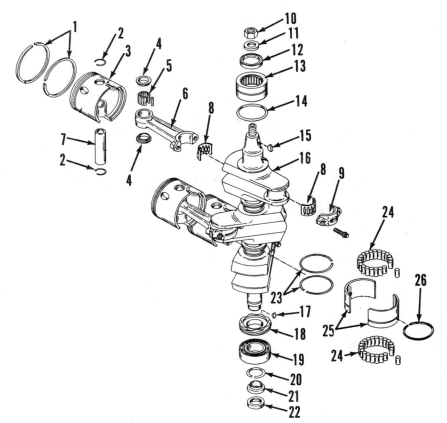

Fig. MR25-16—Exploded view of crankshaft assembly. Some models are equipped with a wear sleeve and "O" ring in place of carrier (21) and seal (22).

1. Piston rings	7. Piston pin	14. "O" ring	20. Retaining ring
2. Retaining ring	8. Crankpin bearing	15. Flywheel key	21. Seal carrier
3. Piston	9. Connecting rod cap	16. Crankshaft	22. Seal
4. Locating washers	10. Nut	17. Oil pump drive gear	23. Seal rings
5. Piston pin bearing	11. Washer	key	24. Main bearing rollers
rollers	12. Seal	18. Oil pump drive gear	25. Main bearing race
6. Connecting rod	13. Bearing	19. Bearing	26. Retaining ring

Mariner 75 & 90 HP 3 cyl. (After 1986)

OUTBOARD MOTOR

out-of-round or excessively worn. Renew connecting rod(s) if big end bearing surface is rough, scored, excessively worn or shows evidence of overheating. Use crocus cloth ONLY to clean the connecting rod big end bearing surface.

Install main bearings with oil holes in outer race facing toward bottom of engine. Install crankshaft seal rings (23) with end gaps 180 degrees apart. Use only Quicksilver Needle Bearing Assembly Grease or a suitable gasoline soluble grease to hold loose bearing rollers in place. Always renew rod cap bolts when reassembling power head. Threads are cut into both the connecting rod and rod cap. To properly align cap and rod during reassembly, proceed as follows: Place rod cap (9) on bearing half (8) and hold tightly against connecting rod while threading in bolt. Finger tighten rod bolts then check rod and cap alignment. Cap and rod must be perfectly aligned. After all rod caps and bolts are installed and aligned, tighten bolts to 15 in.-lbs. (1.7 N·m) and recheck alignment. Then tighten bolts to 30 ft.-lbs. (40.7 N·m) and recheck alignment. If rods and caps are perfectly aligned, tighten rod bolts an additional 90 degrees to complete procedure. Reassemble crankcase assembly as previously outlined.

ELECTRICAL SYSTEM

CHARGING SYSTEM. Refer to Fig. MR25-11 for wiring diagram. To test alternator output, disconnect red lead from rectifier (6) and connect a suitable ammeter between rectifier and red lead. Note that rectifier must be operating properly for accurate test results. Ammeter should indicate 7-9 amperes at 3000 rpm. If not, disconnect stator yellow leads from rectifier and connect a suitable ohmmeter between yellow leads. Stator resistance should be 0.05-1.1 ohms. No continuity should be present between yellow leads and engine ground (or stator black lead if stator is removed from power head). Renew stator if output or resistance is not as specified.

To test rectifier (6), connect ohmmeter alternately between each rectifier terminal and between each terminal and ground. Refer to Fig. MR25-22. Reverse ohmmeter leads after each connection. Ohmmeter should indicate continuity with leads connected one direction but not the other. If ohmmeter shows continuity both directions or no continuity both directions, renew rectifier.

STARTER MOTOR. If starter motor malfunction occurs, perform a visual inspection for corroded or loose connections. Check fuse (17—Fig. MR25-11) and make sure battery is fully charged.

Renew brushes if worn to less than ¹/₄ inch (6.4 mm). Undercut insulation between commutator bars to ¹/₃₂ inch (0.8 mm). Armature should be tested using an armature growler.

LOWER UNIT

PROPELLER. Protection for lower unit is provided by a splined rubber hub built into propeller. Various propellers are available and should be selected to allow motor to operate within the recommended speed range 4750-5250 rpm on 75 hp models and 5000-5500 rpm on 90 hp models at full throttle. The manufacturer recommends propping outboard motor to the high end of full throttle rpm range.

R&R AND OVERHAUL. To remove lower unit, first remove and ground spark plug leads to prevent accidental starting. Shift engine into forward gear and tilt unit to full up position. Remove two screws and washers on each side of lower unit and one nut and washer under antiventilation plate. Remove gear case and secure in a suitable holding fixture.

Note location and size of all shims and thrust washers during disassembly for reference during reassembly.

Remove propeller (66—Fig. MR25-23), thrust hub (65), vent screws (35 and 36) and drain plug (37). Allow gearcase oil to drain while inspecting for water or other contamination.

Remove water pump assembly and screws (11). Using screwdrivers or similar tools placed on each end of water pump base (13), carefully pry base (13) from gearcase. Remove and discard seals (14 and 15). Remove nuts (61 [screws on some models]). Using a suitable puller

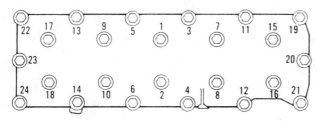

Fig. MR25-18—Tighten inner (large) crankcase cover screws first, in sequence shown, then tighten outer (small) screws. Use three steps to obtain final tightness. Refer to text and CONDENSED SERVICE DATA.

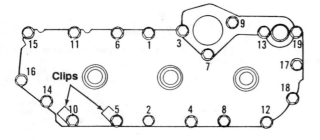

Fig. MR25-19—Tighten exhaust cover screws in sequence shown to 165 in.-lbs. (18.6 N·m).

Fig. MR25-20—Tighten cylinder block cover screws to 165 in.-lbs. (18.6 N·m) in sequence shown. Note location of clips.

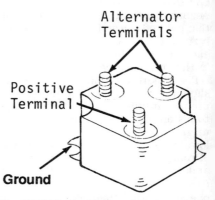

Fig. MR25-22—Rectifier must be connected as shown. Refer to text for rectifier test procedure.

SERVICE MANUAL

Mariner 75 & 90 HP 3 cyl. (After 1986)

break loose carrier-to-gearcase seal then remove bearing carrier (59) and propeller shaft components (46-64) as a unit. Do not lose balls (48) or cam follower (46). Remove and discard seals (63 and 64) and "O" ring (55) from carrier (59). Do not remove bearings (58 and 62) unless renewal is required. Remove retainer spring (52) from dog clutch (50). To remove pin (51), depress cam follower (46) by pushing propeller shaft against a solid object, then push out pin (51) using a small punch. Remove follower (46), sliding pin (47), balls (48), spring (49) and slide dog clutch (50) off propeller

shaft. Place Drive Shaft Holding Tool 91-56755 or similar splined adapter on drive shaft splines or clamp drive shaft into a soft jawed vise then remove pinion nut (38). Remove drive shaft assembly from gearcase. After drive shaft is removed, forward gear (45) and bearing (43) can be removed. Use a suitable expanding jaw type puller to remove race (42), if necessary. Note location and thickness of shims (41). Remove upper drive shaft bearing (17) and bearing carrier (18) if necessary, using expanding jaw type puller. Note that bearing (17) and carrier (18) must be removed before

sleeve (19) removal is possible. If necessary, remove sleeve (19) using a suitable puller. Quicksilver Bearing Race Tool 91-14308A1 is required to drive lower drive shaft bearing race (31) from gearcase. Bearing race (31) can be driven from gearcase with bearing (17), carrier (18) and sleeve (19) installed. Note location and thickness of shims (30). Remove coupler (23), shift shaft retainer (26) and shift shaft (28). Reach into gear cavity and remove shift cam (40). Remove and discard seal (25) and "O" ring (27) from retainer (26) to complete disassembly.

1. Water tube seal
2. Screw
3. Washer
4. Insulator
5. Cover
6. Impeller
7. Key
8. Gasket
9. Plate
10. Gasket
11. Screw
12. Washer
13. Base
14. Seal
15. Seal
16. Gasket
17. Needle bearing
18. Carrier
19. Sleeve
20. Wear sleeve
21. Seal ring
22. Drive shaft
23. Coupler
25. Seal
26. Retainer
27. "O" ring
28. Shift shaft
29. "E" ring
30. Shim
31. Bearing race
32. Bearing
33. Gearcase
34. Gasket
35. Plug
36. Plug
37. Plug
38. Nut
39. Pinion gear
40. Shift cam
41. Shim
42. Bearing race
43. Bearing
44. Bearing
45. Forward gear
46. Cam follower
47. Slide pin
48. Balls
49. Spring
50. Dog clutch
51. Pin
52. Retaining spring
53. Propeller shaft
54. Reverse gear
55. "O" ring
56. Thrust bearing
57. Thrust washer
58. Bearing
59. Bearing carrier
60. Washer
61. Nut
62. Bearing
63. Seal
64. Seal
65. Thrust hub
66. Propeller
67. Locking tab washer
68. Nut

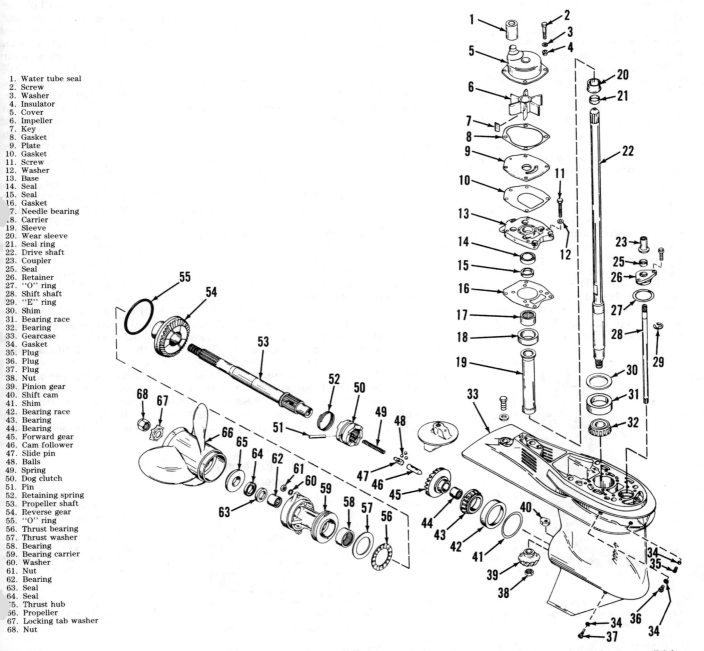

Fig. MR25-23—Exploded view of lower unit gearcase assembly. Shift shaft coupler (23) is equipped with reverse lockout cam on models without power tilt/trim.

Mariner 75 & 90 HP 3 cyl. (After 1986)

OUTBOARD MOTOR

Inspect all components for excessive wear or damage. Check straightness of propeller shaft using a dial indicator and "V" blocks and renew shaft if runout exceeds 0.006 inch (0.15 mm). Inspect all bearings for roughness, pits, rust or other damage and renew as necessary. Inspect sealing area of wear sleeve (20) for grooves and renew as necessary. Renew bearings and races as an assembly. Renew gears if teeth are chipped, broken or excessively worn. Renew all seals, "O" rings and gaskets. Lubricate all friction surfaces with clean gear lubricant. Apply Loctite 271 or equivalent to threads of all screws and outer diameter of all metal cased seals. Lubricate "O" ring (55) and outer diameter of carrier (50) with Quicksilver Special Lubricant 101 (part 92-13872A-1). Lubricate other seals and "O" rings with Quicksilver 2-4-C Marine Lubricant (part 92-90018A12) or Quicksilver Needle Bearing Assembly Grease (part 92-42649A-1).

When reassembling gearcase, place original shim pack (41) into gearcase and install bearing race (42) using a suitable mandrel.

NOTE: If original shims (41) are damaged or lost, install shim pack 0.010 inch (0.25 mm) thick.

Install seal (25) into retainer (26) until flush with top of retainer. Place shift cam (40) into gearcase with numbers facing up and install shift rod making sure splines in shift shaft properly align with cam. Install bearing (62) into carrier (59) with lettered side facing propeller end. Install seal (63) into carrier (59) with lip facing forward and seal (64) with lip facing propeller. Install dog clutch (50) on propeller shaft with

grooved end of clutch facing rearward. Install spring (49), slider (47), balls (48) and cam follower (46) into propeller shaft. Depress follower (46) against spring pressure and align holes in dog clutch and propeller shaft using a suitable punch, then insert pin (51).

If installing a new wear sleeve (20) on drive shaft (22), install seal ring (21), coat inner diameter of sleeve (20) with Loctite 271 and press onto shaft (22) until bottomed. Install original shim pack (30) and draw race (31) into gearcase using suitable mandrels and a threaded rod. If original shims (30) are damaged or lost, start with shim pack 0.025 inch (0.64 mm) thick. Install sleeve (19) making sure antirotation tab properly engages gearcase. Install bearing (43), forward gear (45), drive shaft (22), pinion bearing (32), pinion gear (39) and original pinion nut (38).

NOTE: Pinion nut (38) should be renewed and secured with a suitable thread locking compound after gearcase shimming operation has been properly performed.

Drive shaft assembly must be preloaded to properly adjust pinion gear depth and forward gear backlash. Special Bearing Preload Tool 91-14311A1 and Pinion Gear Locating Tool 91-12349A2 are required for shim selection procedure.

To preload drive shaft and bearing assembly, assemble Bearing Preload Tool 91-14311A1 as shown in Fig. MR25-25 and tighten set screws (2). With nut (3) fully threaded on bolt (1), measure distance (D) between bottom of bolt head to top of nut, then turn nut (3) to increase distance (D) by one inch (25.4 mm). Rotate drive shaft several turns to ensure lower drive shaft bearing is properly seated. Assemble Pinion Gear Location Tool 91-12349A2 as shown in Fig. MR25-26. Install locating disc marked number "3" making sure access hole is facing up. Position sliding collar (4) so gaging block (3) is directly under

pinion gear (39) teeth and flat on gaging block marked "8" is adjacent to pinion gear (39). Clearance between gaging block (3) and pinion gear should be 0.025 inch (0.64 mm) measured with a suitable feeler gage as shown. Vary thickness of shim pack (30—Fig. MR25-23) to adjust. Changing thickness of shims (30) by 0.001 inch (0.03 mm) will change pinion gear thickness by 0.001 inch (0.03 mm).

Insert assembled propeller shaft assembly into bearing carrier (59—Fig. MR25-23) and install carrier and propeller shaft assembly into gearcase. Position carrier (59) so "TOP" mark is facing up. Outward pressure should be applied to propeller shaft to hold reverse gear (54) tight against thrust bearing (56) and washer (57) to prevent thrust washer and bearing from being dislodged. A tool can be fabricated out of 1¼ to 1½ inch (31.7-38.1 mm) PVC pipe cut off to 6 inches (152.4 mm) long. Place pipe over propeller shaft and secure with washer (67) and nut (68). Tighten nut (68) so reverse gear (54) is pulled securely against thrust bearing (56) and washer (57). Securely tighten nuts (61) or screws if so equipped.

To check forward gear backlash, proceed as follows: Allow bearing preload tool (Fig. MR25-25) to remain installed. Preload propeller shaft by installing suitable puller as shown in Fig. MR25-27. Tighten puller center bolt to 25 in.-lbs. (2.8 N·m), rotate propeller shaft several turns, then retighten puller bolt to 25 in.-lbs. (2.8 N·m). Again, rotate propeller shaft several turns and recheck torque on puller bolt. Refer to Fig. MR25-28 and assemble a suitable threaded rod to gearcase using nuts and washers as shown. Affix a suitable dial indicator to threaded rod. Install Backlash Indicator 91-78473 on drive shaft and align dial indicator plunger with the mark "4" on backlash indicator. Check backlash by carefully rotating drive shaft back-and-forth. Note that if any movement is noted at propeller shaft,

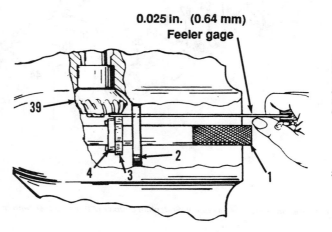

Fig. MR25-25—View of Bearing Preload Tool 91-14311A1 assembled over drive shaft (22). Refer to text for gearcase shim selection procedure.

1. Bolt
2. Set screws
3. Nut
4. Spring
5. Thrust washer
6. Thrust bearing
7. Adapter
22. Drive shaft

0.025 in. (0.64 mm) Feeler gage

Fig. MR25-26—Assemble Pinion Gear Locating Tool 91-12349A2 as shown. Make sure sliding collar (4) is positioned so gaging block is located under pinion gear (39) as shown.

1. Arbor
2. Locating disc (number 3)
3. Gaging block
4. Sliding collar
39. Pinion gear

SERVICE MANUAL

repeat propeller shaft preloading procedure as previously outlined. Backlash should be 0.012-0.019 inch (0.31-0.48 mm). Vary thickness of shim pack (41) to adjust. Note that changing thickness of shims (41) by 0.001 inch (0.03 mm) will result in approximately 0.00125 inch (0.032 mm) change in backlash.

After shim selection procedure is completed, remove carrier and drive shaft assembly. Remove pinion nut, apply Loctite 271 to a NEW pinion nut, install nut with beveled side facing up and tighten to 70 ft.-lbs. (95 N·m). Reinstall carrier and propeller shaft assembly, apply Loctite 271 to nuts (61—Fig. MR25-23) or screws if so equipped, and tighten nuts (61) to 275 in.-lbs. (31.1 N·m) or screws to 150 in.-lbs. (17 N·m). Complete reassembly by reversing disassembly procedure. Tighten propeller nut to 55 ft.-lbs. (75 N·m).

To reinstall gearcase on drive shaft housing, proceed as follows: Position shift block on power head in the forward gear position. Shift block should extend past forward side of shift rail by $^1/_{32}$ inch (3.2 mm) if properly positioned. Shift lower unit into forward gear. Lubricate inner diameter of water tube seal (1) with Quicksilver 2-4-C Marine Lubricant. Lightly lubricate drive shaft splines with 2-4-C Marine lubricant. Do not apply grease to top of drive shaft or drive shaft may not fully engage crankshaft.

NOTE: On models not equipped with power tilt/trim, position shift shaft coupler (23) with reverse lock cam facing forward.

Install gearcase in drive shaft housing making sure drive shaft aligns with crankshaft, upper shift shaft aligns with coupler (23) and water tube aligns with water tube seal (1). Apply Loctite 271 to threads of gearcase mounting screws and tighten to 40 ft.-lbs. (54.2 N·m). After installing gearcase, make sure shift linkage operates properly as follows: Shift outboard into forward gear. Propeller shaft should lock into gear when rotated counterclockwise and ratchet

when rotated clockwise. When shifted into reverse gear, propeller shaft should be locked into gear when rotated either direction. If shift linkage does not operate as specified, lower unit must be removed and shift linkage malfunction repaired.

POWER TILT/TRIM

FLUID AND BLEEDING. Recommended fluid is Quicksilver Power Trim & Steering Fluid or a suitable Type F, FA or Dextron II automatic transmission fluid.

NOTE: Hydraulic system is under pressure. Fill plug (Fig. MR25-29) must not be removed unless outboard is in full up position and tilt lock lever is engaged. Be sure to securely tighten fill plug prior to lowering outboard motor.

To check fluid level, tilt motor to full up position, engage tilt lock lever and slowly remove fill plug (Fig. MR25-29). Fluid should be visible in fill tube. Fill as necessary and securely tighten fill plug.

To determine if air is present in hydraulic system, trim motor out until both trim rods are slightly extended. Apply downward pressure on lower unit. If trim rods retract into cylinders more than $^1/_8$ inch (3.2 mm), air is present and bleeding is required.

The hydraulic circuit is self-bleeding as the tilt/trim system is operated through several cycles. After servicing system, be sure to check reservoir level after filling and operating system.

Trim limit adjustment is not required. Port trim rod and piston assembly (15—Fig. MR25-30) is equipped with a check

valve designed to open at a specific pressure, limiting trim range to 20 degrees when engine speed exceeds 2,000 rpm. If engine speed falls below 2,000 rpm, trim angle may exceed 20 degrees; however, once engine speed exceeds 2,000 rpm, propeller thrust will increase pressure in trim cylinders causing check valve in port side trim rod to unseat, bypassing hydraulic fluid to the reservoir and lowering trim angle to 20 degrees maximum. Except for cleaning valve and strainer (16), check valve in port trim rod is not serviceable and should not be removed. If check valve malfunction is evident, renew port trim rod.

HYDRAULIC TESTING. The system can be checked by connecting a 5000 psi (34.5 MPa) test gage to the UP (U—Fig. MR25-32) and DOWN (D—Fig. MR25-33) ports. Prior to connecting test gage, place outboard motor in the full up position and engage tilt lock lever. Unscrew reservoir fill plug and rotate manual release valve (21—Fig. MR25-32) three to four turns counterclockwise to release pressure on system. Remove UP or DOWN Allen head test port plug and connect test gage with suitable adapter and hose. Install fill plug and rotate manual release valve clockwise until seated. System pressure when testing at UP (U) port should be a minimum of 1300 psi (8.9 MPa). System pressure when testing at DOWN (D—Fig. MR25-33) port should be a minimum of 500 psi (3.5 MPa). Release pressure on system as previously outlined prior to removing test gage. Reinstall Allen head plug.

OVERHAUL. Refer to Fig. MR25-30 for exploded view of manifold and trim

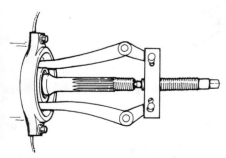

Fig. MR25-27—When checking forward gear backlash, preload propeller shaft by installing a suitable puller as shown. Refer to text.

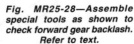

Fig. MR25-28—Assemble special tools as shown to check forward gear backlash. Refer to text.

1. Dial indicator & adapater assy.
2. Backlash indicator tool 91-78473
3. Nuts
4. Threaded rod
5. Washers

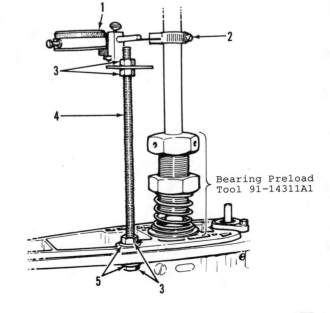

Bearing Preload Tool 91-14311A1

Mariner 75 & 90 HP 3 cyl. (After 1986)

OUTBOARD MOTOR

cylinder components, and Fig. MR25-31 for exploded view of tilt cylinder components. Special socket 91-44487A1 and a spanner wrench is required to service trim and tilt cylinders. Keep all components clean and away from contamination. Keep components separated and label if necessary for correct reassembly. Lubricate all "O" rings or seal lips with Quicksilver Power Trim & Steering Fluid, Dexron II, Type F or Type FA automatic transmission fluid during reassembly.

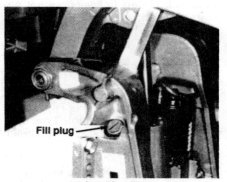

Fig. MR25-29—View showing location of fill plug on power tilt/trim system.

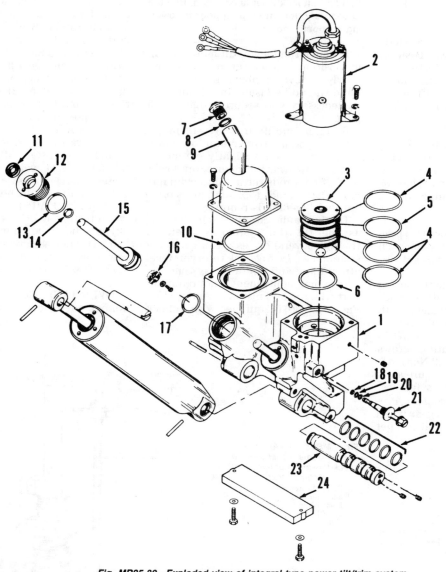

Fig. MR25-30—Exploded view of integral type power tilt/trim system.

1. Manifold		
2. Motor	8. "O" ring	14. "O" ring	20. "O" ring
3. Pump assy.	9. Reservoir cover	15. Trim piston & rod	21. Manual release
4. "O" rings	10. Seal ring	16. Strainer	valve
5. "O" ring	11. Seal	17. "O" ring	22. "O" ring
6. "O" ring	12. Cap	18. "O" ring	23. Shaft
7. Fill plug	13. "O" ring	19. "O" ring	24. Anode plate

SERVICE MANUAL

Mariner 75 & 90 HP 3 cyl. (After 1986)

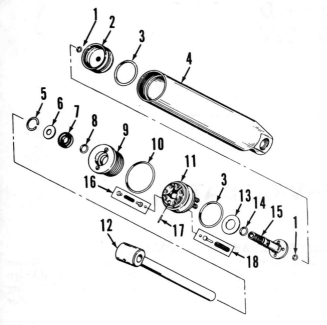

Fig. MR25-31—Exploded view of tilt cylinder assembly.

1. "O" ring
2. Cup
3. "O" ring
4. Cylinder
5. Circlip
6. Washer
7. Scraper
8. "O" ring
9. Cap
10. "O" ring
11. Piston
12. Rod
13. Washer
14. "O" ring
15. Rod end
16. Check valve assy.
17. Pin
18. Check valve assy.

Fig. MR25-32—Release pressure on system, then remove Allen head plug (U) and install a 5000 psi (34.5 MPa) test gage with a suitable adapter and hose to test system pressure when operated in the "UP" direction. View identifies location of manual release valve (21).

Fig. MR25-33—Release pressure on system, then remove Allen head plug (D) and install a 5000 psi (34.5 MPa) test gage with a suitable adapter and hose to test system pressure when operated in the "DOWN" direction.

MARINER 90, 115 AND 140 HP
(PRIOR TO 1986)

CONDENSED SERVICE DATA

TUNE-UP

Hp/rpm:
  Model 90 .90/4500-5000
  Model 115 . . . . .115/5000-5500
  Model 140 . . . . .140/5300-5800
Bore . . . . .2-7/8 in.
                     (73.03 mm)
Stroke . . . . .2-9/16 in.
                     (65.09 mm)
Displacement .99.8 cu. in.
                     (1635 cc)
Compression at Cranking Speed . . . . *
Firing Order 1-4-5-2-3-6
Ignition Type .Breakerless
Spark Plug . . . . .See Text
Idle Speed:
  Model 90 (in gear) . . . . .500-600 rpm
  Models 115 & 140 (in gear) . . . . .550-600 rpm
Fuel:Oil Ratio 50:1

*Not more than 15 psi (103.5 kPa) variation between cylinders.

SIZES—CLEARANCES

Piston Rings:
  End Gap . . . .*
  Side Clearance . . . .*
Piston Skirt Clearance . . . . *
Crankshaft Bearing Type:
  Top Main Bearing .Ball Bearing
  Main Bearing (2) . . . . .Bushing with Reed Valve
  Main Bearing (3) . . . . .Roller
  Center Main Bearing . . . . .Bushing with Reed Valve

SIZES—CLEARANCES CONT.

  Main Bearing (5) . . . . .Roller
  Main Bearing (6) . . . . .Bushing with Reed Valve
  Bottom Main Bearing . . . . .Ball Bearing
  Crankpin . . . . .Roller
Piston Pin Bearing:
  Type . . . . .Roller
  Number of Rollers 29

**Publication not authorized by manufacturer.

TIGHTENING TORQUES

Connecting Rod .180 in.-lbs.
                     (20.3 N·m)
Crankcase Screws . . . . .200 in.-lbs.
                     (22.6 N·m)
Cylinder Cover . . . . .85 in.-lbs.
                     (9.6 N·m)
Exhaust Cover . . . . .250 in.-lbs.
                     (28.2 N·m)
Flywheel Nut . . . . .100 ft.-lbs.
                     (136 N·m)
Reed Screws . . . . .25 in.-lbs.
                     (2.8 N·m)
Spark Plugs . . . . .240 in.-lbs.
                     (27.1 N·m)
Transfer Port Covers . . . . .85 in.-lbs.
                     (9.6 N·m)
Water Jacket Cover:
  Early Models .200 in.-lbs.
                     (22.6 N·m)
  Late Models . . . . .150 in.-lbs.
                     (16.9 N·m)

LUBRICATION

The power head is lubricated by oil mixed with the fuel. Fuel should be regular leaded, low lead or unleaded gasoline with a minimum pump octane rating of 86. Recommended oil is Quicksilver Formula 50-D Outboard Lubricant. Normal fuel:oil ratio is 50:1; during engine break-in, fuel:oil ratio should be 25:1.

Lower unit gears and bearings are lubricated by oil contained in the gearcase. Recommended oil is Mariner Super Duty Gear Lube. Lubricant is drained by removing vent and drain plugs in the gearcase. Refill through drain plug hole until oil has reached level of vent plug. Then allow 1 ounce (30 mL) to drain from gearcase.

FUEL SYSTEM

CARBURETOR. Three "Back Drag" type carburetors are used on all 6-cylinder motors. Refer to Fig. MR26-1 for exploded view of caburetor typical of type used on all models. Initial setting for the idle mixture screw (12) is one turn open from the closed position. Run motor until operating temperature is reached, then shift to forward gear and allow motor to run at idle speed. Slowly turn idle mixture screw (12) out (counterclockwise) until motor runs unevenly (loads up). Turn needle in (clockwise) until motor picks up speed and again runs evenly and continue turning until motor slows down and misses. Needle should be set between the two extremes. Turning screw (12) in (clockwise) leans the mixture. Slightly rich idle mixture is more desirable than too lean.

NOTE: Mixture adjustment should not be attempted in neutral.

Standard main jet (13) size is 0.070 inch (1.78 mm) on 90 hp models, 0.072 inch (1.83 mm) on 115 hp models below serial number 5050763, 0.074 inch (1.88 mm) on 115 hp models serial number 5050763 and above, 0.080 inch (2.03 mm) on 140 hp models below serial number 5327663 and 0.074 inch (1.88 mm) on 140 hp models serial number 5327663 and above for operation below 2500 feet (762 m) altitude. Standard

vent jet (V – Fig. MR26-2) size is 0.092 inch (2.34 mm) on 90 hp models, 0.092 inch (2.34 mm) on 115 hp models below serial number 5050763, 0.096 inch (2.44 mm) on 115 hp models serial number 5050763 and above, 0.092 inch (2.34 mm) on 140 hp models below serial number 5327663 and 0.090 inch (2.29 mm) on 140 hp models serial number 5327663 and above for operation below 2500 feet (762 m) altitude. Other jet sizes are available for adjusting the calibration for altitude or other special conditions.

To determine the float level, invert bowl cover (1 – Fig. MR26-3) with inlet needle and seat (5) primary lever (6) and secondary lever (7) installed. Measure distance (A) from carburetor body surface to top of secondary lever (7). Distance (A) should be 13/32 inch (10.32 mm). Adjust distance (A) by bending curved end of primary lever (6). Turn bowl cover (1 – Fig. MR26-4) upright and measure distance (D) between primary lever (6) and end of secondary lever (7). Distance (D) should be ¼ inch (6.4 mm). Bend tab (T) to adjust. The contact spring located in center of float (9 – Fig. MR26-1) should extend 3/32 inch (2.38 mm) above top of float. Check to see if spring has been stretched or damaged.

SPEED CONTROL LINKAGE. The speed control linkage must be synchronized to advance the ignition timing and open the carburetor throttles in a precise manner. Because the two actions are interrelated, it is important to check the complete system following the sequence outlined in the following paragraphs.

Models With Distributor. Refer to the special precautions listed in the IGNITION section before servicing these motors. Incorrect servicing procedures can damage the ignition system.

NOTE: Do not disconnect any part of the ignition system while engine is running or while checking the speed control linkage adjustments.

Connect a power timing light to number 1 (top) spark plug wire. Mount motor in test tank and start engine with timing light installed. Slowly advance speed control until 4°-6° BTDC throttle pickup timing marks are aligned.

Timing grid is marked on cowl support bracket and three punch marks on flywheel are used as timing mark on these models. A white dot is painted on top side of flywheel adjacent to three timing dots.

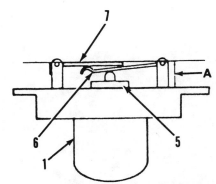

Fig. MR26-3—Distance (A) should be 13/32 inch (10.32 mm). Refer to text for adjustment procedure and Fig. MR26-1 for parts identification.

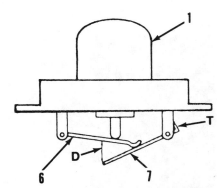

Fig. MR26-4—With bowl cover (1) upright, distance (D) between primary lever (6) and end of secondary lever (7) should be ¼ inch (6.4 m). Bend tab (T) to adjust.

Fig. MR26-6—View of throttle pickup cams and lever typical of models equipped with a distributor. Primary pickup should occur at (1) and secondary pickup at (2). Refer to text for adjustment.

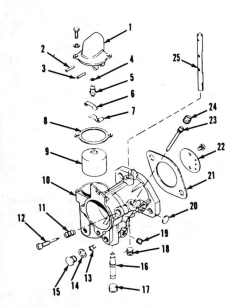

Fig. MR26-1—Exploded view of typical carburetor used on all models. A different cover (1) with a fuel strainer located under the cover is used on some early models.

1. Cover
2. Pin
3. Pin
4. Gasket
5. Inlet needle & seat
6. Primary lever
7. Secondary lever
8. Gasket
9. Float
10. Body
11. Spring
12. Idle mixture screw
13. Main jet
14. Gasket
15. Plug
16. Main nozzle
17. Plug
18. Spring
19. Plug
20. Welch plug
21. Gasket
22. Throttle plate
23. Idle tube
24. Plug
25. Throttle shaft

Fig. MR26-2—View showing vent jet (V), idle mixture screw (12) and main jet access plug (15).

The primary cam on the throttle pickup plate should just contact the primary pickup lever as shown at (1 – Fig. MR26-6) when the speed control is advanced to 4°-6° BTDC pickup position. If clearance at (1) is not 0-0.005 inch (0-0.13 mm), loosen the two attaching screws (P – Fig. MR26-7) and move the throttle pickup plate. Recheck pickup point after tightening the two attaching screws.

To check maximum spark advance, start engine and advance speed control until distributor touches spark advance stop screw (A – Fig. MR26-8). Timing

light should indicate full spark advance at 21° BTDC. Turn spark advance stop screw to adjust full advance timing if necessary.

Secondary throttle pickup should be checked after maximum spark advance is adjusted. With engine stopped, advance speed controls until distributor is just touching spark advance stop screw. Secondary pickup on throttle cam should be just touching secondary pickup on carburetor cluster (2 – Fig. MR26-6) at this point. Turn throttle pickup screw (S – Fig. MR26-7) to adjust secondary throttle pickup.

Maximum throttle stop screw (T – Fig. MR26-8) should be adjusted so throttles are fully opened at maximum speed position of speed control. Linkage should have a small amount of free play at maximum speed position to prevent binding.

Adjust idle speed screw (I) so idle speed is 500-600 rpm on 90 hp models and 550-650 rpm on 115 and 140 hp models with outboard in gear.

Models Without Distributor. Refer to special precautions listed in the IGNITION section before servicing these motors. Incorrect servicing procedures can damage the ignition system.

NOTE: Do not disconnect any part of the ignition system while engine is running or while checking the speed control linkage adjustment.

Check ignition timing pointer alignment as follows: Install a dial indicator gage in number 1 (top) spark plug hole and turn flywheel clockwise until piston is 0.464 inch (12 mm) BTDC. Loosen retaining screw and position timing pointer so it is aligned with ".464 BTDC" mark on flywheel.

If engine is equipped with an idle stabilizer module (M – Fig. MR26-9), disconnect white/black module wire from switch box terminal. Tape end of wire to prevent grounding. Reconnect other white/black wire between switch boxes to switch box terminal. Remove all spark plugs except number 1 (top) cylinder spark plug to prevent engine starting. Detach throttle cable barrel from retainer of cable anchor bracket. Adjust idle stop screw (I – Fig. MR26-10) so idle marks (M – Fig. MR26-11) on throttle cam and bracket are aligned as shown; retighten stop screw locknut. Loosen screw (W) in top carburetor lever (V). Hold idle stop screw (I – Fig. MR26-10) against stop then turn carburetor lever (V – Fig. MR26-11) so throttle valves are completely closed and cam (C) just contacts roller (R). Connect a power timing light to number 1 cylinder spark plug. With outboard in neutral, position throttle lever so idle stop screw is against stop. Crank engine using starter motor and adjust primary pickup screw (P – Fig. MR26-12) so ignition timing is 1°-3° BTDC on 90 hp models, 5°-7° ATDC on 115 hp models and 4°-6° ATDC on 140 hp models.

Open throttle and crank engine using starter motor. Adjust maximum ignition advance screw (A) so ignition timing is 20° BTDC.

NOTE: Due to electronic characteristics of ignition system, maximum advance is set at 20° BTDC but ignition will retard to 18° BTDC at high engine speed.

Fig. MR26-7—View of secondary pickup adjusting screws (S) and primary pickup plate attaching screws (P) typical of models equipped with a distributor.

Fig. MR26-8—View showing location of maximum advance screw (A), idle speed screw (I) and throttle stop screw (T) on models equipped with a distributor.

Fig. MR26-9—View showing location of idle stabilizer module (M) used on some models.

Fig. MR26-10—View of idle speed screw (I) on models without a distributor.

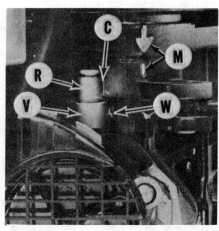

Fig. MR26-11—View of pickup cam (C) and throttle roller (R) on models without a distributor.

C. Pickup cam
M. Idle speed marks
R. Throttle roller
V. Carburetor lever
W. Screw

Fig. MR26-12—Adjust primary pickup screw (P) and maximum advance screw (A) on models without distributor as outlined in text.

Without engine running, move throttle lever to maximum throttle position and adjust full throttle stop screw (T – Fig. MR26-9) so there is 0.010-0.015 inch (0.25-0.38 mm) clearance between roller (R – Fig. MR26-11) and cam (C). Be sure carburetor throttle plates are not acting as stops.

Reconnect idle stabilizer module wire to switch box. Install throttle cable barrel in retainer while adjusting barrel so it fits into retainer and places a very light preload on throttle lever against idle speed screw. Excessive throttle cable preload will result in difficult shifting from forward to neutral.

Adjust idle speed screw (I – Fig. MR26-10) so idle speed is 500-600 rpm on 90 hp models and 550-650 rpm on 115 and 140 hp models with outboard in gear.

REED VALVES. The inlet reed valves are located on the crankshaft second, fourth and sixth main bearings. Each reed valve unit passes fuel mixture from one of the carburetors to the two adjoining cylinders.

Reed petals (2 – Fig. MR26-14) should be perfectly flat and have no more than 0.007 inch (0.178 mm) clearance between free end of reed petal seating surface of center main bearing. The reed stop (1) must be carefully adjusted to 0.162 inch (4.11 mm). This clearance is measured between end of stop and seating surface of reed plate. Seating surface of bearing must be smooth and flat, and may be refinished on a lapping plate after removing reed stops, reed valves and dowels. Do not attempt to bend or straighten a reed petal to modify performance or to salvage a damaged reed. Never install a bent reed. Lubricate the reed valve units with "Quicksilver" Multipurpose Lubricant or a light distributor cam grease when reassembling.

FUEL PUMP. A diaphragm type fuel pump is used. Pressure and vacuum pulsations from the crankcases alternate to pull fuel from the supply tank and supply the carburetor. Most of the work is performed by the main supply chamber (5 – Fig. MR26-16). Vacuum in the crankcase pulls the diaphragm (2) downward causing fuel to be drawn through inlet line (8), past inlet check valve (7) into main pump chamber (5). The alternate pressure forces diaphragm out and fuel leaves the chamber through outlet check valve (6). The booster pump chamber (3) serves to dampen the action of the larger, main pump chamber (5), and increase the maximum potential fuel flow.

When overhauling the fuel pump, renew all defective or questionable parts.

When assembling fuel pump, install check valves as shown in Fig. MR26-17 with tips of retainer (R) pointing away from check valves. Fuel pressure should be at least 2 psi (13.8 kPa) at carburetor when running motor at full throttle.

IGNITION SYSTEM

All models are equipped with a capacitor discharge ignition system. Refer to the appropriate following paragraphs for service.

Models With Distributor

This ignition is extremely durable in normal operation but can be easily damaged by improper testing or servicing procedures. Observe the following list of cautions and use **only** the approved methods for checking the system to prevent damage to the components.
1. DO NOT reverse battery terminals.
2. DO NOT check polarity of battery by sparking the lead wires.
3. DO NOT install resistor type spark plugs or lead wires other than those specified.
4. DO NOT disconnect **any** wires while engine is running.
5. DO NOT ground any wires to engine block when checking. Ground only to front cover plate or bottom cowl to which switch box is mounted as described.
6. DO NOT use tachometer except for those designed or approved for this system.

TROUBLESHOOTING. Use only approved procedures when testing to prevent damage to components.

SPARK TEST. Do not remove spark plug wire while motor is running. Cut off the ground electrode from a stand-

ard spark plug (such as Champion J4J or L4J) and connect one of the spark plug wires to the test plug. Ground the test plug to the support bracket using a clamp or jumper wire.

CAUTION: Do not hold spark plug or wire in hand.

Make certain that test plug is properly grounded, then crank motor with electric starter. If test plug fires but engine will not start, check for incorrect installation of timing belt as outlined in the following TRIGGER AND DISTRIBUTOR paragraphs. Fuel system problems can also prevent starting. If test plug does not fire, check wiring and connections.

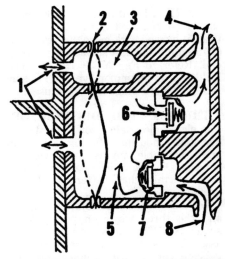

Fig. MR26-16—Schematic view of diaphragm type fuel pump. Pump body mounts on side of cylinder block and is ported to two crankcases as shown.

1. Pressure ports	5. Main fuel chamber
2. Diaphragm	6. Outlet check valve
3. Booster chamber	7. Inlet check valve
4. To carburetor	8. Fuel inlet

Fig. MR26-17—View showing installation of outlet check valve (6) and inlet check valve (7) in fuel pump body. Install retainer (R) so tips are away from check valves.

Fig. MR26-14—View of intermediate main bearing and reed valve assembly. Inspect reed stops (1) and reed petals (2) as outlined in text.

TRIGGER COIL AND SWITCH BOX TEST. To check trigger coil and switch box, manufacturer recommends use of Thunderbolt Ignition Analyzer (C-91-62563A1). Follow instructions accompanying tester.

COIL TEST. The ignition coil can be checked using an ignition tester available from several sources, including the following:

GRAHAM TESTERS, INC.
4220 Central Ave. N.E.
Minneapolis, Minn. 55421

MERC-O-TRONIC
INSTRUMENTS CORP.
215 Branch St.
Almont, Mich. 48003

SPARK PLUGS. The spark plugs should be removed if the center electrode is burned back more than 1/32 inch (0.79 mm) below flat surface of the plug end. Refer to Fig. MR26-19. AC type V40FFM or Champion type L76V, surface gap spark plugs should be used.

TRIGGER AND DISTRIBUTOR. The electronic trigger coil is located in distributor housing (10 – Fig. MR26-20) and is available only as a unit with the housing. Before removing any wires, make certain that battery is disconnected.

To disassemble, disconnect battery and the three wires on port side of switch box. The wires are from trigger assembly and terminals are marked to indicate correct wire connections. Remove cover (18), drive belt pulley (19) and spacer (20). Bend tabs of washer (23) away from nut (21), remove nut and withdraw the distributor from adapter and economizer (25 and 29). Remove clamp (3) and cap (1). Carefully press bearing (15) out of housing by working through the two holes provided.

NOTE: Do not damage nut (17) or shaft when removing bearing.

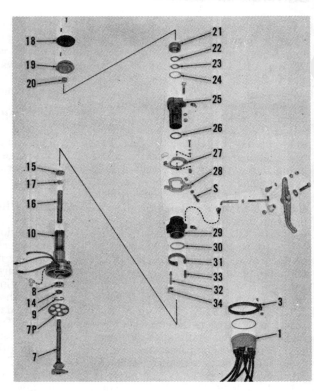

Fig. MR26-20—Exploded view of the ignition distributor and drive used on some models.

1. Distributor cap
3. Clamp
7. Rotor & shaft
7P. Timer plate
8. Ball bearing
9. Snap ring
10. Distributor housing & trigger assy.
14. Spacer
15. Ball bearing
16. Spacer
17. Nut
18. Flange plate
19. Drive pulley
20. Spacer
21. Cap nut
22. Wave washer
23. Tang washer
24. Washer
25. Adapter
26. Washer
27. Throttle cam plate (primary pickup)
28. Throttle cam (secondary pickup)
29. Economizer collar
30. Washer
31. Spring
32. Spring anchor stud
33. Spring anchor pin
34. Spark advance stop

Remove nut (17) then bump the rotor shaft (7) out of bearing (8). The shaft should slide easily out of timer plate (7P) and spacer (14). Bearing (8) can be removed after extracting snap ring (9).

When reassembling, install bearing (8) and snap ring (9). Position spacer (14) then insert the timer plate (7P) into the trigger coil slot. Insert the rotor shaft (7) through the timer plate (7P), spacer (14) and bearing (8).

CAUTION: Make certain that tab on timer plate (7P) correctly engages slot in rotor shaft (7) before pressing shaft into bearing (8).

Install spacer (16) and tighten nut (17) to 75-80 in-lbs. (8.5-9.0 N·m). Rotate rotor shaft and note any interference as timer plate turns. If necessary, install shims between bearing (8) and spacer (14) to adjust timer plate height. Press ball bearing (15) around shaft and into housing (10). Install distributor cap (1) and clamp (3). Joint of clamp should be positioned under the trigger coil wires. Assemble distributor to the economizer collar (29) and adapter (25), then install washers (22, 23 and 24). Tighten cap nut (21), back nut off until the nearest notch lines up with tang of washer (23), then bend tang into notch. Install spacer (20) and pulley (19) over the drive key. Firing order is 1-4-5-2-3-6.

To renew the distributor drive belt, it is first necessary to remove pulley flange plate (18), disengage belt from pulley, then remove flywheel. When installing, position drive belt under alternator stator and around the crankshaft. Install flywheel being careful not to damage the belt. Turn the flywheel and distributor pulley as shown in (Fig. MR26-21) so timing dot (D) is aligned with pulley arrow (A), then install drive belt over the pulley. Recheck timing marks after belt is installed. Marks must be on center line between crankshaft and distributor shaft. Refer to SPEED CONTROL LINKAGE paragraphs for adjusting linkage and ignition timing.

Fig. MR26-19—Surface gap plug snould be renewed if center electrode is 1/32 inch (0.79 mm) below the end of plug.

Fig. MR26-21—Distributor drive belt (B) should be installed with cast arrow (A) on drive pulley (P) aligned with dot (D) on flywheel as shown.

Models Without Distributor

These models are equipped with a solid-state, capacitor discharge ignition system consisting of trigger coils, stator, switch boxes and ignition coils. The trigger coils are contained in a trigger ring module under the flywheel. Diodes, SCR's and capacitors are contained in the switch boxes. Switch boxes, trigger ring module and stator must be serviced as unit assemblies.

Check all wires and connections before troubleshooting ignition circuit. The following test specifications will aid troubleshooting.

STATOR

Tests	Ohms
Blue and red stator leads	5400-6200
Blue/white and red/white stator leads	5400-6200
Red stator lead and engine ground*	125-175
Red/white stator lead and engine ground*	125-175

*If stator has a black ground wire, be sure ground wire is properly connected to engine.

Note when testing the trigger module that yellow sleeves enclose wires from the trigger module to the lower switch box. The lower switch box serves the even-numbered cylinders while the upper switch box serves the odd-numbered cylinders.

TRIGGER MODULE

Tests	Ohms
Brown trigger lead (no yellow sleeve) and white trigger lead (with yellow sleeve)	1100-1400
White trigger lead (no yellow sleeve) and violet trigger lead (with yellow sleeve)	1100-1400
Violet trigger lead (no yellow sleeve) and brown trigger lead (with yellow sleeve)	1100-1400

COOLING SYSTEM

WATER PUMP. The rubber impeller type water pump is housed in the gearcase housing. The impeller is mounted on and driven by the lower unit drive shaft.

When cooling system problems are encountered, first check the water inlet for plugging or partial stoppage, then if not corrected, remove the gearcase housing as outlined in LOWER UNIT section and examine the water pump, water tubes and seals.

POWER HEAD

R&R AND DISASSEMBLE. To remove the power head assembly, first disconnect the battery and remove the top and side cowling. Remove electric starter, then disconnect all interfering wires and linkage. Remove the stud nuts which secure the power head to lower unit then jar power head on exhaust side to loosen gasket. Lift power head from lower unit and install on a suitable stand. Remove the flywheel, distributor, alternator-generator and the carburetors. Exhaust manifold cover, cylinder block cover and transfer port covers should be removed for cleaning and inspection.

Remove screws securing upper and lower crankcase end caps. Remove the main bearing locking bolts from front crankcase half, remove the flange bolts; then remove crankcase front half by inserting screwdriver in the recesses provided on side flanges. Use extra care not to spring the parts or to mar the machined, mating surfaces. Use a mallet or soft faced hammer to tap crankcase end caps from cylinder block assembly. Be careful not to damage adjustment shims on end caps. The crankcase half (6 – Fig. MR26-23) and cylinder assembly (15) are matched and align bored, and are available only as an assembly.

Crankshaft, pistons, bearings and connecting rods may now be removed for service as outlined in the appropriate following paragraphs. When assembling, follow the procedures outlined in the ASSEMBLY paragraph.

ASSEMBLY. When assembling, the crankcase must be completely sealed against both vacuum and pressure. Exhaust manifold and water passages must be sealed against pressure leakage.

Whenever power head is disassembled, it is recommended that all gasket surfaces and machined joints without gaskets be carefully checked for nicks and burrs which might interfere with a tight seal. Make certain that threaded holes in cylinder for attaching the water jacket cover (20 – Fig. MR26-23) are cleaned.

Lubricate all bearing and friction surfaces with engine oil. Loose needle bearings may be held in place during assembly using a light, nonfibrous grease.

After the crankcase, connecting rods, pistons and main bearings are positioned in the cylinder, check the crankshaft end play. Temporarily install the crankshaft end caps (2 and 13) omitting the sealing rings (4 and 9), but using the shims (3 and 10) that were originally installed. Tighten the end cap to cylinder retaining screws. Use a soft hammer to bump the crankshaft each way to seat bearings, then measure the end play.

Bump the crankshaft toward top, and measure clearance between the top crankshaft counterweight and the end cap as shown in Fig. MR26-24. Bump the crankshaft toward bottom and again measure clearance between counterweight and end cap. Subtract the first (minimum) clearance from the second clearance which will indicate the amount of end play. If end play is not within limits of 0.004-0.012 inch (0.102-0.305 mm), add or remove shims (3 or 10 – Fig. MR26-23) as necessary, then recheck. The crankshaft should be centered by varying the amount of shims between upper (3) and lower (10) shim stacks. When centering the crankshaft, make certain that end play is correct.

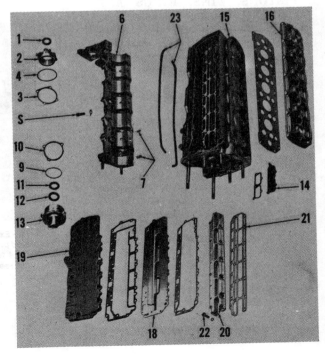

Fig. MR26-23—Exploded view of typical crankcase assembly.

S. Main bearing screw
1. Oil seal
2. End cap
3. Shim
4. "O" ring
6. Crankcase half
7. Dowel pins
9. "O" ring
10. Shim
11. Oil seal
12. Oil seal
13. End cap
14. Transfer port cover
15. Cylinder half
16. Cylinder cover
18. Exhaust plate
19. Exhaust cover
20. Water jacket cover
21. Gasket
22. Screws
23. Sealing strips

Gasket and sealing surfaces should be lightly and carefully coated with an impervious liquid sealer. Surface must be completely coated, using care that excess sealer does not squeeze out into bearings, crankcase or other passages.

Clean the gasket surfaces and threaded holes of water jacket cover (20) and cylinder (15). Coat the first four threads of all screws (22) with Resiweld and allow to set for 10 minutes. Coat gasket surface of water jacket cover and mating surface of cylinder with gasket sealer, then install gasket (21) and water jacket cover (20). Tighten the screws (22) evenly from the center outward to a torque of 200 in.-lbs. (22.6 N·m) on early models and 150 in.-lbs. (16.9 N·m) on late models.

Check the assembly by turning the crankshaft after each step to check for binding or locking which might indicate improper assembly. Remove the cause before proceeding. Rotate the crankshaft until each piston ring in turn appears in one of the exhaust or transfer ports, then check by pressing on ring with a blunt tool. Ring should spring back when released; if it does not, a broken or binding ring is indicated, and the trouble should be corrected.

Tighten the crankcase exhaust cover and cylinder cover cap screws by first tightening the center screws, then tightening screws evenly working toward top of power head. When upper half is tightened, again start at the center and tighten screws alternately toward bottom of power head. Tightening torques are given in the CONDENSED SERVICE DATA table.

PISTONS, PINS, RINGS AND CYLINDERS. Before detaching connecting rods from crankshaft, make sure that rod and cap are properly identified for correct assembly to each other and in the correct cylinder.

Maximum allowable cylinder bore wear or out-of-round is 0.004 inch (0.102 mm). Worn or slightly damaged standard size cylinders may be repaired by boring and honing to fit an oversize piston. Pistons and rings are available in 0.015 inch (0.38 mm) oversize on early models and 0.015 inch (0.38 mm) and 0.030 inch (0.76 mm) oversizes on later models.

Two or three piston rings are used on each piston. Piston rings are interchangeable in the ring grooves and are pinned to prevent rings from rotating in grooves.

Piston pin is pressed in piston bosses and secured with retaining rings. The retaining rings should not be reused. Two types of retaining rings (4 – Fig. MR26-25) have been used and must NOT be interchanged. Some late models use "C" rings and other models use "G" type retaining rings. Piston end of connecting rod is fitted with loose needle rollers. Refer to the CONNECTING RODS, BEARINGS AND CRANKSHAFT paragraphs for number of rollers used. The piston pin needle rollers use the connecting rod bore and the piston pin as bearing races. When assembling, install bearing washers and needle bearings in piston end of connecting rod using light nonfibrous grease to hold them in place. A Mariner special tool may be used to hold needles in position while positioning piston for installation. Piston must be installed so sharp, vertical side of

deflector will be to starboard (intake) side of cylinder block. Heat piston to approximately 135°F (57°C) on early models and 190°F (88°C) on late models, then press piston pin into place. Pin should be centered in piston. Use new retaining rings on each reassembly of engine.

Assemble the connecting rod and piston assemblies, together with the main bearing units to the crankshaft; then install the complete assembly in cylinder half of block. Numbers 2 and 4 pistons should be started first. Use the Ring Compressor Kit (C-91-47844A2), if available; or carefully compress each ring with the fingers if kit is not available. Thoroughly lubricate pistons and rings during assembly.

CONNECTING RODS, BEARINGS AND CRANKSHAFT. Upper and lower ends of crankshaft are carried by ball bearings. The second, fourth and sixth main bearings (Fig. MR26-14) also contain the inlet reed valves. The third and fifth main bearings (13 – Fig. MR26-25), contain loose needle rollers (15) which ride in a split type outer race (14), held together by a retaining ring (16).

The connecting rod uses 29 loose needle rollers at piston end. The crankpin end of connecting rod uses a caged needle bearing. Check rod for alignment by placing rod on a surface plate and checking with a light. Rod is bent or distorted if 0.002 inch (0.05 mm) feeler gage can be inserted between rod and surface plate.

If bearing surface of rod and cap is rough, scored, worn or shows evidence of overheating, renew the connecting rod. Inspect crankpin and main bearing journals. If scored, out-of-round or worn, renew the crankshaft. Check the crankshaft for straightness using a dial indicator and "V" blocks.

Inspect and adjust the reed valves as outlined in REED VALVE paragraph, and reassemble as outlined in ASSEMBLY paragraph.

ELECTRICAL SYSTEM

Refer to Fig. MR26-27 or MR26-28 for a typical wiring diagram. Note the following cautions when servicing electrical components:

DO NOT reverse battery connections. Battery negative (−) terminal is grounded.

DO NOT "spark" battery connections to check polarity.

DO NOT disconnect battery cable while engine is running.

DO NOT crank engine if ignition switch boxes are not grounded to engine.

Fig. MR26-24—Refer to text for method of checking crankshaft end play. The crankshaft should be centered in the cylinder block.

Fig. MR26-25—Exploded view of the crankshaft and associated parts typical of all models. Refer to Fig. MR26-14 for intermediate main bearings and reed valve assemblies.

1. Piston rings
2. Piston
3. Piston pin
4. Retainers
5. Bearing washers
6. Needle rollers
7. Connecting rod
8. Needle rollers
9. Crankshaft
10. Top main bearing
11. Bottom main bearing
12. Bearing alignment dowel
13. Bearing housing
14. Main bearing race
15. Needle rollers
16. Retaining ring

LOWER UNIT

PROPELLER AND DRIVE CLUTCH. Protection for the motor is built into a special cushioning clutch in the propeller hub. No adjustment is possible on the propeller or clutch. Various pitch propellers are available and propeller should be selected to provide full throttle engine operation within rpm range listed below. Propellers other than those designed for the motor must not be used.

Model	RPM Range
90 hp	4500-5000
115 hp	5000-5500
140 hp	5300-5800

R&R AND OVERHAUL. Most service on the lower unit can be performed by detaching the gearcase housing from the drive shaft housing. To remove housing, remove plastic plug and Allen head screw from location (1–Fig. MR26-30). Remove trim tab (2) and screw from under trim tab. Remove stud nut from location (3), and stud nuts (4) on each side and stud nut (5), if so equipped then withdraw the lower unit gearcase assembly.

Remove plugs and drain oil from housing, then secure the gearcase in a soft jawed vise with propeller up. Wedge a piece of wood between propeller and antiventilation plate, remove propeller nut, then remove propeller.

Disassemble gearcase by removing gearcase housing cover nut (61–Fig. MR26-31). Clamp the outer end of pro-

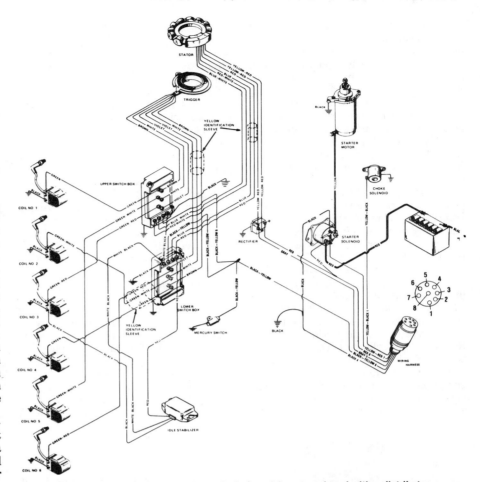

Fig. MR26-28—Wiring diagram typical of models not equipped with a distributor.

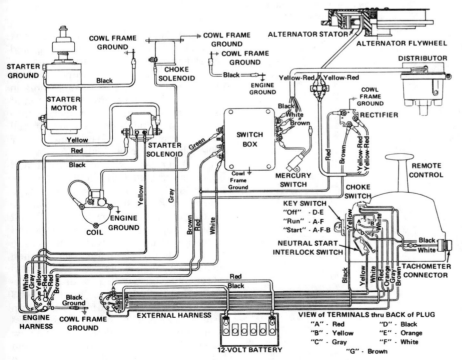

Fig. MR26-27—Wiring schematic for models equipped with a distributor.

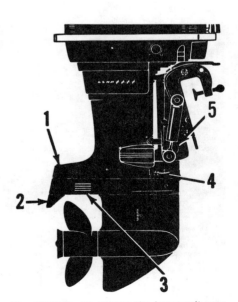

Fig. MR26-30—To remove the lower unit gearcase assembly, remove the attaching screws and stud nuts from positions indicated.

Illustrations courtesy Mariner

187

peller shaft in a soft jawed vise and remove gearcase by tapping with a rubber mallet. Be careful not to lose key (59) or shims (47) on early models. Forward gear (40) will remain in housing. Withdraw propeller shaft from bearing carrier (56) and reverse gear (46).

Clamp bearing carrier (56) in a soft jawed vise and remove reverse gear (46) and bearing (49) with an internal expanding puller and slide hammer. Remove and discard propeller shaft rear seals (58).

To remove dog clutch (43) from propeller shaft, remove retaining ring (44). Insert cam follower (8) in hole in shaft and apply only enough pressure on end of cam follower to remove spring pressure, then push out pin (42) with a small punch. The pin passes through drilled holes in dog clutch and operates in slotted holes in propeller shaft.

To disassemble drive shaft and associated parts, reposition gearcase in vise with drive shaft projecting upward. Remove rubber slinger (11), water pump body (16), impeller (19) and impeller drive key (20). Remove flushing screw and withdraw remainder of water pump parts. Clamp upper end of drive shaft in a soft jawed vise, remove pinion retain-

ing nut or screw (37); then tap gearcase off drive shaft and bearing. Note position and thickness of shims (30 and 30A) on drive shaft upper bearing. On all models, mesh position of pinion is controlled by shims (30) placed underneath the bearing. On models with ball type upper bearing, shims (30A) control shaft end play. The shims are identical but should not be interchanged or mixed, except to adjust the mesh position of drive pinion.

After drive shaft has been removed, forward gear (40) and bearing cone can be withdrawn. Use an internal expanding type puller to withdraw bearing cup if removal is required. Remove and save shim pack (38).

Shift shaft (5) and cam (7) can be removed after removing forward gear and unscrewing bushing (3) from gearcase housing.

If gear wear was abnormal or if any parts that affect gear alignment were renewed, check and adjust gear mesh as follows: Install forward gear (40) and bearing (39) using shims (38) that were originally installed. Position shims (30) that were originally installed at bottom of bearing bore. On late models with taper bearing (32) and spiral gear teeth,

install bearing cup (32) in housing bore against shims (30). On all models, position drive pinion (35) in housing and insert drive shaft (33), with bearing (32) installed, into housing, bearing (34) and gear (35). On all models with ball type upper bearing, the bearing must be firmly seated in housing bore. On all models, install retaining screw or nut (37). Coat gears (35 and 40) with bearing blue and check mesh position. On models with straight-cut gears, pull up on drive shaft gears to check mesh position. On models with spiral gears, it will be necessary to push down on end of drive shaft while checking mesh position. On all models, if gears do not mesh in center of teeth, add or remove shims (30) under bearing as necessary. After setting mesh position, check backlash between teeth of gears (35 and 40). Backlash should be 0.014-0.016 inch (0.356-0.406 mm). To increase clearance (backlash), remove part of shim stack (38) behind bearing cup. If gears are too loose, add shims. After changing thickness of shims (38), gears should be recoated with bearing blue and mesh position should be rechecked. Install bearing (49), thrust washer (48) and reverse gear (46) in bearing carrier (56). To check reverse gear (46) backlash on all early models with straight-cut gear teeth, install bearing carrier and gear assembly using shims (47) that were originally installed. If backlash is not within limits of 0.006-0.008 inch (0.152-0.203 mm), add or remove shims (47) as required. Adding shims at (47) increases backlash (clearance). Reverse gear backlash is not adjustable on models with spiral gears.

When reassembling, long splines on shift rod (5) should be toward top. Shift cam (7) is installed with notches up and toward rear. Assemble shifting parts (9, 8S, 43, 42 and 44) into propeller shaft (45). Pin (42) should be through hole in slide (8S). Position follower (8) in end of propeller shaft and insert shaft into bearing (41) and forward gear. Install the reverse gear and bearing carrier assembly using new seals (55 and 58). Lip of inner seal (58) should face in and lip of outer seal (58) should face propeller (out). On models with ball type bearing at (32), install shims (30A) above bearing and position new gasket (29) and water pump base (23) on housing. Add shims (30A) until the water pump base stands out slightly from gasket, then measure clearance between gasket and water pump base with a feeler gage. Remove shims (30A) equal to 0.002-0.003 inch (0.051-0.076 mm) less than clearance measured. When water pump is tightened down, compression of a new gasket (29) will be sufficient to hold bearing (32) in position with zero clearance.

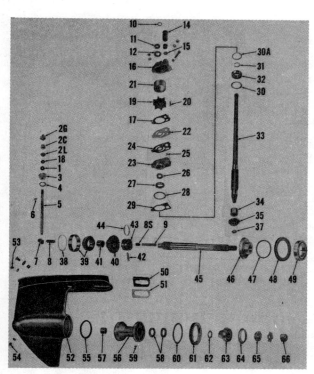

Fig. MR26-31—Exploded view of gearcase assembly typical of all models. Shim (47) is not used on later models. Some models use a tapered bearing in place of ball bearing (32), snap ring (31) and shim (30A).

25. Dowel
26. Oil seal
27. Spring loaded oil seal
28. "O" ring
29. Gasket
30. & 30A. Shims
31. Snap ring
32. Ball bearing
33. Drive shaft
34. Roller bearing
35. Drive pinion
37. Nut
38. Shim
39. Tapered roller bearing
40. Forward gear
41. Roller bearing
42. Cross pin
43. Dog clutch
44. Retaining ring
45. Propeller shaft
46. Reverse gear
47. Shim
48. Thrust washer
48. Ball bearing
50. Exhaust tube seal
51. Support plate
52. Gear housing
53. Vent screw
54. Filler screw
55. "O" ring
56. Bearing carrier
57. Roller bearing
58. Oil seals
59. Key
60. Washer
61. Housing cover nut
62. Thrust washer
63. Thrust hub
64. Cupped washer
65. Splined washer
66. Propeller nut

1. Oil seal
2C. Reverse locking cam
2G. Push rod guide
2L. Lower spacer
3. Bushing
4. "O" ring
5. Shift shaft
6. Snap ring
7. Shift cam
8. Cam follower
8S. Slide
9. Spring
10. "O" ring
11. Rubber ring (slinger)
12. Oil seal
14. Seal
15. Nylon washer
16. Water pump body
17. Gasket
19. Impeller
20. Key
21. Insert
22. Plate
23. Pump base
24. Gasket

Upper oil seal (26) should be installed with lips facing up (toward engine) and lower oil seal (27) should be pressed into water pump base with lips facing down toward propeller shaft. Install remainder of water pump assembly and tighten the screws or nuts to the following recommended torque. Torque ¼-28 nuts to 30 in.-lbs. (3.4 N·m). Torque 5/16-24 nuts to 40 in.-lbs. (4.5 N·m). Torque ¼-20 screws to 20 in.-lbs. (2.2 N·m).

The lower spacer (2L) should be installed with groove down. Reverse locking cam (2C) should be installed on shaft splines so flat on cam is in center toward front when shift shaft (5) is in reverse position. When in neutral, reverse locking cam should be positioned as shown in Fig. MR26-32. The push rod guide (2G – Fig. MR26-31) is located in the drive shaft housing.

Before attaching gearcase housing to the drive shaft housing, make certain that shift cam (7) and the shift lever (on motor) are in forward gear position on early models and neutral position on late models. In forward gear position, shift shaft (5) should be in clockwise position (viewed from top end of shaft). Complete assembly by reversing disassembly.

POWER TILT/TRIM

Non-Integral Type

FLUID. Recommended fluid is SAE 10W-30 or 10W-40 automotive oil. With outboard in full up position, oil level should reach bottom of fill plug hole threads. Do not overfill.

BLEEDING. To bleed air from hydraulic system, position outboard at full tilt and engage tilt lock lever. Without disconnecting hoses, remove hydraulic trim cylinders. Be sure fluid reservoir is full and remains so during bleeding operation. Remove down circuit bleed screw (D – Fig. MR26-35) and "O" ring. Press "IN" control button for a few seconds, release button and wait approximately one minute. Repeat until expelled oil is air-free. Install "O" ring and bleed screw (D) and repeat procedure on opposite cylinder. Place cylinder in a horizontal position so bleed port (P – Fig. MR26-36) is up and remove up circuit bleed screw (U). Press "UP" and "UP/OUT" control buttons for a few seconds, release buttons and wait approximately one minute. Repeat until expelled oil is air-free. Install "O" ring and bleed screw (U) and repeat procedure on opposite cylinder. Reinstall cylinders.

ADJUST TRIM LIMIT SWITCH. Operate trim control so outboard is in full down position. Press "UP/OUT" or "UP" control button and hold until pump motor stops. Outboard should tilt up and stop so there is ½ inch (12.7 mm) overlap (L – Fig. MR26-37) between swivel bracket flange (W) and clamp bracket flange (M). Pull up on lower unit to remove slack when checking overlap (L). Note that if cylinder rods enter cylinders more than an additional ⅛ inch (3.17 mm), that hydraulic system should be bled of air as outlined in BLEEDING section. If overlap (L) is incorrect, loosen retainer screw (R – Fig. MR26-38) then turn adjusting nut (N)

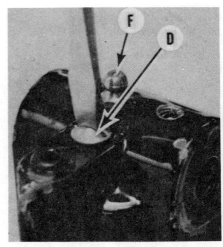

Fig. MR26-35—View showing location of down circuit bleed screw (D) and grease fitting (F).

Fig. MR26-36—View showing location of up circuit bleed screw (U) and bleed port (P).

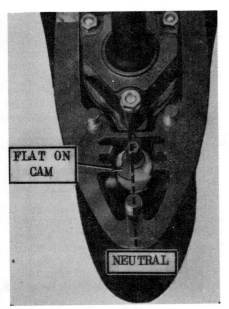

Fig. MR26-32—The reverse locking cam must be in position shown when lower unit (and the shift shaft) are in neutral.

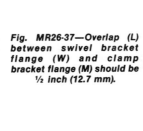

Fig. MR26-37—Overlap (L) between swivel bracket flange (W) and clamp bracket flange (M) should be ½ inch (12.7 mm).

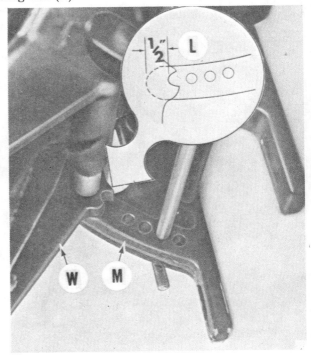

Fig. MR26-38—Loosen retainer screw (R) and turn trim limit adjusting nut (N) to adjust trim limit switch.

counterclockwise to increase overlap or clockwise to decrease overlap. Retighten retainer screw (R) and recheck adjustment.

PRESSURE TEST. To check hydraulic system pressure, disconnect four hoses attached to control valve as shown in Fig. MR26-39; small hoses are for up circuit while large hoses are for down circuit. Connect a pressure gage to one up circuit port (small) of control valve and another pressure gage to one down circuit port (large). Screw plugs into remaining ports. Check fluid reservoir and fill if necessary. Operate trim control in up direction and note pressure

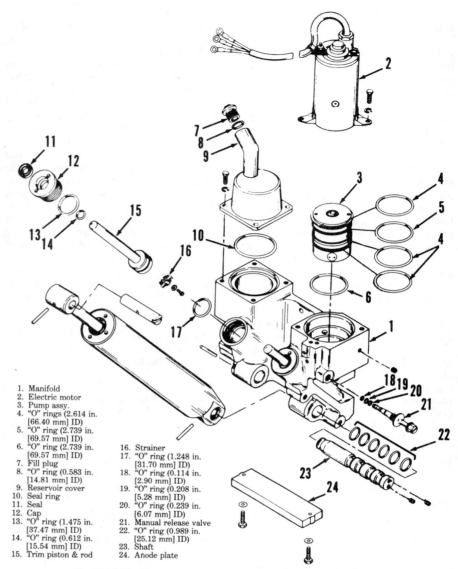

1. Manifold
2. Electric motor
3. Pump assy.
4. "O" rings (2.614 in. [66.40 mm] ID)
5. "O" ring (2.739 in. [69.57 mm] ID)
6. "O" ring (2.739 in. [69.57 mm] ID)
7. Fill plug
8. "O" ring (0.583 in. [14.81 mm] ID)
9. Reservoir cover
10. Seal ring
11. Seal
12. Cap
13. "O" ring (1.475 in. [37.47 mm] ID)
14. "O" ring (0.612 in. [15.54 mm] ID)
15. Trim piston & rod
16. Strainer
17. "O" ring (1.248 in. [31.70 mm] ID)
18. "O" ring (0.114 in. [2.90 mm] ID)
19. "O" ring (0.208 in. [5.28 mm] ID)
20. "O" ring (0.239 in. [6.07 mm] ID)
21. Manual release valve
22. "O" ring (0.989 in. [25.12 mm] ID)
23. Shaft
24. Anode plate

Fig. MR26-45—Exploded view of integral type power tilt/trim system.

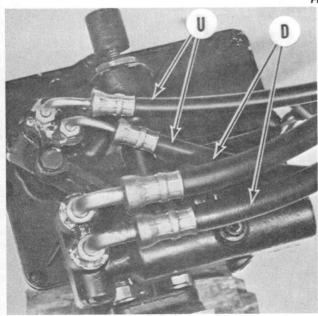

Fig. MR26-39—View of control valve showing location of up circuit hoses (U) and down circuit hoses (D).

gage reading. Minimum pressure should be 3500 psi (24.1 MPa) on new pumps with a red sleeve on wires or 3200-3500 psi (22.0-24.1 MPa) minimum on used pumps with red sleeve on wires. Minimum pressure on all other new pumps is 3000 psi (20.7 MPa) while minimum pressure on used pumps is 2700-3000 psi (18.6-20.7 MPa). Release trim control button. Pressure will drop slightly after stabilizing but should not drop faster than 100 psi (690 kPa) every 15 seconds. Operate trim control in down direction and note pressure gage reading. Minimum pressure is 500-1000 psi (3.4-6.9 MPa). Release trim control button. Pressure will drop slightly after stabilizing but should not drop faster than 100 psi (690 kPa) every 15 seconds. If pressure is normal, inspect trim cylinders and hoses for leakage. If pressure is abnormal, install a good control valve and recheck pressure. If

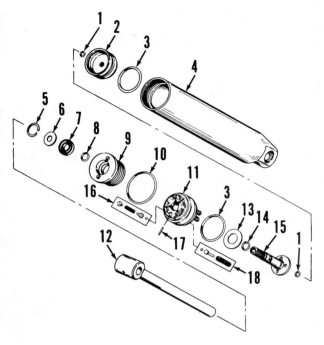

Fig. MR26-46—Exploded view of tilt cylinder components.

1. "O" ring (0.307 in. [7.79 mm] ID)
2. Cup
3. "O" ring (1.957 in. [49.71 mm] ID)
4. Cylinder
5. Circlip
6. Washer
7. Scraper
8. "O" ring (0.854 in. [21.69 mm] ID)
9. Cap
10. "O" ring (2.067 in. [52.5 mm] ID)
11. Piston
12. Rod
13. Washer
14. "O" ring (0.661 in. [16.79 mm] ID)
15. Rod end
16. Check valve assy.
17. Pin
18. Check valve assy.

Fig. MR26-47—Release pressure on system, then remove Allen head plug (U) and install a 5000 psi (34.5 MPa) test gage with a suitable adapter and hose to test system pressure when operated in the "UP" direction. View identifies location of manual release valve (21).

pressure remains abnormal, install a new pump body.

Integral Type

FLUID AND BLEEDING. Recommended fluid is Dexron II or Type AF automatic transmission fluid. Remove fill plug (7 – Fig. MR26-45) and fill reservoir until fluid is visible in fill tube with the outboard motor in the full-up position.

The hydraulic circuit is self-bleeding as the tilt/trim system is operated through several cycles. After servicing system, be sure to check reservoir level after filling and operating system.

HYDRAULIC TESTING. The system can be checked by connecting a 5000 psi (34.5 MPa) test gage to the UP (U – Fig. MR26-47) and DOWN (D – Fig. MR26-48) ports. Prior to connecting test gage, place outboard motor in the full-up position and engage tilt lock lever. Unscrew reservoir fill plug and rotate manual release valve (21 – Fig. MR26-47) three to four turns counterclockwise to release pressure on system. Remove UP

or DOWN Allen head test port plug and connect test gage with suitable adapter and hose. Install fill plug and rotate manual release valve clockwise until seated. System pressure when testing at UP (U) port should be a minimum of 1300 psi (8.9 MPa). System pressure when testing at DOWN (D – Fig. MR26-48) port should be a minimum of 500 psi (3.5 MPa). Release pressure on system as previously outlined prior to removing test gage. Reinstall Allen head plug.

OVERHAUL. Refer to Fig. MR26-45 for an exploded view of manifold and trim cylinder components, and Fig. MR26-46 for an exploded view of tilt cylinder components. Special socket 91-44487A1 and a spanner wrench is required to service trim and tilt cylinders. Keep all components clean and away from contamination. Keep components separated and label if needed for correct reassembly. Note "O" ring sizes as stated in legends of Figs. MR26-45 and MR26-46. Lubricate all "O" rings or seal lips with Dexron II or Type AF

automatic transmission fluid during reassembly.

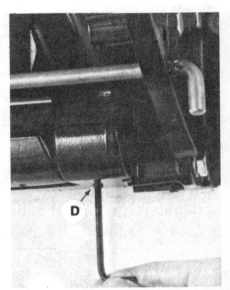

Fig. MR26-48—Release pressure on system, then remove Allen head plug (D) and install a 5000 psi (34.5 MPa) test gage with a suitable adapter and hose to test system pressure when operated in the "DOWN" direction.

MARINER 100 HP (After 1987)
AND 115 HP (After 1988) Four-Cylinders

CONDENSED SERVICE DATA

TUNE-UP

Hp/rpm	100/4750-5250
	(74.6 kW)
	115/4750-5250
	(85.8 kW)
Bore	3.375 in.
	(85.72 mm)
Stroke	2.930 in.
	(74.42 mm)
Displacement	105 cu. in.
	(1720.6 cc)
Compression at Cranking Speed	*
Firing Order	1-3-2-4
Ignition Type	CDI

Spark Plug:
- NGK ....BUHW
- AC. V40FFM
- Champion L76V

Idle Speed (in gear)	650-700 rpm
Fuel:Oil Ratio	See Text
Gearcase Oil Capacity	22.5 fl. oz.
	(665.3 mL)

*Compression should not vary more than 15 psi (103.5 kPa) between cylinders.

SIZES-CLEARANCES

Piston Rings:
- End Gap. ....*
- Side Clearance ....*

Piston Skirt Clearance	0.005 in.
	(0.13 mm)

Crankshaft Bearing Type:
- Top Main Bearing..............Caged Roller
- Center Main Bearings ....Loose Roller
  - Number of Rollers ....32 Each
- Bottom Main Bearing ....Ball Bearing
- Crankpin ....Caged Roller

Piston Pin Bearing:
- Type ....Loose Roller
- Number of Rollers ....29 Each

*Publication not authorized by manufacturer.

TIGHTENING TORQUES

Connecting Rod	*
Crankcase Cover	†
Crankcase End Cap (Lower)	150 in.-lbs.
	(17 N·m)
Cylinder Block Cover	180 in.-lbs.
	(20.3 N·m)
Exhaust Cover	180 in.-lbs.
	(20.3 N·m)
Flywheel Nut	120 ft.-lbs.
	(162.7 N·m)
Fuel Pump Screws	40 in.-lbs.
	(4.5 N·m)
Intake Manifolds	180 in.-lbs.
	(20.3 N·m)
Oil Injection Pump Screws	60 in.-lbs.
	(6.8 N·m)
Power Head-to-Drive Shaft Housing	350 in.-lbs.
	(39.5 N·m)
Reed Block	60 in.-lbs.
	(6.8 N·m)
Spark Plugs	20 ft.-lbs.
	(27.1 N·m)

*Tighten connecting rod screws to 15 in.-lbs. (1.7 N·m), check rod-to-cap alignment then tighten to 30 ft.-lbs. (40.7 N·m). After tightening to 30 ft.-lbs. (40.7 N·m), tighten screws an additional 90 degrees. Refer to text.
†Tighten large inner crankcase cover screws to 25 ft.-lbs. (33.9 N·m) and small outer screws to 180 in.-lbs. (20.3 N·m).

LUBRICATION

The power head is lubricated by oil mixed with the fuel. All models are equipped with oil injection. The oil injection pump delivers oil relative to crankshaft speed and throttle position. The recommended fuel is regular leaded, premium low-lead or unleaded gasoline with minimum octane rating of 86. The recommended oil is Quicksilver 2-Cycle Outboard Oil.

During break-in of a new or rebuilt engine (initial 30 gallons [113.6 L] of fuel), use a 50:1 fuel and oil mixture in the fuel tank in combination with the oil injection system to ensure sufficient power head lubrication. After using the first 30 gallons (113.6 L) of fuel, switch to straight gasoline in the fuel tank.

The lower unit gears and bearings are lubricated by oil contained in the gearcase. The recommended gearcase oil is Quicksilver Super Duty Gear Lubricant. Gearcase capacity is 22.5 fl. oz. (665.3 mL). The lower unit gearcase should be drained and refilled after initial 25 hours of operation, then after every 100 hours or seasonally thereafter. Fill gearcase through drain/fill plug hole until oil reaches the first vent plug hole. Refer to Fig. MR27-1. Install first vent plug and continue filling until oil reaches second vent plug hole. When oil reaches second vent plug hole, drain approximately one ounce (30 mL) to allow for oil expansion.

Make sure vent and fill plugs are securely tightened with new gaskets if necessary.

FUEL SYSTEM

CARBURETOR. Refer to Fig. MR27-2 for exploded view of typical WME carburetor. Four WME-11 carburetors are used. Carburetor model number may be stamped on face of air box mounting flange on early models or is stamped on top of mounting flange on all other models. Note that carburetor model numbers contain the suffix 1, 2, 3 and 4 for installation on their respective cylinder.

On models 100 and 115, cylinders number 3 and 4 are inoperative at engine speeds below approximately 1800 rpm due to reduced fuel flow from their respective carburetors. On carburetors used on cylinders number 3 and 4, the off idle discharge ports are relocated farther from the power head so the fuel:air mixture at idle speeds is too lean for combustion to occur, yet adequate to lubricate the cylinders. As engine speed reaches approximately 1800 rpm and air flow through carburetors increases, the fuel:air mixture to cylinders 3 and 4 becomes sufficient to support combustion and all four cylinders become operational.

Initial setting of slow speed mixture screw (5) is 1¼ turns open from a lightly seated position. Only top two carburetors are equipped with slow speed mixture screws. Final slow speed mixture adjustment should be performed with engine running at normal operating temperature, in forward gear, with the correct propeller installed and boat in the water, or with the correct test wheel installed and lower unit submersed in a suitable test tank.

Air calibration screw (20) is preset and sealed by the manufacturer, and should not require further adjustment. Conventional carburetor cleaning solutions should not affect the sealant used to secure the factory adjustment.

To check float level, remove float bowl (19) and gasket (13), invert carburetor and measure from float bowl mating surface to float as shown in Fig. MR27-3. Float level should be 7/16 inch (11.1 mm) measured as shown. Carefully bend metal tab (T) to adjust.

Standard main jet (16) size for normal operation at elevations up to 2500 feet (762 m) is 0.054 inch (1.73 mm) on 100 hp models and 0.074 inch (1.83 mm) on 115 hp models. Main jet (16) size should be reduced from standard size by 0.002 inch (0.05 mm) for operation at elevations of 2500-5000 feet (762-1524 m), 0.004 inch (0.10 mm) at elevations of 5000-7500 feet (1524-2286 m) and 0.006 inch (0.15 mm) at elevations of 7500 feet (2286 m) and up.

All models are equipped with an electrically operated enrichment valve to provide additional fuel to aid cold starting. Enrichment valve is activated by pushing in on ignition key. Pressurized fuel is fed to the enrichment valve from a "T" fitting between carburetors number 1 and 2. When valve is opened, fuel is fed to all four carburetors through "T" fittings on the intake manifolds of cylinders number 2 and 4, then to cylinders number 1 and 3 through internal passages. Enrichment valve can be operated manually by depressing button located on the valve.

If enrichment system malfunction is noted, make sure battery voltage is present at valve (yellow/black wire) when key (or choke button) is depressed and that sufficient fuel is being delivered to the valve.

ACCELERATOR PUMP. A diaphragm type linkage operated accelerator pump attached to the side of the power head provides additional fuel to cylinders 3 and 4 during rapid acceleration. Fuel from the accelerator pump passes

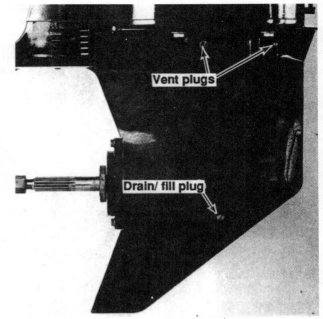

Fig. MR27-1—View of drain/fill and vent plugs. Refer to text when refilling gearcase.

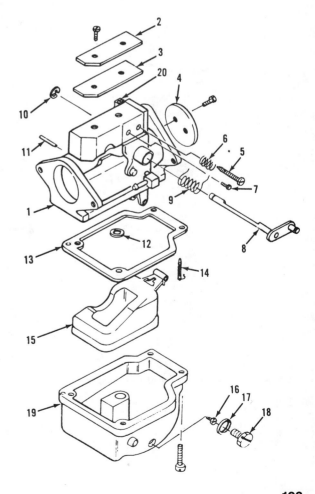

Fig. MR27-2—Exploded view of typical WME carburetor.
1. Body
2. Cover
3. Gasket
4. Throttle valve
5. Low speed mixture screw
6. Spring
7. Vent jet (back drag jet)
8. Throttle shaft
9. Spring
10. "E" ring
11. Pin
12. Gasket
13. Gasket
14. Inlet needle
15. Float
16. Main jet
17. Gasket
18. Plug
19. Float bowl
20. Air calibration screw

through an inline filter and then to the injectors located in the transfer ports of cylinders 3 and 4. The injectors are equipped with check valves that unseat at approximately 11-14 psi (75.8-96.5 kPa) allowing fuel to flow into cylinders. To test check valves, remove injectors from cylinder block and lubricate valve by spraying a small amount of WD-40 or

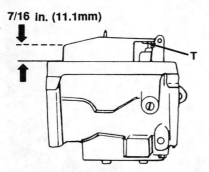

7/16 in. (11.1mm)

Fig. MR27-3—Check float level as shown. Bend metal tab (T) to adjust.

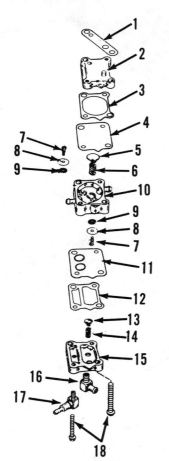

Fig. MR27-5—Exploded view of fuel pump assembly.

1. Gasket	10. Pump body
2. Pump base	11. Boost diaphragm
3. Gasket	12. Gasket
4. Diaphragm	13. End cap
5. End cap	14. Spring
6. Spring	15. Chamber plate
7. Retainer	16. Fitting
8. Check valve	17. Check valve
9. Rubber disc	18. Screws

equivalent into barbed end of valve. Remove excess WD-40 using compressed air. Using a suitable hand-held pump, apply pressure to injector until check valve unseats (approximately 11-14 psi [75.8-96.5 kPa]). After check valve unseats, pressure should not drop below 5 psi (34.5 kPa) in 30 seconds. Renew injector if not as specified.

Accelerator pump adjustment is critical to the proper operation of outboard motor. Refer to SPEED CONTROL LINKAGE section for adjustment.

FUEL PUMP. The diaphragm type fuel pump is activated by crankcase pulsations. Test pump by installing a clear fuel hose between pump and carburetors. Start engine and check for air bubbles in fuel line. Fuel pump output should be approximately 4-6 psi (27.6-41.4 kPa) at full throttle.

Remove fuel pump from power head by unscrewing two Phillips head screws. Disassemble pump by unscrewing two hex head screws. Inspect all components for wear or damage and renew as necessary. Make sure check valve (17—Fig. MR27-5) is functioning properly. When reassembling pump, lubricate check valve retainers (7) with engine oil or soapy water to ease installation. Trim end of retainer (7) at ridge to prevent retainer from contacting pump diaphragm.

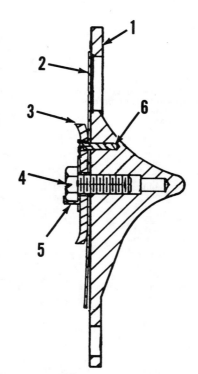

Fig. MR27-6—Sectional view of reed valve assembly.

1. Reed block	4. Screw
2. Reed petal	5. Locking tab washer
3. Retainer	6. Pin

NOTE: Fuel pump components have a "V" tab on one side for directional reference during assembly. Be CERTAIN "V" tabs on all components are aligned.

The manufacturer recommends assembling fuel pump using 1/4-inch bolts or dowels as guides to ensure that all components are properly aligned. Be especially careful with gasket (12) and diaphragm (11). The two large holes in diaphragm (11) are provided for oil from injection pump to enter the gasoline flow. Failure to properly align gasket (12) and diaphragm (11) may result in power head damage.

REED VALVES. Reed valve assemblies are located between crankcase cover and intake manifolds. Reed valves can be removed for inspection after removing carburetors and intake manifolds.

Do not disassemble reed valve assembly unless necessary. Screw (4—Fig. MR27-6) is installed at the factory using Loctite. Reed petals (2) should be flat and smooth along entire seating surface. Renew reed petals if cracked, chipped or damaged, or if petals stand open in excess of 0.020 inch (0.51 mm). Never attempt to bend or straighten a damaged reed petal.

Make sure reed petals are properly positioned over pins (6) when assembling reed valves. Renew locking tab washer (5) and tighten screw (4) to 60 in.-lbs. (6.8 N·m). It may be necessary to continue tightening screw (4) to align locking tab with flat area of screw, but, do not exceed 100 in.-lbs. (11.3 N·m). Be sure to bend locking tab to secure screw (4).

SPEED CONTROL LINKAGE. To verify timing pointer alignment, install a suitable dial indicator into number 1 (top) spark plug hole. Rotate flywheel clockwise until number 1 piston is at TDC. Zero dial indicator and rotate flywheel counterclockwise until dial indicator indicates approximately 0.600 inch (15.24 mm) BTDC, then rotate flywheel clockwise until dial indicator indicates exactly 0.554 (14.07 mm) BTDC. With flywheel in this position, timing pointer should be aligned with .554 timing mark on flywheel. If not, loosen pointer screws and move pointer as necessary to align pointer with .491 timing mark. Tighten timing pointer screws to 20 in.-lbs. (2.3 N·m).

Ignition timing may be adjusted at cranking speed if desired. To adjust ignition timing at cranking speed, proceed as follows: Remove all spark plugs to prevent engine from starting and install a suitable spark gap tool to spark plug leads. Disconnect throttle cable from throttle lever (2—Fig. MR27-8) and connect a suitable timing light to number 1 (top) spark plug lead. Shift outboard into neutral gear. While holding throttle lever (2) in idle position, crank engine while noting timing marks. Adjust idle timing screw (6) to obtain 3 degrees BTDC timing at cranking speed. Next, hold lever (2) so maximum advance screw (10) is against stop. Crank engine while observing timing marks and adjust screw (10) so maximum spark advance is 27 degrees BTDC.

NOTE: Maximum spark advance with engine running at 3000-5000 rpm should be 23 degrees BTDC. Due to the electronic spark advance characteristics of the ignition system, timing adjustment at cranking speed should be set as previously described to obtain the specified spark advance with engine running at 3000-5000 rpm. Timing adjustments performed at cranking speed should be verified, and readjusted if necessary, with engine running at 3000-5000 rpm.

When reinstalling throttle cable on lever (2), adjust throttle cable barrel so cable applies a slight preload (toward idle position) on throttle lever (2). Note that excessive preload will result in difficult forward gear to neutral shifting. Readjust if necessary.

Carburetor throttle valves must be synchronized to open and close at exactly the same time. Proceed as follows to synchronize carburetors and adjust speed control linkage: Loosen cam follower screw (13—Fig. MR27-8). Loosen synchronizing screws (4). Make sure all carburetor throttle valves are fully closed, then apply light downward pressure on vertical shaft (3) and tighten screws (4) starting with top screw and working down. Verify that all throttle valves are fully closed after tightening screws (4) and readjust if necessary.

Loosen idle stop screw (5) locknut and hold throttle lever (2) so idle stop screw (5) is against the stop. Hold cam follower roller (8) against throttle cam (7) and adjust idle stop screw (5) to align throttle cam mark (12) with center of roller (8). While holding throttle lever (2) in the idle position, adjust cam follower (9) to provide a clearance of 0.005-0.020 inch (0.13-0.51 mm) between roller (8) and throttle cam (7), then retighten screw (13). Loosen full throttle stop screw (11) locknut. While holding throttle lever (2) in the full throttle position, adjust full throttle stop screw (11) so carburetor throttle valves are fully open while allowing approximately 0.015 inch (0.38 mm) free play in throttle linkage to prevent throttle valves from bottoming out. Retighten full throttle stop screw locknut.

To adjust accelerator pump, hold throttle cam in the full throttle position, loosen accelerator mounting screws and adjust pump to provide a clearance of 0.020-0.040 inch (0.51-1.02 mm) between throttle cam and top of accelerator pump casting (not plunger) as shown in Fig. MR27-9.

With throttle lever in the idle position, stamped mark on oil injection pump lever should align with stamped mark on oil pump body. Disconnect and adjust length of oil pump control rod to adjust.

NOTE: Some models may have two stamped marks on oil injection pump body.

On models so equipped, disregard the mark on the right side (looking straight at pump) and reference mark on left.

OIL INJECTION SYSTEM

BLEEDING OIL PUMP. Make sure carburetors and oil pump are properly synchronized as outlined in SPEED CONTROL LINKAGE section. To bleed air from oil injection system, loosen bleed screw (B—Fig. MR27-10) three or four turns and allow oil to flow from bleed hole (with engine NOT running) until air bubbles are no longer present in oil pump inlet hose. Retighten bleed

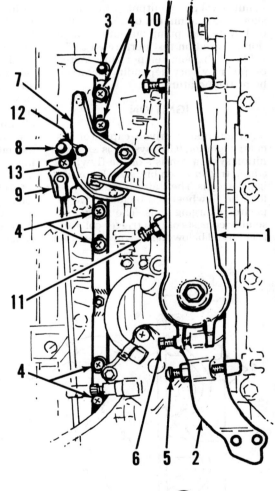

Fig. MR27-8—View of speed control linkage. Refer to text for synchronization procedure.

1. Spark advance lever
2. Throttle lever
3. Vertical shaft
4. Synchronizing screws
5. Idle stop screw
6. Idle timing screw
7. Throttle cam
8. Cam follower roller
9. Cam follower
10. Maximum spark advance screw
11. Full throttle stop screw
12. Throttle cam mark
13. Cam follower screw

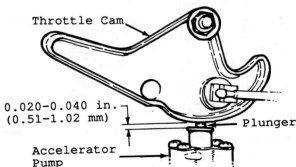

Fig. MR27-9—With throttle cam in full throttle position, clearance between cam and top of accelerator pump casting should be as shown. Loosen accelerator pump mounting screws to adjust.

screw (B) to 25 in.-lbs. (2.8 N·m). Start engine and run at idle speed until no air bubbles are noted in pump outlet hose.

CHECKING OIL PUMP OUTPUT. A 50:1 (25:1 if during break-in period) fuel and oil mixture must be used in fuel tank while checking pump output.

Remove oil pump output hose from fuel pump and plug fuel pump fitting. Place disconnected end of oil pump outlet hose into a graduated container. Remove oil pump control rod (6—Fig. MR27-10) from pump lever and rotate pump lever to full throttle position (counterclockwise). Connect an accurate tachometer to engine, start engine and allow to run at 700 rpm for 15 minutes. Oil pump output in 15 minutes should be a minimum of 25.5 mL (0.86 oz.). Note that pump output specification is based on test performed at 70° F (21.1° C) room temperature. Actual output may vary depending upon ambient temperature.

IGNITION

An alternator driven capacitor discharge ignition (CDI) system is used. Ignition system consists of the flywheel, stator, trigger assembly, switch box and ignition coils. The stator is mounted below the flywheel and includes two capacitor charging coils. The trigger assembly consists of two trigger coils and is mounted below the flywheel. Ignition timing is advanced and retarded by rotating trigger assembly in relation to the inner flywheel magnets. Refer to SPEED CONTROL LINKAGE section for timing adjustment procedures. Diodes, capacitors and SCR's are contained in the switch box. Switch box, trigger assembly and stator must be serviced as unit assemblies. Refer to Fig. MR27-12 for wiring diagram.

If engine malfunction is noted, and the ignition system is suspected, make sure the spark plugs and all electrical wiring are in acceptable condition and all electrical connections are clean and tight prior to trouble-shooting CDI system.

To properly test the switch box and ignition coils require the use of Quicksilver Multi-Meter DVA Tester part 91-99750 or a suitable voltmeter capable of measuring a minimum of 400 DC volts used with Quicksilver Direct Voltage Adaptor (DVA) part 91-89045. Follow instructions provided by tester manufacturer when performing tests. If these testers are not available, a process of elimination must be used when testing the ignition system. Stator and trigger assemblies can be effectively tested using a suitable ohmmeter.

NOTE: All tests that involve cranking or running the engine must be performed with lead wires connected. Switch box case MUST be grounded to engine for all tests or switch box may be damaged.

To test ignition system, proceed as follows:

IGNITION COILS. Connect DVA red test lead to ignition coil positive (+) terminal and black test lead to coil negative (−) terminal. Position tester selector switch to 400 VDC. Tester should read 150-250 volts at cranking or idle speed (300-1000 rpm) and 180-280 volts at 1000-4000 rpm. If voltage readings are below specified reading, refer to SWITCH BOX STOP CIRCUIT test. If readings are within specifications, connect a suitable spark tester to ignition coil high tension leads, crank engine and note spark. If weak or no spark is noted, renew ignition coil(s). If normal spark is noted, renew spark plugs. If malfunction is still evident after renewing spark plugs, check ignition timing. If ignition timing is erratic, inspect trigger advance linkage for excessive wear or damage and inner flywheel magnets (shifted position or other damage). If timing is within specifications, problem is not in ignition system.

SWITCH BOX STOP CIRCUIT. Connect DVA black test lead to engine ground and red test lead to black/yellow switch box terminal (orange terminal on early models). Refer to Fig. MR27-12. Set DVA selector switch to 400 VDC. Voltage reading at cranking and all running speeds should be 200-360 volts. If reading is within specifications, refer to STATOR tests. If reading is above specified voltages, connect a suitable ohmmeter between trigger brown and white/black leads, then white and white/black leads. Trigger resistance should be 700-1000 ohms at both test connections. If not, renew trigger assembly. If trigger resistance is acceptable, renew switch box and repeat SWITCH BOX STOP CIRCUIT test. If SWITCH BOX STOP CIRCUIT test reading is below specified voltage, disconnect ignition switch, stop switch and mercury switch from black/yellow switch box terminal (orange switch box terminal on early models). With stop switch, ignition switch and mercury switch isolated, repeat SWITCH BOX STOP CIRCUIT test. If reading is now within specification, ignition switch, stop switch or mercury switch is defective. If reading remains below specification, refer to STATOR test.

STATOR. Connect DVA black lead to engine ground and red lead to blue switch box terminal. Set DVA selector switch to 400 VDC. Voltage reading should be 210-310 volts at cranking and idle speeds and 190-310 volts at 1000-4000 rpm. Switch DVA red test lead to red switch box terminal. Leave black test lead connected to engine ground. Voltage reading should be 20-100 volts

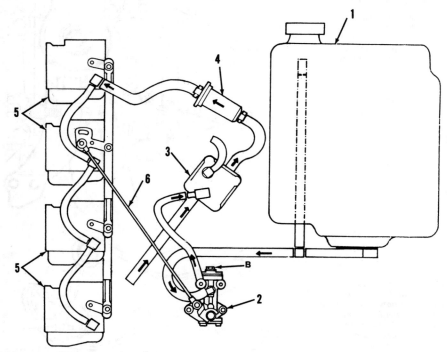

Fig. MR27-10—View of oil injection system.

B. Bleed screw	4. Filter
1. Oil tank	5. Carburetors
2. Oil pump	6. Oil pump control
3. Fuel pump	rod

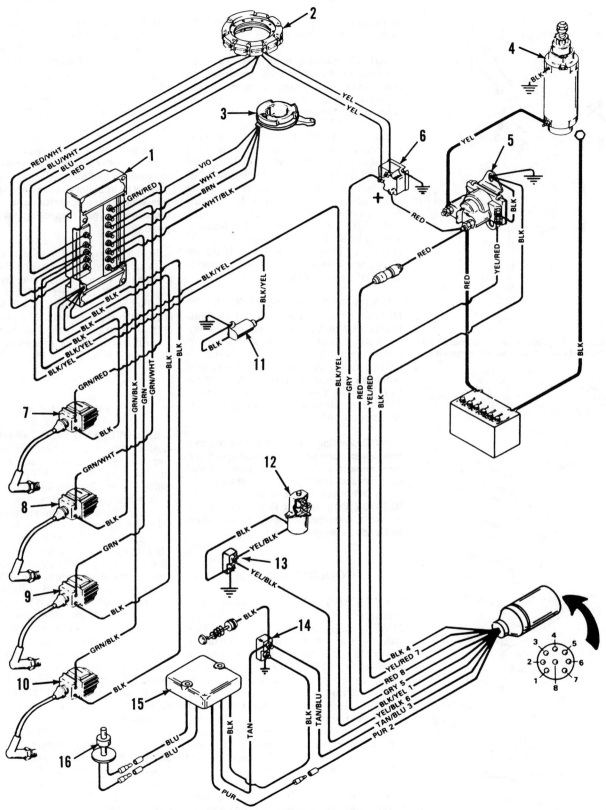

Fig. MR27-12—Wiring diagram of ignition and electrical system.

1. Switch box
2. Stator
3. Trigger
4. Starter motor
5. Starter solenoid
6. Rectifier
7. Ignition coil (no. 1)
8. Ignition coil (no. 2)
9. Ignition coil (no. 3)
10. Ignition coil (no. 4)
11. Mercury switch
12. Enrichment valve
13. Terminal block
14. Terminal block
15. Low oil warning module
16. Low oil sensor

V. Violet
W. White
Y. Yellow
Bl. Blue
Br. Brown
B. Black
G. Green
R. Red
T. Tan
Gr. Gray
Pr. Purple
B/Y. Black with yellow tracer

G/B. Green with black tracer
G/R. Green with red tracer
G/W. Green with white tracer
R/W. Red with white tracer

Y/B. Yellow with black tracer
Y/R. Yellow with red tracer
W/B. White with black tracer
Bl/W. Blue with white tracer
T/Bl. Tan with blue tracer

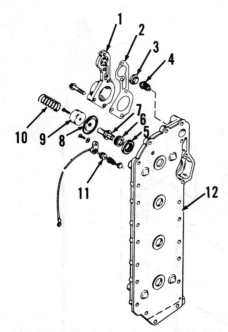

Fig. MR27-13—Exploded view of thermostat (4), pressure relief valve (7) and related components.

1. Cover	8. Diaphragm
2. Gasket	9. Cup
3. Seal	10. Spring
4. Thermostat	11. Temperature sensor
5. Grommet	12. Cylinder block
6. Gasket	cover
7. Pressure relief valve	

Fig. MR27-14—Exploded view of water pump assembly.

1. Water tube seal	
2. Screw	9. Plate
3. Washer	10. Gasket
4. Insulator	11. Screw
5. Cover	12. Washer
6. Impeller	13. Base
7. Key	14. Seal
8. Gasket	15. Seal

at cranking or idle speeds and 140-310 volts at 1000-4000 rpm.

NOTE: A shorted or open capacitor inside switch box will result in faulty stator voltage readings during cranking and running tests. Stator resistance should be checked as follows before failing stator.

If either STATOR test is not to specification, proceed as follows: Connect a suitable ohmmeter between blue and blue/white stator leads. Resistance between blue and blue/white stator leads should be 6000-7000 ohms. Next, connect ohmmeter between red and red/white stator leads. Resistance should be 90-140 ohms. Renew stator if resistance is not as specified. If stator resistance is as specified, renew switch box and repeat STATOR tests.

IGNITION COILS RESISTANCE TEST. Disconnect wires and high tension lead from coil. Connect a suitable ohmmeter between coil positive (+) and negative (−) terminals. Resistance should be 0.02-0.04 ohm. Connect ohmmeter between coil high tension terminal and negative (−) terminal. Resistance should be 800-1100 ohms. Renew ignition coil(s) if resistance is not as specified.

NOTE: Ignition coil resistance tests can only detect open or shorted windings. If coil resistance is within specification and still suspected as defective, coil must be tested using DVA meter as previously outlined in IGNITION COIL test. If DVA meter is not available, substitute a known good ignition coil and run engine to test.

COOLING SYSTEM

THERMOSTAT. All models are equipped with a thermostat (4—Fig. MR27-13) and pressure relief valve (7) located under cover (1) in cylinder block cover (12). Thermostat should begin to open at 140°-145° F (60°-63° C). Temperature sensor (11) is provided to activate a warning horn should power head overheat. Be sure the correct sensor (11) is used. Identify sensor (11) by the length of sensor lead; the lead on 190° F (87.8° C) sensor is 18.5 inches (470 mm) long and 15.5 inches (394 mm) long on 240° F (115.6° C) sensor.

WATER PUMP. The rubber impeller type water pump is housed in the gearcase housing. The impeller is mounted on and driven by the lower unit drive shaft.

If cooling system malfunction occurs, first check the water inlet for plugging or partial restriction. If necessary, remove the gearcase as outlined in LOW-

ER UNIT section and inspect water pump, water tubes and seals.

Renew cover (5—Fig. MR27-14) if thickness at discharge ports is 0.060 inch (1.5 mm) or less, or if grooves in excess of 0.030 inch (0.76 mm) are noted in top of cover (5). Renew plate (9) if grooves are noted in excess of 0.030 inch (0.76 mm).

NOTE: Sealing bead surrounding center hub of impeller (6) will wear circular grooves in cover (5) and plate (9). Circular grooves caused by impeller sealing bead will not affect water pump operation and should be disregarded when inspecting cover (5) and plate (9).

Rotate drive shaft in clockwise direction when installing cover (5) over impeller (6). Coat outer diameter of seals (14 and 15) with Loctite 271 or a suitable locking compound. Install seals into base (13) back-to-back. Apply Loctite 271 or suitable thread locking compound to threads of screws (11 and 2). Tighten screws (11 and 2) to 60 in.-lbs. (6.8 N·m).

POWER HEAD

REMOVE AND DISASSEMBLE. To remove power head, proceed as follows: Remove engine cowl and rear cowl bracket. Remove spark plugs, ignition plate cover, disconnect battery leads, power trim leads and power trim fuse. Remove two screws and clamp securing wiring harness to power head. Disconnect fuel lines, throttle cable, shift cable and disconnect shift arm from shift block (16—Fig. MR27-15). Remove eight screws securing power head to drive shaft housing, attach a suitable lifting fixture to power head and remove power head from drive shaft housing. Place power head on a suitable stand.

To disassemble power head, proceed as follows: Label and disconnect all wires interfering with power head disassembly. Remove starter motor. Remove two cowl support screws at top of air box, two bottom cowl support screws at front of power head, disconnect vapor hose from "T" fitting next to fuel pump, remove fuel connector screw, remove bottom cowl support bracket, air box cover and air box. Disconnect and remove carburetors as an assembly. Disconnect and remove oil reservoir, disconnect fuel hose from accelerator pump, disconnect link rod between throttle lever and throttle cam and unscrew and lay enrichment valve to the side with hoses and wires attached. Remove intake manifolds as an assembly. Note that pry points are provided on starboard side of power head for intake manifold removal. Remove reed valve assemblies. Remove flywheel nut and washer, place a suitable protector cap over crankshaft and remove flywheel using flywheel puller 91-73687A1 or a suitable equivalent.

NOTE: Do not strike puller bolt to dislodge flywheel from crankshaft or crankshaft or main bearing damage may result.

Remove ignition system components. Ignition plate, stator and trigger may be removed as an assembly. Remove fuel pump, accelerator pump, oil injection pump and related hoses. Remove throttle and spark advance lever assembly. Remove shift block assembly. Remove three screws securing lower end cap (8—Fig. MR27-15), 26 screws securing crankcase cover (5) and remove cover (5) and end cap (8). Note that pry points are provided between cover (5) and block (10) to prevent damaging mating surfaces. Remove thermostat cover, thermostat, pressure relief valve and related components. Remove cylinder block cover (12). Pry points are provided at top and bottom of cover (12) to prevent damage to mating surfaces. Remove 35 exhaust cover screws and remove exhaust cover (1). Pry points are provided at front top and bottom of cover. Crankshaft, pistons, bearings and connecting rods may now be removed for service as outlined in the appropriate following sections. Refer to ASSEMBLY section for reassembly procedures.

ASSEMBLY. When reassembling the power head, the crankcase must be completely sealed against both vacuum and pressure. All gasket surfaces and machined joints without gaskets should be carefully checked for nicks and burrs which might interfere with a tight seal. Cylinder block and crankcase cover are matched and align bored assembly and not available separately.

Lubricate all bearing and friction surfaces with engine oil. Loose needle bearings should be held in place during reassembly using Quicksilver Needle Bearing Assembly Grease (part C-92-42649A-1) or a suitable gasoline soluble grease. Lubricate all seal lips using needle bearing assembly grease or suitable gasoline soluble grease.

Prior to assembling crankcase, inspect check valves (13—Fig. MR27-15) by looking through valve. If light is noted while looking through valve, check ball has failed (melted) or is missing. If check ball is present in valve, make sure ball is free to move slightly inside valve. Remove check valves by carefully driving out using a suitable punch. Install check valves with single hole facing crankshaft.

Apply Loctite 271 or a suitable equivalent thread locking compound to outer diameter of all metal cased seals and any fastener used on moving or rotating components.

Apply a continuous bead, $\frac{1}{16}$ inch (1.6 mm) diameter, of Loctite Master Gasket Sealer (part 92-12564-1) to mating surface of crankcase cover (5) to seal crankcase assembly. Run bead to the inside of all screw holes. Make sure bead is continuous but avoid excess application.

Tighten large inner crankcase cover screws, in three steps, in sequence shown in Fig. MR27-18 to final tightness of 25 ft.-lbs. (33.9 N·m). After tightening inner cover screws, tighten small outer screws to final tightness of 180 in.-lbs. (20.3 N·m) in sequence shown. While tightening cover screws, check rotation of crankshaft for binding or unusual noise. If binding or noise is noted, repair cause before proceeding. Coat mating surface of lower end cap (8—Fig. MR27-15) with Quicksilver Perfect Seal or equivalent. Rotate crankshaft so each piston ring in turn is visible in exhaust or transfer ports, then check by pressing on rings with a blunt tool. Ring should spring back when released. If

not, a broken or binding ring is indicated and must be repaired before proceeding. Tighten exhaust and cylinder block cover screws to 180 in.-lbs. (20.3 N·m) in sequence shown in Figs. MR27-19 and MR27-20 respectively.

Renew gasket (9—Fig. MR27-15) when installing power head on drive shaft housing. Lubricate drive shaft splines with a small amount of Quicksilver 2-4-C or equivalent. Apply Loctite 271 or equivalent to threads of power head mounting screws and tighten to 350 in.-lbs. (39.5 N·m). Remainder of assembly and reinstallation is the reverse of removal procedure. Note the following tightening torques: Trigger and stator assemblies, 60 in.-lbs. (6.8 N·m); Electrical component mounting plate, 180 in.-lbs. (20.3 N·m); Starter motor, 180 in.-lbs. (20.3 N·m); Air box nuts, 100 in.-lbs. (11.3 N·m).

PISTONS, PINS, RINGS AND CYLINDERS. Prior to detaching connecting rods from crankshaft, make sure that rod, rod cap and pistons are properly marked for correct reassembly to each other, in the correct cylinder and in the correct direction.

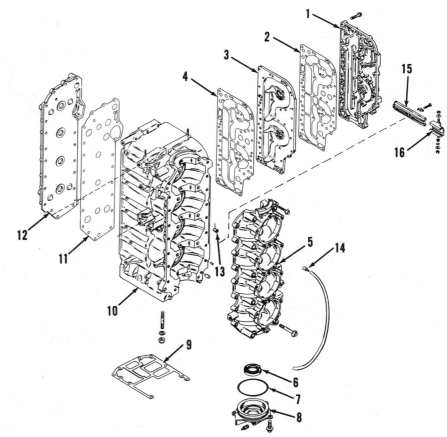

Fig. MR27-15—Exploded view of crankcase assembly.

1. Exhaust cover	6. Seal	10. Cylinder block	13. Check valve
2. Gasket	7. "O" ring	11. Gasket	14. Check valve
3. Baffle plate	8. Lower end cap	12. Cylinder block	15. Shift rail
4. Gasket	9. Gasket	cover	16. Shift block
5. Crankcase cover			

Standard cylinder bore diameter is 3.375 inch (85.72 mm). Piston skirt-to-cylinder bore clearance should be 0.005 inch (0.13 mm). Measure piston skirt diameter at right angle to piston pin bore 0.50 inch (12.7 mm) up from bottom of skirt. Maximum allowable cylinder bore wear, taper or out-of-round is 0.003 inch (0.08 mm). Pistons and rings are available in 0.015 inch (0.38 mm) and 0.030 inch (0.76 mm) oversize. Note that oversize pistons weigh approximately the same as standard size pistons. All cylinders do not require oversize boring if one cylinder is excessively worn or damaged. If installing 0.015 inch (4.38 mm) oversize piston, finished cylinder diameter should be 3.390 inch (86.11 mm). If installing 0.030 inch (4.76 mm) oversize piston, finished cylinder diameter should be 3.405 inch (86.49 mm).

Piston rings are semi-keystone shaped and are pinned to prevent rotation. Install rings with "T" mark facing up.

Always renew piston pin retaining rings (2—Fig. MR27-16) if removed. Piston pin rides in 29 loose needle bearing rollers (5). The manufacturer recommends renewing piston pin bearing rollers (5) when reassembling power head. Piston pin is a snug fit in piston and can be tapped out using a suitable driver and soft-face mallet. When reassembling, hold needle bearing rollers in place with a suitable gasoline soluble grease. Install locating washers (4) with large diameter facing away from pin (7).

Cylinder block is designed to allow piston installation without the use of a piston ring compressor. Install pistons into cylinders with "UP" mark on piston crown facing flywheel end of power head.

CONNECTING RODS, BEARINGS AND CRANKSHAFT. Refer to Fig. MR27-16 for exploded view of crankshaft, connecting rods and bearings. Be sure connecting rods (6), rod caps (9), pistons (3) and all wearing components are marked for reference during reassembly. Top main bearing (13) is a caged roller bearing and bottom main bearing (19) is a ball bearing. Each center main bearing consist of 32 loose bearing rollers (24) and race (25).

Do not remove bearing (19) from crankshaft unless bearing (19) or oil pump drive gear (18) require renewal. Note location of key (17).

On models equipped with a wear sleeve and "O" ring, carefully heat wear sleeve to remove on models so equipped. To install wear sleeve, apply Loctite 271 or equivalent to inner diameter of sleeve and drive sleeve squarely on crankshaft until bottomed using a suitable wooden block and hammer. On models equipped with a seal and seal carrier in place of wear sleeve (21) and "O" ring (22), renew seal anytime power head is disassembled.

Inspect crankshaft splines for excessive wear and crankshaft for straightness using a dial indicator and "V" blocks. Inspect crankshaft bearing surfaces and renew crankshaft if scored, out-of-round or excessively worn. Renew connecting rod(s) if big end bearing surface is rough, scored, excessively worn or shows evidence of overheating. Use crocus cloth ONLY to clean the connecting rod big end bearing surface.

Install main bearings with oil holes in outer race facing toward bottom of engine. Install crankshaft seal rings (23) with end gaps 180 degrees apart. Use only Quicksilver Needle Bearing Assembly Grease or a suitable gasoline soluble grease to hold loose bearing rollers in place. Always renew rod cap bolts when reassembling power head.

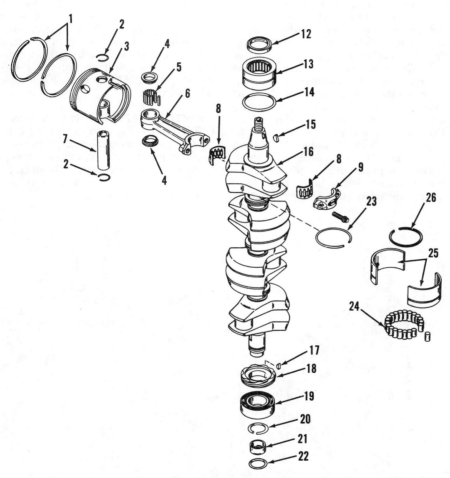

Fig. MR27-16—Exploded view of crankshaft assembly. Note that some models are equipped with a seal and seal carrier in place of wear sleeve (21) and "O" ring (22).

1. Piston rings
2. Retaining rings
3. Piston
4. Locating washers
5. Piston pin bearing rollers
6. Connecting rod
7. Piston pin
8. Crankpin bearing
9. Connecting rod cap
12. Seal
13. Main bearing
14. "O" ring
15. Flywheel key
16. Crankshaft
17. Oil pump drive gear key
18. Oil pump drive gear
19. Main bearing
20. Retaining ring
21. Wear sleeve
22. "O" ring
23. Seal ring
24. Main bearing rollers
25. Main bearing race
26. Retaining ring

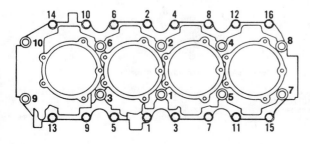

Fig. MR27-18—Crankcase cover tightening sequence. Tighten inner (large) screws first, then tighten outer (small) screws. Tighten inner screws in three steps to final value of 25 ft.-lbs. (33.9 N·m) and outer screws in three steps to final value of 180 in.-lbs. (20.3 N·m).

Threads are cut into both the connecting rod and rod cap. To properly align cap and rod during reassembly, proceed as follows: Place rod cap (9) on bearing half (8) and hold tightly against connecting rod while threading in bolt. Finger tighten rod bolts then check rod and cap alignment. Cap and rod must be perfectly aligned. After all rod caps and bolts are installed and aligned, tighten bolts to 15 in.-lbs. (1.7 N·m) and recheck alignment. Then tighten bolts to 30 ft.-lbs. (40.7 N·m) and recheck alignment. If rods and caps are perfectly aligned, tighten rod bolts an additional 90 degrees to complete procedure. Reassemble crankcase assembly as previously outlined.

ELECTRICAL SYSTEM

CHARGING SYSTEM. Refer to Fig. MR27-12 for wiring diagram. To test alternator output, disconnect red lead from rectifier (6) and connect a suitable ammeter between rectifier and red lead. Note that rectifier must be operating properly for accurate test results. Ammeter should indicate 7-9 amperes at 3000 rpm. If not, disconnect stator yellow leads from rectifier and connect a suitable ohmmeter between yellow leads. Stator resistance should be 0.05-1.1 ohms. No continuity should be present between yellow leads and engine ground with stator installed on power head. Renew stator if output or resistance is not as specified.

To test rectifier (6), connect ohmmeter alternately between each rectifier terminal and ground and between each terminal and ground. Refer to Fig. MR27-22. Reverse ohmmeter leads after each connection. Ohmmeter should indicate continuity with leads connected one direction but not the other. If ohmmeter shows continuity both directions or no continuity both directions, renew rectifier.

STARTER MOTOR. If starter motor malfunction occurs, perform a visual inspection for corroded or loose connections. Check inline fuse in red lead at starter solenoid and make sure battery is fully charged.

Renew brushes if worn to less than ¼ inch (6.4 mm). Undercut insulation between commutator bars to 1/32 inch (0.8 mm). Armature should be tested using an armature growler.

LOWER UNIT

PROPELLER. Protection for lower unit is provided by a splined rubber hub built into propeller. Various propellers are available and should be selected to allow motor to operate within the rec-

ommended speed range 4750-5250 rpm at full throttle. The manufacturer recommends propping outboard motor to the high end of full throttle rpm range.

R&R AND OVERHAUL. To remove lower unit, first remove and ground spark plug leads to prevent accidental starting. Shift engine into forward gear and tilt unit to full up position. Remove two screws and washers on each side of lower unit and one nut and washer under antiventilation plate. Remove gearcase and secure in a suitable holding fixture.

Note location and size of all shims and thrust washers during disassembly for reference during reassembly.

Remove propeller (66—Fig. MR27-23), thrust hub (65), vent screws (35 and 36) and drain plug (37). Allow gearcase oil to drain while inspecting for water or other contamination.

Remove water pump assembly and screws (11). Using screwdrivers or similar tools placed on each end of water pump base (13), carefully pry base (13)

from gearcase. Remove and discard seals (14 and 15). Remove nuts (61 [screws on some models]). Using a suitable puller, break loose carrier-to-gearcase seal then remove bearing carrier (59) and propeller shaft components (46-64) as a unit. Do not lose balls (48) or cam follower (46). Remove and discard seals (63 and 64) and "O" ring (55) from carrier (59). Do not remove bearings (58 and 62) unless renewal is required. Remove retainer spring (52) from dog clutch (50). To remove pin (51), depress cam follower (46) by pushing propeller shaft against a solid object, then push out pin (51) using a small punch. Remove follower (46), sliding pin (47), balls (48), spring (49) and slide dog clutch (50) off propeller shaft. Place Drive Shaft Holding Tool 91-56755 or similar splined adapter on drive shaft splines or clamp drive shaft into a soft jawed vise then remove pinion nut (38). Remove drive shaft assembly from gearcase. After drive shaft is removed, forward gear (45) and bearing (43) can be removed. Use a suitable expanding jaw type puller to remove race (42), if necessary. Note location and

Fig. MR27-19—Tighten exhaust cover screws in sequence shown to 180 in.-lbs. (20.3 N·m).

Fig. MR27-20—Tighten cylinder block cover screws in sequence shown to 180 in.-lbs. (20.3 N·m).

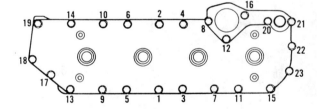

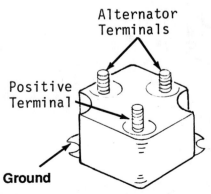

Fig. MR27-22—Rectifier must be connected as shown. Refer to text for rectifier test procedure.

thickness of shims (41). Remove upper drive shaft bearing (17) and bearing carrier (18) if necessary, using expanding jaw type puller. Note that bearing (17) and carrier (18) must be removed before sleeve (19) removal is possible. If necessary, remove sleeve (19) using a suitable puller. Quicksilver Bearing Race Tool 91-14308A1 is required to drive lower drive shaft bearing race (31) from gearcase. Bearing race (31) can be driven from gearcase with bearing (17), carrier (18) and sleeve (19) installed. Note location and thickness of shims (30). Remove coupler (23), shift shaft retainer (26) and shift shaft (28). Reach into gear cavity and remove shift cam (40). Remove and discard seal (25) and "O" ring

(27) from retainer (26) to complete disassembly.

Inspect all components for excessive wear or damage. Check straightness of propeller shaft using a dial indicator and "V" blocks and renew shaft if runout exceeds 0.006 inch (0.15 mm). Inspect all bearings for roughness, pits, rust or other damage and renew as necessary. Inspect sealing area of wear sleeve (20) for grooves and renew as necessary. Renew bearings and races as an assembly. Renew gears if teeth are chipped, broken or excessively worn. Renew all seals, "O" rings and gaskets. Lubricate all friction surfaces with clean gear lubricant. Apply Loctite 271 or equivalent to threads of all screws and outer diame-

ter of all metal cased seals. Lubricate "O" ring (55) and outer diameter of carrier (59) with Quicksilver Special Lubricant 101 (part 92-13872A-1). Lubricate other seals and "O" rings with Quicksilver 2-4-C Marine Lubricant (part 92-90018A12) or Quicksilver Needle Bearing Assembly Grease (part 92-42649A-1).

When reassembling gearcase, place original shim pack (41) into gearcase and install bearing race (42) using a suitable mandrel. If original shims (41) are damaged or lost, install shim pack 0.010 inch (0.25 mm) thick.

Install seal (25) into retainer (26) until flush with top of retainer. Place shift cam (40) into gearcase with numbers facing up and install shift rod making

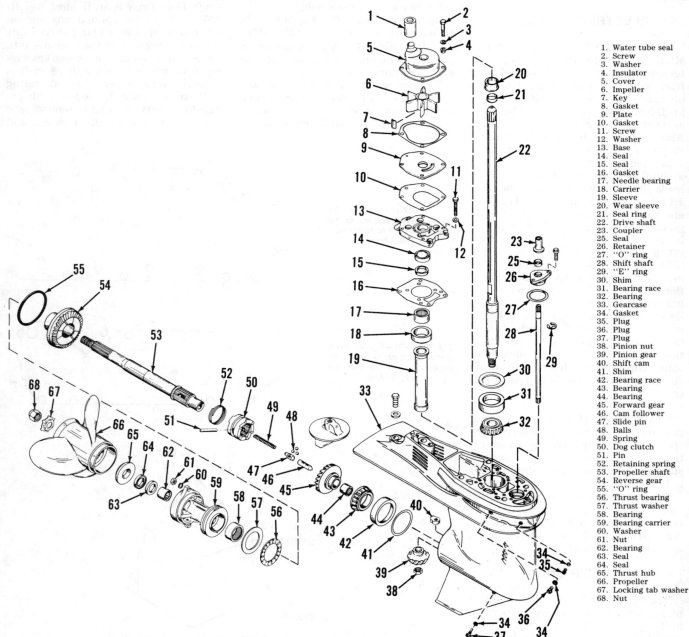

1. Water tube seal
2. Screw
3. Washer
4. Insulator
5. Cover
6. Impeller
7. Key
8. Gasket
9. Plate
10. Gasket
11. Screw
12. Washer
13. Base
14. Seal
15. Seal
16. Gasket
17. Needle bearing
18. Carrier
19. Sleeve
20. Wear sleeve
21. Seal ring
22. Drive shaft
23. Coupler
25. Seal
26. Retainer
27. "O" ring
28. Shift shaft
29. "E" ring
30. Shim
31. Bearing race
32. Bearing
33. Gearcase
34. Gasket
35. Plug
36. Plug
37. Plug
38. Pinion nut
39. Pinion gear
40. Shift cam
41. Shim
42. Bearing race
43. Bearing
44. Bearing
45. Forward gear
46. Cam follower
47. Slide pin
48. Balls
49. Spring
50. Dog clutch
51. Pin
52. Retaining spring
53. Propeller shaft
54. Reverse gear
55. "O" ring
56. Thrust bearing
57. Thrust washer
58. Bearing
59. Bearing carrier
60. Washer
61. Nut
62. Bearing
63. Seal
64. Seal
65. Thrust hub
66. Propeller
67. Locking tab washer
68. Nut

Fig. MR27-23—Exploded view of lower unit gearcase assembly.

sure splines in shift shaft properly align with cam. Install bearing (62) into carrier (59) with lettered side facing propeller end. Install seal (63) into carrier (59) with lip facing forward and seal (64) with lip facing propeller. Install dog clutch (50) on propeller shaft with grooved end of clutch facing rearward. Install spring (49), slider (47), balls (48) and cam follower (46) into propeller shaft. Depress follower (46) against spring pressure and align holes in dog clutch and propeller shaft using a suitable punch, then insert pin (51).

If installing a new wear sleeve (20) on drive shaft (22), install seal ring (21), coat inner diameter of sleeve (20) with Loctite 271 and press onto shaft (22) until bottomed. Install original shim pack (30) and draw race (31) into gearcase using suitable mandrels and a threaded rod. If original shims (30) are damaged or lost, start with shim pack 0.025 inch (0.64 mm) thick. Install sleeve (19) making sure antirotation tab properly engages gearcase. Install bearing (43), forward gear (45), drive shaft (22), pinion bearing (32), pinion gear (39) and original pinion nut (38).

NOTE: Pinion nut (38) should be renewed and secured with a suitable thread locking compound after gearcase shimming operation has been properly performed.

Drive shaft assembly must be preloaded to properly adjust pinion gear depth and forward gear backlash. Special Bearing Preload Tool 91-14311A1 and Pinion gear Locating Tool 91-12349A2 are required for shim selection procedure.

To preload drive shaft and bearing assembly, assemble Bearing Preload Tool 91-14311A1 as shown in Fig. MR27-25 and tighten set screws (2). With nut (3) fully threaded on bolt (1), measure distance (D) between bottom of bolt head to top of nut, then turn nut (3) to increase distance (D) by one inch (25.4 mm). Rotate drive shaft several turns to ensure lower drive shaft bearing is properly seated. Assemble Pinion Gear Location Tool 91-12349A2 as shown in Fig. MR27-26. Install locating disc marked number "3" making sure access hole is facing up. Position sliding collar (4) so gaging block (3) is directly under pinion gear (39) teeth and flat on gaging block marked "8" is adjacent to pinion gear (39). Clearance between gaging block (3) and pinion gear should be 0.025 inch (0.64 mm) measured with a suitable feeler gage as shown. Vary thickness of shim pack (30—Fig. MR27-23) to adjust. Changing thickness of shims (30) by 0.001 inch (0.03 mm) will

change pinion gear thickness by 0.001 inch (0.03 mm).

Insert assembled propeller shaft assembly into bearing carrier (59) and install carrier and propeller shaft assembly into gearcase. Position carrier (59) so "TOP" mark is facing up. Outward pressure should be applied to propeller shaft to hold reverse gear (54) tight against thrust bearing (56) and washer (57) to prevent thrust washer and bearing from being dislodged. A tool can be fabricated out of $1\frac{1}{4}$ to $1\frac{1}{2}$ inch (31.7-38.1 mm) PVC pipe cut off to 6 inches (152.4 mm) long. Place pipe over propeller shaft and secure with washer (67) and nut (68). Tighten nut (68) so reverse gear (54) is pulled securely against thrust bearing (56) and washer (57). Securely tighten nuts (61) or screws if so equipped.

To check forward gear backlash, proceed as follows: Allow bearing preload tool (Fig. MR27-25) to remain installed. Preload propeller shaft by installing a suitable puller as shown in Fig. MR27-27. Tighten puller center bolt to 25 in.-lbs. (2.8 N·m), rotate propeller shaft several turns, then retighten puller bolt to 25 in.-lbs. (2.8 N·m). Again, rotate propeller shaft several turns and recheck torque on puller bolt. Refer to Fig. MR27-28 and assemble a suitable threaded rod to gearcase using nuts and washers as shown. Affix a suitable dial indicator to threaded rod. Install Backlash Indicator 91-19660 on drive shaft and align dial indicator plunger with the mark "1" on backlash indicator. Check backlash by carefully rotating drive shaft back-and-forth. Note that if any movement is noted at propeller shaft, repeat propeller shaft preloading procedure as previously outlined. Backlash should be 0.012-0.019 inch (0.31-0.48 mm). Vary thickness of shim pack (41) to adjust. Note that changing thickness of shims (41) by 0.001 inch (0.03 mm) will result in approximately 0.00125 inch (0.032 mm) change in backlash.

After shim selection procedure is completed, remove carrier and drive shaft assembly. Remove pinion nut, apply Loctite 271 to a NEW pinion nut, install nut with beveled side facing up and tighten to 70 ft.-lbs. (95 N·m). Reinstall carrier and propeller shaft assembly, apply Loctite 271 to nuts (61—Fig. MR27-23) or screws if so equipped, and tighten nuts (61) to 275 in.-lbs. (31.1 N·m) or screws to 150 in.-lbs. (17 N·m). Complete reassembly by reversing disassembly procedure. Tighten propeller nut to 55 ft.-lbs. (75 N·m).

To reinstall gearcase on drive shaft housing, proceed as follows: Position shift block (16—Fig. MR27-15) on power head in the forward gear position. Shift block (16) should extend past forward side of shift rail (15) by $\frac{1}{32}$ inch (3.2 mm) if properly positioned. Shift lower unit into forward gear. Lubricate inner diameter of water tube seal (1—Fig. MR27-23) with Quicksilver 2-4-C Marine Lubri-

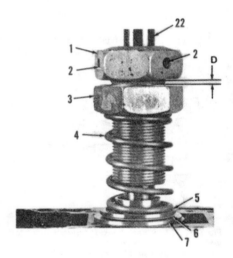

Fig. MR27-25—View of Bearing Preload Tool 91-14311A1 assembled over drive shaft (22). Refer to text for gearcase shim selection procedure.

1. Bolt	5. Thrust washer
2. Set screws	6. Thrust bearing
3. Nut	7. Adapter
4. Spring	22. Drive shaft

Fig. MR27-26—Assemble Pinion Gear Locating Tool 91-12349A2 as shown. Make sure sliding collar (4) is positioned so gaging block is located under pinion gear (39) as shown.

1. Arbor
2. Locating disc (number 3)
3. Gaging block
4. Sliding collar
39. Pinion gear

0.025 in. (0.64 mm) Feeler gage

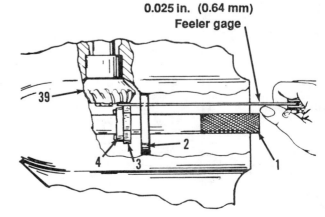

cant. Lightly lubricate drive shaft splines with 2-4-C Marine Lubricant. Do not apply grease to top of drive shaft or drive shaft may not fully engage crankshaft.

Install gearcase in drive shaft housing making sure drive shaft aligns with crankshaft, upper shift shaft aligns with coupler (23) and water tube aligns with water tube seal (1). Apply Loctite 271 to threads of gearcase mounting screws and tighten to 40 ft.-lbs. (54.2 N·m). After installing gearcase, make sure shift linkage operates properly as follows: Shift outboard into forward gear. Propeller shaft should lock into gear when rotated counterclockwise and ratchet when rotated clockwise. When shifted into reverse gear, propeller shaft should be locked into gear when rotated either direction. If shift linkage does not operate as specified, lower unit must be removed and shift linkage malfunction repaired.

POWER TILT/TRIM

FLUID AND BLEEDING. Recommended fluid is Quicksilver Power Trim

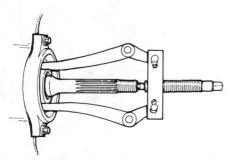

Fig. MR27-27—When checking forward gear backlash, preload propeller shaft by installing a suitable puller as shown. Refer to text.

& Steering Fluid or a suitable Type F, FA or Dextron II automatic transmission fluid.

NOTE: Hydraulic system is under pressure. Fill plug (Fig. MR27-29) must not be removed unless outboard is in full up position and tilt lock lever is engaged. Be sure to securely tighten fill plug prior to lowering outboard motor.

To check fluid level, tilt motor to full up position, engage tilt lock lever and slowly remove fill plug. Fluid should be visible in fill tube. Fill as necessary and securely tighten fill plug.

To determine if air is present in hydraulic system, trim motor out until both trim rods are slightly extended. Apply downward pressure on lower unit. If trim rods retract into cylinders more than $1/8$ inch (3.2 mm), air is present and bleeding is required.

The hydraulic circuit is self-bleeding as the tilt/trim system is operated through several cycles. After servicing system, be sure to check reservoir level after filling and operating system.

Trim limit adjustment is not required. Port trim rod and piston assembly (15—Fig. MR27-30) is equipped with a check valve designed to open at a specific pressure, limiting trim range to 20 degrees when engine speed exceeds 2,000 rpm. If engine speed falls below 2,000 rpm, trim angle may exceed 20 degrees; however, once engine speed exceeds 2,000 rpm, propeller thrust will increase pressure in trim cylinders causing check valve in port side trim rod to unseat, bypassing hydraulic fluid to the reservoir and lowering trim angle to 20 degrees maximum. Except for cleaning valve and strainer (16), check valve in

port trim rod is not serviceable and should not be removed. If check valve malfunction is evident, renew port trim rod.

HYDRAULIC TESTING. The system can be checked by connecting a 5000 psi (34.5 MPa) test gage to the UP (U—Fig. MR27-32) and DOWN (D—Fig. MR27-33) ports. Prior to connecting test gage, place outboard motor in the full up position and engage tilt lock lever. Unscrew reservoir fill plug and rotate manual release valve (21—Fig. MR27-32) three to four turns counterclockwise to release pressure on system. Remove UP or DOWN Allen head test port plug and connect test gage with suitable adapter and hose. Install fill plug and rotate manual release valve clockwise until seated. System pressure when testing at UP (U) port should be a minimum of 1300 psi (8.9 MPa). System pressure when testing at DOWN (D—Fig. MR27-33) port should be a minimum of 500 psi (3.5 MPa). Release pressure on system as previously outlined prior to removing test gage. Reinstall Allen head plug.

OVERHAUL. Refer to Fig. MR27-30 for exploded view of manifold and trim cylinder components, and Fig. MR27-31 for exploded view if tilt cylinder components. Special socket 91-44487A1 and a spanner wrench is required to service trim and tilt cylinders. Keep all components clean and away from contamination. Keep components separated and label if necessary for correct reassembly. Lubricate all "O" rings or seal lips with Quicksilver Power Trim & Steering Fluid, Dexron II, Type F or Type FA automatic transmission fluid during reassembly.

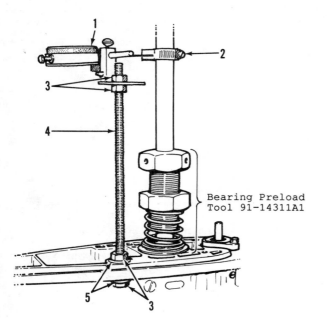

Bearing Preload
Tool 91-14311A1

Fig. MR27-28—Assemble special tools as shown to check forward gear backlash. Refer to text.

1. Dial indicator & adapter assy.
2. Backlash indicator tool 91-19660
3. Nuts
4. Threaded rod
5. Washers

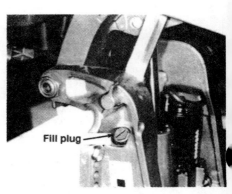

Fill plug

Fig. MR27-29—View showing location of fill plug on power tilt/trim system.

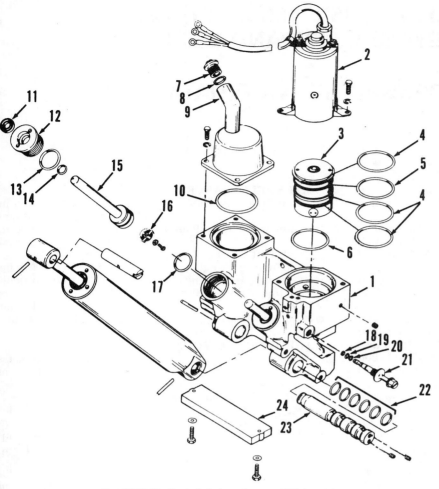

Fig. MR27-30—Exploded view of power tilt/trim system.

1. Manifold
2. Motor
3. Pump assy.
4. "O" rings
5. "O" ring
6. "O" ring
7. Fill plug
8. "O" ring
9. Reservoir cover
10. Seal ring
11. Seal
12. Cap
13. "O" ring
14. "O" ring
15. Trim piston & rod
16. Strainer
17. "O" ring
18. "O" ring
19. "O" ring
20. "O" ring
21. Manual release valve
22. "O" ring
23. Shaft
24. Anode plate

Fig. MR27-32—Release pressure on system, then remove Allen head plug (U) and install a 5000 psi (34.5 MPa) test gage with a suitable adapter and hose to test system pressure when operated in the "UP" direction. View identifies location of manual release valve (21).

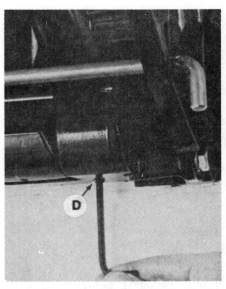

Fig. MR27-33—Release pressure on system, then remove Allen head plug (D) and install a 5000 psi (34.5 MPa) test gage with a suitable adapter and hose to test system pressure when operated in the "DOWN" direction.

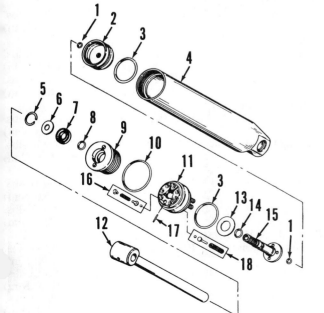

Fig. MR27-31—Exploded view of tilt cylinder assembly.

1. "O" ring
2. Cup
3. "O" ring
4. Cylinder
5. Circlip
6. Washer
7. Scraper
8. "O" ring
9. Cap
10. "O" ring
11. Piston
12. Rod
13. Washer
14. "O" ring
15. Rod end
16. Check valve assy.
17. Pin
18. Check valve assy.

MARINER 135, 150, 150 MAGNUM, 150 MAGNUM II, 175 AND 200 HP

CONDENSED SERVICE DATA

TUNE-UP

Hp/rpm:

Model 135 . . . . 135/5000-5500
(100.7 kW)

Model 150 . . . . 150/5000-5500
(111.9 kW)

Model 150 Magnum 150/5500-6000
(111.9 kW)

Model 150 Magnum II 150/5000-5500
(111.9 kW)

Model 175 . . . . 175/5300-5800
(130.5 kW)

Model 200 . . . . 200/5300-5800
(149.2 kW)

Bore:

135 Hp, 150 Hp, 150 Magnum & 175 Hp
(prior to serial no. 6618751) . . . . 3.125 in.
(79.38 mm)

150 Magnum II, 175 Hp (after serial
no. 6618750) & 200 Hp . . . . 3.375 in.
(85.73 mm)

Stroke . . . . 2.650 in.
(67.31 mm)

Displacement:

135 Hp, 150 Hp, 150 Magnum & 175 Hp
(prior to serial no. 6618751) . . . . 122 cu. in.
(1999.2 cc)

150 Magnum II, 175 Hp (after serial
no. 6618750) & 200 Hp . . . . 142.2 cu. in.
(2330.2 cc)

Firing Order 1-2-3-4-5-6

Number System (top to bottom):

Port 2-4-6

Starboard 1-3-5

Spark Plug:

All Models Prior to Serial No.
5464486 . . . . Champion L76V

All Models After Serial No.
5464485 . . . . NGK BU8H

Idle Speed (in forward gear):

All Models Prior to Serial No.
5464486 . . . . 550-650 rpm

All Models After Serial No. 5464485

Except 150 Magnum II . . . . 600-700 rpm

150 Magnum II . . . . 625-700 rpm

Compression . . . . *

Ignition Type . . . . CDI

Fuel:Oil Ratio . . . . See Text

*Compression should not vary more than 15 psi (103.4 kPa)
between cylinders.

SIZES—CLEARANCES

Piston Rings End Gap . . . . 0.018-0.025 in.
(0.46-0.63 mm)

Maximum Cylinder Tolerance . . . . 0.006 in.
(0.15 mm)

Crankshaft Bearing Type:

Top Main Bearing . . . . Caged Roller

Center Main Bearing . . . . Caged Roller

Bottom Main Bearing . . . . Ball Bearing

Crankpin . . . . Caged Roller

Piston Pin Bearing . . . . 29 Loose Rollers

TIGHTENING TORQUES

Connecting Rod . . . . 30 ft.-lbs.
(40.7 N·m)

Crankcase Screws—

Prior to Serial No. C100861:

$^5/_{16}$ . . . . 200 in.-lbs.
(22.6 N·m)

$^3/_8$ . . . . 35 ft.-lbs.
(47.4 N·m)

After Serial No. C100860:

$^5/_{16}$ . . . . 180 in.-lbs.
(20.3 N·m)

$^3/_8$ . . . . 45 ft.-lbs.
(61.0 N·m)

Cylinder Head:

Prior to Serial No. C100861 . . . . See Text

After Serial No. C100860 . . . . 30 ft.-lbs.
(40.7 N·m)

Cylinder Head Cover:

Prior to Serial No. C100861 . . . . 150 in.-lbs.
(16.9 N·m)

End Cap:

Upper . . . . 150 in.-lbs.
(16.9 N·m)

Lower . . . . 80 in.-lbs.
(9.0 N·m)

Exhaust Cover:

Prior to Serial No. C100861 . . . . 180 in.-lbs.
(20.3 N·m)

After Serial No. C100860 . . . . 200 in.-lbs.
(22.6 N·m)

Flywheel Nut:

Prior to Serial No. C100861 . . . . 100 ft.-lbs.
(135.6 N·m)

After Serial No. C100860 . . . . 120 ft.-lbs.
(162.7 N·m)

Reed Block Mounting Screws:

Prior to Serial No. C100861 . . . . 60 in.-lbs.
(6.8 N·m)

After Serial No. C100860 . . . . 105 in.-lbs.
(11.9 N·m)

Spark Plugs . . . . 20 ft.-lbs.
(27.1 N·m)

LUBRICATION

The power head is lubricated by oil mixed with the fuel. Fuel should be regular leaded, low lead or unleaded gasoline with a minimum pump octane rating of 86. Recommended oil is Quicksilver Formula 50-D Outboard Lubricant. Normal fuel:oil ratio for models not equipped with oil injection is 50:1; during engine break-in (initial 10 hours of operation) fuel:oil ratio should be 25:1.

On 1984 and later models, an oil injection system is used. Fuel:oil ratio is varied from approximately 50:1 at full throttle to approximately 100:1 at idle. The crankshaft driven oil pump is synchronized with carburetor throttle opening by mechanical linkage. As the carburetor throttle opens or closes, the oil being supplied to the fuel pump is varied, thus matching the proper fuel:oil ratio to engine demand.

On oil injection equipped models, a 50:1 fuel and oil mixture should be used in the fuel tank in combination with the oil injection system to ensure proper lubrication during engine break-in period (initial 30 gallons [114 L] of fuel used). After the first 30 gallons (114 L) of fuel and oil mixture is used, switch to straight gasoline in the fuel tank.

Lower unit gears and bearings are lubricated by oil contained in the gearcase. Recommended oil is Quicksilver Premium Blend Gear Lube. Lubricant is drained by removing vent and drain plugs in the gearcase. Refill through drain plug hole until oil reaches level of vent plug hole, then drain one ounce (30 mL) of oil to allow for expansion. Lower unit oil capacity is 21 fl. oz. (625 mL) on 150 Magnum II models and 24¼ fl. oz. (717 mL) on all other models.

FUEL SYSTEM

CARBURETOR. Three ''dual float center bowl'' type carburetors are used. Carburetor identification numbers are stamped on each carburetor mounting flange. Standard jet sizes are dependent upon the carburetor identification numbers. Use the standard carburetor jet sizes as recommended by the manufacturer for normal operation when used at altitudes of 2500 feet (762 m) and below. Main jets (23—Fig. MR28-1) and vent jets (5) should be reduced in size by 0.002 inch (0.05 mm) at altitudes of 2500-5000 feet (762-1524 m). Idle jets (8) should be increased in size by 0.002 inch (0.05 mm) at altitudes of 2500-5000 feet (762-1524 m). Main jets (23) and vent jets (5) should be reduced in size by 0.004 inch (0.10 mm) at altitudes of 5000-7500 feet (1524-2286 m). Idle jets (8) should be increased in size by 0.004 inch (0.10 mm) at altitudes of 5000-7500 feet (1524-2286 m). Main jets (23) and vent jets (5) should be reduced in size by 0.006 inch (0.15 mm) at altitudes of 7500 feet (2286 m) and above. Idle jets (8) should be increased in size by 0.006 inch (0.15 mm) at altitudes of 7500 feet (2286 m) and above.

NOTE: Vent jets (5) are not used on some models. If vent jets are not noted, do not try to install jets.

No idle mixture screw adjustment is provided. Idle jet (8) size must be altered to change idle air:fuel ratio. Refer to CONDENSED SERVICE DATE for recommended idle speeds.

To measure float setting, invert float bowl (6) with inlet needle and seat (20) and float (18) installed. On each float chamber, measure distance (D—Fig. MR28-2) from float bowl surface to top of float (18). Distance (D) should be ¹/₁₆ inch (1.6 mm). Adjust distance (D) by bending tang at rear of float arm.

On some models, a choke plate containing choke valves is positioned in the air silencer. The choke valves are actuated by a solenoid mounted on the reed housing.

SPEED CONTROL LINKAGE (Early Model 175 Hp Prior to Serial Number C100861). To synchronize ignition and carburetor opening, proceed as follows: To verify timing pointer alignment, install a dial indicator into number 1 (top starboard) cylinder spark plug hole. Position number 1 piston at TDC and zero dial indicator.

NOTE: To prevent accidental starting from flywheel rotation, remove all spark plugs and ground plug leads.

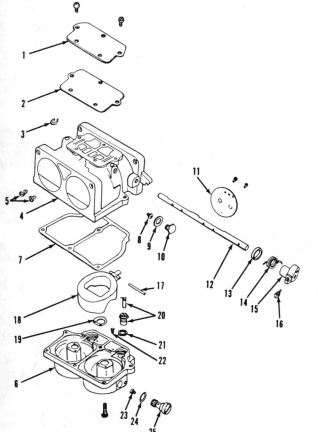

Fig. MR28-1 — Exploded view of carburetor used on all models. Note that idle jet components (8 through 10) and main jet components (23 through 25) are also located on the starboard side of carburetor.

1. Cover
2. Gasket
3. Clip
4. Body
5. Vent jets
6. Float bowl
7. Gasket
8. Idle jet
9. Gasket
10. Plug
11. Throttle plate
12. Throttle shaft
13. Spacer
14. Spring
15. Lever
16. Screw
17. Float pin
18. Float
19. Gasket
20. Inlet needle & seat
21. Gasket
22. Screw
23. Main jet
24. Gasket
25. Plug

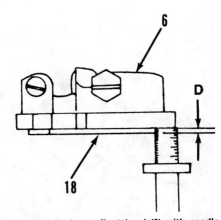

Fig. MR28-2 — Invert float bowl (6) with needle and seat (20—Fig. MR28-1) and float (18) installed. Distance (D) should be 1/16 inch (1.6 mm) for proper float setting.

Rotate flywheel counterclockwise approximately ¼ turn past the .462 mark on flywheel, then rotate flywheel clockwise until indicator reads exactly 0.462 inch (11.73 mm) BTDC. Note position of timing pointer and reposition pointer to align with .462 mark on flywheel if necessary.

Be sure link rod (L—Fig. MR28-4) protrudes ¹¹/₁₆ inch (17.46 mm) from link body as shown. If engine is equipped with an idle stabilizer module (M—Fig. MR28-5), disconnect the white/black module wire from switch box terminal. Tape end of wire to prevent grounding. Be sure the other white/black wire remains connected to switch box terminal.

NOTE: To prevent engine from starting, make sure only the number 1 (top, starboard) spark plug is installed and its plug wire attached.

Disconnect fuel tank supply hose at the outboard motor connector. Detach throttle cable barrel from retainer of the cable anchor bracket. Remove choke knob and wing nuts, then withdraw air intake cover from the front of the carburetors. Loosen carburetor synchronizing screws (S—Fig. MR28-4) and allow carburetor throttle plates to close freely. With light pressure, hold cam follower roller (R—Fig. MR28-6) against throttle cam (T). At the same time, lift up on bottom carburetor throttle shaft (H—Fig. MR28-4) to remove slack in linkage components. Adjust idle speed screw (I) so short mark (M—Fig. MR28-6) on

throttle cam (T) is centered on cam follower roller (R) as shown. Retighten stop screw locknut. While maintaining light pressure, retighten all screws (S—Fig. MR28-4). Check to be sure that carburetor throttle plates are completely closed when cam follower roller (R—Fig. MR28-6) is aligned with short mark (M) on throttle cam (T). Repeat adjustment procedure if setting is incorrect. Reinstall air intake cover.

Connect a power timing light to number 1 cylinder spark plug lead. With outboard motor in neutral, position throttle lever (C—Fig. MR28-4) so idle speed screw (I) is against stop. Crank engine with starter motor and adjust primary screw (P) so that ignition timing is 14 degrees ATDC.

Open throttle until maximum spark advance screw (A) is against stop. Crank engine with starter motor and adjust maximum spark advance screw (A) so ignition timing is 20 degrees BTDC.

NOTE: Due to electronic characteristics of the ignition system, maximum advance is set at 20 degrees BTDC, but ignition will retard to 18 degrees BTDC at high engine speed.

The carburetor throttle plate must not act as the wide open throttle stop. To prevent damage to the carburetors, move speed control linkage to the maximum speed position and adjust maximum throttle stop screw (N) so a clearance (C—Fig. MR28-7) of 0.010-0.015 inch (0.25-0.38 mm) is between throttle cam (T) and cam follower roller (R).

Reconnect idle stabilizer module wire to switch box. Reinstall spark plugs then adjust idle speed screw (I—Fig. MR28-4) as outlined in the CARBURETOR section.

Hold idle speed screw (I) against stop and install throttle cable barrel in retainer while adjusting throttle cable barrel so it fits into retainer and a very light preload between idle speed screw and its stop is established. Excessive throttle cable preload will result in difficult shifting from forward to neutral.

Fig. MR28-5—View showing location of idle stabilizer module (M) used on some models. Some models are equipped with a spark advance or combination low speed/high speed spark advance module.

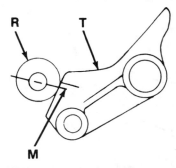

Fig. MR28-6—Cam follower roller (R) should align with short mark (M) on throttle cam (T) when speed control linkage is set as outlined in text.

Fig. MR28-4—View showing speed control linkage components used on 135, 150, 175, 150 Magnum, 150 Magnum II and early 200 hp models. Refer to text for adjustment procedures.

A. Maximum spark advance screw
B. Maximum spark advance lever
C. Throttle lever
H. Throttle shaft
I. Idle speed screw
L. Link rod
N. Maximum throttle stop screw
P. Primary screw
S. Screws
T. Throttle cam

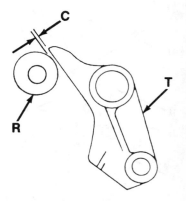

Fig. MR28-7—Clearance (C) should exist between cam follower (R) and throttle cam (T) when speed control linkage is set as outlined in text.

(Models 135, 150 Hp, 150 Magnum, 150 Magnum II, 175 Hp After Serial Number 100860 and Early 200 Hp). To synchronize ignition and carburetor opening, proceed as follows: To verify timing pointer alignment, a dial indicator must be installed in the number 1 (top, starboard) cylinder and the indicator synchronized with the piston position (dial indicator reads zero when piston is at top dead center).

NOTE: To prevent accidental starting from flywheel rotation, remove all spark plugs and properly ground plug wires.

Rotate the flywheel counterclockwise approximately $1/4$ turn past the 0.462 inch (12 mm) BTDC reading, then rotate flywheel clockwise until indicator face reads 0.462 inch (12 mm) BTDC. Note the position of the timing pointer. Reposition pointer if it is not aligned with the .462 BTDC mark on flywheel. Remove dial indicator assembly from number 1 cylinder after adjustment is completed and reinstall spark plug and plug lead.

Be sure link rod (L—Fig. MR28-4) protrudes $11/16$ inch (17.5 mm) from link body as shown. If the engine is equipped with an idle stabilizer module (M—Fig. MR28-5), three-wire spark advance module, or combination low speed/high speed spark advance module, disconnect white/black module wire from outer switch box terminal. Tape end of wire to prevent grounding. Be sure the other white/black wire remains connected to switch box terminal. On models equipped with a four-wire module, do not disconnect white/black wire.

NOTE: To prevent engine from starting, make sure only the number 1 (top, starboard) spark plug is installed and its plug wire attached.

Disconnect fuel tank supply hose at the outboard motor connector. Detach throttle cable barrel from the retainer of the cable anchor bracket. Adjust idle speed screw (I—Fig. MR28-4) so bottom edge of throttle cam (T—Fig. MR28-8) is a distance (D) of $1/8$ inch (3.2 mm) from top edge of mounting boss (B) for maximum throttle stop screw.

Withdraw air intake cover from the front of the carburetors. Position throttle lever (C—Fig. MR28-4) so idle speed screw (I) is against its stop. Loosen carburetor synchronizing screws (S) and allow carburetor throttle plates to close freely. With light pressure, hold the cam follower roller against throttle cam (T). At the same time, lift up on bottom carburetor throttle shaft (H) to remove slack in linkage components. Then retighten screws (S). Check to be sure that carburetor throttle plates are com-

pletely closed and operate freely. Repeat adjustment procedure if setting is incorrect. Reinstall air intake cover.

Connect a power timing light to number 1 cylinder spark plug lead. With outboard motor in neutral, position throttle lever (C) so idle speed screw (I) is against stop. Crank engine with starter motor and adjust primary screw (P) so ignition timing is 5-7 degrees ATDC on 135 hp models, 6-12 degrees ATDC on 150 hp and 150 Magnum models, 4-6 degrees ATDC on 150 Magnum II models, 3-5 degrees ATDC on 175 hp models and 10 degrees ATDC on 200 hp models.

Open throttle until maximum spark advance screw (A) is against stop. Crank engine with starter motor and adjust maximum spark advance screw (A) so ignition timing is 18 degrees BTDC on 135 hp, 150 hp and 150 Magnum; 22 degrees BTDC on 150 Magnum II and 20 degrees BTDC on 175 hp and 200 hp models.

NOTE: Due to electronic spark advance characteristics of the ignition systems, maximum advance timing set at cranking speed will be advanced by 6 degrees on 150 Magnum II models and retarded by 2 degrees on all other models when engine is running at full throttle. Maximum advance timing with engine running at full throttle should be 16 degrees BTDC on 135 hp, 150 hp and 150 Magnum models, 26 degrees BTDC on 150 Magnum II models and 18 degrees BTDC on 175 and 200 models. On 150 Magnum II models equipped with low speed/high speed/spark advance/excessive rpm spark retard module, timing is electronically advanced by 6 degrees at 5000 rpm, then retarded 4 degrees if engine speed exceeds approximately 5700 rpm. Timing will remain retarded by 4 degrees until engine speed falls below approximately 5700 rpm.

The carburetor throttle plate must not act as the wide open throttle stop. To prevent damage to the carburetors, move speed control linkage to the maximum speed position and adjust maximum throttle stop screw (N) so a clearance (C—Fig. MR28-7) of 0.010-0.015 inch (0.25-0.38 mm) is between throttle cam (T) and cam follower roller (R).

Make sure carburetors and oil injection pump are properly synchronized as outlined in OIL INJECTION SYSTEM section.

Reconnect idle stabilizer module or spark advance module wire to switch box. Reinstall spark plugs, then adjust idle speed screw (I—Fig. MR28-4) to idle speed specified in CONDENSED SERVICE DATA.

Hold idle speed screw (I) against stop and install throttle cable barrel in the retainer while adjusting throttle cable barrel so it fits into retainer and a very

light preload between idle speed screw and its stop is established. Excessive throttle cable preload will result in difficult shifting from forward to neutral.

(Late Model 200 HP). To synchronize ignition and carburetor opening, proceed as follows: To verify timing pointer alignment, a dial indicator must be installed in number 1 (top, starboard) cylinder and synchronized with the piston position (dial indicator reads zero when piston is at top dead center).

NOTE: To prevent accidental starting from flywheel rotation, remove all spark plugs and properly ground plug wires.

Rotate flywheel counterclockwise approximately $1/4$ turn past the 0.462 inch (12 mm) BTDC reading, then rotate flywheel clockwise until indicator face reads 0.462 inch (12 mm) BTDC. Note position of timing pointer. Reposition pointer if the timing pointer is not aligned with ''.462 BTDC'' mark on flywheel. Remove the dial indicator assembly from number 1 cylinder after adjustment is completed and reinstall spark plug and plug lead.

Be sure link rod (L—Fig. MR28-9) protrudes $11/16$ inch (17.46 mm) from link body as shown. A spark advance module is located above the top carburetor and is mounted to the air intake cover. If the module is equipped with four wires, no wires need to be disconnected to time the engine. However, if the module is equipped with three wires, disconnect the white/black module wire from switch box terminal. Tape end of wire to prevent grounding. Be sure the other white/black wire remains connected to switch box terminal.

NOTE: To prevent engine from starting, make sure only number 1 (top, starboard) spark plug is installed and its plug wire attached.

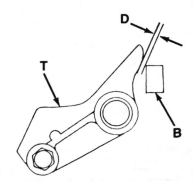

Fig. MR28-8 — Distance (D) should exist between throttle cam (T) and boss (B) when speed control linkage is set as outlined in text.

Fig. MR28-9 — View showing speed control linkage components used on late 200 hp models. Refer to text for adjustment procedures.

A. Maximum spark advance screw
B. Maximum spark advance lever
L. Link rod
P. Primary screw

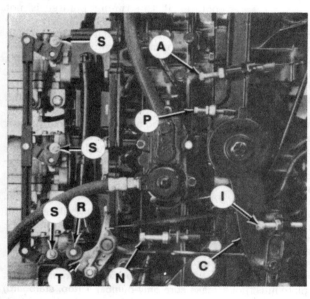

Fig. MR28-10 — View showing speed control linkage components used on late 200 hp models. Refer to text for adjustment procedures.

A. Maximum spark advance screw
C. Throttle lever
I. Idle speed screw
N. Maximum throttle stop screw
P. Primary screw
R. Cam follower roller
S. Screws
T. Throttle cam

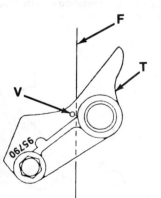

Fig. MR28-11 — A ⅛ inch (3 mm) diameter rod or drill bit must be installed in hole (V) on models with the numbers "95790" cast on throttle cam (T). The rod or drill bit should just contact edge of carburetor adapter flange (F) when speed control linkage is set and adjusted as outlined in text.

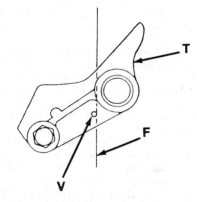

Fig. MR28-12 — A ⅛ inch (3 mm) diameter rod or drill bit must be installed in hole (V) on models with no numbers cast on throttle cam (T). The rod or drill bit should just contact edge of carburetor adapter flange (F) when speed control linkage is set and adjusted as outlined in text.

Disconnect fuel tank supply hose at the outboard motor connector. Detach throttle cable barrel from the retainer of the cable anchor bracket.

Install a ⅛ inch (3 mm) diameter rod or drill bit in hole (V—Fig. MR28-11) on models equipped with the casting numbers "95790" on throttle cam (T). Install a ⅛ inch (3 mm) diameter rod or drill bit in hole (V—Fig. MR28-12) on models not equipped with numbers cast on throttle cam (T). While holding rod or drill bit perpendicular to throttle cam (T—Fig. MR28-11 or Fig. MR28-12), adjust idle speed screw (I—Fig. MR28-10) until rod or drill bit just contacts edge of carburetor adapter flange (F—Fig. MR28-11 or Fig. MR28-12).

Withdraw air intake cover from front of the carburetors. Position throttle lever (C—Fig. MR28-10) so idle speed screw (I) is against its stop. Loosen carburetor synchronizing screws (S) and allow carburetor throttle plates to close freely. With light pressure, hold cam follower roller (R) against throttle cam (T). At the same time, lift up on bottom carburetor throttle shaft to remove slack in linkage components. Then retighten screws (S). Be sure carburetor throttle plates are completely closed and operate freely. Repeat adjustment procedure if setting is incorrect. Reinstall air intake cover.

Connect a power timing light to number 1 cylinder spark plug lead. With outboard motor in neutral, position throttle lever (C) so idle speed screw (I) is against stop. Crank engine with starter motor and adjust primary screw (P) so ignition timing is 12 degrees ATDC on models prior to serial number C100861 and 2-7 degrees ATDC on models after serial number C100860.

Open throttle until maximum spark advance screw (A) is against stop. Crank engine with starter motor and adjust maximum spark advance screw (A) so ignition timing is 22 degrees BTDC.

NOTE: Due to electronic characteristics of ignition system, maximum advance is set at 22 degrees BTDC, but ignition will retard to 20 degrees BTDC at 5400 rpm and increase to 26 degrees BTDC over 5600 rpm.

The carburetor throttle plate must not act as the wide open throttle stop. To prevent damage to carburetors, move speed control linkage to maximum speed position and adjust maximum throttle stop screw (N) so a clearance (C—Fig. MR28-7) of 0.010-0.015 inch (0.25-0.38 mm) is between throttle cam (T) and cam follower roller (R).

Make sure carburetors and oil injection pump are properly synchronized as outlined in OIL INJECTION SYSTEM section.

Reconnect spark advance module wire to outer switch box. Reinstall spark plugs, then adjust idle speed screw (I—Fig. MR28-10) to idle speed specified in CONDENSED SERVICE DATA.

Hold idle speed screw (I) against stop and install throttle cable barrel in retainer while adjusting throttle cable barrel so it fits into retainer and a very light preload between idle screw and its stop is established. Excessive throttle cable preload will result in difficult shifting from forward to neutral.

REED VALVES. The fuel:air mixture for each cylinder is directed through a reed valve assembly. Six reed valve assemblies are attached to the intake manifold. Reed block assemblies may be either mounted horizontally or vertically on intake manifold.

Reed petals shown in Fig. MR.28-14 should be flat and have no more than 0.007 inch (0.18 mm) clearance between free end of reed petal and seating sur-

face of reed block. On vertical mounted reed blocks, reed petals should not stand open more than 0.020 inch (0.51 mm). Do not attempt to bend or straighten a reed petal or turn reed petals around on reed block. Reed block seating surface must be flat. Reed block should be renewed if indented by reed petals or damaged. Reed petals are available in sets for each reed block only.

Note reed petal shapes in Fig. MR28-14. Early 150 hp engines are equipped with "straight-cut" reed petals (A) and late 150 and 200 hp engines are equipped with "teardrop" reed petals (B). Early 175 hp engines used both types of reed petals; later 175 hp engines are equipped with "teardrop" reed petals (B). Install reed blocks of early 175 hp engines so "teardrop" reed petals are toward center side of reed housing. When renewing reed petals on early 175 hp engines, always install a "teardrop" reed petal, even if the old reed was "straight-cut" type.

Reed stop setting on models so equipped is 0.020 inch (0.51 mm) on 150 hp models and 0.300 inch (7.62 mm) on 175 and 200 hp models. Measure reed stop opening from reed stop to reed petal seating surface as shown in Fig. MR28-15.

FUEL PUMP. A diaphragm type fuel pump is mounted on the intake manifold. Early models are equipped with an "oval" design pump and later models are equipped with a "square" design pump. Crankcase pulsations actuate the fuel pump diaphragm to pump fuel on all models. Fuel pump pressure on early "oval" design pump should be 4.0-5.5 psi (28-38 kPa) at full throttle and 3 psi (21 kPa) at idle. Full throttle fuel pump pressure on later "square" design pump should be a minimum of 3 psi (20.7 kPa) and should not exceed 10 psi (68.9 kPa). Normal idle speed pressure on "square" pump is 2-3 psi (13.8-20.7 kPa) with a minimum of 1 psi (6.9 kPa).

If the fuel pump malfunctions due to a split diaphragm on early 175 hp models, drill a 0.078 inch (1.98 mm) hole (B—Fig. MR28-17) through the pulse chamber so the hole is ⅜ inch (9.5 mm) from centerline of hole (A) as shown, and bevel edge of hole (A).

When overhauling the fuel pump, renew all defective or questionable components. The manufacturer recommends renewing pump gaskets and diaphragms if pump is disassembled. When assembling early "oval" pump, install check valves as shown in Fig. MR28-18 with tips of retainer (R) pointing away from check valves. After installing check valve retainers (6—Fig. MR28-19) on "square" pump, break off

stem of retainer (6) by bending over. Then, insert stem into retainer and tap down until flush with top of retainer. Tighten mounting screws on "square" pump to 50-60 in.-lbs. (5.7-6.8 N·m).

OIL INJECTION. Some 1984 and all 1985 and later models are equipped with oil injection. The fuel:oil ratio is varied from approximately 50:1 at full throttle to approximately 100:1 at idle. The oil injection pump is synchronized with carburetor throttle opening by mechanical linkage. As the carburetor throttle opens or closes, oil delivered to the fuel pump is matched to power head demand. The oil injection pump is driven by a gear secured to the engine crankshaft.

Oil tank (2—Fig. MR28-21) is pressurized by crankcase pressure and feeds oil to reservoir (5). Check valve (3) will unseat allowing air to enter oil line should oil line between tank (2) and reservoir (5) become restricted, preventing oil pump (7) from creating a vacu-

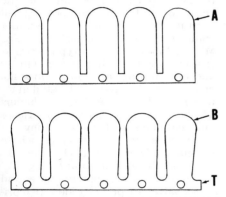

Fig. MR28-14—View of "straight-cut" (A) and "teardrop" (B) reed petals. Note tang (T) on "teardrop" reed petals.

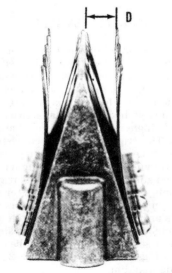

Fig. MR28-15 — Reed stop setting (D) should be 0.200 inch (5.08 mm) for 150 hp models and 0.300 inch (7.62 mm) for 175 and 200 hp models.

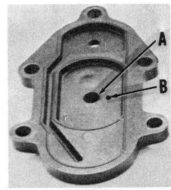

Fig. MR28-17—Modify the fuel pump on early 175 hp models with a split diaphragm as outlined in text.

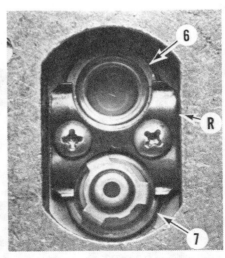

Fig. MR28-18—View showing installation of outlet check valve (6) and inlet check valve (7) in early "oval" design fuel pump body. Install retainer (R) so tips are facing away from check valves.

um in reservoir (5). Check valve (12) prevents fuel pump from pumping gasoline into oil line (13). Motion sensor (8) detects movement of a magnet inside pump coupler and triggers warning module (9) to sound a warning horn if pump movement stops. Note that if removed, the north end of the magnet must be installed into the coupler first. The north end of the magnet can be determined by holding magnet close to a suitable camping (directional) compass. Do not use the boat compass. The end of the magnet that attracts the north arrow of the compass is the north end of magnet.

BLEEDING OIL INJECTION PUMP. With engine not started, loosen bleed screw (B—Fig. MR28-20) three to four turns. Allow oil to drain from around bleed screw until no air bubbles are noted. Securely retighten bleed screw (B).

THROTTLE ARM AND OIL INJECTION PUMP SYNCHRONIZATION. Place throttle linkage in idle position, then note if mark (M—Fig. MR28-20) on oil pump control lever aligns with mark (R) on pump body. If not, disconnect and adjust length of pump control rod as necessary to align marks.

OIL PUMP OUTPUT TEST. Proceed as follows to check oil injection pump output: Connect a remote fuel tank containing a 50:1 fuel and oil mixture to fuel pump. Disconnect the clear oil pump output line from the fuel pump inlet line "T" fitting and plug fitting. Place disconnected end of oil output line into a suitable graduated container. Start engine and run at 1500 rpm for 3 minutes. Then stop engine and note pump output in container. Next, disconnect oil pump control rod and move pump lever to full throttle position.

Again, start engine and run at 1500 rpm for three minutes, stop engine and note pump output. On 122 cu. in. (1999.2 cc) engines, output should be 6.1-7.5 mL (0.21-0.25 oz.) with pump control rod connected to oil pump and 15.3-18.7 mL (0.52-0.63 oz.) with pump lever in full throttle position. On 142 cu. in (2330.2 cc) engines, pump output should be 7.4-9.0 mL (0.25-0.30 oz.) with pump control rod connected to oil pump and 17.3-21.1 mL (0.59-0.71 oz.) with pump control lever at full throttle position.

DRIVE GEAR. If a new oil injection pump drive gear is installed on crankshaft, the maximum allowable misalignment at split line of gear is 0.030 inch (0.76 mm). Tighten gear retaining Allen head screw to 8 in.-lbs. (0.9 N·m). Zero clearance should be noted at split line of gear.

CRANKCASE BLEED SYSTEM

A crankcase bleed system is used to remove unburned oil residue from the crankcase and lower main bearing and burn it or direct it to the three upper main bearings. See diagram in Fig. MR28-22 for a view of a typical crankcase bleed system. The number of hoses and hose routing may differ on some models. Check valves are located in intake manifold while fittings to cylinders are located in cylinder block. Hoses must be connected between fitting and check valve with same letter, i.e., a hose is connected between check valve "B" on reed valve housing and fitting "B" on cylinder block. Make sure hoses and check valves are properly identified prior to components being separated. Engine will not operate properly if hoses are connected incorrectly. Check operation of check valves.

IGNITION SYSTEM

An alternator driven capacitor discharge ignition (CDI) system is used. Ignition system consists of the flywheel, stator, trigger assembly, switch box and ignition coils. The stator is mounted below the flywheel and contains two (low-speed, high-speed) capacitor charging coils. The trigger assembly consists of three trigger coils and is mounted below the flywheel. Ignition timing is advanced and retarded by rotating trigger assembly in relation to the inner flywheel magnets. Diodes, capacitors and SCR's are contained in the switch box. Switch box, trigger assembly and stator must be serviced as unit assemblies. Refer to Figs. MR28-23 and MR28-24 for wiring diagrams.

If engine malfunction is noted, and ignition system is suspected, make sure

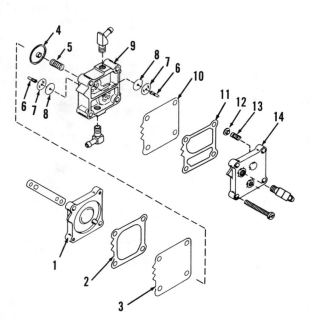

Fig. MR28-19—Exploded view of "square" design fuel pump used on late models.

1. Base
2. Gasket
3. Diaphragm
4. Cap
5. Boost spring
6. Retainer
7. Plastic disc
8. Check valve
9. Body
10. Diaphragm
11. Gasket
12. Cap
13. Spring
14. Cover

Fig. MR28-20—View showing oil injection pump used on some 1984 and all later models. Refer to text for adjustment procedures and identification of components.

spark plugs and all electrical wiring are in acceptable condition and all electrical connections are clean and tight prior to trouble-shooting CDI system.

To properly test the switch box and ignition coils requires the use of Quicksilver Multi-Meter DVA Tester part 91-99750 or a suitable voltmeter capable of measuring a minimum of 400 DC volts used with Quicksilver Direct Voltage Adaptor (DVA) part 91-89045. Follow instructions provided by tester manufacturer when performing tests. If these testers are not available, a process of elimination must be used when testing ignition system. Stator and trigger as-

semblies can be effectively tested using a suitable ohmmeter.

NOTE: All tests that involve cranking or running the engine must be performed with lead wires connected. Switch boxes MUST be grounded to engine for all tests or switch box may be damaged. If switch box is removed from power head to ease access, connect a separate ground lead from switch box to power head.

To test ignition system, proceed as follows:

IGNITION COILS PRIMARY VOLTAGE. Connect DVA red test lead to ignition coil positive (+) terminal and black test lead to coil negative (−) ter-

minal. Position tester selector switch to DVA/400. Tester should read 150-250 volts at cranking or idle speed (300-1000 rpm) and 180-280 volts at 1000-4000 rpm. If voltage readings are below specified reading, refer to SWITCH BOX STOP CIRCUIT test. If readings are within specifications, connect a suitable spark tester to ignition coil high tension leads, crank engine and note spark. If weak or no spark is noted, renew ignition coil(s). If normal spark is noted, renew spark plugs. If malfunction is still evident after renewing spark plugs, check ignition timing. If ignition timing is within specification, malfunction is not in ig-

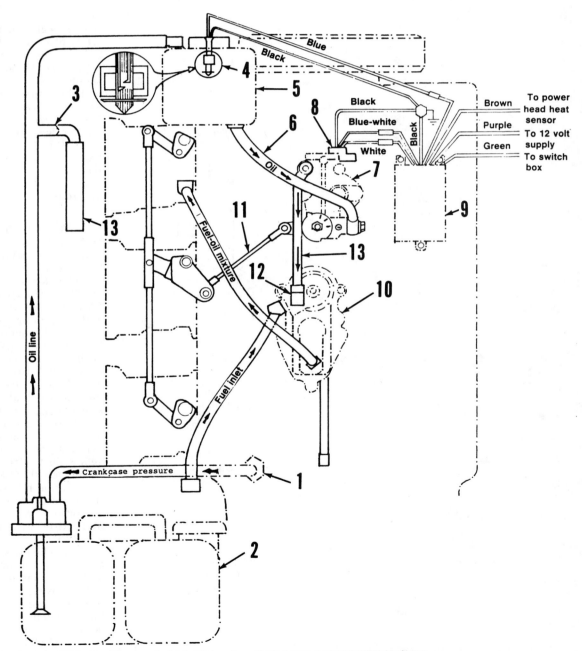

1. One-way check valve
2. Remote oil tank
3. Check valve
4. Low oil sensor
5. Oil reservoir
6. Oil pump supply line
7. Oil pump assy.
8. Motion sensor
9. Warning module
10. Fuel pump
11. Oil pump control rod
12. Check valve
13. Oil pump output line
B. Black
G. Green
W. White
Bl. Blue
Br. Brown
Pr. Purple
Bl/W. Blue with white tracer

Fig. MR28-21—Diagram of oil injection system. Early design fuel pump (10) is shown.

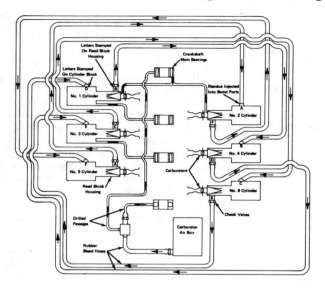

Fig. MR28-22—Diagram of typical crankcase bleed system.

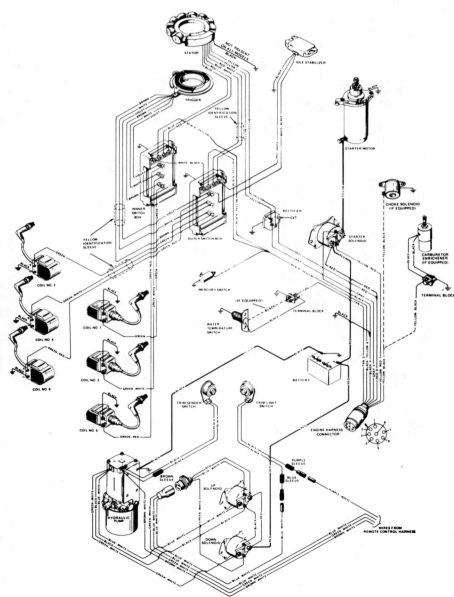

Fig. MR28-23—Wiring diagram of models prior to serial number C100861.

nition system. If ignition timing is not to specification, such as a sudden timing change, inspect trigger advance linkage for excessive wear or damage and inner flywheel magnets (shifted position or other damage). If timing is erratic or unstable, disconnect idle stabilizer or spark advance module and recheck timing. If timing is now within specification, idle stabilizer or spark advance module is defective and must be renewed. If timing is still erratic or unstable with idle stabilizer or spark advance module isolated, refer to SWITCH BOX BIAS section.

SWITCH BOX BIAS. Check switch box bias as follows: Connect a red test lead of a suitable voltmeter (not DVA meter) to engine ground and black test lead to white/black switch box terminal. Voltage at cranking or idle speed should be 2-10 volts. Voltage at 1000-4000 rpm should be 10-30 volts. If voltage reading is below specification, one or both switch boxes are defective. If switch box bias voltage is within specification, check trigger resistance as outlined in SWITCH BOX STOP CIRCUIT section. If trigger resistance is acceptable, one or both switch boxes may be defective. Substitute known good switch box(es) and retest.

SWITCH BOX STOP CIRCUIT. Connect DVA black test lead to engine ground and red test lead to black/yellow switch box terminal (orange terminal on early models). Refer to Figs. MR28-23 and MR28-24. Set DVA selector switch to DVA/400. Voltage reading at cranking and all running speeds should be 200-360 volts. If reading is within specifications, refer to STATOR tests. If reading is above specified voltages, disconnect trigger leads from switch boxes. Check resistance between brown (without yellow sleeve) and white (with yellow sleeve) trigger leads, then white (without yellow sleeve) and violet (with yellow sleeve) trigger leads, then violet (without yellow sleeve) and brown (with yellow sleeve) trigger leads. Resistance should be 1100-1400 ohms at all connections. If not, renew trigger assembly. If trigger resistance is acceptable, renew one or both switch box(es) and repeat SWITCH BOX STOP CIRCUIT test.

If SWITCH BOX STOP CIRCUIT test reading is below specified voltage, disconnect ignition switch, stop switch and mercury switch from black/yellow switch box terminal (orange switch box terminal on early models). Be sure ignition switch lead is disconnected from both switch boxes. With stop switch, ignition switch and mercury switch isolated, repeat SWITCH BOX STOP CIR-

CUIT test. If reading is now within specification, ignition switch, stop switch or mercury switch is defective. If reading remains below specification refer to STATOR test.

STATOR. Disconnect idle stabilizer or spark advance module leads from switch box prior to testing stator. Connect DVA black test lead to engine ground and red test lead to blue/white terminal on outer switch box. Set DVA selector switch to DVA/400. Voltage reading should be 200-300 volts at cranking and idle speeds and 200-330 volts at 1000-4000 rpm. Switch DVA red test lead to red/white outer switch box terminal. Leave black test lead connected to engine ground. Voltage reading should be 20-90 volts at cranking or idle speeds and 130-300 volts at 1000-4000 rpm. Next, connect black tester lead to engine ground and red tester lead to blue switch box terminal on inner switch box.

1. Inner switch box
2. Trigger
3. Stator
4. Starter motor
5. Warning module
6. Idle stabilizer
7. Oil tank cap
8. Oil pump motion sensor
9. Enrichment valve
10. Starter solenoid
11. Outer switch box
12. Temperature sensor
13. Water temperature switch
14. Mercury (tilt) switch
15. Voltage regulator
16. No. 1 ignition coil
17. No. 2 ignition coil
18. No. 3 ignition coil
19. No. 4 ignition coil
20. No. 5 ignition coil
21. No. 6 ignition coil
B. Black
G. Green
R. Red
T. Tan
V. Vilot
W. White
Y. Yellow
Br. Brown
Bl. Blue
Gr. Gray
Pr. Purple
B/Y. Black with yellow tracer
G/R. Green with red tracer
G/W. Green with white tracer
R/W. Red with white tracer
W/B. White with black tracer
Y/B. Yellow with black tracer
Y/R. Yellow with red tracer
Bl/W. Blue with white tracer
T/Bl. Tan with blue tracer

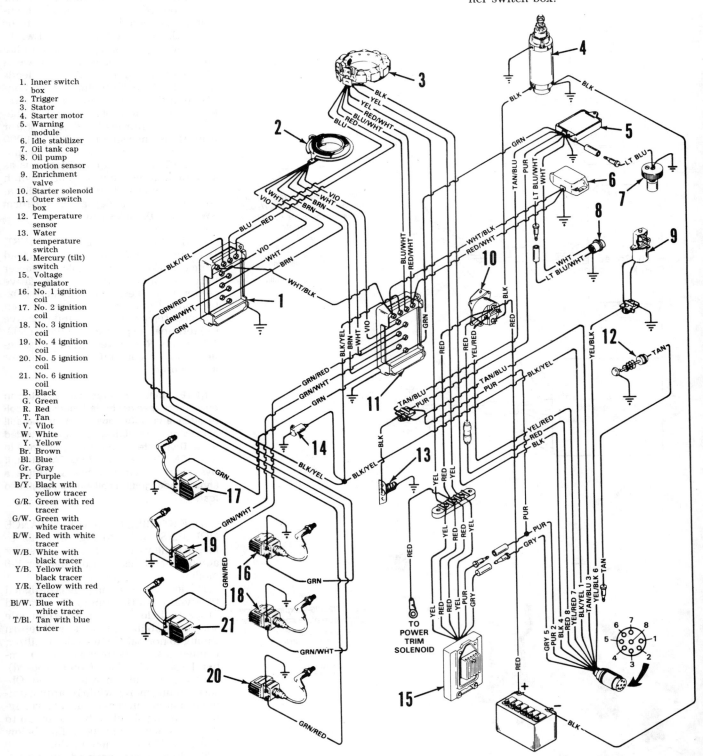

Fig. MR28-24—Wiring diagram on models after serial number C100860. Models 150 Magnum II and 200 hp are equipped with a low speed/high speed spark advance module or low speed/high speed/spark advance/excessive rpm spark retard module in place of idle stabilizer (6).

NOTE: Outer switch box should be removed to gain access to inner switch box. Be sure to connect a ground lead from both switch boxes to engine ground prior to cranking engine to prevent damage to ignition system.

Tester selector switch should be set at DVA/400. Voltage reading should be 200-

300 volts at cranking and idle speeds and 200-330 volts at 1000-4000 rpm. Remove red tester lead from blue switch box terminal and connect to red terminal on inner switch box. Voltage reading at cranking and idle speeds should be 20-90 volts and 130-300 volts at 1000-4000 rpm.

NOTE: A shorted or open capacitor inside switch box will result in faulty stator voltage readings during cranking and running tests. Stator resistance should be checked as follows before failing stator.

If any STATOR voltage reading is below specification, proceed as follows: Disconnect leads from inner and outer switch boxes. Connect a suitable ohmmeter between blue and red stator leads, then blue/white and red/white stator leads. Resistance between blue and red stator leads and between blue/white and red/white stator leads should be 3600-4200 ohms. Next, connect ohmmeter between red/white stator lead and stator black lead, then between red stator lead and black stator lead. Resistance should be 9000-14,000 ohms. Renew stator if resistance is not as specified. If stator resistance is as specified, renew one or both switch boxes and repeat STATOR tests. If all stator tests are acceptable, perform SWITCH BOX BIAS test.

IGNITION COILS RESISTANCE TEST. Disconnect wires and high tension lead from coil. Connect a suitable ohmmeter between coil positive (+) and negative (−) terminals. Resistance should be 0.02-0.04 ohm. Connect ohmmeter between coil high tension terminal and negative (−) terminal. Resistance should be 800-1100 ohms. Repeat test on all coils. Renew ignition coil(s) if resistance is not as specified.

NOTE: Ignition coil resistance tests can only detect open or shorted windings. If coil resistance is within specification and still suspected as defective, coil must be tested using DVA meter as previously outlined in IGNITION COILS PRIMARY VOLTAGE test. If DVA meter is not available, substitute a known good ignition coil and run engine to test.

IDLE STABILIZER/SPARK ADVANCE MODULES. Refer to Fig. MR28-25 to identify the various idle stabilizer/spark advance modules used on Mariner V-6 models.

The idle stabilizer module is designed to advance ignition timing if idle speed drops to below 550 rpm. When idle speed is stabilized, module will return timing to normal. To test idle stabilizer, connect a suitable timing light to number 1 spark plug lead (top starboard), start engine and run at idle speed. Observe timing marks while retarding timing by pulling on spark control lever. Ignition timing should advance by up to 9 degrees when idle speed falls below 550 rpm. If not, renew module.

The high-speed spark advance module is designed to advance ignition tim-

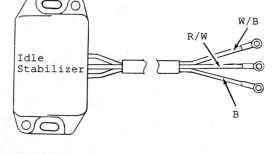

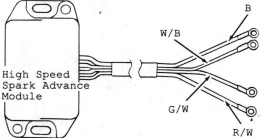

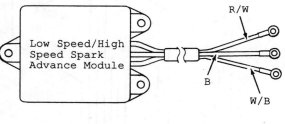

Fig. MR28-25—View of the various idle stabilizer/spark advance modules used on V-6 models.

   B. Black
G/W. Green with white tracer
R/W. Red with white tracer
W/B. White with black tracer

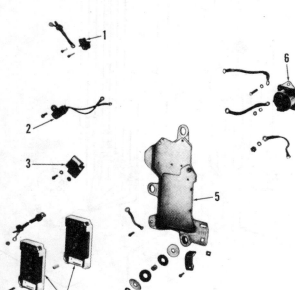

Fig. MR28-26—Exploded view of ignition plate components.

  1. Terminal block
  2. Mercury switch
  3. Rectifier
  4. Switch boxes
  5. Ignition plate
  6. Starter solenoid

ing when engine speed reaches approximately 5600 rpm. Timing will remain advanced until engine speed drops to approximately 5400 rpm. To test spark advance module, connect a suitable timing light to number 1 spark plug lead (top starboard). Start engine and slowly increase engine speed to 5600 rpm while observing timing marks. Ignition timing should advance by 6 degrees at approximately 5600 rpm and return to normal setting at approximately 5400 rpm. If not, renew module.

Low speed/high speed spark advance module combines the functions of an idle stabilizer and high-speed spark advance module. Test module by performing idle stabilizer and high-speed spark advance module tests as previously outlined.

COOLING SYSTEM

THERMOSTAT. All models are equipped with a thermostat in each cylinder head cover. Thermostat should begin to open at 140°-145° F (60°-63° C). A temperature sender is installed in the starboard cylinder head either below number one spark plug or in the outer portion of the cylinder head between number one and number three spark plug. The temperature sender will activate an alarm horn should engine overheating occur. Temperature sender may be checked with a continuity tester and a high-temperature thermometer. Place sender and thermometer in water that is being heated. Sender positioned in the outer portion of the cylinder head should show a closed circuit when water temperature reaches 180°-200° F (82°-93° C) and then reopen when temperature drops to 160°-180° F (71°-82° C). Sender positioned below number 1 spark plug should show a closed circuit when water temperature reaches 230°-250° F (110°-121° C) and then reopen when temperature starts dropping below 230° F (110° C).

A water pressure relief valve is located on starboard side of cylinder block. Note cross section of valve shown in Fig. MR28-29. Diaphragm is renewable. Inspect components for nicks, cracks or other damage which may cause leakage.

WATER PUMP. The rubber impeller type water pump is housed in the gearcase housing. The impeller is mounted on and driven by the lower unit drive shaft. Water pump is accessible after separating gearcase housing from drive shaft housing as outlined in LOWER UNIT section.

POWER HEAD

R&R AND DISASSEMBLE. To remove power head assembly, disconnect all wires and hoses and remove all cowling which will interfere with power head separation from drive shaft housing. Detach shift rod from control cable bracket. Unscrew 10 locknuts securing power head to drive shaft housing and lift power head off drive shaft housing and install on a suitable stand. If equipped, remove oil injection pump reservoir and plug hose fittings. Remove flywheel, stator, trigger plate and starter motor. Remove choke solenoid, temperature sender, ignition coils, switch box plate assembly and speed control linkage. If equipped, remove oil injection pump. Remove fuel pump and disconnect and label interfering bleed hoses. Remove carburetors and airbox as an assembly. Remove intake manifold with reed valve assemblies, cylinder head cover, cylinder heads and exhaust manifold assembly.

Remove screws securing end caps to crankcase and loosen end cap to cylinder block screws. Remove crankcase mounting screws, then remove crankcase by using recesses under crankcase to pry against. Use extra care not to damage machined mating surfaces of cylinder block and crankcase. Mark connecting rods with cylinder numbers so they can be reinstalled in original cylinders and remove rod and piston assemblies. Unscrew end cap to cylinder block screws and remove end caps. Crankcase and cylinder block are matched and align bored and can be renewed as a set only.

Refer to following paragraphs to service pistons, rods, crankshaft and bearings. When assembling, follow the procedures outlined in the ASSEMBLY paragraphs.

ASSEMBLY. When assembling, the crankcase must be sealed against both vacuum and pressure. Exhaust manifold

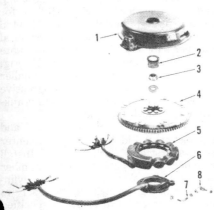

Fig. MR28-27—View of flywheel and ignition components.

1. Flywheel cover
2. Plug
3. Nut
4. Flywheel
5. Stator
6. Trigger plate
7. Trigger plate link rod
8. Ball joint

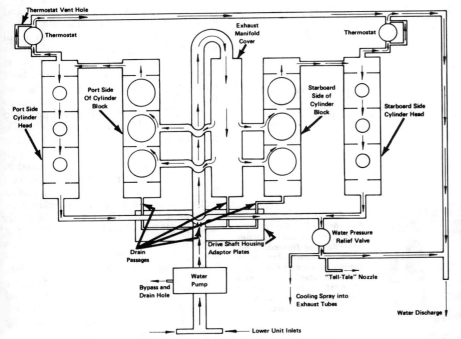

Fig. MR28-28 — Typical diagram of coolant flow. Refer to Fig. MR28-29 for cross section of water pressure relief valve.

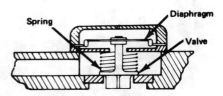

Fig. MR28-29—Cross-sectional view of water pressure relief valve.

and water passage must be sealed against pressure leakage. Whenever power head is disassembled, it is recommended that all gasket surfaces and machined joints without gaskets be carefully checked for nicks and burrs which might interfere with a tight seal.

Install seals in lower end cap with lips down (away from cylinder block). Install seal in upper end cap with lip down (toward cylinder block). Be sure seal does not block bleed passage in end cap. Loctite 271 or 290 should be applied to seal bore of end caps. Lubricate all bearing and friction surfaces with engine oil. Loose needle bearings may be held in place during assembly using a light, non-fibrous grease.

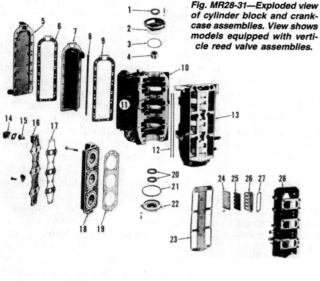

Fig. MR28-31—Exploded view of cylinder block and crankcase assemblies. View shows models equipped with vertical reed valve assemblies.

1. Oil seal
2. Upper end cap
3. "O" ring
4. Roller bearing
5. Exhaust manifold cover
6. Gasket
7. Divider plate
8. Seal
9. Gasket
10. Cylinder block
11. Bearing locating dowel pins
12. Sealing strips
13. Crankcase
14. Thermostat housing
15. Thermostat
16. Cylinder head cover
17. Gasket
18. Cylinder head
19. Gasket
20. Oil seals
21. "O" ring
22. Lower end cap
23. Gasket
24. Reed petal stop
25. Reed petal
26. Reed block
27. Gasket
28. Intake manifold

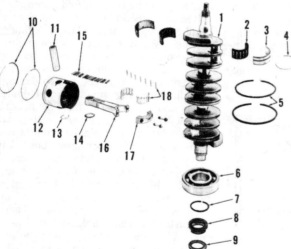

Fig. MR28-32 — Exploded view of crankshaft assembly.

1. Crankshaft
2. Roller bearing
3. Bearing race
4. Retaining ring
5. Seal rings
6. Ball bearing
7. Snap ring
8. Seal carrier
9. Oil seal
10. Piston rings
11. Piston pin
12. Piston
13. Retaining ring
14. Spacer
15. Bearing rollers (29)
16. Connecting rod
17. Rod cap
18. Roller bearing

Fig. MR28-33 — On models prior to serial number 5464486, use tightening sequence shown for large crankcase screws (C). Tighten small crankcase screws (S) next. Note position of long seal screw (B) used on early models.

Install pistons, rod and crankshaft assemblies as outlined in appropriate following paragraphs. End caps should be in place with screws installed but not tightened. Rotate crankshaft and check for binding. Cut gasket strips off flush with edge of crankcase bores. Apply a thin coat of sealer such as Permatex 2C-12 to mating surfaces of crankcase and cylinder block using care to prevent excess sealer from entering bearings, crankcase or passages.

Progressively tighten eight large crankcase screws until crankshaft seal rings are compressed and crankcase mates with cylinder block. Tighten eight large crankcase screws in three progressive steps to specified torque and using tightening sequence in Fig. MR28-33 for models prior to serial number 5464486 and Fig. MR28-34 for models after serial number 5464485. On early models, note location of long seal screw (B–Fig. MR28-33) and then tighten six smaller crankcase screws in three progressive steps to specified torque. Rotate crankshaft and check for binding.

When installing intake manifold and exhaust manifold cover, tighten center screws first and work outward. Install cylinder head gaskets with number stamped in gasket up (away from cylinder block). Tighten cylinder head screws in three progressive steps to specified torque and using tightening sequence in Fig. MR28-35.

PISTONS, PINS, RINGS AND CYLINDERS. Before detaching connecting rods from crankshaft, make sure that rod and cap are marked so rods and caps are not interchanged and may be returned to original cylinders.

Piston pin is pressed into piston on all models. On early models, manufacturer recommends discarding piston if pin is pressed out of piston. Piston pin boss marked "UP" has smaller piston pin hole than other pin boss. Press pin out so pin exits "UP" boss first and press pin in so pin enters "UP" boss last. Pistons are marked on piston pin boss and piston crown according to their location in cylinder block. "S" pistons must be used in starboard cylinders while "P" pistons must be used in port cylinders. Install piston on connecting rods so side with alignment bumps (B–Fig. MR28-36) is nearer "UP" piston pin boss. Piston pin is supported by 29 loose rollers. Rollers may be held in connecting rod with non-fibrous grease during piston installation. Install piston and rod assembly in engine so "UP" pin boss is towards flywheel end of engine. Be sure piston ring ends are properly located around pins in ring grooves during installation.

On late models, the manufacturer recommends renewing piston pin needle bearings if piston pin is removed from piston. A torch lamp or suitable equivalent should be used to heat piston dome to approximately 190° F (88° C) prior to removal or installation of piston pin. Piston pin is supported by 29 loose rollers. Rollers may be held in connecting rod with nonfibrous grease during piston installation. Use recommended Mariner tools or suitable equivalents when pressing piston pin in to or out of piston. Renew piston pin retaining clips during reassembly. Install piston and rod assembly in cylinder identified on rod during disassembly. Piston must be installed with "UP" stamped on piston dome toward fly-

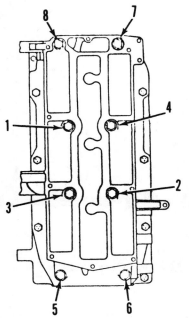

Fig. MR28-34 — Tighten crankcase screws following sequence shown on vertical and horizontal reed models after serial number 5464485.

wheel end of crankshaft. Pistons are marked "P" for port and "S" for starboard on piston domes for correct installation in port or starboard cylinder bank.

Maximum allowable cylinder tolerance is 0.006 inch (0.15 mm). Cylinders on 122 cu. in. (1999.2 cc) models can be bored to accommodate 0.015 inch (0.38 mm) and 0.030 inch (0.76 mm) oversize pistons. Cylinders on 142.2 cu. in. (2330.2 cc) models are chrome plated and no oversize pistons are available. Chrome cylinder bores can be replated to original size if excessively worn, scored or damaged. On some chrome bore models, a cast iron sleeve can be installed in one or more cylinders to restore cylinders to standard size. Note that cylinder block and crankcase must be renewed as an assembly.

CONNECTING RODS, BEARINGS AND CRANKSHAFT. Connecting rod has 29 loose rollers in small end and caged roller bearings in big end. Install piston on connecting rod so side with alignment bumps (B—Fig. MR28-36) is nearer "UP" piston pin boss on early models or bumps (B) and "UP" stamped on piston dome both face flywheel end of crankshaft on late models. Be sure alignment bumps (B) and marks (M) are correctly positioned when installing rod on crankshaft. Connecting rod big end is fractured type and rod and cap must be mated perfectly before tightening cap screws.

Inspect crankshaft crankpin and main bearing journal surfaces. If scored, out-of-round or worn, renew crankshaft. Check crankshaft for straightness. Do not interchange main bearings.

ELECTRICAL SYSTEM

Refer to Figs. MR28-23 and MR28-24 for wiring diagrams. Early models are equipped with a 9 ampere alternator. On 19861988 models, a 15 ampere alternator with a voltage regulator is used. Models after serial number C100860 are equipped with a 40 ampere alternator with a voltage regulator.

The rectifier on early models can be checked by disconnecting wires to rectifier and using a continuity tester or ohmmeter as follows: Connect a tester lead to ground and then alternately connect other tester lead to alternator terminals of rectifier. Note reading then reverse tester leads. Tester should indicate a short or open circuit with first test and opposite reading when tester leads are reversed. Connect a tester lead to positive rectifier terminal and alternately connect other tester lead to alternator terminals of rectifier. Note reading then reverse tester leads. Tester should show opposite reading when tester leads are reversed. Renew rectifier if testing indicates faulty circuits. No ohmmeter tests are possible on rectifier/regulator assembly used with 40 ampere alternator system.

To check alternator stator on all models, disconnect yellow stator leads at rectifier (Fig. MR28-23) or voltage regulator (Fig. MR28-24). Connect ohmmeter between yellow leads. Stator resistance should be less than 1 ohm. No continuity should be present between either stator yellow lead and ground.

Regulated voltage measured at the battery should be 14-14.5 volts at 1000 rpm.

Normal starter motor current draw on early models equipped with starter part A-50-86976 is 190 amperes. On later models equipped with starter part A-50-79472, normal current draw is 175 amperes. Renew starter brushes when worn to less than 1/4 inch (6.4 mm) long.

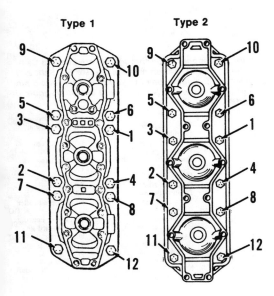

Type 1   Type 2

Fig. MR28-35—Tighten cylinder head in sequence shown on all models. Tighten type 1 cylinder head to 40 in.-lbs. (4.5 N·m). Tighten type 2 cylinder head and all late models to 30 in.-lbs. (3.4 N·m).

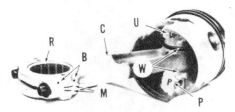

Fig. MR28-36 — View of piston and connecting rod assembly. Note location of alignment bumps (B), alignment marks (M), and washers (W) used on all models. "P" locating mark (P) and "UP" mark (U) are used on early models. "P" locating mark indicates port side piston while a starboard piston will have an "S" locating mark.

LOWER UNIT

Early models and Model 150 Magnum II are equipped with Cam-Shift lower unit and later models and all 200 hp models are equipped with E-Z Shift lower unit.

To identify Cam-Shift and E-Z Shift lower unit, note the following: With lower unit attached to engine and shifted into reverse gear, propeller shaft on E-Z Shift lower unit will ratchet in one direction and propeller shaft on Cam-Shift unit will be locked in gear in both directions. Also, with lower unit removed, shift shaft on Cam-Shift lower unit will rotate 360 degrees in counterclockwise direction and shift shaft on E-Z Shift lower unit will only rotate 30 degrees in either direction.

All Models

PROPELLER AND DRIVE CLUTCH. Protection for the motor and lower unit is provided by a special cushioning clutch in the propeller hub in early models and by a splined rubber hub in propeller on later models. Various pitch propellers are available. Select a propeller that will allow outboard motor to operate within the specified speed range at full throttle. Refer to CONDENSED SERVICE DATA.

Cam-Shift Models

R&R AND OVERHAUL. Most service on the lower unit can be performed by detaching the gearcase from the drive shaft housing. To remove gearcase, remove plastic plug and Allen screw from location (1—Fig. MR28-38). Remove trim tab (2) and screw from under trim tab. Remove stud nuts from location (3), stud nuts (4) on each side and stud nut (5), then remove the lower unit gearcase assembly.

Remove the gearcase plugs and drain the gearcase lubricant, then secure the gearcase in a vise between two blocks of soft wood, with propeller up. Wedge a piece of wood between propeller and antiventilation plate, remove the propeller nut, then remove the propeller.

Disassemble gearcase by removing gearcase cover nut (55—Fig. MR28-39).

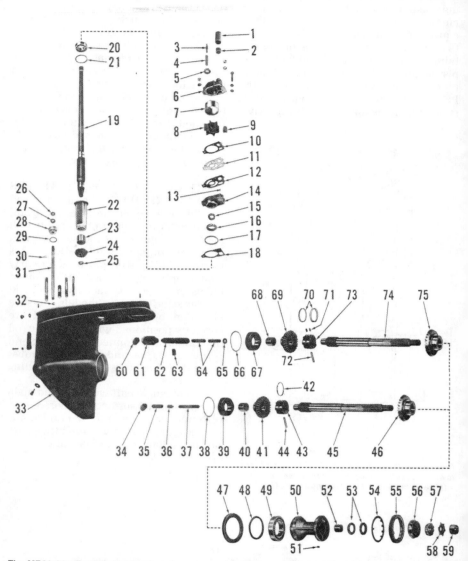

Fig. MR28-39—Exploded view of gearcase assembly. Components (34 through 46) are used on Cam-Shift models while components (60 through 75) are used on E-Z Shift models. On late E-Z Shift and 150 Magnum II models, a threaded bearing retainer located above bearing (20) is used. Preload pin (3) and spring (4) are absent on late models. Reverse gear bearing (49) is absent on 150 Magnum II models.

1. Water tube guide	20. Bearing	39. Tapered roller bearing
2. Seal	21. Shim	40. Roller bearing
3. Pin	22. Sleeve	41. Forward gear
4. Spring	23. Roller bearing	42. Spring clip
5. Rubber ring (slinger)	24. Pinion gear	43. Dog clutch
6. Water pump body	25. Nut	44. Pin
7. Insert	26. Rubber washer	45. Propeller shaft
8. Impeller	27. Oil seal	46. Reverse gear
9. Key	28. Bushing	47. Thrust washer
10. Gasket	29. "O" ring	48. "O" ring
11. Plate	30. "E" ring	49. Ball bearing
12. Gasket	31. Shift shaft	50. Bearing carrier
13. Dowel pin	32. Circlip	51. Key
14. Pump base	33. Gearcase	52. Roller bearing
15. Oil seal	34. Shift cam	53. Oil seals
16. Oil seal	35. Cam follower	54. Washer
17. "O" ring	36. Slide	55. Nut
18. Gasket	37. Spring	56. Thrust hub
19. Drive shaft	38. Shim	

57. Thrust piece
58. Tab washer
59. Nut
60. Shift cam
61. Cam follower
62. Shift rod
63. Pin
64. Springs
65. Shim
66. Shim
67. Tapered roller bearing
68. Roller bearing
69. Forward gear
70. Spring clips
71. Detent pins
72. Pin
73. Dog clutch
74. Propeller shaft
75. Reverse gear

Fig. MR28-38—To remove the lower unit gearcase assembly, remove the attaching screws and stud nuts from positions indicated.

Clamp outer end of propeller shaft in a soft-jawed vise and remove the gearcase by tapping with a rubber mallet. Be careful not to lose key (51). Forward gear (41) will remain in gearcase. Withdraw propeller shaft from bearing carrier (50) and reverse gear (46).

Clamp bearing carrier (50) in a soft-jawed vise and remove reverse gear (46) and bearing (49) with an internal expanding puller and slide hammer. Reverse gear bearing (49) is not used on 150 Magnum II models. Remove and discard propeller shaft seals (53).

To remove clutch (43) from propeller shaft, remove retaining ring (42). Insert cam follower (35) into end of shaft (45) and apply sufficient pressure on cam follower (35) to relieve spring pressure, then push out pin (44) with a suitable punch. Pin (44) passes through drilled holes in clutch and operates in slotted holes in propeller shaft. On 150 Magnum II models, three loose ball bearings are present between follower (35) and slide (36).

To disassemble drive shaft and associated parts, reposition gearcase in vise with drive shaft projecting upward. Remove rubber slinger (5), water pump body (6), impeller (8) and impeller drive key (9). Remove flushing screw and withdraw remainder of water pump parts. Clamp upper end of drive shaft in a soft-jawed vise, remove pinion retaining nut (25), then tap gearcase off drive shaft and bearing. Note position and thickness of shims (21) on drive shaft upper bearing. Mesh position of pinion is controlled by shims (21) placed underneath the bearing.

After drive shaft has been removed, forward gear (41) and bearing cone can be extracted. Use an internal expanding-type puller to extract bearing cup if removal is required. Remove and save shim pack (38).

Shift shaft (31) and cam (34) can be removed after removing forward gear and unscrewing bushing (28) from gearcase.

If gear wear was abnormal or if any parts that affect gear alignment were renewed, install bearings on gears and drive shaft, and in gearcase (including shims 21 and 38). To determine gear mesh and forward gear backlash, proceed as follows: Install drive shaft components (19 through 25) and forward gear components (38 through 41). Tighten pinion nut (25) to 70 ft.-lbs. (95 N·m). Install tool C-91-74776 in gear cavity of gearcase so it bottoms against shoulder of gearcase. Apply approximately 15 pounds (66.7 N) of downward pressure (toward pinion gear) and rotate drive shaft several times to seat drive shaft bearing. While maintaining downward pressure on drive shaft, measure clearance between pinion gear and tool.

Clearance should be 0.025 inch (0.63 mm). Add or delete shims (21) to obtain desired clearance. Apply "Loctite" to drive shaft threads during final assembly.

With drive shaft and forward gear assemblies installed, install propeller shaft (without shift components) and bearing carrier (50), then install nut (55) until snug, but do not tighten. Attach a suitable puller to bearing carrier as shown in Fig. MR28-40 and tighten puller screw to 45 in.-lbs. (5.1 N·m). Rotate drive shaft several times to seat forward gear bearing and recheck tightness on puller screw. Install backlash indicator tool C-91-78473 (C-91-19660 on 150 Magnum II) on drive shaft as shown in Fig. MR28-41 and set up a dial indicator to read movement at the "2" mark on backlash indicator tool. Recheck torque on bearing carrier puller (45 in.-lbs. [5.1 N·m]). Measure forward gear backlash by applying downward pressure and turning drive shaft. Forward gear backlash should be 0.016-0.019 inch (0.41-0.48 mm) on 150 Magnum II models and 0.008-0.013 inch (0.20-0.33 mm) on all other models. Adjust backlash by varying thickness of shims (38—Fig. MR28-39).

When reassembling, long splines of shift shaft (31) should be toward top. Shift cam (34) is installed with long side on port side of gearcase. On 150 Magnum II, make sure three loose ball bearings are installed between slide (36) and follower (35). On 150 Magnum II models, install thrust washer (47), with beveled outer diameter facing carrier (50). Install reverse gear and bearing carrier assembly using new seals (48 and 53). Lip of inner seal (53) should face inward and lip of outer seal (53) should face propeller.

Upper oil seal (15) should be installed with lips facing up (toward engine) and lower oil seal (16) should be pressed into water pump base with lips facing down toward propeller shaft. Install remainder of water pump assembly and tighten screws or nuts to following recommended torque: Torque 1/4-28 nuts to 25-30 in.-lbs. (2.8-3.4 N·m). Torque 5/16-24 nuts to 35-40 in.-lbs. (3.9-4.5 N·m).

Torque 1/4-20 screws to 15-20 in.-lbs. (1.7-2.2 N·m).

Do not apply excessive grease to drive shaft splines; there must not be grease on tops of drive shaft or shift shaft. Shift lower unit to forward gear and move guide block anchor pin on engine to forward gear position. Tighten gearcase fasteners with 3/8-16 threads to 55 ft.-lbs. (75 N·m) and fasteners with 7/16-20 threads to 65 ft.-lbs. (88 N·m).

E-Z Shift Models

R&R AND OVERHAUL. Most service on the lower unit can be performed by detaching the gearcase from the drive shaft housing. To remove gearcase, shift outboard to neutral gear, then detach propeller and drain gearcase lubricant. Remove the plastic plug and Allen screw from location (1—Fig. MR28-38). Remove trim tab (2) and stud nut from under trim tab. Remove stud nut from location (3), two stud nuts (4) from each side and stud nut (5) if so equipped, then withdraw the lower unit gearcase assembly.

To disassemble gearcase, remove rubber slinger (5—Fig. MR28-39), water tube guide (1) and seal (2). Unscrew and remove water pump components (6 through 18). Position gearcase in a soft-jawed vise so propeller shaft is horizontal. Check to be sure gearcase is in neutral gear. Unscrew but do not remove shift shaft bushing (28) and withdraw shift shaft (31) from gearcase. DO NOT turn shift shaft during removal or gearcase may be shifted into forward or reverse gear position. Bend back lockwasher (54) tabs, unscrew nut (55) and use a suitable puller to remove bearing carrier (50).

NOTE: Do not apply side load or strike side of propeller shaft during or after removal of bearing carrier as shift rod (62) may break.

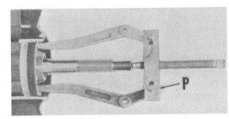

Fig. MR28-40—Install a puller (P) as shown to preload forward gear bearing when determining gear backlash as outlined in text.

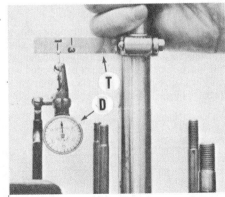

Fig. MR28-41—Install backlash measuring tool C-91-78473 (T) and a dial indicator (D) set to read movement at number on tool as described in text.

Withdraw propeller shaft from gearcase, but do not use excessive force or a puller. If shaft is lodged in gearcase, proceed as follows: Push propeller shaft inward so it contacts forward gear, reinstall shift shaft and be sure gears are in neutral. Remove shift shaft and attempt to withdraw propeller shaft. If propeller shaft remains stuck, push shaft inward so it contacts forward gear. Reinstall bearing carrier and lay gearcase on its port side. Strike upper forward end of gearcase with a rubber mallet so shift cam (60) is dislodged and falls into a cavity in side of gearcase. Remove bearing carrier and propeller shaft.

To remove shift rod (62) from propeller shaft, remove spring clips (70), being careful not to lose detent pins (71). Drive out pin (72) and remove shift rod (62), being careful not to lose pin (63), which may fall from rod. Slide dog clutch (73) off shaft.

To disassemble drive shaft and associated parts, clamp upper end of drive shaft in a soft-jawed vise and remove pinion gear nut (25).

NOTE: On late models not equipped with pin (3) and spring (4), unscrew and remove bearing retainer above bearing assembly (20).

Tap gearcase off drive shaft and bearing. Note position and thickness of shims (21) and bearing. Remove pinion gear (24) and forward gear (69). Use a suitable puller to extract cups of bearings (20 and 67). Note number and thickness of shims (21 and 66) and save for reassembly. Pull out sleeve (22) then drive roller bearing (23) down into gear cavity for removal.

Inspect all components for excessive wear and damage. If water pump insert (7) must be renewed, use a punch and drive out old insert. It may be necessary to drill two holes in top of water pump body (6) to drive out insert – do not drill through insert. Apply RTV sealant to holes after installing the new insert.

Install bearings on gears and drive shaft, and in gearcase (including shims 21 and 66). To determine gear mesh and forward gear backlash, note number of pinion gear (24) teeth, then proceed as follows: Install drive shaft components (19 through 25) and forward gear components (66 through 69). Tighten bearing retainer above bearing assembly (20), if so equipped, to 100 ft.-lbs. (136 N·m) with side of retainer marked "OFF" facing toward top of gearcase housing. Tighten pinion nut (25) to 70 ft.-lbs. (95 N·m) on early models and 80 ft.-lbs. (109 N·m) on late models. Install tool C-91-74776 in gear cavity of gearcase so it bottoms against shoulder of gearcase. Apply approximately 15 pounds (67 N) of downward pressure (toward pinion gear) and rotate drive shaft several times to seat drive shaft bearing. While maintaining downward pressure on drive shaft, measure clearance between pinion gear and tool. Clearance should be 0.025 inch (0.64 mm). Add or delete shims (21) to obtain desired clearance. Apply Loctite to drive shaft threads during final assembly.

With drive shaft and forward gear assemblies installed, install propeller shaft (without shift components) and bearing carrier (50), then install nut (55) until snug, but do not tighten. Attach a suitable puller to bearing carrier as shown in Fig. MR28-40 and apply 45 in.-lbs. (5.1 N·m) torque to puller screw. Rotate drive shaft several times to seat forward gear bearing. Install backlash measuring tool C-91-78473 on drive shaft as shown in Fig. MR28-41 and set up a dial indicator to read movement at "1" on backlash tool for models with a 15-tooth pinion gear or at "2" for models with a 14-tooth pinion gear. Recheck torque on bearing carrier puller (45 in.-lbs. [5.1 N·m]). Measure forward gear backlash by applying downward pressure and turning drive shaft. Dial indicator should measure 0.008-0.013 inch (0.20-0.33 mm) backlash on models equipped with preload type drive shaft and 0.018-0.027 inch (0.46-0.69 mm) on models without preload type drive shaft. Adjust backlash by adding or deleting shims (66 – Fig. MR28-39). Changing shim thickness by 0.001 inch (0.025 mm) will alter backlash by 0.0015 inch (0.038 mm).

To properly adjust spring tension in shift rod (62), install springs (64) and pin (63) in shift rod. Insert tool C-91-86642, or an old pin (72) with a ground-down end, between springs as shown in Fig. MR28-42. Tool (T) or pin should be centered in shift rod slot within 1/64 inch (0.397 mm). Adjust tool position by installing shims (65) at ends of springs (64).

Assemble remainder of lower unit by reversing disassembly procedure while noting the following points: Install thrust washer (47) so larger diameter side is nearer reverse gear (75) then press bearing (49) on gear. Lip of inner seal (53) should face in and lip of outer seal (53) should face propeller (out). In-

stall spring clips (70) so bent end of each spring engages the hole in one of the detent pins (71). Spring clips should be wound in opposite directions around dog clutch (73) and must not overlap. Use heavy grease to hold shift cam (60) in cam follower (61) with "UP" side facing up. Be sure "E" ring (30) and circlip (32) are seated on shift shaft (31) before inserting shaft. Tighten bushing (28) after tightening bearing carrier nut (55). Tighten bearing carrier nut (55) to 210 ft.-lbs. (284 N·m).

Upper oil seal (15) is installed with lips facing (toward engine) while lower oil seal (16) lips should face down towards gearcase. If reusing old impeller (8), install impeller so vanes rotate in same direction during previous operation. Be sure key (9) is properly installed. Tighten water pump fasteners to following torques: 1/4-28 nuts to 25-30 in.-lbs. (2.8-3.4 N·m), 5/16-24 nuts to 35-40 in.-lbs. (3.9-4.5 N·m) and 1/2-20 screws to 15-20 in.-lbs. (1.7-2.2 N·m).

Do not apply excessive grease to drive shaft splines; there must not be grease on tops of drive shaft or shift shaft. Shift lower unit to forward gear and move guide block anchor pin on engine to forward gear position. Tighten gearcase fasteners with 3/8-16 threads to 55 ft.-lbs. (75 N·m) and 7/16-20 threads to 65 ft.-lbs. (88 N·m).

POWER TILT/TRIM

Non-Integral Type

Two types of hydraulic power tilt/trim systems have been used. Early models are identified by the rectangular oil reservoir while later models use a circular fluid reservoir. Refer to the following sections for service.

Early Models

FLUID. Recommended fluid is SAE 10W-30 or 10W-40 automotive oil. With outboard in full down position, oil level should reach "Full" mark on dipstick. Do not overfill.

BLEEDING. Check fluid level in reservoir and fill if required. Operate trim system several times to purge air in system. Recheck fluid level and fill if required.

HYDRAULIC TESTING. Disconnect cylinder hoses from control valve and connect a pressure gage to outlets of control valve as shown in Fig. MR28-45. Note that large outlet is "up" circuit and small outlet is "down" circuit. Close appropriate pressure gage valve circuit.

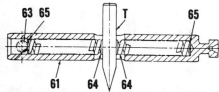

Fig. MR28-42 — Cross section of shift rod on E-Z Shift models. Center tool (T) using shims (64) as outlined in text.

Make sure manual tilt valve (M) is tightly closed. Close and open appropriate pressure gage valves while operating system to check pressure in up and down circuits. Hydraulic pressure should be 3100 psi (21.4 MPa) minimum for up circuit and 1200 psi (8.3 MPa) minimum for down circuit. Pressure may drop slightly but should remain steady. If pressure is normal, inspect trim cylinders and hoses for leakage. If pressure is abnormal, install a good control valve and recheck pressure. If pressure remains abnormal, install a new pump body.

Later Models

FLUID AND BLEEDING. Recommended fluid is SAE 10W-40 with an API rating of SE. Fill reservoir to "FULL" mark on dipstick.

The hydraulic circuit is self-bleeding as the trim system is operated several times. Be sure to check reservoir level after filling and operating system after system has been serviced.

HYDRAULIC TESTING. The pump may be checked by connecting a 5000 psi (34.5 MPa) test gage alternately to the "UP" and "DOWN" ports. Note that the pump motor blue wire is the positive battery connection to pressurize the "UP" port and connecting the positive battery terminal to the pump motor green wire will pressurize the "DOWN" port. Pressure at the "UP" port should be 3100-3500 psi (21.4-24.1 MPa) and should not drop lower than 1500 psi (10.3 MPa) after pumping stops. Pressure at the "DOWN" port should be 1500-1900 psi (10.3-13.1 MPa) and should not drop lower than 750 psi (5.2 MPa) after pumping stops.

Integral Type

FLUID AND BLEEDING. Recommended fluid is Dexron II or Type AF automatic transmission fluid. Remove fill plug (7 – Fig. MR28-50) and fill reservoir until fluid is visible in fill tube with the outboard motor in the full-up position.

The hydraulic circuit is self-bleeding as the tilt/trim system is operated through several cycles. After servicing system, be sure to check reservoir level after filling and operating system.

HYDRAULIC TESTING. The system can be checked by connecting a 5000 psi (34.5 MPa) test gage to the UP (U – Fig. MR28-52) and DOWN (D – Fig. MR28-53) ports. Prior to connecting test gage, place outboard motor in the full-up position and engage tilt lock lever. Unscrew reservoir fill plug and rotate man-

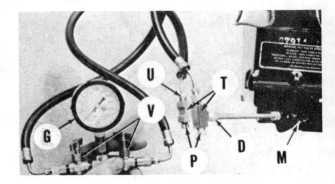

Fig. MR28-45 — Connect a pressure gage (G) as shown for hydraulic testing of non-integral type power tilt/trim.
D. "Down" line
G. Pressure gage
M. Manual tilt valve
P. Plugs
T. Tees
U. "Up" line
V. Valves

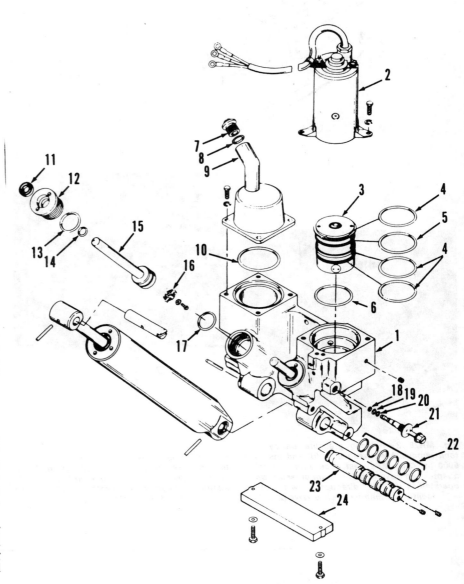

Fig. MR28-50 — Exploded view of integral type power tilt/trim system.

1. Manifold	9. Reservoir cover	18. "O" ring (0.114 in. [2.90 mm] ID)
2. Electric motor	10. Seal ring	19. "O" ring (0.208 in. [5.28 mm] ID)
3. Pump assy.	11. Seal	20. "O" ring (0.239 in. [6.07 mm] ID)
4. "O" rings (2.614 in. [66.40 mm] ID)	12. Cap	21. Manual release valve
5. "O" ring (2.739 in. [69.57 mm] ID)	13. "O" ring (1.475 in. [37.47 mm] ID)	22. "O" rings (0.989 in. [25.12 mm] ID)
6. "O" ring (2.739 in. [69.57 mm] ID)	14. "O" ring (0.612 in. [15.54 mm] ID)	23. Shaft
7. Fill plug	15. Trim piston & rod	24. Anode plate
8. "O" ring (0.583 in. [14.81 mm] ID)	16. Strainer	
	17. "O" ring (1.248 in. [31.70 mm] ID)	

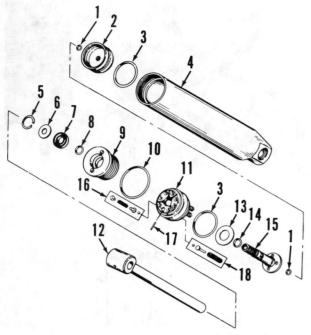

Fig. MR28-51 — Exploded view of tilt cylinder components.

1. "O" ring (0.307 in. [7.79 mm] ID)
2. Cup
3. "O" ring (1.957 in. [49.71 mm] ID)
4. Cylinder
5. Circlip
6. Washer
7. Scraper
8. "O" ring (0.854 in. [21.69 mm] ID)
9. Cap
10. "O" ring (2.067 in. [52.5 mm] ID)
11. Piston
12. Rod
13. Washer
14. "O" ring (0.661 in. [16.79 mm] ID)
15. Rod end
16. Check valve assy.
17. Pin
18. Check valve assy.

ual release valve (21 – Fig. MR28-52) three to four turns counterclockwise to release pressure on system. Remove UP or DOWN Allen head test port plug and connect test gage with suitable adapter and hose. Install fill plug and rotate manual release valve clockwise until seated. System pressure when testing at UP (U) port should be a minimum of 1300 psi (8.9 MPa). System pressure when testing at DOWN (D – Fig. MR28-53) port should be a minimum of 500 psi (3.5 MPa). Release pressure on system as previously outlined prior to removing test gage. Reinstall Allen head plug.

OVERHAUL. Refer to Fig. MR28-50 for an exploded view of manifold and trim cylinder components, and Fig. MR28-51 for an exploded view of tilt cylinder components. Special socket 91-44487A1 and a spanner wrench is required to service trim and tilt cylinders. Keep all components clean and away from contamination. Keep components separated and label if needed for correct reassembly. Note "O" ring sizes as stated in legends of Figs. MR28-50 and MR28-51. Lubricate all "O" rings or seal lips with Dexron II or Type AF automatic transmission fluid during reassembly.

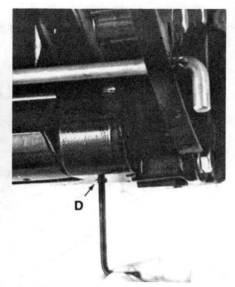

Fig. MR28-52 — Release pressure on system, then removo Allen head plug (U) and install a 5000 psi (34.5 MPa) test gage with a suitable adapter and hose to test system pressure when operated in the "UP" direction. View identifies location of manual release valve (21).

Fig. MR28-53 — Release pressure on system, then remove Allen head plug (D) and install a 5000 psi (34.5 MPa) test gage with a suitable adapter and hose to test system pressure when operated in the "DOWN" direction.

MERCURY

**Mercury Marine
Div. Brunswick Corp.
Fond du Lac, Wisconsin 54935**

TWO-CYLINDER MODELS

Year Produced	Model
1970-1971	400
1972-1978	402
1978-1983	40
1984-1985	35

CONDENSED SERVICE DATA

TUNE-UP

Hp/rpm:
Model 35 ....35/5400-6000
Models 40, 400 & 402 ....40/5000-5500
Bore...2.870 in.
(72.9 mm)
Stroke ....2.562 in.
(65.1 mm)
Displacement ....33.3 cu. in.
(546 cc)
Compression At Cranking Speed ....*
Spark Plug:
AC...V40FFM†
Champion.......................................L76V
Electrode Gap ....Surface Gap
Ignition:
Type................................Solid State
Trigger Gap (Model 400) ....0.050-0.060 in.
(1.27-1.52 mm)
Carburetor Pickup Timing...................See Text
Maximum Advance ....See Text
Fuel:Oil Ratio.............................See Text

*Not more than 15 psi (103.5 kPa) variations between cylinders.
†AC type M40FFX spark plugs gapped at 0.030 inch (0.76 mm) are recommended for use on 1971 400 models if rough low speed operation is noted.

SIZES—CLEARANCES

Piston Rings:
End Gap ....*
Side Clearance...............................*
Piston Skirt Clearance ....*

SIZES—CLEARANCES CONT.

Crankshaft Bearings:
Top Main Bearing..............Roller or Ball Bearing
Center Main Bearing ....Bushing With Reed Valve
Lower Main Bearing ....Ball Bearing
Crankpin ....Caged Rollers
Piston Pin Bearing In Rod ....Loose Rollers
Number of Rollers Per Rod 29

*Publication not authorized by manufacturer.

TIGHTENING TORQUES

Connecting Rod ....180 in.-lbs.
(20.3 N·m)
Crankcase Screws ....200 in.-lbs.
(22.6 N·m)
Cylinder Cover:
35 HP ....100 in.-lbs.
(11.3 N·m)
40 HP ....70 in.-lbs.
(7.9 N·m)
Exhaust Cover ....200 in.-lbs.
(22.6 N·m)
Flywheel Nut ....70-75 ft.-lbs.
(95.2-102 N·m)
Reed Screws ....25 in.-lbs.
(2.8 N·m)
Spark Plugs ....240 in.-lbs.
(27.1 N·m)
Transfer Port Cover:
35 HP ....50 in.-lbs.
(5.6 N·m)
40 HP ....60 in.-lbs.
(6.8 N·m)

LUBRICATION

The engine is lubricated by oil mixed with the fuel. Fuel should be regular leaded, low lead or unleaded gasoline with a minimum pump octane rating of 86. Premium gasoline may be used if desired regular gasoline is not available. Recommended oil is Quicksilver Formula 50 or 50-D. A good quality NMMA cer-

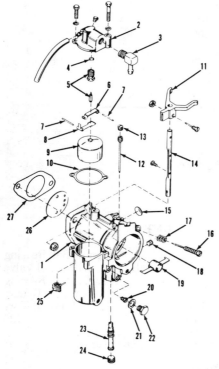

Fig. M10-1—Exploded view of Mercarb "WMK" carburetor. Tillotson carburetor is similar.

1. Body	
2. Bowl cover	14. Throttle shaft
3. Inlet fitting	15. Welch plug
4. Gasket	16. Idle mixture screw
5. Inlet needle & seat	17. Spring
6. Primary lever	18. Plug
7. Pin	19. Venturi
8. Secondary lever	20. Main jet
9. Float	21. Gasket
10. Gasket	22. Plug
11. Follower	23. Main nozzle
12. Idle tube	24. Plug
13. Plug	25. Spring

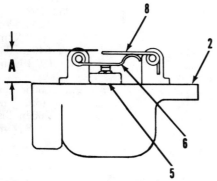

Fig. M10-2—Distance (A) should be 13/32 inch (10.32 mm). Refer to text for adjustment procedure and Fig. M10-1 for parts identification.

tified TC-WII oil may be used. Fuel:oil ratio should be 50:1 when using Formula 50 or 50-D oil. Follow fuel:oil ratio recommended by oil manufacturer if Formula 50 or 50-D is not used.

To break in new or overhauled motors, observe the following: Vary throttle opening during first hour of operation while avoiding extended idling in cold water and prolonged full throttle operation.

The lower unit gears and bearings are lubricated by oil contained in the gearcase. Only Quicksilver Super Duty Gear Lubricant should be used. Gearcase is filled through the lower plug hole on port side of case, with motor in an upright position. The vent plug (located aft and above the fill plug) should be removed when filling. Lubricant should be maintained at level of vent plug.

FUEL SYSTEM

CARBURETOR. Standard make of carburetor is a Tillotson KD-5A on Model 400 prior to serial number 2979679. Standard make of carburetor on all other models is a MerCarb WMK. Standard main jet (20—Fig. M10-1) size on early models is 0.0785 inch (2 mm) and 0.072 inch (1.83 mm) on later models (after serial number 5823917). Various main jet (20) sizes are available for adjusting the calibration for elevations or other special conditions. Preliminary adjustment of idle mixture screw (16) is 1 to $1\frac{1}{4}$ turns out from a lightly seated position. Recommended idle speed is 650-750 rpm on early models and 500-650 on later models. Adjust idle speed with engine running at normal operating temperature in forward gear.

With the outboard motor properly mounted on a boat or suitable tank, immerse the lower unit. Connect a tachometer and set it on the appropriate range scale. Start the engine and allow it to warm up to normal operating temperature. With the engine running at idle speed and forward gear engaged, turn idle mixture screw (16) until smooth engine operation is noted. Readjust engine idle speed screw (IS—Fig. M10-8, Fig. M10-13 or Fig. M10-14) to recommended idle speed if required.

To determine float level, invert bowl cover (2—Fig. M10-2) with inlet needle and seat (5), primary lever (6) and secondary lever (8) installed. On early models, measure distance (A) from carburetor body surface to top of secondary lever (8). Distance (A) should be $\frac{13}{32}$ inch (10.3 mm). Adjust distance (A) by bending curved end of primary lever (6). On later models (after serial number 5823917) bend curved end of primary lever (6) so secondary lever (8) is parallel to bowl cover (2) mating surface.

To check float drop, position bowl cover upright (Fig. M10-3) and measure distance (D) between primary lever (6) and end of secondary lever (8). Distance (D) should be $\frac{1}{4}$ inch (6.4 mm). Bend tab (T) to adjust. The contact spring located in center of float (9—Fig. M10-1) should extend $\frac{3}{32}$ inch (2.4 mm) above top of float. Inspect spring and renew if stretching or other damage is noted.

SPEED CONTROL LINKAGE. The speed controls change ignition timing and the amount of carburetor throttle opening. The timing and throttle opening must be correctly synchronized to provide proper operation. When checking, the complete system should be tested in sequence to ensure desired results. Speed control linkage used on 400 models is different from linkage used on 35, 40 and 402 models. Refer to the appropriate following paragraphs.

Model 400

Before attempting any test, check all linkage for free movement. Make certain that spark advance arm (Fig. M10-5) remains aligned with the throttle arm throughout its full movement, from idle until the spark control arm contacts the

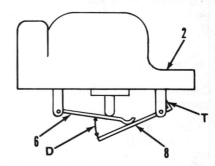

Fig. M10-3—With bowl cover (2) upright, distance (D) between primary lever (6) and end of secondary lever (8) should be $\frac{1}{4}$ inch (6.4 mm). Bend tab (T) to adjust.

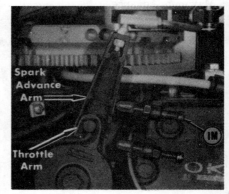

Fig. M10-5—Merc 400 spark advance arm and throttle arm should be aligned as shown from idle until the spark advance arm contacts stop screw (IM). The throttle arm should still be able to move until carburetor throttle is completely open.

maximum advance stop screw. The spark advance arm is attached to the throttle arm with a spring which allows further movement of the throttle arm after ignition reaches maximum advance. Excessive friction in linkage, incorrect routing of pickup coil wires, etc., may prevent free movement and result in inaccurate checks and adjustments.

Check clearance between trigger pickup coil (C – Fig. M10-6) and trigger magnets in flywheel. Trigger gap (clearance) should be 0.050-0.060 inch (1.27-1.52 mm). If incorrect, loosen screws (S) and add or remove shims between plate (P) and starter housing. Make certain that trigger gap remains within limits throughout operating slot length. Screws (S) should be centered in elongated holes in plate (P).

Connect a suitable tachometer to the engine and a timing light to the top cylinder. Start the engine and shift into forward gear. Increase engine speed until the two ignition timing dots (D – Fig. M10-7) are in center of timing window. With controls set as outlined, the primary pickup edge of throttle plate should just contact throttle follower (11 – Fig. M10-8). If the primary pickup is not in contact with the follower or if the throttle is partially open, loosen the two screws that attach the throttle plate to the bottom of the actuator and move the throttle plate. Repeat the above procedure to confirm the proper adjustment.

Increase engine speed to 5000-5200 rpm and check maximum advance timing marks in window (W – Fig. M10-7). If the straight line timing mark is not in the center of the timing window, loosen locknut and turn ignition maximum advance stop screw (IM – Fig. M10-5) to stop movement of the spark advance arm when maximum advance timing is correct.

With the engine stopped, move speed controls slowly from idle toward fast position and stop just as the spark advance arm contacts ignition maximum advance stop screw (IM).

NOTE: It is important that maximum advance is correct before attempting this check. Just as the spark advance arm touches stop screw (IM), the secondary throttle pickup should just contact the secondary arm of follower as shown in Fig. M10-9. If the secondary pickup is not yet touching or if the primary arm is away from cam at (X), carefully bend the secondary pickup until correct. If corrections are necessary, recheck by again moving speed controls from idle toward fast until spark advance arm just contacts stop screw (IM – Fig. M10-5).

Carefully move the speed controls toward maximum speed position while checking for play at the carburetor throttle follower. The throttle stop screw (Fig. M10-10) should stop movement of throttle arm just before all play is removed from the throttle and follower (11 – Fig. M10-9). With throttle arm against stop screw (Fig. M10-10), throttle follower (11 – Fig. M10-9) should have approximately 0.010-0.015 inch (0.25-0.38 mm) play to prevent damage. If speed controls are forced after throttle is completely open, the secondary pickup may be bent or other damage may result.

Idle speed is adjusted at stop screw (IS – Fig. M10-8). Refer to the CARBURETOR section for idle speed adjustment.

Fig. M10-6 — View of Model 400 trigger coil (C) installed. The coil moves in the slot to change ignition timing. Plate (P) should be centered in screws (S).

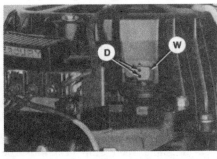

Fig. M10-7 — View showing timing dots (D) and window (W) used on Model 400. Refer to text.

Fig. M10-8 — View showing throttle follower (11), idle mixture screw (16) and idle speed screw (IS) used on Model 400.

Models 35, 40 And 402

To synchronize ignition timing and throttle opening, proceed as follows: Connect a power timing light to the top cylinder spark plug lead and attach a suitable tachometer to the engine. With the engine running, shift into "Forward" gear. On manual start models, view window (A – Fig. M10-11) on all 35 and 40 models and 402 models with serial number 4726798 and above, and window

Fig. M10-9 — On Model 400, view of the throttle follower (11) attached to top of carburetor throttle shaft. Refer to text for checking the secondary throttle pickup.

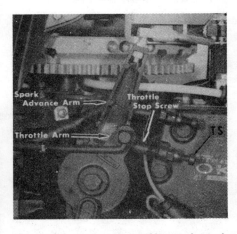

Fig. M10-10 — View of Model 400 control arms in maximum speed position. The spark advance arm contacts the ignition maximum advance screw before the throttle arm contacts the throttle stop screw (TS). Refer to text for adjustment.

Fig. M10-11 — On manual start models, view window (A) on all 35 and 40 models and 402 models with serial number 4726798 and above, and window (B) on 402 models prior to serial number 4726798.

(B) on 402 models prior to serial number 4726798. On electric start models, refer to timing pointer and numbered degree marks on flywheel. Increase the engine speed until the two ignition timing dots (D–Fig. M10-12), on manual start models, are aligned with timing window notch (N). On electric start models, timing pointer should align with 2°-5° BTDC timing mark on flywheel. At this point, on 402 models and early 40 models, adjust turnbuckle (T–Fig. M10-13) so throttle cam just contacts follower (11) at point (P). On 35 models and late 40 models, adjust primary throttle pickup screw (PP–Fig. M10-14) so throttle cam just contacts follower (11–Fig. M10-13) at point (P).

Increase engine speed to 5000-5500 rpm on 40 models and 5400-6000 rpm on 35 models and check maximum advance timing at timing pointer on electric start models and look for mark in window (W–Fig. M10-12) on manual start models. If the straight line timing mark is not aligned with notch (N) on manual start models or 27° BTDC mark on electric start models, loosen locknut and turn ignition maximum advance stop screw (IM–Fig. M10-4 or Fig. M10-15) to stop movement of the spark advance arm (S) when maximum advance timing is correct. Tighten locknut on screw.

Stop the engine and remove the timing light. Position spark advance arm (S) so it touches maximum advance stop screw (IM). Adjust throttle pickup screw (TP–Fig. M10-14 or Fig. M10-16) so it just contacts secondary pickup arm (PA–Fig. M10-13) on carburetor follower.

Move speed control to maximum speed position and check carburetor to make sure throttle valve is completely open. The throttle stop screw (TS–Fig. M10-14 or Fig. M10-15) should stop movement of throttle arm just before all play is removed from the throttle and follower (11–Fig. M10-13). With throttle arm against stop screw (TS–Fig. M10-14 or Fig. M10-15), throttle follower (11–Fig. M10-13) should have approximately 0.010-0.015 inch (0.25-0.38 mm) play to prevent damage.

Idle speed is adjusted at stop screw (IS–Fig. M10-13 or Fig. M10-14). Refer to the CARBURETOR section for idle speed adjustment.

REED VALVES. The inlet reed valves are located on the center main bearing assembly. The crankshaft must be removed before reed valves can be serviced.

Reed petals (18–Fig. M10-27) should be perfectly flat and have no more than 0.007 inch (0.18 mm) clearance between free end and seating surface of main bearing. The reed stop (17) must be carefully adjusted to provide 5/32 inch (3.97 mm) clearance between end of stop and reed seating surface. Seating sur-

face on bearing must be smooth and flat, and may be refinished on a lapping plate after removing reed valves. Do not attempt to bend or straighten a reed petal and never install a bent petal. Reeds and reed plates are secured by either short screws threaded into main bearing or by screws extending through the bearing and having nuts on the ends. Lubricate reed valve before assembly. On models so equipped, install screws (21) with heads toward top and nuts (16) toward bottom to provide proper clearance for crankshaft.

FUEL PUMP. A diaphragm type fuel pump is used. Pressure and vacuum pulsations from the crankcase alternate to pull fuel from supply tank and fill carburetor float bowl. Most of the work is performed by the main supply chamber (5–Fig. M10-18). Vacuum in the crankcase pulls diaphragm (2) downward causing fuel to be drawn through inlet line (8), past inlet check valve (7) into main pump chamber (5). The alternate pressure forces diaphragm out and fuel leaves the chamber through outlet check valve (6). The booster pump chamber (3)

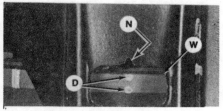

Fig. M10-12 — View showing timing dots (D), timing window (W) and notch (N) used on Models 35, 40 and 402 with manual start. Refer to text.

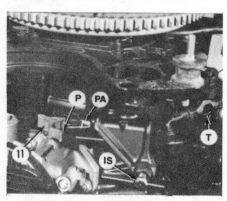

Fig. M10-13 — View of speed control components used on 402 models and early 40 models. Refer to text.

11. Throttle follower
P. Contact point
T. Turnbuckle
IS. Idle speed screw
PA. Secondary pickup arm

Fig. M10-14 — View of speed control components used on 35 models and late 40 models. Refer to text.

S. Spark advance arm
IM. Maximum advance stop screw
IS. Idle speed screw
PP. Primary throttle pickup screw
TP. Secondary throttle pickup screw
TS. Throttle stop screw

Fig. M10-15 — View identifying spark advance arm (S), maximum advance stop screw (IM) and throttle stop screw (TS) used on 402 models and early 40 models. Refer to text.

Fig. M10-16 — View identifying secondary throttle pickup screw (TP) used on 402 models and early 40 models. Refer to text for adjustment procedures.

Illustrations courtesy Mercury

serves to dampen the action of the larger, main pump chamber (5), and increase maximum potential fuel flow.

When overhauling fuel pump, renew all defective or questionable components. On pump equipped with one red and one white color check valve, be sure red color check valve is installed on intake side of pump.

IGNITION SYSTEM

Early Models

Refer to Fig. M10-20 for wiring diagram on Model 400 and Fig. M10-21 for wiring diagram on Model 402 and early Model 40. All models are equipped with Thunderbolt breakerless ignition. Refer to the appropriate SPEED CONTROL LINKAGE section for checking and adjusting ignition timing and speed control linkage.

Check all wires and connections before trouble-shooting ignition system. Make sure all connections are clean and tight.

Test ignition components using a suitable ohmmeter. The following specifications will aid trouble-shooting:

Model 400
STATOR
Manual Start—Blue lead and
    ground . . . . 2100-2500 ohms
Electric Start—White lead and
    ground . . . . 115-130 ohms

IGNITION COIL
Part A-332-4075A1
    Primary—Positive terminal and
      ground . . . . .0 ohms
    Secondary—High tension tower and
      ground . . . . 2400-3000 ohms
Part A-336-4592A2
    Primary—Positive terminal and
      ground . . . . 0.01-0.015 ohm
    Secondary—High tension tower and
      ground . . . . 9000-10500 ohms

TRIGGER
Part A-332-4315A1
    Brown and black leads .27-41 ohms
Part A-332-4608A2 . No resistance test
possible

Model 402 (1972-1974)
STATOR
Manual Start—Red and blue
    leads . . . . 5000-6400 ohms
Electric Start—Red lead and
    ground . . . . 45-60 ohms

IGNITION COIL
    Primary—Positive and negative
      terminals . . . . 0.02-0.04 ohm
    Secondary—High tension tower and
      ground . . . . 9000-11000 ohms

TRIGGER
    White and brown
      leads . . . . 700-1000 ohms

Model 402 (1975-1978)
STATOR
    Blue lead and
      ground . . . . 5000-6000 ohms
    Red lead and ground . . . 50-60 ohms

IGNITION COIL
    Primary— Positive and negative
      terminals . . . . 0.02-0.4 ohm
    Secondary—High tension tower and
      ground . . . . 900-1200 ohms

TRIGGER
    Between trigger
      leads . . . . 800-1000 ohms

Models 35 and 40 Hp

IGNITION. An alternator driven capacitor discharge ignition (CDI) system is used. Ignition system consists of the flywheel, stator, trigger assembly, switch box and ignition coils. The stator is mounted below the flywheel and includes two capacitor charging coils. The trigger assembly consists of two trigger coils and is mounted below the flywheel. Ignition timing is advanced and retarded by rotating trigger assembly in relation to the inner flywheel magnets. Refer to SPEED CONTROL LINKAGE section for timing adjustment procedures. Diodes, capacitors and SCR's are contained in the switch box. Switch box, trigger assembly and stator must be serviced as unit assemblies. Re-

fer to Fig. M10-21 for wiring diagram on early model 40 and Fig. M10-22 for 35 hp and late 40 models.

If engine malfunction is noted, and the ignition system is suspected, make sure the spark plugs and all electrical wiring are in acceptable condition and all electrical connections are clean and tight prior to trouble-shooting CDI system.

Proper testing of the switch box and ignition coils requires the use of Quicksilver Multi-Meter DVA Tester part 91-99750, or a suitable voltmeter capable of measuring a minimum of 400 DC volts

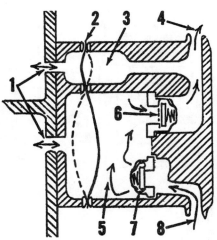

Fig. M10-18 — Schematic view of diaphragm type fuel pump. Pump body mounts on side of cylinder block and is ported to two crankcases as shown.

1. Pressure ports
2. Diaphram
3. Booster chamber
4. To carburetor
5. Main fuel chamber
6. Outlet check valve
7. Inlet check valve
8. Fuel inlet

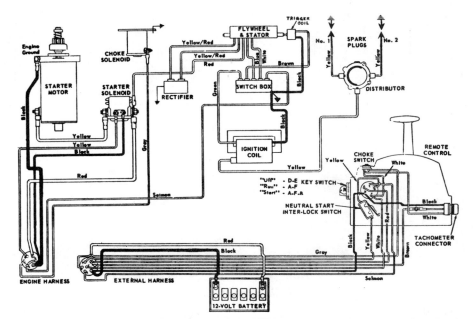

Fig. M10-20 — Wiring diagram of electric starting 400 models. Ignition is similar on manual start 400 models.

used with Quicksilver Direct Voltage Adaptor (DVA) part 91-89045. Follow instructions provided by tester manufacturer when performing tests. If these testers are not available, a process of elimination must be used when testing the ignition system. Stator and trigger assemblies can be effectively tested using a suitable ohmmeter.

NOTE: All tests that involve cranking or running the engine must be performed with lead wires connected. Switch box case

MUST be grounded to engine for all tests or switch box may be damaged.

To test ignition system, proceed as follows:

IGNITION COILS PRIMARY CIRCUIT. On models after serial number 5823917, connect DVA red test lead to ignition coil negative (−) terminal and black test lead to coil positive (+) terminal. On earlier models, connect red test lead to ignition coil positive (+) terminal and black test lead to coil negative (−) terminal. Position tester selector switch to 400 DVA. On early models, tester should read 150-250 volts at cranking or idle speed (300-1000 rpm) and 180-280 volts at 1000-4000 rpm. On models after serial number 5823917, tester should read 100-250 volts at cranking or idle speed (300-1000 rpm) and 150-300 volts at 1000-4000 rpm. If voltage readings are below specified reading, refer to SWITCH BOX STOP CIRCUIT test. If readings are within specifications, connect a suitable spark tester to ignition coil high tension leads, crank engine and note spark. If weak or no spark is noted, renew ignition coil(s). If normal spark is noted, renew spark plugs. If malfunction is still evident after renewing spark plugs, check ignition timing. If ignition timing is erratic, such as a sudden timing change, inspect trigger advance linkage for excessive wear or damage and inner flywheel magnets (shifted position or other damage). If timing is within specifications, problem is not in ignition system.

SWITCH BOX STOP CIRCUIT. On early models, connect DVA black test lead to engine ground and red test lead to black/yellow switch box terminal (orange terminal on some early models). On models after serial number 5823917, connect red test lead to engine ground and black test lead to black/yellow switch box terminal. Set DVA selector

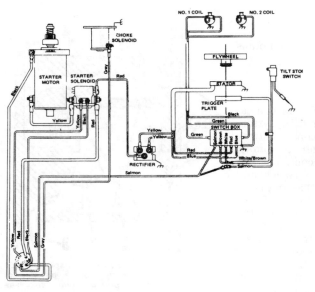

Fig. M10-21 — Wiring diagram of electric starting on early 40 models and 402 models. Ignition for manual start 40 and 402 is similar. External wiring harness in Fig. M10-20 is common to all electric start models.

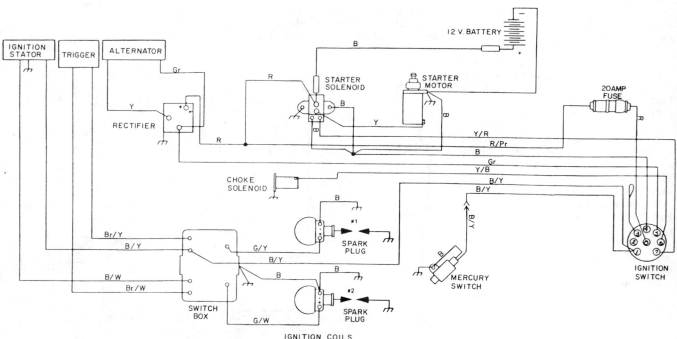

Fig. M10-22 — Wiring diagram of electric starting on late 40 models and 35 models. Ignition system on manual start models is similar.

B. Black					
R. Red						Y/R. Yellow with red tracer
Y. Yellow						R/Pr. Red with purple tracer
Gr. Gray	B/Y. Black with yellow tracer	G/Y. Green with yellow	
B/W. Black with white tracer	G/W. Green with white tracer	Y/B. Yellow with black tracer	Br/Y. Brown with yellow tracer

switch to 400 DVA. Voltage reading at cranking and all running speeds should be 200-360 volts on all models. If reading is within specifications, refer to STATOR tests. If reading is above specified voltages, disconnect trigger leads at switch box and connect a suitable ohmmeter between trigger leads. Trigger resistance should be 800-1000 on early models and 650-8500 ohms on models after serial number 5823917. If not, renew trigger assembly. If trigger resistance is acceptable, renew switch box and repeat SWITCH BOX STOP CIRCUIT test. If SWITCH BOX STOP CIRCUIT test reading is below specified voltage, disconnect ignition switch, stop switch and mercury switch from black/yellow switch box terminal (orange switch box terminal on early models). Make sure black/yellow stator lead remains connected to switch box. With stop switch, ignition switch and mercury switch isolated, repeat SWITCH BOX STOP CIRCUIT test. If reading is now within specification, ignition switch, stop switch or mercury switch is defective. If reading remains below specification refer to STATOR test.

STATOR. On early models, connect DVA black lead to engine ground and red lead to blue switch box terminal. On models after serial number 5823917, connect red test lead to engine ground and black test lead to black/yellow switch box terminal. Set DVA selector switch to 400 DVA. Voltage reading on early models should be 210-310 volts at cranking and idle speeds and 190-310 volts at 1000-4000 rpm. Voltage reading on models after serial number 5823917 should be 200-360 volts at all cranking and running speeds. Next, on early models, switch DVA red test lead to red switch box terminal or on models after serial number 5823917, switch black test lead to black/white switch box terminal. Voltage reading on early models should be 20-100 volts at cranking or idle speeds and 140-310 volts at 1000-4000 rpm. Voltage reading on models after serial number 5823917 should be 10-100 volts at cranking or idle speeds and 100-300 volts at 1000-4000 rpm.

NOTE: A shorted or open capacitor inside switch box will result in faulty stator voltage readings during cranking and running tests. Stator resistance should be checked as follows before failing stator.

If either STATOR test is not to specification, check stator resistance as follows: On early models, resistance between blue stator lead and engine ground should be 5000-6000 ohms and between red stator lead and ground resistance should be 50-60 ohms. On

models after serial number 5823917, resistance between black/white stator lead and ground should be 120-180 ohms, between black/yellow stator lead and ground should be 3200-3800 ohms and between black/yellow and black/white stator leads should be 3100-3700 ohms. Renew stator if resistance is not as specified. If stator resistance is as specified, renew switch box and repeat STATOR tests.

IGNITION COILS RESISTANCE TEST. Disconnect wires and high tension lead from coil. Connect a suitable ohmmeter between coil positive (+) and negative (−) terminals. Resistance should be 0.02-0.04 ohm on all models. On early models, connect ohmmeter between coil high tension terminal and ground. Resistance should be 900-1200 ohms. On models after serial number 5823917, connect ohmmeter between coil high tension terminal and coil negative terminal. Resistance should be 800-1100 ohms. Renew ignition coil(s) if resistance is not as specified.

NOTE: Ignition coil resistance tests can only detect open or shorted windings. If coil resistance is within specification and still suspected as defective, coil must be tested using DVA meter as previously outlined in IGNITION COIL test. If DVA meter is not available, substitute a known good ignition coil and run engine to test.

All Models

Recommended spark plug is AC V40FFM or Champion L76V. Champion QL76V may be used if radio noise suppression is required. Renew surface gap spark plugs if the center electrode is more than $1/32$ inch (0.79 mm) below flush with flat surface of plug end. If rough low speed operation is noted on 1971 400 models, AC M40FFX or Champion L77J spark plugs gapped at 0.030 inch (0.76 mm) can be used.

COOLING SYSTEM

WATER PUMP. The rubber impeller type water pump is housed in the gearcase housing. The impeller is mounted on and driven by the lower unit drive shaft. Model 402 is equipped with a thermostat and a poppet type pressure relief valve (Fig. M10-24) mounted under the ignition coil bracket on top of the power head.

When cooling system problems are encountered, first check the water inlet for plugging or partial stoppage, then, if not corrected, remove the gearcase housing as outlined in LOWER UNIT section and examine the water pump, water tubes and seals.

When assembling, observe the assembly notes, cautions and tightening torques listed in the LOWER UNIT section.

POWER HEAD

R&R AND DISASSEMBLE. To remove the power head assembly, first remove the top cowl and disconnect stop switch wire, speed control linkage and choke linkage. Remove nuts securing power head to lower unit; then lift off the complete power head assembly.

Place the unit on power head stand or equivalent and remove fuel pump, carburetor, flywheel and ignition components. Exhaust cover plate (1 – Fig. M10-26), cylinder block cover plate (3) and transfer port cover (4) should be removed for inspection and cleaning.

Remove cap screws that retain top end cap (5). Remove screws (20) that secure lower end cap (16) on 35, 40 and 402 models and bearing retainer (10 – Fig. M10-27) on 35, 40, 400 and 402 models. Unbolt and remove crankcase half (11 – Fig. M10-26). Use extra care not to spring parts or to mar machined

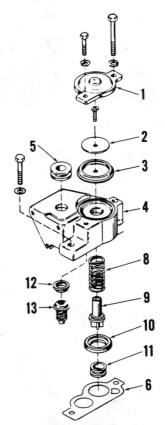

Fig. M10-24—Exploded view of typical thermostat and relief valve installation used on Model 402. Thermostat (13) is used on some 35 and 40 models.

1. Cover	8. Spring
2. Washer	9. Poppet valve
3. Diaphragm	10. Washer
4. Coil mount bracket	11. Grommet
5. Grommet	12. Gasket
6. Gasket	13. Thermostat

mating surfaces. Crankcase half (11) and cylinder block (13) are matched and align bored, and are available only as an assembly.

The crankshaft and bearings assembly, with pistons and connecting rods attached can now be lifted out of cylinder block for service or overhaul as outlined in the appropriate following paragraphs. Assemble by following the procedures outlined in the ASSEMBLY paragraph.

ASSEMBLY. When assembling, the crankcase must be completely sealed against both vacuum and pressure. Exhaust manifold and water passages must be sealed against pressure leakage. Whenever power head is disassembled, it is recommended that all gasket surfaces and machined joints without gaskets be carefully checked for nicks and burrs which might interfere with a tight seal.

Completely assemble the crankshaft main bearings, connecting rods, piston and rings. Lip of lower end seals (15 – Fig. M10-26) should be down. Install screws (21 – Fig. M10-27) with heads toward top. Install the crankshaft assembly by inserting pistons in lower end of cylinders. Two special Mercury ring compressors should be used. If ring compressor kit is not available, two men must work together and use extreme care in installing the crankshaft and pistons assembly. Thoroughly lubricate the pistons, rings and bearings using new engine oil and make sure that ring end gaps are aligned with the locating pins in the ring grooves.

Make certain that end cap (5 – Fig. M10-26) correctly engages dowel (10) and that retainer (10 – Fig. M10-27) engages dowel (21 – Fig. M10-26). Sealing strips (12) are used between halves of crankcase (11 and 13) on all models. Apply a thin bead of Permatex 2C-12 or a suitable equivalent to mating surface of crankcase half prior to installation. On models so equipped, seals (18) should be installed on the retainer attaching screws (20). After crankcase is assembled, turn the crankshaft until each piston ring has been visible in the exhaust and transfer ports and check for damage during assembly. Turn crankshaft several revolutions to make certain that all parts are free and do not bind.

PISTONS, PINS RINGS AND CYLINDERS. Before detaching connecting rods from crankshaft assembly, make sure that rod and cap are properly identified for correct assembly to each other and in the correct cylinder.

Maximum allowable cylinder bore wear or out-of-round is 0.004 inch (0.102 mm) on 400, 402 and early 40 models and 0.006 inch (0.152 mm) on late 40 models and 35 models.

Piston pin is pressed in piston bosses and secured with retaining rings. Piston end of connecting rod is fitted with 29 loose bearing rollers which use the connecting rod bore and the piston pin as bearing races. Install bearing washers and needle bearings in piston end of connecting rod using light nonfibrous grease to hold them in place. Heat piston to 190° F (88° C), then install the piston pin using Mercury special tool 91-76159A1. Pistons must be installed so sharp vertical side of deflector will be toward intake side and long sloping side of piston will be toward exhaust port in cylinder. Thoroughly lubricate all friction surfaces during assembly.

CONNECTING RODS, BEARINGS AND CRANKSHAFT. Upper end of crankshaft is carried by ball bearing (8—Fig. M10-26). The unbushed center main bearing also contains the inlet reed valves. Lower main bearing (11—Fig. M1027) is not interchangeable with the upper ball bearing.

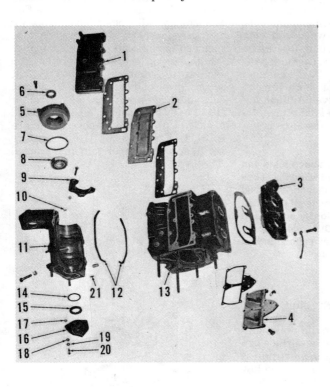

Fig. M10-26 – Exploded view of crankcase and cylinder block assembly typical of all models. Refer to text.

1. Exhaust cover
2. Exhaust baffle
3. Cylinder cover
4. Transfer port cover
5. Top end cap
6. Oil seal
7. "O" ring
8. Ball bearing
9. Starter motor bracket
10. Dowel
11. Crankcase half
12. Sealing strips
13. Cylinder block
14. "O" ring
15. Lower seal
16. Lower end cap
17. "O" ring
18. Seal
19. Washer
20. Screw
21. Dowel

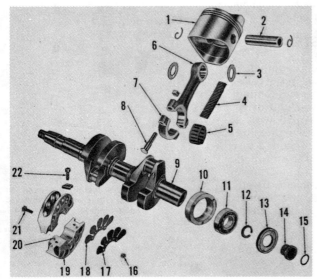

Fig. M10-27 – View of crankshaft and center main bearing assembly typical of the type used on all models. Bearing retainer (12) and spacer (13) are not used on early 402 models. Components (12 through 15) are not used on 400 models. Components (13 through 15) are not used on 35 and late 40 models.

1. Piston
2. Piston pin
3. Washer
4. Needles
5. Bearing cage
6. Connecting rod
7. Rod cap
8. Rod screw
9. Crankshaft
10. Bearing retainer
11. Ball bearing
12. Retainer ring
13. Retainer spacer
14. "O" ring carrier
15. "O" ring
16. Nut
17. Reed stop
18. Reeds
19. Center main bearing
20. Dowel pin
21. Reed stop screw
22. Bearing clamp screw

Each connecting rod rides on 29 loose bearing rollers (4) at piston pin end and caged rollers (5) at crankpin end. Check rod for alignment, using Mercury Alignment Tool C-91-2844A2, or by placing rod on a surface plate and checking with a light. Make certain that alignment marks on connecting rods are both on same side of rod during assembly.

Crankpin bearing surface of connecting rods should be cleaned with crocus cloth only. Piston pin bearing surface of connecting rod should be cleaned with #320 carborundum paper only.

If bearing surface of rod and cap is rough, scored, worn, or shows evidence of overheating, renew the connecting rod. Inspect crankpin and main bearing journals. If scored, out-of-round, or worn, renew the crankshaft. Check the crankshaft for straightness using a dial indicator and "V" blocks.

Inspect and adjust the reed valves as outlined in REED VALVE paragraph, and reassemble as outlined in ASSEMBLY paragraph.

MANUAL STARTER

Early Type

Refer to Fig. M10-30 for exploded view of rewind starter assembly. To disassemble, remove three stud nuts securing motor top cowl to power head, pry rope anchor (22) out of starter handle and remove top cowl. Tie a slip knot in start rope to keep it from winding into housing. Remove ignition trigger assembly on 400 models. Disconnect shift interlock cable (Fig. M10-32) on late 400 models and 40 and 402 models. Detach starter housing from top of motor. Insert a screwdriver in slot in top in sheave shaft (19 – Fig. M10-30) and loosen the left hand thread nut (3). Allow the screwdriver and shaft (19) to turn clockwise until recoil spring unwinds. Remove nut (3), invert the assembly and remove the parts, making sure that recoil spring (7) remains in housing recess as sheave (10) is removed. Protect hands with gloves or a cloth, grasp the recoil spring (7), remove spring and allow it to unwind slowly.

Lubricate the parts with Multipurpose Lubricant, and assemble by reversing the disassembly procedure. Install spring guide bushing (8) with chamfered end toward sheave (10). Make sure that pawls (12) are all installed the same way, with radius to outside and identification mark away from sheave (10). Install retainer (15) with cup end out and position washer (16) and wave washer (17) in cup. Make certain that tang on spring retainer (6) engages slot in sheave shaft (19). Position starter with end of shaft

(19) through housing (15) and install lockwasher (4) and nut (3). Pull free end of recoil rope through cowl or starter housing and install handle (21) and anchor (22). Turn sheave shaft (19) counterclockwise until handle is pulled against cowl, plus an additional 1¼ turns; then tighten nut (3). Pull cord out and check for sticking and full return.

NOTE: When checking, it will be necessary to hold starter lock (24) up.

The starter lockout (23, 24 and 25) used on early 400 models prevents manual starter from being pulled at high speed throttle settings. To adjust, locate the locknut cam with ⅛ inch (3.175 mm) clearance as shown in Fig. M10-31. The top screw should be located at front of slot in cam. Adjustment is accomplished by moving cam on bottom screw. The ignition control rod should push the lockout cam and lever up at slow speed settings.

The shift interlock (Fig. M10-32) used on late 400 models and 40 and 402 models is used to prevent starting with motor in forward or reverse gear. Loosen screw holding cable clamp (C) and move cable until pin of toggle (T) is at mid-point of cam on sliding cam (SC) with motor in neutral. Tighten cable clamp screw.

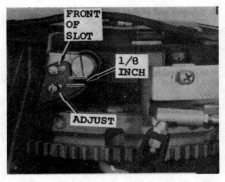

Fig. M10-30 — Exploded view of the recoil starter used on 400 models. Unit used on Models 40 and 402 is similar.

1. Pulley	14. Spacer
2. Spacer	15. Retainer
3. Nut	16. Washer
4. Lockwasher	17. Wave washer
5. Housing	18. Plate
6. Retainer	19. Sheave shaft
7. Rewind spring	21. Handle
8. Bushing	22. Anchor
10. Sheave	23. Spring
11. Wave washers	24. Lockout lever
12. Pawls	25. Cam
13. Bushing	

Late Type

To remove the manual rewind starter, first remove the engine cover assembly. Remove the starter rope from the handle anchor and allow the rope to rewind into the starter. Remove the starter interlock cable at the starter housing. Remove the screws retaining the manual starter to the engine. Withdraw the starter assembly.

To disassemble, bend tabs of tab washer (4 – Fig. M10-33) away from nut (3). Insert a screwdriver in slot of sheave shaft (19) and loosen the left-hand thread nut (3). Remove nut (3), invert starter housing (5) and remove manual starter components. Make sure that the rewind spring remains in pulley recess as the starter pulley is removed. Use

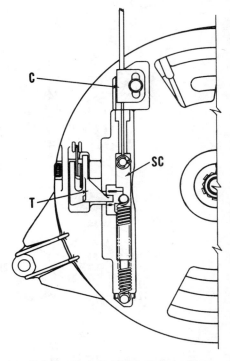

Fig. M10-31 — Refer to text for adjusting the manual starter lockout cam.

Fig. M10-32 — View of shift interlock used on early Model 40, Model 402 and late Model 400.

suitable hand protection and extract the rewind spring from the starter pulley. Allow the rewind spring to uncoil in a safe area.

Inspect all components for damage and excessive wear and renew if needed.

NOTE: During reassembly, lubricate all friction surfaces with a suitable low temperature grease.

Assemble by reversing the disassembly procedure. Be sure that pawl (12) is installed with the radius toward the outside and the identification mark (dot) away from sheave (10). On early models, install washer (25) with cupped side facing away from sheave (10). Make certain that tab on spring retainer plate (6) properly engages rewind spring (7) loop during installation.

With the manual starter assembly properly assembled, install tab washer (4) and nut (3). Pull free end of starter rope (27) through housing (5) and secure with a knot approximately 1 foot (30 cm) from rope end. Place a suitable size screwdriver blade in sheave shaft (19) slot. Turn sheave shaft counterclockwise until starter rope knot is pulled against the rope guide, then continue to turn the sheave shaft an additional 2 full turns. Tighten nut (3) and bend tabs of tab washer (4) to secure nut (3) in place. Bend one tab on tab washer (4) into

starter housing hole. Pull the starter out to full length while checking for freedom of travel, then allow the starter rope to rewind slowly onto the starter pulley.

Remount the manual starter assembly. Adjust starter lockout assembly by varying position of operation cable. Starter should engage when gear shift lever is in the neutral position, but not engage when gear shift lever is in the forward or reverse position.

Install the engine cover assembly. Feed the starter rope through the engine cover opening and starter handle. Secure rope end with handle anchor.

LOWER UNIT

PROPELLER AND DRIVE CLUTCH. Protection for the motor is built into a special cushioning clutch in the propeller hub. No adjustment is possible on the propeller or clutch. Various pitch propellers are available and propeller should be selected for the best performance under applicable conditions. With speed control linkage correctly adjusted propeller should be selected to provide maximum speed of 5400-6000 rpm on 35 hp models and 5000-5500 rpm on 40 hp models. Propellers other than those designed for the motor must not be used.

R&R AND OVERHAUL. Most service on the lower unit can be performed by detaching the gearcase housing from the drive shaft housing. To remove the housing, remove the plastic plug and Allen head screw from location (1–Fig. M10-35). Remove trim tab (2) and stud nut from under trim tab. Remove the stud nut from location (3) and the two stud nuts (4) from each side then withdraw the lower unit gearcase assembly.

NOTE: Do not lose plunger or spring (67 and 68—Fig. M10-36).

Remove the housing plugs and drain the housing, then secure the gearcase in a vise between two blocks of soft wood, with propeller up. Wedge a piece of wood between propeller and antiventilation plate, remove the propeller nut, then remove the propeller.

Disassemble the gearcase by removing the gearcase housing cover nut (61–Fig. M10-36). Clamp the outer end of propeller shaft in a soft jawed vise and remove the gearcase by tapping with a rubber mallet. Be careful not to lose key (59) or shims (47) on early models. Forward gear (40) will remain in housing. Withdraw the propeller shaft from bearing carrier (56) and reverse gear (46).

Clamp the bearing carrier (56) in a soft-jawed vise and remove reverse gear (46) and bearing (49) with an internal expanding puller and slide hammer. Remove and discard the propeller shaft rear seal or seals (58).

To remove dog clutch (43) from propeller shaft, remove retaining ring (44). Insert cam follower (8) in hole in shaft and apply only enough pressure on end of cam follower to remove the spring pressure, then push out pin (42) with a small punch. The pin passes through

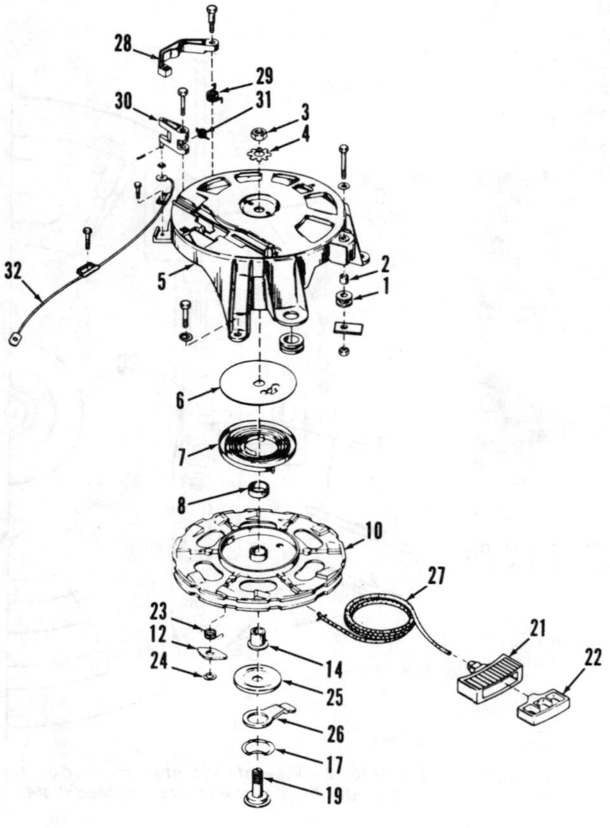

Fig. M10-33 – Exploded view of manual rewind starter used on late Model 40 and Model 35.

1. Pulley
2. Spacer
3. Nut
4. Tab washer
5. Housing
6. Retainer
7. Rewind spring
8. Bushing
10. Sheave
12. Pawl
14. Spacer
17. Wave washer
19. Sheave shaft
21. Handle
22. Anchor
23. Spring
24. Clip
25. Washer
26. Lever
27. Starter rope
28. Interlock cam
29. Spring
30. Interlock actuator
31. Spring
32. Interlock cable

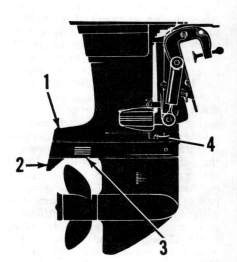

Fig. M10-35 – To remove the lower unit gearcase assembly, remove the Allen head screw and stud nuts from location indicated.

drilled holes in dog clutch and operates in slotted holes in propeller shaft.

To disassemble the drive shaft and associated parts, reposition gearcase in vise with drive shaft projecting upward. Remove rubber slinger (11), water pump body (16), impeller (19) and impeller drive pin (20). Remove the flushing screw and withdraw the remainder of the water pump parts. Clamp upper end of drive shaft in a soft jawed vise, remove pinion retaining cap screw or nut (37); then tap gearcase off drive shaft and bearing. Note the position and thickness of shims (30) on drive shaft upper bearing. Mesh position of pinion is controlled by shims (30) placed underneath the bearing.

After drive shaft has been removed, the forward gear (40) and bearing cone can be withdrawn. Use an internal expanding type puller to withdraw bearing cup if removal is required. Remove and save the shim pack (38).

Shift shaft (5) and cam (7) can be removed after removing forward gear and unscrewing bushing (3) from gearcase housing.

If gear wear is abnormal or if any parts that affect gear alignment were renewed, check and adjust gear mesh as follows: Install forward gear (40) and bearing (39) using shims (38) that were originally installed. Position shims (30) that were originally installed at bottom of bearing bore, then install bearing cup (32) in housing bore against shims (30). Position the drive pinion in housing and insert drive shaft (33), with bearing (32) installed, into housing, bearing (34) and gear (35). Install the retaining nut (37). Coat gears (35 and 40) with bearing blue and check mesh position. It will be necessary to push down on end of drive shaft while checking mesh position. If gears do not mesh in center of teeth, add or remove shims (30) under bearing as necessary. After setting mesh position, check backlash between teeth of gears (35 and 40). Backlash should be within limits of 0.003-0.005 inch (0.076-0.127 mm) on 400, 402 and early 40 models and 0.007-0.010 inch (0.178-0.254 mm) on 35 and late 40 models. To increase clearance (backlash), remove part of shim stack (38) behind bearing cup. If gears are too loose, add shims. After changing thickness of shims (38), gears should be recoated with bearing blue and mesh position should be rechecked. Install bearings (49), thrust washer (48) and reverse gear (46) in bearing carrier (56). Then, install bearing carrier and gear assembly using shims (47), on early models, that were originally installed and check backlash between gears (35 and 46). If backlash is not within the limits of 0.003-0.005 inch (0.076-0.127

mm), add or remove shims (47) as required. Adding shims (47) increases backlash (clearance).

When reassembling, long splines on shift rod (5) should be toward top. Shift cam (7) is installed with notches up and toward rear. Assemble shifting parts (9, 8S, 43, 42 and 44) into propeller shaft (45). Pin (42) should be through hole in slide (8S). Position follower (8) in end of propeller shaft and insert shaft into bearing (41) and forward gear. Install the reverse gear and bearing carrier assembly using new seals (55 and 58). Lip of seal (58) should face propeller (out) on single seal models. On two seal models, install inner seal with lip toward reverse gear and outer seal with lip toward propeller.

Upper oil seal (26) should be installed with lips facing up (toward engine) and lower oil seal (27) should be pressed into water pump base with lips facing down toward propeller shaft. Install remainder of water pump assembly and tighten the screws or nuts to the following recommended torque. Torque 1/4-28 nuts to 25-30 in.-lbs. (2.8-3.4 N·m). Torque 5/16-24 nuts to 35-40 in.-lbs. (3.9-4.5 N·m). Torque 1/4-20 screws to 15-20 in.-lbs. (1.7-2.2 N·m).

On early models, the reverse locking cam must be installed on shaft splines so the two tabs are aligned with the left front stud when in FORWARD gear (clockwise) position. Refer to Fig. M10-37. On later models, place shift shaft (5—Fig. M10-36) in neutral position. Install nylon washer with grooved side down and position reverse lock cam (2C—Fig. M10-38) with high point (H) of cam positioned as shown in Fig. M10-38.

Later models are equipped with two seals which fit over upper drive shaft splines. Install splined seal on drive shaft splines with splined seal end toward top of drive shaft, then install remaining seal with small end toward top of drive shaft.

Before attaching gearcase housing to the drive shaft housing, make certain that shift cam (7—Fig. M10-36) and the shift lever (on motor) are in forward gear position on models with reverse locking cam shown in Fig. M10-37 and neutral position on models with reverse locking cam shown in Fig. M10-38. Complete assembly by reversing disassembly procedure.

Make certain that spring (68—Fig. M10-36) and plunger (67) are positioned before attaching gearcase to drive shaft housing.

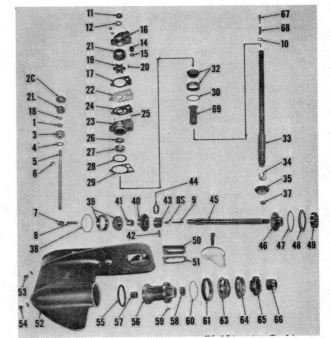

Fig. M10-36 — Exploded view of typical gearcase assembly. Two oil seals (1) are used on some models. Two seals (58) are used on later models. Shim (47) is not used on later models. On later models, a nylon washer replaces spacer (2L).

1. Oil seal
2C. Reverse locking cam
2L. Spacer
3. Bushing
4. "O" ring
5. Shift shaft
6. Snap ring
7. Shift cam
8. Cam follower
8S. Slide
9. Spring
10. "O" ring
11. Rubber ring (slinger)
12. Oil seal
14. Seal
15. Nylon washer
16. Water pump body
17. Gasket
18. Rubber washer
19. Impeller
20. Key
21. Insert
22. Plate
23. Pump base
24. Gasket
25. Dowel
26. Oil seal
27. Spring loaded oil seal
28. "O" ring
29. Gasket
30. Shims
32. Tapered bearing
33. Drive shaft
34. Roller bearing
35. Drive pinion
37. Nut
38. Shim
39. Tapered roller bearing
40. Forward gear
41. Roller bearing
42. Cross pin
43. Dog clutch
44. Retaining ring
45. Propeller shaft
46. Reverse gear
47. Shim
48. Thrust washer
49. Ball bearing
50. Exhaust tube seal
51. Support plate
52. Gear housing
53. Vent screw
54. Filler screw
55. "O" ring
56. Bearing carrier
57. Roller bearing
58. Oil seal
59. Key
60. Washer
61. Housing cover nut
63. Thrust hub
64. Cupped washer
65. Spline washer
66. Propeller nut
67. Plunger
68. Spring
69. Lubrication sleeve

Fig. M10-37—On early models, the reverse lock cam must be installed on shift splines as shown when in forward gear position.

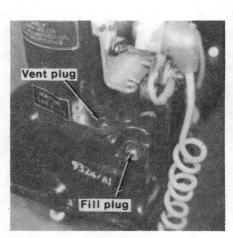

Fig. M10-38—On later models, the reverse lock cam (2C) must be installed on shift splines with high point (H) of cam positioned as shown when in neutral position.

POWER TILT/TRIM

FLUID. Recommended fluid is SAE 10W-30 automotive oil. With outboard in full up position, oil level should reach bottom of fill plug hole threads (Fig. M10-40). Do not overfill.

BLEEDING. To determine if air is present in tilt/trim hydraulic system, trim outboard out to trim limit position, then pull up on lower unit. If trim cylinder pistons retract into cylinders in excess of $\frac{1}{8}$ inch (3.2 mm), air is present and should be purged from system.

Make sure manual release valve is in full counterclockwise position and open vent screw (Fig. M10-40) two turns. Make sure pump reservoir is full of oil. To bleed system, operate tilt/trim system through several full up and full in cycles, checking oil level in reservoir at each full up position.

ADJUST TRIM LIMIT SWITCH. Operate trim control so outboard is in full down position. Press "UP/OUT" or "UP" control button and hold it until pump motor stops. Outboard should tilt up and stop so there is $\frac{1}{2}$ inch (12.7 mm) overlap (L—Fig. M10-41) between swivel bracket flange (W) and clamp bracket flange (M). Pull up on lower unit to remove slack when checking overlap (L). Note that if cylinder rods enter cylinders more than an additional $\frac{1}{8}$ inch (3.2 mm), air is present in hydraulic system and should be purged as outlined in BLEEDING section. If overlap (L) is incorrect, loosen retainer screw

(R—Fig. M10-42), then turn adjusting nut (N) counterclockwise to increase overlap or clockwise to decrease overlap. Retighten retainer screw (R) and recheck adjustment.

PRESSURE TEST. To check hydraulic system pressure, disconnect four hoses attached to control valve as shown in Fig. M10-43; small hoses are for up circuit while large hoses are for down circuit. Connect a pressure gage to one up circuit port of control valve and another pressure gage to one down circuit port. Screw plugs into remaining ports. Check fluid reservoir and fill if

Fig. M10-42—Loosen retainer screw (R) and turn trim limit adjusting nut (N) to adjust trim limit switch.

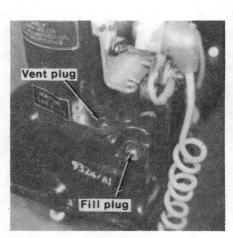

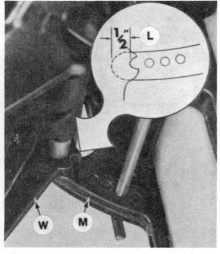

Fig. M10-41—Overlap (L) between swivel bracket flange (W) and clamp bracket flange (M) should be $\frac{1}{2}$ inch (12.7 mm) minimum.

Fig. M10-40—View showing power tilt/trim system fill plug and reservoir vent plug.

Fig. M10-43—View of control valve showing location of up circuit hoses (U) and down circuit hoses (D).

necessary. Operate trim control in up direction until maximum pressure is indicated on gage. Minimum up pressure is 2700 psi (18.6 MPa). After releasing trim control button, pressure will drop slightly after stabilizing but should not drop faster than 100 psi (689.5 kPa) eve-ry 15 seconds. Operate trim control in the down direction until the maximum pressure is indicated on the gage. Down pressure should be within 500-1000 psi (3.4-6.9 MPa). After releasing trim control button, pressure will drop slightly after stabilizing but should not drop faster than 100 psi (689.5 kPa) every 15 seconds. If pressure is normal, inspect trim cylinders and hoses for leakage. If pressure is abnormal, install a known good control valve and recheck pressure. If pressure remains abnormal, install a new pump body.

MERCURY
THREE-CYLINDER MODELS

Year Produced	Models
1972-1976	650
1977-1978	700
1979-1983	70
1984-1985	60
1984-1989	60
1986-1989	50

Letters after model number indicate equipment variations.
E – Electric starter and alternator
L – Long shaft
XS – High performance
PT – Power trim

CONDENSED SERVICE DATA

TUNE-UP

Hp/rpm:
Model 650 ....65/4800-5300*
Models 700 & 70 ....70/5000-5500
Model 50 ....50/5300-5800
Model 60 ....60/5000-5500
Bore ....2⁷⁄₈ in.

Stroke ....2-9/16 in.

Displacement ....49.8 cu. in.

Firing Order ....1-3-2†
Compression At Cranking Speed ....‡
Ignition ....Solid State
Spark Plugs ....See Text
Fuel:Oil Ratio 50:1

*Model 650XS is rated 70 hp at 6000-7000 rpm.
†On models prior to serial number 5579017, firing order is
1-2-3.
‡Not more than 15 psi (103.5 kPa) variation between
cylinders.

SIZES—CLEARANCES

Piston Rings:
End Gap ....*
Side Clearance...................................*
Piston Skirt Clearance ....*
Crankshaft Bearing Type:
Top Main................................Ball Bearing
Main Bearing (2)....................Loose Rollers

SIZES—CLEARANCES CONT.

No. of Rollers..................................56
Main Bearing (3)....................Loose Rollers
No. of Rollers..................................56
Bottom Main Bearing ....Ball Bearing
Crankpin ....Caged Roller
Piston Pin Bearing ....Loose Rollers
No. of Rollers (each rod) 29

*Publication not authorized by manufacturer.

TIGHTENING TORQUES

Connecting Rods ....180 in.-lbs.
(20.3 N·m)
Crankcase Screws ....200 in.-lbs.
(22.6 N·m)
Cylinder Cover ....70 in.-lbs.
(7.9 N·m)
Exhaust Cover:
¼ inch ....115 in.-lbs.
(13 N·m)
5/16 inch.............................200 in.-lbs.
(22.6 N·m)
Flywheel Nut ....85 ft.-lbs.
(115.2 N·m)
Reed Screws ....30 in.-lbs.
(3.4 N·m)
Spark Plugs............................20 ft.-lbs.
(27.1 N·m)
Transfer Port Covers ....160 in.-lbs.
(18.1 N·m)

LUBRICATION

The engine is lubricated by oil mixed with the fuel. Fuel should be regular leaded, low lead or unleaded gasoline with a minimum pump octane rating of 86. Premium gasoline may be used if desired regular gasoline is not available. Recommended oil is Quicksilver Formula 50 or 50-D. A good quality NMMA certified TC-WII oil may be used. Fuel:oil ratio should be 50:1 when using Formula 50 or 50-D oil. Follow fuel:oil ratio recommended by oil manufacturer if Formula 50 or 50-D is not used.

AutoBlend fuel and oil mixing system is used on Models 50 and 60 after 1985. The AutoBlend system is designed to deliver a constant 50:1 fuel and oil mixture to the power head at all engine speeds. To provide sufficient lubrication during break-in (first 30 gallons [114 L] of fuel used) of a new or rebuilt engine, a 50:1 fuel and oil mixture should be used in fuel tank in combination with the AutoBlend system. After initial 30 gallons (114 L) of fuel is consumed, switch to straight gasoline in fuel tank.

Translucent filter (1—Fig. MR11-1) behind cover (2) should be inspected once per month and renewed each boating season or if sediment inside filter is evident. AutoBlend diaphragm plate should be inspected for cracking, swelling or deterioration once per year. To inspect diaphragm plate, remove eight screws securing main body cover (6) to main body (7), then remove clip securing diaphragm plate to pump shaft.

NOTE: Remove inner ring of screws to remove cover from main body. Outer ring of screws secures main body to reservoir.

Renew diaphragm plate as necessary. Reverse disassembly procedure to reassemble unit. Tighten eight main body cover screws in a crossing pattern to 30 in.-lbs. (3.4 N·m).

To check for proper operation of pump check valves, remove fuel hose and plug outlet (O). Remove fuel hose from inlet (I) and connect a suitable hand-held vacuum pump with gage to inlet (I). Check valves should hold steady vacuum with 8 inches HG (27 kPa) applied and allow leakage when 10 inches HG (33.8 kPa) is applied. Check valves can be removed for inspection or renewal by removing main body (7) from reservoir (5). Check valves are located under cover secured to top of pump by two screws. When reassembling, tighten main body screws in a crossing pattern to 30 in.-lbs. (3.4 N·m).

The lower unit gears and bearings are lubricated by oil contained in the gearcase. Only Quicksilver Super Duty Gear Lubricant should be used. Gearcase is filled through the lower filler plug hole until lubricant reaches the upper vent plug hole. Then allow 1 ounce (30 mL) of oil to drain from gearcase. On most models, both plugs are on port side of gearcase.

FUEL SYSTEM

CARBURETOR. Two WMK type carburetors (Fig. M11-2) are used on early 650 models; two MerCarb center bowl type carburetors (Fig. M11-6) are used on late 650 models and all 50, 60, 70 and 700 models. Refer to the appropriate following paragraphs for service information.

EARLY MODEL 650. Initial setting of idle mixture needle (A—Fig. M11-3) is one turn open from a lightly seated position. Final idle mixture adjustment should be performed with motor running at normal operating temperature in forward gear. Turning needle (A) clockwise leans idle mixture.

The high speed mixture may be adjusted for elevations or other special conditions by changing the size of main jet (20—Fig. M11-2). Standard main jet (20) size is 0.074 inch (1.88 mm) and should be used for elevations below 4000 feet (1219 m).

NOTE: If main jet (20) is too small, high speed mixture will be excessively lean and may result in damage to power head.

To adjust the fuel level, remove inlet cover (2) and invert the cover assembly.

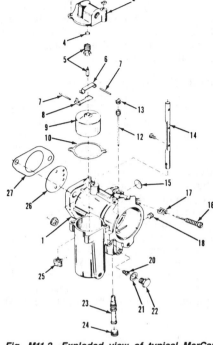

Fig. M11-2—Exploded view of typical MerCarb WMK type carburetor.

1. Body	15. Welch plug
2. Bowl cover	16. Idle mixture screw
4. Gasket	17. Spring
5. Inlet needle & seat	18. Plug
6. Primary lever	20. Main jet
7. Pin	21. Gasket
8. Secondary lever	22. Plug
9. Float	23. Main nozzle
10. Gasket	24. Plug
12. Idle tube	25. Spring
13. Plug	26. Throttle plate
14. Throttle shaft	27. Gasket

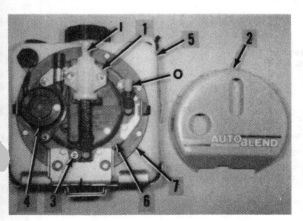

Fig. M11-1—View of AutoBlend fuel and oil mixing unit with cover (2) removed.

1. Filter
2. Cover
3. Drain plug
4. Warning horn
5. Reservoir
6. Main body cover
7. Main body
I. Inlet (gasoline)
O. Outlet (fuel & oil mixture)

Fig. M11-3—Idle mixture needles (A) should be one turn out from a lightly seated position for initial adjustment.

Measure distance (A—Fig. M11-4) between secondary lever (8) and gasket surface of bowl cover with inlet valve (5) closed. Distance (A) should be $^{13}/_{32}$ inch (10.3 mm). Bend curved tang on primary lever (6) to adjust. Turn bowl cover (2—Fig. M11-5) upright and measure distance (D) between primary lever (6) and end of secondary lever (8). Distance (D) should be $^1/_4$ inch (6.4 mm). Bend tab (T) to adjust. The contact spring located in center of float (9—Fig. M11-2) should extend $^3/_{32}$ inch (2.4 mm) above top of float. Inspect spring for stretching or other damage.

MODELS 50, 60, 70, 700 AND LATE 650. Standard make of carburetor is a center bowl type MerCarb. Two carburetors are used. Note that these carburetors are equipped with an enrichment valve (24—Fig. MR11-6) in place of a choke plate. Preliminary adjustment of idle mixture screw (19) is one turn out from a lightly seated position on all models. Recommended idle speed is 550-650 rpm on 650 models and 650-750 rpm on all other models. Adjust idle speed with engine running at normal operating temperature in forward gear.

Standard main jet (10) size is 0.080 inch (2.03 mm) for 650 short shaft models, 0.088 inch (2.24 mm) for 650 long shaft models, 0.086 inch (2.18 mm) for 650 extra long shaft and all other models prior to serial number 4576237. Standard main jet (10) size on 50 and 70 hp models after serial number 4576236 is 0.058 inch (1.47 mm). Standard main jet (10) size on 60 hp models after serial number 4576236 is 0.0785 inch (2.0 mm) on top carburetor and 0.072 inch (1.83 mm) on bottom carburetor.

Standard vent jet (4) size is 0.072 inch (1.83 mm) on 650 short shaft models, 0.052 inch (1.32 mm) on 650 long shaft models and 0.066 inch (1.68 mm) on all other models prior to serial number 4576237. Standard vent jet (4) size on all models after serial number 4576236 is 0.096 inch (2.44 mm).

NOTE: Standard size jets are designed for operation at elevations up to 2500 feet (762 m).

Various jet sizes are available for adjusting carburetor calibration for operation at higher elevations or other special conditions.

When overhauling carburetor, drive float pins (16) and fuel inlet lever pin (18) out toward knurled end of pin. Insert plain end of pin first during reassembly. Note that strong throttle return spring (0.034 inch diameter wire) must be used on top carburetor throttle shaft. Numbers on throttle plate (29) must face outward at closed throttle. Be sure rubber insert in fuel inlet valve seat (6) is installed so flat end of insert is toward inlet valve.

To determine the fuel level, invert carburetor body and measure distance (D—Fig. MR11-7) from the carburetor body to base of float (15). Distance (D) should be $^{11}/_{16}$ inch (17.5 mm) on solid type float and $^{19}/_{32}$ inch (15.1 mm) on hollow type float. Adjust distance (D) by bending fuel inlet lever (17—Fig. MR11-8) within area (A).

SPEED CONTROL LINKAGE. The speed control linkage must be synchronized to advance the ignition timing and open the carburetor throttles in a precise manner. Because the two actions are interrelated, it is important to check the complete system in the sequence outlined in the appropriate following paragraphs.

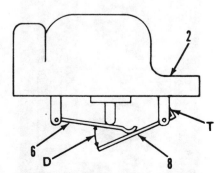

Fig. M11-4—Distance (A) should be $^{13}/_{32}$ inch (10.3 mm). Refer to text for adjustment procedure and Fig. M11-2 for component identification.

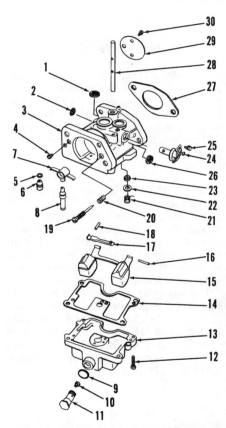

Fig. M11-6—Exploded view of center bowl type MerCarb carburetor used on late 650, 700, 70 and all 50 and 60 models.

1. Welch plug (9/16 inch)	16. Pin
2. Fuel inlet strainer	17. Fuel inlet lever
3. Body	18. Pin
4. Vent jet	19. Idle mixture screw
5. Gasket	20. Spring
6. Inlet needle & seat	21. Spring
assy.	22. Flat washer
7. Venturi	23. Rubber seal
8. Nozzle	24. Enrichment valve
9. Gasket	assy.
10. Main jet	25. Screw & lockwasher
11. Main jet plug	26. Welch plug (7/16 inch)
12. Screw	27. Gasket
13. Float bowl	28. Throttle shaft
14. Gasket	29. Throttle plate
15. Float	30. Screw

Fig. M11-7—To determine float level, invert carburetor body and measure distance (D) from carburetor body to base of float (15). Distance (D) should be $^{11}/_{16}$ inch (17.5 mm) on solid type float and $^{19}/_{32}$ inch (15.1 mm) on hollow type float.

Fig. M11-8—Adjust float level by bending fuel inlet lever (17) within area (A).

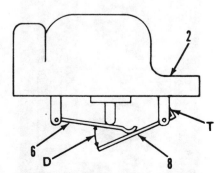

Fig. M11-5—With bowl cover (2) upright, distance (D) between primary lever (6) and end of secondary lever (8) should be $^1/_4$ inch (6.4 mm). Bend tab (T) to adjust.

Refer to the special precautions listed in the IGNITION section before servicing these motors. Incorrect servicing procedures can damage the ignition system.

NOTE: Do not disconnect any part of the ignition system while engine is running or while checking the speed control linkage adjustments.

MODEL 650 WITH DISTRIBUTOR. Disconnect the fuel tank and allow motor to run until all fuel is out of the carburetors. If any fuel remains, motor can start while checking the speed control linkage and may prevent accurate adjustments.

Connect an approved Mercury tachometer and timing light to the engine. Slowly advance speed controls while cranking engine with electric starter. Throttle cam should just contact throttle lever (A—Fig. M11-10) as timing pointer aligns with specified primary pickup point on flywheel decal.

Primary pickup point is 0-2 degrees BTDC on models before serial number 3552906 and 3-5 degrees BTDC on models after serial number 3552905. Adjust primary pickup point (initial contact of the throttle cam and lever) by turning adjustment screw (S). Be sure to tighten locknut on screw (S) when adjustment is complete.

To adjust maximum spark advance, crank engine with electric starter and move speed controls toward full speed position. Timing pointer should align with 23 degrees BTDC mark on flywheel decal as full advance stop screw (C—Fig. M11-11) just touches spark control

arm. If full advance is incorrect, loosen locknut on stop screw (C) and turn screw until timing light indicates full advance timing at 23 degrees BTDC. Tighten locknut when adjustment is completed and recheck full advance timing.

Adjust stop screw (B) so carburetor throttles are fully opened when throttle control arm touches stop screw (B). Throttle shutters should have 0.010-0.015 inch (0.25-0.38 mm) free play when fully opened to prevent binding in linkage. Adjust free play in carburetor shutters by turning stop screw (B). Be sure to tighten locknut on throttle stop screw when adjustment is completed.

MODEL 650 WITHOUT DISTRIBUTOR. Disconnect fuel tank and run engine out of fuel to prevent engine starting while adjusting timing.

Connect a power timing light to number 1 (top) cylinder. Primary pickup point is 6-8 degrees BTDC. Crank engine with starter and position speed control so timing pointer and timing decal are aligned at 6-8 degrees BTDC. Turn pickup adjusting screw (P—Fig. M11-12) so carburetor throttle roller just contacts cam.

Crank engine with starter and position speed control so ignition timing advances to 28 degrees BTDC. Turn stop screw (A) so screw just touches boss with ignition timing at 28 degrees BTDC. Due to design of ignition system, maximum advance of 28 degrees at cranking speed will provide a desired maximum advance of 23 degrees BTDC at 5300 rpm.

Adjust stop screw (B) so carburetor throttle plates are fully opened when throttle arm stop screw (B) contacts boss. There should be 0.010-0.015 inch (0.25-0.38 mm) clearance between cam and carburetor throttle roller to prevent throttle plates from sticking in bores.

MODELS 50, 60, 70 AND 700. To synchronize ignition and carburetor opening, proceed as follows: On models with an adjustable timing pointer, a dial indicator must be installed in the top cylinder and the indicator synchronized with the piston position.

Rotate the flywheel counterclockwise approximately ¼ turn past the 0.464 inch (12 mm) BTDC reading, then rotate

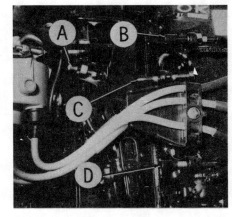

Fig. M11-11 — View of primary pickup screw (A), throttle stop screw (B), spark stop screw (C) and idle stop screw (D). Refer to text for adjustment procedures.

Fig. M11-10 — Primary pickup of throttle lever (A), should occur when ignition is advanced to specification listed in text. Refer to text for adjustment procedures.

Fig. M11-12 — View of throttle and spark control linkage. Refer to text for adjustment.

A. Max. advance stop screw
B. Throttle stop screw
I. Idle speed screw
P. Pickup screw
S. Spark control lever
T. Throttle control arm

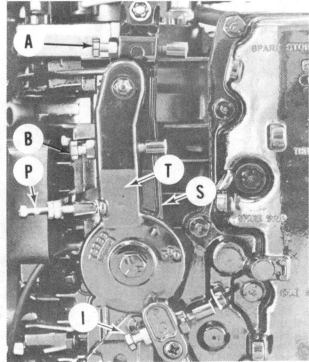

flywheel clockwise until indicator face reads 0.464 inch (12 mm) BTDC. Note position of the timing pointer and reposition if timing pointer (P—Fig. M11-13) is not aligned with dot (D) on timing decal. Loosen screw (S) to reposition. Remove the dial indicator assembly from the top cylinder after adjustment is completed and reassemble.

Connect a suitable power timing light to number 1 (top) spark plug wire. With the lower unit properly immersed, start the engine and shift outboard motor into forward gear. While running engine at 5000-5500 rpm (5300-5800 rpm after serial number 4576236), adjust maxi-

mum ignition advance screw (A—Fig. M11-12) until timing pointer is aligned with the 23 degrees BTDC mark on the timing decal. Secure screw position with locknut.

Move the spark lever until maximum advance screw (A) just contacts the stop boss and adjust secondary pickup screw (P) so carburetor cluster pin (R—Fig. M11-14) is located on throttle actuator cam (C) as shown. To prevent damage to the carburetor throttle plate at full throttle, adjust full throttle stop screw (B—Fig. M11-12) so a clearance of 0.010-0.015 inch (0.25-0.38 mm) is between throttle actuator cam (C—Fig. M11-14) and cluster pin (R) when throttle lever is moved to the wide open position.

Adjust idle speed screw (I—Fig. M11-12) as outlined in the previous CARBURETOR section.

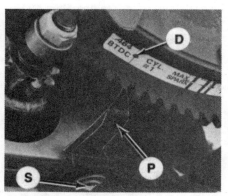

Fig. M11-13—On models equipped with an adjustable timing pointer, timing pointer (P) must align with dot (D) on flywheel timing decal when the piston of the top cylinder is 0.464 inch (12 mm) BTDC. Loosen screw (S) to reposition pointer (P).

Fig. M11-14—Adjust secondary pickup screw (P—Fig. M11-12) so carburetor cluster pin (R) is located on throttle actuator cam (C) as shown when maximum ignition advance screw (A—Fig. M11-12) just contacts the stop boss.

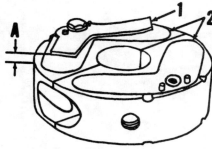

Fig. M11-16—View of intermediate main bearing housing and reed valve assembly. Height (A) of reed stop should be 0.180 inch (4.57 mm).

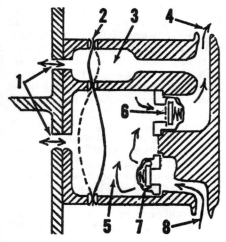

Fig. M11-17—Schematic view of diaphragm type fuel pump used on early models. Pump body mounts on side of cylinder block.

1. Pressure ports
2. Diaphragm
3. Booster chamber
4. To carburetor
5. Main fuel chamber
6. Outlet check valve
7. Inlet check valve
8. Fuel inlet

Fig. M11-18—View of early "triangle" shape fuel pump showing inlet (8) and discharge (9) check valves installed. Retainer (R) is secured by screws (10) and retainer tips must point away from check valves. Later design "triangle" shape fuel pump is similar except a filler block is used to retain check valves (8 and 9) in place of retainer (R).

REED VALVES. The inlet reed valves are located on the intermediate main bearing assemblies. Two reed valve assemblies are used, one for each carburetor. The center cylinder receives a partial fuel-air charge from each reed valve and carburetor.

Reed petals (2—Fig. M11-16) should be perfectly flat and have no more than 0.007 inch (0.18 mm) clearance between free end of reed petal and seating surface of main bearing/reed block assembly. The reed stop (18) must be carefully adjusted to 0.180 inch (4.57 mm). This clearance is measured between end of stop and seating surface of reed plate as shown at (A—Fig. M11-16). Seating surface of bearing must be smooth and flat, and may be refinished on a lapping plate after removing reed stops, reed valves and dowels. Do not attempt to bend or straighten a reed petal to modify performance or to salvage a damaged reed. Never install a bent reed. Lubricate the reed valve units with Quicksilver Multipurpose Lubricant or a light distributor cam grease when reassembling.

Each valve unit has four reeds which are available only as a matched set. Crankshaft must be removed before reed valve units can be serviced.

FUEL PUMP. All models are equipped with a diaphragm type fuel pump mounted on power head. Fuel pump is actuated by crankcase pulsations. Early models are equipped with first, second or third design "triangle" shaped pump and later models are equipped with a "square" shaped pump.

First, second and third design "triangle" shaped fuel pumps are similar. Third design pump is equipped with a filler block to retain check valves in pump housing in place of retainer (R—Fig. M11-18).

Fuel pressure on "triangle" shaped pump should be minimum of 2 psi (13.8 kPa) at idle and 4 to 4½ psi (27.6-31.0 kPa) at wide-open throttle. Fuel pressure on "square" style pump should be minimum of 3 psi (20.7 kPa) at idle and 6-8 psi (41.4-55.2 kPa) at wide-open throttle.

When assembling first and second design "triangle" shaped pump, make sure tips of retainer (R) are facing away from check valves. On all "triangle" shaped pumps, install red colored check valve on inlet side of pump.

After installing check valve retainer (4—Fig. M11-19) on "square" shape fuel pump, trim off excess end of retainer (4) at ridge to prevent retainer from contacting pump diaphragm.

IGNITION SYSTEM

Models Equipped With Distributor

"Thunderbolt" electronic ignition used on three-cylinder 650 models uses an electronic triggering device and does not use breaker points. This ignition is extremely durable in normal operation, but can be easily damaged by improper testing or servicing procedures.

Observe the following list of cautions and use only the approved methods for checking the system to prevent damage to the components.
1. DO NOT reverse battery terminals.
2. DO NOT check polarity of battery by sparking the lead wires.
3. DO NOT install resistor type spark plugs or lead wires other than those specified by the manufacturer.
4. DO NOT disconnect any wires while engine is running.
5. DO NOT ground any wire to engine block when checking. Ground only to front cover plate or bottom cowl to which switch box is mounted as described.
6. DO NOT use tachometer except those designed for this system.

TROUBLESHOOTING. Use only approved procedures when testing to prevent damage to components.

SPARK TEST. Do not remove spark plug wire while motor is running. Cut off the ground electrode from a standard 14 mm spark plug (not surface gap type) and connect one of the spark plug wires to the test plug. Ground the test plug to the support bracket using a clamp or jumper wire.

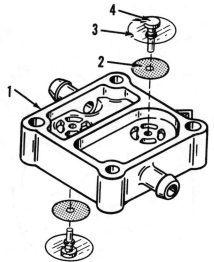

Fig. M11-19—View of "square" style fuel pump used on late models.

1. Body
2. Check valve (black rubber)
3. Check valve (clear plastic)
4. Retainer

CAUTION: Do not hold spark plug or wire in hand.

Make certain that the test plug is properly grounded; then, crank motor with electric starter. If test plug fires but engine will not start, check for incorrect installation of timing belt as outlined in the following TRIGGER AND DISTRIBUTOR paragraph. Fuel system problems can also prevent starting. If test plug does not fire, check the wiring as follows.

WIRING AND CONNECTION TEST. Turn the key switch OFF. Connect one lead of voltmeter to red terminal of switch box (Fig. M11-33) and ground other lead to front cover plate. If red terminal is dead (no voltage), check battery, battery connections or for broken wiring harness. If red terminal has voltage, proceed as follows:

Connect one lead of voltmeter to the white terminal and ground other lead to front cover plate. Turn key to the RUN position. If white terminal is dead (no voltage), key switch or wiring is defective. If white terminal has voltage, check the remaining components of system as follows:

Turn key switch OFF. Disconnect the black, white/black and blue trigger wires from the distributor assembly and connect them to a distributor with a trigger that is known to be good. Disconnect the coil secondary lead from the distributor center terminal, then connect a test spark plug (or gap tester) to the coil secondary lead and ground the tester to the cowl support bracket. Turn the key switch to RUN position and rotate the test distributor by hand. If a spark jumps at test plug, the original trigger assembly is faulty and should be renewed. If spark does not jump at test plug, listen for "click" around area of the high tensions coil as the test distributor is turned. "Clicking" indicated shorted high tension coils or high tension (secondary) lead wire. If the lead wire is not shorted, the high tension coil should be checked further as outlined in the following paragraph. If spark does not jump the test plug and coil is not damaged, the switch box should be renewed.

NOTE: A faulty switch box is nearly always caused by reversing battery leads, which damages the rectifier and in turn damages the switch box.

If switch box is suspected, check rectifier before renewing the switch box. If tests indicate that rectifier is damaged, renew the rectifier and again test the ignition system.

NOTE: Before disconnecting any wires, make certain that motor is not running and disconnect battery.

COIL TEST. The ignition coil can be tested using an ignition tester available from several sources including the following:

GRAHAM TESTERS, INC.
4220 Central Ave. N.E.
Minneapolis, Minn. 55421

MERC-O-TRONIC
INSTRUMENTS CORP.
215 Branch St.
Almont, Mich. 48003

An alternate method of checking is possible as follows: Disconnect the coil secondary lead and the green lead to the switch box. Resistance between the CONV (green lead) terminal and the GRD (black lead) terminal should be 0 ohms on the Rx1 scale of an ohmmeter. Resistance between the GRD terminal and the secondary voltage tower should be 8-12 ohms on the Rx100 scale. If either of these resistances are incorrect, renew the high tension coil.

SPARK PLUGS. The spark plugs should be renewed if the center electrode is burned back more than 1/32 inch (0.79 mm) below flat surface of the plug end. Refer to Fig. M11-20. Standard recommended spark plugs are Champion type L77V or AC type V40FFM surface gap spark plugs. Radio noise suppression, AC type, VR40FFM spark plug may also be used.

TRIGGER AND DISTRIBUTOR. The electronic trigger coil is located in the distributor housing (18 – Fig. M11-21) and is available only as an assembly with the housing. Before removing any of the components or disconnecting any wires, make certain that battery is disconnected.

Fig. M11-20 — Surface gap spark plugs should be renewed if center electrode is 1/32 inch (0.79 mm) below the end of plug.

Disassemble as follows: Disconnect battery and trigger wires. Remove flange (2 – Fig. M11-21), then unbolt and remove adapter (13). Pry pulley (5) off shaft, then remove key (3) and spacer (6). Bend tabs of washer (9) away from nut (7). Remove nut and withdraw distributor from adapter (13). Carefully press bearing (35 – Fig. M11-22) out of housing by working through two holes provided. Use caution to prevent damage to nut (36) or to distributor rotor shaft (46). Remove nut (36) and bump distributor shaft out of bearing (41). Bearing (41) is retained by snap ring (44).

Inspect distributor parts, especially bearings for wear and cleanliness. Renew or clean and lubricate parts as necessary. Inspect distributor cap for cracks or evidence of corrosion or carbon build up. Renew distributor cap if cracked or if evidence of leakage is found.

When reassembling, install shim (40), bearing (41) and snap ring bearing retainer (44). Position shim (42) and spacer (43), then insert timing disc (45) as shown in Fig. M11-23.

NOTE: If the timing disc is installed incorrectly it will be impossible to set ignition timing.

Insert distributor rotor shaft (46—Fig. M11-22) through timing disc (45), spacer (43) and shim (42).

CAUTION: Make sure that tab (Fig. M11-23) is aligned with slot in distributor shaft before pressing shaft into bearing (41—Fig. M11-22).

Install sleeve (37) and tighten nut (36) to 70 in.-lbs. (7.9 N·m). Press upper ball bearing (35) into housing around shaft. Install gasket (48) and brush spring (49), then assemble distributor cap (50) to housing with clamp (47).

NOTE: Joint of clamp (47) should be positioned next to trigger wires coming out of distributor housing.

Place wave washer (17—Fig. M11-21) on distributor housing (18) and insert housing in adapter (13). Install flat washer (10), tab washer (9) and washer (8) with raised portion next to nut (7). Install and tighten nut (7), back it out just enough to align tabs on tab washer (9), then bend tabs into slots in nut. Install spacer (6), then install pulley (5) over drive key (3).

Align BELT ALIGNING MARK on flywheel with plastic timing pointer on engine, then align cast timing point on pulley (5) with cast timing boss on adapter (13). Place distributor drive belt over pulley (5) and bolt adapter to engine while maintaining alignment of all marks. Make sure that locating pin (15) is installed between engine block and adapter. Install flange (2) and secure in position with pin (4) and screw (1). Refer to SPEED CONTROL LINKAGE paragraphs for adjusting linkage and timing ignition.

Models Without Distributor

IGNITION. An alternator driven capacitor discharge ignition (CDI) system is used. Ignition system consists of the flywheel, stator, trigger assembly, switch box and ignition coils. The stator is mounted below the flywheel and includes two capacitor charging coils. The trigger assembly consists of three trigger coils and is mounted below the flywheel. Ignition timing is advanced and retarded by rotating trigger assembly in relation to the inner flywheel magnets. Diodes, capacitors and SCR's are contained in the switch box. Switch box, trigger assembly and stator must be serviced as unit assemblies. Refer to Fig. MR11-34 for wiring diagram typical of early models. Later models are similar.

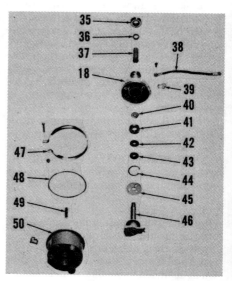

Fig. M11-22—Exploded view of distributor assembly. Refer to text for disassembly procedure.

18. Distributor housing	35. Upper ball bearing	43. Spacer
	36. Nut	44. Snap ring
	37. Sleeve	45. Timing disc
	38. Ground strap	46. Rotor & shaft assy.
	39. Flame arrestor	47. Clamp
	40. Shim	48. Gasket
	41. Lower ball bearing	49. Brush & spring
	42. Shim	50. Distributor cap

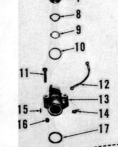

Fig. M11-21—Exploded view of distributor drive and control components.

1. Screw
2. Flange
3. Key
4. Pin
5. Pulley
6. Spacer
7. Nut
8. Wave washer
9. Tab washer
10. Washer
11. Bolt
12. Ground strap
13. Adapter
14. Grease fitting
15. Locating pin
16. Nut
17. Washer
18. Distributor housing
19. Spark advance link
20. Washer
21. Primary pickup screw
22. Rubber cap
23. Spark advance lever
24. Return spring
25. Spring
26. Control lever bushing
27. Throttle control lever
28. Latch
29. Screw
30. Bushing
31. Throttle cam housing
32. Throttle cam
33. Link
34. Timing belt

Fig. M11-23 — Timing disc must be installed with side shown toward distributor cap (down).

Recommended spark plugs are AC V40FFM or Champion L76V. Renew surface gap spark plugs if center electrode is $1/_{32}$ inch (0.79 mm) below end of plug as shown in Fig. M11-20.

If engine malfunction is noted, and the ignition system is suspected, make sure the spark plugs and all electrical wiring are in acceptable condition and all electrical connections are clean and tight prior to trouble-shooting CDI system.

To properly test the switch box and ignition coils require the use of Quicksilver Multi-Meter DVA Tester part 91-99750 or a suitable voltmeter capable of measuring a minimum of 400 DC volts used with Quicksilver Direct Voltage Adaptor (DVA) part 91-89045. Follow instructions provided by tester manufacturer when performing tests. If these testers are not available, a process of elimination must be used when testing the ignition system. Stator and trigger assemblies can be effectively tested using a suitable ohmmeter.

NOTE: All tests that involve cranking or running the engine must be performed with lead wires connected. Switch box case MUST be grounded to engine for all tests or switch box may be damaged.

To test ignition system, proceed as follows:

IGNITION COILS PRIMARY TEST. Connect DVA red test lead to ignition coil positive (+) terminal and black test lead to coil negative (−) terminal. Position tester selector switch to DVA/400. Tester should read 150-250 volts at cranking or idle speed (300-1000 rpm) and 180-280 volts at 1000-4000 rpm. If voltage readings are below specified reading, refer to SWITCH BOX STOP CIRCUIT test. If readings are within specifications, connect a suitable spark tester to ignition coil high tension leads, crank engine and note spark. If weak or no spark is noted, renew ignition coil(s). If normal spark is noted, renew spark plugs. If malfunction is still evident after renewing spark plugs, check ignition timing. If ignition timing is erratic, such as a sudden timing change, inspect trigger advance linkage for excessive wear or damage and inner flywheel magnets (shifted position or other damage). If timing is within specifications, problem is not in ignition system.

SWITCH BOX STOP CIRCUIT. Connect DVA black test lead to engine ground and red test lead to black/yellow switch box terminal (orange terminal on early models). Set DVA selector switch to DVA/400. Voltage reading at cranking and all running speeds should be 200-360 volts. If reading is within specifica-

tions, refer to STATOR tests. If reading is above specified voltages, connect a suitable ohmmeter between trigger brown and white/black leads, white and white/black leads and purple and white/black leads. Trigger resistance should be 1100-1400 ohms at all three connections. If not, renew trigger assembly. If trigger resistance is acceptable, renew switch box and repeat SWITCH BOX STOP CIRCUIT test. If SWITCH BOX STOP CIRCUIT test reading is below specified voltage, disconnect ignition switch, stop switch and mercury switch from black/yellow switch box terminal (orange switch box terminal on early models). With stop switch, ignition switch and mercury switch isolated, repeat SWITCH BOX STOP CIRCUIT test. If reading is now within specification, ignition switch, stop switch or mercury switch is defective. If reading remains below specification refer to STATOR test.

STATOR. Connect DVA black lead to engine ground and red lead to blue switch box terminal. Set DVA selector switch to DVA/400. Voltage reading should be 200-300 volts at cranking and idle speeds and 200-330 volts at 1000-4000 rpm. Switch DVA red test lead to red switch box terminal. Leave black test lead connected to engine ground. Voltage reading should be 20-90 volts at cranking or idle speeds and 130-300 volts at 1000-4000 rpm.

NOTE: A shorted or open capacitor inside switch box will result in faulty stator voltage readings during cranking and running tests. Stator resistance should be checked as follows before failing stator.

If either STATOR test is not to specification, proceed as follows: Connect a suitable ohmmeter between blue and red stator leads. Resistance between blue and red stator leads should be 5400-6200 ohms. Next, connect ohmmeter between red stator lead and engine ground, or stator black lead (ground). Resistance should be 125-175 ohms. Renew stator if resistance is not as specified. If stator resistance is as specified, renew switch box and repeat STATOR tests.

IGNITION COILS RESISTANCE TEST. Disconnect wires and high tension lead from coil. Connect a suitable ohmmeter between coil positive (+) and negative (−) terminals. Resistance should be 0.02-0.04 ohm. Connect ohmmeter between coil high tension terminal and negative (−) terminal. Resistance should be 800-1100 ohms. Renew ignition coil(s) if resistance is not as specified.

NOTE: Ignition coil resistance tests can detect only open or shorted windings. If coil resistance is within specification and still suspected as defective, coil must be tested using DVA meter as previously outlined in IGNITION COIL test. If DVA meter is not available, substitute a known good ignition coil and run engine to test.

COOLING SYSTEM

WATER PUMP. The rubber impeller type water pump is housed in the gearcase housing. The impeller is mounted on and driven by the lower unit drive shaft.

When cooling system problems are encountered, first check the water inlet for plugging or partial stoppage, then if not corrected, remove the gearcase housing as outlined in LOWER UNIT section and examine the water pump, water tubes and seals.

Water pump housing is plastic. Refer to assembly notes, cautions and tightening torques listed in the LOWER UNIT section when assembling.

POWER HEAD

R&R AND DISASSEMBLE. To remove the power head assembly, first disconnect the battery and remove the top side cowling. Remove electric starter, then disconnect all interfering wires and linkage. Remove the stud nuts that secure the power head to lower unit, then jar power head on exhaust side to loosen gasket. Lift power head from lower unit and install on a suitable stand. Remove the flywheel, distributor, alternator-generator and the carburetors. Exhaust manifold cover, cylinder block cover and transfer port covers should be removed for cleaning and inspection.

Remove the upper and lower crankcase end caps by using a suitable puller attached to threaded holes in caps. Remove the main bearing locking bolts from front crankcase half, remove the flange bolts; then remove crankcase front half by inserting screwdriver in the recesses provided on side flanges. Use extra care not to spring the parts or to mar the machined mating surfaces. The crankcase half (25—Fig. M11-25 and Fig. M11-26) and cylinder assembly (6) are matched and align bored, and are available only as an assembly.

Crankshaft, pistons, bearings and connecting rods may now be removed for service as outlined in the appropriate following paragraphs. When assembling, follow the procedures outlined in the ASSEMBLY paragraph.

ASSEMBLY. When assembling, the crankcase must be completely sealed

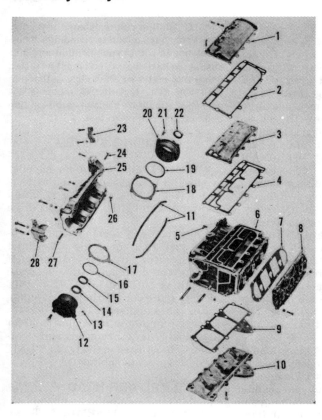

Fig. M11-25 — Exploded view of early type crankcase assembly.

1. Exhaust cover
2. Gasket
3. Baffle
4. Gasket
5. Dowel
6. Cylinder block
7. Gasket
8. Head cover
9. Gasket
10. Transfer cover
11. Sealing strips
12. Lower end cap
13. Check valve assy.
14. Oil seal
15. Oil seal
16. "O" ring
17. Shim
18. Shim
19. "O" ring
20. Upper end cap
21. Screw
22. Oil seal
23. Start motor retainer
24. Plastic timing pointer
25. Crankcase half
26. Dowel
27. Stud
28. Start motor cover

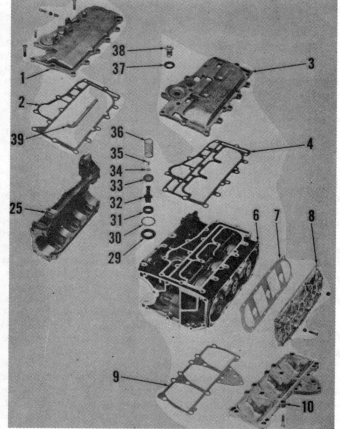

9. Gasket
29. Grommet
30. Retainer
31. Relief valve grommet
32. Relief valve
33. Diaphragm
34. Washer
35. Screw
36. Spring
37. Gasket
38. Thermostat
39. Gasket

Fig. M11-26 — View of late type crankcase components with thermostat. Diaphragm components (33, 34 & 35) are not used on all models with thermostat in block assembly. Refer to Fig. M11-25 and the following for legend.

against both vacuum and pressure. Exhaust manifold and water passages must be sealed against pressure leakage. Whenever power head is disassembled, it is recommended that all gasket surfaces and machined joints without gaskets be carefully checked for nicks and burrs that might interfere with a tight seal.

Lubricate all bearing and friction surfaces with engine oil. Loose needle bearings may be held in place during assembly using a light, nonfibrous grease.

After the crankshaft, connecting rods, pistons and main bearings are positioned in the cylinder, check the crankshaft end play. Temporarily install the crankshaft end caps (20 and 12 – Fig. M11-25) omitting sealing rings (19 and 16), but using shims (18 and 17) that were originally installed. Tighten the end cap to cylinder retaining screws. Use a soft hammer to bump the crankshaft each way to seat bearings, then measure end play.

Bump the crankshaft toward top and measure clearance between the top crankshaft counterweight and the end cap as shown in Fig. M11-27. Bump the crankshaft toward bottom and again measure clearance between counterweight and top end cap. Subtract the first (minimum) clearance from the second clearance which will indicate the amount of end play. If end play is not within limits of 0.004-0.012 inch (0.102-0.305 mm), add or remove shims (18 and 17 – Fig. M11-25) as necessary, then recheck. The crankshaft should be centered by varying the amount of shims between upper (18) and lower (17) shim stacks. When centering the crankshaft, make certain that end play is correct.

Shims (18 and 17) are available in thicknesses of 0.002, 0.003, 0.005, 0.006, 0.008 and 0.010 inch.

All gaskets and sealing surfaces should be lightly and carefully coated

Fig. M11-27 — Refer to text for method of checking crankshaft end play. The crankshaft should be centered in the cylinder.

with an impervious liquid sealer such as Mercury Gasket Sealer Compound (C-92-28804). Surface must be completely coated, using care that excess sealer does not squeeze out into bearings, crankcase or other passages.

Check the assembly by turning the crankshaft after each step to check for binding or locking which might indicate improper assembly. Remove the cause before proceeding. Rotate the crankshaft until each piston ring in turn appears in one of the exhaust or transfer ports, then check by pressing on ring with a blunt tool. Ring should spring back when released; if it does not, a broken or binding ring is indicated, and the trouble should be corrected.

Tighten the crankcase exhaust cover and cylinder cover cap screws by first tightening center screws, then tightening screws evenly working outward, away from center of crankcase. Tightening torques are given in the CONDENSED SERVICE DATA table.

PISTONS, PINS, RINGS AND CYLINDERS. Before detaching connecting rods from crankshaft, make sure that rod and cap are properly identified for correct assembly to each other and in the correct cylinder.

Piston rings are interchangeable in the ring grooves and are pinned in place.

Maximum allowable cylinder bore wear or out-of-round is 0.004 inch (0.102 mm). Excessively worn or slightly damaged, standard size cylinders may be repaired by boring and honing to fit an oversize piston. Pistons and rings are available in 0.015 inch (0.38 mm) oversize on early models and 0.015 inch (0.38 mm) and 0.030 inch (0.76 mm) oversizes on later models.

Piston pin is pressed in piston bosses and secured with retaining rings. The retaining rings should not be reused. Piston end of connecting rod is fitted with 29 loose needle rollers.

The piston pin needle rollers use the connecting rod bore and the piston pin as bearing races. When assembling, install bearing washers and needle bearings in piston end of connecting rod using light nonfibrous grease to hold them in place. A Mercury special tool may be used to hold needles in position while positioning piston for installation. Piston must be installed so sharp, vertical side of deflector will be to starboard (intake) side of cylinder bore. Heat piston to approximately 135°F (57°C) and press piston pin into place. Pin should be centered in piston. Use new piston retaining rings on each assembly.

CONNECTING RODS, BEARINGS AND CRANKSHAFT. Upper and lower ends of crankshaft are carried by ball bearings. The two center main bearings (21 – Fig. M11-28) also contain the inlet reed valve assemblies. Two split type outer races (25) each contain 56 loose bearing rollers in two rows. The outer race is held together by a retaining ring (27). The reed valve assembly (21) fits around outer race (25).

The connecting rod uses 29 loose rollers at the piston end and a caged roller bearing at the crankpin end.

Check rod for alignment, using Mercury Alignment Tool, or by placing rod on a surface plate and checking with a light.

If bearing surface of rod and cap is rough, scored, worn or shows evidence of overheating, renew the connecting rod. Inspect crankpin and main bearing journals. If scored, out-of-round or worn, renew the crankshaft. Check the crankshaft for straightness using a dial indicator and "V" blocks.

Inspect and adjust the reed valves as outlined in REED VALVE paragraph, and reassemble as outlined in ASSEMBLY paragraph.

ELECTRICAL SYSTEM

Refer to Fig. M11-33 or Fig. M11-34 for wiring diagram of electrical system. Before any servicing, refer to precautions listed in ignition paragraphs.

The rectifier assembly is designed to protect the ignition switch box if battery terminal or harness plug becomes loose with motor running. However, the rectifier assembly (Fig. M11-35) will be damaged. If battery terminals are reversed, the rectifier and the ignition switch box will be damaged. The motor can be operated without rectifier if the two yellow/red wires (from the alternator) are disconnected from the rectifier and taped separately.

Refer to Fig. M11-35 for correct rectifier connections.

Alternator output should be 7-9 amperes measured at the battery. To test alternator, disconnect stator yellow leads from rectifier and connect a suitable ohmmeter between yellow leads. Resistance should be 0.5-1.0 ohm. No continuity should be present between either stator yellow lead and engine ground (or stator frame if removed).

Models are equipped with Prestolite or Bosch starter motor. Renew brushes if worn to less than $1/4$ inch (6.4 mm) long. Undercut insulation between commutator segments to $1/32$ inch (0.8 mm). Starter motor through-bolts should be tightened to 70 in.-lbs. (7.9 N·m). On Prestolite starter, armature end play should be 0.010-0.035 inch (0.25-0.89 mm). Adjust end play by varying thickness of shims on commutator end of armature.

LOWER UNIT

PROPELLER AND DRIVE CLUTCH. Protection for the motor is built into a special cushioning clutch in the propeller hub. No adjustment is possible on the propeller or clutch. Various pitch propellers are available and propeller

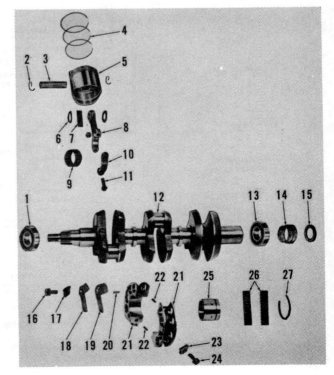

Fig. M11-28 — Exploded view of typical crankshaft assembly. On later models, a shim is used between crankshaft and ball bearing (13).

1. Ball bearing
2. Piston pin retaining clip
3. Piston pin
4. Piston rings
5. Piston
6. Side washer
7. Needle rollers
8. Connecting rod
9. Caged roller bearing
10. Rod cap
11. Screw
12. Crankshaft
13. Ball bearing
14. "O" ring carrier
15. "O" ring
16. Screw
17. Clamp nut
18. Reed stop
19. Reed petal
20. Locating dowel
21. Reed plate & main bearing housing
22. Pin
23. Nut
24. Screw
25. Outer race
26. Needle rollers
27. Outer race holding clip

should be selected for best performance under applicable conditions. Propellers other than those designed for the motor must not be used.

R&R AND OVERHAUL. Most service on the lower unit can be performed by detaching the gearcase housing from the drive shaft housing. To remove the housing, remove the plastic plug and Allen head screw from location (1—Fig. M11-38). Remove trim tab (2) and stud

nut from under trim tab. Remove stud nut from location (3), two stud nuts (4) from each side and stud nut (5) if so equipped, then withdraw the lower unit gearcase assembly.

NOTE: Use caution to prevent loss of spring (68—Fig. M11-40) or plunger (67).

Remove the housing plugs and drain the housing, then secure the gearcase in a vise between two blocks of soft

wood, with propeller up. Wedge a piece of wood between propeller and anti-ventilation plate, remove the propeller nut, then remove the propeller.

Disassemble the gearcase by removing the gearcase housing cover nut (61—Fig. M11-40). Clamp the outer end of propeller shaft in a soft jawed vise and remove the gearcase by tapping with a rubber mallet. Be careful not to lose key (59) or shims (47) on early models. Forward gear (40) will remain in housing. Withdraw the propeller shaft from bearing carrier (56) and reverse gear (46).

Clamp the bearing carrier (56) in a soft jawed vise and remove reverse gear (46) and bearing (49) with an internal expanding puller and slide hammer. Remove and discard the propeller shaft rear seal or seals (58).

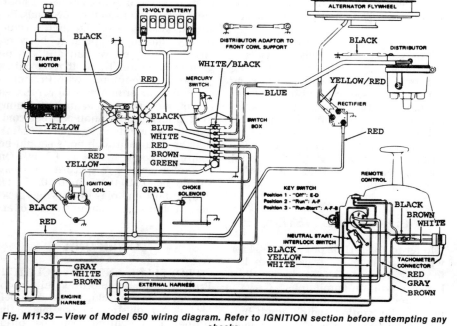

Fig. M11-33—View of Model 650 wiring diagram. Refer to IGNITION section before attempting any checks.

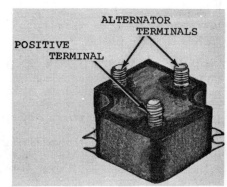

Fig. M11-35—Rectifier must be connected as shown or damage to the electrical system will result.

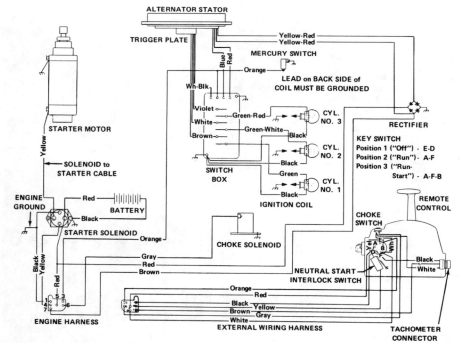

Fig. M11-34—Wiring schematic for early models not equipped with ignition distributor. Later models are similar.

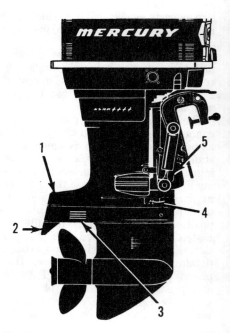

Fig. M11-38 — To remove the lower unit gearcase assembly, remove the attaching screws and stud nuts from positions indicated.

To remove dog clutch (43) from propeller shaft, remove retaining ring (44). Insert cam follower (8) in hole in shaft and apply only enough pressure on end of cam follower to remove the spring pressure, then push out pin (42) with a small punch. The pin passes through drilled holes in dog clutch and operates in slotted holes in propeller shaft.

To disassemble the drive shaft and associated parts, reposition gearcase in vise with drive shaft projecting upward. Remove rubber slinger (11), water pump body (16), impeller (19) and impeller drive pin (20). Remove the flushing screw and withdraw the remainder of the water pump parts. Clamp upper end of drive shaft in a soft jawed vise, remove pinion retaining nut (37); then tap gearcase off drive shaft and bearing. Note the position and thickness of shims (30) on drive shaft upper bearing. Mesh position of pinion is controlled by shims (30) placed underneath the bearing.

After drive shaft has been removed, the forward gear (40) and bearing cone can be withdrawn. Use an internal expanding type puller to withdraw bearing cup if removal is required. Remove and save the shim pack (38).

Shift shaft (5) and cam (7) can be removed after removing forward gear and

unscrewing bushing (3) from gearcase housing.

If gear wear was abnormal or if any parts that affect gear alignment were renewed, check and adjust gear mesh as follows: Install forward gear (40) and bearing (39) using shims (38) that were originally installed. Position shims (30) that were originally installed at bottom of bearing bore. Install bearing assembly (32) in housing bore against shims (30). Position the drive pinion (35) in housing and insert drive shaft (33), with bearing assembly (32) installed, into housing, bearing (34) and gear (35). Install retaining nut (37). Coat gears (35 and 40) with bearing blue and check mesh position. Due to the spiral cut gears, it will be necessary to press down on end of drive shaft while checking position. If gears do not mesh in center of teeth, add or remove shims (30) under bearing as necessary. After setting mesh position of gears, check backlash between teeth of gears (35 and 40). Backlash should be within limits of 0.003-0.005 inch (0.076-0.127 mm). To increase clearance (backlash), remove part of shim stack (38) behind bearing cup. If gears are too loose, add shims. After changing thickness of shims (38), gears should be recoated with bearing

blue and mesh position should be rechecked. Install bearing (49), thrust washer (48) and reverse gear (46) in bearing carrier (56). Then, install bearing carrier and gear assembly using shims (47), on early models that were originally installed and check backlash between gears (35 and 46). If backlash is not within limits of 0.003-0.005 inch ((0.076-0.127 mm), add or remove shims (47) as required. Adding shims (47) increases backlash (clearance).

When reassembling, long splines on shift rod (5) should be toward top. Shift cam (7) is installed with notches up and toward rear. Assemble shifting parts (9, 8S, 43, 42 and 44) into propeller shaft (45). Pin (42) should be through hole in slide (8S). Position follower (8) in end of propeller shaft and insert shaft into bearing (41) and forward gear. Install the reverse gear and bearing carrier assembly using new seals (55 and 58). Lip of seal (58) should face propeller (out) on single seal models. On two seal models, install inner seal with lip toward reverse gear and outer seal with lip toward propeller.

Upper oil seal (26) should be installed with lips facing up (toward engine) and lower oil seal (27) should be pressed into water pump base with lips facing down toward propeller shaft. Install remainder of water pump assembly and tighten the screws or nuts to the following recommended torque. Torque 1/4-28 nuts to 30 in.-lbs (3.4 N·m). Torque 5/16-24 nuts to 40 in.-lbs. (4.5 N·m).

On early models, the reverse locking cam (2C) must be installed on shaft splines so the two tabs are aligned with the left front stud when in forward gear (full clockwise) position. Refer to Fig. M11-42. On later models, place shift shaft (5 – Fig. M11-40) in neutral position. Install nylon washer with grooved side down and position reverse lock cam (2L – Fig. M11-43) with high point (H) of cam positioned as shown in Fig. M11-43.

Later models are equipped with two seals which fit over upper drive shaft

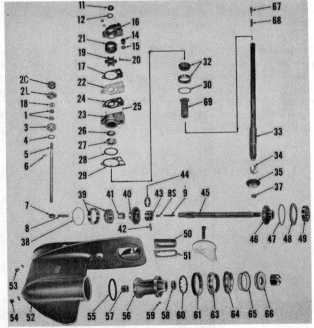

Fig. M11-40 – Exploded view of lower unit gearcase assembly used. Two seals (58) are used on later models. Shim (47) is not used on later models. On later models, a nylon washer replaces spacer (2L). One oil seal (1) is used on later models.

1. Oil seals	18. Rubber washer
2C. Reverse locking cam	19. Impeller
2L. Lower spacer	20. Key
3. Bushing	21. Insert
4. "O" ring	22. Plate
5. Shift shaft	23. Pump base
6. Snap ring	24. Gasket
7. Shift cam	25. Dowel
8. Cam follower	26. Oil seal
8S. Slide	27. Spring loaded oil seal
9. Spring	28. "O" ring
11. Rubber ring (slinger)	29. Gasket
12. Oil seal	30. Shims
14. Seal	32. Taper roller bearing
15. Nylon washer	33. Drive shaft
16. Water pump body	34. Roller bearing
17. Gasket	35. Drive pinion
	37. Nut
	38. Shim
	39. Tapered roller bearing
	40. Forward gear
	41. Roller bearing
	42. Cross pin
	43. Dog clutch
	44. Retaining rings
	45. Propeller shaft
	46. Reverse gear
	47. Shim
	48. Thrust washer
	49. Ball bearing
	50. Exhaust tube seal
	51. Support plate
	52. Gear housing
	53. Vent screw
	54. Filler screw
	55. "O" ring
	56. Bearing carrier
	57. Roller bearing
	58. Oil seals
	59. Key
	60. Tab washer
	61. Nut
	63. Thrust hub
	64. Cupped thrust washer
	65. Cupped thrust washer
	66. Thrust hub
	67. Plunger
	68. Spring

Fig. M11-42 – On early models, the reverse lock cam must be installed on splines as shown when in FORWARD gear position.

splines. Install splined seal on drive shaft splines with splined seal end toward top of drive shaft, then install re-

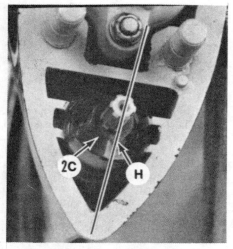

Fig. M11-43—On later models, the reverse lock cam (2C) must be installed on shift shaft splines with high point (H) of cam positioned as shown when in neutral position.

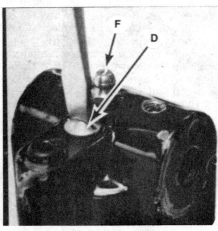

Fig. M11-50—View showing location of down circuit bleed screw (D) and grease fitting (F).

Fig. M11-51—View showing location of up circuit bleed screw (U) and bleed port (P).

maining seal with small end towards top of drive shaft.

Before attaching gearcase housing to the driveshaft housing, make certain that shift cam (7 – Fig. M11-40) and the shift lever (on motor) are in forward gear position on models with reverse locking cam shown in Fig. M11-42 and neutral position on models with reverse locking cam shown in Fig. M11-43. Complete assembly by reversing disassembly procedure. Make certain that spring (68 – Fig. M11-40) and plunger (67) are positioned before attaching gearcase to drive shaft housing.

POWER TILT/TRIM

Non-Integral Type

FLUID. Recommended fluid is SAE 10W-30 or 10W-40 automotive oil. With outboard in full up position, oil level should reach bottom of fill plug hole. Do not overfill.

BLEEDING. To bleed air from hydraulic system on early non-integral system, position outboard at full tilt and engage tilt lock lever. Without disconnecting hoses, remove hydraulic trim cylinders. Be sure fluid reservoir is full and remains so during bleeding operation. Remove down circuit bleed screw (D—Fig. M11-50) and "O" ring. Press "IN" control button for a few seconds, release button and wait approximately one minute. Repeat until expelled oil is air-free. Install "O" ring and bleed screw (D) and repeat procedure on opposite cylinder. Place cylinder in a horizontal position so bleed port (P—Fig. M11-51) is facing up and remove up circuit bleed screw (U). Press "UP" and

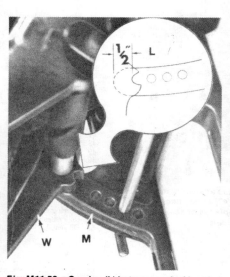

Fig. M11-52—Overlap (L) between swivel bracket flange (W) and clamp bracket flange (M) should be ½ inch (12.7 mm).

"UP/OUT" control buttons for a few seconds, release buttons, wait approximately one minute, then repeat procedure until expelled oil is air-free. Install "O" ring and bleed screw (U) and repeat procedure on opposite cylinder.

Late non-integral hydraulic system is essentially self-bleeding. Make sure reservoir is full of oil and open reservoir vent screw (adjacent to fill plug) two turns. Operate system through several full-out and full-in cycles to purge air from system. Recheck reservoir and refill as necessary.

ADJUST TRIM LIMIT SWITCH. Operate trim control so outboard is in full down position. Press "UP/OUT" or "UP" control button and hold it until pump motor stops. Outboard should tilt up and stop so there is ½ inch (12.7 mm) overlap (L—Fig. M11-52) between swivel bracket flange (W) and clamp bracket flange (M). Pull up on lower unit to remove slack when checking overlap (L). Note that if cylinder rods enter cylinders more than an additional ⅛ inch (3.17 mm), that hydraulic system should be bled of air as outlined in BLEEDING section. If overlap (L) is incorrect, loosen retainer screw (R – Fig. M11-53) then turn adjusting nut (N) counterclockwise to increase overlap or clockwise to decrease overlap. Retighten retainer screw (R) and recheck adjustment.

PRESSURE TEST. To check hydraulic system pressure, disconnect four hoses attached to control valve as shown in Fig. M11-54; small hoses are for up

Fig. M11-53—Loosen retainer screw (R) and turn trim limit adjusting nut (N) to adjust trim limit switch.

circuit while large hoses are for down circuit. Connect a pressure gage to one up circuit port (small) of control valve and another pressure gage to one down circuit port (large). Screw plugs into remaining ports. Check fluid reservoir and fill if necessary. Operate trim control in up direction and note pressure gage reading. Minimum pressure should be 3500 psi (24.1 MPa) on new pumps with a red sleeve on wires or 3200-3500 psi (22.0-24.1 MPa) minimum on used pumps with red sleeve on wires. Minimum pressure on all other new pumps is 3000 psi (20.7 MPa) while minimum pressure on all other used pumps is 2700-3000 psi (18.6-20.7 MPa). Release trim control button. Pressure will drop slightly after stabilizing but should not drop faster than 100 psi (690 kPa) every 15 seconds. Operate trim control in down direction and note pressure gage reading. Minimum pressure is 500-1000 psi (3.4-6.9 MPa). Release trim control button. Pressure will drop slightly after stabilizing but should not drop faster than 100 psi (690 kPa) every 15 seconds. If pressure is normal, inspect trim cylinders and hoses for leakage. If pressure is abnormal, in-

stall a good control valve and recheck pressure. If pressure remains abnormal, install a new pump body.

Integral Type

FLUID AND BLEEDING. Recommended fluid is Quicksilver Power Trim & Steering Fluid or a suitable Type F, FA or Dextron II automatic transmission fluid.

NOTE: Hydraulic system is under pressure. Fill plug (Fig. M11-56) must not be removed unless outboard is in full up position and tilt lock lever is engaged. Be sure to securely tighten fill plug prior to lowering outboard motor.

To check fluid level, tilt motor to full up position, engage tilt lock lever and

slowly remove fill plug (Fig. M11-56). Fluid should be visible in fill tube. Fill as necessary and securely tighten fill plug.

To determine if air is present in hydraulic system, trim motor out until both trim rods are slightly extended. Apply downward pressure on lower unit. If trim rods retract into cylinders more than $1/8$ inch (3.2 mm), air is present and bleeding is required.

The hydraulic circuit is self-bleeding as the tilt/trim system is operated through several cycles. After servicing system, be sure to check reservoir level after filling and operating system.

Trim limit adjustment is not required. Port trim rod and piston assembly (15—Fig. M11-57) is equipped with a check valve designed to open at a specific pressure, limiting trim range to 20 de-

Fig. M11-54—View of control valve showing location of up circuit hoses (U) and down circuit hoses (D).

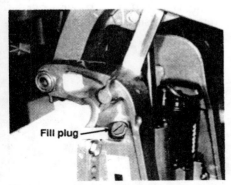

Fig. M11-56—View showing location of fill plug on integral type tilt/trim system.

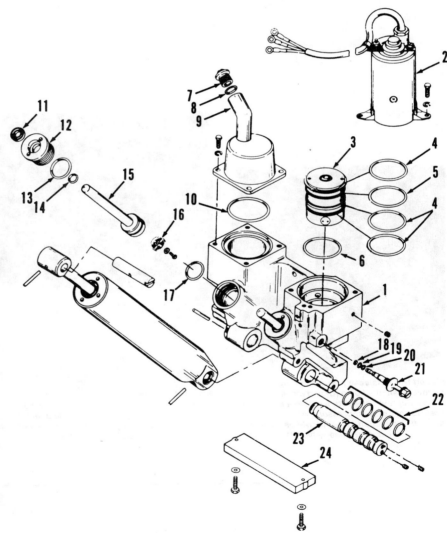

Fig. M11-57—Exploded view of integral type power tilt/trim system.

1. Manifold	8. "O" ring	14. "O" ring	20. "O" ring
2. Motor	9. Reservoir cover	15. Trim piston & rod	21. Manual release
3. Pump assy	10. Seal ring	16. Strainer	valve
4. "O" rings	11. Seal	17. "O" ring	22. "O" ring
5. "O" ring	12. Cap	18. "O" ring	23. Shaft
6. "O" ring	13. "O" ring	19. "O" ring	24. Anode plate
7. Fill plug			

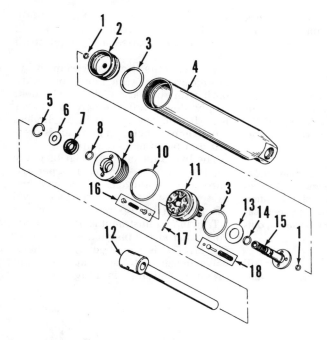

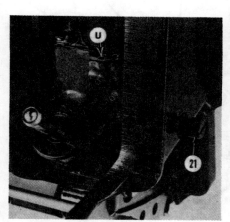

Fig. M11-58—Exploded view of tilt cylinder assembly.

1. "O" ring
2. Cup
3. "O" ring
4. Cylinder
5. Circlip
6. Washer
7. Scraper
8. "O" ring
9. Cap
10. "O" ring
11. Piston
12. Rod
13. Washer
14. "O" ring
15. Rod end
16. Check valve assy.
17. Pin
18. Check valve assy.

grees when engine speed exceeds 2,000 rpm. If engine speed falls below 2,000 rpm, trim angle may exceed 20 degrees. However, once engine speed exceeds 2,000 rpm, propeller thrust will increase pressure in trim cylinders, causing check valve in port side trim rod to unseat, bypassing hydraulic fluid to the reservoir and lowering trim angle to 20 degrees maximum. Except for cleaning valve and strainer (16), check valve in port trim rod is not serviceable and should not be removed. If check valve malfunction is evident, renew port trim rod.

HYDRAULIC TESTING. The system can be checked by connecting a 5000 psi (34.5 MPa) test gage to the UP (U—Fig. M11-59) and DOWN (D—Fig. M11-60) ports. Prior to connecting test gage, place outboard motor in the full up position and engage tilt lock lever. Unscrew reservoir fill plug and rotate manual release valve (21—Fig. M11-57) three to four turns counterclockwise to release pressure on system. Remove UP or DOWN Allen head test port plug and connect test gage with suitable adapter and hose. Install fill plug and rotate manual release valve clockwise until seated. System pressure when testing at UP (U—Fig. M11-59) port should be a minimum of 1300 psi (8.9 MPa). System pressure when testing at DOWN (D—Fig. M11-60) port should be a minimum of 500 psi (3.5 MPa). Release pressure on system as previously outlined prior to removing test gage. Reinstall Allen head plug.

OVERHAUL. Refer to Fig. M11-57 for exploded view of manifold and trim cylinder components, and Fig. M11-58 for exploded view if tilt cylinder components. Special socket 91-44487A1 and a spanner wrench is required to service trim and tilt cylinders. Keep all components clean and away from contamination. Keep components separated and label if necessary for correct reassembly. Lubricate all "O" rings or seal lips with Quicksilver Power Trim & Steering Fluid, Dexron II, Type F or Type FA automatic transmission fluid during reassembly.

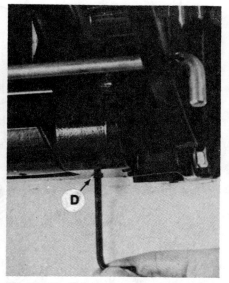

Fig. M11-59—Release pressure on system, then remove Allen head plug (U) and install a 5000 psi (34.5 MPa) test gage with a suitable adapter and hose to test system pressure when operated in the "UP" direction. View identifies location of manual release valve (21).

Fig. M11-60—Release pressure on system, then remove Allen head plug (D) and install a 5000 psi (34.5 MPa) test gage with a suitable adapter and hose to test system pressure when operated in the "DOWN" direction.

MERCURY THREE-CYLINDER MODELS
(After Serial Number A719280)

Year Produced	Models
1987-1989	70
1987-1989	80
1987-1989	90

Letters after model number indicate equipment variations.
E—Electric start
L—Long shaft
O—Oil injection
PT—Power tilt/trim

CONDENSED SERVICE DATA

TUNE-UP
Hp/rpm:
  Model 70 ....70/4750-5250
             (52.2 kW)
  Model 80 ....80/4750-5250
             (59.7 kW)
  Model 90 ....90/5000-5500
             (67.1 kW)
Bore ....3.375 in.
             (85.72 mm)
Stroke.................................2.650 in.
             (67.31 mm)
Displacement.......................71.12 cu. in.
             (1165.4 cc)
Compression at Cranking Speed ....*
Firing Order 1-3-2
Ignition Type ....CDI
Spark Plug:
  NGK BUHW-2
  AC. V40FFK
  Champion L78V
Idle Speed (in gear) ....650-700 rpm
Fuel:Oil Ratio.......................See Text
Gearcase Oil Capacity ....22.5 fl. oz.
             (665.3 mL)

*Compression should not vary more than 15 psi (103.5 kPa) between cylinders.

SIZES-CLEARANCES
Piston Rings:
  End Gap. ....*
  Side Clearance ....*
Piston Skirt Clearance ....0.005 in.
             (0.13 mm)
Crankshaft Bearing Type:
  Top Main Bearing ....Caged Roller
  Center Main Bearings ....Loose Roller

Number of Rollers ....32 Each
Bottom Main Bearing ....Ball Bearing
Crankpin ....Caged Roller
Piston Pin Bearing:
  Type ....Loose Roller
  Number of Rollers ....29 Each
*Publication not authorized by manufacturer.

TIGHTENING TORQUES
Connecting Rod ....*
Crankcase Cover ....†
Crankcase End Cap (Lower) ....150 in.-lbs.
             (17 N·m)
Cylinder Block Cover ....165 in.-lbs.
             (18.6 N·m)
Exhaust Cover ....165 in.-lbs.
             (18.6 N·m)
Flywheel Nut ....120 ft.-lbs.
             (162.7 N·m)
Fuel Pump Screws.......................40 in.-lbs.
             (4.5 N·m)
Intake Manifolds ....150 in.-lbs.
             (17 N·m)
Power Head-to-Drive Shaft Housing ....165 in.-lbs.
             (18.6 N·m)
Reed Block ....60 in.-lbs.
             (6.8 N·m)
Spark Plugs............................20 ft.-lbs.
             (27.1 N·m)

*Tighten connecting rod screws to 15 in.-lbs. (1.7 N·m), check rod-to-cap alignment then tighten to 30 ft.-lbs. (40.7 N·m). After tightening to 30 ft.-lbs. (40.7 N·m), tighten screws an additional 90 degrees.
†Tighten large inner crankcase cover screws to 25 ft.-lbs. (33.9 N·m) and small screws to 165 in.-lbs. (18.6 N·m).

LUBRICATION

The power head is lubricated by oil mixed with the fuel. All models are equipped with oil injection. The oil injection pump delivers oil relative to crankshaft speed and throttle position. The recommended fuel is regular leaded, premium low-lead or unleaded gasoline with minimum octane rating of 86. The recommended oil is Quicksilver 2-Cycle Outboard Oil.

During break-in of a new or rebuilt engine (initial 30 gallons [113.6 L] of fuel), use a 50:1 fuel and oil mixture in the fuel tank in combination with the oil injection system to ensure sufficient power head lubrication. After using the first

30 gallons (113.6 L) of fuel, switch to straight gasoline in the fuel tank.

The lower unit gears and bearings are lubricated by oil contained in the gearcase. The recommended gearcase oil is Quicksilver Super Duty Gear Lubricant. Gearcase capacity is 22.5 fl. oz. (665.3 mL). The lower unit gearcase should be drained and refilled after initial 25 hours of operation, then after every 100 hours or seasonally thereafter. Fill gearcase through drain/fill plug hole until oil reaches the first vent plug hole. Refer to Fig. M11-70. Install first vent plug and continue filling until oil reaches second vent plug hole. When oil reaches second vent plug hole, drain approximately one ounce (30 mL) to allow for oil expansion. Make sure vent and fill plugs are securely tightened with new gaskets if necessary.

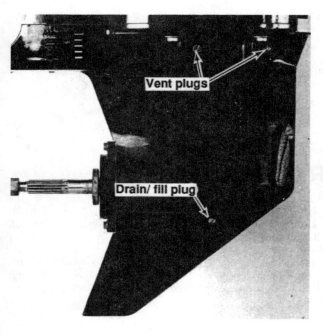

Fig. M11-70—View of drain/fill and vent plugs. Refer to text when refilling gearcase.

FUEL SYSTEM

CARBURETOR. Refer to Fig. M11-71 for exploded view of typical WME carburetor. Three WME-8 carburetors are used on 75 hp models and three WME-10 carburetors are used on 90 hp models. Carburetor model number may be stamped on face of air box mounting flange on early models or is stamped on top of mounting flange on all other models.

Initial setting of slow speed mixture screw (5) is $1\frac{1}{4}$ turns open from a lightly seated position on each carburetor. Final slow speed mixture adjustment should be performed with engine running at normal operating temperature, in forward gear, with the correct propeller installed and boat in the water, or with the correct test wheel installed and lower unit submersed in a suitable test tank.

Air calibration screw (20) is preset and sealed by the manufacturer, and should not require further adjustment. Conventional carburetor cleaning solutions should not affect the sealant used to secure the factory adjustment.

To check float level, remove float bowl (19) and gasket (13), invert carburetor and measure from float bowl mating surface to float as shown in Fig. M11-72. Float level should be $\frac{7}{16}$ inch (11.1 mm) measured as shown. Carefully bend metal tab (T) to adjust.

Standard main jet (16) size for normal operation at elevations up to 2500 feet (762 m) is 0.068 (1.73 mm) on 75 hp models and 0.072 (1.83 mm) on 90 hp models. Standard vent jet (7) size for

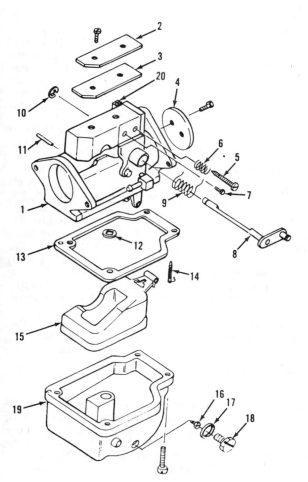

Fig. M11-71—Exploded view of WME carburetor used on all models.

1. Body
2. Cover
3. Gasket
4. Throttle valve
5. Low speed mixture screw
6. Spring
7. Vent jet (back drag jet)
8. Throttle shaft
9. Spring
10. "E" ring
11. Pin
12. Gasket
13. Gasket
14. Inlet needle
15. Float
16. Main jet
17. Gasket
18. Plug
19. Float bowl
20. Air calibration screw

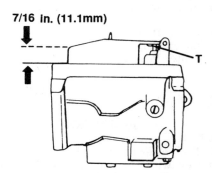

7/16 in. (11.1mm)

Fig. M11-72—Check float level as shown. Bend metal tab (T) to adjust.

normal operation at elevations up to 2500 feet (762 m) is 0.094 on all models. Main jet (16) size should be reduced from standard size by 0.002 inch (0.05 mm) for operation at elevations of 2500-5000 feet (762-1524 m), 0.004 inch (0.10 mm) at elevations of 5000-7500 feet (1524-2286 m) and 0.006 inch (0.15 mm) at elevations of 7500 feet (2286 m) and up.

All models are equipped with an electrically operated enrichment valve to provide additional fuel to aid cold starting. Enrichment valve is activated by pushing in on ignition key or by choke button if so equipped. Fuel is gravity fed to the enrichment valve from the float bowl of the top carburetor and is supplied to the power head through fittings in the intake manifold at each carburetor. Enrichment valve can be operated manually by depressing button located on the bottom of the valve.

If enrichment system malfunction is noted, make sure battery voltage is present at valve (yellow/black wire) when key (or choke button) is depressed and that sufficient fuel is being delivered to top fitting of valve.

FUEL PUMP. The diaphragm type fuel pump is activated by crankcase pulsations. Test pump by installing a clear fuel hose between pump and carburetors. Start engine and check for air bubbles in fuel line and fuel output.

Remove fuel pump from power head by unscrewing two Phillips head screws. Disassemble pump by unscrewing two hex head screws. Inspect all components for wear or damage and renew as necessary. Make sure check valve (17—Fig. M11-74) is functioning properly. When reassembling pump, lubricate check valve retainers (7) with engine oil or soapy water to ease installation. Trim end of retainer (7) at ridge to prevent retainer from contacting pump diaphragm.

NOTE: Fuel pump components have a "V" tab on one side for directional reference during assembly. Be CERTAIN "V" tabs on all components are aligned.

The manufacturer recommends assembling fuel pump using ¼-inch bolts or dowels as guides to ensure that all components are properly aligned. Be especially careful with gasket (12) and diaphragm (11). The two large holes in diaphragm (11) are provided for oil from injection pump to enter the gasoline flow. Failure to properly align gasket (12) and diaphragm (11) may result in power head damage.

REED VALVES. Reed valve assemblies are located between crankcase cover and intake manifolds. Reed valves may be removed for inspection after removing carburetors and intake manifolds.

Do not disassemble reed valve assembly unless necessary. Screw (4—Fig. M11-75) is installed at the factory using Loctite. Reed petals (2) should be flat and smooth along entire seating surface. Renew reed petals if cracked, chipped or damaged, or if petals stand open in excess of 0.020 inch (0.51 mm). Never attempt to bend or straighten a damaged reed petal.

Make sure reed petals are properly positioned over pins (6) when assembling reed valves. Renew locking tab washer (5) and tighten screw (4) to 60 in.-lbs. (6.8 N·m). It may be necessary to continue tightening screw (4) to align locking tab with flat area of screw, but, do not exceed 100 in.-lbs. (11.3 N·m). Be sure to bend locking tab to secure screw (4).

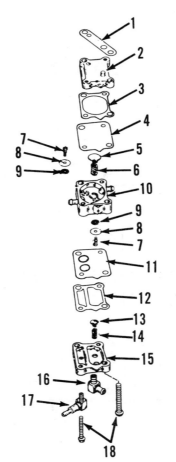

Fig. M11-74—Exploded view of fuel pump assembly.

1. Gasket	10. Pump body
2. Pump base	11. Boost diaphragm
3. Gasket	12. Gasket
4. Diaphragm	13. End cap
5. End cap	14. Spring
6. Spring	15. Chamber plate
7. Retainer	16. Fitting
8. Check valve	17. Check valve
9. Rubber disc	18. Screws

SPEED CONTROL LINKAGE. To verify timing pointer alignment, install a suitable dial indicator into number 1 (top) spark plug hole. Rotate flywheel clockwise until number 1 piston is at TDC. Zero dial indicator and rotate flywheel counterclockwise until dial indicator indicates 0.550 inch (13.97 mm) BTDC, then rotate flywheel clockwise until dial indicator indicates exactly 0.491-inch (12.47 mm) BTDC. With flywheel in this position, timing pointer should be aligned with .491 timing mark on flywheel. If not, loosen pointer screws and move pointer as necessary to align pointer with .491 timing mark. Tighten timing pointer screws to 20 in.-lbs. (2.3 N·m).

Ignition timing may be adjusted at cranking speed if desired. To adjust ignition timing at cranking speed, proceed as follows: Remove all spark plugs to prevent engine from starting and install a suitable spark gap tool to spark plug leads. Disconnect throttle cable from power head and connect a suitable timing light to number 1 (top) spark plug lead. Shift outboard into neutral gear. While holding throttle arm (10—Fig. M11-77) in idle position, crank engine while noting timing marks. Adjust idle timing screw (1) to obtain 2 degrees BTDC timing at cranking speed. Next, hold arm (10) so maximum advance screw (2) is against stop. Crank engine while observing timing marks and adjust screw (2) so maximum spark ad-

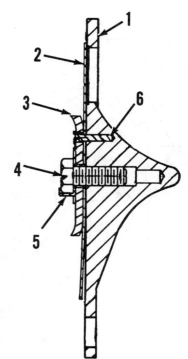

Fig. M11-75—Sectional view of reed valve assembly.

1. Reed block	4. Screw
2. Reed petal	5. Locking tab washer
3. Retainer	6. Pin

vance is 24 degrees BTDC on models prior to serial number B239242 and 28 degrees BTDC on models after serial number B239241.

NOTE: Maximum spark advance with engine running 5000 rpm should be 22 degrees BTDC on models prior to serial number B239242 and 26 degrees BTDC on models after serial number B239241. Due to the electronic spark advance characteristics of the ignition system, timing adjustment at

cranking speed should be set as previously described to obtain the specified spark advance with engine running at 5000 rpm. Timing adjustments performed at cranking speed should be verified, and readjusted if necessary, with engine running at 5000 rpm.

Carburetor throttle valves must be synchronized to open and close at exactly the same time. Proceed as follows to synchronize carburetors: Loosen cam follower screw (3—Fig. M11-77). Loosen

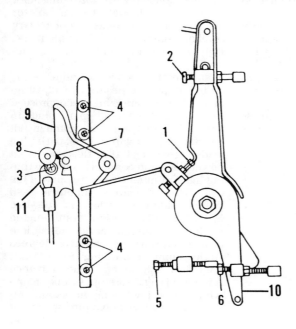

Fig. M11-77—View of speed control linkage.
1. Idle timing screw
2. Maximum spark advance screw
3. Cam follower screw
4. Carburetor synchronizing screws
5. Full throttle stop screw
6. Idle stop screw
7. Throttle cam mark
8. Cam follower roller
9. Throttle cam
10. Throttle arm
11. Cam follower

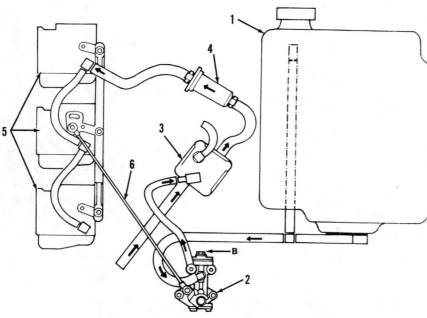

Fig. M11-78—View of oil injection system.
B. Pump bleed screw
1. Oil tank
2. Oil pump
3. Fuel pump
4. Filter
5. Carburetors
6. Oil pump control rod

synchronizing screws (4). Make sure all carburetor throttle valves are fully closed and tighten screws (4). Verify that all throttle valves are fully closed after tightening screws (4) and readjust if necessary. Loosen idle stop screw (6) locknut and hold throttle arm (10) so idle stop screw (6) is against the stop. Hold cam follower roller (8) against throttle cam (9) and adjust idle stop screw (6) to align throttle cam mark (7) with center of roller (8). While holding throttle arm (10) in the idle position, adjust cam follower (11) to provide a clearance of 0.025-0.050 inch (0.64-1.27 mm) between roller (8) and throttle cam (7), then retighten screw (3). Loosen full throttle stop screw (5) locknut. While holding throttle arm (10) in the full throttle position, adjust full throttle stop screw (5) so carburetor throttle valves are fully open while allowing approximately 0.015 inch (0.38 mm) free play in throttle linkage to prevent throttle valves from bottoming out. Retighten full throttle stop screw locknut. Make sure stamped mark on oil injection pump body aligns with stamped mark on oil pump control lever with throttle arm in the idle position.

NOTE: Some models may have two stamped marks on oil injection pump body. On models so equipped, disregard the mark on the right side (looking straight at pump) and reference mark on left.

If marks do not align, disconnect and adjust length of oil pump control rod so marks align.

OIL INJECTION SYSTEM

BLEEDING OIL PUMP. Make sure carburetors and oil pump are properly synchronized as outlined in SPEED CONTROL LINKAGE section. To bleed air from oil injection system, loosen bleed screw (B—Fig. M11-78) three or four turns and allow oil to flow from bleed hole (with engine NOT running) until air bubbles are no longer present in oil pump inlet hose. Retighten bleed screw (B) to 25 in.-lbs. (2.8 N·m). Start engine and run at idle speed until no air bubbles are noted in pump outlet hose.

CHECKING OIL PUMP OUTPUT. A 50:1 (25:1 if during break-in period) fuel and oil mixture must be used in fuel tank while checking pump output.

Remove oil pump output hose from fuel pump and plug fuel pump fitting. Place disconnected end of oil pump outlet hose into a graduated container. Remove oil pump control rod (6—Fig. M11-78) from pump lever and rotate pump lever to full throttle position (counterclockwise). Connect an accurate tachometer to engine, start engine and allow to run at 700 rpm for 15 minutes. Oil pump output in 15 minutes should be a minimum of 0.63 oz. (18.7 mL). Note that pump output specification is based on test performed at 70° F (21.1° C) room temperature. Actual output may vary depending upon ambient temperature.

IGNITION

An alternator driven capacitor discharge ignition (CDI) system is used. Ignition system consists of the flywheel, stator, trigger assembly, switch box and ignition coils. The stator is mounted below the flywheel and includes two capacitor charging coils. The trigger assembly consists of three trigger coils and is mounted below the flywheel. Ignition timing is advanced and retarded by rotating trigger assembly in relation to the inner flywheel magnets. Diodes, capacitors and SCR's are contained in the switch box. Switch box, trigger assembly and stator must be serviced as unit assemblies. Refer to Fig. M11-79 for wiring diagram.

If engine malfunction is noted, and the ignition system is suspected, make sure the spark plugs and all electrical wiring are in acceptable condition and all electrical connections are clean and tight prior to trouble-shooting CDI system.

To properly test the switch box and ignition coils require the use of Quicksilver Multi-Meter DVA Tester part 91-99750 or a suitable voltmeter capable of measuring a minimum of 400 DC volts used with Quicksilver Direct Voltage Adaptor (DVA) part 91-89045. Follow instructions provided by tester manufacturer when performing tests. If these testers are not available, a process of elimination must be used when testing the ignition system. Stator and trigger assemblies can be effectively tested using a suitable ohmmeter.

NOTE: All tests that involve cranking or running the engine must be performed with lead wires connected. Switch box case MUST be grounded to engine for all tests or switch box may be damaged.

To test ignition system, proceed as follows:

IGNITION COILS PRIMARY TEST. Connect DVA red test lead to ignition coil positive (+) terminal and black test lead to coil negative (−) terminal. Position tester selector switch to DVA/400. Tester should read 150-250 volts at cranking or idle speed (300-1000 rpm) and 180-280 volts at 1000-4000 rpm. If voltage readings are below specified

reading, refer to SWITCH BOX STOP CIRCUIT test. If readings are within specifications, connect a suitable spark tester to ignition coil high tension leads, crank engine and note spark. If weak or no spark is noted, renew ignition coil(s). If normal spark is noted, renew spark plugs. If malfunction is still evident after renewing spark plugs, check ignition timing. If ignition timing is erratic, inspect trigger advance linkage for excessive wear or damage and inner flywheel magnets (shifted position or other damage). If timing is within specifications, problem is not in ignition system.

SWITCH BOX STOP CIRCUIT. Connect DVA black test lead to engine ground and red test lead to black/yellow switch box terminal (orange terminal on early models). Refer to Fig. M11-79. Set DVA selector switch to DVA/400. Voltage reading at cranking and all running speeds should be 200-360 volts. If reading is within specifications, refer to STATOR tests. If reading is above specified voltages, connect a suitable ohmmeter between trigger brown and white/black leads, white and white/black leads and purple and white/black leads. Trigger resistance should be 1100-1400 ohms at all three connections. If not, renew trigger assembly. If trigger resistance is acceptable, renew switch box and repeat SWITCH BOX STOP CIRCUIT test. If SWITCH BOX STOP CIRCUIT test reading is below specified voltage, disconnect ignition switch, stop switch and mercury switch from black/yellow switch box terminal (orange switch box terminal on early models). With stop switch, ignition switch and mercury switch isolated, repeat SWITCH BOX STOP CIRCUIT test. If reading is now within specification, ignition switch, stop switch or mercury switch is defective. If reading remains below specification refer to STATOR test.

STATOR. Connect DVA black lead to engine ground and red lead to blue switch box terminal. Set DVA selector switch to DVA/400. Voltage reading should be 200-300 volts at cranking and idle speeds and 200-330 volts at 1000-4000 rpm. Switch DVA red test lead to red switch box terminal. Leave black test lead connected to engine ground. Voltage reading should be 20-90 volts at cranking or idle speeds and 130-300 volts at 1000-4000 rpm.

NOTE: A shorted or open capacitor inside switch box will result in faulty stator voltage readings during cranking and running tests. Stator resistance should be checked as follows before failing stator.

If either STATOR test is not to specification, proceed as follows: Connect a suitable ohmmeter between blue and red stator leads. Resistance between blue and red stator leads should be 3600-4200 ohms. Next, connect ohmmeter between red stator lead and engine ground, or stator black lead (ground). Resistance should be 90-140 ohms. Renew stator if resistance is not as specified. If stator resistance is as specified, renew switch box and repeat STATOR tests.

IGNITION COILS RESISTANCE TEST. Disconnect wires and high tension lead from coil. Connect a suitable ohmmeter between coil positive (+) and negative (−) terminals. Resistance should be 0.02-0.04 ohm. Connect ohmmeter between coil high tension terminal and negative (−) terminal. Resistance should be 800-1,100 ohms. Renew ignition coil(s) if resistance is not as specified.

NOTE: Ignition coil resistance tests can only detect open or shorted windings. If coil resistance is within specification and still suspected as defective, coil must be tested using DVA meter as previously outlined in IGNITION COIL test. If DVA meter is not available, substitute a known good ignition coil and run engine to test.

COOLING SYSTEM

THERMOSTAT. All models are equipped with a thermostat (4—Fig. M11-81) and pressure relief valve (7) located under cover (1) in cylinder block cover (12). Thermostat should begin to open at 140°-145° F (60°-63° C). Temperature sensor (11) is provided to activate a warning horn should power head overheat. Be sure the correct sensor (11) in used. Identify sensor (11) by the length of sensor lead; the lead on 190° F (87.8° C) sensor is 18.5 inches (470 mm) long and 15.5 inches (394 mm) long on 240° F (115.6° C) sensor.

WATER PUMP. The rubber impeller type water pump is housed in the gearcase housing. The impeller is mounted on and driven by the lower unit drive shaft.

If cooling system malfunction occurs, first check the water inlet for plugging or partial restriction. If necessary, remove the gearcase as outlined in LOWER UNIT section and inspect water pump, water tubes and seals.

Renew cover (5—Fig. M11-82) if thickness at discharge ports is 0.060 inch (1.5 mm) or less, or if grooves in excess of 0.030 inch (0.76 mm) are noted in top of cover (5). Renew plate (9) if grooves are noted in excess of 0.030 inch (0.76 mm).

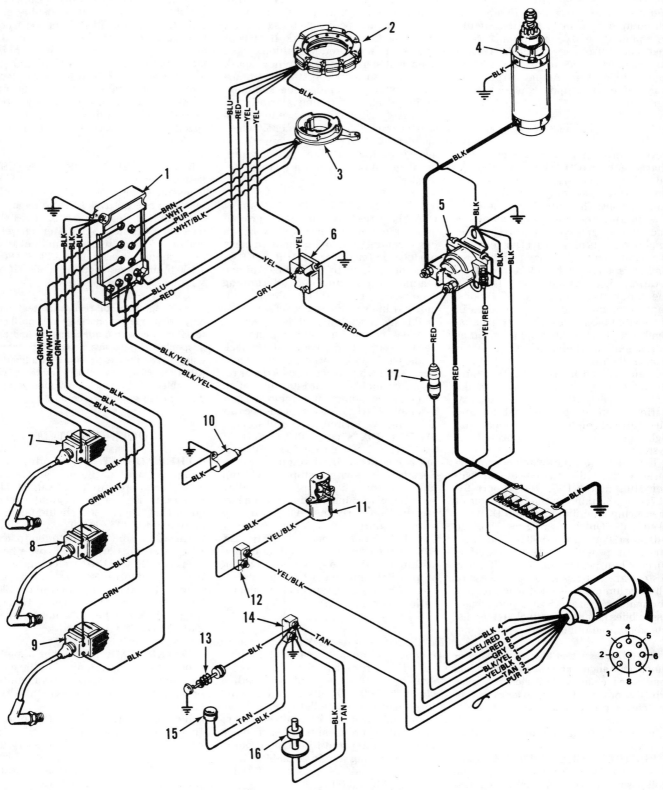

Fig. M11-79—Wiring diagram on models not equipped with low oil warning module.

1. Switch box
2. Stator
3. Trigger assy.
4. Starter motor
5. Starter solenoid
6. Rectifier
7. Ignition coil (no. 1 cyl)

8. Ignition coil (no. 2 cyl)
9. Ignition coil (no. 3 cyl)
10. Mercury switch
11. Enrichment valve
12. Terminal block

13. Temperature switch
14. Terminal block
15. Test button
16. Low oil sensor
17. Fuse (20 ampere)

G. Green
R. Red
T. Tan
W. White
Y. Yellow
Bl. Blue
Br. Brown

Gr. Gray
Pr. Purple
B/Y. Black with yellow tracer
G/R. Green with red tracer

G/W. Green with white tracer
W/B. White with black tracer
Y/B. Yellow with black tracer
Y/R. Yellow with red tracer

NOTE: Sealing bead surrounding center hub of impeller (6) will wear circular grooves in cover (5) and plate (9). Circular grooves

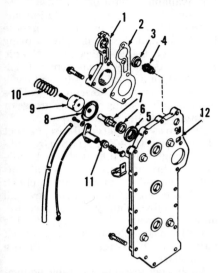

Fig. M11-81—Exploded view of thermostat (4) pressure relief valve (7) and related components.

1. Cover	8. Diaphragm
2. Gasket	9. Cup
3. Seal	10. Spring
4. Thermostat	11. Temperature sensor
5. Grommet	assy.
6. Gasket	12. Cylinder block
7. Pressure relief valve	cover

caused by impeller sealing bead will not affect water pump operation and should be disregarded when inspecting cover (5) and plate (9).

Rotate drive shaft in clockwise direction when installing cover (5) over impeller (6). Coat outer diameter of seals (14 and 15) with Loctite 271 or a suitable locking compound. Install seals into base (13) back-to-back. Apply Loctite 271 or suitable thread locking compound to threads of screws (11 and 2). Tighten screws (11 and 2) to 60 in.-lbs. (6.8 N·m).

POWER HEAD

REMOVE AND DISASSEMBLE. To remove power head, proceed as follows: Remove front cowl bracket and air box cover. Remove air box, disconnect oil lines and remove oil reservoir. Disconnect throttle linkage and remove carburetors as an assembly. Remove intake manifolds and reed valves. Remove flywheel nut and place a suitable protector cap over crankshaft. Remove flywheel using flywheel puller part 91-73687A1 or a suitable equivalent puller.

NOTE: Do not strike puller bolt to dislodge flywheel from crankshaft or crankshaft or main bearing damage may result.

Remove ignition system components. Remove wiring harness and related components as an assembly. Remove shift linkage. Remove eight screws securing power head to drive shaft housing, install a suitable lifting fixture to power head and lift power head off drive shaft housing.

Remove fuel pump, oil injection pump and related hoses. Remove oil pump driven gear and housing. Refer to Fig. M11-81 and remove thermostat cover, thermostat, pressure relief valve and related components. Remove cylinder block cover (12—Fig. M11-84) screws and carefully pry off cover (12). Pry points are provided in cover (12) to prevent damage to mating surfaces. Remove exhaust cover (1) and divider plate (3). Remove lower end cap (8) screws, crankcase cover (5) screws and carefully pry crankcase cover (5) from cylinder block (10). Remove lower end cap (8). Crankshaft, pistons, bearings and connecting rods may now be removed for service as outlined in the appropriate following

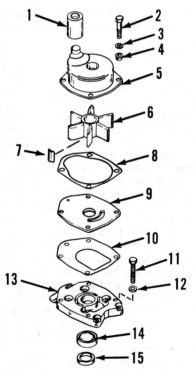

Fig. M11-82—Exploded view of water pump assembly.

1. Water tube seal	
2. Screw	9. Plate
3. Washer	10. Gasket
4. Insulator	11. Screw
5. Cover	12. Washer
6. Impeller	13. Base
7. Key	14. Seal
8. Gasket	15. Seal

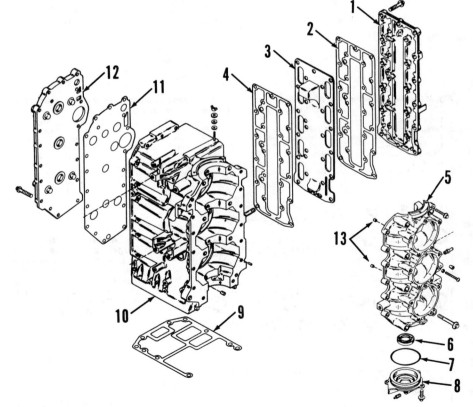

Fig. M11-84—Exploded view of crankcase assembly.

1. Exhaust cover	6. Seal	11. Gasket	
2. Gasket	7. "O" ring	12. Cylinder block	
3. Divider plate	8. Lower end cap	cover	
4. Gasket	9. Gasket	13. Check valves	
5. Crankcase cover	10. Cylinder block		

sections. Refer to ASSEMBLY section for reassembly procedures.

ASSEMBLY. When reassembling the power head, the crankcase must be completely sealed against both vacuum and pressure. All gasket surfaces and machined joints without gaskets should be carefully checked for nicks and burrs which might interfere with a tight seal.

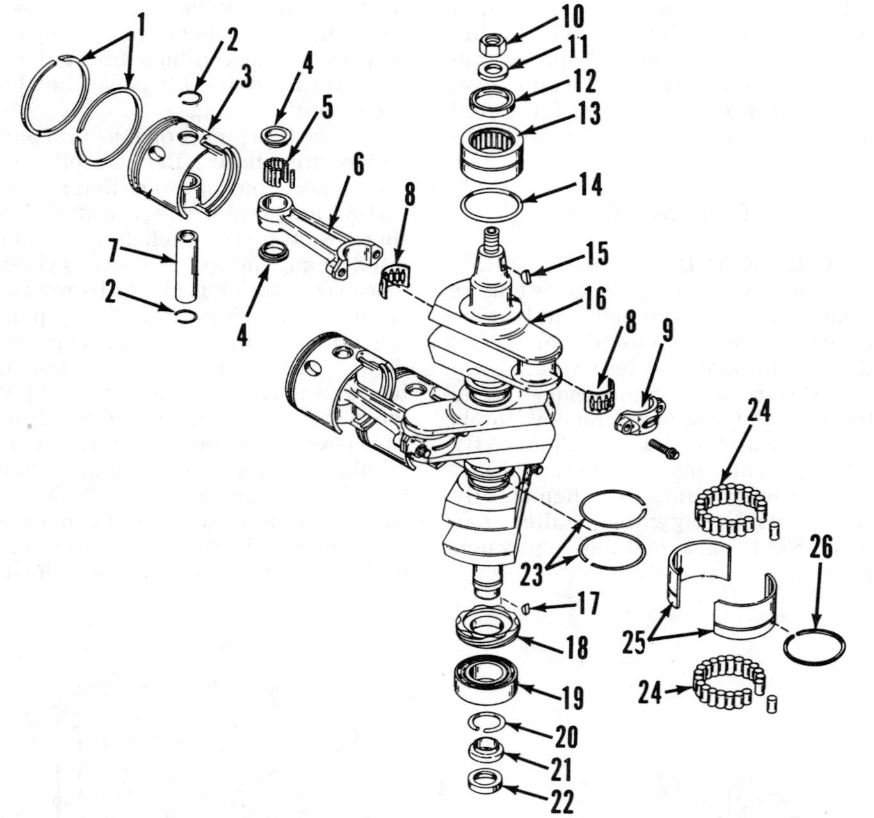

Cylinder block and crankcase cover are matched and align bored assembly and not available separately.

Lubricate all bearing and friction surfaces with engine oil. Loose needle bearings should be held in place during reassembly using Quicksilver Needle Bearing Assembly Grease (part C-92-42649A-1) or a suitable equivalent gasoline soluble grease. Lubricate all seal lips using needle bearing assembly grease or suitable gasoline soluble grease.

Prior to assembling crankcase, inspect check valves (13—Fig. M11-84) by looking through valve. If light is noted while looking through valve, check ball has failed (melted) or is missing. If check ball is present in valve, make sure ball is free to move slightly inside valve. Remove check valves by carefully driving out using a suitable punch. Install check valves with single hole facing crankshaft.

Apply Loctite 271 or a suitable equivalent thread locking compound to outer diameter of all metal cased seals and any fastener used on moving or rotating components.

Apply a continuous bead, $\frac{1}{16}$ inch (1.6 mm) diameter, of Loctite Master Gasket Sealer (part 92-12564-1) to mating surface of crankcase cover (5—Fig. M11-84) to seal crankcase assembly. Run bead to the inside of all screw holes. Make sure bead is continuous but avoid excess application.

Tighten large inner crankcase cover screws, in three steps, in sequence shown in Fig. M11-86 to final tightness of 25 ft.-lbs. (33.9 N·m). After tightening inner cover screws, tighten small outer screws to final tightness of 165 in.-lbs. (18.6 N·m) in sequence shown. While tightening cover screws, check rotation of crankshaft for binding or unusual noise. If binding or noise is noted, repair cause before proceeding. Coat mating surface of lower end cap (8—Fig. M11-84) with Quicksilver Perfect Seal or equivalent. Rotate crankshaft so each piston ring in turn is visible in exhaust or transfer ports, then check by pressing on rings with a blunt tool. Ring should spring back when released. If not, a broken or binding ring is indicated and must be repaired before proceeding. Tighten exhaust and cylinder block cover screws to 165 in.-lbs. (18.6 N·m) in sequence shown in Figs. M11-87 and M11-88 respectively.

Renew gasket (9—Fig. M11-84) when installing power head on drive shaft housing. Lubricate drive shaft splines with a small amount of Quicksilver 2-4-C or equivalent. Apply Loctite 271 or equivalent to threads of power head mounting screws and tighten to 165 in.-lbs. (18.6 N·m). Remainder of assembly and reinstallation is the reverse of

Fig. M11-85—Exploded view of crankshaft assembly. Some models are equipped with a wear sleeve and "O" ring in place of carrier (21) and seal (22).

1. Piston rings	7. Piston pin	14. "O" ring	20. Retaining ring
2. Retaining ring	8. Crankpin bearing	15. Flywheel key	21. Seal carrier
3. Piston	9. Connecting rod cap	16. Crankshaft	22. Seal
4. Locating washers	10. Nut	17. Oil pump drive gear	23. Seal rings
5. Piston pin bearing	11. Washer	key	24. Main bearing rollers
rollers	12. Seal	18. Oil pump drive gear	25. Main bearing race
6. Connecting rod	13. Bearing	19. Bearing	26. Retaining ring

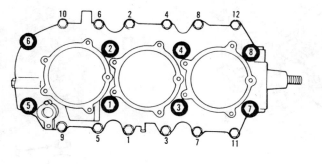

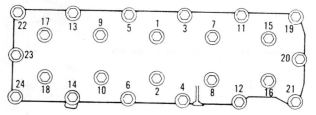

Fig. M11-86—Tighten inner (large) crankcase cover screws first, in sequence shown, then tighten outer (small) screws. Use three steps to obtain final tightness. Refer to text and CONDENSED SERVICE DATA.

Fig. M11-87—Tighten exhaust cover screws in sequence shown to 165 in.-lbs. (18.6 N·m).

removal procedure. Note the following tightening torques: Trigger and stator assemblies, 60 in.-lbs. (6.8 N·m); Electrical component mounting plate, 165 in.-lbs. (18.6 N·m); Starter motor, 165 in.-lbs. (18.6 N·m); Air box screws, 100 in.-lbs. (11.3 N·m).

PISTONS, PINS, RINGS AND CYLINDERS. Prior to detaching connecting rods from crankshaft, make sure that rod, rod cap and pistons are properly marked for correct reassembly to each other, in the correct cylinder and in the correct direction.

Piston skirt-to-cylinder bore clearance should be 0.005 inch (0.13 mm). Measure piston skirt diameter at right angle to piston pin bore 0.50 inch (12.7 mm) up from bottom of skirt. Maximum allowable cylinder bore wear, taper or out-of-round is 0.003 inch (0.08 mm). Pistons and rings are available in 0.015 inch (0.38 mm) and 0.030 inch (0.76 mm) oversize. Note that oversize pistons weigh approximately the same as standard size pistons. All cylinders do not require oversize boring if one cylinder is excessively worn or damaged.

Piston rings are semikeystone shaped and are pinned to prevent rotation. Install rings with "T" mark facing up.

Always renew piston pin retaining rings (2—Fig. M11-85) if removed. Piston pin rides in 29 loose needle bearing rollers (5). The manufacturer recommends renewing piston pin bearing rollers (5) when reassembling power head. Piston pin is a snug fit in piston and can be tapped out using a suitable driver and soft-face mallet. When reassembling, hold needle bearing rollers in place with a suitable gasoline soluble grease. Install locating washers (4) with large diameter facing away from pin (7).

Cylinder block is designed to allow piston installation without the use of a piston ring compressor. Install pistons into cylinders with "UP" mark on piston crown facing flywheel end of power head.

CONNECTING RODS, BEARINGS AND CRANKSHAFT. Refer to Fig. M11-85 for exploded view of crankshaft, connecting rods and bearings. Be sure connecting rods (6), rod caps (9), pistons (3) and all wearing components are marked

for reference during reassembly. Top main bearing (13) is a caged needle bearing and bottom main bearing (19) is a ball bearing. Each center main bearing consist of 32 loose bearing rollers (24) and race (25).

Do not remove bearing (19) from crankshaft unless bearing (19) or oil pump drive gear (18) require renewal. Note location of key (17).

Some models are equipped with a wear sleeve and "O" ring in place of carrier (21) and seal (22). Carefully heat wear sleeve to remove on models so equipped. To install wear sleeve, apply Loctite 271 or equivalent to inner diameter of sleeve and drive sleeve squarely on crankshaft until bottomed using a suitable wooden block and hammer.

Inspect crankshaft splines for excessive wear and crankshaft for straightness using a dial indicator and "V" blocks. Inspect crankshaft bearing surfaces and renew crankshaft if scored, out-of-round or excessively worn. Renew connecting rod(s) if big end bearing surface is rough, scored, excessively worn or shows evidence of overheating. Use crocus cloth ONLY to clean the connecting rod big end bearing surface.

Install main bearings with oil holes in outer race facing toward bottom of engine. Install crankshaft seal rings (23) with end gaps 180 degrees apart. Use only Quicksilver Needle Bearing Assembly Grease or a suitable gasoline soluble grease to hold loose bearing rollers in place. Always renew rod cap bolts when reassembling power head. Threads are cut into both the connecting rod and rod cap. To properly align cap and rod during reassembly, proceed as follows: Place rod cap (9) on bearing half (8) and hold tightly against connecting rod while threading in bolt. Finger tighten rod bolts then check rod and cap alignment. Cap and rod must be perfectly aligned. After all rod caps and bolts are installed and aligned, tighten bolts to 15 in.-lbs. (1.7 N·m) and recheck alignment. Then tighten bolts to 30 ft.-lbs. (40.7 N·m) and recheck alignment. If rods and caps are perfectly aligned, tighten rod bolts an additional 90 degrees to complete procedure. Reassemble crankcase assembly as previously outlined.

ELECTRICAL SYSTEM

CHARGING SYSTEM. Refer to Fig. M11-79 for wiring diagram. To test alternator output, disconnect red lead from rectifier (6) and connect a suitable ammeter between rectifier and red lead. Note that rectifier must be operating properly for accurate test results. Ammeter should indicate 7-9 amperes at 3000 rpm. If not, disconnect stator yellow leads from rectifier and connect a suitable ohmmeter between yellow leads. Stator resistance should be 0.05-1.1 ohms. No continuity should be present between yellow leads and engine ground (or stator black lead if stator is removed from power head). Renew stator if output or resistance is not as specified.

To test rectifier (6), connect ohmmeter alternately between each rectifier terminal and between each terminal and ground. Refer to Fig. M11-89. Reverse ohmmeter leads after each connection. Ohmmeter should indicate continuity with leads connected one direction but not the other. If ohmmeter shows continuity both directions or no continuity both directions, renew rectifier.

STARTER MOTOR. If starter motor malfunction occurs, perform a visual inspection for corroded or loose connections. Check fuse (17—Fig. M11-79) and make sure battery is fully charged.

Renew brushes if worn to less than $1/4$ inch (6.4 mm). Undercut insulation between commutator bars to $1/32$ inch (0.8 mm). Armature should be tested using an armature growler.

LOWER UNIT

PROPELLER. Protection for lower unit is provided by a splined rubber hub built into propeller. Various propellers are available and should be selected to allow motor to operate within the recommended speed range 4750-5250 rpm

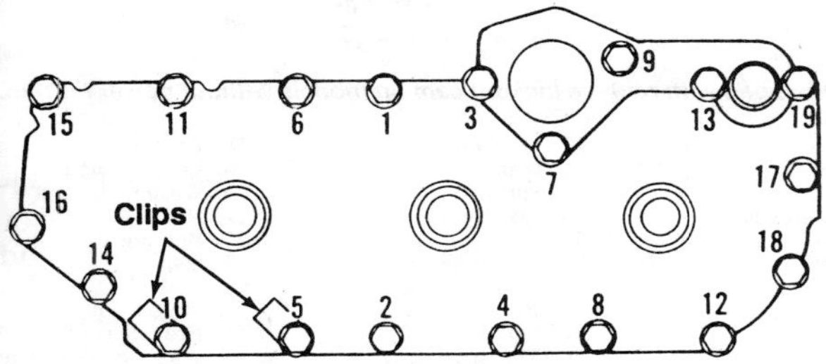

Fig. M11-88—Tighten cylinder block cover screws to 165 in.-lbs. (18.6 N·m) in sequence shown. Note location of clips.

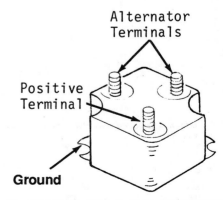

Fig. M11-89—Rectifier must be connected as shown. Refer to text for rectifier test procedure.

on 75 hp models and 5000-5500 rpm on 90 hp models at full throttle. The manufacturer recommends propping outboard motor to the high end of full throttle rpm range.

R&R AND OVERHAUL. To remove lower unit, first remove and ground spark plug leads to prevent accidental starting. Shift engine into forward gear and tilt unit to full up position. Remove two screws and washers on each side of lower unit and one nut and washer under antiventilation plate. Remove gearcase and secure in a suitable holding fixture.

Note location and size of all shims and thrust washers during disassembly for reference during reassembly.

Remove propeller (66—Fig. M11-90), thrust hub (65), vent screws (35 and 36) and drain plug (37). Allow gearcase oil to drain while inspecting for water or other contamination.

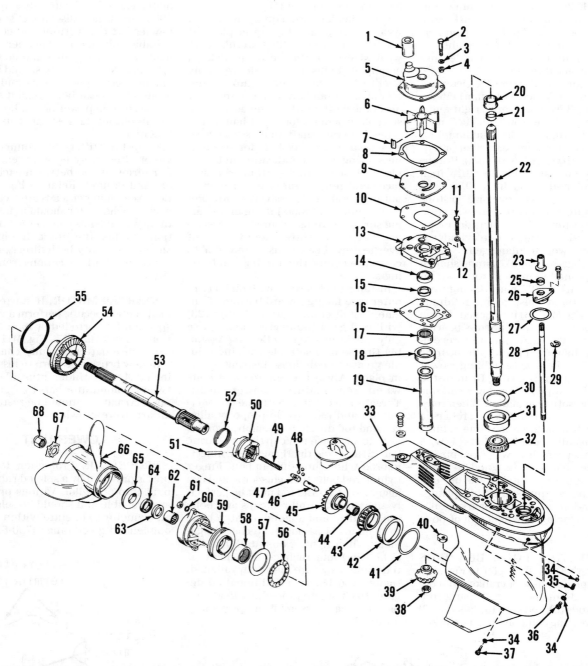

Fig. M11-90—Exploded view of lower unit gearcase assembly. Shift shaft coupler (23) is equipped with reverse lockout cam on models without power tilt/trim.

1. Water tube seal
2. Screw
3. Washer
4. Insulator
5. Cover
6. Impeller
7. Key
8. Gasket
9. Plate
10. Gasket
11. Screw
12. Washer
13. Base
14. Seal
15. Seal
16. Gasket
17. Needle bearing
18. Carrier
19. Sleeve
20. Wear sleeve
21. Seal ring
22. Drive shaft
23. Coupler
25. Seal
26. Retainer
27. "O" ring
28. Shift shaft
29. "E" ring
30. Shim
31. Bearing race
32. Bearing
33. Gearcase
34. Gasket
35. Plug
36. Plug
37. Plug
38. Nut
39. Pinion gear
40. Shift cam
41. Shim
42. Bearing race
43. Bearing
44. Bearing
45. Forward gear
46. Cam follower
47. Slide pin
48. Balls
49. Spring
50. Dog clutch
51. Pin
52. Retaining spring
53. Propeller shaft
54. Reverse gear
55. "O" ring
56. Thrust bearing
57. Thrust washer
58. Bearing
59. Bearing carrier
60. Washer
61. Nut
62. Bearing
63. Seal
64. Seal
65. Thrust hub
66. Propeller
67. Locking tab washer
68. Nut

Remove water pump assembly and screws (11). Using screwdrivers or similar tools placed on each end of water pump base (13), carefully pry base (13) from gearcase. Remove and discard seals (14 and 15). Remove nuts (61 [screws on some models]). Using a suitable puller, break loose carrier-to-gearcase seal then remove bearing carrier (59) and propeller shaft components (46-64) as a unit. Do not lose balls (48) or cam follower (46). Remove and discard seals (63 and 64) and "O" ring (55) from carrier (59). Do not remove bearings (58 and 62) unless renewal is required. Remove retainer spring (52) from dog clutch (50). To remove pin (51), depress cam follower (46) by pushing propeller shaft against a solid object, then push out pin (51) using a small punch. Remove follower (46), sliding pin (47), balls (48), spring (49) and slide dog clutch (50) off propeller shaft. Place Drive Shaft Holding Tool 91-56755 or similar splined adapter on drive shaft splines or clamp drive shaft into a soft jawed vise then remove pinion nut (38). Remove drive shaft assembly from gearcase. After drive shaft is removed, forward gear (45) and bearing (43) can be removed. Use a suitable expanding jaw type puller to remove race (42), if necessary. Note location and thickness of shims (41). Remove upper drive shaft bearing (17) and bearing carrier (18) if necessary, using expanding jaw type puller. Note that bearing (17) and carrier (18) must be removed before sleeve (19) removal is possible. If necessary, remove sleeve (19) using a suitable puller. Quicksilver Bearing Race Tool 91-14308A1 is required to drive lower drive shaft bearing race (31) from gearcase. Bearing race (31) can be driven from gearcase with bearing (17), carrier (18) and sleeve (19) installed. Note location and thickness of shims (30). Remove coupler (23), shift shaft retainer (26) and shift shaft (28). Reach into gear cavity and remove shift cam (40). Remove and discard seal (25) and "O" ring (27) from retainer (26) to complete disassembly.

Inspect all components for excessive wear or damage. Check straightness of propeller shaft using a dial indicator and "V" blocks and renew shaft if runout exceeds 0.006 inch (0.15 mm). Inspect all bearings for roughness, pits, rust or other damage and renew as necessary. Inspect sealing area of wear sleeve (20) for grooves and renew as necessary. Renew bearings and races as an assembly. Renew gears if teeth are chipped, broken or excessively worn. Renew all seals, "O" rings and gaskets. Lubricate all friction surfaces with clean gear lubricant. Apply Loctite 271 or equivalent to threads of all screws and outer diameter of all metal cased seals. Lubricate

"O" ring (55) and outer diameter of carrier (50) with Quicksilver Special Lubricant 101 (part 92-13872A-1). Lubricate other seals and "O" rings with Quicksilver 2-4-C Marine Lubricant (part 92-90018A12) or Quicksilver Needle Bearing Assembly Grease (part 92-42649A-1).

When reassembling gearcase, place original shim pack (41) into gearcase and install bearing race (42) using a suitable mandrel.

NOTE: If original shims (41) are damaged or lost, install shim pack 0.010 inch (0.25 mm) thick.

Install seal (25) into retainer (26) until flush with top of retainer. Place shift cam (40) into gearcase with numbers facing up and install shift rod making sure splines in shift shaft properly align with cam. Install bearing (62) into carrier (59) with lettered side facing propeller end. Install seal (63) into carrier (59) with lip facing forward and seal (64) with lip facing propeller. Install dog clutch (50) on propeller shaft with grooved end of clutch facing rearward. Install spring (49), slider (47), balls (48) and cam follower (46) into propeller shaft. Depress follower (46) against spring pressure and align holes in dog clutch and propeller shaft using a suitable punch, then insert pin (51).

If installing a new wear sleeve (20) on drive shaft (22), install seal ring (21), coat inner diameter of sleeve (20) with Loctite 271 and press onto shaft (22) until bottomed. Install original shim pack (30) and draw race (31) into gearcase using suitable mandrels and a threaded rod. If original shims (30) are damaged or lost, start with shim pack 0.025 inch (0.64 mm) thick. Install sleeve (19) making sure antirotation tab properly engages gearcase. Install bearing (43), forward gear (45), drive shaft (22), pinion bearing (32), pinion gear (39) and original pinion nut (38).

NOTE: Pinion nut (38) should be renewed and secured with a suitable thread locking compound after gearcase shimming operation has been properly performed.

Drive shaft assembly must be preloaded to properly adjust pinion gear depth and forward gear backlash. Special Bearing Preload Tool 91-14311A1 and Pinion Gear Locating Tool 91-12349A2 are required for shim selection procedure.

To preload drive shaft and bearing assembly, assemble Bearing Preload Tool 91-14311A1 as shown in Fig. M11-91 and tighten set screws (2). With nut (3) fully threaded on bolt (1), measure distance (D) between bottom of bolt head to top of nut, then turn nut (3) to increase distance (D) by one inch (25.4 mm). Rotate drive shaft several turns to ensure lower drive shaft bearing is properly seated. Assemble Pinion Gear Locating Tool 91-12349A2 as shown in Fig. M11-92. Install locating disc marked number "3" making sure access hole is

Fig. M11-91—View of Bearing Preload Tool 91-14311A1 assembled over drive shaft (22). Refer to text for gearcase shim selection procedure.

1. Bolt
2. Set screws
3. Nut
4. Spring
5. Thrust washer
6. Thrust bearing
7. Adapter
22. Drive shaft

Fig. M11-92—Assemble Pinion Gear Locating Tool 91-12349A2 as shown. Make sure sliding collar (4) is positioned so gaging block is located under pinion gear (39) as shown.

1. Arbor
2. Locating disc (number 3)
3. Gaging block
4. Sliding collar
39. Pinion gear

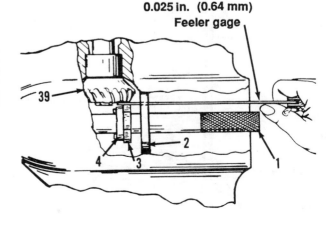

0.025 in. (0.64 mm) Feeler gage

facing up. Position sliding collar (4) so gaging block (3) is directly under pinion gear (39) teeth and flat on gaging block marked "8" is adjacent to pinion gear (39). Clearance between gaging block (3) and pinion gear should be 0.025 inch (0.64 mm) measured with a suitable feeler gage as shown. Vary thickness of shim pack (30—Fig. M11-90) to adjust. Changing thickness of shims (30) by 0.001 inch (0.03 mm) will change pinion gear clearance by 0.001 inch (0.03 mm).

Insert assembled propeller shaft assembly into bearing carrier (59) and install carrier and propeller shaft assembly into gearcase. Position carrier (59) so "TOP" mark is facing up. Outward pressure should be applied to propeller shaft to hold reverse gear (54) tight against thrust bearing (56) and washer (57) to prevent thrust washer and bearing from being dislodged. A tool can be fabricated out of 1¼ to 1½ inch (31.7-38.1 mm) PVC pipe cut off to 6 inches (152.4 mm) long. Place pipe over propeller shaft and secure with washer (67) and nut (68). Tighten nut (68) so reverse gear (54) is pulled securely against

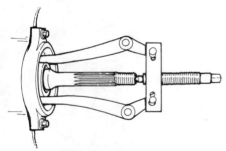

Fig. M11-93—When checking forward gear backlash, preload propeller shaft by installing a suitable puller as shown. Refer to text.

thrust bearing (56) and washer (57). Securely tighten nuts (61) or screws if so equipped.

To check forward gear backlash, proceed as follows: Allow bearing preload tool (Fig. M11-91) to remain installed. Preload propeller shaft by installing a suitable puller as shown in Fig. M11-93. Tighten puller center bolt to 25 in.-lbs. (2.8 N·m), rotate propeller shaft several turns, then retighten puller bolt to 25 in.-lbs. (2.8 N·m). Again, rotate propeller shaft several turns and recheck torque on puller bolt. Refer to Fig. M11-94 and assemble a suitable threaded rod to gearcase using nuts and washers as shown. Affix a suitable dial indicator to threaded rod. Install Backlash Indicator 91-78473 on drive shaft and align dial indicator plunger with the mark "4" on backlash indicator. Check backlash by carefully rotating drive shaft back-and-forth. Note that if any movement is noted at propeller shaft, repeat propeller shaft preloading procedure as previously outlined. Backlash should be 0.012-0.019 inch (0.31-0.48 mm). Vary thickness of shim pack (41—Fig. M11-90) to adjust. Note that changing thickness of shims (41) by 0.001 inch (0.03 mm) will result in approximately 0.00125 inch (0.032 mm) change in backlash.

After shim selection procedure is completed, remove carrier and drive shaft assembly. Remove pinion nut, apply Loctite 271 to a NEW pinion nut, install nut with beveled side facing up and tighten to 70 ft.-lbs. (95 N·m). Reinstall carrier and propeller shaft assembly, apply Loctite 271 to nuts (61—Fig. M11-90) or screws if so equipped, and tighten nuts (61) to 275 in.-lbs. (31.1 N·m) or screws to 150 in.-lbs. (17 N·m). Complete reassembly by reversing disassembly

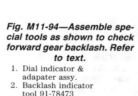

Fig. M11-94—Assemble special tools as shown to check forward gear backlash. Refer to text.

1. Dial indicator & adapater assy.
2. Backlash indicator tool 91-78473
3. Nuts
4. Threaded rod
5. Washers

Bearing Preload Tool 91-14311A1

procedure. Tighten propeller nut to 55 ft.-lbs. (75 N·m).

To reinstall gearcase on drive shaft housing, proceed as follows: Position shift block on power head in the forward gear position. Shift block should extend past forward side of shift rail by ¹⁄₃₂ inch (3.2 mm) if properly positioned. Shift lower unit into forward gear. Lubricate inner diameter of water tube seal (1) with Quicksilver 2-4-C Marine Lubricant. Lightly lubricate drive shaft splines with 2-4-C Marine lubricant. Do not apply grease to top of drive shaft or drive shaft may not fully engage crankshaft.

NOTE: On models not equipped with power tilt/trim, position shift shaft coupler (23) with reverse lock cam facing forward.

Install gearcase in drive shaft housing making sure drive shaft aligns with crankshaft, upper shift shaft aligns with coupler (23) and water tube aligns with water tube seal (1). Apply Loctite 271 to threads of gearcase mounting screws and tighten to 40 ft.-lbs. (54.2 N·m). After installing gearcase, make sure shift linkage operates properly as follows: Shift outboard into forward gear. Propeller shaft should lock into gear when rotated counterclockwise and ratchet when rotated clockwise. When shifted into reverse gear, propeller shaft should be locked into gear when rotated either direction. If shift linkage does not operate as specified, lower unit must be removed and shift linkage malfunction repaired.

POWER TILT/TRIM

FLUID AND BLEEDING. Recommended fluid is Quicksilver Power Trim & Steering Fluid or a suitable Type F, FA or Dextron II automatic transmission fluid.

NOTE: Hydraulic system is under pressure. Fill plug (Fig. M11-95) must not be removed unless outboard is in full up position

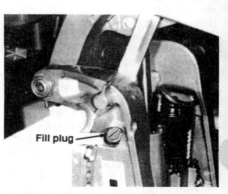

Fill plug

Fig. M11-95—View showing location of fill plug on power tilt/trim system.

and tilt lock lever is engaged. Be sure to securely tighten fill plug prior to lowering outboard motor.

To check fluid level, tilt motor to full up position, engage tilt lock lever and slowly remove fill plug (Fig. M11-95). Fluid should be visible in fill tube. Fill as necessary and securely tighten fill plug.

To determine if air is present in hydraulic system, trim motor out until both trim rods are slightly extended. Apply downward pressure on lower unit. If trim rods retract into cylinders more than $1/8$ inch (3.2 mm), air is present and bleeding is required.

The hydraulic circuit is self-bleeding as the tilt/trim system is operated through several cycles. After servicing system, be sure to check reservoir level after filling and operating system.

Trim limit adjustment is not required. Port trim rod and piston assembly (15—Fig. M11-96) is equipped with a check valve designed to open at a specific pressure, limiting trim range to 20 degrees when engine speed exceeds 2,000 rpm. If engine speed falls below 2,000 rpm, trim angle may exceed 20 degrees; however, once engine speed exceeds 2,000 rpm, propeller thrust will increase pressure in trim cylinders causing check valve in port side trim rod to unseat, bypassing hydraulic fluid to the reservoir and lowering trim angle to 20 degrees maximum. Except for cleaning valve and strainer (16), check valve in port trim rod is not serviceable and should not be removed. If check valve malfunction is evident, renew port trim rod.

HYDRAULIC TESTING. The system can be checked by connecting a 5000 psi (34.5 MPa) test gage to the UP (U—Fig. M11-98) and DOWN (D—Fig. M11-99) ports. Prior to connecting test gage, place outboard motor in the full up position and engage tilt lock lever. Unscrew reservoir fill plug and rotate manual release valve (21—Fig. M11-98) three to four turns counterclockwise to release pressure on system. Remove UP or DOWN Allen head test port plug and connect test gage with suitable adapter and hose. Install fill plug and rotate manual release valve clockwise until seated. System pressure when testing at UP (U) port should be a minimum of 1300 psi (8.9 MPa). System pressure when testing at DOWN (D—Fig. M11-99) port should be a minimum of 500 psi (3.5 MPa). Release pressure on system as previously outlined prior to removing test gage. Reinstall Allen head plug.

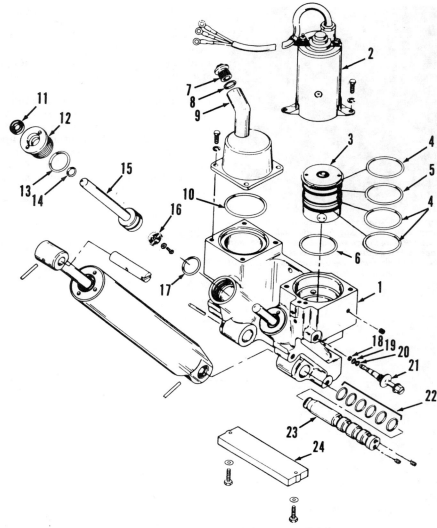

Fig. M11-96—Exploded view of integral type power tilt/trim system.

1. Manifold	6. "O" ring	11. Seal
2. Motor	7. Fill plug	12. Cap
3. Pump assy.	8. "O" ring	13. "O" ring
4. "O" rings	9. Reservoir cover	14. "O" ring
5. "O" ring	10. Seal ring	15. Trim piston & rod
16. Strainer	21. Manual release
17. "O" ring	valve
18. "O" ring	22. "O" ring
19. "O" ring	23. Shaft
20. "O" ring	24. Anode plate

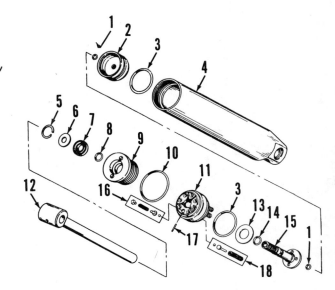

Fig. M11-97—Exploded view of tilt cylinder assembly.

1. "O" ring
2. Cup
3. "O" ring
4. Cylinder
5. Circlip
6. Washer
7. Scraper
8. "O" ring
9. Cap
10. "O" ring
11. Piston
12. Rod
13. Washer
14. "O" ring
15. Rod end
16. Check valve assy.
17. Pin
18. Check valve assy.

Fig. M11-98—Release pressure on system, then remove Allen head plug (U) and install a 5000 psi (34.5 MPa) test gage with a suitable adapter and hose to test system pressure when operated in the "UP" direction. View identifies location of manual release valve (21).

OVERHAUL. Refer to Fig. M11-96 for exploded view of manifold and trim cylinder components, and Fig. M11-97 for exploded view of tilt cylinder components. Special socket 91-44487A1 and a spanner wrench is required to service trim and tilt cylinders. Keep all components clean and away from contamination. Keep components separated and label if necessary for correct reassembly. Lubricate all "O" rings or seal lips with Quicksilver Power Trim & Steering Fluid, Dexron II, Type F or Type FA automatic transmission fluid during reassembly.

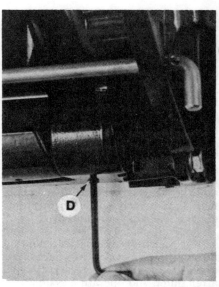

Fig. M11-99—Release pressure on system, then remove Allen head plug (D) and install a 5000 psi (34.5 MPa) test gage with a suitable adapter and hose to test system pressure when operated in the "DOWN" direction.

MERCURY
FOUR-CYLINDER MODELS (1969-1989)

Year Produced						Year Produced					
1969	500	650	....	800	....	1980	50	....	....	80	....
1970	500	650	....	800	....	1981	50	....	....	80	....
1971	500	650	....	800	....	1982	50	....	....	80	....
1972	500	....	....	800	....	1983	50	....	....	80	....
1973	500	....	....	....	850	1984	50	....	75	....	....
1974	500	....	....	....	850	1985	50	....	75	....	....
1975	500	....	....	....	850	1986	45	75	....	....	....
1976	500	....	....	....	850	1987	45	....	....	....	....
1977	500	....	....	....	850	1988	45	....	....	....	....
1978	500	....	....	800	....	1989	45	....	....	....	....
1979	50	....	....	80	....						

Letter after model number indicates variation of equipment: M—Manual starter, S—Electric starter without alternator, E—Electric starter and alternator, L—Long shaft, PT—Power trim, SS—Solid state ignition, XS—High performance.

CONDENSED SERVICE DATA

TUNE-UP
Hp/rpm

Model 45 ....45/5000-5500
　　　　　　　　　　　　　　　(33.6 kW)

Models 500 & 50 ....50/4800-5500
　　　　　　　　　　　　　　　(37.3 kW)

Model 650 ....65/4800-5300
　　　　　　　　　　　　　　　(48.5 kW)

Model 75 ....75/5000-5500
　　　　　　　　　　　　　　　(55.9 kW)

Models 800 & 80 ....80/4800-5500
　　　　　　　　　　　　　　　(59.7 kW)

Model 850 ....85/4800-5500*
　　　　　　　　　　　　　　　(63.4 kW)

Bore:

Models 45, 50 & 500 ....2.565 in.
　　　　　　　　　　　　　　　(65.15 mm)

Model 650 ....$2^{15}/_{16}$ in.
　　　　　　　　　　　　　　　(74.61 mm)

Models 800, 850, 80 & 75 ....$2^7/_8$ in.
　　　　　　　　　　　　　　　(73.03 mm)

Stroke:

Models 45, 50 & 500 ....$2^1/_8$ in.
　　　　　　　　　　　　　　　(53.98 mm)

Model 650 ....$2^{19}/_{64}$ in.
　　　　　　　　　　　　　　　(58.42 mm)

Models 800, 850, 80 & 75 ....$2^9/_{16}$ in.
　　　　　　　　　　　　　　　(65.09 mm)

Firing Order 1-3-2-4
Compression At Cranking Speed ....†
Spark Plug ....See Text
Ignition.........................See Text
Idle Speed ....See Text
Fuel:Oil Ratio ‡.....................50:1‡

*Full throttle speed range is 4800-6000 rpm on Model 850XS.

†Compression should not vary more than 15 psi (103.4 kPa) between cylinders.

‡Models after 1985 may be equipped with AutoBlend fuel and oil mixing system.

SIZES—CLEARANCES
Piston Rings:
End Gap...........................*
Side Clearance.....................*
Piston Skirt Clearance................*
Crankshaft Bearing Type:
Top Main Bearing...................Ball Bearing
Main Bearing (2)............Bushing With Reed Valve
Center Main Bearing..................Roller †
Main Bearing (4)............Bushing With Reed Valve
Bottom Main Bearing..............Ball Bearing
Crankpin......................Roller†
Piston Pin Bearing..................Roller†

*Publication not authorized by manufacturer.
†Refer to text for number of rollers at center main bearing, crankpin and piston pin.

TIGHTENING TORQUES
Connecting Rod....................180 in.-lbs.
　　　　　　　　　　　　　　　(20.3 N·m)

Crankcase Screws:
Models 650 & 800 (Prior to 1973)...........150 in.-lbs.
　　　　　　　　　　　　　　　(16.9 N·m)
All Other Models....................200 in.-lbs.
　　　　　　　　　　　　　　　(22.6 N·m)

Cylinder Cover:
Models 45, 50 & 500 ....70 in.-lbs.
　　　　　　　　　　　　　　　(7.9 N·m)
Models 650 & 800 (Prior to 1973)...........100 in.-lbs.
　　　　　　　　　　　　　　　(11.3 N·m)
Models 800 (After 1972), 850,
　　80 & 75.......................85 in.-lbs.
　　　　　　　　　　　　　　　(9.6 N·m)

Exhaust Cover:
Models 45, 50 & 500 ....200 in.-lbs.
　　　　　　　　　　　　　　　(22.6 N·m)
Models 650 & 800 (Prior to 1973)...........150 in.-lbs.
　　　　　　　　　　　　　　　(16.9 N·m)
Models 800 (After 1972), 850,
　　80 & 75.......................250 in.-lbs.
　　　　　　　　　　　　　　　(28.2 N·m)

TIGHTENING TORQUES CONT.

Flywheel:
Models 800 (After 1972), 850,
  80 & 75 . . . . 100 ft.-lbs.
                                               (136 N·m)
  All Other Models . . . . 65 ft.-lbs.
                                               (88.4 N·m)
Reed Screws:
  Models 45, 50 & 500 . . . . 30 in.-lbs.
                                               (3.4 N·m)
  Models 650 & 800 (Prior to 1973) . . . . 35 in.-lbs.
                                               (3.9 N·m)

TIGHTENING TORQUES CONT.

Models 800 (After 1972), 850,
  80 & 75 . . . . 25 in.-lbs.
                                               (2.8 N·m)
Spark Plugs . . . . 240 in.-lbs.
                                               (27.1 N·m)
Transfer Port Covers:
Models 800 (After 1972), 850,
  80 & 75 . . . . 85 in.-lbs.
                                               (9.6 N·m)
  All Other Models . . . . 60 in.-lbs.
                                               (6.8 N·m)

LUBRICATION

The engine is lubricated by oil mixed with the fuel. Fuel should be regular leaded, low leaded or unleaded gasoline with a minimum octane rating of 86. Recommended oil is Quicksilver Premium Blend Outboard Motor Oil or a good quality NMMA certified TC-W or TC-WII oil.

On models not equipped with AutoBlend fuel and oil mixing system, fuel:oil ratio should be 25:1 during engine break-in and 50:1 during normal operation.

Models after 1985 may be equipped with AutoBlend fuel and oil mixing system. The AutoBlend system is designed to deliver a constant 50:1 fuel:oil mixture to power head at all engine speeds. To provide sufficient lubrication during break-in of a new or rebuilt engine, a 50:1 fuel and oil mixture should be used in fuel tank in combination with the AutoBlend system.

Translucent filter (1—Fig. M12-1) behind cover (2) should be inspected once per month and renewed each boating season or if sediment inside filter is evident. AutoBlend diaphragm plate should be inspected for cracking, swelling or deterioration once per year. To inspect diaphragm plate, remove eight screws securing main body cover (6) to main body (7), then remove clip securing diaphragm plate to pump shaft.

NOTE: Remove inner ring of screws to remove cover from main body. Outer ring of screws secures main body to reservoir.

Renew diaphragm plate as necessary. Reverse disassembly procedure to reassemble unit. Tighten eight main body cover screws in a crossing pattern to 30 in.-lbs. (3.4 N·m).

To check for proper operation of pump check valves, remove fuel hose and plug outlet (O). Remove fuel hose from inlet (I) and connect a suitable vacuum pump with gage to inlet (I). Check valves should hold steady vacuum with 8 inches HG (27 kPa) vacuum applied and allow leakage with 10 inches HG (33.8 kPa) vacuum applied. Check valves can be removed for inspection or renewal by removing main body (7) from reservoir (5). Check valves are located under cover secured to top of pump by two screws. When reassembling, tighten main body screws in a crossing pattern to 30 in.-lbs. (3.4 N·m).

Lower unit gears and bearings are lubricated by oil contained in the gearcase. Recommended oil is Quicksilver Super Duty Gear Lubricant or Quicksilver Premium Blend Gear Lubricant. Remove vent plug and fill gearcase through drain plug opening until oil is level with vent plug hole, then allow one ounce (30 mL) of oil to drain out to allow for expansion.

FUEL SYSTEM

All Models Prior To 1976

CARBURETOR. Refer to Fig. M12-2 for exploded view of carburetor typical of models prior to 1976.

Initial setting for the idle mixture screw (14) is one turn open from the

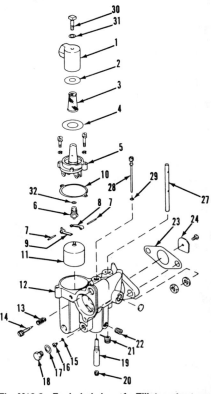

Fig. M12-2—Exploded view of a Tillotson type carburetor. MerCarb WMK type carburetor is similar. Main jet (16) has a tapered seat and does not use gasket (15) on KD and WMK type carburetors.

1. Strainer cover
2. Gasket
3. Strainer
4. Gasket
5. Bowl cover
6. Inlet needle & seat
7. Pins
8. Primary lever
9. Secondary lever
10. Gasket
11. Float
12. Body
13. Spring
14. Idle mixture screw
15. Gasket
16. Main jet
17. Gasket
18. Plug
19. Main nozzle
20. Plug
21. Spring
22. Plug
23. Gasket
24. Throttle valve
27. Throttle shaft
28. Idle tube
29. Gasket
30. Cap screw
31. Gasket
32. Gasket

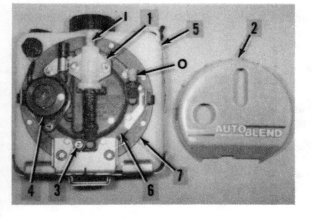

Fig. M12-1—View of AutoBlend fuel and oil mixing unit with cover (2) removed.
1. Filter
2. Cover
3. Drain plug
4. Warning horn
5. Reservoir
6. Main body cover
7. Main body
I. Inlet (gasoline)
O. Outlet (fuel & oil mixture)

Illustrations courtesy Mercury

closed position. Run motor until operating temperature is reached, then shift to Forward gear and allow motor to run at idle speed. Slowly turn idle screw (14) out (counterclockwise) until motor runs unevenly (loads up). Turn needle in (clockwise) until motor picks up speed and again runs evenly and continue turning until motor slows down and misses. Needle should be set between the two extremes. Turning screw (14) in (clockwise) leans the idle mixture. Slightly rich idle mixture is more desirable than too lean.

NOTE: Mixture adjustment should not be attempted in neutral.

The high speed mixture may be adjusted for altitude or other special conditions by changing the size of main jet (16). The standard main jet should normally be correct for altitudes below 4000 feet (1220 m). Refer to the following for standard main jet size (diameter).

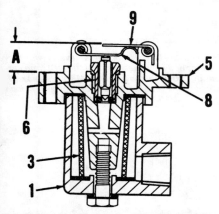

Fig. M12-3—Float height is adjusted by bending primary lever (8) until distance (A) is ¹³/₃₂ inch (10.3 mm) with inlet valve (6) closed.

Fig. M12-4—With bowl cover (5) upright, distance (D) between primary lever (8) and end of secondary lever (9) should be ¹/₄ inch (6.4 mm). Bend tab (T) to adjust.

Model 500

Carburetor	Main Jet
KA-21A	0.057 in. (1.45 mm)
KA-21B	0.061 in. (1.55 mm)
KA-21C	0.065 in. (1.65 mm)
KA-21D & KA-24A	0.063 in. (1.60 mm)

Model 650

KA-5A	0.071 in. (1.80 mm)
KC-5B, KC-5C, KC-11A and KC-15A	0.061 in. (1.55 mm)

Model 800

KD-4A and WMK-2	0.074 in. (1.88 mm)

NOTE: If main jet (16—Fig. M12-2) is too small, high speed mixture will be excessively lean and power head damage may result.

To adjust the fuel level, remove bowl cover (5) and invert the cover assembly. Measure distance (A—Fig. M12-3) between secondary lever (9) and gasket surface of bowl cover with inlet valve (6) closed. Distance (A) should be ¹³/₃₂ inch (10.3 mm). Bend curved tang on primary lever (8) to adjust.

Position bowl cover (5—Fig. M12-4) upright and measure distance (D) between primary lever (8) and end of secondary lever (9). Distance (D) should

be ¹/₄ inch (6.4 mm). Bend tab (T) to adjust.

Models 45, 50 And Model 500 After 1975

Models 45 and 50 and Model 500 after 1975 are equipped with two Mer-Carb carburetors. Refer to Fig. M12-5 for exploded view of carburetor used. Some 45 models may be equipped with a similar carburetor without integral fuel pump.

Standard main jet (24) size for normal operation below 2500 feet (762 m) elevations is 0.055 inch (1.40 mm) on Model 500 and Model 50 prior to serial number 4576237, and 0.057 inch (1.45 mm) on Models 45 and 50 after serial number 4576236.

Initial setting of idle mixture screw (21) is 1¹/₂ turns open on carburetor with integral fuel pump and two turns open on carburetor without integral fuel pump.

To adjust fuel level, remove float bowl and invert carburetor. Measure distance from float to gasket surface as shown in Fig. M12-6. Float level should be ¹⁵/₆₄ to ¹⁷/₆₄ inch (6.0-6.8 mm). To check float drop, position carburetor upright and measure from float to highest point on main jet (24). Float drop should be ¹/₃₂ to ¹/₁₆ inch (0.8-1.6 mm).

Idle speed should be 550-650 rpm on early models and 600-700 rpm on later models (after serial number 4576236).

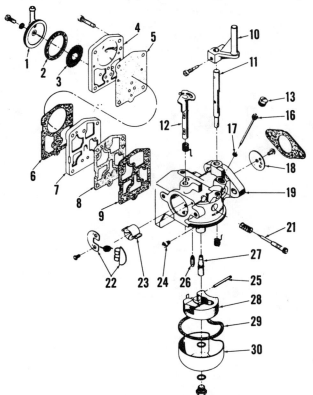

Fig. M12-5—Exploded view of MerCarb type carburetor used on Models 45 and 50, and Model 500 after 1975. Some 45 models are equipped with carburetor without integral fuel pump.

1. Inlet fitting
2. Gasket
3. Screen
4. Cover
5. Diaphragm
6. Gasket
7. Pump body
8. Check valve diaphragm
9. Gasket
10. Throttle lever
11. Throttle shaft
12. Choke shaft
13. Plug
16. Idle tube
17. Gasket
18. Throttle plate
19. Body
21. Idle mixture screw
22. Choke shutter plates
23. Boost venturi
24. Main jet
25. Float pin
26. Inlet needle
27. Main nozzle
28. Float
29. Gasket
30. Float bowl

Adjust idle speed with outboard motor running at normal operating temperature in forward gear.

Models 75, 80, 800 and 850 After 1975

Two MerCarb carburetors are used. Refer to Fig. M12-7 for exploded view of carburetor used. Note that these carburetors are equipped with an enrichment valve (24) in place of a choke plate. Initial adjustment of idle mixture screw (19) is one turn open. Standard main jet (10) size for operation below 2500 feet (762 m) elevations is 0.088 inch (2.23 mm) for models with serial number 4366802-4423111 and 0.090 inch (2.29 mm) on models after serial number 4423111. Vent jet (4) size for operation below 2500 feet (762 m) elevations is 0.080 inch (2.03 mm) on models with serial number 4366802-4423111 and 0.072 inch (1.83 mm) on models after serial number 4423111.

When overhauling carburetor, drive float pins (16) and fuel inlet drive lever pin (18) out toward knurled end of pin. Insert plain end of pin first during reassembly. Note that the stronger throttle return spring (0.034 in. diameter wire) must be used on top carburetor throttle shaft.

Numbers on throttle plate (29) must face outward at closed throttle. Be sure rubber insert in fuel inlet valve seat (6) is installed so flat end of insert is toward inlet needle (26).

To determine fuel level, invert carburetor body and measure distance (D—Fig. M12-8) from carburetor body to base of float (15). Distance (D) should

be $^{11}/_{16}$ inch (17.5 mm) on solid float, $^{19}/_{32}$ inch (15.1 mm) on hollow float and is adjusted by bending fuel inlet lever (17—Fig. M12-9) within area (A).

SPEED CONTROL LINKAGE. The speed control linkage must be synchronized to advance the ignition timing and open the carburetor throttles in a precise manner. Because the two actions are interrelated, it is important to check the complete system in the sequence outlined in the appropriate following paragraphs. Examine the motor to establish which type of ignition is used. Original system application is listed in the IGNITION SYSTEM section.

Model 500 and Model 650 With "Thunderbolt" Ignition. Refer to special precautions listed in the "Thunderbolt" IGNITION section before servicing these motors. Incorrect service procedures can damage the ignition system.

NOTE: Do not disconnect any part of the ignition system while engine is running or while checking the speed control linkage.

Disconnect the fuel tank and allow motor to run until all fuel is used out of the carburetors. If any fuel remains, motor can start while checking the speed control linkage and prevent accurate adjustments.

Connect a power timing light (such as Mercury part C-91-35507) to the top (No. 1) spark plug.

Turn ignition key on and crank motor with electric starter. Advance the

Fig. M12-8—To determine float level, invert carburetor body and measure distance (D) from carburetor body to base of float (15). Distance (D) should be $^{11}/_{16}$ (17.5 mm) on solid float and $^{19}/_{32}$ inch (15.1 mm) on hollow float.

Fig. M12-9—Adjust float level by bending fuel inlet lever (17) within area (A).

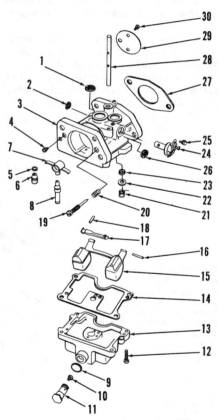

Fig. M12-6—Float level should be $^{15}/_{64}$ to $^{17}/_{64}$ inch (6.0-6.8 mm) from float to gasket surface. Float drop is measured with carburetor upright from top of main jet (24) to float. Refer to text.

Fig. M12-7—Exploded view of center bowl type MerCarb carburetor used on Models 75, 80, 800 and 850 after 1975.

1. Welch plug (9/16 inch)	16. Pin
2. Fuel inlet strainer	17. Fuel inlet lever
3. Body	18. Pin
4. Vent jet	19. Idle mixture screw
5. Gasket	20. Spring
6. Inlet needle & seat assy.	21. Spring
7. Venturi	22. Flat washer
8. Nozzle	23. Rubber seal
9. Gasket	24. Enrichment valve assy.
10. Main jet	25. Screw & lockwasher
11. Main jet plug	26. Welch plug (7/16 inch)
12. Screw	27. Gasket
13. Float bowl	28. Throttle shaft
14. Gasket	29. Throttle plate
15. Float	30. Screw

Fig. M12-10—When controls are in maximum speed position, stop should be against screw (T) and lever (L) should have less than 1/64 inch (0.4 mm) free movement.

Illustrations courtesy Mercury

speed controls until timing light flashes when the flywheel timing mark is aligned with the correct maximum advance degree mark (Fig. M12-14). Maximum ignition advance should be 35 degrees BTDC for Model 500SS and should be 38 degrees BTDC for Model 650SS. If maximum advance timing is incorrect, turn the stop screw (A–Fig. M12-13) to stop the ignition advance at correct position.

With the timing light still connected, synchronize the carburetor throttle opening to the ignition timing as follows: Crank motor with the electric starter and slowly advance speed control from the idle position. On Model 500SS, the timing light should flash when the flywheel mark passes the "CYL #1TDC" mark (Fig. M12-14). On Model 650SS, timing light should flash when flywheel mark passes the "PICKUP" mark (Fig. M12-14). With controls correctly set as outlined, the pickup tab should just contact the carburetor throttle lever as shown in Fig. M12-11. If throttle is partly open or if lever is not touching the tab, loosen the two screws (S–Fig. M12-12) and move the pickup plate in the elongated holes. Throttle pickup should be rechecked after tightening the pickup plate retaining screws (S).

Move the speed control handle to the maximum speed position until the throttle stop contacts the throttle stop screw (T–Fig. M12-10). The carburetor should be completely open. If the stop does not contact screw (T), turn the screw in to prevent damage to linkage. If throttle lever (L) has more than 1/64 inch (0.4 mm) free movement, turn the throttle stop screw (T) out.

Model 500 and Model 650 With "Lightning Energizer" Ignition. Refer to the special precautions listed under "Lightning Energizer" IGNITION before servicing these motors. Incorrect servicing procedures can damage the ignition system.

NOTE: It is important that an approved tachometer is used. Do NOT disconnect any part of the ignition system while engine is running or while checking the speed control linkage.

Use a Mercury timing light (part C-91-35507) or equivalent.

NOTE: A jumper wire (ground) must be connected from negative terminal of battery to the motor lower cowl or front cover plate on manual start motors.

Start engine and adjust the idle speed screw (I–Fig. M12-15) to provide 550-650 rpm in forward gear while holding the ignition unit at full retard.

Advance the ignition until timing occurs between 7° and 9° BTDC. The throttle actuator plate should be just touching the carburetor primary pickup as shown at (1–Fig. M12-16). If throttle is slightly open or if pickup is not touching, loosen the two attaching screws (P–Fig. M12-17) and move throttle actuator plate so it just touches the primary pickup lever when ignition is set at 7°-9° BTDC.

With motor running at maximum speed, check the ignition timing. Ignition timing should be within the limits as follows for the operating rpm.

Model 500

RPM	Degrees BTDC
2000-4000	38-39
4000-4800	37-38
5200-5600	35

Model 650

2000-4000	41-42
4000-4800	40-41
4800-5200	38

If maximum ignition timing is incorrect, loosen the locknut and turn the advance stop screw (A–Fig. M12-13) until timing is correct for the rpm. After adjusting, be sure to recheck.

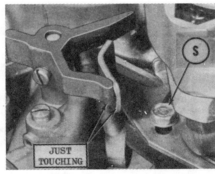

Fig. M12-11—Refer to text for method of determining throttle pickup point. Two screws (S) retain the pickup plate.

Fig. M12-12—When adjusting clearance (C), refer to text. Clearance is adjusted by bending at (X).

NOTE: It is important to know engine speed (rpm) when checking maximum ignition timing because of the characteristics of the electronic ignition. Timing may be checked on boat or test tank, but must be accomplished at maximum throttle opening.

To adjust the throttle secondary pickup, advance the ignition unit until it contacts the advance stop (A–Fig. M12-13).

NOTE: Do not move the economizer collar after the ignition unit contacts stop screw (A).

Check clearance at (2–Fig. M12-17) between secondary pickup lever and screw. The screw should be just contacting the secondary pickup lever and is adjusted by turning screw (S–Fig. M12-15). Make certain that the primary end of the throttle pickup lever is still against the primary pickup cam (1–Fig. M12-17).

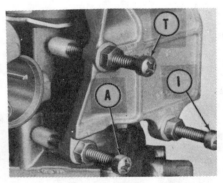

Fig. M12-13—Maximum ignition advance is adjusted by stop screw (A); idle speed by screw (I); and throttle stop screw (T) prevents damage to linkage. Position of these three screws is similar for all models.

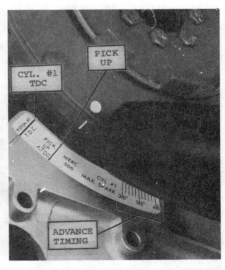

Fig. M12-14—Refer to text for method used for setting the speed control linkage before adjusting. Timing marks shown are typical.

To adjust the throttle stop screw (T–Fig. M12-13), move the speed control handle to maximum speed position. The carburetor throttles should be completely open when the throttle stop contacts screw (T). If the throttles are not

Fig. M12-15 – Refer to text for adjusting speed control linkage on Models 500 and 650 with "Lightning Energizer" ignition system.

I. Idle stop screw   S. Secondary pickup screw

Fig. M12-16 – View of the throttle actuator plate just contacting the primary pickup lever (1). Refer to text.

completely open, turn stop screw (T) out. If the throttle stop does not contact screw (T), turn the screw in to prevent damage to linkage.

Model 800 And Model 850 (Below Ser. No. 386595). Refer to the special precautions listed in the **"Thunderbolt"** IGNITION section before servicing these motors. Incorrect servicing procedures can damage the ignition system.

NOTE: Do not synchronize any part of the ignition system while engine is running or while checking the speed control linkage adjustments.

Disconnect the fuel tank and allow motor to run until all fuel is used out of the carburetors. If any fuel remains, motor can start while checking the speed control linkage and may prevent accurate adjustments. Connect a power timing light to number 1 (top) spark plug wire.

To adjust the spark advance stop screw (A–Fig. M12-20), the speed control must be in the maximum speed position. Turn on the key switch, crank engine with starter and check the ignition timing. The timing mark on flywheel (dots) should be aligned with 23° BTDC mark when the timing light flashes. If incorrect, loosen the locknut and turn stop screw (A) as required to stop ignition advance at 23° BTDC. Recheck timing after tightening locknut.

The primary cam on the throttle pickup plate should just contact the primary pickup lever as shown at (1–Fig. M12-18) when the speed control lever is advanced to provide 5°-7° BTDC ignition timing. To check, crank engine with starter while checking ignition timing. Advance the speed control until the ignition timing is within 5°-7° BTDC, then check the throttle pickup at

Fig. M12-17 – View of the secondary pickup lever just contacting the screw (2). Refer to text. The primary pickup lever should still be contacting cam at (1).

(1). If clearance is not 0-0.005 inch (0-0.13 mm), loosen the two attaching screws (P–Fig. M12-19) and move the throttle pickup plate. Recheck pickup point after moving plate and tightening the two attaching screws.

To adjust the secondary pickup, rotate the distributor against the maximum advance stop screw (A–Fig. M12-20) and check the secondary pickup between

Fig. M12-18 – View of throttle pickup cams and lever used on Models 800 and 850. Primary pickup should occur at (1) and secondary pickup at (2). Refer to text for adjusting.

Fig. M12-19 – View of secondary pickup adjusting screws (S) and primary pickup plate attaching screws (P) typical of Model 800 and Model 850 with distributor.

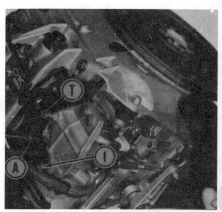

Fig. M12-20 – View of Model 800 showing location of ignition advance stop screw (A), idle speed stop screw (I) and throttle stop screw (T). Model 850 with distributor is similar.

cam and throttle lever at (2 – Fig. M12-18).

NOTE: Do not advance speed control past the point that distributor just touches stop screw (A – Fig. M12-20) when checking the secondary pickup. If the secondary pickup is not touching, loosen the locknut and turn screw (S – Fig. M12-19) in until secondary cam just touches throttle lever. If secondary cam is contacting the throttle lever, back screw (S) out until cam is away from lever, then readjust to make certain that cam is just touching.

Move the speed control toward maximum speed position until throttle stop contacts screw (T – Fig. M12-20). The carburetor throttles should be completely open. If stop does not contact screw (T), turn the stop screw in to prevent damage to linkage. If throttles are not completely open, turn stop screw (T) out.

Model 850 (Ser. No. 3865695-4366800). Refer to the special precautions listed in the "Thunderbolt" IGNITION section before servicing these motors. Incorrect servicing procedures can damage the ignition system.

NOTE: Do not disconnect any part of the ignition system while engine is running or while checking the speed control linkage adjustments.

Ignition timing pointer alignment may be checked as follows: Install a dial indicator in number 1 (top) spark plug hole and turn flywheel clockwise until number 1 piston is 0.464 inch (11.8 mm) BTDC. Loosen retaining screw and align timing pointer (P – Fig. M12-21) with ".464 BTDC" mark on flywheel.

Connect a power timing light to number 1 (top) spark plug wire. The primary cam on the throttle pickup plate should just contact the primary pickup lever as shown at (1 – Fig. M12-18) when the speed control lever is advanced to provide BTDC ignition timing. To check, crank engine with starter while checking ignition timing. Advance the speed

control until the ignition timing is within 3°-5° BTDC, then check the throttle pickup at (1). If clearance is not 0-0.005 inch (0-0.13 mm), loosen the two attaching screws (P – Fig. M12-19) and move the throttle pickup plate. Recheck pickup point after moving plate and tightening the two attaching screws.

To check maximum spark advance, start motor in test tank with timing light attached. Hold timing light on pointer (P – Fig. M12-21) and advance speed control until pointer is aligned with 27° mark on flywheel. Distributor should be just touching maximum advance stop screw (A – Fig. M12-20) at this point. To adjust, loosen locknut and turn screw (A) until it is just touching distributor with timing pointer and 27° mark on flywheel aligned. Recheck maximum spark advance after tightening locknut on adjustment screw.

To adjust the secondary pickup, rotate the distributor against the maximum advance stop screw (A – Fig. M12-20) and check the secondary pickup between cam and throttle lever at (2 – Fig. M12-18).

NOTE: Do not advance speed control past the point that distributor just touches stop screw (A – Fig. M12-20) when checking the secondary pickup. If the secondary pickup is not touching, loosen the locknut and turn screw (S – Fig. M12-19) in until secondary cam just touches throttle lever. If secondary cam is contacting the throttle lever, back screw (S) out until cam is away from lever. then readjust to make certain that cam is just touching.

Move the speed control to the maximum speed position until throttle stop contacts screw (T – Fig. M12-20). The carburetor throttles should be completely open. If the stop does not contact screw (T), turn the stop screw in to prevent damage to linkage. If throttles are

not completely open, turn the stop screw (T) out.

Models 45, 50 And 500 After Serial Number 4357640. To synchronize ignition and carburetor opening, connect a power timing light to number 1 (top) spark plug lead. Start engine and run outboard in forward gear. Open throttle until ignition timing is 7-9 degrees BTDC on models prior to serial number 5531630 or 2 degrees BTDC to 2 degrees ATDC on models after serial number 5531629. Then loosen actuator plate screws (S—Fig. M12-22) and rotate actuator plate (P) so primary pickup arm (A—Fig. M12-23) just contacts primary cam (C). Retighten actuator plate screws and return engine to idle speed. Open throttle (in forward gear) and adjust maximum ignition advance screw (A—Fig. M12-24) so ignition timing is 32 degrees BTDC, then stop engine.

Fig. M12-23 — Primary pickup arm (A) should just contact primary cam (C) at point (P) with 7°-9° BTDC ignition timing.

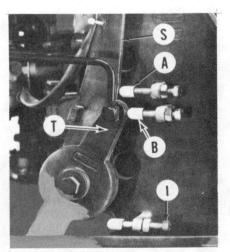

Fig. M12-24—View of throttle (T) and spark (S) control arms on Model 500 after serial number 4357640. On 500 models after 1977 and all 45 and 50 models, screws (A, B and I) are located on arms (T and S).

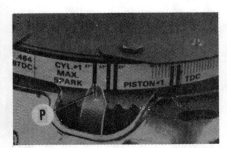

Fig. M12-21 — View of flywheel and timing pointer (P) used on late 850 models.

Fig. M12-22—View of actuator plate (P) and secondary pickup adjusting screw (W) on 45 and 50 models, and Model 500 after serial number 4357640. Refer to text for adjustment procedure.

NOTE: Due to electronic characteristics of ignition system, maximum advance is set at 32 degrees BTDC, but ignition system will electronically retard timing to 30 degrees BTDC at 5000 rpm.

Fig. M12-25—Adjust full throttle stop screw (B—Fig. M12-24) so there is 0.010-0.015 inch (0.25-0.38 mm) clearance between secondary pickup arm (R) and screw (W) at full throttle.

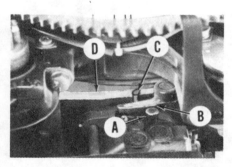

Fig. M12-26 — View of throttle pickup pins (A & C) and cams (B & D) used on Models 75, 80, 800 and 850 after serial number 4366801.

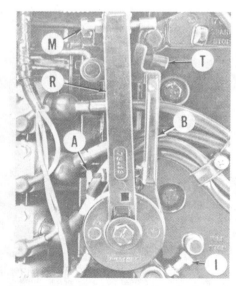

Fig. M12-27—View of throttle (B) and spark (R) control arms on Models 75, 80, 800 and 850 after serial number 4366801.

With engine not running, open throttle so spark arm (S) just contacts maximum advance screw (A) and adjust actuator plate secondary pickup screw (W—Fig. M12-22) so screw just touches secondary pickup arm as shown in Fig. M12-25.

To prevent damage to carburetor throttle plate at full throttle, lightly hold carburetor throttle plate in full open (engine not running) position by turning secondary pickup arm (R—Fig. M12-25). Adjust full throttle stop screw (B—Fig. M12-24) so a clearance of 0.010-0.015 inch (0.25-0.38 mm) is between secondary pickup screw (W—Fig. M12-25) and pickup arm (R) when throttle arm (T—Fig. M12-24) just touches full throttle stop screw (B). Adjust idle speed screw (I), with outboard running in forward gear, to obtain 550-650 rpm on early models and 600-700 rpm on later models (after serial number 4576236).

Models 75, 80, 800 And 850 After Serial Number 4366801. Check ignition timing pointer alignment as follows: Install a dial indicator gage in number 1 (top) spark plug hole and turn flywheel clockwise until piston is 0.464 inch (12 mm) BTDC. Loosen retaining screw and position timing pointer so that it is aligned with ".464 BTDC" mark on flywheel.

Connect a power timing light to number 1 (top) spark plug wire. Run engine with outboard in forward gear and open throttle until primary cam (B—Fig. M12-26) just touches throttle lever primary pin (A). Primary cam should contact primary pin at 2-4 degrees BTDC on models below serial number 4423112 or 2 degrees BTDC to 2 degrees ATDC on models after serial number 4423111. Turn pickup adjustment screw (A—Fig. M12-27) to obtain desired pickup point. Open throttle and turn maximum advance adjustment screw (M) so spark arm (R) movement will stop at 27 degrees BTDC. Stop engine.

Carburetor throttle plate must not act as stop for wide open throttle. To prevent damage to carburetor, lightly hold carburetor throttle plate in full open position by turning upper carburetor throttle lever. Adjust full throttle stop screw (T) so there is 0.010-0.015 inch (0.25-0.38 mm) between throttle lever secondary pin (C—Fig. M12-26) and secondary cam (D) when throttle arm (B—Fig. M12-27) is in wide open position.

Idle speed should be 550-650 rpm with outboard in forward gear. Turn idle speed screw (I) to adjust idle speed.

REED VALVES. The inlet reed valves are located on the crankshaft second and fourth main bearing assemblies. Each reed valve unit supplies fuel mixture from one of the carburetors to the two adjoining cylinders.

Reed petals (2—Fig. M12-30 or M12-31) should be perfectly flat and have not more than 0.007 inch (0.18 mm) clearance between free end of reed petal and seating surface of center main bearing. The reed stop opening (A—Fig. M12-30) must be carefully adjusted to $^3/_{16}$ inch (4.76 mm) on 650 models, 0.180 inch (4.57 mm) on 500, 800 and early 50 models, $^5/_{32}$ inch (3.97 mm) on 45 and late 50 models (after serial number 4576236) and 0.162 inch (4.11 mm) on 75, 80 and 850 models.

Seating surface of bearing must be smooth and flat, and may be refinished on a lapping plate after removing reed stops, reed valves and dowels. Do not attempt to bend or straighten a damaged reed. Never install a bent reed. Lubricate reed valve assemblies with Quicksilver Multipurpose Lubricant when reassembling.

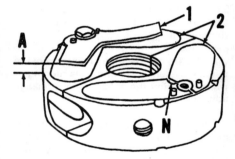

Fig. M12-30—Intermediate main bearing and reed valve for Models 45, 50, 500 and 650. Reed petals (2) are right- and left-hand units. When installing reed petals, place the reed with the cut-out notch (N) on left side as shown. Refer to Fig. M12-31.

Fig M12-31 — View of intermediate main bearing and reed valve assembly used on Models 75, 80, 800 and 850. Later models use nuts and three bolts to secure reeds (2) and reed stops (1) to valve assembly.

On 45, 50, 500 and 650 models, each reed valve assembly has eight reeds, which are right-hand and left-hand units. Reeds are available only as a matched set. When installing reed valves, place the reed petal with cut-out notch (N) to the left as shown. Crankshaft must be removed before reed valve units can be serviced.

FUEL PUMP. Diaphragm type fuel pump is used. Fuel pump is actuated by crankcase pulsations. Early models are equipped with "triangle" shaped fuel pumps. Later models are equipped with "square" shaped pumps. Model 50 and some 45 models are equipped with carburetor and integral fuel pump assembly shown in Fig. M12-5.

Fuel pressure on early "triangle" shaped pumps should be 2 psi (13.8 kPa) minimum with motor running at full throttle. Fuel pressure on later "square" shaped pumps should be 2 psi (13.8 kPa) at idle speed and 5.5-6.5 psi (37.9-44.8 kPa) at full throttle.

Renew gaskets and diaphragms whenever fuel pump is disassembled. On early "triangle" shaped pumps, install check valve retainer with tips of retainer pointing away from check valves. Be sure check valves are installed into the correct bore. On some models, check valves are color-coded red and white. Red check valve must be installed into intake side of pump.

On "square" shaped pumps, install check valves as shown in Fig. M12-33. After installing check valve retainers (4), cut retainer off at ridge to prevent contacting pump diaphragm.

IGNITION SYSTEM

Various types of ignition systems have been used. Make certain of type used, then refer to the appropriate following paragraphs for service. Original ignition system application is as follows:

MODEL	IGNITION TYPE
500 Ser. No. 251419-4357639	Lightning Energizer
45, 50 and 500 after Ser. No. 4357639	Thunderbolt Without Distributor
650 Ser. No. 2503991-2803561	Lightning Energizer
650 Ser. No. 2803562-4382056	Thunderbolt With Distributor
650 After Ser. No. 4382056	Thunderbolt With Distributor
800 Prior To Ser. No. 4831999	Thunderbolt With Distributor
75, 80 and 800 After Ser. No. 4831998	Thunderbolt Without Distributor
850 Prior To Ser. No. 4366802	Thunderbolt With Distributor
850 After Ser. No. 4366801	Thunderbolt Without Distributor

Thunderbolt Models With Distributor

Models with Thunderbolt ignition and a distributor vary slightly. When variations in service procedures are necessary, notation will be made.

The Thunderbolt ignition system uses an electronic triggering device and does not use breaker points. This ignition is extremely durable in normal operation but can be easily damaged by improper testing or servicing procedures.

Observe the following list of cautions and use **only** the approved methods for checking the system to prevent damage to the components.
1. DO NOT reverse battery terminals.
2. DO NOT check polarity of battery by sparking the lead wires.
3. DO NOT install resistor type spark plugs or lead wires.
4. DO NOT disconnect **any** wires while engine is running.
5. DO NOT ground any wires to engine block when checking. Ground only to front cover plate or bottom cowl to which switch box is mounted as described.
6. DO NOT use tachometer except those designed for this system.

TROUBLESHOOTING. Use only approved procedures when testing to prevent damage to components.

SPARK TEST. Do not remove spark plug wire **while motor is running.** Cut off the ground electrode from a standard spark plug (such as Champion J4J or L4J) and connect one of the spark plug wires to the test plug. Ground the test plug to the support bracket using a clamp or jumper wire.

CAUTION: Do not hold spark plug or wire in hand.

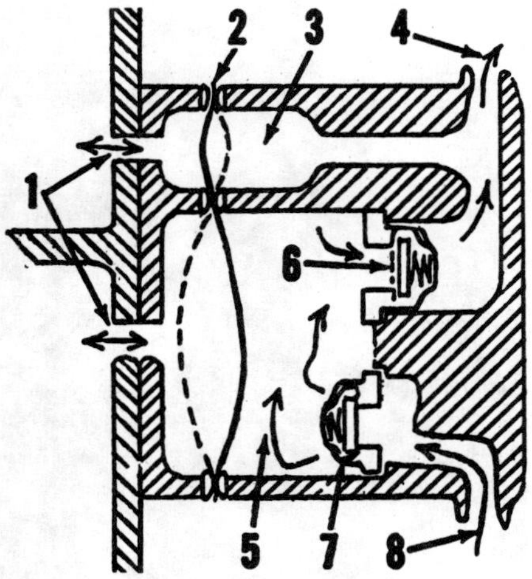

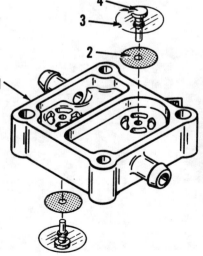

Fig. M12-32 — Schematic view of diaphragm type fuel pump. Pump body mounts on side of cylinder block and is ported to two crankcases as shown.

1. Pressure ports
2. Diaphragm
3. Booster chamber
4. To carburetor
5. Main fuel chamber
6. Outlet check valve
7. Inlet check valve
8. Fuel inlet

Fig. M12-33—Install check valves as shown on models equipped with "square" shape fuel pump. Check valve retainers (4) should be cut off at the ridge after installation to prevent contact with diaphragm.

1. Body
2. Check valve (black rubber)
3. Check valve (clear plastic)
4. Retainer

Fig. M12-34—Refer to text for timing instructions when installing drive belt or ignition unit. Dots (I) are marked on flywheel on some models that are timed by aligning straight line and arrow (TM). Be sure to use proper alignment marks.

Make certain that test plug is properly grounded; then, crank motor with electric starter. If test plug fires but engine will not start, check for incorrect installation of timing belt as outlined in the appropriate following TRIGGER AND DISTRIBUTOR paragraph. Fuel system problems can also prevent starting. If test plug does not fire, check the wiring as follows.

WIRING AND CONNECTION TEST (Model 800 Ser. No. 3051041 through 3052380 and Model 800 Ser. No. 3144219 through 3192962 ONLY). Turn key switch "OFF." Make certain that all connections are tight. Make certain that all bonding straps are in position.

NOTE: Switch box damage will result if bonding strap from cylinder head to cowl is disconnected with engine running.

Connect one voltmeter lead to white wire terminal on high tension lead retainer and other lead to ground. Battery voltage should be indicated with key switch in "RUN" position. Check wiring to key switch and battery if no voltage is found. If battery voltage is available, proceed as follows:

Turn key switch "OFF" and connect a test plug to top cylinder plug wire as

Fig. M12-35—When installing ignition drive belt on 650 models with Thunderbolt or Lightning Energizer ignition, or on late 800 or 850 models, the three ignition timing dots should be aligned with arrow on pulley. Refer to text.

Fig. M12-36—Surface gap plugs should be renewed if center electrode is 1/32 inch (0.79 mm) below the end of plug.

described in SPARK TEST section. Turn engine by hand to place number 1 (top) piston in TDC position. Disconnect blue wire at switch box that comes from distributor. Attach a jumper wire to ground on motor and and turn key switch to "RUN" position. Hold jumper wire to blue terminal on switch box (Fig. M12-57). Spark plug firing when jumper is removed from blue terminal will indicate that trigger assembly is faulty. No spark when jumper is lifted will indicate a faulty high tension coil or a faulty switch box.

WIRING AND CONNECTION TEST (ALL OTHER MOTORS WITH THUNDERBOLT IGNITION AND DISTRIBUTOR). Turn the key switch OFF. Connect one lead of voltmeter to red terminal of switch box (R–Fig. M12-37) and ground other lead to front cover plate. If red terminal is dead (no voltage), check battery, battery connections or for broken wire in wiring harness. If red terminal has voltage, proceed as follows:

Connect one lead of voltmeter to the white terminal (W–Fig. M12-37) and ground other lead to front cover plate. Turn key switch ON. If white terminal is dead (no voltage), key switch or wiring is defective. If white terminal has voltage, check the remaining components of system as follows:

Turn the key switch OFF. Disconnect the black (BL—Fig. M12-39), white (W)

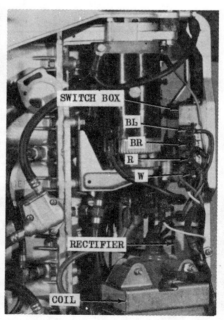

Fig. M12-37—View of electrical connections used on most models with Thunderbolt ignition. Refer to text for motor identification. Six-cylinder motor is shown, however, four-cylinder models are similar.

BL. Black (green on
    some models)
BR. Brown

R. Red
W. White

and brown (BR) wires from switch box and connect the three wires from a trigger assembly that is known to be good. Refer to Fig. M12-40. Disconnect the coil secondary lead from the distributor center terminal, then connect a test spark plug (or gap tester) to the coil secondary lead.

NOTE: Spark plug or spark tester must also be grounded to engine.

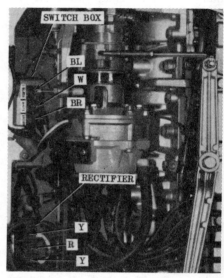

Fig. M12-39—Wires to port side of switch box and rectifiers must be connected as shown on motors with Thunderbolt ignition shown in Fig. M12-56.

BL. Black
BR. Brown
R. Red

W. White
Y. Yellow

Fig. M12-40—Refer to text when testing Thunderbolt ignition system. Spark tester is shown at (ST).

Turn key switch ON, then pass a metal feeler gage through the trigger coil as shown. If a spark jumps at test plug, the original trigger assembly is faulty and should be renewed. If spark does not jump at test plug, listen for "click" around area of high tension coil as the feeler gage passes through the trigger coil. "Clicking" indicates shorted high tension coil or high tension (secondary) lead wire. If the lead wire is not shorted, the high tension coil should be checked further as outlined in the following paragraph. If spark does not jump the test plug and coil is not damaged, the switch box should be renewed.

NOTE: A faulty switch box is nearly always caused by reversing battery leads, which damages the rectifier and in turn damages the switch box.

If switch box is suspected, check rectifier before renewing the switch box. If tests indicate that rectifier is damaged, renew the rectifier and again test the ignition system.

NOTE: Before disconnecting any wires, make certain that motor is not running and disconnect battery.

COIL TEST. The ignition coil can be tested using an ignition tester available from several sources including the following:

GRAHAM TESTERS, INC.
4220 Central Ave., N.E.
Minneapolis, Minn. 55421

MERC-O-TRONIC
INSTRUMENTS CORP.
215 Branch St.
Almont, Mich. 48003

SPARK PLUGS. The spark plugs should be renewed if the center electrode is burned back more than 1/32 inch (0.79 mm) below flat surface of the plug end. Refer to Fig. M12-36. AC type V40FFM or radio noise suppression type VR40FFM surface gap spark plugs should be used.

TRIGGER AND DISTRIBUTOR (Model 650 After Ser. No. 2803561, Model 800 And Model 850). The electronic trigger coil (A – Fig. M12-43) is contained in the distributor housing (10) on Model 800 serial number 3051041 through 3052380 and 800 serial number 3144219 through 3192962. The trigger coil may be purchased separately for these motors. The trigger coil on other motors is built into the distributor housing (10 – Fig. M12-42) and is available only as a unit with the housing. Before removing any of the components or

Fig. M12-42 – Exploded view of the Thunderbolt ignition distributor and drive used on Model 850 and most 800 models. Late 650 models are similar except for parts (27 & 28).

1. Distributor cap
2. Brush & spring
3. Clamp
7. Rotor & shaft
7P. Timer plate
8. Ball bearing
9. Snap ring
10. Distributor housing & trigger assy.
14. Spacer
15. Ball bearing
16. Spacer
17. Nut
18. Cover
19. Drive pulley
20. Spacer
21. Cap nut
22. Wave washer
23. Tang washer
24. Washer
25. Adapter
26. Washer
27. Throttle cam plate (primary pickup)
28. Throttle cam (secondary pickup)
29. Economizer collar
30. Washer
31. Spring
32. Spring anchor stud
33. Spring anchor pin
34. Spark advance stop

disconnecting any wires, make certain that battery is disconnected.

To disassemble, disconnect battery, and the three wires that lead from distributor. Remove cover (18 – Fig. M12-42), drive belt, pulley (19) and spacer (20). Bend tabs of washer (23) away from nut (21), remove nut and withdraw the distributor from adapter and economizer (25 and 29). Remove clamp (3) and cap (1). Carefully press bearing (15) out of housing by working through the two holes provided.

NOTE: Do not damage nut (17) or shaft when removing bearing.

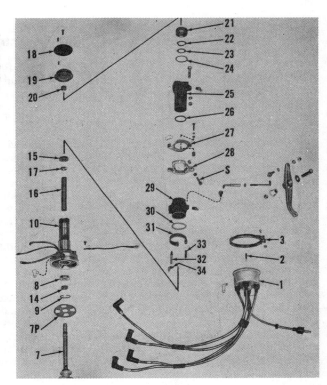

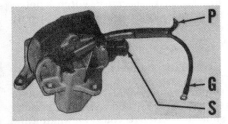

Fig. M12-41 – View of high tension ignition coil used on some Thunderbolt ignition motors. Primary lead (P) is green on late models, black on other models. Ground wire (G) is black on all models. The secondary (high tension) terminal is at (S).

Fig. M12-43 – View of removable trigger coil (A) and trigger wheel (B) used on some Model 800 distributor housings. Refer to Fig. M12-42 for parts common to all motors.

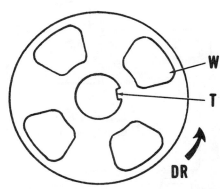

Fig. M12-44 – Install the timer plate with side shown, out toward the distributor cap. If the timer is installed incorrectly, it will be impossible to time the ignition.

T. Tab   W. Window

Remove nut (17) then bump the rotor shaft (7) out of bearing (8). The shaft should slide easily out of timer plate (7P) or trigger wheel (B–Fig. M12-43) and spacer (14–Fig. M12-42). Bearing (8) can be removed after extracting snap ring (9).

When reassembling, install bearing (8) and snap ring (9). Position spacer (14) then insert the timer plate (7P) into the trigger coil slot. Make certain that the side of timer plate shown in Fig. M12-44 is out (toward distributor cap).

NOTE: If the timer plate is incorrectly installed it will be impossible to set ignition timing.

Insert the rotor shaft (7–Fig. M12-42) through the timer plate (7P), spacer (14) and bearing (8).

CAUTION: Make certain tab (T—Fig. M12-44) correctly engages slot in rotor shaft before pressing shaft into bearing (8—Fig. M12-42).

Install spacer (16) and tighten nut (17) to 75-80 in.-lbs. (8.5-9 N·m). Press ball bearing (15) around shaft and into housing (10). Install brush and spring (2), distributor cap (1) and clamp (3). Joint of clamp should be positioned under the trigger coil wires as shown in Fig. M12-45. Assemble distributor to the economizer collar (29–Fig. M12-42) and adapter (25), then install washers (22, 23 and 24). Tighten cap nut (21), back nut off until nearest notch lines up with tang of washer (23), then bend tang into notch. Install spacer (20) and pulley (19) over drive key.

Turn flywheel and distributor pulley until index mark on flywheel is aligned with arrow on distributor pulley.

Flywheel index mark on 800 models prior to serial number 2881082 is a

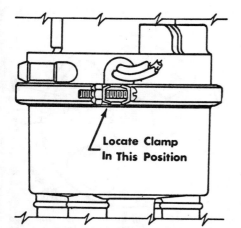

Fig. M12-45 — The joint of distributor cap clamp should be located below the wires from the timing coil.

straight white line (Fig. M12-34). Flywheel index mark on all other models is three dots (Fig. M12-35). Dots are on flywheel decal on late 850 models. When flywheel index mark and arrow on distributor pulley are aligned, install drive belt over pulley.

Make certain that index marks on flywheel and arrow on distributor pulley are correctly aligned and on center line of crankshaft and distributor shaft. Install cover (18—Fig. M12-42)and tighten the retaining screw to 60 in.-lbs. (6.8 N·m). Refer to the SPEED CONTROL LINKAGE paragraphs for adjusting linkage and ignition timing.

Thunderbolt Models Without Distributor

An alternator driven capacitor discharge ignition (CDI) system is used. Ignition system consists of flywheel, stator, trigger assembly, switch box and ignition coils. The stator is mounted below the flywheel and includes two capacitor charging coils. The trigger assembly consists of two trigger coils and is mounted below the flywheel. Ignition timing is advanced and retarded by rotating trigger assembly in relation to the inner flywheel magnets. Refer to SPEED CONTROL LINKAGE section for timing adjustment procedures. Diodes, capacitors and SCR's are in the switch box. Switch box, trigger assembly and stator must be serviced as unit assemblies. Refer to Figs. M12-58 and M12-59 for wiring diagram.

If engine malfunction is noted, and the ignition system is suspected, make sure the spark plugs and all electrical wiring are in acceptable condition and all electrical connections are clean and tight prior to trouble-shooting CDI system.

To properly test switch box and ignition coils, use Quicksilver Multi-Meter DVA Tester part 91-99750 or a suitable voltmeter capable of measuring a minimum of 400 DC volts used with Quicksilver Direct Voltage Adaptor (DVA) part 91-89045. Follow instructions provided by tester manufacturer when performing tests. If these testers are not available, use a process of elimination when testing the ignition system. Stator and trigger assemblies can be effectively tested using a suitable ohmmeter.

NOTE: All tests that involve cranking or running the engine must be performed with lead wires connected. Switch box case MUST be grounded to engine for all tests or switch box may be damaged.

To test ignition system, proceed as follows:

IGNITION COILS PRIMARY TEST. Connect DVA red test lead to ignition coil positive (+) terminal and black test lead to coil negative (−) terminal. Position tester selector switch to DVA/400. Tester should read 150-250 volts at cranking or idle speed (300-1000 rpm) and 180-280 volts at 1000-4000 rpm. If voltage readings are below specified reading, refer to SWITCH BOX STOP CIRCUIT test. If readings are within specifications, connect a suitable spark tester to ignition coil high tension leads, crank engine and note spark. If weak or no spark is noted, renew ignition coil(s). If normal spark is noted, renew spark plugs. If malfunction is still evident after renewing spark plugs, check ignition timing. If ignition timing is erratic, inspect trigger advance linkage for excessive wear or damage and inner flywheel magnets (shifted position or other damage). If timing is within specifications, problem is not in ignition system.

SWITCH BOX STOP CIRCUIT. Connect DVA black test lead to engine ground and red test lead to black/yellow switch box terminal (orange terminal on early models). Set DVA selector switch to DVA/400. Voltage reading at cranking and all running speeds should be 200-360 volts. If reading is within specifications, refer to STATOR tests. If reading is above specified voltages, connect a suitable ohmmeter between trigger brown and white/black leads, then white and violet leads. Trigger resistance should be 700-1000 ohms at both test connections. If not, renew trigger assembly. If trigger resistance is acceptable, renew switch box and repeat SWITCH BOX STOP CIRCUIT test. If SWITCH BOX STOP CIRCUIT test reading is below specified voltage, disconnect ignition switch, stop switch and mercury switch from black/yellow switch box terminal (orange switch box terminal on early models). With stop switch, ignition switch and mercury switch isolated, repeat SWITCH BOX STOP CIRCUIT test. If reading is now within specification, ignition switch, stop switch or mercury switch is defective. If reading remains below specification refer to STATOR test.

STATOR. Connect DVA black lead to engine ground and red lead to blue switch box terminal. Set DVA selector switch to DVA/400. Voltage reading should be 210-310 volts at cranking and idle speeds and 190-310 volts at 1000-4000 rpm. Switch DVA red test lead to red switch box terminal. Leave black test lead connected to engine ground. Voltage reading should be 20-100 volts at cranking or idle speeds and 140-310 volts at 1000-4000 rpm.

NOTE: A shorted or open capacitor inside switch box will result in faulty stator voltage readings during cranking and running tests. Stator resistance should be checked as follows before failing stator.

If either STATOR test is not to specification, proceed as follows: Connect a suitable ohmmeter between blue and blue/white stator leads. Resistance between blue and blue/white stator leads should be 5700-8000 ohms (5900-6900 ohms on stator with part number 398-5454A21). Next, connect ohmmeter between red and red/white stator leads. Resistance should be 56-76 ohms (125-175 ohms on stator with part number 398-5454A21). No continuity should be present between blue or red stator lead and engine ground. Renew stator if resistance is not as specified. If stator resistance is as specified, renew switch box and repeat STATOR tests.

IGNITION COILS RESISTANCE TEST. Disconnect wires and high tension lead from coil. Connect a suitable ohmmeter between coil positive (+) and negative (−) terminals. Resistance should be 0.02-0.04 ohm. On orange colored coil, no continuity should be present between high tension tower and either positive (+) or negative (−) terminal. On blue or black colored coil, resistance between high tension tower and either positive (+) or negative (−) terminal, or between high tension tower and engine ground should be 800-1100 ohms. Renew ignition coil(s) if resistance is not as specified.

NOTE: Ignition coil resistance tests can detect only open or shorted windings. If coil resistance is within specification and still suspected as defective, coil must be tested using DVA meter as previously outlined in IGNITION COIL test. If DVA meter is not available, substitute a known good ignition coil and run engine to test.

Recommended spark plugs for Model 500 prior to serial number 4576237 and Model 650 is AC V40FFM or Champion L76V. Recommended spark plug for Model 500 after serial number 4576236 and Models 45, 50 75, 80, 800 and 850 is AC V40FFK or Champion L78V.

"Lightning Energizer" Ignition

The "Lightning Energizer" ignition system consists of the drive unit, switch box and the high tension coil. Refer to Fig. M12-46. Electrical current for ignition is generated within driver unit (A). Wire (S) is connected to the ignition switch and is grounded to stop engine.

Observe the following cautions and use only approved methods for checking the system to prevent damage to the components.
1. DO NOT install incorrect spark plugs or lead wires.
2. DO NOT disconnect any wires while engine is running.
3. DO NOT use any tachometer except those approved for use with this system. (Mercury A-91-45294A3 or A-91-4816A6 with module A-52552A3 for boat or C-91-31591 for use while servicing.)

TROUBLESHOOTING. Failure of one (or more) of the "Lightning Energizer" ignition components will normally prevent the motor from running at all. Some ignition problems that will cause an engine to lack performance are:
1. Incorrectly adjusted speed control linkage.
2. Faulty (or incorrect) spark plugs.
3. Faulty (or incorrect) high tension wires.
4. Intermittent short (ground) in the mercury safety switch (D−Fig. M12-46), ignition key switch, tachometer or ignition low tension wires (1 through 7).
If engine will not start, disconnect the salmon and brown wires (6 and 7) from the blue terminal of switch box (B).

NOTE: Leave blue wire (2) attached.

Attempt to start engine. If engine starts, grounding the blue switch box terminal to the cowl frame will stop engine and fault is in the disconnected wires, switches or tachometer. If engine will not start, proceed with remaining tests.
Disconnect red, white and blue wires (1, 2 and 3−M12-46) from switch box and check continuity using an ohmmeter. Resistance between red wire (1) and white wire (3) should be 4.1-4.3 ohms when tested on Rx100 scale of ohmmeter. Resistance between blue wire (2) and white wire (3) should be 10.0-11.0 ohms when tested on Rx100 scale. Test resistance between each of the three wires (1, 2 and 3) and housing of driver (A) using the Rx100 scale. Resistance should be infinite. If any resistance is incorrect, the driver unit (A) should be disassembled and tested further. If resistance is correct, check the high tension coil (C) as follows:
Disconnect the black and green wires (4 and 5) from switch box terminals and the coil secondary wire (8) from coil. The resistance between the two leads (4 and 5) should be zero when tested on Rx1 ohmmeter scale. Resistance between one (either) of the leads (4 or 5) and the

secondary terminal should be 3.0-3.6 ohms when tested on Rx1000 scale. Check resistance between each of the three leads (4, 5 and secondary terminal) to the coil bracket. Resistance should be infinite when checked on the Rx1000 scale. If any resistance is incorrect, the high tension coil should be renewed. If resistance tests of ignition driver (A) and coil (C) are correct, the switch box (B) should be renewed.

DRIVER UNIT. If resistance checks listed in the TROUBLESHOOTING section indicate that drive unit is faulty, proceed as follows:
Unbolt and remove driver from the pilot assembly (13 − Fig. M12-47). Remove cap (1−Fig. M12-48), rotor (4) and cover (6). Remove the four retaining screws (15), clamp (17) and terminal block (14), then withdraw coils (12 and 13).

NOTE: The rotor (4) and the retaining screws (15) are installed with Loctite. The housing (16) should be heated slightly before attempting to remove screws (15).

The coils (12 and 13) can be checked and renewed (if necessary) individually after detaching wires from soldered connections of terminal block (14). Rotating magnet (10) and bearings (9 and 11) can be removed after removing bearing cap (8).
When assembling, Loctite should be used on the screws attaching bearing cap (8) to housing (16). After bearings (9 and 11), rotating magnet (10) and bearing cap (8) are assembled in housing (16), rotate the shaft to check for binding. When assembling coil, make certain that the RED coil (410-430 ohms

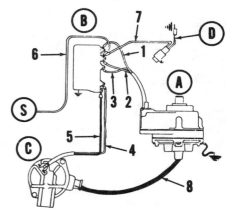

Fig. M12-46 — Schematic of components used on models with Lightning Energizer ignition system. Wire (S) is attached to the ignition switch and tachometer.

A. Ignition driver unit	3. White
B. Switch box	4. Green
C. High tension coil	5. Black
D. Mercury safety switch	6. Salmon
1. Red	7. Brown
2. Blue	8. High tension (secondary) wire

resistance) is installed at (R). The BLUE coil (10-11 ohms resistance) is installed at (B). Apply Loctite to the four coil retaining screws (15) and tighten to 22-25 in.-lbs. (2.5-2.8 N·m). After the coil wires are soldered to the terminal block, coat the terminals with liquid neoprene (Mercury C-92-25711-1). Cover gasket (7) should be renewed if damaged, before installing cover (6). Clean the splines of rotating magnet shaft (10) and make certain that clip (5) is pressed into bottom of rotor (4). Apply three drops of Loctite to bottom of hole in rotor and install on shaft. Check condition of brush and spring (2), cap (1) and gasket (3), before assembling. Mating splines on shafts (19 – Fig. M12-47) and (10 – Fig. M12-48) are provided with a blind spline to facilitate installation. Because of the electronic timing characteristics, the speed control linkage adjustment should be checked after the ignition drive unit is repaired or renewed.

To remove the ignition drive belt (24—Fig. M12-47), remove pulley flange (15) and disengage belt from pulley (17). Remove flywheel using a suitable puller and withdraw the belt. When installing, position drive belt under the alternator stator (if so equipped) and around crankshaft. Install flywheel being careful not to damage the belt. On Model 500, turn the flywheel and ignition driven pulley until the straight line on flywheel is aligned with arrow on driven pulley as shown in Fig. M12-34, then install drive belt over the pulley. On Model 650, turn the flywheel and driven pulley until the three ignition timing dots on flywheel are aligned with the arrow on ignition driven pulley as shown in Fig. M12-35, then install drive belt over the pulley. On all models, the correct mark on flywheel must be toward the arrow on pulley and both must be on center line between the crankshaft and ignition drive shaft, as shown in Fig. M12-34 or M12-35, after belt is installed.

SPARK PLUGS. The spark plugs should be renewed if the center electrode is burned back more than $1/32$ inch (0.79 mm) below flat surface of plug end. Refer to Fig. M12-36. AC type V40FFM or radio noise suppression type VR40FFM surface gap spark plugs should be used.

COOLING SYSTEM

WATER PUMP. The rubber impeller type water pump is housed in the gearcase housing. The impeller is mounted on and driven by the lower unit drive shaft.

When cooling system problems are encountered, first check the water inlet for plugging or partial stoppage, then if not corrected, remove the gearcase housing as outlined in LOWER UNIT section and examine the water pump, water tubes and seals.

Early models were originally equipped with aluminum water pump housings; however, on later models, the water pump housings are plastic. The later type pump can be installed on early models. When assembling, observe the assembly notes, cautions and tightening torques listed in the LOWER UNIT section.

POWER HEAD

R&R AND DISASSEMBLE. To remove the power head assembly, first disconnect the battery and remove the top and side cowling. Remove electric starter, then disconnect all interfering wires and linkage. Remove the stud nuts which secure the power head to lower unit then jar power head on exhaust side to loosen gasket. Lift power head from lower unit and install on a suitable stand. Remove the flywheel, magneto or distributor, alternator-generator and the carburetors. Exhaust manifold cover, cylinder block cover and transfer port covers should be removed for cleaning and inspection.

Remove the main bearing locking bolts from front crankcase half, remove the flange bolts; then remove crankcase front half by inserting screwdriver in the recesses provided on side flanges. Use extra care not to spring the parts or to mar the machined, mating surfaces. Gently tap end caps off crankshaft. The crankcase half (6 – Fig. M12-50 or M12-51) and cylinder assembly (15) are matched and align bored, and are available only as an assembly.

Crankshaft, pistons, bearings and connecting rods may now be removed for service as outlined in the appropriate following paragraphs. When assembling, follow the procedures outlined in the ASSEMBLY paragraph.

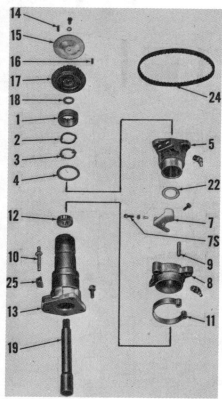

Fig. M12-47 — Exploded view of ignition drive and mounting bracket used on models with Lightning Energizer ignition system.

1. Cap nut	12. Ball bearing
2. Wave washer	13. Pilot assy.
3. Tab washer	14. Pulley drive key
4. Thrust washer	15. Pulley flange
5. Adapter	16. Flange pin
7. Throttle pickup	17. Pulley
7S. Secondary pickup screw	18. Thrust washer
8. Advance collar	19. Drive shaft
9. Pin	22. Washer
10. Pin	24. Drive belt
11. Retard spring	25. Ignition advance stop

Fig. M12-48 — Exploded and partially assembled views of the Lightning Energizer ignition driver. The coils (12 & 13) are color coded and must be correctly assembled as shown in the partially assembled view. Refer to text.

B. Blue coil	9. Bearing
R. Red coil	10. Rotating magnet
1. Cap	11. Bearing
2. Brush & spring	12. Blue coil
3. Gasket	13. Red coil
4. Rotor	14. Terminal block
5. Rotor clip	15. Coil retaining screw
6. Cover	16. Housing
7. Gasket	17. Wire retaining clamp
8. Bearing cap	

ASSEMBLY. When assembling, the crankcase must be completely sealed against both vacuum and pressure. Exhaust manifold and water passages must be sealed against pressure leakage. Whenever power head is disassembled, it is recommended that all gasket surfaces and machined joints without gaskets be carefully checked for nicks and burrs which might interfere with a tight seal. On Models 75, 80, 800 and 850, make certain that threaded holes in cylinder for attaching the water jacket cover (20 – Fig. M12-51) are cleaned.

Lubricate all bearing and friction surfaces with engine oil. Loose needle bearings may be held in place during assembly using a light, nonfibrous grease.

After the crankshaft, connecting rods, pistons and main bearings are positioned in the cylinder, check crankshaft end play. Temporarily install crankshaft end caps (2 and 13 – Fig. M12-50 or M12-51) omitting sealing rings (4 and 9), but using shims (3 and 10) that were originally installed. Tighten end cap to cylinder retaining screws. Use a soft hammer to bump crankshaft each way to seat bearings, then measure end play. To measure end play, (M12-50 or M12-51), bump the crankshaft toward top, and measure clearance between top crankshaft counterweight and end cap as shown in Fig. M12-53. Bump crankshaft toward bottom and again measure clearance between counterweight and end cap. Subtract first (minimum) clearance from second clearance, which will indicate the amount of end play. If end play is not within limits of 0.004-0.012 inch (0.102-0.305 mm) on Model 75 or 0.008-0.012 inch (0.203-0.305 mm) on all other models, add or remove shims (3 or 10—Fig. M12-50 or M12-51) as necessary, then recheck. The crankshaft should be centered by varying the amount of shims between upper (3) and lower (10) shims stacks. When centering crankshaft, make certain the end play is correct. Shims are available in thicknesses of 0.005 and 0.010 inch for Models 50, 75 and 80. Shims (3) are available in thicknesses of 0.006, 0.008 and 0.010 inch for Models 800 and 850, and thicknesses of 0.002, 0.003, 0.005 and 0.010 inch for all other models.

On models equipped with gasket sealing strips (23—Fig. M12-51), use only Permatex #2 Form-a-Gasket (part 92-72592-1) to seal crankcase assembly. Apply sealer to mating surface of crankcase cover (6) making sure sealer covers entire mating surface. Avoid excess application. On models without gasket sealing strips (Fig. M12-50), use only Loctite Master Gasket Sealer (part 92-12564-1) to seal crankcase assembly. Apply sealer to crankcase cover (6) in

a continuous $\frac{1}{16}$ inch (1.6 mm) bead. Run bead to inside of all screw holes. Make sure bead is continuous, but avoid excess application.

On Models 75, 80, 800 and 850, clean the gasket surfaces and threaded holes of the water jacket cover (20—Fig. M12-51) and cylinder (15). Coat the first four threads of all screws (22) with Resiweld and allow to set for 10 minutes. Coat gasket surface of water jacket cover and mating surface of cylinder with gasket sealer, then install gasket (21) and water jacket cover (20). Tighten screws (22) evenly from the center outward to a torque of 200 in.-lbs. (22.6 N·m) on early models and 150 in.-lbs. (16.9 N·m) on later models.

On all models, check the assembly by turning the crankshaft after each step to

check for binding or locking which might indicate improper assembly. Remove the cause before proceeding. Rotate the crankshaft until each piston ring in turn appears in one of the exhaust or transfer ports, then check by pressing on ring with a blunt tool. Ring should spring back when released; if it does not, a broken or binding ring is indicated, and the trouble should be corrected.

Tighten the crankcase, exhaust cover and cylinder cover cap screws beginning with screws in center of crankcase and working outward. Tightening torques are given in the CONDENSED SERVICE DATA table.

PISTONS, PINS, RINGS AND CYLINDERS. Before detaching connecting rods from crankshaft, make

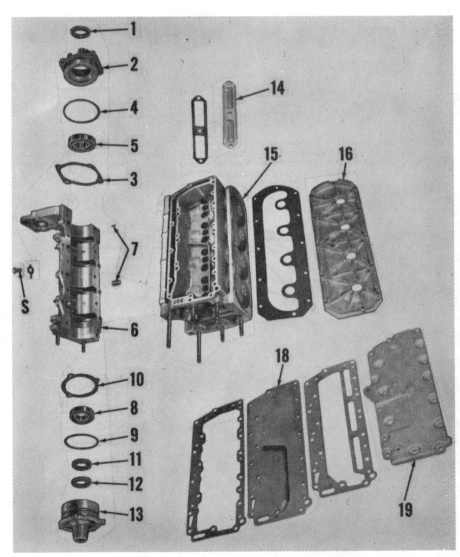

Fig. M12-50—Exploded view of crankcase and related components used on Model 650; Models 45, 50 and 500 are similar. Refer to Fig. M12-51.

S. Main bearing screw	5. Ball bearing
1. Oil seal	6. Crankcase half
2. End cap	7. Dowel pins
3. Shim	8. Ball bearing
4. "O" ring	9. "O" ring

10. Shim	15. Cylinder half
11. Oil seal	16. Cylinder cover
12. Oil seal	18. Exhaust plate
13. End cap	19. Exhaust cover
14. Transfer port cover	

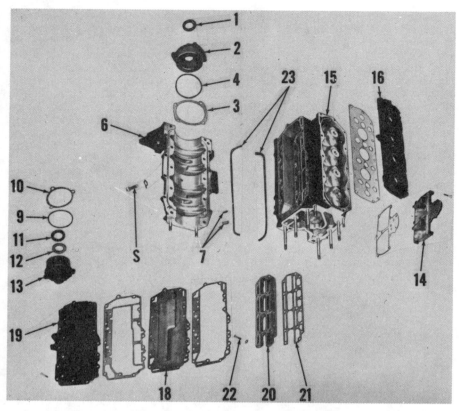

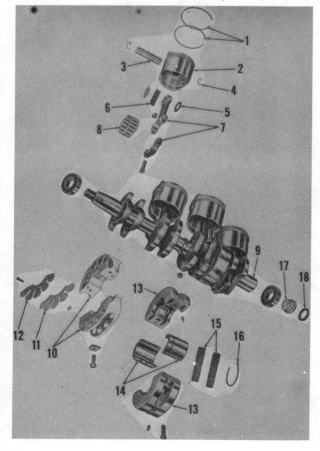

Fig. M12-51 — Exploded view of Model 800 prior to 1978 crankcase and associated parts showing the water jacket cover (20), gasket (21) and attaching screws (22). Sealing strips are shown at (23). Model 800 after 1977 and Models 75, 80 and 850 crankcase assembly have similar construction. Refer to Fig. M12-50 for parts identification.

Fig. M12-52 — Exploded view of Model 850 crankshaft and associated parts. Other motors are similar.

1. Piston rings
2. Piston
3. Piston pin
4. Retainers
5. Bearing washers
6. Needle rollers
7. Connecting rod
8. Caged needle bearing
9. Crankshaft
10. Intermediate main bearing
11. Reed petals
12. Reed stop
13. Main bearing
14. Outer race
15. Needle rollers
16. Retaining ring
17. Seal retainer
18. Seal

sure that rod and cap are properly identified for correct assembly to each other and in the correct cylinder.

Maximum allowable cylinder bore wear or out-of-round is 0.004 inch (0.102 mm). Worn or slightly damaged, standard size, cylinders may be repaired by boring and honing to fit an oversize piston. Pistons and rings are available in 0.015 inch (0.38 mm) oversize on early models and 0.015 inch (0.38 mm) and 0.030 inch (0.76 mm) oversizes on later models.

Piston rings are interchangeable in the ring grooves and are pinned in place.

Piston pin is pressed in piston bosses and secured with retaining rings. The retaining rings should not be reused. Two types of retaining rings have been used and must NOT be interchanged. Models 75, 80, 800 and 850 use "C" rings and other models use "G" type retaining rings. Piston end of connecting rod is fitted with loose needle rollers. Refer to the CONNECTING RODS, BEARINGS AND CRANKSHAFT paragraphs for number of rollers used.

The piston pin needle rollers use the connecting rod bore and the piston pin as bearing races. When assembling, install bearing washers and needle bearings in piston end of connecting rod using light nonfibrous grease to hold them in place. Use a torch lamp or suitable equivalent to heat piston to approximately 135°F (57°C) on early models and 190°F (88°C) on late models, then install and center the piston pin. Special tools are available from Mercury Marine for installing and centering the piston pin. Piston must be installed so that sharp, vertical side of deflector will be to starboard (intake) side of cylinder block.

Assemble the connecting rod and piston assemblies, together with the main bearing units to the crankshaft; then install the complete assembly in cylinder half of block. Number 2 and number 3 piston should be started into

Fig. M12-53 — Refer to text for method of checking crankshaft end play. The crankshaft should be centered in the cylinder block.

cylinders first. Use the Mercury Ring Compressor Kit (C-91-47844A2), if available; or carefully compress each ring with the fingers if kit is not available. Thoroughly lubricate pistons and rings during assembly.

CONNECTING RODS, BEARINGS AND CRANKSHAFT. Upper and lower ends of crankshaft are carried by ball bearings. The second and fourth main bearings (10–Fig. M12-52) also contain the inlet reed valves. The third main bearing (13) contains loose needle rollers (15) which ride in a split type outer race (14), held together by a retaining ring (16).

The connecting rod uses loose needle rollers at piston end. The crankpin end of connecting rod contains loose needle rollers in Models 45, 50, 500 and 650. A caged roller bearing is used at crankpin end of connecting rod in Models 75, 80, 800 and 850. Refer to the following table for number of rollers used.

PISTON PIN BEARINGS

Model	No. of Rollers
45, 50 and 500	27
75, 80, 650, 800 and 850	29

CRANKPIN BEARINGS

Model	No. of Rollers
45, 50 and 500	25
650	32
75, 80 and 800	Caged Rollers
850	Caged Rollers

MAIN BEARINGS

Model	No. of Rollers
45, 50 and 500:	
Single Row	28
Double Row	56
All other models (each main bearing)	56

Check rod for alignment, using Mercury Alignment Tool, or by placing rod on a surface plate and checking with a light.

If bearing surface of rod and cap is rough, scored, worn or shows evidence of overheating, renew the connecting rod. Inspect crankpin and main bearing journals. If scored, out-of-round or worn, renew the crankshaft. Check the crankshaft for straightness using a dial indicator and "V" blocks.

Inspect and adjust the reed valves as outlined in REED VALVE paragraph, and reassemble as outlined in ASSEMBLY paragraph.

MANUAL STARTER

Refer to Fig. M12-54 for rewind starter used on Models 45, 50 and 500. Remove the top cowl and rewind starter assembly from power head. Insert a

screwdriver in slot in top of sheave shaft (19) and loosen the left-hand threaded nut (3). Allow the screwdriver and shaft (19) to turn clockwise until rewind spring unwinds. Pry anchor (22) out of starter handle and remove anchor and handle from rope. Remove nut (3), invert starter assembly and remove the starter components, making sure that rewind spring (7) remains in housing recess as sheave (10) is removed. Remove spring (7) and allow it to unwind slowly. Care must be taken during spring removal to prevent injury.

Lubricate components with Quicksilver Multipurpose Lubricant and reassemble by reversing disassembly procedure. Install spring guide bushing (8) with chamfered end toward pulley (10). Make sure that pawls (12) are all installed the same way, with radius to outside and identification mark away from sheave (10). Install retainer (15) with cup end out and position washer (16) and wave washer (17) in cup. Make certain that tang on spring retainer (6) engages slot in sheave shaft (19). Position starter with end of shaft (19) through housing (5) and install lockwasher (4) and nut (3). Pull free end of rewind rope through housing and install handle (21) and anchor (22). Turn sheave shaft (19) counterclockwise until handle is pulled against starter housing, plus an additional 1¼ to 2 turns, then tighten nut (3). Pull rope out and check for proper operation.

Adjust starter interlock cable on 45 and 50 models so starter cannot operate unless outboard is in neutral gear.

ELECTRICAL SYSTEM

Refer to Figs. M12-56, M12-57, M12-58 and M12-59 for wiring diagrams. Be-

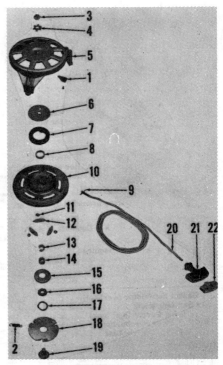

Fig. M12-54—Exploded view of Model 500 rewind starter assembly. Starter used on Models 45 and 50 is similar.

1. Rope guide		12. Pawls	
2. Spring		13. Bushing	
3. Nut		14. Spacer	
4. Lockwasher		15. Retainer	
5. Starter housing		16. Washer	
6. Retainer		17. Wave washer	
7. Recoil spring		18. Plate	
8. Bushing		19. Sheave shaft	
9. Rope retaining pin		20. Rope	
10. Sheave		21. Handle	
11. Wave washers		22. Anchor	

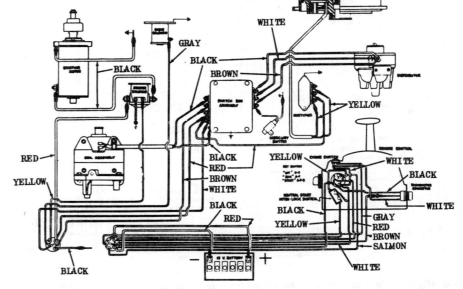

Fig. M12-56 — Wiring diagram typical of most models with Thunderbolt ignition and a distributor.

fore servicing motors with Thunderbolt ignition system, refer to cautions listed in the applicable ignition paragraphs.

On all motors equipped with flywheel alternator, the rectifier will be damaged if battery leads are disconnected while motor is running or leads are reversed.

On motors with Thunderbolt ignition and a distributor, the rectifier assembly is designed to protect the ignition switch box if battery terminals or har-

ness plug becomes loose with motor running. However, the rectifier assembly will be damaged. If battery terminals are reversed, the rectifier and the ignition switch box will be damaged. The motor can be operated without rectifier if the two yellow or yellow/red wires (from the alternator) are disconnected from rectifier and taped separately.

LOWER UNIT

PROPELLER AND DRIVE CLUTCH. Protection for the motor is built into a special cushioning clutch in the propeller hub. No adjustment is possible on the propeller or clutch. Various pitch propellers are available and propeller should be selected to provide full throttle engine operation within rpm range listed in CONDENSED SERVICE DATA table at the beginning of section. Propellers other than those designed for the motor must not be used.

R&R AND OVERHAUL. Most service on lower unit can be performed by detaching gearcase housing from driveshaft housing. To remove housing, remove plastic plug and Allen screw from location (1 – Fig. M12-60). Remove trim tab (2) and screw from under trim tab. Remove stud nut from location (3), stud nuts (4) on each side and stud nut (5) if so equipped, then withdraw the lower unit gearcase assembly.

NOTE: On late models with spiral cut gears and tapered bearing, do not lose plunger or spring (67 & 68 – Fig. M12-61).

Remove plugs and drain oil from housing, then secure gearcase in a soft jawed vise, with propeller up. Wedge a piece of wood between propeller and antiventilation plate, remove propeller nut, then remove propeller.

Disassemble gearcase by removing gearcase housing cover nut (61 – Fig. M12-61 or M12-62). Clamp outer end of propeller shaft in a soft jawed vise and remove the gearcase by tapping with a rubber mallet. Be careful not to lose key (59) or shims (47) on early models. Forward gear (40) will remain in housing. Withdraw propeller shaft from bearing carrier (56) and reverse gear (46).

Clamp bearing carrier (56) in a soft jawed vise and remove reverse gear (46) and bearing (49) with an internal expanding puller and slide hammer. Remove and discard propeller shaft rear seals (58).

To remove dog clutch (43) from propeller shaft, remove retaining ring (44). Insert cam follower (8) in hole in shaft and apply only enough pressure on end of cam follower to remove spring pressure, then push out pin (42) with a small punch. The pin passes through drilled holes in dog clutch and operates in slotted holes in propeller shaft.

To disassemble the drive shaft and associated parts, reposition gearcase in vise with drive shaft projecting upward. Remove rubber slinger (11), water pump body (16), impeller (19) and impeller

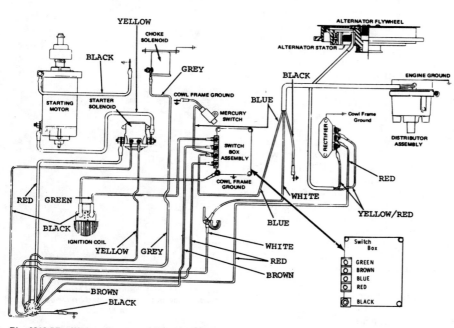

Fig. M12-57 — Wiring diagram of Thunderbolt ignition system with distributor used on some motors. Refer to text for particular motor serial numbers. Remote control unit in Fig. M12-56 is common to all Thunderbolt ignition models. Brown switch box terminal does not exist on some models and brown or orange wire from E and G ignition switch terminals connects to blue switch box terminal.

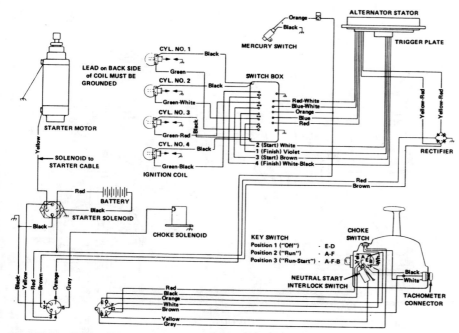

Fig. M12-58 — Wiring schematic for Model 800 (after 1977), Model 500 and Model 850 Thunderbolt models without a distributor. Models 50, 75 and 80 are similar.

drive key (20). Remove flushing screw and withdraw remainder of water pump parts. Clamp upper end of drive shaft in a soft jawed vise, remove pinion retaining nut or screw (37); then tap gearcase off drive shaft and bearing. Note position and thickness of shims (30 and 30A) on drive shaft upper bearing.

On all models, mesh position of pinion is controlled by shims (30) placed underneath the bearing. On models with ball type upper bearing, shims (30A) control shaft end play. The shims are identical but should not be interchanged or mixed, except to adjust mesh position of drive pinion.

After drive shaft has been removed, forward gear (40) and bearing cone can be withdrawn. Use an internal expanding type puller to withdraw bearing cup if removal is required. Remove and save shim pack (38).

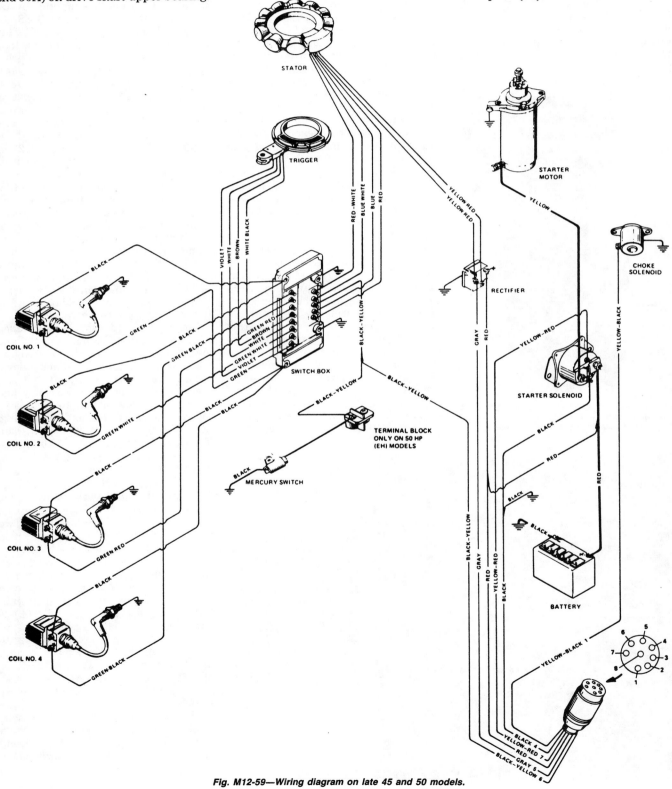

Fig. M12-59—Wiring diagram on late 45 and 50 models.

Shift shaft (5) and cam (7) can be removed after removing forward gear and unscrewing bushing (3) from gearcase housing.

If gear wear was abnormal or if any parts that affect gear alignment were renewed, check and adjust gear mesh as follows: Install forward gear (40—Figs. M12-61 or M12-62) and bearing (39) using shims (38) that were originally installed. Position shims (30) that were originally installed at bottom of bearing bore. On models with taper bearing (32—Fig. M12-61) and spiral gear teeth,

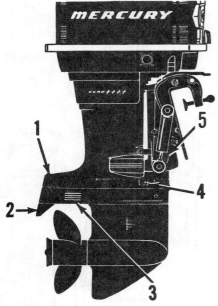

Fig. M12-60 — To remove the lower unit gearcase assembly, remove the attaching screws and stud nuts from position indicated.

install bearing cup (32) in housing bore against shims (30). On all models, position drive pinion (35—Fig. M12-61 or M12-62) in housing and insert drive shaft (33), with bearing (32) installed, into housing, bearing (34) and gear (35). On all models with ball type bearing, the bearing must be firmly seated in housing bore. On all models, install retaining screw or nut (37). Coat gears (35 and 40) with bearing blue and check mesh position. On models with spiral gears, it will be necessary to push down on end of drive shaft while checking mesh position. On all models, if gears do not mesh in center of teeth, add or remove shims (30) under bearing as necessary. After setting mesh position, check backlash between teeth of gears (35 and 40). Backlash should be 0.003-0.005 inch (0.08-0.13 mm) on models 45, 50 and 500 with spiral cut gears and 0.006-0.008 inch (0.15-0.20 mm) on models 500, 650 and 800 models with straight cut gears. Backlash should be 0.014-0.016 inch (0.36-0.41 mm) on 850 models and 0.008-0.012 inch (0.20-0.30 mm) on Models 75 and 80. Adjust backlash by varying thickness of shim pack (38) behind bearing cup. Pinion gear (35) and forward gear (40) mesh pattern should be rechecked if backlash is adjusted. Install bearing (49), thrust washer (48) and reverse gear (46) in bearing carrier (56). To check reverse gear (46) backlash on all early models except Model 850 with spiral gears, install bearing carrier and gear assembly using original shims (47). If backlash is not within 0.003-0.005 inch (0.08-0.13 mm) on Models 45, 50 and 500, or 0.006-0.008 inch (0.15-0.20 mm) on all other

models, vary thickness of shims (47) as necessary. Reverse gear backlash is not adjustable on models with spiral cut gears, but may be checked to ensure gearcase is assembled properly.

When reassembling, long splines on shift rod (5—Figs. M12-61 or M12-62) should be toward top. Shift cam (7) is installed with notches up and toward rear. Assemble shifting parts (9, 8S, 43, 42 and 44) into propeller shaft (45). Pin (42) should be through hole in slide (8S). Position follower (8) in end of propeller shaft and insert shaft into bearing (41) and forward gear. Install the reverse gear and bearing carrier assembly using new seals (55 and 58). Lip of inner seal (58) should face in and lip of outer seal (58) should face propeller (out). On models with ball type bearing at (32), install shims (30A) above bearing and position new gasket (29) and water pump base (23) on housing. Add shims (30A) until the water pump base stands out slightly from gasket, then measure clearance between gasket and water pump base with a feeler gage. Remove shims (30A) equal to 0.002-0.003 inch (0.051-0.076 mm) less than clearance measured. When water pump is tightened down, compression of a new gasket (29) will be sufficient to hold bearing (32) in position with zero clearance.

Upper oil seal (26) should be installed with lips facing up (toward engine) and lower oil seal (27) should be pressed into water pump base with lips facing down toward propeller shaft. Install remainder of water pump assembly and tighten the screw or nuts to the following recommended torque. Torque ¼-28 nuts to 25-30 in.-lbs. (2.8-3.4 N·m). Torque 5/16-24 nuts to 35-40 in.-lbs. (3.9-4.5 N·m). Torque ¼-20 screws to 15-20 in.-lbs. (1.7-2.2 N·m).

Lower spacer (2L – Fig. M12-61 or M12-62) is installed with groove down. Note two types of reverse locking cam (2C) in Figs. M12-63 and M12-64. Two tabs of reverse locking cam shown in Fig. M12-63 must be aligned with left front stud when unit is in forward gear. Install reverse locking cam shown in Fig. M12-64 with high part of cam aligned as shown with unit in neutral. Push rod guide (2G – Fig. M12-62) is located in drive shaft housing.

Before attaching gearcase housing to the drive shaft housing, make certain that shift cam (7 – Fig. M12-61 or M12-62) and the shift lever (on motor) are in forward gear position on early models and neutral position on late models. In forward gear position, shift shaft (5) should be in clockwise position (viewed from top end of shaft). Complete assembly by reversing disassembly procedure.

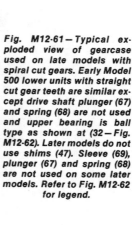

Fig. M12-61 — Typical exploded view of gearcase used on late models with spiral cut gears. Early Model 500 lower units with straight cut gear teeth are similar except drive shaft plunger (67) and spring (68) are not used and upper bearing is ball type as shown at (32 – Fig. M12-62). Later models do not use shims (47). Sleeve (69), plunger (67) and spring (68) are not used on some later models. Refer to Fig. M12-62 for legend.

Later models are equipped with two seals which fit over upper drive shaft splines. Install splined seal on drive shaft splines with splined seal end toward top of drive shaft, then install remaining seal with small end towards top of drive shaft.

On models so equipped, make certain that spring (68–Fig. M12-61) and plunger (67) are positioned before attaching gearcase to drive shaft housing.

POWER TILT/TRIM

Non-Integral Type

FLUID. Recommended fluid is SAE 10W-30 or 10W-40 automotive oil. With outboard in full up position, oil level should reach bottom of fill plug hole threads. Do not overfill.

BLEEDING. To bleed air from hydraulic system, position outboard at full tilt and engage tilt lock lever. Without disconnecting hoses, remove hydraulic trim cylinders. Be sure fluid reservoir is full and remains so during bleeding operation. Remove down circuit bleed screw (D–Fig. M12-70) and "O" ring. Press "IN" control button for a few seconds, release button and wait approximately one minute. Repeat until

expelled oil is air-free. Install "O" ring and bleed screw (D) and repeat procedure on opposite cylinder. Place cylinder in a horizontal position so bleed port (P–Fig. M12-71) is up and remove up circuit bleed screw (U). Press "UP" and "UP/OUT" control buttons for a few seconds, release buttons and wait approximately one minute. Repeat until expelled oil is air-free. Install "O" ring and bleed screw (U) and repeat procedure on opposite cylinder. Reinstall cylinders.

Late models are not equipped with bleed screws (Figs. M12-70 and M12-71) and are essentially self-bleeding. Loosen reservoir vent screw (adjacent to fill plug) two turns and operate system through several full in/full out cycles while making sure reservoir remains full of oil.

ADJUST TRIM LIMIT SWITCH. Operate trim control so outboard is in full down position. Press "UP/OUT" or "UP" control button and hold until pump motor stops. Outboard should tilt up and stop so there is ½ inch (12.7 mm) overlap (L–Fig. M12-72) between swivel bracket flange (W) and clamp bracket flange (M). Pull up on lower unit to remove slack when checking overlap (L). Note that if cylinder rods enter

cylinders more than an additional ⅛ inch (3.17 mm), hydraulic system should be bled of air as outlined in BLEEDING section. If overlap (L) is incorrect, loosen retainer screw (R—Fig. M12-73), then turn adjusting nut (N) counterclockwise to increase overlap or clock-

Fig. M12-63 – View of reverse lock cam with two tangs. The reverse lock cam must be installed on splines as shown when in forward gear position.

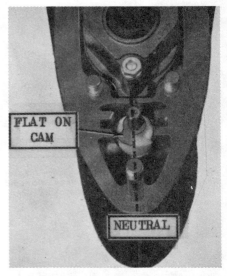

Fig. M12-64 – View of reverse lock cam with a single cam. Cam must be in position when lower unit (and shift-shaft) is in neutral.

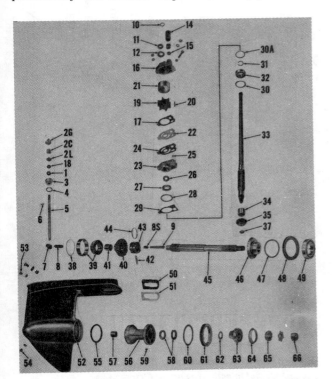

Fig. M12-62 – Exploded view of gearcase assembly typical of Model 650 before serial number 2997339 and Model 800 before serial number 3059821.

1. Oil seal	4. "O" ring	8S. Slide
2C. Reverse locking cam	5. Shift shaft	9. Spring
2G. Push rod guide	6. Snap ring	10. "O" ring
2L. Lower spacer	7. Shift cam	11. Rubber ring (slinger)
3. Bushing	8. Cam follower	12. Oil seal

14. Seal
15. Nylon washer
16. Water pump body
17. Gasket
18. Rubber washer
19. Impeller
20. Drive key
21. Insert
22. Plate
23. Pump base
24. Gasket
25. Dowel
26. Oil seal
27. Spring loaded oil seal
28. "O" ring
29. Gasket
30. & 30A. Shims
31. Snap ring
32. Ball bearing
33. Drive shaft
34. Roller bearing
35. Drive pinion
37. Nut
38. Shim
39. Tapered roller bearing
40. Forward gear
41. Roller bearing
42. Cross pin
43. Dog clutch
44. Retaining ring
45. Propeller shaft
46. Reverse gear
47. Shim
48. Thrust washer
49. Ball bearing
50. Exhaust tube seal
51. Support plate
52. Gear housing
53. Vent screw
54. Filler screw
55. "O" ring
56. Bearing carrier
57. Roller bearing
58. Oil seals
59. Key
60. Washer
61. Housing cover nut
62. Thrust washer
63. Thrust hub
64. Cupped washer
65. Splined washer
66. Propeller nut

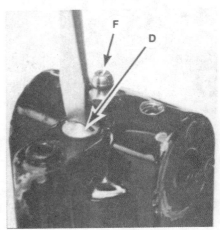

Fig. M12-70 – View showing location of down circuit bleed screw (D) and grease fitting (F).

Fig. M12-71 — View showing location of up circuit bleed screw (U) and bleed port (P).

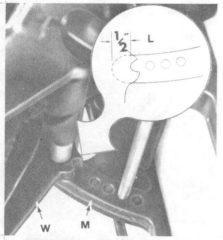

Fig. M12-72 — Overlap (L) between swivel bracket flange (W) and clamp bracket flange (M) should be ½ inch (12.7 mm).

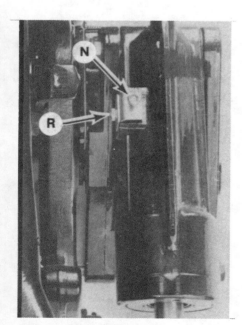

Fig. M12-73 — Loosen retainer screw (R) and turn trim limit adjusting nut (N) to adjust trim limit switch.

wise to decrease overlap. Retighten retaining screw (R) and recheck adjustment.

PRESSURE TEST. To check hydraulic system pressure, disconnect four hoses attached to control valve as shown in Fig. M12-74; small hoses are for up circuit and large hoses are for down circuit. Connect a pressure gage to one up circuit port (small) of control valve and another pressure gage to one down circuit port (large). Screw plugs into remaining ports. Check fluid reservoir and fill if necessary. Operate trim control in up direction and note pressure gage reading. Minimum pressure should be 3500 psi (24.1 MPa) on new pumps with a red sleeve on wires, 3200-

Fig. M12-74 — View of control valve showing location of up circuit hoses (U) and down circuit hoses (D).

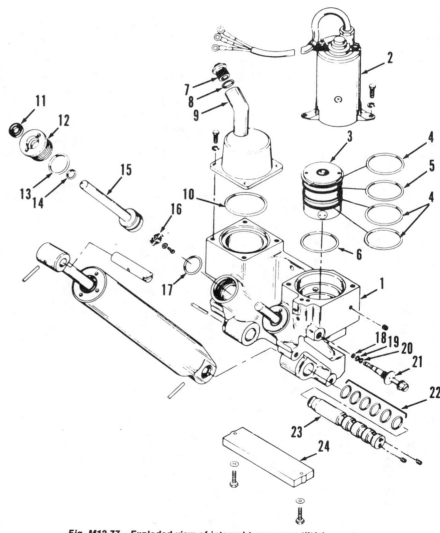

Fig. M12-77 — Exploded view of integral type power tilt/trim system.

1. Manifold	7. Fill plug	14. "O" ring (0.612 in. [15.54 mm] ID)
2. Electric motor	8. "O" ring (0.583 in. [14.81 mm] ID)	15. Trim piston & rod
3. Pump assy.	9. Reservoir cover	16. Strainer
4. "O" rings (2.614 in. [66.40 mm] ID)	10. Seal ring	17. "O" ring (1.248 in. [31.70 mm] ID)
5. "O" ring (2.739 in. [69.57 mm] ID)	11. Seal	18. "O" ring (0.114 in. [2.90 mm] ID)
6. "O" ring (2.739 in. [69.57 mm] ID)	12. Cap	
	13. "O" ring (1.475 in. [37.47 mm] ID)	

19. "O" ring (0.208 in. [5.28 mm] ID)
20. "O" ring (0.239 in. [6.07 mm] ID)
21. Manual release valve
22. "O" rings (0.989 in. [25.12 mm] ID
23. Shaft
24. Anode plate

3500 psi (22.0-24.1 MPa) minimum on used pumps with red sleeve on wires or 2700 psi (18.6 MPa) on late model pump with no bleed screws on cylinders. Minimum pressure on all other new pumps is 3000 psi (20.7 MPa) and minimum pressure on all other used pumps is 2700-3000 psi (18.6-20.7 MPa). Release trim control button. Pressure will drop slightly after stabilizing, but should not drop faster than 100 psi (690 kPa) every 15 seconds. Operate trim control in down direction and note pressure gage reading. Minimum pressure is 500-1000 psi (3.4-6.9 MPa) on all models. Release trim control button. Pressure will drop slightly after stabilizing, but should not drop faster than 100 psi (690 kPa) every 15 seconds. If pressure is normal, in-

Fig. M12-78 — Release pressure on system, then remove Allen head plug (U) and install a 5000 psi (34.5 MPa) test gage with a suitable adapter and hose to test system pressure when operated in the "UP" direction. View identifies location of manual release valve (21).

spect trim cylinders and hoses for leakage. If pressure is abnormal, install a known good control valve and recheck pressure. If pressure remains abnormal, renew pump body.

Integral Type

FLUID AND BLEEDING. Recommended fluid is Dexron II or Type AF automatic transmission fluid. Remove fill plug (7—Fig. M12-77) and fill reservoir until fluid is visible in fill tube with the outboard motor in the full-up position.

The hydraulic circuit is self-bleeding as the tilt/trim system is operated through several cycles. After servicing system, be sure to check reservoir level after filling and operating system.

HYDRAULIC TESTING. The system can be checked by connecting a 5000 psi (34.5 MPa) test gage to the UP (U–Fig. M12-78) and DOWN (D–Fig. M12-80) ports. Prior to connecting test gage, place outboard motor in the full-up position and engage tilt lock lever. Unscrew reservoir fill plug and rotate manual release valve (21–Fig. M12-78) three to four turns counterclockwise to release pressure on system. Remove UP or DOWN Allen head test port plug and connect test gage with suitable adapter and hose. Install fill plug and rotate manual release valve clockwise until seated. System pressure when testing at UP (U) port should be a minimum of 1300 psi (8.9 MPa). System pressure when testing at DOWN (D–Fig. M12-80) port should be a minimum of 500 psi (3.5 MPa). Release pressure on

system as previously outlined prior to removing test gage. Reinstall Allen head plug.

OVERHAUL. Refer to Fig. M12-77 for an exploded view of manifold and trim cylinder components, and Fig. M12-79 for an exploded view of tilt cylinder components. Special Mercury socket 91-44487A1 and a spanner wrench is required to service trim and tilt cylinders. Keep all components clean and away from contamination. Keep components separated and label if needed for correct reassembly. Note "O" ring sizes as stated in legends of Figs. M12-77 and M12-79. Lubricate all "O" rings or seal lips with Dexron II or Type AF automatic transmission fluid during reassembly.

Fig. M12-80 — Release pressure on system, then remove Allen head plug (D) and install a 5000 psi (34.5 MPa) test gage with a suitable adapter and hose to test system pressure when operated in the "DOWN" direction.

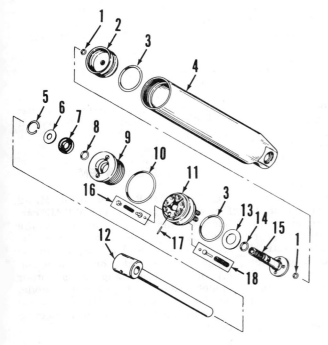

Fig. M12-79 — Exploded view of tilt cylinder components.

1. "O" ring (0.307 in. [7.79 mm] ID)
2. Cup
3. "O" ring (1.957 in. [49.71 mm] ID)
4. Cylinder
5. Circlip
6. Washer
7. Scraper
8. "O" ring (0.854 in. [21.69 mm] ID)
9. Cap
10. "O" ring (2.067 in. [52.5 mm] ID)
11. Piston
12. Rod
13. Washer
14. "O" ring (0.661 in. [16.79 mm] ID)
15. Rod end
16. Check valve assy.
17. Pin
18. Check valve assy.

MERCURY 100 HP (After 1987)
AND 115 HP (After 1988) FOUR-CYLINDER MODELS

CONDENSED SERVICE DATA

TUNE-UP

Hp/rpm	100/4750-5250
	(74.6 kW)
	115/4750-5250
	(85.8 kW)
Bore	3.375 in.
	(85.72 mm)
Stroke	2.930 in.
	(74.42 mm)
Displacement	105 cu. in.
	(1720.6 cc)
Compression at Cranking Speed	*
Firing Order	1-3-2-4
Ignition Type	CDI
Spark Plug:	
NGK	BUHW
AC	V40FFM
Champion	L76V
Idle Speed (in gear)	650-700 rpm
Fuel:Oil Ratio	See Text
Gearcase Oil Capacity	22.5 fl. oz.
	(665.3 mL)

*Compression should not vary more than 15 psi (103.5 kPa) between cylinders.

SIZES-CLEARANCES

Piston Rings:	
End Gap	*
Side Clearance	*
Piston Skirt Clearance	0.005 in.
	(0.13 mm)
Crankshaft Bearing Type:	
Top Main Bearing	Caged Roller
Center Main Bearings	Loose Roller
Number of Rollers	32 Each
Bottom Main Bearing	Ball Bearing
Crankpin	Caged Roller

Piston Pin Bearing:	
Type	Loose Roller
Number of Rollers	29 Each

*Publication not authorized by manufacturer.

TIGHTENING TORQUES

Connecting Rod	*
Crankcase Cover	†
Crankcase End Cap (Lower)	150 in.-lbs.
	(17 N·m)
Cylinder Block Cover	180 in.-lbs.
	(20.3 N·m)
Exhaust Cover	180 in.-lbs.
	(20.3 N·m)
Flywheel Nut	120 ft.-lbs.
	(162.7 N·m)
Fuel Pump Screws	40 in.-lbs.
	(4.5 N·m)
Intake Manifolds	180 in.-lbs.
	(20.3 N·m)
Oil Injection Pump Screws	60 in.-lbs.
	(6.8 N·m)
Power Head-to-Drive Shaft Housing	350 in.-lbs.
	(39.5 N·m)
Reed Block	60 in.-lbs.
	(6.8 N·m)
Spark Plugs	20 ft.-lbs.
	(27.1 N·m)

*Tighten connecting rod screws to 15 in.-lbs. (1.7 N·m), check rod-to-cap alignment then tighten to 30 ft.-lbs. (40.7 N·m). After tightening to 30 ft.-lbs. (40.7 N·m), tighten screws an additional 90 degrees. Refer to text.
†Tighten large inner crankcase cover screws to 25 ft.-lbs. (33.9 N·m) and small outer screws to 180 in.-lbs. (20.3 N·m).

LUBRICATION

The power head is lubricated by oil mixed with the fuel. All models are equipped with oil injection. The oil injection pump delivers oil relative to crankshaft speed and throttle position. The recommended fuel is regular leaded, premium low-lead or unleaded gasoline with minimum octane rating of 86. The recommended oil is Quicksilver 2-Cycle Outboard Oil.

During break-in of a new or rebuilt engine (initial 30 gallons [113.6 L] of fuel), use a 50:1 fuel and oil mixture in the fuel tank in combination with the oil injection system to ensure sufficient power head lubrication. After using the first 30 gallons (113.6 L) of fuel, switch to straight gasoline in the fuel tank.

The lower unit gears and bearings are lubricated by oil contained in the gearcase. The recommended gearcase oil is Quicksilver Super Duty Gear Lubricant. Gearcase capacity is 22.5 fl. oz. (665.3 mL). The lower unit gearcase should be drained and refilled after initial 25 hours of operation, then after every 100 hours or seasonally thereafter. Fill gearcase through drain/fill plug hole until oil reaches the first vent plug hole. Refer to Fig. M13-1. Install first vent plug and continue filling until oil reaches second vent plug hole. When oil reaches second vent plug hole, drain approximately one ounce (30 mL) to allow for oil expansion.

Make sure vent and fill plugs are securely tightened with new gaskets if necessary.

FUEL SYSTEM

CARBURETOR. Refer to Fig. M13-2 for exploded view of typical WME carburetor. Four WME-11 carburetors are used. Carburetor model number may be stamped on face of air box mounting flange on early models or is stamped on top of mounting flange on all other models. Note that carburetor model numbers contain the suffix 1, 2, 3 and 4 for installation on their respective cylinder.

On models 100 and 115, cylinders number 3 and 4 are inoperative at engine speeds below approximately 1800 rpm due to reduced fuel flow from their respective carburetors. On carburetors used on cylinders number 3 and 4, the off idle discharge ports are relocated farther from the power head so the fuel:air mixture at idle speeds is too lean for combustion to occur, yet adequate to lubricate the cylinders. As engine speed reaches approximately 1800 rpm and air flow through carburetors increases, the fuel:air mixture to cylinders 3 and 4 becomes sufficient to support combustion and all four cylinders become operational.

Initial setting of slow speed mixture screw (5) is 1¼ turns open from a lightly seated position. Only top two carburetors are equipped with slow speed mixture screws. Final slow speed mixture adjustment should be performed with engine running at normal operating temperature, in forward gear, with the correct propeller installed and boat in the water, or with the correct test wheel installed and lower unit submersed in a suitable test tank.

Air calibration screw (20) is preset and sealed by the manufacturer, and should not require further adjustment. Conventional carburetor cleaning solutions should not affect the sealant used to secure the factory adjustment.

To check float level, remove float bowl (19) and gasket (13), invert carburetor and measure from float bowl mating surface to float as shown in Fig. M13-3. Float level should be ⁷⁄₁₆ inch (11.1 mm) measured as shown. Carefully bend metal tab (T) to adjust.

Standard main jet (16—Fig. M13-2) size for normal operation at elevations up to 2500 feet (762 m) is 0.054 (1.73 mm) on 100 hp models and 0.074 (1.83 mm) on 115 hp models. Main jet (16) size should be reduced from standard size by 0.002 inch (0.05 mm) for operation at elevations of 2500-5000 feet (762-1524 m), 0.004 inch (0.10 mm) at elevations of 5000-7500 feet (1524-2286 m) and 0.006 inch (0.15 mm) at elevations of 7500 feet (2286 m) and up.

All models are equipped with an electrically operated enrichment valve to provide additional fuel to aid cold starting. Enrichment valve is activated by pushing in on ignition key. Pressurized fuel is fed to the enrichment valve from a "T" fitting between carburetors number 1 and 2. When valve is opened, fuel is fed to all four carburetors through "T" fittings on the intake manifolds of cylinders number 2 and 4, then to cylinders number 1 and 3 through internal passages. Enrichment valve can be operated manually by depressing button located on the valve.

Fig. M13-1—View of drain/fill and vent plugs. Refer to text when refilling gearcase.

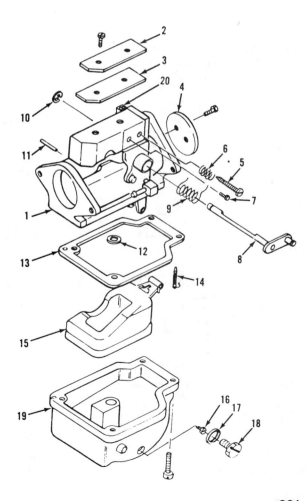

Fig. M13-2—Exploded view of typical WME carburetor.

1. Body
2. Cover
3. Gasket
4. Throttle valve
5. Low speed mixture screw
6. Spring
7. Vent jet (back drag jet)
8. Throttle shaft
9. Spring
10. "E" ring
11. Pin
12. Gasket
13. Gasket
14. Inlet needle
15. Float
16. Main jet
17. Gasket
18. Plug
19. Float bowl
20. Air calibration screw

If enrichment system malfunction is noted, make sure battery voltage is present at valve (yellow/black wire) when key (or choke button) is depressed and that sufficient fuel is being delivered to the valve.

ACCELERATOR PUMP. A diaphragm type linkage operated accelerator pump

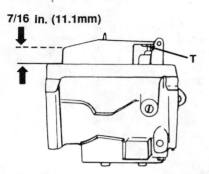

7/16 in. (11.1mm)

Fig. M13-3—Check float level as shown. Bend metal tab (T) to adjust.

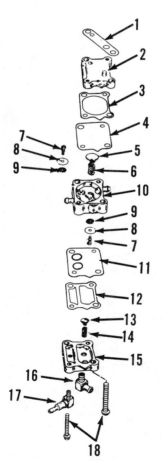

Fig. M13-5—Exploded view of fuel pump assembly.

1. Gasket	10. Pump body
2. Pump base	11. Boost diaphragm
3. Gasket	12. Gasket
4. Diaphragm	13. End cap
5. End cap	14. Spring
6. Spring	15. Chamber plate
7. Retainer	16. Fitting
8. Check valve	17. Check valve
9. Rubber disc	18. Screws

attached to the side of the power head provides additional fuel to cylinders 3 and 4 during rapid acceleration. Fuel from the accelerator pump passes through an inline filter and then to the injectors located in the transfer ports of cylinders 3 and 4. The injectors are equipped with check valves that unseat at approximately 11-14 psi (75.8-96.5 kPa) allowing fuel to flow into cylinders. To test check valves, remove injectors from cylinder block and lubricate valve by spraying a small amount of WD-40 or equivalent into barbed end of valve. Remove excess WD-40 using compressed air. Using a suitable hand-held pump, apply pressure to injector until check valve unseats (approximately 11-14 psi [75.8-96.5 kPa]). After check valve unseats, pressure should not drop below 5 psi (34.5 kPa) in 30 seconds. Renew injector if not as specified.

Accelerator pump adjustment is critical to the proper operation of outboard motor. Refer to SPEED CONTROL LINKAGE section for adjustment.

FUEL PUMP. The diaphragm type fuel pump is activated by crankcase pulsations. Test pump by installing a clear fuel hose between pump and carburetors. Start engine and check for air bubbles in fuel line. Fuel pump output should be approximately 4-6 psi (27.6-41.4 kPa) at full throttle.

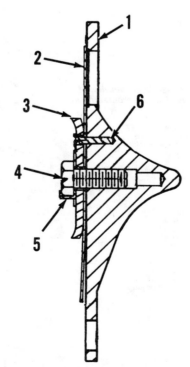

Fig. M13-6—Sectional view of reed valve assembly.

1. Reed block	4. Screw
2. Reed petal	5. Locking tab washer
3. Retainer	6. Pin

Remove fuel pump from power head by unscrewing two Phillips head screws. Disassemble pump by unscrewing two hex head screws. Inspect all components for wear or damage and renew as necessary. Make sure check valve (17—Fig. M13-5) is functioning properly. When reassembling pump, lubricate check valve retainers (7) with engine oil or soapy water to ease installation. Trim end of retainer (7) at ridge to prevent retainer from contacting pump diaphragm.

NOTE: Fuel pump components have a "V" tab on one side for directional reference during assembly. Be CERTAIN "V" tab on all components are aligned.

The manufacturer recommends assembling fuel pump using ¼-inch bolts or dowels as guides to ensure that all components are properly aligned. Be especially careful with gasket (12) and diaphragm (11). The two large holes in diaphragm (11) are provided for oil from injection pump to enter the gasoline flow. Failure to properly align gasket (12) and diaphragm (11) may result in power head damage.

REED VALVES. Reed valve assemblies are located between crankcase cover and intake manifolds. Reed valves can be removed for inspection after removing carburetors and intake manifolds.

Do not disassemble reed valve assembly unless necessary. Screw (4—Fig. M13-6) is installed at the factory using Loctite. Reed petals (2) should be flat and smooth along entire seating surface. Renew reed petals if cracked, chipped or damaged, or if petals stand open in excess of 0.020 inch (0.51 mm). Never attempt to bend or straighten a damaged reed petal.

Make sure reed petals are properly positioned over pins (6) when assembling reed valves. Renew locking tab washer (5) and tighten screw (4) to 60 in.-lbs. (6.8 N·m). It may be necessary to continue tightening screw (4) to align locking tab with flat area of screw, but, do not exceed 100 in.-lbs. (11.3 N·m). Be sure to bend locking tab to secure screw (4).

SPEED CONTROL LINKAGE. To verify timing pointer alignment, install a suitable dial indicator into number 1 (top) spark plug hole. Rotate flywheel clockwise until number 1 piston is at TDC. Zero dial indicator and rotate flywheel counterclockwise until dial indicator indicates approximately 0.600 inch (15.24 mm) BTDC, then rotate flywheel clockwise until dial indicator indicates exactly 0.554 (14.07 mm) BTDC. With flywheel in this position, timing pointer should be aligned with .554 timing mark on flywheel. If not, loosen pointer screws and move pointer as necessary to align pointer with .554 timing mark. Tighten timing pointer screws to 20 in.-lbs. (2.3 N·m).

Ignition timing may be adjusted at cranking speed if desired. To adjust ignition timing at cranking speed, proceed as follows: Remove all spark plugs to prevent engine from starting and install a suitable spark gap tool to spark plug leads. Disconnect throttle cable from throttle lever (2—Fig. M13-8) and connect a suitable timing light to number 1 (top) spark plug lead. Shift outboard into neutral gear. While holding throttle lever (2) in idle position, crank engine while noting timing marks. Adjust idle timing screw (6) to obtain 3 degrees BTDC timing at cranking speed. Next, hold lever (2) so maximum advance screw (10) is against stop. Crank engine while observing timing marks and adjust screw (10) so maximum spark advance is 27 degrees BTDC.

NOTE: Maximum spark advance with engine running at 3000-5000 rpm should be 23 degrees BTDC. Due to the electronic spark advance characteristics of the ignition system, timing adjustment at cranking speed should be set as previously described to obtain the specified spark advance with engine running at 3000-5000 rpm. Timing adjustments performed at cranking speed should be verified, and readjusted if necessary, with engine running at 3000-5000 rpm.

When reinstalling throttle cable on lever (2), adjust throttle cable barrel so cable applies a slight preload (toward idle position) on throttle lever (2). Note that excessive preload will result in difficult forward gear to neutral shifting. Readjust if necessary.

Carburetor throttle valves must be synchronized to open and close at exactly the same time. Proceed as follows to synchronize carburetors and adjust speed control linkage: Loosen cam follower screw (13—Fig. M13-8). Loosen synchronizing screws (4). Make sure all carburetor throttle valves are fully closed, then apply light downward pressure on verticle shaft (3) and tighten screws (4) starting with top screw and working down. Verify that all throttle valves are fully closed after tightening screws (4) and readjust if necessary.

Loosen idle stop screw (5) locknut and hold throttle lever (2) so idle stop screw (5) is against the stop. Hold cam follower roller (8) against throttle cam (7) and adjust idle stop screw (5) to align throttle cam mark (12) with center of roller (8). While holding throttle lever (2) in the idle position, adjust cam follower (9)

to provide a clearance of 0.005-0.020 inch (0.13-0.51 mm) between roller (8) and throttle cam (7), then retighten screw (13). Loosen full throttle stop screw (11) locknut. While holding throttle lever (2) in the full throttle position, adjust full throttle stop screw (11) so carburetor throttle valves are fully open while allowing approximately 0.015 inch (0.38 mm) free play in throttle linkage to prevent throttle valves from bottoming out. Retighten full throttle stop screw locknut.

To adjust accelerator pump, hold throttle cam in the full throttle position, loosen accelerator mounting screws and

adjust pump to provide a clearance of 0.020-0.040 inch (0.51-1.02 mm) between throttle cam and top of accelerator pump casting (not plunger) as shown in Fig. M13-9.

With throttle lever in the idle position, stamped mark on oil injection pump lever should align with stamped mark on oil pump body. Disconnect and adjust length of oil pump control rod to adjust.

NOTE: Some models may have two stamped marks on oil injection pump body. On models so equipped, disregard the mark on the right side (looking straight at pump) and reference mark on left.

Fig. M13-8—View of speed control linkage. Refer to text for synchronization procedure.

1. Spark advance lever
2. Throttle lever
3. Vertical shaft
4. Synchronizing screws
5. Idle stop screw
6. Idle timing screw
7. Throttle cam
8. Cam follower roller
9. Cam follower
10. Maximum spark advance screw
11. Full throttle stop screw
12. Throttle cam mark
13. Cam follower screw

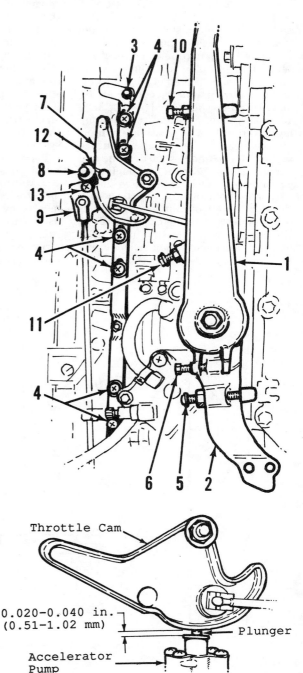

Fig. M13-9—With throttle cam in full throttle position, clearance between cam and top of accelerator pump casting should be as shown. Loosen accelerator pump mounting screws to adjust.

Throttle Cam

0.020-0.040 in. (0.51-1.02 mm)

Plunger

Accelerator Pump

OIL INJECTION SYSTEM

BLEEDING OIL PUMP. Make sure carburetors and oil pump are properly synchronized as outlined in SPEED CONTROL LINKAGE section. To bleed air from oil injection system, loosen bleed screw (B—Fig. M13-10) three or four turns and allow oil to flow from bleed hole (with engine NOT running) until air bubbles are no longer present in oil pump inlet hose. Retighten bleed screw (B) to 25 in.-lbs. (2.8 N·m). Start engine and run at idle speed until no air bubbles are noted in pump outlet hose.

CHECKING OIL PUMP OUTPUT. A 50:1 (25:1 if during break-in period) fuel and oil mixture must be used in fuel tank while checking pump output.

Remove oil pump output hose from fuel pump and plug fuel pump fitting. Place disconnected end of oil pump outlet hose into a graduated container. Remove oil pump control rod (6—Fig. M13-10) from pump lever and rotate pump lever to full throttle position (counterclockwise). Connect an accurate tachometer to engine, start engine and allow to run at 700 rpm for 15 minutes. Oil pump output in 15 minutes should be a minimum of 25.5 mL (0.86 oz.). Note that pump output specification is based on test performed at 70° F (21.1° C) room temperature. Actual output may vary depending upon ambient temperature.

IGNITION

An alternator driven capacitor discharge ignition (CDI) system is used. Ignition system consists of the flywheel, stator, trigger assembly, switch box and ignition coils. The stator is mounted below the flywheel and includes two capacitor charging coils. The trigger assembly consists of two trigger coils and is mounted below the flywheel. Ignition timing is advanced and retarded by rotating trigger assembly in relation to the inner flywheel magnets. Refer to SPEED CONTROL LINKAGE section for timing adjustment procedures. Diodes, capacitors and SCR's are contained in the switch box. Switch box, trigger assembly and stator must be serviced as unit assemblies. Refer to Fig. M13-12 for wiring diagram.

If engine malfunction is noted, and the ignition system is suspected, make sure the spark plugs and all electrical wiring are in acceptable condition and all electrical connections are clean and tight prior to trouble-shooting CDI system.

To properly test the switch box and ignition coils require the use of Quicksilver Multi-Meter DVA Tester part 91-99750 or a suitable voltmeter capable of measuring a minimum of 400 DC volts used with Quicksilver Direct Voltage Adaptor (DVA) part 91-89045. Follow instructions provided by tester manufacturer when performing tests. If these testers are not available, a process of elimination must be used when testing the ignition system. Stator and trigger assemblies can be effectively tested using a suitable ohmmeter.

NOTE: All tests that involve cranking or running the engine must be performed with lead wires connected. Switch box case MUST be grounded to engine for all tests or switch box may be damaged.

To test ignition system, proceed as follows:

IGNITION COILS. Connect DVA red test lead to ignition coil positive (+) terminal and black test lead to coil negative (−) terminal. Position tester selector switch to DVA/400. Tester should read 150-250 volts at cranking or idle speed (300-1000 rpm) and 180-280 volts at 1000-4000 rpm. If voltage readings are below specified reading, refer to SWITCH BOX STOP CIRCUIT test. If readings are within specifications, connect a suitable spark tester to ignition coil high tension leads, crank engine and note spark. If weak or no spark is noted, renew ignition coil(s). If normal spark is noted, renew spark plugs. If malfunction is still evident after renewing spark plugs, check ignition timing. If ignition timing is erratic, inspect trigger advance linkage for excessive wear or damage and inner flywheel magnets (shifted position or other damage). If timing is within specifications, problem is not in ignition system.

SWITCH BOX STOP CIRCUIT. Connect DVA black test lead to engine ground and red test lead to black/yellow switch box terminal (orange terminal on early models). Refer to Fig. M13-12. Set DVA selector switch to DVA/400. Voltage reading at cranking and all running speeds should be 200-360 volts. If reading is within specifications, refer to STATOR tests. If reading is above specified voltages, connect a suitable ohmmeter between trigger brown and white/black leads, then white and white/black leads. Trigger resistance should be 700-1000 ohms at both test connections. If not, renew trigger assembly. If trigger resistance is acceptable, renew switch box and repeat SWITCH BOX STOP CIRCUIT test. If SWITCH BOX STOP CIRCUIT test reading is below specified voltage, disconnect ignition switch, stop switch and mercury switch from black/yellow switch box terminal (orange switch box terminal on early models). With stop switch, ignition switch and mercury switch isolated, repeat SWITCH BOX STOP CIRCUIT test. If reading is now within specification, ignition switch, stop switch or mercury switch is defec-

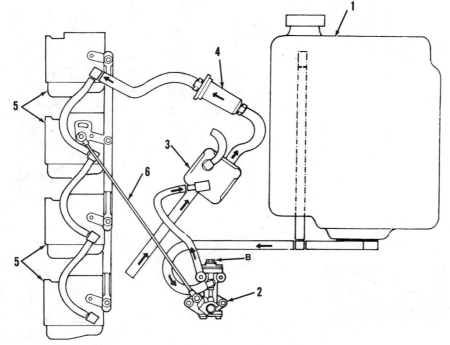

Fig. M13-10—View of oil injection system.

B. Bleed screw	3. Fuel pump	
1. Oil tank	4. Filter	6. Oil pump control
2. Oil pump	5. Carburetors	rod

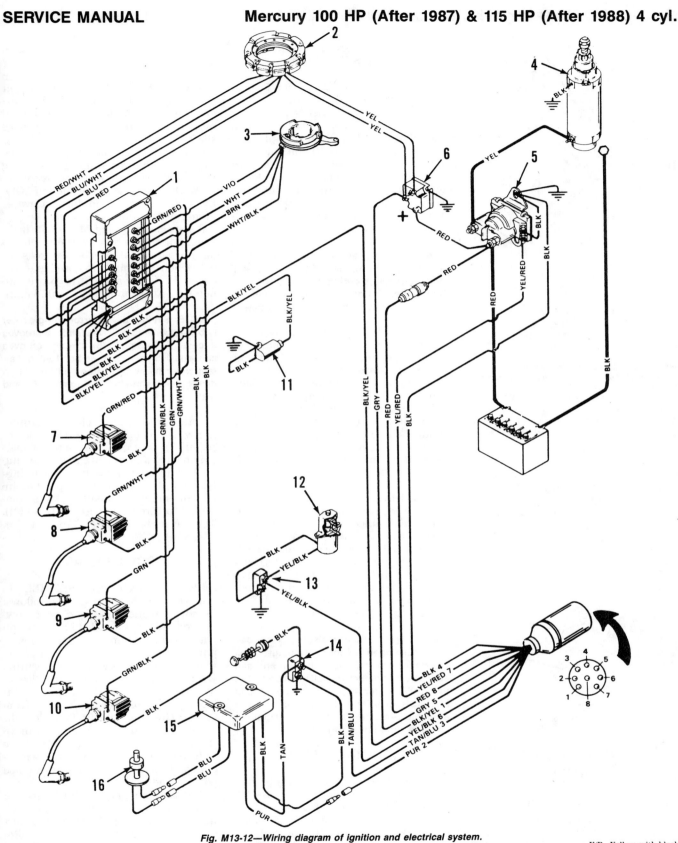

Fig. M13-12—Wiring diagram of ignition and electrical system.

1. Switch box
2. Stator
3. Trigger
4. Starter motor
5. Starter solenoid
6. Rectifier
7. Ignition coil (no. 1)
8. Ignition coil (no. 2)
9. Ignition coil (no. 3)
10. Ignition coil (no. 4)
11. Mercury switch
12. Enrichment valve
13. Terminal block
14. Terminal block
15. Low oil warning module
16. Low oil sensor

W. White
Y. Yellow
Bl. Blue
Br. Brown
Gr. Gray
Pr. Purple
B/Y. Black with yellow tracer

G/B. Green with black tracer
G/R. Green with red tracer
G/W. Green with white tracer
R/W. Red with white tracer

Y/B. Yellow with black tracer
Y/R. Yellow with red tracer
W/B. White with black tracer
Bl/W. Blue with white tracer
T/Bl. Tan with blue tracer

B. Black
G. Green
R. Red
T. Tan
V. Violet

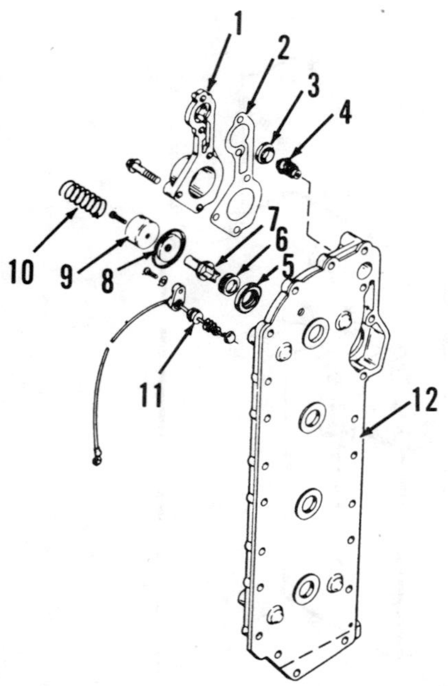

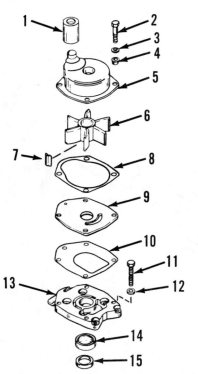

Fig. M13-13—Exploded view of thermostat (4), pressure relief valve (7) and related components.

1. Cover
2. Gasket
3. Seal
4. Thermostat
5. Grommet
6. Gasket
7. Pressure relief valve
8. Diaphragm
9. Cup
10. Spring
11. Temperature
12. Cylinder block cover

Fig. M13-14—Exploded view of water pump assembly.

1. Water tube seal
2. Screw
3. Washer
4. Insulator
5. Cover
6. Impeller
7. Key
8. Gasket
9. Plate
10. Gasket
11. Screw
12. Washer
13. Base
14. Seal
15. Seal

tive. If reading remains below specification refer to STATOR test.

STATOR. Connect DVA black lead to engine ground and red lead to blue switch box terminal. Set DVA selector switch to DVA/400. Voltage reading should be 210-310 volts at cranking and idle speeds and 190-310 volts at 1000-4000 rpm. Switch DVA red test lead to red switch box terminal. Leave black test lead connected to engine ground. Voltage reading should be 20-100 volts at cranking or idle speeds and 140-310 volts at 1000-4000 rpm.

NOTE: A shorted or open capacitor inside switch box will result in faulty stator voltage readings during cranking and running tests. Stator resistance should be checked as follows before failing stator.

If either STATOR test is not to specification, proceed as follows: Connect a suitable ohmmeter between blue and blue/white stator leads. Resistance between blue and blue/white stator leads should be 6000-7000 ohms. Next, connect ohmmeter between red and red/white stator leads. Resistance should be 90-140 ohms. Renew stator if resistance is not as specified. If stator resistance is as specified, renew switch box and repeat STATOR tests.

IGNITION COILS RESISTANCE TEST. Disconnect wires and high tension lead from coil. Connect a suitable ohmmeter between coil positive (+) and negative (−) terminals. Resistance should be 0.02-0.04 ohm. Connect ohmmeter between coil high tension terminal and negative (−) terminal. Resistance should be 800-1100 ohms. Renew ignition coil(s) if resistance is not as specified.

NOTE: Ignition coil resistance tests can only detect open or shorted windings. If coil resistance is within specification and still suspected as defective, coil must be tested using DVA meter as previously outlined in IGNITION COIL test. If DVA meter is not available, substitute a known good ignition coil and run engine to test.

COOLING SYSTEM

THERMOSTAT. All models are equipped with a thermostat (4—Fig. M13-13) and pressure relief valve (7) located under cover (1) in cylinder block cover (12). Thermostat should begin to open at 140°-145° F (60°-63° C). Temperature sensor (11) is provided to activate a warning horn should power head overheat. Be sure the correct sensor (11) in used. Identify sensor (11) by the length of sensor lead; the lead on 190° F (87.8° C) sensor is 18.5 inches (470 mm)

long and 15.5 inches (394 mm) long on 240° F (115.6° C) sensor.

WATER PUMP. The rubber impeller type water pump is housed in the gearcase housing. The impeller is mounted on and driven by the lower unit drive shaft.

If cooling system malfunction occurs, first check the water inlet for plugging or partial restriction. If necessary, remove the gearcase as outlined in LOWER UNIT section and inspect water pump, water tubes and seals.

Renew cover (5—Fig. M13-14) if thickness at discharge ports is 0.060 inch (1.5 mm) or less, or if grooves in excess of 0.030 inch (0.76 mm) are noted in top of cover (5). Renew plate (9) if grooves are noted in excess of 0.030 inch (0.76 mm).

NOTE: Sealing bead surrounding center hub of impeller (6) will wear circular grooves in cover (5) and plate (9). Circular grooves caused by impeller sealing bead will not affect water pump operation and should be disregarded when inspecting cover (5) and plate (9).

Rotate drive shaft in clockwise direction when installing cover (5) over impeller (6). Coat outer diameter of seals (14 and 15) with Loctite 271 or a suitable locking compound. Install seals into base (13) back-to-back. Apply Loctite 271 or suitable thread locking compound to threads of screws (11 and 2). Tighten screws (11 and 2) to 60 in.-lbs. (6.8 N·m).

POWER HEAD

REMOVE AND DISASSEMBLE. To remove power head, proceed as follows: Remove engine cowl and rear cowl bracket. Remove spark plugs, ignition plate cover, disconnect battery leads, power trim leads and power trim fuse. Remove two screws and clamp securing wiring harness to power head. Disconnect fuel lines, throttle cable, shift cable and disconnect shift arm from bracket (16—Fig. M13-15). Remove eight screws securing power head to drive shaft housing, attach a suitable lifting fixture to power head and remove power head from drive shaft housing. Place power head on a suitable stand.

To disassemble power head, proceed as follows: Label and disconnect all wires interfering with power head disassembly. Remove starter motor. Remove two cowl support screws at top of air box, two bottom cowl support screws at front of power head, disconnect vapor hose from "T" fitting next to fuel pump, remove fuel connector screw, remove bottom cowl support bracket, air box cover and air box. Disconnect and remove all carburetors as an assembly. Disconnect and remove oil reservoir, disconnect fuel hose from accelerator pump, disconnect link rod between throttle lever and throttle cam and unscrew and lay enrichment valve to the side with hoses and wires attached. Remove intake manifolds as an assembly. Note that pry points are provided on starboard side of power head for intake manifold removal. Remove reed valve assemblies. Remove flywheel nut and washer, place a suitable protector cap over crankshaft and remove flywheel using flywheel puller 91-73687A1 or a suitable equivalent.

NOTE: Do not strike puller bolt to dislodge flywheel from crankshaft or crankshaft or main bearing damage may result.

Remove ignition system components. Ignition plate, stator and trigger may be removed as an assembly. Remove fuel pump, accelerator pump, oil injection pump and related hoses. Remove throttle and spark advance lever assembly. Remove shift bracket assembly. Remove three screws securing lower end cap (8—Fig. M13-15), 26 screws securing crankcase cover (5) and remove cover (5) and end cap (8). Note that pry points are provided between cover (5) and block (10) to prevent damaging mating surfaces. Remove thermostat cover, thermostat, pressure relief valve and related components. Remove cylinder block cover (12). Pry points are provided at top and bottom of cover (12) to prevent damage to mating surfaces. Remove 35 exhaust cover screws and remove exhaust cover (1). Pry points are provided at front top and bottom of cover. Crankshaft, pistons, bearings and connecting rods may now be removed for service as outlined in the appropriate following sections. Refer to ASSEMBLY section for reassembly procedures.

ASSEMBLY. When reassembling the power head, the crankcase must be completely sealed against both vacuum and pressure. All gasket surfaces and machined joints without gaskets should be carefully checked for nicks and burrs that might interfere with a tight seal. Cylinder block and crankcase cover are matched and align bored assembly and not available separately.

Lubricate all bearing and friction surfaces with engine oil. Loose needle bearings should be held in place during reassembly using Quicksilver Needle Bearing Assembly Grease (part C-92-42649A-1) or a suitable gasoline soluble grease. Lubricate all seal lips using needle bearing assembly grease or suitable gasoline soluble grease.

Prior to assembling crankcase, inspect check valves (13—Fig. M13-15) by looking through valve. If light is noted while looking through valve, check ball has failed (melted) or is missing. If check ball is present in valve, make sure ball is free to move slightly inside valve. Remove check valves by carefully driving out using a suitable punch. Install check valves with single hole facing crankshaft.

Apply Loctite 271 or a suitable equivalent thread locking compound to outer diameter of all metal cased seals and any fastener used on moving or rotating components.

Apply a continuous bead, 1/16 inch (1.6 mm) diameter, of Loctite Master Gasket Sealer (part 92-12564-1) to mating surface of crankcase cover (5) to seal crankcase assembly. Run bead to the inside of all screw holes. Make sure bead is continuous but avoid excess application.

Tighten large inner crankcase cover screws, in three steps, in sequence shown in Fig. M13-18 to final tightness of 25 ft.-lbs. (33.9 N·m). After tightening inner cover screws, tighten small outer screws to final tightness of 180 in.-lbs. (20.3 N·m) in sequence shown. While tightening cover screws, check rotation of crankshaft for binding or unusual noise. If binding or noise is noted, repair cause before proceeding. Coat mating surface of lower end cap (8—Fig. M13-15) with Quicksilver Perfect Seal or equivalent. Rotate crankshaft so each piston ring in turn is visible in exhaust or transfer ports, then check by pressing on rings with a blunt tool. Ring should spring back when released. If not, a broken or binding ring is indicated and must be repaired before proceeding. Tighten exhaust and cylinder block cover screws to 180 in.-lbs. (20.3 N·m) in sequence shown in Figs. M13-19 and M13-20 respectively.

Renew gasket (9—Fig. M13-15) when installing power head on drive shaft housing. Lubricate drive shaft splines with a small amount of Quicksilver 2-4-C or equivalent. Apply Loctite 271 or equivalent to threads of power head mounting screws and tighten to 350 in.-lbs. (39.5 N·m). Remainder of assembly and reinstallation is the reverse of removal procedure. Note the following tightening torques: trigger and stator as-

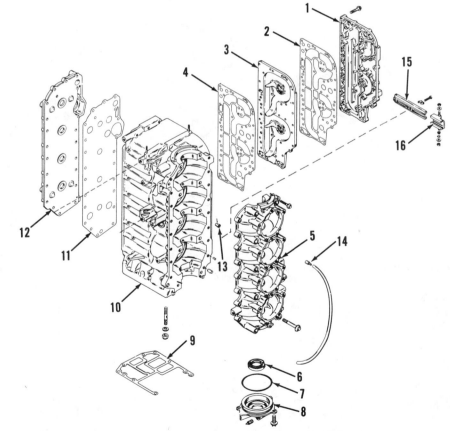

Fig. M13-15—Exploded view of crankcase assembly.

1. Exhaust cover	8. Lower end cap
2. Gasket	9. Gasket
3. Baffle plate	10. Cylinder block
4. Gasket	11. Gasket
5. Crankcase cover	12. Cylinder block
6. Seal	cover
7. "O" ring	13. Check valve
	14. Check valve
	15. Shift rail
	16. Shift block

semblies, 60 in.-lbs. (6.8 N·m); electrical component mounting plate, 180 in.-lbs. (20.3 N·m); starter motor, 180 in.-lbs. (20.3 N·m); air box nuts, 100 in.-lbs. (11.3 N·m).

PISTONS, PINS, RINGS AND CYLINDERS. Prior to detaching connecting rods from crankshaft, make sure that rod, rod cap and pistons are properly marked for correct reassembly to each other, in the correct cylinder and in the correct direction.

Standard cylinder bore diameter is 3.375 inch (85.72 mm). Piston skirt-to-cylinder bore clearance should be 0.005 inch (0.13 mm). Measure piston skirt diameter at right angle to piston pin bore 0.50 inch (12.7 mm) up from bottom of skirt. Maximum allowable cylinder bore wear, taper or out-of-round is 0.003 inch (0.08 mm). Pistons and rings are available in 0.015 inch (0.38 mm) and 0.030 inch (0.76 mm) oversize. Note that oversize pistons weigh approximately the same as standard size pistons. All cylinders do not require oversize boring if one cylinder is excessively worn or damaged. If installing 0.015 inch (4.38 mm) oversize piston, finished cylinder diameter should be 3.390 inch (86.11 mm). If installing 0.030 inch (0.76 mm) oversize piston, finished cylinder diameter should be 3.405 inch (86.49 mm).

Piston rings are semi-keystone shaped and are pinned to prevent rotation. Install rings with "T" mark facing up.

Always renew piston pin retaining rings (2—Fig. M13-16) if removed. Piston pin rides in 29 loose needle bearing rollers (5). The manufacturer recommends renewing piston pin bearing rollers (5) when reassembling power head. Piston pin is a snug fit in piston and can be tapped out using a suitable driver and soft-face mallet. When reassembling, hold needle bearing rollers in place with a suitable gasoline soluble grease. Install locating washers (4) with large diameter facing away from pin (7).

Cylinder block is designed to allow piston installation without the use of a piston ring compressor. Install pistons into cylinders with "UP" mark on piston crown facing flywheel end of power head.

CONNECTING RODS, BEARINGS AND CRANKSHAFT. Refer to Fig. M13-16 for exploded view of crankshaft, connecting rods and bearings. Be sure connecting rods (6), rod caps (9), pistons (3) and all wearing components are marked for reference during reassembly. Top main bearing (13) is a caged roller bearing and bottom main bearing (19) is a ball bearing. Each center main bearing consist of 32 loose bearing rollers (24) and race (25).

Do not remove bearing (19) from crankshaft unless bearing (19) or oil pump drive gear (18) require renewal. Note location of key (17).

On models equipped with a wear sleeve and "O" ring, carefully heat wear sleeve to remove sleeve (21) from crankshaft. To install wear sleeve, apply Loctite 271 or equivalent to inner diameter of sleeve and drive sleeve squarely on crankshaft until bottomed using a suitable wooden block and hammer. On models equipped with a seal and seal carrier in place of wear sleeve (21) and "O" ring (22), renew seal anytime power head is disassembled.

Inspect crankshaft splines for excessive wear and crankshaft for straightness using a dial indicator and "V" blocks. Inspect crankshaft bearing surfaces and renew crankshaft if scored, out-of-round or excessively worn. Renew connecting rod(s) if big end bearing surface is rough, scored, excessively worn or shows evidence of overheating. Use crocus cloth ONLY to clean the

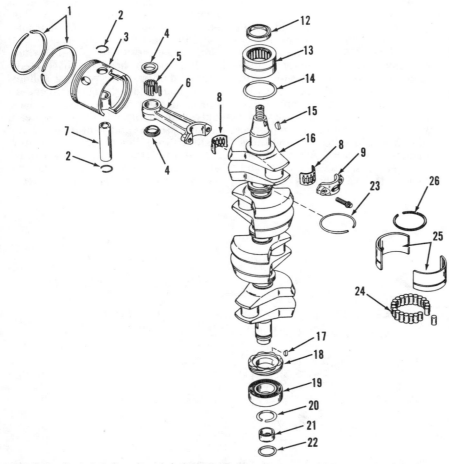

Fig. M13-16—Exploded view of crankshaft assembly. Note that some models are equipped with a seal and seal carrier in place of wear sleeve (21) and "O" ring (22).

1. Piston rings	7. Piston pin	16. Crankshaft	21. Wear sleeve
2. Retaining rings	8. Crankpin bearing	17. Oil pump drive gear	22. "O" ring
3. Piston	9. Connecting rod cap	key	23. Seal ring
4. Locating washers	12. Seal	18. Oil pump drive gear	24. Main bearing rollers
5. Piston pin bearing	13. Main bearing	19. Main bearing	25. Main bearing race
rollers	14. "O" ring	20. Retaining ring	26. Retaining ring
6. Connecting rod	15. Flywheel key		

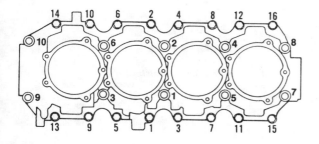

Fig. M13-18—Crankcase cover tightening sequence. Tighten inner (large) screws first, then tighten outer (small) screws. Tighten inner screws in three steps to final value of 25 ft.-lbs. (33.9 N·m) and outer screws in three steps to final value of 180 in.-lbs. (20.3 N·m).

connecting rod big end bearing surface.

Install main bearings with oil holes in outer race facing toward bottom of engine. Install crankshaft seal rings (23) with end gaps 180 degrees apart. Use only Quicksilver Needle Bearing Assembly Grease or a suitable gasoline soluble grease to hold loose bearing rollers in place. Always renew rod cap bolts when reassembling power head. Threads are cut into both the connecting rod and rod cap. To properly align cap and rod during reassembly, proceed as follows: Place rod cap (9) on bearing half (8) and hold tightly against connecting rod while threading in bolt. Finger tighten rod bolts then check rod and cap alignment. Cap and rod must be perfectly aligned. After all rod caps and bolts are installed and aligned, tighten bolts to 15 in.-lbs. (1.7 N·m) and recheck alignment. Then tighten bolts to 30 ft.-lbs. (40.7 N·m) and recheck alignment. If rods and caps are perfectly aligned, tighten rod bolts an additional 90 degrees to complete procedure. Reassemble crankcase assembly as previously outlined.

ELECTRICAL SYSTEM

CHARGING SYSTEM. Refer to Fig. M13-12 for wiring diagram. To test alternator output, disconnect red lead from rectifier (6) and connect a suitable ammeter between rectifier and red lead. Note that rectifier must be operating properly for accurate test results. Ammeter should indicate 7-9 amperes at 3000 rpm. If not, disconnect stator yellow leads from rectifier and connect a suitable ohmmeter between yellow leads. Stator resistance should be 0.05-1.1 ohms. No continuity should be present between yellow leads and engine ground with stator installed on power

head. Renew stator if output or resistance is not as specified.

To test rectifier (6), connect ohmmeter alternately between each rectifier terminal and between each terminal and ground. Refer to Fig. M13-22. Reverse ohmmeter leads after each connection. Ohmmeter should indicate continuity with leads connected one direction but not the other. If ohmmeter shows continuity both directions or no continuity both directions, renew rectifier.

STARTER MOTOR. If starter motor malfunction occurs, perform a visual inspection for corroded or loose connections. Check inline fuse in red lead at starter solenoid and make sure battery is fully charged.

Renew brushes if worn to less than $\frac{1}{4}$ inch (6.4 mm). Undercut insulation between commutator bars to $\frac{1}{32}$ inch (0.8 mm). Armature should be tested using an armature growler.

LOWER UNIT

PROPELLER. Protection for lower unit is provided by a splined rubber hub built into propeller. Various propellers are available and should be selected to allow motor to operate within the recommended speed range 4750-5250 rpm at full throttle. The manufacturer recommends propping outboard motor to the high end of full throttle rpm range.

R&R AND OVERHAUL. To remove lower unit, first remove and ground spark plug leads to prevent accidental starting. Shift engine into forward gear and tilt unit to full up position. Remove two screws and washers on each side of

lower unit and one nut and washer under antiventilation plate. Remove gearcase and secure in a suitable holding fixture.

Note location and size of all shims and thrust washers during disassembly for reference during reassembly.

Remove propeller (66—Fig. M13-23), thrust hub (65), vent screws (35 and 36) and drain plug (37). Allow gearcase oil to drain while inspecting for water or other contamination.

Remove water pump assembly and screws (11). Using screwdrivers or similar tools placed on each end of water pump base (13), carefully pry base (13) from gearcase. Remove and discard seals (14 and 15). Remove nuts (61 [screws on some models]). Using a suitable puller, break loose carrier-to-gearcase seal then remove bearing carrier (59) and propeller shaft components (46-64) as a unit. Do not lose balls (48) or cam follower (46). Remove and discard seals (63 and 64) and "O" ring (55) from carrier (59). Do not remove bearings (58 and 62) unless renewal is required. Remove retainer spring (52) from dog clutch (50). To remove pin (51), depress cam follower (46) by pushing propeller shaft against a solid object, then push out pin (51) using a small punch. Remove follower (46), sliding pin (47), balls (48), spring (49) and slide dog clutch (50) off propeller shaft. Place Drive Shaft Holding Tool 91-56755 or similar splined adapter on drive shaft splines or clamp drive shaft into a soft jawed vise then remove pinion nut (38). Remove drive shaft assembly from gearcase. After drive shaft is removed, forward gear (45) and bearing (43) can be removed. Use a suitable expanding jaw type puller to remove race (42), if necessary. Note location and thickness of shims (41). Remove upper drive shaft bearing (17) and bearing carrier (18) if necessary, using expanding jaw type puller. Note that bearing (17) and carrier (18) must be removed before sleeve (19) removal is possible. If necessary, remove sleeve (19) using a suitable

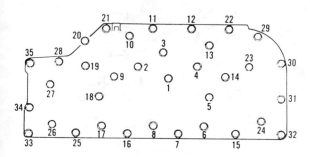

Fig. M13-19—Tighten exhaust cover screws in sequence shown to 180 in.-lbs. (20.3 N·m).

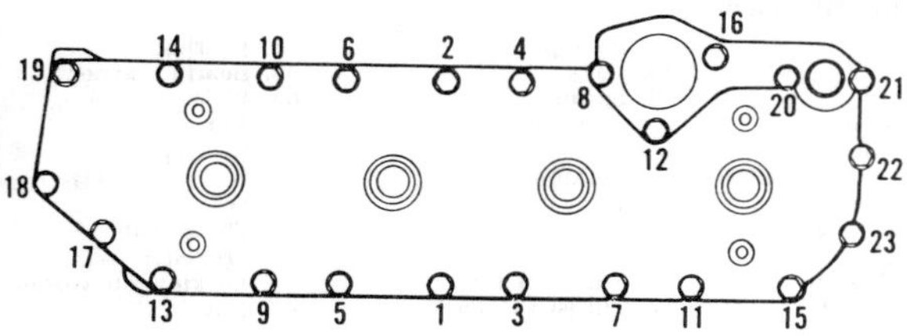

Fig. M13-20—Tighten cylinder block cover screws in sequence shown to 180 in.-lbs. (20.3 N·m).

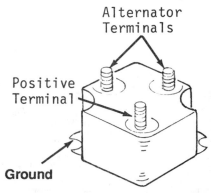

Fig. M13-22—Rectifier must be connected as shown. Refer to text for rectifier test procedure.

puller. Quicksilver Bearing Race Tool 91-14308A1 is required to drive lower drive shaft bearing race (31) from gearcase. Bearing race (31) can be driven from gearcase with bearing (17), carrier (18) and sleeve (19) installed. Note location and thickness of shims (30). Remove coupler (23), shift shaft retainer (26) and shift shaft (28). Reach into gear

cavity and remove shift cam (40). Remove and discard seal (25) and "O" ring (27) from retainer (26) to complete disassembly.

Inspect all components for excessive wear or damage. Check straightness of propeller shaft using a dial indicator and "V" blocks and renew shaft if runout exceeds 0.006 inch (0.15 mm). Inspect all

bearings for roughness, pits, rust or other damage and renew as necessary. Inspect sealing area of wear sleeve (20) for grooves and renew as necessary. Renew bearings and races as an assembly. Renew gears if teeth are chipped, broken or excessively worn. Renew all seals, "O" rings and gaskets. Lubricate all friction surfaces with clean gear lubricant.

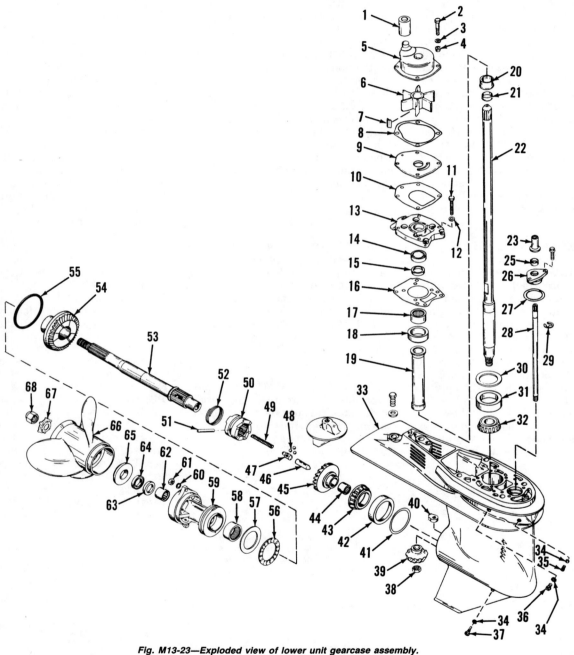

Fig. M13-23—Exploded view of lower unit gearcase assembly.

1. Water tube seal	12. Washer	23. Coupler	35. Plug	47. Slide pin	58. Bearing
2. Screw	13. Base	25. Seal	36. Plug	48. Balls	59. Bearing carrier
3. Washer	14. Seal	26. Retainer	37. Plug	49. Spring	60. Washer
4. Insulator	15. Seal	27. "O" ring	39. Pinion gear	50. Dog clutch	61. Nut
5. Cover	16. Gasket	28. Shift shaft	40. Shift cam	51. Pin	62. Bearing
6. Impeller	17. Needle bearing	29. "E" ring	41. Shim	52. Retaining spring	63. Seal
7. Key	18. Carrier	30. Shim	42. Bearing race	53. Propeller shaft	64. Seal
8. Gasket	19. Sleeve	31. Bearing race	43. Bearing	54. Reverse gear	65. Thrust hub
9. Plate	20. Wear sleeve	32. Bearing	44. Bearing	55. "O" ring	66. Propeller
10. Gasket	21. Seal ring	33. Gearcase	45. Forward gear	56. Thrust bearing	67. Locking tab washer
11. Screw	22. Drive shaft	34. Gasket	46. Cam follower	57. Thrust washer	68. Nut

Apply Loctite 271 or equivalent to threads of all screws and outer diameter of all metal cased seals. Lubricate "O" ring (55) and outer diameter of carrier (50) with Quicksilver Special Lubricant 101 (part 92-13872A-1). Lubricate other seals and "O" rings with Quicksilver 2-4-C Marine Lubricant (part 92-90018A12) or Quicksilver Needle Bearing Assembly Grease (part 92-42649A-1).

When reassembling gearcase, place original shim pack (41) into gearcase and install bearing race (42) using a suitable mandrel. If original shims (41) are damaged or lost, install shim pack 0.010 inch (0.25 mm) thick.

Install seal (25) into retainer (26) until flush with top of retainer. Place shift cam (40) into gearcase with numbers facing up and install shift rod making sure splines in shift shaft properly align with cam. Install bearing (62) into carrier (59) with lettered side facing propeller end. Install seal (63) into carrier (59) with lip facing forward and seal (64) with lip facing propeller. Install dog clutch (50) on propeller shaft with grooved end of clutch facing rearward.

Fig. M13-25—View of Bearing Preload Tool 91-14311A1 assembled over drive shaft (22). Refer to text for gearcase shim selection procedure.

1. Bolt	5. Thrust washer
2. Set screws	6. Thrust bearing
3. Nut	7. Adapter
4. Spring	22. Drive shaft

Install spring (49), slider (47), balls (48) and cam follower (46) into propeller shaft. Depress follower (46) against spring pressure and align holes in dog clutch and propeller shaft using a suitable punch, then insert pin (51).

If installing a new wear sleeve (20) on drive shaft (22), install seal ring (21), coat inner diameter of sleeve (20) with Loctite 271 and press onto shaft (22) until bottomed. Install original shim pack (30) and draw race (31) into gearcase using suitable mandrels and a threaded rod. If original shims (30) are damaged or lost, start with shim pack 0.025 inch (0.64 mm) thick. Install sleeve (19) making sure antirotation tab properly engages gearcase. Install bearing (43), forward gear (45), drive shaft (22), pinion bearing (32), pinion gear (39) and original pinion nut (38).

NOTE: Pinion nut (38) should be renewed and secured with a suitable thread locking compound after gearcase shimming operation has been properly performed.

Drive shaft assembly must be preloaded to properly adjust pinion gear depth and forward gear backlash. Special Bearing Preload Tool 91-14311A1 and Pinion Gear Locating Tool 91-12349A2 are required for shim selection procedure.

To preload drive shaft and bearing assembly, assemble Bearing Preload Tool 91-14311A1 as shown in Fig. M13-25 and tighten set screws (2). With nut (3) fully threaded on bolt (1), measure distance (D) between bottom of bolt head to top of nut, then turn nut (3) to increase distance (D) by one inch (25.4 mm). Rotate drive shaft several turns to ensure lower drive shaft bearing is properly seated. Assemble Pinion Gear Locating Tool 91-12349A2 as shown in Fig. M13-26. Install locating disc marked number "3" making sure access hole is facing up. Position sliding collar (4) so gaging block (3) is directly under pinion gear (39) teeth and flat on gaging block marked "8" is adjacent to pinion gear (39). Clearance between gaging block (3)

and pinion gear should be 0.025 inch (0.64 mm) measured with a suitable feeler gage as shown. Vary thickness of shim pack (30—Fig. M13-23) to adjust. Changing thickness of shims (30) by 0.001 inch (0.03 mm) will change pinion gear clearance by 0.001 inch (0.03 mm).

Insert assembled propeller shaft assembly into bearing carrier (59) and install carrier and propeller shaft assembly into gearcase. Position carrier (59) so "TOP" mark is facing up. Outward pressure should be applied to propeller shaft to hold reverse gear (54) tight against thrust bearing (56) and washer (57) to prevent thrust washer and bearing from being dislodged. A tool can be fabricated out of 1¼ to 1½ inch (31.7-38.1 mm) PVC pipe cut off to 6 inches (152.4 mm) long. Place pipe over propeller shaft and secure with washer (67) and nut (68). Tighten nut (68) so reverse gear (54) is pulled securely against thrust bearing (56) and washer (57). Securely tighten nuts (61) or screws if so equipped.

To check forward gear backlash, proceed as follows: Allow bearing preload tool (Fig. M13-25) to remain installed. Preload propeller shaft by installing a suitable puller as shown in Fig. M13-27. Tighten puller center bolt to 25 in.-lbs. (2.8 N·m), rotate propeller shaft several turns, then retighten puller bolt to 25 in.-lbs. (2.8 N·m). Again, rotate propeller shaft several turns and recheck torque on puller bolt. Refer to Fig. M13-28 and assemble a suitable threaded rod to gearcase using nuts and washers as shown. Affix a suitable dial indicator to threaded rod. Install Backlash Indicator 91-19660 on drive shaft and align dial indicator plunger with the mark "1" on backlash indicator. Check backlash by carefully rotating drive shaft back-and-forth. Note that if any movement is noted at propeller shaft, repeat propeller shaft preloading procedure as previously outlined. Backlash should be 0.012-0.019 inch (0.31-0.48 mm). Vary thickness of shim pack (41—Fig. M13-23) to adjust. Note that changing thickness of shims (41) by 0.001 inch (0.03 mm) will result in approximately 0.00125 inch (0.032 mm) change in backlash.

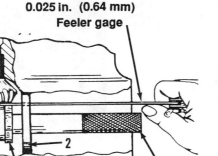

0.025 in. (0.64 mm) Feeler gage

Fig. M13-26—Assemble Pinion Gear Locating Tool 91-12349A2 as shown. Make sure sliding collar (4) is positioned so gaging block is located under pinion gear (39) as shown.

1. Arbor
2. Locating disc (number 3)
3. Gaging block
4. Sliding collar
39. Pinion gear

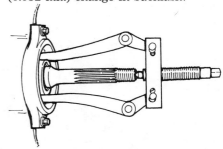

Fig. M13-27—When checking forward gear backlash, preload propeller shaft by installing a suitable puller as shown. Refer to text.

After shim selection procedure is completed, remove carrier and drive shaft assembly. Remove pinion nut, apply Loctite 271 to a NEW pinion nut, install nut with beveled side facing up and tighten to 70 ft.-lbs. (95 N·m). Reinstall carrier and propeller shaft assembly, apply Loctite 271 to nuts (61—Fig. M13-23) or screws if so equipped, and tighten nuts (61) to 275 in.-lbs. (31.1 N·m) or screws to 150 in.-lbs. (17 N·m). Complete reassembly by reversing disassembly procedure. Tighten propeller nut to 55 ft.-lbs. (75 N·m).

To reinstall gearcase on drive shaft housing, proceed as follows: Position shift block (16—Fig. M13-15) on power head in the forward gear position. Shift block (16) should extend past forward side of shift rail (15) by 1/32 inch (3.2 mm) if properly positioned. Shift lower unit into forward gear. Lubricate inner diameter of water tube seal (1—Fig. M13-23) with Quicksilver 2-4-C Marine Lubricant. Lightly lubricate drive shaft splines with 2-4-C Marine lubricant. Do not apply grease to top of drive shaft or drive shaft may not fully engage crankshaft.

Install gearcase in drive shaft housing making sure drive shaft aligns with crankshaft, upper shift shaft aligns with coupler (23) and water tube aligns with water tube seal (1). Apply Loctite 271 to threads of gearcase mounting screws and tighten to 40 ft.-lbs. (54.2 N·m). After installing gearcase, make sure shift linkage operates properly as follows: Shift outboard into forward gear. Propeller shaft should lock into gear when rotated counterclockwise and ratchet when rotated clockwise. When shifted into reverse gear, propeller shaft should be locked into gear when rotated either direction. If shift linkage does not operate as specified, lower unit must be removed and shift linkage malfunction repaired.

POWER TILT/TRIM

FLUID AND BLEEDING. Recommended fluid is Quicksilver Power Trim & Steering Fluid or a suitable Type F, FA or Dextron II automatic transmission fluid.

NOTE: Hydraulic system is under pressure. Fill plug (Fig. M13-29) must not be removed unless outboard is in full up position and tilt lock lever is engaged. Be sure to securely tighten fill plug prior to lowering outboard motor.

To check fluid level, tilt motor to full up position, engage tilt lock lever and slowly remove fill plug. Fluid should be visible in fill tube. Fill as necessary and securely tighten fill plug.

To determine if air is present in hydraulic system, trim motor out until both trim rods are slightly extended. Apply downward pressure on lower unit. If trim rods retract into cylinders more than 1/8 inch (3.2 mm), air is present and bleeding is required.

The hydraulic circuit is self-bleeding as the tilt/trim system is operated through several cycles. After servicing system, be sure to check reservoir level after filling and operating system.

Trim limit adjustment is not required. Port trim rod and piston assembly (15—Fig. M13-30) is equipped with a check valve designed to open at a specific pressure, limiting trim range to 20 degrees when engine speed exceeds 2,000 rpm. If engine speed falls below 2,000 rpm, trim angle may exceed 20 degrees; however, once engine speed exceeds 2,000 rpm, propeller thrust will increase pressure in trim cylinders causing check valve in port side trim rod to unseat, bypassing hydraulic fluid to the reservoir and lowering trim angle to 20 degrees maximum. Except for cleaning valve and strainer (16), check valve in port trim rod is not serviceable and should not be removed. If check valve malfunction is evident, renew port trim rod.

HYDRAULIC TESTING. The system can be checked by connecting a 5000 psi (34.5 MPa) test gage to the UP (U—Fig. M13-32) and DOWN (D—Fig. M13-33) ports. Prior to connecting test gage, place outboard motor in the full up position and engage tilt lock lever. Unscrew reservoir fill plug and rotate manual release valve (21—Fig. M13-32) three to four turns counterclockwise to release pressure on system. Remove UP or DOWN Allen head test port plug and connect test gage with suitable adapter and hose. Install fill plug and rotate manual release valve clockwise until seated. System pressure when testing at UP (U) port should be a minimum of 1300 psi (8.9 MPa). System pressure when testing at DOWN (D—Fig. M13-33) port should be a minimum of 500 psi (3.5 MPa). Release pressure on system as previously outlined prior to removing test gage. Reinstall Allen head plug.

OVERHAUL. Refer to Fig. M13-30 for exploded view of manifold and trim cylinder components, and Fig. M13-31 for exploded view of tilt cylinder components. Special socket 91-44487A1 and a spanner wrench are required to service trim and tilt cylinders. Keep all components clean and away from contamination. Keep components separated and label if necessary for correct reassembly. Lubricate all "O" rings or seal lips with Quicksilver Power Trim & Steering Fluid, Dexron II, Type F or Type FA automatic transmission fluid during reassembly.

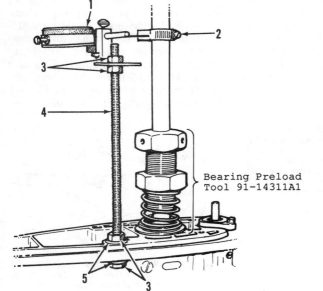

Fig. M13-28—Assemble special tools as shown to check forward gear backlash. Refer to text.
1. Dial indicator & adapter assy.
2. Backlash indicator tool 91-19660
3. Nuts
4. Threaded rod
5. Washers

Bearing Preload Tool 91-14311A1

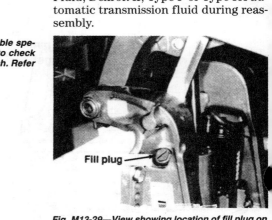

Fill plug

Fig. M13-29—View showing location of fill plug on power tilt/trim system.

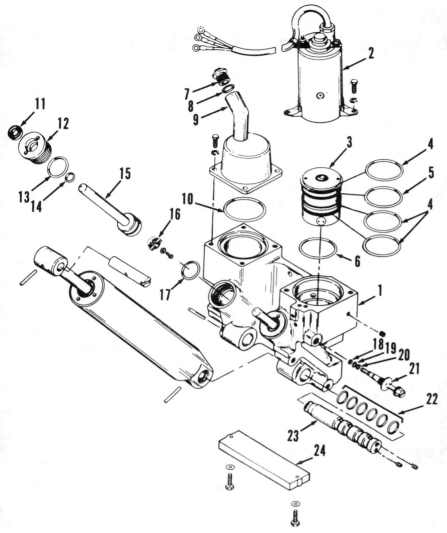

Fig. M13-30—Exploded view of power tilt/trim system.

1. Manifold	8. "O" ring	14. "O" ring
2. Motor	9. Reservoir cover	15. Trim piston & rod
3. Pump assy.	10. Seal ring	16. Strainer
4. "O" rings	11. Seal	17. "O" ring
5. "O" ring	12. Cap	18. "O" ring
6. "O" ring	13. "O" ring	19. "O" ring
7. Fill plug		

20. "O" ring
21. Manual release
valve
22. "O" ring
23. Shaft
24. Anode plate

Fig. M13-32—Release pressure on system, then remove Allen head plug (U) and install a 5000 psi (34.5 MPa) test gage with a suitable adapter and hose to test system pressure when operated in the "UP" direction. View identifies location of manual release valve (21).

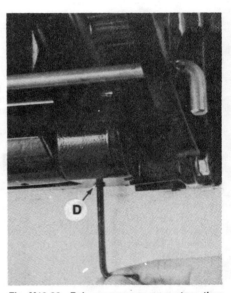

Fig. M13-33—Release pressure on system, then remove Allen head plug (D) and install a 5000 psi (34.5 MPa) test gage with a suitable adapter and hose to test system pressure when operated in the "DOWN" direction.

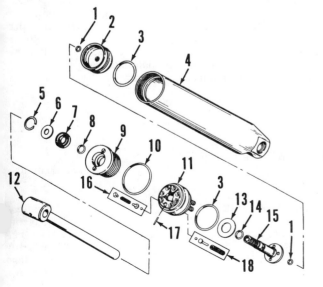

Fig. M13-31—Exploded view of tilt cylinder assembly.

1. "O" ring
2. Cup
3. "O" ring
4. Cylinder
5. Circlip
6. Washer
7. Scraper
8. "O" ring
9. Cap
10. "O" ring
11. Piston
12. Rod
13. Washer
14. "O" ring
15. Rod end
16. Check valve assy.
17. Pin
18. Check valve assy.

MERCURY IN-LINE
SIX-CYLINDER MODELS (1969-1988)

Year Produced	Model	Year Produced	Model
1969	1000	1979	90
	1250		115
1970	1150		140
	1350	1980	90
1971	1150		115
	1350		140
1972	1150	1981	90
	1400		115
1973	1150		140
	1500	1982	90
1974	1150		115
	1500	1983	90
1975	150		115
	1500	1984	90
1976	1150		115
	1500	1985	90
1977	1150		115
	1500	1986	90
1978	900		115
	1150	1987	115
	1400	1988	115
	1500XS		

Letter after model number indicates variation of equipment.
BP – Racing models, E – Electric starter and alternator, L – Long shaft,
SS – Solid state ignition, PT – Power trim, XS – High performance.

CONDENSED SERVICE DATA

TUNE-UP
Hp/rpm:
Models 90 & 900 .... 90/4500-5000
Model 1000 .... 100/4800-5300
Models 115 & 1150 .... 115/5000-5500
Model 1250 .... 125/4800-5300
Model 1350 .... 135/4800-5300
Models 140 & 1400 .... 140/5300-5800
Model 1500 .... 150/5300-5800
Model 1500XS 155/5800-6300
Bore .... 2⅞ in.
(73.03 mm)
Stroke:
Model 1000 .... 2.3 in.
(58.42 mm)
All Other Models .... 2-9/16 in.
(65.09 mm)
Displacement:
Model 1000 .... 89.6 cu. in.
(1469 cc)
All Other Models .... 99.8 cu. in.
(1635 cc)
Compression At Cranking Speed .... *
Firing Order 1-4-5-2-3-6
Ignition Type .... Breakerless
Spark Plug .... See Text
Idle Speed:
Model 90 (in gear) .... 500-600 rpm
All Other Models (in gear) .... 550-600 rpm
Fuel:Oil Ratio 50:1
*Not more than 15 psi (103.5 kPa) variation between cylinders.

SIZES – CLEARANCES
Piston Rings:
End Gap .... *
Side Clearance .... *
Piston Skirt Clearance .... *
Crankshaft Bearing Type:
Top Main Bearing .... Ball Bearing
Main Bearing (2) .... Bushing With Reed Valve
Main Bearing (3) .... Roller
Center Main Bearing .... Bushing With Reed Valve
Main Bearing (5) .... Roller
Main Bearing (6) .... Bushing With Reed Valve
Bottom Main Bearing .... Ball Bearing
Crankpin .... Roller
Piston Pin Bearing .... Roller†
*Publication not authorized by manufacturer.
†Refer to text for number of piston pin rollers.

TIGHTENING TORQUES
Connecting Rod .... 180 in.-lbs.
(20.3 N·m)
Crankcase Screws:
Models 1000 & 1250 .... 150 in.-lbs.
(16.9 N·m)
All Other Models .... 200 in.-lbs.
(22.6 N·m)
Cylinder Cover .... 85 in.-lbs.
(9.6 N·m)

TIGHTENING TORQUES CONT.

Exhaust Cover:
Models 1000 & 1250 ....150 in.-lbs.
(16.9 N·m)
All Other Models ....250 in.-lbs.
(28.2 N·m)
Flywheel Nut ....100 ft.-lbs.
(136 N·m)
Reed Screws ....25 in.-lbs.
(2.8 N·m)

TIGHTENING TORQUES CONT.

Spark Plugs ....240 in.-lbs.
(27.1 N·m)
Transfer Port Covers....................85 in.-lbs.
(9.6 N·m)
Water Jacket Cover:
Early Models ....200 in.-lbs.
(22.6 N·m)
Late Models ....150 in.-lbs.
(16.9 N·m)

LUBRICATION

The engine is lubricated by oil mixed with the fuel. Fuel should be regular leaded, low lead or unleaded gasoline with a minimum pump octane rating of 86. Premium gasoline may be used if desired regular gasoline is not available. Recommended oil is Quicksilver Formula 50 or 50D. A good quality BIA certified TC-W oil may be used. Fuel:oil ratio should be 50:1 when using Formula 50 or 50-D oil. Follow fuel:oil ratio recommended by oil manufacturer if Formula 50 or 50-D is not used.

The lower unit gears and bearings are lubricated by oil contained in the gearcase. Only Quicksilver Super Duty Gear Lubricant should be used. Gearcase is filled through the lower filler plug hole until lubricant reaches the upper vent plug hole. Then allow 1 ounce (30 mL) to drain from gearcase. On most models, both plugs are on port side of gearcase.

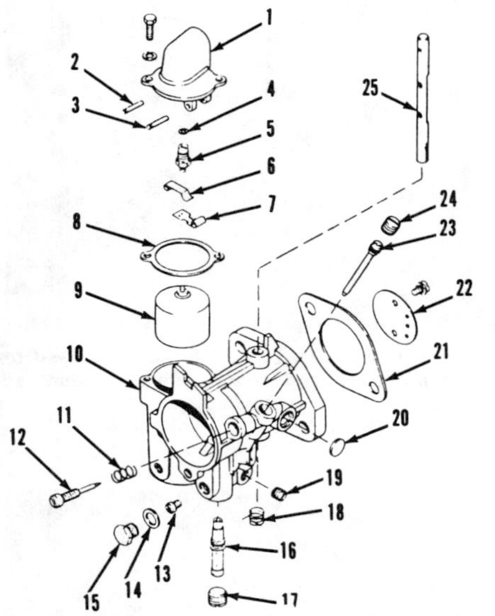

FUEL SYSTEM

CARBURETOR. Three "Back Drag" type carburetors are used. Refer to Fig. M14-1 for exploded view of carburetor, typical of type used on all models. Initial setting for the idle mixture screw (12) is one turn open from the closed position. Run motor until operating temperature is reached, then shift to forward gear and allow motor to run at idle speed. Slowly turn idle mixture screw (12) out (counterclockwise) until motor runs unevenly (loads up). Turn needle in (clockwise) until motor picks up speed and again runs evenly and continue turning until motor slows down and misses. Needle should be set between the two extremes. Turning screw (12) in (clockwise) leans the mixture. Slightly rich idle mixture is more desirable than too lean.

NOTE: Mixture adjustment should not be attempted in neutral.

Standard main jet (13) size is 0.070 inch (1.78 mm) on Model 90, 0.072 inch (1.83 mm) on Model 115 below serial number 5050763, 0.074 inch (1.88 mm) on Model 115 serial number 5050763 and above, 0.080 inch (2.03 mm) on Model 140 below serial number 5327663 and 0.074 inch (1.88 mm) on Model 140 serial number 5327663 and above for operation below 2500 feet (762 m) altitude. Standard vent jet (V – Fig. M14-2) size is 0.092 inch (2.34 mm) on Model 90, 0.092 inch (2.34 mm) on Model 115 below serial number 5050763, 0.096 inch (2.44 mm) on Model 115 serial number 5050763 and above, 0.092 inch (2.34 mm) on Model 140 below serial number 5327663 and 0.090 inch (2.29 mm) on Model 140 serial number 5327663 and above for operation below 2500 feet (762 m) altitude. Other jet sizes are available for adjusting the calibration for altitude or other special conditions.

Refer to the following for standard main jet (13 – Fig. M14-1) sizes on all early models operated below 4000 feet (1220 m).

Model 900

All Carburetors ....0.070 in.
(1.78 mm)

Model 1000

KA-10A, KC-7B1 and
KC-14A ....0.059 in.
(1.5 mm)

Fig. M14-1 – Exploded view of typical carburetor used on all models. A different cover (1) with a fuel strainer located under the cover is used on some early models.

1. Cover
2. Pin
3. Pin
4. Gasket
5. Inlet needle & seat
6. Primary lever
7. Secondary lever
8. Gasket
9. Float
10. Body
11. Spring
12. Idle mixture screw
13. Main jet
14. Gasket
15. Plug
16. Main nozzle
17. Plug
18. Spring
19. Plug
20. Welch plug
21. Gasket
22. Throttle plate
23. Idle tube
24. Plug
25. Throttle shaft

Fig. M14-2 – View showing vent jet (V), idle mixture screw (12) and main jet access plug (15).

Model 1150

KD-6A, KD-6B and WMK-3 . . . 0.066 in.
(1.67 mm)
WMK-10 . . . . 0.072 in.
(1.83 mm)

Model 1250

KD-1A and KD-1B . . . . 0.082 in.
(2.08 mm)
KD-1BR1 . . . . 0.080 in.
(2.03 mm)
KD-2A . . . . 0.076 in.
(1.93 mm)

Model 1350

KD-7A, KD-7B and WMK-4 . . 0.0785 in.
(1.99 mm)

Model 1400

(Serial no. 3293234-3295133 and
serial no. 3425632-345672)
Top carburetor . . . . 0.084 in.
(2.13 mm)
Lower and center carburetor . . 0.082 in.
(2.08 mm)
(All 1400 models not included in
above serial numbers)
All carburetors . . . . 0.080 in.
(2.03 mm)

Model 1500

WMK-11 and WMK-14
Model 1500 . . . . 0.080 in.
(2.03 mm)
Model 1500XS . . . . 0.082 in.
(2.08 mm)

To determine the float level, invert bowl cover (1–Fig. M14-3) with inlet needle and seat (5), primary lever (6) and secondary lever (7) installed. Measure distance (A) from carburetor body surface to top of secondary lever (7). Distance (A) should be 13/32 inch (10.32 mm). Adjust distance (A) by bending curved end of primary lever (6). Turn bowl cover (1–Fig. M14-4) upright and measure distance (D) between primary lever (6) and end of secondary lever (7). Distance (D) should be ¼ inch (6.4 mm). Bend tab (T) to adjust. The contact spring located in center of float (9–Fig. M14-1) should extend 3/32 inch (2.38 mm) above top of float. Check to see if spring has been stretched or damaged.

SPEED CONTROL LINKAGE. The speed control linkage must be synchronized to advance the ignition timing and open the carburetor throttles in a precise manner. Because the two actions are interrelated, it is important to check the complete system following the sequence outlined in the appropriate following paragraphs.

Model 1000SS With "Thunderbolt Ignition." Refer to the special precautions listed in the **"Thunderbolt"** IGNITION section before servicing these motors. Incorrect service procedures can damage the ignition system.

NOTE: Do not disconnect any part of the ignition system while engine is running or while checking the speed control linkage.

Disconnect the fuel tank and allow motor to run until all fuel is used out of the carburetors. If any fuel remains, motor can start while checking the speed control linkage and may prevent accurate adjustments.

Connect a power timing light to the number 1 (top) spark plug. Turn ignition key on and crank motor with electric starter. Advance the speed controls until the timing light flashes when flywheel timing mark dots are aligned with the 36½° advance timing mark (Fig. M14-8). If advance timing is incorrect, turn the stop screw (A–Fig. M14-5) to stop the ignition advance at the correct position.

With the timing light still connected, synchronize the carburetor throttle opening to the ignition timing as follows: Crank motor with the electric starter and slowly advance speed control from idle position. The timing light should flash when dots on flywheel are between 5° and 7° BTDC.

With controls correctly set as outlined, the pickup tab should just contact the carburetor throttle lever. Refer to Fig. M14-9. If throttle is partly open or if lever is not touching the tab, loosen the two screws securing pickup plate and reposition plate for proper alignment.

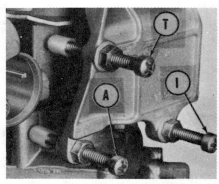

Fig. M14-5 — Maximum ignition advance is adjusted by stop screw (A) and idle speed by screw (I). Throttle stop screw (T) prevents damage to linkage.

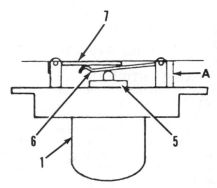

Fig. M14-3 — Distance (A) should be 13/32 inch (10.32 mm). Refer to text for adjustment procedure and Fig. M14-1 for parts identification.

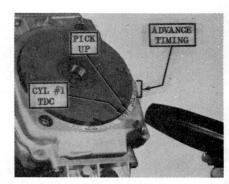

Fig. M14-8 — Refer to text for method used for setting the speed control linkage before adjusting.

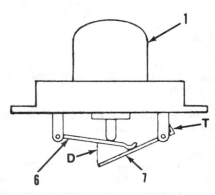

Fig. M14-4 — With bowl cover (1) upright, distance (D) between primary lever (6) and end of secondary lever (7) should be ¼ inch (6.4 mm). Bend tab (T) to adjust.

Fig. M14-9 — View of the throttle actuator plate just contacting the primary pickup lever (1). A four-cylinder motor is shown; however, Model 1000 is similar.

Throttle pickup should be rechecked after tightening the pickup plate retaining screws.

To adjust the throttle secondary pickup, advance the ignition distributor until it contacts the advance stop (A – Fig. M14-5).

NOTE: Do not move the economizer collar after the distributor contacts screw (A).

Check clearance at (2 – Fig. M14-10) between secondary pickup lever and screw. The screw should be just contacting the secondary pickup lever and is adjusted by turning screw (S – Fig. M14-11). Make certain that the primary end of the throttle pickup lever is still against the primary pickup cam (1 – Fig. M14-10).

To adjust the throttle stop screw (T – Fig. M14-5), move the speed control handle to maximum speed position. The carburetor throttles should be completely open when the throttle stop contacts screw (T). If the throttles are not completely open, turn stop screw (T) out. If the throttle stop does not contact screw (T), turn the screw in to prevent damage to linkage.

Model 1250. Refer to the special precautions listed in the **"Thunderbolt"** IGNITION section before servicing these motors. Incorrect servicing procedures can damage the ignition system.

NOTE: Do not disconnect any part of the ignition system while engine is running or while checking the speed control linkage adjustments.

Disconnect the fuel tank and allow motor to run until all fuel is used out of carburetors. If any fuel remains, motor

can start while checking the speed control linkage and may prevent accurate adjustments.

Connect a power timing light to number 1 (top) spark plug wire. Back the throttle stop screw (T – Fig. M14-12) out and move the speed control to the maximum speed position until the carburetor throttle valves are completely open. Turn screw (T) in until it just touches the throttle stop, then turn the screw in an additional ¾ turn to prevent damage to the linkage.

To adjust the spark advance linkage, the speed control should be in the maximum speed position. Turn the key switch on, crank engine with starter and check the ignition timing. The mark on flywheel (dots) should be aligned with the correct degree mark when the timing light flashes. Advance timing should occur at 34° BTDC. If timing is incorrect, vary the length of link rod by turning nuts (N – Fig. M14-12). Make certain to recheck after nuts are tightened against the swivel.

The primary cam on the throttle pickup plate should just contact the primary pickup lever as shown at (1 – Fig. M14-13) when the speed control lever is advanced to provide 7°-9° BTDC ignition timing. To check, crank the engine with the starter while checking the ignition timing. Advance the speed control until the ignition timing is within 7°-9° BTDC, then check the throttle pickup at (1). If clearance at (1) is not 0-0.005 inch (0-0.13 mm), loosen the two attaching screws (P – Fig. M14-14) and move the throttle pickup plate. Recheck pickup point after moving plate and tightening the two attaching screws.

To adjust the secondary throttle pickup, move the speed control to maximum speed position, then turn screw (S – Fig. M14-14) until the carburetor throttles are fully open and the maximum speed stop contacts stop screw (T – Fig. M14-12). At maximum speed, carburetor throttles should have slight play and should not bind, but all carburetor throttles should be fully open.

Fig. M14-11 — Refer to text for adjusting speed control linkage.

Fig. M14-12 — View of throttle stop screw (T) and idle stop screw (I) for 1250 models.

Fig. M14-10 — View of the secondary pickup lever just contacting the screw (2). The primary pickup lever should still be contacting cam at (1). A four cylinder motor is shown; however, Model 1000 is similar.

Fig. M14-13 — View of throttle pickup cams and lever typical of all models except Model 1000. Primary pickup should occur at (1) and secondary pickup at (2). Refer to text for adjusting.

Fig. M14-14—Typical view of secondary pickup adjusting screws (S) and primary pickup plate attaching screws (P) used on Models 900, 1150, 1250, 1350, 1400 and 1500.

Models 900, 1150, 1350, 1400 And 1500. Refer to the special precautions listed in the **"Thunderbolt"** IGNITION section before servicing these motors. Incorrect servicing procedures can damage the ignition system.

NOTE: Do not disconnect any part of the ignition system while engine is running or while checking the speed control linkage adjustments.

Connect a power timing light to number 1 (top) spark plug wire. Mount motor in test tank and start engine with timing light installed. Slowly advance speed control until proper throttle pickup timing marks are aligned. Refer to the following for throttle pickup timing specifications:

Model	Throttle Pickup Timing
900	4°-6° BTDC
1150 (Below Ser. No. 2928768)	5°-7° BTDC
1150 (Ser. No. 2928768-3761035)	2° BTDC-TDC
1150 (Above Ser. No. 3761035)	1°-3° BTDC
1350 (Below Ser. No. 2928768)	5°-7° BTDC
1350 (Above Ser. No. 2928767)	2° BTDC-TDC
1400 (1972)	2° BTDC-TDC
1400 (1978)	4°-6° BTDC
1500 (Below Ser. No. 3628318)	2° BTDC-TDC
1500 (Ser. No. 3628318-3751849)	2°-4° BTDC
1500 (Above Ser. No. 3751850)	4°-6° BTDC

Timing grid is marked on cowl support bracket on Model 1150 before serial number 3761035, Model 1350, Model 1400 and Model 1500 before serial number 3628318. Three punch marks on flywheel are used as timing mark on these models. A white dot is painted on top side of flywheel adjacent to three timing dots.

A metal timing pointer is secured to engine and a timing decal is placed on flywheel of Model 900, late Model 1150 and late Model 1500.

The primary cam on the throttle pickup plate should just contact the primary pickup lever as shown at (1 – Fig. M14-13) when the speed control is advanced to specified pickup position. If clearance at (1) is not 0-0.005 inch (0-0.13 mm), loosen the two attaching screws (P – Fig. M14-14) and move the throttle pickup plate. Recheck pickup point after tightening the two attaching screws.

To check maximum spark advance, start engine and advance speed control until distributor touches spark advance stop screw (A – Fig. M14-10). Timing light should indicate full spark advance at 21° BTDC. Turn spark advance stop screw to adjust full advance timing if necessary.

Secondary throttle pickup should be checked after maximum spark advance is adjusted. With engine stopped, advance speed controls until distributor is just touching spark advance stop screw. Secondary pickup on throttle cam should be just touching secondary pickup on carburetor cluster (2 – Fig. M14-13) at this point. Turn throttle pickup screw (S – Fig. M14-11) to adjust secondary throttle pickup.

Maximum throttle stop screw (T – Fig. M14-10) should be adjusted so throttles are fully opened at maximum speed position of speed control. Linkage should have a small amount of free play at maximum speed position to prevent binding.

Models 90, 115 And 140. Refer to special precautions listed in the IGNITION section before servicing these motors. Incorrect servicing procedures can damage the ignition system.

NOTE: Do not disconnect any part of the ignition system while engine is running or while checking speed control linkage adjustments.

Check ignition timing pointer alignment as follows: Install a dial indicator gage in number 1 (top) spark plug hole and turn flywheel clockwise until piston is 0.464 inch (12 mm) BTDC. Loosen retaining screw and position timing pointer so it is aligned with ".464 BTDC" mark on flywheel.

If engine is equipped with an idle stabilizer module (M – Fig. M14-15), disconnect white/black module wire from switch box terminal. Tape end of wire to prevent grounding. Reconnect other white/black wire between switch boxes to switch box terminal. Remove all spark plugs except number 1 (top) cylinder spark plug to prevent engine starting. Detach throttle cable barrel from retainer of cable anchor bracket. Adjust idle stop screw (I – Fig. M14-16) so idle marks (M – Fig. M14-17) on throttle cam and bracket are aligned as shown; retighten stop screw locknut. Loosen screw (W) in top carburetor lever (V). Hold idle stop screw (I – Fig. M14-16) against stop then turn carburetor lever (V – Fig. M14-17) so throttle valves are completely closed and cam (C) just contacts roller (R). Connect a power timing light to number 1 cylinder spark plug. With outboard in neutral, position throttle lever so idle stop screw is against stop. Crank engine using starter motor and adjust primary pickup screw (P – Fig. M14-18) so ignition timing is 1°-3° BTDC on Model 90, 5°-7° ATDC on Model 115 and 4°-6° ATDC on Model 140.

Open throttle and crank engine using starter motor. Adjust maximum ignition advance screw (A) so ignition timing is 20° BTDC.

NOTE: Due to electronic characteristics of ignition system, maximum advance is set at 20°BTDC but ignition will retard to 18° BTDC at high engine speed.

Fig. M14-15—View showing location of idle stabilizer module (M) used on some models.

Fig. M14-16—View of idle speed screw (I) on 90, 115 and 140 models.

Without engine running, move throttle lever to maximum throttle position and adjust full throttle stop screw T – Fig. M14-15) so there is 0.010-0.015 inch (0.25-0.38 mm) clearance between roller (R – Fig. M14-17) and cam (C). Be sure carburetor throttle plates are not acting as stops.

Reconnect idle stabilizer module wire to switch box. Install throttle cable barrel in retainer while adjusting barrel so it fits into retainer and places a very light preload on throttle lever against idle speed screw. Excessive throttle cable preload will result in difficult shifting from forward to neutral.

Adjust idle speed screw (I – Fig. M14-16) so idle speed is 500-600 rpm on Model 90 and 550-600 rpm on Models 115 and 140 with outboard in gear.

REED VALVES. The inlet reed valves are located on the crankshaft second, fourth and sixth main bearings. Each reed valve unit supplies fuel mixture from one of the carburetors to the two adjoining cylinders.

Reed petals (2 – Fig. M14-19 or M14-20) should be perfectly flat and have no more than 0.007 inch (0.178 mm) clearance between free end of reed petal and seating surface of center main bearing. The reed stop (1) must be

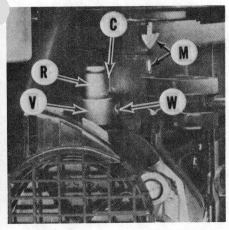

Fig. M14-17 – View of pickup cam (C) and throttle roller (R) on Merc 90, 115 and 140.

C. Pickup cam
M. Idle speed marks
R. Throttle roller
V. Carburetor lever
W. Screw

Fig. M14-18 – Adjust primary pickup screw (P) and maximum advance screw (A) 90, 115 and 140 models.

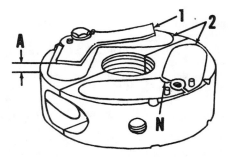

Fig. M14-19 – Intermediate main bearing and reed valve for 1000 models. Reed petals are right and left hand units. When installing reed petals, place reed with the cutout notch (N) on left as shown. Refer also to Fig. M14-20.

carefully adjusted to 3/16 inch (4.76 mm) on Model 1000; 5/32 inch on Models 1150, 1250, 1350 and 1400; and 0.162 inch (4.11 mm) on Models 90, 115, 140, 900, 1150 and 1500. This clearance is measured between end of stop and seating surface of reed plate as shown at (A – Fig. M14-19). Seating surface of bearing must be smooth and flat, and may be refinished on a lapping plate after removing reed stops, reed valves and dowels. Do not attempt to bend or straighten a reed petal to modify performance or to salvage a damaged reed. Never install a bent reed. Lubricate the reed valve units with "Quicksilver" Multipurpose Lubricant or a light distributor cam grease when reassembling.

On Model 1000, each reed valve unit has eight reeds which are right-hand and left-hand units, and are available only as a matched set. When installing reed valves, place the reed petal with the cutout notch (N) to the left as shown. Crankshaft must be removed before reed valve units can be serviced.

Fig. M14-20 – View of the intermediate main bearing and reed valve assembly use on 90, 115, 140, 900, 1500, 1250 and 1350 models. Reed petals are shown at (2) and reed stops at (1). In addition to small retaining screw shown, Models 90, 115 and 140, late Model 1150, Model 1400 and Model 1500 have through-bolts securing reed plates and petals to valve assemblies.

FUEL PUMP. Diaphragm type fuel pumps are used. Pressure and vacuum pulsations from the crankcase alternate to pull fuel from the supply tank and supply the carburetor. Most of the work is performed by the main supply chamber (5 – Fig. M14-21). Vacuum in the crankcase pulls the diaphragm (2) downward causing fuel to be drawn through inlet line (8), past inlet check valve (7) into main pump chamber (5). The alternate pressure forces diaphragm out and fuel leaves the chamber through outlet check valve (6). The booster pump chamber (3) serves to dampen the action of the larger, main pump chamber (5), and increase the maximum potential fuel flow.

When overhauling the fuel pump, renew all defective or questionable parts. Fuel pressure should be at least 2 psi (13.8 kPa) at carburetor when running motor at full throttle.

IGNITION SYSTEM

All models are equipped with Thunderbolt ignition system. Refer to the appropriate following paragraphs for service.

The breakerless Thunderbolt ignition system uses an electronic triggering device and does not use breaker points. This ignition is extremely durable in normal operation but can be easily damaged by improper testing or servicing procedures.

Observe the following list of cautions and use **only** the approved methods for checking the system to prevent damage to the components.
1. DO NOT reverse battery terminals.

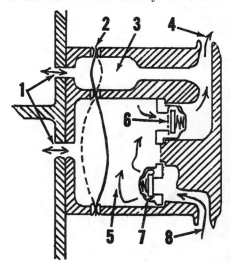

Fig. M14-21 – Schematic view of diaphragm type fuel pump. Pump body mounts on side of cylinder block and is ported to two crankcases as shown.

1. Pressure ports
2. Diaphragm
3. Booster chamber
4. To carburetor
5. Main fuel chamber
6. Outlet check valve
7. Inlet check valve
8. Fuel inlet

2. DO NOT check polarity of battery by sparking the lead wires.

3. DO NOT install resistor type spark plugs or lead wires other than those specified.

4. DO NOT disconnect **any** wires while engine is running.

5. DO NOT ground any wires to engine block when checking. Ground only to front cover plate or bottom cowl to which switch box is mounted as described.

6. DO NOT use tachometer except for those designed for this system.

All Models Except Models 90, 115 And 140

TROUBLESHOOTING. Use only approved procedures when testing to prevent damage to components.

SPARK TEST. Do not remove spark plug wire while motor is running. Cut off the ground electrode from a standard spark plug (such as Champion J4J or L4J) and connect one of the spark plug wires to the test plug. Ground the test plug to the support bracket using a clamp or jumper wire.

CAUTION: Do not hold spark plug or wire in hand.

Make certain that test plug is properly grounded, then crank motor with electric starter. If test plug fires but engine will not start, check for incorrect installation of timing belt as outlined in the following TRIGGER AND DISTRIBUTOR paragraphs. Fuel system problems can also prevent starting. If test plug does not fire, check the wiring as follows.

WIRING AND CONNECTION TEST (Models Prior To 1976.) Turn the key switch OFF. Connect one lead of voltmeter to red terminal of switch box (R – Fig. M14-27) and ground other lead

to front cover plate. If red terminal is dead (no voltage), check battery, battery connections or for broken wire in wiring harness. If red terminal has voltage, proceed as follows:

Connect one lead of voltmeter to the white terminal (W) and ground other lead to front cover plate. Turn key switch ON. If white terminal is dead (no voltage), key switch or wiring is defective. If white terminal has voltage, check the remaining components of system as follows:

Turn the key switch OFF. Disconnect the black (BL – Fig. M14-29), white (W) and brown (BR) wires from switch box and connect the three wires from a trigger assembly that is known to be good. Refer to Fig. M14-30. Disconnect the coil secondary lead from the distributor center terminal, then connect a test spark plug (or gap tester) to the coil secondary lead.

NOTE: Spark plug or spark tester must also be grounded to engine.

Turn key switch ON, then pass a metal feeler gage through the trigger coil as shown in Fig. M14-30. If a spark jumps at test plug, the original trigger assembly is faulty and should be renewed. If spark does not jump at test plug, listen for "click" around area of the high tension coil as the feeler gage passes through the trigger coil. "Clicking" indicates shorted high tension coil or high tension (secondary) lead wire. If the lead wire is not shorted, the high tension coil should be checked further as outlined in the following paragraph. If spark does not jump the test plug and coil is not damaged, the switch box should be renewed.

NOTE: A faulty switch box is nearly always caused by reversing battery leads, which damages the rectifier and in turn damages the switch box.

If switch box is suspected, check rectifier before renewing the switch box. If tests indicate that rectifier is damaged, renew the rectifier and again test the ignition system.

NOTE: Before disconnecting any wires, make certain that motor is not running and disconnect battery.

Models After 1975. To check trigger coil and switch box, manufacturer recommends use of Thunderbolt Ignition Analyzer (C-91-62563A1). Follow instructions accompanying tester.

Fig. M14-26 – Surface gap plus should be renewed if center electrode is 1/32 inch (0.79 mm) below the end of plug.

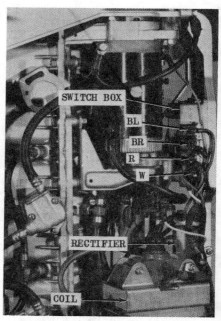

Fig. M14-27 – Wires to starboard side of switch box must be connected as shown on motors with breakerless Thunderbolt ignition.

BL. Black or green   R. Red
BR. Brown   W. White

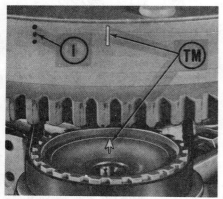

Fig. M14-22 – Refer to text for timing instructions when installing drive belt or ignition unit. Straight line mark on flywheel is used as belt aligning mark on 1000 and 1250 models. Refer to Fig. M14-33 for belt aligning marks on later models.

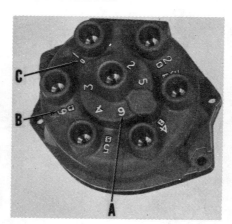

Fig. M14-23 – The distributor cap is marked for installation on several 6-cylinder motors. Inside numbers (A) are used for early 60 cu.-in. (983 cc) and 66 cu.-in. (1081 cc) motors. The outside numbers (B) are used for 76 cu.-in. (1245 cc) and larger motors except those with Thunderbolt ignition. Numbers (C) inside the squares are for early models (before 1970) with Thunderbolt ignition.

COIL TEST. The ignition coil can be checked using an ignition tester available from several sources, including the following:

GRAHAM TESTERS, INC.
4220 Central Ave. N.E.
Minneapolis, Minn. 55421

MERC-O-TRONIC
INSTRUMENTS CORP.
215 Branch St.
Almont, Mich. 48003

SPARK PLUGS. The spark plugs should be removed if the center electrode is burned back more than 1/32 inch

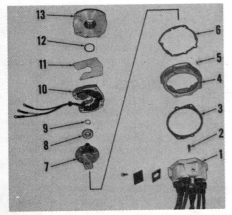

Fig. M14-28 — Exploded view of ignition distributor typical of breakerless Thunderbolt ignition models before 1970.

1. Distributor cap
2. Brush & spring
3. Gasket
4. Adapter
5. Dowel pin (2 used)
6. Gasket
7. Shaft, rotor & timer assy.
8. Ball bearing (2 used)
9. Snap ring (2 used)
10. Trigger assy.
11. Shims
12. Wave washer
13. Primary housing

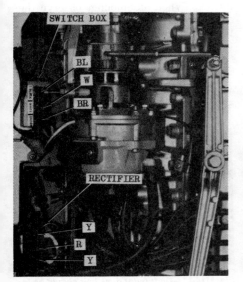

Fig. M14-29 — Wires to port side of switch box and rectifier on models prior to 1976 must be connected as shown.

BL. Black
BR. Brown
R. Red
W. White
Y. Yellow

(0.79 mm) below flat surface of the plug end. Refer to Fig. M14-26. AC type V40FFM or Champion type L77V, surface gap spark plugs should be used. Radio noise suppression spark plugs, AC type VR40FFM or Champion types QL76V or QL77V, may also be used.

TRIGGER AND DISTRIBUTOR (Models 1000 and 1250). The electronic trigger assembly is mounted in the distributor assembly as shown in Fig. M14-28. Before disconnecting any wires, disconnect the battery. The three wires from the trigger assembly (10) are connected to three terminals on port side of the switch box. The three terminals are marked to indicate correct wire connections. When installing trigger assembly, install shims (11) between trigger housing (10) and primary housing (13) until the timer disc on rotor shaft (7) is centered in trigger slot. Recheck after trigger housing screws are tightened to make certain that timer disc is centered in slot.

NOTE: The rotor and timer disc cannot be removed from shaft.

Connect wires from trigger assembly to terminals on port side of switch box. Switch box terminals are marked for correct installation of wires as shown in Fig. M14-29.

To install the distributor to the drive pulley and housing, turn drive end of distributor shaft so tang is forward.

Firing order is 1-4-5-2-3-6. The distributor cap is marked for installing

Fig. M14-30 — Refer to text when testing Thunderbolt ignition system. Spark tester is shown at (ST).

spark plug wires. The numbers (C – Fig. M14-23) inside the squares are for Thunderbolt ignition models.

To remove the distributor drive belt, it is first necessary to remove the pulley flange plate. Disengage belt from the distributor pulley, then remove flywheel using a suitable puller. When installing, position drive belt under the alternator stator and around the crankshaft. Install flywheel being careful not to damage to the belt. Turn the flywheel and distributor until the straight line on flywheel is aligned with the arrow on distributor pulley as shown in (TM – Fig. M14-22), then install drive belt over the pulley.

NOTE: Do not use the ignition timing mark dots (I). Recheck marks (TM) after belt is installed. Marks must be on center line between crankshaft and distributor shaft.

TRIGGER AND DISTRIBUTOR (Models 900, 1150, 1350, 1400 and 1500). The electronic trigger coil is located in distributor housing (10 – Fig. M14-32) and is available only as a unit with the housing. Before removing any wires, make certain that battery is disconnected.

To disassemble, disconnect battery and three wires on port side of switch box. The wires from trigger assembly and terminals are marked to indicate correct wire connections. Remove cover (18), drive belt pulley (19) and spacer (20). Bend tabs of washer (23) away from nut (21), remove nut and withdraw the distributor from adapter and economizer (25 and 29). Remove clamp (3) and cap (1). Carefully press bearing (15) out of housing by working through the two holes provided.

NOTE: Do not damage nut (17) or shaft when removing bearing.

Remove nut (17) then bump the rotor shaft (7) out of bearing (8). The shaft should slide easily out of timer plate (7P) and spacer (14). Bearing (8) can be removed after extracting snap ring (9).

When reassembling, install bearing (8) and snap ring (9). Position spacer (14) then insert the timer plate (7P) into the trigger coil slot. Insert the rotor shaft (7) through the timer plate (7P), spacer (14) and bearing (8).

CAUTION: Make certain that tab on timer plate (7P) correctly engages slot in rotor shaft (7) before pressing shaft into bearing (8).

Install spacer (16) and tighten nut (17) to 75-80 in.-lbs. (8.5-9.0 N·m). Rotate rotor shaft and note any interference as timer plate turns. If necessary, install shims between bearing plate (8) and spacer (14) to adjust timer plate height. Press ball bearing (15) around shaft and into housing (10). Install distributor cap (1) and clamp (3). Joint of clamp should be positioned under the trigger coil wires. Assemble distributor to the economizer collar (29) and adapter (25), then install washers (22, 23 and 24). Tighten cap nut (21), back nut off until the nearest notch lines up with tang of washer (23), then bend tang into notch. Install spacer (20) and pulley (19) over the drive key. Firing order is 1-4-5-2-3-6.

To renew the distributor drive belt, it is first necessary to remove pulley flange plate (18), disengage belt from pulley, then remove flywheel. When installing, position drive belt under alternator stator and around the crankshaft. Install flywheel being careful not to damage the belt. Turn the flywheel and distributor pulley as shown in (Fig. M14-33), then install drive belt over the pulley. Dots are punched into flywheel and painted white on early models. Recheck timing marks after belt is installed. Marks must be on center line between crankshaft and distributor shaft. Refer to SPEED CONTROL LINKAGE. Paragraphs for adjusting linkage and ignition timing.

Models 90, 115 And 140

These models are equipped with a solid-state, capacitor discharge ignition system consisting of trigger coils, stator, switch boxes and ignition coils. The trigger coils are contained in a trigger ring module under the flywheel. Diodes, SCR's and capacitors are contained in the switch boxes. Switch boxes trigger ring module and stator must be serviced as unit assemblies.

Check all wires and connections before troubleshooting ignition circuit. The following test specifications will aid troubleshooting.

STATOR

Tests	Ohms
Blue and red stator leads	5400-6200
Blue/white and red/white stator leads	5400-6200
Red stator lead and engine ground*	125-175
Red/white stator lead and engine ground*	125-175

*If stator has a black ground wire, be sure ground wire is properly connected to engine.

Note when testing the trigger module that yellow sleeves enclose wires from the trigger module to the lower switch box. The lower switch box serves the even-numbered cylinders while the upper switch box serves the odd-numbered cylinders.

TRIGGER MODULE

Tests	Ohms
Brown trigger lead (no yellow sleeve) and white trigger lead (with yellow sleeve	1100-1400
White trigger lead (no yellow sleeve) and violet trigger lead (with yellow sleeve)	1100-1400
Violet trigger lead (no yellow sleeve) and brown trigger lead (with yellow sleeve)	1100-1400

COOLING SYSTEM

WATER PUMP. The rubber impeller type water pump is housed in the gearcase housing. The impeller is mounted on and driven by the lower unit drive shaft.

When cooling system problems are encountered, first check the water inlet for plugging or partial stoppage, then if not corrected, remove the gearcase housing as outlined in LOWER UNIT section and examine the water pump, water tubes and seals.

Early models were originally equipped with aluminum water pump housings; however, on later models, the water pump housings are plastic. The later type pump can be installed on early models. When assembling, observe the assembly notes, cautions and tightening torques listed in the LOWER UNIT section.

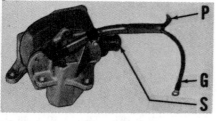

Fig. M14-31 — View of typical high tension ignition coil. Primary lead (P) may be green or black. Ground wire (G) is black on all models. The secondary (high tension) terminal is at (S).

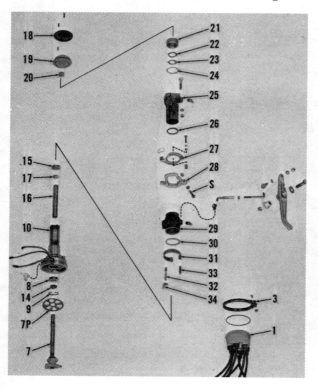

Fig. M14-32 — Exploded view of the Thunderbolt ignition distributor and drive used on 1970 and later models.

  1. Distributor cap
  3. Clamp
  7. Rotor & shaft
 7P. Timer plate
  8. Ball bearing
  9. Snap ring
10. Distributor housing & trigger assy.
14. Spacer
15. Ball bearing
16. Spacer
17. Nut
18. Flange plate
19. Drive pulley
20. Spacer
21. Cap nut
22. Wave washer
23. Tang washer
24. Washer
25. Adapter
26. Washer
27. Throttle cam plate (primary pickup)
28. Throttle cam (secondary pickup)
29. Economizer collar
30. Washer
31. Spring
32. Spring anchor stud
33. Spring anchor pin
34. Spark advance stop

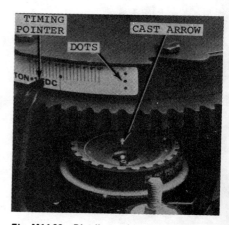

Fig. M14-33 — Distributor drive belt should be installed with cast arrow on drive pulley aligned with dots on flywheel of 900, 1150, 1350, 1400 and 1500 models. Dots are stamped into flywheel and painted white on early models not equipped with timing decal on flywheel.

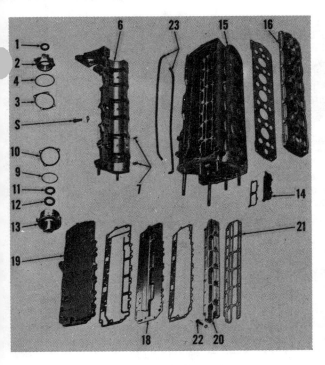

Fig. M14-41 – Exploded view of Model 1250 crankcase assembly. Other models are similar; however, parts (20, 21, 22 & 23) are not used on Model 1000.

S. Main bearing screw
1. Oil seal
2. End cap
3. Shim
4. "O" ring
6. Crankcase half
7. Dowel pins
9. "O" ring
10. Shim
11. Oil seal
12. Oil seal
13. End cap
14. Transfer port cover
15. Cylinder half
16. Cylinder cover
18. Exhaust plate
19. Exhaust cover
20. Water jacket cover
21. Gasket
22. Screws
23. Sealing strips

POWER HEAD

R&R AND DISASSEMBLE. To remove the power head assembly, first disconnect the battery and remove the top and side cowling. Remove electric starter, then disconnect all interfering wire and linkage. Remove the stud nuts which secure the power head to lower unit then jar power head on exhaust side to loosen gasket. Lift power head from lower unit and install on a suitable stand. Remove the flywheel, distributor, alternator-generator and the carburetors. Exhaust manifold cover, cylinder block cover and transfer port covers should be removed for cleaning and inspection.

Remove screws securing upper and lower crankcase end caps. Remove the main bearing locking bolts from front crankcase half, remove the flange bolts;

Fig. M14-42 – Refer to text for method of checking crankshaft end play. The crankshaft should be centered in the cylinder block.

then remove crankcase front half by inserting screwdriver in the recesses provided on side flanges. Use extra care not to spring the parts or to mar the machined, mating surfaces. Use a mallet or soft faced hammer to tap crankcase end caps from cylinder block assembly. Be careful not to damage adjustment shims on end caps. The crankcase half (6 – Fig. M14-41) and cylinder assembly (15) are matched and align bored, and are available only as an assembly.

Crankshaft, pistons, bearings and connecting rods may now be removed for service as outlined in the appropriate following paragraphs. When assembling, follow the procedures outlined in the ASSEMBLY paragraph.

ASSEMBLY. When assembling, the crankcase must be completely sealed against both vacuum and pressure. Exhaust manifold and water passages must be sealed against pressure leakage. Whenever power head is disassembled, it is recommended that all gasket surfaces and machined joints without gaskets be carefully checked for nicks and burrs which might interfere with a tight seal.

On all models so equipped, make certain that threaded holes in cylinder for attaching the water jacket cover (20 – Fi.g M14-41) are cleaned.

Lubricate all bearing and friction surfaces with engine oil. Loose needle bearings may be held in place during assembly using a light, nonfibrous grease.

After the crankcase, connecting rods, pistons and main bearings are positioned in the cylinder, check the crank-

shaft end play. Temporarily install the crankshaft end caps (2 and 13) omitting the sealing rings (4 and 9), but using the shims (3 and 10) that were originally installed. Tighten the end cap to cylinder, retaining screws. Use a soft hammer to bump the crankshaft each way to seat bearings, then measure the end play.

Bump the crankshaft toward top, and measure clearance between the top crankshaft counterweight and the end cap as shown in Fig. M14-42. Bump the crankshaft toward bottom and again measure clearance between counterweight and end cap. Subtract the first (minimum) clearance from the second clearance which will indicate the amount of end play. If end play is not within limits of 0.004-0.012 inch (0.102-0.305 mm), add or remove shims (3 or 10 – Fig. M14-41) as necessary, then recheck. The crankshaft should be centered by varying the amount of shims between upper (3) and lower (10) shim stacks. When centering the crankshaft, make certain that end play is correct.

On all models, all of the gasket and sealing surfaces should be lightly and carefully coated with an impervious liquid sealer. Surface must be completely coated, using care that excess sealer does not squeeze out into bearings, crankcase or other passages.

On models so equipped, clean the gasket surfaces and threaded holes of water jacket cover (20) and cylinder (15). Coat the first four threads of all screws (22) with Resiweld (C-92-65150-1) and allow to set for 10 minutes. Coat gasket surface of water jacket cover and mating surface of cylinder with gasket sealer, then install gasket (21) and water jacket cover (20). Tighten the screws (22) evenly from the center outward to a torque of 200 in.-lbs. (22.6 N·m) on early models and 150 in.-lbs. (16.9 N·m) on late models.

On all models, check the assembly by turning the crankshaft after each step to check for binding or locking which might indicate improper assembly. Remove the cause before proceeding. Rotate the crankshaft until each piston ring in turn appears in one of the exhaust or transfer ports, then check by pressing on ring with a blunt tool. Ring should spring back when released; if it does not, a broken or binding ring is indicated, and the trouble should be corrected.

Tighten the crankcase exhaust cover and cylinder cover cap screws by first tightening the center screws, then tightening screws evenly working toward top of power head. When upper half is tightened, again start at the center and tighten screws alternately toward bottom of power head. Tightening torques are given in the CONDENSED SERVICE DATA table.

PISTONS, PINS, RINGS AND CYLINDERS. Before detaching connecting rods from crankshaft, make sure that rod and cap are properly identified for correct assembly to each other and in the correct cylinder.

Maximum allowable cylinder bore wear or out-of-round is 0.004 inch (0.102 mm). Worn or slightly damaged standard size cylinders may be repaired by boring and honing to fit an oversize piston. Pistons and rings are available in 0.015 inch (0.38 mm) oversize on early models and 0.015 inch (0.38 mm) and 0.030 inch (0.76 mm) oversizes on later models.

Piston rings are interchangeable in the ring grooves and are pinned to prevent rings from rotating in grooves. Some motors use two rings on each piston while others use three rings.

Piston pin is pressed in piston bosses and secured with retaining rings. The retaining rings should not be reused. Two types of retaining rings (4–Fig. M14-43) have been used and must NOT be interchanged. Some late models use "C" rings and other models use "G" type retaining rings. Piston end of connecting rod is fitted with loose needle rollers. Refer to the CONNECTING RODS, BEARINGS AND CRANKSHAFT paragraphs for number of rollers used. The piston pin needle rollers use the connecting rod bore and the piston pin as bearing races. When assembling, install bearing washers and needle bearings in piston end of connecting rod using light nonfibrous grease to hold them in place. A Mercury special tool may be used to hold needles in position while positioning piston for installation.

Piston must be installed so sharp, vertical side of deflector will be to starboard (intake) side of cylinder block. Heat piston to approximately 135°F (57°C) on early models and 190°F (88°C) on late models, then press piston pin into place. Pin should be centered in piston. Use new retaining rings on each reassembly of engine.

Assemble the connecting rod and piston assemblies, together with the main bearing units to the crankshaft; then install the complete assembly in cylinder half of block. Numbers 2 and 4 pistons should be started first. Use the Mercury Ring Compressor Kit (C-91-47844A2), if available; or carefully compress each ring with the fingers if kit is not available. Thoroughly lubricate pistons and rings during assembly.

CONNECTING RODS, BEARINGS AND CRANKSHAFT. Upper and lower ends of crankshaft are carried by ball bearings. The second, fourth and sixth main bearings (Fig. M14-19 or M14-20) also contain the inlet reed valves. The third and fifth main bearings (13–Fig. M14-43), contain both loose needle rollers (15) which ride in a split

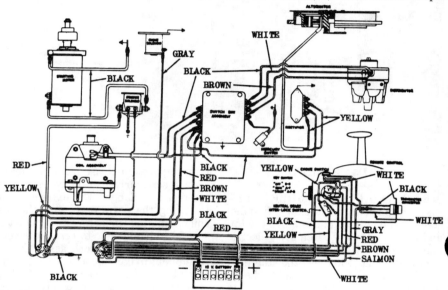

Fig. M14-47—Wiring diagram typical of all models with breakerless Thunderbolt ignition prior to 1976.

Fig. M14-43—Exploded view of the crankshaft and associated parts typical of all models. Refer to Fig. M14-19 or M14-20 for intermediate main bearings and reed valve assemblies.

1. Piston rings
2. Piston
3. Piston pin
4. Retainers
5. Bearing washers
6. Needle rollers
7. Connecting rod
8. Needle rollers
9. Crankshaft
10. Top main bearing
11. Bottom main bearing
12. Bearing alignment dowel
13. Bearing housing
14. Main bearing race
15. Needle rollers
16. Retaining ring

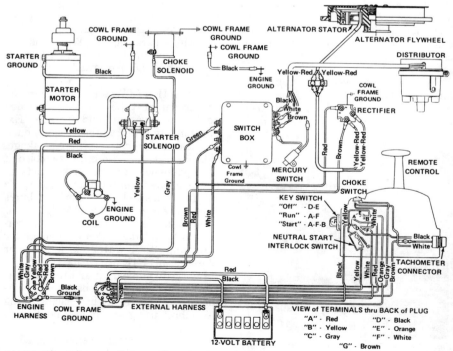

Fig. M14-48—Wiring schematic for models between 1975 and 1979 equipped with Thunderbolt ignition.

type outer race (14), held together by a retaining ring (16).

The connecting rod uses 29 loose needle rollers at piston end. The crankpin end of connecting rod uses a caged needle bearing on all models except Model 1000. Model 1000 motors were equipped with 32 loose needle roller bearings at crankpin end of connecting rod.

Check rod for alignment using Mercury Alignment tool, or by placing rod on a surface plate and checking with a light.

If bearing surface of rod and cap is rough, scored, worn or shows evidence of overheating, renew the connecting rod. Inspect crankpin and main bearing journals. If scored, out-of-round or worn, renew the crankshaft. Check the crankshaft for straightness using a dial indicator and "V" blocks.

Inspect and adjust the reed valves as outlined in REED VALVE paragraph, and reassemble as outlined in ASSEMBLY paragraph.

ELECTRICAL SYSTEM

Refer to Figs. M14-47, M14-48 or M14-49 for a typical wiring diagram.

Note the following cautions when servicing electrical components:

DO NOT reverse battery connections. Battery negative (–) terminal is grounded.

DO NOT "spark" battery connections to check polarity.

DO NOT disconnect battery cables while engine is running.

DO NOT crank engine if ignition switch boxes are not grounded to engine.

LOWER UNIT

PROPELLER AND DRIVE CLUTCH. Protection for the motor is built into a special cushioning clutch in the propeller hub. No adjustment is possible on the propeller or clutch. Various pitch propellers are available and propeller should be selected to provide full throttle engine operation within rpm range listed below. Propellers other than those designed for the motor must not be used.

Model	RPM Range
90,900	4500-5000
1000, 1250 and 1350	4800-5300
115, 1150	5000-5500
140, 1400 and 1500	5300-5800
1500XS	5800-6300

R&R AND OVERHAUL. Most service on the lower unit can be performed by detaching the gearcase housing from the drive shaft housing. To remove housing, remove plastic plug and Allen screw from location (1–Fig. M14-51. Remove trim tab (2) and screw from under trim tab. Remove stud nut from location (3), stud nuts (4) on each side and stud nut (5), if so equipped, then withdraw the lower unit gearcase assembly.

Remove plugs and drain oil from housing, then secure the gearcase in a soft jawed vise with propeller up. Wedge a piece of wood between propeller and antiventilation plate, remove propeller nut, then remove propeller.

Disassemble gearcase by removing gearcase housing cover nut (61–Fig. M14-52). Clamp the outer end of propeller shaft in a soft jawed vise and remove gearcase by tapping with a rubber mallet. Be careful not to lose key (59) or shims (47) on early models. Forward gear (40) will remain in housing. Withdraw propeller shaft from bearing carrier (56) and reverse gear (46).

Clamp bearing carrier (56) in a soft jawed vise and remove reverse gear (46) and bearing (49) with an internal expanding puller and slide hammer. Remove and discard propeller shaft rear seals (58).

To remove dog clutch (43) from propeller shaft, remove retaining ring (44). Insert cam follower (8) in hole in shaft and apply only enough pressure on end of cam follower to remove spring pressure, then push out pin (42) with a small punch.The pin passes through drilled

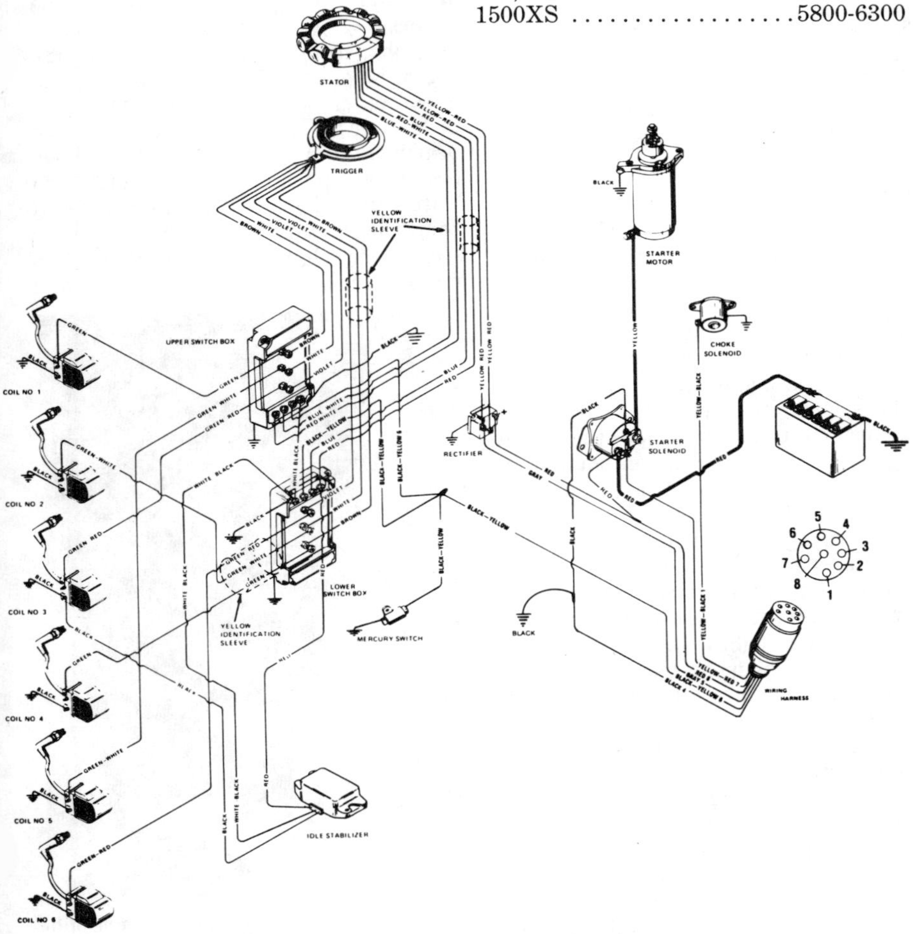

Fig. M14-49—Wiring diagram typical of 90, 115 and 140 models.

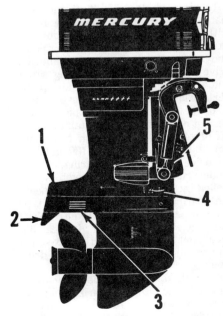

Fig. M14-51 — To remove the lower unit gearcase assembly, remove the attaching screws and stud nuts from positions indicated.

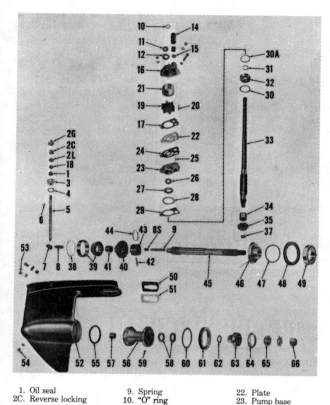

Fig. M14-52 — Exploded view of gearcase assembly typical of all models. Shim (47) is not used on later models. Some models use a tapered bearing in place of ball bearing (32), snap ring (31) and shim (30A).

1. Oil seal
2C. Reverse locking cam
2G. Push rod guide
2L. Lower spacer
3. Bushing
4. "O" ring
5. Shift shaft
6. Snap ring
7. Shift cam
8. Cam follower
8S. Slide
9. Spring
10. "O" ring
11. Rubber ring (slinger)
12. Oil seal
14. Seal
15. Nylon washer
16. Water pump body
17. Gasket
19. Impeller
20. Key
21. Insert
22. Plate
23. Pump base
24. Gasket
25. Dowel
26. Oil seal
27. Spring loaded oil seal
28. "O" ring
29. Gasket
30. & 30A. Shims
31. Snap ring
32. Ball bearing
33. Drive shaft
34. Roller bearing
35. Drive pinion
37. Nut
38. Shim
39. Tapered roller bearing
40. Forward gear
41. Roller bearing
42. Cross pin
43. Dog clutch
44. Retaining ring
45. Propeller shaft
46. Reverse gear
47. Shim
48. Thrust washer
49. Ball bearing
50. Exhaust tube seal
51. Support plate
52. Gear housing
53. Vent screw
54. Filler screw
55. "O" ring
56. Bearing carrier
57. Roller bearing
58. Oil seals
59. Key
60. Washer
61. Housing cover nut
62. Thrust washer
63. Thrust hub
64. Cupped washer
65. Splined washer
66. Propeller nut

necessary. After setting mesh position, check backlash between teeth of gears (35 and 40). Backlash should be 0.014-0.016 inch (0.356-0.406 mm). To increase clearance (backlash), remove part of shim stack (38) behind bearing cup. If gears are too loose, add shims. After changing thickness of shims (38), gears should be recoated with bearing blue and mesh position should be rechecked. Install bearing (49), thrust washer (48) and reverse gear (46) in bearing carrier (56). To check reverse gear (46) backlash on all early models with straight-cut gear teeth, install bearing carrier and gear assembly using shims (47) that were originally installed. If backlash is not within limits of 0.006-0.008 inch (0.152-0.203 mm), add or remove shims (47) as required. Adding shims at (47) increases backlash (clearance). Reverse gear backlash is not adjustable on models with spiral gears.

When reassembling, long splines on shift rod (5) should be toward top. Shift cam (7) is installed with notches up and toward rear. Assemble shifting parts (9, 8S, 43, 42 and 44) into propeller shaft (45). Pin (42) should be through hole in slide (8S). Position follower (8) in end of propeller shaft insert shaft into bearing (41) and forward gear. Install the reverse gear and bearing carrier assembly using new seals (55 and 58). Lip of inner seal (58) should face in and lip of outer seal (58) should face propeller (out). On models with ball type bearing at (32), install shims (30A) above bearing and position new gasket (29) and water pump base (23) on housing. Add shims (30A) until the water pump base stands out slightly from gasket, then measure clearance between gasket and

holes in clutch and operates in slotted holes in propeller shaft.

To disassemble drive shaft and associated parts, reposition gearcase in vise with drive shaft projecting upward. Remove rubber slinger (11), water pump body (16), impeller (19) and impeller drive key (20). Remove flushing screw and withdraw remainder of water pump parts. Clamp upper end of drive shaft in a soft jawed vise, remove pinion retaining nut or screw (37); then tap gearcase off drive shaft and bearing. Note position and thickness of shims (30 and 30A) on drive shaft upper bearing. On all models, mesh portion of pinion is controlled by shims (30) placed underneath the bearing. On models with ball type upper bearing, shims (30A) control shaft end play. The shims are identical but should not be interchanged or mixed, except to adjust the mesh portion of drive pinion.

After drive shaft has been removed, forward gear (40) and bearing cone can be withdrawn. Use an internal expanding type puller to withdraw bearing cup if removal is required. Remove and save shim pack (38).

Shift shaft (5) and cam (7) can be removed after removing forward gear and unscrewing bushing (3) from gearcase housing.

If gear wear was abnormal or if any parts that affect gear alignment were renewed, check and adjust gear mesh as follows: Install forward gear (40) and bearing (39) using shims (38) that were originally installed. Position shims (30) that were originally installed at bottom of bearing bore. On late models with taper bearing (32) and spiral gear teeth, install bearing cup (32) in housing bore against shims (30). On all models, position drive pinion (35) in housing and insert drive shaft (33), with bearing (32) installed, into housing, bearing (34) and gear (35). On models with ball type bearing, the bearing must be firmly seated in housing bore. On all models, install retaining screw or nut (37). Coat gears (35 and 40) with bearing blue and check mesh position. On models with spiral gears, it will be necessary to push down on end of drive shaft while checking mesh position. On all models, if gears do not mesh in center of teeth, add or remove shims (30) under bearing as

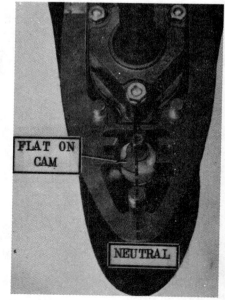

Fig. M14-53 — The reverse locking cam must be in position shown when lower unit (and the shift shaft) are in neutral.

water pump base with feeler gage. Remove shims (30A) equal to 0.002-0.003 inch (0.051-0.076 mm) less than clearance measured. When water pump is tightened down, compression of a new gasket (29) will be sufficient to hold bearing (32) in position with zero clearance.

Upper oil seal (26) should be installed with lips facing up (toward engine) and lower oil seal (27) should be pressed into water pump base with lips facing down toward propeller shaft. Install remainder of water pump assembly and tighten the screws or nuts to the following recommended torque. Torque ¼-28 nuts to 30 in.-lbs. (3.4 N·m). Torque 5/16-24 nuts to 40 in.-lbs. (4.5 N·m). Torque ¼-20 screws to 20 in.-lbs. (2.2 N·m).

The lower spacer (2L) should be installed with groove down. Reverse locking cam (2C) should be installed on shaft splines so flat on cam is in center toward front when shift shaft (5) is in reverse position. When in neutral, reverse locking cam should be positioned as shown in Fig. M14-53. The push rod guide (2G—

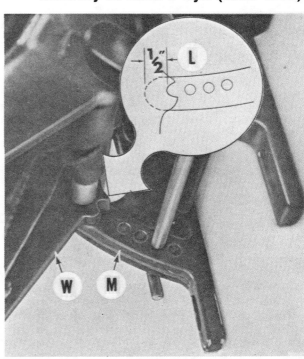

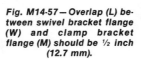

Fig. M14-57 — Overlap (L) between swivel bracket flange (W) and clamp bracket flange (M) should be ½ inch (12.7 mm).

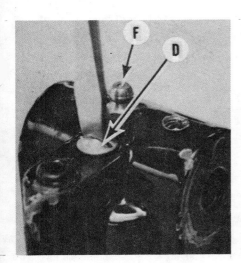

Fig. M14-55 — View showing location of down circuit bleed screw (D) and grease fitting (F).

Fig. M14-56 — View showing location of up circuit bleed screw (U) and bleed port (P).

Fig. M14-52) is located in the drive shaft housing.

Before attaching gearcase housing to the drive shaft housing, make certain that shift cam (7) and the shift lever (on motor) are in forward gear position on early models and neutral position on late models. In forward gear position, shift shaft (5) should be in clockwise position (viewed from top end of shaft). Complete assembly by reversing disassembly.

POWER TILT/TRIM

Non-Integral Type

FLUID. Recommended fluid is SAE 10W-30 or 10W-40 automotive oil. With outboard in full up position, oil level should reach bottom of fill plug hole threads. Do not overfill.

BLEEDING. To bleed air from hydraulic system, position outboard at full tilt and engage tilt lock lever. Without disconnecting hoses, remove hydraulic trim cylinders. Be sure fluid reservoir is full and remains so during bleeding operation. Remove down circuit bleed screw (D—Fig. M14-55) and "O" ring. Press "IN" control button for a few seconds, release button and wait approximately one minute. Repeat until expelled oil is air-free. Install "O" ring and bleed screw (D) and repeat procedure on opposite cylinder. Place cylinder in horizontal position so bleed port (P—Fig. M14-56) is up and remove up circuit bleed screw (U). Press "UP" and "UP/OUT" control buttons for a few

seconds, release buttons and wait approximately one minute. Repeat until expelled oil is air-free. Install "O" ring and bleed screw (U) and repeat procedure on opposite cylinder. Reinstall cylinders.

ADJUST TRIM LIMIT SWITCH. Operate trim control so outboard is in full down position. Press "UP/OUT" or "UP" control button and hold until pump motor stops. Outboard should tilt up and stop so there is ½ inch (12.7 mm) overlap (L—Fig. M14-57) between swivel bracket flange (W) and clamp bracket flange (M). Pull up on lower unit to remove slack when checking overlap (L). Note that if cylinder rods enter cylinders more than an additional ⅛ inch (3.17 mm), that hydraulic system should be bled of air as outlined in BLEEDING section. If overlap (L) is incorrect, loosen retainer screw (R—Fig. M14-58) then turn adjusting nut (N) counterclockwise to increase overlap or clockwise to decrease overlap. Retighten retainer screw (R) and recheck adjustment.

PRESSURE TEST. To check hydraulic system pressure, disconnect four hoses attached to control valve as shown in Fig. M14-59; small hoses are for up circuit while large hoses are for down circuit. Connect a pressure gage to one up circuit port (small) of control valve and another pressure gage to one down circuit port (large). Screw plugs into remaining ports. Check fluid reservoir and fill if necessary. Operate trim control in up direction and note pressure gage reading. Minimum pressure should be 3500 psi (24.1 MPa) on new pumps with a red sleeve on wires or 3200-3500 psi (22.0-24.1 MPa) minimum on used pumps with red sleeve on wires. Minimum pressure on all other new pumps is 3000 psi (20.7 MPa) while minimum pressure on all other used pumps is 2700-3000 psi (18.6-20.7 MPa). Release trim control button. Pressure will drop slightly after stabilizing but should not drop faster than 100 psi (690 kPa) every 15 seconds. Operate trim control in down direction and note pressure gage reading. Minimum pressure is 500-1000 psi (3.4-6.9 MPa). Release trim control button. Pressure

Fig. M14-58 — Loosen retainer screw (R) and turn trim limit adjusting nut (N) to adjust trim limit switch.

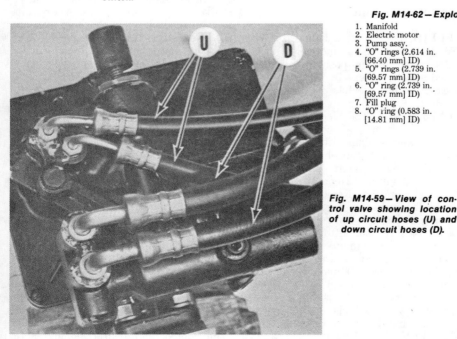

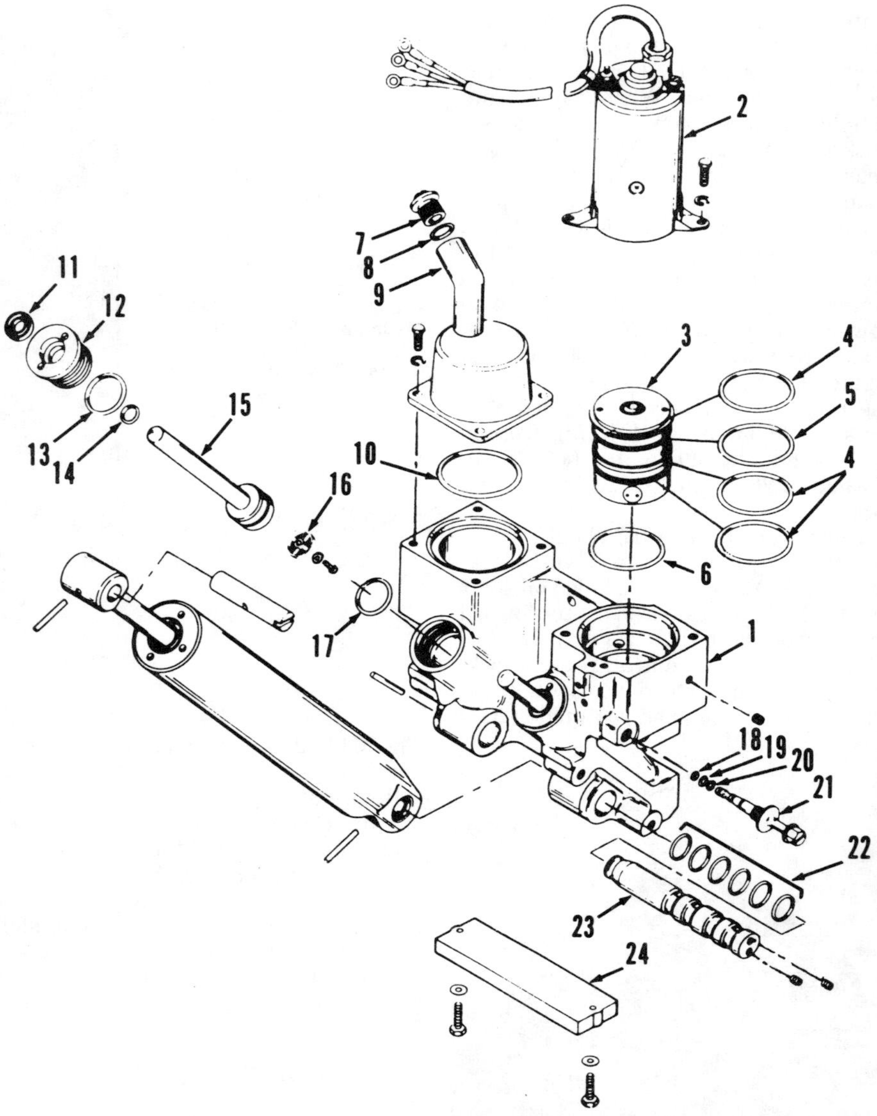

Fig. M14-62 — Exploded view of integral type power tilt/trim system.

1. Manifold	9. Reservoir cover	18. "O" ring (0.114 in. [2.90 mm] ID)
2. Electric motor	10. Seal ring	
3. Pump assy.	11. Seal	19. "O" ring (0.208 in. [5.28 mm] ID)
4. "O" rings (2.614 in. [66.40 mm] ID)	12. Cap	
	13. "O" ring (1.475 in. [37.47 mm] ID)	20. "O" ring (0.239 in. [6.07 mm] ID)
5. "O" rings (2.739 in. [69.57 mm] ID)	14. "O" ring (0.612 in. [15.54 mm] ID)	21. Manual release valve
6. "O" ring (2.739 in. [69.57 mm] ID)	15. Trim piston & rod	22. "O" rings (0.989 in. [25.12 mm] ID)
7. Fill plug	16. Strainer	23. Shaft
8. "O" ring (0.583 in. [14.81 mm] ID)	17. "O" ring (1.248 in. [31.70 mm] ID)	24. Anode plate

Fig. M14-59 — View of control valve showing location of up circuit hoses (U) and down circuit hoses (D).

will drop slightly after stabilizing but should not drop faster than 100 psi (690 kPa) every 15 seconds. If pressure is normal, inspect trim cylinders and hoses for leakage. If pressure is abnormal, install a good control valve and recheck pressure. If pressure remains abnormal, install a new pump body.

Integral Type

FLUID AND BLEEDING. Recommended fluid is Dexron II or Type AF automatic transmission fluid. Remove fill plug (7 – Fig. M14-62) and fill reser-

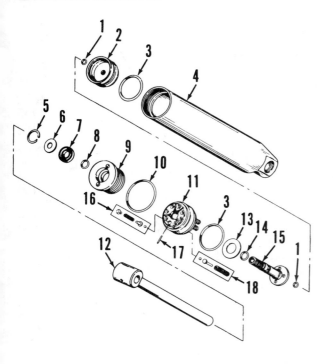

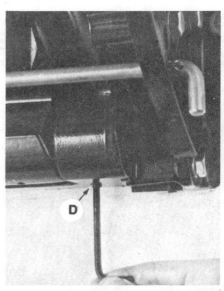

Fig. M14-63 — Exploded view of tilt cylinder components.

1. "O" ring (0.307 in. [7.79 mm] ID)
2. Cup
3. "O" ring (1.957 in. [49.71 mm] ID)
4. Cylinder
5. Circlip
6. Washer
7. Scraper
8. "O" ring (0.854 in. [21.69 mm] ID)
9. Cap
10. "O" ring (2.067 in. [52.5 mm] ID)
11. Piston
12. Rod
13. Washer
14. "O" ring (0.661 in. [16.79 mm] ID)
15. Rod end
16. Check valve assy.
17. Pin
18. Check valve assy.

Fig. M14-65 — Release pressure on system, then remove Allen head plug (D) and install a 5000 psi (34.5 MPa) test gage with a suitable adapter and hose to test system pressure when operated in the "DOWN" direction.

Fig. M14-64 — Release pressure on system, then remove Allen head plug (U) and install a 5000 psi (34.5 MPa) test gage with a suitable adapter and hose to test system pressure when operated in the "UP" direction. View identifies location of manual release valve (21).

voir until fluid is visible in fill tube with the outboard motor in the full-up position.

The hydraulic circuit is self-bleeding as the tilt/trim system is operated through several cycles. After servicing system, be sure to check reservoir level after filling and operating system.

HYDRAULIC TESTING. The system can be checked by connecting a 5000 psi (34.5 MPa) test gage to the UP (U – Fig. M14-64) and DOWN (D – Fig. M14-65) ports. Prior to connecting test gage, place outboard motor in the full-up position and engage tilt lock lever. Unscrew reservoir fill plug and rotate manual release valve (21 – Fig. M14-64) three to four tu.. counterclockwise to release pressure on system: Remove UP and DOWN Allen head test port plug and connect test gage with suitable adapter and hose. Install fill plug and rotate manual release valve clockwise until seated. System pressure when testing at

UP (U) port should be a minimum of 1300 psi (8.9 MPa). System pressure when testing at DOWN (D – Fig. M14-65) port should be a minimum of 500 psi (3.5 MPa). Release pressure on system as previously outlined prior to removing test gage. Reinstall Allen head plug.

OVERHAUL. Refer to Fig. M14-62 for an exploded view of manifold and trim cylinder components, and Fig. M14-63 for an exploded view of tilt cylinder components. Special Mercury socket 91-44487A1 and a spanner wrench is required to service trim and tilt cylinders. Keep all components clean and away from contamination. Keep components separated and label if needed for correct reassembly. Note "O" ring sizes as stated in legends of Figs. M14-62 and M14-63. Lubricate all "O" rings or seal lips with Dexron II or Type AF automatic transmission fluid during reassembly.

MERCURY V-6
(EXCEPT 300 AND 3.4L)

Year Produced	Model
1976 1750	
1977 1750	
1978 1500	
	1750
	2000
1979 150	
	175
	200
1980 150	
	175
	200
1981 150	
	175
	200
	225
1982 150	
	200
1983 150	
	200
1984 150	
	200
1985 150	
	175
	200

Year Produced	Model
1986 135	
	150
	175
	150 XR2
	200
1987 135	
	150
	150 XR2
	175
	200
1988 135	
	150
	150 XR4
	175
	200
1989 135	
	150
	150 XR4
	175
	200

Letter suffix indicates equipment variation: E – Electric starter and alternator, L – Long shaft, O – Oil injection and PT – Power trim.

CONDENSED SERVICE DATA

TUNE-UP

Hp/rpm:

Model 135 . . . . .135/5000-5500
(100.7 kW)

Models 150 & 1500 . . . . .150/5000-5500
(111.9 kW)

Model 150 XR2 . . . . .150/5500-6000
(111.9 kW)

Model 150 XR4 . . . . .150/5000-5500
(111.9 kW)

Models 175 & 1750 . . . . .175/5300-5800
(130.5 kW)

Models 200 and 2000 . . . . .200/5300-5800
(149.2 kW)

Model 225 . . . . .225/5300-5800
(167.8 kW)

Bore:

135 Hp, 150 Hp, 150 XR2 & 175 Hp (prior to serial no. 6618751) . . . . .3.125 in.
(79.38 mm)

150 XR4, 175 Hp (after serial no. 6618750), 200 Hp & 225 Hp . . . . .3.375 in.
(85.73 mm)

Stroke . . . . .2.650 in.
(67.31 mm)

Displacement:

135 Hp, 150 Hp, 150 XR2 & 175 Hp (prior to serial no. 6618751) . . . . .122 cu. in.
(1999.2 cc)

150 XR4 175 Hp (after serial no. 6618750), 200 Hp & 225 Hp . . . . . . .142.2 cu. in.
(2330.2 cc)

Firing Order 1-2-3-4-5-6

Number System (top to bottom):

Port 2-4-6

Starboard 1-3-5

Spark Plug:

All Models Prior to Serial No. 5464486 . . . . .Champion L76V

All Models After Serial No. 5464485 . . . . .NGK BU8H

Idle Speed (in forward gear):

All Models Prior to Serial No. 5464486 . . . . .550-650 rpm

All Models After Serial No. 5464485

Except 150 XR4 .600-700 rpm

150 XR4 . . . . .625-700 rpm

Compression . . . .*

Ignition Type . . . . .CDI

Fuel:Oil Ratio . . . . .See Text

*Compression should not vary more than 15 psi (103.4 kPa) between cylinders.

SIZES—CLEARANCES

Piston Rings End Gap . . . . .0.018-0.025 in.
(0.46-0.63 mm)

Maximum Cylinder Tolerance . . . . .0.006 in.
(0.15 mm)

Illustrations courtesy Mercury

Crankshaft Bearing Type:
Top Main Bearing . . . . .Caged Roller
Center Main Bearing . . . . .Caged Roller
Bottom Main Bearing . . . . .Ball Bearing
Crankpin . . . . .Caged Roller
Piston Pin Bearing . . . . .29 Loose Rollers

TIGHTENING TORQUES

Connecting Rod . . . . .30 ft.-lbs.
(40.7 N·m)

Crankcase Screws—
Prior to Serial No. C100861:
$^5/_{16}$ . . . . .200 in.-lbs
(22.6 N·m)
$^3/_8$ . . . . .35 ft.-lbs.
(47.4 N·m)
After Serial No. C100860:
$^5/_{16}$ . . . . .180 in.-lbs.
(20.3 N·m)
$^3/_8$ . . . . .45 ft.-lbs.
(61.0 N·m)

Cylinder Head:
Prior to Serial No. C100861 . . . . .See Text
After Serial No. C100860 . . . . .30 ft.-lbs.
(40.7 N·m)

Cylinder Head Cover:
Prior to Serial No. C100861 . . . . .150 in.-lbs.
(16.9 N·m)

End Cap:
Upper . . . . .150 in.-lbs.
(16.9 N·m)
Lower . . . . .80 in.-lbs.
(9.0 N·m)

Exhaust Cover:
Prior to Serial No. C100861 . . . . .180 in.-lbs.
(20.3 N·m)
After Serial No. C100860 . . . . .200 in.-lbs.
(22.6 N·m)

Flywheel Nut:
Prior to Serial No. C100861 . . . . .100 ft.-lbs.
(135.6 N·m)
After Serial No. C100860 . . . . .120 ft.-lbs.
(162.7 N·m)

Reed Block Mounting Screws:
Prior to Serial No. C100861 . . . . .60 in.-lbs.
(6.8 N·m)
After Serial No. C100860 . . . . .105 in.-lbs.
(11.9 N·m)

Spark Plugs . . . . .20 ft.-lbs.
(27.1 N·m)

LUBRICATION

The power head is lubricated by oil mixed with the fuel. Fuel should be regular leaded, low lead or unleaded gasoline with a minimum pump octane rating of 86. Recommended oil is Quicksilver Formula 50-D Outboard Lubricant. Normal fuel:oil ratio for models not equipped with oil injection is 50:1; during engine break-in (initial 10 hours of operation) fuel:oil ratio should be 25:1.

On 1984 and later models, an oil injection system is used. Fuel:oil ratio is varied from approximately 50:1 at full throttle to approximately 100:1 at idle. The crankshaft driven oil pump is synchronized with carburetor throttle opening by mechanical linkage. As the carburetor throttle opens or closes, the oil being supplied to the fuel pump is varied, thus matching the proper fuel:oil ratio to engine demand.

On oil injection equipped models, a 50:1 fuel and oil mixture should be used in the fuel tank in combination with the oil injection system to ensure proper lubrication during engine break-in period (initial 30 gallons [114 L] of fuel used). After the first 30 gallons (114 L) of fuel and oil mixture is used, switch to straight gasoline in the fuel tank.

Lower unit gears and bearings are lubricated by oil contained in the gearcase. Recommended oil is Quicksilver Premium Blend Gear Lube. Lubricant is drained by removing vent and drain plugs in the gearcase. Refill through drain plug hole until oil reaches level of vent plug hole, then drain one ounce (30 mL) of oil to allow for expansion. Lower unit oil capacity is 21 fl. oz. (625 mL) on 150 XR4 models and 24¼ fl. oz. (717 mL) on all other models.

FUEL SYSTEM

CARBURETOR. Three "dual float center bowl" type carburetors are used. Carburetor identification numbers are stamped on each carburetor mounting flange. Standard jet sizes are dependent upon carburetor identification numbers. Use the standard carburetor jet sizes as recommended by the manufacturer for normal operation when used at altitudes of 2500 feet (762 m) and below. Main jets (23—Fig. M15-1) and vent jets (5) should be reduced in size by 0.002 inch (0.05 mm) at altitudes of 2500-5000 feet (762-1524 m). Idle jets (8) should be increased in size by 0.002 inch (0.05 mm) at altitudes of 2500-5000 feet (762-1524 m). Main jets (23) and vent jets (5) should be reduced in size by 0.004 inch (0.10 mm) at altitudes of 5000-7500 feet (1524-2286 m). Idle jets (8) should be increased in size by 0.004 inch (0.10 mm) at altitudes of 5000-7500 feet (1524-2286 m). Main jets (23) and vent jets (5) should be reduced in size by 0.006 inch (0.15 mm) at altitudes of 7500 feet (2286 mm) and above. Idle jets (8) should be increased in size by 0.006 inch (0.15 mm) at altitudes of 7500 feet (2286 m) and above.

NOTE: Vent jets (5) are not used on some models. If vent jets are not noted, do not try to install jets.

No idle mixture screw adjustment is provided. Idle jet (8) size must be altered to change idle air:fuel ratio. Refer to CONDENSED SERVICE DATA for recommended idle speeds.

To measure float setting, invert float bowl (6) with inlet needle and seat (20) and float (18) installed. On each float chamber, measure distance (D—Fig. M15-2) from float bowl surface to top of float (18). Distance (D) should be ¹/₁₆ inch (1.6 mm). Adjust distance (D) by bending tang at rear of float arm.

On some models, a separate choke plate containing choke valves is positioned in the air silencer. The choke valves are actuated by a solenoid mounted on the reed housing.

SPEED CONTROL LINKAGE (Early Model 175 Hp Prior to Serial Number C100861). To synchronize ignition and carburetor opening, proceed as follows: To verify timing pointer alignment, install a dial indicator into number 1 (top starboard) cylinder spark plug hole. Position number 1 piston at TDC and zero dial indicator.

NOTE: To prevent accidental starting from flywheel rotation, remove all spark plugs and ground plug leads.

Rotate flywheel counterclockwise approximately ¼ turn past the .462 mark on flywheel, then rotate flywheel clockwise until indicator reads exactly 0.462 inch (11.73 mm) BTDC. Note position of timing pointer and reposition pointer to align with .462 mark on flywheel if necessary.

Be sure link rod (L—Fig. M15-4) protrudes $^{11}/_{16}$ inch (17.46 mm) from link body as shown. If engine is equipped with an idle stabilizer module (M—Fig. M15-5), disconnect the white/black module wire from switch box terminal. Tape end of wire to prevent grounding. Be sure the other white/black wire remains connected to switch box terminal.

NOTE: To prevent engine from starting, make sure only the number 1 (top, starboard) spark plug is installed and its plug wire attached.

Disconnect the fuel tank supply hose at the connector. Detach the throttle cable barrel from the retainer of the cable anchor bracket. Remove the choke knob and wing nuts, then withdraw the air intake cover from the front of the carburetors. Loosen carburetor synchronizing screws (S–Fig. M15-4) and allow the carburetor throttle plates to close freely. With light pressure, hold cam follower roller (R–Fig. M15-6) against throttle cam (T). At the same time, lift up on bottom carburetor throttle shaft (H–Fig. M15-4) to remove slack in linkage components. Adjust idle speed screw (I) so short mark (M–Fig. M15-6) on throttle cam (T) is centered on

follower roller (R) as shown. Retighten stop screw locknut. While maintaining light pressure, retighten all screws (S–Fig. M15-4). Check to be sure that carburetor throttle plates are completely closed when cam follower roller (R–Fig. M15-6) is aligned with short mark (M) on throttle cam (T). Repeat adjustment procedure if setting is incorrect. Reinstall air intake cover.

Connect a power timing light to number 1 cylinder spark plug lead. With the outboard motor in neutral, position throttle lever (C–Fig. M15-4) so idle speed screw (I) is against stop. Crank the engine over with the starter motor and adjust primary screw (P) so the ignition timing is 14° ATDC.

Open the throttle until the maximum spark advance screw (A) is against stop. Crank the engine over with the starter motor and adjust maximum spark advance screw (A) so ignition timing is 20° BTDC.

NOTE: Due to electronic characteristics of the ignition system, maximum advance is set at 20° BTDC but ignition will retard to 18° BTDC at high engine speed.

The carburetor throttle plate must not act as the wide open throttle stop. To prevent damage to the carburetors,

move speed control linkage to the maximum speed position and adjust maximum throttle stop screw (N) so a clearance (C–Fig. M15-7) of 0.010-0.015 inch (0.25-0.38 mm) is between throttle cam (T) and cam follower roller (R).

Reconnect idle stabilizer module wire to switch box. Reassemble and adjust idle speed screw (I–Fig. M15-4) as outlined in the CARBURETOR section.

Hold idle speed screw (I) against stop and install the throttle cable barrel in the retainer while adjusting barrel so it fits into retainer and a very light preload between idle speed screw and its stop is established. Excessive throttle cable preload will result in difficult shifting from forward to neutral.

(Models 150 Hp, 150 XR2, 150 XR4, 175 Hp After Serial Number 100860 and Early 200 Hp). To synchronize ignition and carburetor opening, proceed as follows: To verify timing pointer alignment, a dial indicator must be installed in the number 1 (top, starboard) cylinder and the indicator zeroed when the piston is positioned at TDC.

NOTE: To prevent accidental starting from flywheel rotation, remove all spark plugs and properly ground plug wires.

Rotate the flywheel counterclockwise approximately $^1/_4$ turn past the 0.462 inch (12 mm) BTDC reading, then rotate flywheel clockwise until indicator face reads 0.462 inch (12 mm) BTDC. Note position of timing pointer. Reposition pointer if the timing pointer is not aligned with ".462 BTDC" mark on flywheel. Remove the dial indicator assembly from the number 1 cylinder after adjustment is completed and reinstall spark plug and plug lead.

Be sure link rod (L—Fig. M15-4) protrudes $^{11}/_{16}$ inch (17.5 mm) from link body as shown. If the engine is equipped with an idle stabilizer module

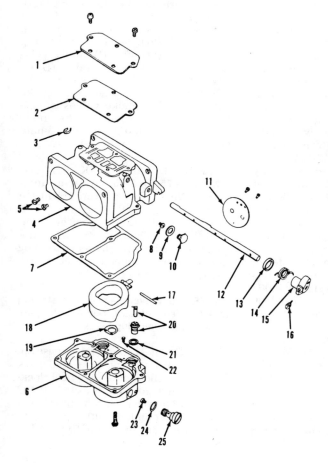

Fig. M15-1—Exploded view of carburetor used on all models. Note that idle jet components (8 through 10) and main jet components (23 through 25) are located on the carburetor starboard side.

1. Cover
2. Gasket
3. Clip
4. Body
5. Vent jets
6. Float bowl
7. Gasket
8. Idle jet
9. Gasket
10. Plug
11. Throttle plate
12. Throttle shaft
13. Spacer
14. Spring
15. Lever
16. Screw
17. Float pin
18. Float
19. Gasket
20. Inlet needle & seat
21. Gasket
22. Screw
23. Main jet
24. Gasket
25. Plug

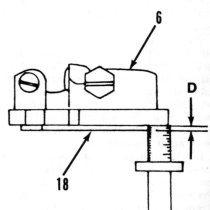

Fig. M15-2—Invert float bowl (6) with needle and seat (20—Fig. M15-1) and float (18) installed. Distance (D) should be 1/16 inch (1.6 mm) for proper float setting.

(M—Fig. M15-5), three-wire spark advance module, or combination low speed/high speed spark advance module, disconnect the white/black module wire from the outer switch box terminal. Tape end of wire to prevent grounding. Be sure the other white/black wire remains connected to switch box terminal. On models equipped with a four-wire module, do not disconnect white/black wire.

NOTE: To prevent engine from starting, make sure only the number 1 (top, starboard) spark plug is installed and its plug wire attached.

Disconnect the fuel tank supply hose at the outboard motor connector. Detach the throttle cable barrel from the retainer of the cable anchor bracket. Adjust idle speed screw (I—Fig. M15-4) so bottom edge of throttle cam (T—Fig. M15-8) is a distance (D) of ¹⁄₈ inch (3.2 mm) from top edge of mounting boss (B) for maximum throttle stop screw.

Withdraw air intake cover from the front of the carburetors. Position throttle lever (C—Fig. M15-4) so idle speed screw (I) is against its stop. Loosen carburetor synchronizing screws (S) and allow the carburetor throttle plates to close freely. With light pressure, hold the cam follower roller against throttle cam (T). At the same time, lift up on the bottom carburetor throttle shaft (H) to remove slack in linkage components. Then retighten screws (S). Be sure carburetor throttle plates are completely closed and operate freely. Repeat adjustment procedure if setting is incorrect. Reinstall air intake cover.

Connect a power timing light to number 1 cylinder spark plug lead. With the outboard motor in neutral, position throttle lever (C) so idle speed screw (I) is against stop. Crank engine with starter motor and adjust primary screw (P) so ignition timing is 5-7 degrees ATDC on 135 hp models, 6-12 degrees ATDC on 150 hp and 150 XR2 models, 4-6 degrees ATDC on 150 XR4, 3-5 degrees ATDC on 175 hp models and 10 degrees ATDC on 200 hp models.

Open the throttle until maximum spark advance screw (A) is against stop. Crank engine with starter motor and adjust maximum spark advance screw (A) so ignition timing is 18 degrees BTDC on 135 hp, 150 hp and 150 XR2, 22 degrees BTDC on 150 XR4, and 20 degrees BTDC on 175 hp and 200 hp models.

NOTE: Due to electronic spark advance characteristics of the ignition systems, maximum advance timing set at cranking speed will be advanced up to 6 degrees on 150 XR4 models and retarded by 2 degrees on all other models when engine is running at full throttle. Maximum advance timing with engine running at full throttle should be 16 degrees BTDC on 135 hp, 150 hp and 150 XR2 models, 26 degrees BTDC on 150 XR4 models, and 18 degrees BTDC on 175 and 200 models. On 150 XR4 models equipped with low speed/high speed/spark advance/excessive rpm spark retard module, timing is electronically advanced by 6 degrees at 5000 rpm, then retarded 4 degrees if engine speed exceeds approximately 5700 rpm. Timing will remain retarded by 4 degrees until engine speed falls below approximately 5700 rpm.

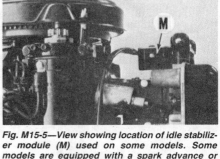

Fig. M15-5—View showing location of idle stabilizer module (M) used on some models. Some models are equipped with a spark advance or combination low speed/high speed spark advance module.

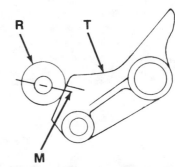

Fig. M15-6—Cam follower roller (R) should align with short mark (M) on throttle cam (T) when speed control linkage is set as outlined in text.

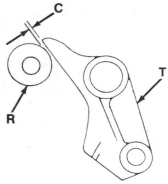

Fig. M15-7—Clearance (C) should exist between cam follower (R) and throttle cam (T) when speed control linkage is set as outlined in text.

Fig. M15-4—View showing speed control linkage components used on 135 hp, 150 hp, 150 XR2, 175, 150 XR4 and early 200 hp models. Refer to text for adjustment procedures.

  A. Maximum spark advance screw
  B. Maximum spark advance lever
  C. Throttle lever
  H. Throttle shaft
  I. Idle speed screw
  L. Link rod
  N. Maximum throttle stop screw
  P. Primary screw
  S. Screws
  T. Throttle cam

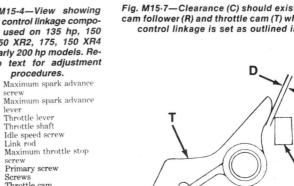

Fig. M15-8—Distance (D) should exist between throttle cam (T) and boss (B) when speed control linkage is set as outlined in text.

Fig. M15-9—View showing speed control linkage components used on late 200 hp and 225 hp models. Refer to text for adjustment procedures.

A. Maximum spark advance screw
B. Maximum spark advance lever
L. Link rod
P. Primary screw

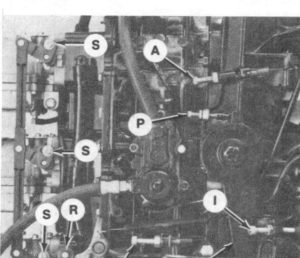
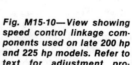

Fig. M15-10—View showing speed control linkage components used on late 200 hp and 225 hp models. Refer to text for adjustment procedures.

A. Maximum spark advance screw
C. Throttle lever
I. Idle speed screw
N. Maximum throttle stop screw
P. Primary screw
R. Cam follower roller
S. Screws
T. Throttle cam

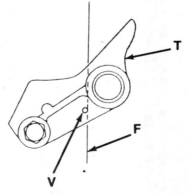

Fig. M15-11—A ⅛ inch (3mm) diameter rod or drill bit must be installed in hole (V) on models with the numbers "95790" cast on throttle cam (T). The rod or drill bit should just contact edge of carburetor adapter flange (F) when speed control linkage is set and adjusted as outlined in text.

Fig. M15-12—A ⅛ inch (3 mm) distance rod or drill bit must be installed in hole (V) on models with no numbers cast on throttle cam (T). The rod or drill bit should just contact edge of carburetor adapter flange (F) when speed control linkage is set and adjusted as outlined in text.

The carburetor throttle plate must not act as the wide open throttle stop. To prevent damage to carburetors, move speed control linkage to maximum speed position and adjust maximum throttle stop screw (N) so a clearance (C—Fig. M15-7) of 0.010-0.015 inch (0.25-0.38 mm) is between throttle cam (T) and cam follower roller (R).

Make sure carburetors and oil injection pump are properly synchronized as outlined in OIL INJECTION SYSTEM section.

Reconnect idle stabilizer module or spark advance module wire to switch box. Reinstall spark plugs, then adjust idle speed screw (I—Fig. M15-4) to idle speed specified in CONDENSED SERVICE DATA.

Hold idle speed screw (I) against stop and install throttle cable barrel in retainer while adjusting barrel so it fits into retainer and a very light preload between idle speed screw and its stop is established. Excessive throttle cable preload will result in difficult shifting from forward to neutral.

(Late Models 200 HP And All 225 HP). To synchronize ignition and carburetor opening, proceed as follows: To verify timing pointer alignment, a dial indicator must be installed in the number 1 (top, starboard) cylinder and the indicator zeroed when the piston is positioned at TDC.

NOTE: To prevent accidental starting from flywheel rotation, remove all spark plugs and properly ground plug wires.

Rotate the flywheel counterclockwise approximately ¼ turn past the 0.462 inch (12 mm) BTDC reading, then rotate flywheel clockwise until indicator face reads 0.462 inch (12 mm) BTDC. Note the position of the timing pointer. Reposition pointer if the timing pointer is not aligned with ".462 BTDC" mark on flywheel. Remove the dial indicator assembly from the number 1 cylinder after adjustment is completed and reinstall spark plug and plug lead.

Be sure link rod (L–Fig. M15-9) protrudes 11/16 inch (17.46 mm) from link body as shown. A spark advance module is located above the top carburetor and is mounted to the air intake cover. If the module is equipped with four wires, no wires need to be connected to time the engine. But if the module is equipped with three wires, disconnect the white/black module wire from the switch box terminal. Tape the end of the wire to prevent grounding. Be sure the other white/black wire remains connected to switch box terminal.

NOTE: To prevent engine from starting, make sure only the number 1 (top, starboard) spark plug is installed and its plug wire attached.

Disconnect the fuel tank supply hose at the outboard motor connector. Detach the throttle cable barrel from the retainer of the cable anchor bracket.

Install a ⅛ inch (3 mm) diameter rod or drill bit in hole (V–Fig. M15-11) on models equipped with the casting numbers "95790" on throttle cam (T). Install a ⅛ inch (3 mm) diameter rod or drill bit in hole (V–Fig. M15-12) on models not equipped with numbers cast on throttle cam (T). While holding rod or drill bit perpendicular to throttle cam (T—Fig. M15-11 or Fig. M15-12), adjust idle speed screw (I—Fig. M15-10) until rod or drill bit just contacts edge of carburetor adapter flange (F—Fig. M15-11 or Fig. M15-12).

Withdraw the air intake cover from the front of the carburetors. Position throttle lever (C–Fig. M15-10) so idle speed screw (I) is against its stop. Loosen carburetor synchronizing screws (S) and allow the carburetor throttle plates to close freely. With light pressure, hold cam follower roller (R) against throttle cam (T). At the same time, lift up on bottom carburetor throttle shaft to remove slack in linkage components. Then retighten screws (S). Be sure carburetor throttle plates are completely closed and operate freely. Repeat adjustment procedure if setting is incorrect. Reinstall air intake cover.

Connect a power timing light to the number 1 cylinder spark plug lead. With outboard motor in neutral, position throttle lever (C) so idle speed screw (I) is against stop. Crank engine with starter motor and adjust primary screw (P) so ignition timing is 12 degrees ATDC on models prior to serial number C100861 and 2-7 degrees ATDC on models after serial number C100860.

Open throttle until maximum spark advance screw (A) is against stop. Crank engine with starter motor and adjust maximum spark advance screw (A) so ignition timing is 22 degrees BTDC.

NOTE: Due to electronic characteristics of ignition system, maximum advance is set at 22 degrees BTDC, but ignition will retard to 20 degrees BTDC at 5400 rpm and increase to 26 degrees BTDC over 5600 rpm.

The carburetor throttle plate must not act as the wide open throttle stop. To prevent damage to carburetors, move speed control linkage to the maximum speed position and adjust maximum throttle stop screw (N) so a clearance (C–Fig. M15-7) of 0.010-0.015 inch

(0.25-0.38 mm) is between throttle cam (T) and cam follower roller (R).

Be sure carburetors and oil injection pump are properly synchronized as outlined in OIL INJECTION SYSTEM section.

Reconnect spark advance module wire to outer switch box. Reinstall spark plugs, then adjust idle speed screw (I—Fig. M15-10) to idle speed specified in CONDENSED SERVICE DATA.

Hold idle speed screw (I) against stop and install the throttle cable barrel in the retainer while adjusting barrel so it fits into retainer and a very light preload between idle speed screw and its stop is established. Excessive throttle cable preload will result in difficult shifting from forward to neutral.

REED VALVES. The fuel:air mixture for each cylinder is directed through a reed valve assembly. Six reed valve assemblies are attached to the intake manifold. Reed block assemblies may be either mounted horizontally or vertically on intake manifold.

Reed petals shown in Fig. M15-14 should be flat and have no more than 0.007 inch (0.18 mm) clearance between free end of reed petal and seating surface of reed block. On vertical mounted reed blocks, reed petals should not stand open more than 0.020 inch (0.51 mm). Do not attempt to bend or straighten a reed petal or turn reed petals around on reed block. Reed block seating surface must be flat. Reed block should be renewed if indented by reed petals or damaged. Reed petals are available in sets for each reed block only.

Note reed petal shapes in Fig. M15-14. Early 150 hp engines are equipped with "straight-cut" reed petals (A) while late 150, 200 and 225 hp engines are equipped with "teardrop" reed petals (B). Early 175 hp engines used both types of reed petals and later 175 hp engines are equipped with "teardrop" reed petals (B). Install reed blocks of early 175 hp engines so "teardrop" reed petals are toward center side of reed housing. When renewing reed petals on early 175 hp engines, always install a "teardrop" reed petal, even if the old reed was "straight-cut" type.

Reed stop setting on models so equipped is 0.200 inch (5.08 mm) on 150 hp models and 0.300 inch (7.62 mm) on 175 and 200 hp models. Measure reed stop opening from reed stop to reed petal seating surface as shown in Fig. M15-15.

FUEL PUMP. A diaphragm type fuel pump is mounted on the intake manifold. Early models are equipped with an "oval" design pump; later models are equipped with a "square" design pump.

Fuel pump is actuated by crankcase pulsations on all models. Fuel pump pressure on early "oval" design pump should be 4.0-5.5 psi (28-38 kPa) at full throttle and 3 psi (21 kPa) at idle. Full throttle fuel pump pressure on later "square" design pump should be a minimum of 3 psi (20.7 kPa) and should not exceed 10 psi (68.9 kPa). Normal fuel pump pressure at idle speed on "square" pump is 2-3 psi (13.8-20.7 kPa) with a minimum of 1 psi (6.9 kPa).

If the fuel pump malfunctions due to a split diaphragm on early 175 hp models, drill a 0.078 inch (1.98 mm) hole (B–Fig. M15-17) through the pulse chamber so the hole is ⅜ inch (9.5 mm) from centerline of hole (A) as shown, and bevel edge of hole (A).

When overhauling the fuel pump, renew all defective or questionable components. The manufacturer recommends renewing pump gaskets and diaphragms if pump is disassembled.

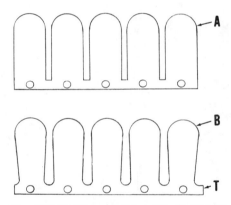

Fig. M15-14—View of "straight-cut" (A) and "teardrop" (B) reed petals. Note tang (T) on "teardrop" reed petals.

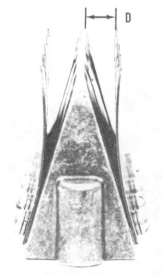

Fig. M15-15—Reed stop setting (D) on models so equipped, should be 0.200 inch (5.08 mm) on 150 hp models and 0.300 inch (7.62 mm) on all other models.

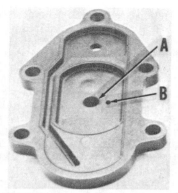

Fig. M15-17—Modify fuel pump on early 175 hp models with a split diaphragm as outlined in text.

Fig. M15-18—View showing installation of outlet check valve (6) and inlet check valve (7) in early "oval" design fuel pump body. Install retainer (R) so tips are facing away from check valves.

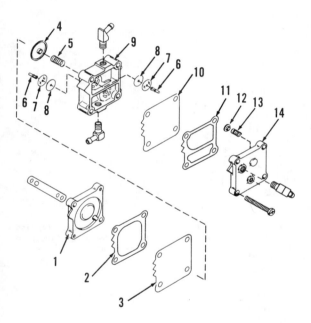

Fig. M15-19—Exploded view of "square" design fuel pump used on late models.

1. Base
2. Gasket
3. Diaphragm
4. Cap
5. Boost spring
6. Retainer
7. Plastic disc
8. Check valve
9. Body
10. Diaphragm
11. Gasket
12. Cap
13. Spring
14. Cover

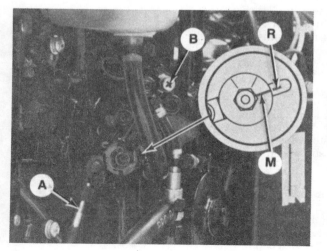

Fig. M15-20—View showing oil injection pump used on some 1984 and all later models. Refer to text for adjustment procedures and identification of components.

When assembling early "oval" pump, install check valves as shown in Fig. M15-18 with tips of retainer (R) pointing away from check valves. After installing check valve retainers (6—Fig. M15-19) on "square" pump, break off stem of retainer (6) by bending over. Then, insert stem into retainer and tap down until flush with top of retainer. Tighten mounting screws on "square" pump to 50-60 in.-lbs. (5.7-6.8 N·m).

OIL INJECTION. Some 1984 and all 1985 and later models are equipped with oil injection. The fuel:oil ratio is varied from approximately 50:1 at full throttle to approximately 100:1 at idle. The oil injection pump is synchronized with carburetor throttle opening by mechanical linkage. As the carburetor throttle opens or closes, the oil delivered to the fuel pump is matched to power head demand. The oil injection pump is driven by a gear secured to the engine crankshaft.

The oil tank (2—Fig. M15-21) is pressurized by crankcase pressure and feeds oil to reservoir (5). Check valve (3) will unseat allowing air to enter oil line should oil line between tank (2) and reservoir (5) become restricted, preventing oil pump (7) from creating a vacuum in reservoir (5). Check valve (12) prevents fuel pump from pumping gasoline into oil line (13). Motion sensor (8) detects movement of a magnet inside pump coupler and triggers warning module (9) to sound a warning horn if pump movement stops. Note that if removed, the North end of the magnet must be installed into the coupler first. The North end of the magnet can be determined by holding magnet close to a suitable camping (directional) compass. Do not use the boat compass. The end of the magnet that attracts the North arrow of the compass is the North end of magnet.

BLEEDING OIL INJECTION PUMP. With engine not started, loosen bleed screw (B—Fig. M15-20) three to four turns. Allow oil to drain from around bleed screw until no air bubbles are noted. Securely retighten bleed screw (B).

THROTTLE ARM AND OIL INJECTION PUMP SYNCHRONIZATION. Place throttle linkage in idle position, then note if mark (M—Fig. M15-20) on oil pump control lever aligns with mark (R) on pump body. If not, disconnect and adjust length of pump control rod as necessary to align marks.

OIL PUMP OUTPUT TEST. Proceed as follows to check oil injection pump output: Connect a remote fuel tank containing a 50:1 fuel and oil mixture to fuel pump. Disconnect the clear oil pump output line from the fuel pump inlet line "T" fitting and plug fitting. Place disconnected end of oil output line into a suitable graduated container. Start engine and run at 1500 rpm for 3 minutes, then stop engine and note pump output in container. Next, disconnect oil pump control rod and move pump lever to full throttle position. Again, start engine and run at 1500 rpm for 3 minutes, stop engine and note pump output. On 122 cu. in. (1999.2 cc) engines, output should be 6.1-7.5 mL (0.21-0.25 oz.) with pump control rod connected to oil pump and 15.3-18.7 mL

(0.52-0.63 oz.) with pump lever in full throttle position. On 142 cu. in (2330.2 cc) engines, pump output should be 7.4-9.0 mL (0.25-0.30 oz.) with pump control rod connected to oil pump and 17.3-21.1 mL (0.59-0.71 oz.) with pump control lever at full throttle position.

DRIVE GEAR. If a new oil injection pump drive gear is installed on crankshaft, the maximum allowable misalignment at split line of gear is 0.030 inch (0.76 mm). Tighten gear retaining Allen head screw to 8 in.-lbs. (0.9 N·m). Zero clearance should be noted at split line of gear.

CRANKCASE BLEED SCREW

A crankcase bleed system is used to remove unburned oil residue from the crankcase and lower main bearing and burn it or direct it to the three upper main bearings. See diagram in Fig. M15-22 for a view of a typical crankcase bleed system. The number of hoses and hose routing may differ on some models. Check valves are located in intake manifold while fittings to cylinders are located in cylinder block. Hoses must be connected between fitting and check valve with same letter, *i.e.*, a hose is connected between check valve

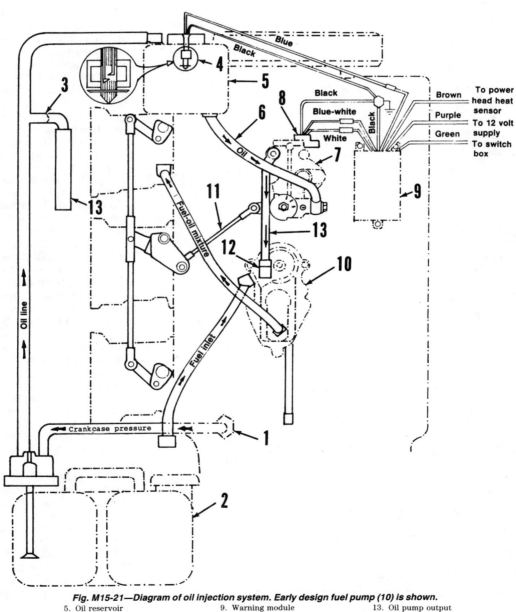

Fig. M15-21—Diagram of oil injection system. Early design fuel pump (10) is shown.

1. One-way check valve	5. Oil reservoir	9. Warning module	13. Oil pump output line
2. Remote oil tank	6. Oil pump supply line	10. Fuel pump	B. Black
3. Check valve	7. Oil pump assy.	11. Oil pump control rod	G. Green
4. Low oil sensor	8. Motion sensor	12. Check valve	W. White

Bl. Blue
Br. Brown
Pr. Purple
Bl/W. Blue with white tracer

"B" on reed valve housing and fitting "B" on cylinder block. Make sure hoses and check valves are properly identified prior to components being separated. Engine will not operate properly if hoses are incorrectly connected. Check operation of check valves.

IGNITION SYSTEM

An alternator driven capacitor discharge ignition (CDI) system is used. Ignition system consists of the flywheel, stator, trigger assembly, switch box and ignition coils. The stator is mounted below the flywheel and contains two (low speed/high speed) capacitor charging coils. The trigger assembly consists of three trigger coils and is mounted below the flywheel. Ignition timing is advanced and retarded by rotating trigger assembly in relation to the inner flywheel magnets. Diodes, capacitors and SCR's are contained in the switch box. Switch box, trigger assembly and stator must be serviced as unit assemblies. Refer to Figs. M15-23, M15-24 and M15-25 for wiring diagrams.

If engine malfunction is noted, and the ignition system is suspected, make sure the spark plugs and all electrical wiring are in acceptable condition and all electrical connections are clean and tight prior to trouble-shooting CDI system.

To properly test the switch box and ignition coils, use a Quicksilver Multi-Meter DVA Tester part 91-99750 or a suitable voltmeter capable of measuring a minimum of 400 DC volts used with Quicksilver Direct Voltage Adaptor (DVA) part 91-89045. Follow instructions provided by tester manufacturer when performing tests. If these testers are not available, a process of elimination must be used when testing the ignition system. Stator and trigger assemblies can be effectively tested using a suitable ohmmeter.

NOTE: All tests that involve cranking or running the engine must be performed with lead wires connected. Switch boxes MUST be grounded to engine for all tests or switch box may be damaged. If switch box is removed from power head to ease access, connect a separate ground lead from switch box to power head.

To test ignition system, proceed as follows:

IGNITION COILS PRIMARY VOLTAGE. Connect DVA red test lead to ignition coil positive (+) terminal and black test lead to coil negative (−) terminal. Position tester selector switch to DVA/400. Tester should read 150-250 volts at cranking or idle speed (300-1000 rpm) and 180-280 volts at 1000-4000 rpm. If voltage readings are below specified reading, refer to SWITCH BOX STOP CIRCUIT test. If readings are within specifications, connect a suitable spark tester to ignition coil high tension leads, crank engine and note spark. If weak or no spark is noted, renew ignition coil(s). If normal spark is noted, renew spark plugs. If malfunction is still evident after renewing spark plugs, check ignition timing. If ignition timing is within specification, malfunction is not in ignition system. If ignition timing is not to specification such as a sudden timing change, inspect trigger advance linkage for excessive wear or damage and inner flywheel magnets (shifted position or other damage). If timing is erratic or unstable, disconnect idle stabilizer or spark advance module and recheck timing. If timing is now within specification, idle stabilizer or spark advance module is defective and must be renewed. If timing is still erratic or unstable with idle stabilizer or spark advance module isolated, refer to SWITCH BOX BIAS section.

SWITCH BOX BIAS. Check switch box bias as follows: Connect a red test lead of a suitable voltmeter (not DVA meter) to engine ground and black test lead to white/black switch box terminal. Voltage at cranking or idle speed should be 2-10 volts. Voltage at 1000-4000 rpm should be 10-30 volts. If voltage reading is below specification, one or both switch boxes are defective. If switch box bias voltage is within specification, check trigger resistance as outlined in SWITCH BOX STOP CIRCUIT section. If trigger resistance is acceptable, one or

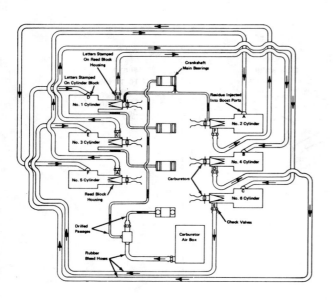

Fig. M15-22—Diagram of a typical crankcase bleed system.

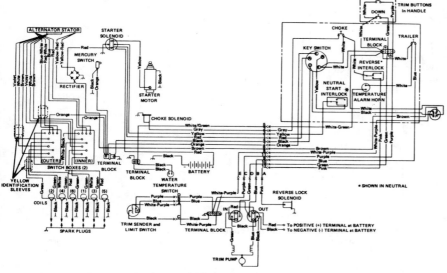

Fig. M15-23—Wiring diagram typical of models prior to 1980.

both switch boxes may be defective. Substitute known good switch box(es) and retest.

SWITCH BOX STOP CIRCUIT. Connect DVA black test lead to engine ground and red test lead to black/yellow switch box terminal (orange terminal on early models). Set DVA selector switch to DVA/400. Voltage reading at cranking and all running speeds should be 200-360 volts. If reading is within specifications, refer to STATOR tests. If reading is above specified voltages, disconnect trigger leads from switch boxes. Check resistance between brown (without yellow sleeve) and white (with yellow sleeve) trigger leads, then white (without yellow sleeve) and violet (with yellow sleeve) trigger leads, then violet (without yellow sleeve) and brown (with yellow sleeve) trigger leads. Resistance should be 1100-1400 ohms at all connections. If not, renew trigger assembly. If trigger resistance is acceptable, renew one or both switch box(es) and repeat SWITCH BOX STOP CIRCUIT test.

If SWITCH BOX STOP CIRCUIT test reading is below specified voltage, disconnect ignition switch, stop switch and mercury switch from black/yellow switch box terminal (orange switch box terminal on early models). Be sure ignition switch lead is disconnected from both switch boxes. With stop switch, ignition switch and mercury switch isolated, repeat SWITCH BOX STOP CIRCUIT test. If reading is now within specification, ignition switch, stop switch or mercury switch is defective. If reading remains below specification refer to STATOR test.

STATOR. Disconnect idle stabilizer or spark advance module leads from switch box prior to testing stator. Connect DVA black test lead to engine ground and red test lead to blue/white terminal on outer switch box. Set DVA selector switch to DVA/400. Voltage reading should be 200-300 volts at cranking and idle speeds and 200-330 volts at 1000-4000 rpm. Switch DVA red test lead to red/white outer switch box terminal. Leave black test lead connected to engine ground. Voltage reading should be 20-90 volts at cranking or idle speeds and 130-300 volts at 1000-4000 rpm. Next, connect black tester lead to engine ground and red tester lead to blue switch box terminal on inner switch box.

NOTE: Outer switch box should be removed to gain access to inner switch box. Be sure to connect a ground lead from both switch boxes to engine ground prior to

cranking engine to prevent damage to ignition system.

Tester selector switch should be set at DVA/400. Voltage reading should be 200-300 volts at cranking and idle speeds and 200-330 volts at 1000-4000 rpm. Remove red tester lead from blue switch box terminal and connect to red terminal on inner switch box. Voltage reading at cranking and idle speeds should be 20-90 volts and 130-300 volts at 1000-4000 rpm.

NOTE: A shorted or open capacitor inside switch box will result in faulty stator voltage readings during cranking and running tests. Stator resistance should be checked as follows before failing stator.

If any STATOR voltage reading is below specification, proceed as follows: Disconnect leads from inner and outer switch boxes. Connect a suitable ohmmeter between blue and red stator leads, then blue/white and red/white stator leads. Resistance between blue and red stator leads and between blue/white and red/white stator leads should be 3600-4200 ohms. Next, connect ohmmeter between red/white stator lead and stator black lead, then between red stator lead and black stator lead. Resistance should be 9000-14,000 ohms. Renew stator if resistance is not as specified. If stator resistance is as specified, renew one or both switch boxes and repeat STATOR tests. If all stator tests are acceptable, perform SWITCH BOX BIAS test.

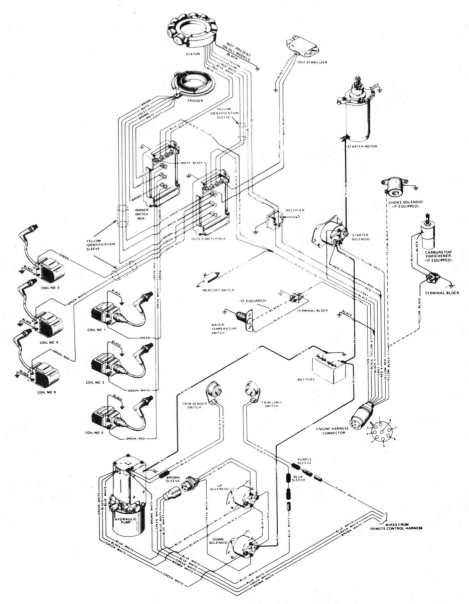

Fig. M15-24—Wiring diagram typical of models after 1979 but prior to serial number C100861.

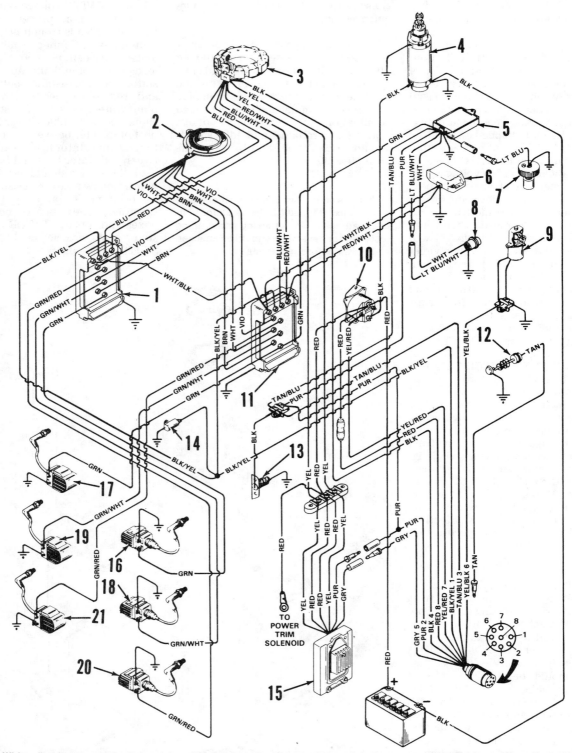

Fig. M15-25—Wiring diagram on models after serial number C100860. Models 150 XR4 and 200 hp are equipped with a low speed/high speed spark advance module or low speed/high speed/spark advance/excessive rpm spark retard module in place of idle stabilizer (6).

1. Inner switch box
2. Trigger
3. Stator
4. Starter motor
5. Warning module
6. Idle stabilizer
7. Oil tank cap
8. Oil pump motion sensor
9. Enrichment valve
10. Starter solenoid
11. Outer switch box
12. Temperature sensor
13. Water temperature switch
14. Mercury (tilt) switch
15. Voltage regulator
16. No. 1 ignition coil
17. No. 2 ignition coil
18. No. 3 ignition coil
19. No. 4 ignition coil
20. No. 5 ignition coil
21. No. 6 ignition coil

B. Black
G. Green
R. Red
T. Tan
V. Vilot
W. White
Y. Yellow
Br. Brown
Bl. Blue
Gr. Gray
Pr. Purple

B/Y. Black with yellow tracer
G/R. Green with red tracer
G/W. Green with white tracer
R/W. Red with white tracer
W/B. White with black tracer

Y/B. Yellow with black tracer
Y/R. Yellow with red tracer
Bl/W. Blue with white tracer
T/Bl. Tan with blue tracer
LtBl. Light blue
LtBl/W. Light blue with white tracer

IGNITION COILS RESISTANCE TEST. Disconnect wires and high tension lead from coil. Connect a suitable ohmmeter between coil positive (+) and negative (−) terminals. Resistance should be 0.02-0.04 ohm. Connect ohmmeter between coil high tension terminal and negative (−) terminal. Resistance should be 800-1100 ohms. Repeat test on all coils. Renew ignition coil(s) if resistance is not as specified.

NOTE: Ignition coil resistance tests can detect only open or shorted windings. If coil resistance is within specification and still suspected as defective, coil must be tested using DVA meter as previously outlined in IGNITION COILS PRIMARY VOLTAGE test. If DVA meter is not available, substitute a known good ignition coil and run engine to test.

IDLE STABILIZER/SPARK ADVANCE MODULES. Refer to Fig. M15-26 to identify the various idle stabilizer/spark advance modules used on Mercury V-6 models.

The idle stabilizer module is designed to advance ignition timing if idle speed drops to below 550 rpm. When idle speed is stabilized, module will return timing to normal. To test idle stabilizer, connect a suitable timing light to number 1 spark plug lead (top starboard), start engine and run at idle speed. Observe timing marks while retarding timing by pulling on spark control lever. Ignition timing should advance by up to 9 degrees when idle speed falls below 550 rpm. If not, renew module.

The high speed spark advance module is designed to advance ignition timing when engine speed reaches approximately 5600 rpm. Timing will remain advanced until engine speed drops to approximately 5400 rpm. To test spark advance module, connect a suitable timing light to number 1 spark plug lead (top starboard). Start engine and slowly increase engine speed to 5600 rpm while observing timing marks. Ignition timing should advance by 6 degrees at approximately 5600 rpm and return to normal setting at approximately 5400 rpm. If not, renew module.

Low speed/high speed spark advance module combines the functions of an idle stabilizer and high speed spark advance module. Test module by performing idle stabilizer and high speed spark advance module tests as previously outlined.

COOLING SYSTEM

THERMOSTAT. All models are equipped with a thermostat in each cylinder head cover. Thermostat should begin to open at 140°-145°F (60°-63°C). A temperature sender is installed in the starboard cylinder head either below number one spark plug or in the outer portion of the cylinder head between number one and number three spark plug. The temperature sender will activate an alarm horn should engine overheating occur. Temperature sender may be checked with a continuity tester and a high temperature thermometer. Place sender and thermometer in water that is being heated. Sender positioned in the outer portion of the cylinder head should show a closed circuit when water temperature reaches 180°-200°F (82°-93°C) and then reopen when

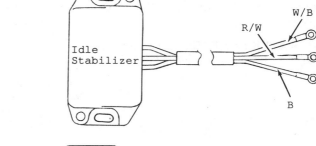

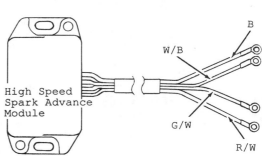

Fig. M15-26—View of the various idle stabilizer/spark advance modules used on V-6 models.

B. Black
G/W. Green with white tracer
R/W. Red with white tracer
W/B. White with black tracer

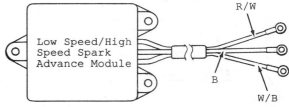
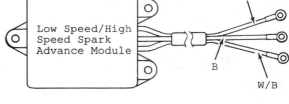

Fig. M15-27—Exploded view of ignition plate components.

1. Terminal block
2. Mercury switch
3. Rectifier
4. Switch boxes
5. Ignition plate
6. Starter solenoid

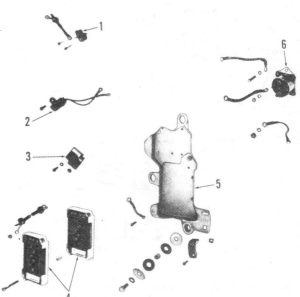
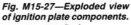

temperature drops to 160°-180°F (71°-82°C). Sender positioned below number one spark plug should show a closed circuit when water temperature reaches 230°-250°F (110°-121°C) and then reopen when temperature starts dropping below 230°F (110°C).

A water pressure relief valve is located on starboard side of cylinder block. Note cross section of valve shown in Fig. M15-30. Diaphragm is renewable. Inspect components for nicks, cracks or other damage which may cause leakage.

WATER PUMP. The rubber impeller type water pump is housed in the gear-case housing. The impeller is mounted on and driven by the lower unit drive shaft. Water pump is accessible after separating gearcase housing from drive shaft housing as outlined in LOWER UNIT section.

POWER HEAD

R&R AND DISASSEMBLE. To remove power head assembly, disconnect all wires and hoses and remove all cowling which will interfere with power head separation from drive shaft housing. Detach shift rod from control cable bracket. Unscrew 10 locknuts securing power head to drive shaft housing and lift power head off drive shaft housing and install on a suitable stand. If equipped, remove oil injection pump reservoir and plug hose fittings. Remove flywheel, stator, trigger plate and starter motor. Remove choke solenoid, temperature sender, ignition coils, switch box plate assembly and speed control linkage. If equipped, remove oil injection pump. Remove fuel pump and disconnect and label interfering bleed hoses. Remove carburetors and airbox as an assembly. Remove intake manifold with reed valve assemblies, cylinder head cover, cylinder heads and exhaust manifold assembly.

Remove screws securing end caps to crankcase and loosen end cap to cylinder block screws. Remove crankcase mounting screws, then remove crankcase by using recesses under crankcase to pry against. Use extra care not to damage machined mating surfaces of cylinder block and crankcase. Mark connecting rods with cylinder numbers so they can be reinstalled in original cylinders and remove rod and piston assemblies. Unscrew end cap to cylinder block screws and remove end caps. Crankcase and cylinder block are matched and align bored and can be renewed as a set only.

Refer to following paragraphs to service pistons, rods, crankshaft and bearings. When assembling, follow the procedures outlined in the ASSEMBLY paragraphs.

ASSEMBLY. When assembling, the crankcase must be sealed against both vacuum and pressure. Exhaust manifold and water passage must be sealed against pressure leakage. Whenever power head is disassembled, it is recommended that all gasket surfaces and machined joints without gaskets be carefully checked for nicks and burrs which might interfere with a tight seal.

Install seals in lower end cap with lips down (away from cylinder block). Install seal in upper end cap with lip down (toward cylinder block). Be sure seal does not block bleed passage in end cap. Loctite 271 or 290 should be applied to seal bore of end caps. Lubricate all bearing and friction surfaces with engine oil. Loose needle bearings may be held in place during assembly using light, nonfibrous grease. Gaps of seal rings (5 – Fig. 15-34) must be towards crankcase.

Install piston, rod and crankshaft assemblies as outlined in appropriate following paragraphs. End caps should be in place with screws installed but not tightened. Rotate crankshaft and check for binding. Cut gasket strips off flush with edge of crankcase bores. Apply a thin coat of sealer such as Permatex 2C-12 to mating surfaces of crankcase and cylinder block using care to prevent excess sealer from entering bearings, crankcase or passages.

Progressively tighten eight large crankcase screws until crankshaft seal rings are compressed and crankcase mates with cylinder block. Tighten eight large crankcase screws in three progressive steps to specified torque and using tightening sequence in Fig. M15-35 for models prior to serial number 5464486 and Fig. M15-36 for

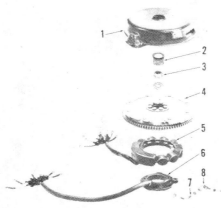

Fig. M15-28—View of flywheel and ignition components.

1. Flywheel cover	5. Stator
2. Plug	6. Trigger plate
3. Nut	7. Trigger plate link rod
4. Flywheel	8. Ball joint

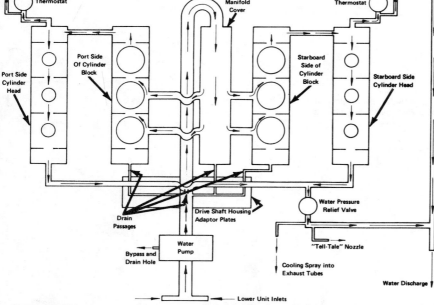

Fig. M15-29 — Typical diagram of coolant flow. Refer to Fig. M15-30 for cross section of water pressure relief valve.

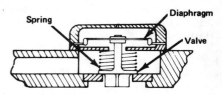

Fig. M15-30—Cross-sectional view of water pressure relief valve.

models after serial number 5464485. On early models note location of long seal screw (B – Fig. M15-35) and then tighten six smaller crankcase screws in three progressive steps to specified torque. Rotate crankshaft and check for binding.

When installing intake manifold and exhaust manifold cover, tighten center screws first and work outward. Install cylinder head gaskets with number stamped in gasket up (away from cylinder block). Tighten cylinder head screws in three progressive steps to specified torque and using tightening sequence in Fig. M15-37.

PISTONS, PINS, RINGS AND CYLINDERS. Before detaching connecting rods from crankshaft, make sure that rod and cap are marked so rods and caps are not interchanged and may be returned to original cylinders.

Piston pin is pressed into piston on all models. On early models, manufacturer recommends discarding piston if pin is pressed out of piston. Piston pin boss marked "UP" has smaller piston pin hole than other pin boss. Press pin out so pin exits "UP" boss first and press pin in so pin enters "UP" boss last. Pistons are marked on piston pin boss and piston crown according to their location in cylinder block. "S" pistons must be used in starboard cylinders while "P" pistons must be used in port cylinders. Install piston on connecting rods so side with alignment bumps (B – Fig. M15-38) is nearer "UP" piston pin boss. Piston pin is supported by 29 loose rollers. Rollers may be held in connecting rod with non-fibrous grease during piston installation. Install piston and rod assembly in engine so "UP" pin boss is towards flywheel end of engine. Be sure piston ring ends are properly located around pins in ring grooves during installation.

On late models, the manufacturer recommends renewing piston pin needle bearings if piston pin is removed from piston. A torch lamp or suitable equivalent should be used to heat piston dome to approximately 190° F (88° C) prior to removal or installation of piston pin. Piston pin is supported by 29 loose rollers. Rollers may be held in connecting rod with nonfibrous grease during piston installation. Use recommended Mercury tools or suitable equivalents when pressing piston pin into or out of piston. Renew piston pin retaining clips during reassembly. Install piston and rod assembly in cylinder identified on rod during disassembly. Piston must be installed with "UP" stamped on piston dome toward flywheel end of crankshaft. Pistons are marked "P" for port and "S" for starboard on piston domes for correct in-

stallation in port or starboard cylinder bank.

Maximum allowable cylinder tolerance is 0.006 inch (0.15 mm). Cylinders on 122 cu. in. (1999.2 cc) models can be bored to accommodate 0.015 inch (0.38 mm) and 0.030 inch (0.76 mm) oversize pistons. Cylinders on 142.2 cu. in. (2330.2 cc) models are chrome plated and no oversize pistons are available. Chrome cylinder bores can be replated

to original size if excessively worn, scored or damaged. On some chrome bore models a cast iron sleeve can be installed in one or more cylinders to restore cylinders to standard size. Note that cylinder block and crankcase must be renewed as an assembly.

CONNECTING RODS, BEARINGS AND CRANKSHAFT. Connecting rod has 29 loose rollers in small end and

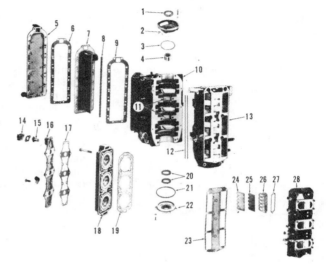

Fig. M15-32—Exploded view of cylinder block and crankcase assemblies.

1. Oil seal
2. Upper end cap
3. "O" ring
4. Roller bearing
5. Exhaust manifold cover
6. Gasket
7. Divider plate
8. Seal
9. Gasket
10. Cylinder block
11. Bearing locating dowel pin
12. Sealing strips
13. Crankcase
14. Thermostat housing
15. Thermostat
16. Cylinder head cover
17. Gasket
18. Cylinder head
19. Gasket
20. Oil seals
21. "O" ring
22. Lower end gap
23. Gasket
24. Reed petal stop
25. Reed petal
26. Reed block
27. Gasket
28. Intake manifold

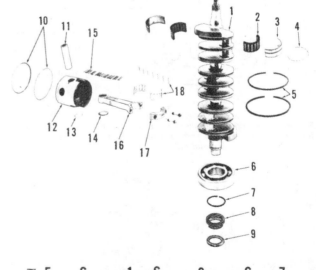

Fig. M15-34—Exploded view of crankshaft assembly.

1. Crankshaft
2. Roller bearing
3. Bearing race
4. Retaining ring
5. Seal rings
6. Ball bearings
7. Snap ring
8. Seal carrier
9. Oil seal
10. Piston rings
11. Piston pin
12. Piston
13. Retaining ring
14. Spacer
15. Bearing rollers (29)
16. Connecting rod
17. Rod cap
18. Roller bearing

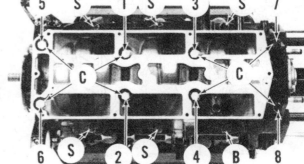

Fig. M15-35—On models prior to serial number 5464486, use tightening sequence shown for large crankcase screws (C). Reverse tightening sequence of screws one and three on 225 hp models. Tighten small crankcase screws (S) next. Note position of long seal screw (B) used on early models except 225 hp models.

caged roller bearings in big end. Install piston on connecting rod so side with alignment bumps (B—Fig. M15-38) is nearer "UP" piston pin boss (early models) or "UP" stamped on piston dome (late models). On all models, piston and rod must be installed with alignment bumps and "UP" mark facing flywheel end of crankshaft. Be sure alignment bumps (B) and marks (M) are correctly positioned when installing rod on crankshaft. Connecting rod big end is fractured type and rod cap must be mated perfectly before tightening cap screws.

Inspect crankshaft crankpin and main bearing journal surfaces. If scored, out-of-round or worn, renew crankshaft.

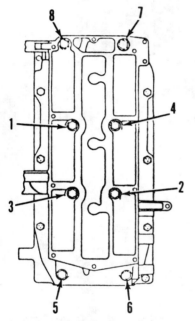

Fig. M15-36—Tighten crankcase screws following sequence shown on vertical and horizontal reed models after serial number 5464485.

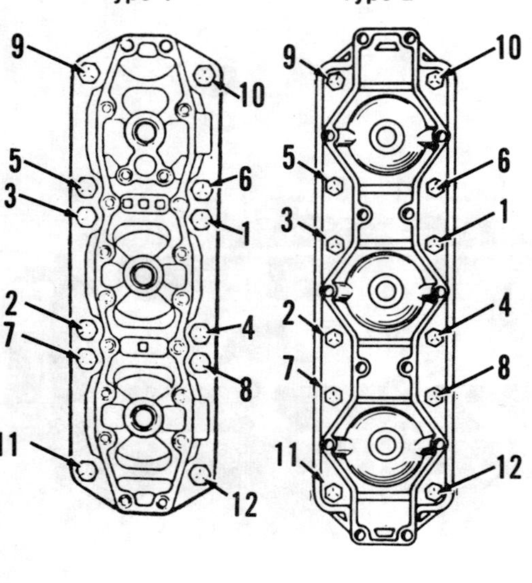

Check crankshaft or straightness. Do not interchange main bearings.

ELECTRICAL SYSTEM

Refer to Figs. M15-23, M15-24 and M15-25 for wiring diagrams. Early models are equipped with a 9 ampere alternator. On 1986-1988 models, a 15 ampere alternator with a voltage regulator is used. Models after serial number C100860 are equipped with a 40 ampere alternator with a voltage regulator.

The rectifier on early models can be checked by disconnecting wires to rectifier and using a continuity tester or ohmmeter as follows: Connect a tester lead to ground and then alternately connect other tester lead to alternator terminals of rectifier. Note reading, then reverse tester leads. Tester should indicate a short or open circuit with first test and opposite reading when tester leads are reversed. Connect a tester lead to positive rectifier terminal and alternately connect other tester lead to alternator terminals of rectifier. Note reading, then reverse tester leads. Tester should show opposite reading when tester leads are reversed. Renew rectifier if testing indicates faulty circuits. No ohmmeter tests are possible on rectifier/regulator assembly used with 40 ampere alternator system.

To check alternator stator on all models, disconnect yellow stator leads at rectifier or voltage regulator. Connect ohmmeter between yellow leads. Stator resistance should be under 1 ohm. No continuity should be present between either stator yellow lead and ground.

Regulated voltage, measured at the battery, should be 14-14.5 volts at 1000 rpm.

Normal starter motor current draw on early models equipped with starter part A-50-86976 is 190 amperes. On later models equipped with starter part A-50-79472, normal current draw is 175 amperes. Renew starter brushes when worn to less than ¼ inch (6.4 mm) long.

LOWER UNIT

Early models and Model 150 XR4 are equipped with Cam-Shift lower unit. Later models, and all 200 hp models, are equipped with E-Z Shift lower unit.

To identify Cam-Shift and E-Z Shift lower units, note the following: With lower unit attached to engine and shifted into reverse gear, propeller shaft on E-Z Shift lower unit will ratchet in one direction, but propeller shaft on Cam Shift unit will be locked in gear in both directions. Also, with lower unit removed, shift shaft on Cam Shift lower unit will rotate 360 degrees in counterclockwise direction, but shift shaft on E-Z Shift lower unit will only rotate 30 degrees in either direction.

All Models

PROPELLER AND DRIVE CLUTCH. Protection for the motor and lower unit is provided by a special cushioning clutch in the propeller hub in early models and by a splined rubber hub in propeller on later models. Various pitch propellers are available. Select a propeller that will allow outboard motor to operate within the specified speed range at full throttle. Refer to CONDENSED SERVICE DATA.

Cam-Shift Models

R&R AND OVERHAUL. Most service on the lower unit can be performed by detaching the gearcase from the drive shaft housing. To remove gearcase, remove plastic plug and Allen screw from location (1—Fig. M15-40). Remove trim tab (2) and screw from under trim tab. Remove stud nuts from location (3), stud nuts (4) from each side and stud

---

Type 1   **Type 2**

Fig. M15-37—Tighten cylinder head in sequence shown on all models. Tighten type 1 cylinder head to 40 in.-lbs. (4.5 N·m). Tighten type 2 cylinder head and all late models to 30 in.-lbs. (3.4 N·m).

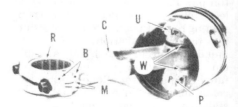

Fig. M15-38—View of piston and connecting rod assembly. Note location of alignment bumps (B), alignment marks (M) and washers (W) used on all models. "P" locating mark (P) and "UP" mark (U) are used on early models. "P" locating mark indicates port side while a starboard piston will have an "S" locating mark.

nut (5), then remove the lower unit gearcase assembly.

Remove the gearcase plugs and drain the gearcase lubricant, then secure the gearcase in a vise between two blocks of soft wood with propeller up. Wedge a piece of wood between propeller and antiventilation plate, remove the propeller nut, then remove the propeller.

Disassemble gearcase by removing gearcase cover nut (55—Fig. M15-41). Clamp outer end of propeller shaft in a soft-jawed vise and remove the gearcase by tapping with a rubber mallet. Be careful not to lose key (51). Forward gear (41) will remain in gearcase. Withdraw propeller shaft from bearing carrier (50) and reverse gear (46).

Clamp bearing carrier (50) in a soft-jawed vise and remove reverse gear (46) and bearing (49) with an internal expanding puller and slide hammer. Reverse gear bearing (49) is not used on 150 XR4 models. Remove and discard propeller shaft seals (53).

To remove clutch (43) from propeller shaft, remove retaining ring (42). Insert cam follower (35) into end of shaft (45) and apply sufficient pressure on cam follower (35) to relieve spring pressure, then push out pin (44) with a suitable punch. Pin (44) passes through drilled holes in clutch and operates in slotted holes in propeller shaft. On 150 XR4 models, three loose ball bearings are present between follower (35) and slide (36).

To disassemble drive shaft and associated parts, reposition gearcase in vise with drive shaft projecting upward. Remove rubber slinger (5), water pump

body (6), impeller (8) and impeller drive key (9). Remove flushing screw and withdraw remainder of water pump parts. Clamp upper end of drive shaft in a soft-jawed vise, remove pinion retaining nut (25); then tap gearcase off drive shaft and bearing. Note position and thickness of shims (21) on drive shaft upper bearing. Mesh position of

pinion is controlled by shims (21) placed underneath the bearing.

After drive shaft has been removed, forward gear (41) and bearing cone can be extracted. Use an internal expanding type puller to extract bearing cup if removal is required. Remove and save shim pack (38).

Shift shaft (31) and cam (34) can be

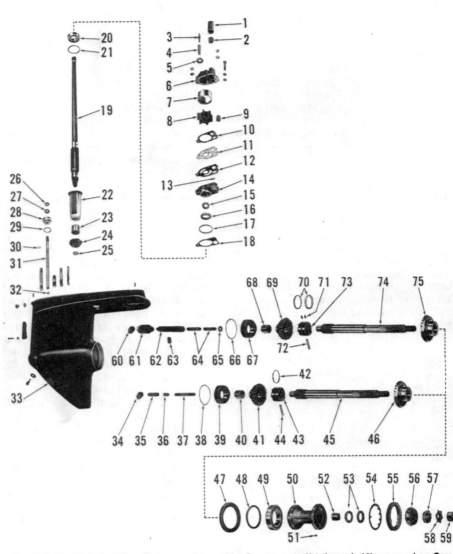

Fig. M15-41—Exploded view of gearcase assembly. Components (34 through 46) are used on Cam-Shift models. Components (60 through 75) are used on E-Z Shift models. On late E-Z Shift and 150 XR4 models, a threaded bearing retainer located above bearing (20) is used. Preload pin (3) and spring (4) are absent on late models. Reverse gear bearing (49) is absent on 150 XR4 models.

1. Water tube guide
2. Seal
3. Pin
4. Spring
5. Rubber ring (slinger)
6. Water pump body
7. Insert
8. Impeller
9. Key
10. Gasket
11. Plate
12. Gasket
13. Dowel pin
14. Pump base
15. Oil seal
16. Oil seal
17. "O" ring
18. Gasket
19. Drive shaft
20. Bearing
21. Shim
22. Sleeve
23. Roller bearing
24. Pinion gear
25. Nut
26. Rubber washer
27. Oil seal
28. Bushing
29. "O" ring
30. "E" ring
31. Shift shaft
32. Circlip
33. Gearcase
34. Shift cam
35. Cam follower
36. Slide
37. Spring
38. Shim
39. Tapered roller bearing
40. Roller bearing
41. Forward gear
42. Spring clip
43. Dog clutch
44. Pin
45. Propeller shaft
46. Reverse gear
47. Thrust washer
48. "O" ring
49. Ball bearing
50. Bearing carrier
51. Key
52. Roller bearing
53. Oil seals
54. Washer
55. Nut
56. Thrust hub
57. Thrust piece
58. Tab washer
59. Nut
60. Shift cam
61. Cam follower
62. Shift rod
63. Pin
64. Springs
65. Shim
66. Shim
67. Tapered roller bearing
68. Roller bearing
69. Forward gear
70. Spring clips
71. Detent pins
72. Pin
73. Dog clutch
74. Propeller shaft
75. Reverse gear

Fig. M15-40 — To remove the lower unit gearcase assembly, remove the attaching screws and stud nuts from positions indicated.

removed after removing forward gear and unscrewing bushing (28) from gearcase.

If gear wear is abnormal or if any parts that affect gear alignment were renewed, install bearings on gears and drive shaft, and in gearcase (including shims 21 and 38). To determine gear mesh and forward gear backlash, proceed as follows: Install drive shaft components (19 through 25) and forward gear components (38 through 41). Tighten pinion nut (25) to 70 ft.-lbs. (95 N·m). Install tool C-91-74776 in gear cavity of gearcase so it bottoms against shoulder of gearcase. Apply approximately 15 pounds (66.7 N) of downward pressure (toward pinion gear) and rotate drive shaft several times to seat drive shaft bearing. While maintaining downward pressure on drive shaft, measure clearance between pinion gear and tool. Clearance should be 0.025 inch (0.63 mm). Add or delete shims (21) to obtain desired clearance. Apply Loctite to drive shaft threads during final assembly.

With drive shaft and forward gear assemblies installed, install propeller shaft (without shift components) and bearing carrier (50), then install nut (55) until snug, but do not tighten. Attach a suitable puller to bearing carrier as shown in Fig. M15-42 and tighten puller screw to 45 in.-lbs. (5.1 N·m). Rotate drive

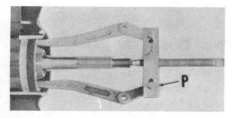

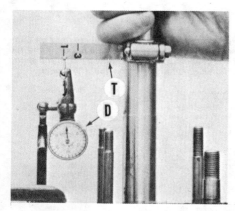

Fig. M15-42—Install a puller (P) as shown to preload forward gear bearing when determining gear backlash as outlined in text.

Fig. M15-43—Install backlash measuring tool C-91-78473 (T) and a dial indicator (D) set to read movement at number on tool as described in text.

shaft several times to seat forward gear bearing and recheck tightness on puller screw. Install backlash indicator tool C-91-78473 (C-91-19660 on 150 XR4) on drive shaft as shown in Fig. M15-43 and set up a dial indicator to read movement at the "2" mark on backlash indicator tool. Recheck torque on bearing carrier puller (45 in.-lbs. [5.1 N·m]). Measure forward gear backlash by applying downward pressure and turning drive shaft. Forward gear backlash should be 0.016-0.019 inch (0.41-0.48 mm) on 150 XR4 models and 0.008-0.013 inch (0.20-0.33 mm) on all other models. Adjust backlash by varying thickness of shims (38—Fig. M15-41).

When reassembling, long splines of shift shaft (31) should be toward top. Shift cam (34) is installed with long side on port side of gearcase. On 150 XR4, make sure three loose ball bearings are installed between slide (36) and follower (35). On 150 XR4 models, install thrust washer (47), with beveled outer diameter facing carrier (50). Install reverse gear and bearing carrier assembly using new seals (48 and 53). Lip in inner seal (53) should face inward and lip of outer seal (53) should face propeller.

Upper oil seal (15) should be installed with lips facing up (toward engine) and lower oil seal (16) should be pressed into water pump base with lips facing down toward propeller shaft. Install remainder of water pump assembly and tighten the screws or nuts to the following recommended torque. Torque $\frac{1}{4}$-28 nuts to 24-30 in.-lbs. (2.7-3.4 N·m). Torque $\frac{5}{16}$-24 nuts to 35-40 in.-lbs. (3.9-4.5 N·m). Torque $\frac{1}{4}$-20 screws to 15-20 in.-lbs. (1.7-2.2 N·m).

Do not apply excessive grease to drive shaft splines; there must not be grease on tops of drive shaft or shift shaft. Shift lower unit to forward gear and move guide block anchor pin on engine to forward gear position. Tighten gearcase fasteners with $\frac{3}{8}$-16 threads to 55 ft.-lbs. (75 N·m) and fasteners with 7/16-20 threads to 65 ft.-lbs. (88 N·m).

E-Z Shift Models

R&R AND OVERHAUL. Most service on the lower unit can be performed by detaching the gearcase from the drive shaft housing. To remove gearcase, shift outboard to neutral gear, then detach propeller and drain gearcase lubricant. Remove the plastic plug and Allen screw from location (1—Fig. M15-40). Remove trim tab (2) and stud nut from under trim tab. Remove stud nut from location (3), two stud nuts (4) from each side and stud nut (5) if so equipped, then withdraw the lower unit gearcase assembly.

To disassemble gearcase, remove rubber slinger (5—Fig. M15-41), water tube guide (1) and seal (2). Unscrew and remove water pump components (6 through 18). Position gearcase in a soft-jawed vise so propeller shaft is horizontal. Check and be sure gearcase is in neutral gear. Unscrew but do not remove shift shaft bushing (28) and withdraw shift shaft (31) from gearcase. DO NOT turn shift shaft during removal or gearcase may be shifted into forward or reverse gear position. Bend back lockwasher (54) tabs, unscrew nut (55) and use a suitable puller to remove bearing carrier (50).

NOTE: Do not apply side load or strike side of propeller shaft during or after removal of bearing carrier as shift rod (62) may break.

Withdraw propeller shaft from gearcase, but do not use excessive force or a puller. If shaft is lodged in gearcase proceed as follows: Push propeller shaft inward so it contacts forward gear, reinstall shift shaft and be sure gears are in neutral. Remove shift shaft and attempt to withdraw propeller shaft. If propeller shaft remains stuck, push shaft inward so it contacts forward gear. Reinstall bearing carrier and lay gearcase on its port side. Strike upper forward end of gearcase with a rubber mallet so shift cam (6) is dislodged and falls into a cavity in side of gearcase. Remove bearing carrier and propeller shaft.

To remove shift rod (62) from propeller shaft, remove spring clips (70) while being careful not to lose detent pins (71). Drive out pin (72) and remove shift rod (62) while being careful not to lose pin (63) which may fall from rod. Slide dog clutch (73) off shaft.

To disassemble drive shaft and associated parts, clamp upper end of drive shaft in a soft-jawed vise and remove pinion gear nut (25).

NOTE: On late models not equipped with pin (3) and spring (4), unscrew and remove bearing retainer above bearing assembly (20).

Tap gearcase off drive shaft and bearing. Note position and thickness of shims (21) and bearing. Remove pinion gear (24) and forward gear (69). Use a suitable puller to extract cups of bearings (20 and 67). Note number and thickness of shims (21 and 66) and save for reassembly. Pull out sleeve (22) then drive roller bearing (23) down into gear cavity for removal.

Inspect all components for excessive wear and damage. If water pump insert (7) must be renewed, use a punch and drive out old insert. It may be necessary to drill two holes in top of water pump body (6) to drive out insert – do not drill through insert. Apply RTV sealant to holes after installing the new insert.

Install bearings on gears and drive shaft, and in gearcase (including shims 21 and 66). To determine gear mesh and forward gear backlash, note number of pinion gear (24) teeth, then proceed as follows: Install drive shaft components (19 through 25) and forward gear components (66 through 69). Tighten bearing retainer above bearing assembly (20), if so equipped, to 100 ft.-lbs. (136 N·m) with side of retainer marked "OFF" facing toward top of gearcase housing. Tighten pinion gear nut (25) to 70 ft.-lbs. (95 N·m) on early models and 80 ft.-lbs. (109 N·m) on later models. Install tool C-91-74776 in gear cavity of gearcase so it bottoms against shoulder of gearcase. Apply approximately 15 pounds (67 N) of downward pressure (toward pinion gear) and rotate drive shaft several times to seat drive shaft bearing. While maintaining downward pressure on drive shaft, measure clearance between pinion gear and tool. Clearance should be 0.025 inch (0.64 mm). Add or delete shims (21) to obtain desired clearance. Apply Loctite to drive shaft threads during final assembly.

With drive shaft and forward gear assemblies installed, install propeller shaft (without shift components) and bearing carrier (50), then install nut (55) until snug, but do not tighten. Attach a suitable puller to bearing carrier as shown in Fig. M15-42 and apply 45 in.-lbs. (5.1 N·m) torque to puller screw. Rotate drive shaft several times to seat forward gear bearing. Install backlash measuring tool C-91-78473 on drive shaft as shown in Fig. M15-43 and set up a dial indicator to read movement at "1" on backlash tool for models with a 15-tooth pinion gear or at "2" for models with a 14-tooth pinion gear. Recheck torque on bearing carrier puller (45 in.-lbs. [5.1 N·m]). Measure forward gear backlash by applying downward pressure and turning drive shaft. Dial indicator should measure 0.008-0.013 inch (0.20-0.33 mm) backlash on models equipped with preload type drive shaft and 0.018-0.027 inch (0.46-0.69 mm) on

models without preload type drive shaft. Adjust backlash by adding or deleting shims (66 – Fig. M15-41). Changing shim thickness by 0.001 inch (0.025 mm) will alter backlash by 0.0015 inch (0.038 mm).

To properly adjust spring tension in shift rod (62), install springs (64) and pin (63) in shift rod. Insert tool C-91-86642, or an old pin (72) with a ground-down end, between springs as shown in Fig. M15-44. Tool (T) or pin should be centered in shift rod slot within 1/64 inch (0.397 mm). Adjust tool position by installing shims (65) at ends of springs (64).

Assemble remainder of lower unit by reversing disassembly procedure while noting the following points: Install thrust washer (47 – Fig. M15-41) so larger diameter side is nearer reverse gear (75), then press bearing (49) on gear. Lip of inner seal (53) should face in and lip of outer seal (53) should face propeller (out). Install spring clips (70) so bent end of each spring engages the hole in one of the detent pins (71). Wind spring clips in opposite directions around dog clutch (73); they must not overlap.

Use heavy grease to hold shift cam (60) in cam follower (61) with "UP" side facing up. Be sure "E" ring (30) and circlip (32) are seated on shift shaft (31) before installing shaft. Tighten bushing (28) after tightening bearing carrier nut (55). Tighten bearing carrier nut (55) to 210 ft.-lbs. (284 N·m).

Upper oil seal (15) is installed with lips facing up (toward engine) while lower oil seal (16) lips should face down towards gearcase. If reusing old impeller (8), install impeller so vanes rotate in same direction during previous operation. Be sure key (9) is properly installed. Tighten water pump fasteners to following torques: 1/4-28 nuts to 25-30 in.-lbs. (2.8-3.4 N·m), 5/16-24 nuts to 35-40 in.-lbs. (3.9-4.5 N·m) and 1/2-20 screws to 15-20 in.-lbs. (1.7-2.2 N·m).

Do not apply excessive grease to drive shaft splines; there must not be grease on tops of drive shaft or shift shaft. Shift lower unit to forward gear and move guide block anchor pin on engine to for-

ward gear position. Tighten gearcase fasteners with 3/8-16 threads to 55 ft.-lbs. (75 N·m) and 7/16-20 threads to 65 ft.-lbs. (88 N·m).

POWER TILT/TRIM

Non-Integral Type

Two types of non-integral hydraulic power tilt/trim systems have been used. Early models are identified by the rectangular oil reservoir and later models use a circular fluid reservoir. Refer to the following sections for service.

Early Models

FLUID. Recommended fluid is SAE 10W-30 or 10W-40 automotive oil. With outboard in full down position, oil level should reach "Full" mark on dipstick. Do not overfill.

BLEEDING. Check fluid level in reservoir and fill if required. Operate trim system several times to purge air in system. Recheck fluid level and fill if required.

HYDRAULIC TESTING. Disconnect cylinder hoses from control valve and connect a pressure gage to oulets of control valve as shown in Fig. M15–50. Note that large outlet is "up" circuit and small outlet is "down" circuit. Close appropriate pressure gage valve circuit. Make sure manual tilt valve (M) is tightly closed. Close and open appropriate pressure gage valves while operating system to check pressure in up and down circuits. Hydraulic pressure should be 3100 psi (21.4 MPa) minimum for up circuit and 1200 psi (8.3 MPa) minimum for down circuit. Pressure may drop slightly but should remain steady. If pressure is normal, inspect trim cylinders and hoses for leakage. If pressure is abnormal, install a good control valve and recheck pressure. If pressure remains abnormal, install a new pump body.

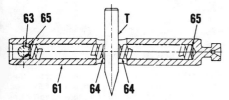

Fig. M15-44 — Cross section of shift rod on E-Z Shift models. Center tool (T) using shims (64) as outlined in text.

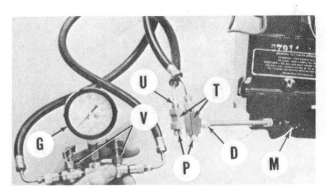

Fig. M15-50 — Connect a pressure gage (G) as shown for hydraulic testing of non-integral type power tilt/trim.

   D. "Down" line
   G. Pressure gage
   M. Manual tilt valve
   P. Plugs
   T. Tees
   U. "Up" line
   V. Valves

Later Models

FLUID AND BLEEDING. Recommended fluid is SAE 10W-40 with an API rating of SE. Fill reservoir to "FULL" mark on dipstick.

The hydraulic circuit is self-bleeding as the trim system is operated several times. Be sure to check reservoir level after filling and operating system after system has been serviced.

HYDRAULIC TESTING. The pump may be checked by connecting a 5000 psi (34.5 MPa) test gage alternately to the "UP" and "DOWN" ports. Note that the pump motor blue wire is the positive battery connection to pressurize the "UP" port and connecting the positive battery terminal to the pump motor green wire will pressurize the "DOWN" port. Pressure at the "UP" port should be 3100-3500 psi (21.4-24.1 MPa) and should not drop lower than 1500 psi (10.3 MPa) after pumping stops. Pressure at the "DOWN" port should be 1500-1900 psi (10.3-13.1 MPa) and should not drop lower than 750 psi (5.2 MPa) after pumping stops.

Integral Type

FLUID AND BLEEDING. Recommended fluid is Dexron II or Type A automatic transmission fluid. Remove fill plug (7—Fig. M15-55) and fill reservoir until fluid is visible in fill tube with the outboard motor in the full-up position.

The hydraulic circuit is self-bleeding as the tilt/trim system is operated through several cycles. After servicing system, be sure to check reservoir level after filling and operating system.

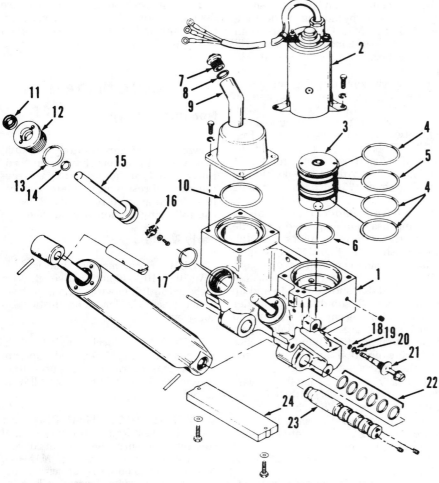

Fig. M15-55—Exploded view of integral type power tilt/trim system.

1. Manifold	7. Fill plug	14. "O" ring (0.612 in. [15.54 mm] ID)
2. Electric motor	8. "O" ring (0.583 in. [14.81 mm] ID)	15. Trim piston & rod
3. Pump assy.	9. Reservoir cover	16. Strainer
4. "O" rings (2.614 in. [66.40 mm] ID)	10. Seal ring	17. "O" ring (1.248 in. [31.70 mm] ID)
5. "O" ring (2.739 in. [69.57 mm] ID)	11. Seal	18. "O" ring (0.114 in. [2.90 mm] ID)
6. "O" ring (2.739 in. [69.57 mm] ID)	12. Cap	19. "O" ring (0.208 in. [5.28 mm] ID)
	13. "O" ring (1.475 in. [37.47 mm] ID)	20. "O" ring (0.239 in. [6.07 mm] ID)
		21. Manual release valve
		22. "O" rings (0.989 in. [25.12 mm] ID)
		23. Shaft
		24. Anode plate

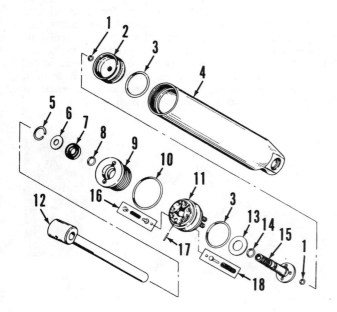

Fig. M15-56—Exploded view of tilt cylinder components.

1. "O" ring (0.307 in. [7.9 mm] ID)
2. Cup
3. "O" ring (1.957 in. [49.71 mm] ID)
4. Cylinder
5. Circlip
6. Washer
7. Scraper
8. "O" ring (0.854 in. [21.69 mm] ID)
9. Cap
10. "O" ring (2.067 in. [52.5 mm] ID)
11. Piston
12. Rod
13. Washer
14. "O" ring (0.661 in. [16.79 mm] ID)
15. Rod end
16. Check valve assy.
17. Pin
18. Check valve assy.

Fig. M15-57—Release pressure on system, then remove Allen head plug (U) and install a 5000 psi (34.5 MPa) test gage with suitable adapter and hose to test system pressure when operated in the "UP" direction. View identifies location of manual release valve (21).

HYDRAULIC TESTING. The system can be checked by connecting a 5000 psi (34.5 MPa) test gage to the UP (U – Fig. M15-57) and DOWN (D – Fig. M15-58) ports. Prior to connecting test gage, place outboard motor in the full-up position and engage tilt lock lever. Unscrew reservoir fill plug and rotate manual release valve (21 – Fig. M15-57) three to four turns counterclockwise to release pressure on system. Remove UP or DOWN Allen head test port plug and connect test gage with suitable adapter and hose. Install fill plug and rotate manual release valve clockwise until seated. System pressure when testing at UP (U) port should be a minimum of 1300 psi (8.9 MPa). System pressure when testing at DOWN (D – Fig.

M15-58) port should be a minimum of 500 psi (3.5 MPa). Release pressure on system as previously outlined prior to removing test gage. Reinstall Allen head plug.

Fig. M15-58—Release pressure on system, then remove Allen head plug (D) and install a 5000 psi (34.5 MPa) test gage with a suitable adapter and hose to test system pressure when operated in the "DOWN" direction.

OVERHAUL. Refer to Fig. M15-55 for an exploded view of manifold and trim cylinder components, and Fig. M15-56 for an exploded view of tilt cylinder components. Special Mercury socket 91-44487A1 and a spanner wrench is required to service trim and tilt cylinders. Keep all components clean and away from contamination. Keep components separated and label if needed for correct reassembly. Note "O" ring sizes as stated in legends of Figs. M15-55 and M15-56. Lubricate all "O" rings or seal lips with Dexron II or Type AF automatic transmission fluid during assembly.

MERCURY 300 AND 3.4L

Year Produced	Model
1980	300
1981	300
1982	....
1983	300
1984	3.4L
1985	3.4L
1986	3.4L

Letter suffix indicates equipment variation: E–Electric starter and alternator, L–Long shaft, XL–Extra long shaft and PT–Power trim.

CONDENSED SERVICE DATA

TUNE-UP
Hp/rpm:
Model 300 . . . . .300/5300-5800
Model 3.4L 275/5300-5800
Bore. . . . . .3.74 in.
(95 mm)
Stroke . . . . .3.14 in.
(80 mm)
Number of Cylinders 6
Displacement . . . . .207 cu. in.
(3393 cc)
Firing Order 1-2-3-4-5-6
Number System (top to bottom):
Port 2-4-6
Starboard 1-3-5
Spark Plug:
Champion. L76V
AC. V40FFM
Electrode Gap . . . . .Surface Gap
Idle Speed (in gear) . . . . .550-600 rpm
Fuel:Oil Ratio 50:1

SIZES—CLEARANCES
Piston Ring End Gap . . . . .0.018-0.025 in.
(0.457-0.635 mm)
Maximum Cylinder Tolerance . . . . .0.006 in.
(0.152 mm)

SIZES—CLEARANCES CONT.
Crankshaft Bearing Type:
Top Main Bearing . . . . .Caged Roller
Center Main Bearings . . . . .Caged Roller
Bottom Main Bearing . . . . .Ball Bearing
Crankpin . . . . .Caged Roller
Piston Pin Bearing . . . . .34 Loose Rollers

TIGHTENING TORQUES
Carburetor Adapter Plate . . . . .150 in.-lbs.
(17 N·m)
Connecting Rod . . . . .See Text
Crankcase Screws . . . . .30 ft.-lbs.
(40 N·m)
Cylinder Head. . . . . .150 in.-lbs.
(17 N·m)
Lower End Cap . . . . .150 in.-lbs.
(17 N·m)
Exhaust Cover . . . . .150 in.-lbs.
(17 N·m)
Flywheel Nut . . . . .125 ft.-lbs.
(169 N·m)
Reed Block to Reed Plate Mounting Screws . . . . .60 in.-lbs.
(6.7 N·m)
Reed Plate to Carburetor Adapter
Plate Mounting Screws. . . . . .60 in.-lbs.
(6.7 N·m)
Spark Plugs . . . . .204 in.-lbs.
(17 N·m)

LUBRICATION

The engine is lubricated by oil mixed with the fuel. The fuel should be regular leaded, low lead or unleaded gasoline with a minimum pump octane rating of 86. Recommended oil is Quicksilver Formula 50-D Outboard Lubricant or a BIA certified TC-W motor oil. The recommended fuel:oil ratio for normal operation is 50:1. During engine break-in, the fuel:oil ratio should be increased to 25:1.

The lower unit gears and bearings are lubricated by oil contained in the gearcase. The recommended oil is Quicksilver Super Duty Gear Lubricant or a suitable EP90 outboard gear oil. The gearcase should be refilled periodically and the lubricant renewed after every 30 hours of operation or more frequently if needed. The gearcase is drained and filled through the same plug port. An upper and lower oil level (vent) port are used in the gearcase filling procedure and to ease in oil drainage. Drain plug and level plugs are

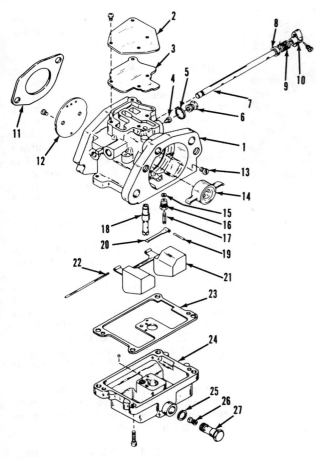

Fig. M17-1—Exploded view of carburetor.

1. Body
2. Cover plate
3. Gasket
4. Idle jet
5. Gasket
6. Plug
7. Throttle shaft
8. Spacer
9. Spring
10. Lever
11. Gasket
12. Throttle plate
13. Vent jet
14. Venturi
15. Gasket
16. Seat
17. Needle
18. Main nozzle
19. Pin
20. Inlet lever
21. Float
22. Pin
23. Gasket
24. Float bowl
25. Gasket
26. Main jet
27. Main jet plug

SPEED CONTROL LINKAGE. To synchronize ignition and carburetor opening, proceed as follows: To verify timing pointer alignment, a dial indicator must be installed in the number 1 (top, starboard) cylinder and the indicator synchronized with the piston position (dial indicator reads zero when piston is at top dead center).

NOTE: To prevent accidental starting from flywheel rotation, remove all spark plugs and properly ground plug wires.

Rotate the flywheel counterclockwise approximately ¼ turn past the 0.557 inch (14.15 mm) BTDC reading, then rotate flywheel clockwise until indicator face reads 0.557 inch (14.15 mm) BTDC. Note position of the timing pointer and reposition if the timing pointer is not

Fig. M17-2—To determine float level, invert the carburetor body and measure distance (D) from the carburetor body to base of float (21). Distance (D) should be 11/16 inch (17.5 mm).

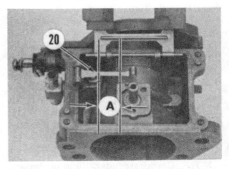

Fig. M17-3—Adjust float level by bending fuel inlet lever (20) within area (A).

Fig. M17-5—Link rod (L) should protrude 11/16 inch (17.46 mm) from link body. Refer to text for procedures to adjust maximum spark advance screw (A).

located on starboard side of gearcase. To fill gearcase with oil, place the outboard motor in a vertical position. Add oil through drain plug opening until oil begins to overflow from lower oil level plug port. Reinstall lower oil level plug, then continue to add oil until the oil begins to overflow from upper oil level plug port. Allow 1 ounce (30 mL) to drain from gearcase, then reinstall upper oil level plug and drain plug.

FUEL SYSTEM

CARBURETOR. Standard make of carburetor is a center bowl type Mercarb. Six carburetors are used. For operation below 2500 feet (762 m) altitude, the standard jet sizes are as follows:

WO-3 Carburetor

Main jet	0.072 in. (1.83 mm)
Vent jet	0.080 in. (2.03 mm)
Idle jet	0.052 in. (1.32 mm)

WO-5 Carburetor

Main jet	0.076 in. (1.93 mm)
Vent jet	0.080 in. (2.03 mm)
Idle jet	0.062 in. (1.57 mm)

NOTE: Carburetor indentification letters and number are stamped on the top side of carburetor mounting flange.

Other jet sizes are available for adjusting the calibration for altitude or other special conditions. No idle mixture screw adjustment is provided. Idle jet (4–Fig. MY13-9) size must be altered to change idle air:fuel ratio. The idle jet meters air, therefore installing an idle jet with a smaller orifice will enrich the idle air:fuel ratio and installing an idle jet with a larger orifice will lean the idle air:fuel ratio. Recommended idle speed is 550-600 rpm with engine at normal operating temperature and forward gear engaged. After engine idle speed adjustment, hold idle speed screw against stop and install the throttle cable barrel in the retainer while adjusting barrel so it fits into retainer and a very light preload between idle speed screw and its stop is established. Excessive throttle cable preload will result in difficult shifting from forward to neutral.

To determine the float level, invert the carburetor body and measure distance (D–Fig. MY13-10) from the carburetor body to base of float (21). Distance (D) should be ¹¹⁄₁₆ inch (17.5 mm) and is adjusted by bending fuel inlet lever (20–Fig. MY13-11) within area (A).

aligned with ".557 BTDC" mark on flywheel. Loosen the two cap screws retaining the timing pointer and reposition, if needed, then retighten cap screws. Remove the dial indicator assembly from the top cylinder after adjustment is completed and reinstall number 1 (top) spark plug and lead.

Be sure link rod (L – Fig. M17-5) protrudes 11/16 inch (17.46 mm) from link body as shown.

NOTE: To prevent engine from starting, make sure only the number 1 (top, starboard) spark plug is installed and its plug wire attached.

Disconnect the fuel tank supply hose at the outboard motor connector. Detach the throttle cable barrel from the retainer of the cable anchor bracket. Adjust idle speed screw (I – Fig. M17-6) so idle mark (M) on throttle cam (C) is in contact with roller (R) as shown.

Withdraw the air intake cover from the front of the carburetors. Position throttle lever (T) so idle speed screw (I) is against its stop. Loosen carburetor synchronizing screws (S) and allow the carburetor throttle plates to close freely. With light pressure, hold cam follower roller (R) against throttle cam (C). Then retighten screws (S). Check to be sure that carburetor throttle plates are completely closed and operate freely. Repeat adjustment procedure if setting is incorrect. Reinstall air intake cover.

Connect a suitable timing light to number 1 cylinder spark plug lead. With the outboard motor in neutral, position throttle lever (T) so idle speed screw (I) is against stop. Crank the engine with the electric starter and adjust primary screw (P) so the ignition timing is 7° ATDC on engines equipped with WO-5 carburetors and 13° ATDC on engines equipped with WO-3 carburetors.

NOTE: Carburetor identification letters and number are stamped on the top side of carburetor mounting flange.

Open the throttle until maximum spark advance screw (A – Fig. M17-5) is against stop. Crank the engine with the starter motor and adjust maximum spark advance screw (A) so ignition timing is 22° BTDC.

NOTE: Due to electronic characteristics of the ignition system, maximum advance is set at 22° BTDC, but ignition will retard to 20° BTDC at 5500 rpm.

The carburetor throttle plates must not act as the wide open throttle stop. To prevent damage to the carburetors, move speed control linkage to the max-

Fig. M17-6 – View showing speed control components.

B. Maximum throttle stop screw
C. Throttle cam
I. Idle speed screw
M. Idle mark
P. Primary screw
R. Roller
S. Screw
T. Throttle lever

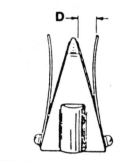

Fig. M17-8 – Reed stop setting (D) should be 0.300 inch (7.62 mm) on all models.

imum speed position and adjust maximum throttle stop screw (B – Fig. M17-6) so a clearance of 0.010-0.015 inch (0.25-0.38 mm) is between throttle cam (C) and cam follower roller (R).

Reassemble and adjust idle speed screw (I) as outlined in the following CARBURETOR section.

Hold idle speed screw (I) against stop and install the throttle cable barrel in the retainer while adjusting barrel so it fits into retainer and a very light preload between idle speed screw and its stop is

established. Excessive throttle cable preload will result in difficult shifting from forward to neutral.

REED VALVES. The fuel:air mixture for each cylinder is directed through a reed plate assembly containing two reed blocks with 10 reed petals on each block. Reed plate assemblies are mounted to a carburetor adapter plate. The carburetor adapter plate is mounted to the crankcase. The upper reed block is retained to the reed plate by two screws reaching through carburetor adapter plate. The reed plate must be removed from carburetor adapter plate before lower reed block can be separated from reed plate.

Reed petals should be flat and have no more than 0.020 inch (0.51 mm) clearance between free end of reed petal and seating surface of reed block. Do not attempt to bend or straighten a reed petal or turn reed petals around on reed block. Reed block seating surface must be flat. Reed block should be renewed if indented by reed petals or damaged. Reed petals are available in sets for each reed block only.

Reed stop setting is 0.300 inch (7.62 mm) for all models. Measure from reed stop to reed petal seating surface as shown in Fig. M17-8.

FUEL PUMP. Two fuel pump assemblies are used. The fuel pumps operate in series, the starboard mounted fuel pump pumps fuel to the port mounted fuel pump, which pumps fuel to the carburetors.

Pulse hoses connected between the crankcase and fuel pump mounting plate (20 – Fig. M17-10) are used to transfer crankcase pulsating pressure. Make sure hoses are airtight and in good condition.

A booster chamber is used on pump discharge side to dampen the action of the larger main pump diaphragm, thus

Fig. M17-10 – Exploded view of fuel pump assembly.
1. Cap screw
2. Plastic washer
3. Filter cover
4. "O" ring
5. Strainer
6. Housing
7. Gaskets
8. Inlet check valve
9. Discharge check valve
10. Retainer
11. Retainer
12. Spring
13. Cap
14. Gaskets
15. Diaphragm
16. Booster chamber
17. Gasket
18. Base
19. Gasket
20. Mounting plate

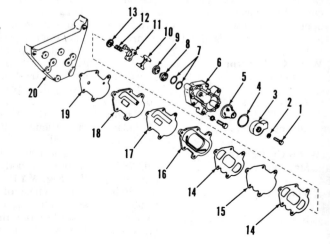

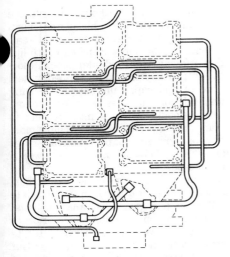

Fig. M17-12—View showing correct routing of crankcase bleed system hoses and fuel pump pulse hoses.

increasing the maximum potential fuel flow.

Spring (12) and cap (13) are used to load the diaphragm, thus allowing the diaphragm to respond more quickly to crankcase pressure changes.

When overhauling the fuel pump or pumps, renew all defective or questionable parts. When assembling fuel pump, retainer (10) must be installed with tips pointing away from the check valves.

CRANKCASE BLEED SYSTEM

A crankcase bleed system is used to remove unburned oil residue from the crankcase and lower main bearing and burn or direct the unburned oil residue to the three upper main bearings. Refer to Fig. M17-12 for the correct routing of crankcase bleed system hoses.

IGNITION SYSTEM

All models are equipped with a Thunderbolt solid state capacitor discharge ignition system consisting of trigger coils, stator, switch boxes and ignition coils. The trigger coils are contained in a trigger ring module under the flywheel. Diodes, SCR's and capacitors are contained in the switch boxes. Switch boxes, trigger ring module and stator must be serviced as unit assemblies.

Check all wires and connections before troubleshooting ignition circuit. The following test specifications will aid troubleshooting. Resistance between blue and red stator leads or blue/white and red/white stator leads should be 5400-6200 ohms. Resistance between red stator lead and ground or red/white stator lead and ground should be 125-175 ohms. Resistance should be 1200-1400 ohms between the following

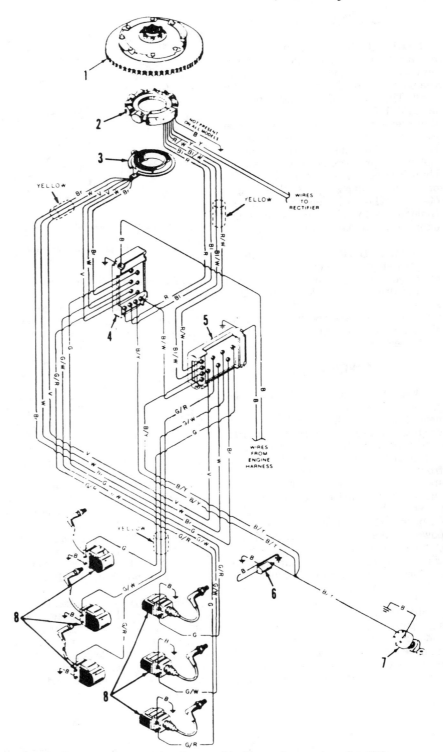

Fig. M17-14—Typical wiring diagram of ignition system used on all models.

1. Flywheel	7. Ignition switch	Y. Yellow
2. Stator	8. Ignition coils	Bl. Blue
3. Trigger ring		Br. Brown
4. Upper switch box		B/W. Black with white tracer
5. Lower switch box		
6. Mercury stop switch		B/Y. Black with white tracer

B. Black	
G. Green	G/R. Green with red tracer
R. Red	G/W. Green with white tracer
V. Violet	R/W. Red with white tracer
W. White	Bl/W. Blue with white tracer

trigger coil leads; between brown (in yellow sleeve) and violet (without yellow sleeve), between white (in yellow sleeve) and brown (without yellow sleeve), between violet (in yellow sleeve) and white

(without yellow sleeve). Ignition coils may be checked using a suitable coil checker.

Recommended spark plugs are AC V40FFM or Champion L76V.

COOLING SYSTEM

THERMOSTAT. All models are equipped with a thermostat positioned on both the starboard and port side of the power head adjacent to the cylinder head. Thermostat should begin to open at 140°-145°F (60°-63°C). A temperature sender is installed in the starboard cylinder head which activates an alarm horn should engine overheating occur.

A water pressure relief valve assembly is located in port and starboard side of exhaust adapter plate. Diaphragm (4 – Fig. M17-16) is renewable. Inspect components for nicks, cracks or other damage which may cause leakage.

WATER PUMP. The rubber impeller type water pump is housed in the gearcase housing. The impeller is mounted on and driven by the lower unit drive shaft. Water pump is accessible after separating gearcase housing from drive shaft housing as outlined in LOWER UNIT section.

POWER HEAD

R&R AND DISASSEMBLE. To remove power head assembly, disconnect all wires and hoses and remove all cowling which will interfere with power head separation from drive shaft housing. Detach shift arm from shift shaft at front of exhaust adapter plate. Remove six nuts and one screw securing exhaust adapter plate to drive shaft housing and lift power head off drive shaft housing. Remove exhaust adapter plate from power head and install power head on a suitable stand. Remove flywheel, stator, trigger ring and starter motor. Remove carburetor enrichener, temperature sender, ignition coils, switch boxes and speed control linkage. Remove fuel pumps and disconnect and label interfering pulse hoses. Remove carburetors and label for proper reassembly. Remove carburetor adapter plates with reed valve assemblies and disconnect and label interfering bleed hoses.

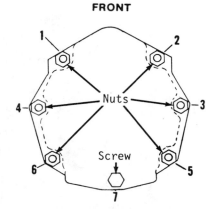

FRONT

Fig. M17-18 — Tighten exhaust adapter plate to drive shaft housing screw and nuts to 30 ft.-lbs. (40 N·m) following sequence shown.

Remove cylinder heads and exhaust cover.

Remove screws securing lower end cap. Remove crankcase mounting screws and nut, then remove crankcase by using a soft-faced mallet to tap crankcase free. Use extra care not to damage machined mating surfaces of cylinder block and crankcase. Mark connecting rods with cylinder numbers so they can be reinstalled in original cylinders and remove rod and piston assemblies. Remove lower end cap. Crankcase and cylinder block are matched and align bored and can be renewed only as a set.

Refer to following paragraphs to service pistons, rods, crankshaft and bearings. When assembling, follow the procedures outlined in the ASSEMBLY paragraphs. Tighten exhaust adapter plate to drive shaft housing screw and nuts to 30 ft.-lbs. (40 N·m) following sequence shown in Fig. M17-18.

ASSEMBLY. When assembling, the crankcase must be sealed against both vacuum and pressure. Exhaust cover and water passages must be sealed against pressure leakage. Whenever power head is disassembled, it is recommended that all gasket surfaces and

machined joints without gaskets be carefully checked for nicks and burrs which might interfere with a tight seal.

Install seals in lower end cap with lips down (away from cylinder block). Loctite 271 or 290 should be applied to seal bore of end cap. Lubricate all bearing and friction surfaces with engine oil. Loose needle bearings may be held in place during assembly using a light, nonfibrous grease. Gaps of seal rings (15 – Fig. M17-19) must be towards crankcase.

Install piston, rod and crankshaft assemblies as outlined in appropriate following paragraphs. Crankcase must be installed on cylinder block prior to tightening lower end cap screws. Rotate crankshaft and check for binding. Cut gasket strips off flush with edge of crankcase bores. Apply a thin coat of sealer such as Permatex 2C-12 to mating surfaces of crankcase and cylinder block using care to prevent excess sealer from entering bearings, crankcase or passages.

Progressively tighten crankcase seven main bearing screws and one nut until crankshaft seal rings are compressed and crankcase mates with cylinder block. Tighten seven screws and one nut in three progressive steps to a final torque of 30 ft.-lbs. (40 N·m) using a criss-cross tightening sequence starting in center of crankcase and working out to ends. Tighten six crankcase flange screws in three progressive steps to 30 ft.-lbs. (40 N·m). Rotate crankshaft and check for binding.

Complete reassembly in reverse order of disassembly and tighten components to torque values shown in CONDENSED SERVICE DATA.

PISTONS, PINS, RINGS AND CYLINDERS. Before detaching connecting rods from crankshaft, make sure that rod and cap are marked so rods and caps are not interchanged and can be returned to original cylinders.

The manufacturer recommends renewing piston pin needle bearings if piston pin is removed from piston. Piston pin is supported by 34 loose needle bearings. Needle bearings can be held in connecting rod with nonfibrous grease during piston pin installation. Use recommended Mercury tools or suitable equivalents when installing or removing piston pin. Renew piston pin retaining clips during reassembly.

Piston rings must be installed on piston with dot side facing top of piston. Piston ring gap should be 0.018-0.025 inch (0.45-0.64 mm).

Install piston and rod assembly in cylinder identified on rod during disassembly. Piston must be installed with letter on piston dome toward

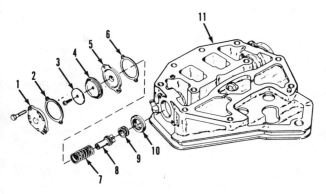

Fig. M17-16 — Exploded view of water pressure relief valve assembly located in port and starboard side of exhaust adapter plate.

1. Cover
2. Gasket
3. Washer
4. Diaphragm
5. Plate
6. Gasket
7. Spring
8. Relief valve
9. Carrier
10. Grommet
11. Exhaust adapter plate

flywheel end of crankshaft. Pistons are marked "P" for port and "S" for starboard on piston domes for correct installation in port or starboard cylinder bank.

Maximum allowable cylinder tolerance is 0.006 inch (0.152 mm). Cylinders are chrome plated and no service other than renewal of cylinder block and crankcase assembly is recommended by the manufacturer.

CONNECTING RODS, BEARINGS AND CRANKSHAFT.

Connecting rod has 34 loose needle bearings in small end and caged roller bearings in big end. Connecting rod big end is fractured type and rod and cap must be mated perfectly before tightening screws. Tighten 5/16-18 rod cap screws to 180 in.-lbs. (20.3 N·m), then rotate screws an additional ½ turn. Tighten ⅜-24 rod cap screws to 360 in.-lbs. (40.6 N·m), then rotate screws an additional ¼ turn.

Inspect crankshaft crankpin and main bearing journal surfaces; if scored, out-of-round or worn, renew crankshaft. Check crankshaft for straightness. Do not interchange main bearings.

ELECTRICAL SYSTEM

Refer to Fig. M17-14 for a typical wiring diagram of ignition and starter components for all models. Note the following cautions when servicing electrical components:

DO NOT reverse battery connections. Battery negative (−) terminal is grounded.

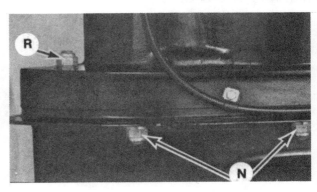
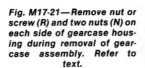

Fig. M17-21—Remove nut or screw (R) and two nuts (N) on each side of gearcase housing during removal of gearcase assembly. Refer to text.

DO NOT "spark" battery connections to check polarity.

DO NOT disconnect battery cables while engine is running.

DO NOT crank engine if ignition switch boxes are not grounded to engine.

The rectifier may be checked by disconnecting wires to rectifier and using a continuity tester or ohmmeter as follows: Connect a tester lead to ground and then alternately connect other tester lead to alternator terminals of rectifier. Note reading then reverse tester leads. Tester should indicate a short or open circuit with first test and opposite reading when tester leads are reversed. Connect a tester lead to positive rectifier terminal and alternately connect other tester lead to alternator terminals of rectifier. Note reading then reverse tester leads. Tester should show opposite reading when tester leads are reversed. Renew rectifier if testing indicated faulty circuits.

To check alternator stator, disconnect alternator leads from rectifier and connect an ohmmeter to alternator leads. Resistance reading should be approximately 0.30 ohms. There should be infinite resistance between either alternator lead and ground. Alternator output should be 13.5-15.5 amps.

LOWER UNIT

PROPELLER AND DRIVE CLUTCH. Protection for the motor is built into a special cushioning clutch in the propeller hub. No adjustment is possible on the propeller or clutch. Various pitch propellers are available and propeller should be selected to provide full throttle engine operation within range of 5300-5800 rpm. Propellers other than those recommended should not be used.

R&R AND OVERHAUL. Most service on the lower unit can be performed by detaching the gearcase from the drive shaft housing. To remove gearcase, shift outboard motor to neutral gear, then detach propeller and drain gearcase lubricant. Disconnect hydrasteer cables from rudder arm (26–Fig. M17-22) and remove rudder arm (26) and rudder (30). Remove anode plate (31) and nut under anode plate. Remove two screws from bottom of antiventilation plate. Remove nut or screw (R–Fig. M17-21) and two nuts (N) in equal increments from each side of gearcase. Disconnect speedometer hose, if needed, then withdrawn the lower unit gearcase assembly.

To disassemble gearcase, remove water tube guide (1–Fig. M17-22) and seal (2). Unscrew and remove water pump components (3 through 8). Use two water pump screws to extract seal carrier (9) with oil seal (10) and "O" ring (11). Position gearcase in a soft-jawed vise so propeller shaft is horizontal. Check and be sure gearcase is in neutral gear. Unscrew shift shaft bushing (20) and withdraw shift shaft (23) with bushing (20) from gearcase. DO NOT turn shift shaft during removal or gearcase may be shifted into forward or

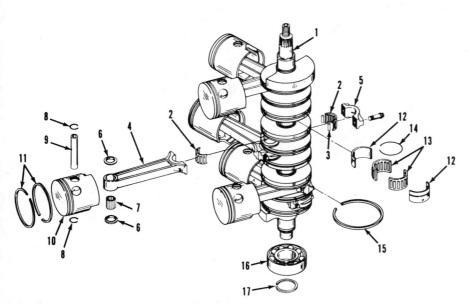

Fig. M17-19-Exploded view of crankshaft, connecting rod and piston assemblies.

1. Crankshaft	6. Spacers	10. Piston	14. Retaining ring
2. Bearing cage	7. Needle bearings	11. Piston rings	15. Seal ring
3. Roller	8. Clips	12. Bearing race	16. Ball bearing
4. Connecting rod	9. Piston pin	13. Bearing	17. Snap ring
5. Rod cap			

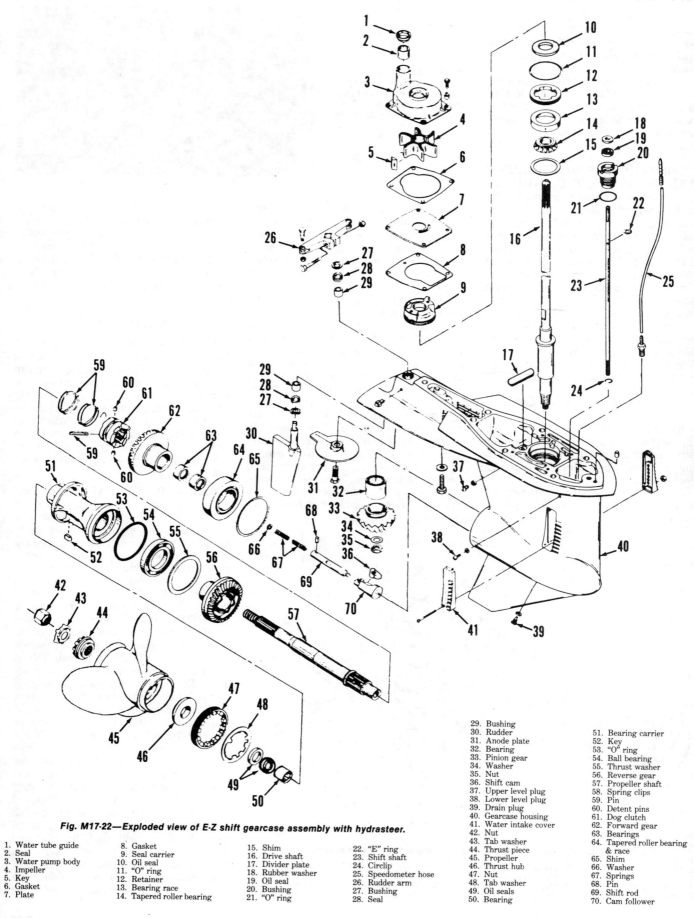

Fig. M17-22—Exploded view of E-Z shift gearcase assembly with hydrasteer.

1. Water tube guide	8. Gasket	15. Shim	22. "E" ring
2. Seal	9. Seal carrier	16. Drive shaft	23. Shift shaft
3. Water pump body	10. Oil seal	17. Divider plate	24. Circlip
4. Impeller	11. "O" ring	18. Rubber washer	25. Speedometer hose
5. Key	12. Retainer	19. Oil seal	26. Rudder arm
6. Gasket	13. Bearing race	20. Bushing	27. Bushing
7. Plate	14. Tapered roller bearing	21. "O" ring	28. Seal

29. Bushing	43. Tab washer	51. Bearing carrier
30. Rudder	44. Thrust piece	52. Key
31. Anode plate	45. Propeller	53. "O" ring
32. Bearing	46. Thrust hub	54. Ball bearing
33. Pinion gear	47. Nut	55. Thrust washer
34. Washer	48. Tab washer	56. Reverse gear
35. Nut	49. Oil seals	57. Propeller shaft
36. Shift cam	50. Bearing	58. Spring clips
37. Upper level plug		59. Pin
38. Lower level plug		60. Detent pins
39. Drain plug		61. Dog clutch
40. Gearcase housing		62. Forward gear
41. Water intake cover		63. Bearings
42. Nut		64. Tapered roller bearing
		& race
		65. Shim
		66. Washer
		67. Springs
		68. Pin
		69. Shift rod
		70. Cam follower

reverse gear position. Bend back tabs on tab washer (48) and unscrew nut (47), then use a suitable puller to remove bearing carrier (51).

NOTE: Do not apply side load or strike side of propeller shaft during or after removal of bearing carrier as shift rod (69) could break.

Withdraw propeller shaft from gearcase, but do not use excessive force or a puller. If shaft is lodged in gearcase, proceed as follows: Push propeller shaft inward so it contacts forward gear. Reinstall shift shaft and be sure gears are in neutral. Remove shift shaft and attempt to withdraw propeller shaft. If propeller shaft remains stuck, push shaft inward so it contacts forward gear. Reinstall bearing carrier and lay gearcase on its port side. Strike upper forward end of gearcase with a rubber mallet so shift cam (36) is dislodged and falls into a cavity in side of gearcase. Remove bearing carrier and propeller shaft.

To remove shift rod (69) from propeller shaft, remove spring clips (58) while being careful not to lose detent pins (60). Drive out pin (59) and remove shift rod (69) while being careful not to lose pin (68) which may fall from rod. Slide dog clutch (61) off shaft.

To disassemble drive shaft and associated parts, clamp upper end of drive shaft in a soft-jawed vise and remove retainer (12) and pinion gear nut (35). Tap gearcase off drive shaft and bearing. Note position and thickness of shims (15). Remove pinion gear (33) and forward gear (62). Use a suitable puller to extract cup of bearing (64). Note number and thickness of shims (65) and save for reassembly. Drive roller bearing (32) down into gear cavity for removal.

Inspect all components for excessive wear and damage. Install bearings on gears and drive shaft, and in gearcase (including shims 15 and 65). To determine gear mesh and forward gear backlash, proceed as follows: Install drive shaft components (12 through 16 and 32 through 35) and forward gear components (62 through 65). Tighten retainer (12) to 55 ft.-lbs. (75 N·m) and pinion nut (25) to 70 ft.-lbs. (95 N·m). Install tool 91-74776 in gear cavity of gearcase so it bottoms against shoulder of gearcase. Apply approximately 15 pounds (67 N) of upward pressure on drive shaft and rotate drive shaft several times to seat drive shaft bearing. While maintaining upward pressure on drive shaft, measure clearance between pinion gear and tool. Clearance should be 0.025 inch (0.64 mm). Add or delete shims (15) to obtain desired clearance.

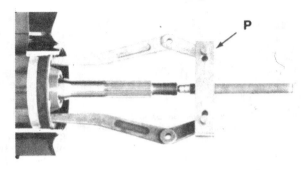

Fig. M17-23—Install a puller (P) as shown to preload forward gear bearing when determining gear backlash as outlined in text.

Apply Loctite 271 or 290 to drive shaft threads during final assembly.

With drive shaft and forward gear assemblies installed, install propeller shaft (without shift components) and bearing carrier (51), then install nut (47) until snug, but do not tighten. Attach a suitable puller to bearing carrier as shown in Fig. M17-23 and apply 45 in.-lbs. (5.1 N·m) torque to puller screw. Rotate drive shaft several times to seat forward gear bearing. Install backlash measuring tool 91-53459 on drive shaft as shown in Fig. M17-24 and set up a dial indicator to read movement at "I" on backlash tool. Recheck torque on bearing carrier puller (45 in.-lbs. [5.1 N·m]). Measure forward gear backlash by applying upward pressure and turning drive shaft. Dial indicator should measure 0.010-0.015 inch (0.25-0.38 mm) backlash. Adjust backlash by adding or deleting shims (65 – Fig. M17-22). Changing shim thickness by 0.001 inch (0.025 mm) will alter backlash by 0.0015 inch (0.038 mm).

To properly adjust spring tension in shift rod (69), install springs (67) and pin (68) in shift rod. Insert tool 91-86642, or an old pin (59) with a ground-down end, between springs as shown in Fig. M17-25. Tool (T) or pin should be centered in shift rod slot within 1/64 inch (0.397 mm). Adjust tool position by installing washers (66) at ends of springs (67).

Assemble remainder of lower unit by reversing disassembly procedure while noting the following points: Install thrust washer (55 – Fig. M17-22) so larger diameter side is nearer reverse gear (56), then press bearing (54) on gear. Lip of inner seal (49) should face in and lip of outer seal (49) should face propeller (out). Install spring clips (58) so bent end of each spring engages the hole in one of the detent pins (60). Spring clips should be wound in opposite directions around dog clutch (61) and must not overlap. Use heavy grease to hold shift cam (36) in cam follower (70) with "UP" side facing up. Be sure "E" ring (22) and circlip (24) are seated on shift shaft (23) before inserting shaft. Tighten

bushing (20) after tightening bearing carrier nut (47). Tighten bearing carrier nut (47) to 210 ft.-lbs. (284 N·m).

Assemble oil seal (10) to seal carrier (9) so spring end of oil seal is toward top of seal carrier. If reusing old impeller (4), install impeller so vanes rotate in same direction as previous operation. Be sure key (5) is properly installed. Tighten water pump screws to 30 in.-lbs. (3.4 N·m).

Do not apply excessive grease to drive shaft splines; there must not be grease on tops of drive shaft or shift shaft. Install splined seal on drive shaft splines with splined seal end towards top of drive shaft, then install remaining seal with small end towards top of drive shaft. Shift lower unit to forward gear and move shift lever on engine to forward gear position. Tighten gearcase fasteners to 40 ft.-lbs. (54 N·m).

POWER TILT/TRIM

FLUID AND BLEEDING. Recommended fluid is SAE 10W-30 or 10W-40. Fill reservoir to "FULL" mark on dipstick with the outboard motor in the full-down position.

Fig. M17-24—Install backlash measuring tool 91-53459 (T) and a dial indicator (D) using a suitable adapter kit (A). Position dial indicator pointer on the "I" line of tool (T). Proceed as outlined in text.

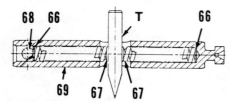

Fig. M17-25—Cross section of shift rod (69). Center tool (T) using washers (66) at ends of springs (67).

The hydraulic circuit is self-bleeding as the tilt/trim system is operated through several cycles. After servicing system, be sure to check reservoir level after filling and operating system.

HYDRAULIC TESTING. The pump can be checked by connecting a 5000 psi (34.5 MPa) test gage alternately to the UP (U–Fig. M17-27) and DOWN (D) pump ports. Note that the pump motor blue wire with white tracer is the positive battery connection to pressurize the UP (U) port and connecting the positive battery lead to the pump motor green wire with white tracer will pressurize the DOWN (D) port. Pressure at the UP (U) port should be 3100-3500 psi (21.4-24.1 MPa) and should not drop lower than 1500 psi (10.3 MPa) after pumping stops. Pressure at the DOWN (D) port should be 1500-1900 psi (10.3-13.1 MPa) and should not drop lower than 750 psi (5.2 MPa) after pumping stops.

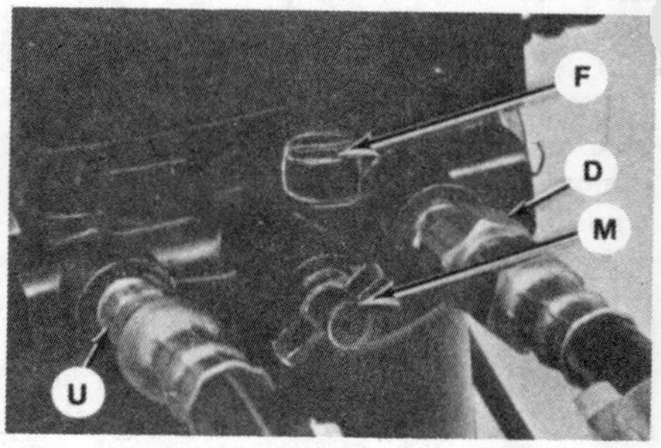

Fig. M17-27—View identifying reservoir fill screw (F), manual release valve (M), up port (U) and down port (D) on power tilt/trim pump.

Illustrations courtesy Mercury

OUTBOARD MARINE CORPORATION

EVINRUDE MOTORS	JOHNSON MOTORS
4143 N. 27th Street	200 Sea-horse Drive
Milwaukee, Wisconsin 53216	Waukegan, Illinois 60085

EVINRUDE AND JOHNSON
28 HP (1987-1989), 30 HP AND 35 HP (1976-1989)

EVINRUDE MODELS

Year Produced	30 HP	35 HP
1976	....	35602, 35603, *35652, *35653
1977	....	35702, 35703, *35752, *35753
1978	....	35802, 35803, *35852, *35853
1979	....	35902, 35903, *35952, *35953
1980	....	35RCS, 35RLCS, *35ECS, *35ELCS
1981	....	35RCI, 35RLCI, *35ECI, *35ELCI
1982	....	35RCN, 35RLCN, *35ECN, *35ELCN
1983	....	35RCT, 35RLCT, *35ECT, *35ELCT, *35TELCT
1984	*30ECR, *30ELCR	35RCR, 35RLCR, *35ECR, *35ELCR, *35TELCR
1985	30RCO, 30RLCO, *30ECO, *30ELCO, *30TECO, *30TELCO	....
1986	30RCD, 30RLCD, *30ECD, *30ELCD, *30TECD, *30TELCD	....

	28 HP	30 HP	35 HP
1987	E28ESLCU*	E30ECU* E30RLCU, E30ELCU*, E30BACU, E30TECU*, E30BALCU, E30TELCU*	. . . . .
1988	E28ESLCC*	E30RCC, E30ECC* E30RLCC, E30ELCC*, E30BACC,	. . . . .

JOHNSON MODELS

Year Produced	30 HP	35 HP
1976	....	35602, 35603, *35652, *35653
1977	....	35702, 35703, *35752, *35753
1978	....	35802, 35803, *35852, *35853
1979	....	35902, 35903, *35952, *35953
1980	....	35RCS, 35RLCS, *35ECS, *35ELCS
1981	....	35RCI, 35RLCI, *35ECI, *35ELCI
1982	....	35RCN, 35RLCN, *35ECN, *35ELCN
1983	....	35RCT, 35RLCT, *35ECT, *35ELCT, *35TELCT
1984	*30ECR, *30ELCR	35RCR, 35RLCR, *35ECR, *35ELCR, *35TELCR
1985	30RCO, 30RLCO, *30ECO, *30ELCO, *30TECO, *30TELCO	....
1986	30RCD, 30RLCD, *30ECD, *30ELCD, *30TECD, *30TELCD	....

	28 HP	30 HP	35 HP
1987	J28ESLCU*	J30RCU, J30ECU* J30RLCU, J30ELCU*, J30BACU, J30TECU*, J30BALCU, J30TELCU*	. . . . .
1988	J28ESLCC*	J30RCC, J30ECC* J30RLCC, J30ELCC*,	. . . . .

Year Produced	28 HP	30 HP	35 HP	Year Produced	28 HP	30 HP	35 HP
		E30TECC*, E30BALCC, E30TELCC*				J30BACC, J30TECC*, J30BALCC, J30TELCC*	
1989	E28ESLCE*	E30RCE, E30ECE* E30RLCE, E30ELCE*, E30BACE, E30TECE*, E30BALCE, E30TELCE*	....	1989	J28ESLCE*	J30RCE, J30ECE* J30RLCE, J30ELCE*, J30BACE, J30TECE*, J30BALCE, J30TELCE*	....

Electric start models.

CONDENSED SERVICE DATA

TUNE-UP

Hp/rpm 28/5000
  30/5500
  35/5200-5800
Bore . . . . .3.000 in.
  (76.20 mm)
Stroke . . . . .2.250 in.
  (57.15 mm)
Number of Cylinders 2
Spark Plug—Champion:
  1976 . . . . .UL81J
  Electrode Gap . . . . .0.030 in.
  (0.76 mm)
  1977-1985 . . . . .QL77J4*
  Electrode Gap . . . . .0.040 in.
  (1.0 mm)
  1986-1989 . . . . .QL77JC4*
  Electrode Gap . . . . .0.040 in.
  (1.0 mm)
Ignition Type:
  1976 . . . . .Breaker Point
  Breaker Point Gap . . . . .0.020 in.
  (0.51 mm)
  1977-1989 . . . . .CDI
Carburetor Make . . . . .OMC
Idle Speed (in gear):
  Prior to 1986 . . . . .650 rpm
  After 1985 . . . . .650-700 rpm
Fuel:Oil Ratio . . . . .See Text

*Champion QL78V spark plugs are recommended 1985 and later models when operated at sustained high speeds. Renew surface gap spark plug if center electrode is more than 1/32 inch (0.79 mm) below flat surface of the plug end.

SIZES—CLEARANCES

Piston Ring End Gap . . . . .0.007-0.017 in.
  (0.18-0.43 mm)
Lower Piston Ring Side Clearance:
  1976-1984 . . . . .0.0015-0.0040 in.
  (0.038-0.102 mm)
  1985-1989 . . . . .0.004 in. Max.
  (0.102 mm)

SIZES—CLEARANCES CONT.

Piston Skirt Clearance:
  1976-1978 . . . . .0.0030-0.0050 in.
  (0.076-0.127 mm)
  1979-1982 . . . . .0.0035-0.0065 in.
  (0.089-0.165 mm)
  1983-1984 . . . . .0.0024-0.0044 in.
  (0.061-0.118 mm)
  1985-1989 . . . . .See Text
Standard Cylinder Bore Diameter . . . . .2.9995-3.0005 in.
  (76.187-76.213 mm)
Max. Allowable Out-of-Round . . . . .0.003 in.
  (0.08 mm)
Max. Allowable Taper .0.002 in.
  (0.05 mm)
Crankshaft Journal Diameters—
  Top Main:
  1969-1976 .0.9995-1.0000 in.
  (25.387-25.400 mm)
  1977 . . . . .1.2495-1.2500 in.
  (31.737-31.750 mm)
  1978-1989 .1.2510-1.2515 in.
  (31.775-31.788 mm)
  Center Main:
  1969-1977 .0.9995-1.0000 in.
  (25.387-25.400 mm)
  1978-1982 .1.1805-1.1810 in.
  (29.985-29.997 mm)
  1983-1989 .1.1833-1.1838 in.
  (30.056-30.068 mm)
  Bottom Main:
  1969-1976 .0.9995-1.0000 in.
  (25.387-25.400 mm)
  1977-1989 .0.9842-0.9846 in.
  (24.999-25.009 mm)
Crankpin . . . . .1.1823-1.1828 in.
  (30.030-30.043 mm)
Crankshaft End Play:
  1969-1976 . . . . .0.009-0.023 in.
  (0.23-0.58 mm)
  1977-1978 . . . . .0.003-0.011 in.
  (0.08-0.28 mm)
  1979-1984 . . . . .0.000-0.025 in.
  (0.00-0.63 mm)

SIZES—CLEARANCES CONT.

Lower Unit Diametral Clearances –
1976-1984:

Propeller Shaft to Forward
Gear Bushing . . . . .0.0010-0.0020 in.
(0.025-0.051 mm)

Propeller Shaft to Reverse
Gear Bushing . . . . .0.0005-0.0015 in.
(0.013-0.038 mm)

Bushing to Reverse Gear . . . . .0.0005-0.0020 in.
(0.013-0.051 mm)

TIGHTENING TORQUES

Connecting Rod:

Prior to 1977 . . . . .180-186 in.-lbs.
(20.3-21.0 N·m)

1976-1987 . . . . .29-31 ft.-lbs.
(39.3-42.0 N·m)

1988-1989 . . . . .30-32 ft.-lbs.
(40.7-43.4 N·m)

Crankcase Halves:

Six Main Bearing Screws . . . . .168-192 in.-lbs.
(19-22 N·m)

Eight Outer Screws .60-84 in.-lbs.
(7-9 N·m)

Cylinder Head . . . . .216-240 in.-lbs.
(24-27 N·m)

Flywheel . . . . .100-105 ft.-lbs.
(136-143 N·m)

Spark Plug . . . . .216-240 in.-lbs.
(24-27 N·m)

Standard Screws:

No. 6 . . . . .7-10 in.-lbs.
(0.8-1.2 N·m)

No. 8 . . . . .15-22 in.-lbs.
(1.6-2.4 N·m)

No. 10 . . . . .25-35 in.-lbs.
(2.8-4.0 N·m)

No. 12 . . . . .35-40 in.-lbs.
(4.0-4.6 N·m)

¼ Inch . . . . .60-80 in.-lbs.
(7-9 N·m)

5/16 Inch . . . . .120-140 in.-lbs.
(14-16 N·m)

⅜ Inch . . . . .220-240 in.-lbs.
(24-27 N·m)

7/16 Inch . . . . .340-360 in.-lbs.
(38-40 N·m)

LUBRICATION

The power head is lubricated by oil mixed with the fuel. The recommended fuel is regular leaded or unleaded gasoline with a minimum octane rating of 67 on models produced after 1980, and 86 on models prior to 1981. If the recommended fuel is not available, gasoline containing not more than 10 percent ethanol alcohol or gasoline containing not more than 5 percent methanol alcohol with 5 percent co-solvent additives may be used. Do not use gasoline exceeding the specified alcohol content regardless of octane rating. Discontinue the use of alcohol extended gasoline if fuel system problems are encountered.

The recommended oil is Evinrude or Johnson Outboard Lubricant or a suitable equivalent NMMA (formerly known as BIA) certified TC-W or TC-WII engine oil. The manufacturer recommends using only oil certified TC-WII on models after 1988. The recommended fuel:oil ratio for normal service and during engine break-in is 50:1.

NOTE: OMC service bulletin 2211, issued September 1988, recommends using a 50:1 fuel:oil ratio on all recreational outboard motors that were previously recommended for a 100:1 fuel:oil mixture. For 1989, Accumix and Accumix R fuel and oil mixing systems have been changed to a 50:1 ratio.

On models so recommended, a 100:1 fuel:oil mixture may be used if an approved oil formulated for 100:1 mixture is used, but only after the engine is completely broken-in and if the motor is used on a frequent basis. Do not use a 100:1 mixture if motor is used infrequently or, if during nonuse, the motor is stored in a high-humidity area or an area of wide-scale temperature changes, or if motor is operated at constant high speeds.

The lower unit gears and bearings are lubricated by oil contained in the gearcase. The recommended oil is OMC HI-VIS Gearcase Lube. The gearcase oil level should be checked after every 50 hours of operation and the gearcase should be drained and filled with new oil every 100 hours or once each season, whichever occurs first.

The gearcase oil is drained and filled through the same plug port. An oil level (vent) port is used to indicate the full level of the gearcase with oil and to ease oil drainage.

To drain the oil, place the outboard motor in a vertical position. Remove drain plug and oil level plug and allow the lubricant to drain into a suitable container.

To fill the gearcase with oil, place the outboard motor in a vertical position. Add oil through drain plug opening with an oil feeder until the oil begins to overflow from oil level plug port. Reinstall oil level plug with a new gasket, if needed, and tighten. Remove oil feeder, then reinstall drain plug with a new gasket, if needed, and tighten.

FUEL SYSTEM

CARBURETOR. Refer to Fig. OM11-1 for view of carburetor typical to all models prior to 1989. Carburetor used on 1989 models is similar. Refer to Fig. OM11-2.

NOTE: The manufacturer does not recommend submerging carburetor components in carburetor or parts cleaning solutions. An aerosol type carburetor cleaner is recommended to clean carburetor. The float and other components made of plastic and rubber should not be subjected to some cleaning solutions. Safety eyewear and hand protection are recommended when working with solvent.

Initial setting of low speed needle (5—Figs. OM11-1 or OM11-2) is one turn open from a lightly seated position on models prior to 1977, 1¼ turns open on 1977-1986 models, one turn open on 1987 and 1988 models and 1¾ turns open on 1989 models. Make final idle mixture adjustment with engine running in gear at normal operating temperature. High speed fuel mixture is metered by fixed high speed jet (23). Note that 1989 models are equipped with intermediate jet (I—Fig. OM11-2). Idle speed should be 650 rpm on models prior to 1987 and 650-700 rpm on all other models. For optimum results when adjusting idle speed, boat should be in the water with the correct propeller installed. Engine should be running in forward gear at normal operating temperature with boat movement unrestrained.

To check float level, remove float bowl and invert carburetor. Place OMC Float Gage 324891 on float bowl gasket surface as shown in Fig. OM11-3. Make sure float gage is not pushing down on float. Float should be between notches on side of float gage marked 25 THRU 75 HP. Carefully bend float arm to adjust level. If float gage 324891 is not available, adjust float so float is level and parallel with float gage surface. To check float drop, hold carburetor upright and allow float to hang by its own weight. Measure from float bowl gasket surface to bottom of float 180 degrees from inlet needle. Carefully bend tang on float arm (adjacent to inlet needle) to set float drop to $1^{1}/_{8}$ to $1^{5}/_{8}$ inches (28.6-41.3 mm) on 1989 models and $1^{1}/_{8}$ to $1^{1}/_{2}$ inches (28.6-38.1 mm) on earlier models. Apply a suitable thread locking compound to float bowl screws upon reassembly.

SPEED CONTROL LINKAGE. The speed control lever rotates the magneto armature plate and the carburetor throttle valve is synchronized to open as ignition timing is advanced. A cam attached to the bottom of the magneto armature plate moves cam follower (16 and 17—Fig. OM11-1), which opens the throttle plate (12), via link (15) and lever (14). It is very important that the ignition timing and throttle plate opening be correctly synchronized to obtain satisfactory operation.

Before adjusting the speed control linkage, make certain that roller (17) is contacting the cam and that choke linkage is not holding throttle partially open. Turn the speed control grip until the cam follower roller is centered be-

tween the two index marks as shown in Fig. OM11-4. Loosen throttle shaft screw (S—Fig. OM11-5), hold throttle closed and retighten screw (S). Check to make certain that throttle begins to open as marks on cam (Fig. OM11-4) pass the follower roller when speed control is advanced. Adjust throttle control rod by shifting unit to forward gear, then advance throttle so throttle lever is against cylinder stop. Push throttle control rod (R—Fig. OM11-6) to full open position

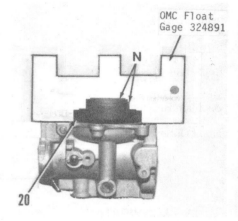

Fig. OM11-3—To check float level, invert carburetor and place OMC Float Gage 324891 on carburetor body as shown. Make sure float gage is not pushing down on float (20). Float should be between notches (N) on side of gage marked 25 THRU 75 HP. Bend float arm to adjust.

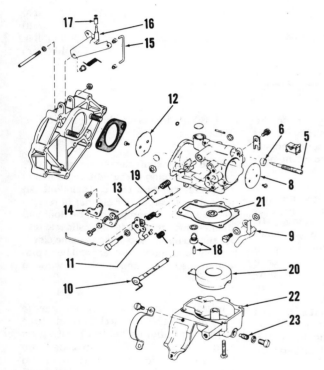

Fig. OM11-1—Exploded view of carburetor typical of all models. Choke components are not used on models after 1983.

5. Idle mixture needle
6. Retainer
8. Choke plate
9. Choke lever
10. Choke shaft
11. Choke bellcrank
12. Throttle plate
13. Throttle shaft
14. Throttle lever
15. Link
16. Follower
17. Follower roller
18. Inlet valve
19. Float pivot
20. Float
21. Nozzle gasket
22. Float chamber
23. Main jet

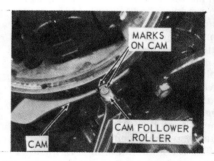

Fig. OM11-4—Refer to text when checking the speed control linkage.

Fig. OM11-2—View of carburetor used on 1989, 20 and 25 hp models. Refer to Fig. OM11-1 for component identification, except intermediate jet (I).

Fig. OM11-5—Loosen throttle shaft screw (S) to adjust linkage as outlined in text.

and move collar (C) so it is against pivot block (B). Tighten collar screw securely. Note that offset on pivot block (B) must face toward front of engine for proper operation.

Idle speed stop screw (Fig. OM11-7) should be adjusted to approximately 650 rpm on models prior to 1986 and 650-700 rpm on 1986 and later models. For optimum results when adjusting idle speed, boat should be in the water with the correct propeller installed. Engine should be running in forward gear at normal operating temperature with boat movement unrestrained.

REED VALVES. The reed type inlet valves (6—Fig. OM11-8) and reed stops (7) are attached to reed plate (5). Reed plate assembly is attached to power head with screw (3).

The reed petals (6) should seat very lightly against reed plate (5) throughout the entire length of reed with the least possible tension. Renew reed petals if broken, cracked, warped or bent, Do not attempt to repair reed petals (6). Seating surface of reed plate (5) must be smooth and flat and reeds must be centered over inlet holes in plate. Alignment recesses are provided at one location for each set of reed petals to assist in centering the reed petals. Make certain that reed stops (7) are not damaged and that stops are centered behind the reed petals. Damage to the reed petals (6) may result if reed stops (7) are dam-

aged or improperly centered over reed petals.

The oil drain valve reed petal (4) should be centered over hole on outside of reed plate. Check petal and seating surface of reed plate (5) carefully and make certain that hole is clean and open.

FUEL PUMP. The diaphragm type fuel pump is mounted on one of the cylinder transfer port covers and is actuated by vacuum and pressure pulsations in the crankcase. Service parts for the pump are not available and damage to the pump can be corrected only by renewing the pump and fuel filter assembly.

If fuel delivery problems are noted, first remove and clean fuel filter located under fuel pump cover. Install filter with lip of element facing away from pump cover. Remove and blow through fuel lines to ensure lines are clean and open. Test fuel lines and remote tank installation using a suitable vacuum pump and gage. If over 4 inches (13.5 kPa) vacuum is required to draw fuel from tank, check for restrictions in fuel tank and lines. Note that remote fuel tank must not be more than 24 inches (61 cm) below fuel pump.

To test fuel pump, install a suitable pressure gage between fuel pump and carburetor and start engine. Fuel pump pressure should be 1 psi (7 kPa) at 600 rpm, 1.5 psi (10.3 kPa) at 2500-3000 rpm and 2.5 psi (17 kPa) at 4500 rpm. Fuel pump mounting screws should be treated with OMC Nut Lock or a suitable equivalent thread locking compound and tightened to 24-36 in.-lbs. (3-4 N·m). Tighten fuel pump cover screws to 10-15 in.-lbs. (1-2 N·m).

IGNITION

Models Prior to 1977

Breaker point gap should be 0.020 inch (0.51 mm) and both sets of points should be synchronized so they open exactly 180 degrees apart. The manufac-

turer provides a timing fixture (OMC part 386635) to be used for adjusting and synchronizing breaker points. The fixture is installed on crankshaft in place of flywheel as shown in Fig. OM11-9, and used in conjunction with a timing light (with battery) or continuity meter.

To synchronize the points using the timing fixture and light, remove flywheel and install timing fixture, making sure it is properly fitted over flywheel key. Disconnect condenser and magneto coil leads from both sets of breaker points. Attach test light or meter to the opening set of breaker points and to a suitable ground. Bulb should go out when points are opened. Turn crankshaft until fixture pointer rests midway between the two embossed armature plate timing marks shown in Fig. OM11-9. Adjust the gap until points just open when timing fixture pointer is between the two marks (TM) on armature plate. Turn the crankshaft exactly $\frac{1}{2}$ turn until the opposite pointer of timing fixture is aligned; then adjust the other set of points.

NOTE: Timing fixture pointer legs are marked "T" and "B" to indicate upper and lower cylinders, respectively.

Side of breaker point cam marked "TOP" should face up. Face of coil shoes should be flush with machined surfaces on armature plate. One of the three points is shown at (F). The drive key for flywheel and cam should be installed with marked end down and edge parallel with center of crankshaft.

Timing mark shown in Fig. OM11-10 or Fig. OM11-11 should align with 34 degrees flywheel mark at full throttle. Turn timing stop screw (S—Fig. OM11-12) to adjust full throttle ignition timing.

Models After 1976

OPERATION. Models produced during 1977-1988 are equipped with CD2 breakerless capacitor discharge ignition system. Refer to Fig. OM11-13 for wir-

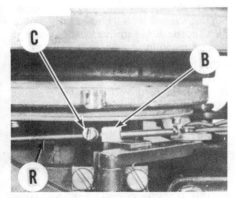

Fig. OM11-6—Collar (C) should touch pivot block (B) when throttle control rod (R) is in full forward position. Refer to text.

Fig. OM11-7—Idle speed stop screw should be set to provide an idle speed of approximately 650 rpm.

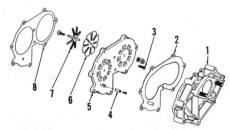

Fig. OM11-8—Exploded view of reed valve and inlet manifold.

1. Inlet manifold
2. Manifold to plate gasket
3. Plate retaining screw
4. Oil drain valve
5. Reed plate
6. Reed petals
7. Reed stop
8. Crankcase to plate gasket

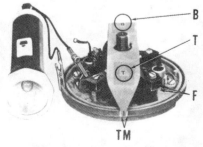

Fig. OM11-9—View showing timing fixture and timing test light attached. Refer to Text for setting breaker point gap.

Fig. OM11-10—On manual rewind start models, timing mark (TM) should align with 34-degree mark on flywheel of 1976 models, 30-31-degree mark on 1977-1985 models and 29-31-degree mark on 1986 and later models. Thirty-four degree mark is identified. Turn screw (S—Fig. OM11-12) to adjust timing.

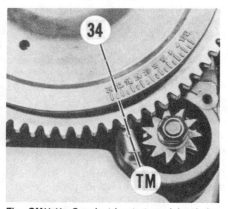

Fig. OM11-11—On electric start models, timing mark (TM) should align with 34-degree mark on flywheel on 1976 models, 30-31-degree mark on 1977-1985 models and 29-31-degree mark on 1986 and later models. Thirty-four degree mark is identified. Turn screw (S—Fig. OM11-12) to adjust timing.

Fig. OM11-12—View of ignition timing adjusting screw.

ing schematic. A charge coil and sensor coil are located under the flywheel. Two magnets in flywheel induce a current in the charge coil which is rectified and directed to a capacitor for storage. The two flywheel magnets also induce current in the sensor coil to provide a positive charge on the gate of one of two silicone controlled rectifiers (SCR'S). The positive charge opens the SCR and allows the charged capacitor to discharge through the SCR and primary circuit of the ignition coil. The rapid coil field buildup induces a secondary voltage that fires the spark plug. Diodes, SCR'S and capacitor are contained in the power pack assembly and are not available individually.

Models after 1988 are equipped with CD2USL ignition system. Except for the ignition coils, all CD2U components are located under the flywheel. Refer to Fig. OM11-14 for wiring schematic. The breakdown of the CD2USL model number is as follows: CD—capacitor discharge; 2—two cylinders; U—under flywheel ignition; L—engine speed limiter; S-S.L.O.W. (speed limiting overheat warning) function. The S.L.O.W. function limits engine speed to approximately 2000 rpm if engine temperature exceeds 180° F (82° C). Ignition system model number is printed on top of ignition module located under flywheel. The power pack and sensor coil are integrated into a single ignition module assembly instead of separate components as in earlier CD2 systems.

All Models

IGNITION TIMING. To check the ignition timing, first mount the outboard motor on a boat or a suitable test tank and immerse the lower unit. Connect a suitable timing light to the top cylinder (No. 1) spark plug lead. Start the engine and adjust the speed control until the engine is running at full throttle. On manual rewind start models, timing mark (TM—Fig. OM11-10) should align with the flywheel 34-degree mark on models prior to 1982, 30-31-degree mark on 1982-1985 models and 29-31-degree mark on 1986 and later models. On electric start models, timing mark (TM—Fig. OM11-11) should align with the flywheel 34-degree mark on models prior to 1982, 30-31-degree mark on 1982-1985 models and 29-31-degree mark on 1986 and later models.

NOTE: Two sets of timing grids are located on flywheel. Use grid marked "CD" for rope start models and grid marked "ELEC CD" for models equipped with electric start.

To adjust timing on all models, turn timing stop screw (S—Fig. OM11-12).

Each complete turn is equivalent to approximately one degree. Turing screw (S) clockwise advances ignition timing. Backfiring and popping may be due to improperly connected wiring. Refer to wiring schematics in Figs. OM11-13 and OM11-14.

CD2 Ignition

TROUBLE-SHOOTING. On models prior to 1985, the 4-wire connector plugs connect the charge and sensor coil leads to the power pack. The 3-wire connector plugs connect the power pack and ignition coils. On models after 1984, a 5-wire connector is used between the power pack and armature plate. On models prior to 1985, check to make sure the black/white wire in the 4-wire connector is positioned in connector terminal B. Also check to make sure the number 1 coil (orange) wire is in the 3-wire connector B terminal and that it connects with the power pack orange/blue wire in the other connector B terminal. On models after 1984, check to make sure the black/white wire in the 5-wire connector is positioned in connector terminal B of both connector halves. Also check to make sure the orange/blue power pack lead is connected to the number 1 ignition coil.

NOTE: Outer edges of charge coil and sensor coil must be flush with machined surface of armature plate to provide the proper clearance between coils and flywheel magnets. OMC locating ring 317001 may be used to simplify this procedure. Place locating ring over machined bosses on armature plate, push coil out against locating ring and tighten mounting screws.

To check charge coil output, use Merc-O-Tronic Model 781, Stevens Model CD77 or a suitable peak voltage tester. Disconnect connector between armature plate and power pack. Connect black tester lead to stator lead connector terminal A and red tester lead to terminal D. Turn tester knobs to Negative and 500. Crank engine while observing tester. If tester reading is below 230 volts, check condition of charge coil wiring and connectors, and verify pin location in connector. If wiring and connectors are in acceptable condition, check charge coil resistance as follows: Connect an ohmmeter to terminals A and D in stator plate lead connector. Renew charge coil if resistance is not 500-650 ohms on models prior to 1986, or 550-600 ohms on 1986-1988 models. Connect negative ohmmeter lead to stator plate (ground) and positive ohmmeter lead to connector terminal A, then to connector terminal D. Infinite resistance should exist between A terminal and stator plate and D terminal and stator plate. If not, charge coil or charge coil lead is shorted to ground.

To check sensor coil, connect an ohmmeter to terminals B and C in stator plate lead connector. Renew sensor coil if resistance is not 30-50 ohms. Connect negative ohmmeter lead to stator plate (ground) and positive ohmmeter lead to connector terminal B, then to connector terminal C. Infinite resistance should exist between B terminal and stator plate and C terminal and stator plate. If not, sensor coil or sensor coil lead is shorted to ground. To check sensor coil output, use Merc-O-Tronic Model 781, Stevens Model CD77 or a suitable peak voltage tester. Connect black tester lead to stator lead connector terminal C and red tester lead to terminal B. On Merc-O-Tronic Model 781, turn knobs to Positive and 5, and on Stevens Model CD77, turn knobs to S and 5. Crank engine while observing tester. Reverse tester leads and repeat test. Sensor coil output on both tests should be 2 volts or more on models prior to 1987 and 1.5 volts or more on 1987 and 1988 models. Renew sensor coil if output is not as specified.

To check power pack output, first reconnect connector between armature plate and power pack. Use Merc-O-Tronic Model 781, Stevens Model CD77 or a suitable peak voltage tester. Connect black tester lead to a suitable engine ground. Connect red tester lead to wire leading to either ignition coil. Turn tester knobs to Negative and 500. Crank engine while observing tester. Repeat test on other lead. Renew power pack if readings are not at least 180 volts or higher on models prior to 1985 or 200 volts or higher on models after 1984.

To test ignition coils, disconnect high tension lead at ignition coil. On models prior to 1985, disconnect 3-wire connector and insert a jumper lead in terminal B of the ignition coil end of connector. Connect ohmmeter positive lead to the B terminal jumper wire and ohmmeter negative lead to a good engine ground. On models after 1984, disconnect coil primary wire at coil and connect ohmmeter positive lead to coil primary terminal and negative lead to a good engine ground or to coil ground tab. Ignition coil primary resistance should be 0.05-0.15 ohm on all models.

To check coil secondary resistance, move ohmmeter negative lead to the high tension terminal. Secondary resistance should be 225-325 ohms on models prior to 1986 and 250-300 ohms on models after 1985. Repeat procedure on number 2 ignition coil.

CD2USL Ignition System

TROUBLE-SHOOTING. Disconnect

spark plug leads from spark plugs and connect a suitable spark tester. Set tester spark gap to ½ inch (12.7 mm). On models so equipped, install emergency ignition cutoff clip and lanyard. Crank engine and observe spark tester. If an acceptable spark is noted at each spark gap, perform RUNNING OUTPUT TEST.

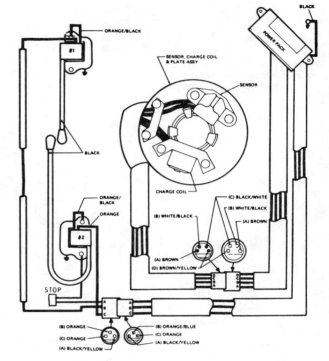

Fig. OM11-13—Typical wiring schematic of ignition circuit on models prior to 1989. Electric start models have a key switch in place of STOP button.

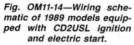

Fig. OM11-14—Wiring schematic of 1989 models equipped with CD2USL ignition and electric start.

B. Black
R. Red
Y. Yellow
Br. Brown
Y/R. Yellow with red tracer
R/Br. Red with brown tracer
R/Or. Red with orange tracer
Y/Bl. Yellow with blue tracer
Or/G. Orange with green tracer
Gr/Y. Gray with yellow tracer
Or/Bl. Orange with blue tracer

If spark is noted at only one spark gap, perform IGNITION PLATE OUTPUT TEST as described in this section. If no spark is noted at either spark gap, perform STOP CIRCUIT TEST.

NOTE: If acceptable spark is noted at each spark gap during spark output test but en-

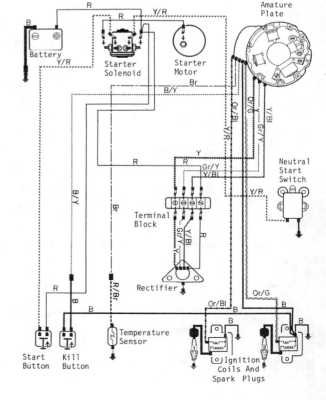

gine pops and backfires during starting or running, ignition system may be out of time. Be sure orange/blue primary wire is connected to number 1 ignition coil, spark plug high tension leads are properly connected, flywheel is properly located on crankshaft and speed control linkage is properly adjusted.

STOP CIRCUIT TEST. Remove spark plug leads from spark plugs and connect a suitable spark tester. Disconnect stop circuit connector (Fig. OM11-15). Make sure ignition emergency cutoff clip and lanyard are installed on models so equipped. Crank engine and observe spark tester. If no spark is noted, per-

form IGNITION PLATE OUTPUT TEST. If normal spark is noted, connect ohmmeter between engine ground and the one-pin stop circuit connector (Fig. OM11-15). Ohmmeter should show infinite resistance. If meter shows continuity, repair short in wiring or renew stop button. Depress stop button or remove emergency cutoff clip and note ohmmeter. If ohmmeter does not indicate continuity, repair open in wiring or renew stop button.

IGNITION PLATE OUTPUT TEST. Disconnect spark plug leads to prevent accidental starting. Remove primary leads from ignition coils. Connect number 1 ignition coil primary lead to the red lead of Stevens load adapter PL-88 and black lead of load adapter to engine ground.

NOTE: If Stevens load adapter is not available, fabricate load adapter using a 10 ohm, 10 watt resistor (Radio Shack part 271-132) or equivalent.

Connect red test lead of CD77 or equivalent peak reading voltmeter to red lead of Stevens load adapter PL-88 and black test lead to engine ground. Set CD voltmeter to Positive and 500. Crank engine and note meter. Repeat test procedure on number 2 ignition coil primary lead. If CD voltmeter indicates 175 volts or higher on both tests, perform IGNITION COIL TESTS. If one primary lead shows no output, renew ignition module. If both tests indicate no output, perform CHARGE COIL RESISTANCE TEST.

CHARGE COIL RESISTANCE TEST. Remove manual starter and flywheel. Remove two ignition module mounting screws and disconnect module brown and brown/yellow bullet connectors. Connect ohmmeter between brown and brown/yellow charge coil connectors. Renew charge coil if resistance is not within 535-585 ohms. Connect one ohmmeter lead to engine ground and connect other ohmmeter lead to brown charge coil lead, then to brown/yellow charge coil lead. Renew charge coil if ohmmeter shows continuity between engine ground and either wire. If charge coil tests acceptable, renew ignition module.

NOTE: When installing charge coil or ignition module, use OMC Locating Ring 334994 to properly position components on armature plate. Place ring over machined surfaces on armature plate, push component outward against locating ring and tighten mounting screws to 30-40 in.-lbs. (3.4-4.5 N·m).

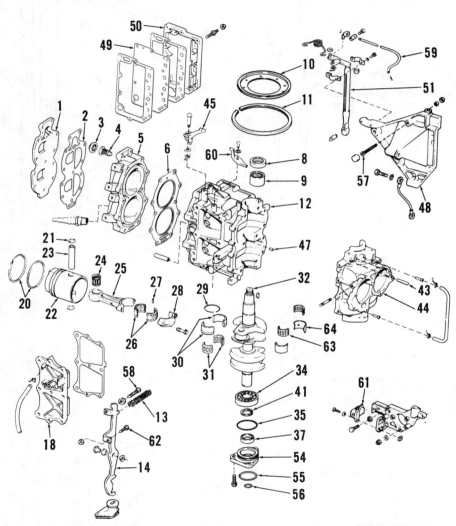

Fig. OM11-16—Exploded view of early model power head. Later models are similar.

1. Cover	21. Retaining rings	35. "O" ring
2. Gasket	22. Piston	37. Lower bearing seal
3. Seal	23. Piston pin	41. Snap ring
4. Thermostat	24. Needle bearing	43. Taper pin
5. Cylinder head	25. Connecting rod	44. Crankcase front half
6. Gasket	26. Bearing cage	45. Lockout assy.
8. Upper seal	27. Roller	47. Bearing retaining
9. Top main bearing	28. Rod cap	dowel
10. Support	29. Retaining ring	48. Starter bracket
11. Retainer	30. Center bearing	49. Exhaust inner cover
12. Cylinder	outer race	50. Outer cover
13. Spring	31. Center main	51. Speed control shaft
14. Shift lock	bearings & cage	54. Seal housing
18. Transfer port cover	32. Crankshaft	55. "O" ring
20. Piston rings	34. Lower main bearing	56. "O" ring

57. Timing adjusting screw
58. Shifter lock adjusting screw
59. Throttle control rod
60. Lockout lever
61. Electric start safety switch
62. Safety switch adjusting screw
63. Bearing
64. Bearing race

RUNNING OUTPUT TEST. Remove propeller and install the correct test wheel, then mount outboard motor in a suitable test tank. Remove ignition coil primary wires and install suitable terminal extenders (Stevens TS-77 or equivalent) on coil primary terminals, then install primary wires on terminal extenders. Connect peak reading voltmeter red test lead to number 1 coil terminal extender and black test lead to engine ground. Set voltmeter to Positive and 500. Start engine and run at rpm where ignition malfunction is evident while noting meter. Repeat test procedure on number 2 ignition coil. If either cylinder shows less than 200 volts, perform CHARGE COIL RESISTANCE TEST. If charge coil test results are acceptable, renew ignition module.

IGNITION COIL RESISTANCE TEST. To check ignition coil primary resistance, connect ohmmeter between primary terminal and coil ground. Resistance should be 0.05-0.15 ohm. To check secondary resistance, connect ohmmeter between coil high tension terminal and primary terminal. Resistance should be 250-300 ohms. Renew coil if resistance is not as specified.

S.L.O.W. (Speed Limiting Overheat Warning). To test S.L.O.W. function, place outboard motor in a suitable test tank with the correct test wheel, or place boat in the water. Start engine and run at 3,500 rpm. Disconnect brown temperature sensor lead and touch lead to engine ground. Engine speed should slow to approximately 2,000 rpm when brown sensor lead is grounded. If not, inspect wiring harness or renew ignition module.

COOLING SYSTEM

A rubber impeller type water pump located around the drive shaft is used to circulate water to the power head.

When cooling system problems are encountered, first check water inlet for plugging or partial stoppage, then if not corrected, check water pump and thermostat.

WATER PUMP. To remove the water pump, refer to the LOWER UNIT section and remove the gearcase assembly. Water pump is located at top of gearcase as shown in Fig. OM11-25. Make certain water passages and tubes are not damaged or plugged. Refer to LOWER UNIT section for installation and assembly instructions.

THERMOSTAT. The thermostat (4—Fig. OM11-16) is located behind cylinder head cover (1) at top of cylinder head.

Operating temperature can be checked using "Thermomelt" sticks. With outboard motor operating in forward gear and under 1000 rpm, a 125° F (52° C) stick applied to cylinder head should melt; a 163° F (73° C) stick should not melt.

POWER HEAD

R&R AND DISASSEMBLE. It is usually desirable, depending upon work to be done, to remove the rewind starter (electric starter, if so equipped), magneto assembly, carburetor, inlet manifold, reed valves, fuel pump and covers before removing the power head. Remove the port and starboard starter mounting brackets, remove the power head attaching screws, then lift power head off drive shaft housing.

Remove cylinder head (5—Fig. OM11-16). Drive the taper alignment pin (43) out of crankcase toward front (carburetor) side of power head. Remove armature support (10) and retainer (11), then remove crankcase front half (44).

NOTE: Two of the crankcase screws are accessible through intake passages in front of crankcase.

If crankcase half is stuck, tap it lightly with a soft hammer. DO NOT pry between crankcase and cylinders.

Pistons, rods and crankshaft are now accessible for removal and overhaul as outlined in the following paragraphs.

When assembling, follow the procedures outlined in the following paragraphs.

ASSEMBLY. Before assembling, check all sealing surfaces of crankcase and covers making certain that all sealing surfaces are clean, smooth and flat. Small nicks or burrs may be polished out on a lapping plate, but sealing surfaces MUST NOT be lowered.

When reassembling crankcase, make sure mating surfaces of crankcase halves are completely clean and free of old cement, nicks and burrs. On 1976 models, install sealing strips and trim ends to extend approximately 1/32 inch (0.79 mm) into bearing bores, then sparingly apply OMC Adhesive "M" to cylinder half of crankcase only. On models after 1976, apply OMC Gel-Seal II to one crankcase mating surface. Do not use sealers that will harden and prevent contact between crankcase mating surfaces. Immediately assemble crankcase halves after applying sealer and position halves by installing locating taper pin; then install and tighten crankcase screws.

Refer to CONDENSED SERVICE DATA for recommended tightening

values. Refer to Fig. OM11-17 for cylinder head tightening sequence. Cylinder head screws should be retightened after motor has been test run and allowed to cool.

PISTONS, RINGS AND CYLINDERS. Mark pistons, connecting rods and caps for reinstallation in original location. Each piston is fitted with two piston rings. Top ring is semi-keystone shape. Refer to CONDENSED SERVICE DATA for piston ring service specifications. Pistons are equipped with locating pins to prevent ring rotation.

Refer to CONDENSED SERVICE DATA for piston skirt-to-cylinder clearance on models prior to 1985. The manufacturer does not specify piston skirt clearance on models after 1984. If cylinder bore and piston are within tolerance, piston-to-cylinder clearance should be acceptable. Pistons and rings are available in 0.030 inch (0.76 mm) oversize for all models.

On models prior to 1983, measure piston diameter 1/8 inch (3.2 mm) up from bottom of skirt. Take one measurement parallel to piston pin bore and another at 90 degrees to pin bore. Renew piston if difference between measurements exceeds 0.002 inch (0.05 mm).

Models produced during 1983-1988 are equipped with cam ground pistons. To check wear on cam ground pistons, proceed as follows: Measure piston diameter 90 degrees to piston pin bore, 1/8 to 1/4 inch (3.2-6.3 mm) up from bottom of skirt. This dimension is the major piston diameter. Renew piston if major diameter is less than 2.9940 inch (76.048 mm) on standard size piston or 3.0240 inch (76.810 mm) for oversize piston. Next, measure piston skirt diameter parallel to piston pin bore. This measurement is the minor diameter. Renew piston if difference between major and minor diameters exceeds 0.0045 inch (0.114 mm), or if minor diameter is larger than major diameter.

On 1989 models, two piston designs are used. Refer to Fig. OM11-19 to visually identify pistons. Both piston designs are cam ground. On both designs, meas-

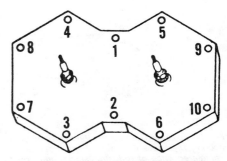

Fig. OM11-17—Tighten cylinder head screws in sequence shown.

ure piston at a point $1/8$ to $1/4$ inch (3.2-6.3 mm) up from bottom of skirt. Measure piston at 90 degrees to pin bore (major diameter) and parallel to pin bore (minor diameter). Subtract minor diameter from major diameter to obtain piston cam dimension. Cam dimension

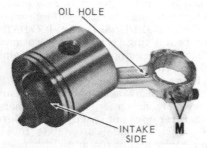

Fig. OM11-18—The piston and connecting rod must be assembled to each other with sharp deflector toward intake side of cylinder. On models so equipped, oil hole in connecting rod small end must face toward top of engine. Match marks (M) on rod and cap must be aligned. Refer to text.

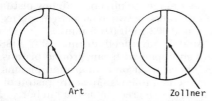

Fig. OM11-19—To identify Art or Zollner pistons used on 1989 models, view top of piston crown. Art piston will have half-circle in center of deflector as shown. Refer to text for piston measuring procedure.

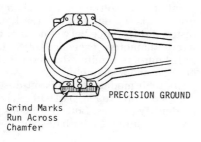

Grind Marks Run Across Chamfer

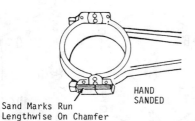

Sand Marks Run Lengthwise On Chamfer

Fig. OM11-20—To identify precision ground connecting rod, note direction of grind marks on chamfered edge of rod. Precision ground rods have grind marks running across chamfer as shown. Refer to text.

should be 0.0015-0.0025 inch (0.038-0.063 mm) on Art type piston and 0.005-0.007 inch (0.13-0.18 mm) on Zollner type piston. Renew piston if cam dimension is not as specified. Refer to CONDENSED SERVICE DATA for standard cylinder bore diameter. Maximum allowable cylinder bore out-of-round is 0.003 inch (0.08 mm) on all models. Maximum allowable cylinder bore taper is 0.002 inch (0.05 mm) on models after 1976 and 0.003 inch (0.08 mm) on all earlier models. To determine cylinder bore oversize diameter when reboring cylinder block, add piston oversize dimension (0.030 inch [0.08 mm]) to standard cylinder bore diameter.

On models prior to 1978, one pin bore is press fit and the other bore is a slip fit. The loose fit bore is marked on underside of piston. Piston pin must be removed from piston toward press fit side and reinstalled in loose fit side first. Piston may be heated to ease pin removal and installation. On later models, piston pin is loose fit on both piston bores and rides on 28 loose needle bearing rollers. Always renew piston pin retaining rings if removed. On all models, piston must be assembled to connecting rod with the long tapered side of piston crown facing exhaust ports. On models so equipped, oil hole (Fig. OM11-18) in connecting rod must face top of engine. Connecting rod with two holes in rod small end has no specific directional orientation, but, if reused, should be installed in same direction as removed.

CONNECTING RODS, BEARINGS AND CRANKSHAFT. Prior to detaching connecting rods from crankshaft, make sure that rod, cap and piston are marked for correct location during reassembly.

Connecting rod small end is fitted with caged needle bearing on models prior to 1985 and with 28 loose bearing rollers and washers on 1985 and later models. Install washers with flat surface facing outward.

Crankshaft is supported by three main bearings. Refer to Fig. OM11-16. Top main bearing (9) will slide off crankshaft for inspection. Do not remove lower main bearing (34) unless bearing renewal is required.

When assembling main bearings and seals to crankshaft on models prior to 1977, observe the following: Position center main bearing rollers (31) around crankshaft journal and install outer bearing race halves (30) with retaining ring groove facing down. Make sure retaining ring (29) is properly installed in groove. Install lower bearing (34) on crankshaft with groove facing up and install "O" ring (35) around bearing (34). Lip of top seal (8—Fig. OM11-16) should

face down. Be sure bearings properly engage dowel pins when installing crankshaft in cylinder block.

When assembling crankshaft and bearings on 1977 and later models, press lower bearing (34) on crankshaft from lettered side of bearing. Make sure snap ring (41) is properly seated in groove of crankshaft. Install upper bearing (9) on crankshaft with lettered end of bearing facing down. Install seal (8) with lip facing down. Install center main bearing rollers (31) around crankshaft journal and install outer race with retaining ring facing down. Lubricate "O" ring (56) with OMC Moly Lube and install in lower end of crankshaft. Apply OMC Gasket Sealing Compound to outer diameter of seal (37) and press into housing (54) until seated. Make sure lip of seal (37) faces upward. Make sure dowel pin on bearing (9) properly engages notch in cylinder block and dowel (47) properly engages center main bearing outer race. Note that center main alignment dowel (47) may be renewed if damaged or loose in cylinder block.

Joint between connecting rod and cap is fractured and not machined. When assembling connecting rods to crankpins, first determine if engine is equipped with hand-sanded or precision-ground connecting rods by referring to Fig. OM11-20. On models equipped with hand-sanded connecting rods (some 1985 and all earlier models), install rod cap making sure match marks on rod and cap are aligned and tighten cap screws finger tight. Check cap-to-rod alignment by running a pencil point or similar tool over joint between rod and cap. Align cap by carefully tapping with a suitable mallet. If rod and cap are properly aligned, joint between rod and cap should be nearly invisible. When proper alignment is obtained, tighten cap screws to the recommended value (CONDENSED SERVICE DATA). If acceptable alignment cannot be obtained, rod and cap assembly must be renewed.

Models equipped with precision ground connecting rods (Fig. OM11-20) require the use of OMC Rod Cap Alignment Fixture 396749 to assemble connecting rod and cap. Follow instructions provided with special tool and refer to Fig. OM11-21. Make sure rod and cap match marks are aligned. When rod and cap are correctly aligned, tighten cap screws using OMC Socket 331638. Refer to CONDENSED SERVICE DATA for recommended torque value.

On all models, be certain of the following: All bearing rollers are installed; oil hole (Fig. OM11-18) on models so equipped is facing up; long sloping side of piston crown is toward exhaust ports and match marks on rod and cap are aligned.

MANUAL REWIND STARTER

Fig. OM11-22 shows an exploded view of the manual starter typical of all models. Starter can be removed from power head after removing three mounting screws and detaching starter lockout cable from starter housing, if so equipped.

To disassemble starter, remove rope handle (13) and allow pulley (4) to unwind until all tension is removed from rewind spring (3). Remove nut on top of housing, screw, spindle, and on later models, spring washer and friction ring (not shown). Remove retainers (8), pawls (7) and links (6). To remove pulley (4) and rewind spring (3), hold housing (1) upright and strike housing against a bench or other suitable flat surface to dislodge pulley and spring.

Inspect all components for excessive wear or other damage and renew as necessary. Reassemble starter by reversing disassembly. Apply OMC Triple-Guard grease or Lubriplate 777 to rewind spring, spindle and spindle area in housing. Wind rewind spring into housing in counterclockwise direction starting with outer coil. Preload rewind spring by winding pulley (4) counterclockwise until rewind spring is tight, back off pulley (4) ½ to 1 full turn, then allow rewind spring to wind rope into housing. Apply a suitable thread locking compound to starter assembly mounting screws and tighten to 96-120 in.-lbs. (10.8-13.6 N·m). Starter lockout mechanism should prevent manual starter operation if shift handle is in forward or reverse gear position.

ELECTRIC STARTER

Electric starter motor (Fig. OM11-23) is typical of all models. On early model starter, no-load motor speed should be a minimum of 8000 rpm with maximum current draw of 60 amps at 10 volts. On late model starter, no-load speed should be 6500-7500 rpm with maximum current draw of 30 amps at 12-12.4 volts.

Seal joints between starter frame, brush holder and head assembly with OMC Black Neoprene Dip or equivalent. Tighten through-bolts to 95-110 in.-lbs. (10.7-12.4 N·m). Nut (1) should be renewed if removed and tightened to 20-25 ft.-lbs. (27-34 N·m).

On models equipped with electric start, battery must maintain a minimum of 9.6 volts under cranking load for 15 seconds. If not, battery must be charged or renewed.

AC LIGHTING COIL

Manual Start Models

To test lighting coil, disconnect three pin connector leading from armature plate. Connect a suitable ohmmeter between yellow wire with gray tracer and yellow wire. Renew lighting coil if resistance is not within 0.81-0.91 ohm. Next, connect ohmmeter between yellow wire with gray tracer and yellow wire with blue tracer. Renew lighting coil if resistance is not within 1.19-1.23 ohms. Connect ohmmeter between engine ground and alternately to each pin in three pin connector (yellow, yellow/gray and yellow/blue). Ohmmeter should read infinity at each connection. If not, inspect for shorted lighting coil or coil wires.

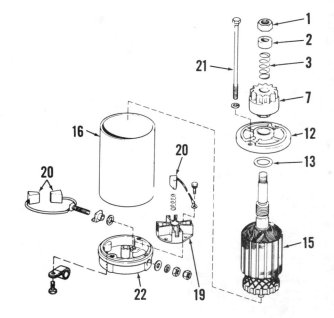

Fig. OM11-21—View showing OMC Rod Cap Alignment Fixture properly assembled on connecting rod. Follow instructions provided with special tool.

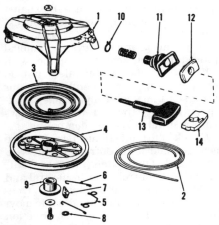

Fig. OM11-22—Exploded view of manual rewind starter typical of all models. Late type starter is equipped with two drive pawls (7). A spring washer, friction ring, friction plate, shim and bushing are located between spindle (9) and pulley (4) on later models.

1. Housing	8. Retainer
2. Rope	9. Spindle
3. Recoil spring	10. Clamp
4. Pulley	11. Cover
5. Spring	12. Cover
6. Link	13. Handle
7. Pawl	14. Anchor

Fig. OM11-23—Exploded view of electric starter motor typical of all models.

1. Stop nut
2. Pinion stop
3. Antidrift spring
7. Drive pinion
12. Head assy.
13. Thrust washer
15. Armature
16. Frame
19. Brush holder
20. Brush
21. Through-bolt

BATTERY CHARGING SYSTEM

Electric Start Models

To test alternator output, connect a suitable ammeter in series with the red rectifier lead and red wiring harness lead. At 5500 rpm, alternator output should be approximately 4.5 amps. If not, proceed as follows: Disconnect battery cables from battery. Disconnect all stator leads from the terminal board. Using a suitable ohmmeter, connect red tester lead to stator yellow lead. Connect black tester lead to stator yellow/blue lead. Resistance should be 0.22-0.32 ohm. Move red tester lead to stator yellow/gray lead. Resistance should be 0.22-0.32 ohm. Renew or repair stator if resistance is not as specified.

To check for shorted stator or stator wiring, connect black tester lead to engine ground. Connect red tester lead to stator yellow/blue lead, then to stator yellow and yellow/gray leads. If ohmmeter does not read infinity at all connections, stator or stator wiring is shorted to ground and must be repaired or renewed.

To test rectifier, disconnect battery cables at battery and proceed as follows: Connect ohmmeter black test lead to engine ground and red test lead to rectifier yellow/gray lead. Note ohmmeter reading, then reverse tester lead connections. A very high reading should result in one connection and a very low reading should result in the other connection. Repeat test with ohmmeter connected between engine ground and rectifier yellow lead, then between ground and yellow/blue lead. One connection should show high resistance, the other low resistance. Next, connect ohmmeter between rectifier red lead and yellow/gray lead. Note reading and reverse tester connections. Repeat test between rectifier red lead and yellow lead, then red lead and yellow/blue lead. As before, one connection should show high resistance and the other low resistance. Renew rectifier if not as specified.

LOWER UNIT

PROPELLER AND HUB. Protection for propeller and drive unit is provided by a cushioning hub built into the propeller. Service consists of propeller renewal if hub is damaged.

REMOVE AND REINSTALL. Drain lubricant and remove propeller if gearcase disassembly is necessary. On models prior to 1980, remove exhaust housing side cover (10—Fig. OM11-24) and unscrew lower screw in shift rod connector (17—Fig. OM11-25). On models after 1979, detach water inlet screens (22—Fig. OM11-26) on both gearcase sides and unscrew upper shift rod connector (56). Note that keeper (57) under connector (56) may be dislodged when gearcase is removed. Unscrew fasteners retaining gearcase to exhaust housing and separate gearcase from exhaust housing.

To install gearcase, reverse removal procedure. Coat drive shaft splines with OMC Moly Lube or equivalent but do not apply lubricant to end of shaft or drive shaft may not fully engage crankshaft. Coat gearcase retaining screws with a suitable sealing compound.

Check shift mechanism to be sure gearcase and shift control lever are synchronized. On models prior to 1981, place shift control lever in neutral and make certain that propeller turns freely. Rotate propeller by hand while moving shift handle slowly in each direction to the point where lower unit dog clutch engages gears. Mark shift handle location on shroud at point of engagement. Travel should be the same distance each side of neutral position to point of engagement. If not, loosen clamp screw and adjustment screw, then move shift handle as required and retighten screws. There should be 0.03-0.06 inch (0.8-1.5 mm) gap (G—Fig. OM11-28) between

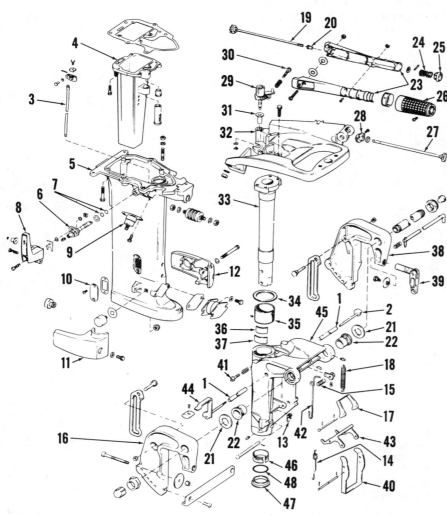

Fig. OM11-24—Typical view of stern bracket, exhaust housing, drive shaft housing and related components.

1. Bushings	14. Spring	26. Throttle grip	37. Plate
2. Tilt cam	15. Spring	27. Throttle shaft	38. Stern bracket
3. Shift rod	16. Stern bracket	28. Throttle pinion	39. Clamp
4. Exhaust plate	17. Reverse lock	29. Throttle gear	40. Link
5. Exhaust housing	18. Spring	30. Idle speed adjusting	41. Friction adjusting
6. Shifter shaft	19. Throttle shaft	screw	screw
7. "O" rings	20. Bushing	31. Bushing	42. Link
8. Shift handle	21. Washer	32. Steering bracket	43. Link
9. Rubber mount	22. Bushing	33. Pilot shaft	44. Tilt lever
10. Cover plate	23. Steering handle	34. Thrust washer	45. Swivel bracket
11. Lower mount	24. Spring	35. Liner	46. Bushing
12. Lower mount	25. Friction block	36. Spacer	47. Thrust washer
13. Spring			48. "O" ring

shift lock (14—Fig. OM11-16) and stop on stator plate retainer with unit in reverse. Install spacers between shift control lever (8—Fig. OM11-24) and shift shaft (6) to obtain desired gap.

Adjust shift mechanism on models after 1980 by adjusting shift control lever position so neutral in gearcase is synchronized with neutral on shift control detent plate.

WATER PUMP. Refer to previous section and remove gearcase. Unscrew pump housing screws and lift up pump housing (7—Fig. OM11-25 or Fig. OM11-26) and impeller (8) while holding drive shaft down. Remove and inspect remainder of water pump components.

To assemble water pump, apply OMC Adhesive "M" or equivalent to grommet (5) and install in pump housing. Apply GE Adhesive Sealant RTV or equivalent to bottom of impeller plate (10). Be sure sealant does not adhere to top of impeller plate. Install impeller key (9) on models prior to 1985 and drive cam on models after 1984. Drive cam must be installed with flat side against drive shaft and sharp edge pointing in a clockwise direction when viewed from crankshaft end of drive shaft. Install impeller (8). Lightly oil impeller tips and turn drive shaft clockwise while installing impeller housing. Apply sealing compound to impeller housing screws.

GEARCASE. Note: If OMC special tools are not used, exact position of seals and bearings should be noted during disassembly.

Remove water pump as previously outlined and withdraw drive shaft. Remove screws which retain housing (34—Fig. OM11-25 or Fig. OM11-26), then use OMC tool 378103 or other suitable puller to withdraw bearing housing (34) from gearcase. Remove snap ring (38) and retainer plate (39). Unscrew and remove shift rod (18). Remove shift yoke (44) and unscrew pivot pin (24). Withdraw propeller shaft assembly. Remove shift lever (46), pinion gear (28), thrust bearing (26), thrust washers (25 and 27), forward gear (50) and bearing (52). Using a suitable puller, remove seals (13), bearing (15) and bearing and seal housing (14). Drive bearing or bearings (16) into propeller shaft cavity of gearcase and remove. Use a suitable puller to remove shift rod washer (21), "O" ring (20) and bushing (19). Remove "O" ring (55—Fig. OM11-26) on models after 1979. Using suitable pullers, remove bearing (52—Fig. OM11-25 or Fig. OM11-26) cup from gearcase and seals (32) and bearings (33 and 36) from bearing housing (34).

Inspect components for excessive wear or damage. Chipped or excessively rounded engagement surfaces of dog clutch dog (48) or gears (41 and 50) may cause shifting malfunction. Be sure gearcase and exhaust housing mating surfaces are flat and free of nicks.

To reassemble gearcase proceed as follows: Use OMC Gasket Sealing Compound or equivalent around outside of seals. Lubricate bearings, shafts and gears with recommended lubricant before assembly. Install shift rod washer (21), "O" ring (20) and bushing (19) using OMC Tool 304515. Install "O" ring (55—Fig. OM11-26) on models after 1979. Install pinion bearing or bearings (16—Fig. OM11-25 or Fig. OM11-26) into gearcase to correct depth with letter end of bearing up. OMC Tool 391257 can be used when assembled with correct spacer to install pinion bearing or bearings. Pinion bearing is at correct depth when plate bottoms against gearcase. Press bearing (15) into housing (14) so bearing is flush with housing. Using OMC Tool 322923, drive housing (14) into gearcase until plate bottoms against gearcase. Install seals (13) back-to-back in housing (14). Drive bearing (33) into bearing housing (34) with OMC Tool 321429 until tool abuts housing. Install seals (32) so inner seal lip is towards inside of bearing housing and outer seal lip is towards outside of housing. Drive bearing (36) into bearing housing with

OMC Tool 321428 until tool abuts housing. Install bearing and cap (52) in gearcase. Place lower thrust washer (27) on pinion gear (28) with inner bevel towards gear. Install thrust bearing (26) and thrust washer (25) on pinion gear (28). External bevel on thrust washer (25) should be toward top of gearcase. Install pinion gear assembly in gearcase. Install forward gear (50), thrust washer (49)—models so equipped and shift lever (46) in gearcase. Place detent spring (29) and detent balls (30) in propeller shaft (43) and slide dog clutch (48) with groove towards propeller end of shaft onto shaft while making sure detent grooves in dog clutch are aligned with detent balls. Grease cradle (47) and install on dog clutch (48). Install propeller shaft and dog clutch assembly in gearcase with slots in cradle (47) facing shift lever (46). Engage shift lever (46) fingers in cradle slots. Install thrust washers (42), models so equipped, and reverse gear (41).

Install shift yoke (44) with open end of hook towards gears and engage hook with shift lever pin (45). Thread shift rod (18) into yoke (44). Install pivot pin (24) in shift lever (46) hole by moving shift rod (18). Remainder of assembly is evident after inspection of unit and referral to Fig. OM11-25 or Fig. OM11-26. On models after 1984, install drive cam (9—Fig. OM11-26) with flat side against drive shaft and sharp edge pointing in a

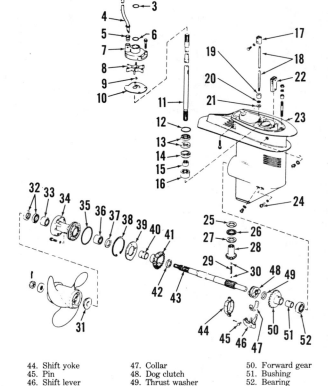

Fig. OM11-25 — Exploded view of gearcase assembly used on 35 models prior to 1980.

3. "O" ring
4. Water tube
5. Grommet
6. "O" ring
7. Impeller housing
8. Impeller
9. Impeller drive key
10. Plate
11. Drive shaft
12. "O" ring
13. Seals
14. Bearing housing
15. Bearing
16. Bearing
17. Shift rod connector
18. Shift rod
19. Shift rod bushing
20. "O" ring
21. Washer
22. Intake screen
23. Gearcase
24. Pivot pin
25. Thrust washer
26. Thrust bearing
27. Thrust washer
28. Pinion gear
29. Spring
30. Detent balls
31. Thrust bearing
32. Seals
33. Bearing
34. Bearing housing
35. "O" ring
36. Bearing
37. Thrust washer
38. Snap ring
39. Retainer
40. Bushing
41. Reverse gear
42. Thrust washer
43. Propeller shaft
44. Shift yoke
45. Pin
46. Shift lever
47. Collar
48. Dog clutch
49. Thrust washer
50. Forward gear
51. Bushing
52. Bearing

clockwise direction when viewed from crankshaft end of drive shaft. Install water pump, attach gearcase to exhaust housing and fill gearcase with lubricant

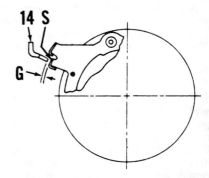

Fig. OM11-28—Gap (G) should be 0.03-0.06 inch (0.76-1.52 mm) between shift lock (14) and stop (S) on stator plate retainer. Refer to text.

Fig. OM11-26—Exploded view of gearcase assembly used on models after 1979. Shims (42 and 49—Fig. OM11-25) are used on models prior to 1984. One bearing (16) is used on models prior to 1984. A gasket in place of seal (2) is used on models prior to 1983. An impeller key is used instead of drive cam (9) on models prior to 1985.

1. Liner	15. Bearing	27. Thrust washer	39. Retainer	54. "O" ring
2. Seal	16. Bearings	28. Pinion gear	40. Bushing	55. "O" ring
3. Gasket	17. Nut	29. Spring	41. Reverse gear	56. Connector
4. Water tube	18. Shift rod	30. Detent balls	43. Propeller shaft	57. Keeper
5. Grommet	19. Bushing	31. Spacer	44. Shift yoke	58. Gasket
6. "O" ring	20. "O" ring	32. Seals	45. Pin	59. Level plug
7. Impeller housing	21. Washer	33. Bearing	46. Shift lever	60. Drain plug
8. Impeller	22. Water inlet screen	34. Bearing housing	47. Cradle	61. "O" ring
9. Drive cam	23. Gearcase	35. "O" ring	48. Dog clutch	62. Propeller & drive hub
10. Plate	24. Pivot pin	36. Bearing	50. Forward gear	63. Spacer
11. Drive shaft	25. Thrust washer	37. Thrust washer	52. Bearing	64. Nut
13. Seals	26. Thrust bearing	38. Snap ring	53. Bushing	65. Cotter pin
14. Bearing housing				

EVINRUDE AND JOHNSON

33 & 40 HP (1969-1976)

EVINRUDE

Year Produced	33 HP	40 HP
1969	33902, 33903, 33952, 33953	40902, 40903, 40952, 40953, 40972, 40973
1970	33002, 33003, 33052, 33053	40002, 40003, 40052, 40053, 40072, 40073
1971	....	40102, 40103, 40152, 40153
1972	....	40202, 40203, 40252, 40253
1973	....	40304, 40305, 40354, 40355
1974	....	40404, 40405 40454, 40455
1975	....	40504, 40505, 40554, 40555
1976	....	40604, 40605, 40654, 40655

JOHNSON

Year Produced	33 HP	40 HP
1969	33R69, 33E69	40R69, 40E69, 40ES69
1970	33R70, 33E70	40R70, 40E70, 40E70
1971	....	40R71, 40RL71,
	....	40E71, 40EL71
1972	....	40R72, 40RL72, 40E72, 40EL72
1973	....	40R73, 40RL73, 40E73, 40EL73
1974	....	40R74, 50RL74, 40E74, 40EL74
1975	....	40R75, 40RL75, 40E75, 40EL75
1976	....	40R76, 40RL76, 40E76, 40EL76

CONDENSED SERVICE DATA

TUNE-UP	33 HP	40 HP
Hp/rpm	33/4500	40/4500
Bore – Inches	3-1/16	3-3/16
Stroke – Inches	2¾	2¾
Number of Cylinders	2	2
Displacement – Cu. In. . . .	40.5	43.9
Spark Plug:		
Champion	J4J	J4J**
Auto-Lite	A21X	....
AC	M42K	....
Electrode Gap	0.030	0.030
Magneto:		
Point Gap	0.020	0.020
Carburetor:		
Make	Own	Own
Fuel:Oil Ratio	50:1	50:1

SIZES – CLEARANCES	33 HP	40 HP
Piston Rings:		
End Gap	0.007-0.017	0.007-0.017
Side Clearance		
(1969-1970)	0.0045-0.007	0.002-0.0045
Side Clearance		
(1971-1976)	....	0.0015-0.004
Piston Skirt Clearance . . .	0.003-0.0045	0.003-0.005
Crankshaft Bearing		
Diameters:		
Top Main Bearing	1.2495-1.250	1.4974-1.4979#
Center Main Bearing . . .	0.9995-1.000	1.3748-1.3752#
Bottom Main Bearing . .	0.9995-1.000	1.1810-1.1815#
Crankpin	1.1823-1.1828	1.1823-1.1828
Crankshaft End Play	0.007-0.011	0.003-0.011

TIGHTENING TORQUES
(All Values In Inch-Pounds

Unless Noted)	33 HP	40 HP
Connecting Rod	348-372	348-372
Crankcase Halves:		
Center Screws	162-168	162-168
Flange Screws	150-170	150-170
Cylinder Head	168-192	168-192
Inlet Manifold	24-36	24-36
Exhaust Manifold	60-84	60-84
Flywheel (Ft.-Lbs.)	100-105	100-105
Spark Plug	240-246	240-246

**Champion L4J is used in 1974, 1975 and 1976 models.
#Crankshaft bearing diameters on 40 hp models prior to
1974 are same as 33 hp models.

LUBRICATION

The power head is lubricated by oil mixed with the fuel. Use 1/6 pint of BIA certified TC-W outboard oil with each gallon of unleaded or low lead gasoline with octane rating on pump greater than 85 octane. Mix oil and gasoline thoroughly, using a separate container, before pouring mixture into fuel tank.

The lower unit of gears and bearings are lubricated by oil contained in the gearcase. Special OMC Sea-Lube Premium Blend Gearcase Lube should be used. This lubricant is supplied in a tube and filling procedures are as follows: Remove lower plug from gear case and attach tube. Remove upper (vent) plug from case and, with motor in an upright position, fill gearcase until lubricant reaches level of upper (vent) plug hole. Reinstall vent plug, then remove lubricant tube and reinstall lower plug. Tighten both plugs securely, using new gaskets if necessary, to assure a water-tight seal. Lower gear lubricant should be maintained at level of vent plug, and drained and renewed every 100 hours of operation or once a year.

FUEL SYSTEM

CARBURETOR. The carburetor used on 33 hp models is provided with both high speed and idle speed mixture adjustment needles. Inital setting is ⅜-¼ turn open for the high speed needle (26 – Fig. OM12-4) and 1¼ turns open for the idle mixture needle (20). Knob (23) and lever (25) must be disconnected before adjusting the mixture needles. The high speed needle must be adjusted to provide best operation at high speed

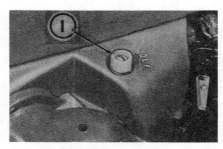

Fig. OM12-2—Idle speed stop screw (I) is located on port side of front motor cover on some 40 hp models. Refer also to Figs. OM12-1, OM12-2A, OM12-2B and OM12-2C.

(in forward gear) before adjusting the idle mixture needle. After needles are adjusted, attach knob (23) and lever (25) so that both knobs (22 and 23) are pointing up. Idle speed stop screw (I – Fig. OM12-1) should be adjusted to provide 650 rpm at minimum speed in forward gear.

The carburetor used on 40 hp models is provided with a 0.064 inch main jet (26A – Fig. OM12-5) on early models and a 0.067 inch main jet on later models. Initial setting for the idle mixture needle (20) is approximately 1-⅛ turns open. Adjustment is accomplished in forward gear after knob (23) is removed. After needle is adjusted, attach knob (23) so that it points up. Idle speed stop screw is located at (I – Fig. OM12-1, OM12-2, OM12-2A, OM12-2B or OM12-2C). Idle speed should be 650 rpm in forward gear.

To set the carburetor float level, remove the carburetor, then remove and invert the throttle body (5 – Fig. OM12-4 or OM12-5) with float installed. With body inverted, nearest surface of float should be parallel and flush with gasket surface of carburetor body. If it is not, carefully bend float lever; then check after reassembly to be sure float does not stick or bind.

Fig. OM12-1 – Idle speed screw (I) is located on throttle control gear on 33 hp and 40 hp (1972-1975) models.

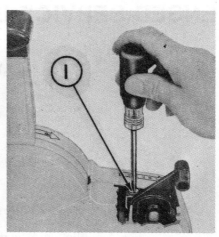

Fig. OM12-2A – On some 40 hp models, the idle speed stop screw (I) is located as shown in the remote control unit.

Fig. OM12-2B – On some late 40 hp motors, the idle speed stop screw (I) is located above the carburetor as shown.

To adjust the electric choke on 33 hp models so equipped, refer to Fig. OM12-6. Loosen band (A) securing solenoid housing to float chamber and pull out manual choke control until choke is fully closed. Push solenoid housing through band in direction indicated by arrow, until plunger bottoms in housing; then tighten band (A). Open the manual choke and check to see that choke operates properly when choke button is pressed.

On models with hot-air actuated automatic choke, a heat exchanger unit is built into the outer exhaust cover shown in Fig. OM12-7, and a vacuum passage (P – Fig. OM12-5) is built into carburetor body, gasket and intake manifold. When the engine is running, manifold vacuum draws air through the intake passage (11 – Fig. OM12-7) into the heat exchanger, then through the air transfer tube (10) to the choke housing, where engine heat controls the tension of the bimetal choke spring. The degree of choking action can be adjusted by loosening the three screws which secure cover (39 – Fig. OM12-5) to choke housing (41), then turning over counterclockwise to decrease choke action, or clockwise to increase choking. Service in addition to choke adjustment consists of making sure passages are kept open and clean and/or renewing choke parts. The air passage in manifold (at passage P – Fig. OM12-5) should be 0.020 and can be checked with a #76 drill.

NOTE: Do not enlarge hole.

In addition to the hot-air actuated bimetal unit, the automatic choke contains a solenoid unit (32, 33, 34, 37, 43 and 44) which fully closes choke when key is turned to "START" position and returns

control to the bimetal strip when key is released to "ON" position. A toggle switch is locted on the control panel (adjacent to the key switch) which permits manual interruption of the solenoid circuit and thus prevents over-choking when attempting to start a warm motor. Service on the solenoid consists of checking the circuit and renewal of malfunctioning units. Make certain that plunger (33) moves freely in solenoid coil (34).

NOTE: Do not lubricate plunger or solenoid coil, because this will later cause plunger to stick. The solenoid coil (34) should have a resistance of 3 ohms.

SPEED CONTROL LINKAGE. The

1. Throttle plate
2. Throttle shaft
3. Spring
4. Choke detent spring
5. Throttle body
6. Lever
7. Bellcrank
8. Spring
9. Choke shaft
10. Gasket
11. Fuel inlet valve
12. Float
13. Pivot pin
14. Nozzle
15. Float chamber
16. Choke rod
17. Choke plate
18. Packing
19. Nut
20. Idle mixture needle
21. Control panel
22. Knob
23. Knob
24. Link
25. Lever
26. High speed mixture needle
27. Nut
28. Packing
29. Stud
30. Choke bellcrank
31. Cover
32. Spring
33. Plunger
34. Solenoid cell
35. Clamp
36. Choke link

carburetor throttle valve is synchronized to open as the ignition timing is advanced. It is important that ignition timing and throttle valve opening be checked and adjusted, if necessary.

To check the linkage, refer to Fig. OM12-8. Remove upper motor cover and move speed control lever until index on armature cam is aligned with index pointer on intake manifold as shown. With index marks aligned, all slack should be removed from throttle linkage with throttle plate just beginning to move from closed position. On 33 hp models, adjust by loosening the clamp screw (A – Inset), and turning the Nylon eccentric bushing (B) until slack is removed and throttle shaft just begins to move. On 40 hp models, adjust by

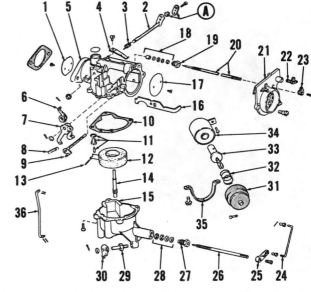

Fig. OM12-4—Exploded view of carburetor used on 33 hp models with electric starter. Manual starting models are similar except choke solenoid (29 through 36) is not used.

Fig. OM12-2C — On some control units, the idle speed stop screw (I) is located as shown.

Fig. OM12-5—Exploded view of carburetor and associated parts used on electric starting, 40 hp models. Hot air actuated choke and solenoid are not used on manual start models. Refer to Fig. OM12-4 for legend except for the following:

   A. Throttle arm
   B. Clamp screw
   P. Vacuum port
   26A. High speed jet
   27A. Plug
   37. Spring
   38. Air-transfer tube
   39. Cover
   40. Gasket
   41. Body
   42. Lever
   43. Washer
   44. Spring guide
   45. Sleeve

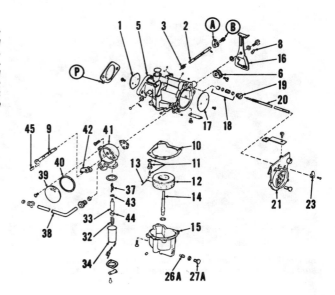

loosening clamp screw (B – Fig. OM12-8A) and moving throttle arm (A). On all models, retighten clamp screw when adjustment is correct.

All models are equipped with a fuel-saver linkage which permits partial throttle opening with full magneto advance. The linkage includes a spring which allows speed control lever to move in a slot after the armature plate reaches full advance position. Movement of the speed control after reaching full ignition advance, continues to open the carburetor throttle. To adjust the linkage first rotate the armature plate until plate contacts stop.

NOTE: Do not move the speed control linkage, rotate the armature plate only.

Fig. OM12-8 – On 33 hp motors, speed control linkage is adjusted by loosening clamp screw (A-inset) and turning eccentric bushing (B). Method of control is similar on all models. Refer to text.

Fig. OM12-6 – To adjust the choke solenoid on 33 hp motors so equipped, loosen band (A), pull out manual choke linkage and with choke fully closed, push solenoid housing in direction shown by arrow.

With advance plate against stop, measure clearance between moveable stop (C – Fig. OM12-10) and pivot (P). If clearance is not 1/32 inch, loosen the clamp screw in the moveable stop and reposition on the link (L). Tighten the clamp screw to retain the moveable stop 1/32 inch from pivot (P).

Electric starting models are equipped with a safety switch (22 – Fig. OM12-11) which prevents starter actuation at wide-open throttle. To adjust the switch, disconnect the white lead at switch and connect a continuity meter or light to the disconnected terminal on switch and ground the other lead to bracket (21). With armature plate in fully retarded position, the test light should light or meter should show continuity. Slowly

move armature plate in direction indicated by arrow (advance direction) until the point where continuity is broken as indicated by meter or light. When continuity is broken, distance (D) between shifter lock bracket and cast stop on cylinder should measure 7/32-9/32 inch; if it does not, loosen clamp screw (A) and reposition bracket (21) and switch (22) until distance (D) is correct.

INLET REED VALVES. Two sets of reed valves (2 – Fig. OM12-12) are used; one for each cylinder. Reed valve plate (1) is located between intake manifold and the power head crankcase, and should be checked whenever carburetor is removed for service. Reed petals (2) should seat very lightly against reed plate (1) throughout their entire length with the least possible tension. Do not attempt to straighten a bent reed or bend a reed in order to modify performance; always renew a bent or damaged reed. Seating surface of reed plate (1)

Fig. OM12-7 – On models with hot-air actuated automatic choke, a heat exchanger is inside the exhaust cover (4) and air is drawn through transfer tube (10) to choke housing. Make sure inlet port (11) is not plugged.

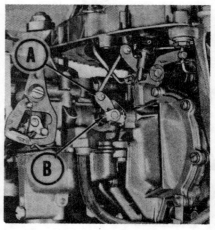

Fig. OM12-8A – On 40 hp motors, speed control linkage is adjusted by loosening clamp screw (B) and moving throttle arm (A),

should be smooth and flat and reed petals should be centered over ports. Reed stop (3) must center over reed petals.

FUEL PUMP. The diaphragm type fuel pump (Fig. OM12-13) is available only as an assembly which also contains the fuel filter (4 through 7). If fuel pump troubles are encountered, first remove and clean the filter (5) and check to be sure fuel lines are open and clean. If trouble is not corrected, renew the fuel pump assembly.

RECIRCULATING VALVE. Late model motors are equipped with a fuel

Fig. OM12-10—When adjusting the fuel saver linkage, refer to text. The movable stop and the clamp screw on early models are shown at (C). Later models are similar.

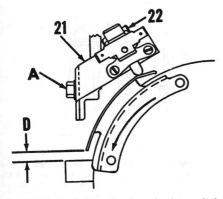

Fig. OM12-11—Schematic view of safety switch and actuating linkage which interrupts starter current at fast throttle.

A. Cap screw
D. Adjustment (see text)
21. Bracket
22. Switch

recirculating valve (Fig. OM12-14A). The recirculating valve allows liquid fuel or oil which may gather in the crankcase at slow operating speeds to be drawn back into the engine at the transfer port covers. Small passages in the bottom of each crankcase lead to the recirculating valve location at the bottom of the power head. Any condensed liquid accumulates in the bleed pocket and passage until the piston travels its downward stroke, when crankcase pressure forces the check valve off its seat and feeds the liquid back into the transfer cover of the same cylinder.

When engine is overhauled, passages to recirculating valve should be blown out with compressed air. Clean any accumulated gum or varnish from valve with solvent. Make certain that hoses to transfer covers are installed as per instructions on recirculating valve body.

CRANKCASE BLEEDER VALVE. All motors not equipped with a recirculating valve are equipped with a crankcase bleed valve as shown in Fig. OM12-14. The bleeder valve is designed to remove any liquid fuel or oil which might build up in crankcase, thus providing smoother operation at all speeds and lessening the possibility of spark plug fouling during slow-speed operation. There is a small passage leading

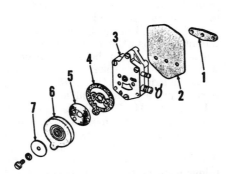

Fig. OM12-13—Typical diaphragm type fuel pump showing filter exploded. Component parts of pump (3) are not serviced.

1. Gasket
2. Plate
3. Fuel pump
4. Gasket
5. Filter
6. Cover
7. Washer

Fig. OM12-12—Exploded view of the inlet reed valves, manifold and throttle linkage. Screw (11) attaches reed plate to crankcase. Economizer linkage (C, L & P) are shown in Fig. OM12-10.

1. Reed plate
2. Reed petals
3. Stop
4. Gasket
5. Cam roller
6. Bellcrank
7. Link
8. Spring
9. Inlet manifold
10. Gasket

from the bottom of each crankcase to the bleeder valve location, at bottom of power head. Any condensed liquid accumulates in the bleeder pocket and passage until the piston travels its downward stroke, when crankcase pressure forces bleeder valve off its seat

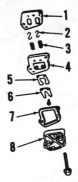

Fig. OM12-14—The crankcase bleeder valve may be serviced without disassembly of power head after removing the valve cover plate.

1. Gasket
2. Screen retainer
3. Screen
4. Valve plate
5. Valve leaf
6. Leaf stop
7. Gasket
8. Cover plate

Fig. OM12-14A—A recirculating valve is fitted to all late model 40 hp motors. Condensed liquid (gas or oil) is fed back into engine instead of overboard.

and blows the accumulated liquid out into the exhaust passage. When engine is overhauled, bleeder passages should be blown out with compressed air. Valve leaf petals should exert a slight pressure against seating surface of crankcase. Seating surface should be smooth and flat. Renew any parts which are badly worn, broken or otherwise damaged.

IGNITION

Breaker point gap should be 0.020 and both sets of points must be adjusted to open exactly 180° apart. Adjustment or

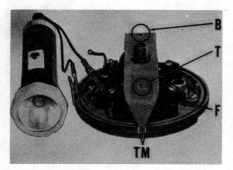

Fig. OM12-15—Timing fixture installed and aligned with armature plate timing marks (TM) for adjusting points. Refer to text.

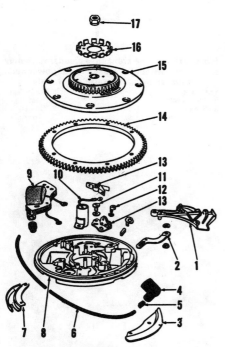

Fig. OM12-16—Exploded view of armature (stator) plate and associated parts used on models prior to 1971.

1. Anchor & pin	
2. Link	10. Condenser
3. Throttle cam	11. Screw
4. Cover	12. Adjusting screw
5. Terminal	13. Point set
6. Wire	14. Ring gear
7. Shift stop	15. Flywheel
8. Plate	16. Starter cap
9. Coil & lamination	17. Nut

inspection of points requires removal of flywheel.

The recommended method of breaker point adjustment and synchronization requires the use of a special timing fixture (OMC Part No. 378966 for models prior to 1974 or Part No. 386635 for later models) as shown in Fig. OM12-15, and a timing test light or continuity meter. To adjust the points using the special tools, first remove flywheel and disconnect the leads from both sets of points. Install the timing fixture and turn the crankshaft until either pointer is centered between the embossed timing marks (TM) on armature plate as shown. Attach the timing test light or meter to the insulated terminal of the opening set of points and to a suitable ground. Loosen the breaker point anchor screw and turn the adjusting screw until points are closed as indicated by the timing test light or meter; then, turn adjusting screw in the opposite direction until points barely open. Tighten the anchor screw and recheck by turning crankshaft, to be sure points open when timing pointer is midway between embossed timing marks (TM). Turn crankshaft ½ turn until opposite leg of timing fixture is properly aligned with timing marks, attach timing test light to the other set of points and adjust by following the same procedure.

Use Fig. OM12-16 or OM12-16A as a guide for overhaul of magneto armature (stator) plate. The ends of coil laminations (9) should be flush with machined mounting pads of armature plate when coil is installed. Also check for broken or worn insulation, broken wires or loose or corroded connections. Renew any parts which are questionable.

If support (34 – Fig. OM12-21) and retainer (33) on early models is removed, make certain that magneto retainer is installed with tapered (rounded) side down toward crankcase. Flat side of retainer must be toward support (34) and magneto armature plate.

Fig. OM12-16A—Exploded view of magneto assembly used on models after 1970. Alternator stator (1) is only used on electric start models.

1. Alternator stator
2. Breaker points
3. Condenser
4. Armature plate
5. Ring
6. Plate support
7. Cam & link assy.
8. Ignition coil
9. Magneto coil
10. Nut
11. Starter cup
12. Flywheel

When installing the flywheel, make sure that mating surfaces of flywheel and crankshaft are completely free from dirt, oil or grease. Remove any nicks or burrs which might interfere with flywheel seating. Outer edge of flywheel key must be parallel with centerline of crankshaft as shown in Fig. OM12-17 (not parallel with crankshaft taper). Tighten the flywheel retaining nut to a torque of 100-105 ft.-lbs.

AUTOMATIC CUT-OUT SWITCH. All motors are equipped with a vacuum actuated cut-out (overspeed) switch (S – Fig. OM12-18). The switch prevents erratic overspeed when motor is suddenly cut back from high speed to idle, with gear shift lever in neutral. One side of switch diaphragm is connected to intake manifold via vent tube (V) while a ground (kill) wire (3) leads from switch terminal to breaker terminal on one set of points. When overspeed occurs with throttle closed, high manifold vacuum momentarily closes the switch, shorting out one spark plug until engine speed again comes under control.

To service the automatic cut-out switch, refer to Fig. OM12-19. Check

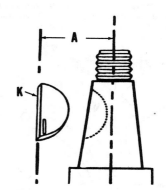

Fig. OM12-17—When installing flywheel, make sure outer edge of key (K) is parallel with centerline of crankshaft as shown at (A).

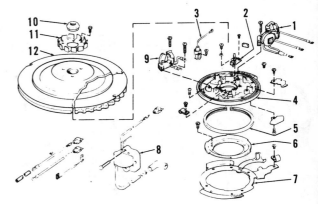

Fig. OM12-18—The vacuum actuated overspeed switch (S) grounds the ignition primary for the lower cylinder when throttle is closed suddenly.

S. Overspeed switch	1. Wire from safety switch (T) to wire (2)	3. Wire to breaker points (lower cylinder)	5. Wire from breaker points (upper cylinder to ignition switch
T. Starting safety switch			
V. Vacuum hose	2. Wire to starter solenoid	4. Wire to ignition switch	

electronically for grounds, if indicated, before disassembly. Disassemble the unit Fig. OM12-19 as a guide. Renew diaphragm (3) if leaks are apparent or if otherwise damged. Make sure that terminal screw is tight and well insulated when reassembling, that diaphragm chamber is air-tight, and that breather passage is open to rear of diaphragm.

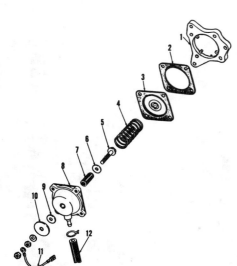

Fig. OM12-19—Exploded view of vacuum actuated overspeed switch.

1. Adapter	7. Insulator
2. Gasket	8. Body
3. Diaphragm	9. Insulator washer
4. Spring	10. Washer
5. Screw	11. Wire
6. Insulator washer	12. Tube

COOLING SYSTEM

WATER PUMP. All models are equipped with a rubber impeller type water pump. Impeller is mounted on and driven by the lower unit drive shaft. The main water inlet scoop is located below the exhaust outlet, above and behind the propeller as shown in Fig. OM12-20.

When cooling system problems are encountered, first check the water inlet for plugging or partial stoppage. On 40 hp models, check thermostat operation. If the trouble is not corrected, remove the lower unit gearcase as outlined in the appropriate section, and check the condition of water pump, water passages, gaskets and sealing surfaces.

THERMOSTAT. Forty horsepower models are equipped with a recirculating type thermostat as shown in Fig. OM12-20. Before coolant liquid reaches operating temperature, the main flow of coolant is recirculated through the return tube and water pump, as shown; little additional coolant water is introduced into the system. Thermostat (31) should open at a temperature of 130°-150°F; and spring (27) should maintain a pressure of approximately one psi in cooling system passages.

To service the thermostat, remove the motor cover and refer to Fig. OM12-21. Remove thermostat cover (32) and withdraw thermostat (31), housing (30), gasket (29), pressure valve (28) and spring (27). Renew any parts which are

damaged or questionable, and reassemble by reversing the disassembly procedure.

POWER HEAD

R&R AND DISASSEMBLE. To overhaul the power head, clamp the motor on a stand or support and remove the motor cover, rear exhaust housing cover, carburetor and intake manifold. Remove starter unit or units, flywheel, magneto armature plate and fuel pump.

Remove armature plate support (34 – Fig. OM12-21) and retainer (33), speed control lever (39) and outer and inner exhaust covers (20 and 18). Remove cylinder head (24 or 24A) and port and starboard brackets (7 and 10), then unbolt and remove power head from lower unit.

Tap out the two tapered crankcase aligning pins (12), working from cylinder side of crankcase flange; then, unbolt and remove front crankcase half (8).

NOTE: The two center main bearing cap screws are accessible through intake ports and must be removed.

Remove seal housing (29 – Fig. OM12-23A) and snap ring (28) on 40 hp models after 1973.

Pistons, rods and crankshaft are now accessible for removal and overhaul as

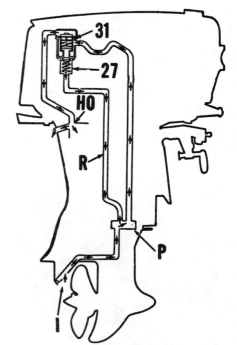

Fig. OM12-20—Schematic view of cooling system used on 40 hp models with recirculating type thermostat.

HO. Hot water oulet	R. Cold water return
I. Inlet	27. Spring
P. Water pump	31. Thermostat

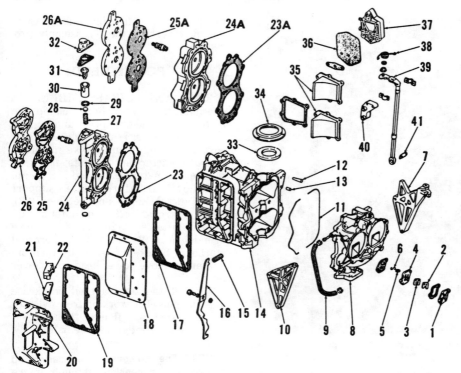

Fig. OM12-21 — Exploded view of crankcase and associated parts typical of all models.

1. Cover	12. Taper pin	22. Safety switch	32. Cover
2. Stop	13. Dowel	23. Gasket	33. Retainer
3. Bleeder valve	14. Cylinder half	24. Cylinder head	34. Support
4. Plate	15. Spring	25. Gasket	35. Transfer port cover
5. Screen	16. Lockout lever	26. Cover	36. Shield
6. Retainer	17. Gasket	27. Spring	37. Fuel pump
7. Bracket	18. Inner exhaust cover	28. Valve	38. Spring
8. Crankcase half	19. Gasket	29. Seal	39. Lever
9. Oil tube	20. Outer cover	30. Housing	40. Bracket
10. Bracket	21. Bracket	31. Thermostat	41. Pin
11. Seal strip			

outlined in the appropriate following paragraphs. Remove crankcase bleeder valve (4) or recirculating valve if installed and oil line (9). Blow oil lines and passages out using compressed air. When reassembling, follow the procedures outlined in the ASSEMBLY paragraph which follows.

ASSEMBLY. Because of the two-stroke design, crankcase and intake

manifold must be completely sealed against vacuum and pressure. The exhaust manifold and cylinder head must be sealed against water leakage and pressure. Mating surfaces of power head and exhaust housing must form a tight seal.

Fig. OM12-23 — Exploded view of crankshaft, bearings, pistons, rings and associated parts used on models prior to 1974.

1. Snap ring
2. Retainer
3. Spring
4. Washer
5. Seal
6. Quad ring
7. "O" ring
8. Bearing
9. Crankshaft
10. Key
11. Bearing
12. Seal
13. "O" ring
14. Retaining ring
15. Bearing race
16. Bearing cage
17. Bearing roller
18. Rod bolt
19. Rod cap
20. Bearing cage
21. Bearing roller
22. Connecting rod
23. Bearing
24. Piston
25. Ring set
26. Piston pin
27. Retainer

Whenever power head is disassembled, it is recommended that all gasket surfaces and the mating surfaces of crankcase halves be carefully checked for nicks and burrs or warped surfaces which might interfere with at tight seal. The cylinder head, head end of cylinder block or mating surfaces of manifold and crankcase may be lapped if necessary, to provide a smooth surface. Do not remove any more metal than is necessary.

Mating surfaces of crankcase may be checked for smoothness on the lapping block, and high spots and nicks removed; but surfaces must not be lowered. If extreme care is used, a slightly damaged crankcase may be salvaged in this manner. In case of doubt, renew the crankcase.

The crankcase halves are positively located during assembly by the use of two tapered dowel pins. Check to make sure that the dowel pins are not bent, nicked or distorted, and that dowel pin holes are clean and true. When installing dowel pins, make sure they are fully seated, but do not use excessive force.

When reassembling the crankcase, install the sealing strips (11 – Fig. OM12-21) and trim the ends to extend approximately 1/16 inch into bearing bores. Make sure mating surfaces of crankcase halves are completely clean and free from old cement or from nicks or burrs. Apply a non-hardening cement such as OMC Adhesive "M" to cylinder half of crankcase only. Apply cement sparingly and evenly, making sure entire surface is covered. Immediately install front half of crankcase and position

Fig. OM12-22 — One piston boss is a slip fit for easier assembly and proper expansion control. Loose boss is marked as shown.

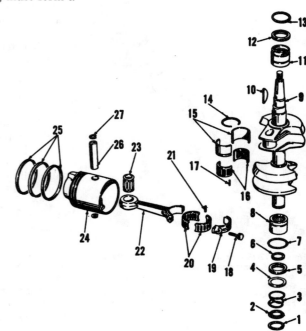

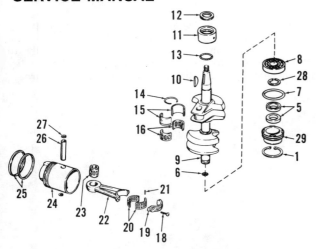

Fig. OM12-23A — Exploded view of crankshaft assembly used on models after 1973. Refer to Fig. OM12-23 for parts identification except for (28) snap ring; (29) seal housing.

on underneath side as shown in Fig. OM12-22. When servicing the piston or rod, press pin out or in, working through the "LOOSE" boss to keep from distorting piston. When assembling the piston to connecting rods, the oil hole (H – Fig. OM12-24) must be toward top of motor and the long tapering side of piston head toward exhaust side of motor.

When reassembling, all engine parts should be well coated with engine oil. Piston should be installed in cylinder with the long, tapering side of piston head toward exhaust port side of cylinder.

CONNECTING RODS, BEARINGS, AND CRANKSHAFTS. Before detaching connecting rods from crankshaft, make sure rods and pistons are properly marked for reinstallation in correct cylinder. Also note alignment marks on rod and and center main bearing cages.

Connecting rods are fitted with needle rollers in a two-piece bearing cage at crankpin end and a caged needle bearing at piston end. The bores at each end of the steel rod are hardened and ground to serve as the bearing outer race. All models are equipped with a cartridge type roller bearing at top main bearing and a split cage roller bearing for the center main bearing. Lower main bearing is a ball bearing on models after 1973 and a cartridge type roller bearing on all other models. The upper bearing on early models contains a recess for crankshaft upper seal. The center main bearing uses a split cage (16 – Fig. OM12-23

by installing the locating dowel pins; then install and tighten the crankcase screws.

Magneto retainer (33 – Fig. OM12-21) on early models must be installed with tapered (rounded) side down toward crankcase. Flat side is toward support (34) and magneto armature plate.

Install seals (5 – Fig. OM12-23A) back to back in seal housing (29) on 40 hp models after 1973.

When installing gaskets, check to make sure correct gasket is used and that ALL water passage holes are open. All gasket surfaces and cap screw threads must be sealed using a non-hardening cement such as OMC Gasket Sealing Compound. Tightening torques are given in the CONDENSED SERVICE DATA table. When installing the flywheel, refer to the special instructions given in IGNITION section.

PISTONS, PINS, RINGS AND CYLINDERS. Before detaching connecting rods from crankshaft, make sure that rod and cap are marked for

correct assembly to each other and in the proper cylinder.

Each aluminum piston on early models is fitted with three identical rings which are interchangeable and which may be installed either side up. Piston on later models has two piston rings which are not interchangeable. Piston and rings are available in standard size and oversizes. Refer to CONDENSED SERVICE DATA for piston and ring specifications. Renew pistons, rings, and/or cylinder assembly if parts are scored or otherwise damaged, or if clearances are excessive.

Piston pin is a transition fit (0.0001-0.0006 clearance) in one piston pin boss and a press fit in other boss at room temperature. The looser boss is marked

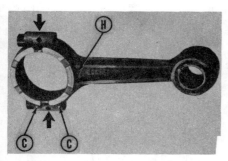

Fig. OM12-24 — Connecting rod is "fractured" at point of arrows. When installing cap, make sure correlation marks (C) are aligned, then work cap back and forth a slight amount until fracture lines match. Oil hole (H) must be toward top of motor.

Fig. OM12-25 — Exploded view of manual starter.

1. Screw
2. Washer
3. Spindle
4. Dowel
5. Wave washer
6. Friction ring
7. Bushing
8. Retainer
9. Pawl
10. Pulley
11. Recoil spring
12. Housing
13. Pin
14. Bushing
15. Spring
16. Ball
17. Nut
18. Guard
19. Rope
20. Lock
21. Spring
22. Anchor
23. Spring
24. Rod
25. Collar
26. Handle
27. Anchor

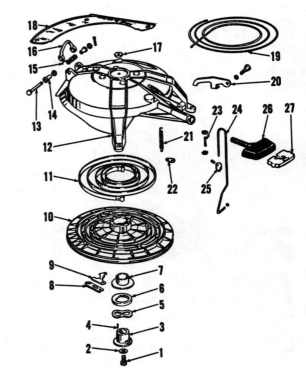

or OM12-23A) and outer race (15), held together at assembly by retaining ring (14).

When assembling the pistons to connecting rods, the oil hole (H–Fig. OM12-24) must be toward top of motor and the long tapering side of piston head toward exhaust side of motor.

The connecting rod is drilled and finished, then carefully fractured at points shown by arrows (Fig. OM12-24). The parting line is not machined, the uneven fractured surfaces serving to align rod and cap assembly. When installing the cap, align the index marks (C), then move rod cap back and forth slightly as rod screws are tightened, until uneven fracture lines mesh. Test the alignment after assembly, by scratching a fingernail across the parting line.

The main bearing outer races are prevented from turning in crankcase by locating dowels (13–Fig. OM12-21) in cylinder half of bearing bore. The dowel must fit hole in bearing race. To renew the dowel, first center-punch end of dowel; then drill with a No. 25 drill. Tap the hole using a No. 10-24 thread tap and use a puller plate and jack screw to remove the dowel.

Thoroughly lubricate all friction surfaces during assembly, using engine oil. Use petroleum jelly or Lubriplate to retain the loose needle bearings. Renew all crankcases seals whenever motor is disassembled.

MANUAL STARTER

Figure OM12-25 shows an exploded view of the manual starter. A new starter cord may be installed after starter is removed without disassembly of the unit. A 73¾ inch, 7/32 inch diameter nylon cord is used. Invert the removed starter in a vise and wind the recoil spring by inserting a punch in hole in pulley and turning pulley counterclock-

wise until spring is completely wound. Reverse the pulley one turn and install the cord.

To disassemble the starter for spring renewal or other service, remove center

bolt (1) and nut (17) and lift off pulley (10) leaving spring (11) in recess in housing (12). Remove spring carefully to avoid personal injury. Assemble by reversing the disassembly procedure.

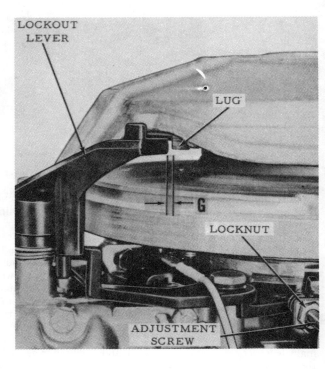

Fig. OM12-26A—Lockout lever on models after 1972 should be 0.030-0.060 inch (G) from lugs on starter pulley with outboard in neutral.

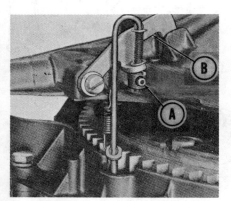

Fig. OM12-26—To adjust the starter latch on models prior to 1973 first set speed control grip at the fast speed recommended for starting. Loosen stop collar (A) and adjust latch (B) until it just clears cast lugs on starter pulley.

2. Drive shaft
3. Upper race
4. Thrust bearing
5. Lower race
6. Bearing
7. Drive pinion
8. Bearing cup
9. Bearing cone
10. Forward gear
11. Thrust washer
12. Shift lever
13. Pivot screw
14. Cradle
15. Dog clutch
16. Propeller shaft
17. Lower gearcase
18. Plug
19. Dowel
20. Seal strip
21. Thrust washer
23. Reverse gear
24. Thrust washer
25. Snap ring
26. Bearing
27. Seal
28. Housing
29. "O" ring
30. Propeller
31. Drive pin
32. Washer
33. Nut
34. Extension
35. Adapter
36. Grommet
37. Housing
38. Impeller
39. Plate
40. Seal
41. Bushing
42. Bearing
43. Gearcase
44. Screen
46. Bearing
47. Shift rod
48. Connector
53. Spring
54. Detent balls
55. Bushing

Fig. OM2-27—Exploded view of lower unit gearcase and associated parts used on models with manual shift. Snap ring (25) is not used on models after 1971. One seal (40) is used on models prior to 1974. Refer to Fig. OM12-27A for installation of detent balls (54) and spring (53). Pinion bearing (46) is not used on later models.

Models prior to 1973 are equipped with a starter latch which is mechanically linked to carburetor cam to prevent starting the motor when throttle is set for high speed. To adjust the starter latch, set shift lever in neutral position and the speed control lever to the fast limit (against neutral stop). Loosen the set screw in stop collar (A–Fig. OM12-26) and adjust the collar up or down on link until inner end of latch (B) just clears the cast lugs on starter pulley. Tighten the set screw (A) and check to make sure the latch disengages throughout the throttle range recommended for starting.

The starter lockout on models after 1972 is linked to the gearshift mechanism to prevent starter operation when outboard is in gear. To adjust starter lockout, place gearshift lever in neutral and turn adjustment screw shown in Fig. OM12-26A so that locknut lever is 0.030-0.060 inch from lugs (G) on starter pulley.

LOWER UNIT

Manual Shift Models

PROPELLER AND DRIVE PIN. Protection for the propeller and drive unit is provided by a cushion and slip clutch built into the propeller hub. Use only a propeller especially designed for the motor.

Propeller clutch slippage can be tested using a torque wrench and a suitable holding fixture and adapter. Slippage should occur at a torque of 185-225 ft.-lbs. Service consists of renewing the propeller. A 10½ inch diameter 3-blade 12 or 13 inch pitch propeller is normally used.

REMOVE AND REINSTALL. Most service on the lower unit can be performed by detaching the gearcase housing from exhaust housing. When servicing the lower unit, pay particular attention to water pump and water tubes with respect to air or water leaks. Leaky connections may interfere with proper cooling of the motor.

When overhauling the lower unit, use appropriate exploded views Fig. OM12-27 through OM12-30A as a guide, together with the special service information which follows. All gasket surfaces must be smooth, free from nicks and burrs, and assembled using a nonhardening sealer such as OMC Gasket Sealing Compound. All joints without gaskets must be smooth and free from nicks, burrs and old cement, and sealed with a nonhardening sealer such as OMC Adhesive "M." Refer to CONDENSED SERVICE DATA table for recommended tightening torques.

The propeller shaft (16–Fig. OM12-27) and drive gears (10 and 23) can be removed after first draining lubricant from gear compartment, removing pivot screw (13), and unbolting and removing gearcase lower housing (17). The drive pinion (7) and bearings (3 through 6) can also be withdrawn.

Make certain that the two ¼ inch hardened steel balls (54) and spring (53) are not lost when dog clutch (15) is pulled from propeller shaft (16).

To separate gearcase from exhaust housing, first remove cover (36–Fig. OM12-28) or covers (35 and 38–Fig. OM-29) and remove the lower screw in shift rod clamp (48–Fig. OM12-27). Gearcase can then be unbolted and separated from exhaust housing.

A slight difference will be noted in the two drive pinion thrust bearing races (3 and 5). The race with the larger hole should be installed above thrust bearing (4).

NOTE: Make certain that dog clutch (15 – Fig. OM12-27A) is correctly installed. if detent balls (54) do not exactly align with center of notches (N) turn dog clutch 180° and reinstall.

When reassembling gearcase, install a new sealing strip (20–Fig. OM12-27) in lower housing groove and trim ends of strip evenly to extend approximately 1/16 inch beyond ends of seal groove. Coat mating surfaces of housings with a nonhardening cement such as OMC Adhesive "M."

Shift linkage must be adjusted to provide full engagement of shifter collar

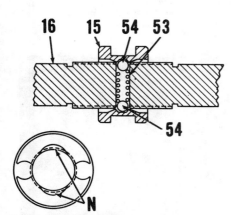

Fig. OM12-27A—The clutch is equipped with spring loaded detent balls as shown. When assembling, make certain that balls (54) are centered in notches (N).

15. Dog clutch
16. Propeller shaft
53. Detent spring
54. Detent balls

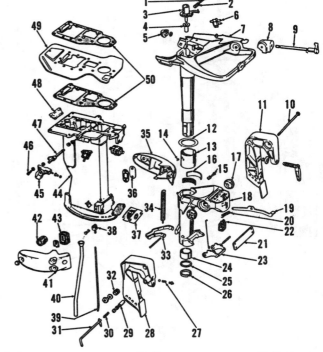

Fig. OM12-28—Exploded view of stern bracket, exhaust housing, swivel bracket and associated parts used on 33 hp and 40 hp (1971-1975) models.

1. Adjusting screw
2. Spring
3. Speed control gear
4. Bushing
5. Pinion
6. Connector
7. Steering bracket
8. Throttle cover
9. Throttle control
10. Tilt bolt
11. Stern bracket
12. Thrust washer
13. Liner
14. Pin
15. Adjusting screw
16. Friction plate
17. Bushing
18. Swivel bracket
19. Lever arm
20. Spring
21. Strap
22. Bumper
23. Link
24. Liner
25. "O" ring
26. Spacer
27. Detent
28. Stern bracket
29. Pin
30. Spring
31. Thrust rod
32. Tilt spring
33. Reverse lock
34. Spring
35. Lower mount

41. Lower mount	36. Cover	46. Clamp screw
42. Mount	37. Mount	47. Shift arm
43. Bumper	38. Clevis	48. Deflector
44. Exhaust housing	39. Shift rod	49. Plate
45. Shift lever	40. Water tube	50. Gasket

with the forward and reverse gears. To adjust the linkage, refer to Fig. OM12-30 or OM12-30A and proceed as follows: Loosen clamp screw (A) if necessary, and with lockout pin (P) setting in neutral detent as shown, adjust shift lever (L) to a vertical position. Tighten clamp screw and while turning propeller shaft by hand move shift lever in each direction and check to make sure that clutch dogs start to engage on high points of shifter lock (S) an equal distance from neutral detent.

On late models, neutral detent assembly (Fig. OM12-27A) in lower unit must be in neutral when pin (P–Fig. OM12-30 or OM12-30A) is in neutral position on shifter lock (S).

Steering tension can be adjusted by turning tension screw (15–Fig. OM12-28 or 5–Fig. OM12-29) until motor is easy to steer but will maintain a set course.

Electric Shift Models

PROPELLER AND DRIVE PIN. Protection for the propeller and drive unit is provided by a cushion and slip clutch built into the propeller hub. Use only a propeller especially designed for the motor.

Propeller clutch slippage can be tested using a torque wrench and a suitable holding fixture and adapter. Slippage should occur at a torque of 185-225 ft.-lbs. Service consists of renewing the propeller. A 10½ inch diameter 3-blade 12- or 13-inch pitch propeller is normally used.

REMOVE AND REINSTALL. Most service on the lower unit can be performed by detaching the gearcase housing from exhaust housing. When servicing the lower unit, pay particular attention to water pump and water tubes with respect to air or water leaks. Leaky connections may interfere with proper cooling of the motor.

When overhauling the lower unit, use appropriate exploded views Fig. OM12-32 through OM12-34 as a guide, together with the special service information which follows. All gasket surfaces must be smooth, free from nicks and burrs, and assembled using a nonhardening sealer such as OMC Gasket Sealing Compound. All joints without gaskets must be smooth and free from nicks, burrs and old cement, and sealed with a nonhardening sealer such as OMC "Adhesive M." Refer to CONDENSED SERVICE DATA table for

recommended tightening torques.

The driving mechanism of electric shift models consists of two driven gears which turn freely on the propeller shaft, two clutch coils, two clutch hubs splined to propeller shaft; and a forward drive and reverse drive electromagnet.

The clutch coils are anchored to their respective driven gears by three headless, Allen set screws, and the gear and clutch assembly secured to the splined clutch hub by snap ring. Energizing either the electromagnets attracts the free end of the clutch coil, causing it to drag on friction surface of the splined, clutch hub. The resultant friction causes the coil to wrap around hub, gripping it firmly and locking the propeller shaft to the selected drive gear. When the magnetic attraction is broken, the grip of the coil is released and both driven gears again turn independently of the propeller shaft.

Malfunction of the unit could result in clutch slippage in one or both directions of travel; complete loss of ability to engage in either or both of the gears;

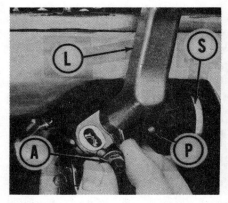

Fig. OM12-30 — View of shift linkage for 33 hp and 40 hp (1971-1975) motors. Adjust so that lower unit is in neutral when pin (P) is in neutral detent or shifter lock (S).

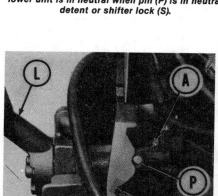

Fig. OM12-30A — View of shift linkage for manual shift of 40 hp motors prior to 1971. Refer to text for adjustment.

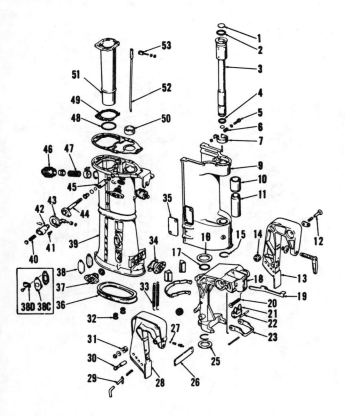

1. Plug
2. "O" ring
3. Pivot shaft
4. "O" ring
5. Adjusting screw
6. Spring
7. Friction band
9. Exhaust cover
10. Bushing
11. Bushing
12. Tilt bolt
13. Stern clamp
14. Bushing
15. Snap ring
16. Thrust ring
17. "O" ring
18. Swivel bracket
19. Lever arm
20. Spring
21. Bumper
22. Shaft
23. Link
25. Thrust ring
26. Strap
27. Detent
28. Stern bracket
29. Thrust pad
30. Tilt lock pin
31. Spring
32. Grommet
33. Spring
34. Mount
35. Cover
36. Seal
37. Mount
38. Cover
38C. Cover for electric shift
38D. Clamp
39. Exhaust housing
40. Spring
41. Screw
42. Shift lever
43. Lockout lever
44. Shift shaft
45. Spacer
46. Boot
47. Spring
48. "O" ring
49. Gasket
50. Bushing
51. Inner housing
52. Shift rod
53. Yoke

Fig. OM12-29 — Exploded view of exhaust housing, drive shaft housing and mounting bracket used on 40 hp models prior to 1971.

failure to release in one of the gears; or complete lock-up, in which drive shaft or propeller shaft could not be turned. Malfunction could be either electrical or mechanical in nature, and the cause should be determined as nearly as possible before disassembly is attempted.

The shift wiring consists of a hot wire leading from "A" terminal on starting switch to the remote control unit; the control switches; connecting wires leading from switches to the electromagnets; the electromagnets; and the ground running back through motor housings to the battery. Malfunction of an electrical nature usually results in failure of one or both clutch units to engage. Failure to disengage could be caused by malfunction of the control switch. Similar troubles could also be of a mechanical nature.

An electrical system test can be accomplished using an ohmmeter at the pins of the motor quick disconnect plug. The reverse shift wire is color coded light blue and the forward shift wire is light green. Attach one ohmmeter lead to motor ground and check resistance of each shift lead. Resistance should be approximately eight ohms. A zero ohms reading indicates a short circuit to ground while an infinite reading indicates an open circuit. An extremely high reading could indicate loose or corroded connections. To further check, connect one ohmmeter lead to the reverse shift wire and the other ohmmeter lead to the forward shift wire. Zero resistance indicates the two wires are shorted together, which will engage both clutches at the same time and lock up the lower end. If any case of unsatisfactory resistance is noted, the lower unit must be removed for further testing.

If a satisfactory reading was obtained, use a voltmeter to check continuity of circuits and available current with remote control unit and a battery connected. Current should flow at battery voltage from the proper shift wire to a suitable ground, when ignition switch is in "ON" position and control lever is moved to a forward or reverse operating position. There should be no current flow when switch is in "OFF" position or when control lever is in neutral or the opposite directional position.

To remove the lower unit, first remove the engine cover and the rear exhaust cover. Disconnect shift cable leads from motor wiring harness at the quick disconnects. Remove cover (35 – Fig. OM12-29) from the front exhaust cover (9). Remove the two attaching screws, then remove clamp (38D) and inner cover (38C).

NOTE: Apply oil or liquid soap to wires when withdrawing wires from cover (38C) and grommet. Be careful not to damage cable insulation. Refer to Fig. OM12-33.

After upper cable is free, remove propeller then unbolt upper gearcase assembly from exhaust housing. Remove gearcase while feeding cable through cable support opening. When installing, note that two series of ridges are molded into cable cover about five inches apart. When long shaft unit is installed, engage support in upper set of ridges. Engage support in lower rides on short shaft models, pulling slack into upper exhaust housing. The series of ridges form an exhaust gas seal.

To disassemble the gearcase, unbolt and remove the water pump and drive shaft, then remove and discard the two stud nuts (25 – Fig. OM12-32) retaining lower gearcase to upper housing. New self-locking nuts should be used when reassembling.

Invert the assembly and separate lower gearcase (35) from upper case (27). Tap lower gearcase lightly with a soft hammer, if necessary, to free lower case from its doweled position. Separate the housings 2-3 inches, then disconnect the two coil leads from upper shift cable (30). The connectors are covered by an insulating rubber sleeve which must first be pushed up the cable wires. After wiring is disconnected, the lower gearcase may be withdrawn.

Remove four screws from rear surface of gearcase head (41). Thread puller legs into both threaded holes and remove

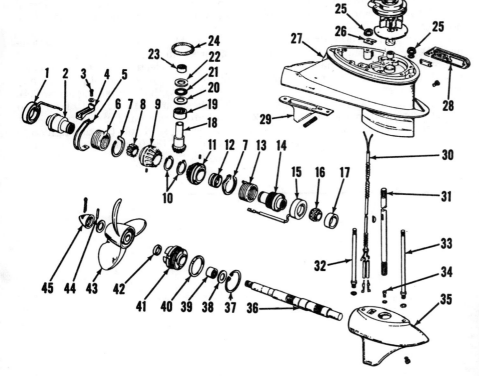

Fig. OM12-32 – Exploded view of gearcase and associated parts used on electric shift models.

1. Reverse electro-magnet	12. Forward bushing	23. Needle bearing
2. Reverse hub	13. Clutch roll	24. "O" ring
3. Screw	14. Forward hub	25. Self-locking nut
4. Retainer	15. Forward electro-magnet	26. Clip
5. Wire guard	16. Bearing cone	27. Upper housing
6. Clutch coil	17. Bearing cup	28. Water inlet
7. Spacer	18. Drive pinion	29. Water inlet
8. Needle bearing	19. Needle bearing	30. Upper wiring
9. Reverse gear	20. Washer (small holes)	31. Drive shaft
10. Snap ring	21. Thrust bearing	32. Stud
11. Forward gear	22. Washer (large hole)	33. Stud
		34. Clamp screw

35. Lower gearcase
36. Propeller shaft
37. Snap ring
38. Thrust washer
39. Needle bearing
40. "O" ring
41. Gearcase head
42. Seal
43. Propeller
44. Drive pin
45. Propeller nut

Fig. OM12-33 – Before lower unit can be removed, upper cable must be disconnected. Refer to text.

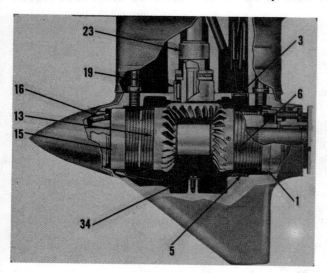

Fig. OM12-34 — Cross section of the assembled gearcase and associated parts used on electric shift models. Refer to Fig. OM12-32.

gearcase head, using a suitable puller. Remove snap ring (37), clamp screw (3) and coil wire retaining clamp (4). Insert a small punch into drive pin hole in propeller shaft and tap lightly on side of punch, pulling propeller shaft out of gearcase enough to dislodge the reverse electromagnet (1); then remove the electromagnet, being careful not to damage the coil lead.

Withdraw propeller shaft (36) with the reverse gear and hub assembly remaining on shaft. Tilt the pinion gear (18) toward the rear and withdraw through rear opening of gearcase; then, tilt the gearcase and remove forward gear and hub assembly.

Reach down through drive pinion opening with a screwdriver and remove the screw (34) which retains the forward

coil lead shield to bottom of gearcase. Refer to Fig. OM12-34. After the screw is removed, insert an internal expanding gear puller into bearing cone (16 – Fig. OM12-32), and pull the bearing cone and forward electromagnet (15). Bearing cup (17) can be removed with an internal expanding puller and slide hammer, or by heating the gearcase (35) to approximately 200°F. and jarring cup from housing.

Forward and reverse drive gears (9 and 11) are identical, but should not be interchanged once they have been used. Clutch coils (6 and 13) and spacers (7) are also identical for forward and reverse drive units. The forward clutch hub (14) differs from the reverse hub (2) by being knurled on the friction surface. These two hubs must not be inter-

changed. The reverse driving gear (9) is fitted with a needle roller bearing (8), while forward gear contains a bushing (12). These must also be installed in the indicated positions.

The spacers (7) are wedge-shaped, and designed to fill up the space between the last winding of clutch coil and the pocket of the driving gear. The projecting lugs of coil and spacer are placed side by side to completely fill the driving slot of gear. Apply one drop of Grade D "Loctite" to the threads of the retaining set screws and tighten the screws to a torque of 15-20 inch-pounds, using a torque wrench and suitable adapter. Forward bushing (12) should have a diametral clearance of 0.0003-0.0011 on the hub (14) and in the bore of driving gear (11). Because of the close clearance, extreme care must be used in assembly. Make sure parts are absolutely clean, and do not use force. Perfect alignment is required when assembling the gear and hub unit. Use a light oil as a lubricant when assembling the forward gear and bushing assembly; and needle bearing assembly grease or equivalent, when assembling the reverse gear. If clutch coil tends to bind, turn gear counterclockwise while applying gentle pressure until gear is fully installed on hub. Install snap ring (10) with the sharp edge to the outside.

Assemble by reversing the disassembly procedure, making sure that the lead for forward electromagnet (15) properly fits in groove in bottom of gearcase and is secured with the retaining screw (34). Fit the guard (5) over tail of forward lead after gear units are installed. Use self-locking stud nuts (25) and tighten to a torque of 18-20 ft.-lbs.

EVINRUDE AND JOHNSON
TWO-CYLINDER MODELS
40 HP (1985-1989)
48 HP (1987-1989)
50 HP (1971-1975 & 1978-1989)
55 HP (1976-1981)
60 HP (1980-1985)

EVINRUDE

Year Produced	40 HP	50 HP	55 HP	60 HP
1971	....	50172, 50173	....	....
1972	....	50202, 50203, 50272, 50273	....	....
1973	....	50302, 50303, 50372, 50373	....	....
1974	....	50442, 50443, 50472, 50473	....	....
1975	....	50542, 50543, 50572, 50573	....	....
1976	....	....	55642, 55643, 55672, 55673	....
1977	....	....	55742, 55743, 55772, 55773	....
1978	....	50802, 50803	55874, 55875	....
1979	....	50902, 50903	55974, 55975	....
1980	....	50ECS, 50ELCS	55RCS, 55RLCS	60ECS, 60ELCS
1981	....	50BECI, 50BELCI	55RCI, 55RLCI	60ECI, 60ELCI, 60TLCI
1982	....	50BECN, 50BELCN	....	60ECN, 60ELCN, 60TLCN
1983	....	50BECT, 50BELCT, 50TELCT	....	60ECT, 60ELCT, 60TLCT
1984	....	50BECR, 50BELCR, 50TLCR, 50TELCR	....	60ECR, 60ELCR, 60TLCR
1985	40RCO, 40RLCO, 40ECO, 40ELCO, 40TECO, 40TELCO	50BECO, 50BELCO, 50TLCO, 50TELCO	....	60ECO, 60ELCO, 60TLCO
1986	40RCD, 40RLCD, 40ECD, 40ELCD, 40TECD, 40TELCD	50BECD, 50BELCD, 50TLCD, 50TELCD	....	....

Year Produced	40 HP	48 HP	50 HP	55 HP	60 HP
1987	E40RCU E40RLCU E40BACU E40BALCU	E48ESLCU*	E50BECU* E50BELCU* E50TELCU* E50TLCU	. . . . .	. . . . .

Year Produced	40 HP	48 HP	50 HP	55 HP	60 HP
1988	E40ECU* E40ELCU* E40TECU* E40TELCU* E40RCC E40RLCC E40BACC E40BALCC E40ECC* E40ELCC* E40TECC* E40TELCC* E40TLCC	E48ESLCC*	E50BECC* E50BELCC* E50TELCC* E50TLCC	.....	.....
1989	E40RCE E40RLCE E40BACE E40BALCE E40ECE* E40ELCE* E40TECE* E40TELCE* E40TLCE E40TTLCE	E48ESLCE*	E50BECE* E50BELCE* E50TELCE* E50TLCE	.....	.....

JOHNSON

Year Produced	40 HP	50 HP	55 HP	60 HP
1971	...	50ES71, 50ESL71	....	....
1972	....	50ES72, 50ESL72, 50R72,50RL70	....	....
1973	....	50ES73, 50ESL73	....	....
1974	....	50ES74, 50ESL74	....	....
1975	....	50ES75, 50ESL75	....	....
1976	....	....	55E76, 55EL76	....
1977	....	....	55E77, 55EL77	....
1978	....	50MR78, 50MLR78	55E78, 55EL78	....
1979	....	50R79, 50RL79	55E79, 55EL79	....
1980	....	50ECS, 50ELCS	55RCS, 55RLCS	60ECS, 60ELCS
1981	....	50BECI, 50BELCI	55RCI, 55RLCI	60ECI, 60ELCI, 60TLCI
1982	....	50BECN, 50BELCN	55RCN, 55RLCN	60ECN, 60ELCN, 60TLCN
1983	....	50BECT, 50BELCT, 50TELCT	55RCT, 55RLCT	60ECT, 60ELCT, 60TLCT
1984	....	50BECR, 50BELCR, 50TLCR, 50TELCR	55RSF, 55RSLF	60ECR, 60ELCR, 60TLCR
1985	40RCO, 40RLCO, 40ECO, 40ELCO, 40TECO,	50BECO, 50BELCO, 50TLCO, 50TELCO,	....	60ECO, 60ELCO, 60TLCO

		40TELCO			
1986		40RCD,	50BECD,	....	....
		40RLCD,	50BELCD,		
		40ECD,	50TLCD,		
		40ELCD,	50TELCD,		
		40TECD,			
		40TELCD			

Year Produced	40 HP	48 HP	50 HP	55 HP	60 HP
1987	J40RCU	J48ESLCU*	J50BECU*	. . . . .	. . . . .
	J40RLCU		J50BELCU*		
	J40BACU		J50TELCU*		
	J40BALCU		J50TLCU		
	J40ECU*				
	J40ELCU*				
	J40TECU*				
	J40TELCU*				
1988	J40RCC	J48ESLCC*	J50BECC*	. . . .	. . . .
	J40RLCC		J50BELCC*		
	J40BACC		J50TELCC*		
	J40BALCC		J50TLCC		
	J40ECC*				
	J40ELCC*				
	J40TECC*				
	J40TELCC*				
	J40TLCC				
1989	J40RCE	J48ESLCE*	J50BECE*	. . . . .	. . . . .
	J40RLCE		J50BELCE*		
	J40BACE		J50TELCE*		
	J40BALCE		J50TLCE		
	J40ECE*				
	J40ELCE*				
	J40TECE*				
	J40TELCE*				
	J40TLCE				
	J40TTLCE				

CONDENSED SERVICE DATA

TUNE-UP

Hp/rpm	40/5000
	48/5000
	50/5500 (prior to 1976)
	50/5000 (after 1977)
	55/5500 (prior to 1980)
	55/5000 (after 1979)
	60/5500
Bore	3.1875 in.
	(80.963 mm)
Stroke.	2.820 in.
	(71.63 mm)
Number of Cylinders	2
Displacement	45 cu. in.*
	(737 cc)

Spark Plug:
1971-1985	L77J4†
Electrode Gap	0.040 in.
	(1.0 mm)
1986-1988	QL77JC4†
Electrode Gap	0.040 in.
	(1.0 mm)
1989	QL78C†
Electrode Gap	0.030 in.
	(0.76 mm)

Ignition Type	CDI
Carburetor Make	OMC

Idle Speed (in gear):
Prior to 1989	700-750 rpm
After 1988	770-830 rpm
Fuel:Oil Ratio	50:1‡

*On 50 hp models prior to 1976, bore is 3.06 inches (77.7 mm) and displacement is 41.5 cu. in. (680 cc).

†When operated at sustained high speeds, Champion QL78V spark plugs are recommended for 1985-1988 models, or QL16V for 1989 models. Renew surface gap spark plug if center electrode is more than $1/_{32}$ inch (0.79 mm) below flat surface of plug end.

‡On 1985 and later models equipped with variable ratio oiling (VRO), the VRO pump varies the fuel:oil ratio from approximately 50:1 to approximately 150:1 by sensing engine power output.

SIZES—CLEARANCES
Piston Ring End Gap	0.007-0.017 in.
	(0.18-0.43 mm)

SIZES—CLEARANCES

Lower Piston Ring Side Clearance:
1971-1984 . . . . 0.015-0.0040 in.
(0.038-0.102 mm)
1985-1989 . . . . 0.004 in. Max.
(0.10 mm)

Piston Skirt Clearance:
1971-1978 . . . . 0.0045-0.0065 in.
(0.114-0.165 mm)
1979-1981 . . . . 0.0055-0.0095 in.
(0.140-0.241 mm)
1982-1984 . . . . 0.0018-0.0049 in.
(0.046-0.124 mm)
1985-1989 . . . . See Text

Maximum Cylinder Bore Tolerance
(Prior to 1987) . . . . 0.003 in.
(0.08 mm)

Standard Cylinder Bore Diameter
(After 1984) . . . . 3.1870-3.1880 in.
(80.950-80.975 mm)
Maximum Allowable Taper . . . . 0.002 in.
(0.05 mm)
Maximum Allowable Out-of-Round . . . . 0.003 in.
(0.08 mm)

Crankshaft Journal Diameters:
Top Main . . . . 1.4974-1.4979 in.
(38.03-38.04 mm)
Center Main . . . . 1.3748-1.3752 in.
(34.92-34.93 mm)
Bottom Main . . . . 1.1810-1.1815 in.
(30.00-30.11 mm)
Crankpin . . . . 1.1823-1.1828 in.
(30.03-30.04 mm)

Crankshaft End Play:
1971-1981 . . . . 0.0006-0.0165 in.
(0.015-0.419 mm)

TIGHTENING TORQUES

Connecting Rod Cap:
Prior to 1987 . . . . 29-31 ft.-lbs.
(39.3-42.0 N·m)
After 1986 . . . . 30-32 ft.-lbs.
(40.7-43.4 N·m)

Crankcase Halves:
Six Main Bearing Screws . . . . 216-240 in.-lbs.
(24-27 N·m)
Eight Outer Screws . . . . 60-84 in.-lbs.
(7-9 N·m)

Cylinder Head . . . . 216-240 in.-lbs.
(24-27 N·m)

Flywheel:
1978-1982 . . . . 80-85 ft.-lbs.
(110-115 N·m)
All Other Models . . . . 100-105 ft.-lbs.
(136-143 N·m)

Spark Plug . . . . 216-240 in.-lbs.
(24-27 N·m)

Standard Screws:
No. 6 . . . . 7-10 in.-lbs.
(0.8-1.2 N·m)
No. 8 . . . . 15-22 in-lbs.
(1.6-2.4 N·m)
No. 10 . . . . 25-35 in.-lbs.
(2.8-4.0 N·m)
No. 12 . . . . 35-40 in.-lbs.
(4.0-4.6 N·m)
¼ Inch . . . . 60-80 in.-lbs.
(7-9 N·m)
5/16 Inch . . . . 120-140 in.-lbs.
(14-16 N·m)
⅜ Inch . . . . 220-240 in.-lbs.
(24-27 N·m)
7/16 Inch . . . . 340-360 in.-lbs.
(38-40 N·m)

LUBRICATION

The power head is lubricated by oil mixed with the fuel. The recommended fuel is regular leaded or unleaded gasoline with a minimum octane rating of 87 on 1987-1989 models, 86 on 1976-1986 models and 89 on 1971-1975 models. If the recommended fuel is not available, gasoline containing not more than 10 percent ethanol alcohol, or gasoline containing not more than 5 percent methanol alcohol with 5 percent co-solvent additives, may be used. Do not use gasoline exceeding the specified alcohol content regardless of octane rating. Discontinue using alcohol extended gasoline if fuel system problems are encountered.

The recommended oil for all models is Evinrude/Johnson Outboard Lubricant, OMC 2-Cycle Motor Oil or a suitable equivalent NMMA (formerly known as BIA) certified TC-W or TC-WII engine oil. The manufacturer recommends using only oil certified TC-WII on models after 1988. On models not equipped with variable ratio oiling (VRO) the recommended fuel:oil ratio for normal service and during engine break-in is 50:1.

NOTE: OMC service bulletin 2211 issued September 1988, recommends using a 50:1 fuel:oil ratio on all recreational outboard motors that were previously recommended for a 100:1 fuel:oil mixture. For 1989, Accumix and Accumix R fuel and oil mixing systems have been changed to a 50:1 ratio.

On models so recommended, a 100:1 fuel:oil mixture may be used under the following circumstances: an approved oil formulated for 100:1 mixture is used; the engine is completely broken-in; the motor is used on a frequent basis. Do not use a 100:1 mixture if motor is used infrequently or if during nonuse, the motor is stored in areas of high humidity or wide-scale temperature changes, or if motor is operated at constant high speeds.

On 1985 and later models equipped with VRO, the VRO pump varies the fuel:oil ratio from approximately 150:1 at idle to approximately 50:1 at full throttle by sensing engine power output. During engine break-in (initial 10 hours of operation) on VRO equipped models, a 100:1 fuel and oil mixture (50:1 on 1985 models) should be added to the fuel tank and used in combination with the VRO system. During break-in, oil level in VRO tank should be observed to ensure oil level is dropping, indicating VRO system is functioning. After initial 10 hours of operation, make sure oil in VRO tank is being consumed, then switch to straight gasoline in fuel tank. If oil in VRO tank is not being consumed, refer to VRO section for testing procedure.

The lower unit gears and bearings are lubricated by oil contained in the gearcase. The recommended oil is OMC Sea-Lube Premium Blend Gearcase Lube on models prior to 1977 and OMC HI-VIS Gearcase Lube on models after 1976. The gearcase oil level should be checked after every 50 hours of operation and the gearcase should be drained and filled with new oil every 100 hours or once each season, whichever occurs first.

The gearcase is drained and filled through the same plug port. An oil level (vent) port is used to indicate the full oil level of the gearcase and for ease in oil drainage.

To drain the oil, place the outboard motor in a vertical position. Remove the drain plug and oil level plug and allow the lubricant to drain into a suitable container.

To fill the gearcase with oil, place the outboard motor in a vertical position. Add oil through the drain plug opening with an oil feeder until the oil begins to overflow from oil level plug port.

Reinstall oil level plug with a new gasket, if needed, and tighten. Remove oil feeder, then reinstall drain plug with a new gasket, if needed, and tighten.

FUEL SYSTEM

CARBURETOR. Carburetors used on models prior to 1977 are equipped with a low speed mixture screw (5A—Fig. OM13-1). Models after 1976 are equipped with fixed idle mixture jet (4). On models after 1978 (except 1980 50 hp and 1985 and later models), orifice (25) is the idle jet and orifice (4) is the intermediate mixture jet. On 1989 models, a slow speed mixture needle is used in place of idle jet (25). High speed mixture is metered by fixed jet (11) on all models.

NOTE: The manufacturer does not recommend submerging carburetor components in carburetor or parts cleaning solutions. An aerosol type carburetor cleaner is recommended to clean carburetor. The float and other components made of plastic and rubber should not be subjected to some cleaning solutions. Safety eyewear and hand protection are recommended when working with solvent.

Initial setting of idle mixture needle (5A) is $^5/_8$ turn open on models prior to 1975, $1^1/_8$ turns open on 1975 models, $2^1/_4$ turns open on 1989 40 hp models and $2^3/_4$ turns open on 1989 48 and 50 hp models. Final slow speed mixture adjustment should be performed with motor running in forward gear at normal operating temperature. If so equipped, arms should be detached from idle mixture screws before making individual adjustments. Reinstall arms so levers are pointing straight to port after adjustment.

To check float level, remove float bowl and invert carburetor. Place OMC Float Gage 324891 on float bowl gasket surface as shown in Fig. OM13-4. Make sure float gage is not pushing down on

float. Float should be between notches on side of float gage marked 25 THRU 75 HP. Carefully bend float arm to adjust. If float gage 324891 is not available, adjust float so float is level and parallel with float bowl gasket surface. To check float drop, hold carburetor upright and allow float to hang by its own weight. Measure from float bowl gasket surface to bottom of float 180 degrees from inlet valve. Carefully bend tang on float arm (adjacent to inlet valve) to adjust float drop to $1^1/_8$ to $1^5/_8$ inches (28.6-41.3 mm). Apply a suitable thread lock-

ing compound to float bowl screws upon reassembly.

Refer to CONDENSED SERVICE DATA for recommended idle speed. For optimum results when adjusting idle speed, boat should be in the water with the correct propeller installed. Engine should be running in forward gear at normal operating temperature with boat movement unrestrained.

Electric start models (prior to 1983) are provided with a choke solenoid (9— Fig. OM13-2). Solenoid is usually controlled by a thermo switch in exhaust

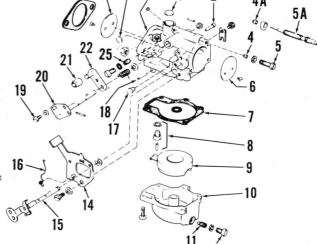

Fig. OM13-1—Exploded view of carburetor. Idle jet (4) is used on models after 1976. Idle mixture needle (5A) is used on models prior to 1977. On some later models, orifice (4) is the intermediate mixture jet and orifice (25) is the idle mixture jet. On 1989 models, a slow speed mixture needle and adapter sleeve is used in place of idle jet (25). Choke components are not used on models after 1982. Refer to text.

1. Core plug
2. Fuel nipple
3. Carburetor body
4. Idle jet or intermediate jet
4A. Bushing
5. Screw
5A. Idle mixture needle
6. Choke valve
7. Gasket
8. Inlet valve
9. Float
10. Float bowl
11. Main jet
12. Plug
14. Manual choke lever
15. Choke shaft
16. Override spring
17. Detent pin
18. Float pivot pin
19. Screw
20. Throttle shaft
21. Roller
22. Lever
23. Core plug
24. Throttle plate
25. Idle jet

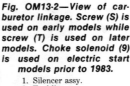

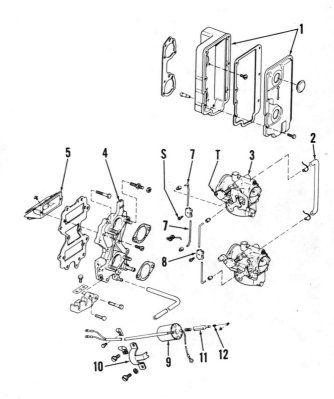

Fig. OM13-2—View of carburetor linkage. Screw (S) is used on early models while screw (T) is used on later models. Choke solenoid (9) is used on electric start models prior to 1983.

1. Silencer assy.
2. Fuel line
3. Carburetor
4. Intake manifold
5. Reed valve
7. Throttle links
8. Choke link fastener
9. Choke solenoid
10. Clamp
11. Plunger
12. Spring

cover. However, manual control is possible at motor. A switch is provided at the remote control box for additional choke control. Choke should be installed so top of plunger (11) is held $^{3}/_{16}$ inch (4.76 mm) from top of solenoid (9) as shown in Fig. OM13-5. Choke spring (12—Fig. OM13-2) is installed on plunger $2^{1}/_{2}$-$3^{1}/_{2}$ turns. Service to the choke solenoid consists of checking the circuit and renewal of malfunctioning parts. Make certain plunger moves freely in solenoid coil.

NOTE: Do not lubricate plunger as eventual sticking will result.

Models after 1982 use a manual primer system on manual rewind start models, and an electric primer system on electric start models.

SPEED CONTROL LINKAGE

All Models Prior to 1984 And Some 1984 Models. The carburetor throttle valves are synchronized to open as the ignition is advanced. It is important that throttle valve opening and ignition timing synchronization be checked and adjusted if necessary.

Use the following procedure to check and adjust linkage synchronization: Move speed control to full stop position.

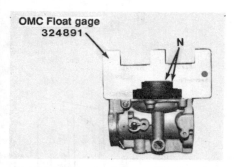

Fig. OM13-4—To check float level, invert carburetor and place OMC Float Gage 324891 on carburetor body as shown. Make sure float gage is not pushing down on float (9). Float should be between notches (N) on side of gage marked 25 THRU 75 HP. Bend float arm to adjust.

Fig. OM13-5—Choke solenoid should be installed so plunger is 3/16 inch (4.76 mm) from casing.

On early models, loosen set screw (S—Fig. OM13-6) and, on later models, screw located in top carburetor throttle shaft cam. Use a small amount of hand pressure to hold throttle plates fully closed while screw is retightened. Slowly advance speed control until throttle cam (TC) contacts cam roller (CR) and all slack is taken up. Lower mark on throttle cam should align with center of cam roller. Loosen screw (A) to adjust cam roller. Connect a power timing light to top cylinder and start the engine. Turn idle speed screw (I) until spark advance at idle speed is 2-4 degrees BTDC. If necessary, stop engine and remove pin (P) in throttle cam yoke. Turn yoke (Y) to realign mark on throttle cam with center of cam roller. Full advanced ignition timing should be 21 degrees BTDC on 60 hp models and 18-20 degrees BTDC on other models, at a minimum of 3500 rpm. One clockwise turn of full advance stop screw (AS) will retard ignition timing approximately 1 degree. Stop engine and check full throttle carburetor stop. Free play (A—Fig. OM13-7) between throttle cam and throttle cam roller should be 0.000-0.020 inch (0.00-0.50 mm) with speed controls in full speed position. Turning

Fig. OM13-6—View of speed control linkage used on all models prior to 1984 and some 1984 models. Refer to text for identification of components and adjustment procedures.

stop screw (B—Fig. OM13-6) adjusts free play.

A safety starting switch (SS) is located on electric start models prior to 1976 to prevent starter operation with speed control set at high throttle settings. Switch is not adjustable but may be inspected with an ohmmeter or continuity light. Switch must show a closed circuit if throttle is set in the "START" position or below. On models after 1975, the safety start switch is located in the remote control.

Some 1984 Models And 1985-1988 Tiller Handle Models. The carburetor throttle valves are synchronized to open as the ignition is advanced. It is important that throttle valve opening and ignition timing synchronization be checked and adjusted if necessary.

The following procedure should be used to check and adjust synchronization of linkage. Turn idle speed adjustment knob, located at the end of the steering handle, counterclockwise to complete slow speed position. While turning the twist grip from full closed position to full open position, check the clearance (C—Fig. OM13-8) between roller (1) and end of slot in cam (2).

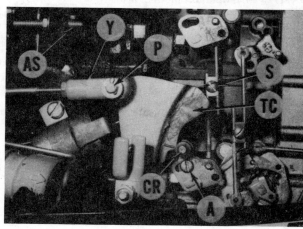
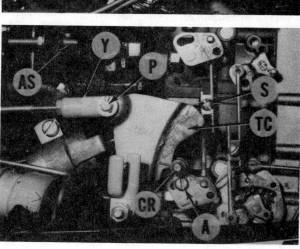
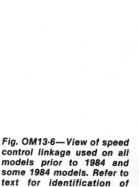

Clearance should be ¼ inch (6.35 mm) at both ends of slot. If not, remove screw (3) and rotate connector (4) until the correct adjustment is obtained, then reinstall screw (3).

Rotate twist grip to closed position. Loosen the screw located in top carburetor throttle shaft cam (5). Use a small amount of hand pressure to hold the throttle plates fully closed and retighten screw (5). Rotate the twist grip until throttle cam (6) contacts cam roller (7) and all slack is taken up. Lower mark on throttle cam (6) should align with center of cam roller (7) just as throttle plates begin to open. Loosen screw (8) to adjust cam roller.

Connect a power timing light to engine top cylinder. Rotate the twist grip until the throttle plates just start to open. Start the engine and note the spark advance with the timing light. The spark advance at idle speed should be 2-4 degrees BTDC. If not, stop the engine and remove pin (9). Rotate yoke (10) clockwise to increase the pickup timing degrees and counterclockwise to decrease. One turn will equal approximately 2 degrees.

Full advanced ignition timing should be 18-20 degrees BTDC on all models at a minimum of 3500 rpm. Spark advance rod (11) must be removed and the ends

Fig. OM13-7—Free play of throttle lever (A) should be 0.000-0.020 inch (0.00-0.50 mm) at full throttle position.

bent to adjust. The wide-open throttle adjustment screw (12) must be adjusted so the carburetor throttle shaft pins (port side of carburetor) are exactly vertical when throttle control is placed in full throttle position.

Remote Control Models 1985-1988. The carburetor throttle valves should open and close at exactly the same time and be synchronized to open as the ignition is advanced. Use the following procedure to check and adjust speed control linkage.

To synchronize carburetor throttle valves, remove both remote control cables from the power head and place throttle lever in the idle position. Loosen throttle cam roller screw (8—Fig. OM13-9) and push cam roller (7) away from throttle cam (6). Loosen adjusting screw (S) located in upper carburetor throttle lever (5). Making sure throttle valves are completely closed, rotate upper carburetor throttle lever (5) counterclockwise to remove any play in linkage, then retighten screw (S). Recheck adjustment to be sure throttle valves open and close at the same time.

To adjust throttle pickup point, advance throttle cam (6) until cam just contacts cam follower roller (7). Lower mark on throttle cam (6) should align with center of roller (7) just as throttle valves begin to open. Loosen screw (8) and move roller (7) to adjust.

To adjust pickup timing, connect a suitable timing light to number 1 (top) spark plug lead and advance throttle until throttle cam (6) contacts cam follower roller (7). While holding throttle in this position, start engine and note timing.

NOTE: On some models, it may be necessary to adjust idle stop screw (12—Fig. OM13-10) so center of cam follower roller (7—Fig. OM13-9)) is aligned with top mark on cam (6) to keep engine running. If so, be sure to return idle speed stop screw to original position after timing adjustment.

Pickup timing should be 2-4 degrees BTDC. To adjust, stop engine and loos-

en jamb nut (N) and turn thumb screw (9) as necessary. Note that turning top of thumb screw (9) toward crankcase advances timing.

Full throttle stop screw (11-Fig. OM13-10) should be adjusted so throttle shaft roll pins (port side of carburetors) are positioned exactly vertical when throttle control is advanced to full throttle (engine not running). Make sure roll pins do not rotate past vertical.

Full throttle maximum timing should be 18-20 degrees BTDC at a minimum of 5000 rpm. To check, connect a suitable timing light to number 1 (top) spark plug lead. Lower unit should be submersed in a suitable test tank with the proper test wheel installed to check maximum timing advance. Start engine and run at 5000 rpm or more while noting ignition timing. To adjust, stop engine and turn maximum advance screw (10—Fig. OM13-9) as necessary. Note that turning screw (10) clockwise retards timing.

Fig. OM13-9—View of speed control linkage on 1985-1988 models equipped with remote control.

N. Jamb nut	8. Screw
S. Screw	9. Thumb screw
5. Throttle lever	10. Maximum spark
6. Throttle cam	advance screw
7. Cam follower roller	

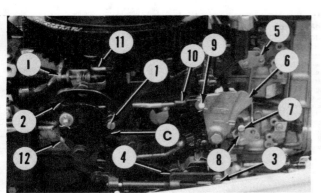

Fig. OM13-8—View of speed control linkage used on some 1984 models and all 1985-1988 tiller handle models. Refer to text for identification of components and adjustment procedures.

Fig. OM13-10—View of full throttle stop screw (11) and idle speed stop screw (12) on 1985-1988 models equipped with remote control.

The manufacturer recommends adjusting idle speed with the boat in the water with the correct propeller installed. Outboard motor should be running in forward gear at normal operating temperature with boat movement unrestrained. Turn idle speed stop screw (12—Fig. OM13-10) to obtain idle speed of 700-750 rpm.

Models After 1988. To synchronize throttle valves, remove throttle cable from throttle lever and loosen screw (S—Fig. OM13-9) on upper carburetor throttle lever (5). Open both carburetor throttle valves and allow valves to snap shut, then rotate upper carburetor throttle lever counterclockwise removing play in linkage and retighten screw (5). Recheck adjustment to be sure carburetor throttle valves open and close at exactly the same time.

Proceed as follows to adjust throttle pickup point: Loosen cam follower roller screw (3—Fig. OM13-11) and push cam (1) and roller (2) together until they contact. With cam (1) and roller (2) just touching and carburetor throttle valves closed, align mark on cam (1) with center of roller (2), then retighten screw (3). Next, push idle speed screw (5) against the stop. With idle speed screw (5) against its stop, spark lever cam follower (10) should be centered between marks on throttle lever (8) and a clearance of 0.010 inch (0.25 mm) should be between cam (1) and roller (2). If not, adjust length of throttle control rod (4) as necessary. With throttle pickup properly adjusted, idle speed timing should be 1-5 degrees ATDC. If idle speed timing is not as specified, make sure engine is running within the proper temperature range, carburetors are properly adjusted and calibrated, power head is in acceptable condition and flywheel and key are not damaged or excessively worn.

NOTE: Lower unit should be submersed in a suitable test tank with the correct test

propeller installed to check or adjust maximum timing advance.

Check maximum timing advance as follows: Connect a suitable timing light to the number 1 (top) spark plug lead, start engine and note timing at full throttle. Full throttle timing should be 18-20 degrees BTDC at a minimum of 5000 rpm. If adjustment is required, stop engine, remove spark control rod (6) and adjust length of rod (6) as necessary.

The manufacturer recommends adjusting idle speed with the boat in the water with the correct propeller installed. Outboard motor should be running in forward gear at normal operating temperature with boat movement unrestrained. Turn idle speed screw (5) to obtain idle speed of 700-750 rpm. If throttle speed adjustment is required, throttle pickup point must be readjusted as previously outlined. Carburetor throttle shaft pins (starboard side) should be pointing exactly vertical with carburetors in the full throttle position. If not, adjust full throttle stop screw (9) as necessary. Install throttle cable in upper hole in throttle lever (8) on tiller handle models and lower hole on remote control models.

REED VALVES. Two sets of reed (leaf) valves (1—Fig. OM13-12) are used, one for each cylinder. The reed plate assembly is located between intake manifold (5) and crankcase and should be inspected whenever the carburetors are removed. Reed petals should be centered over reed plate openings and seat lightly against reed plate throughout their entire length with the least possible tension. Reed petals should be smooth, flat and completely free of nicks, cracks or other damage. Intake manifold mating surface must be flat to within 0.004 inch (0.10 mm).

Do not disassemble reed valve assemblies unless renewal is required. Never attempt to straighten or repair a bent

or damaged reed petal. Never turn a used reed petal over and return to service. Apply a suitable thread locking compound to reed petal attaching screws and tighten to 25-35 in.-lbs. (2.8-4.0 N·m). Tighten reed plate-to-manifold screws to 25-35 in.-lbs. (2.8-4.0 N·m). Tighten manifold-to-crankcase screws to 60-84 in.-lbs. (6.8-9.5 N·m).

FUEL PUMP (WITHOUT VRO). The diaphragm type fuel pump (5—Fig. OM13-13) is available only as an assembly. If fuel delivery malfunction is noted, make sure filter element (3) and fuel lines are clean. Fuel pump pressure should be as follows: 1 psi (6.9 kPa) at 600 rpm; 1.5 psi (10.3 kPa) at 2500-3000 rpm; 2.5 psi (17.2 kPa) at 4500 rpm. If fuel pump pressure is not as specified, renew pump assembly. Tighten pump mounting screws to 24-36 in.-lbs. (2.7-4.1 N·m). Install filter (3) with lip facing pump (5). Tighten screw (1) to 10-15 in.-lbs. (1.1-1.7 N·m).

VRO TYPE FUEL PUMP. The VRO type fuel pump (1—Fig. OM13-14) meters the fuel:oil mixture in the prop-

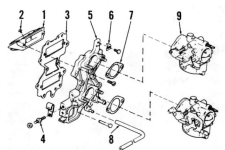

Fig. OM13-12—Carburetor and intake manifold typical of all models. Early type intake manifold (5) is shown.

1. Reed plate	
2. Screw	6. Timing pointer
3. Gasket	7. Gasket
4. Pivot bolt	8. Hose
5. Manifold	9. Carburetor

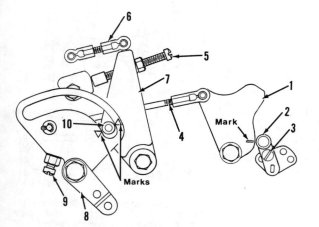

Fig. OM13-11—View of speed control linkage on 1989 models.

1. Throttle cam
2. Throttle cam follower roller
3. Screw
4. Throttle control rod
5. Idle speed screw
6. Spark control rod
7. Spark control lever
8. Throttle lever
9. Full throttle stop screw
10. Spark lever cam follower

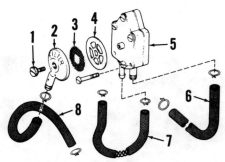

Fig. OM13-13—View of fuel pump on models without variable ratio oiling (VRO).

1. Screw	6. Pump to "T" fitting hose
2. Cap	
3. Screen	7. Pump to manifold hose
4. Gasket	
5. Pump assy.	8. Inlet hose

er ratio depending upon power output. Fuel:oil ratio varies from approximately 150:1 at idle to approximately 50:1 at full throttle.

NOTE: If the VRO system is not being used, the inlet nozzle at the outboard motor connector must be plugged to prevent fuel system contamination. A 50:1 fuel and oil mixture must be added to the fuel tank to ensure the proper engine lubrication.

TESTING. Using a "T" fitting, connect a suitable vacuum gage and a length of clear plastic hose to fuel inlet fitting at lower engine cover. All connections should be clamped to prevent leakage. Start engine and allow to warm to normal operating temperature.

NOTE: When performing VRO system tests that require full throttle operation, install outboard motor in a suitable test tank with the correct test wheel installed.

Run motor at full throttle for two minutes minimum while observing clear hose and note vacuum reading. Vacuum reading should not exceed 4 inches Hg (13.5 kPa) and air bubbles should not be present in clear hose. Excessive vacuum indicates a restricted fuel line between fuel tank and motor. Air bubbles in clear hose indicates an air leak in fuel line between fuel tank and motor.

If vacuum reading is within 1-4 inches Hg (3.4-13.5 kPa) and no bubbles were noted in clear hose, proceed as follows: Remove clear hose and install a suitable 0-15 psi (0-103.4 kPa) pressure gage between VRO pump discharge port (5) and carburetors. Start engine and run at 800 rpm in forward gear. Pump output pressure should stabilize at not less than 3 psi (20.7 kPa).

If pressure is less than 3 psi (20.7 kPa), inspect pulse fitting (4) for plugging or other damage. Pulse fitting on models prior to 1988 is equipped with an integral flame arrestor. On 1988 and later models, pulse fitting is equipped with an integral check valve. Clean both type fittings by back-flushing with a suitable solvent. On 1988 and later models, install pulse fitting with black side facing VRO pump.

If pump pressure is low and pulse fitting is in acceptable condition, renew VRO pump assembly.

MANUAL PRIMER. Some later models are equipped with a manually operated fuel primer pump to assist in cold starting. Fuel can be pumped into the intake ports by actuating primer pump knob located at front control panel. With the primer pump knob in the warm-up position, fuel can be drawn into the intake ports through the prim-

er pump when the engine is operating to enrich the fuel mixture. Push primer pump knob fully in to stop primer enrichment.

Remove retainer clip to remove and disassemble primer pump for inspection of check valves and "O" rings. Renew any components found to be defective.

IGNITION SYSTEM

Models Prior To 1978

OPERATION. A breakerless capacitor discharge ignition (CDI) is used. Refer to Fig. OM13-15. The alternator produces approximately 300 volts, which is stored in a capacitor. Sensor magnets induce a small current in the sensor coil that is used to trigger the electronic switches (SCR'S) to release voltage stored in the capacitor to the ignition coils. The system is independent and requires no battery to operate.

The CDI system is extremely durable in normal use, but can be easily damaged by improper operating, testing and servicing procedures. The following precautions should be observed:

1. Make certain all wiring connections are clean and tight.
2. Make certain wires do not bind moving parts or contact sharp metal edges creating a short circuit.
3. DO NOT open or close any electrical circuits while engine is running.

4. DO NOT use an electric tachometer other than those recommended by the manufacturer.
5. DO NOT hold spark plug wires while checking for spark.

TROUBLE-SHOOTING. Use only approved methods to prevent damage to components. Before inspecting ignition system, make sure the trouble is not because of contaminated fuel or other fuel system malfunction.

CHECKING FOR SPARK. Disconnect spark plug leads at spark plugs and con-

Fig. OM13-14—View of VRO type fuel pump.
1. VRO fuel pump assy.
2. Oil inlet nipple
3. Fuel inlet nipple
4. Crankcase pulse nipple
5. Fuel mixture discharge nipple

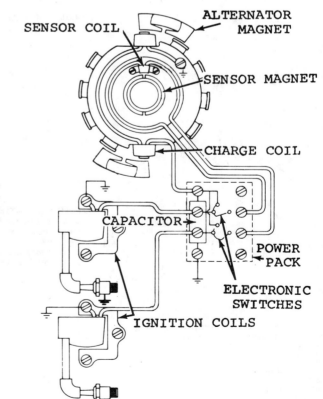

Fig. OM13-15—Schematic of ignition system on models prior to 1978. Charge coil is grounded to power head on later models.

nect a suitable spark tester as shown in Fig. OM13-16. Set spark gap at ½ inch (12.7 mm). Crank engine and note spark.

A strong steady spark indicates system is functioning properly; suspect spark plugs, timing or improper wiring routing.

Weak inconsistent spark or spark from only one coil indicates possible faulty sensor coil or ignition coil. Weak inconsistent spark from both coils indicates possible faulty charge coils. No spark indicates possible faulty ignition switch, ignition switch circuit or power pack.

WIRING. Engine missing, surging and failure to start or run can be caused by loose or corroded electrical connections. Check all terminals and connectors for

Fig. OM13-16—Use a spark tester as shown to check total ignition output.

clean tight contact. Also check all wiring for open or shorted circuits.

SENSOR COIL. The sensor coil may be checked with an ohmmeter. Disconnect black/white leads from number 6 terminals on power pack (11—Fig. OM13-17). Tag disconnected leads for reference during reassembly. Ohmmeter should indicate 10-20 ohms between sensor coil leads. No continuity should be present between sensor coil leads and engine ground. Sensor coil is not available separately from timer base (3).

CHARGE COILS. To test charge coils, disconnect light brown lead from number 1 terminal on power pack. Resistance between light brown wire and engine ground should be 800-950 ohms. Charge coils and stator (2—Fig. OM13-17) are renewed as an assembly after removing flywheel.

SHIFT DIODE (1971 and 1972 Models). Failure of the shift diode (5—Fig. OM13-17) may cause the lower unit to shift into forward gear immediately after ignition switch is turned OFF.

Shift diode may be inspected with an ohmmeter or continuity light with not more than a 12 volt power source. Disconnect diode leads at terminal block (12). Connect tester leads to purple/green wire and to yellow wire from diode. Reverse tester connections. Tester should indicate continuity in one connection and infinity in the other. Repeat test with purple/green wire and yellow/gray wire.

STATOR AND TIMER BASE ASSEMBLY. Stator (2—Fig. OM13-17) and timer base (3) may be serviced after removal of flywheel (1). Stator assembly is secured to the power head by four screws. The timer base may be removed after the stator by removing four screws and clips along the outer edge.

Disconnect stator leads from power pack and test with a suitable ohmmeter. Resistance between stator leads should be 0.8-1.2 ohms on 1971-1975, 6-ampere charging system; 0.3-0.7 on 1971-1975, 12-ampere charging system; and 1.0-1.6 ohms on all 1976 and 1977 models.

When reassembling unit, make certain wiring does not restrict free movement of timer base. Inspect taper on crankshaft and taper in flywheel. Taper should be absolutely clean and dry when installing flywheel. Install flywheel key with flat of key parallel to center line of crankshaft—NOT surface of taper. Tighten flywheel nut to 100-105 ft.-lbs. (135.6-142.4 N·m).

Models After 1977

OPERATION. Models produced during 1977-1988 are equipped with CD2 breakerless capacitor discharge ignition system. Refer to Fig. OM13-18 for wiring schematic. A charge coil and sensor coil are located under the flywheel. Two magnets in flywheel induce a current in the charge coil that is rectified and directed to a capacitor for storage. The two flywheel magnets also induce current in the sensor coil to provide a positive charge on the gate of one of

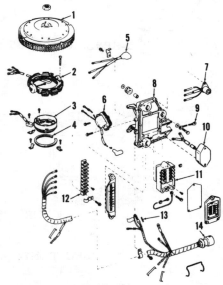

Fig. OM13-17—Component parts of ignition system used on models prior to 1978.

1. Flywheel	9. Ground strap
2. Stator	10. Voltage regulator
3. Timer base	(electric start
4. Retainer ring	models)
5. Diode	11. Power pack
6. Ignition coil	12. Terminal block
7. Rectifier	13. Fuse (20 amp)
8. Bracket	14. Connector

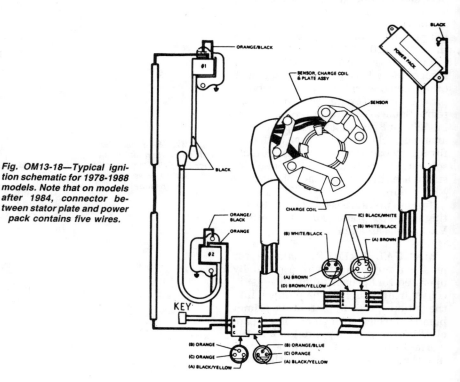

Fig. OM13-18—Typical ignition schematic for 1978-1988 models. Note that on models after 1984, connector between stator plate and power pack contains five wires.

two silicone-controlled rectifiers (SCR'S). The positive charge opens the SCR and allows the charged capacitor o discharge through the SCR and primary circuit of the ignition coil. The rapid coil field buildup induces a secondary voltage that fires the spark plug. Diodes, SCR'S and capacitor are contained in the power pack assembly and are not available individually.

Models after 1988 are equipped with CD2USL ignition system. Except for the ignition coils, all CD2U components are located under the flywheel. Refer to Fig. OM13-19 for wiring schematic. The breakdown of the CD2USL model number is as follows: CD—capacitor discharge; 2—two cylinders; U—under flywheel ignition; L—engine speed limiter; S—S.L.O.W. (speed limiting overheat warning) function. The S.L.O.W. function limits engine speed to approximately 2,000 rpm if engine temperature exceeds 203° F (95° C). Ignition system model number is printed on top of ignition module located under flywheel. The power pack and sensor coil are integrated into a single ignition module assembly instead of separate components as in earlier CD2 systems.

CD2 Ignition (Models Prior to 1989)

TROUBLE-SHOOTING. On models prior to 1985, the 4-wire connector plugs connect the charge and sensor coil leads to the power pack. The 3-wire connector plugs connect the power pack and ignition coils. On models after 1984, a 5-wire connector is used between the power pack and armature

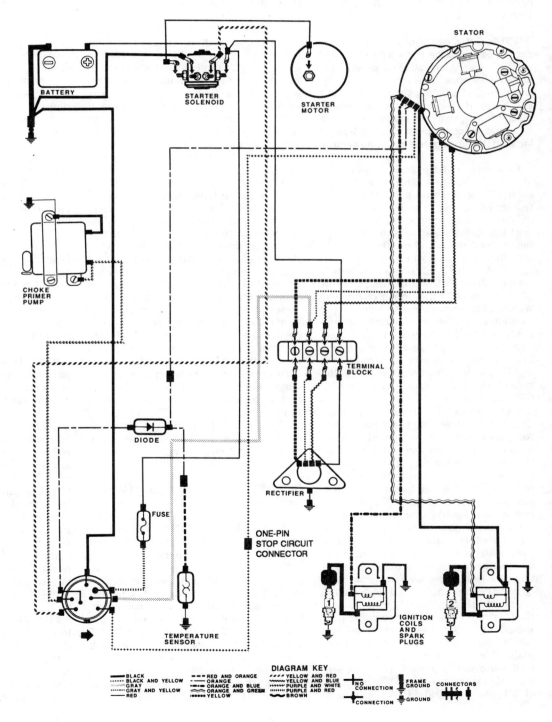

Fig. OM13-19—Wiring schematic on 1989 (CD2USL ignition) models equipped with remote electric start.

B. Black
R. Red
T. Tan
Y. Yellow
Gr. Gray
Or. Orange
B/Y. Black with yellow tracer
Gr/Y. Gray with yellow tracer
Or/G. Orange with green tracer
Pr/R. Purple with red tracer
Pr/W. Purple with white tracer
Y/Bl. Yellow with blue tracer
Or/Bl. Orange with blue tracer

plate. On models prior to 1985, check to make sure the white/black wire in the 4-wire connector is positioned in connector terminal B. Also check to make sure the number 1 coil primary wire is in the 3-wire connector B terminal and that it connects with the power pack orange/blue wire in the other connector B terminal. On models after 1984, check to make sure the white/black wire in the 5-wire connector is positioned in connector terminal B of both connector halves. Also check to make sure the orange/blue power pack lead is connected to the number 1 ignition coil.

NOTE: Outer edges of charge coil and sensor coil must be flush with machined surface of armature plate to provide the proper clearance between coils and flywheel magnets. OMC locating ring 317001 can be used to simplify this procedure. Place locating ring over machined bosses on armature plate, push coil out against locating ring and tighten mounting screws.

To check charge coil output, use Merc-O-Tronic Model 781, Stevens Model CD77 or a suitable peak voltage tester. Disconnect connector between armature plate and power pack. Connect black tester lead to stator lead connector terminal A and red tester lead to terminal D. Turn tester knobs to Negative and 500. Crank engine while observing tester. If tester reading is below 230 volts, check condition of charge coil wiring and connectors, and verify pin location in connector. If wiring and connectors are in acceptable condition check charge coil resistance as follows: Connect an ohmmeter to terminals A and D in stator plate lead connector. Renew charge coil if resistance is not 500-650 ohms on models prior to 1986, or 550-600 ohms on 1986-1988 models. Connect negative ohmmeter lead to stator plate (ground) and positive ohmmeter lead to connector terminal A, then to connector terminal D. Infinite resistance should exist between A terminal and stator plate and D terminal and stator plate. If not, charge coil or charge coil lead is shorted to ground.

To check sensor coil, connect an ohmmeter to terminals B and C in stator plate lead connector. Renew sensor coil if resistance is not 30-50 ohms. Connect negative ohmmeter lead to stator plate (ground) and positive ohmmeter lead to connector terminal B, then to connector terminal C. Infinite resistance should exist between B terminal and stator plate and C terminal and stator plate. If not, sensor coil or sensor coil lead is shorted to ground. To check sensor coil output, use Merc-O-Tronic Model 781, Stevens Model CD77 or a suita-

ble peak voltage tester. Connect black tester lead to stator lead connector terminal C and red tester lead to terminal B. On Merc-O-Tronic Model 781, turn knobs to Positive and 5, and on Stevens Model CD77, turn knobs to S and 5. Crank engine while observing tester. Reverse tester leads and repeat test. Sensor coil output on both tests should be 2 volts or more on models prior to 1987 and 1.5 volts or more on 1987 and 1988 models. Renew sensor coil if output is not as specified.

To check power pack output, first reconnect connector between armature plate and power pack. Use Merc-O-Tronic Model 781, Stevens Model CD77 or a suitable peak voltage tester. Connect black tester lead to a suitable engine ground. Connect red tester lead to wire leading to either ignition coil. Turn tester knobs to Negative and 500. Crank engine while observing tester. Repeat test on other coil lead. Renew power pack if readings are not at least 180 volts or higher on models prior to 1985 or 200 volts or higher on models after 1984.

To test ignition coils, disconnect high tension lead at ignition coil. On models prior to 1985, disconnect 3-wire connector and insert a jumper lead in terminal B of the ignition coil end of connector. Connect ohmmeter positive lead to the B terminal jumper wire and ohmmeter negative lead to a good engine ground. On models after 1984, disconnect coil primary wire at coil and connect ohmmeter positive lead to coil primary terminal and negative lead to a good engine ground or to coil ground tab. Ignition coil primary resistance should be 0.05-0.15 ohm on all models.

To check coil secondary resistance, move ohmmeter negative lead to the high tension terminal. Secondary resistance should be 225-325 ohms on models prior to 1986 and 250-300 ohms on models after 1985. Repeat procedure on number 2 ignition coil.

CD2USL Ignition System (1989 Models)

TROUBLE-SHOOTING. Disconnect spark plug leads from spark plugs and connect a suitable spark tester. Set tester spark gap to $\frac{1}{2}$ inch (12.7 mm). On models so equipped, install emergency ignition cutoff clip and lanyard. Crank engine and observe spark tester. If an acceptable spark is noted at each spark gap, perform RUNNING OUTPUT TEST. If spark is noted at only one spark gap, perform IGNITION PLATE OUTPUT TEST as described in this section. If no spark is noted at either spark gap, perform STOP CIRCUIT TEST.

NOTE: If acceptable spark is noted at each spark gap during spark output test, but engine pops and backfires during starting or running, ignition system may be out of time. Be sure orange/blue primary wire is connected to number 1 ignition coil, spark plug high tension leads are properly connected, flywheel is properly located on crankshaft and speed control linkage is properly adjusted.

STOP CIRCUIT TEST. Remove spark plug leads from spark plugs and connect a suitable spark tester. Disconnect stop circuit connector (Fig. OM13-19). Make sure ignition emergency cutoff clip and lanyard are installed on models so equipped. Crank engine and observe spark tester. If no spark is noted, perform IGNITION PLATE OUTPUT TEST. If normal spark is noted, connect ohmmeter between engine ground and the one-pin stop circuit connector. On remote control models, turn key to "ON" position. Ohmmeter should show infinite resistance. If meter shows continuity, repair short in wiring or renew stop button. Depress stop button or turn key "OFF" and note ohmmeter. If ohmmeter does not indicate continuity, repair open in wiring or renew stop button.

IGNITION PLATE OUTPUT TEST. Disconnect spark plug leads to prevent accidental starting. Remove primary leads from ignition coils. Connect number 1 ignition coil primary lead to the red lead of Stevens load adapter PL-88 and black lead of load adapter to engine ground.

NOTE: If Stevens load adapter is not available, fabricate load adapter using a 10 ohm, 10 watt resistor (Radio Shack part 271-132) or equivalent.

Connect red test lead of CD77 or equivalent peak reading voltmeter to red lead of Stevens load adapter PL-88 and black test lead to engine ground. Set CD voltmeter to Positive and 500. Crank engine and note meter. Repeat test procedure on number 2 ignition coil primary lead. If CD voltmeter indicates 175 volts or higher on both tests, perform IGNITION COIL TESTS. If one primary lead shows no output, renew ignition module. If both tests indicate no output, perform CHARGE COIL RESISTANCE TEST.

CHARGE COIL RESISTANCE TEST. Remove manual starter and flywheel. Remove two ignition module mounting screws and disconnect module brown and brown/yellow bullet connectors. Connect ohmmeter between brown and brown/yellow charge coil connectors.

Renew charge coil if resistance is not within 535-585 ohms. Connect one ohmmeter lead to engine ground and connect other ohmmeter lead to brown charge coil lead, then to brown/yellow charge coil lead. Renew charge coil if ohmmeter shows continuity between engine ground and either wire. If charge coil tests acceptable, renew ignition module.

NOTE: When installing charge coil or ignition module, use OMC Locating Ring 334994 to properly position components on armature plate. Place ring over machined surfaces on armature plate, push component outward against locating ring and tighten mounting screws to 30-40 in.-lbs. (3.4-4.5 N·m).

RUNNING OUTPUT TEST. Remove propeller and install the correct test wheel, then mount outboard motor in a suitable test tank. Remove ignition coil primary wires and install suitable terminal extenders (Stevens TS-77 or equivalent) on coil primary terminals, then install primary wires on terminal extenders. Connect peak reading voltmeter red test lead to number 1 coil terminal extender and black test lead to engine ground. Set voltmeter to Positive and 500. Start engine and run at rpm where ignition malfunction is evident while noting meter. Repeat test procedure on number 2 ignition coil. If either cylinder shows less than 200 volts, perform CHARGE COIL RESISTANCE TEST. If charge coil test results are acceptable, renew ignition module.

IGNITION COIL RESISTANCE TEST. To check ignition coil primary resistance, connect ohmmeter between primary terminal and coil ground. Resistance should be 0.05-0.15 ohm. To check secondary resistance, connect

ohmmeter between coil high tension terminal and primary terminal. Resistance should be 250-300 ohms. Renew coil if resistance is not as specified.

S.L.O.W. (Speed Limiting Overheat Warning). To test S.L.O.W. function, place outboard motor in a suitable test tank with the correct test wheel, or place boat in the water. Start engine and run at 3,500 rpm. Disconnect tan temperature sensor lead (Fig. OM13-19) and touch lead to engine ground. Engine speed should slow to approximately 2000 rpm when tan sensor lead is grounded. If not, inspect wiring harness or renew ignition module. If engine speed slows to approximately 2000 rpm, but S.L.O.W. function is inoperative, renew temperature sensor.

COOLING SYSTEM

The cooling system is controlled by both temperature and pressure. At slow operating speeds, the thermostat opens when the temperature in the cooling system reaches approximately 145° F (63° C). At high operating speeds, water pump pressure forces pressure relief valve (11—Fig. OM13-22) off its seat and allows cool water to circulate through the power head, bypassing the thermostat. This allows the motor to run cooler at high operating speeds.

Cooling system operation can be checked by applying a heat sensitive stick, such as "Markal Thermomelt Stik" to top of cylinder head. A 125° F (52° C) stick and a 163° F (73° C) stick will be needed. At speeds below 1000 rpm and in forward gear, the 125° F (52° C) stick should melt, but the 163° F (73° C) stick should not. At engine speeds over 4000 rpm, the 163° F (73° C) stick should not melt. If the 125° F (52° C) stick does not melt at slow speeds, pressure relief valve or thermostat may be stuck open. Overheating may be caused by damaged thermostat, damaged relief valve, exhaust cover gaskets leaking, head gaskets leaking, water passages obstructed, water passages leaking or faulty water pump. A hot horn in remote control panel should sound when engine is overheated. Temperature switch (3) should close circuit to hot horn at 205°-217° F (96°-102° C).

Thermostat (13), pressure relief valve and temperature switch may be serviced after removing cylinder head cover. Install new gaskets when reassembling.

WATER PUMP. The water pump is mounted on top surface of gearcase housing. The rubber impeller is mounted on, and driven by, the drive shaft. Water pump may be serviced after separating the lower unit gearcase from the drive shaft/exhaust housing. Refer to Fig. OM13-40, Fig. OM13-48 or Fig. OM13-51 for exploded view of water pump. Seals (9 and 10) are identical. Install lower seal with lip down to prevent loss of gearcase grease and upper

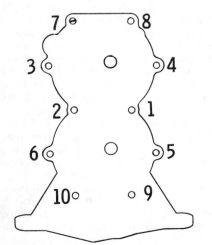

Fig. OM13-21—Cylinder head tightening sequence should be used to prevent head warpage.

Fig. OM13-22 — Exploded view typical of crankcase and cylinder assembly used on all models. Sealing strips (17) are not used on later models.

1. Cylinder head cover
2. Gasket
3. Temperature switch
4. Thermo switch
5. Exhaust cover
6. Exhaust deflector
7. Gasket
8. Lifting ring
9. Cylinder head
10. Valve spring
11. Pressure relief valve
12. Grommet
13. Thermostat
14. Head gasket
15. Cylinder block
16. Spark advance stop screw
17. Sealing strip
18. Crankcase half
19. Locating dowel
20. Frame
21. Throttle lever bracket
22. Throttle cam
23. Yoke
24. Throttle rod
25. Idle adjustment screw
26. Bushing
27. Throttle lever spring
28. Throttle stop screw
29. Throttle lever
30. Lever screw
31. Cable clamp
32. Throttle link
33. Rod retainer
34. Rod
35. Safety starting switch
36. Idle adjustment stop

seal with lip up to prevent water from entering gearcase. Coat bottom of impeller plate (8) with OMC Adhesive "M" or equivalent before installation. On models prior to 1986, install key (7) in drive shaft.

On 1986 and later models, install drive cam with flat side against drive shaft and sharp edge pointing in a clockwise direction when viewed from crankshaft end of drive shaft. Install impeller (6). A NEW impeller may be installed either side up. Apply a suitable grease to impeller blades and rotate drive shaft in a clockwise direction while installing pump housing (5) over impeller. The manufacturer recommends renewing water tube grommet (4) upon reassembly. Pump housing (5) screws should be coated with a suitable gasket sealing compound during reassembly.

POWER HEAD

R&R AND DISASSEMBLE. Place motor on a suitable stand and remove engine cover and forward and aft exhaust covers. Disconnect remote shift control wires on electric start models or shift rod screw (Fig. OM13-51) on all other models. Unscrew four nuts from each side of exhaust housing and single nut from aft stud. Power head and lower motor cover may be lifted from exhaust housing adapter as an assembly.

To disassemble power head, remove shift lever on manual start models and four bolts that secure lower motor cover on all models. Remove air intake, carburetors and starter assembly. Remove flywheel, stator and stator plate assembly. Note position of wires as they are disconnected and mark them if necessary to ensure proper replacement. Remove throttle linkage, spark advance linkage and choke solenoid (models prior to 1983). Remove lower main bearing

seal housing (20 – Fig. OM13-24) and inspect seal (19) and "O" ring (18). Cylinder head (9 – Fig. OM13-22) may be removed without unbolting head cover (1). Removal of the head cover is necessary to service thermostat (13), pressure relief valve (11) and temperature switch (3).

Drive taper pin (19) out toward front of motor and remove fourteen screws securing lower crankcase half to cylinder block. Tap side of crankshaft with a rawhide mallet to break seal between crankcase sections.

Primary internal engine parts are now accessible for removal and overhaul as outlined in the appropriate following paragraphs. When reassembling, follow the procedures outlined in the ASSEMBLY paragraphs that follow.

ASSEMBLY. Because of the two-stroke design, crankcase and intake manifold must be completely sealed against vacuum and pressure. The exhaust manifold and cylinder head must be sealed against water leakage and pressure. Mating surfaces of power head and exhaust housing must form a tight seal.

Whenever power head is disassembled, it is recommended that all gasket surfaces and the mating surfaces of crankcase halves be carefully checked for nicks and burrs or warped surfaces which might interfere with a tight seal. The cylinder head, head end of cylinder block and mating surfaces of manifold and crankcase may be lapped if necessary, to provide a smooth surface. Do not remove any more metal than is necessary.

Mating surfaces of crankcase may be checked for smoothness on the lapping block, and high spots and nicks removed; but surfaces must not be lowered. If extreme care is used, a slightly

damaged crankcase may be salvaged in this manner. In case of doubt, renew the crankcase.

The crankcase halves are positively located during assembly by the use of a tapered dowel pin (19 – Fig. OM13-22). Make sure that pin is not bent or distorted and that dowel pin hole is clean and true. Make certain that pin is fully seated on reinstallation.

When reassembling crankcase, make sure mating surfaces of crankcase halves are completely clean and free of old cement, nicks and burrs. On models prior to 1979, install sealing strips (17) and trim ends to extend approximately 1/32 inch (0.79 mm) into bearing bores, then sparingly apply OMC Adhesive "M" to cylinder half of crankcase only. On models after 1978, apply OMC Gel-Seal II to one crankcase mating surface. Do not use sealers which will harden and prevent contact between crankcase mating surfaces. Immediately assemble crankcase halves after applying sealer and position halves by installing locating dowel pin; then install and tighten crankcase screws.

When installing gaskets, check to make sure correct gasket is used and that ALL water passage holes are open. All gasket surfaces and cap screw threads must be sealed using a non-hardening cement such as OMC Gasket Sealing Compound.

Tighten cylinder head screws to 216-240 in.-lbs. (24-27 N·m) using sequence shown in Fig. OM13-21 for initial tightening. After engine has been run up to normal operating temperature and allowed to cool, repeat tightening procedure. General tightening torques are given in the CONDENSED SERVICE DATA table. When installing the flywheel, make sure key is properly installed in crankshaft groove.

PISTONS, RINGS AND CYLINDERS. Mark pistons, connecting rods and caps for reinstallation in original location. Each piston is fitted with two piston rings. Top ring is semi-keystone shape. Refer to CONDENSED SERVICE DATA for piston ring service specifications. Pistons are equipped with locating pins to prevent ring rotation.

Refer to CONDENSED SERVICE DATA for piston skirt-to-cylinder clearance on models prior to 1985. The manufacturer does not specify piston skirt clearance on models after 1984. If cylinder bore and piston are within tolerance, piston-to-cylinder clearance should be acceptable. Pistons and rings are available in 0.030 inch (0.76 mm) oversize for all models.

On models prior to 1983, measure piston diameter $\frac{1}{8}$ inch (3.2 mm) up from

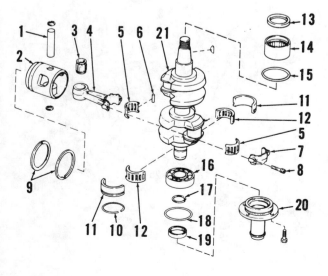

Fig. OM13-24 — Exploded view typical of crankshaft and related parts used on all models. On models after 1983, loose needle bearings and thrust washers are used in place of caged needle bearing (3).

1. Piston pin
2. Piston
3. Needle bearing
4. Connecting rod
5. Bearing cage
6. Bearing roller
7. Rod cap
8. Rod bolt
9. Piston rings
10. Bearing retainer
11. Bearing sleeve
12. Bearing cage
13. Seal
14. Needle bearing
15. "O" ring
16. Ball bearing
17. Snap ring
18. "O" ring
19. Seal
20. Seal housing

bottom of skirt. Take one measurement parallel to piston pin bore and another at 90 degrees to pin bore. Renew piston if difference between measurements exceeds 0.002 inch (0.05 mm).

On 1984-1989 models, measure piston diameter ⅛ inch (3.2 mm) up from bottom of skirt directly inline with piston ring locating pin in top ring groove. This dimension is the major piston diameter. Renew piston if major diameter is less than 3.1381 inches (79.708 mm) on standard size piston or 3.2131 inches (81.613 mm) for oversize piston. Next, measure piston skirt diameter in several locations, ⅛ inch (3.2 mm) up from bottom of skirt. Renew piston if any measurement is in excess of 0.004 inch (0.10 mm) smaller than major diameter previously measured, or if any measurement is larger than major diameter.

Maximum allowable cylinder bore out-of-round is 0.003 inch (0.08 mm) for all models. Maximum allowable cylinder bore taper is 0.002 inch (0.05 mm) for models after 1976 and 0.003 inch (0.08 mm) for all earlier models. To determine cylinder bore oversize diameter when reboring cylinder block, add piston oversize dimension (0.030 inch [0.76 mm]) to cylinder bore diameter.

On models prior to 1978, one pin bore is press fit and the other bore is a slip fit. The loose fit bore is marked "L" on underside of piston. Piston pin must be removed from piston toward press fit side and reinstalled in loose fit side first. Piston may be heated to ease pin removal and installation. On later models, piston pin is loose fit on both

piston bores and rides on 28 loose needle bearing rollers. Always renew piston pin retaining rings if removed. On all models, piston must be assembled to connecting rod with the long tapered side of piston crown facing exhaust ports. On models so equipped, oil hole (Fig. OM13-25) in connecting rod must face top of engine. Connecting rod with two holes in rod small end has no specific directional orientation but, if reused, should be installed in same direction as removed.

CONNECTING RODS, BEARINGS AND CRANKSHAFT. Before detaching connecting rods from crankshaft, make sure that rods and pistons are marked for reinstallation in correct cylinder. Also note alignment marks (M – Fig. OM13-25) on rods and rod caps.

Connecting rods are fitted with a two-piece roller bearing cage containing 16 rollers at crankpin end and a caged needle bearing at the piston end on models prior to 1984 and loose needle bearings and thrust washers on models after 1983. The split cage needle bearing at crankshaft center main may be disassembled for cleaning and inspection by working retaining ring (10 – Fig. OM13-24) out of groove and off end of retainers (11). Lower main bearing (16) may be removed with a bearing puller. Caged needle top main bearing will slide off shaft.

Assemble connecting rods on crankshaft with oil hole (Fig. OM13-25), models prior to 1985, toward threaded end of crankshaft (top).

On 1985 and later models equipped with precision ground rods, OMC Alignment Fixture 396749 is recommended to properly align connecting rod with rod cap during tightening of connecting rod screws.

NOTE: Precision ground rods are identified by grind marks running ACROSS

corners on ears of connecting rod and rod cap.

Make certain that dowels in crankcase align with recesses in top and center main bearings.

Crankcase seals and "O" rings should be renewed at each reassembly. Lubricate all friction surfaces with engine oil on reassembly.

MANUAL STARTER

Early Type

Refer to Fig. OM13-28 for exploded view of early type manual rewind starter. Start rope may be renewed without disassembling starter. If rope has been broken, remove remnants and proceed as follows: Cut a new length of nylon starter rope 75¾ inches (192.4 cm) long and burn ends to facilitate reassembly and prevent fraying. Insert a suitable tool in top or rewind spool (16) and rewind spring until tight. Allow spring to unwind far enough to gain access to rope hole in spool. Lift starter pinion (2) to engage flywheel teeth and place a wrench or other suitable tool beneath pinion to hold it in this position. Tie a knot in one end of start rope and thread it into hole in spool. Thread end of rope through lower motor cover, attach handle and allow rope to slowly rewind.

If start rope is not severed, simply pull rope all the way out, allow it to rewind far enough to gain access to rope hole in spool and lock pinion (2) as described previously. Rope may now be renewed as per previous instructions.

To disassemble starter for further service, remove air intake cover to gain access to two screws holding rope guide (10) and single screw holding bracket (9). Remove starter handle and allow rope to wind fully onto spool. Loosen lower screw in lock-out link (13) and release

HEAD OF PISTON MARKED "UP"

OIL HOLE

M

Fig. OM13-25 – Connecting rods must be reinstalled in original position, with oil hole up (models prior to 1985) and rod cap correctly installed.

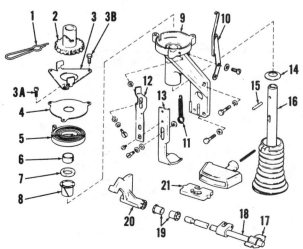

Fig. OM13-28 – Exploded view of early type manual rewind starter.

1. Drag spring
2. Pinion
3. Pinion latch
3A. Flat head screw
3B. Hex head screw
4. Spring cover
5. Rewind spring
6. Spring retainer
7. Thrust washer
8. Bushing
9. Starter bracket
10. Rope guide
11. Lockout spring
12. Lockout cam
13. Lockout link
14. Spring washer
15. Pinion pin
16. Rewind spool
17. Lever
18. Lever & shaft assy.
19. Bushings
20. Shift interlock cam

throttle cable from clamp. Do not disturb two smaller screws on lock-out link as readjustment will be required. Remove two remaining bolts securing starter bracket from port side and remove starter assembly.

NOTE: Safety glasses or goggles are recommended for further disassembly.

Use a punch to remove roll pin (15). Note position of drag spring (1) before removing pinion gear (2). Starter bracket should be mounted in a vise and recoil spring pulled out as far as possible (approximately 12 inches [30.5 cm]) before removing spring cover. Note position of latch (3) and flat head screw (3A). Slide spring retainer (6) up shaft to remove spring. Spool (16) may be pulled from bracket for access to bushing (8) in bracket or wave washer (14) between bracket and spool. When installing rewind spring, install spring cover and place a punch or other object through loop of spring inside spool to keep spring from pulling out while rewinding. Wedge a large screwdriver in spool with punch and rewind spring until end is seated in starter bracket. Use caution when releasing tension on screwdriver, make sure that end of spring is seated and will not snap back. Once spring is properly seated, remove cover and fill compartment with grease.

Adjust lock-out links (12 and 13) so starter pinion cannot engage flywheel in forward or reverse gear.

Late Type

A starter lockout slide (S–Fig. OM13-31) is used to prevent starter engagement when the gear shift lever is in the forward or reverse position.

To overhaul the manual starter, proceed as follows: Remove engine top cover. Remove cap screw (C) and disconnect starter lockout cable (L) from lockout slide (S). Move lockout slide (S) to align with disassembly notches in starter housing and withdraw. Remove the screws retaining the manual starter to the engine. Withdraw the starter assembly.

Check pawl (13–Fig. OM13-30) for freedom of movement, excessive wear of engagement area and damage. Renew or lubricate pawl (13) with OMC TRIPLE-GUARD GREASE or Lubriplate 777 and reinstall the starter assembly if additional service is not required.

To disassemble, detach starter rope (9) at anchor (3) and allow the rope to wind into the starter. Remove nut (22), bolt (19), washer (18), pawl plate (21), pawl return spring (23), pawl (13), pawl wave washer and spring (20). Remove snap ring (17), friction plate (16) and wave washer. Insert a suitable screwdriver blade through hole (A) to hold rewind spring (7) securely in housing (1) Carefully lift pulley (10) with starter rope (9) from housing (1). BE CAREFUL when removing pulley (10)

to prevent possible injury from rewind spring (7). Remove starter rope (9) from pulley (10) if renewal is required. T remove rewind spring (7) from housing (1), invert housing so it sets upright on a flat surface, then tap the housing top until rewind spring (7) falls free and uncoils.

Inspect all components from damage and excessive wear and renew if needed.

To reassemble, install plate (6) and apply a coating of OMC TRIPLE-GUARD GREASE or Lubriplate 777 to rewind spring area of housing (1). Install rewind spring (7) in housing (1) so spring coils wind in a counterclockwise direction from the outer end. Make sure spring outer hook is properly secured over starter housing pin. Install plate (8). If needed, a new starter rope (9) cut to a length of 96½ inches (245 cm) should be installed on pulley (10).

NOTE: Lubricate all friction surfaces with OMC TRIPLE-GUARD GREASE or Lubriplate 777 during reassembly.

Install pulley (10) in starter housing making sure that pulley slot engages hook end in rewind spring (7). Insert a suitable screwdriver through hole (A) to guide spring (7) if needed. Complete reassembly in the reverse order of disassembly.

Turn pulley (10) eight turns counterclockwise when viewed from the flywheel side. Thread starter rope (9) through starter housing (1) and handle (2) and secure in anchor (3). Release pulley (10) and allow starter rope to slowly wind onto pulley.

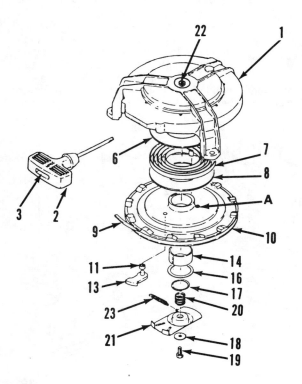

Fig. OM13-30 — Exploded view of rewind starter similar to the type used on later models so equipped. A wave washer is located under drive pawl (13) and friction plate (16).

1. Starter housing
2. Handle
3. Anchor
6. Plate
7. Rewind spring
8. Plate
9. Starter rope
10. Pulley
11. Bushing
13. Drive pawl
14. Bushing
16. Friction plate
17. Snap ring
18. Washer
19. Bolt
20. Spring
21. Pawl plate
22. Nut
23. Pawl return spring

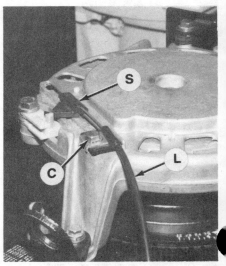

Fig. 13-31 — View showing starter lockout assembly used on later models.

C. Cap screw
L. Cable   S. Slide

NOTE: Do not apply any more tension on rewind spring (7) than required to draw starter handle (2) back into the proper released position.

Adjust starter lockout assembly by adjusting cable (L–Fig. OM13-31) so starter will engage when gear shift lever is in neutral position, but will not engage when gear shift lever is in forward or reverse position. Secure cable (L) by tightening cap screw (C).

PROPELLER

An aluminum, three-blade propeller with built-in cushion clutch is standard on most motors while some motors are equipped with a stainless steel propeller. Optional propellers are available. Only propellers designed for use on these motors should be used. Refer to CONDENSED SERVICE DATA for desired engine speed at full throttle.

LOWER UNIT

Electric Shift Lower Unit

REMOVE AND REINSTALL. An electric shift lower unit is used on 1971 and 1972 models with an electric starter. Most service of the lower unit can be accomplished after separating gearcase from exhaust housing.

Disconnect spark plug wires. Disconnect blade type connectors on remote shift wires and tie a length of string to loose wires as an assembly aid. Mark trim tab (22–Fig. OM13-40) to ensure proper relocation and remove. Remove screw in trim tab cavity and screw just forward of trim tab area. Remaining two screws on port and two screws on starboard side secure gearcase to exhaust housing.

Reassemble gearcase to exhaust housing in following manner: Make sure that "O" ring (1) is in good condition and in place on the drive shaft. Coat mating surfaces of gearcase and exhaust housing with OMC Adhesive "M" or equivalent and run string tied to shift wires through exhaust housing into engine compartment. Make certain water tube enters pump grommet (4) and pull shift wires through exhaust housing and power head adapter. Drive shaft and crankshaft splines may be aligned by turning flywheel clockwise.

GEARCASE. Gearcase may be disassembled in the following manner: Drain lubricant and remove gearcase as described in previous section. Remove screws securing water pump housing (5–Fig. OM13-40); lift housing, impeller (6) and remove pump drive key. Remove

plate (8) and bearing housing (11). Remove solenoid cover (24) and wave washer (27) then carefully lift out solenoid and plunger assembly. Dismount propeller and unscrew four screws holding bearing housing (69). Use a puller attached with two 8-inch long 5/16-18 bolts to remove bearing housing. Slide thrust washer (64) and thrust bearing (63) off shaft and remove

retaining rings (66). Propeller shaft can now be removed with reverse gear (62), dog clutch (54) and associated parts. A special socket (OMC Special Tool 316612) is available to hold drive shaft so that nut securing pinion gear (18) can be removed. Drive shaft can be lifted free of gearcase and forward gear (52) removed after removing pinion gear. Use slide hammers and two 16-inch long

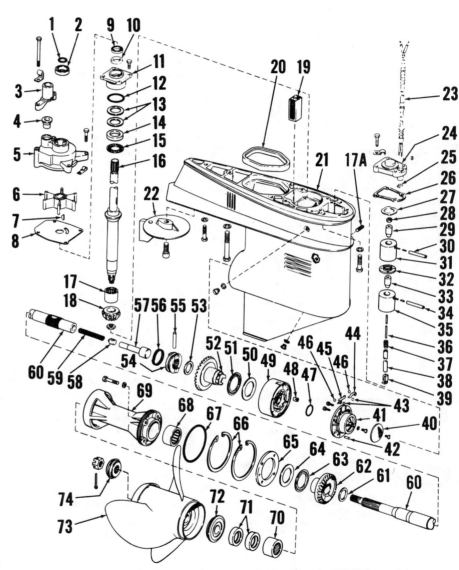

Fig. OM13-40 — View of lower unit gearcase used on electric shift 50 hp models.

1. "O" ring	19. Water screen	38. Shift rod casing
2. Grommet	20. Exhaust seal	39. Cap
3. Water tube bracket	21. Gearcase	40. Oil screen
4. Grommet	22. Trim tab	41. Valve housing
5. Impeller housing	23. Shift control wires	42. Locating dowel
6. Impeller	24. Solenoid cover	43. Shift valve balls
7. Drive key	25. Retainer	44. Neutral lever
8. Plate	26. Gasket	45. Reverse lever
9. Seal	27. Wave washer	46. Valve seats
10. Seal	28. Locknut	47. "O" ring
11. Bearing & housing assy.	29. Upper plunger	48. Plug
12. "O" ring	30. Heat shrink tube	49. Oil pump assy.
13. Adjustment shims	31. Upper solenoid	50. Thrust washer
14. Thrust washer	32. Spacer	51. Thrust bearing
15. Thrust bearing	33. Lower plunger	52. Forward gear
16. Drive shaft	34. Heat shrink tube	53. Thrust washer
17. Needle bearing	35. Lower solenoid	54. Dog clutch
17A. Set screw	36. Shift rod	55. Pin
18. Pinion gear	37. Lock screw	

56. Pin retaining spring
57. Oil pump piston
58. Dog clutch retainer
59. Spring
60. Propeller shaft
61. Thrust washer
62. Reverse gear
63. Thrust bearing
64. Thrust washer
65. Retainer plate
66. Snap rings
67. "O" ring
68. Needle bearing
69. Bearing housing
70. Needle bearing
71. Seals
72. Thrust bushing
73. Propeller
74. Prop nut spacer

rods with ¼-20 threads on the ends to remove oil pump (49).

Inspect drive shaft splines, bearing surfaces and seal surfaces for wear or damage. Damaged splines may be caused by striking a submerged object and bending the exhaust housing. Check parallelism of top and bottom surfaces if questionable. If surfaces are not parallel, renew housing, do not attempt to straighten it.

Lower drive shaft bearing (17) should only be removed if renewal is intended. Do not reinstall a used bearing. Removal and installation procedure varies between 1971 and 1972 models, refer to the following paragraphs for correct method: Bearing removal on 1971 models is accomplished by driving bearing out toward bottom of gearcase. OMC Special Tool 383173 (A—Fig. OM13-41) should be used to install new bearing. Assemble bearing and tool in gearcase with lettered side of bearing down and pull bearing up into case.

On 1972 models, bearing is held in position by a set screw (17A—Fig. OM13-40) as well as a press fit in gearcase. Set screw is located on starboard side in area of water intake. After removing set screw, install OMC Special Tool 385546, with shouldered side of puller piece against bearing and pull bearing out of case toward top. New bearing is installed by assembling special tool with the sleeve provided and driving bearing into gearcase with let-

tered side of bearing up (Fig. OM13-42) and shouldered side of pusher piece against bearing. Bearing will be properly positioned when plate of tool touches top of gearcase. Apply "Loctite" to set screw (17A—Fig. OM13-40) and install.

Shift solenoids (31 and 35) should be checked with an ohmmeter. Resistance should be 5-6 ohms when checked between each of the wires and solenoid case. If solenoid or wires (23) are renewed, use new heat shrink insulating tubes (30 and 34) to seal wire connections.

The shift pump valve balls (43) and seats (46) for these balls can be renewed. The surfaces of rotor set in housing should be checked for wear and scoring. Renew complete pump assembly if any part of rotor set is damaged excessively. The front surfaces of rotor set should be flush with front face of pump housing, when parts (50, 51 and 52) are in position. Make certain that locating pin (42) is fully seated in recess in forward end of gear housing on reassembly.

Pinion gear (18) mesh position is not adjustable on 1971 models. The different arrangement of thrust bearing assembly (14 and 15) on 1972 models makes exact positioning of pinion gear (18) necessary. The mesh position is adjusted by varying shims (13). The following procedure may be used to determine proper shimming for 1972 models. Place pinion gear (18) on drive shaft and torque retaining nut to 40-45 ft.-lbs. Install shims (13) that were removed during disassembly and leave thrust washer (14) or thrust bearing (15) off shaft. Hold shim gage (OMC Special Tool 315767) firmly against shims and measure clearance between end of gage and pinion gear (Fig. OM13-44). Proper clearance is 0.000-0.002 inch (0.00-0.05 mm).

NOTE: If clearance appears to be 0, make certain that enough shims are installed for an accurate check.

Shims are available in thicknesses of 0.002 and 0.005 inch and may be used in

any quantity to obtain proper clearance. Set the correct shims aside until drive shaft is installed.

Seals (9 and 10 – Fig. OM13-40) should be installed with lip of bottom seal (10) down and lip of top seal (9) up.

Needle bearings (68 and 70) should not be removed from propeller shaft housing unless renewal is intended. Do not install used bearings. OMC Special Tool 317061 should be used to press aft bearing into propeller shaft housing (69) to ensure proper positioning. OMC Special Tool 314641 should be used to properly position forward bearing (68) in bore of housing. Seals (71) should be installed so lip on aft seal is toward propeller and lip on forward seal is facing forward.

Gearcase may be assembled in the following manner: Position oil pump assembly (parts 40 through 49 and 57) in gearcase, making sure that locating pin (42) is fully seated in recess provided. Install drive shaft (16) and pinion gear (18). Refer to Fig. OM13-43 for 1971 motors and Fig. OM13-40 for 1972 motors. Torque pinion gear retaining nut to 40-45 ft.-lbs. (54-61 N·m). Assemble dog clutch (54) on propeller shaft, placing side of dog clutch marked "PROP END" toward rear. Place thrust washer (61), reverse gear (62) and retainer plate (65) on propeller shaft and install in gearcase. Install snap rings (66) and place thrust bearing parts (63 and 64) in position on shaft. Make certain that "O" ring (67) is correctly seated in groove of

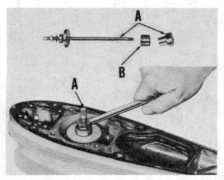

Fig. OM13-41—Lower drive shaft bearing (B) used on 1971 models should be pulled into position in gearcase with OMC Tool 383173 (A).

SCREW
WASHER
PLATE
GUIDE
SLEEVE
INSTALLER
DRIVESHAFT
LOWER
BEARING

Fig. OM13-42 — Installer/removal tool (OMC Tool 385546) may be used to drive lower drive shaft bearing into gearcase of 1972 and some later models. Refer to text for procedure.

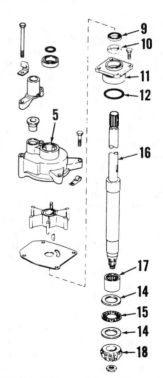

Fig. OM13-43 — Arrangement of thrust bearing parts (14 & 15) common to 1971 models. Refer to Fig. OM13-40 for legend.

bearing housing (69) and is free of any nicks or tears. Lubricate "O" ring and slide bearing housing into gearcase making certain that "UP" mark on housing is toward top. Coat screws that secure bearing housing with a sealing compound and install them.

Install and adjust shift solenoids in the following manner: Screw plunger (with large hole) into tubular shift rod casing (Fig. OM13-45), then install and tighten lock screw. Insert plunger and shift rod into reverse solenoid (blue wire) and push cap onto bottom of shift rod casing. Insert lower solenoid assembly into gearcase bore. Make sure end of shift rod is against the shift valve lever on pump and solenoid is against bottom of bore in housing. Check distance from top of plunger to top of solenoid. Top of plunger must be flush with top of solenoid. Adjustment is accomplished by removing assembly, loosening lock screw, and turning shift rod casing. The lock screw should be torqued to 9-11 in.-lbs. (1.0-1.2 N·m) when adjustment is complete. Install lower solenoid assembly. Position spacer (32 – Fig. OM13-40) on top of lower solenoid with flat side down. Assemble small shift rod (Fig. OM13-46), plunger with small hole and locknut. Position the plunger and shift rod in neutral (upper) solenoid. Insert the neutral solenoid and shift rod assembly into gearcase bore above the reverse shift assembly and spacer. Make sure end of rod is through hole in top valve lever (44 – Fig. OM13-40) and solenoids are tight against bottom of bore. Check distance between top of plunger and top of solenoid. Top of plunger must be flush with top of solenoid. Adjustment is accomplished after loosening locknut and turning shift rod. Locknut should be torqued to 3-5

inch-pounds when adjustment is completed.

NOTE: Improper shifting will result if adjustment of shift rods and plungers is not correct.

Install solenoids and shift rods, position wave washer (27) on top of solenoids, coat both sides of gasket (26) with OMC Gasket Sealing Compound or equivalent and install cover (24). Apply OMC Adhesive "M" or equivalent to bottom of impeller plate (8), install key (7) in drive shaft and locate impeller (6) over key. Lubricate impeller, hold blades in and install water pump housing (5).

NOTE: Drive shaft can be rotated clockwise while assembling pump housing, but should never be turned backwards.

Coat screws attaching water pump housing with OMC Gasket Sealing Compound or equivalent before installing. Reinstall shift cable clamps in original position (aft, starboard screw in water pump housing and solenoid cover) and make certain that drive shaft "O" ring (1) is in position.

Hydraulic Shift Lower Unit

A hydraulically shifted lower unit is used on 1973 and 1974 models with an electric starter. To service lower unit, refer to following sections.

SHIFT LINKAGE ADJUSTMENT. Shift linkage is adjusted by disconnecting clevis (C – Fig. OM13-47) from bellcrank (R). Turn clevis (C) to obtain measurement (D) of 5-3/16 to 5-5/16 inches (13.18-13.49 cm) between center of bellcrank pin (P) and center of shift cable bracket (B).

REMOVE AND REINSTALL. To remove gearcase, disconnect spark plug leads, remove electric starter and detach upper end of shift rod by removing screw shown in Fig. OM13-52. Mark trim tab (22 – Fig. OM13-48) to ensure proper relocation and remove trim tab. Remove screw in trim tab cavity and screw just forward of trim tab area.

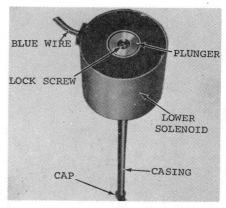

Fig. OM13-45 — View of lower (reverse) solenoid assembly. Refer to text for adjustment.

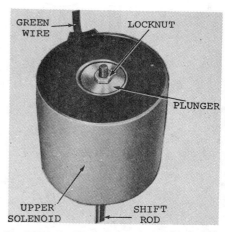

Fig. OM13-46 — View of upper (neutral) solenoid.

Fig. OM13-44 — Shim gage (OMC Tool 315767) should be used to properly set mesh position of pinion gear on drive shaft. Refer to text for procedure.

GAGE FIRM AGAINST SHIMS

0.000-0.002 in. CLEARANCE

Fig. OM13-47 – View of gear shift mechanism on hydraulic shift models. Refer to text for adjustment.

Unscrew two screws on port and starboard sides and separate gearcase from exhaust housing. Be careful not to bend shift rod during disassembly.

Reassemble gearcase to exhaust housing using following procedure: Make certain that "O" ring (1) is in good condition and in position on end of drive shaft. Check length of gear shift rod (27). With shifter in neutral, distance from mating surface of gearcase (21) to center of hole in top of shift rod should be 16-3/16 to 16¼ inches (41.12-41.27 cm) for standard models and 21-3/16 to 21¼ inches (53.82-53.97 cm) for long shaft models. Flattened area on end of shift rod should slant toward front on reassembly. Apply OMC Adhesive "M" or equivalent to mating surface of exhaust housing and gearcase. Install gearcase while observing proper alignment of water tube in water tube grommet on water pump. Turn flywheel clockwise to align crankshaft splines with those on drive shaft.

GEARCASE. To disassemble gearcase, drain lubricant, remove propeller and separate gearcase from exhaust housing as outlined in previous section. Remove water pump housing (5 – Fig. OM13-48), impeller (6), key (7) and lower plate (8). Remove four screws holding propeller shaft bearing housing (69) and using a suitable puller, withdraw bearing housing from gearcase. Remove snap rings (66), thrust washer (64), thrust bearing (63) and shift rod cover (28). Remove shift rod and propeller shaft components by withdrawing shift rod (27) and propeller shaft simultaneously. Hold drive shaft with OMC Tool 316612 or another suitable tool and unscrew pinion nut. Remove pinion (18), unscrew bearing housing (11) screws and withdraw drive shaft and components from gearcase. Bearing in housing (11) is not renewable but must be obtained as a unit assembly with housing. Remove forward gear (53). Using a suitable puller and two 16 inch rods with ¼-20 threads, remove oil pump (43) from gearcase.

To disassemble oil pump, unscrew four screws securing cover (42) and remove cover. Remove snap ring (48), plug (47), spring (46), guide (45) and pressure relief valve ball (44). Inspect pressure relief valve components and renew if worn or damaged. Inspect oil pump assembly for wear or damage. Dots on rotors must be up and surfaces of rotors and housing must be flat across ends when forward gear, thrust bearing and washer are installed in pump. Rotors, housing and bearing are not available separately and must be renewed as a unit assembly.

Seals (9 and 10) should be installed with lip of bottom seal (10) down and lip of top seal (9) up.

Needle bearings (68 and 70) should not be removed from propeller shaft housing unless renewal is intended. Do not install used bearings. OMC Special Tool 317061 should be used to press aft bearing into propeller shaft housing (69) to ensure proper positioning. OMC Special Tool 314641 should be used to properly position forward bearing (68) in bore of housing. Seals (71) should be installed so that lip on aft seal is toward propeller and lip on forward seal is facing forward.

Thicknesses of shims (13) is varied to adjust mesh position of pinion gear (18) in forward and reverse gear. A shim gage, OMC Special Tool 315767, should be used to determine proper shimming.

Fig. OM13-48 — Exploded view of hydraulic shift lower unit used on 1973 models with electric starter and all 1974 models.

1. "O" ring	17A. Set screw	36. Pin	55. Pin
2. Grommet	18. Pinion gear	37. Piston	56. Retaining spring
3. Water tube bracket	19. Water screen	38. Plug	59. Spring
4. Grommet	20. Exhaust seal	39. Push rod	60. Propeller shaft
5. Impeller housing	21. Gearcase	40. Screen	61. Thrust washer
6. Impeller	22. Trim tab	41. Locating dowel	62. Reverse gear
7. Drive key	23. Seal	42. Cover	63. Thrust bearing
8. Plate	24. Grommet	43. Oil pump & housing	64. Thrust washer
9. Seal	25. Tie strap	44. Relief valve ball	65. Retainer plate
10. Seal	26. Seal	45. Ball guide	66. Snap rings
11. Bearing & housing assy.	27. Shift rod	46. Spring	67. "O" ring
12. "O" ring	28. Shift rod cover	47. Plug	68. Needle bearing
13. Shims	29. "O" ring	48. Snap ring	69. Bearing housing
14. Thrust washer	30. Gasket	49. Shift plunger	70. Needle bearing
15. Thrust bearing	31. Piston cap	50. Detent balls	71. Seals
16. Drive shaft	32. "O" ring	51. Thrust washer	72. Thrust bushing
17. Needle bearing	33. Cylinder	52. Thrust bearing	73. Propeller
	34. "O" ring	53. Forward gear	74. Spacer
	35. Valve	54. Dog clutch	

Place pinion gear (18) on drive shaft and torque retaining nut to 40-45 ft.-lbs. (54-61 N·m). Install shims (13) that were removed during disassembly and leave thrust washer (14) and thrust bearing (15) off shaft. Hold shim gage firmly against shims and measure clearance between end of gage and pinion gear (Fig. OM13-44). Proper clearance is 0.000-0.002 inch (0.00-0.051 mm).

NOTE: If clearance appears to be 0, make certain that enough shims are installed for an accurate check.

Shims are available in thicknesses of 0.002 inch and 0.005 inch and may be installed in any quantity to obtain proper clearance. Set the correct shims aside until drive shaft is installed.

Inspect drive shaft splines, bearing surfaces and seal surfaces for wear or damage. Damaged splines may be caused by striking a submerged object and bending the exhaust housing. Check parallelism of top and bottom surfaces if questionable. If surfaces are not parallel, renew housing. Do not attempt to straighten it.

Lower drive shaft bearing (17 – Fig. OM13-48) should only be removed if renewal is intended. Do not reinstall a used bearing. Drive shaft bearing is held in position by a set screw (17A) as well as a press fit in gearcase. Set screw is located on starboard side in area of water intake. After removing set screw, install OMC Special Tool 385546, with shouldered side of puller piece against bearing and pull bearing out of case toward top. New bearing is installed by assembling special tool with sleeve provided and puller piece turned over so that shouldered side will again be next to bearing. Drive bearing (with lettered side up) into case (Fig. OM13-42). Bearing will be properly positioned when plate of tool touches top of gearcase. Apply Loctite to set screw and install.

Hydraulic shift components (31 and 39 – Fig. OM13-48) may be disassembled with OMC Tool 386112 by engaging pins on tool with holes in piston (37) and piston cap (31) and unscrewing cap from piston. Be careful not to bend or damage push rod (39) during disassembly. Remove pin (36) to separate valve (35), piston (37) and push rod. Cap (31) should be tightened to 12-15 ft.-lbs. (16.3-20.4 N·m) during reassembly.

To assist in installing shift plunger components in propeller shaft, grind away the end of a 9/32-inch rod to form a long flat taper on one side. Rod should be approximately 2⅝ inches (66.67 mm) long. Position dog clutch (54 – Fig. OM13-48) on propeller shaft with pin hole in dog clutch and slot in shaft aligned. Place three detent balls (50) and

spring (59) in plunger (49) as shown in Fig. OM13-49 and install plunger in propeller shaft so detent balls match grooves in propeller shaft. Align holes in dog clutch (54 – Fig. OM13-48) and shift plunger (48) and insert tapered end of tool through holes to properly position detent spring. Carefully push tool out with retaining pin (55) and install pin retaining spring (56) in outer groove of dog clutch. Coils of spring must not overlap.

To reassemble gearcase, install oil pump (43), forward gear (53), thrust bearing (52) and thrust washer (51) so that locating pin (41) aligns with pin hole in gearcase. Install drive shaft (16) and pinion gear (18) and tighten pinion nut to 40-45 ft.-lbs. (54-61 N·m). Lay gearcase on starboard side and install propeller shaft with flat side of shift plunger (49) up until propeller shaft is bottomed. Install hydraulic shift assembly with flat on end of push rod (39) down. Insert shift assembly until flats on push rod (39) and shift plunger (49) are engaged (push rod will not turn). Place light pressure against shift cylinder (33) and slowly withdraw propeller shaft until key on end of push rod meshes with keyway in shift plunger as shown in Fig. OM13-50. When key and keyway are meshed, push shift assembly and propeller shaft in to complete engagement. Complete remainder of assembly noting the following points: Install snap ring (66) with flat side out. Install bearing housing (69) with "UP" mark towards water pump. Apply OMC Gasket Sealing Compound to threads of screws securing retainer plate (65) and bearing housing (69).

Manual Shift Lower Unit (Prior to 1989)

REMOVE AND REINSTALL. Most service of the lower unit can be accomplished after separating gearcase from exhaust housing. Gearcase may be removed in the following manner: Disconnect spark plug leads, remove manual starter (if equipped with early type) and remove shift rod screw (Fig. OM13-52). Mark trim tab (22 – Fig. OM13-51) to ensure proper relocation and remove. Remove screw in trim tab cavity and screw just forward of trim tab area. Remaining two screws on port and two screws on starboard side secure gearcase to exhaust housing.

Reassemble gearcase to exhaust housing in the following manner: Make sure that "O" ring (1) is in good condition and in position on end of drive shaft. Check length of gear shift rod (25). With shifter in neutral, distance from mating surface

of gearcase (21) to center of hole in top of shift rod on pre-1974 models should be 16-7/32 inches (41.19 cm) for standard models and 21-7/32 inches (53.89 cm) for long-shaft models. Shift rod height for 1975-1978 models should be set using OMC Tool 321200. Shift rod height for models after 1978 is 15-29/32 inches (40.4 cm) for standard models and 20-29/32 inches (53.1 cm) for long-shaft models. Flattened area on end of shift rod should slant toward drive shaft on reassembly. Apply OMC Adhesive "M" or equivalent to mating surface of exhaust housing and gearcase. Install gearcase while observing proper alignment of water tube in water tube grommet on water pump. Turn flywheel clockwise to align crankshaft splines with those on drive shaft.

GEARCASE. Gearcase may be disassembled in the following manner: Remove propeller, drain lubricant and remove gearcase as described in previous section. Remove screws securing shift rod cover (29 – Fig. OM13-51), unscrew shift rod (25) and remove shift rod and cover as an assembly. Remove water pump housing (5), impeller (6), key (7) and lower plate (8). Remove four screws holding propeller shaft bearing housing (69) and using a suitable puller, remove bearing housing. Discard seals (71) and "O" ring (67). Remove snap rings (66), thrust washer assembly (64 and 63) and slide reverse gear (62) off propeller shaft. A special socket (OMC Special Tool 316612) is available to hold drive shaft so nut securing pinion gear (18)

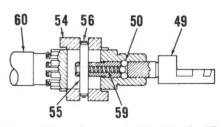

Fig. OM13-49—Cross-sectional view of shift plunger (49) and dog clutch (54) components. Refer to Fig. OM13-48 for parts identification.

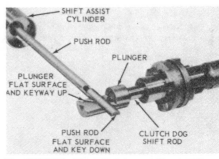

Fig. OM13-50 — View showing relative positions of shift assemblies when installed in gearcase. Refer to text for installation.

can be removed. After pinion gear (18) retaining nut is removed, unscrew the four screws securing upper drive shaft bearing housing (11). Pull drive shaft and associated parts out of gearcase. A puller is necessary to remove drive shaft assembly on 1975 and later models. Bearing in housing (11) on models prior to 1974 is not renewable. If bearing is worn, renew entire housing. A taper

roller bearing is used on 1975 and later model drive shaft. Propeller shaft (60) may now be pulled from gearcase complete with forward gear (52), forward bearing housing (38), and all associated parts.

Inspect drive shaft splines, bearing surfaces and seal surfaces for wear or damage. Damaged splines may be caused by striking a submerged object

and bending the exhaust housing. Check parallelism of top and bottom surfaces if questionable. If surfaces are not parallel, renew housing. Do not attempt to straighten it.

Lower drive shaft bearing (17) should only be removed if renewal is intended. Do not reinstall a used bearing. Drive shaft bearing is held in position by a set screw (17A) as well as a press fit in gearcase. Set screw is located on starboard side in area of water intake. After removing set screw, use a suitable puller and pull bearing out of case toward top. New bearing is installed by assembling special tool with sleeve provided and puller piece turned over so shouldered side will again be next to drive bearing (with lettered side up) into case. Apply Loctite to set screw and install.

Forward gear (52) and propeller shaft (60) may be removed from propeller shaft bearing housing (38) after dislodging spring (56) and removing dog clutch assembly (55 and 54). Bearing housing and shifter mechanism assembly (38) may be disassembled by driving out shift lever pin (36) on all models and unscrew-

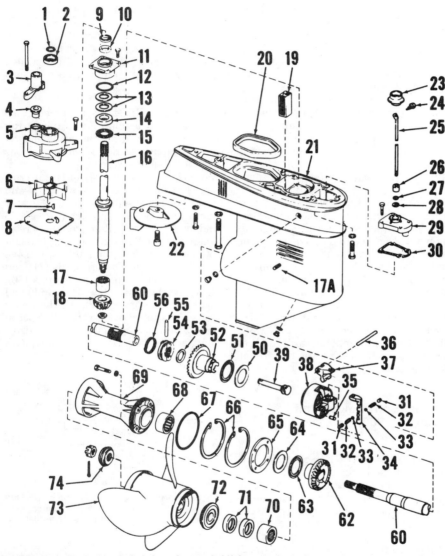

Fig. OM13-52—Shift rod screw (24—Fig. OM13-51) must be removed before removing manual shift lower unit.

Fig. OM13-51—Typical exploded view of manual shift lower unit used on models prior to 1989. Some models use tapered roller bearings in place of thrust bearings and washers (14, 15, 50 and 51). Later models do not use thrust washer (53).

1. "O" ring	16. Drive shaft	30. Gasket
2. Grommet	17. Needle bearing	31. Set screw
3. Water tube bracket	17A. Set screw	32. Detent springs
4. Grommet	18. Pinion gear	33. Detent balls
5. Impeller housing	18. Water screen	34. Detent
6. Impeller	20. Exhaust seal	35. Locating dowel
7. Drive key	21. Gearcase	36. Shift lever pin
8. Plate	22. Trim tab	37. Shift lever
9. Seal	23. Shift rod seal	38. Bearing housing
10. Seal	24. Shift rod screw	39. Shift shaft
11. Bearing & housing assy.	25. Shift rod	50. Thrust washer
12. "O" ring	26. Bushing	51. Thrust bearing
13. Adjustment shims	27. "O" ring	52. Forward gear
14. Thrust washer	28. Gasket	53. Thrust washer
15. Thrust bearing	29. Shift rod cover	54. Dog clutch

55. Pin	
56. Pin retaining spring	
60. Propeller shaft	
62. Reverse gear	
63. Thrust bearing	
64. Thrust washer	
65. Retainer plate	
66. Snap rings	
67. "O" ring	
68. Needle bearing	
69. Bearing housing	
70. Needle bearing	
71. Seals	
72. Thrust bushing	
73. Propeller	
74. Prop nut spacer	

Fig. OM13-53 — Measure gap between shift tool gage (G) and pinion gear to determine thickness of shims (13 — Fig. OM13-53). Refer to text.

ing set screws (31) on models prior to 1974.

Thickness of shims (13) is varied to adjust mesh position of pinion gear (18) in forward and reverse gears. An OMC shim tool should be used to determine proper shimming.

Place pinion gear (18) on drive shaft and torque retaining nut to 40-45 ft.-lbs. (54-61 N·m). On models prior to 1974, install shims (13) that were removed during disassembly and leave thrust washer (14) and thrust bearing (15) off shaft. On 1975 and later models, only pinion gear, nut, taper bearing cone and cup should be on drive shaft. Hold shim gage firmly against shims and measure distance between end of gage and pinion gear (Fig. OM13-53). Install shims (13) so there is zero clearance between shim tool and gear.

NOTE: On models prior to 1974, if clearance appears to be 0, make certain that enough shims are installed for an accurate check.

Shims are available in thicknesses of 0.002 inch and 0.005 inch for pre-1974 models and from 0.003 to 0.007 inch for 1975 and later models, and may be installed in any quantity to obtain proper clearance. Set the correct shims aside until drive shaft is installed.

Needle bearings (68 and 70 – Fig. OM13-51) should not be removed from propeller shaft housing (69) unless renewal is intended. Do not reinstall used bearings. OMC Special Tool 317061 (pre-1974 models) or 320738 (1975 and later models) should be used to press aft bearing into propeller shaft housing to ensure proper positioning. OMC Special Tool 314641 (pre-1974 models) or 320669 (1975 and later models) should be used to position bearing (70) in forward bore of propeller shaft housing. Seals (71) should be installed so lip on aft seal is toward propeller and lip on forward seal is facing forward.

Assemble gearcase in the following manner: Renew all gaskets, seals and "O" rings. If lower drive shaft bearing (17) or propeller shaft bearings (68 and 70) have been removed, they too should be renewed. Assemble shift lever (37), shift detent (34) and shift shaft (39) in bearing housing (38). Install detent balls and springs, then apply Loctite to set screws (31) on pre-1974 models. Assemble forward gear (52) with bearing in bearing housing (38). Place thrust washer (53), on models so equipped, and dog clutch (54) on propeller shaft (60). Make sure that hole in dog clutch is aligned with slot in propeller shaft. Insert propeller shaft in forward gear and bearing housing assembly, then insert pin (55) through dog clutch propeller

shaft and hole in shift shaft (39). Install pin retaining spring (56). Press shift detent (34) down and place propeller shaft, forward gear and bearing housing assembly (38) into position in gearcase. Make sure locating pin (35) is seated in recess provided in gearcase. Install shift rod (25) and shift rod cover (29) as an assembly. Thread shift rod fully into detent (34), pull rod to neutral (middle detent) and adjust for proper length. Refer to shift rod adjustment in LOWER UNIT REMOVE AND REINSTALL section for specifications. Pull rod up into forward gear position on completion of adjustment.

Pinion gear (18) may be positioned for reinstallation after turning gearcase upside down. Insert drive shaft (16). Install pinion gear retaining nut and torque it to 40-45 ft.-lbs. (54-61 N·m). Assemble thrust bearing (64 and 63) on reverse gear (62) and slide onto propeller shaft (60). Position bearing retainer plate (65) and install snap rings (66). Make sure that "O" ring (67) is fully seated in groove of bearing housing (69) and that seals (71) are properly installed. Lip of forward seal should be toward front and lip of aft seal should be toward propeller.

Installation of bearing housing (69) will be eased by using two guide pins 10 inches long with ¼-20 threads on one end. Thread guide pins into bearing retainer plate (65) and slide bearing housing (69) into position. Coat bearing housing screws with sealing compound and install. Turn gearcase right side up.

Install seals (9 and 10) in upper drive shaft bearing housing (11) with lip of lower seal (10) down and lip of upper seal (9) up. Place thrust bearing assembly (14 and 15) on drive shaft of pre-1974 models and install previously selected shims or shims (13). Coat screws that secure bearing housing (11) with sealing compound and install. Bottom edge of impeller plate (8) should be coated with OMC Adhesive "M" or equivalent and placed in position. Install key (7), lubricate edges of impeller (6) and install on drive shaft. Drive shaft should be turned clockwise while installing water pump housing (5). Coat screws that secure water pump housing and water tube bracket with sealing compound and install.

**Models 40, 48 and 50 Hp
After 1988**

REMOVE AND REINSTALL. Remove and ground spark plug leads to prevent accidental starting. Remove screw securing shift rod (20—Fig. OM13-55) to shift link. Remove five screws securing gearcase to exhaust housing (two on each side and one forward of

trim tab). Separate gearcase from exhaust housing and place into a suitable holding fixture. Remove oil drain and level plugs and allow oil to drain while inspecting for contamination.

To reinstall gearcase, coat drive shaft splines with OMC Moly Lube or equivalent water resistant grease. Do not lubricate top of drive shaft or drive shaft may not properly engage crankshaft. Install gearcase on exhaust housing making sure water tube properly engages water pump housing. Coat threads of gearcase retaining screws with OMC Nut Lock or a suitable equivalent thread locking compound and tighten ⅜ inch diameter screws to 18-20 ft.-lbs. (24.4-27.1 N·m) and ⁷/₁₆ inch diameter screws to 28-30 ft.-lbs. (38.0-40.7 N·m). Make sure power head shift linkage is in neutral position with gearcase in neutral.

OVERHAUL GEARCASE. Note location and thickness of all shims and thrust washers for reference during reassembly. Remove water pump assembly (1 through 7—Fig. OM13-55). Remove anode (58) and bearing housing screws and retainers (55). Pull bearing housing (54) from gearcase using a universal-type puller with two ¼-20 screws approximately 8 inches (20 cm) long. Remove and discard "O" ring (52). Remove reverse gear (49) and thrust bearing (50) from gearcase. Remove shift lever pivot screw (34) and shift rod housing screws (23). Pull shift rod assembly (20, 21, 22, 24, 25, 26 and 28) out top of gearcase. Remove and discard "O" rings (22 and 25). Pull propeller shaft assembly and shift yoke (29) from gearcase. To disassemble propeller shaft, pry retainer spring (41) from dog clutch (40), push out pin (39), remove dog clutch (40) from shaft (42) and pull plunger (36) from shaft (42). Be sure to retrieve three detent balls (37) and spring (38). Remove three screws securing bearing housing (10) to gearcase. Place OMC Drive Shaft Holding Socket 316612 or a suitable spline adapter on upper drive shaft splines, reach into gearcase with an ¹¹/₁₆ inch open-end wrench and remove pinion nut (19). Pinion gear (18) is a taper fit on drive shaft (16). OMC Puller 387206 and Backing Plate 325867 may be necessary to separate gear (18) from drive shaft. Reach into gearcase and retrieve pinion gear (18), then pull drive shaft (16) from gearcase. Remove forward gear (47), thrust bearing (46) and thrust washer (45). Pinion bearing (17) should not be removed unless bearing renewal is required. If necessary, remove bearing retaining screw (34) and drive bearing (17) down into gear cavity using OMC Pinion Bearing Remover and Installer 391257 and Pinion Service Kit 433033, or suitable equivalent driver. Do not remove forward gear bearings (44 and 43) unless renewal is required. OMC Forward Gear Bearing Service Kit 433034 or equivalent is required to remove bearings (44 and 43). Do not remove bearings (53 and 56) from bearing housing (54) unless renewal is required. If necessary, use a suitable slide hammer type puller to remove bearings (53 and 56).

Inspect all components for excessive wear or other damage. Renew all seals, gaskets and ''O'' rings during reassembly. Bearings (53 and 56) should be driven into housing (54) from lettered side of bearing. Apply OMC Gasket Sealing Compound to outer diameter of seals (57) and install seals into housing with lips facing away from each other. Lubricate seal lips with OMC Triple-Guard Grease or equivalent. Bearing housing

(10) and bearing (12) are not available separately. Renew housing (10) assembly if bearing requires renewal. Apply OMC Gasket Sealing Compound to outer diameter of seals (8 and 9) and install into housing (10) with lips facing away from each other. Lubricate seal lips with OMC Triple-Guard grease or equivalent.

If renewing thrust bearing (15), thrust washers (14), bearing housing (10), pin-

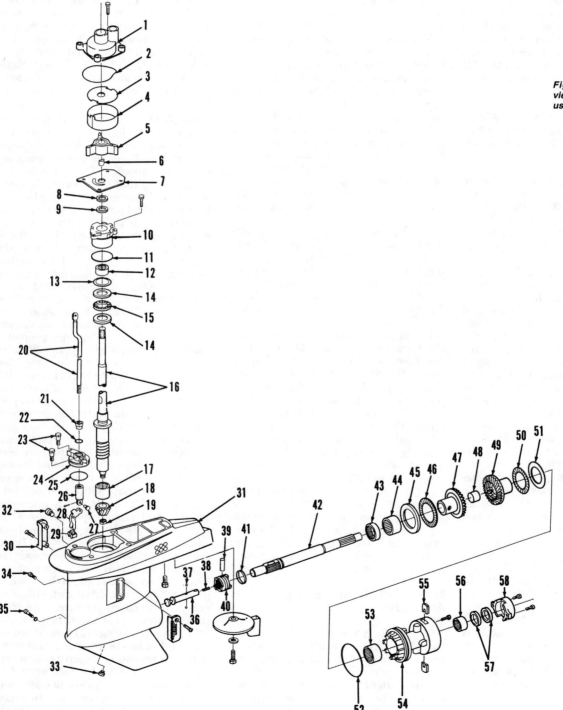

Fig. OM13-55—Exploded view of gearcase assembly used on 1989 40, 48 and 50 hp models.

1. Housing
2. Seal
3. Plate
4. Liner
5. Impeller
6. Key
7. Plate
8. Seal
9. Seal
10. Bearing housing
11. ''O'' ring
12. Bearing
13. Shim
14. Thrust washers
15. Thrust bearing
16. Drive shaft
17. Pinion bearing
18. Pinion gear
19. Pinion nut
20. Shift rod
21. Nut
22. ''O'' ring
23. Shoulder screws
24. Shift rod housing
25. ''O'' ring
26. Coupler
27. Pin
28. Lever
29. Yoke
30. Water inlet
31. Gearcase
32. Oil level plug
33. Drain plug
34. Pinion bearing retaining screw
35. Shift lever pivot screw
36. Shift plunger
37. Detent balls
38. Spring
39. Pin
40. Dog clutch
41. Retainer
42. Propeller shaft
43. Bearing
44. Bearing
45. Thrust washer
46. Thrust bearing
47. Forward gear
48. Bearing
49. Reverse gear
50. Thrust washer
51. Thrust washer
52. ''O'' ring
53. Bearing
54. Bearing housing
55. Retainer
56. Bearing
57. Seals
58. Anode

ion gear (18) or drive shaft (16), the correct shim (13) thickness must be determined to provide the proper clearance between pinion gear (18) and drive gears (47 and 49). OMC Drive Shaft Shimming Tool 393185 and Service Kit 433032 is required to select shim (13) thickness. Proceed as follows to determine shim thickness: Assemble thrust washers (14), thrust bearing (15) and bearing housing (10) on drive shaft (16). Do not install shim (13). Install pinion gear (18) on drive shaft and tighten nut (19) to 40-45 ft.-lbs. (54.2-61.0 N·m). Place collar (OMC part 334985) over drive shaft so large end of collar contacts bearing housing (10). Position drive shaft and collar assembly into OMC Shimming Tool 393185 as shown in Fig. OM13-56. Tighten preload screw (S) against drive shaft until groove on plunger (P) is flush with end of threads, then tighten retaining nut (N). Place OMC Shim Gage 334984 (G) on guide pins of tool base. While holding end shim gage (G) against pinion gear, rotate drive shaft housing (10—Fig. OM13-55) and measure clearance between shim gage (G—Fig. OM13-56) and mating surface of bearing housing (10—Fig. OM13-55). Renew housing (10) if clearance varies more than 0.004 inch (0.10 mm). Next, abut end of shim gage with mating surface of bearing housing (10). While holding shim gage (G—Fig. OM13-56) against bearing housing, rotate drive shaft (not bearing housing) and measure clearance between end of shim gage (G) and pinion gear. Subtract average clearance from 0.030 inch (0.76 mm). Remainder equals the correct thickness of shims (13—Fig. OM13-55).

NOTE: If clearance measured between shim gage (G—Fig. OM13-56) and pinion gear varies more than 0.002 inch (0.05 mm), drive shaft and/or pinion and forward gear set should be renewed.

Check shim selection by reassembling drive shaft using the correct thickness shims (13), place into shimming tool and measure clearance between gage and pinion gear as previously outlined. Clearance should be 0.030 inch (0.76 mm).

Reassemble in the reverse order of disassembly while noting the following: Bearing (17—Fig. OM13-55) should be driven into gearcase from lettered side of bearing. After bearing (17) installation, install a new seal and apply OMC Nut Lock to threads of retaining screw (34) and tighten to 48-80 in.-lbs. (5.4-9.0 N·m). Bearings (43 and 44) should be driven into gearcase from lettered side. Thinner bearing (43) must be installed first. Slide dog clutch (40) on propeller shaft (42) with end marked PROP END facing propeller. Place two detent balls

(37) into hole in side of plunger (36), then place third ball and then spring (38) into hole in end of plunger (36). Align holes in plunger (36) and dog clutch (40) with slot in propeller shaft (42) and insert plunger (36) into propeller shaft until detent balls engage with groove in propeller shaft. With holes aligned, place a suitable wedge shaped tool through holes as shown in Fig. OM13-57. Angled side of tool should be installed toward plunger (36).

NOTE: Wedge tool should be ⁹/₃₂ inch (7.1 mm) diameter and 2⁵/₈ inches (75 mm) long. Sharp end of tool should be ground at 20 degree angle.

Push wedge tool through propeller shaft using pin (39) as shown. Install a new retainer spring (41—Fig. OM13-55) making sure coils of retainer do not overlap.

Install thrust washers (14) with chamfered edges facing away from each other. Tighten pinion nut to 40-45 ft.-lbs. (54.2-61.0 N·m). Reassemble shift rod and housing and lubricate shift rod housing "O" rings (22 and 25) with OMC Triple-Guard Grease. Tighten nut (21) to 48-60 in.-lbs. (5.4-6.8 N·m). Screw shift rod (20) into coupler (26) nine turns. Place shift yoke (29) on shift plunger (36) with part number facing up. Secure yoke (29) with a suitable grease. Carefully insert propeller shaft assembly into gearcase until rear edge of yoke (29) is even with front edge of forward gear, then install shift rod assembly with shift lever (28) positioned as shown in Fig. OM13-58. Make sure tangs on lever (28) properly engage yoke (29—Fig. OM13-55), apply OMC Nut Lock to threads of pivot screw (35) and install screw (35) while moving shift rod to align hole in lever (28) with hole in gearcase. Tighten screw (35) to 48-80 in.-lbs. (5.4-9.0 N·m). Apply OMC Gasket Sealing Compound to screws (23) and tighten screws (23) to 60-84 in.-lbs. (6.8-9.5 N·m). Install thrust bearing (50) on reverse gear (49) and install gear and bearing over propeller shaft and into gearcase. Place thrust washer (51) on housing (54) and secure with a suitable grease. Seal housing (54) and "O" ring (53) with OMC Gasket Sealing Compound, install housing assembly (54) into gearcase and tighten retainer (55) screws to 120-144 in.-lbs. (13.8-16.3 N·m). Tighten anode (58) securing screws to 108-132 in.-lbs. (12.2-14.9 N·m). Do not use sealer on anode screws.

With offset on upper end of shift rod (20) facing front of gearcase, measure from gearcase-to-exhaust housing mating surface to center of hole in top of shift rod (20). Distance should be 16²⁹/₃₂

to 16³¹/₃₂ inches (429.4-431.0 mm) on standard shaft models and 21²⁹/₃₂ to 21³¹/₃₂ inches (556.4-558.0 mm) on long shaft models. Screw shift rod (20) in or out of coupler (26) as necessary to adjust. Fill gearcase with 16.4 fl. oz. of OMC Hi-Vis gear lube and install on exhaust housing as outlined in REMOVE AND REINSTALL section to complete reassembly.

POWER TILT AND TRIM

So Equipped Models After 1981

OPERATION. Some models after 1981 are equipped with a hydraulically

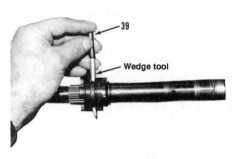

Fig. OM13-57—Refer to text to reassemble propeller shaft.

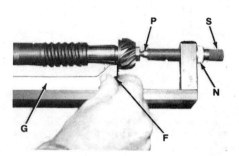

Fig. OM13-56—View showing drive shaft positioned in OMC Shim Tool 393185. Refer to text for shim (13—Fig. OM13-55) selection procedure.
F. Feeler gage
G. Shim gage (part 334984)
N. Retaining nut
P. Plunger
S. Preload screw

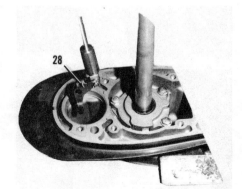

Fig. OM13-58—Position shift lever (28) as shown when installing shift rod assembly into gearcase. Make sure tangs on lever (28) properly engage shift yoke (29—Fig. OM13-55).

actuated power tilt and trim system. An oil pump driven by a reversible electric motor provides oil pressure. One hydraulic cylinder trims the outboard motor while another hydraulic cylinder tilts the outboard motor. A rocker control switch determines motor and pump rotation thereby retracting or extending tilt and trim cylinders. The pump motor is equipped with a thermal overload switch which resets after approximately one minute. Turn slotted manual release valve screw (S–Fig. OM13-65) at bottom of pump to manually raise or lower outboard. Tighten manual release valve clockwise to operate hydraulic tilt and trim.

Hydraulic system contains approximately 25 oz. (740 mL) of oil. Recommended oil is OMC Power Trim and Tilt Fluid or DEXRON Automatic Transmission Fluid. Do not run pump without oil in reservoir. Fill plug (R) is located in side of pump reservoir. Oil level should reach fill plug hole threads with outboard tilted in full up position. Hydraulic tilt should be cycled several times and oil level rechecked if system has been drained or lost a large amount of oil.

TROUBLESHOOTING. The following specifications should be noted when a malfunction occurs in tilt and trim system. Current draw should be 45 amps when operating either up or down. Current draw with unit stalled in up or down position should be 55 amps. To check oil pressure, first momentarily cycle system "UP" and "DOWN" a few times. Remove manual release valve screw (S–Fig. OM13-65) and install OMC gage "A." Operate system in the "UP" direction and observe gage after system stalls out at full extension. Gage reading should not drop below 100-200 psi (700-1400 kPa). Install OMC gage "B." Operate system in the "DOWN" direction and observe gage after system is fully retracted and stalls out. Gage reading should not drop below 100-200 psi (700-1400 kPa).

OVERHAUL. Oil pump must be serviced as a unit assembly. Motor components are available. Refer to Figs. OM13-66 and OM13-67 for exploded views of trim and cylinders. To check operation of trim gage sending unit, connect ohmmeter leads to sender (3–Fig. OM13-66) and elbow (1). Resistance should be 2.5-3.5 ohms with cylinder rod fully extended and 84-96 ohms with rod fully retracted.

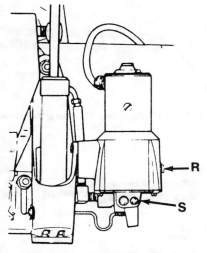

Fig. OM13-65—View identifying manual release valve screw (S) and reservoir fill plug (R) location.

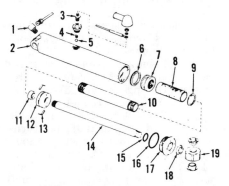

Fig. OM13-66—Exploded view of hydraulic trim cylinder.

1. Elbow	11. Stop
2. Trim cylinder	12. Carrier bearing
3. Sender	13. Sender ground
4. Spring	springs
5. Ball	14. Shaft
6. "O" ring	15. "O" ring
7. Piston	16. "O" ring
8. Sender bobbin	17. End cap
9. Retaining ring	18. Wiper
10. Piston carrier	19. Shaft end

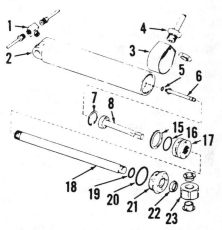

Fig. OM13-67—Exploded view of hydraulic tilt cylinder.

1. Tee	16. "O" ring
2. Tilt cylinder	17. Piston
3. Band	18. Shaft
4. Oil line	19. "O" ring
5. "O" ring	20. "O" ring
6. Stem valve	21. End cap
7. Snap ring	22. Wiper
8. Relief valve assy.	23. Shaft end
15. Piston ring	

EVINRUDE AND JOHNSON
3-CYLINDER MODELS
55, 60, 65, 70 AND 75 HP

EVINRUDE	
Year Produced	**Model**
1969	55972, 55973
1970	60072, 66073
1971	60172, 60173
1972	65272, 65273
1973	65372, 65373
1974	70442, 70443,
	70472, 70473
1975	70572, 70573,
	75542, 75543
1976	70673, 74642, 75643
1977	70773, 75742, 75743
1978	70873, 75842, 75843
1979	70973, 75942, 75943
1980	70ELCX, 75ERCS, 75ERLCS, 75TRLCS
1981	70ELC1, 75ERCI, 75TRLCI
1982	70ELCN, 75ERCN, 75TRLCN
1983	70ELCT, 75ERCT, 75TRLCT
1984	70ELCR, 70TLCR, 75ECR, 75TLCR
1985	70ELCO, 70TLCO, 75ECO
1986	60ELCD, 60TLCD, 70ELCD, 70TLCD, 75ECD
1987	E60ELCU, E60TLCU, E70ELCU, E70TLCU
1988	E60ELCC, E60TLCC, E60TTLCC, E70ELCC, E70TLCC
1989	E60ELCE, E60TLCE, E60TTLCE, E70ELCE, E70TLCE

JOHNSON	
Year Produced	**Model**
1969	55ES69, 55ESL9
1970	60ES70, 60ESL70
1971	60ES71, 60ESL71
1972	65ES72, 65ESL72
1973	65ES73, 65ESL73, 65ESLR73
1974	70ES74, 70ESL74, 70ESLR74
1975	70ES75, 70ESL75, 74ERS75, 75ESLR75
1976	70EL76, 75ER76, 75ELR76
1977	70EL77, 75ER77, 75ELR77
1978	70EL78, 75ER78, 75ELR78
1979	70EL79, 75ER79, 75ELR79
1980	70ELCS, 75ERCS, 75ERLCS, 75TRLCS
1981	70ELCI, 75ERCI, 75TRLCI
1982	70ELCN, 75ERCN, 75TRLCN
1983	70ELCT, 75ERCT, 75TRLCT
1984	70ELCR, 70TLCR, 75ECR, 75TLCR
1985	70ELCO, 70TLCO, 75ECO
1986	60ELCD, 60TLCD, 70ELCD, 70TLCD, 75ECD
1987	J60JLCU, J60TLCU, J70JLCU, J70TLCU
1988	J60JLCC, J60TLCC, J60TTLCC, J70JLCC, J70TLCC
1989	J60JLCE, J60TLCE, J60TTLCE, J70ELCE, J70TLCE

CONDENSED SERVICE DATA

TUNE-UP

Hp/rpm 55/5000
60/5000*
65/5000
70/5500†
75/5500‡

Bore:
55, 60 (prior to 1989), 65, 70 (prior
to 1986) & 75 hp . . . . 3.000 in.
(76.20 mm)
60 (1989) & 70 (after 1985) . . . . 3.188 in.
(80.97 mm)
Stroke . . . . 2.344 in.
(59.54 mm)
Number of Cylinders 3
Displacement:
55, 60 (prior to 1989), 65,
70 (prior to 1986) & 75 . . . . 49.7 cu. in.
(814.4 cc)
60 (1989) & 70 (after 1985) . . . . 56.1 cu. in.
(919.3 cc)
Spark Plug:
55 & 60 (prior to 1971) . . . . AC V40FF
Champion L20V
60 (1971) . . . . Champion L76V
65 & 70 (1972-1974) . . . . AC VB40FFM
Champion UL77V
All Models (1975-1982) . . . . AC M40FFX
Champion L77JC4

Electrode Gap . . . . 0.040 in.
(1.0 mm)
All Models (1983-1989) . . . . AC M40FFX
Champion QL77JC4§
Electrode Gap . . . . 0.040 in.
(1.0 mm)

Ignition:
55 & 60 (prior to 1972) . . . . . CDI—With Breaker Points
Point Gap . . . . 0.010 in.
(0.25 mm)

All Models
(after 1971) . . . . CDI—Without Breaker Points
Carburetor Make . . . . OMC
Idle Speed (in gear):
All Models (prior to 1987) . . . . 750 rpm
All Models (after 1986) . . . . 700-750 rpm
Fuel:Oil Ratio 50:1**

*On 1989 60 hp models, engine is rated at 60 hp at 5500 rpm.
†On 70 hp models prior to 1986, engine is rated at 70 hp at 5000 rpm.
‡On 1978-1985 75 hp models, engine is rated at 75 hp at 5200 rpm.
§Champion QL78V surface gap spark plugs are recommended for 1985 and later models when operated at sustained high speeds. Surface gap spark plugs should be re-

newed if center electrode is more than $1/_{32}$ inch (0.79 mm) below flat surface of plug end.

**On 1985 and later models equipped with Variable Ratio Oiling (VRO), the VRO pump varies fuel:oil ratio from approximately 150:1 at idle to approximately 50:1 at full throttle.

SIZES — CLEARANCES
Piston Ring End Gap .0.007-0.017 in.
(0.18-0.43 mm)

Piston Ring Side Clearance (1969-1984)*:
55 Hp (1969) . . . . .0.0045-0.0070 in.
(0.114-0.178 mm)
60 Hp (1970) .0.0015-0.0045 in.
(0.038-0.114 mm)
60 Hp (1971) .0.0015-0.0040 in.
(0.038-0.102 mm)
65, 70 & 75 Hp . . . . .0.0015-0.0040 in.
(0.038-0.102 mm)

Lower Piston Ring Side Clearance:
All Models (after 1984) . . . . .0.004 in. max.
(0.10 mm)

Piston Skirt Clearance:
55 Hp . . . . .0.0040-0.0055 in.
(0.102-0.140 mm)
1970-1978 .0.0035-0.0055 in.
(0.090-0.140 mm)
1979-1981 .0.0045-0.0065 in.
(0.114-0.165 mm)
1982-1984 .0.0045-0.0055 in.
(0.114-0.140 mm)
1985-1989 . . . .†

Maximum Cylinder Tolerance:
All Models (prior to 1986) . . . . .0.003 in.
(0.08 mm)

All Models (after 1985)
Max. Taper . . . . .0.002 in.
(0.05 mm)
Max. Out-of-Round . . . . .0.003 in.
(0.08 mm)

Standard Cylinder Diameter (after 1984):
60 (prior to 1989) & 75 . . . . .2.9995-3.0005 in.
(76.187-76.213 mm)
60 (after 1988) & 70 . . . . .3.1870-3.1880 in.
(80.950-80.975 mm)

Standard Piston Diameter:
All Models (prior to 1986) . . . . .See Text
60 (prior to 1989) & 75 . . . . .2.9940-2.9950 in.
(76.048-76.073 mm)
60 (after 1988) & 70 . . . . .3.1806-3.1841 in.
(80.787-80.876 mm)

Crankshaft Diameters:
Top Main . . . . .1.4974-1.4979 in.
(38.03-38.05 mm)
Center Mains . . . . .1.3748-1.3752 in.
(34.92-34.93 mm)
Lower Main . . . . .1.1810-1815 in.
(30.00-30.01 mm)

SIZES — CLEARANCES CONT.
Crankpin . . . . .1.1823-1.1828 in.
(30.03-30.04 mm)

Crankshaft End Play:
55 Hp (1969) .0.00055-0.01635 in.
(0.0140-0.4153 mm)
60 Hp (1970 & 1971) . . . . .0.0006-0.0156 in.
(0.015-0.396 mm)
65, 70 & 75 Hp (Prior to 1982) . . . . .0.0006-0.0165 in.
(0.015-0.419 mm)

Forward Gear Bushing to Propeller
Shaft Clearance (Prior to 1985) . . . . .0.001-0.002 in.
(0.03-0.05 mm)

*Ring side clearance is not applicable to semi-keystone type ring.

†The manufacturer does not specify piston skirt clearance on models after 1984. If cylinder bore and piston are within tolerance, clearance should be acceptable.

TIGHTENING TORQUES
Connecting Rod:
Prior to 1988 . . . . .29-31 ft.-lbs.
(39.3-42.0 N·m)
After 1987 .30-32 ft.-lbs.
(40.7-43.4 N·m)

Crankcase Halves:
Main Bearing Screws . . . . .216-240 in.-lbs.
(24-27 N·m)
Flange Screws . . . . .60-84 in.-lbs.
(7-9 N·m)

Cylinder Head . . . . .216-240 in.-lbs.
(24-27 N·m)

Flywheel:
1969-1971 . . . . .70-85 ft.-lbs.
(95-115 N·m)
All Other Models . . . . .100-105 ft.-lbs.
(136-143 N·m)

Spark Plug . . . . .216-240 in.-lbs.
(24-27 N·m)

Standard Screws:
No. 6 . . . . .7-10 in.-lbs.
(0.8-1.2 N·m)
No. 8 . . . . .15-22 in.-lbs.
(1.6-2.4 N·m)
No. 10 . . . . .25-35 in.-lbs.
(2.8-4.0 N·m)
No. 12 . . . . .35-40 in.-lbs.
(4.0-4.6 N·m)
¼ Inch . . . . .60-80 in.-lbs.
(7-9 N·m)
5/16 Inch . . . . .120-140 in.-lbs.
(14-16 N·m)
⅜ Inch . . . . .220-240 in.-lbs.
(24-27 N·m)
7/16 Inch . . . . .340-360 in.-lbs.
(38-40 N·m)

LUBRICATION

The engine is lubricated by oil mixed with the fuel. On 1969-1975 models, fuel should be regular unleaded or premium leaded with a minimum pump octane rating of 89. On all models after 1975, the fuel should be regular leaded, regular unleaded, premium leaded or premium unleaded gasoline with a minimum pump octane rating of 86.

On models prior to 1985, recommended oil is Evinrude or Johnson 50/1 Lubricant or a NMMA certified TC-WII motor oil. The recommended fuel:oil ratio for normal operation and engine break-in is 50:1.

On 1985 and later models equipped with variable ratio oiling (VRO), recommended oil is Evinrude or Johnson Outboard Lubricant, OMC 2-Cycle Motor Oil or a suitable NMMA (formerly BIA) certified TC-WII motor oil. The VRO pump varies the fuel:oil ratio from approximately 150:1 at idle to approximately 50:1 at full throttle by sensing engine power output. During engine break-in (first 10 hours of operation), the fuel in the fuel tank must be mixed at a fuel:oil ratio of 50:1 and used in combination with the VRO system to ensure proper lubrication. Oil level in the VRO tank should be observed during engine break-in to be sure oil level is dropping, indicating VRO system is functioning. After the first 10 hours of operation, re-fill VRO tank with recommended oil and switch to straight gasoline in the fuel tank. If VRO system is not used on models so equipped, mix fuel and oil at a 50:1 ratio.

The lower unit gears and bearings are lubricated by oil contained in the gear-case. The recommended oil is OMC Sea-Lube Premium Blend Gearcase Lube on models prior to 1977, and OMC HI-VIS Gearcase Lube on models after 1976. The gearcase oil level should be checked after every 50 hours of operation and the gearcase should be drained and refilled with new oil every 100 hours or once each season, whichever occurs first.

The gearcase is drained and filled through the same plug port. An oil lev-el (vent) port is used to indicate the full oil level of the gearcase and to ease in oil drainage.

To drain the oil, place the outboard motor in a vertical position. Remove the drain plug and oil level plug and allow the lubricant to drain into a suitable con-tainer.

To fill the gearcase with oil, place the outboard motor in a vertical position. Add oil through the drain plug opening with an oil feeder until the oil begins to overflow from oil level plug port. Reinstall oil level plug with a new gas-ket, if needed, and tighten. Remove oil feeder, then reinstall drain plug with a new gasket, if needed, and tighten.

FUEL SYSTEM

CARBURETORS. Three single-barrel, float type carburetors are used. Each carburetor provides fuel for one cylinder and each is equipped with low speed and high speed (main) metering components.

ADJUSTMENT. The idle mixture ad-justing needles on models prior to 1976 are linked together and can be external-ly adjusted within a limited range by turning the adjustment knob behind the control panel door on front of motor. If further adjustment is necessary, remove the motor cover and proceed as follows: Pull knob (1–Fig. OM14-1) off, then remove silencer cover (2). Pull levers (3 and 5) off idle mixture needles. Normal setting for idle needles (IN) is 5/8 turn open. Run motor until normal operating temperature is reached, then adjust

each of the three idle mixture needles to provide the smoothest operation at 700-750 rpm, in gear with motor on boat (or in test tank). After adjustment is complete, install levers (3 and 5) and connecting link (4) making certain that levers are horizontal and toward star-board.

NOTE: Make certain idle needles are not moved when installing levers.

Idle speed should be adjusted to 750 rpm in forward gear and is adjusted at stop screw (I–Fig. OM14-3).

NOTE: If throttle valves are not synchro-nized to be open exactly the same amount, it may be impossible to obtain a smooth idle. If difficulty is encountered, close throttle and make certain that the follower roller (F) is not touching throt-tle cam (T). Loosen clamp screws (B) on throt-tle shafts of top and bottom carburetors, hold all three throttle shafts closed, then tighten screws (B).

On models without idle needle (IN—Figs. OM14-1 or OM14-2), change size of idle jet (8—Fig. OM14-2) to adjust idle mixture. On models equipped with idle

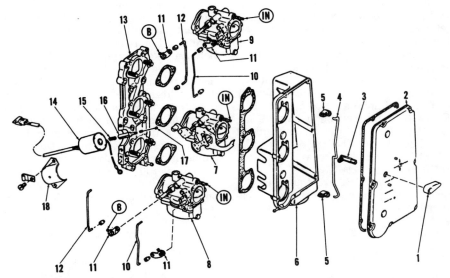

Fig. OM14-1 — View of early carburetors, inlet manifold and silencer. Later models are similar. Refer to Fig. OM14-2 for exploded view of carburetor.

B. Set screws (top & bottom carburetors only)
IN. Idle mixture needles
1. External adjustment knob
2. Cover

3. Lever for center carburetor
4. Link rod
5. Lever (top & bottom carburetors)
6. Silencer

7. Center carburetor
8. Bottom carburetor
9. Top carburetor
10. Choke links
11. Choke & throttle levers

12. Throttle links
13. Inlet manifold
14. Choke solenoid
15. Spring
16. Plunger
17. Connector spring
18. Retainer plate

IN. Idle mixture needle
1. Fuel inlet valve
2. Float
3. Float pivot pin
4. Float bowl
5. Orifice plug
6. Gasket
7. Plug
8. Idle jet or intermediate jet
8A. Bearing
9. Retainer
10. Throttle plate
11. Throttle shaft
12. Follower lever
13. Follower roller
14. Screw
15. Choke manual control lever
16. Override spring
17. Choke shaft
18. Shoulder (pivot) screw
19. Spring washer
20. Washer
22. Idle jet
29. Roll pin
30. Washer

Fig. OM14-2—Exploded view of carburetor. On early models, the top and bottom carburetors are the same; components (11 through 20) are different for center carburetor. On early models, note linkage for top and bottom carburetors in Fig. OM14-1. Choke components are not used on models after 1982. On 1989 models, a slow speed mixture needle and adapter sleeve is used in place of jet (22).

mixture needle (IN), mark position of needle (IN) prior to removing for reference during reassembly. Adjust idle mixture with screw (IN) on models so equipped. Note that 1989 models are equipped with a slow speed mixture screw and adapter sleeve in place of idle jet (22). Slow speed mixture screw is adjusted at the factory and should not require further adjustment. Mark position of mixture screw on adapter sleeve prior to removing screw for reference during reassembly.

Models in 1979-1984 (except 1983 and 1984 75 hp) are equipped with an intermediate jet (8) and idle jet (22). Both jets (8 and 22) may be removed so another jet size can be installed to alter carburetor fuel mixture.

On models prior to 1983, the choke solenoid should be positioned so choke plates open and close fully. The solenoid plunger should protrude approximately ¼ inch (6.35 mm) as shown at (P–Fig. OM14-3). Make certain linkage is adjusted to close all three choke plates at the same time. The spring (17–Fig. OM14-1) should be screwed onto the solenoid plunger 2½-3½ turns.

Models after 1982 are equipped with an electric primer system on recreational models.

R&R AND OVERHAUL. The carburetor can be removed after removing silencer (6–Fig. OM14-1), linkage and fuel lines. The top and bottom carburetors are the same; however, the center carburetor is equipped with different controls, linkage, choke shaft and throttle shaft. Disassembly procedure is self evident. The screws attaching choke and throttle plates are staked after assembly and should be renewed if removed from shafts.

NOTE: On models after 1979, the manufacturer does not recommend submerging the parts in carburetor or parts cleaning solutions. An aerosol type carburetor cleaner is recommended. The float and other components made of plastic and rubber should not be subjected to some cleaning solutions. Safety eyewear and solvent resistant gloves are recommended.

To check float level, remove float bowl and invert carburetor. Place OMC Float Gage 324891 on float bowl gasket surface as shown in Fig. OM14-4. Make sure float gage is not pushing down on float. Float should be between notches on side of float gage marked 25 THRU 75 HP. Carefully bend float arm to adjust. If float gage 324891 is not available, adjust float so float is level and parallel with float bowl gasket surface. To check float drop, hold carburetor upright and allow float to hang by its own weight. Measure from float bowl gasket surface to bottom of float 180 degrees from inlet valve. Carefully bend tang on float arm (adjacent to inlet valve) to adjust float drop to 1⅛ to 1⅝ inches (28.6-41.3 mm). Apply a suitable thread locking compound to float bowl screws upon reassembly.

The choke control lever (15–Fig. OM14-2) has three positions. When control is pushed up, the choke is manually off (open). When control is pushed down, choke is manually on (closed). The center position provides automatic operation. When in automatic position and ignition switch ON, battery current is supplied to the solenoid (14–Fig. OM14-1) via a thermal switch located at bottom of cylinder head. If motor is cool, current passes through the thermal switch, energizes the solenoid and closes the choke plates, but when motor reaches 145°F (63°C), the thermal switch should open and stop current flow to the solenoid.

Refer to ADJUSTMENT paragraphs after carburetors are assembled and installed.

SPEED CONTROL LINKAGE (Early Models). The carburetor throttle valves must be correctly synchronized to open as the ignition timing is advanced. To adjust the speed control linkage, it is necessary to first check (and adjust if required) the ignition maximum advance using a power timing light as outlined in the previous IGNITION SYSTEM section. Move the speed control to the idle position and make sure follower roller (F–Fig. OM14-3) is not touching throttle cam (T). Loosen top and bottom carburetor clamp screws (B) and make certain that all three throttle plates are closed, then tighten clamp screws (B). Move the speed control lever slowly from idle position toward fast position and note the point at which throttle cam (T) contacts follower roller (F). The cam should just contact roller (F) when throttle cam (T) lower alignment mark (T–Fig. OM14-5) is exactly centered with roller (F) as shown. If incorrect, loosen screw (14) and reposition the roller. Move the speed control lever to the maximum speed position and check the carburetor throttle plates. If the throttle plates are not completely open, reposition yoke (Y–Fig. OM14-3) on rod (R). Make sure the carburetor linkage cannot be damaged by attempting to open the throttle too far. Normally, length from end of rod (R) to the rear face of yoke (Y) should be 4-31/32 inches (126.2 mm).

All Later Models. The carburetor throttle valves are synchronized to open as the ignition timing is advanced. Throttle valve opening and ignition advance synchronization should be checked and adjusted if necessary.

Fig. OM14-3—View of speed control linkage used on early models. Refer to text.

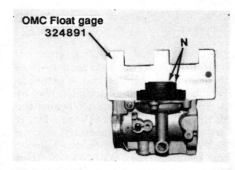

Fig. OM14-4—To check float level, invert carburetor and place OMC Float Gage 324891 on carburetor body as shown. Make sure float gage is not pushing down on float. Float should be between notches (N) on side of gage marked 25 THRU 75 HP. Bend float arm to adjust.

The following procedure should be used to check and adjust speed control linkage: Remove remote control cables from power head. Make sure timing pointer is aligned with TDC mark on flywheel when number one piston is positioned at TDC. Loosen timing pointer securing screw and move pointer as necessary if adjustment is required.

NOTE: The flywheel is equipped with two timing grids. Be sure to reference timing grid NOT marked "ROPE" for remote control models.

To synchronize carburetor throttle valves (all models), move the speed control lever to the idle position. Loosen cam follower roller screw (14—Fig. OM14-6) so follower roller (F) does not contact throttle cam (T). Loosen top and bottom carburetor lever screws (L) and make certain that all three throttle valves are completely closed, then tighten screws (L). Recheck adjustment to be sure all throttle valves open and close at exactly the same time.

NOTE: Two style throttle cams (T—Fig. OM14-6) are used on late models. One cam has two embossed marks and part number 394466. Other cam has one embossed mark and part number 431707. Inspect throttle cam and refer to appropriate following sections for adjustment procedures.

Throttle Cam With Two Marks (Part 394466)

Advance throttle cam (T—Fig. OM14-6) until cam (T) just contacts cam follow-

er roller (F). Lower (short) mark on cam (T) should be aligned with center of follower roller (F) when cam and roller contact. To adjust, loosen screw (14) and position follower roller (F) as necessary.

Connect a suitable timing light to number 1 spark plug lead. Start engine and advance throttle until carburetor throttle valves just begin to open and hold in this position. With linkage in this position, ignition timing should be 1 degree ATDC to 1 degree BTDC on models prior to 1987, 3-5 degrees ATDC on 70 hp models after 1986 and 0-2 degrees ATDC on 1988 and later 60 and 70 hp models. To adjust, stop engine, loosen locknut (N) and rotate adjustment nut (A) as necessary. Note that turning screw (A) clockwise (as viewed from front of motor) advances pickup timing. One complete turn equals approximately 2 degrees timing change.

Open throttle to full throttle position (engine not running) and adjust full throttle stop screw (W) so carburetor throttle shaft pins (port side of carburetor) are positioned exactly vertical.

NOTE: The throttle shaft pins must not advance past the vertical position or carburetor damage may result.

Outboard motor should be properly submersed in a suitable test tank and correct test wheel installed to adjust full throttle, maximum timing advance. Connect a suitable timing light to the number 1 spark plug lead, start engine and advance throttle to 5000 rpm minimum.

NOTE: Accurate maximum timing advance can not be obtained unless engine speed is 5000 rpm or more.

Maximum timing advance should be 18-20 degrees BTDC. To adjust, stop engine, loosen locknut and adjust full throttle timing screw (located under flywheel adjacent to starter motor) as necessary. Note that turning screw clockwise retards timing. One full turn

equals approximately 1 degree timing change.

To adjust idle speed, boat should be in the water running in forward gear, at normal operating temperature with the correct propeller installed. Boat movement should be unrestrained. Rotate idle speed screw (I) as necessary to obtain the recommended idle speed (CONDENSED SERVICE DATA).

Throttle Cam With One Mark (Part 431707)

Make sure timing pointer is properly adjusted and synchronize throttle plates as previously outlined. Next, adjust idle speed to 800 rpm with boat in the water, running in forward gear with correct propeller installed. Boat movement should be unrestrained. Adjust idle speed screw (I—Fig. OM14-6) as necessary.

Advance throttle cam (T) until cam (T) just contacts cam follower roller (F). Mark on cam (T) should be aligned with center of roller (F) as carburetors just begin to open. To adjust, loosen screw (14), align mark and roller, then retighten screw.

Loosen locknut (N). While holding throttle arm against the idle speed stop screw, rotate nut (A) until cam (T) and roller (F) contact. With carburetor throttle valves closed and throttle arm against idle stop screw, mark on cam (T) should be aligned with center of roller (F). Next, turn idle speed stop screw (I) exactly ½ turn counterclockwise. Idle speed should now be 700-750 rpm in forward gear with a clearance of 0.005-0.010 inch (0.13-0.25 mm) between throttle cam (T) and roller (F).

Open carburetors to full throttle position (engnine not running) and adjust full throttle stop screw (W) so throttle shaft pins (port side of carburetors) are exactly vertical.

NOTE: Throttle shaft pins must not travel past vertical position or carburetor damage may result.

Fig. OM14-5 — On early models, the throttle cam should just contact roller (F) when throttle cam lower alignment mark (T) is exactly centered with the roller as shown. If incorrect, loosen screw (14) and reposition the roller.

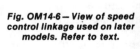

Fig. OM14-6 — View of speed control linkage used on later models. Refer to text.

Outboard motor should be properly submersed in a suitable test tank and the correct test wheel installed to adjust full throttle, maximum timing advance. Connect a suitable timing light to the number 1 spark plug lead, start engine and advance throttle to 5000 rpm minimum.

NOTE: Accurate maximum timing advance can not be obtained unless engine rpm is 5000 rpm or more.

Full throttle timing advance should be 18-20 degrees BTDC. To adjust, stop engine, loosen locknut and adjust full throttle timing screw (located under flywheel adjacent to starter motor) as necessary. Note that turning screw clockwise retards timing. One full turn equals approximately 1 degree timing change.

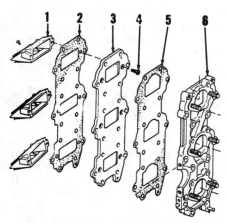

Fig. OM14-7 — Exploded view of the reed valves and inlet manifold. Base (3) and gasket (5) are not used on later models.

1. Leaf valve assy.
2. Gasket (leaf plate base to valves & crankcase)
3. Leaf plate base
4. Valve assy. retaining screw (6 used)
5. Gasket (inlet manifold to leaf plate base)
6. Inlet manifold

Fig. OM14-8 — View of a VRO type fuel pump.

1. VRO fuel pump assy.
2. Oil inlet nipple
3. Fuel inlet nipple
4. Crankcase pulse nipple
5. Fuel mixture discharge nipple

REED VALVES. Three sets of leaf (reed) valves are used, one for each cylinder. The three valves are attached to the leaf plate base (3 – Fig. OM14-7). The leaf petals should seat very lightly against the valve block throughout their entire length with the least possible tension. The individual parts of the leaf valve assembly are not available separately. Renew the complete valve assembly if petals are broken, cracked, warped or bent.

NON-VRO FUEL PUMP. The fuel pump is operated by the pressure and vacuum pulsations in the crankcase. Repair parts for the fuel pump are not available. Complete pump must be renewed if unit fails. Make certain pump filter screen is clean and fuel lines, air lines and filter are not leaking air or fuel.

VRO TYPE FUEL PUMP. The VRO type fuel pump (1 – Fig. OM14-8) meters the fuel:oil ratio from approximately 50:1 up to approximately 150:1 by sensing the engine power output. During engine break-in or after any procedure that permitted air to enter VRO system, the fuel in the fuel tank must be mixed at a fuel:oil ratio of 50:1 to ensure the engine of proper lubrication.

To check the VRO system for proper operation, first fill the VRO oil tank with a recommended two-stroke motor oil and note oil level for future reference. Install a fuel:oil mixture of 50:1 in the fuel tank. After the recommended engine break-in period or after a suitable test period for other conditions, note the oil level in the VRO oil tank. If the oil level has dropped and the VRO system is operating properly, refill the VRO oil tank and switch to straight fuel.

NOTE: When the VRO system is not used, the inlet nozzle at the outboard motor connector must be capped and clamped to prevent dirt or moisture from entering the fuel system. The fuel in the fuel tank must be mixed at a fuel:oil ratio of 50:1.

TESTING. Using a "T" fitting, connect a suitable vacuum gage and a length of clear plastic hose to fuel inlet fitting at lower engine cover. All connections should be clamped to prevent leakage. Start engine and allow to warm to normal operating temperature.

NOTE: When performing VRO system tests that require full throttle operation, install outboard motor in a suitable test tank with the correct test wheel installed.

Run motor at full throttle for two minutes minimum while observing clear

hose and note vacuum reading. Vacuum reading should not exceed 4 inches Hg (13.5 kPa) and air bubbles should not be present in clear hose. Excessive vacuum indicates a restricted fuel line between fuel tank and motor. Air bubbles in clear hose indicates an air leak in fuel line between fuel tank and motor.

If vacuum reading is within 1-4 inches Hg (3.4-13.5 kPa) and no bubbles are noted in clear hose, proceed as follows: Remove clear hose and install a suitable 0-15 psi (0-103.4 kPa) pressure gage between VRO pump discharge port (5— Fig. OM14-8) and carburetors. Start engine and run at 800 rpm in forward gear. Pump output pressure should stabilize at not less than 3 psi (20.7 kPa).

If pressure is less than 3 psi (20.7 kPa), inspect pulse fitting (4) for plugging or other damage. Pulse fitting on models prior to 1988 is equipped with an integral flame arrestor and on 1988 and later models, pulse fitting is equipped with an integral check valve. Clean both type fittings by back-flushing with a suitable solvent.

NOTE: A plugged pulse fitting may result in power head damage due to inadequate lubrication. If excessive carbon deposits are noted, renew pulse fitting and repair cause of excessive carbon before returning outboard motor to service.

If pump pressure is low and pulse fitting is in acceptable condition, renew VRO pump assembly.

IGNITION SYSTEM

A capacitor discharge ignition (CDI) system is used on all models. CDI with breaker points is used on models prior to 1972. Later models are equipped with breakerless CDI. Refer to the appropriate following paragraphs.

Breaker Point Models

Two sets of breaker points operate against a cam at top of crankshaft to trigger the unit.

The ignition is extremely durable in normal operation, but can be easily damaged by improper operating, testing or servicing procedures. To prevent damage to the components, observe the following list of cautions and use only approved methods for checking and servicing the system.

1. DO NOT reverse battery terminals.
2. DO NOT disconnect battery while motor is running or attempt to start motor without a battery in the system.
3. DO NOT disconnect **any** wires while motor is running or while ignition switch is ON.

4. DO NOT use any tachometer except those approved for use with this system.

TROUBLESHOOTING. Use only approved procedures to prevent damage to the components. The fuel system should be checked first to make certain that faulty running is not caused by incorrect fuel mixture or contaminated fuel. If the motor continues to run after ignition switch is turned OFF, check the blocking diode as outlined in appropriate paragraphs.

CHECKING FOR SPARK. Connect a spark tester to the three spark plug leads as shown in Fig. OM14-11, attempt to start motor and check for spark at the tester.

NOTE: A neon spark tester or three conventional spark plugs with the ground electrode removed can be used in place of the tester shown.

Spark gap must not be more than 3/8 inch (9.5 mm). The coil wire is molded into coil and screwed into the distributor

cap. Do not attempt to pull the coil wire out of either end.

If spark occurs at all three connected points of ignition tester, check ignition timing. Also check condition of the spark plugs and make certain that leads are connected to the correct spark plugs.

If spark is erratic, check gap and condition of breaker points.

WIRING. Engine missing, surging and failure to start or run can be caused by loose or corroded electrical connections. Check all terminals and connectors for clean tight contact. Also check all wir-

ing for short circuit to ground, especially the black wire with white tracer leading from breaker points to the amplifier. A voltmeter can be used to make certain that battery voltage is supplied to

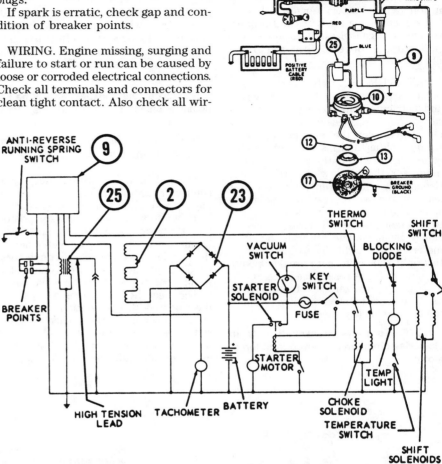

Fig. OM14-10 — The top view shows the basic parts of the capacitor discharge ignition system used in 55 hp motors. The lower view is schematic of the complete electrical system. Refer to Fig. OM14-12 for legend.

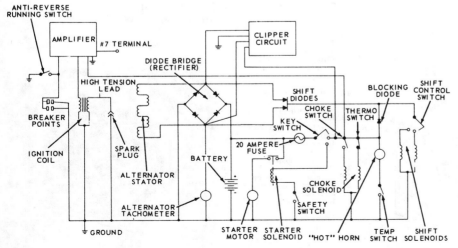

Fig. OM14-9 — Top view shows the basic parts of the ignition system used in 1971 60 hp motors. Lower view is a diagram of the complete system. Wiring is similar for 1970 motors except for the deletion of the clipper circuit. Refer to Fig. OM14-12 for legend.

Fig. OM14-11 — View showing a spark tester connected to spark plug leads. A four prong tester is shown with only three being used.

the amplifier. Disconnect the connector to the amplifier and insert one lead of voltmeter into terminal of purple (power supply) wire. Ground other lead and turn ignition switch ON. Battery voltage should be indicated. If not, check the 20 ampere fuse, which is located on the wire that supplies voltage to the ignition switch battery terminal. If fuse is good, check lead-in wires and connectors. If voltage is present at power supply wire, proceed with remaining checks.

BREAKER POINTS. The breaker points are located under the flywheel and distributor cap; however, some tests can be accomplished without disassembly. Disconnect the plug-in connector from amplifier and insert an ohmmeter or test light (with battery) lead into terminal for the black/white stripe wire. Ground the other ohmmeter or test light lead to the motor, remove the three spark plugs and move the speed control to the fast position. Turn the flywheel slowly by hand and observe the ohmmeter or test light. The ohmmeter or test light should indicate breaker points opening (infinite resistance or light off) and closing (near zero resistance or light on) three times during one revolution of the crankshaft (flywheel).

NOTE: Turn the crankshaft only in clockwise direction as viewed from top of motor.

The breaker points should just open when the straight "A" mark on flywheel is in center of the square mark on edge of ring gear guard as shown in Fig. OM14-15 (or 22° BTDC) if the speed control is in fast position. If breaker points do not open when timing marks align, refer to TIMING paragraphs.

When making this test, the black with white stripe wire should be carefully inspected and moved in an effort to locate any intermittent short circuit to ground or open circuit such as loose connections.

NOTE: Complete inspection will be impossible unless the distributor is disassembled.

If no malfunction is noted, proceed with remaining tests.

AMPLIFIER. Disconnect the plug-in connector from amplifier on 55 hp motors and connect jumper wires for the black/white stripe wire (breaker points) and the gray wire (tachometer lead). Connect a low reading ammeter across the purple wire terminals of connectors. On 60 hp motors, merely disconnect the purple lead wires at the terminal board and connect the low reading ammeter to the leads. With the ignition switch ON but motor not running, current draw should be 0.2 amperes. If possible, start motor and operate at 4500 rpm. Ammeter should indicate 1.5-3.0 amperes.

Unsteady meter reading with motor running indicates trouble with breaker points. If current draw is steady but incorrect (either running or not running), the amplifier should be renewed.

NOTE: Use extreme caution to make certain that test connections are not disconnected or shorted. Clip on test connectors should not be used with motor running.

An alternate method of testing the amplifier is as follows: Connect one lead of a neon test light to the coil blue lead wire and ground other test light lead to the motor. Turn ignition switch ON, crank motor with electric starter and observe the neon bulb. If the bulb flickers while motor is cranking, the amplifier is operating correctly and the high tension coil, distributor cap, rotor, spark plug leads or spark plugs should be suspected. If the neon bulb does not light, disconnect the black/white wire (from breaker points to amplifier), turn ignition switch ON and ground the black/white wire (from amplifier) to the motor. When the black/white wire is lifted from contact with motor, the neon bulb should flicker. If the bulb lights, check condition of breaker points connecting wires and antireverse switch. If the neon test light does not flicker, renew the amplifier.

COIL. The ignition high tension coil can be tested using an ignition tester available from several sources, including the following:

GRAHAM TESTERS, INC.
4220 Central Ave. N.E.
Minneapolis, Minn. 55421

MERC-O-TRONIC
INSTRUMENTS CORP.
215 Branch St.
Almont, Mich. 48003

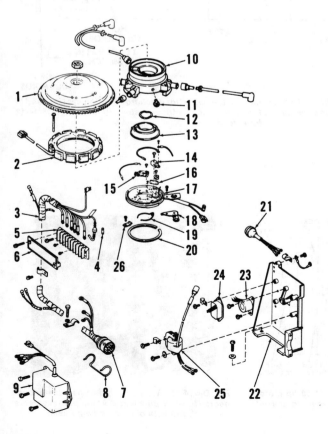

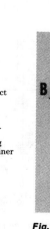

Fig. OM14-12—View of component parts of ignition and alternator system typical of 55 and 60 hp (prior to 1972) models. Terminal block (5) and clipper (24) are not used on early models.

1. Flywheel
2. Stator
3. Wiring harness
4. Fuse (20 amp)
5. Terminal block
6. Cover
7. Connector
8. Clamp
9. Amplifier
10. Distributor cap assy.
11. Vent
12. Wave washer
13. Rotor
14. Reverse cutoff contact assy.
15. Breaker points
16. Oiler wick
17. Distributor base assy.
18. Clamp
19. Reverse cutoff spring
20. Distributor base retainer
21. Shift diode
22. Bracket
23. Rectifier
24. Clipper assy.
25. Ignition coil
26. Clips

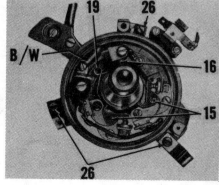

Fig. OM14-13—View of breaker base with cap and rotor removed. Refer to Fig. OM14-12 for legend.

Coil test procedures and specifications are available from the manufacturers of the tester.

NOTE: The high tension coil lead is molded into coil and screwed into distributor cap.

SHIFT DIODE. Failure of shift diode (21 – Fig. OM14-12) used on 60 hp motors may cause lower unit to shift to forward gear immediately after ignition switch is turned "OFF".

To check shift diode, disconnect yellow, yellow/gray and purple/green wires at terminal block that leads from shift diode. Use a battery powered (not more that 12 volts) continuity light or ohmmeter for testing. Attach one test lead to purple/green wire and other lead to yellow wire, then reverse test leads. Tester should indicate continuity in one connection and no continuity with tester leads reversed. Attach tester leads between yellow/gray wire and purple/green wire, then reverse leads. Continuity should be noted in one test connection and no continuity with test leads reversed. If either test is not as specified, renew shift diode.

CLIPPER. A clipper circuit is installed in all 1971 motors to prevent damage to CD ignition components in the event of an open circuit or intermittent battery current when engine is running.

Failure of the clipper unit (24 – Fig. OM14-12) should be suspected if any of the following occurs: Battery current is momentarily interrupted with motor running; charge low when charging system checks OK; CD amplifier inoperative; fuses blow repeatedly.

Clipper unit may be checked with an ohmmeter in the following manner: Disconnect **all** leads from the clipper to the terminal block before making any checks. Correct ohmmeter test lead polarity must be determined before inspecting clipper unit. Ohmmeter polarity may be determined by connecting meter leads to yellow lead and purple/green lead of a good **shift diode.** Refer to SHIFT DIODE check in previous section. If ohmmeter shows little or no resistance through shift diode, lead attached to yellow wire will be ground lead for purposes of checking clipper. If resistance is high, opposite lead will be ground.

Depending on date of production, clipper units may have three or four wires attached. The fourth wire is black and is used to ground unit. Unit will ground through case if no ground wire is fitted.

To check clipper, momentarily touch the purple lead to the case of the clipper. Connect ohmmeter ground lead (previously determined) to the clipper

case or black ground wire if so equipped. Connect other ohmmeter lead to yellow wire of clipper. Renew clipper if resistance is less than 300 ohms. If an infinite resistance reading is obtained, disconnect ohmmeter lead from yellow wire, momentarily short purple wire against case and connect ohmmeter to yellow/gray wire while retaining original ground connection. Renew clipper if resistance is less than 300 ohms. If infinite resistance is noted, remove test lead from yellow/gray wire, momentarily short purple wire against case and connect ohmmeter lead to purple wire. If ohmmeter needle moves and returns to infinity or registers less than 300 ohms, renew clipper. If infinite resistance is noted, disconnect ohmmeter, momentarily short purple wire against case, connect ohmmeter ground lead to purple wire and other ohmmeter lead to ground of clipper. Clipper is good if meter swings toward zero resistance and returns to infinity. Renew clipper if meter needle does not move or if meter needle moves to zero and remains.

BLOCKING DIODE. Failure of the blocking diode may allow motor to continue running after ignition switch is turned OFF. The blocking diode is located near the ignition switch and the purple wire is attached to the "IGNITION" terminal of switch. The purple with green stripe wire from diode is equipped with a quick release connector which attaches to a wire leading to the shift control switch.

To check the blocking diode, first remove the diode. Attach one lead of ohmmeter or continuity test light (with a battery of less than 12 volts) to each wire from diode. Observe ohmmeter reading or test light, then reverse the test connections. Current should pass through diode with one connection (low resistance or light on) but should not pass current with leads reversed. If current passes both directions or does not pass in either direction, renew the blocking diode.

If the blocking diode checks OK but motor continues to run after switch is turned OFF and Forward gear is engaged until motor starts, check for open circuits or short circuits at switches, wires and connectors.

DISTRIBUTOR. To service components of the distributor, remove flywheel (1—Fig. OM14-12) and stator (2). The distributor cap (10) is retained by the same three screws that attach stator. Note that the three screws are secured with thread locking compound. The coil high tension lead and spark plug leads are screwed into the distrib-

utor cap. Remove the wave washer (12) and rotor (13).

Reverse cutoff spring (19) is clipped to crankshaft and when crankshaft is turning in normal direction of rotation, the coiled projection is against the oiler felt (16). If the crankshaft turns in opposite direction, reverse cutoff spring (19) turns with the crankshaft until it grounds the ignition system through reverse cutoff contact assembly (14). When installing the reverse cutoff spring (19), the crankshaft should be lubricated lightly and the flat side of spring should be facing down as shown in Fig. OM14-14.

Breaker point gap should be set at 0.010 inch (0.25 mm) for used breaker points, or 0.012 inch (0.30 mm) if new breaker points are installed. After breaker point gap is correctly set, install rotor (13—Fig. OM14-12) making certain lug engages slot in crankshaft. Install wave washer (12), then position distributor cap (10) over breaker plate. Make certain the coil high tension lead and spark plug wires are screwed into distributor cap and are correctly positioned. Locate alternator stator (2) over distributor cap, coat the three retaining screws with Loctite and tighten screws to 48-60 in.-lbs. (5.4-6.7 N·m). Check ignition advance timing as outlined in TIMING paragraphs. Make certain tapers in flywheel and on end of crankshaft are clean and dry before installing flywheel. Flywheel drive key should be parallel to crankshaft center line, NOT aligned with taper. Tighten flywheel nut to 70-85 ft.-lbs. (95.2-115.6 N·m).

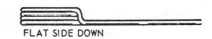

FLAT SIDE DOWN

Fig. OM14-14 — The antireverse spring should be installed with flat side down.

Fig. OM14-15 — View of advance timing marks aligned. The straight mark on flywheel should be used. On 1970 motors, flywheel mark should align with 22° mark. The wedge shaped mark is not for use on these motors.

TIMING. Timing marks on flywheels of pre-1971 models, and 1971 motors with model numbers ending in "E," consist of a straight line with an "A" or a triangle next to it. A timing mark or small timing grid will be on the ring gear guard of these models. Flywheels on later models (1971 motors with model numbers ending in "C") have a timing pointer attached to the intake manifold and a grid marked off in degrees on the flywheel. Timing procedure is basically the same for all versions. To check the maximum advance ignition timing, connect a power timing light to the top cylinder spark plug and run motor at full speed in gear. The straight line on the flywheel of models so equipped should be aligned with timing mark (22 degrees) on ring gear guard as shown in Fig. OM14-15. Timing pointer should align with 22 degree mark on flywheel of later models as shown in Fig. OM14-16. If timing is incorrect, loosen locknut and turn the spark advance stop screw (Fig. OM14-17) as necessary. Make certain that wires do not prevent free movement of base plate.

Fig. OM14-16 — View of flywheel with timing marks aligned properly for full advance ignition on 60 (prior to 1972) hp three-cylinder motors. This is a "C" type flywheel, refer to text.

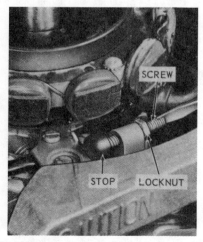

Fig. OM14-17 — View of the ignition advance stop screw. The flywheel is removed so screw can be easily seen. Removal of flywheel is not necessary for adjustment.

Breakerless Ignition Models Prior to 1979

The capacitor discharge ignition system used on 65, 70 and 75 hp motors prior to 1979 does not have breaker points. Magnets built into central portion of flywheel are used to trigger the ignition unit.

This ignition is extremely durable in normal operation, but can be easily damaged by improper operating, testing or servicing procedures. To prevent damage to components, observe the following list of precautions and use only approved methods for checking and servicing system.

DO NOT disconnect any wires while motor is running or while ignition switch is ON.

DO NOT use any tachometer except those approved for use with this system.

DO NOT hold spark plug wires while checking for spark.

DO make certain that all wiring connections are clean and tightly joined.

DO make certain that wires do not bind moving parts or touch metal edges where they may chafe through insulation.

TROUBLESHOOTING. Use only approved procedures to prevent damage to the components. The fuel system should be checked first to make certain that faulty running is not caused by incorrect mixture or contaminated fuel. If motor continues to run after ignition switch is turned OFF, check the blocking diode as outlined in appropriate paragraphs.

CHECKING FOR SPARK. Disconnect spark plug leads at spark plugs and connect them to a needle point spark checker, similar to unit in Fig. OM14-11, with three gaps used set at ½ inch (12.7 mm). Consistent, strong spark indicates ignition system functioning properly; suspect spark plugs, timing, improper wiring to ignition coils or to spark plugs.

Weak inconsistent spark or spark from only one or two ignition coils; suspect sensor coils or ignition coils. Weak, inconsistent spark from all three ignition coils; suspect charge coils. No spark at all; suspect power pack.

WIRING. Engine missing, surging and failure to start or run can be caused by loose or corroded electrical connections. Check all terminals and plug-in connectors for tight clean contact. Also check all wiring for short to ground.

SENSOR COILS. Sensor coils may be checked by disconnecting the white/black lead wires from terminals #8, #9 and #10 (see Fig. OM14-19) and the common sensor lead (black/white wire) from terminal #11. Resistance between the common lead and each of the three sensor leads should be 7.5-9.5 ohms. Sensor coils should also be checked for a short to ground. Defective sensor coils are not renewable separately, timer base assembly (11 – Fig. OM14-18) must be renewed.

CHARGE COILS. Charge coils may be checked by reading resistance between brown wire attached to terminal #4 and brown/orange wire attached to terminal #5. Correct resistance is 870-930 ohms on models prior to 1976 and 555-705 ohms on models after 1975. Stator assembly (12 – Fig. 14-18) must be renewed if charge coils are defective.

IGNITION COILS. Ignition coils may be checked with standard ignition coil test equipment. Complete operating instructions and coil test specifications will be included with tester.

SHIFT DIODE. Failure of the shift diode (2 — Fig. OM14-18) on 1972, 65 hp models may cause the lower unit to shift into forward gear immediately after ignition switch is turned off.

Shift diode may be inspected with an ohmmeter or a continuity light with no more than a 12 volt power source. Disconnect diode leads at terminal block (8). Connect tester leads to purple/green wire and to yellow wire from diode. Reverse connection. Tester reading with a good shift diode will indicate inifinite resistance with one connection and no resistance in other direction. Repeat this test with purple/green wire and yellow/gray wire. Again, diode should show no resistance in one direction and infinite resistance in other direction.

STATOR AND TIMER BASE ASSEMBLY. Stator (12 – Fig. OM14-18) and timer base (11) may be serviced after removal of the flywheel. Stator assembly is secured to the power head by three screws. The timer base may be removed after the stator by removing the three screws and clips along the outside edge.

When reassembling unit, make certain wiring does not restrict free movement of timer base. Inspect taper on crankshaft and taper in flywheel. Install flywheel key with flat of key parallel to center line of crankshaft, NOT with surface of taper. Tighten flywheel nut to 100-105 ft.-lbs. (135.6-142.4 N·m).

TIMING. Connect a suitable timing light to number 1 (top) spark plug lead and note degree mark on flywheel with motor running at full speed in gear (Fig.

OM14-21). Ignition should occur at 16 degrees BTDC on all 75 hp models, 17 degrees BTDC on 70 hp models after 1974, 20 degrees BTDC on all 1974 models, 22 degrees BTDC on all other models. Stop engine and turn spark advance stop screw (A—Fig. OM14-22) if timing adjustment is required. Turning screw clockwise one full turn will retard ignition timing approximately 1 degree.

Breakerless Ignition After 1978

All 70 and 75 hp models after 1978, and 1986 and later 60 hp models, are equipped with a capacitor discharge ignition (CDI) system. To prevent damage to components, note the following precautions:

1. DO NOT disconnect any wires while motor is running or while ignition switch is ON.
2. DO NOT use any tachometer except those approved for use with this system.
3. DO NOT hold spark plug wires while checking for spark.
4. DO make certain that all wiring connections are clean and tightly joined.
5. DO make certain that wires do not bind moving parts or touch metal edges where they may chafe through insulation.

TROUBLESHOOTING. Use only approved procedures to prevent damage to the components. The fuel system should be checked first to make certain that faulty running is not caused by fuel starvation, incorrect mixture or contaminated fuel.

CHECKING FOR SPARK. Disconnect spark plug leads at spark plugs and connect them to a needle point spark checker, similar to unit in Fig. OM14-11, with three gaps used at ½ inch (12.7 mm). Consistent, strong spark indicates ignition system functioning properly; suspect spark plugs, timing, improper wiring to ignition coils or to spark plugs.

Weak, inconsistent spark or spark from only one or two ignition coils; suspect sensor coils or ignition coils. Weak, inconsistent spark from all three ignition coils; suspect charge coils. No spark at all; suspect power pack.

WIRING. Engine missing, surging and failure to start or run can be caused by loose or corroded electrical connections. Check all terminals and plug-in connectors for tight clean contact. Also check all wiring for short circuit to ground.

CHARGE COILS. The three charge coils are contained in the stator assembly. To test charge coils, disconnect the

two-pin connector on models prior to 1985, three-pin connector on 1985-1988 models and five-pin connector on 1989 models. Refer to Fig. OM14-23.

To check charge coil output, use Merc-O-Tronic Model 781, Stevens Model CD77 or a suitable equivalent peak reading voltmeter. Connect black tester lead to terminal A and red tester lead to terminal B in connector leading to stator. On models prior to 1989, set tester knobs to "NEG" (−) and "500." On 1989 models, set tester knobs to "POS" and "500." Crank engine and note tester reading. If charge coil output is 220 volts or more on models prior to 1985 or 250

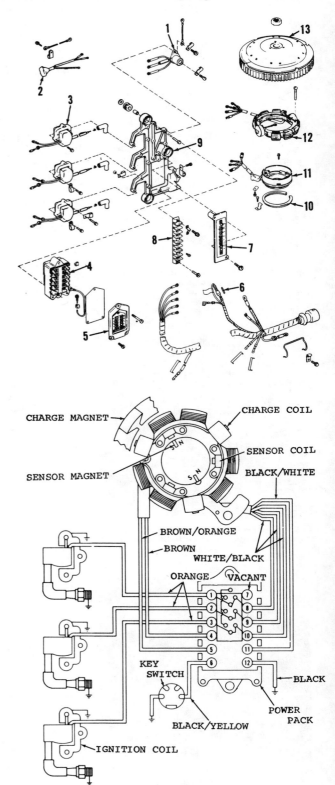

Fig. OM14-18 — View of component parts of ignition system used on 65, 70 and 75 hp motors prior to 1979. Shift diode is used on 1972 65 hp models.

1. Rectifier
2. Diode
3. Ignition coil
4. Power pack
5. Cover
6. Fuse (20 amp)
7. Cover
8. Terminal block
9. Mount bracket
10. Retainer ring
11. Timer base assy.
12. Stator
13. Flywheel

Fig. OM14-19 — Simplified wiring diagram of CD magneto used on 65, 70 and 75 hp outboards prior to 1979.

CHARGE MAGNET
CHARGE COIL
SENSOR COIL
BLACK/WHITE
SENSOR MAGNET
BROWN/ORANGE
BROWN
WHITE/BLACK
ORANGE
VACANT
KEY SWITCH
BLACK
POWER PACK
BLACK/YELLOW
IGNITION COIL

volts or more on 1985-1989 models, proceed to SENSOR COILS. If charge coil output is less than specified, test charge coil resistance. Connect a suitable ohmmeter between terminals A and B (Fig. OM14-23) in connector leading to stator. Renew stator assembly (or repair stator leads) if resistance is not 475-625 ohms on models prior to 1985, 535-585 ohms

on 1985-1988 models and 455-505 ohms on 1989 models. No continuity should be present between either terminal A or B and engine ground. If continuity is noted, check stator lead for short or renew stator assembly.

SENSOR COILS. The three sensor coils are contained in the timer base assembly. To test sensor coil output, use Merc-O-Tronic Model 781, Stevens Model CD77 or a suitable equivalent peak reading voltmeter. Disconnect four-pin connector between timer base and power pack. Refer to Fig. OM14-23. Connect black tester lead to timer base connector terminal D and red tester lead to terminal A. Set tester knobs to "POS" (+) and "5" on Merc-O-Tronic tester or "S" and "5" on Stevens tester. Crank engine and note tester reading. Then alternately connect red tester lead to terminals B and C. Sensor coil output should be 0.3 volt or more at all three test connections. If sensor coil output is 0.3 volt or more, proceed to POWER PACK section. If output is less than 0.3 volt, inspect sensor coil leads and connections. If leads and connections are in acceptable condition, test sensor coil resistance. Connect one ohmmeter lead to timer base connector terminal D. Alternately connect other ohmmeter lead to terminal A, B and C. Resistance should be 12-22 ohms on models prior to 1989 and 8-14 ohms on 1989 models. No continuity should be present between engine ground and terminals A, B, C and D. If resistance is not as specified, repair faulty wiring or renew timer base.

POWER PACK. To check power pack output, reconnect stator and timer base

connectors. Test power pack using Merc-O-Tronic Model 781, Stevens Model CD77 or a suitable equivalent peak reading voltmeter. On models prior to 1989, connect black tester lead to good engine ground and red tester lead to number 1 coil primary lead. Note that coil primary lead must remain connected to ignition coil. A terminal extender may be required to connect tester to coil. Set tester knobs to "NEG" (−) and "500." Crank engine while noting tester, then repeat test at number 2 and 3 ignition coils. Power pack output should be 230 volts or more at each ignition coil. If output is 230 volts or more, proceed to IGNITION COILS section. If output is less than 230 volts, and all wiring and connections are in acceptable condition, renew power pack.

On 1989 models, Stevens Load Adapter PL-88 is required to test power pack output.

NOTE: If Stevens load adapter is not available, fabricate load adapter using a 10 ohm, 10 watt resistor (Radio Shack part 271-132) or equivalent.

Connect load adapter PL-88 red lead to number 1 ignition coil primary lead and load adapter black lead to good engine ground. Connect peak reading voltmeter red lead to load adapter red lead and black lead to good engine ground. Crank engine and note voltmeter reading. Repeat test on primary lead of number 2 and 3 ignition coils. Power pack output should be 230 volts or more. If not, renew power pack(s). If output is 230 volts or more, refer to IGNITION COILS section.

IGNITION COILS. Ignition coils may be tested using a suitable ignition analyzer available from tester manufacturers. Follow instructions included with analyzer for operation and specifications.

To test ignition coil resistance, connect ohmmeter between coil primary terminal and ground. Resistance should be 0.05-0.15 ohm. Next, connect ohmmeter between coil primary terminal and high tension terminal. Resistance should be 250-300 ohms.

IGNITION TIMING. Timing pointer position is adjustable; be sure pointer is aligned with TDC mark on flywheel when number 1 piston is positioned at TDC.

Maximum timing advance should be 18-20 degrees BTDC. Adjust maximum advance by turning full advance timing screw (A—Fig. OM14-22). Refer to SPEED CONTROL LINKAGE section.

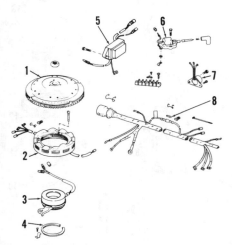

Fig. OM14-20—View of igniton components typical of the type used on models after 1978.

1. Flywheel
2. Stator
3. Timer base
4. Retainer ring
5. Power pack
6. Ignition coil
7. Rectifier
8. Fuse (20 amp)

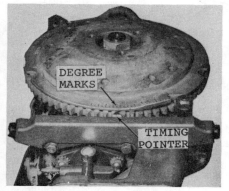

Fig. OM14-21 — Timing pointer should align with appropriate degree mark on flywheel at full advance.

Fig. OM14-22 — Full advance timing stop screw (A) may be turned after loosening locknut (B).

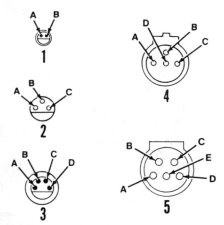

Fig. OM14-23—View of ignition wiring harness connectors and identification of terminals.

1. Two-pin connector used on models prior to 1985.
2. Three-pin connector used on 1985-1988 models.
3. Four-pin connector used on models prior to 1986.
4. Four-pin connector used on 1986-1989 models.
5. Four-pin connector used on 1989 models.
6. Five-pin connector used on 1989 models.

COOLING SYSTEM

THERMOSTAT. A cooling system thermostat is used to maintain an even temperature of 130°-150°F. Temperature can be checked using heat sensitive sticks such as "Markal Thermomelt Stick." A 125°F (52°C) stick should melt, but a 163°F (73°C) stick should not melt, after engine reaches normal operating temperature. If the 125°F (52°C) stick does not melt, the thermostat may be stuck open. Overheating could be caused by damaged thermostat, damaged pressure contol valve, exhaust cover gaskets leaking, head gasket leaking, water passages obstructed, water passages leaking or water pump failure.

The thermostat is located at top of cylinder head under the small cover. When assembling thermostat and cover, use a new gasket and make certain that gasket is correctly positioned.

WATER PUMP. The water pump is mounted on top of the gearcase with the rubber impeller driven by the drive

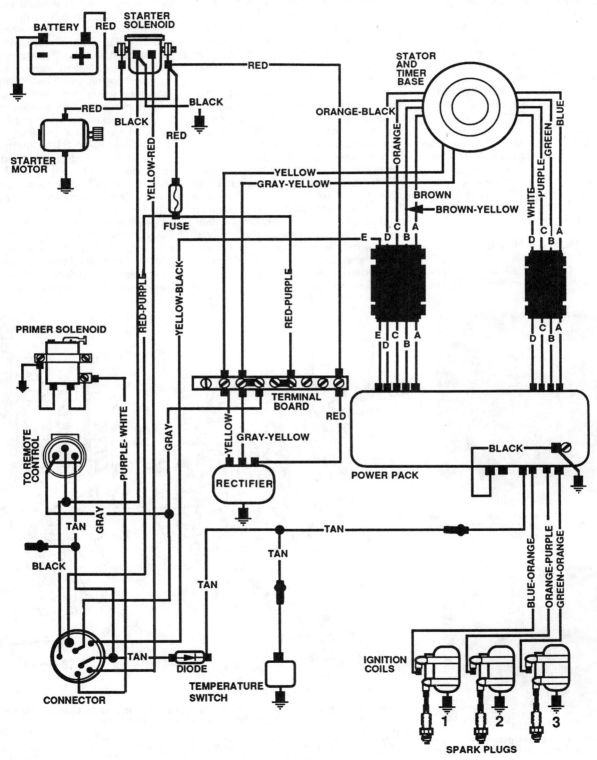

Fig. OM14-24—Wiring diagram on late 60 and 70 hp models.

shaft. Separate gearcase from exhaust housing for access to water pump.

Refer to Fig. OM14-37, Fig. OM14-40, Fig. OM14-43, Fig. OM14-47 and Fig. OM14-51 for an exploded view of water pump. On early models, install seal (16–Fig. OM14-37 or 5–Fig. OM14-40 and Fig. OM14-43) with lip towards top. Some later models are equipped with a renewable liner in the water pump housing. Later models are equipped with a gasket or "O" ring to seal between the pump housing and lower plate. On models after 1984, an impeller drive cam is used in place of drive key (7–Fig. OM14-51). Install drive cam with flat side against drive shaft and sharp edge pointing in a clockwise direction when viewed from crankshaft end of drive shaft. Apply OMC Adhesive "M" or equivalent between pump housing and lower plate. Lubricate impeller and hold blades in while installing housing. Drive shaft can be rotated clockwise while assembling, but should not be turned backwards. Apply a suitable sealant to water pump screws.

POWER HEAD

R&R AND DISASSEMBLE. If so desired, remove carburetors, fuel pump or VRO pump, inlet manifold and reed valve assembly. On non-VRO equipped 1973 and later models, remove remote cables and disconnect shift rod from shift arm as shown in Fig. OM14-31. On VRO equipped models, remove remote cables and hairpin clip at base of shift lever (L–Fig. OM14-32). Push shift lever (L) towards power head, then slide shift rod off pin head of shift rod lever on port side of engine. Disconnect interfering wires and remove flywheel and ignition components. Remove starter and withdraw the red cable from crankcase web. Remove the two screws from the front brackets to the lower cover (Fig. OM14-25). Remove attaching screws, then remove the two halves of exhaust housing cover. Remove the six screws and one nut (Fig. OM14-26) and lift power head from lower unit.

To disassemble power head, remove the lower main bearing seal housing, cylinder head and exhaust cover. Drive taper pin out toward front and remove the screws and stud nuts attaching crankcase halves together. Do not damage crankcase when separating halves. Pistons, rods, rod caps, rod bearings and main bearings should be marked as they are removed for assembly in their original location.

ASSEMBLY. Refer to individual sections for checking and assembling pistons, rings, piston pins, connecting rods, crankshaft and bearings. Make certain that connecting rods are assembled to piston with "UP" mark on piston head and the oil hole in connecting rod at piston pin and both toward top.

Check all sealing surfaces of crankcase, cylinder head, exhaust covers for absolutely flat, smooth surfaces. Crankcase halves must seal both vacuum and pressure. The cylinder head and exhaust covers must seal against water leakage and pressure. Mating surface of crankcase and lower unit must form an exhaust and water tight seal.

Mating surfaces of crankcase halves may be checked on a lapping block and localized high spots or nicks removed, but surface must **NOT** be lowered. If extreme care is used, a slightly damaged crankcase can be salvaged; however, crankcase should be renewed in case of doubt. Other surfaces of crankcase, cylinder head and exhaust cover can be lapped if necessary to provide a smooth, flat surface. Do not remove any more metal than absolutely necessary.

When reassembling crankcase, make sure mating surfaces of crankcase halves are completely clean and free of

Fig. OM14-25 – View of bracket at front, port side of motor. Another bracket is similarly located on starboard side.

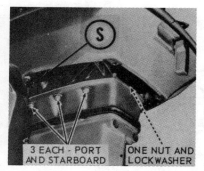

Fig. OM14-26 – View showing exhaust housing cover removed. Power head is attached by six screws (3 shown) and one nut.

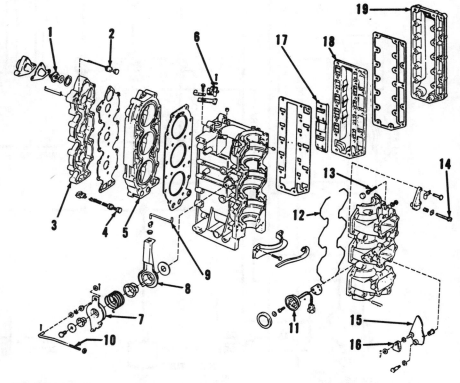

Fig. OM14-27 – Exploded view of early crankcase and associated parts. Later models are similar. Sealing strips (12) are not used on later models.

1. Thermostat
2. Temperature switch
3. Cylinder head cover
4. Automatic choke thermal switch
5. Cylinder head
6. Safety starting switch
7. Throttle lever
8. Spark advance lever
9. Ignition control link
10. Throttle control link
11. Vacuum switch
12. Sealing strips
13. Ignition advance stop screw
14. Idle speed stop screw
15. Throttle cam
16. Yoke
17. Exhaust deflector
18. Inner exhaust cover
19. Outer exhaust cover

old cement or from nicks or burrs. On models prior to 1979, install sealing strips (12 – Fig. OM14-27) and trim ends to extend approximately 1/32 inch (0.79 mm) into bearing bores, then sparingly apply OMC Adhesive "M" to cylinder half of crankcase only. On models after 1978, apply OMC Gel-Seal II to one crankcase mating surface. Do not use sealers which will harden and prevent contact between crankcase mating surfaces. Immediately assemble crankcase halves after applying sealer and position halves by installing locating dowel pin; then install and tighten main bearing crankcase screws to 216-240 in.-lbs. (24-27 N·m) and flange screws to 60-84 in.-lbs. (7-9 N·m). Install the cylinder head, making certain that temperature indicator switch and choke control thermal unit are installed. Tighten the cylinder head screws in sequence shown in Fig. OM14-28 to 216-240 in.-lbs. (24-27 N·m) when assembling.

NOTE: Cylinder head screws should be retightened after motor has been operated and allowed to cool.

Install the lower main bearing seal housing, using new seal and "O" rings. Securely tighten the four retaining screws.

PISTONS, PINS, RINGS AND CYLINDERS. Before detaching rods from crankshaft, be sure rod, cap and piston are all marked for correct assembly to each other and in correct cylinder. Separate bearings and cages for correct assembly to the original crankpin and connecting rod.

On 1969 models, each piston is fitted with three rings that are interchangeable and may be installed either side up. On 1970 and later models, the top ring is the semi-keystone type and the second ring is conventional type. When installing the top ring on these models, use caution not to damage ring groove in piston and install ring with beveled side toward top.

Refer to CONDENSED SERVICE DATA for piston skirt clearance on models prior to 1985. The manufacturer does not specify piston skirt clearance on models after 1984. If cylinder bore and piston are within tolerance, piston-to-cylinder clearance should be acceptable. Pistons and rings are available in 0.030 inch (0.76 mm) oversize.

Measure piston diameter in two locations, 90 degrees apart, 1/4 inch (6.4 mm) up from bottom of skirt. Renew piston if difference between measurements exceeds 0.003 inch (0.08 mm).

Maximum allowable cylinder bore out-of-round is 0.003 inch (0.08 mm) on all models. Maximum allowable cylinder bore taper is 0.002 inch (0.05 mm) on models after 1976, and 0.003 inch (0.08 mm) on earlier models. To determine cylinder bore oversize diameter when reboring cylinder block, add piston oversize dimension (0.030 in. [0.08 mm]) to cylinder bore diameter.

The piston pin is retained in piston by snap rings in piston pin bore. Small end of connecting rod is fitted with a caged needle roller bearing on models prior to 1985 and with 28 loose needle bearings and thrust washers on 1985 and later models. The piston pin and connecting rod bore are used as bearing races. Check bearing and bearing race surfaces for excessive wear, scoring or overheating. On models prior to 1976, install piston pin retaining snap rings with lettered side toward outside of piston.

On some models after 1975, one pin boss is press fit and the other is a slip fit. The loose pin boss is marked "L." When removing piston pin, remove both retaining rings, heat piston and press pin out toward the tight piston pin boss. Install pin through loose side first.

When reassembling, pistons and connecting rods must be assembled so "UP" mark on piston head and the oil hole for piston pin in connecting rod are both toward top of motor. Refer to Fig. OM14-29. Thoroughly lubricate all friction surfaces when assembling and tighten the connecting rod retaining screws to 348-372 in.-lbs. (40-42 N·m).

CONNECTING RODS, BEARINGS AND CRANKSHAFT. Before detaching connecting rods from crankshaft, make certain that piston, rod and cap are marked for correct assembly to each

other and in original cylinder. Separate bearings and bearing cages for installation in original location.

Connecting rods ride on roller bearings at both ends. The lower bearing consists of 16 rollers located in a split retainer cage. The piston pin bearing uses a one-piece cage on models prior to 1985 and 28 loose needle rollers on 1985 and later models. When reassembling piston and connecting rod, make certain that "UP" mark on piston crown and oil hole in connecting rod are

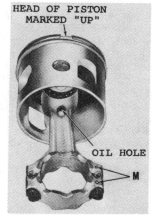

Fig. OM14-29 — Connecting rods must be assembled to pistons with "UP" mark on piston head and oil hole toward top of motor.

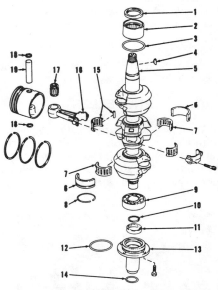

Fig. OM14-30—Exploded view of crankshaft, pistons, connecting rods and related components. Two piston rings per piston are used on models after 1969. Loose needle bearings and thrust washers are used in place of caged piston pin bearing (17) on 1985 and later models.

　1. Top seal
　2. Top main bearing
　3. "O" ring
　4. Flywheel key
　5. Crankshaft
　6. Center bearing outer race
　7. Bearing & retainer
　8. Retainer ring
　9. Lower bearing
10. Snap ring
11. Seal
12. "O" ring
13. Seal housing
14. "O" ring
15. Crankpin bearing & retainer
16. Connecting rod
17. Piston pin bearing
18. Snap ring
19. Piston pin

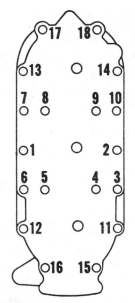

Fig. OM14-28 — The cylinder head retaining screws should be tightened in sequence shown.

both facing top of engine as shown in Fig. OM14-29.

The two center main bearings use a split retainer and a two-piece outer race. The outer race is held together by a retaining ring and is positioned in cylinder block by a dowel pin. The top main bearing is a roller type with rollers contained in the one-piece outer race. The outer race is also provided with a bore at top end to accept a lip type seal. The sealing "O" ring should be installed around top bearing. The ball type lower main bearing should be renewed if any looseness or roughness is detected.

When positioning crankshaft in main bearing bores, make certain that the top and two center main bearing races correctly engage locating dowel pins. Also make certain that "O" ring around top main bearing is aligned with groove in bearing bore.

When assembling connecting rod cap to rod, make certain that index marks (M – Fig. OM14-29) are aligned and all machined surfaces of rod and cap are smooth. Do not interchange rod caps. On 1985 and later models equipped with precision ground rods, OMC Alignment Fixture 396749 is recommended to properly align connecting rod with rod cap during tightening of connecting rod screws.

NOTE: Precision ground rods are identified by grind marks running ACROSS corners on ears of connecting rod and rod cap.

Refer to ASSEMBLY paragraphs for assembling the crankcase halves.

PROPELLER

An aluminum, three-blade propeller with built-in cushion clutch is standard on most motors while some motors are equipped with a stainless steel propeller. Optional propellers are available. Only propellers designed for use on these motors should be used. Refer to CONDENSED SERVICE DATA for desired engine speed at full throttle.

LOWER UNIT

REMOVE AND REINSTALL. Most service on the lower unit can be performed after detaching the gearcase housing from the drive shaft and exhaust housing. When servicing the lower unit pay particular attention to water pump and water tubes with respect to air or water leaks. Leaky connections may interfere with proper cooling and performance of motor.

To remove the gearcase, disconnect the two shift wires at connectors on side of power head exhaust cover on pre-1973 models. Disconnect shift rod from shift arm on non-VRO equipped 1973 and later models as shown in Fig. OM14-31. On VRO equipped models, remove hairpin clip at base of shift lever (L – Fig. OM14-32). Push shift lever (L) towards power head, then slide shift rod off pin head of shift rod lever on port side of engine. Remove the lower cover and drive shaft exhaust housing on pre-1973 models, apply liquid soap to cable sleeve (S – Fig. OM14-26) and push cables into exhaust housing. Mark location of trim tab to aid reassembly, then remove the trim tab. Remove the two screws from each side of gearcase and two screws at rear.

NOTE: One of the rear screws is under trim tab. Carefully withdraw the gearcase and drive shaft.

CAUTION: Do not damage shift wires and do not lose the two plastic water tube guides.

When installing lower unit on models prior to 1973, renew "O" ring at top of drive shaft. Coat both gasket surfaces of gearcase and exhaust housing with OMC Adhesive "M" or equivalent. Insert a wire through hole (S – Fig. OM14-26) down through exhaust housing and attach to end of shift wires. Coat the shift wire grommet with liquid soap and slide the plastic water tube guides onto ends of water tubes. Install gearcase, while aligning water tube guides with pump grommets and pulling shift wires up through hole (S). Drive shaft splines can be aligned by turning flywheel clockwise. Dip the six attaching screws in OMC Gasket Sealing Compound or equivalent before installing. Make certain that shift cable grommet is through hole (S) and attach shift cable leads. Install trim tab, aligning the previously affixed marks.

To install lower unit on models after 1972, renew "O" ring at top of drive shaft. Coat both gasket surfaces of gearcase and exhaust housing with OMC Adhesive "M." Screw in shift rod (27 – Fig. OM14-47 or 25 – Fig. OM14-51) until seated, then unscrew shift rod so offset at top of shift rod is located on port side of gearcase so it will mate with shift rod arm. On 1974 and later models, measure distance from gearcase mating surface to center of hole in upper shift rod with gearcase in neutral. Distance for 1974 and 1975 models should be $16^{11}/_{32}$ inches (41.5 cm) for standard models and $21^{11}/_{32}$ inches (54.2 cm) for long shaft models. Distance should be $21^{25}/_{64}$ inches (54.3 cm) on long shaft 1976 and 1977 70 and 75 hp models, $21^{23}/_{32}$ inches (55.2 cm) on long shaft 1978-1989 60, 70 and 75 hp models and $16^{13}/_{32}$ inches (41.7 cm) on all standard 75 hp models. Install gearcase while aligning water tube guide with pump grommet and shift rod with grommet in lower motor cover. Turn engine clockwise to align crankshaft and drive shaft splines. Apply OMC Gasket Sealing Compound to six gearcase screws. Install trim tab with marks aligned and connect upper end of shaft rod to clevis. Move shift lever to forward gear while turning propeller shaft and check for full engagement of dog clutch with forward gear. On models prior to 1983, refer to Figs. OM14-33 or OM14-34 and check shift linkage adjustment. If distance is incorrect, remove clevis pin and turn clevis until desired distance is obtained.

Due to construction differences in the lower units used on 55, 60, 65, 70 and 75 hp motors, disassembly and overhaul of each unit will be covered separately.

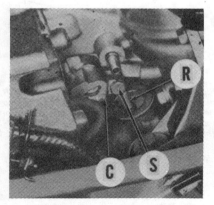

Fig. OM14-31 – Shift rod (R) on non-VRO equipped models after 1972 is disconnected from shift arm (C) by unscrewing screw (S).

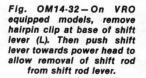

Fig. OM14-32 – On VRO equipped models, remove hairpin clip at base of shift lever (L). Then push shift lever towards power head to allow removal of shift rod from shift rod lever.

55 HP GEARCASE. To disassemble, remove gearcase, drain lubricant, remove propeller (2 – Fig. OM14-37) and detach shift cable (5) from clamps (6). Remove the four attaching screws, then withdraw pump housing (7), impeller (8), drive key (9) and plate (10). Remove screws attaching bearing housing (19) and solenoid cover (23). Remove solenoid and valve assembly (28 through 32). Remove the four screws (34) using a long ¼-inch Allen wrench, then pull bearing housing (35) out using a slide hammer puller with a hook. Remove the two snap rings (40) and withdraw propeller shaft (44). Remove nut (50), then lift drive shaft (55) and bearing housing (19) out top and gear (51), bearing (52) and thrust washer (53) out bottom. Remove forward gear (56), thrust bearing (57) and washer (58), then remove snap ring (59). The oil pump (60 through 70) can now be withdrawn from housing. If bearing (54) is to be renewed, drive the bearing down and remove from bottom.

Inspect drive shaft splines, bearing surfaces and seal surfaces for wear or damage. Damaged splines may be

caused by striking a submerged object and bending a housing. Check parallelism of top and bottom gasket surfaces of the exhaust and drive shaft housing. If surfaces are not parallel, renew housing, do not attempt to straighten. Shift solenoids should be checked with an ohmmeter. Resistance should be 5-6 ohms when checked between each of the two wires and ground. If solenoids (28) or wires (5) are renewed, use new heat shrink insulating tubes (29). Before assembling oil pump, install the pump rotor set, bearing (62), thrust washer (58), thrust bearing (57) and forward gear (56) in the pump housing (63). When checked with a straightedge as shown in Fig. OM14-38, the inner rotor, outer rotor and surface of housing

should be flush. If the inner rotor is too high, inspect surface of thrust washer (58 – Fig. OM14-37), bearing (57) and forward gear (56). Also, make certain rotor is installed with correct side against drive lugs on gear.

NOTE: Most pumps have dots etched on sides of inner and outer rotors. If provided with these dots, they should both be toward cover (68).

Guide (65) should be on small end of spring (64) and ball (66) should be in open end of guide. Clearance between bushing in forward gear (56) and end of propeller shaft (44) should be 0.001-0.002 inch (0.025-0.051 mm). If clearances are excessive, renew propeller shaft and/or gears. When install-

Fig. OM14-33 – Distance (D) between center of holes in shift arms should be 4-3/32 to 4-5/32 inches (10.4-10.5 cm) with lower unit in forward gear on models with manual shift lower unit. Turn clevis on shift link to obtain desired distance.

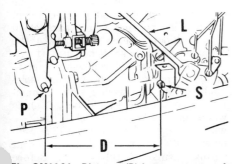

Fig. OM14-34 – Distance (D) between center of shift arm pin (P) and center of bracket screw (S) on hydraulic shift models should be 4¾ to 4⅞ inches (12.1-12.4 cm) with lower unit in forward gear. Turn clevis at upper end of shift link (L) until desired distance is obtained.

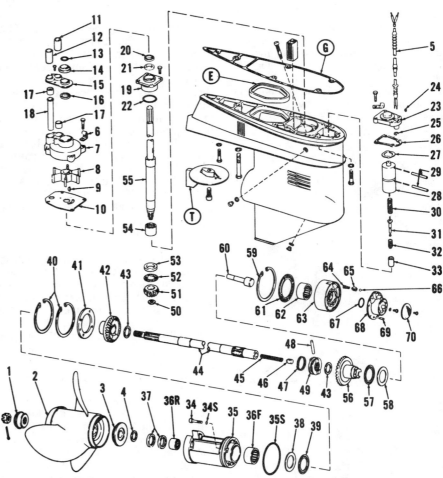

Fig. OM14-37 – Exploded view of the gearcase assembly used on 55 hp motors.

E. Exhaust seal	13. Drive shaft "O" ring	26. Gasket
G. Gasket	14. Seal	27. Wave washer
T. Trim tab	15. Cover	28. Solenoid
1. Spacer	16. Seal	29. Heat shrink tubes (wire covers)
2. Propeller	17. Grommets	30. Spring
3. Thrust bushing sleeve	18. Water tube	31. Valve
4. Thrust washer	19. Bearing housing	32. Spring
5. Shift cable	20. Upper seal	33. Sleeve
6. Clamps	21. Lower seal	34. Allen screws
7. Water pump housing	22. "O" ring	34S. Seal
8. Impeller	23. Solenoid cover	35. Bearing housing
9. Drive key	24. Wire connector clamp	35S. "O" ring
10. Impeller plate	25. Wire grommet retaining ring	36F. Bearing
11. Short guide tube		36R. Bearing
12. Long guide tube		37. Seals

38. Thrust washer	55. Drive shaft
39. Thrust bearing	56. Forward gear
40. Snap rings	57. Thrust bearing
41. Retainer plate	58. Thrust washer
42. Reverse gear	59. Snap ring
43. Thrust washers	60. Shift plunger
44. Propeller shaft	61. Screen
45. Spring	62. Bearing
46. Retainer	63. Pump housing & rotor set
47. Retainer spring	64. Spring
48. Pin	65. Guide
49. Dog clutch	66. Valve ball
50. Nut	67. "O" ring
51. Drive pinion	68. Cover
52. Thrust bearing	69. Dowel pin
53. Thrust washer	70. Screen
54. Bearing	

ing bearing (54), use special tool 383173 to pull bearing up into position. The lettered end of bearing should be down. Seals (20 and 21) should be installed with lip of bottom seal (21) down and lip of top seal (20) up. Seals (37) should be installed with lip of inside seal toward front (inside) and lip of outside seal toward rear (out).

To assemble the gearcase, position the oil pump (62 through 70) in forward end of gearcase.

NOTE: Make certain that dowel (69) engages hole in gearcase and pump is completely seated.

If pump is not correctly installed, plunger (31) will not fit into pump housing and solenoids will be impossible to install. Position screen (61) against pump with loops on screen toward rear (outside). Install snap ring (59) with flat side toward pump. Assemble thrust bearing (57) and washer (58) to forward gear (56) and insert into pump housing, making sure that lugs on gear engage lugs on pump rotor. Install the drive shaft and drive pinion (50, 51, 52, 53 and 55). The pinion nut (50) should be torqued to 40-45 ft.-lbs. (54.4-61.2 N·m) using

THRUST WASHER AND BEARING NOT VISIBLE

FORWARD GEAR

Fig. OM14-38 — Refer to text when checking installation of pump rotor set. Note the dots on rotor set should both be up as shown.

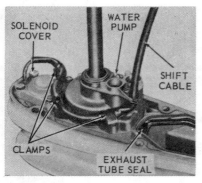

SOLENOID COVER

WATER PUMP

SHIFT CABLE

CLAMPS

EXHAUST TUBE SEAL

Fig. OM14-39 — View showing correct installation of the shift control cable and clamps.

special socket 312752 on the drive shaft splines. Position "O" ring (22) in groove of housing (19) and install housing in gearcase bore around drive shaft. Coat the four retaining screws with OMC Gasket Sealing Compound or equivalent before installing. If the clutch (49) has been removed from propeller shaft, insert spring (45) and retainer (46) into propeller shaft bore with hole in retainer aligned with hole in propeller shaft (at splines). Slide the clutch (49) on shaft splines with side marked "PROP END" toward rear and hole aligned with hole in propeller shaft. Compress retainer (46) and spring (45) enough to align holes in retainer, propeller shaft and clutch, then insert pin (48). Wrap the retainer spring (47) around clutch to keep the pin in position. Install thrust washers (43) around propeller shaft and insert piston (60) in end of shaft. Carefully slide the propeller shaft (44) including parts (43, 45, 46, 47, 48 and 49) into the gearcase. Slide reverse gear (42) onto propeller shaft and position retaining plate (41) in housing. Install the two snap rings (40), then position thrust bearing (39) and thrust washer (38) over the reverse gear hub. Position retaining plate (41) in bearing housing (35) and lubricate outer edge of "O" ring . Slide bearing housing (35) into gearcase, with exhaust cut out toward top. The "Bottom" marking should be down. Coat the retaining Allen screws with OMC Gasket Sealing Compound or equivalent before installing and make certain that seals (34S) are correctly installed on screws.

NOTE: Installation of bearing housing will be easier if two long guide studs are used to locate holes in retainer plate (41) as the bearing housing is installed and the other two screws are installed.

Install solenoid assembly (27 through 33) making certain that valve plunger (31) enters hole in pump housing.

CAUTION: Do not attempt to force.

Position wave washer (27) on top of solenoids, coat both sides of gasket (26) with OMC Gasket Sealing Compound or equivalent and install cover (23). Apply OMC Adhesive "M" or equivalent to bottom of impeller plate (10), install key (9) in drive shaft and locate impeller (8) over key. Lubricate impeller, hold blades in and install water pump housing (7).

NOTE: Drive shaft can be rotated clockwise while assembling pump housing, but should not be turned backwards.

Coat the screws attaching water pump housing with OMC Gasket Sealing Compound or equivalent before installing.

Refer to Fig. OM14-39 for location of clamps and routing of shift cable. The "O" ring for sealing the top splines of drive shaft is shown at (13 – Fig. OM14-37).

60 HP GEARCASE. (Prior to 1972). To disassemble, remove propeller (79 – Fig. OM14-40), drain lubricant and remove gearcase. Remove screws securing water pump housing (8) to gearcase, slide housing up off drive shaft, then remove impeller (9), key (10) and pump plate (11). Remove screws holding upper bearing housing (14). Remove screws in solenoid cover (26), lift cover and remove wave washer (29) and then carefully lift solenoid assembly (24 through 40) out of gearcase. Remove propeller shaft bearing housing screws (73). Propeller shaft bearing housing (71) is used on models with "E" at end of the serial number. Housing may be removed with a pair of slide hammers with hooks on the ends. Models with "C" serial number suffix are equipped with housing (71A) which is provided with two 5/16-18 threaded holes in rear. A puller attached with two bolts approximately eight inches long may be used to remove housing (71A). On all models, slide thrust bearing assembly (66 and 65) off propeller shaft. Reverse gear (64), propeller shaft (62) and dog clutch assembly (56 through 61) can be removed after snap rings (68) are removed from gearcase. Remove nut (21), then lift drive shaft (16) and bearing housing (14) out top and pinion gear (20) and thrust bearing assembly (18 and 19) out bottom. Forward gear (54) and thrust bearing (52 and 53) may now be removed. Some models are equipped with a snap ring (51) which must be removed before oil pump assembly (41 through 50) can be pulled from gearcase. Bearing (17) should only be removed if renewal is intended. Drive bearing out of bore from top if renewal is necessary.

Inspect drive shaft splines, bearing surfaces and seal surfaces for wear or damage. Damaged splines may be caused by striking a submerged object and bending housing. Check parallelism of top and bottom gasket surfaces of the exhaust and drive shaft housing. If surfaces are not parallel, renew housing, do not attempt to straighten. Shift solenoids should be checked with an ohmmeter. Resistance should be 5-6 ohms when checked between each of the two wires and ground. If solenoids (32 or 36) or wires (24) are renewed, use new heat shrink insulating tubes (33). Before assembling oil pump, install the rotor set, bearing assembly (52 and 53), forward gear (54) in the pump housing (50). When checked with a straightedge as shown in Fig. OM14-38, the inner rotor, outer rotor and surface of housing should be flush. If the inner rotor is too high, inspect surface of thrust washer (52 – Fig. OM14-40), bearing (53) and forward gear (54). Also, make certain rotor is installed with correct side against drive lugs on gear. Clearance between bushing in forward gear (54) and end of propeller shaft (62) should be 0.001-0.002 inch (0.025-0.051 mm). If clearance is excessive, renew propeller shaft and/or gear.

When installing new bearing (17), use OMC Special Tool 383173 to pull bearing up into position. The lettered end of bearing should be down. Bearings (70 and 74) should only be removed from propeller shaft bearing housing if renewal is intended. OMC Special Tools should be used to press new bearings into housing to ensure proper positioning. Use tool 314642 to install aft bearing (74) in housing (71) of "E" models. Use tool 314643 to install aft bearing (74) in housing (71A) of "C" models. Forward bearing (70) may be installed in either housing with tool 314641. Seals (75 and 76) should be installed with lip of forward seal toward front and lip of aft seal toward propeller.

Gearcase may be assembled in the following manner: Assemble oil pump (parts 41 through 50 and 59) and position in gearcase. Make sure that aligning dowel (42) is fully seated in recess provided in forward end of gearcase. Install snap ring (51), used on "E" models, with flat side of snap ring against oil pump. Position forward gear (54), thrust bearing (53) and thrust washer (52) in oil pump. Place drive shaft (16) in gearcase and assemble thrust washer (18), bearing (19) and pinion (20). Install retaining nut (21) and torque to 40-45 ft.-lbs. (54.4-61.2 N·m). Upper drive shaft bearing in housing (14) should be renewed if bearing is defective. Renew "O" ring (15) and seals (12 and 13). Install lower seal (13) with lip down and upper seal (12) with lip toward top. Coat screws used to secure bearing housing (14) with sealing compound and install. Assemble propeller shaft and dog clutch components with side of dog clutch (56) marked "PROP END" toward rear. Place thrust washer (63), reverse gear (64) and retainer plate (67) on propeller shaft bearing housing (71) and oil the outer edge. Guide pins can be threaded into retainer plate (67) to ease alignment of bearing housing (71 or 71A) on installation. Make certain that directional marking is ...itioned properly when installing ...earing housing (71 or 71A). Coat screws (73) with sealing compound and secure housing in position.

Solenoid assembly (24 through 40)

may be installed and adjusted in the following manner: Screw plunger (with large hole) into tubular shift rod casing (Fig. OM14-41), then install and tighten lock screw. Insert plunger and shift rod into reverse solenoid (blue wire) and push cap onto bottom of shift rod casing. Insert lower solenoid assembly into gearcase bore. Make sure end of shift rod is against the shift valve lever on pump and solenoid is against bottom of bore in housing. Check distance from

top of plunger to top of solenoid. Top of plunger must be flush to 1/64 inch (0.4 mm) below top of solenoid. Adjustment is accomplished by removing assembly, loosening lock screw, and turning shift rod casing. The lock screw should be torqued to 9-11 in.-lbs. (1.0-1.2 N·m) after adjustment is completed. Install lower solenoid assembly. Position spacer (34 – Fig. OM14-40) on top of lower solenoid with flat side down. Assemble small shift rod (Fig. OM14-42), plunger

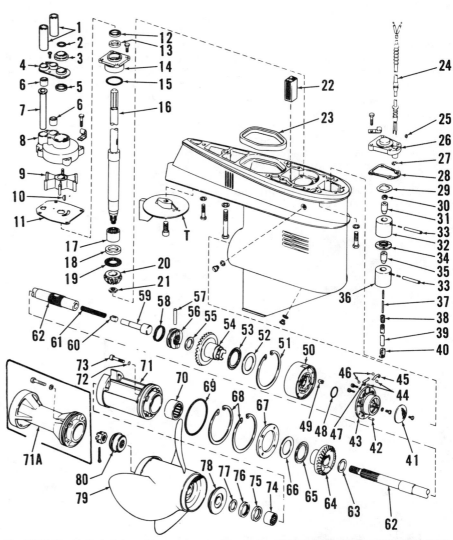

Fig. OM14-40 — Exploded view of gearcase assembly used on 60 hp (prior to 1972) models. Inset (71A) shows type of propeller shaft bearing housing used on late production units.

T. Trim tab	16. Drive shaft	33. Heat shrink tube	50. Oil pump assy.	67. Retainer plate
1. Water tube guides	17. Needle bearing	34. Spacer	51. Snap ring	68. Snap rings
2. "O" ring	18. Thrust washer	35. Lower plunger	52. Thrust washer	69. "O" ring
3. Grommet	19. Thrust bearing	36. Lower (Reverse)	53. Thrust bearing	70. Needle bearing
4. Cover	20. Pinion gear	solenoid	54. Forward gear	71. Bearing housing
5. Seal	21. Retaining nut	37. Shift rod	55. Thrust washer	("E" models)
6. Grommet	22. Water screen	38. Lock screw	56. Dog clutch	71A. Bearing housing
7. Water tube	23. Exhaust gasket	39. Shift rod casing	57. Pin	("C" models)
extension	24. Shift wires	40. Cap	58. Pin retaining	72. Seal
8. Impeller cover	25. Splice	41. Screen	spring	73. Screw
9. Impeller	26. Solenoid cover	42. Locating dowel	59. Shift shaft	74. Needle bearing
10. Drive key	27. Retainer	43. Valve housing	60. Dog clutch retainer	75. Seal
11. Plate	28. Gasket	44. Shift valve balls	61. Spring	76. Seal
12. Seal	29. Wave washer	45. Neutral lever	62. Propeller shaft	77. Thrust washer
13. Seal	30. Locknut	46. Shift valve seats	63. Thrust washer	("E" models only)
14. Bearing & housing	31. Upper plunger	47. Reverse lever	64. Reverse gear	78. Thrust bearing
assy.	32. Upper (Neutral)	48. "O" ring	65. Thrust bearing	79. Propeller
15. "O" ring	solenoid	49. Plug	66. Thrust washer	80. Prop nut spacer

with small hole and locknut. Position the plunger and shift rod in neutral (upper) solenoid. Insert the neutral solenoid and shift rod assembly into gearcase bore above the reverse shift assembly and spacer. Make sure end of rod is through hole in top valve lever (47 – Fig. OM14-40) and solenoids are tight against bottom of bore. Check distance between top of plunger and top of solenoid. Top of plunger must be flush to 1/64 inch (0.4 mm) below top of solenoid. Adjustment is accomplished after loosening locknut and turning shift rod. Locknut should be torqued to 3-5 in.-lbs. (0.3-0.5 N·m) when adjustment is completed.

NOTE: Improper shifting will result if adjustment of shift rods and plungers is not correct.

Install solenoids and shift rods, position wave washer (29 – Fig. OM14-40) on top of solenoids, coat both sides of gasket (28) with OMC Gasket Sealing Compound or equivalent and install cover (26). Apply OMC Adhesive "M" or equivalent to bottom of impeller plate (11), install key (10) in drive shaft and locate impeller (9) over key. Lubricate

impeller, hold blades in and install water pump housing (8).

NOTE: Drive shaft can be rotated clockwise while assembling pump housing, but should never be turned backwards.

Coat screws attaching water pump housing with OMC Gasket Sealing Compound or equivalent before installing. Make certain that drive shaft "O" ring (2) is in position.

65 HP GEARCASE (1972) MODELS). Gearcase may be disassembled as follows: Drain lubricant and remove gearcase. Remove screws securing water pump housing (8 – Fig. OM14-43); lift housing, impeller (9) and remove pump drive key. Remove plate (11) and bearing housing (14). Remove screws securing solenoid cover (26), remove wave washer (29) and carefully lift out solenoid and plunger assembly.

Dismount propeller and unscrew four screws holding bearing housing (71). Use a puller attached with two 8-inch long 5/16-18 bolts to remove bearing housing. Slide thrust washer (66) and thrust bearing (65) off shaft and remove retaining rings (68). Propeller shaft can now be removed with reverse gear (64), dog clutch (56) and associated parts. A special socket (OMC Special Tool 316612) is available to hold drive shaft so that nut (21) securing pinion gear can be removed. Drive shaft can be lifted free of gearcase and forward gear (54) removed after removing pinion gear. Use slide hammers and two 16 inch long rods with ¼-20 threads on the ends to remove oil pump (50).

Inspect drive shaft splines, bearing surfaces and seal surfaces for wear or damage. Damaged splines may be caused by striking a submerged object and bending the exhaust housing. Check

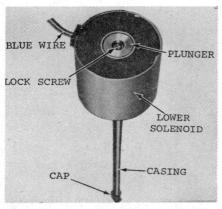

Fig. OM14-41 — View of lower (reverse) solenoid assembly. Refer to text for adjustment.

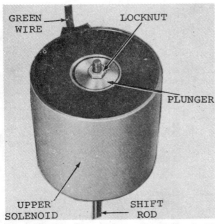

Fig. OM14-42 — View of upper (neutral) solenoid assembly.

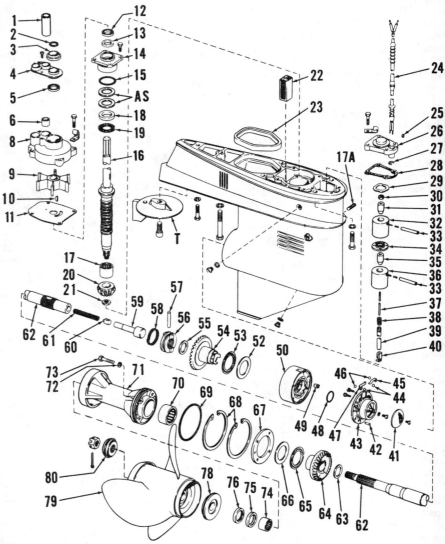

Fig. OM14-43—Exploded view of lower unit gearcase used on 1972 65-hp models. Drive shaft mesh position is adjusted by varying the number of shims (AS). Refer to Fig. OM14-40 for legend, except set screw (17A) and adjusting shims (AS).

parallelism of top and bottom surfaces if questionable. If surfaces are not parallel, renew housing, do not attempt to straighten it.

Lower drive shaft bearing (17) should only be removed if renewal is intended. Do not reinstall a used bearing. Lower drive shaft bearing is held in position by a set screw (17A – Fig. OM14-43) as well as a press fit in gearcase. Set screw is located on starboard side in area of water intake. After removing set screw, install OMC Special Tool 385546, with shouldered side of puller piece against bearing and pull bearing out of case toward top. New bearing is installed by assembling special tool with sleeve provided and driving bearing into gearcase with lettered side of bearing up (Fig. OM14-44) and shouldered side of pusher piece against bearing. Bearing will be properly positioned when plate of tool touches top of gearcase. Apply Loctite to set screw (17A – Fig. OM14-43) and install.

Shift solenoids (32 and 36) should be checked with an ohmmeter. Resistance should be 5-6 ohms when checked between each of the wires and case of solenoid. If solenoid wires (24) are renewed, use new heat shrink insulating tubes (33) to seal wire connections.

The shift pump valve balls (44 and 46) and seats can be renewed. The surfaces of rotor set in housing should be checked for wear or scoring. Renew complete pump assembly if any part of rotor set is damaged excessively. The front surfaces of rotor set should be flush with front face of pump housing, when parts (54, 53 and 52) are in position. Make certain that locating pin (42) is fully seated in recess in forward end of rear housing on reassembly.

Mesh position of pinion gear (20) is determined by thickness of adjusting shims (AS). The following procedure may be used to determine proper shimming. Place pinion gear (20) on drive shaft and torque retaining nut to 40-45 ft.-lbs. (54.4-61.2 N·m). Install shims (AS) that were removed during disassembly without installing thrust washer (18) or thrust bearing (19). Hold shim gage (OMC Special Tool 315767) firmly

against shims and measure clearance between end of gage and pinion gear (Fig. OM14-45). Proper clearance is 0.000-0.002 inch (0.00-0.051 mm).

NOTE: If clearance appears to be zero, make certain that enough shims are installed for an accurate check.

Shims are available in thicknesses of 0.002 and 0.005 inch and may be used in any quantity to obtain proper clearance. Set the correct shims aside until drive shaft is installed.

Seals (12 and 13 – Fig. OM14-43) should be installed with lip of bottom seal (13) down and lip of top seal (12) up.

Needle bearings (70 and 74) should not be removed from propeller shaft housing unless renewal is intended. Do not install used bearings. OMC Special Tool 317061 should be used to press aft bearing into propeller shaft housing (71) to ensure proper positioning. OMC Special Tool 314641 should be used to properly position forward bearing (70) in bore of housing. Seals (76 and 75) should be installed so that lip on aft seal is toward propeller and lip on forward seal is facing forward.

Gearcase may be assembled in the following manner: Position oil pump assembly in gearcase, making sure that locating pin (42) is fully seated in recess provided. Install drive shaft (16) and pinion gear (20). Torque pinion gear retaining nut to 40-45 ft.-lbs. (54.4-61.2 N·m). Assemble dog clutch (56) on propeller shaft, placing side of dog clutch marked "PROP END" toward rear. Assemble thrust washer (63), reverse gear (64) and retainer plate (67) on propeller shaft and install in gearcase. Install snap rings (68) and place thrust bearings parts (66 and 65) in position on shaft. Make certain that "O" ring (69) is correctly seated in groove of bearing housing (71) and is free of any nicks or tears. Lubricate "O" ring and slide bearing housing into gearcase making certain that "UP" mark on housing is toward top. Coat bearing housing screws with sealing compound before installation.

Install and adjust shift solenoids in the following manner: Screw plunger (with

large hole) into tubular shift rod casing (Fig. OM14-42), then install and tighten lock screw. Insert plunger and shift rod into reverse solenoid (blue wire) and push cap onto bottom of shift rod casing. Insert lower solenoid assembly into gearcase bore. Make sure end of shift rod is against the shift valve lever on pump and solenoid is against bottom of bore in housing. Check distance from top of plunger to top of solenoid. Top of plunger must be flush with top of solenoid. Adjustment is accomplished by removing assembly, loosening lock screw, and turning shift rod casing. The lock screw should be torqued to 9-11 in.-lbs. (1.0-1.2 N·m) after adjustment is completed. Install lower solenoid assembly. Position spacer (34 – Fig. OM14-43) on top of lower solenoid with flat side down. Assemble small shift rod (Fig. OM14-42), plunger with small hole and locknut. Position the plunger and shift rod in neutral (upper) solenoid. Insert the neutral solenoid and shift rod assembly into gearcase bore above the reverse shift assembly and spacer. Make sure end of rod is through hole in valve lever (47 – Fig. OM14-43) and solenoids are tight against bottom of bore. Check distance between top of plunger and top of solenoid. Top of plunger must be flush with top of solenoid. Adjustment is accomplished after loosening locknut and turning shift rod. Locknut should be torqued to 3-5 in.-lbs. (0.3-0.5 N·m) when adjustment is completed.

NOTE: Improper shifting will result if adjustment of shift rods and plungers is not correct.

Install solenoids and shift rods, position wave washer (29 – Fig. OM14-43) on top of solenoids, coat both sides of gasket (28) with OMC Gasket Sealing Compound or equivalent and install

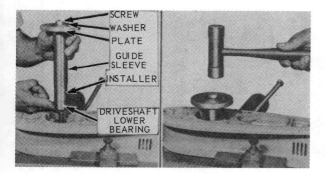

Fig. OM14-44 — Installer/removal tool 385546 should be used to drive lower drive shaft bearing into gearcase. Refer to text for procedure.

GAGE FIRM AGAINST SHIMS

0.000-0.002 in. CLEARANCE

Fig. OM14-45 — Shim gage (OMC Tool 315767) should be used to properly set mesh position of pinion gear on drive shaft.

cover (26). Apply OMC Adhesive "M" or equivalent to bottom of impeller plate (11), install key (10) in drive shaft and locate impeller (9) over key. Lubricate impeller, hold blades in and install water pump housing (8).

NOTE: Drive shaft can be rotated clockwise while assembling pump housing, but should never be turned backwards.

Coat screws attaching water pump housing with OMC Gasket Sealing Compound or equivalent before installing.

Reinstall shift cable clamps in original position and make certain that drive shaft "O" ring (2) is in position.

65 AND 70 HP WITH HYDRAULIC SHIFT GEARCASE. To disassemble gearcase, drain lubricant, remove propeller and separate gearcase from exhaust housing as outlined in previous section. Remove water pump housing (5 – Fig. OM14-47), impeller (6), key (7) and lower plate (8). Remove four screws holding propeller shaft bearing housing (69) and using a suitable puller, with-

draw bearing housing from gearcase. Remove snap rings (66), thrust washer (64), thrust bearing (63) and shift rod cover (28). Remove shift rod and propeller shaft components by withdrawing shift rod (27) and propeller shaft simultaneously. Hold drive shaft with OMC Tool 316612 or another suitable tool and unscrew pinion nut. Remove pinion (18), unscrew bearing housing (11) screws and withdraw drive shaft and components from gearcase. Bearing in housing (11) is not renewable but must be obtained as a unit assembly with housing. Remove forward gear (53). Using a suitable puller and two 16 inch long rods with ¼-20 threads, remove oil pump (43) from gearcase.

Inspect drive shaft splines, bearing surfaces and seal surfaces for wear or damage. Damaged splines may be caused by striking a submerged object and bending the exhaust housing. Check parallelism of top and bottom surfaces if questionable. If surfaces are not parallel, renew housing. Do not attempt to straighten it.

Lower drive shaft bearing (17) should only be removed if renewal is intended. Do not reinstall a used bearing. Drive shaft bearing is held in position by a set screw (17A) as well as a press fit in gearcase. Set screw is located on starboard side in area of water intake. After removing set screw, install OMC Special Tool 385546, with shouldered side of puller piece against bearing and pull bearing out of case toward top. New bearing is installed by assembling special tool with sleeve provided and puller piece turned over so shouldered side will again be next to bearing. Drive bearing (with lettered side up) into case (Fig. OM14-44). Bearing will be properly positioned when plate of tool touches top of gearcase. Apply Loctite to set screw and install.

Hydraulic shift components (31 through 39 – Fig. OM14-47) may be disassembled with OMC Tool. 386112 by engaging pins on tool with holes in piston (37) and piston cap (31) and unscrewing cap from piston. Be careful not to bend or damage push rod (39) during disassembly. Remove pin (36) to separate valve (35), piston (37) and push rod. Cap (31) should be tightened to 12-15 ft.-lbs. (16.3-20.4 N·m) during reassembly.

To disassemble oil pump, unscrew four screws securing cover (42) and remove cover. Remove snap ring (48), plug (47), spring (46), guide (45) and pressure relief valve ball (44). Inspect pressure relief valve components and renew if worn or damaged. Inspect oil pump assembly for wear or damage. Dots on rotors must be up and surfaces of rotors and housing must be flat across ends

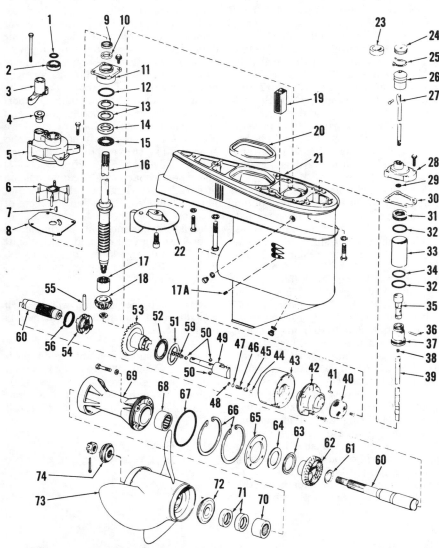

Fig. OM14-47 — Exploded view of hydraulic shift lower unit used on some 65 and 70 hp models.

1. "O" ring	15. Thrust bearing	29. "O" ring	44. Relief valve ball
2. Grommet	16. Drive shaft	30. Gasket	45. Ball guide
3. Water tube bracket	17. Needle bearing	31. Piston cap	46. Spring
4. Grommet	17A. Set screw	32. "O" ring	47. Plug
5. Impeller housing	18. Pinion gear	33. Cylinder	48. Snap ring
6. Impeller	19. Water screen	34. "O" ring	49. Shift plunger
7. Drive key	20. Exhaust seal	35. Valve	50. Detent balls
8. Plate	21. Gearcase	36. Pin	51. Thrust washer
9. Seal	22. Trim tab	37. Piston	52. Thrust bearing
10. Seal	23. Seal	38. Plug	53. Forward gear
11. Bearing & housing assy.	24. Grommet	39. Push rod	54. Dog clutch
12. "O" ring	25. Tie strap	40. Screen	55. Pin
13. Shims	26. Seal	41. Locating dowel	56. Retaining spring
14. Thrust washer	27. Shift rod	42. Cover	59. Spring
	28. Shift rod cover	43. Oil pump & bearing	60. Propeller shaft

61. Thrust washer	
62. Reverse gear	
63. Thrust bearing	
64. Thrust washer	
65. Retainer plate	
66. Snap rings	
67. "O" ring	
68. Needle bearing	
69. Bearing housing	
70. Needle bearing	
71. Seals	
72. Thrust bushing	
73. Propeller	
74. Spacer	

when forward gear, thrust bearing and washer are installed in pump. Rotors, housing and bearing are not available separately and must be renewed as a unit assembly.

Seals (9 and 10 – Fig. OM14-47) should be installed with lip of bottom seal (10) down and lip of top seal (9) up.

Needle bearings (68 and 70) should not be removed from propeller shaft housing unless renewal is intended. Do not install used bearings. OMC Special Tool 317061 should be used to press aft bearing into propeller shaft housing (69) to ensure proper positioning. OMC Special Tool 314641 should be used to properly position forward bearing (68) in bore of housing. Seals (71) should be installed so that lip on aft seal is toward propeller and lip on forward seal is facing forward.

Thickness of shims (13) is varied to adjust mesh position of pinion gear (18) in forward and reverse gear. A shim gage, OMC Special Tool 315767, should be used to determine proper shimming.

Place pinion gear (18) on drive shaft and torque retaining nut to 40-45 ft.-lbs. (54.4-61.2 N·m). Install shims (13) that were removed during disassembly and leave thrust washer (14) and thrust bearing (15) off shaft. Hold shim gage firmly against shims and measure clearance between end of gage and pinion gear (Fig. OM14-45). Proper clearance is 0.000-0.002 inch. (0.000-0.05 mm).

NOTE: If clearance appears to be zero make certain that enough shims are installed for an accurate check.

Shims are available in thicknesses of 0.002 inch and 0.005 inch and may be installed in any quantity to obtain proper clearance. Set the correct shims aside until drive shaft is installed.

To assist in installing shift plunger components in propeller shaft, grind away the end of a 9/32 inch (7.14 mm) rod to form a long flat taper on one side. Rod should be approximately 2⅝ inches (6.67 cm) long. Position dog clutch (54 – Fig. OM14-47) on propeller shaft with pin hole in dog clutch and slot in shaft aligned. Place three shift balls (50) and spring (59) in plunger (49) as shown in Fig. OM14-48 and install plunger in propeller shaft so that detent balls match grooves in propeller shaft. Align holes in dog clutch (54 – Fig. OM14-47) and shift plunger (49) and insert tapered end of tool through holes to properly position detent spring. Carefully push tool out with retaining pin (55) and install pin retaining spring (56) in outer groove of dog clutch. Coils of spring must not overlap.

To reassemble gearcase, install oil pump (43), forward gear (53) and thrust

bearing (52) and thrust washer (51) so that locating pin (41) aligns with pin hole in gearcase. Install drive shaft (16) and pinion gear (18) and tighten pinion nut to 40-45 ft.-lbs. (54.4-61.2 N·m). Lay gearcase on starboard side and install propeller shaft with flat side of shift plunger (49) up until propeller shaft is bottomed. Install hydraulic shift assembly with flat on end of push rod (39) down. Insert shift assembly until flats on push rod (39) and shift plunger (49) are engaged (push rod will not turn). Place light pressure against shift cylinder (33) and slowly withdraw propeller shaft until key on end of push rod meshes with keyway in shift plunger as shown in Fig. OM14-49. When key and keyway are meshed, push shift assembly and propeller shaft in to complete engagement. Complete remainder of assembly noting the following points: Install snap rings (66) with flat side out. Install bearing housing (69) with "UP" mark towards water pump. Apply OMC Gasket Sealing Compound to threads of screws securing retainer plate (65) and bearing housing (69).

60, 70 AND 75 HP WITH MANUAL SHIFT GEARCASE. Gearcase may be disassembled in the following manner: Remove propeller, drain lubricant and remove gearcase as described in previous section. Remove screws securing shift rod cover (29 – Fig. OM14-51), unscrew shift rod (25) and remove shift rod and cover as an assembly. Remove water pump housing (5), impeller (6), key (7) and lower plate (8). Remove four screws holding propeller shaft bearing housing (69) and using a suitable puller, remove bearing housing. Discard seals (71) and "O" ring (67). Remove snap rings (66), thrust washer assembly (64 and 63) and slide reverse gear (62) off propeller shaft. A special socket is available to hold drive shaft so that nut securing pinion gear (18) can be removed. After pinion gear retaining nut is removed, unscrew the four screws securing upper drive shaft housing (11). Lift drive shaft and associated parts from gearcase. A puller may be necessary to remove drive shaft assembly if drive shaft does not lift out easily. Upper drive shaft bearing on all models except standard length 75 hp models is contained in housing (11) and is not renewable. If bearing is worn, renew housing with bearing. A taper roller upper drive shaft bearing is used on standard length 75 hp models. Propeller shaft (60) may now be pulled from gearcase complete with forward gear (52), forward bearing housing (38) and all associated parts.

Inspect drive shaft splines, bearing surfaces and seal surfaces for wear or damage. Damaged splines may be caused by striking a submerged object and bending the exhaust housing. Check parallelism of top and bottom surfaces if questionable. If surfaces are not parallel, renew housing. Do not attempt to straighten it.

Lower drive shaft bearing (17) should only be removed if renewal is intended. Do not reinstall a used bearing. Drive shaft bearing is held in position by a set screw (17A) as well as a press fit in gearcase. Set screw is located on starboard side in area of water intake. After removing set screw, install a suitable puller or OMC special tool 391257 with correct adapter. Place shouldered side of puller adapter against bearing and pull bearing out of case toward top. New bearing is installed by properly assembling special tool 391257 and forcing bearing into gearcase. Install bearing with lettered side toward drive shaft housing end of gearcase. Apply OMC Gasket Sealing Compound to set screw and install.

Forward gear (52) and propeller shaft (60) may be removed from propeller shaft bearing housing (38) after dislodging spring (56) and removing dog clutch assembly (55 and 54). Bearing housing and shifter mechanism assembly (39) may be disassembled by driving out shift lever pin (36) on all models and unscrewing set screws (31) on models prior to 1982 except standard length 75 hp models.

Thickness of shims (13) is varied to adjust mesh position of pinion gear (18) in

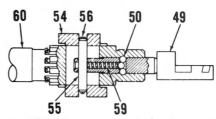

Fig. OM14-48 – Cross-sectional view of shift plunger (49) and dog clutch (54) components. Refer to Fig. OM14-47 for parts identification.

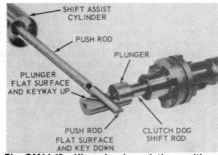

Fig. OM14-49 – View showing relative positions of shift assemblies when installed in gearcase. Refer to text for installation.

forward and reverse gear. A shim gage, OMC Special Tool 320739 for standard length 75 hp models or 315767 for all other models, should be used to determine proper shimming.

Place pinion gear (18) on drive shaft and torque retaining nut to 40-45 ft.-lbs. (54.4-61.2 N·m). On all models except standard length 75 hp models install

shims (13) that were removed during disassembly and leave thrust washer (14) and thrust bearing (15) off shaft. On standard length 75 hp models, only pinion gear, nut, taper roller bearing cone and cup should be on drive shaft. Hold shim gage firmly against shims and measure clearance between end of gage and pinion gear (Fig. OM14-45). Proper

clearance is 0.00-0.002 inch (0.00-0.05 mm) on models prior to 1977 and 0.000 inch (0.00 mm) on models after 1976.

NOTE: If clearance appears to be zero, make certain that enough shims are installed for accurate check.

Shims are available from 0.002 through 0.007 inch sizes for standard length 75 hp models and 0.002 inch and 0.005 inch sizes for all other models. Set the correct shims aside until drive shaft is installed.

Needle bearings (68 and 70 – Fig. OM14-51) should not be removed from propeller shaft housing (69) unless renewal is intended. Do not reinstall used bearings. OMC special tools should be used to press bearings into propeller shaft housing to ensure proper positioning. Seals (71) should be installed so lip on aft seal is toward propeller and lip on forward seal is facing forward.

Assemble gearcase in the following manner: Renew all gaskets, seals and "O" rings. If lower drive shaft bearing (17) or propeller shaft bearings (68 and 70) have been removed, they too should be renewed. Assemble shift lever (37), shift detent (34) and shift shaft (39) in bearing housing (38) on models prior to 1982 other than standard length 75 hp models. Install detent balls and springs, then apply Loctite to set screws (31) and install screws. On models after 1981 and on standard length 75 hp models, install detent spring (32) and detent ball (33) in blind hole of housing (38). Hold spring and ball in position while installing detent (34). Assemble shift shaft (39), shift lever yoke (37A), shift lever (37) and pin (36). On all models, assemble forward gear (52) with thrust bearing (51) and thrust washer (50), models so equipped, in bearing housing. Place dog clutch (54) on propeller shaft (60) making sure hole in dog clutch is aligned with slot in propeller shaft. Insert propeller shaft in forward gear and bearing housing assembly, then insert pin (55) through dog clutch propeller shaft and hole in shift shaft (39). Install pin retaining spring (56). Press shift detent (34) down and place propeller shaft, forward gear and bearing housing assembly (38) into position in gearcase. Make sure locating pin (35) is seated in recess provided in gearcase. Install shift rod (25) and shift rod cover (29) as an assembly. Thread shift rod fully into detent (34), pull rod to neutral (middle detent) and adjust for proper length. Refer to shift rod adjustment in LOWER UNIT REMOVE AND REINSTALL section for specifications. Pull rod up into forward gear position on completion of adjustment.

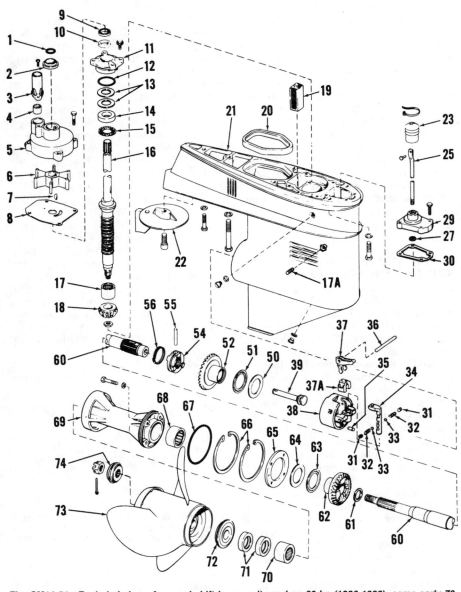

Fig. OM14-51—Exploded view of manual shift lower unit used on 60 hp (1986-1989), some early 70 hp, all late 70 hp (1986-1989) and all 75 hp models. Only one detent spring (32) and one detent ball (33) are used on 60 and 70 hp (1986-1989), standard length 75 hp and long shaft models after 1981. Shift lever yoke (37A) is used on 60 and 70 hp (1986-1989), standard shaft 75 hp and long shaft models after 1981. Drive key (7) is replaced with a drive cam on models after 1984.

1. "O" ring	12. "O" ring	23. Shift rod seal	37A. Shift lever yoke	63. Thrust bearing
2. Grommet	13. Adjustment shims	25. Shift rod	38. Bearing housing	64. Thrust washer
3. Water tube bracket	14. Thrust washer	27. "O" ring	39. Shift shaft	65. Retainer plate
4. Grommet	15. Thrust bearing	29. Shift rod cover	50. Thrust washer	66. Snap rings
5. Impeller housing	16. Drive shaft	30. Gasket	51. Thrust bearing	67. "O" ring
6. Impeller	17. Needle bearing	31. Set screw	52. Forward gear	68. Needle bearing
7. Drive key	17A. Set screw	32. Detent springs	54. Dog clutch	69. Bearing housing
8. Plate	18. Pinion gear	33. Detent balls	55. Pin	70. Needle bearing
9. Seal	19. Water screen	34. Detent	56. Pin retaining spring	71. Seals
10. Seal	20. Exhaust seal	35. Locating dowel	60. Propeller shaft	72. Thrust bushing
11. Bearing & housing assy.	21. Gearcase	36. Shift lever pin	61. Thrust washer	73. Propeller
	22. Trim tab	37. Shift lever	62. Reverse gear	74. Prop nut spacer

Pinion gear (18) may be positioned for reinstallation after turning gearcase upside down. Insert drive shaft (16). Install pinion gear retaining nut and torque it to 40-45 ft.-lbs. (54.4-61.2 N·m). Assemble thrust bearing (64 and 63) on reverse gear (62) and slide onto propeller shaft (60). Position bearing retainer plate (65) and install snap rings (66). Make sure that "O" ring (67) is fully seated in groove of bearing housing (69) and that seals (71) are properly installed. Lip of forward seal should be toward front and lip of aft seal should be toward propeller.

Installation of bearing housing (69) will be eased by using two guide pins 10 inches long with ¼-28 threads on one end. Thread guide pins into bearing retainer plate (65) and slide bearing housing (69) into position. Coat bearing housing screws with sealing compound and install. Turn gearcase right side up.

Install seals (9 and 10) in upper drive shaft bearing housing (11) with lip of lower seal (10) down and lip of upper seal (9) up. Place thrust bearing assembly (14 and 15) on drive shaft of all models except standard length 75 hp models and install previously selected shim or shims (13). Coat screws that secure bearing housing (11) with sealing compound and install. Bottom edge of impeller plate (8) should be coated with OMC Adhesive "M" or equivalent and placed in position. Install key (7), lubricate edges of impeller (6) and install on drive shaft. On models after 1984, key (7) is replaced with a drive cam. Install drive cam with flat side against drive shaft and sharp edge pointing in a clockwise direction when viewed from crankshaft end of drive shaft. Drive shaft should be turned clockwise while installing water pump housing (5). Coat screws that secure water pump housing and water tube bracket with sealing compound and install.

POWER TILT AND TRIM

So Equipped Models After 1979

OPERATION. A hydraulically actuated power tilt and trim system is used. Manifold (50 – Fig. OM14-55) contains valves, oil pump and trim cylinders. Oil pump motor, oil reservoir and tilt cylinder are attached to manifold. Electric oil pump motor is reversible and oil pump rotation is thereby changed to extend or retract trim and tilt cylinders. Note position of valves in Fig. OM14-55. Turn manual release valve counterclockwise to manually raise or lower outboard.

Hydraulic system contains approximately 25 fl. oz. (740 mL) of oil. Recommended oil is OMC Power Trim/Tilt

Fluid or DEXRON II automatic transmission fluid. Do not run pump without oil in reservoir. Oil level should reach fill plug (11) hole threads when tilt and trim pistons are fully extended. System should be cycled several times prior to checking oil level if system has been drained or lost a large amount of oil.

TROUBLESHOOTING. Be sure battery is fully charged, electrical connections are good, oil reservoir is full and air is not trapped in system before testing components.

To check oil pressure, first momentarily cycle system "UP" and "DOWN" a few times. Remove snap ring (39 – Fig. OM14-55) and manual release valve (37), then install OMC gage "A" as shown in Fig. OM14-56. Operate system in the "UP" direction and observe gage after system stalls out at full extension. Gage reading should not drop below 100-200 psi (700-1400 kPa). Install OMC gage "B." Operate system in the "DOWN" direction and observe gage after system stalls out at fully retracted. Gage reading should not drop below 100-200 psi (700-1400 kPa).

To test check valves, screw each valve into OMC check valve tester 390063 (T – Fig. OM14-57). Use a suitable pressure tester (P) and apply 30 psi (207

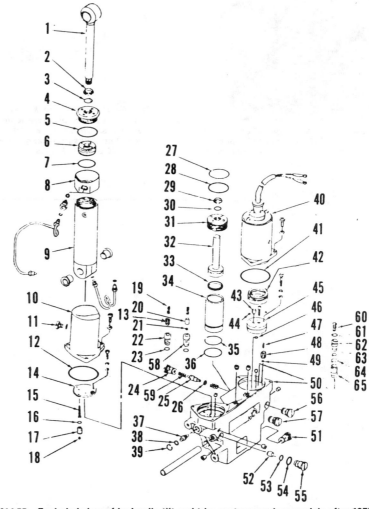

Fig. OM14-55 — Exploded view of hydraulic tilt and trim system used on models after 1979. A three-wire pump motor is used on 1980 and 1981 models.

1. Shaft	28. "O" ring	42. Oil pump filter
2. Wiper	29. Wiper	43. Drive coupling
3. "O" ring	30. "O" ring	44. Ball
4. End cap	31. End cap	45. Oil pump
5. "O" ring	32. Piston	46. "O" ring
6. Piston	33. Piston ring	47. Spring
7. "O" ring	34. Trim cylinder	48. Trim down pump
8. Band	35. Retaining ring	relief valve
9. Tilt cylinder	36. "O" ring	49. Seal
10. Reservoir	37. Manual release valve	50. Manifold
11. Fill plug	38. "O" ring	51. Separation valve
12. "O" ring	39. Snap ring	52. Valve piston
13. Needle	40. Pump motor	53. "O" ring
14. Plate	41. "O" ring	54. "O" ring
15. Screen		55. Impact letdown valve
16. "O" ring		56. Trim check valve
17. Check valve		57. Tilt check valve
18. Valve ball		58. Impact sensor valve
19. Spring		59. Spring
20. Spring seat		60. Spring
21. Ball		61. "O" ring
22. Trim up relief valve		62. Expansion relief valve
23. "O" ring		core
24. Reverse lock check		63. "O" ring
valve		64. "O" ring
25. Piston		65. Expansion relief valve
26. "O" ring		seat
27. Retaining ring		

kPa) of pressure to check valve. Check valve can be considered good if no pressure leakage is noted.

Refer to the following for a list of symptoms and probable causes:

Symptoms	Probable Causes
Tilt Leakdown	1, 2, 3, 4, 5 or 6
Trim and Tilt Both Leak	7, 8 or 9
Reverse Lock Does Not Hold	2, 3, 6, 10, 11 or 12
Will Not Trim Out Under Load or Will Not Tilt	1, 2, 7 or 9
Will Not Trim or Tilt Down	2, 8, 10, 11 or 13

Key to Probable Causes
1. Trim Up Relief Valve
2. Manual Release Valve
3. Tilt Cylinder Valve or Seals
4. Tilt Check Valve
5. Impact Letdown Valve
6. Oil Line
7. Trim Cylinders Sleeve "O" Rings or Piston Seals
8. Trim Check Valve
9. Expansion Relief Valve or "O" Rings
10. Filter Valve Seat
11. Impact Sensor Valve
12. Reverse Lock Check Valve
13. Trim Down Pump Relief Valve

Fig. OM14-56—Install OMC gage "A" or "B" into manual release valve (37 — Fig. OM14-55) port as shown to test system oil pressure. Refer to text.

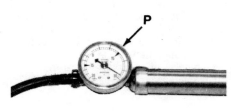

Fig. OM14-57—Use OMC check valve tester 390063 (T) and a suitable pressure tester (P) to test check valves. Check valve can be considered good if no pressure leakage at approximately 30 psi (207 kPa) is noted.

OVERHAUL. Oil pump must be serviced as a unit assembly. Motor is not serviceable with the exception of brushes. Refer to Fig. OM14-55 for exploded view of trim and tilt cylinders and manifold components. Keep all components separated during disassembly and identify each component, if needed, to assure correct position during reassembly.

EVINRUDE AND JOHNSON
4-CYLINDER MODELS
85, 90, 100, 110, 115, 120, 125, 135 and 140 HP
(PRIOR TO 1987)

Year Produced	EVINRUDE	JOHNSON	Year Produced	EVINRUDE	JOHNSON	Year Produced	EVINRUDE	JOHNSON
1969	85993	85ESL69	1978	85890	85ML78	1982	90MLCN	90MLCN
	115983	115ESL69		85895	85ETLR78		90TLCN	90TLCN
1970	85093	85ESL70		85899	85TXLR78		90TXCN	90TXCN
	115083	115ESL70		115890	115ML78		115MLCN	115MLCN
1971	85193	85ESL71		115893	115ETL78		115TLCN	115TLCN
	100193	100ESL71		115899	115TXL78		115TXCN	115TXCN
	125183	125ESL71		140840	140ML78		140MLCN	140MLCN
1972	85293	85ESL72		140843	140TL78		140TRLCN	140TLCN
	100293	100ESL72		140883	140TXL78		140TRXCN	140TXCN
	125283	125ESL72	1979	85990	85ML79	1983	90MLCT	90MLCT
1973	85393	85ESL73		85995	85TL79		90TLCT	90TLCT
	115393	115ESL73		85999	85TXL79		90TXCT	90TXCT
	135383	135ESL73		100990	100ML79		115MLCT	115MLCT
1974	85493	85ESL74		100993	100TLR79		115TLCT	115TLCT
	115493	115ESL74		100999	100TXLR79		115TXCT	115TXCT
	135483	115ETL74		115990	115ML79		140TRLCT	140TRLCT
	135443	135ESL74		115993	115TL79		140TRXCT	140TRXCT
	135489	135ETL74		115999	115TXL79	1984	90MLCR	90MLCR
1975	85593	85ESL75		140940	140ML79		90TLCR	90TLCR
	115593	115ESL75		140943	140TL79		90TXCR	90TXCR
	135583	115ETL75		140983	140TXL79		115MLCR	115MLCR
	135543	135ESL75	1980	85MLCS	85MLCS		115TLCR	115TLCR
	135589	135ETL75		85TLCS	85TLCS		115TXCR	115TXCR
1976	85693	85EL76		85TXCS	85TXCS		140TLCR	140TLCR
	85699	85ETL76		100MLCS	100MLCS		140TXCR	140TXCR
	115693	115EL76		100TLCS	100TRLCS	1985	90MLCO	90MLCO
	115699	115ETL76		100TXCS	100TRXCS		90TLCO	90TLCO
	135643	135EL76		115MLCS	115MLCS		90TXCO	90TXCO
	135683	135ETL76		115TLCS	115TLCS		120TLCO	120TLCO
1977	85790	85EL77		115TXCS	115TXCS		120TXCO	120TXCO
	85793	85ETL77		140MLCS	140MLCS		140TLCO	140TLCO
	85799	85TXLR77		140TRLCS	140TLCS		140TXCO	140TXCO
	115790	115EL77		140TRXCS	140TXCS	1986	90MLCD	90MLCD
	115793	115ETL77	1981	90MLCI	90MLCI		90TLCD	90TLCD
	115799	115TXL77		90TLCI	90TLCI		90TXCD	90TXCD
	140740	140ML77		90TXCI	90TXCI		110MLCD	110MLCD
	140743	140TL77		115MLCI	115MLCI		110TLCD	110TLCD
	140783	140TXL77		115TLCI	115TLCI		120TLCD	120TLCD
				115TXCI	115TXCI		120TXCD	120TXCD
				140MLCI	140MLCI		140TLCD	140TLCD
				140TRLCI	140TLCI		140TXCD	140TXCD
				140TRXCI	140TXCI			

CONDENSED SERVICE DATA

TUNE-UP

Hp/rpm 85/5000
90/5000
100/5000
110/5000
115/5000
120/5500
125/5000
135/5000
140/5000 (Prior to 1985)
140/5500 (After 1984)

TUNE-UP CONT.

Bore:
85 HP (Prior to 1979) .... 3.375 in.
(85.73 mm)
100 HP (Prior to 1973) .... 3.375 in.
(85.73 mm)
115 HP (Prior to 1973) .... 3.438 in.
(87.33 mm)
All Other Models .... 3.500 in.
(88.90 mm)

TUNE-UP CONT.
Stroke:
120 and 140 HP (After 1984) . . . . .2.860 in.
(72.60 mm)
All Other Models . . . . .2.588 in.
(65.74 mm)

Number of Cylinders 4
Displacement:
85 HP (Prior to 1979) .92.6 cu. in.
(1517 cc)
100 HP (Prior to 1973) . . . . .92.6 cu. in.
(1517 cc)
115 HP (Prior to 1973) . . . . .96.1 cu. in.
(1575 cc)
120 and 140 HP (After 1984) . . . . .110 cu. in.
(1800 cc)
All Other Models . . . . .99.6 cu. in.
(1632 cc)

Spark Plug – Champion:
85 HP and 90 HP (Prior to 1986) L77J4
90 HP (1986) QL77JC4*
100 HP L77V
110 HP QL77JC4*
115 HP L77J4
120 HP (Prior to 1986) L77J4*
120 HP (1986) QL77JC4*
125 HP L77V
135 HP UL77V
140 HP (Prior to 1985) UL77V
140 HP (1985) L77J4*
140 HP (1986) QL77JC4*
Ignition – 85 HP and 100 HP (1971):
Type . . . . .CDI – With Breaker Points
Point Gap . . . . .0.010 in.
(0.25 mm)

Ignition – All Other Models:
Type . . . . .CDI – Without Breaker Points
Carburetor Make . . . . .Own
Idle Speed (in gear) . . . . .600-650 rpm
Fuel:Oil Ratio . . . . .50:1†

*A Champion QL78V is recommended when used at sustained high speeds. Renew surface gap spark plug if center electrode is more than 1/32 inch (0.79 mm) below the flat surface of the plug end.
†On 1984 and later models equipped with variable ratio oiling (VRO), the VRO pump meters the fuel:oil ratio from approximately 50:1 up to approximately 150:1 by sensing the engine power output.

SIZES – CLEARANCES
Piston Ring End Gap . . . . .0.007-0.017 in.
(0.18-0.43 mm)
Piston Ring Side Clearance (1969-1984):
85, 100 and 115 HP (Prior to 1973) . . . . .0.0045-0.0070 in.
(0.114-0.178 mm)
85, 100 and 115 HP (After 1972) . . . . .0.002-0.004 in.
(0.051-0.102 mm)
90, 135 and 140 HP . . . . .0.002-0.004 in.
(0.051-0.102 mm)
125 HP . . . . .0.0045-0.0070 in.
(0.114-0.178 mm)
Lower Piston Ring Side Clearance
(1985 and 1986) . . . . .0.004 in. Max.
(0.102 mm)
Piston Skirt Clearance:
125 HP . . . . .0.0030-0.0045 in.
(0.076-0.114 mm)
135 and 140 HP (1973-1978) . . . . .0.0035-0.0055 in.
(0.089-0.140 mm)

SIZES – CLEARANCES CONT.
All Other Models (1969-1978) . . . . .0.0025-0.0040 in.
(0.063-0.102 mm)
All Models (1979-1984) . . . . .0.0045-0.0075 in.
(0.114-0.190 mm)
Crankshaft Diameters:
Top Main (1969-1972) . . . . .1.4975-1.4980 in.)
(38.036-38.049 mm)
(After 1972) . . . . .1.6199-1.6204 in.
(41.145-41.158 mm)
Center Main (1969-1978) . . . . .1.3748-1.3752 in.
(34.920-34.930 mm)
(After 1978) . . . . .2.1870-2.1875 in.
(55.550-55.562 mm)
Lower Main (1969-1972) . . . . .1.1810-1.1815 in.
(29.997-30.010 mm)
(After 1972 Except 1985 and 1986
120 and 140 HP) . . . . .1.3779-1.3784 in.
(34.998-35.011 mm)
(1985 and 1986 120 and 140 HP) . . . . . .1.5747-1.5752 in.
(39.997-40.010 mm)
Crankpin (1969-1973) . . . . .1.1823-1.1828 in.
(30.030-30.043 mm)
(After 1973 Except 1985 and 1986
120 and 140 HP) . . . . .1.3757-1.3762 in.
(34.942-34.955 mm)
(1985 and 1986 120 and 140 HP) . . . . . .1.4995-1.5000 in.
(38.087-38.100 mm)
Crankshaft End Play:
1969 and 1970 . . . . .0.003-0.011 in.
(0.076-0.279 mm)
1971 and 1972 . . . . .0.0006-0.0335 in.
(0.015-0.851 mm)
1973-1980 . . . . .0.0017-0.0347 in.
(0.043-0.881 mm)
1981-1984 . . . . .0.008-0.011 in.
(0.203-0.279 mm)
Forward Gear Bushing to Propeller
Shaft Clearance (Prior to 1985) . . . . .0.001-0.002 in.
(0.03-0.05 mm)

TIGHTENING TORQUES
Connecting Rod:
All Models Except 1985 and 1986
120 and 140 HP . . . . .348-372 in.-lbs.
(39-42 N·m)
1985 and 1986 120 and 140 HP . . . . .504-528 in.-lbs.
(57-60 N·m)
Crankcase Halves:
Main Bearing Screws –
(1969-1972) . . . . .162-168 in.-lbs.
(18-19 N·m)
After 1972 Except 1985 and
1986 120 and 140 HP) . . . . .216-240 in.-lbs.
(24-27 N·m)
(1985 and 1986 120 and 140 HP) . . . . .312-360 in.-lbs.
(35-41 N·m)
Flange Screws –
(1969-1972) . . . . .144-168 in.-lbs.
(16-19 N·m)
(After 1972) . . . . .60-84 in.-lbs.
(7-9 N·m)
Crankcase Head:
Upper –
(All Models Except 1985 and 1986
120 and 140 HP) . . . . .120-144 in.-lbs.
(13-16 N·m)
(1985 and 1986 120 and 140 HP) . . . . .72.96 in.-lbs.
(8-11 N·m)

TIGHTENING TORQUES CONT.

Lower Bearing Head –
(All Models Except 1985 and
1986 120 and 140 HP) . . . . 96-120 in.-lbs.
(11-13 N·m)
(1985 and 1986 120 and 140 HP) . . . . 72-96 in.-lbs.
(8-11 N·m)
Cylinder Head . . . . 216-240 in.-lbs.
(24-27 N·m)
Flywheel Nut:
1969-1971 . . . . 70-85 ft.-lbs.
(95-116 N·m)
After 1971 Except 1985 and 1986
120 and 140 HP . . . . 100-105 ft.-lbs.
(136-143 N·m)
1985 and 1986 120 and 140 HP . . . . 140-145 ft.-lbs.
(190-197 N·m)
Lower Main Bearing Retainer
Plate Screws . . . . 96-120 in.-lbs.
(11-13 N·m)

TIGHTENING TORQUES CONT.

Spark Plug . . . . 216-240 in.-lbs.
(24-27 N·m)
Standard Screws:
No. 6 . . . . 7-10 in.-lbs.
(0.8-1.2 N·m)
No. 8 . . . . 15-22 in.-lbs.
(1.6-2.4 N·m)
No. 10 . . . . 25-35 in.-lbs.
(2.8-4.0 N·m)
No. 12 . . . . 35-40 in.-lbs.
(4.0-4.6 N·m)
¼ Inch . . . . 60-80 in.-lbs.
(7-9 N·m)
5/16 Inch . . . . 120-140 in.-lbs.
(14-16 N·m)
⅜ Inch . . . . 220-240 in.-lbs.
(24-27 N·m)
7/16 Inch . . . . 340-360 in.-lbs.
(38-40 N·m)

LUBRICATION

The engine is lubricated by oil mixed with the fuel. On 1969-1975 models, fuel should be regular leaded or premium leaded with a minimum pump octane rating of 89. On 1976-1986 models except 1981-1984 140 hp models, fuel should be regular leaded or regular unleaded with a minimum pump octane rating of 86. On 1981-1984 140 hp models, fuel should be regular leaded or premium leaded with a minimum pump octane rating of 88.

On models prior to 1984, recommended oil is Evinrude or Johnson 50/1 Lubricant or a BIA certified TC-W motor oil. The recommended fuel:oil ratio for normal operation and engine break-in is 50:1.

On 1984 and later models equipped with variable ratio oiling (VRO), recommended oil is Evinrude or Johnson Outboard Lubricant, OMC 2 Cycle Motor Oil or a BIA certified TC-W motor oil. The VRO pump meters the fuel:oil ratio from approximately 50:1 up to approximately 150:1 by sensing the engine power output. During engine break-in, the fuel in the fuel tank must be mixed at a fuel:oil ratio of 50:1 to assure the engine of proper lubrication and the oil level in the VRO oil tank must be monitored. If, after engine break-in, oil level has dropped indicating the VRO system is operating, refill the VRO oil tank and switch to straight fuel.

On 1984 and later recreational models when VRO is not being used, the recommended fuel:oil ratio for normal operation and engine break-in is 50:1.

The lower unit gears and bearings are lubricated by oil contained in the gearcase. The recommended oil is OMC Sea-Lube Premium Blend Gearcase Lube on models prior to 1977 and OMC HI-VIS Gearcase Lube on models after 1976. The gearcase oil level should be checked after every 50 hours of operation and the gearcase should be drained and filled with new oil every 100 hours or once each season, whichever occurs first.

The gearcase is drained and filled through the same plug port. An oil level (vent) port is used to indicate the full oil level of the gearcase and to ease in oil drainage.

To drain the oil, place the outboard motor in a vertical position. Remove the drain plug and oil level plug and allow the lubricant to drain into a suitable container.

To fill the gearcase with oil, place the outboard motor in a vertical position. Add oil through the drain plug opening with an oil feeder until the oil begins to overflow from oil level plug port. Reinstall oil level plug with a new gasket, if needed, and tighten. Remove oil feeder, then reinstall drain plug with a new gasket, if needed, and tighten.

FUEL SYSTEM

All Models Except 1985 And 1986 120 And 140 HP Models

CARBURETORS. Two carburetors are used and each is of the two-barrel type with one (common) float chamber. Each of the four carburetor barrels provides fuel for one of the cylinders and is equipped with individual metering components.

Carburetors on models prior to 1980 are equipped with choke plates actuated by an electric solenoid through linkage. On models after 1979, additional fuel to aid starting is injected into the engine's transfer ports through tubes in the transfer port covers. A key-controlled, electric solenoid valve directs fuel from the fuel pump to the transfer port covers. The valve may be opened manually if rope starting is required.

Adjustment. Throttle valves must be synchronized for optimum performance. To synchronize throttle valves, close the throttle and make certain that follower roller (F – Fig. OM16-3 or OM16-7) is not touching throttle cam (T). Loosen clamp screw (B), hold both throttle shafts closed, then tighten screw (B).

Fig. OM16-1 – The silencer cover (C) on early models is attached to base by the three screws (S). Rod (R) attaches the idle mixture external adjustment knob to the outer lever (L) on models prior to 1972.

High speed mixture on all models is controlled by high speed jets (30–Fig. OM16-5) located in opposite sides of the float bowl. On 1980 through early 1983 models an intermediate speed jet (31) is located just above high speed jet (30). On late 1983 and later models, intermediate speed jet (31) is mounted vertically in float bowl (29).

Idle mixture on models after 1971 is controlled by low speed jets (13) located in opposite sides of the carburetor. Models prior to 1972 are equipped with four idle mixture adjusting needles that are connected together with linkage and can be externally adjusted within a limited range by turning the adjustment knob at front of motor lower cover. If further adjustment is necessary, proceed as follows: Remove the motor top cover. Pull lever (L–Fig. OM16-1) off shaft, remove three screws (S) and lift the silencer cover (C). Pull the four levers from the idle mixture needles (N—Fig. OM16-2) and remove levers, linkage and bellcrank. Normal setting for idle mixture needles (N) is 7/8-turn

open. Run motor until normal operating temperature is reached, then adjust each of the four needles to provide the smoothest operation at 700-750 rpm, in gear with motor on boat or in test tank. After adjustment is complete, install levers, links and bellcrank, making certain that needle setting is not changed and that levers are exactly horizontal as shown in Fig. OM16-2. After installing the silencer cover (C–Fig. OM16-1), install lever (L) so the external adjustment knob is in center of adjusting range.

NOTE: If throttle valves are not synchronized to open exactly the same amount, it may be impossible to adjust the idle mixture needles for a smooth idle.

Idle speed on all models should be adjusted to 600-650 rpm in gear and is adjusted by turning stop screw (I–Fig. OM16-3 or OM16-7).

Refer to SPEED CONTROL LINKAGE section for synchronizing carburetor throttle opening to the ignition timing.

The choke solenoid on models prior to 1980 should be positioned so choke plates open and close fully. The solenoid plunger (P–Fig. OM16-3) should protrude approximately 5/16 inch (7.9 inch). Make certain that the choke linkage is adjusted to close both choke plates at the same time. The spring should be screwed onto the solenoid plunger 2½-3½ turns.

Fig. OM16-2—Each of the four idle mixture adjustment needles (N) on models prior to 1972 can be individually adjusted after removing connecting links.

Fig. OM16-3—Idle speed is adjusted at stop screw (I) on early models. Refer to Fig. OM16-7 for linkage on later models.

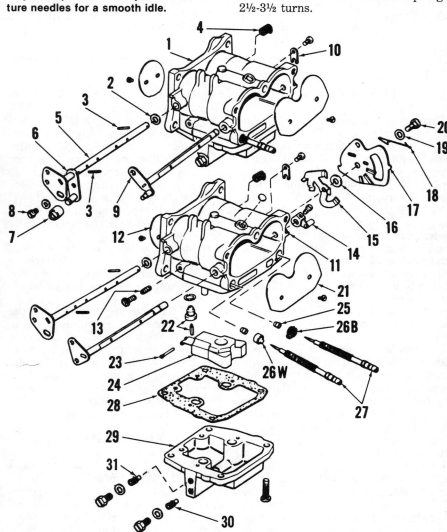

Fig. OM16-5—Exploded view of carburetor typical of the type used on all models except 1985 and 1986 120 and 140 hp models. Carburetors on models after 1979 are not equipped with choke components. Low speed jets (13) are used on 1972-1979 models in place of idle mixture screws (27). Low speed jets are located in each carburetor barrel on models after 1979. On 1980 through early 1983 models, an intermediate speed jet (31) is located just above high speed jet (30). On late 1983 and later models, intermediate speed jet (31) is mounted vertically in float bowl (29).

1. Top carburetor
2. Washer
3. Pins
4. Return spring
5. Throttle shaft
6. Cam follower lever
7. Follower roller
8. Set screw
9. Choke shaft (top)
10. Choke shaft retainer
11. Body
12. Throttle plate
13. Low speed jet
14. Choke arm
15. Detent spring
16. Washer
17. Manual choke lever
18. Manual choke spring
19. Washer
20. Shoulder bolt
21. Choke plate
22. Fuel inlet valve
23. Pivot pin
24. Float
25. Bushing
26B. Black retainer (Port)
26W. White retainer (Starboard)
27. Idle mixture needle
28. Gasket
29. Float bowl
30. High speed jet
31. Intermediate jet

R&R And Overhaul. The carburetors can be removed after after removing the air silencer assembly and linkage. The top and bottom carburetors are slightly different as shown in Fig. OM16-5. Disassembly procedure is self-evident. The screws attaching choke and throttle plates are staked after assembly and should be renewed if removed from shafts.

The float should be parallel to carburetor body gasket surface as shown in Fig. OM16-6. The black retainers (26B – Fig. OM16-5) must be installed on port side and the white retainers (26W) must be on starboard as shown.

The fuel mixture on models prior to 1980 is enriched for starting using carburetor choke plates. The carburetor choke may be actuated manually by moving the choke control knob or lever, or by activating a solenoid controlled by the ignition key switch. On early models the solenoid regulates choke plate opening according to a signal from the thermal switch in the engine's water bypass cover. On later models the thermal switch is not used and the solenoid moves the choke plate to fully closed position when activated. Refer to ADJUSTMENT paragraphs for choke adjustment.

The fuel mixture on models after 1979 is enriched for starting using a key-controlled, electric solenoid valve which directs fuel from the fuel pump to the transfer port covers where fuel is injected into the transfer port passages. Inspect valve and renew any damaged components.

SPEED CONTROL LINKAGE. The carburetor throttle valves are synchronized to open as the ignition is advanced. It is important that throttle valve opening and ignition timing synchronization be checked and adjusted if necessary.

The following procedure should be used to check and adjust synchronization of linkage. Move the speed control lever to the idle position and make sure follower roller (F – Fig. OM16-3 or OM16-7) is not touching throttle cam (T).

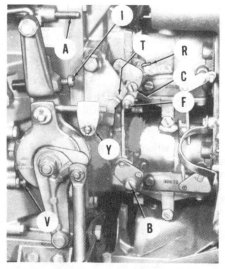

Fig. OM16-7 – View of speed control linkage typical of the type used on all later models except 1985 and 1986 120 and 140 hp models. Models after 1979 do not use the choke linkage. Refer to text.

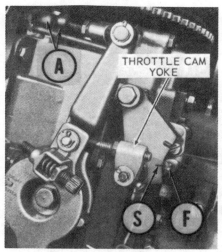

Fig. OM16-8 – Lower mark (S) should be aligned with center of roller (F) when ignition advance screw just contacts maximum stop (A).

Loosen clamp screw (B) and make certain that throttle plates are closed, then tighten clamp screw (B). Move the speed control lever slowly from the idle position toward the fast position and note the point at which throttle cam (T) con-

tacts follower roller (F). The cam should just contact roller (F) when throttle cam (T) larger (upper) alignment mark is exactly centered with roller (F) as shown. If incorrect, loosen screw (C) and reposition the roller.

On models prior to 1971, move the speed control lever toward the fast position until the ignition advance just contacts the stop as shown at (A – Fig. OM16-8). The lower alignment mark (S) should be exactly aligned with the center of follower roller (F). If mark (S) is not in center of roller (F), reposition the throttle cam yoke on the rod.

On models after 1970 but prior to 1984, there should be 0.001-0.003 inch (0.02-0.07 mm) clearance between roll pin (R – Fig. OM16-7) and stop at wide-open throttle. Turn wide-open throttle stop screw (V) to obtain desired clearance.

On models after 1983, the wide-open throttle stop screw (V) must be adjusted so the carburetor throttle shaft pins are exactly vertical when engine throttle lever is manually advanced to wide-open throttle.

NOTE: The throttle shaft pin must not go past vertical or damage to the carburetors may result.

REED VALVES. Four sets of leaf (reed) valves are used, one for each cylinder. The four valves (15 – Fig. OM16-9) are attached to the intake manifold (14) with a gasket between each reed block and manifold. The leaf petals should seat very lightly against the valve block throughout their entire length with the least possible tension. The individual parts of the reed valve assembly are not available separately. Renew the reed valve assembly if petals are broken, cracked, warped or bent.

NON-VRO TYPE FUEL PUMP. The fuel pump is operated by the pressure and vacuum pulsations in the crankcase. Repair parts for the fuel pump (16 – Fig. OM16-9) are not available and the complete pump must be renewed if the unit fails. Make certain that filter screen (17)

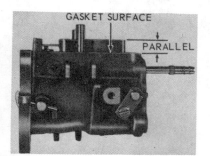

Fig. OM16-6 – The float should be parallel to the gasket surface of carburetor body when fuel inlet valve is closed.

Fig. OM16-9 – Typical view of silencer, carburetors, fuel pump and intake manifold used on early models. Later models are similar.

1. Idle adjust lever
2. Silencer cover
3. Bushing
4. Spring
5. Bellcrank
6. Needle levers (4 used)
7. Bushing
8. Silencer base
9. Choke solenoid
10. Choke connecting link
11. Throttle connecting link
12. Top carburetor
13. Bottom carburetor
14. Intake manifold
15. Reed valve assy. (4 used)
16. Fuel pump
17. Fuel filter screen
18. Cover

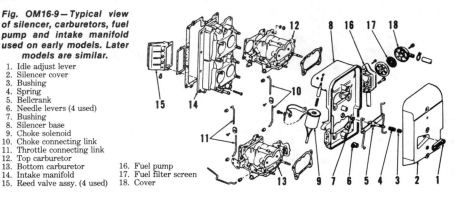

is clean and that fuel lines, air lines and filter are not leaking air or fuel.

VRO TYPE FUEL PUMP. The VRO type fuel pump (1–Fig. OM16-10) meters the fuel:oil ratio from approximately 50:1 up to approximately 150:1 by sensing the engine power output. During engine break-in or after any procedure that permitted air to enter VRO system, the fuel in the fuel tank must be mixed at a fuel:oil ratio of 50:1 to ensure the engine of proper lubrication.

To check the VRO system for proper operation, first fill the VRO oil tank with

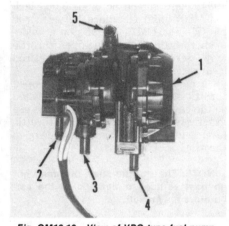

Fig. OM16-10— View of VRO type fuel pump.

1. VRO fuel pump assy.
2. Oil inlet nipple
3. Fuel inlet nipple
4. Crankcase pulse nipple
5. Fuel mixuture discharge nipple

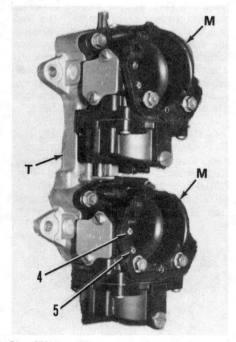

Fig. OM16-11— View showing two-barrel type carburetors used on 1985 and 1986 120 and 140 hp models. A common throttle body assembly (T) with separate main body assemblies (M) are used. View identifies position of intermediate air bleed jet (4) and low speed air bleed jet (5). Refer to text.

a recommended two-stroke motor oil and note oil level for future reference. Install a fuel:oil mixture of 50:1 in the fuel tank. After the recommended engine break-in period or after a suitable test period for other conditions, note the oil level in the VRO oil tank. If the oil level has dropped and the VRO system is operating properly, refill the VRO oil tank and switch to straight fuel.

NOTE: When the VRO system is not used, the inlet nozzle at the outboard motor connector must be capped and clamped to prevent dirt or moisture from entering the fuel system. The fuel in the fuel tank must be mixed at a fuel:oil ratio of 50:1.

TESTING. Stop the engine. Disconnect fuel mixture discharge hose at VRO pump nipple (4–Fig. OM16-10). Connect a tee fitting in hose end. Connect one end of a clear hose to one tee outlet and connect remaining hose end to pump discharge fitting. Connect a 0-15 psi (0-103 kPa) pressure gage to the remaining tee outlet. Start the engine and run at wide open throttle. The VRO pump should develop between 3 psi (21 kPa) and 15 psi (103 kPa) at wide-open throttle. The fuel pressure will drop 1-2 psi (6.8-13.7 kPa) and a clicking sound should be heard with each oil discharge. A small squirt of oil should be noticed every time the pump pulses.

If fuel pump (1) malfunction is noted, the fuel pump must be renewed as a complete assembly.

1985 And 1986 120 And 140 HP Models

CARBURETOR. Two two-barrel type carburetors are used. Each carburetor assembly has a common throttle body assembly (T–Fig. OM16-11) with

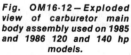

Fig. OM16-12—Exploded view of carburetor main body assembly used on 1985 and 1986 120 and 140 hp models.

1. Main body
2. Gasket
3. Plate
4. Intermediate air bleed jet
5. Low speed air bleed jet
6. Seal
7. Inlet needle & seat
8. Gasket
9. High speed jet
10. Gasket
11. Plug
12. Float bowl
13. Pin
14. Float

separate main body assemblies (M). Recommended low speed air bleed jet (5) size is #14 on 1985 120 and 140 hp models, #16 on 1986 120 hp models and #28 on 1986 140 hp models. Recommended intermediate air bleed jet (4) size is #43 on 1985 120 hp models, #40 on 1985 140 hp models, #45 on port carburetors on 1986 120 hp models, #42 on starboard carburetors on 1986 120 hp models, #20 on port carburetors on 1986 140 hp models and #16 on starboard carburetors on 1986 140 hp models. Recommended high speed jet (9–Fig. OM16-12) size is #57D on 1985 120 hp models, #59D on 1985 140 hp models and 1986 120 hp models and #61D on 1986 140 hp models.

NOTE: Starboard carburetors supply fuel to port cylinders and port carburetors supply fuel to starboard cylinders.

The main body assemblies are constructed of a nonmetallic type material. Care must be used when working with the main body assembly. DO NOT overtighten any screws. Tighten each screw in small increments using a criss-cross tightening sequence.

If service is performed, note the following: Keep carburetor components for each carburetor separate from the others. The manufacturer does not recommend submerging the parts in carburetor or parts cleaning solutions. An aerosol type carburetor cleaner is recommended. The float and other components made of plastic and rubber should not be subjected to some cleaning solutions. Safety eyewear and solvent resistant gloves are recommended.

To determine the float level, invert float bowl (12–Fig. OM16-13) with the fuel inlet valve and float installed. The float should be flush with the float bowl gasket surface. Use a straightedge as

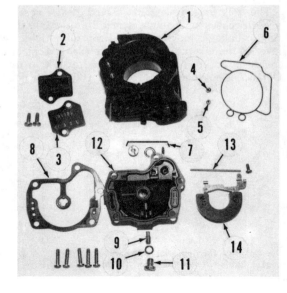

Fig. OM16-13 — With float bowl (12) inverted and fuel inlet valve and float installed, float should just touch straightedge (S). Refer to text.

shown in Fig. OM16-13 to check float setting. Remove the float and carefully bend the float tang to adjust.

Recommended idle speed is 600-650 rpm with the engine at normal operating temperature and forward gear engaged. Loosen nut (N – Fig. OM16-14) and turn screw (I) to adjust engine idle speed.

SPEED CONTROL LINKAGE. The carburetor throttle valves are synchronized to open as the ignition is advanced. it is important that throttle valve opening and ignition timing synchronization be checked and adjusted if necessary.

The following procedure should be used to check and adjust sychronization of linkage. Move the speed control lever to the idle position and make sure follower roller (F – Fig. OM16-14) is not touching throttle cam (T). Loosen follower roller screw (C) and move roller away from throttle cam (T). Loosen screw (S) two complete turns and make certain that throttle plates are closed, then tighten screw (S). Leave screw (C) loose. Hold follower roller (F) against throttle cam (T) and adjust throttle arm stop screw (D) until alignment mark (M) is centered with follower roller (F). Withdraw roller (F) away from throttle cam (T) enough to allow throttle plates to close at idle and tighten screw (C). Adjust wide-open throttle (WOT) stop screw (W) so WOT mark (0) on follower roller bracket points directly front-to-rear when the speed control lever is at WOT.

REED VALVES. Four sets of leaf (reed) valves are used, one for each cylinder. The four valves are positioned horizontally and are attached to the intake manifold with a gasket between each reed block and manifold. The leaf petals should seat very lightly against the valve block throughout their entire length with the least possible tension. The individual parts of the reed valve assembly are not available separately. Renew the reed valve assembly if petals are broken, cracked, warped or bent.

VRO TYPE FUEL PUMP. The VRO type fuel pump (1 – Fig. OM16-10) meters the fuel:oil ratio from approximately 50:1 up to approximately 150:1 by sensing the engine power output. During engine break-in or after any procedure that permitted air to enter VRO system, the fuel in the fuel tank must be mixed at fuel:oil ratio of 50:1 to ensure the engine of proper lubrication.

To check the VRO system for proper operation, first fill the VRO oil tank with a recommended two-stroke motor oil and note oil level for future reference. Install a fuel:oil mixture of 50:1 in the fuel tank. After the recommended engine break-in period or after a suitable test period for other conditions, note the oil level in the VRO oil tank. If the oil level has dropped and the VRO system is operating properly, refill the VRO oil tank and switch to straight fuel.

NOTE: When the VRO system is not used, the inlet nozzle at the outboard motor connector must be capped and clamped to prevent dirt or moisture from entering the fuel system. The fuel in the fuel tank must be mixed at a fuel:oil ratio of 50:1.

Fig. OM16-14 — View of speed control linkage used on 1985 and 1986 120 and 140 hp models. Refer to text.

TESTING. Stop the engine. Disconnect fuel mixture discharge hose at VRO pump nipple (4 – Fig. OM16-10). Connect a tee fitting in hose end. Connect one end of a clear hose to one tee outlet and connect remaining hose end to pump discharge fitting. Connect a 0-15 psi (0-103 kPa) pressure gage to the remaining tee outlet. Start the engine and run at wide-open throttle. The VRO pump should develop between 3 psi (21 kPa) and 15 psi (103 kPa) at wide-open throttle. The fuel pressure will drop 1-2 psi (6.8-13.7 kPa) and a clicking sound should be heard with each oil discharge. A small squirt of oil should be noticed every time the pump pulses.

If fuel pump (1) malfunction is noted, the fuel pump must be renewed as a complete assembly.

IGNITION SYSTEM

The ignition systems are of the capacitor discharge type; however, 85 hp models prior to 1973 and 1971 100 hp models use breaker points to trigger the ignition and all 90, 110, 115, 120, 125, 135 and 140 hp models and late 100 hp models are triggered by an electronic sensor. Refer to the appropriate following paragraphs when servicing.

BREAKER POINT MODELS

The capacitor discharge ignition is triggered by two sets of breaker points located in the distributor unit under the flywheel. The ignition is extremely durable in normal operation, but can be easily damaged by improper operating, testing or servicing procedures. To prevent damage to the components, observe the following list of cautions and use only approved methods for checking and servicing the system.

1. DO NOT reverse battery terminals.
2. DO NOT disconnect battery while motor is running or attempt to start motor without a battery in the system.
3. DO NOT disconnect any wires while motor is running or while ignition switch is ON.
4. DO NOT use any tachometer except those approved for use with this system.

TROUBLESHOOTING. Use only approved procedures to prevent damage to the components. The fuel system should be checked first to make certain that faulty running is not caused by incorrect fuel mixture or contaminated fuel. If the motor continues to run after ignition switch is turned OFF, check the blocking diode as outlined in the appropriate paragraphs.

CHECKING FOR SPARK. Connect a spark tester to the four plug leads as shown in Fig. OM16-15, attempt to start motor and check for spark at the tester.

NOTE: A neon spark tester or four conventional spark plugs with the ground electrodes removed can be used in place of the tester shown.

Spark gap must not be more than 3/8 inch (9.5 mm). The coil wire is molded into coil and screwed into the distributor cap. **Do not attempt to pull the coil wire out of either end.**

If spark occurs at all four points of ignition tester, check ignition timing. Also check condition of spark plugs and make certain the leads are connected to the correct spark plugs.

If spark occurs at only two of the four tester points, check condition and gap of the breaker points.

If spark does not occur at any of the four tester points, continue with remainder of tests.

WIRING. Engine missing, surging and failure to start or run can be caused by loose or corroded electrical connections. Check all terminals and plug-in connectors for tight clean contact. Also check all wiring for short circuit to ground, especially the black wire with white stripe leading from the breaker

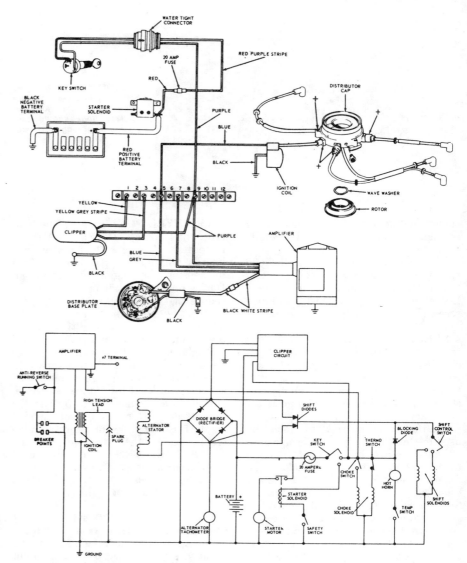

Fig. OM16-16 — The top shows the basic parts and color of connecting wires for ignition system used on breaker point ignition models. Lower view is a schematic of the complete electrical system. Early 85 hp motors were not equipped with a clipper, but wiring was otherwise the same.

Fig. OM16-15 — View showing a spark tester (T) connected to the spark plug leads. Refer to text for recommended gap.

points in distributor to the amplifier. Make certain that all wires are connected to the terminal block as shown in Fig. OM16-17 or Fig. OM16-18. A voltmeter or 12 volt test light can be used to check wiring. Connect one lead of voltmeter (or test light) to purple lead terminal (13, 13A, 14 or 15) and ground other lead. With ignition switch ON, battery voltage should be indicated. If this terminal is dead, check the 20 amp fuse located at (F – Fig. OM16-19), battery and all lead in wires and connectors.

NOTE: The fuse may be in a different location than shown.

If current is available, proceed with remaining checks.

BREAKER POINTS. The breaker points are located under the flywheel

and distributor cap; however, some tests can be accomplished without disassembly. Disconnect the plug-in connector (B – Fig. OM16-17) and attach one ohmmeter or test light (with battery) lead to the wire from the breaker points. Ground the other ohmmeter or test light lead to the motor, remove the four spark plugs and move the speed control to fast position. Turn flywheel slowly by hand and observe ohmmeter or test light. The ohmmeter or test light should indicate breaker points opening (infinite resistance or light off) and closing (near zero resistance or light on) four times during one revolution of the crankshaft (flywheel).

NOTE: Turn crankshaft only in clockwise direction as viewed from top of motor to prevent damage to water pump impeller.

The breaker points should just open when each of the two "B" marks on flywheel align with timing lug on lifting bracket if the speed control is in fast position. If breaker points open, but not when "B" marks align with timing lug, refer to the ignition timing paragraph.

When making this test, the black with white stripe wire should be carefully inspected and moved in an effort to locate any intermittent short circuit to ground or open circuit such as loose connections.

NOTE: Complete inspection will be impossible unless the distributor is disassembled.

If no malfunction is noted, proceed with remaining tests.

AMPLIFIER. Disconnect the purple wire (15 – Fig. OM16-17) to the amplifier and attach a low reading ammeter between the disconnected wire (to amplifier) and power supply terminal (13). With ignition switch ON but motor not running, maximum current draw should be 0.2 amperes. If possible, start motor and operate at 4500 rpm. Ammeter should indicate 2.0-4.0 amperes. Unsteady meter reading with motor running indicates trouble with breaker points. If current draw is incorrect, either running or not running, the amplifier should be renewed.

NOTE: Use extreme caution to make certain that test connections are not disconnected or shorted. Clip on test connectors should not be used with motor running.

As an alternate method of testing the amplifier, connect one lead from a neon test light to terminal (8 and 9) and attach other lead from neon tester to motor ground. Turn ignition switch ON, crank motor with electric starter and observe the neon bulb. If the bulb flickers while motor is cranking, the amplifier is operating correctly and the high tension coil, distributor cap, rotor, spark plug leads or spark plugs should be suspected. If the neon bulb does not light, disconnect plug (B), turn ignition switch ON, and ground the amplifier end of connector (B) to the motor. When the connector (B) is lifted from contact with motor, the neon bulb should flicker. If the bulb lights, check condition of breaker points, connecting wires and antireverse switch. If the neon test light does not flicker, renew the amplifier.

COIL. The ignition high tension coil can be tested using an ignition tester available from several sources, including the following:

GRAHAM TESTERS INC.
4220 Central Ave. N.E.
Minneapolis, Minn. 55421

MERC-O-TRONIC
INSTRUMENTS CORP.
215 Branch St.
Almont, Mich. 48003

Coil test procedures and specifications are available from the manufacturers of the tester.

NOTE: The high tension coil lead is molded into coil and screwed into distributor cap.

SHIFT DIODE. Failure of the shift diode (D—Fig. OM16-17) may cause the lower unit to shift into forward gear immediately after ignition switch is turned OFF.

To check the shift diode, disconnect the yellow (3), yellow/gray (7) and purple/green (16) wires from the terminal block and remove the shift diode (D). Use a continuity light (with battery of less than 12 volts) or ohmmeter for checking. Attach one test light (or ohmmeter) lead to the purple/green wire and other lead to the yellow wire; then, reverse the test leads. The test light or ohmmeter should indicate continuity with one connection and NO continuity with leads reversed. Attach test leads similarly to the yellow/gray wire and the purple/green wire; then, reverse leads. Continuity should again exist with one connection; but not when leads are reversed. If either of the two tests allow current to pass in both directions or prevent current from passing in either direction, renew the shift diode.

CLIPPER. Models produced after 1970 were equipped with a clipper circuit to prevent damage to CD ignition components in the event of an open circuit or intermittent battery current when engine is running.

Failure of the clipper unit (C—Fig. OM16-17) should be suspected if any of the following occurs: Battery current is momentarily interrupted with motor running; battery charge low when charging system check OK; CD amplifier inoperative; fuses blow repeatedly.

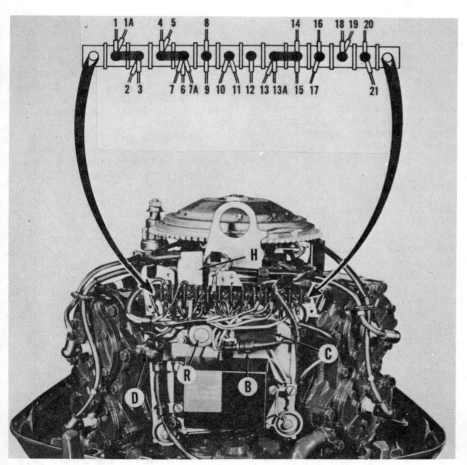

Fig. OM16-17 — Rear view of 1972 85 hp motor. Other breaker timed motors are similar. Inset shows location of wires on terminal block.

1, 1A, 2 & 3. Yellow		13, 13A, 14 & 15. Purple
4 & 5. Yellow/gray stripe		16 & 17. Purple/green stripe
6. Gray	8 & 9. Blue	18 & 19. Purple/yellow stripe
7 & 7A. Yellow/gray stripe	10 & 11. Red	20 & 21. Purple/white stripe
	12. Gray	

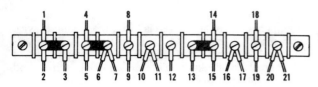

1, 2 & 3. Yellow
4 & 5. Yellow/gray stripe
6. Gray
7. Yellow/gray stripe
8 & 9. Blue
10 & 11. Red

Fig. OM16-18 – View of terminal block showing location of wires used on early 85 hp motors.

12. Gray
13, 14 & 15. Purple
16 & 17. Purple/green stripe
18 & 19. Purple/yellow stripe
20 & 21. Purple/white stripe

Clipper unit may be checked with an ohmmeter in the following manner: Disconnect **all** leads from clipper to terminal block before making any checks. Correct ohmmeter test lead polarity must be determined before inspecting clipper unit. Ohmmeter polarity may be determined by connecting meter leads to the yellow lead and the purple/green lead of a good **shift diode**. Refer to Shift Diode check in previous section. If ohmmeter shows little or no resistance through shift diode, lead attached to yellow wire will be "ground lead" for purposes of checking clipper. If resistance is high, opposite lead will be ground.

To check clipper, momentarily touch the purple lead to the case of the clipper. Connect the ohmmeter "ground lead" to ground (either the case or the black wire) of the clipper. Connect other ohmmeter lead to yellow wire of clipper. Renew clipper if reading is less than 300 ohms. If an infinite resistance reading is obtained, disconnect ohmmeter lead from yellow wire, momentarily short purple wire against case and connect ohmmeter to yellow/gray wire while retaining original ground connection. Renew clipper if reading is less than 300 ohms. If an infinite reading is obtained, remove lead from yellow/gray wire, momentarily short purple wire against case and connect ohmmeter lead to purple wire. If meter moves and then returns to infinity or registers less than 300 ohms, renew clipper unit. If an infinite reading is obtained, disconnect ohmmeter, momentarily short purple wire against case, connect "ground lead" from ohmmeter to purple wire and other ohmmeter lead to ground of clipper. Clipper is good if meter swings toward zero and returns to infinity. Renew clipper if meter needle does not move or if meter needle moves to zero and stays.

BLOCKING DIODE. Failure of the blocking diode may allow motor to continue running after ignition switch is turned OFF or the lower unit may remain in Forward gear until after motor starts.

The blocking diode is located near the ignition switch and the purple wire is attached to "IGNITION" terminal of switch. The purple/green wire from diode is equipped with a quick release connector which attaches to a wire leading to the shift control switch.

To check the blocking diode, first remove the diode. Attach one lead of ohmmeter or continuity test light (with a battery of less than 12 volts) to each wire from diode. Observe ohmmeter reading or test light, then reverse the test connections. Current should pass through diode with one connection (low resistance or light on) but should not pass current with leads reversed. If current passes both directions or does not pass in either direction, renew the blocking diode.

If the blocking diode checks OK but motor continues to run after switch is turned OFF or Forward gear is not engaged until after motor starts, check the switches, wires and connectors for short or open circuits.

RECTIFIER. To check the rectifier (R – Fig. OM16-17), disconnect the yellow (2), yellow/gray (5) and red (10) wires from the terminal block. Connect one lead of ohmmeter to yellow wire from rectifier and attach other ohmmeter lead to motor ground. Check continuity, then reverse the ohmmeter leads. The ohmmeter should indicate low resistance (near zero) with one connection and high resistance (near infinity) with leads reversed. Repeat this test (including reversing the ohmmeter leads) at the ground connection and

yellow/gray lead; between the yellow ane red leads; then, between the red and yellow/gray leads.

If any of the tests indicate near zero resistance in both directions or near infinite resistance in both directions, renew the rectifier.

NOTE: A continuity test light (with battery of less than 12 volts) can be used to check condition of rectifier instead of ohmmeter. Light should glow with one connection, but should not when leads are reversed.

DISTRIBUTOR. To service components of the distributor, remove the flywheel (24 – Fig. OM16-20) and alternator stator (23). The distributor cap is retained by the same three screws which attach the alternator stator and these screws are coated with Loctite. The coil high tension wire and the spark plug wires are screwed into the distributor cap. Remove the spring washer (22) and rotor (4).

The antireverse spring (16 – Fig. OM16-21) is clipped onto crankshaft and when crankshaft is turning in normal direction, the coiled projection is against the oiler felt (18). If the crankshaft turns in counterclockwise direction, the antireverse spring turns with the crankshaft until it grounds the ignition system through contact (17). When installing the antireverse spring, the crankshaft should be lubricated lightly and the flat side of spring should be down as shown in Fig. OM16-22.

Breaker point gap should be set at 0.010 inch (0.25 mm) for used breaker points, or 0.012 inch (0.30 mm) if new breaker points are installed. After breaker point gap is correctly set, install rotor (4 – Fig. OM16-20) making certain that lug engages slot in crankshaft. Install spring washer (22), then position distributor cap (5) over breaker plate. Make certain that coil high tension lead and spark plug wires are screwed into distributor cap and are correctly positioned. Locate the alternator stator (23) over distributor cap, coat the three retaining screws with Loctite and tighten screws to 48-60 in.-lbs. (5.4-6.7 N·m) torque. Initial timing can be set using the timing marks shown in Fig. OM16-23; however, a power timing light and the flywheel timing marks should be used for final setting. Refer to TIMING paragraphs. Make certain that tapers in flywheel (and top of crankshaft) are clean and dry before installing flywheel. The flywheel drive key should be parallel with crankshaft center line, NOT aligned with taper. Tighten the flywheel retaining nut to 70-85 ft.-lbs. (95-116 N·m) torque.

Fig. OM16-19 – View of port side of late model engine showing location of fuse (F) and start solenoid (S).

IGNITION TIMING. To check the

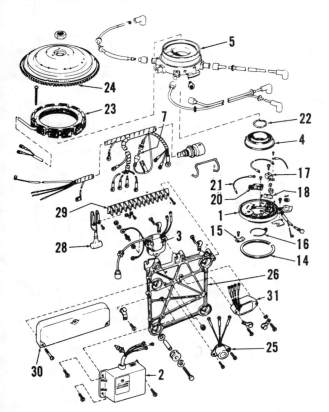

Fig. OM16-20 — Exploded view of the ignition and alternator system components used on breaker point ignition 85 and 100 hp models. Ignition cam is part of crankshaft. Clipper (31) is used on 1971 and later models only.

1. Distributor base plate
2. Amplifier
3. High tension coil
4. Rotor
5. Distributor cap
7. Fuse (20 amp)
14. Retaining ring
15. Clip
16. Antireverse spring
17. Antireverse contact
18. Oiler felt
20. Breaker points
21. Ground wire
22. Wave washer
23. Alternator stator
24. Flywheel
25. Rectifier
26. Bracket
28. Shift diodes
29. Terminal block
30. Cover
31. Clipper

in gear and running at 4500 rpm. If timing is incorrect, loosen locknut and turn the spark advance adjustment screw (Fig. OM16-23). One turn of the screw clockwise will retard ignition approximately one degree.

BREAKERLESS IGNITION

Models Prior to 1973

All 125 hp motors, 1972 100 hp motors and 115 hp motors prior to 1971 are equipped with breakerless capacitor ignition systems which use a distributor. The systems used are primarily the same. Testing and trouble-shooting procedures will be the same except when special note is made.

The capacitor discharge ignition is triggered electronically by a sensor coil located in the distributor unit under the flywheel. The ignition system is extremely durable in normal operation, but can be easily damaged by improper operating, testing or servicing procedures. To prevent damage to the components, observe the following list of cautions and use only approved methods for checking and servicing the system.

1. DO NOT reverse battery terminals.
2. DO NOT disconnect battery while motor is running or attempt to start motor without a battery in the system.

maximum advance ignition timing, connect a power timing light to number 1 (top starboard) cylinder spark plug and run motor at 4500 rpm in forward gear. Different flywheels were used on motors built in 1969 and 1970 than those used on later models. Refer to Fig. OM16-24, Fig. OM16-25 and the appropriate following paragraphs.

1969 And 1970 Models. The "B" timing mark with straight line must align with timing lug on hoisting bracket as shown in Fig. OM16-24. If timing is incorrect, loosen locknut and turn the spark advance adjustment screw (Fig. OM16-23) as required. Make certain that

wires do not prevent free movement of base plate.

The timing light can be attached to the number 2 (top port) cylinder spark plug to check timing of that cylinder. The light should flash as the "B" mark with wedge aligns with timing lug when motor is running at 4500 rpm. If timing is correct for number 1 cylinder but not for number 2, the breaker point gap should be rechecked.

1971 And Later Models. Timing pointer (A – Fig. OM16-25) must align with 28° mark on flywheel with engine

FLAT SIDE DOWN

Fig. OM16-22 — The antireverse spring should be clipped onto crankshaft with the flat side down as shown.

Fig. OM16-24 — When timing light flashes, the "B" mark on flywheel used on 1969 and 1970 models should be aligned with lug on hoisting bracket. Ignition timing is at maximum advance. The "A" mark is not used on these motors.

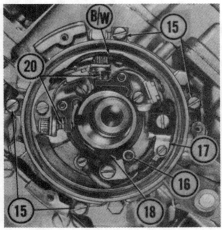

Fig. OM16-21 — View of breaker base with cap and rotor removed. Refer to Fig. OM16-20 for legend.

Fig. OM16-23 — View of maximum advance adjustment screw and initial timing marks. Speed control should be in fast position with base plate lever against stop screw.

Fig. OM16-25 — View of flywheel used after 1970. Full advanced ignition timing should occur when engine speed is above 4500 rpm.

3. DO NOT disconnect **any** wires while motor is running or while ignition switch is ON.

4. DO NOT use any tachometer except those approved for use with this system.

TROUBLE-SHOOTING. Use only approved procedures to prevent damage to the components. The fuel system should be checked first to make certain that faulty running is not caused by incorrect fuel mixture or contaminated fuel. If the motor continues to run after ignition switch is turned OFF, check the blocking diode as outlined in the appropriate paragraphs.

CHECKING FOR SPARK. Connect a spark tester to the four spark plug leads as shown in Fig. OM16-15, attempt to start motor and check for spark at the tester.

NOTE: A neon spark tester or four conventional spark plugs with the ground electrodes removed can be used in place of the tester shown.

Spark gap must not be more than ⅜ inch (9.5 mm). The coil wire is molded into coil and screwed into distributor cap. Do not attempt to pull the wire out of either end.

If spark occurs at all four points of ignition tester, check ignition timing. Also check condition of spark plugs and make certain that leads are connected to correct spark plugs.

If spark occurs regularly at some of the points and irregularly or not at all at other points, check condition of the spark plug leads.

If spark does not occur at any of the tester points, continue with remainder of tests.

WIRING. Engine missing, surging and failure to start or run can be caused by loose or corroded electrical connections. Check all terminals and plug-in connectors for tight clean contact. Also check all wiring for short circuit to ground. Make certain that wires are connected to the terminal block as shown in Fig. OM16-28 or Fig. OM16-29. A voltmeter or 12 volt test light can be used to check wiring. Connect one lead of voltmeter (or test light) to purple lead terminal (16, 17 and 18 – Fig. OM16-28 or 14, 15, 16 and 17 – Fig. OM16-29) and ground other lead. With ignition switch ON, battery voltage should be indicated. If these terminals are dead, check the 20 amp fuse, battery and all lead in wires and connectors.

If battery voltage is available at the terminal block on 115 hp motors, connect a jumper wire between terminal (14 and 15 – Fig. OM16-28) and terminal (16, 17 and 18), then attempt to start motor. If motor does not start, one or more of the ignition components (1, 2, 3, 4 and 5 – Fig. OM16-26 or related wiring are faulty.

CAUTION: Exercise care when making test with jumper wire attached; because, motor may start immediately before lower unit is in Neutral.

If the motor starts and runs properly with jumper wire connected (safety circuit bypassed), the ignition system is OK and one or more of the following components or connecting wires are faulty: Ignition safety circuit (9 – Fig. OM16-26), rectifier, shift diodes, alternator stator, tachometer or flywheel magnets. The ignition safety circuit is actuated by alternator output. Refer to the appropriate paragraphs for further testing of charging system and ignition safety circuit.

If battery voltage is available at the terminal block on 125 and 100 hp models, attempt to start motor. If motor does not start, any of the following components may be at fault; power pack, sensor, ignition coil, distributor cap, rotor or related wiring. Refer to the following paragraphs for inspection of individual components.

SENSOR. The sensor is used to actuate (trigger) the ignition circuit in much the same way as the breaker points of a standard ignition system. Any difficulty with the sensor or connecting wires will affect ignition of this system in a way similar to malfunctions of breaker points.

The air gap between the sensor and the trigger wheel should be 0.028 inch (0.71 mm) as checked in the DISTRIBUTOR paragraphs. To set the air gap, the flywheel, alternator stator,

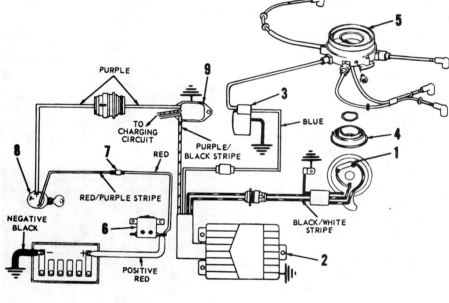

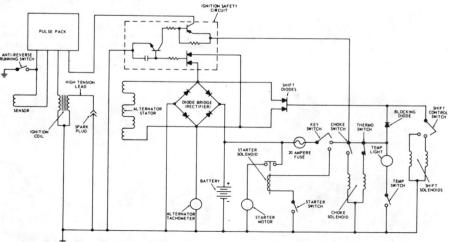

Fig. OM16-26 — The top view shows the basic parts and color of connecting wires for ignition system used on 1969 and 1970 115 hp motors. Lower view is schematic of complete electrical system.

1. Sensor unit	3. High tension coil	5. Distributor cap	7. Fuse (20 amp)
2. Amplifier	4. Rotor	6. Starter solenoid	8. Ignition switch	9. Ignition safety circuit

distributor cap and rotor must be removed.

After sensor air gap is correctly set, disconnect sensor wires at connector plug (S–Fig. OM16-28 or Fig. OM16-29) and attach one ohmmeter lead to each of the two connectors (2–Fig. OM16-30). The resistance through the sensor should be 4-6 ohms.

NOTE: Move the speed control linkage and the sensor wires while testing resistance to check for intermittent open circuit.

If resistance is within 4-6 ohms, detach one ohmmeter lead from connector plug and attach to ground. The test should indicate infinite resistance to ground.

NOTE: Move the wires and speed control linkage to check for short circuit to ground.

If the resistance through sensor is not 4-6 ohms or sensor circuit is shorted to ground, carefully check all wiring. If wires are not faulty, renew the sensor unit. Also, check the condition of the antireverse spring and the ground wire between distributor base and motor.

The ignition system can be triggered for test purposes by opening and closing the connection at (S–Fig. OM16-28 or Fig. OM16-29).

If the sensor circuit is not faulty, proceed with remaining tests.

POWER PACK. The power pack may be inspected with a low reading ammeter. Disconnect the 12 volt wire which provides power to the power pack. This wire will be purple with black stripe (15–Fig. OM16-28) on 115 hp motors or purple (14, 15, 16 or 17–Fig. OM16-29) on 100 and 125 hp motors.

NOTE: Wire to power pack may be at any one of the four locations (14, 15, 16 or 17) and must be isolated before detaching.

On all models, attach ammeter between terminal and disconnected wire. On 115 hp motors it is necessary to attach a jumper wire between terminal (14 and 15–Fig. OM16-28) and terminal (16, 17 and 18) in order to bypass the ignition safety circuit. On all models, maximum current draw should be 0.7 amperes with key switch "ON." Current draw should be between 1.5 and 2.5 amperes with engine running at 4500 rpm. Do not attempt to run motor with clip-on type connectors holding ammeter in circuit as possible poor connection may damage ignition units. Unsteady meter reading indicates faulty sensor, incorrect distributor base ground or faulty sensor wires. If current draw is higher or lower than specified, power pack is defective.

NOTE: Use extreme caution to make sure that test connections are not disconnected or shorted while power is "ON".

As an alternate method for testing the power pack, first make certain that the sensor circuit is checked completely as previously outlined. Remove blue lead (11–Fig. OM16-28 or Fig. OM16-29) from terminal and connect one lead from a neon test light to wire and other test light lead to motor ground. Turn the ignition switch ON, crank motor with electric starter and observe the neon bulb. If the bulb flickers while motor is cranking, the power pack is operating correctly and the high tension coil, distributor cap, rotor, spark plug leads or spark plugs should be suspected. If the neon bulb does not light, disconnect the high tension leads from spark plugs and proceed as follows:

Connect a jumper wire between terminal (14 and 15–Fig. OM16-28) and terminal (16, 17 and 18) if working on a 115 hp motor. On all models, keep the neon light connected and ignition switch "ON"; open and close connector plug (S–Fig. OM16-28 or Fig. OM16-29) several times while observing the neon test light. If the neon bulb flickers, check the sensor air gap and the ignition safety circuitry on models so equipped. Renew power pack if the neon test light still does not glow and the sensor is known to be OK.

COIL. The ignition high tension coil can be tested using an ignition tester available from several sources, including the following:

GRAHAM TESTERS, INC.
4220 Central Ave. N.E.
Minneapolis, Minn. 55421

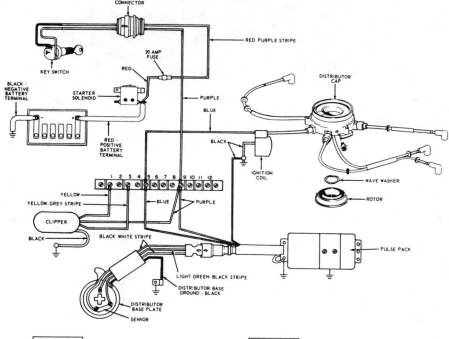

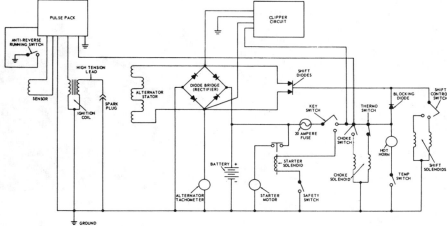

Fig. OM16-27 — The top view shows the basic parts and color of connecting wires for ignition system used on 125 hp motors. Lower view is schematic of complete electrical system.

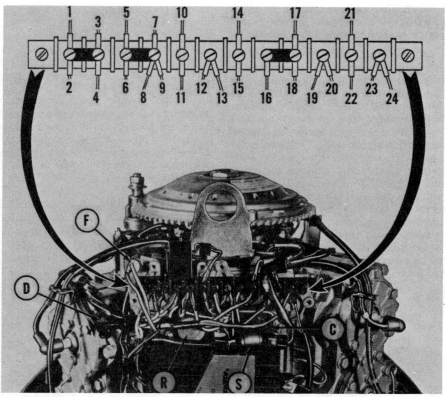

Fig. OM16-28 — Rear view of 115 hp motor showing location of terminal block. Inset shows location of wires. Refer to Fig. OM16-29 for wiring used on early 100 and 125 hp motors.

1, 2, 3 & 4. Yellow	10 & 11. Blue	16, 17 & 18. Purple
5. Yellow/gray stripe	12. Red	19 & 20. Purple/green stripe
6. Gray	13. Red/yellow stripe	21 & 22. Purple/yellow stripe
7, 8 & 9. Yellow/gray stripe	14 & 15. Purple/black stripe	23 & 24. Purple/white stripe

minal (14 and 15) and ground other lead. If light glows only when motor is being cranked, the ignition safety circuit is operating correctly. If the light does not glow, proceed with remaining tests.

Attach one test light lead to ground and other lead to terminal (1, 2, 3 and 4), then attempt to start motor. Disconnect lead from terminal (1, 2, 3 and 4) and attach to terminal (5, 6, 7, 8 and 9). Attempt to start motor again. If the light glows when attached to terminal (1, 2, 3 and 4) and terminal (5, 6, 7, 8 and 9); but does not glow when attached to terminal (14 and 15), the ignition safety circuit unit (C) is faulty and should be renewed. If the test light glows only when attached to terminal 16, 17 and 18) and does not glow when attached as described in other tests, check alternator stator, shift diodes and rectifier.

Disconnect the purple with black stripe wire (15) which leads to the ignition safety circuit (C). Attach one lead from test light to the disconnected wire and ground other lead. Turn the ignition switch ON. If the light glows, without cranking motor, disconnect the yellow wire to rectifier (2), yellow/gray to rectifier (8), yellow wire to shift diode (3). If the test light glows when ignition switch is turned on after wires are disconnected, renew the ignition safety circuit (C). If the test light does not glow after wires (2, 3 and 8) are disconnected, the shift diode (D) or rectifier (R) is faulty and

MERC-O-TRONIC
INSTRUMENTS CORP.
215 Branch St.
Almont, Mich. 48003

Coil test procedures and specifications are available from the manufacturers of the tester.

NOTE: The high tension coil lead is molded into coil and screwed into distributor cap.

IGNITION SAFETY CIRCUIT. The ignition safety circuit (9 – Fig. OM16-26) is installed on 115 hp motors to prevent motor from starting before the lower unit is supplied with current to shift into neutral. The safety circuit is actuated by alternator output. Refer to the WIRING paragraphs in this trouble-shooting section for a preliminary check of the ignition safety circuit using a 12 volt test bulb with wires for attaching to the test points.

Attach one lead from test light to terminal (16, 17 and 18 – Fig. OM16-28), ground the other lead and turn the ignition switch ON. If light does not glow, check battery, ignition switch, fuse (F) and connecting wires. If light glows, proceed with remaining tests.

Attach one lead from test light to ter-

Fig. OM16-29 — Rear view of wiring and ignition system components common to 125 hp models and early 100 hp models.

	9. Yellow/gray stripe	
1, 2, 3 & 4. Yellow	10 & 11. Blue	
5, 6 & 7. Yellow/gray stripe	12 & 13. Red	18 & 19. Purple/green stripe
8. Gray	14, 15, 16 & 17. Purple	20 & 21. Purple/yellow stripe
		22 & 23. Purple/white stripe

should be checked as outlined in the following paragraphs.

SHIFT DIODE. Failure of the shift diode (D – Fig. OM16-28 or Fig. OM16-29) may prevent motor from starting or may cause the lower unit to shift to forward gear immediately after ignition switch is turned OFF.

To check the shift diode, disconnect the wires (yellow, yellow/gray stripe and purple/green) from terminal block, then remove diode (D). Use a continuity light (with a battery of less than 12 volts) or ohmmeter for checking. Attach one test light (or ohmmeter) lead to the purple/green wire and other lead to the yellow wire; then, reverse the test leads. The test light or ohmmeter should indicate continuity with one connection and NO continuity with leads reversed. Attach test leads similarly to the yellow/gray wire and the purple/green wire; then, reverse leads. Continuity should again exist with one connection; but not when leads are reversed. If either of the two tests allow current to pass in both directions or prevent current from passing in either direction, renew the shift diode.

CLIPPER. Failure of the clipper unit (31 – Fig. OM16-32) should be suspected if any of the following occur: Battery current is momentarily interrupted with motor running; battery charge is low and charging system checks OK; CD power pack inoperative; fuses blow repeatedly.

Clipper unit may be checked with an ohmmeter in the following manner: Disconnect **all** leads from clipper to terminal block before making any checks. Correct ohmmeter test lead polarity must be determined by connecting meter leads to the yellow lead and the purple/green lead of a good **shift diode**. Refer to Shift Diode check in previous section. If ohmmeter shows little or no

Fig. OM16-30 – The sensor circuit can be checked at terminals (2) using an ohmmeter.

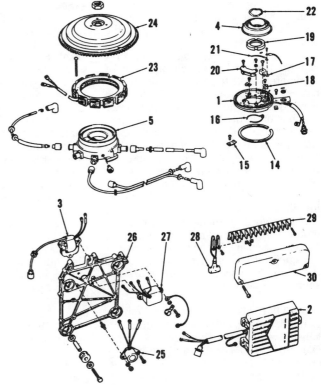

Fig. OM16-31 – Exploded view of the ignition and alternator system components used on 1969 and 1970 115 hp motors.

1. Distributor base plate
2. Amplifier
3. High tension coil
4. Rotor
5. Distributor cap
14. Retainer ring
15. Clip
16. Antireverse spring
17. Antireverse contact
18. Stop
19. Trigger wheel
20. Sensor
21. Sensor leads
22. Wave washer
23. Alternator stator
24. Flywheel
25. Rectifier
26. Bracket
27. Ignition safety circuit
28. Shift diode
29. Terminal block
30. Cover

resistance through shift diode, lead attached to yellow wire will be "ground lead" for purposes of checking clipper. If resistance is high, opposite lead will be ground.

To check clipper, momentarily touch the purple lead to the case of the clipper. Connect the ohmmeter "ground lead" to ground (either the case or the black wire) of the clipper. Connect other ohmmeter lead to yellow wire of clipper. Renew clipper if reading is less than 300 ohms. If an infinite resistance reading is obtained, disconnect ohmmeter lead from yellow wire, momentarily short purple wire against case and connect ohmmeter to yellow/gray wire while retaining original ground connection. Renew clipper if reading is less than 300 ohms. If an infinite reading is obtained, remove lead from yellow/gray wire, momentarily short purple wire against case and connect ohmmeter lead to purple wire. If meter moves and then returns to infinity or registers less than 300 ohms, renew clipper unit. If an infinite resistance reading is obtained, disconnect ohmmeter, momentarily short purple wire against case, connect "ground lead" from ohmmeter to purple wire and other ohmmeter lead to ground of clipper. Clipper is good if meter swings toward zero and returns to infinity. Renew clipper if meter needle does not move or if meter needle moves to zero and stays.

RECTIFIER. Failure of the rectifier should prevent motor from starting

unless the ignition safety circuit is bypassed.

To check the rectifier (R – Fig. OM16-28 or Fig. OM16-29), disconnect wires at terminal block from rectifier (yellow, yellow/gray, and red/yellow). Connect one lead of ohmmeter to yellow wire from rectifier and attach other ohmmeter lead to motor ground. Check continuity, then reverse the ohmmeter leads. The ohmmeter should indicate low resistance (near zero) with one connection and high resistance (near infinity) with leads reversed. Repeat this test (including reversing the ohmmeter leads) at the ground connection and yellow/gray lead; between the yellow and red/yellow leads; then, between red/yellow and yellow/gray leads.

If any of the tests indicate near zero resistance in both directions or near infinite resistance in both directions, renew the rectifier.

NOTE: A continuity test (with a battery of less than 12 volts) can be used to check condition of rectifier instead of ohmmeter. Light should glow with one connection, but should not when leads are reversed.

BLOCKING DIODE. Failure of the blocking diode may allow motor to continue running after ignition switch is turned OFF or the lower unit may remain in forward gear until after motor starts.

The blocking diode is located near the ignition switch with the purple wire attached to the "IGN." terminal of switch.

The purple/green wire from diode is equipped with a quick release connector which attaches to a wire leading to the shift control switch.

To check the blocking diode, first remove the diode. Attach one lead of ohmmeter or continuity test light (with a battery of less than 12 volts) to each wire from diode. Observe ohmmeter reading or light, then reverse the test connections. Current should pass through diode with one connection (low resistance or light on) but should not pass current with leads reversed. If current passes both directions or does not pass in either direction, renew the blocking diode.

If the blocking diode checks OK but motor continues to run after ignition switch is turned OFF or Forward gear is engaged until after motor starts, check the switches, wires and connectors for shorts or open circuits.

DISTRIBUTOR. To service components of the distributor, including the sensor, remove the flywheel (24—Figs. OM16-31 or OM16-32) and alternator stator (23). The distributor is retained by the same three screws that attach alternator stator and these screws are coated with Loctite. The coil high-tension wire and the spark plug wires are screwed into distributor cap. Remove the spring washer (22) and rotor (4). If the trigger wheel (19) is to be removed, carefully pry unit off crankshaft using two screwdrivers. Remainder of disassembly will be self-evident.

The antireverse spring (16) is clipped onto crankshaft and when crankshaft is turning in normal direction, the coiled projection is against stop (18). If the crankshaft turns in counterclockwise direction, the antireverse spring turns with the crankshaft until it grounds the ignition sensor system through contact (17).

When assembling, lubricate the crankshaft lightly, then clip the antireverse spring onto crankshaft with flat side down (Fig. OM16-22). Install retainer (14—Fig. OM16-31 or Fig. OM16-32) in groove with flat side toward base (1). Position base assembly around crankshaft with coil or antireverse spring (16) between stop (18) and contact (17). Make certain that the speed control link can be connected to distributor base. Install the clips (15) and be sure that base rotates freely with no binding. The base retainer (14) and bushing surface of base (1) can be oiled lightly before assembling. Install trigger wheel (19) with notch aligned with drive pin in crankshaft. Install sensor (20) with 0.028 inch (0.71 mm) clearance between sensor surface and trigger wheel (19). Make certain that sensor wires are correctly positioned and not shorted or broken.

Install rotor (4) making certain that lug engages notch in crankshaft. Install wave washer (22), then position distributor cap (5) and alternator stator over the distributor base plate. Make certain that the coil high tension lead and spark plug wires are screwed into cap and correctly positioned. Coat the three alternator stator and distributor cap retaining screws with Loctite and tighten the

screws evenly to 48-60 in.-lbs. (5.4-6.7 N·m) torque. Initial timing can be set using the timing marks shown in Fig. OM16-23; however, a power timing light and the flywheel timing marks should be used for final setting. Refer to TIMING paragraphs. Make certain that tapers in flywheel and on crankshaft are clean and dry before installing flywheel. The flywheel drive key should be parallel with crankshaft center line, NOT aligned with taper. Flywheel nut on all 1972 models should be torqued to 100-105 ft.-lbs. (136-143 N·m). Flywheel nut on all earlier models should be torqued to 70-85 ft.-lbs. (95-116 N·m).

IGNITION TIMING. To check the maximum advance ignition timing, connect a power timing light to the number 1 (top starboard) cylinder spark plug and run motor at 4500 rpm in forward gear.

When timing 1969 and 1970 motors, the "B" timing mark with straight line must align with timing lug on hoisting bracket as shown in Fig. OM16-24. If timing is incorrect, loosen locknut and turn the spark advance adjusting screw (Fig. OM16-23) as required. Make certain that wires do not prevent free movement of base plate. When timing 1971 and 1972 motors, the 28 degree mark on the flywheel must align with timing pointer (A—Fig. OM16-25). If timing is incorrect, loosen locknut and turn spark advance adjusting screw (Fig. OM 16-23). One turn of screw will change ignition approximately 1 degree. Be sure wires do not prevent free movement of distributor base plate.

1973-1977 Models

The capacitor discharge ignition system used on motors from 1973 to 1977 does not have a distributor or breaker points. Magnets built into central portion of flywheel and two sensor coils are used to trigger the ignition unit.

This ignition is extremely durable in normal operation, but can be easily damaged by improper operating, testing or servicing procedures. To prevent damage to components, observe the following list of precautions and use only approved methods for checking and servicing system.

1. DO NOT disconnect any wires while motor is running or while ignition switch is ON.
2. DO NOT use any tachometer except those approved for use with this system.
3. DO NOT hold spark plug wires while checking for spark.
4. DO make certain that all wiring connections are clean and tightly joined.

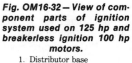

Fig. OM16-32—View of component parts of ignition system used on 125 hp and breakerless ignition 100 hp motors.

1. Distributor base
2. Amplifier
3. Ignition coil
4. Rotor assy.
5. Distributor cap assy.
14. Distributor base retainer
15. Clip
16. Reverse cut off spring
17. Antireverse contact
18. Stop
19. Trigger wheel
20. Sensor
21. Sensor leads
22. Spring washer
23. Stator
24. Flywheel
25. Rectifier
26. Mount bracket
28. Shift diode
29. Terminal block
30. Cover
31. Clipper
32. Fuse (20 amp)

5. DO make certain that wires do not bind moving parts or touch metal edges where they may chafe through insulation.

TROUBLE-SHOOTING. Use only approved procedures to prevent damage to the components. The fuel system should be checked first to make certain that faulty running is not caused by incorrect mixture or contaminated fuel.

CHECKING FOR SPARK. Disconnect spark plug leads at spark plugs and connect them to a needle point spark checker, similar to unit in Fig. OM16-15, with four gaps used set at 7/16 inch (11.1 mm). Consistent, strong spark indicates ignition system functioning properly; suspect spark plugs, timing, improper wiring to ignition coils or to spark plugs.

Weak, inconsistent spark or spark from only one or two ignition coils; suspect sensor coils or ignition coils. Weak, inconsistent spark from all four ignition coils; suspect charge coils. No spark at all; suspect power pack.

WIRING. Engine missing, surging and failure to start or run can be caused by loose or corroded electrical connections. Check all terminals and plug-in connectors for tight clean contact. Also check all wiring for short to ground.

SENSOR COILS. Two sensor coils (1 and 2 – Fig. OM16-34) are used to trigger ignition at each cylinder. Sensor coil 1/3 (1) controls ignition for cylinders 1 and 3 while sensor 2/4 (2) controls ignition for cylinders 2 and 4. Sensor coils may be checked by disconnecting the white/black and black/white lead wires from terminal #2, #4, #9 and #12 (see Fig. OM16-34). Resistance between the leads of sensor coils 1/3 or sensor coil 2/4 should be 6.5-10.5 ohms. Sensor coils should also be checked for a short to ground. Defective sensor coils are not renewable separately, timer base assembly (7 – Fig. OM16-33) must be renewed.

CHARGE COILS. Charge coils may be checked by reading resistance between brown wire attached to terminal #7 and brown/yellow wire attached to terminal #8. Correct resistance is 555-705 ohms. There must also be infinite resistance between either lead and ground. Stator assembly (6 – Fig. OM16-33) must be renewed if charge coils are defective.

IGNITION COILS. Ignition coils may be checked with standard ignition coil test equipment. Complete operating instructions and coil test specifications will be included with tester.

POWER PACK. Power pack contains storage capacitor, rectifier and SCR (silicone controlled rectifiers) switches for ignition operation. Misfire in one or more cylinders or complete ignition system failure may be caused by malfunction of power pack components. If power pack is suspected cause of ignition trouble, install a known-to-be-good power pack into ignition system and check operation. Power pack is available only as a unit assembly.

STATOR AND TIMER BASE ASSEMBLY. Stator (6 – Fig. OM16-33) and timer base (7) may be serviced after removal of the flywheel. Stator assembly is secured to the power head by four screws. The timer base may be removed after the stator by removing the four screws and clips along the outside edge.

When reassembling unit, make certain that wiring does not restrict free movement of timer base. Inspect taper on crankshaft and taper in flywheel. Install flywheel key with flat of key parallel to center line of crankshaft, NOT surface of taper. Tighten flywheel nut to 100-105 ft.-lbs. (136-143 N·m) torque.

IGNITION TIMING. Connect a power timing light to number 1 (top) cylinder spark plug. Timing pointer should align with appropriate degree mark on flywheel with motor running at full speed in gear (Fig. OM16-25). Stop engine and turn spark advance stop screw (A – Fig. OM16-8) if timing is incorrect. Turning screw clockwise one full turn will retard ignition timing approximately one degree.

Refer to following table for full advance ignition timing:

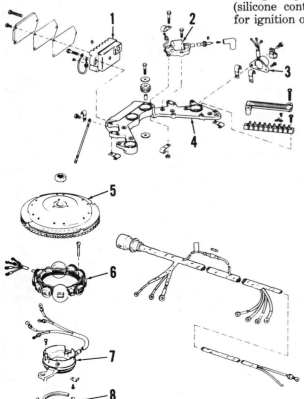

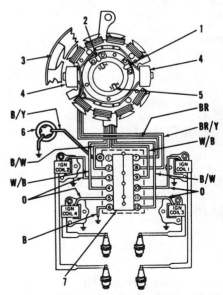

Fig. OM16-33 – Exploded view of ignition components used on models from 1973 through 1977.

1. Power pack
2. Ignition coils
3. Rectifier
4. Bracket
5. Flywheel
6. Stator
7. Timer base assy.
8. Retainer ring

Fig. OM16-34 – Schematic of breakerless ignition system used on 1973-1977 models.

1. Sensor coil 1/3	7. Power pack
2. Sensor coil 2/4	B. Black
3. Charge magnet	BR. Brown
4. Charge coils	O. Orange
5. Sensor magnet	W. White
6. Ignition switch	Y. Yellow

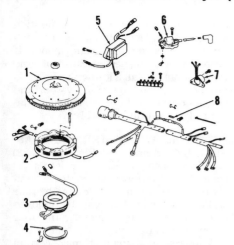

Fig. OM16-35 — View of ignition components typical of the type used on models after 1977.

1. Flywheel
2. Stator
3. Timer base
4. Retainer ring
5. Power pack
6. Ignition coil
7. Rectifier
8. Fuse (20 amp)

Models	Degrees BTDC
85 hp	
1973, 1974	28
1975, 1976, 1977	26
115 hp	
1973, 1974	26
1975, 1976	24
1977	28
135 and 140 hp	
1973, 1974	22
1975, 1976	20
1977	28

Models After 1977

All models are equipped with a capacitor discharge ignition system which is triggered by sensor coils on stator plate. To prevent damage to components, note the following list of precautions:

1. DO NOT disconnect any wires while motor is running or while ignition switch is ON.
2. DO NOT use any tachometer except those approved for use with this system.
3. DO NOT hold spark plug wires while checking for spark.
4. DO make certain that all wiring connections are clean and tightly joined.
5. DO make certain that wires do not bind moving parts or touch metal edges where they may chafe through insulation.

TROUBLE-SHOOTING. Use only approved procedures to prevent damage to the components. The fuel system should be checked first to make certain that faulty running is not caused by fuel starvation, incorrect mixture or contaminated fuel.

CHECKING FOR SPARK. Disconnect spark plug leads at spark plugs and connect them to a needle point spark checker, similar to unit in Fig. OM16-15, with four gaps used set at ½ inch (12.7 mm). Consistent, strong spark indicates ignition system functioning properly; suspect spark plugs, timing, improper wiring to ignition coils or to spark plugs.

Weak, inconsistent spark or spark from only one or two ignition coils; suspect sensor coils or ignition coils. Weak, inconsistent spark from all four ignition coils; suspect charge coils. No spark at all; suspect power pack.

WIRING. Engine missing, surging and failure to start or run can be caused by loose or corroded electrical connections. Check all terminals and plug-in connectors for tight clean contact. Also check all wiring for short circuit to ground.

CHARGE COILS. Models after 1977 except 1985 and 1986 120 and 140 hp models use two charge coils contained in the stator assembly. Models with 120 and 140 hp in 1985 and 1986 use one charge coil contained in the stator assembly. To check charge coil or coils, disconnect the two-wire connector (one per bank of cylinders on two charge coil models) and connect an ohmmeter to terminals A and B (Fig. OM16-36) in connector leading to stator. Renew stator assembly if resistance is not 485-635 ohms on two charge coil models and 535-585 ohms on one charge coil models. Connect negative ohmmeter lead to an engine ground and positive ohmmeter lead to connector terminal A, then to connector terminal B. Infinite resistance should exist between A terminal and engine ground and B terminal and engine ground. If not, charge coil or charge coil lead is shorting to ground. To check charge coil output, use Merc-O-Tronic Model 781, Stevens Model CD77 or a suitable peak voltage tester. Connect black tester lead to terminal A in connector leading to stator and red tester lead to terminal B. Turn tester

Fig. OM16-36 — Ignition wiring schematic for models after 1977 except 1985 and 1986 120 and 140 hp models. Models 120 and 140 in 1985 and 1986 use only one power pack (2). First letter indicates connector terminal while letters after dash denote wire color, i.e., A — BR/Y indicates terminal A is connected to a brown/yellow wire.

1. Stator
2. Power packs
3. Ignition switch
4. Ignition coils
B. Black
BL. Blue
BR. Brown
G. Green
O. Orange
W. White
Y. Yellow

knobs to "NEG (−)" and "500." Crank engine while observing tester. Repeat test on other charge coil on two charge coil models. Renew stator assembly if meter reads below 160 volts on either coil test on two charge coil models or 175 volts on one charge coil model.

SENSOR COILS. Models after 1977 except 1985 and 1986 120 and 140 hp models use two sensor coils contained in the timer base assembly. Models with 120 and 140 hp in 1985 and 1986 use four sensor coils contained in the timer base assembly. To check sensor coils on two sensor coil models, connect an ohmmeter to terminals A and B (Fig. OM16-36) and then A and C in four-wire connector leading to timer base. Repeat test on other sensor coil connection. Renew timer base if resistance readings are not 30-50 ohms. Connect negative ohmmeter lead to an engine ground and positive ohmmeter lead to connector terminal A, then B and then C. Repeat test on other sensor coil connection. Infinite resistance should exist between all terminal connections and engine ground. If not, sensor coil or sensor coil lead is shorting to ground. To check sensor coil output, use Merc-O-Tronic Model 781, Stevens Model CD77 or a suitable peak voltage tester. Connect black tester lead to timer base connector terminal A and red tester lead to terminal B. On Merc-O-Tronic Model 781, turn knobs to "POS (+)" and "5" and on Stevens Model CD77, turn knobs to "S" and "5." Crank engine while observing tester. Repeat test with black tester lead still connected to terminal A and connect red tester lead to terminal C. Repeat test on other sensor coil connection. Renew timer base assembly if meter reads below 0.3 volts.

To check sensor coils on four sensor coil models, connect an ohmmeter to terminals A and E (Fig. OM16-37), then B and E, then C and E and then D and E in five-wire connector leading to timer base. Renew timer base if resistance readings are not 30-50 ohms. Connect negative ohmmeter lead to an engine

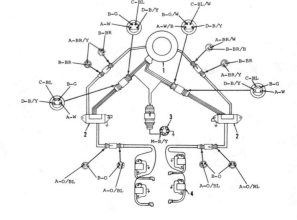

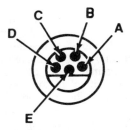

Fig. OM16-37 — View identifying wire terminals in timer base assembly connector on 1985 and 1986 120 and 140 hp models.

ground and positive ohmmeter lead to connector terminal A, then B, then C, then D and then E. Infinite resistance should exist between all terminal connections and engine ground. If not, sensor coil or sensor coil lead is shorting to ground. To check sensor coil output, use Merc-O-Tronic Model 781, Stevens Model CD77 or a suitable peak voltage tester. Connect black tester lead to timer base connector terminal E and red tester lead to terminal A. On Merc-O-Tronic Model 781, turn knobs to "POS (+)" and "5" and on Stevens Model CD77, turns knobs to "S" and "5." Crank engine while observing tester. Repeat test with black tester lead still connected to terminal E and connect red tester lead to terminal B, then C and then to D. Renew timer base if meter reads below 0.3 volts.

POWER PACK. To check power pack output, first reconnect stator and timer base connectors. Use Merc-O-Tronic Model 781, Stevens Model CD77 or a suitable peak voltage tester. Connect black tester lead to a suitable engine ground. Connect red tester lead to wire leading to one of the four ignition coils. Turn tester knobs to "NEG (−)" and "500." Crank engine while observing tester. Repeat test on other leads. Renew power pack on 1985 and 1986 120 and 140 hp models if readings are not at least 175 volts or higher. Renew power pack or packs on all other models

Fig. OM16-40 — View of starting safety switch (S) on models prior to 1973, and speed control lever (L). Refer to text for adjustment.

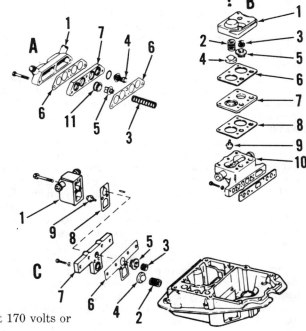

Fig. OM16-41 — Exploded view of the thermostat and pressure relief valve components. Components in (A) are used on all models after 1976 (except 1985 and 1986 120 and 140 hp models). Components in (B) are used on all models prior to 1973. Components in (C) are used on all 1973-1976 models.

1. Cover
2. Thermostat spring
3. Pressure relief valve spring
4. Thermostat
5. Pressure relief valve
6. Gasket
7. Plate
8. Gasket
9. Thermostat control unit
10. Housing
11. Grommet

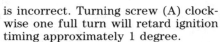

if readings are not at least 170 volts or higher.

NOTE: Power pack on 120 and 140 hp models marked "CDL" have an internal device to limit engine speed to 6100 rpm.

IGNITION COILS. Renew ignition coil or coils if no other ignition component is found faulty.

IGNITION TIMING. The timing pointer is adjustable. If the timing pointer or intake manifold has been disturbed, a dial indicator must be used to verify the timing pointer alignment with flywheel TDC mark when the number 1 (top, starboard) cylinder piston is at TDC. Remove the number 1 cylinder spark plug and install a dial indicator so indicator plunger extends through the plug opening and into the cylinder. Position the number 1 cylinder piston at TDC. Align timing pointer with TDC (0 degree) mark on flywheel and secure pointer position. Remove dial indicator and reassemble.

To check maximum advance ignition timing, connect a power timing light to number 1 cylinder spark plug lead. Start engine and shift into forward gear, then accelerate to full throttle. Note flywheel marks when timing light flashes. Ignition should occur at 26 degrees BTDC on 85-hp models and at 28 degrees BTDC on all other models prior to 1983. On models after 1982, consult engine decal for maximum spark advance specifications. Ignition should occur at 22 degrees BTDC on 1985 120- and 140-hp models and 17-19 degrees BTDC on 1986 120- and 140-hp models. Stop engine and turn spark advance stop screw (A—Figs. OM16-7 or OM16-14) if timing

is incorrect. Turning screw (A) clockwise one full turn will retard ignition timing approximately 1 degree.

On all models except 1985 and 1986 120 and 140 hp models, check pickup timing as follows: Connect a power timing light to number 1 cylinder spark plug lead. Advance speed control lever until throttle plates just start to open. Start engine and note throttle pickup timing with the timing light. Throttle pickup timing should be 0-3 degrees BTDC on 115- and 140-hp models prior to 1979 and 5 degrees BTDC on all other models. If not, stop engine and adjust position of yoke (Y). One complete turn will equal approximately 2 degrees.

STARTING SAFETY SWITCH

The starting safety switch on models prior to 1973 prevents the motor from being started at advanced throttle. The switch (S—Fig. OM16-40) is actuated by a cam on the speed control lever (L) and should close at approximtely midpoint on the cam slope. Continuity should exist through the switch during the low speed section of lever movement and should open as the speed control lever passes the starting position. Adjust by loosening the screws (2) and repositioning the switch.

COOLING SYSTEM

THERMOSTAT. A cooling system thermostat is used to maintain an even temperature of 130°-150°F (54°-65°C). Later models have two thermostats as shown in Fig. OM16-41 and Fig. OM16-42. Temperatures can be checked using heat sensitive sticks such as "Markal Thermomelt Stik." A 125°F (52°C) stick should melt, but a 163°F (73°C). stick should not melt, after engine reaches normal operating temperature. If the 125°F (52°C) stick does not melt, the thermostat may be stuck open. Overheating could be caused by damaged thermostat, damaged pressure control valve, exhaust cover gaskets leaking, head gaskets leaking, water passages obstructed, water passages leaking or water pump failure. The control panel on 1969 and 1970 motors is fitted with a temperature warning light, later motors are fitted with a "hot horn." Either of these, when operating, indicates an overheated condition in the power head. A temperature sensing switch (16–Fig. OM16-45) located in the starboard cylinder head on early models and in both cylinder heads on later models is used to activate these warning devices. Temperature switch operation may be checked with a continuity tester and a high temperature thermometer. Place switch and thermometer in oil that is being heated. Switch should show a closed circuit at 205°-217°F (96°-102°C) and should open again at 168°-182°F (75°-83°C).

On all models except 1985 and 1986 120 and 140 hp models, the thermostat housing is located at rear of adapter plate attaching power head to low unit, below the ignition power pack and bracket. Refer to Fig. OM16-41. On 1985 and 1986 120 and 140 hp models, a thermostat assembly is located at the top of each cylinder head. Refer to Fig. OM16-42.

On later 85, 115 and 140 (prior to 1985) hp models, check valves (3–Fig. OM16-41) open at high engine rpm when high water pump impeller speed increases water pressure. On all other models, check valve (3) closes when ther-

mostat opens to expel water and prevent return of hot water to water pump. Check valve is open when thermostat is closed so water will circulate through engine until water reaches opening temperature of thermostat.

WATER PUMP. The water pump is mounted on top surface of gearcase housing. The rubber impeller is mounted on and driven by the drive shaft. To remove the water pump, separate the lower unit (gearcase) from the drive shaft and exhaust housing.

Lip of seal (16–Fig. OM16-51, 9–Fig. OM16-59 and 4–Fig. OM16-66) should be down. Screws attaching water pump housing and cover should be coated with OMC Gasket Sealing Compound or equivalent. Apply OMC Adhesive M or equivalent to bottom of impeller plate before installing. Lubricate impeller and hold blades in while installing housing. The drive shaft can be rotated clockwise while assembling, but should not be turned backwards.

POWER HEAD

R&R AND DISASSEMBLE. Remove the flywheel and ignition and charging components if needed. Mark wires for identification, disconnect interfering wires, then remove the bracket (26–Fig. OM16-20) on pre-1973 models and electrical components on all models. Mark wires for identification, then disconnect wires from starter solenoid, starting safety switch, starter motor, temperature switch, choke solenoid and shift cables on models prior to 1973. Disconnect upper end of shift rod shown in Fig. OM16-43 on 1973 through 1977 models or Fig. OM16-64 on all models after 1977 except 1985 and 1986 120 and 140 hp models. On 1985 and 1986 120 and 140 hp models, remove threaded pin

from shift cam located at base of intake manifold on the port side. On models so equipped or as needed, proceed as follows: Remove air silencer, carburetors and fuel pump. Remove exhaust housing rear cover, remove screws attaching motor lower covers and disconnect hoses from thermostat housing. Further disassembly may be desirable depending upon type of repairs. On all models except 1985 and 1986 120 and 140 hp models, remove four nuts and eight screws (Fig. OM16-44), then lift power head from lower unit. On 1985 and 1986 120 and 140 hp models, remove four screws and one nut from each side of upper end of drive shaft housing and two screws and one nut at rear of upper end of drive shaft housing. Lift power head from lower unit.

The transfer port covers, exhaust covers, cylinder heads and inlet manifold should be carefully removed, by loosening screws evenly, to prevent warpage. Remove screws attaching crankcase heads (23 and 27–Fig. OM16-46) to crankcase. Drive the crankcase aligning taper pin or pins out toward front, then unbolt and remove the forward crankcase half.

NOTE: Be sure to remove the four Allen head screws located in the inlet passages before attempting to separate crankcase halves.

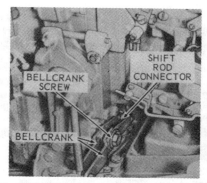

Fig. OM16-43 – Disconnect shift rod connector from bellcrank on 1973 through 1977 models to separate power head and lower unit.

Fig. OM16-44 – View identifying screws and nuts for removal of power head on all models except 1985 and 1986 120 and 140 hp models. Refer to text.

Fig. OM16-42 – On 1985 and 1986 120 and 140 hp models, a thermostat assembly is located behind cover (T) on both the port and starboard cylinder heads. The thermostat and pressure relief valve are a single unit.

Pistons, rods and crankshaft are now accessible for removal and overhaul as outlined in the appropriate following paragraphs. When assembling, follow procedure outline in the ASSEMBLY paragraphs.

ASSEMBLY. When assembling, the crankcase and inlet manifold must be completely sealed against both vacuum and pressure. Exhaust manifold and cylinder heads must be sealed against water leakage and pressure. Mating surfaces of water intake and exhaust areas between lower unit and power head must form a tight seal. It is recommended that all mating surfaces (including joints using gaskets) be carefully inspected for nicks, burrs, erosion and warpage which might interfere with a tight seal. All of these surfaces may be lapped if necessary to provide a smooth, flat surface, but DO NOT remove any more metal than absolutely necessary. The mating surfaces between the crankcase halves (9 and 15 – Fig. OM16-45) **MUST NOT** be lowered, but can be polished to remove imperfections only.

The crankcase halves are positively located during assembly by the use of a tapered dowel pin or pins. Check to make certain that the dowel pin or pins are not bent, nicked or distorted and that dowel pin hole or holes are clean and true. When installing dowel pin or pins, make sure that pin or pins are fully seated, but do not use excessive force.

On models prior to 1979, the mating surfaces of crankcase halves are sealed by means of the sealing strips (14) which fit in grooves in face of front crankcase half (15). When installing these strips, first make certain that the complete surface, including the grooves, is absolutely clean and free from old cement, nicks or foreign matter. Position the crankshaft (32 – Fig. OM16-46) with top main bearing (22 through 25), center main bearing (34 and 35), lower main bearing (26 through 31) and sealing rings (33) assembled into block.

NOTE: The four bearing retainer plate screws (31S) should be installed loosely and should not be tightened until assembly is completed.

Install the piston and connecting rod assemblies to the crankshaft.

NOTE: Make certain that center main bearing outer race is seated correctly on the retaining dowel pin.

When reassembling crankcase, make sure mating surfaces of crankcase halves are completely clean and free of old cement, nicks and burrs. On models

Fig. OM16-45—Exploded view of early crankcase and associated parts. Later models, except for 1985 and 1986 120- and 140-hp models, are similar. Sealing strips (14) are not used after 1978. On 1985 and 1986 120- and 140-hp models, covers (1) and cylinder heads (2) are one piece. Exhaust cover (4) and transfer port covers (10) are cast into cylinder block (9). Refer to Fig. OM16-46 for exploded view of crankshaft and related parts.

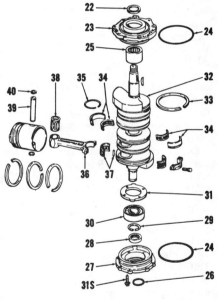

Fig. OM16-46 — Exploded view of the crankshaft and associated parts. Bearing (25) and head (23) are a one-piece unit on models after 1972. Two piston rings are used on later models. Two "O" rings (24) for top and bottom are used on 1985 and 1986 120 and 140 hp models. On 1986 90 and 110 hp models, loose needle bearings and two thrust washers are used in place of caged bearing (38).

1. Cylinder head covers	7. Choke thermo unit	12. Throttle control rod
2. Cylinder heads	8. Hose to thermostat housing	13. Ignition control rod
3. Water passage cover		14. Sealing strips
4. Exhaust cover	9. Cylinder block	15. Crankcase front half
5. Exhaust inner cover	10. Transfer port covers	16. Temperature warning switch
6. Hoisting bracket	11. Speed control lever	17. Ignition control lever
		18. Spring
		19. Throttle cam
		20. Bushing
		21. Bushing

22. Seal	
23. Crankcase upper bearing head	31S. Attaching screws
24. "O" rings	32. Crankshaft
25. Top main bearing	33. Seal rings (6 used)
26. "O" ring	34. Center main bearing
27. Crankcase lower bearing head	35. Retaining ring
28. Seal	36. Connecting rod
29. Snap ring	37. Crankpin bearing & cage
30. Lower main bearing	38. Piston pin bearing
31. Bearing retainer plate	39. Piston pin
	40. Snap ring

449

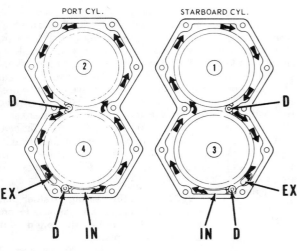

PORT CYL.   STARBOARD CYL.

Fig. OM16-47 — On all models except 1985 and 1986 120 and 140 hp models, water deflectors (D) must be installed in locations shown for proper water flow around cylinders.

prior to 1979, install sealing strips (14) and trim ends to extend approximately 1/32 inch (0.79 mm) into bearing bores, then sparingly apply OMC Adhesive "M" to cylinder half of crankcase only. On models after 1978, apply OMC Gel-Seal II to one crankcase mating surface. Do not use sealers which will harden and prevent contact between crankcase mating surfaces. Immediately assemble crankcase halves after applying sealer and position halves by installing locating taper pin or pins; then install and tighten crankcase retaining screws to the torque listed in the CONDENSED SERVICE DATA table. When tightening the retaining screws, start in the center and work toward ends. Tighten the lower main bearing plate screws (31S – Fig. OM16-46) to the correct torque and check the crankshaft for binding.

On all models except 1985 and 1986 120 and 140 hp models, note location of water deflectors shown in Fig. OM16-47. Deteriorated water deflectors may cause overheating and hot spots. Deflectors are not as tall as water passages so water may drain from water jacket.

On all models except 1985 and 1986 120 and 140 hp models, use a non-hardening sealer on all gasket surfaces and complete assembly of cylinder head and covers. Threads of screws should be coated with nonhardening sealer to prevent water damage to threads, especially on motors operated in salt water. On 1985 and 1986 120 and 140 hp models, install cylinder head gaskets and intake manifold gasket without a sealer.

PISTONS, PINS, RINGS AND CYLINDERS. Before detaching connecting rods from crankshaft, mark piston, rod and cap for correct assembly to each other and for installation into the same cylinder from which they are removed. Separate bearing cages and rollers (37 – Fig. OM16-46) for assembly

into same location if they are to be reinstalled.

Pistons and rings are available in standard size and oversize. Pistons in early models are equipped with three piston rings while later models have two rings. Refer to the CONDENSED SERVICE DATA table for recommended ring end gap, ring side clearance and piston skirt clearance. Rebore cylinder bores or renew cylinder block if cylinder bore taper or out-of-round exceeds 0.003 inch (0.08 mm) on models prior to 1977 and 0.004 inch (0.10 mm) on models after 1976.

The piston pin is retained in piston by snap rings in piston pin bosses. On some models, one piston pin boss is tight on piston pin and the other has slight clearance. When removing or installing piston pin, always press pin from side marked "LOOSE" toward the tight side to prevent damage to piston. The upper end of connecting rod is fitted with a caged needle roller bearing on all models except 1986 90 and 110 hp models. On 1986 90 and 110 hp models, loose needle bearings and two thrust washers are used. The piston pin and connecting rod bore are used as bearing races. Check bearing rollers, cage and bearing race surfaces for wear, scoring or overheating. When assembling, pistons should be heated slightly to facilitate installation of piston pins. The pistons on port side are installed to connecting rods

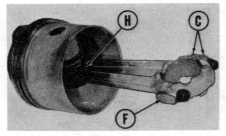

Fig. OM16-48 — The oil hole (H) should be toward top of motor and index marks (C) should be aligned.

differently than for starboard units. The oil hole in side of rod at piston pin end should be up on all connecting rods. On all models except 1985 and 1986 120 and 140 hp models, the long sloping side of pistons must be toward center of cylinder block "V" (exhaust ports). On 1985 and 1986 120 and 140 hp models, the stamping "Exhaust Side" on top of pistons must face cylinder bore exhaust ports. Thoroughly lubricate all bearing surfaces before assembling.

CONNECTING RODS, BEARINGS AND CRANKSHAFT. Before detaching connecting rods from crankshaft, mark rod and cap for correct assembly to each other and in original cylinder. Separate bearing cages and rollers for assembly to original crankpin if units are not renewed.

Connecting rods ride on roller bearings at both ends. The lower bearing consists of a split retainer (cage) and 16 rollers on pre-1974 models and 18 rollers on 1974 and later models except 1985 and 1986 120 and 140 hp models. Sixteen roller bearings per crankpin bearing set are used on 1985 and 1986 120 and 140 hp models. The crankpin end of rod is drilled and finished, then carefully fractured to separate the cap from the rod. The parting line should be nearly invisible. When assembling, make certain that index marks (C – Fig. OM16-48) are aligned, oil hole (H) is toward top of motor and long sloping side or stamping "Exhaust Side" of piston head is toward center of "V." The machined sides (F) of connecting rod and cap should be smooth when assembled. On 1985 and later models equipped with precision ground rods, OMC Alignment Fixture 396749 is recommended to properly align connecting rod with rod cap during tightening of connecting rod screws.

NOTE: Precision ground rods are identified by grind marks running ACROSS corners on ears of connecting rod and rod cap where the components join.

Crankshaft seal rings (33 – Fig. OM16-46) should have 0.0015-0.0025 inch (0.038-0.063 mm) side clearance in crankshaft groove on all models prior to 1985. Seal rings are available in four thicknesses: 0.1565-0.1570 inch (3.975-3.988 mm), 0.1575-0.1580 inch (4.000-4.013 mm), 0.1585-0.1590 inch (4.026-4.039 mm) and 0.1605-0.1610 inch (4.077-4.089 mm). On models after 1984, seal ring (33) should be renewed if thickness is less than 0.154 inch (3.91 mm).

The upper main bearing (25) on models prior to 1973, and seal (22) on all models are located in the upper main bearing head (23). The bearing should be pressed into bearing head with the lettered end of bearing out (toward bottom). Bearing and head (23) are a one-piece assembly on models after 1972 and must be serviced as a unit. Lip of seal (22) should be toward inside and should be pressed in until flush with top surface of bearing head.

The center main bearing (34 and 35) is a split-cage needle bearing. The two-piece outer race is held together with retaining ring (35) and is positioned in cylinder block by a dowel pin. When assembling, make certain that dowel pin in cylinder block bore engages hole in center bearing outer race.

The ball type lower main bearing (30) is located in the lower bearing head (27). The bearing outer race is clamped to the bearing head with retainer plate (31) and screws (31S). To disassemble the lower bearing assembly, remove screws (31S) and pull bearing head (27) from bearing (30). Remove snap ring (29), then remove bearing from crankshaft lower end using a suitable puller. The lower bearing should allow crankshaft end play within the limits specified in the CONDENSED SERVICE DATA table. When assembling, position retainer (31) around crankshaft, then press bearing (30) onto journal and install snap ring (29). Press seal (28) into bore in bearing head using special OMC tool to locate seal at correct depth in the bore. Install new "O" ring or "O" rings (24) in groove or grooves of bearing head and press bearing head onto outer race of bearing. Install screws (31S) into retainer (31), but do not tighten these screws until crankcase is assembled.

Refer to the CONDENSED SERVICE DATA table for dimensional data and recommended torque values. Refer to ASSEMBLY paragraphs for assembling the crankcase halves.

PROPELLER

PROPELLER. An aluminum, three-blade propeller with built in cushion clutch is standard on all motors. Alternates include both two and three blade units with a range in diameter from 12¾

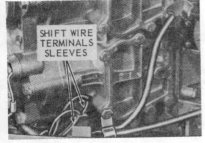

Fig. OM16-50 — View of starboard side of power head showing location of connections for shift wires.

inches (32.4 cm) to 14 inches (35.6 cm) and a range in pitch from 11 inches (27.9 cm) to 23 inches (58.4 cm). Bronze and stainless steel propellers are available in some sizes.

Only propellers designed for use on these motors should be used. Propellers should be selected to place full throttle operation in 5000-6000 rpm range on 1985 and 1986 120 and 140 hp models and 4500-5500 rpm range on all other models.

LOWER UNIT

Models Prior to 1973

REMOVE AND REINSTALL. Most service on the lower unit can be performed after detaching the gearcase housing from the exhaust and drive shaft housing. When servicing the lower unit pay particular attention to water pump and water pump tubes with respect to air or water leaks. Leaky con-

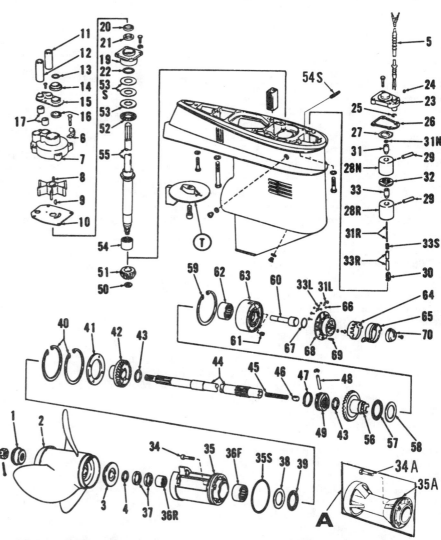

Fig. OM16-51 — Exploded view of typical gearcase assembly prior to 1973. Inset (A) shows rear bearing housing used on 1971 and 1972 motors. Snap ring (59) is used only on 1969 and 1970 motors and set screw (54S) is used only on 1972 motors.

T. Trim tab	19. Bearing housing	31L. Neutral valve lever
1. Spacer	20. Upper seal	31N. Locknut
2. Propeller	21. Lower seal	31R. Neutral shift rod
3. Thrust bearing & sleeve	22. "O" ring	32. Spacer
4. Thrust washer	23. Solenoid cover	33. Reverse solenoid plunger
5. Shift cable	24. Wiring connector clamps	33L. Reverse valve lever (with hole)
6. Clamp	25. Wire grommet retaining ring	33R. Reverse shift rod (tube)
7. Water pump housing	26. Gasket	33S. Lock screw
8. Impeller	27. Wave washer	34. Allen screws
9. Drive key	28N. Neutral solenoid	34A. Hex head screws
10. Impeller plate	28R. Reverse solenoid	35. Bearing housing
11. Short guide tube	29. Heat shrink tubes (wire covers)	35A. Bearing housing
12. Long guide tube	30. Cap	35S. "O" ring
13. Drive shaft "O" ring	31. Neutral solenoid plunger	36F. Bearing
14. Seal		36R. Bearing
15. Cover		
16. Seal		
17. Grommets		

37. Seals	54. Bearing
38. Thrust washer	54S. Set screw
39. Thrust bearing	55. Drive shaft
40. Snap rings	56. Forward gear
41. Retainer plate	57. Thrust bearing
42. Reverse gear	58. Thrust washer
43. Thrust washers	59. Snap ring
44. Propeller shaft	60. Shift plunger
45. Spring	61. Plug
46. Retainer	62. Bearing
47. Retainer spring	63. Pump housing & rotor set
48. Pin	64. Band
49. Dog clutch	65. Seal
50. Nut	66. Valve seats & balls
51. Drive pinion	67. "O" ring
52. Thrust bearing	68. Cover
53. Thrust washer	69. Dowel pin
53S. Shims	70. Screen

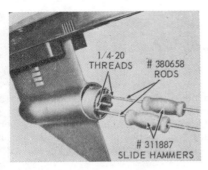

Fig. OM16-52 — View showing method of removing and installing oil pump.

nections may interfere with proper cooling and performance of motor.

To remove the gearcase, disconnect the two shift wires (Fig. OM16-50) at connectors on starboard side of power head. Apply liquid soap to the cable sleeve and push shift wires into exhaust housing. Mark location of the trim tab (T – Fig. OM16-51) to aid reassembly, then remove the trim tab. Remove the two screws from each side of gearcase and two screws at rear.

NOTE: One of the rear screws is under trim tab. Carefully withdraw the gearcase and drive shaft.

CAUTION: Do not damage shift wires and do not lose the two plastic water tube guides.

When installing, renew "O" ring (13) at top of drive shaft. Insert a wire down from the hole in power head adapter plate through the exhaust housing and attach to ends of shift wires. Coat the shift wire grommet with liquid soap and slide the plastic water tube guides onto pump as shown in Fig. OM16-57. Install gearcase while aligning plastic guides with the water tubes and pulling shift wires up through hole in power head adapter. Drive shaft splines can be aligned by turning flywheel. Dip the six gearcase attaching screws in OMC Gasket Sealing Compound or equivalent before installing. Make certain that shift cable grommet is through hole, then attach shift cable leads. Install trim tab, aligning the previously affixed marks.

GEARCASE. To disassemble, remove gearcase, drain lubricant, remove propeller (2 – Fig. OM16-51) and detach shift cable from clamps (6). Remove the attaching screws, then withdraw water pump housing (7), impeller (8), drive key (9) and plate (10). Remove screws attaching bearing housing (19) and solenoid cover (23). Remove solenoid assembly (23 through 33). Remove the four screws (34) using a long ¼ inch Allen wrench, then pull bearing housing (35) out using a slide hammer puller with a hook. Remove the

two snap rings (40) and withdraw propeller shaft (44). Remove nut (50), then lift out drive shaft (55), bearing housing (19), thrust washer (52 and 53) and shims (53S) out top and gear (51) out bottom. Remove forward gear (56), thrust bearing (57) and washer (58), then remove snap ring (59) if fitted. The oil pump (60 through 70) can now be withdrawn from housing using two slide hammer pullers as shown in Fig. OM16-52.

Inspect drive shaft splines, bearing surfaces and seal surfaces for wear or damage. Damaged splines may be caused by striking a submerged object and bending the exhaust and drive shaft housing. Check parallelism of top and bottom surfaces if questionable. If surfaces are not parallel, renew the housing, do not attempt to straighten. Bearing (54 – Fig. OM16-51) is removed through lower (propeller shaft) opening, by pressing from top. On 1972 models it is necessary to remove a set screw (54S) that is used to lock bearing (54) in place before bearing can be driven out of gearcase. Set screw is located on starboard side of gearcase in area of water intake. Install new bearing from top, with lettered end of bearing up and flush with top of bearing bore.

Shift solenoids (28N and 28R) should be checked with an ohmmeter. Resistance should be 5-6 ohms when checked between each of the two wires and case of solenoid. If solenoids or wires (5) are renewed, use new heat shrink insulating tubes (29) to seal wire connections.

The shift pump valve balls (66) and seats for these balls can be renewed. The surfaces of rotor set in housing should be checked for wear or scoring. Renew complete pump assembly if any part of rotor set is damaged excessively. Bearing (62) should be pressed in using special tool (part 314641) to position bearing at correct depth. Before install-

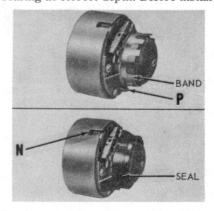

Fig. OM16-53 — Views of gear shift pump. Top view shows installation of band and lower view shows alignment of lug on seal. The control lever with hole should be on top and located on starboard side as shown.

ing cover (68), install pump rotor set in housing with drive lugs on pump inner rotor toward cover (68), install pump rotor set in housing with drive lugs on pump inner rotor toward cover (68).

NOTE: Most pumps have dots etched on sides of inner and outer rotors. If provided with these dots, they should both be toward cover (68).

If installation of rotors is questioned, assemble thrust bearing (57), washer (58) and forward gear (56), then insert into pump housing. If rotor is incorrectly installed, the inner rotor will be pushed out of pump housing. The front surfaces of rotor set should be flush with front face of pump housing, when parts (56, 57 and 58) are in position. Clearance between bushing in forward gear (56) and propeller shaft (44) should be 0.001-0.002 inch (0.03-0.05 mm). If clearances are excessive, renew propeller shaft and/or gears. Refer to Fig. OM16-53 for assembly of control levers, band and seal.

A gage block (part 315767) is required to determine the thickness of shims (53S – Fig. OM16-51) that should be installed. Remove thrust bearing (52) and washer (53) from drive shaft (55). Install pinion gear (51) on end of shaft and tighten nut (50) to 60-65 ft.-lbs (82-88 N·m). Install shims (53S) that were removed against shoulder on drive shaft. Position gage block against shims and surface of pinion gear as shown in Fig. OM16-54. With gage block tight against shims, clearance between end of gage block and top surface of pinion gears should be 0.000 to 0.002 inch (0.00-0.05 mm). If clearance is zero, make certain that enough shims are installed to provide an accurate check. Set the correct shims aside until drive shaft is installed.

Seals (20 and 21 – Fig. OM16-51) should be installed with lip of bottom seal (21) down to prevent gearcase oil from entering water pump and lip of top seal (20) should be up to prevent water from entering gearcase. Special tool (part 315945) should be used to install rear propeller shaft bearing (36R) so

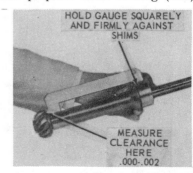

Fig. OM16-54 — View showing use of gage block for determining thickness of drive shaft shims.

bearing is at correct depth. The inner (first) seal (37) should be installed with lip in and outer seal should be installed with lip out.

Refer to the following for assembling the gearcase. Position the oil pump in gearcase, with notch (N – Fig. OM16-53) up and pin (P) correctly engaging hole in gearcase.

NOTE: Use slide hammers as shown in Fig. OM16-52 and make certain that pump is correctly seated.

Snap ring (59 – Fig. OM16-51) used in 1969 and 1970 motors only should be installed with flat side toward pump. Position thrust bearing (57) and washer (58) on forward gear (56), then slide gear into pump. Carefully engage drive lugs on gear with lugs on pump rotor. Position gear (55) and drive shaft (55) in housing and install nut (50). Position thrust bearing (52), washer (53) and shims (53S) over drive shaft and install bearing housing (19). Coat the four screws attaching bearing housing (19) with OMC Gasket Sealing Compound or equivalent before installing. The pinion nut (50) should be tightened to 60-65 ft.-lbs. (82-88 N·m) using special socket (part 312752) on the drive shaft splines. If the dog clutch (49) has been removed from propeller shaft, insert spring (45) and retainer (46) into propeller shaft bore with hole in retainer aligned with hole in propeller shaft (at splines). Slide the dog clutch (49) on shaft splines with the three ramp side toward front (forward gear) and hole aligned with hole in propeller shaft. Compress retainer (46) and spring (45) enough to align holes in retainer, propeller shaft and dog clutch, then insert pin (48). Wrap retainer spring (47) around dog clutch to keep pin in position. Install thrust washers (43) on each end and insert propeller shaft (44) including parts (43, 45, 46, 47, 48

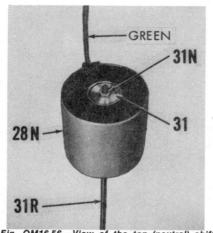

Fig. OM16-56 – View of the top (neutral) shift solenoid and associated parts.

31. Plunger
31N. Locknut
31R. Neutral shift rod

and 49) into the gearcase. Slide reverse gear (42) onto propeller shaft and position retainer plate (41) in housing. Install two snap rings (40), then position thrust bearing (39) and washer (38) over reverse gear hub. Position new "O" ring in groove of bearing housing (35) and lubricate outer edge of "O" ring. Slide bearing housing (35) into gearcase with exhaust cut out toward top. The "BOTTOM" marking should be down. Coat the retaining Allen screws (34) with OMC Gasket Sealing Compound or equivalent before installing.

NOTE: Installation of bearing housing will be easier if two long guide studs are used to locate the holes in retainer plate (41) as the bearing housing is installed and the other two screws are installed.

Install and adjust solenoids as follows: Screw plunger (with large hole) onto tubular shift rod (33R – Fig. OM16-55), then install and tighten lock screw (33S). Insert plunger and shift rod into reverse solenoid (blue wire) and push cap (30) onto bottom of shift rod. Insert the lower solenoid assembly into gearcase bore. Make sure end of shift rod is against the shift valve lever on pump and solenoid is against bottom of bore in housing. Measure distance between top of plunger and top of solenoid. If plunger is not 1/64 inch (0.4 mm) below, to flush with top of solenoid, remove the assembly and adjust by loosening lock screw (33S) and turning shift rod (33R). The lock screw should be torqued to 9-11 in.-lbs. (1-1.2 N·m) after adjustment is correct. Install the lower (reverse) solenoid and shift assembly after adjustment is complete. Position spacer (32 – Fig. OM16-51) on top of the lower solenoid with raised center section toward top. Assemble the small shift rod (31R – Fig. OM16-56), plunger with small hole (31) and locknut (31N). Position the plunger and shift rod in neutral

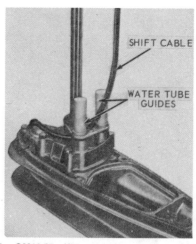

Fig. OM16-57 – View showing position of shift cable and installation of the plastic water tube guides.

solenoid (28N) which has a green wire. Insert the upper solenoid and shift rod assembly into gearcase bore above the reverse shift assembly and spacer. Make sure end of rod is through hole in top valve lever (33L – Fig. OM16-51) and solenoids are tight against bottom of bore. Measure distance between top of plunger and top of upper solenoid. If plunger is not 1/64 inch (0.4 mm) below, to flush with top of solenoid, loosen locknut and turn shift rod. The locknut (31N – Fig. OM16-56) should be tightened to 3-5 in.-lbs. (0.3-0.5 N·m) after adjustment is complete.

NOTE: Improper shifting will result if adjustment of shift rods and plungers is not correct.

Install solenoids and shift rods after adjustment is complete. Position wave washer (27 – Fig. OM16-51) on top of solenoids, coat both sides of gasket (26) with OMC Gasket Sealing Compound or equivalent and install cover (23). Apply OMC Adhesive "M" or equivalent to bottom of impeller plate (10), install key (9) in drive shaft and locate impeller (8) over key. Lubricate impeller, hold blades in and install water pump housing (7).

NOTE: Drive shaft can be rotated clockwise while assembling pump housing, but should never be turned backwards.

Coat screws attaching water pump housing with OMC Gasket Sealing Compound or equivalent before installing. Refer to Fig. OM16-57 for routing of shift cable. The "O" ring for sealing the top splines of drive shaft is shown at (13 – Fig. OM16-51).

1973-1977 Models

REMOVE AND REINSTALL. To remove gearcase, disconnect upper end of shift rod as shown in Fig. OM16-43,

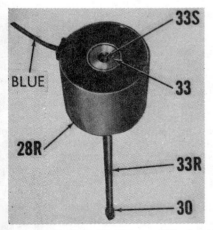

Fig. OM16-55 – View of the reverse shift solenoid and associated parts. Similar parts for neutral shift are shown in Fig. OM16-56.

30. Cap
33. Plunger
33R. Reverse shift rod
33S. Lock screw

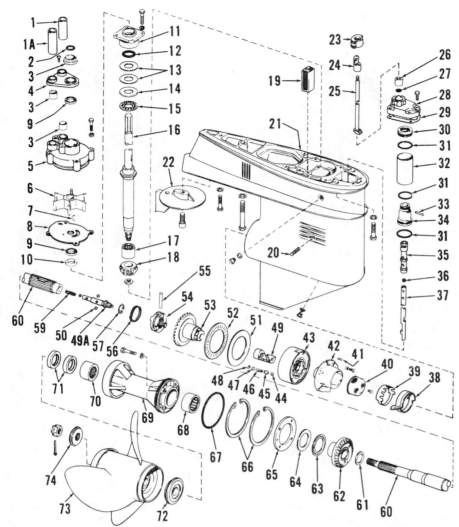

Fig. OM16-59—Exploded view of hydraulic shift lower unit used on 1973-1977 models. Shift rod (49A) and plunger (49) are one piece on models after 1973. Seal (38) and band (39) are not used on some models.

1. Short water tube guide	13. Shims	29. Gasket	45. Ball guide	60. Propeller shaft
1A. Long water tube guide	14. Thrust washer	30. Piston cap	46. Spring	61. Thrust washer
	15. Thrust bearing	31. "O" ring	47. Plug	62. Reverse gear
2. "O" ring	16. Drive shaft	32. Cylinder	48. Snap ring	63. Thrust bearing
3. Grommet	17. Needle bearing	33. Pin	49. Shift plunger	64. Thrust washer
4. Cover	18. Pinion gear	34. Piston	49A. Shift rod	65. Retainer plate
5. Impeller cover	19. Water screen	35. Valve	50. Detent balls	66. Snap rings
6. Impeller	20. Set screw	36. Plug	51. Thrust washer	67. "O" ring
7. Drive key	21. Gearcase	37. Push rod	52. Thrust bearing	68. Needle bearing
8. Plate	22. Trim tab	38. Seal	53. Forward gear	69. Bearing housing
9. Seal	23. Seal	39. Band	54. Dog clutch	70. Needle bearing
10. Seal	24. Shift rod connector	40. Screen	55. Pin	71. Seals
11. Bearing & housing assy.	25. Shift rod	41. Locating dowel	56. Retaining spring	72. Thrust bushing
	26. Seal	42. Pump cover	57. Snap ring	73. Propeller
12. "O" ring	27. "O" ring	43. Oil pump & bearing	59. Spring	74. Spacer
	28. Cover	44. Relief valve ball		

remove propeller and drain lubricant from gearcase. Mark location of trim tab (22–Fig. OM16-59) to aid during reassembly and remove trim tab. Remove two screws on each side of gearcase and two screws at rear.

NOTE: One rear screw is in trim tab cavity.

Separate gearcase from exhaust housing being careful not to bend shift rod or lose water tube guides (1 and 1A).

To install gearcase, reverse removal procedure. Install a new "O" ring in end of drive shaft and coat splines with a suitable antiseize compound. Apply OMC Adhesive "M" to gearcase and exhaust housing gasket surfaces. Be sure water tube guides and water tube are installed properly. Apply OMC Gasket Sealing Compound to threads of gearcase screws.

GEARCASE. To disassemble gearcase, separate gearcase from exhaust housing as outlined in previous section. Remove water pump housing (5–Fig. OM16-59), impeller (6), key (7) and lower plate (8). Remove four screws holding propeller shaft bearing housing (69) and

using a suitable puller, withdraw bearing housing from gearcase. Remove snap rings (66), thrust washer (64) thrust bearing (63), shift rod cover (26) and shift rod (25). Remove hydraulic shift and propeller shaft components by withdrawing push rod (37) and propeller shaft simultaneously. Hold drive shaft with OMC Tool 311875 or another suitable tool and unscrew pinion nut. Remove pinion (18), unscrew bearing housing (11) screws and withdraw drive shaft and components from gearcase. Bearing in housing (11) is not renewable but must be obtained as a unit assembly with housing. Remove forward gear (53). Using a suitable puller and two 16 inch long rods with ¼-20 threads, remove oil pump (43) from gearcase. A two-piece shift plunger (49 and 49A) is used on 1973 models which may be separated by removing snap ring (57). Shift rod (49A) and plunger (49) are one piece on later models.

Inspect drive shaft splines, bearing surfaces and seal surfaces for wear or damage. Damaged splines may be caused by striking a submerged object and bending the exhaust housing. Check parallelism of top and bottom surfaces if questionable. If surfaces are not parallel, renew housing. Do not attempt to straighten it.

Lower drive shaft bearing (17) should only be removed if renewal is intended. Do not reinstall a used bearing. Drive shaft bearing is held in position by a set screw (20) as well as a press fit in gearcase. Set screw is located on starboard side in area of water intake. To remove bearing (17) except on 140 hp and 85790 and 115790 models, install OMC Special Tool 385447, with shouldered side of removal piece against bearing and drive bearing down out of case. New bearing is installed by assembling special tool with sleeve provided and removal piece turned over so that shouldered side will again be next to bearing. Pull bearing (with lettered side against puller) into case (Fig. OM16-60). Bearing will be properly positioned when plate of tool is touching top of gearcase and bolt is tight. Do not overtighten bolt. Apply Loctite to set screw and install.

To remove bearing (17) on 140 hp and 85790 and 115790 models, pull bearing up and out using OMC Special Tool 385546 or other suitable puller. To install bearing, drive bearing down into gearcase with lettered end up using OMC Special Tools 385546 and 321518 assembled as shown in Fig. OM16-61. Bearing is correctly positioned when plate of tool contacts gearcase. Apply Loctite to set screw (20).

Hydraulic shift components (30 through 37–Fig. OM16-59) may be disassembled with OMC Tool 386112 by engaging pins on tool with holes in piston (34) and piston cap (30) and unscrewing cap from piston. Be careful not to bend or damage push rod (37) during disassembly. Remove pin (33) to separate valve (35), piston (34) and push rod. Cap (30) should be tightened to 12-15 ft.-lbs. (16-20 N·m) during reassembly.

To disassemble oil pump, unscrew four screws securing cover (42) and remove cover. Remove snap ring (48), plug (47), spring (46), guide (45) and pressure relief valve ball (44). Inspect pressure relief valve components and renew if worn or damaged. Inspect oil pump assembly for wear or damage. Dots on rotors must be up and surfaces of rotors and housing must be flat across ends when forward gear, thrust bearing and washer are installed in pump. Rotors, housing and bearing are not available separately and r．．it be renewed as a unit assembly.

Seals (9 and 10 – Fig. OM16-59) should be installed with lip of bottom seal (10) down and lips of seals (9) up.

Needle bearings (68 and 70) should not be removed from propeller shaft housing unless renewal is intended. Do not install used bearings. OMC Special Tool 317061 should be used to press aft bearing into propeller shaft housing (69) to ensure proper positioning except on 140 hp and 85790 and 115790 models which should use tool 321517. OMC Special Tool 314641 should be used to properly position forward bearing (68) in bore of housing. Seals (71) should be installed so that lip on aft seal is toward propeller and lip on forward seal is facing forward.

Thickness of shims (13) is varied to adjust mesh position of pinion gear (18) in forward and reverse gear. A shim gage should be used to determine proper shimming. Use OMC shim gage 321520 on 140 hp and 85790 and 115790 models and shim gage 315767 for all other models.

Place pinion gear (18) on drive shaft and torque retaining nut to 60-65 ft.-lbs. (82-88 N·m). Install shims (13) that were removed during disassembly and leave thrust washer (14) and thrust bearing (15) off shaft. Hold shim gage firmly against shims and measure clearance between end of gage and pinion gear (Fig. OM16-54). Clearance should be zero between gear and gage.

NOTE: Make certain that enough shims are installed for an accurate check.

Shims are available in thicknesses of 0.002 inch and 0.005 inch and may be installed in any quantity to obtain proper clearance. Set the correct shims aside until drive shaft is installed.

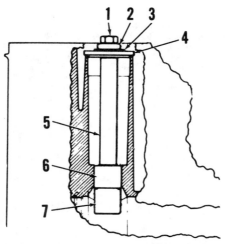

Fig. OM16-60 – View showing arrangement of OMC Tool 385447 for installation of pinion bearing (17 – Fig. OM16-59). Lettered end of bearing must be against puller.

1. Cap screw	4. Step washer
2. Thrust bearing	5. Spacer tube
3. Washer	6. Pinion bearing
	7. Puller

To assist in installing shift plunger components in propeller shaft, grind away the end of a 9/32 inch (7.14 mm) rod to form a long flat taper on one side. Rod should be approximately 2⅝ inches (66.67 mm) long. Position dog clutch (54 – Fig. OM16-59) on propeller shaft with pin hole in dog clutch and slot in shaft aligned. "Prop end" stamped on dog clutch of 1977 models must be towards propeller end of shaft. Place three shift balls (50) and spring (59) in plunger (49) as shown in Fig. OM16-62 and install plunger in propeller shaft so detent balls match grooves in propeller shaft. Align holes in clutch dog (54 – Fig. OM16-59) and shift plunger (49) and insert tapered end of tool through holes to properly position detent spring. Carefully push tool out with retaining pin (55) and install pin retaining spring (56) in outer groove of dog clutch. Coils of spring must not overlap.

To reassemble gearcase, install oil pump (43), forward gear (53), thrust bearing (52) and thrust washer (51) so locating pin (41) aligns with pin hole in gearcase. Install drive shaft (16) and pinion gear (18) and tighten pinion nut to 60-65 ft.-lbs. (82-88 N·m). Lay gearcase on starboard side and install propeller shaft with flat side of shift plunger (49) up until propeller shaft is bottomed. Install hydraulic shift assembly with flat on end of push rod (37) down. Insert shift assembly until flats on push rod (37) and shift plunger (49) are engaged (push rod will not turn). Place light pressure against shift cylinder (32) and slowly withdraw propeller shaft until key on end of push rod meshes with keyway in shift plunger as shown in Fig. OM16-63. When key and keyway are meshed, push shift assembly and pro-

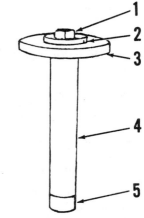

Fig. OM16-61 – View of pinion bearing installation tool.

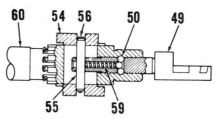

Fig. OM16-62 – Cross-sectional view of shift plunger (49) and dog clutch (54) components. Refer to Fig. OM16-59 for parts identification.

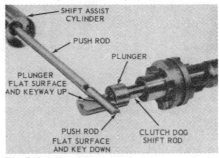

Fig. OM16-63 – View showing relative positions of shift assemblies when installed in gearcase. Refer to text for installation.

peller shaft in to complete engagement. Complete remainder of assembly noting the following points: Install snap rings (66 – Fig. OM16-59) with flat side out. Install bearing housing (69) with "UP" mark towards water pump. Apply OMC Gasket Sealing Compound to threads of screws securing retainer plate (65) and bearing housing (69).

Models After 1977

REMOVE AND REINSTALL. To remove gearcase, disconnect upper end of shift rod shown in Fig. OM16-64 on all models except 1985 and 1986 120 and 140 hp models. On 1985 and 1986 120 and 140 hp models, remove threaded pin from shift cam located at base of intake manifold on the port side. Remove propeller and drain lubricant from gearcase. Mark location of trim tab (22 – Fig. OM16-66) to aid during reassembly and remove trim tab. Remove two screws on each side of gearcase and two screws at rear.

NOTE: One rear screw is in trim tab cavity.

Separate gearcase from exhaust housing being careful not to bend shift rod.

To install gearcase, reverse removal procedure. Install a new "O" ring in end of drive shaft and coat splines with a suitable antiseize compound. Check length of gear shift rod (25). With shifter in neutral, distance from mating surface of gearcase (21) to center of hole in top of shift rod should be 21.843 inches (55.46 cm) on all 20 inch (50.8 cm) transom models except 1985 and 1986 120 and 140 hp models or 26.843 inches (68.16 cm) on all 25 inch (63.5 cm) transom models except 1985 and 1986 120 and 140 hp models. On 1985 and 1986 120 and 140 hp models, shift rod length should be 21.937 inches (55.73 cm) on 20 inch (50.8 cm) transom models and 26.937 inches (68.43 cm) on 25 inch (63.5 cm) transom models. Top of shift rod should slant forward. Apply OMC Adhesive "M" to gearcase and exhaust housing gasket surfaces. Be sure water tube guides and water tube are installed properly. Apply OMC Gasket Sealing Compound to threads of gearcase screws.

GEARCASE. Gearcase may be disassembled in the following manner: Remove propeller, drain lubricant and remove gearcase as described in previous section. Remove screws securing shift rod cover (29 – Fig. OM16-66), unscrew shift rod (25) and remove shift rod and cover as an assembly. Remove water pump housing (5), impeller (6), impeller

Fig. OM16-66 – Exploded view of lower unit used on models after 1977. Shim (33) is used on models prior to 1979. Seal (4) is used on models prior to 1983.

1. "O" ring
2. Grommet
2A. Grommet
3. Water tube bracket
3A. Impeller housing
4. Seal
5. Impeller plate
5A. Impeller lining
6. Impeller
7. "O" ring
8. Plate
9. Seal
10. Seal
11. Bearing & housing assy.
12. "O" ring
13. Adjustment shims
14. Thrust washers
15. Thrust bearing
16. Drive shaft
17. Needle bearing
17A. Set screw
18. Pinion gear
19. Water screen
20. Magnet & spring
21. Gearcase
22. Trim tab
23. Shift rod seal
25. Shift rod
29. Shift rod cover
30. Gasket
31. Detent ball
32. Detent spring
33. Shim
34. Detent
35. Locating dowel
36. Shift lever pin
37. Gear housing
38. Shift lever
39. Shift yoke
40. Shift dog shaft
41. Spring
50. Thrust washer
51. Thrust bearing
52. Forward gear
54. Dog clutch
55. Pin
56. Pin retaining spring
60. Propeller shaft
62. Reverse gear
63. Thrust bearing
64. Thrust washer
65. Retainer plate
66. Snap rings
67. "O" ring
68. Needle bearing
69. Bearing housing
70. Needle bearing
71. Seals
72. Thrust bushing
73. Propeller bushing

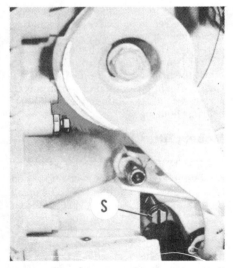

Fig. OM16-64 – View showing location of shift rod screw (S) used on all models after 1977 except 1985 and 1986 120 and 140 hp models.

key and lower plate (8). Remove four screws holding propeller shaft bearing housing (69) and using a suitable puller, remove bearing housing. Discard seals (71) and "O" ring (67). Remove snap rings (66), thrust washer assembly (64 and 63) and slide reverse gear (62) off propeller shaft. A special socket is available to hold drive shaft so nut securing pinion gear (18) can be removed. After pinion gear retaining nut is removed, unscrew the four screws securing upper drive shaft bearing housing (11). Pull drive shaft and associated parts out of gearcase. A puller may be necessary. Propeller shaft (60) may now be pulled from gearcase complete with forward gear (52), forward gear housing (37) and all associated parts.

Inspect drive shaft splines, bearing surfaces and seal surfaces for wear or damage. Damaged splines may be caused by striking a submerged object and bending the exhaust housing. Check parallelism of top and bottom surfaces if questionable. If surfaces are not parallel, renew housing. Do not attempt to straighten it.

Lower drive shaft bearing (17) should only be removed if renewal is intended. Do not reinstall a used bearing. Drive shaft bearing is held in position by a set screw (17A) as well as a press fit in gearcase. Set screw is located on starboard

side in area of water intake. After removing set screw, use OMC Special Tool 318117 or OMC Special Tool 391257 to renew bearing (17). To use OMC Special Tool 318117, place shouldered side of tool against bearing and drive bearing down into propeller shaft cavity. New bearing is installed by assembling special tool with sleeve provided and removal piece turned over so shouldered side will again be next to bearing. Pull bearing (with lettered side against puller) into case (Fig. OM16-67). Bearing will be properly positioned when plate of tool is touching top of gearcase and bolt is tight. Do not overtighten bolt. Apply Loctite to set screw and install.

Forward gear (52 – Fig. OM16-66) and propeller shaft (60) may be removed from propeller shaft gear housing (37) after dislodging spring (56) and removing dog clutch assembly (55 and 54). Bearing housing and shifter mechanism assembly (38) may be disassembled by driving out shift lever pin (36).

Thickness of shims (13) is varied to adjust mesh position of pinion gear (18) in forward and reverse gear. An OMC shim gage should be used to determine proper shimming.

Place pinion gear (18) on drive shaft and torque retaining nut to 60-65 ft.-lbs. (82-88 N·m). Install shims (13) that were removed during disassembly and leave

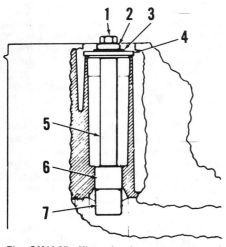

Fig. OM16-67—View showing arrangement of OMC Tool 318117 for installation of pinion bearing (17—Fig. OM16-66). Lettered end of bearing should be against puller.

1. Cap screw
2. Thrust bearing
3. Washer
4. Step washer
5. Spacer tube
6. Pinion bearing
7. Puller

thrust washer (14) and thrust bearing (15) off shaft. Hold shim gage firmly against shims and measure clearance between end of gage and pinion gear (Fig. OM16-54). Install or remove shims to obtain zero clearance between gear and gage.

NOTE: Make certain that enough shims are installed for accurate check.

Shims are available in 0.002, 0.003, 0.004 and 0.005 inch sizes. Set the correct shims aside until drive shaft is installed.

Needle bearings (68 and 70—Fig. OM16-66) should not be removed from propeller shaft housing (69) unless renewal is intended. Do not reinstall used bearings. OMC Special Tool 321517 or Special Tool 326562 should be used to press aft bearing into propeller shaft housing to ensure proper positioning. OMC Special Tool 314641 should be used to position bearing (70) in forward bore of propeller shaft housing. Seals (71) should be installed so lip on aft seal is toward propeller and lip on forward seal is facing forward.

To determine thickness of shims (33) on models prior to 1979, install thrust bearing (51) and washer (50) on face of gear housing (37). Place gear housing (37) on a surface plate with thrust bearing (51) against plate. Position OMC Tool 324797 over housing so step marked "1.902" is directly over outer edge of gear housing and measure gap between tool and housing as shown in Fig. OM16-68. Install shims (33) equal to measured gap.

Assemble gearcase in the following manner: Renew all gaskets, seals and "O" rings. If lower drive shaft bearing (17) or propeller shaft bearings (68 and

Fig. OM16-68—On models prior to 1979, measure gap between OMC Tool 324797 and bearing housing as outlined in text to determine thickness of shims (33—Fig. OM16-66).

70) have been removed, they too should be renewed. Install detent spring (32) and detent ball (31) in blind hole of housing (37). Hold spring and ball in position while installing detent (34). Assemble shift dog shaft (40), shift lever yoke (39), shift lever (38) and pin (36). Assemble forward gear (52) with thrust bearing (51 and 50) and shims (33), on models prior to 1979, into gear housing. Place dog clutch (54) on propeller shaft (60) making sure that hole in dog clutch is aligned with slot in propeller shaft and splined dogs are toward forward gear. Insert propeller shaft into forward gear and bearing housing assembly, then insert pin (55) through dog clutch propeller shaft and hole in shift dog shaft (40). Install pin retaining spring (56). Press shift detent (34) down and place propeller shaft, forward gear and gear housing assembly (37) into position in gearcase. Make sure locating pin (35) is seated in recess provided in gearcase.

Insert drive shaft (16). Install pinion gear retaining nut and tighten to 60-65 ft.-lbs. (82-88 N·m). Install shift rod (25) and shift rod cover (29) as an assembly. Thread shift rod fully into detent (34), back off two turns, pull rod to neutral (middle detent) and adjust for proper length. Refer to shift rod adjustment in REMOVE AND REINSTALL section for specifications.

Assemble thrust bearing (64 and 63)

on reverse gear (62) and slide onto propeller shaft (60). Position bearing retainer plate (65) and install snap rings (66). Make sure "O" ring (67) is fully seated in groove of bearing housing (69) and that seals (71) are properly installed. Lip of forward seal should be toward front and lip of aft seal should be toward propeller.

Installation of bearing housing (69) will be eased by using two guide pins 10 inches long with ¼-20 threads on one end. Thread guide pin into bearing retainer plate (65) and slide bearing housing (69) into position. Coat bearing housing screws with sealing compound and install.

Install seals (9 and 10) in upper drive shaft bearing housing (11) with lip of lower seal (10) down and lip of upper seal (9) up. Place thrust bearing assembly (14 and 15) on drive shaft and install previously selected shim or shims (13). Coat screws that secure bearing housing (11) with sealing compound and install. Bottom edge of impeller plate (8) should be coated with OMC Adhesive "M" or equivalent and placed in position. Install impeller key, lubricate edges of impeller (6) and install on drive shaft. On models after 1984, impeller key is replaced with a drive cam. Install drive cam with flat side against drive shaft and sharp edge pointing in a clockwise direction when viewed from crankshaft end of drive shaft. Drive shaft should be turned clockwise while installing water pump housing (5). Coat screws that secure water pump housing and water tube bracket with sealing compound and install.

POWER TILT AND TRIM

All Models Prior to 1978 Except 85790, 85TXLR77, 115790, 115TXL77 And 140 Hp

OPERATION. These models are equipped with a hydraulically actuated power tilt and trim system. An oil pump

Fig. OM16-75—View of Calco (A) and Prestolite (B) oil pump and motor assemblies.

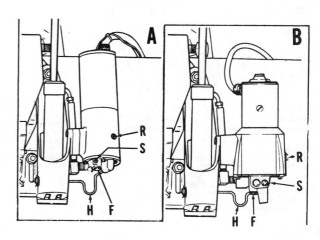

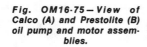

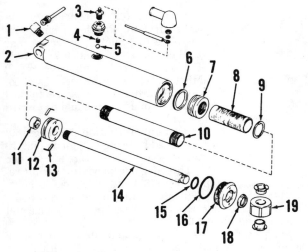

Fig. OM16-76 — Exploded view of hydraulic trim cylinder used on models identified in text.

1. Elbow
2. Trim cylinder
3. Sender
4. Spring
5. Ball
6. "O" ring
7. Piston
8. Sender bobbin
9. Retaining ring
10. Piston carrier
11. Stop
12. Carrier bearing
13. Sender ground springs
14. Shaft
15. "O" ring
16. "O" ring
17. End cap
18. Wiper
19. Shaft end

when operating either up or down. Current draw with unit stalled in up or down position should be 45-55 amps. Torque required to turn oil pump shaft should not exceed 10 in.-ozs. (2.8 N). To check oil pressure, remove fill port plug (F – Fig. OM16-75) and connect a 2000 psi (13.8 MPa) gage to fill port. Oil pressure should be 200 psi (1.4 MPa) when trimming out and 300 psi (2.1 MPa) when tilting up. With 2000 psi (13.8 MPa) gage connected to fill port, disconnect high pressure line (H) from pump and plug hole. Oil pressure should be at least 1450 psi (10 MPa) with unit in tilt position for five seconds.

OVERHAUL. Oil pump must be serviced as a unit assembly and must be matched to Calco or Prestolite motor. Motor components are available. Refer to Fig. OM16-76 and Fig. OM16-77 for exploded views of trim and tilt cylinders. Tighten stem valve (6 – Fig. OM16-77) to 10 in.-lbs. (1.1 N·m). Do not overtighten. To check operation of trim gage sending unit, connect ohmmeter leads to sender (3 – Fig. OM16-76) and elbow (1). Resistance should be 0-3 ohms with

driven by a reversible electric motor provides oil pressure. One hydraulic cylinder trims the outboard motor while another hydraulic cylinder tilts the outboard. A rocker control switch determines motor and pump rotation thereby retracting extending tilt and trim cylinders. The pump motor is equipped with a thermal overload switch which resets after approximately one minute. Turn slotted manual valve screw (S – Fig. OM16-75) at bottom of pump to manually raise or lower outboard. Tighten manual valve screw clockwise to operate hydraulic tilt and trim.

Hydraulic system contains approximately ¾ pint (355 mL) of oil. Recommended oil is OMC Sea-Lube Power Trim/Tilt Fluid. Do not run pump without oil in reservoir. Fill plug (R) is located in side of pump reservoir. Oil level should reach fill plug hole threads with outboard tilted in full up position.

Hydraulic tilt should be cycled several times and oil level rechecked if system has been drained or lost a large amount of oil.

TROUBLE-SHOOTING. The following specifications should be noted when a malfunction occurs in tilt and trim system. Current draw should be 40-45 amps

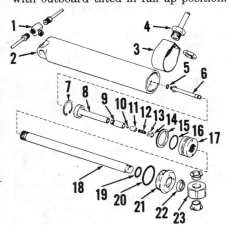

Fig. OM16-77 — Exploded view of tilt cylinder used on models identified in text. Relief valve components (8 through 14) are available as a unit only.

1. Tee	9. Valve seat
2. Tilt cylinder	10. Ball
3. Band	11. Piston
4. Oil line	12. Spring
5. "O" ring	13. Washer
6. Stem valve	14. Snap ring
7. Snap ring	15. Piston ring
8. Relief valve stem	16. "O" ring
17. Piston	
18. Shaft	
19. "O" ring	
20. "O" ring	
21. End cap	
22. Wiper	
23. Shaft end	

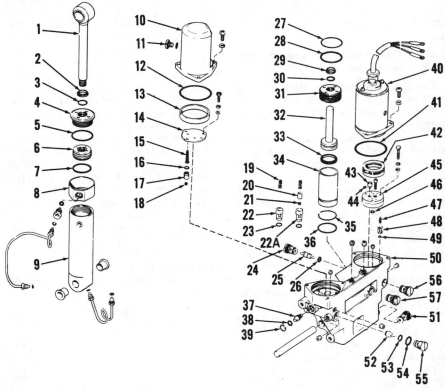

Fig. OM16-78 — Exploded view of hydraulic tilt and trim system used on models identified in text.

1. Shaft	13. Sleeve	24. Valve	35. Retaining ring	46. "O" ring
2. Wiper	14. Plate	25. Piston	36. "O" ring	47. Spring
3. "O" ring	15. Screen	26. "O" ring	37. Manual release valve	48. Pump relief valve
4. End cap	16. "O" ring	27. Retaining ring	38. "O" ring	49. Seal
5. "O" ring	17. Check valve	28. "O" ring	39. Snap ring	50. Manifold
6. Piston	18. Valve ball	29. Wiper	40. Pump motor	51. Valve
7. "O" ring	19. Spring	30. "O" ring	41. "O" ring	52. Valve piston
8. Band	20. Spring seat	31. End cap	42. Oil pump filter	53. "O" ring
9. Tilt cylinder	21. Ball	32. Piston	43. Drive coupling	54. "O" ring
10. Reservoir	22. Relief valve	33. Piston ring	44. Ball	55. Valve
11. Fill plug	22A. Impact relief valve	34. Trim cylinder	45. Oil pump	56. Valve
12. "O" ring	23. "O" ring			57. Valve

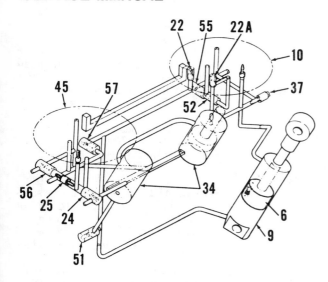

Fig. OM16-79—Schematic of hydraulic tilt and trim system. Refer to Fig. OM16-78 for parts identification.

cylinder rod fully extended and 84-96 ohms with rod fully retracted. Sender ground springs (13) should extend 1/16 inch (1.58 mm) past edge of carrier bearing (12). Apply OMC Nut Lock to stop (11) and bearing (12) threads.

1978 Models And 85790, 85TXLR77, 115790, 115TXL77 And All 140 HP Models Prior to 1979

OPERATION. These models are equipped with a hydraulically actuated power tilt and trim system. Manifold (50–Fig. OM16-78) contains valves, oil pump and trim cylinders. Oil pump motor, oil reservoir and tilt cylinder are attached to manifold. Electric oil pump motor is reversible and oil pump rotation is thereby changed to extend or retract trim and tilt cylinders. Note position of valves in Fig. OM16-78 and Fig. OM16-79. Turn manual release valve (37–Fig. OM16-78) to manually raise or lower outboard.

Hydraulic system contains 25 fl. oz. (740 mL) of oil. Recommended oil is OMC Sea-Lube Power Trim/Tilt Fluid. Do not run pump without oil in reservoir. Oil level should reach fill plug (11) hole threads. Tilt should be cycled several rimes and oil level rechecked if system has been drained or lost a large amount of oil.

TROUBLE-SHOOTING. Be sure battery is fully charged, electrical connections are good, oil reservoir is full and air is not trapped in system before testing components.

OIL PUMP AND MOTOR. To check oil pump, unscrew plug (1–Fig. OM16-80) and install a 2000 psi (13.8 MPa) pressure gage. Oil pressure should be 1300-1600 psi (9-11 MPa) with outboard tilted in full up position. Oil pressure less than specified may indicate

leakage, faulty pressure relief valve (22A–Fig. OM16-78) directional valve (56), oil pump or pump motor. Motor must operate properly in both directions.

VALVES. Faulty valves will cause system malfunction. Note function of valves and carefully inspect valve components which may cause malfunction. Valves (24 and 56–Fig. OM16-78 or Fig. OM16-79) and valve piston (25) direct oil to tilt and trim cylinders from oil pump. Valve (57) directs oil to bottom of tilt cylinder when tilting outboard up and also directs oil to relief valve (22) which relieves system pressure at approximately 1500 psi (10.3 MPa). Valve (22A) relieves pressure during outboard impact and directs oil pressure to letdown valve piston (52) which allows oil to escape from bottom of tilt cylinder so top portion of tilt cylinder can be refilled after impact. Valves in tilt cylinder piston (6) allow oil to transfer from top to bottom of tilt cylinder during outboard impact. Valve (51) allows oil to flow from bottom of tilt cylinder during tilting down operation. Manual release valve (37) allows manual movement of outboard when valve is open.

Fig. OM16-80—View of oil pressure reading points.

TILT AND TRIM CYLINDERS. Tilt and trim system malfunction may be due to leaking "O" rings, seals and fittings in cylinders. Blocked oil lines may cause improper operation. Leaking valves in tilt cylinder piston (6–Fig. OM16-78) may allow unit to leakdown.

OVERHAUL. Filter valve seat (17–Fig. OM16-78) will be damaged if removed. Valves (24, 55, 56 and 57) are identical and may be interchanged. Valve (51) is taller than other valves and must not be interchanged. Motor must be serviced as a unit assembly. Apply OMC Nut Lock to piston shaft (1) threads and install piston (6) on shaft with small holes in piston up.

Models After 1978

OPERATION. A hydraulically actuated power tilt and trim system is used. Manifold (50–Fig. OM16-82) contains valves, oil pump and trim cylinders. Oil pump motor, oil reservoir and tilt cylinder are attached to manifold. Electric oil pump motor is reversible and oil pump rotation is thereby changed to extend or retract trim and tilt cylinders. Note position of valves in Fig. OM16-82. Turn manual release valve counterclockwise to manually raise or lower outboard.

Hydraulic system contains approximately 25 fl. oz. (740 mL) of oil. Recommended oil is OMC Power Trim/Tilt Fluid or DEXRON II automatic transmission fluid. Do not run pump without oil in reservoir. Oil level should reach fill plug (11) hole threads when tilt and trim pistons are fully extended. System should be cycled several times prior to checking oil level if system has been drained or lost a large amount of oil.

TROUBLE-SHOOTING. Be sure battery is fully charged, electrical connections are good, oil reservoir is full and air is not trapped in system before testing components.

To check oil pressure, first momentarily cycle system "UP" and "DOWN" a few times. Remove snap rings (39–Fig. OM16-82) and manual release valve (37), then install OMC gage "A" as shown in Fig. OM16-83 Operate system in the "UP" direction and observe gage after system stalls out at full extension. Gage reading should not drop below 100-200 psi (700-1400 kPa). Install OMC gage "B." Operate system in the "DOWN" direction and observe gage after system stalls out at fully retracted. Gage reading should not drop below 100-200 psi (700-1400 kPa).

To test check valves, screw each valve into OMC check valve tester 390063

(T – Fig. OM16-84). Use a suitable pressure tester (P) and apply 30 psi (207 kPa) of pressure to check valve. Check valve can be considered good if no pressure leakage is noted.

Refer to the following for a list of symptoms and probable causes:

Symptoms   **Probable Causes**
Tilt Leakdown . . . . 1, 2, 3, 4, 5 or 6
Trim and Tilt Both Leak . . . . . . 7, 8 or 9

Reverse Lock
  Does Not Hold . . . . 2, 3, 6, 10, 11 or 12
Will Not Trim Out Under
  Load or Will Not Tilt . . . . . . 1, 2, 7 or 9
Will Not Trim or
  Tilt Down . . . . 2, 8, 10, 11, or 13

Key to Probable Causes
1. Trim Up Relief Valve
2. Manual Release Valve
3. Tilt Cylinder Valve or Seals
4. Tilt Check Valve
5. Impact Letdown Valve
6. Oil Line
7. Trim Cylinders Sleeve "O" Rings or Piston Seals
8. Trim Check Valve
9. Expansion Relief Valve or "O" Rings
10. Filter Valve Seat
11. Impact Sensor Valve
12. Reverse Lock Check Valve
13. Trim Down Pump Relief Valve

OVERHAUL. Oil pump must be serviced as a unit assembly. Motor is not serviceable with the exception of brushes. Refer to Fig. OM16-82 for exploded view of trim and tilt cylinders and manifold components. Keep all components separated during disassembly and identify each component, if needed, to assure correct position during reassembly.

Fig. OM16-83 — Install OMC gage "A" or "B" into manual release valve (37 – Fig. OM16-82) port as shown in test system oil pressure. Refer to text.

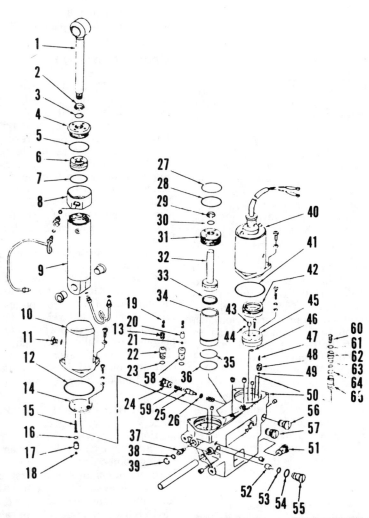

Fig. OM16-82 — Exploded view of hydraulic tilt and trim system used on models after 1978. A three-wire pump motor is used on 1979 and 1980 models.

1. Shaft	18. Valve ball	35. Retaining ring	51. Separation valve
2. Wiper	19. Spring	36. "O" ring	52. Valve piston
3. "O" ring	20. Spring seat	37. Manual release valve	53. "O" ring
4. End cap	21. Ball	38. "O" ring	54. "O" ring
5. "O" ring	22. Trim up relief valve	39. Snap ring	55. Impact letdown valve
6. Piston	23. "O" ring	40. Pump motor	56. Trim check valve
7. "O" ring	24. Reverse lock check valve	41. "O" ring	57. Tilt check valve
8. Band	25. Piston	42. Oil pump filter	58. Impact sensor valve
9. Tilt cylinder	26. "O" ring	43. Drive coupling	59. Spring
10. Reservoir	27. Retaining ring	44. Ball	60. Spring
11. Fill plug	28. "O" ring	45. Oil pump	61. "O" ring
12. "O" ring	29. Wiper	46. "O" ring	62. Expansion relief valve core
13. Needle	30. "O" ring	47. Spring	
14. Plate	31. End cap	48. Trim down pump relief valve	63. "O" ring
15. Screen	32. Piston		64. "O" ring
16. "O" ring	33. Piston ring	49. Seal	65. Expansion relief valve seat
17. Check valve	34. Trim cylinder	50. Manifold	

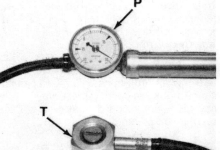

Fig. OM16-84 — Use OMC check valve tester 390063 (T) and a suitable pressure tester (P) to test check valves. Check valve can be considered good if no pressure leakage at approximately 30 psi (207 kPa) is noted.

EVINRUDE AND JOHNSON
4-CYLINDER MODELS
88, 90, 100, 110, 120 and 140 HP (AFTER 1986)

Year Produced	EVINRUDE	JOHNSON
1987	E88MSLCU	J88MSLCU
	E90MLCU	J90MLCU
	E90TLCU	J90TLCU
	E110MLCU	J110MLCU
	E110TLCU	J110TLCU
	E110TXCU	J110TXCU
	E120TLCU	J120TLCU
	E120TXCU	J120TXCU
	E140TLCU	J140TLCU
	E140TXCU	J140TXCU
1988	E88MLSCC	J88MSLCC
	E90MLCC	J90MLCC
	E90TLCC	J90TLCC
	E110MLCC	J110MLCC
	E110TLCC	J110TLCC
	E110TXCC	J110TXCC
	E120TLCC	J120TLCC
	E120TXCC	J120TXCC
	E140TLCC	J140TLCC
	E140TXCC	J140TXCC
	E140CXCC	J140CXCC
1989	E88MSLCE	J88MSLCE
	E90MLCE	J90MLCE
	E90TLCE	J90TLCE
	E90TXCE	J90TXCE
		J90TLCE
	E100STLCE	J100STLCE
	E110MLCE	J110MLCE
	E110TLCE	J110TLCE
	E110TXCE	J110TXCE
		J110MLCE
		J110TLCE
	E120TLCE	J120TLCE
	E120TXCE	J120TXCE
	E140TLCE	J140TLCE
	E140TXCE	J140TXCE
	E140CXCE	J140CXCE

CONDENSED SERVICE DATA

TUNE-UP

Hp/rpm 88/5000
90/5000
100/5000
110/5000
120/5500
140/5500

Bore:
88, 90, 100 & 110 Hp . . . . .3.500 in.
(88.90 mm)
120 & 140 Hp (Prior to 1988) . . . . .3.500 in.
(88.90 mm)
120 & 140 Hp (After 1987) . . . . .3.685 in.
(93.60 mm)

Stroke:
88, 90, 100 & 110 Hp .2.588 in.
(65.74 mm)
120 & 140 Hp . . . . .2.858 in.
(72.59 mm)

Number of Cylinders 4

Displacement:
88, 90, 100 & 110 Hp . . . . .99.6 cu. in.
(1632 cc)
120 & 140 Hp (Prior to 1988) . . . . .110 cu. in.
(1803 cc)
120 & 140 Hp (After 1987) . . . . .122 cu. in.
(1999 cc)

Spark Plug .Champion QL77JC4*
  Electrode Gap:
   Prior to 1989 . . . . .0.040 in.
                     (1.0 mm)
   After 1988 . . . . .0.030 in.
                    (0.76 mm)
Ignition Type . . . . .CDI
Carburetor Make . . . . .OMC
Fuel:Oil Ratio . . . . .See Text

*Champion surface gap spark plug QL77V (Models 88-110 hp) or QL78V (Models 120 and 140 hp) is recommended when operated at sustained high speed. Renew surface gap spark plug if center electrode is more than $^{1}/_{32}$ inch (0.79 mm) below flat surface of plug end.

SIZES—CLEARANCES

Piston Ring End Gap . . . . .0.019-0.031 in.
               (0.48-0.79 mm)
Piston Ring Side Clearance . . . . .0.004 in. Max.
               (1.0 mm)

Piston Skirt Clearance *
Standard Piston Diameter:
  88, 90 100 & 110 Hp . . . . .3.4930-3.4950 in.
           (88.722-88.773 mm)
  120 & 140 Hp (Prior to 1988) . . . . . .3.4958-3.4968 in.
           (88.793-88.819 mm)
  120 & 140 (After 1987) . . . . .3.6803-3.6823 in.
           (93.480-93.530 mm)
Standard Cylinder Bore Diameter:
  88, 90, 100 & 110 Hp and 120 & 140 Hp
  Prior to 1988 . . . . .3.4995-3.5005 in.
           (88.887-88.913 mm)
  120 & 140 Hp (After 1987) . . . . .3.6845-3.6855 in.
           (93.586-93.612 mm)
Crankshaft Journal Diameters:
  Top Main . . . . .1.6199-1.6204 in.
           (41.145-41.158 mm)
  Center Main .2.1870-2.1875 in.
           (55.550-55.562 mm)
  Bottom Main:
  88, 90, 100 & 110 Hp . . . . .1.3779-1.3784 in.
           (34.999-35.011 mm)
  120 & 140 Hp . . . . .1.5747-1.5752 in.
           (39.997-40.010 mm)
  Crankpin:
  88, 90, 100 & 110 Hp . . . . .1.3757-1.3762 in.
           (34.943-34.955 mm)
  120 & 140 Hp . . . . .1.4995-1.5000 in.
           (38.087-38.100 mm)

*The manufacture does not specify piston skirt-to-cylinder clearance. If pistons and cylinders are within wear tolerances, piston skirt clearance should be acceptable. Refer to text.

TIGHTENING TORQUES
Connecting Rod:
  88, 90, 100 & 110 Hp:
  (Prior to 1988) . . . . .29-31 ft.-lbs.
               (39-42 N·m)
  (After 1987) . . . . .30-32 ft.-lbs.
               (41-44 N·m)
  120 & 140 Hp . . . . .42-44 ft.-lbs.
               (57-60 N·m)
Crankcase Halves:
  Main Bearing Screws
  88, 90 100 & 110 Hp . . . . .18-20 ft.-lbs.
               (24-27 N·m)
  120 & 140 Hp . . . . .26-30 ft.-lbs.
               (35-41 N·m)
Flange Screws . . . . .60-84 in.-lbs.
               (7-9 N·m)
Upper Crankcase Head:
  88, 90, 100 & 110 Hp
  (Prior to 1987) .120-144 in.-lbs.
               (13-16 N·m)
  (After 1986) . . . . .96-120 in.-lbs.
               (11-14 N·m)
  120 & 140 Hp . . . . .72-96 in.-lbs.
               (8-11 N·m)
Lower Crankcase Head:
  88, 90, 100 & 110 Hp . . . . .96-120 in.-lbs.
               (11-13 N·m)
  120 & 140 Hp . . . . .72-96 in.-lbs.
               (8-11 N·m)
Cylinder Head:
  88, 90, 100 & 110 Hp . . . . .18-20 ft.-lbs.
               (24-27 N·m)
  120 & 140 Hp . . . . .20-22 ft.-lbs.
               (27-30 N·m)
Flywheel Nut:
  88, 90, 100 & 110 Hp . . . . .100-105 ft.-lbs.
               (136-143 N·m)
  120 & 140 Hp . . . . .140-150 ft.-lbs.
               (190-197 N·m)
Lower Main Bearing Retainer
  Plate Screws . . . . .96-120 in.-lbs.
               (11-13 N·m)
Spark Plug . . . . .18-20 ft.-lbs.
               (24-27 N·m)

LUBRICATION

The engine is lubricated by oil mixed with the fuel. The recommended fuel is regular unleaded gasoline with a minimum pump octane rating of 87. The recommended oil for all models is Evinrude or Johnson Outboard Lubricant, OMC 2-Cycle Motor Oil or a suitable NMMA certified TC-WII oil.

On models not equipped with variable ratio oiling (VRO), the recommended fuel:oil ratio for normal operation, including engine break-in is 50:1.

On models so equipped, the VRO pump varies the fuel:oil ratio from approximately 150:1 at idle to approximately 50:1 at full throttle by sensing power output. During engine break-in (first 10 hours of operation) on VRO equipped models, a 50:1 fuel and oil mixture must be used in the fuel tank in combination with the VRO system to ensure proper engine lubrication. The oil level in the VRO tank should be monitored to be certain the oil level is dropping indicating the VRO system is functioning. After break-in period, switch to straight gasoline in the fuel tank. If the VRO system is not used on models so equipped, a 50:1 fuel and oil mixture must be used in the fuel tank.

The lower unit gears and bearings are lubricated by oil contained in the gearcase. The recommended oil is OMC HI-VIS Gearcase Lubricant. Gearcase oil level should be checked after every 50 hours of operation and drained and refilled with new oil every 100 hours or seasonally, whichever occurs first.

To drain gearcase oil, place outboard motor in a vertical position and remove drain and vent plugs. Allow oil to drain into a suitable container. To fill gearcase, place outboard motor in a vertical position. Add oil through the drain plug hole with an oil feeder until oil overflows from vent plug hole. Install oil level plug first, remove oil feeder then install drain plug. Use new gaskets on plugs and tighten securely.

FUEL SYSTEM

Models 88, 90, 100 And 110 Hp

CARBURETORS. Refer to Fig. OM17-1 for an exploded view of the two-barrel carburetors used. Idle speed is controlled by idle air bleed jet (16) located inside throat of carburetors. High speed mixture is controlled by high speed jets (11). Refer to SPEED CONTROL LINKAGE for idle speed adjustment procedure.

NOTE: The manufacturer does not recommend submerging carburetor components in carburetor or parts cleaning solutions. An aerosol type carburetor cleaner is recommended to clean carburetor. The float and other components made of plastic and rubber should not be subjected to some cleaning solutions. Safety eyewear and hand protection are recommended when working with solvent.

To adjust float level, remove float bowl (10) and invert carburetor. Place OMC Float Gage 324891 on float bowl mating surface as shown in Fig. OM17-2. If properly adjusted, edge of float will rest between notches (N) on side of gage marked V-4 & V-6. Bend float arm to adjust. Float drop (D—Fig. OM17-3) should be $7/8$ to $1\frac{1}{8}$ inches (22.2-28.6 mm) measured as shown in Fig. OM17-3. Bend tang (T) to adjust.

Apply a suitable thread locking compound to threads of float bowl screws and tighten to 24-36 in.-lbs. (2.7-4.1 N·m).

Models 120 And 140 Hp

CARBURETORS. Two two-barrel type carburetors are used. Each carburetor assembly has a common throttle body assembly (T—Fig. OM17-5) with separate main body assemblies (M).

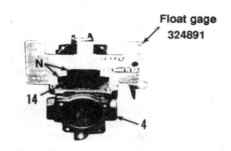

Fig. OM17-2—Check float level on two-barrel carburetors used on 88, 90, 100 and 110 hp models using OMC Float Gage 324891 as shown. Float should be between notches (N) on side of gage marked V-4 and V-6. Refer to text.

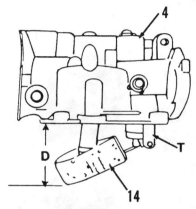

Fig. OM17-3—Float drop (D) should be $7/8$-$1\frac{1}{8}$ inches (22.2-28.6 mm) measured from carburetor body (4) mating surface to bottom of float (14) as shown. Bend tang (T) to adjust.

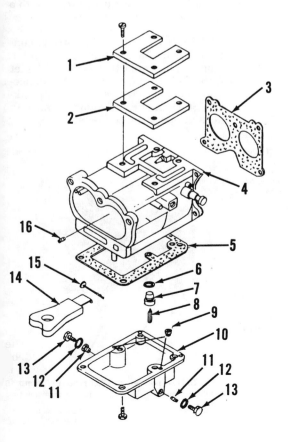

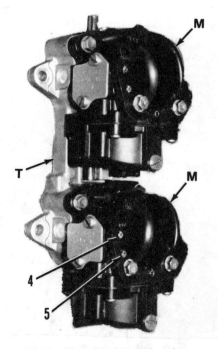

Fig. OM17-1—Exploded view of carburetor used on 88, 90, 100 and 110 hp models.
1. Cover
2. Gasket
3. Gasket
4. Body
5. Gasket
6. Gasket
7. Inlet valve seat
8. Inlet valve needle
9. Intermediate jet
10. Float bowl
11. High speed jet
12. "O" ring
13. Plug
14. Float
15. Pin
16. Idle air bleed jet

Fig. OM17-5—View showing two-barrel type carburetors used on 120 and 140 hp models. A common throttle body assembly (T) with separate main body assemblies (M) are used. View identifies position of intermediate air bleed jet (4) and low speed air bleed jet (5).

The main body assemblies are constructed of a nonmetallic type material. Care must be used when working with the main body assembly. DO NOT overtighten any screws. Tighten each screw in small increments using a crossing pattern.

NOTE: The manufacturer does not recommend submerging carburetor components in carburetor or parts cleaning solutions. An aerosol type carburetor cleaner is recommended to clean carburetor. The float and other components made of plastic and rubber should not be subjected to some cleaning solutions. Safety eyewear and hand protection are recommended when working with solvent.

If service is performed, keep carburetor components for each carburetor separate from the others. To determine float level, invert float bowl (12—Fig. OM17-6) with fuel inlet valve and float installed. The float should be flush with the float bowl gasket surface. Use a straightedge as shown in Fig. OM17-7 to check float level. Remove the float and carefully bend the float tang to adjust.

Refer to SPEED CONTROL LINKAGE section for idle speed adjustment procedure.

FUEL PUMP (WITHOUT VRO). Refer to Fig. OM17-10 for exploded view of the fuel pump used on 88 hp models.

The fuel pump is actuated by crankcase pulsations. Fuel pump (5) is available as an assembly only. If fuel delivery malfunction is noted, inspect and clean filter screen (3) prior to renewing pump assembly.

Check fuel pump operation by connecting a suitable pressure gage inline between pump and carburetors. Pump pressure should be 1 psi (7 kPa) at 600 rpm, 1.5 psi (10 kPa) at 2500-3000 rpm and 2.5 psi (17 kPa) at 4500 rpm. Renew pump assembly (5) if pressure is not as specified. Use thread locking compound on fuel pump mounting screws and tighten to 24-36 in.-lbs. (2.7-4.1 N·m).

VRO TYPE FUEL PUMP. The VRO fuel pump (1—Fig. OM17-11) varies the fuel:oil ratio from approximately 150:1 at idle to approximately 50:1 at full throttle by sensing engine power output. During engine break-in or after any procedure that permitted air to enter VRO system, fuel in the tank must be mixed with a recommended oil at a 50:1 ratio to ensure proper engine lubrication. Prior to switching to straight gasoline in fuel tank, be sure oil level in VRO tank is dropping, indicating VRO system is functioning.

NOTE: When the VRO system is not used, the inlet nozzle at the outboard motor connector must be plugged to prevent dirt or moisture from entering the fuel system. The fuel in the fuel tank must be mixed with a recommended oil at a 50:1 ratio.

TESTING. Using a "T" fitting, connect a suitable vacuum gage and a length of clear plastic hose to fuel inlet fitting at lower engine cover. All connections should be clamped to prevent leakage. Start engine and allow to warm to normal operating temperature.

Fig. OM17-6—Exploded view of carburetor main body assembly used on 120 and 140 hp models.

1. Main body
2. Gasket
3. Plate
4. Intermediate air bleed jet
5. Low speed air bleed jet
6. Seal
7. Inlet needle & gasket
8. Gasket
9. High speed jet
10. Gasket
11. Plug
12. Float bowl
13. Pin
14. Float

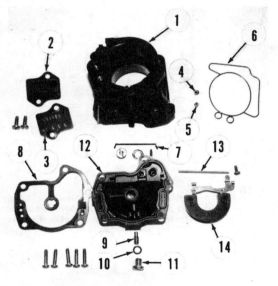

Fig. OM17-7—With float bowl (12) inverted and fuel inlet valve and float installed, float should just touch straightedge (S). Refer to text.

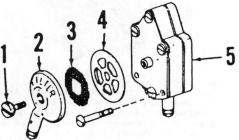

Fig. OM17-10—Exploded view of fuel pump used on 88 hp models.

1. Screw
2. Cover
3. Screen
4. Gasket
5. Pump assy.

Fig. OM17-11—View of VRO type fuel pump.

1. VRO fuel pump assy.	4. Crankcase pulse nipple
2. Oil inlet nipple	5. Fuel & oil mixture discharge nipple
3. Fuel inlet nipple	

NOTE: When performing VRO system tests that require full throttle operation, install outboard motor in a suitable test tank with the correct test wheel installed.

Run motor at full throttle for two minutes minimum while observing clear hose and note vacuum reading. Vacuum reading should not exceed 4 inches Hg (13.5 kPa) and air bubbles should not be present in clear hose. Excessive vacuum indicates a restricted fuel line between fuel tank and motor. Air bubbles in clear hose indicates an air leak in fuel line between fuel tank and motor.

If vacuum reading is within 1-4 inches Hg (3.4-13.5 kPa) and no bubbles were noted in clear hose, proceed as follows: Remove clear hose and install a suitable 0-15 psi (0-103.4 kPa) pressure gage between VRO pump discharge port (5—Fig. OM17-11) and carburetors. Start engine and run at 800 rpm in forward gear. Pump output pressure should stabilize at not less than 3 psi (20.7 kPa).

If pressure is less than 3 psi (20.7 kPa), inspect pulse fitting for plugging or other damage. Pulse fitting is screwed in crankcase at end of hose attached to pulse nipple (4). Pulse fitting on models prior to 1988 is equipped with an integral flame arrestor and on 1988 and later models, pulse fitting is equipped with an integral check valve. Clean both type fittings by back-flushing with a suitable solvent.

NOTE: A plugged pulse fitting may result in power head damage due to inadequate lubrication. If excessive carbon deposits are noted, renew pulse fitting and repair cause of excessive carbon (backfiring) before returning outboard motor to service.

If pump pressure is low and pulse fitting is in acceptable condition, renew VRO pump assembly.

Models 88, 90, 100 And 110 Hp

SPEED CONTROL LINKAGE. Ignition timing advance and throttle opening should be synchronized to occur simultaneously for optimum performance. Use the following procedure to synchronize the speed control linkage.

With number 1 piston (top starboard) at TDC on compression stroke, make sure timing pointer aligns with TDC mark on flywheel. If not, loosen timing pointer screw and move pointer as necessary to align with TDC mark.

To synchronize carburetor throttle valves, remove the air silencer cover. Loosen throttle cam follower screw (1—Fig. OM17-13) and throttle lever adjusting screw (8) on the lower carburetor. Open the throttle valves and allow valves to snap closed. Make sure all throttle valves are completely closed and apply light upward pressure on throttle link (9), then retighten screw (8). Rotate throttle cam follower to be sure all throttle valves open and close at exactly the same time.

Use the following procedure to check and adjust throttle cam follower pick-up point. Slowly advance the throttle cam (3) from the idle position while noting embossed mark on cam (3). The embossed mark should align with the center of cam follower roller (2) when the throttle valves just begin to open. To adjust, loosen cam follower roller screw (1) and adjust cam follower as necessary.

To check maximum timing advance, place outboard motor in a suitable test tank with the correct test wheel installed. Install a timing light to the number 1 cylinder (top starboard) spark plug lead. Start engine and run at full throttle (5000 rpm minimum). Maximum full throttle timing advance should be 27-29 degrees BTDC.

On models prior to 1989, adjust maximum timing by loosening screw (10) and rotating eccentric nut (11) as necessary. If the correct timing can not be obtained by adjusting eccentric nut (11), disconnect spark advance rod (6) and place into the appropriate adjacent hole in rod (6) retainer. Note that each hole in retainer equals approximately four degrees timing change. After changing position of rod (6), recheck timing and finish adjustment using eccentric nut (11).

On 1989 models, adjust maximum timing by loosening jam nut and adjusting length of timing advance rod (6) by turning thumb screw located at rod (6) retainer.

To check pickup timing, start engine and advance throttle until embossed mark on throttle cam (3) is aligned with center of cam follower roller (2). With throttle in this position, timing should be 3-5 degrees BTDC. Adjust pickup timing by loosening jam nut and turning thumb screw (7) as necessary.

To adjust full throttle stop, advance throttle to full throttle position (engine not running). Adjust full throttle stop screw (12) so roll pins in carburetor throttle valve shafts are placed in a vertical position. Be sure roll pins do not travel past vertical or carburetor throttle valve damage may result.

For optimum results when adjusting idle speed, boat should be in the water with the correct propeller installed. Engine should be running in forward gear at normal operating temperature with boat movement unrestrained. Adjust idle speed screw (5) as necessary to obtain 600-700 rpm.

Models 120 And 140 Hp

SPEED CONTROL LINKAGE. Throttle valve opening and ignition timing synchronization should be checked and adjusted as follows: On models prior to 1988, move speed control lever to the idle position and make sure follower roller (F—Fig. OM17-14) is not touching throttle cam (T). Loosen follower roller screw (C) and move roller away from throttle cam (T). Loosen screw (S) two complete turns, make certain that throttle plates are completely closed, then retighten screw (S).

To synchronize throttle valves on 1988 and 1989 models, move throttle lever to idle position and ensure throttle cam (T—Fig. OM17-15) is not touching cam follower roller (F) by loosening cam follower screw (C) and moving cam follower roller (F) away from throttle cam (T). Loosen carburetor link adjustment screws (S) ½ turn maximum. Make sure all carburetor throttle valves are completely closed, then retighten screws (S).

Adjust throttle cam pick-up point on 1987 models as follows: Ensure that cam follower roller screw (C—Fig. OM17-14) is loose. Hold cam follower roller (F) against throttle cam (T) and adjust throttle arm stop screw (D) until alignment mark (M) is centered with follower roller (F). Retighten cam follower roll-

Fig. OM17-13—View of speed control linkage on 88, 90 100 and 110 hp models.

1. Cam follower roller screw
2. Cam follower roller
3. Throttle cam
4. Throttle arm
5. Idle speed screw
6. Spark advance rod
7. Pickup timing adjustment screw
8. Carburetor lever adjusting screw
9. Throttle link
10. Screw
11. Eccentric
12. Full throttle stop screw

er screw (C), then turn throttle arm stop screw (D) one turn counterclockwise to ensure throttle cam (T) does not contact follower roller (F) when engine is at idle speed.

On 1988 and 1989 models, adjust throttle cam pick-up point as follows: Loosen lockring (L—Fig. OM17-15) and turn adjustment knob (K) counterclockwise until internal spring pressure is

completely relieved. With cam follower roller screw (C) loose, hold follower roller (F) against throttle cam (T) and adjust the throttle arm stop screw (D—Fig. OM17-16) until mark (M—Fig. OM17-15) on throttle cam (T) is aligned with center of roller (F). Retighten cam follower roller screw (C).

On 1987 models, adjust full throttle stop screw (W—Fig. OM17-14) so full throttle mark (O) on cam follower bracket is facing directly front-to-rear with throttle arm in the full throttle position (throttle valves wide open).

On 1988 and 1989 models, adjust full throttle stop screw (W—Fig. OM17-16) so full throttle mark (O—Fig. OM17-15)) on cam follower bracket faces directly front-to-rear with throttle arm in the full throttle position.

Prior to checking or adjusting ignition timing on all models, be sure timing pointer aligns with TDC mark on flywheel when number 1 piston is at TDC. If necessary, loosen timing pointer screws and reposition pointer.

NOTE: Outboard motor should be placed into a suitable test tank with the correct test wheel installed when checking or adjusting maximum timing advance. Do not operate at full throttle with a flushing attachment.

To check and adjust maximum timing advance on all models, proceed as follows: Connect a timing light to the number 1 spark (top starboard) plug lead. Start engine and run at 4500-5000 rpm (at normal operating temperature) while noting timing. Adjust full throttle timing advance screw (A—Fig. OM17-14 or OM17-16) as necessary to obtain 17-19 degrees BTDC.

On 1987 models, adjust idle speed screw (I—Fig. OM17-14) to obtain 600-700 rpm with motor running in forward gear. Idle speed adjustment should be performed with the boat in the water with correct propeller installed, at normal operating temperature with boat movement unrestrained.

On 1988 and 1989 models, the correct idle speed is maintained by adjusting idle speed ignition timing. Idle speed timing may be checked or adjusted with outboard motor in a test tank with the correct test wheel installed, or in the water with the correct propeller installed. Loosen lockring (L—Fig. OM17-15) and turn adjustment knob clockwise until knob bottoms. Start engine and allow to warm to normal operating temperature. With outboard motor in forward gear, idle timing should be 8 degrees ATDC. Make sure idle timing screw (Fig. OM17-17) is touching crankcase while checking timing. If necessary, shut off engine and adjust idle timing screw as necessary. Note that turning

Fig. OM17-14—View of speed control linkage on 120 and 140 hp models prior to 1988. Later models are similar. Refer to Fig. OM17-15.

A. Full throttle timing advance screw
C. Cam follower roller screw
D. Throttle arm stop screw
F. Cam follower roller
I. Idle speed screw
M. Mark
N. Nut
O. Full throttle mark
S. Screw
T. Throttle cam
W. Full throttle stop screw

Fig. OM17-15—View of speed control linkage on 120 and 140 hp models after 1987. Earlier models are similar. Refer to Fig. OM17-14.

C. Cam follower roller screw
F. Cam follower roller
K. Adjustment knob
L. Lock ring
M. Mark
O. Full throttle mark
S. Screws
T. Throttle cam

Fig. OM17-16—Speed control linkage on 1988 and 1989 Model 120 and 140 hps. Refer to text.

A. Maximum timing advance screw
D. Throttle arm stop screw
K. Adjustment knob
L. Lockring
W. Full throttle stop screw

idle timing screw clockwise advances timing. Next, restart engine, shift into forward gear and adjust throttle arm stop screw (D—Fig. OM17-16) so engine idles at 950 rpm in forward gear. Stop engine and without moving throttle position, rotate adjustment knob (K—Fig. OM17-15) counterclockwise until timer base just begins to move away from the idle timing screw, then tighten lockring (L). With throttle arm stop screw (D) lightly seated against the crankcase, rotate the stop screw counterclockwise until the original throttle cam pickup point (as previously outlined) is obtained.

All Models

REED VALVES. Four sets of reed (leaf) valves are used, one for each cylinder. The four valves are positioned horizontally and are attached to the intake manifold. To service reed valves, remove carburetors as an assembly, then remove intake manifolds.

The reed petals should seat very lightly against the valve block throughout their entire length with the least possible tension. Individual components of the reed valve assembly are not available separately. Renew reed valve assembly if petals are broken, cracked, warped or bent. Never attempt to repair a damaged reed petal.

Apply OMC Nut Lock or a suitable equivalent thread locking compound to threads of reed block-to-intake manifold screws and tighten to 25-35 in.-lbs. (3-4 N·m). Tighten intake manifold attaching screws to 60-84 in.-lbs. (7-9 N·m).

IGNITION SYSTEM

All models are equipped with capacitor discharge ignition (CDI). Major components of the ignition system are the flywheel, stator and charge coil assembly, timer base assembly, power pack(s) and ignition coils. Refer to Figs. OM17-20 through OM17-23 for wiring diagrams.

Charge coils are located in the stator assembly under the flywheel. Charge coils and stator assembly are not available separately. On 1987 Models 88-110 hp, two charge coils are used. One charge coil is used on 1988 and 1989 Models 88-110 hp and 1987 Models 120 and 140 hp. On 1988 and 1989 Models 120 and 140 hp, one charge coil and one power coil is used.

Sensor coils are located in the timer base under the flywheel. Sensor coils and timer base are not available separately. Two sensor coils are used on 1987 Models 88-110 hp, one sensor for cylinders 1 and 3 and one sensor for cylinders 2 and 4. On 1988 and 1989 Models 88-110 hp and 1987 Models 120 and 140 hp, four sensor coils are used, one per cylinder. Two sensor coils per cylinder are used on 1988 and 1989 Models 120 and 140 hp. One sensor coil is for normal operation and one coil operates the QuickStart electronic timing advance system. The QuickStart system is designed to aid engine starting when engine temperature is below 96° F (36° C) by advancing ignition timing. Ignition timing returns to normal once engine temperature reaches 96° F (36° C). The QuickStart system is also activated for approximately five seconds each time engine is started (regardless of temperature) to ease starting. QuickStart is not functional at engine speeds of 1100 rpm or more.

Two power packs are used on 1987 Models 88-110 hp. All other models are equipped with one power pack. Power packs designated "CDL" are equipped with an integral rpm limiter to prevent power head overspeeding. The rpm limiter prevents engine speed from exceeding 5700 rpm on 1987 Models 88-110 hp, 6700 rpm on 1988 and 1989 Models 120 and 140 hp and 6100 on all other models.

Models 120 and 140 produced in 1988 and 1989 are equipped with S.L.O.W. (speed limiting overheat warning). The S.L.O.W. function limits engine speed to approximately 2500 rpm if engine temperature exceeds 203° F (95° C). If S.L.O.W. function is activated, engine must be stopped and cooled to 162° F (72° C) before normal operation can be resumed.

TROUBLE-SHOOTING. Use only approved procedures to prevent damage to ignition components. The fuel system should be checked first to be certain that malfunction is not the result of fuel delivery problems, incorrect fuel mixture or contaminated fuel.

Trouble-shoot ignition system using a suitable ohmmeter and peak reading voltmeter such as Merc-O-tronic Model 781, Stevens Model CD-77 or Electro-Specialties Model PRV-1. Stevens PL-88 ignition module load adapter and Stevens TS-77 ignition coil terminal extenders may also be required.

NOTE: Resistance specifications are based on measurements taken at ambient temperature of 70° F (21° C). Resistance may change by approximately 10 ohms per one degree temperature variation.

If trouble-shooting an engine that will not start, proceed with TOTAL OUTPUT tests. If engine will start, but is rough running or erratic, refer to INDEXING FLYWHEEL and RUNNING OUTPUT sections.

NOTE: When performing cranking tests, battery must be in good condition and fully charged and spark plugs must be installed.

All Models

INDEXING FLYWHEEL. Power packs with a defective isolation diode or other internal defect can result in erratic ignition system operation. To determine if each cylinder is firing at the proper time, proceed as follows: Remove all spark plugs. Rotate flywheel in clockwise direction until number 2 cylinder is at TDC. With number 2 cylinder at TDC, mark "2" on flywheel directly adjacent to timing pointer. Repeat procedure for all cylinders, placing each cylinder number on flywheel across from timing pointer. Place motor in a suitable test tank, start engine and run at rpm malfunction is evident. Connect a timing light alternately to each spark plug lead and verify cylinders are firing at their respective mark on flywheel. If not, be sure all wiring pins are properly located in connectors or renew power pack.

Models 88-110 hp (1987)

Models 88-110 hp, produced in 1987, are equipped with two separate but identical ignition systems (cylinders 1 and 3 and cylinders 2 and 4). The trouble-shooting procedures must be performed on each ignition system. Note that four-pin connectors connect the timer base and ignition switch leads to the power pack on each side. A two-pin connector connects each charge coil to the power pack on each side.

TOTAL OUTPUT. Disconnect all spark plug leads from spark plugs and install a suitable spark tester to plug leads. Adjust tester spark gap to $\frac{1}{2}$ inch (12.7 mm). Crank engine while noting

Fig. OM17-17—View identifying idle speed timing adjustment screw on 1988 and 1989 Model 120 and 140 hp. Refer to text.

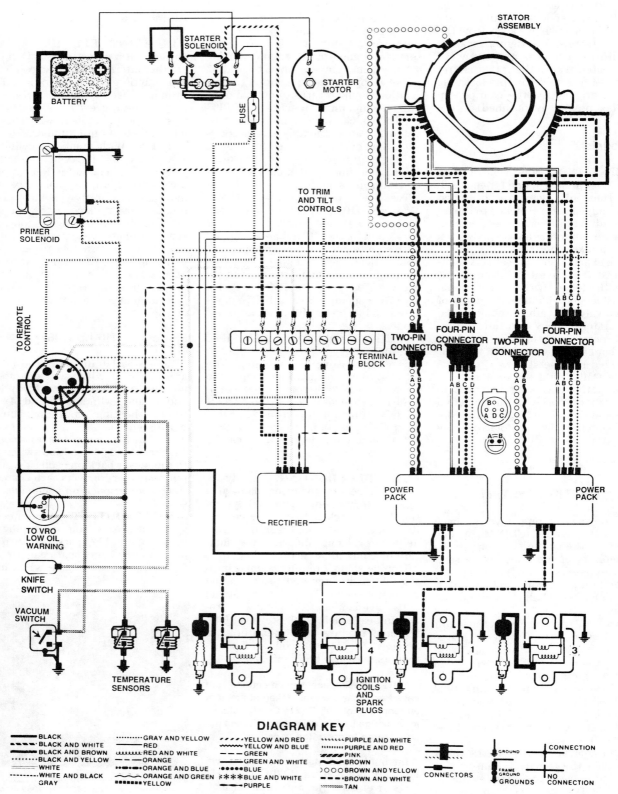

Fig. OM17-20—Wiring diagram of 1987 Models 88-110 hp.

spark tester. If normal spark is noted at all spark gaps, refer to RUNNING OUTPUT section. If weak or no spark is noted, refer to STOP CIRCUIT section.

STOP CIRCUIT. Ignition switch can be isolated by disconnecting four-pin connectors between power packs and timer base. Refer to Fig. OM17-20. Reconnect terminals A, B and C of the four-pin connectors using suitable jumper leads. Install spark tester and adjust spark gap to ½ inch (12.7 mm). Crank engine while noting spark tester. If normal spark is now noted, renew ignition switch, emergency cutoff switch or repair stop switch circuit. If weak or no spark is noted, refer to CHARGE COIL section.

On tiller models, check stop circuit as follows: Disconnect the one-pin connec-

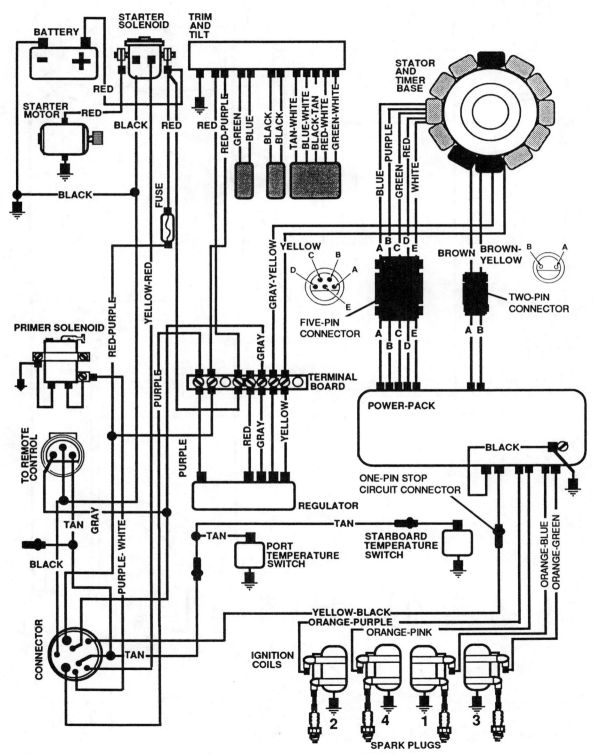

Fig. OM17-21—Wiring diagram of 1988 and 1989 Models 88-110 hp.

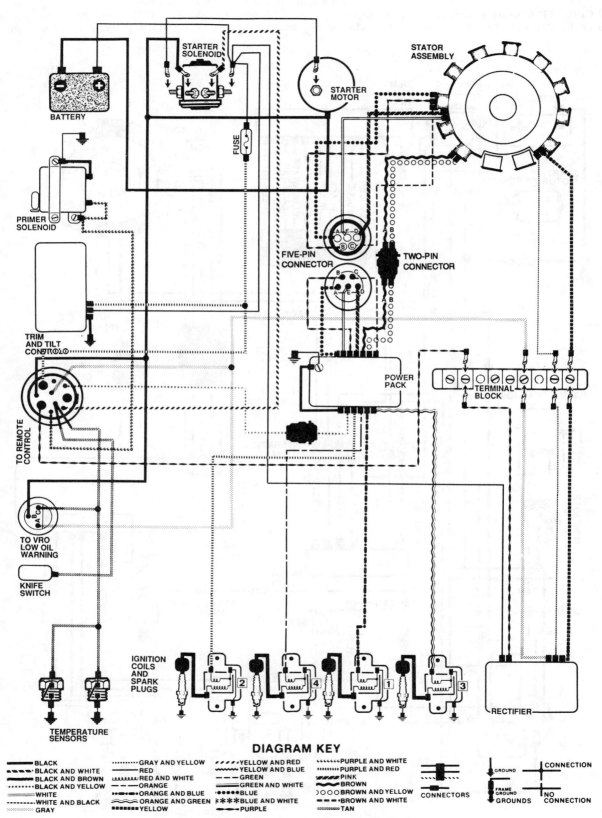

Fig. OM17-22—Wiring diagram of 1987 Models 120 and 140 hp.

tor between stop switch and power packs. Crank engine while noting spark tester. If normal spark is noted at all spark gaps, renew stop switch or repair stop switch circuit. If weak or no spark is noted at spark tester, refer to CHARGE COIL section.

CHARGE COIL. First test charge coils and leads for short to ground. Disconnect the two-pin connectors between power packs and stator. Set peak reading voltmeter control knobs to negative (−) and 500. Insert red lead of voltmeter into terminal A of two-pin connector

and connect black meter lead to engine ground. Crank engine while noting meter. Switch red test lead to terminal B of two-pin connector. Crank engine while noting meter. Any voltage reading on either test indicates grounded charge coils or leads. Repair leads or re-

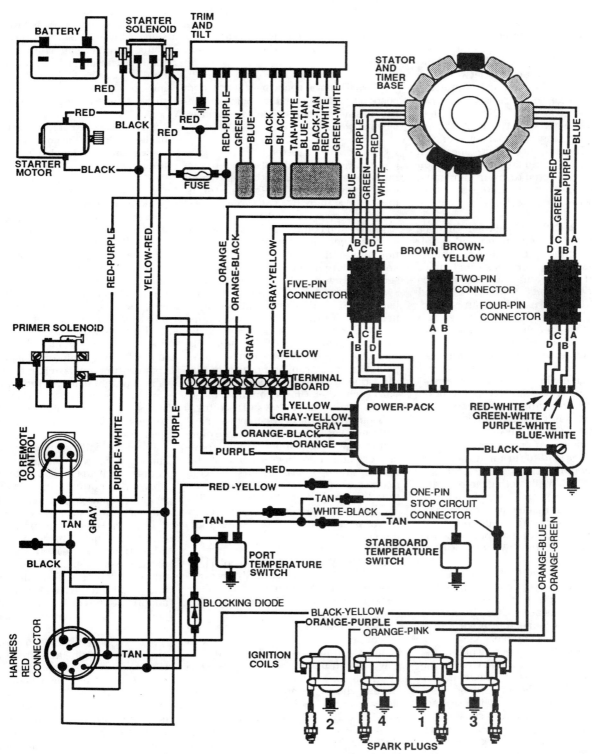

Fig. OM17-23—Wiring diagram of 1988 and 1989 Models 120 and 140 hp.

new stator. Repeat test at other two-pin connector.

To check charge coil output, connect red test lead to terminal B and black test lead to terminal A of two-pin connector. Crank engine while noting meter. Repeat test at other two-pin connector. If meter indicates 150 volts or more, refer to SENSOR COIL section. If meter indicates less than 150 volts, inspect condition of wiring and connectors. Make sure charge coil leads are located in the correct position in connectors. If wiring and connectors are acceptable, check charge coil resistance as follows: Connect a suitable ohmmeter between terminals A and B of two-pin connector. Renew charge coil if resistance is not within 535-585 ohms. Next, connect ohmmeter between terminal A and engine ground, then terminal B and engine ground. If continuity is noted between either terminal and ground, charge coil or leads are shorted to ground and must be repaired or renewed. Repeat test at other two-pin connector.

SENSOR COIL. Check sensor coils and wiring for shorts to ground as follows: Disconnect the four-pin connectors between power packs and timer base. Set peak reading voltmeter knobs to positive (+) and 5. Connect tester red lead to terminal A of four-pin connector and tester black lead to engine ground. Crank engine while noting meter. Move tester red lead to terminal B, crank engine while noting meter then move tester red lead to terminal C and crank engine while noting meter. A voltage reading at terminals A, B or C of either four-pin connector indicates sensor coil or leads are grounded. Renew timer base or repair wiring as necessary.

To check sensor coil output, connect black tester lead to terminal A of four-pin connector. Connect red tester lead to terminal B. While noting meter, crank engine, then move red tester lead to terminal C and crank engine. Be sure to repeat test on other four-pin connector. If sensor coil cranking output is 0.3 volt or more, proceed to POWER PACK OUTPUT section.

If sensor coil cranking output is less than 0.3 volt, inspect condition of sensor coil wiring and connectors. Make sure wiring pins are located in the correct position in connectors. If wiring and connectors are acceptable, check sensor coil resistance by connecting ohmmeter between terminals A and B, then terminals A and C of four-pin connector. Sensor coil resistance should be 30-50 ohms. Renew timer base assembly if resistance is not as specified. Be sure sensor coils are not shorted to ground by connecting ohmmeter between engine ground and alternately to terminals A, B and C

of four-pin connector. Repair sensor coil wiring or renew timer base if continuity is indicated between engine ground and terminal A, B or C.

POWER PACK. Set peak reading voltmeter knobs to negative (−) and 500. Disconnect the orange/blue primary lead from the number 1 (top) ignition coil. Install a Stevens TS-77 Terminal Extender (or suitable equivalent) to coil primary terminal, then connect orange/blue primary lead to terminal extender.

NOTE: Remove spark plug leads from spark plugs and ground to engine or connect to a suitable spark tester to prevent accidental starting.

Connect black tester lead to engine ground. Connect red tester lead to terminal extender at ignition coil. Crank engine while noting meter. If meter indicates less than 150 volts, remove orange/blue primary lead from terminal extender and connect red tester lead to orange/blue lead. Crank engine and note meter. If meter now indicates 150 volts or more, refer to IGNITION COIL section. If meter still indicates less than 150 volts, inspect condition of primary lead and terminal end and repair as necessary. If primary lead and terminal are acceptable, renew power pack. Be sure to repeat test at all ignition coils.

Faulty isolation diode inside power pack can cause rough and erratic running due to power packs interfering with each other. Check condition of isolation diodes as follows: Disconnect four-pin connector between power pack and timer base. Connect a suitable ohmmeter between terminals A and B (power pack side of connector). Note meter reading and reverse test leads. One connection should show very high resistance (infinity) and the other reading should be very low (zero). If not, renew power pack. Repeat test on other four-pin connector.

IGNITION COILS. Ignition coils may be tested using a variety of testers available from various manufacturers. Follow tester manufacturer's instructions when testing coil.

Check ignition coil primary resistance by connecting ohmmeter between coil primary terminal and coil ground. Primary resistance should be 0.05-0.15 ohm. Check secondary resistance between primary terminal and high tension terminal. Secondary resistance should be 225-325 ohms. Renew coil if not as specified. Ignition coil high tension lead (spark plug lead) resistance should be near zero ohm.

RUNNING OUTPUT. Perform running output tests to trouble-shoot intermittent or erratic ignition malfunctions. A CD adapter (junction box) such as Merc-O-Tronic Model 55-861, Stevens Model SA-6 or Electro-Specialties PRV-1A may be used to simplify checking charge coil and sensor coil output while engine is running. Plug connectors into the CD adapter one set at a time to check individual circuits while running engine. If CD adapter is not available, some running tests can be performed using jumper leads to connect peak reading voltmeter in parallel with circuit being tested. Note that all circuits must be connected if using jumper leads to perform running output tests.

NOTE: Place outboard motor into a suitable test tank with the correct test wheel installed when performing running output tests.

To check charge coil running output, peak reading voltmeter must be connected (in parallel) with two-pin connectors between stator and power packs. Connect black tester lead to brown/yellow stator lead and red tester lead to brown stator lead. If using CD adapter separate two-pin connector and plug both ends of connector into CD adapter. Insert voltmeter red test lead into jack A of CD adapter and black test lead into jack B.

Set voltmeter knobs to negative (−) and 500. Start engine and operate at the rpm malfunction is evident. Charge coil is acceptable if meter indicates a continuous reading of 250 volts or more. Test sensor coil running output. Be sure to repeat test on other two-pin connector.

If charge coil running output is less than 250 volts, check charge coil and charge coil leads for shorts to ground as previously outlined in CHARGE COIL section. Repair grounded leads as necessary or renew stator assembly.

To check sensor coil running output, connect voltmeter black test lead to the white timer base lead and red test lead to the green timer base lead. If using CD adapter, separate four-pin connector and plug both halves of connector into adapter. Connect black tester lead to jack A of CD adapter and red tester lead to jack B.

Set voltmeter knobs to positive (+) and 5. Start engine and run at rpm that malfunction is evident. Move red test lead to blue timer base lead or to jack C of CD adapter. Sensor coil running output should be continuous 1.0 volt or more on both tests. If meter indicates 1.0 volt or more, test power pack running output. If meter indicates less than 1.0 volt, check sensor coil and coil leads for short to ground as outlined in SENSOR COIL section. Repair leads as necessary or renew timer base assembly. Repeat test at remaining four-pin connector.

To check power pack running output, disconnect ignition coil primary leads, install terminal extenders (Stevens TS-77 or equivalent) on coil terminals, then connect coil primary leads to terminal extenders. Set voltmeter switches to negative (−) and 500. Connect tester black lead to engine ground. Start engine and run at rpm that malfunction is evident. Alternately, connect red tester lead to terminal extender of each coil. USE CAUTION not to touch metal part of terminal extender or tester lead to prevent shocks. Power pack running output should be a continuous 230 volts. If not, disconnect coil primary lead from terminal extender at top coil and connect tester red lead to primary lead. Disconnect spark plug leads from spark plugs and connect to a suitable spark tester to prevent engine starting. Crank engine while noting voltmeter. If meter indicates 150 volts or more, check ignition coils as outlined in IGNITION COIL section. If meter indicates less than 150 volts, renew power pack. Repeat test at all ignition coils.

Models 88-110 (1988 and 1989)

Refer to Fig. OM17-21 for wiring diagram typical of 1988 and 1989 Models 88-110 hp. A five-pin connector connects the timer base (sensor coils) to the power pack. The timer base contains four sensor coils, one for each cylinder. A two-pin connector connects the charge coil to the power pack. One charge coil is used. A one-pin connector connects power pack to key switch. One power pack is used.

TOTAL OUTPUT. Disconnect all spark plug leads from spark plugs and install a suitable spark tester to plug leads. Adjust tester spark gap to $1/2$ inch (12.7 mm). Crank engine while noting spark tester. If normal spark is noted at all spark gaps, refer to RUNNING OUTPUT section. If no spark output is noted at any spark gap, refer to STOP CIRCUIT section. If spark output is noted on at least one spark gap, refer to SENSOR COIL section.

STOP CIRCUIT. Disconnect one-pin stop circuit connector between power pack and key switch. Refer to Fig. OM17-21. With spark tester still installed, crank engine and note spark gaps. If spark is now present at all spark gaps, check condition of stop circuit and key switch with an ohmmeter and repair as necessary. If weak spark or spark at

some spark gaps is noted, refer to SENSOR COIL section. If no spark is present, refer to CHARGE COIL section.

CHARGE COIL. To check charge coil and coil leads for shorts to ground, disconnect two-pin connector between stator and power pack. Set peak reading voltmeter knobs to positive (+) and 500. Connect black tester lead to engine ground. Connect red tester lead to stator terminal A of two-pin connector. Crank engine while noting voltmeter, then switch red test lead to stator terminal B and crank engine while noting meter. Any voltage reading on either connection indicates charge coil or charge coil leads are grounded. Repair leads or renew stator assembly as necessary.

If no voltage reading is present, connect black test lead to terminal A and red test lead to terminal B of stator two-pin connector. Crank engine while noting meter. If meter indicates 150 volts or more, charge coil output is acceptable. Proceed to SENSOR COIL section.

If charge coil cranking output is less than 150 volts, inspect condition of charge coil wiring and verify pin location in connectors. If wiring and connectors are acceptable, connect a suitable ohmmeter between stator terminals A and B. Charge coil resistance should be 535-585 ohms on models with six ampere battery charging system and 455-505 ohms on models with nine ampere battery charging system. Renew stator assembly if resistance is not as specified.

SENSOR COIL. To check sensor coils and wiring for shorts to ground, connect black test lead to engine ground. Separate five-pin connector. Set peak reading voltmeter knobs to positive (+) and 5. Alternately connect red test lead to each terminal of five-pin connector while cranking engine. Any voltage reading indicates sensor coil or wiring is grounded. Repair wiring or renew timer base.

If no voltage is present, connect black test lead to terminal E and red test lead to terminal A of five-pin connector. Crank engine while noting meter. Repeat test on terminals B, C and D. Sensor coil output is acceptable if output is 0.3 volt or more. Proceed to POWER PACK section. If less than 0.3 volt is present, inspect condition of sensor coil wiring and connectors. Make sure of proper pin location in connectors. If wiring and connectors are in acceptable condition, check sensor coil resistance as follows: Connect ohmmeter black lead to terminal E of five-pin connector. Alternately connect ohmmeter red lead to terminals A, B, C and D. Sensor

coil resistance should be 30-50 ohms at each connection. Renew timer base if resistance is not as specified.

POWER PACK. To test power pack output, disconnect primary leads from ignition coils. Connect number 1 cylinder ignition coil primary lead (orange/blue) to red lead of Stevens Load Adapter No. PL-88. Connect load adapter black lead to engine ground. Connect peak reading voltmeter red test lead to load adapter red lead and voltmeter black test lead to engine ground.

NOTE: If Stevens Load Adapter PL-88 is not available, fabricate adapter using Radio Shack 10 ohm, 10 watt resister, part 271-132, or equivalent.

Set peak reading voltmeter knobs to positive (+) and 500. Crank engine while noting meter. Repeat test on remaining ignition coil primary leads. Power pack cranking output should be 150 volts or more at each coil. If output is acceptable at all coils, test ignition coils as outlined in IGNITION COILS section. If no output is noted at one or more primary lead, renew power pack.

IGNITION COILS. Ignition coils may be tested using a variety of testers available from various manufacturers. Follow tester manufacturer's instructions when testing coil.

Check ignition coil primary resistance by connecting ohmmeter between coil primary terminal and coil ground. Primary resistance should be 0.05-0.15 ohm. Check secondary resistance between primary terminal and high tension terminal. Secondary resistance should be 225-325 ohms. Renew coil if not as specified. Ignition coil high tension lead (spark plug lead) resistance should be near zero ohm.

RUNNING OUTPUT (1988 Models). Perform running output tests to troubleshoot intermittent or erratic ignition malfunctions. A CD adapter (junction box) such as Merc-O-Tronic Model 55-861, Stevens Model SA-6 or Electro-Specialties PRV-1A may be used to simplify checking charge coil and sensor coil output while engine is running. Plug connectors into the CD adapter one set at a time to check individual circuits while running engine. If CD adapter is not available, some running tests can be performed using jumper leads to connect peak reading voltmeter in parallel with circuit being tested. Note that all circuits must be connected if using jumper leads to perform running output tests.

NOTE: Place outboard motor into a suitable test tank with the correct test wheel installed when performing running output tests.

To check charge coil running output, peak reading voltmeter must be connected (in parallel) with two-pin connector between stator and power pack. Connect black tester lead to brown stator lead (terminal A) and red tester lead to brown/yellow stator lead (terminal B). If using CD adapter separate two-pin connector and plug both ends of connector into CD adapter. Insert voltmeter red test lead into jack A of CD adapter and black test lead into jack B.

Set voltmeter knobs to negative (−) and 500. Start engine and operate at the rpm malfunction is evident. Charge coil is acceptable if meter indicates a continuous reading of 250 volts or more. Test sensor coil running output.

If charge coil running output is less than 250 volts, check charge coil and charge coil leads for shorts to ground as previously outlined in CHARGE COIL section. Repair grounded leads as necessary or renew stator assembly.

To check sensor coil running output, connect voltmeter black test lead to the white timer base lead (terminal E) of the five-pin connector and red test lead to the blue timer base lead (terminal A). If using CD adapter, separate five-pin connector and plug both halves of connector into adapter. Connect black tester lead to jack E of CD adapter and red tester lead to jack A.

Set voltmeter knobs to positive (+) and 5. Start engine and run at rpm that malfunction is evident. Note meter reading and move red test lead alternately to the remaining leads of the five-pin timer base connector (terminals B, C and D [or jacks B, C and D of CD adapter]). Sensor coil running output should be continuous 1.0 volt or more on all tests. If meter indicates 1.0 volt or more, test power pack running output. If meter indicates less than 1.0 volt, check sensor coil and coil leads for short to ground as outlined in SENSOR COIL section. Repair leads as necessary or renew timer base assembly.

To check power pack running output, disconnect ignition coil primary leads, install terminal extenders (Stevens TS-77 or equivalent) on coil terminals, then reconnect coil primary leads to terminal extenders. Set voltmeter switches to negative (−) and 500. Connect tester black lead to engine ground. Start engine and run at rpm that malfunction is evident. Alternately, connect red tester lead to terminal extender of each coil. USE CAUTION not to touch metal part of terminal extender or tester lead to prevent shocks. Power pack running

output should be a continuous 230 volts. If not, disconnect coil primary lead from terminal extender at top coil and connect tester red lead to primary lead. Disconnect spark plug leads from spark plugs and connect to a suitable spark tester to prevent engine starting. Crank engine while noting voltmeter. If meter indicates 150 volts or more, check ignition coils as outlined in IGNITION COIL section. If meter indicates less than 150 volts, renew power pack. Repeat test at all ignition coils.

RUNNING OUTPUT (1989 Models). To check running output on 1989 Models 88-110 hp, refer to Fig. OM17-21 and disconnect primary leads from ignition coils. Install terminal extenders (Stevens TS-77 or equivalent) on coil terminals, then reconnect coil primary leads to terminal extenders. Set voltmeter switches to negative (−) and 500. Connect tester black lead to engine ground. Start engine and run at rpm that malfunction is evident. Alternately, connect red tester lead to terminal extender of each coil. USE CAUTION not to touch metal part of terminal extender or tester lead to prevent shocks. Power pack running output should be a continuous 230 volts at each ignition coil. If output is low at one or more coils, test charge coils as previously outlined in CHARGE COIL section. If NO output is noted at one or more coils, test sensor coils as previously outlined in SENSOR COIL section.

Models 120 And 140 (1987)

Refer to Fig. OM17-22 for wiring diagram of 1987 Models 120 and 140 hp. A five-pin connector connects timer base assembly (sensor coils) and power pack. Four sensor coils are used, one per cylinder. A two-pin connector connects stator assembly (charge coils) to power pack. One charge coil and one power pack is used. A one-pin stop circuit connector connects power pack to the key switch.

TOTAL OUTPUT. Disconnect all spark plug leads from spark plugs and install a suitable spark tester to plug leads. Adjust tester spark gap to $\frac{1}{2}$ inch (12.7 mm). Crank engine while noting spark tester. If normal spark is noted at all spark gaps, refer to RUNNING OUTPUT section. If no spark output is noted at any spark gap, refer to STOP CIRCUIT section. If spark output is noted on at least one spark gap, refer to SENSOR COIL section.

STOP CIRCUIT. Disconnect one-pin stop circuit connector (black/yellow) between power pack and key switch. Refer to Fig. OM17-22. With spark tester

still installed, crank engine and note spark gaps. If spark is now present at all spark gaps, check condition of stop circuit and key switch with an ohmmeter and repair as necessary. If no spark is noted at all spark gaps, refer to CHARGE COIL section. If spark is noted at one or more spark gaps, refer to SENSOR COIL section.

CHARGE COIL. To check charge coil and coil leads for shorts to ground, disconnect two-pin connector between stator and power pack. Set peak reading voltmeter knobs to negative (−) and 500. Connect black tester lead to engine ground. Connect red tester lead to stator terminal A of two-pin connector. Crank engine while noting voltmeter, then switch red test lead to stator terminal B and crank engine while noting meter. Any voltage reading on either connection indicates charge coil or charge coil leads are grounded. Repair leads or renew stator assembly as necessary.

If no voltage reading is present, connect black test lead to terminal A and red test lead to terminal B of stator two-pin connector. Crank engine while noting meter. If meter indicates 175 volts or more, charge coil output is acceptable. Proceed to SENSOR COIL section.

If charge coil cranking output is less than 175 volts, inspect condition of charge coil wiring and verify pin location in connectors. If wiring and connectors are acceptable, connect a suitable ohmmeter between stator terminals A and B. Charge coil resistance should be 535-585 ohms. Renew stator assembly if resistance is not as specified. No continuity should be present between either terminal A or B and engine ground.

SENSOR COIL. To check sensor coils and wiring for shorts to ground, separate five-pin connector halves. Set peak reading voltmeter knobs to positive (+) and 5. Connect black test lead to engine ground. Alternately connect red test lead to each terminal of five-pin connector while cranking engine. Any voltage reading indicates sensor coil or wiring is grounded. Repair wiring or renew timer base.

If no voltage is present, connect black test lead to terminal E and red test lead to terminal A of five-pin connector. Crank engine while noting meter. Repeat test on terminals B, C and D. Sensor coil output is acceptable if output is 0.3 volt or more. Proceed to POWER PACK section. If sensor coil output is less than 0.3 volt, inspect condition of sensor coil wiring and connectors. Make sure of proper pin location in connectors. If wiring and connectors are in acceptable condition, check sensor coil resistance as follows: Connect ohmmeter black lead to terminal E of five-pin connector. Alternately connect ohmmeter red lead to terminals A, B, C and D. Sensor coil resistance should be 30-50 ohms at each connection. Renew timer base is resistance is not as specified. No continuity should be present between engine ground and any terminal in five-pin connector.

POWER PACK. Set peak reading voltmeter knobs to negative (–) and 500. Disconnect the orange/blue primary lead from the number 1 (top) ignition coil. Install a Stevens TS-77 Terminal Extender (or suitable equivalent) to coil primary terminal, then connect orange/blue primary lead to terminal extender.

NOTE: Remove spark plug leads from spark plugs and ground to engine or connect to a suitable spark tester to prevent accidental starting.

Connect black tester lead to engine ground. Connect red tester lead to terminal extender at ignition coil. Crank engine while noting meter. Power pack output should be 175 volts or more. If meter indicates less than 175 volts, remove orange/blue primary lead from terminal extender and connect red ·ester lead to orange/blue lead. Crank engine and note meter. If meter now indicates 175 volts or more, refer to IGNITION COIL section. If meter still indicates less than 175 volts, inspect condition of primary lead and terminal end and repair as necessary. If primary lead and terminal are acceptable, renew power pack. Repeat test at all ignition coils.

IGNITION COILS. Ignition coils may be tested using a variety of testers available from various manufacturers. Follow tester manufacturer's instructions when testing coil.

Check ignition coil primary resistance by connecting ohmmeter between coil primary terminal and coil ground. Primary resistance should be 0.05-0.15 ohm. Check secondary resistance between primary terminal and high tension terminal. Secondary resistance should be 225-325 ohms. Renew coil if not as specified. Ignition coil high tension lead (spark plug lead) resistance should be near zero ohm.

RUNNING OUTPUT. Perform running output tests to trouble-shoot intermittent or erratic ignition malfunctions. A CD adapter (junction box) such as Merc-O-Tronic Model 55-861, Stevens Model SA-6 or Electro-Specialties PRV-1A may be used to simplify checking

charge coil and sensor coil output while engine is running. Plug connectors into the CD adapter one set at a time to check individual circuits while running engine. If CD adapter is not available, some running tests can be performed using jumper leads to connect peak reading voltmeter in parallel with circuit being tested. Note that all circuits must be connected if using jumper leads to perform running output tests.

NOTE: Place outboard motor into a suitable test tank with the correct test wheel installed when performing running output tests.

To check charge coil running output, peak reading voltmeter must be connected (in parallel) with two-pin connector between stator and power pack. Connect black tester lead to brown stator lead (terminal A) and red tester lead to brown/yellow stator lead (terminal B). If using CD adapter, separate two-pin connector and plug both ends of connector into CD adapter. Insert voltmeter red test lead into jack A of CD adapter and black test lead into jack B.

Set voltmeter knobs to negative (–) and 500. Start engine and operate at the rpm malfunction is evident. Charge coil is acceptable if meter indicates a continuous reading of 250 volts or more. Test sensor coil running output.

If charge coil running output is less than 250 volts, check charge coil and charge coil leads for shorts to ground as previously outlined in CHARGE COIL section. Repair grounded leads as necessary or renew stator assembly.

To check sensor coil running output, connect voltmeter black test lead to the white timer base lead (terminal E) of the five-pin connector and red test lead to the blue timer base lead (terminal A). If using CD adapter, separate five-pin connector and plug both halves of connector into adapter. Connect black tester lead to jack E of CD adapter and red tester lead to jack A.

Set voltmeter knobs to positive (+) and 5. Start engine and run at rpm that malfunction is evident. Note meter reading and move red test lead alternately to the remaining leads of the five-pin timer base connector (terminals B, C and D [or jacks B, C and D of CD adapter]). Sensor coil running output should be continuous 1.0 volt or more on all tests. If meter indicates 1.0 volt or more, test power pack running output. If meter indicates less than 1.0 volt, check sensor coil and coil leads for short to ground as outlined in SENSOR COIL section. Repair leads as necessary or renew timer base assembly.

To check power pack running output, disconnect ignition coil primary leads,

install terminal extenders (Stevens TS-77 or equivalent) on coil terminals, then reconnect coil primary leads to terminal extenders. Set voltmeter switches to negative (–) and 500. Connect tester black lead to engine ground. Start engine and run at rpm that malfunction is evident. Alternately, connect red tester lead to terminal extender of each coil. USE CAUTION not to touch metal part of terminal extender or tester lead to prevent shocks. Power pack running output should be a continuous 230 volts. If not, disconnect coil primary lead from terminal extender at top coil and connect tester red lead to primary lead. Disconnect spark plug leads from spark plugs and connect to a suitable spark tester to prevent engine starting. Crank engine while noting voltmeter. If meter indicates 175 volts or more, check ignition coils as outlined in IGNITION COIL section. If meter indicates less than 175 volts, renew power pack. Repeat test at all ignition coils.

Models 120 and 140 hp (1988 and 1989)

Refer to Fig. OM17-23 for wiring diagram on 1988 and 1989 Models 120 and 140 hp. The power pack is connected to the timer base (sensor coils) by five-pin and four-pin connectors. Two sensor coils per cylinder are used. One sensor coil is for normal operation and one coil is used to activate the QuickStart function. The power pack is connected to the charge coil with a two-pin connector. One charge coil is used. The power pack is connected to the power coil at a terminal board. A one-pin connector joins the power pack to the key switch.

S.L.O.W. (Speed Limiting Overheat Warning). The S.L.O.W. function is activated when engine temperature exceeds 203° F (95° C). When activated, the S.L.O.W. system limits engine speed to approximately 2500 rpm. To resume normal operation, the engine must be stopped and cooled to 162° F (72° C). The S.L.O.W. system is activated by input from temperature switches located in port and starboard cylinder heads. A blocking diode located in the engine wiring harness is used to isolate the S.L.O.W. system from other warning signals.

To determine if the S.L.O.W. system is functioning properly, disconnect tan temperature switch leads from port and starboard temperature sensors. Place outboard motor in a suitable test tank with the correct test wheel installed. Start engine and run at 3500 rpm. Connect port side temperature switch lead (tan) to engine ground. Engine speed should slow to approximately 2500 rpm.

Repeat test with starboard side temperature switch lead.

If S.L.O.W. system functions properly when tested at both temperature switch tan leads, refer to TEMPERATURE SWITCH section. If proper operation is noted at only one temperature switch lead, inspect condition of wiring harness and connectors and repair as necessary. If neither test indicates proper operation, proceed as follows: Loosen power pack and remove orange and orange/black power coil leads from terminal board. Connect an ohmmeter between orange and orange/black leads. Renew power pack if resistance is within 86-106 ohms. If not, renew stator assembly.

NOTE: DO NOT start engine with power coil leads disconnected.

BLOCKING DIODE. If the S.L.O.W. function is activated by other warning horn systems, test blocking diode located in the wiring harness. Disconnect port and starboard temperature switch tan leads and wiring harness red connector. Connect an ohmmeter between either temperature switch tan lead and tan lead terminal inside harness red connector, then reverse ohmmeter leads. A high reading (infinity) should be indicated in one connection and a low reading (zero) in the other. If not, renew wiring harness assembly.

TEMPERATURE SWITCH. Temperature switches should be open at 147°-177° F (65°-79° C) and should close at 197°-205° F (92°-98° C). Test switches using a suitable continuity light or ohmmeter. Heat switches using a suitable oil bath with an accurate thermometer.

QUICKSTART. The QuickStart circuit is activated each time the engine is started. QuickStart automatically advances ignition timing for approximately five seconds during starting (at all temperatures). QuickStart is also activated any time engine temperature is below 96° F (36° C). QuickStart is inoperative when engine speed exceeds 1100 rpm.

To determine if QuickStart is functioning properly, place outboard motor in a suitable test tank with the correct test wheel installed. Engine temperature must be above 96° F (36° C) before testing.

NOTE: Make sure speed control linkage, idle speed and ignition timing are properly adjusted before attempting to test Quick-Start system. Refer to SPEED CONTROL LINKAGE section.

Place marks on flywheel adjacent to timing pointer indicating TDC for all cylinders. Disconnect white/black lead between power pack and port side temperature switch. Connect a timing light to number 1 cylinder spark plug lead, start engine and run at idle speed in forward gear (not more than 900 rpm). The timing light should flash at the number 1 cylinder TDC mark on flywheel. Reconnect the white/black lead to the power pack. The number 1 cylinder TDC mark should shift to the right approximately 1 inch indicating ignition timing has returned to normal setting. Repeat test for each cylinder. Note that engine must be stopped before testing each remaining cylinder.

If one or more sensor coils do not operate properly, renew timer base assembly. If no sensor coils operate properly, disconnect white/black lead from power pack lead and connect ohmmeter between white/black lead and engine ground. Ohmmeter should indicate continuity with engine temperature below 89° F (32° C). If continuity is noted, test temperature switches. If not, connect ohmmeter between each power coil lead (orange and orange/black) and engine ground. No continuity should be present between power coil leads and ground. Next, check resistance between orange and orange/black power coil leads. Renew power pack if resistance is within 86-106 ohms. If not, renew stator assembly.

If QuickStart system remains activated when engine speed exceeds 1,100 rpm, renew power pack. If QuickStart system remains activated continuously, regardless of temperature, time activated and engine speed, test port side temperature switch white/black lead and connector, test power pack white/black lead and connector, test engine for undercooling condition or renew power pack.

TOTAL OUTPUT. Disconnect all spark plug leads from spark plugs and install a suitable spark tester to plug leads. Adjust tester spark gap to $^1/_2$ inch (12.7 mm). Crank engine while noting spark tester. If normal spark is noted at all spark gaps, refer to RUNNING OUTPUT section. If no spark output is noted at any spark gap, refer to STOP CIRCUIT section. If spark output is noted on at least one spark gap, refer to SENSOR COIL section.

STOP CIRCUIT. Disconnect one-pin stop circuit connector (black/yellow) between power pack and key switch. Refer to Fig. OM17-23. With spark tester still installed, crank engine and note spark gaps. If spark is now present at all spark gaps, check condition of stop circuit and key switch with an ohmmeter

and repair as necessary. If no spark is noted at all spark gaps, refer to CHARGE COIL section. If spark is noted at one or more spark gaps, refer to SENSOR COIL section.

CHARGE COIL. To check charge coil and coil leads for shorts to ground, disconnect two-pin connector between stator and power pack. Set peak reading voltmeter knobs to positive (+) and 500. Connect black tester lead to engine ground. Connect red tester lead to stator terminal A of two-pin connector. Crank engine while noting voltmeter, then switch red test lead to stator terminal B and crank engine while noting meter. Any voltage reading at either connection indicates charge coil or charge coil leads are grounded. Repair leads or renew stator assembly as necessary.

If no voltage reading is present, connect black test lead to terminal A and red test lead to terminal B of stator two-pin connector. Set voltmeter to positive (+) and 500. Crank engine while noting meter. If meter indicates 175 volts or more, charge coil output is acceptable. Proceed to SENSOR COIL section.

If charge coil cranking output is less than 175 volts, inspect condition of charge coil wiring and verify pin location in connectors. If wiring and connectors are acceptable, connect a suitable ohmmeter between stator terminals A and B. Charge coil resistance should be 510-610 ohms on 1988 models and 455-505 ohms on 1989 models. Renew stator assembly if resistance is not as specified. No continuity should be present between either terminal A or B and engine ground.

SENSOR COIL. To check sensor coils and wiring for shorts to ground, separate five-pin and four-pin connectors between timer base and power pack. Set peak reading voltmeter knobs to positive (+) and 5. Connect black test lead to engine ground. Alternately connect red test lead to each timer base terminal while cranking engine. Any voltage reading indicates sensor coil or wiring is grounded. Repair wiring or renew timer base.

To check sensor coil output, connect voltmeter black test lead to terminal E (white) of the five-pin connector. Alternately connect red test lead to the remaining four port and four starboard connector terminals. Crank engine at each connection while noting meter. If sensor coil output is 0.5 volt or more, refer to POWER PACK section. If output is less than 0.5 volt, inspect condition of wiring and connectors. If wiring and connectors are acceptable, connect ohmmeter black lead to terminal E of five-pin connector. Alternately connect ohmmeter red lead to each terminal in four-pin connector. Ohmmeter should indicate 100-160 ohms. Next, check resistance between terminal E and remaining terminals of five-pin connector. Resistance should be 35-55 ohms. No continuity should be present between engine ground and any terminal in five-pin connector or any terminal in four-pin connector. Renew timer base if resistance is not as specified.

POWER PACK. To check power pack output, remove primary leads from ignition coils. Connect primary lead of number 1 cylinder ignition coil (top starboard) to red lead of Stevens Load Adapter PL-88. Connect load adapter black lead to engine ground.

NOTE: If Stevens Load Adapter PL-88 is not available, fabricate adapter using Radio Shack 10 ohm, 10 watt resister, part 271-132, or equivalent.

Set peak reading voltmeter knobs to positive (+) and 500. Connect voltmeter red test lead to load adapter red lead and black test lead to engine ground. Crank engine while noting meter. Power pack output should be 150 volts or more. Repeat test at remaining ignition coils. If 150 volts or more is present at all primary leads, refer to IGNITION COIL section. If no output is noted at any primary lead, renew power pack.

IGNITION COILS. Ignition coils may be tested using a variety of testers available from various manufacturers. Follow tester manufacturer's instructions when testing coil.

Check ignition coil primary resistance by connecting ohmmeter between coil primary terminal and coil ground. Primary resistance should be 0.05-0.15 ohm. Check secondary resistance between primary terminal and high tension terminal. Secondary resistance should be 225-325 ohms. Renew coil if not as specified. Ignition coil high tension lead (spark plug lead) resistance should be near zero ohm.

RUNNING OUTPUT. To check running output, disconnect primary leads from ignition coils. Install terminal extenders (Stevens TS-77 or equivalent) on coil terminals, then reconnect coil primary leads to terminal extenders. Set voltmeter switches to positive (+) and 500. Connect tester black lead to engine ground.

NOTE: Outboard motor should be placed into a suitable test tank with the correct test wheel installed when checking running output.

Start engine and run at rpm that malfunction is evident. Alternately, connect red tester lead to terminal extender of each coil. USE CAUTION not to touch metal part of terminal extender or tester lead to prevent shocks. Power pack running output should be a continuous 180 volts at each ignition coil. If output is low at one or more coils, test charge coils as previously outlined in CHARGE COIL section. If NO output is noted at one or more coils, test sensor coils as previously outlined in SENSOR COIL section.

COOLING SYSTEM

THERMOSTAT. On 88-110 hp models, thermostats and pressure valves are part of the exhaust housing adapter. Refer to Fig. OM17-26 for exploded view. On 120 and 140 hp models, a thermostat and pressure valve are installed in each cylinder head.

Cooling system operation can be checked on all models using heat sensitive sticks such as Markal Thermomelt Stiks. To use Thermomelt Stiks, place outboard motor in test tank with the correct test wheel installed. Start engine and run at 3000 rpm for five minutes minimum. Reduce engine speed to approximately 900 rpm and mark top of both cylinder heads with a 125° F (52° C) and a 163° F (73° C) Thermomelt Stik. At 900 rpm, the 125° F (52° C) Stik should melt but not the 163° F (73° C) Stik.

WATER PUMP. The water pump is mounted on top surface of gearcase housing. The rubber impeller is mounted on and driven by the drive shaft. To remove the water pump, separate the lower unit from the drive shaft and exhaust housing.

Lip of seal (5—Fig. OM17-27) should face down. Screws attaching water pump housing and cover should be coated with OMC Gasket Sealing Compound or equivalent and tightened to 60-84 in.-lbs. (7-9 N·m). Apply OMC Adhesive M or equivalent to bottom of impeller plate before installing. Sharp edge of impeller drive key (11) is leading edge as drive shaft is rotated clockwise (viewed from top). Lubricate impeller and rotate drive shaft clockwise (viewed from top) when installing housing (6) over impeller. Avoid turning drive shaft counterclockwise after water pump is reassembled.

POWER HEAD

Models 88-110 Hp

REMOVE AND REINSTALL. To remove power head, remove screws from two front rubber mounts. Remove shift rod connector clip (Fig. OM17-28). Remove four exhaust cover screws, disconnect thermostat hoses, remove two lower engine cover-to-rear exhaust housing screws, then remove rear exhaust housing cover. Remove power head-to-exhaust housing nuts at rear of exhaust housing. Remove six exhaust housing-to-power head screws. At front of power head, remove one screw and one nut on each side of power head. Disconnect fuel inlet hose from fuel pump on models so equipped. Disconnect VRO

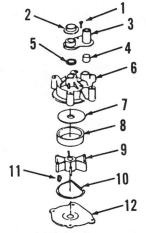

Fig. OM17-27—Exploded view of water pump.

1. Screw	7. Plate
2. Grommet	8. Liner
3. Cover	9. Impeller
4. Water tube seal	10. Seal
5. Seal	11. Drive cam
6. Housing	12. Plate

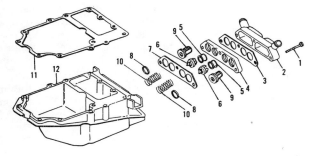

Fig. OM17-26—Exploded view of thermostat, pressure valves and related components on 88-110 hp models.

1. Screw
2. Cover
3. Gasket
4. Valve body
5. Grommet
6. Valve
7. Gasket
8. Gasket
9. Thermostat
10. Spring
11. Gasket
12. Exhaust housing adapter

Fig. OM17-28—View of shift rod connector retainer clip on 88-110 hp models.

pulse hose from power head, unscrew VRO pump and lay aside. Remove power head from exhaust housing and place on a suitable holding fixture.

When reinstalling power head, install a new "O" ring on drive shaft and coat drive shaft splines with OMC Moly Lube or a suitable water-resistance grease. Install a new power head to adapter gasket. Do not use sealer on gasket. Lower power head on adapter while rotating power head slightly to align crankshaft and drive shaft splines. Coat threads of exhaust housing-to-power head screws and adapter-to-power head screws with OMC Gel Seal II. Tighten exhaust housing-to-power head screws to 16-18 ft.-lbs. (22-24 N·m) and adapter-to-power head screws to 10-12 ft.-lbs. (14-16 N·m). Complete remainder of reinstallation by reversing removal procedure.

On VRO equipped models, be sure to bleed air from VRO hoses prior to starting engine. Add a 50:1 fuel and oil mixture to fuel tank and monitor oil in VRO tank to ensure VRO system is functioning. Power head-to-exhaust housing screws should be retightened after running engine, then allowing to cool.

Models 120 And 140 Hp

REMOVE AND REINSTALL. Remove lower engine cover one half at a time. Remove flywheel nut using a $1^7/_{16}$ inch socket and a suitable flywheel holder. Pull flywheel from crankshaft using a suitable universal puller. Remove stator assembly. Disconnect power trim/tilt wiring harness from power head. Unscrew and remove pin securing shift rod to shift lever (under intake manifold). Remove eight screws and two nuts securing exhaust housing to power head. Remove two screws and one nut securing exhaust adapter to power head. Lift power head off exhaust housing and secure in a suitable holding fixture.

When reinstalling power head, coat drive shaft splines with OMC Moly Lube or a suitable equivalent water-resistant grease. Install a new power head base gasket. Do not use sealer on gasket. Lower power head on exhaust housing while rotating power head slightly to align crankshaft and drive shaft splines. Coat threads of power head mounting screws with OMC Gel Seal II. Install all screws loosely, then tighten to 12-14 ft.-lbs. (16-19 N·m).

NOTE: Power head mounting screws should be retighten after engine has been run and allowed to cool.

Tighten power head-to-exhaust adapter screws 12-14 ft.-lbs. (16-19 N·m). Complete remainder of reinstallation by reversing removal procedure. Tighten flywheel nut to 140-150 ft.-lbs. (190-203 N·m).

All Models

DISASSEMBLY AND REASSEMBLY. Remove all carburetion, electrical and ignition components from power head. On 120 and 140 hp models, the complete fuel system can be removed as an assembly by unscrewing carburetors and rotating carburetors to gain access to air silencer screws. Remove VRO pulse hoses from crankcase, remove VRO mounting brackets and lift fuel system assembly from power head.

Note position of all screws, clamps, wires and hoses for reference during reassembly. Transfer port covers, exhaust covers, cylinder heads and intake manifold should be carefully removed, by loosening screws evenly, to prevent

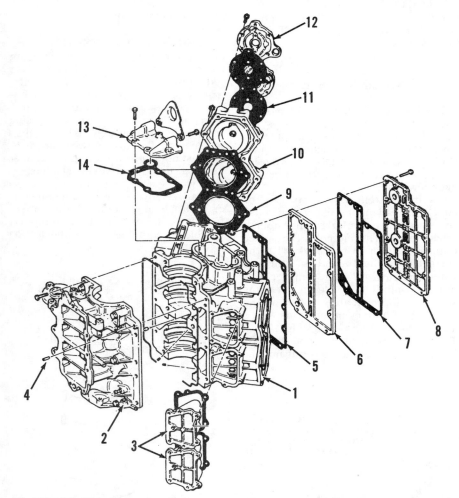

Fig. OM17-29—Exploded view of cylinder block and crankcase assembly on 88-110 hp models. On 120 and 140 hp models, cylinder head covers (12) and transfer port covers (3) are cast into block (1).

1. Cylinder block
2. Crankcase cover
3. Transfer port covers
4. Taper pin
5. Gasket
6. Inner exhaust cover
7. Gasket
8. Exhaust cover
9. Gasket
10. Cylinder head
11. Gasket
12. Cylinder head cover
13. Water passage cover
14. Gasket

warpage. Remove screws attaching crankcase heads (2 and 23—Fig. OM17-30) to crankcase. Drive the crankcase taper pin(s) (4—Fig. OM17-29) out toward front of engine. Use caution not to damage taper pin bore. Unscrew and remove forward crankcase cover (2). Remove the main bearing screws located in intake passages. Loosen screws in several steps to prevent warpage. Separate crankcase cover from cylinder block by gently tapping end of crankshaft with a soft-face mallet, then lift off cover.

Pistons, rods and crankshaft are now accessible for removal and inspection as outlined in the appropriate service sections. All moving and wearing components should be marked for location and direction prior to removal for reference during reassembly.

When reassembling, the crankcase and intake manifold must be completely sealed against both vacuum and pressure. Exhaust manifold and cylinder heads must be sealed against water leakage and pressure. Mating surfaces of water intake and exhaust areas between lower unit and power head must form a tight seal. It is recommended that all mating surfaces be carefully inspected for nicks, burrs, erosion and warping that might interfere with a tight seal. All surfaces may be lapped if necessary to provide a smooth, flat surface, but DO NOT remove any more metal than absolutely necessary.

NOTE: Crankcase cover (2—Fig. OM17-29) and cylinder block (1) mating surfaces MUST NOT be lowered.

Crankcase cover is positively located during reassembly by the use of taper pins. Be certain taper pin(s) are not bent, nicked or distorted and that taper pin bores in crankcase are clean and true. When reassembling crankcase assembly, install all fasteners finger tight, then install taper pin(s). Be sure pins are fully seated, but do not use excessive force.

Make sure crankcase and cylinder block mating surfaces are completely clean and free of old sealer, nicks and burrs. Apply OMC Locquic Primer to mating surface of crankcase cover and allow to dry. Apply OMC Gel Seal II to mating surface of crankcase cover. Be sure entire surface is coated, but avoid excess application. Do not allow Gel Seal II closer than $1/4$ inch (6.3 mm) to seals, seal rings or bearings.

NOTE: If OMC Locquic Primer is not used, power head should be allowed to stand for 24 hours before returning to service.

When tightening crankcase screws, start in the center and work toward

ends. Refer to CONDENSED SERVICE DATA for torque specifications. During reassembly, frequently check rotation of crankshaft for binding or unusual noise.

On 88-110 hp models, note location of water deflectors shown (Fig. OM17-33).

Deteriorated or missing deflectors may cause overheating and hot spots.

PISTONS, PINS, RINGS AND CYLINDERS. Before detaching connecting rods from crankshaft, mark pis-

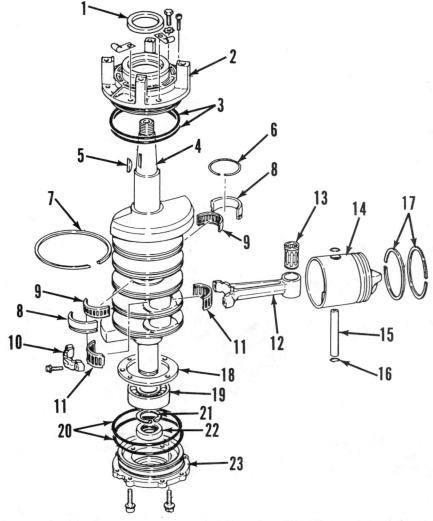

Fig. OM17-30—Exploded view of crankshaft and related components. On 88-110 hp models, piston pin bearing (13) consists of 28 loose needle rollers and two thrust washers. A caged roller bearing (13) is used on 120 and 140 hp models.

1. Seal	9. Main bearing	17. Piston rings
2. Upper crankcase head	10. Connecting rod cap	18. Bearing retainer plate
3. "O" rings	11. Connecting rod bearing	19. Lower main bearing
4. Crankshaft	12. Connecting rod	20. "O" rings
5. Woodruff key	13. Piston pin bearing	21. Snap ring
6. Retaining ring	14. Piston	22. Seal
7. Seal ring	15. Piston pin	23. Lower crankcase head
8. Outer race	16. Snap ring	

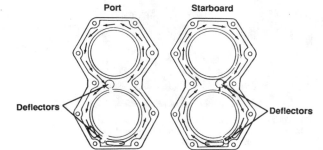

Fig. OM17-33—On 88-110 hp models, water deflectors must be installed in locations shown for proper water flow around cylinders.

ton, rod and cap for correct reassembly to each other and for installation into original cylinder. Pistons and rings are available in standard and 0.030 inch (0.76 mm) oversize. Refer to CONDENSED SERVICE DATA for service specifications. Maximum allowable cylinder bore out-of-round is 0.004 inch

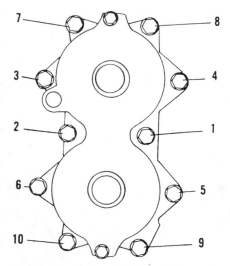

Fig. OM17-34—Tighten cylinder head screws in sequence shown.

Fig. OM17-35—To check clearance of pressure-back (top) piston ring, lay a straightedge across ring groove as shown. If straightedge does not contact piston on both sides of ring, remove ring and clean ring groove.

(0.10 mm). Maximum allowable cylinder bore taper is 0.002 inch (0.05 mm). The manufacturer does not specify piston-to-cylinder clearance. If cylinder and piston are within wear tolerance, clearance should be acceptable. If boring cylinder for oversize piston, add amount of piston oversize (0.030 in. [0.76 mm]) to standard cylinder bore diameter to determine correct cylinder oversize diameter.

Measure cylinder head flatness using a suitable straightedge and feeler gage. Resurface cylinder head if warped in excess of 0.004 inch (0.10 mm). Do not remove more than 0.010 inch (0.25 mm) of metal from head.

The piston pin is retained in piston by snap rings (16—Fig. OM17-30). Snap rings (16) should be renewed once removed. Install snap rings (16) with gap facing down. On 88-110 hp models, piston pin bearing is 28 loose needle rollers with two thrust washers. Thrust washer should be installed with large diameter (flat side) facing outward. A caged roller bearing (13) is used on 120 and 140 hp models.

Refer to CONDENSED SERVICE DATA for piston ring service specifications. Top ring is pressure-back design. To check clearance of pressure-back type ring, place a straightedge across the ring groove as shown in Fig. OM17-35. The straightedge should contact piston on both sides of ring. If not, remove ring and clean ring groove.

Measure piston diameter ¼ inch (6.3 mm) up from bottom of skirt. Take two measurements 90 degrees apart. Renew piston if difference between two measurements exceeds 0.004 inch (0.10 mm). Oil hole in small end of connecting rod must face toward flywheel (up). On 88-110 hp models, install pistons on connecting rods so long sloping side of piston crown faces exhaust ports. On 120 and 140 hp models, piston crown is marked "EXHAUST," "PORT" AND "STBD." Be sure piston is installed in

the appropriate cylinder bank with "EXHAUST" mark facing exhaust ports. Be certain that all wearing surfaces are thoroughly lubricated during reassembly.

CONNECTING RODS, BEARINGS AND CRANKSHAFT. Mark all moving or wearing assemblies for location and direction before removal. Center main bearings consist of split race (8—Fig. OM17-30), retaining ring (6) and bearing (9). Retaining ring groove in split race (8) should be installed facing down. Upper main bearing and upper crankcase head (2) are a unit assembly. Lower main bearing is pressed on crankshaft and retained by snap ring (21). Crankpin bearings consist of bearing halves (11) with connecting rod and cap serving as outer bearing race.

Crankshaft seal rings (7) should be installed in original position if removed. Seal rings (7) should be renewed if worn to less than 0.154 inch (3.91 mm) thick. When installing crankshaft assembly into cylinder block, seal ring end gaps should be facing up.

Connecting rods are cracked-cap design. When properly assembled, parting line between rod and cap should be nearly invisible. When reassembling, make sure match marks on rod and cap are aligned, oil hole in connecting rod small end is facing flywheel and pistons are facing the correct direction. Refer to Fig. OM17-36 and PISTONS, PINS, RINGS AND CYLINDERS section. OMC Alignment Fixture 396749 (Fig. OM17-37) should be used to properly align connecting rod and cap. Follow instructions supplied with tool.

PROPELLER

Lower unit protection is provided by an integral cushion hub in propeller. Various propellers are available from the manufacturer. Select propeller to allow full throttle operation within the recom-

Fig. OM17-36—Oil hole in connecting rod small end should face top of motor and dots on rod and cap should be aligned.

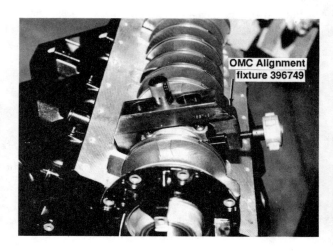

Fig. OM17-37—View showing OMC Alignment Fixture 396749 installed on connecting rod. Refer to text.

mended speed range of 4500-5500 rpm on 88-110 hp models and 5000-6000 rpm on 120 and 140 hp models.

LOWER UNIT

REMOVE AND REINSTALL. To remove gearcase, disconnect upper end of shift rod by removing shift rod retainer (Fig. OM17-28) on 88-110 hp models. On 120 and 140 hp models, remove threaded pin from shift lever located at base of intake manifold on the port side. Remove propeller and drain lubricant from gearcase. Mark location of trim tab (22—Fig. OM17-40) for reference during reassembly, then remove trim tab. Remove two screws on each side of gearcase and two screws at rear.

NOTE: One rear screw is in trim tab cavity.

Separate gearcase from exhaust housing being careful not to bend shift rod.

To install gearcase, reverse removal procedure. Install a new "O" ring in end of drive shaft and coat splines with a suitable water-resistant grease. Check length of gear shift rod (25). With shifter in neutral, distance from mating surface of gearcase (21) to center of hole in top of shift rod should be $21^{13}/_{16}$-$21^{7}/_{8}$ inches (554.04-556.62 mm) on long shaft 88-110 hp models, $26^{13}/_{16}$-$26^{7}/_{8}$ inches (681.04-682.62 mm) on extra long shaft 88-110 hp models, $21^{29}/_{32}$-$21^{31}/_{32}$ inches (556.42-558.00 mm) on 120 and 140 hp models with 20 inch (508 mm) shaft, $24^{13}/_{32}$-$24^{15}/_{32}$ inches (619.92-621.51 mm) on 120 and 140 hp models with 22.5 inch (571 mm) shaft and $26^{29}/_{32}$-$26^{31}/_{32}$ inches (683.42-685.00 mm) on 120 and 140 hp models with 25 inch (635 mm) shaft. Top of shift rod should slant forward. Apply OMC Adhesive M to gearcase and exhaust housing gasket surfaces. Be sure water tube guides and water tube are installed properly. Apply OMC Gasket Sealing Compound to threads of gearcase screws.

GEARCASE. Gearcase may be disassembled using the following procedure: Remove propeller, drain lubricant and remove gearcase as described in previous section. Remove screws securing shift rod cover (29—Fig. OM17-40), unscrew shift rod (25) and remove shift rod and cover as an assembly. Remove water pump housing (3A), impeller (6), impeller drive cam and lower plate (8). Remove four screws holding propeller shaft bearing housing (69) and using a suitable puller, remove bearing housing. Discard seals (71) and "O" ring (67). Remove snap rings (66), thrust washer assembly (64 and 63) and slide reverse gear (62) off propeller shaft. A special socket is available to hold drive shaft so

nut securing pinion gear (18) can be removed. After pinion gear retaining nut is removed, unscrew the four screws securing upper drive shaft bearing housing (11). Pull drive shaft and associated parts out of gearcase. A puller may be necessary. Propeller shaft (60) may now be pulled from gearcase complete with forward gear (52), forward gear housing (37) and all related parts.

Inspect drive shaft spines, bearing surfaces and seal surfaces for wear or damage. Damaged splines may be caused by

striking a submerged object and bending the exhaust housing. Check parallelism of top and bottom surfaces if questionable. If surfaces are not parallel, renew housing. Do not attempt to straighten a bent or damaged exhaust housing.

Lower drive shaft bearing (17) should be removed only if renewal is necessary. Drive shaft bearing is secured in position by set screw (17A) as well as a press fit in gearcase. Set screw (17A) is located on starboard side in area of water in-

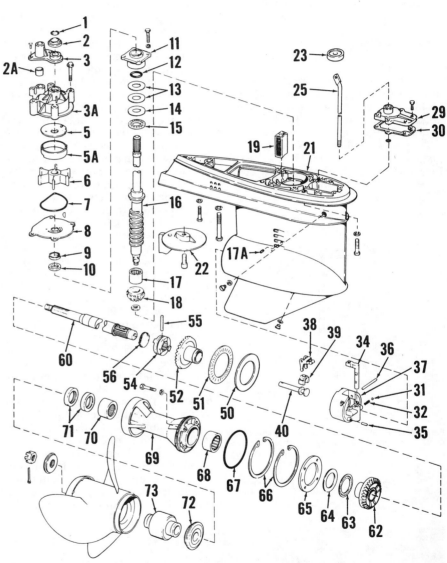

Fig. OM17-40—Exploded view of lower unit assembly.

1. "O" ring	12. "O" ring	31. Detent ball	56. Retaining spring
2. Grommet	13. Adjustment shims	32. Detent spring	60. Propeller shaft
2A. Grommet	14. Thrust washers	34. Detent	62. Reverse gear
3. Water tube	15. Thrust bearing	35. Dowel	63. Thrust bearing
bracket	16. Drive shaft	36. Shift lever pin	64. Thrust washer
3A. Impeller housing	17. Needle bearing	37. Bearing housing	65. Retainer plate
5. Impeller plate	17A. Set screw	38. Shift lever	66. Snap rings
5A. Impeller lining	18. Pinion gear	39. Shift yoke	67. "O" ring
6. Impeller	19. Screen	40. Shift dog shaft	68. Needle bearing
7. "O" ring	21. Gearcase	50. Thrust washer	69. Bearing housing
8. Plate	22. Trim tab	51. Thrust bearing	70. Needle bearing
9. Seal	23. Shift rod seal	52. Forward gear	71. Seals
10. Seal	25. Shift rod	54. Dog clutch	72. Thrust bushing
11. Bearing & housing	29. Shift rod cover	55. Pin	73. Propeller bushing
assy.	30. Gasket		

take. After removing set screw, use OMC Special Tool 318117 or OMC Special Tool 391257 to renew bearing (17). To use OMC Special Tool 318117, place shouldered side of tool against bearing and drive bearing down into propeller shaft cavity. New bearing is installed by assembling special tool with sleeve provided and removal piece turned over so shouldered side will again be next to bearing. Pull bearing (with lettered side against puller) into case (Fig. OM17-41). Bearing will be properly positioned when plate of tool is touching top of gearcase and bolt is tight. Do not overtighten bolt. Apply Loctite to set screw and install.

Forward gear (52—Fig. OM17-40) and propeller shaft (60) may be removed from propeller shaft bearing housing (37) after dislodging spring (56) and removing dog clutch assembly (55 and 54). Bearing housing and shifter mechanism assembly (38) may be disassembled by driving out shift lever pin (36).

Thickness of shims (13) is varied to adjust mesh position of pinion gear (18) in forward and reverse gear. OMC shim gage 393185 should be used to deter-mine proper shimming. To select the proper shims proceed as follows: Place pinion gear (18—Fig. OM17-42)) on drive shaft and tighten retaining nut to 70-75 ft.-lbs. (95-102 N·m). Assemble bearing housing (11), thrust washer (14) and thrust bearing (15) on drive shaft (16) as shown. Place collar 328362 over drive shaft with large diameter facing bearing housing (11). Place assembled drive shaft without shims (13—Fig. OM17-40) into shim tool 393185 as shown and tighten preload screw (S—Fig. OM17-42) until groove in plunger (P) is flush with end of threads. Place shim gage 328366 on guide pins on base of shim tool. Hold shim gage against pinion gear (18) and measure between shim gage and housing (11). Take measurements between each pair of screw holes while rotating housing (11). Renew housing (11) if difference between any measurements exceeds 0.004 inch (0.10 mm). Next, hold shim gage against bearing housing (11). Measure clearance (C) between gage and pinion gear while rotating drive shaft and pinion assembly. If difference between measurements exceeds 0.002 inch (0.05 mm), renew pinion gear (18) and/or drive shaft (16). To determine shim thickness, subtract average clearance (C) from 0.020 (0.51 mm). The remainder is thickness of shims (13—Fig. OM17-40). Use the fewest number of shims to obtain the correct thickness.

Needle bearings (68 and 70) should not be removed from propeller shaft housing (69) unless renewal is required. OMC Special Tool 321517 or Tool 326562 should be used to press aft bearing into propeller shaft housing to ensure proper positioning. OMC Special Tool 314641 should be used to position bearing (70) in forward bore of propeller shaft housing. Seals (71) should be installed so lip on aft seal is toward propeller and lip on forward seal is facing forward.

Reassemble gearcase using the following procedure: Renew all gaskets, seals and "O" rings. If lower drive shaft bearing (17) or propeller shaft bearings (68 and 70) are removed, they should be renewed. Install detent spring (32) and detent ball (31) in blind hole of housing

(37). Hold spring and ball in position while installing detent (34). Assemble shift dog shaft (40), shift lever yoke (39), shift lever (38) and pin (36). Assemble forward gear (52) with thrust bearing (51 and 50) in gear housing. Place dog clutch (54) on propeller shaft (60) making sure that hole in dog clutch is aligned with slot in propeller shaft and splined dogs are toward forward gear. Insert propeller shaft in forward gear and bearing housing assembly, then insert pin (55) through dog clutch, propeller shaft and hole in shift dog shaft (40). Install pin retaining spring (56). Press shift detent (34) down and place propeller shaft, forward gear and bearing housing assembly (37) into position in gearcase. Make sure locating pin (35) is seated in recess provided in gearcase.

Insert drive shaft (16). Install pinion gear retaining nut and tighten to 70-75 ft.-lbs. (95-102 N·m). Install shift rod (25) and shift rod cover (29) as an assembly. Thread shift rod fully into detent (34), back off two turns, pull rod to neutral (middle detent) and adjust for proper length. Refer to shift rod adjustment in REMOVE AND REINSTALL section for shift rod length.

Assemble thrust bearing (64 and 63) on reverse gear (62) and slide onto propeller shaft (60). Position bearing retainer plate (65) and install snap rings (66). Make sure "O" ring (67) is fully seated in groove of bearing housing (69) and that seals (71) are properly installed. Lip of forward seal should be toward front and lip of aft seal should be facing propeller.

Installation of bearing housing (69) will be eased by using two guide pins 10 inches long with 1/4-20 threads on one end. Thread guide pin into bearing retainer plate (65) and slide bearing housing (69) into position. Coat bearing housing screws with sealing compound and install.

Install seals (9 and 10) in upper drive shaft bearing housing (11) with lip of lower seal (10) down and lip of upper seal (9) up. Place thrust bearing assembly (14 and 15) on drive shaft and install previously selected shims (13). Coat screws that secure bearing housing (11) with sealing compound and install. Bottom edge of impeller plate (8) should be coated with OMC Adhesive M or equivalent and placed in position. Install impeller drive cam with sharp edge facing clockwise when viewed from top of drive shaft. Lubricate edges of impeller (6) and install on drive shaft. Rotate drive shaft clockwise when installing water pump housing (3A) over impeller (6). Coat threads of water pump housing screws with OMC Gasket Sealing Compound or a suitable equivalent sealing compound.

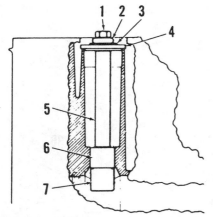

Fig. OM17-41—View showing arrangement of OMC Tool 318117 for installation of pinion bearing (17—Fig. OM17-40). Lettered end of bearing should be against puller.

1. Cap screw
2. Thrust bearing
3. Washer
4. Step washer
5. Spacer tube
6. Pinion bearing
7. Puller

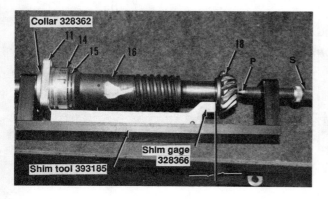

Fig. OM17-42—View showing OMC Shim Tools to select the proper drive shaft shim thickness. Refer to text.

P. Plunger
S. Preload screw
11. Drive shaft bearing & housing assy.
14. Thrust washer
15. Thrust bearing
16. Drive shaft
18. Pinion gear

POWER TILT/TRIM

OPERATION. A hydraulically actuated power trim/tilt system is used. Manifold (50—Fig. OM17-45) contains valves, oil pump and trim cylinders. Oil pump motor, oil reservoir and tilt cylinder are attached to manifold. Electric oil pump motor is reversible and oil pump rotation is therby changed to extend or retract trim and tilt cylinders. Note position of valves in Fig. OM17-45. Turn manual release valve counterclockwise to manually raise or lower outboard motor.

Hydraulic system contains approximately 25 fl. oz. (740 mL) of oil. Recommended oil is OMC Power Trim/Tilt Fluid or Dexron II automatic transmission fluid. Do not run pump without oil in reservoir. Oil level should reach fill plug (11) hole with trim and tilt cylinders fully extended. System should be cycled several times prior to checking oil level if system has been drained or lost a large amount of oil

TROUBLE-SHOOTING. Be sure battery is fully charged, electrical connections are good, oil reservoir is full and air is not trapped in system before testing components.

To check oil pressure, first momentarily cycle system UP and DOWN a few times. Remove snap rings (39—Fig. OM17-45) and manual release valve (37), then install OMC Gage A as shown in Fig. OM17-46. Operate system in the UP direction and observe gage after system stalls out at full extension. Gage reading should not drop below 100-200 psi (690-1379 kPa). Install OMC Gage B. Operate system in the DOWN direction and observe gage after system stalls at fully retracted. Gage reading should not drop below 100-200 psi (690-1379 kPa).

To test check valves, screw each valve into OMC Check Valve Tester 390063 (T—Fig. OM17-47). Use a suitable pressure tester (P) and apply 30 psi (207 kPa) pressure to check valve. Check valve can be considered good if no pressure leakage is noted.

Refer to the following for a list of symptoms and probable causes:

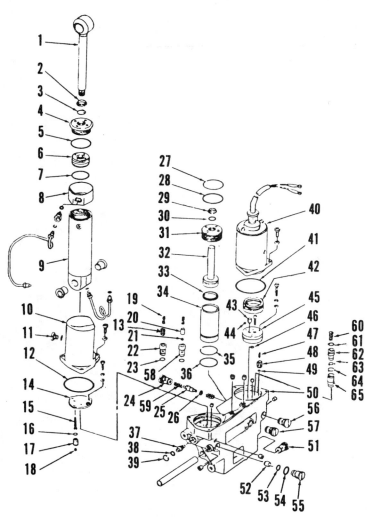

Fig. OM17-45—Exploded view of hydraulic trim and tilt system.

Fig. OM17-46—Install OMC gage A or B into manual release valve (37—Fig. OM17-45) port as shown to test system oil pressure. Refer to text.

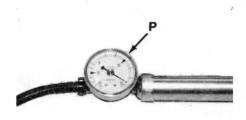

Fig. OM17-47—Use OMC Check Valve Tester 390063 (T) and a suitable pressure tester (P) to test check valves. Check valve can be considered good if no pressure leakage at approximately 30 psi (207 kPa) is noted.

1. Shaft	19. Spring	36. "O" ring
2. Wiper	20. Spring seat	37. Manual release
3. "O" ring	21. Ball	valve
4. End cap	22. Trim up relief valve	38. "O" ring
5. "O" ring	23. "O" ring	39. Snap ring
6. Piston	24. Reverse lock check	40. Pump motor
7. "O" ring	valve	41. "O" ring
8. Band	25. Piston	42. Oil pump filter
9. Tilt cylinder	26. "O" ring	43. Drive coupling
10. Reservoir	27. Retaining ring	44. Ball
11. Fill plug	28. "O" ring	45. Oil pump
12. "O" ring	29. Wiper	46. "O" ring
13. Needle	30. "O" ring	47. Spring
14. Plate	31. End cap	48. Trim down pump
15. Screen	32. Piston	relief valve
16. "O" ring	33. Piston ring	49. Seal
17. Check valve	34. Trim cylinder	50. Manifold
18. Valve ball	35. Retaining ring	51. Separation valve

52. Valve piston
53. "O" ring
54. "O" ring
55. Impact letdown
valve
56. Trim check valve
57. Tilt check valve
58. Impact sensor valve
59. Spring
60. Spring
61. "O" ring
62. Expansion relief
valve core
63. "O" ring
64. "O" ring
65. Expansion relief
valve seat

Symptoms—Probable Causes

Tilt leakdown—1, 2, 3, 4, 5 or 6
Trim and tilt both leak—7, 8 or 9
Reverse lock does not hold—2, 3, 6, 10, 11 or 12
Will not trim out under load or will not tilt—1, 2, 7 or 9
Will not trim or tilt down—2, 8, 10, 11 or 13

Key to Probable Causes

1. Trim up relief valve
2. Manual release valve
3. Tilt cylinder valve or seals
4. Tilt check valve
5. Impact letdown valve
6. Oil line
7. Trim cylinders sleeve "O" rings or piston seals
8. Trim check valve
9. Expansion relief valve or "O" ring
10. Filter valve seat
11. Impact sensor valve
12. Reverse lock check valve
13. Trim down pump relief valve

OVERHAUL. Oil pump must be serviced as a unit assembly. Motor is not serviceable with the exception of brushes. Refer to Fig. OM17-45 for exploded view of trim and tilt cylinders and manifold components. Keep all components separated during disassembly and identify each component, if necessary, to ensure correct position during reassembly.

EVINRUDE AND JOHNSON
6-CYLINDER MODELS

Year Produced	Evinrude Models	Johnson Models
1976	200640, 200649	200TL76, 200TXL76
1977	175740, 175749	175TL77, 175TXL77
	200740, 200749	200TL77, 200TXL77
1978	150849	150TL78
	175840, 175849	175TL78, 175TXL78
	200840, 200849	200TL78, 200TXL78
	235840, 235849	235TL78, 235TXL78
1979	150940, 150949	150TL79, 150TXL79
	175940, 175949	175TL79, 175TXL79
	200940, 200949	200TL79, 200TXL79
	235940, 235949	235TL79, 235TXL79
1980	150TRLCS, 150TRXCS	150TLCS, 150TXCS
	175TRLCS, 175TRXCS	175TLCS, 175TXCS
	200TRLCS, 200TRXCS	200TLCS, 200TXCS
	235TRLCS, 235TRXCS	235TRLCS, 235TXCS
1981	150TRLCI, 150TRXCI	150TLCI, 150TXCI
	175TRLCI, 175TRXCI	175TLCI, 175TXCI
	200TRLCI, 200TRXCI	200TLCI, 200TXCI
	235TRLCI, 235TRXCI	235TLCI, 235TXCI
1982	150TRLCN, 150TRXCN	150TLCN, 150TXCN
	175TRLCN, 175TRXCN	175TLCN, 175TXCN
	200TRLCN, 200TRXCN	200TLCN, 200TXCN
	235TRLCN, 235TRXCN	235TLCN, 235TXCN
1983	150TRLCT, 150TRXCT	150TRLCT, 150TRXCT
	175TRLCT, 175TRXCT	175TRLCT, 175TRXCT
	200TRLCT, 200TRXCT	200TRLCT, 200TRXCT
	235TRLCT, 235TRXCT	235TRLCT, 235TRXCT
1984	150TLCR, 150TXCR	150TLCR, 150TXCR
	150STLCR	150STLCR
	185TLCR, 185TXCR	185TLCR, 185TXCR
	235TLCR, 235TXCR	235TLCR, 235TXCR
	235STLCR	235STLCR
1985	150TLCO, 150TXCO	150TLCO, 150TXCO
	150STLCO	150STLCO
	185TLCO, 185TXCO	185TLCO, 185TXCO
	235TLCO, 235TXCO	235TLCO, 235TXCO
	235STLCO	235STLCO
1986	150TLCD, 150TXCD	150TLCD, 150TXCD
	150STLCD	150STLCD
	175TLCD, 175TXCD	175TLCD, 175TXCD
	200STLCD, 200TXCD	200STLCD, 200TXCD
	225TLCD, 225TXCD	225TLCD, 225TXCD
	225PTLCD, 225PTXCD	225PTLCD, 225PTXCD
1987	E150TLCU, E150TXCU	J150TLCU, J150TXCU
	E150STLCU, E175TLCU	J150STLCU, J175TLCU
	E175TXCU, E200STLCU	J175TXCU, J200STLCU
	E200TXCU, E225TLCU	J200TXCU, J225TLCU
	E225TXCU, E225CLCU	J225TXCU, J225CLCU
	E225CXCU, E225PLCU	J225CXCU, J225PLCU
	E225PXCU	J225PXCU
1988	E150TLCC, E150TXCC	J150TLCC, J150TXCC
	E150CXCC, E150STLCC	J150CXCC, J150STLCC
	E175TLCC, E175TXCC	J175TSCC, J175TXCC
	E175STLCC, E200STLCC	J175STLAC, J200STLCC
	E200TXCC, E200CXCC	J200TXCC, J200CXCC
	E225TLCC, E225TXCC	J225TLCC, J225TXCC
	E225PLCC, E225PXCC	J225PLCC, J225PXCC
1989	E150TLCE, E150TXCE	J150TLCE, J150TXCE
	E150CXCE, E150STLCE	J150CXCE, J150STLCE
	E150SLCE, E150TRLCE	J150TLCE, J150SLCE
	E175TLCE, E175TXCE	J150TRLCE, J175TLCE
	E175STLCE, E200STLCE	J175TXCE, J175STLCE
	E200TXCE, E200CXCE	J200STLCE, J200TXCE

Evinrude Models	Johnson Models
E225TLCE, E225TXCE	J200CXCE, J225TLAE
E225CXCE, E225PLCE	J225TLCE, J225CXCE
E225PXCE, E225SCXCE	J225PLCE, J225PXCE
E225STLCE, E225SPLCE	J225PLAE, J225SCXCE
E225SPXCE	J225STLCE, J225SPLCE
	J225SPXCE

CONDENSED SERVICE DATA

TUNE-UP

Hp/rpm 150/5000
175/5000 (Prior to 1984)
175/5250 (After 1983
185/5250
200/5250 (1984)
200/5500 (After 1984)
225/5500
235/5250

Bore:
175 Hp And 235 Hp . . . . 3.625 in.
(92.07 mm)
200 And 225 Hp (1988 . . . . 3.685 in.
(93.60 mm)
All Other Models . . . . 3.500 in.
(88.90 mm)

Stroke:
200 And 225 Hp Prior to 1988 . . . . 2.860 in.
(72.64 mm)
200 And 225 Hp After 1987 . . . . 2.858 in.
(72.59 mm)
All Other Models . . . . 2.588 in.
(65.73 mm)

Number of Cylinders 6
Displacement:
150 Hp . . . . 149.4 cu. in.
(2448 cc)
175 and 235 Hp . . . . 160.3 cu. in.
(2627 cc)
200 And 225 Hp Prior to 1988 . . . . 165 cu. in.
(2704 cc)
200 And 225 Hp After 1987 . . . . 183 cu. in.
(2999 cc)

Spark Plug:
All Models Prior to 1986 . . . . UL77V
All Models After 1985 . . . . QL77JC4*
Electrode Gap Prior to 1989 . . . . 0.040 in.
(1.0 mm)
Electrode Gap After 1988 . . . . 0.030 in.
(0.76 mm)

Ignition Type . . . . CDI
Carburetor Make . . . . OMC
Idle Speed (in gear):
All Models Prior to 1987 . . . . 650 rpm
All Models After 1986 (Except 1988 & 1989
200 and 225 hp) . . . . 600-700 rpm
1988 & 1989 200 and 225 hp Models . . . . See Text
Fuel:Oil Ratio . . . . 50:1†

*Champion QL78V surface gap spark plug is recommended when operated at sustained high speeds. Renew surface gap spark plug if center electrode is more than 1/32 inch (0.79 mm) below flat surface of plug end.

†On 1984 and later models equipped with variable ratio oiling (VRO), the VRO pump varies the fuel:oil ratio from approximately 150:1 at idle to approximately 50:1 at full throttle by sensing engine power output.

SIZES—CLEARANCES

Piston Ring End Gap:
All Models Prior to 1987 . . . . 0.007-0.017 in.
(0.18-0.43 mm)
All Models After 1986
Except 175 Hp . . . . 0.019-0.031 in.
(0.48-0.78 mm)
175 Hp After 1986 . . . . 0.020-0.033 in.
(0.51-0.84 mm)
Lower Piston Ring Side Clearance:
All Models (1976-1984) . . . . 0.002-0.004 in.
(0.05-0.10 mm)
All Models After 1984 . . . . 0.004 in. Max.
(0.10 mm)
Piston Skirt Clearance:
All Models (1976-1978) . . . . 0.0055-0.0075 in.
(0.140-0.190 mm)
All Models (1979-1984) . . . . 0.0045-0.0075 in.*
(0.114-0.190 mm)
Piston Wear Limit . . . . 0.004 in.
(0.10 mm)
Maximum Allowable Cylinder
Out-of-Round . . . . 0.004 in.
(0.10 mm)
Maximum Allowable Cylinder Taper . . . . 0.002 in.
(0.05 mm)
Maximum Allowable Cylinder Wear Limit . . . . . 0.004 in.
(0.10 mm)
Crankshaft Journal Diameter:
Top Main . . . . 1.6199-1.6204 in.
(41.145-41.158 mm)
Center Mains . . . . 2.1870-2.1875 in.
(55.550-55.562 mm)
Bottom Main:
200 And 225 Hp . . . . 1.5747-1.5752 in.
(39.997-40.010 mm)
All Other Models . . . . 1.3779-1.3784 in.
(34.999-35.011 mm)
Crankpin:
200 And 225 Hp . . . . 1.4995-1.5000 in.
(38.087-38.100 mm)
All Other Models . . . . 1.3757-1.3762 in.
(34.943-34.955 mm)
Crankshaft End Play:
All Models Prior to 1985 . . . . 0.008-0.011 in.
(0.20-0.28 mm)
Forward Gear Bushing to Propeller
Shaft Clearance (Prior to 1985) . . . . 0.001-0.002 in.
(0.03-0.05 mm)

*The manufacturer does not specify piston skirt clearance on models after 1984. If cylinder bore and piston are within wear tolerances, clearance should be acceptable.

TIGHTENING TORQUES
Connecting Rod:
200 And 225 Hp . . . . 42-44 ft.-lbs.
(57-60 N·m)

TIGHTENING TORQUES CONT.

All Other Models Prior to 1988 . . . . .29-31 ft.-lbs.
　　　　　　　　　　　　　　　　　(39-42 N·m)
All Other Models After 1987 . . . . .30-32 ft.-lbs.
　　　　　　　　　　　　　　　　　(41-43 N·m)
Crankcase Halves—
　Main Bearing Screws:
　　200 And 225 Hp . . . . .26-30 ft.-lbs.
　　　　　　　　　　　　　　　　　(35-41 N·m)
　　All Other Models . . . . .18-20 ft.-lbs.
　　　　　　　　　　　　　　　　　(24-27 N·m)
　Flange Screws . . . . .60-84 in.-lbs.
　　　　　　　　　　　　　　　　　(7-9 N·m)
Crankcase Head:
　All Models Except 1987-1989
　　150 And 175 Hp . . . . .72-96 in.-lbs.
　　　　　　　　　　　　　　　　　(8-11 N·m)
　　150 And 175 Hp (1987-1989) . . . . .96-120 in.-lbs.
　　　　　　　　　　　　　　　　　(11-14 N·m)
Cylinder Head:
　150 And 175 Hp . . . . .18-20 ft.-lbs.
　　　　　　　　　　　　　　　　　(24-27 N·m)
　All Other Models . . . . .20-22 ft.-lbs.
　　　　　　　　　　　　　　　　　(27-29 N·m)

Flywheel Nut . . . . .140-145 ft. lbs.
　　　　　　　　　　　　　　　　　(190-197 N·m)
Lower Main Bearing Retainer
　Plate Screws .96-120 in.-lbs.
　　　　　　　　　　　　　　　　　(11-14 N·m)
Spark Plug . . . . .216-240 in.-lbs.
　　　　　　　　　　　　　　　　　(24-27 N·m)
Standard Screws:
　No. 6 . . . . .7-10 in.-lbs.
　　　　　　　　　　　　　　　　　(0.8-1.2 N·m)
　No. 8 . . . . .15-22 in.-lbs.
　　　　　　　　　　　　　　　　　(1.6-2.4 N·m)
　No. 10 . . . . .25-35 in.-lbs.
　　　　　　　　　　　　　　　　　(2.8-4.0 N·m)
　No. 12 . . . . .35-40 in.-lbs.
　　　　　　　　　　　　　　　　　(4.0-4.6 N·m)
　¼ Inch . . . . .60-80 in.-lbs.
　　　　　　　　　　　　　　　　　(7-9 N·m)
　5/16 Inch . . . . .120-140 in.-lbs.
　　　　　　　　　　　　　　　　　(14-16 N·m)
　⅜ Inch . . . . .220-240 in.-lbs.
　　　　　　　　　　　　　　　　　(24-27 N·m)
　7/16 Inch . . . . .340-360 in.-lbs.
　　　　　　　　　　　　　　　　　(38-40 N·m)

LUBRICATION

The engine is lubricated by oil mixed with the fuel. Fuel should be unleaded gasoline with a minimum pump octane rating of 87. Recommended oil for all models is Evinrude or Johnson Outboard Lubricant, Evinrude or Johnson XP Outboard Lubricant or OMC 2-Cycle Motor Oil. If the recommended oil is not available, use a good quality NMMA (formerly BIA) certified TC-WII outboard motor oil. The recommended fuel:oil ratio for models not equipped with variable ratio oiling (VRO) is 50:1 for normal operation and engine break-in.

On models equipped with VRO (1984 and later), the VRO pump varies the fuel:oil ratio from approximately 150:1 at idle to approximately 50:1 at full throttle by sensing engine power output.

During engine break-in (first 10 hours of operation) on VRO equipped models, fuel in the fuel tank must be mixed at a 100:1 fuel:oil mixture and used in combination with the normal VRO system to ensure proper engine lubrication. The oil level in the VRO tank should be monitored to be sure oil level is dropping, indicating VRO system is functioning. After break-in period (first 10 hours of operation), if VRO system is functioning properly, switch to straight gasoline in the fuel tank.

On 1984 and later recreational models originally equipped with VRO, a 50:1 fuel:oil mixture must be used in the fuel tank if VRO system is not used.

The lower unit gears and bearings are lubricated by oil contained in the gearcase. The recommended oil is OMC HI-VIS Gearcase Lube. The gearcase oil level should be checked after every 50 hours of operation and the gearcase should be drained and filled with new oil every 100 hours or once each season, whichever occurs first.

The gearcase is drained and filled through the same plug port. An oil level (vent) port is used to indicate the full oil level of the gearcase and to ease in oil drainage.

To drain the oil, place the outboard motor in a vertical position. Remove the drain plug and oil level plug and allow the lubricant to drain into a suitable container.

To fill the gearcase with oil, place the outboard motor in a vertical position. Add oil through the drain plug opening with an oil feeder until the oil begins to overflow from oil level plug port. Reinstall oil level plug with a new gasket, if needed, and tighten. Remove oil feeder, then reinstall drain plug with a new gasket, if needed, and tighten.

FUEL SYSTEM

All Models Except 200 And 225 Hp Models

CARBURETORS. Three carburetors are used and each is a two-barrel carburetor with a single float. Each carburetor barrel provides fuel for one engine cylinder and is equipped with individual metering components.

Choke plates on models prior to 1980 may be operated manually or by activating choke solenoid. Turn choke con-trol lever on front of outboard to "ON" position to manually close choke plates. Turn choke control lever to "OFF" on 1977 and 1978 models and push ignition key into ignition switch to activate choke solenoid. Turn choke control lever to "Automatic" on 1976 models and push choke switch on control panel to activate choke solenoid.

On models after 1979, additional fuel to aid starting is injected into the engine's transfer ports through tubes in the transfer port covers. A key-controlled, electric solenoid valve directs fuel from the fuel pump to the transfer port covers on early models and intake manifold on later models. The valve may be opened manually if rope starting is required.

Adjustment. Throttle valves must be synchronized for optimum performance. To synchronize throttle valves, close throttle and make sure follower roller (F – Fig. OM18-1) is not touching throttle cam (9). Loosen carburetor throttle arm screws (5) on upper and lower carburetors and allow throttle return springs to close throttle plates. Tighten screws (5).

High speed mixture on all models is controlled by fixed jets (23 – Fig. OM18-2) located in opposite sides of the float bowl. On 1979 through 1982 models, an intermediate speed jet (24) is located just above high speed jet (23). On 1983 and later models, intermediate speed jet (24) is mounted vertically in float bowl (20). The float bowl must be removed to gain access. Low speed fuel mixture on models prior to 1979 is controlled by jet (15) on each side of the carburetor. Low speed fuel mixture on 1979-1983 models is controlled by jet (25) located in each carburetor barrel. On models after 1983, only one low speed jet (25) is used. Carburetor on 1979-1982 235-hp models is equipped with a high-speed pullover jet (26), which supplies additional fuel during high-speed operation. Only one pullover jet is used in each carburetor.

Choke solenoid on models prior to 1980 should be adjusted so choke plates open and close fully. Make certain that choke linkage is adjusted so choke plates close simultaneously. Link (L–Fig. OM18-3) must have open ends up as shown. Loosen choke solenoid clamp screws and close choke plates with manual choke lever. Bottom solenoid plunger (P) in solenoid and position solenoid so slack is removed in solenoid link (L). Move choke solenoid away from plunger an additional 0.016 inch (0.41 mm) so plunger is not bottomed in solenoid and tighten solenoid clamp screws.

Refer to SPEED CONTROL LINKAGE section for synchronizing carburetor throttle opening to ignition timing.

R&R And Overhaul. Carburetors can be removed after removing air silencer assembly and disconnecting linkage. Choke mechanism is slightly different on carburetors. Disassembly procedure is self-evident. Choke and throttle plate screws are staked and must be renewed if removed from shaft.

To check float level, remove float bowl and invert carburetor. Place OMC Float Gage 324891 on carburetor body (6—Fig. OM18-4) as shown. Float (19) should be between, but not touch, notches (N) on side of gage marked V-4 & V-6. To adjust, carefully bend float arm.

The fuel mixture on models prior to 1980 is enriched for starting using carburetor choke plates. The carburetor choke may be actuated manually by moving the choke control knob or lever, or by activating a solenoid controlled by the ignition key switch. On early models the solenoid regulates choke plate opening according to a signal from the thermal switch in the engine's water bypass cover. On later models the thermal switch is not used and the solenoid moves the choke plate to fully closed position when activated. Refer to ADJUSTMENT paragraphs for choke adjustment.

The fuel mixture on models after 1979 is enriched for starting using a key-controlled, electric solenoid valve. On early models, fuel is directed from the fuel pump to the transfer port covers where fuel is injected into the transfer port passages. On later models, fuel is injected directly into intake manifold. Inspect valve and renew any damaged components.

SPEED CONTROL LINKAGE. The carburetor throttle valves must be correctly synchronized to open as the ignition timing is advanced to obtain satisfactory performance. Synchronize throttle valves as previously outlined. Move speed control lever slowly from idle toward fast position and note point of contact between throttle cam and follower roller (F–Fig. OM18-5). Cam should just contact roller when first mark on cam is exactly in center of roller. If incorrect, loosen screw (S) and

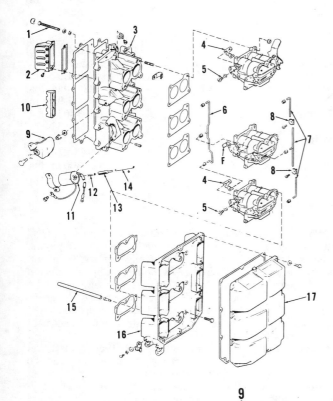

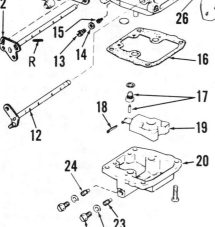

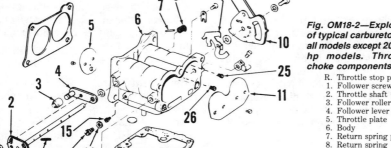

Fig. OM18-1—Exploded view of early carburetor and intake manifold assembly. Later models, except 200 and 225 hp models, are similar.

F. Follower roller
1. Ignition timing adjusting screw
2. Reed valve assy. (6 used)
3. Intake manifold
4. Throttle adjusting lever
5. Screw
6. Throttle link
7. Choke rods
8. Couplers
9. Throttle cam
10. Filler block
11. Choke solenoid
12. Spring
13. Plunger
14. Link
15. Hose
16. Silencer base
17. Silencer cover

Fig. OM18-2—Exploded view of typical carburetor used on all models except 200 and 225 hp models. Throttle and choke components will vary.

R. Throttle stop pin
1. Follower screw
2. Throttle shaft
3. Follower roller
4. Follower lever
5. Throttle plate
6. Body
7. Return spring pin
8. Return spring
9. Detent lever
10. Manual choke lever
11. Choke plate
12. Choke shaft
13. Plug
14. Washer
15. Idle mixture orifice
16. Gasket
17. Fuel needle & seat
18. Float pin
19. Float
20. Float bowl
21. Plug
22. Washer
23. High speed mixture orifice
24. Intermediate orifice
25. Low speed air orifice
26. High speed pullover orifice

reposition roller. Refer to IGNITION SYSTEM and adjust ignition timing. Move speed control lever to full throttle. On models prior to 1984, there should be 0.001-0.003 inch (0.02-0.07 mm) clearance between roll pin (R – Fig. OM18-2) and stop at full throttle. Turn full throttle stop screw (T – Fig. OM18-5) to obtain desired clearance. On models after 1983, the full throttle stop screw (T) must be adjusted so the carburetor throttle shaft pins (R – Fig. OM18-2) are exactly vertical when the engine throttle lever is manually advanced to full throttle.

NOTE: The throttle shaft pins must not go past vertical or damage to the carburetors may result.

REED VALVES. Six sets of reed valves are used, one for each cylinder. The reed valves are attached to the intake manifold as shown in Fig. OM18-1. Reed petals should seat very lightly against reed seat throughout entire length. Individual reed components are not available on models prior to 1985. Renew reed valve assembly if petals are broken, cracked, warped or bent.

Individual components are available on 1985 and later models. Filler block (10) is not used on 1986 and later models.

NON-VRO FUEL PUMP. All models are equipped with two fuel pumps mounted adjacent to carburetors. On 1976 models, both fuel pumps transfer fuel from fuel tank to carburetors; on 1977 and 1978 models, the lower fuel pump transfers fuel from the fuel tank to the upper fuel pump which pumps fuel to the carburetors; on models after 1978, the upper fuel pump supplies the lower fuel pump which pumps fuel to the carburetors. Fuel pumps on all models are operated by crankcase pulsations. Fuel pressure to carburetors should be 2½-6 psi (17.2-41.4 kPa). Fuel pump must be serviced as a unit assembly.

VRO TYPE FUEL PUMP. The VRO type fuel pump (1 – Fig. OM18-6) meters the fuel:oil ratio from approximately 50:1 up to approximately 150:1 by sensing the engine power output. During engine break-in or after any procedure that permitted air to enter the VRO system, the fuel in the fuel tank must be mixed at a fuel:oil ratio of 50:1 to ensure the engine of proper lubrication. On 2.6 GT and XP models, a fuel:oil ratio of 25:1 must be used during testing of system.

To check the VRO system for proper operation, first fill the VRO oil tank with a recommended two-stroke motor oil and note oil level for future reference.

Install correct fuel:oil mixture in the fuel tank. After the recommended engine break-in period or after a suitable test period for other conditions, note the oil level in the VRO oil tank. If the oil level has dropped indicating the VRO system is operating, refill the VRO oil tank and switch to straight fuel or recommended fuel mixture.

NOTE: When the VRO system is not used, the inlet nozzle at the outboard motor connector must be capped and clamped to prevent dirt or moisture from entering the fuel system. The fuel in the fuel tank must be mixed at correct fuel:oil ratio. Refer to LUBRICATION section.

Models Prior To 1987

TESTING. Stop the engine. Disconnect fuel mixture discharge hose at VRO pump nipple (5 – Fig. OM18-6). Connect a tee fitting in hose end. Connect one end of a clear hose to one tee outlet and connect remaining hose to pump discharge fitting. Connect a 0-15 psi (0-103 kPa) pressure gage to the remaining tee outlet. Start the engine and run at wide-open throttle. The VRO pump should develop between 3 psi (21 kPa)

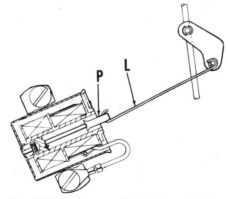

Fig. OM18-3 – Cross-sectional view of choke solenoid used on models prior to 1980. Refer to text to correctly position solenoid.

Fig. OM18-4—To check float level on all models except 200 and 225 hp models, lay OMC Float Gage 324891 on carburetor body (6) as shown. Float (19) should lay between (but not touch) notches (N) on side of gage marked V-4 & V-6. Bend float arm to adjust.

and 15 psi (103 kPa) at wide-open throttle. The fuel pressure will drop 1-2 psi (6.8-13.7 kPa) and a clicking sound should be heard with each oil discharge. A small squirt of oil should be noticed every time the pump pulses.

If fuel pump (1) malfunction is noted, the fuel pump must be renewed as a complete assembly.

Models After 1986

TESTING. Using a "T" fitting, connect a suitable vacuum gage and a length of clear plastic hose to fuel inlet fitting at lower engine cover. All connections should be clamped to prevent leakage. Start engine and allow to warm to normal operating temperature.

NOTE: When performing VRO system tests that require full throttle operation, install outboard motor into a suitable test tank with the correct test wheel installed.

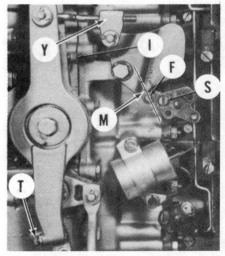

Fig. OM18-5 – View of throttle control linkage. Refer to text for adjustment.

Fig. OM18-6 – View of a VRO type fuel pump.
1. VRO fuel pump assy.
2. Oil inlet nipple
3. Fuel inlet nipple
4. Crankcase pulse nipple
5. Fuel mixture discharge nipple

Run motor at full throttle for two minutes minimum while observing clear hose and note vacuum reading. Vacuum reading should not exceed 4 inches Hg (13.5 kPa) and air bubbles should not be

Fig. OM18-7—View showing two-barrel type carburetors and two one-barrel type carburetors used on 200 and 225 hp models. The top two port and starboard carburetor assemblies have a common throttle body assembly (T) with separate main body assemblies (M). View identifies position of intermediate air bleed jet (4) and low speed air bleed jet (5). Refer to text.

present in clear hose. Excessive vacuum indicates a restricted fuel line between fuel tank and motor. Air bubbles in clear hose indicates an air leak in fuel line between fuel tank and motor.

If vacuum reading is within 1-4 inches Hg (3.4-13.5 kPa) and no bubbles were noted in clear hose, proceed as follows: Remove clear hose and install a suitable 0-15 psi (0-103.4 kPa) pressure gage between VRO pump discharge port (5—Fig. OM18-6) and carburetors. Start engine and run at 800 rpm in forward gear. Pump output pressure should stabilize at not less than 3 psi (20.7 kPa).

If pressure is less than 3 psi (20.7 kPa) inspect pulse fitting for plugging or other damage. Pulse fitting is connected in-line with hose attached to pulse nipple (4). Pulse fitting on models prior to 1988 is equipped with an integral flame arrestor and on 1988 and later models, pulse fitting is equipped with an integral check valve. Clean both type fittings by back-flushing with a suitable solvent. Install pulse fitting with black color nipple facing VRO pump.

NOTE: A plugged pulse fitting may result in power head damage due to inadequate lubrication. Pulse fitting MUST be clean for proper VRO operation. If excessive carbon deposits are noted, renew pulse fitting and repair cause of excessive carbon (backfiring) before returning outboard motor to service.

If pump pressure is low and pulse fitting is in acceptable condition, renew VRO pump assembly.

200 And 225 Hp Models

CARBURETOR. The two-barrel type carburetors and two one-barrel type carburetors are used. The top two port and starboard carburetor assemblies

have a common throttle body assembly (T—Fig. OM18-7) with separate main body assemblies (M).

NOTE: Starboard carburetors supply fuel to port cylinders and port carburetors supply fuel to starboard cylinders.

The main body assemblies are constructed of a nonmetallic type material. Care must be used when working with the main body assembly. DO NOT overtighten any screws. Tighten each screw in small increments using a crisscross tightening sequence.

If service is performed, note the following: Keep carburetor components for each carburetor separate from the others. The manufacturer does not recommend submerging the parts in carburetor or parts cleaning solutions. An aerosol-type carburetor cleaner is recommended. The float and other components made of plastic and rubber should not be subjected to some cleaning solutions. Safety eyewear and solvent resistant gloves are recommended.

To determine the float level, invert float bowl (12—Fig. OM18-9) with the fuel inlet valve and float installed. The float should be flush with the float bowl gasket surface. Use a straightedge as shown in Fig. OM18-9 to check float setting. Remove the float and carefully bend the float tang to adjust.

Recommended idle speed on models prior to 1988 is 600-700 rpm with engine running at normal operating temperature in forward gear. Loosen nut (N—Fig. OM18-10) and turn screw (I) to adjust idle speed.

Idle speed on models after 1987 should be correct (within 575-700 rpm) after correctly adjusting speed control linkage and idle speed ignition timing. Refer to SPEED CONTROL LINKAGE section.

SPEED CONTROL LINKAGE. The carburetor throttle valves are synchronized to open as the ignition is advanced. It is important that throttle valve opening and ignition timing synchronization be checked and adjusted if necessary.

The following procedure should be used to check and adjust speed control. On models prior to 1988, synchronize carburetor throttle valves as follows: Move the speed control lever to idle position and make sure follower roller (F—Fig. OM18-10) is not touching throttle cam (T). Loosen follower roller screw (C) and move roller away from throttle cam (T). Loosen screw (S) two complete turns and make certain all throttle valves are closed, then retighten screw (S). Leave screw (C) loose.

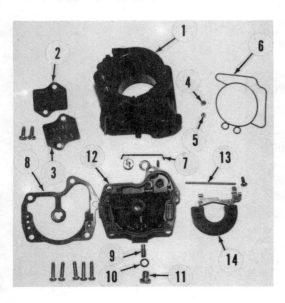

Fig. OM18-8—Exploded view of carburetor main body assembly used on 200 and 225 hp models.
1. Main body
2. Gasket
3. Plate
4. Intermediate air bleed jet
5. Low speed air bleed jet
6. Seal
7. Inlet needle & seat
8. Gasket
9. High speed jet
10. Gasket
11. Plug
12. Float bowl
13. Pin
14. Float

To synchronize carburetor throttle valves on 1988 and 1989 models, move throttle control lever to idle position and ensure throttle cam (T—Fig. OM18-12) is not touching cam follower roller (F) by loosening cam follower screw (C) and moving cam follower roller (F) away from throttle cam (T). Loosen carburetor link adjustment screws (S) ½ turn maximum. Make sure all carburetor throttle valves are completely closed, then retighten screws (S). Leave screw (C) loose.

On models prior to 1988, adjust throttle cam pick-up point as follows: Hold follower roller (F—Fig. OM18-10) against throttle cam (T) and adjust throttle arm stop screw (D) until alignment mark (M) is centered with follower roller (F). Withdraw roller (F) away from throttle cam (T) enough to allow throttle plates to close at idle and tighten screw (C).

On 1988 and 1989 models, adjust throttle cam pick-up point as follows: Loosen lockring (L—Fig. OM18-12) and turn adjustment knob (K) counterclockwise until internal spring pressure is completely relieved. With cam follow-

er roller screw (C) loose, hold follower roller (F) against throttle cam (T) and adjust the throttle arm stop screw (D—Fig. OM18-10) until mark (M—Fig. OM18-12) on throttle cam (T) is aligned with center of roller (F). Retighten cam follower roller screw (C).

On all models, adjust wide-open throttle (WOT) stop screw (W—Fig. OM18-11) so WOT mark (O—Figs. OM18-10 or OM18-12) on follower roller bracket points directly front-to-rear when the speed control lever is at WOT. Refer to IGNITION SYSTEM section to check and adjust ignition timing.

REED VALVES. Six sets of leaf (reed) valves are used, one for each cylinder. The six valves are positioned horizontally and are attached to the upper and lower intake manifolds with a gasket between each reed block and manifold. The leaf petals should seat very lightly against the valve block throughout their entire length with the least possible tension. The individual parts of the reed valve assembly are not available separately. Renew the reed

valve assembly if petals are broken, cracked, warped or bent.

VRO TYPE FUEL PUMP. The VRO type fuel pump (1—Fig. OM18-6) meters the fuel:oil ratio from approximately 50:1 up to approximately 150:1 by sensing the engine power output. During engine break-in or after any procedure that permitted air to enter VRO system, the fuel in the fuel tank must be mixed at a fuel:oil ratio of 50:1 to ensure the engine of proper lubrication. On 200STLCD (XP/GT) models, a fuel:oil ratio of 25:1 must be used during testing of system.

To check the VRO system for proper operation, first fill the VRO oil tank with a recommended two-stroke motor oil and note oil level for future reference. Install the correct fuel:oil mixture in the fuel tank. After the recommended engine break-in period or after a suitable test period for other conditions, note the oil level in the VRO oil tank. If the oil level has dropped and the VRO system is operating properly, refill the VRO oil tank and switch to straight fuel or recommended fuel mixture.

NOTE: When the VRO system is not used, the inlet nozzle at the outboard motor connector must be capped and clamped to prevent dirt or moisture from entering the fuel system. The fuel in the fuel tank must be mixed at correct fuel:oil ratio. Refer to LUBRICATION section.

Models Prior To 1987

TESTING. Stop the engine. Disconnect fuel mixture discharge hose at VRO pump nipple (5—Fig. OM18-6). Connect a tee fitting in hose end. Connect one end of a clear hose to one tee outlet and connect remaining hose end to pump discharge fitting. Connect a 0-15 psi (0-103 kPa) pressure gage to the remain-

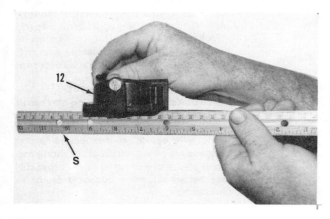

Fig. OM18-9—With float bowl (12) inverted and fuel inlet valve and float installed, float should just touch straightedge (S). Refer to text.

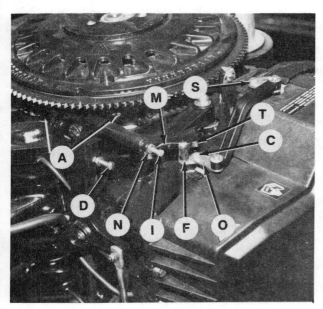

Fig. OM18-10—View of speed control linkage used on 200 and 225 hp models prior to 1988. Later models are similar.

Fig. OM18-11—View identifying wide-open throttle (WOT) stop screw (W) and shift interrupter switch (SI) on 200 and 225 hp models.

ing tee outlet. Start the engine and run at wide-open throttle. The VRO pump should develop between 3 psi (21 kPa) and 15 psi (103 kPa) at wide-open throttle. The fuel pressure will drop 1-2 psi (6.8-13.7 kPa) and a clicking sound should be heard with each oil discharge. A small squirt of oil should be noticed every time the pump pulses.

If fuel pump (1) malfunction is noted, the fuel pump must be renewed as a complete assembly.

Models After 1986

TESTING. Using a ''T'' fitting, connect a suitable vacuum gage and a length of clear plastic hose to fuel inlet fitting at lower engine cover. All connections should be clamped to prevent leakage. Start engine and allow to warm to normal operating temperature.

NOTE: When performing VRO system tests that require full throttle operation, in-

stall outboard motor into a suitable test tank with the correct test wheel installed.

Run motor at full throttle for two minutes minimum while observing clear hose and note vacuum reading. Vacuum reading should not exceed 4 inches Hg (13.5 kPa) and air bubbles should not be present in clear hose. Excessive vacuum indicates a restricted fuel line between fuel tank and motor. Air bubbles in clear hose indicates an air leak in fuel line between fuel tank and motor.

If vacuum reading is within 1-4 inches Hg (3.4-13.5 kPa) and no bubbles were noted in clear hose, proceed as follows: Remove clear hose and install a suitable 0-15 psi (0-103.4 kPa) pressure gage between VRO pump discharge port (5—Fig. OM18-6) and carburetors. Start engine and run at 800 rpm in forward gear. Pump output pressure should stabilize at not less than 3 psi (20.7 kPa).

If pressure is less than 3 psi (20.7 kPa), inspect pulse fitting for plugging or other damage. Pulse fitting is connected in-line with hose attached to pulse nipple (4). Pulse fitting on models prior to 1988 is equipped with an integral flame arrestor and on 1988 and later models, pulse fitting is equipped with an integral check valve. Clean both type fittings by back-flushing with a suitable solvent. Install pulse fitting with black color nipple facing VRO pump.

NOTE: A plugged pulse fitting may result in power head damage due to inadequate lubrication. Pulse fitting MUST be clean for proper VRO operation. If excessive carbon deposits are noted, renew pulse fitting and repair cause of excessive carbon (backfiring) before returning outboard motor to service.

If pump pressure is low and pulse fitting is in acceptable condition, renew VRO pump assembly.

IGNITION SYSTEM

All models are equipped with a capacitor discharge ignition system which is triggered by sensor coils on stator plate. To prevent damage to components, note the following list of precautions:

1. DO NOT disconnect any wires while motor is running or while ignition switch is on.
2. DO NOT use any tachometer except those approved for use with this system.
3. DO NOT hold spark plug wires while checking for spark.
4. DO make certain that all wiring connections are clean and tightly joined.
5. DO make certain that wires do not bind moving parts or touch metal

Fig. OM18-12—View of speed control linkage on late 200 and 225 hp models. Early models are similar.

C. Cam follower roller screw
F. Cam follower roller
I. Idle timing screw (under flywheel)
K. Adjustment knob
L. Lock ring
M. Mark
O. Full throttle mark
S. Screws
T. Throttle cam

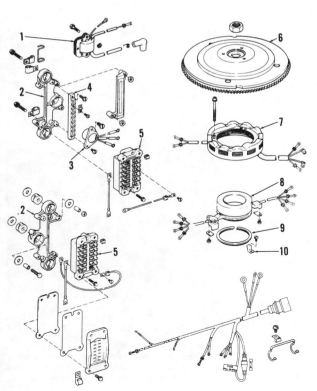

Fig. OM18-13 — Exploded view of early type ignition system.

1. Ignition coil (6 used)
2. Bracket
3. Rectifier
4. Terminal strip
5. Power pack
6. Flywheel
7. Stator
8. Timer base & sensor assy.
9. Retainer
10. Clips (4 used)

edges where they may chafe through insulation.

200 And 225 Hp Models Prior to 1988 And All Other Models Prior to 1989

TROUBLE-SHOOTING. Ignition system consists of two identical but separate ignition systems. One system is used for port side cylinders and one system for starboard cylinders. Trouble-shooting procedures must be performed on each ignition system.

Each power pack is connected to the timer base assembly by a four-pin connector. A two-pin connector joins each power pack to the charge coil. The key switch is connected to the power packs with a single-pin connector.

NOTE: Resistance specifications are based on measurements taken at ambient temperature of 70° F (21° C). Resistance may change by approximately 10 ohms per one degree temperature variation.

Use only approved procedures to prevent damage to ignition components. The fuel system should be checked to make certain faulty running is not the result of fuel starvation, incorrect mixture or contaminated fuel.

INDEXING FLYWHEEL. Power packs with a defective isolation diode or other internal defect can result in erratic ignition system operation. To determine if each cylinder is firing at the proper time, proceed as follows: Remove all spark plugs. Rotate flywheel in clockwise direction until number 2 cylinder is at TDC. With number 2 cylinder at TDC, mark "2" on flywheel directly adjacent to timing pointer. Repeat procedure for all cylinders, placing each cylinder number on flywheel across from timing pointer. Place motor in a suitable test, start engine and run at rpm malfunction is evident. Connect a timing light alternately to each spark plug lead and verify cylinders are firing at their respective mark on flywheel. If not, be sure all wiring pins are properly located in connectors or renew power pack.

CHECKING FOR SPARK. Disconnect spark plug leads at spark plugs and connect them to a needle point spark checker with six gaps set at $7/16$ inch (11 mm). Consistent, strong spark indicates ignition system is functioning properly; suspect spark plugs, timing, improper wiring to ignition coils or to spark plugs.

Weak, inconsistent spark or spark from only one or two ignition coils, suspect sensor coils or ignition coils. Weak, inconsistent spark from all six ignition

coils, suspect charge coils. No spark at all, suspect power pack.

WIRING. Engine missing, surging and failure to start or run can be caused by loose or corroded electrical connections. Check all terminals and plug-in connectors for tight, clean contact. Also, check all wiring for short to ground.

CHARGING COILS. All models are equipped with two charge coils contained in the stator assembly. To check charge coils, proceed as follows: On models prior to 1979, disconnect charge coil wires, as identified in Figs. OM18-14 and OM18-15, from power packs. On models after 1978, disconnect the two-pin connector (one per bank of cylinders). Connect a suitable ohmmeter to wire connectors or terminal ends in connector leading to stator. Renew stator assembly if resistance is not 220-320 ohms on models prior to 1979, 475-625 ohms on 1979-1984 models, 535-585 ohms on 1985 models with 6 and 10 ampere charging systems, 575-625 ohms on 1985 models with 35 ampere charging systems, 535-585 ohms on 1986 and 1987 150 and 175 hp models with 9 ampere charging system, 450-550 ohms on 1988 150 and 175 hp models with 9 ampere charging system, 955-985 ohms on 1986-1988 150 and 175 hp models with 35 ampere charging system and 1986 and 1987 200 and 225 hp models. Connect negative ohmmeter lead to engine ground and positive ohmmeter lead alternately to each stator wire or terminal. No continuity should be present between any stator wire and engine ground. If continuity is noted, charge coil or charge coil leads are shorted to ground.

To check charge coil output on models after 1978, use Merc-O-Tronic Model 781, Stevens Model CD-77 or a suitable equivalent peak reading voltmeter (PRV). Connect black PRV test lead to terminal A in connector leading to stator and red test lead to terminal B. Set tester knobs to negative (−) and 500. Crank engine while noting meter. Repeat test on other charge coil. Renew stator assembly if output is less than 160 volts on 1979-1984 models, 200 volts on 1985-1987 150 and 175 hp models and 130 volts on 1986 and 1987 200 and 225 hp models.

SENSOR COILS. All models are equipped with six sensor coils contained in the timer base assembly. One series of sensor coils are for cylinders 1, 3 and 5; the other series of coils are for cylinders 2, 4 and 6. To test sensor coils, proceed as follows:

On models prior to 1979, disconnect sensor coil wires, as identified in Figs. OM18-14 and OM18-15, from power

packs. Connect an ohmmeter between white common wire and alternately to each sensor coil for one bank of cylinders. Repeat test on other bank of cylinders. Renew timer base if resistance is not 13-23 ohms. Connect ohmmeter between engine ground and alternately between each sensor coil wire for one bank of cylinders. Repeat test on sensor coils for other bank of cylinders. No continuity should be present between engine ground and any sensor coil wire. If continuity is noted, sensor coil or coil lead is shorted to ground.

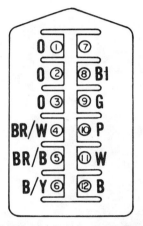

Fig. OM18-14 — Refer to following legend for starboard power pack wire connections on models prior to 1979.

1. Orange – #1 ign. coil
2. Orange – #3 ign. coil
3. Orange – #5 ign. coil
4. Brown/white – charge coil
5. Brown/black – charge coil
6. Black/yellow – ign. switch
7. Vacant
8. Blue – #1 sensor coil
9. Green – #3 sensor coil
10. Purple – #5 sensor coil
11. White – Common sensor coil
12. Black – ground

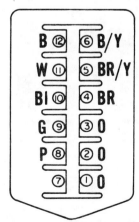

Fig. OM18-15 — Refer to following legend for port power pack wire connections on models prior to 1979.

1. Orange – #6 ign. coil
2. Orange – #4 ign. coil
3. Orange – #2 ign. coil
4. Brown – charge coil
5. Brown/yellow – charge coil
6. Black/yellow – ign. switch
7. Vacant
8. Purple – #6 sensor coil
9. Green – #4 sensor coil
10. Blue – #2 sensor coil
11. White – Common sensor coil
12. Black – ground

To check sensor coil output, use Merc-O-Tronic Models 781, Stevens Model CD-77 or a suitable equivalent peak reading voltmeter (PRV). Connect PRV black test lead to common (white) wire for one bank of cylinders and red test lead to one of three sensor coil wires. On Merc-O-Tronic Model 781, set knobs to positive (+) and 5. On Stevens Model CD-77, set knobs to S and 5. Crank engine while observing PRV. Repeat test with black tester lead still connected to common (white) wire and connect red test lead alternately to each remaining sensor coil wire. Repeat test on other bank of cylinders. Renew timer base if output is less than 0.3 volt.

On models after 1978, disconnect the four-pin connector (one per bank of cylinders). Connect ohmmeter to terminals D and A (Fig. OM18-17), then terminals D and B, then terminals D and C in four-pin connector leading to timer base. Repeat test on other four-pin sensor coil connector. Renew timer base if resistance is not 35-45 ohms on 1986 200 and 225 hp models, 30-50 ohms on 1987 200 and 225 hp models and 12-22 ohms on all other models. Connect ohmmeter between engine ground and alternately to all terminals in four-pin timer base connector. Repeat test on other sensor coil four-pin connector. No resistance should be present between any sensor coil wire and engine ground. If continuity is noted, sensor coil or coil wire is shorted to ground.

To check sensor coil output, use Merc-O-Tronic Model 781, Stevens Model CD-77 or a suitable equivalent peak reading voltmeter (PRV). Connect PRV black test lead to timer base connector terminal D and red test lead to terminal A. On Merc-O-Tronic 781, set tester knobs to positive (+) and 5. On Stevens CD-77, set tester knobs to S and 5. Crank engine while observing tester. Repeat test alternately between terminals D and B, and D and C. Repeat complete test procedure on other timer base four-pin connector. Renew timer base assembly if output is less than 0.3 volt on 200 and 225 hp models and 0.2 volt on all other models.

POWER PACKS. To check power pack output, first reconnect stator and timer base connectors. Use Merc-O-Tronic Model 781, Stevens Model CD-77 or a suitable equivalent peak reading voltmeter (PRV). Connect PRV black test lead to engine ground. Connect red test lead to primary lead of number 1 (top starboard) ignition coil. Note that primary lead must remain connected to ignition coil. Set PRV knobs to negative (−) and 500. Crank engine while observ-

ing meter. Repeat test on all other ignition coils. Renew power pack(s) if output is less than 100 volts on 1985-1987 200 and 225 hp models or 175 volts on all other models.

NOTE: Power packs marked "CDL" are equipped with integral speed limiting device, limiting engine speed to 5800 rpm on 1987 and 1988 150 and 175 hp models, 6700 rpm on 200 and 225 hp models and 6100 rpm on all other models.

SHIFT INTERRUPTER SWITCH. On 1986 and 1987 200 and 225 hp models, shift interrupter switch (SI—Fig. OM18-11) is used to interrupt power supply to starboard power pack during gearcase directional changes. This prevents firing of starboard cylinders, thus lowering engine rpm to allow easier shifting. To check shift interrupter switch (SI), use a suitable ohmmeter placed on high ohms scale. Disconnect the single-pin connector at starboard power pack. Connect black ohmmeter lead to engine ground and red lead to terminal in switch (SI) lead. Low resistance should be noted with switch (SI) engaged and infinite resistance with switch (SI) not engaged. Connect ohmmeter between single-pin connectors of switch, note reading and reverse ohmmeter leads. Infinite resistance should be noted at one connection and low resistance (zero ohm) at other connection. If not, renew shift interrupter switch (SI).

IGNITION TIMING. Connect a power timing light to number 1 (top starboard) cylinder spark plug, start engine and run at 4300-4600 rpm in gear on models prior to 1984, or 5000 rpm or higher in gear on models after 1983. Note timing and stop engine. On all models except 200 and 225 hp models, repeat procedure with timing light connected to number 2 cylinder (top port). Note which cylinder had higher ignition timing and adjust ignition timing stop screw (1—Fig. OM18-1) to obtain ignition timing noted in following table.

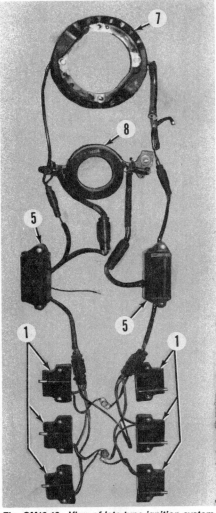

Fig. OM18-16—View of late type ignition system.
1. Ignition coils
5. Power packs
7. Stator
8. Timer base & sensor assy.

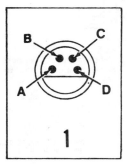

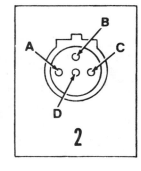

Fig. OM18-17—View "1" identifies terminal ends in timer base connector on 1979-1985 models and view "2" identifies terminal ends in timer base connector on 1986-1988 150 and 175 hp models, and 200 and 225 hp models prior to 1988.

Model	Degrees BTDC
150 Hp	
1979	26
1980	28
1981	
Timer base with black sleeves	28
Timer base with red sleeves	32
1982	28
175 Hp	
1978, 1979, 1980	?
1981	
Timer base with black sleeves	28
Timer base with red sleeves	32
1982	28

200Hp
  1976, 1977, 1978, 1979 28
  1980 26
  1981
    Timer base with black sleeves
      and model suffix "H" 26
    Timer base with black sleeves
      and model suffix "A, B, or M" . 28

Timer base with red sleeves 30
  1982 28
235 Hp
  1978, 1979 28
  1980, 1981, 1982 30

On models after 1982, refer to the engine decal for maximum spark advance

specifications. Turn spark advance stop screw (1—Fig. OM18-1 or A—Fig. OM18-10) to adjust maximum spark advance. Turning spark advance stop screw clockwise one full turn will retard ignition timing approximately one degree.

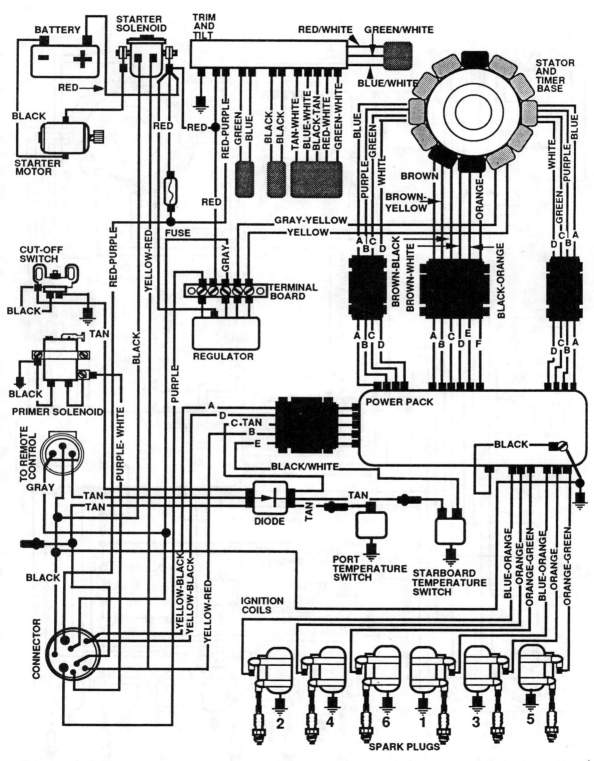

Fig. OM18-18—Wiring diagram typical of late 150 and 175 hp models equipped with 35 ampere charging system. Models equipped with 9 ampere charging system is similar.

On all models except 200 and 225 hp models, adjust throttle cam as outlined in SPEED CONTROL LINKAGE section. Connect a power timing light to number 1 cylinder, start engine and note timing. Idle timing should be 5 degrees BTDC on 175 and 200 hp models prior to 1980 or

6-8 degrees BTDC on all other models. Adjust position of cam yoke (Y—Fig. OM18-5) to align mark and follower roller. On later models, an adjustment nut or a thumb wheel is used to adjust position of cam yoke (Y).

150 And 175 Hp Models After 1988, and 200 and 225 Hp Models After 1987

TROUBLE-SHOOTING. Refer to Fig. OM18-18 for wiring diagram on 150 and 175 hp models and Fig. OM18-19 for wir-

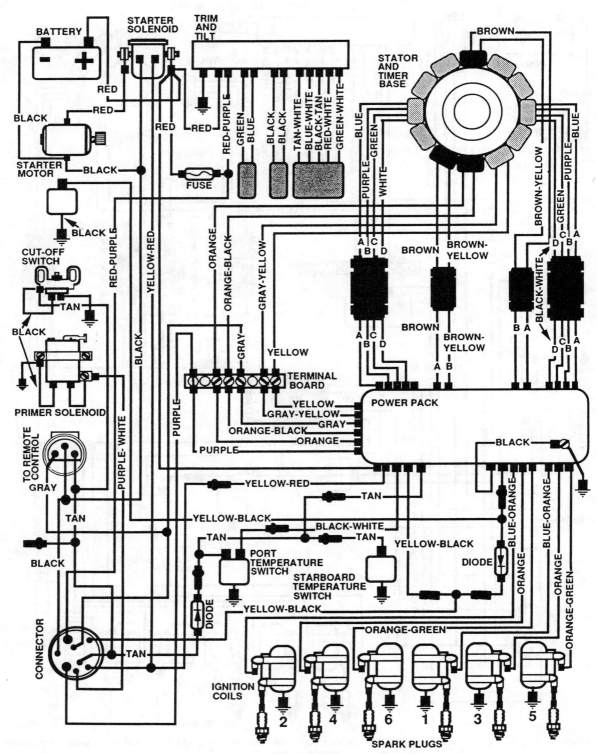

Fig. OM18-19—Wiring diagram typical of late 200 and 225 hp models.

ing diagram on 200 and 225 hp models. Trouble-shoot ignition system using an ohmmeter and a suitable peak reading voltmeter (PRV) such as Merc-O-Tronic Model 781 or Stevens Model CD-77.

NOTE: Resistance specifications are based on measurements taken at ambient temperature of 70° F (21° C). Resistance may change by approximately 10 ohms per one degree temperature variation.

Use only approved procedures to prevent damage to ignition components. The fuel system should be checked to make certain faulty running is not the result of fuel starvation, incorrect mixture or contaminated fuel.

INDEXING FLYWHEEL. Power packs with a defective isolation diode or other internal defect can result in erratic ignition system operation. To determine if each cylinder is firing at the proper time, proceed as follows: Remove all spark plugs. Rotate flywheel in clockwise direction until number 2 cylinder is at TDC. With number 2 cylinder at TDC, mark ''2'' on flywheel directly adjacent to timing pointer. Repeat procedure for all cylinders, placing each cylinder number on flywheel across from timing pointer. Place motor into a suitable test tank, start engine and run at rpm malfunction is evident. Connect a timing light alternately to each spark plug lead and verify cylinders are firing at their respective mark on flywheel. If not, be sure all wiring pins are properly located in connectors or renew power pack.

S.L.O.W. (Speed Limiting Overheat Warning). Models 150 and 175 hp with 35 ampere charging system, and 200 and 225 hp models are equipped with S.L.O.W. (speed limiting overheat warning) system. The S.L.O.W. function is activated when engine temperature exceeds 203° F (95° C). When activated, the S.L.O.W. system limits engine speed to approximately 2500 rpm. To resume normal operation, the engine must be stopped and cooled to 162° F (72° C). The S.L.O.W. system is activated by input from temperature switches located in port and starboard cylinder heads. A blocking diode located in the engine wiring harness is used to isolate the S.L.O.W. system from other warning signals.

To determine if the S.L.O.W. system is functioning properly, disconnect tan temperature switch leads from port and starboard temperature sensors. Place outboard motor into a suitable test tank with the correct test wheel installed. Start engine and run at 3500 rpm. Connect port side temperature switch lead

(tan) to engine ground. Engine speed should slow to approximately 2500 rpm. Repeat test with starboard side temperature switch lead.

If S.L.O.W. system functions properly when tested at both temperature switch tan leads, refer to TEMPERATURE SWITCH section. If proper operation is noted at only one temperature switch lead, inspect condition of wiring harness and connectors and repair as necessary. If neither test indicates proper operation, proceed as follows:

On 150 and 175 hp models, separate six-pin connector between stator and power pack. Connect ohmmeter between engine ground and alternately to terminals E and F of six-pin connector. No continuity should be present between engine ground and terminals E or F. Attach ohmmeter between terminals E and F of six-pin connector leading to power pack. Renew power pack if resistance is within 86-106 ohms. If resistance is not within 86-106 ohms, renew stator assembly.

On 200 and 225 hp models, loosen power pack and remove orange and orange/black power coil leads from terminal board. Connect ohmmeter between engine ground and alternately to orange lead and orange/black lead. No resistance should be present between ground and either orange or orange/black leads. Connect ohmmeter between orange and orange/black leads. Renew power pack if resistance is within 86-106 ohms. If not, renew stator assembly.

NOTE: DO NOT start engine with power coil leads disconnected.

BLOCKING DIODE. If the S.L.O.W. function is activated by other warning horn systems, test blocking diode located in the wiring harness. Disconnect port and starboard temperature switch tan leads and wiring harness red connector. Connect an ohmmeter between either temperature switch tan lead and tan lead terminal inside harness red connector, then reverse ohmmeter leads. A high reading (infinity) should be indicated in one connection and a low reading (zero) in the other. If not, renew wiring harness assembly.

TEMPERATURE SWITCH. On 1987 models, temperature switches should be open at 168°-182° F (75°-83° C) and should close at 205°-216° F (96°-102° C). On 1988 and 1989 models, temperature switch with tan wire should be open at 147°-177° F (65°-79° C) and close at 197°-205° F (92°-96° C). On 1988 and 1989 models, temperature switch with white/black wire should be open at 86°-92° F (30°-34° C) and close at 93°-99° F (34°-38° C). Test switches using a suitable continuity light or ohmmeter. Heat switches using a suitable oil bath with an accurate thermometer.

QUICKSTART. Models 150 and 175 hp equipped with 35 ampere charging system, and 1988 and 1989 Models 200 and 225 hp are equipped with the Quick-

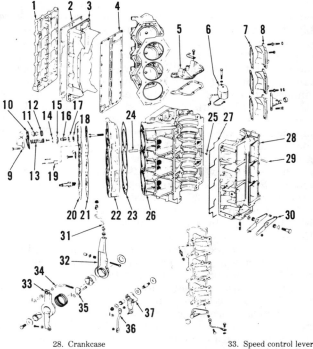

Fig. OM18-20—Exploded view of typical cylinder block and related components used on all models except 200 and 225 hp models. Sealing strips (27) are not used on models after 1978. On 200 and 225 hp models, covers (20) and cylinder heads (22) are one piece. Exhaust cover (1) and transfer port covers (8) are cast into cylinder block (26). Refer to Fig. OM18-21 for view of crankshaft and piston assemblies.

1. Exhaust cover
2. Gasket
3. Exhaust inner cover
4. Gasket
5. Water passage cover
6. Voltage regulator
7. Gasket
8. Transfer port covers
9. Thermostat cover
10. Gasket
11. Thermostat
12. Grommet
13. Relief valve spring
14. Spring seat
15. Seal
16. Relief valve
17. Valve seat
18. Washer
19. Temperature warning switch
20. Cylinder head cover
21. Gasket
22. Cylinder head
23. Gasket
24. Water deflector
25. Main bearing dowel pin
26. Cylinder block
27. Sealing strip
28. Crankcase
29. Taper pin
30. Bellcrank
31. Ignition advance rod
32. Ignition control lever
33. Speed control lever
34. Throttle lever link
35. Yoke
36. Shift rod
37. Shift lever

Start function. The QuickStart circuit is activated each time the engine is started. QuickStart automatically advances ignition timing for approximately five seconds during starting (at all temperatures). QuickStart is also activated any time engine temperature is below 96° F (36° C). QuickStart is inoperative when engine speed exceeds 1100 rpm.

To determine if QuickStart is functioning properly, place outboard motor into a suitable test tank with the correct test wheel installed. Engine temperature must be above 96° F (36° C) before testing.

NOTE: Make sure speed control linkage, idle speed and ignition timing are properly adjusted before attempting to test Quick-Start system. Refer to SPEED CONTROL LINKAGE section.

Place marks on flywheel adjacent to timing pointer indicating TDC for all cylinders. Disconnect white/black lead between power pack and port side temperature switch. Connect a timing light to number 1 cylinder spark plug lead, start engine and run at idle speed in forward gear (not more than 900 rpm). The timing light should flash at the number 1 cylinder TDC mark on flywheel. Reconnect the white/black lead to the power pack. The number 1 cylinder TDC mark should shift to the right approximately 1 inch, indicating ignition timing has returned to normal setting. Repeat test for each cylinder. Note that engine must be stopped before testing each remaining cylinder.

If one or more sensor coils do not operate properly, renew timer base assembly. If no sensor coils operate properly, disconnect white/black lead from power pack lead and connect ohmmeter between white/black lead and engine ground. Ohmmeter should indicate continuity with engine temperature below 89° F (32° C). If continuity is noted, test temperature switches. If not, connect ohmmeter between each power coil lead (orange and orange/black) and engine ground. No continuity should be present between power coil leads and ground. Next, check resistance between orange and orange/black power coil leads. Renew power pack if resistance is within 86-106 ohms. If not, renew stator assembly.

If QuickStart system remains activated when engine speed exceeds 1100 rpm, renew power pack. If QuickStart system remains activated continuously, regardless of temperature, time activated and engine speed, test port side temperature switch, inspect power pack white/black lead and connector, test engine for undercooling condition or renew power pack.

TOTAL OUTPUT. On all models, dis-connect all spark plug leads from spark plugs and install a suitable spark tester to plug leads. Adjust tester spark gap to $^7/_{16}$ inch (11 mm). Refer to the appropriate following paragraphs:

On 150 and 175 hp models with 9 ampere charging system, crank engine while observing spark tester. If normal spark is noted at all spark gaps, refer to RUNNING OUTPUT section. If no spark output is noted at any spark gap, refer to STOP CIRCUIT section. If spark output is noted on at least one spark gap, refer to CHARGE COIL section.

On 150 and 175 hp models with 35 ampere charging system, disconnect five-pin connector between power pack and engine harness. Using jumper leads, connect terminals and A and D in power pack connector half to their respective terminals A and D in wiring harness connector half, then install a jumper lead from terminal E of power pack connector to engine ground. Crank engine while observing spark tester. If normal spark is noted at all spark gaps, refer to RUNNING OUTPUT section. If normal spark is noted at one or more gaps, refer to CHARGE COIL section. If no spark output is noted, refer to STOP CIRCUIT section.

On 200 and 225 hp models, loosen power pack and disconnect yellow/red lead one-pin connector. Ground power pack to engine using a suitable jumper lead. Disconnect white/black lead from port temperature switch and ground white/black lead to engine ground. Crank engine while observing spark tester. If normal spark output is noted at all spark gaps, refer to RUNNING OUTPUT section. If no spark output is noted at cylinders 1, 3, and 5, refer to SHIFT SWITCH section. If normal spark output is noted at one or more cylinders, refer to CHARGE COIL section. If no spark output is noted at all spark gaps, refer to STOP CIRCUIT section.

SHIFT SWITCH. On 200 and 225 hp models, shift switch is used to interrupt power supply to starboard power pack during gearcase shifting. Shift switch prevents starboard cylinders from firing, allowing easier engagement and disengagement of forward and reverse gears.

If during total output test on 200 and 225 hp models, no spark output is present at cylinders 1, 3 and 5, test shift switch as follows: Disconnect both yellow/black one-pin connectors between shift switch and power pack. Connect ohmmeter between engine ground and power pack side of shift switch wiring harness. No continuity should be indicated. Activate shift switch by depressing shift cable pin. Continuity should be indicated. Renew switch and harness if not as specified.

Next, connect ohmmeter between both switch harness one-pin connectors, note reading and reverse ohmmeter leads. A high (infinity) resistance reading should be noted with one connection and a low (zero) resistance reading should be noted with other connection. Renew switch and harness if not as specified.

STOP CIRCUIT. On 150 and 175 hp models with 9 ampere charging system, disconnect one-pin stop circuit connector between power pack and key switch. Crank engine while observing spark tester. If normal spark is now noted, check condition of key switch and stop circuit using a suitable ohmmeter. If no spark output is noted, refer to CHARGE COIL section. If weak spark or spark at one or more spark gaps, refer to SENSOR COIL section.

On 150 and 175 hp models with 35 ampere charging system, disconnect five-pin connector between power pack and engine harness. Connect terminal E of power pack five-pin connector to engine ground with a suitable jumper lead. Crank engine while observing spark tester. Normal spark output at all spark gaps indicate faulty key switch or stop circuit. Refer to CHARGE COIL section if no spark output is noted. If weak spark or spark at some spark gaps is noted, refer to SENSOR COIL section.

On 200 and 225 hp models, disconnect one-pin connector (tan) between power pack and key switch. Crank engine while observing spark tester. Normal spark output at all spark gaps indicate faulty key switch or stop circuit. Refer to CHARGE COIL section if no spark output is noted.

CHARGE COIL. On 150 and 175 hp models, disconnect four-pin connector (9 ampere models) or six-pin connector (35 ampere models) between stator and power pack. Set PRV knobs to positive (+) and 500. Connect PRV between engine ground and terminal A of four-pin connector (9 ampere) or six-pin connector (35 ampere). Crank engine while observing meter. Any voltage reading indicates charge coil or charge coil leads are shorted to ground. Repeat test on remaining terminals B, C and D.

If no voltage reading is noted, connect PRV black test lead to stator terminal A and red test lead to stator terminal B. Crank engine while observing meter. Repeat test with PRV connected between stator terminals C and D. If cranking output is 200 volts or more, refer to SENSOR COIL section. If less than 200 volts are indicated, inspect condition of stator wiring and connectors, and be sure all connector pins are properly located. If wiring and connectors are in acceptable condition, check charge coil resistance by connecting ohmmeter between stator terminals A and B, and terminals C and D. Renew stator assembly if resistance is not within 455-505 ohms on 9 ampere models or 960-1010 ohms on 35 ampere models.

On 200 and 225 hp models, disconnect both (front and rear) two-pin stator connectors. Set PRV knobs to positive (+) and 500. Connect PRV between engine ground and terminal A of either stator two-pin connector. Crank engine while noting meter. Repeat test at remaining terminals of both two-pin connectors. If any voltage output is noted at any stator terminal, charge coil or wiring is shorted to ground.

Attach PRV black test lead to terminal A of forward stator two-pin connector and red test lead to terminal B. Crank engine while observing meter. Repeat test with PRV connected to rear two-pin connector. Charge coil cranking output should be 130 volts or more. If not, inspect condition of stator wiring and connectors. If wiring and connectors are acceptable, connect ohmmeter between terminals A and B of front two-pin connector, then repeat test on rear two-pin connector. Renew stator assembly if resistance is not within 960-1010 ohms.

SENSOR COIL. On all models, disconnect six-pin connector (9 ampere models) or both four-pin connectors (35 ampere models and 200 and 225 hp models) between timer base and power pack. Set PRV knobs to positive (+) and 5. Alternately connect PRV between engine ground and each timer base terminal while cranking engine. Any output indicates sensor coil or wiring is shorted to ground. Repair wiring or renew timer base assembly.

On 9 ampere 150 and 175 hp models, check sensor coil cranking output as follows: Connect PRV black test lead to timer base ground wire. Alternately connect PRV red test lead to each timer base terminal while cranking engine at each connection. If output is 0.2 volt or more, refer to POWER PACK section. If output is less than 0.2 volt, inspect condition of timer base wiring and connectors. If wiring and connectors are acceptable, disconnect timer base ground wire from power head. Alternately connect ohmmeter between timer base ground wire and each timer base terminal in six-pin connector. Renew timer base assembly if sensor coil resistance is not within 30-50 ohms.

Check sensor coil cranking output as follows on 150 and 175 hp models with 35 ampere charging system and 200 and 225 hp models. With PRV set to positive (+) and 5, connect black test lead to ter-

minal D of port four-pin timer base connector. Connect red test lead alternately to terminals A, B and C of starboard timer base connector, then terminals A, B and C of port timer base connector. Crank engine at each test connection and note meter.

If output is less than 0.2 volt, inspect condition of timer base wiring and connectors. If wiring and connectors are acceptable, check sensor coil resistance. If output is 0.2 volt or more, proceed as follows: Install a jumper lead from terminal D in power pack connector to terminal D of harness connector. Connect PRV black test lead to engine ground and alternately connect red test lead to terminals A, B and C of port four-pin connector, then terminals A, B and C of starboard four-pin connector. Crank engine at each test connection. If output is 1.2 volts or more, refer to POWER PACK section. If output is less than 1.2 volts, repair wiring, connectors or renew timer base.

Check sensor coil resistance on 150 and 175 hp models with 35 ampere charging system, and 200 and 225 hp models as follows:

NOTE: Ohmmeter polarity must be determined before proceeding with sensor coil resistance test. Calibrate meter on Rx100 scale and connect leads to a known-good diode, then reverse leads. If first connection indicated very low resistance (zero ohm) and second connection indicated very high resistance (infinity), ohmmeter red lead is positive (+). If opposite result is noted, reverse ohmmeter leads so red lead is positive (+).

Connect ohmmeter red lead to terminal D in port timer base connector. Connect ohmmeter black lead alternately to terminals A, B and C in starboard timer base connector, and terminals A, B and C in port timer base connector.

NOTE: Timer base components may cause resistance readings to vary depending upon individual meter impedance. Readings may be higher or lower. If so, readings should be consistent.

If using Merc-O-Tronic Model M-700 ohmmeter, resistance should be 870-1070 ohms. If using Stevens Model AT-101 ohmmeter resistance should be 330-390 ohms.

Next, connect ohmmeter between D terminals of port and starboard timer base connectors. Ohmmeter should indicate 200-260 ohms. Connect ohmmeter between engine ground and each terminal in port and starboard timer base terminals. No continuity should be present between ground and any timer base terminal. If continuity is noted, re-

pair grounded timer base wires or renew timer base assembly.

POWER PACK. To check power pack output on all models, remove primary leads from ignition coils. Connect primary lead of number 1 cylinder ignition coil (top starboard) to red lead of Stevens Load Adapter PL-88. Connect load adapter black lead to engine ground.

NOTE: If Stevens Load Adapter PL-88 is not available, fabricate adapter using Radio Shack 10 ohm, 10 watt resister, part 271-132, or equivalent.

Set peak reading voltmeter knobs to positive (+) and 500. Connect voltmeter red test lead to load adapter red lead and black test lead to engine ground. Crank engine while noting meter. Power pack output should be 175 volts or more on 150 and 175 hp models or 100 volts or more on 200 and 225 hp models. Repeat test at remaining ignition coils. If the specified voltage or more is present at all primary leads, refer to IGNITION COIL section. If no output is noted at any primary lead, renew power pack.

NOTE: Power packs marked "CDL" are equipped with integral speed limiting device, limiting engine speed to 5800 rpm on 150 and 175 hp models, 6700 rpm on 200 and 225 hp models.

IGNITION COILS. Ignition coils may be tested using a variety of testers available from various manufacturers. Follow tester manufacturer's instructions when testing coil.

Check ignition coil primary resistance by connecting ohmmeter between coil primary terminal and coil ground. Primary resistance should be 0.05-0.15 ohm. Check secondary resistance between primary terminal and high tension terminal. Secondary resistance should be 225-325 ohms. Renew coil if not as specified. Ignition coil high tension lead (spark plug lead) resistance should be near zero ohm.

RUNNING OUTPUT. To check running output, disconnect primary leads from ignition coils. Install terminal extenders (Stevens TS-77 or equivalent) on coil terminals, then reconnect coil primary leads to terminal extenders. Set voltmeter switches to positive (+) and 500. Connect tester black lead to engine ground.

NOTE: Outboard motor should be placed into a suitable test tank with the correct test wheel installed when checking running output.

Start engine and run at rpm that malfunction is evident. Alternately, connect red tester lead to terminal extender of each coil. USE CAUTION not to touch metal part of terminal extender or tester lead to prevent shock hazard. Power pack running output should be a continuous 250 volts or more (150 and 175 hp models) or 130 volts or more (200 and 225 hp models) at each ignition coil. If output is low at one or more coils, test charge coils as previously outlined in CHARGE COIL section. If NO output is noted at one or more coils, test sensor coils as previously outlined in SENSOR COIL section.

IGNITION TIMING (150 And 175 Hp Models). Check pick-up timing as follows: Connect a timing light to number 1 cylinder (top starboard) spark plug lead. Advance throttle control lever until embossed mark on throttle cam is aligned with cam follower roller. Start engine and note timing. Throttle pick-up timing should be 6-8 degrees BTDC. Loosen jam nut and adjust thumb screw at yoke (Y—Fig. OM18-5) to adjust.

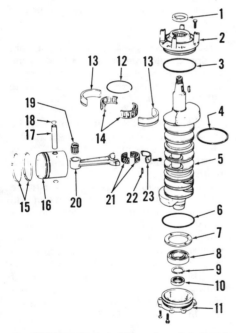

Fig. OM18-21—Exploded view of crankshaft and piston assemblies. Two "O" rings (3 and 6) and two seals (10) are used on 200 and 225 hp models. On 1985 and later models, except 200 and 225 hp models, 28 loose needle bearing rollers and two thrust washers are used in place of caged bearing (19).

1. Seal	
2. Upper crankcase head & bearing	13. Main bearing outer race
3. "O" ring	14. Roller bearing
4. Seal ring (9 used)	15. Piston rings
5. Crankshaft	16. Piston
6. "O" ring	17. Piston pin
7. Retainer plate	18. Snap ring
8. Ball bearing	19. Roller bearing
9. Snap ring	20. Connecting rod
10. Seal	21. Bearing cage
11. Lower crankcase head	22. Bearing rollers
12. Retaining ring	23. Rod cap

NOTE: Outboard motor should be placed into a suitable test tank with the correct test wheel installed, or in the water with the correct propeller installed to check ignition timing. The manufacturer does not recommend checking timing with flushing adapter connected to outboard motor.

To check full throttle timing, connect a timing light to number 1 cylinder spark plug lead. Start engine and run at a minimum of 5000 rpm while noting timing. Repeat procedure with timing light connected to number 2 cylinder spark plug lead. Note cylinder with most advanced timing, stop engine and adjust full throttle timing screw (A—Fig. OM18-10) to obtain 31-33 degrees BTDC on 150 hp and 27-29 degrees BTDC on 150 STL and 175 hp models.

IGNITION TIMING (200 and 225 Hp Models). Idle timing should be 6 degrees ATDC. To check timing, loosen lockring (L—Fig. OM18-12) and turn knob (K) clockwise until knob (K) is seated. Start engine and warm to normal operating temperature. Note timing with outboard motor in forward gear and throttle arm stop screw (D—Fig. OM18-10) contacting crankcase. To adjust idle timing, stop engine and turn idle timing screw (I—Fig. OM18-12), located under flywheel, as necessary.

NOTE: After adjusting idle timing, the engine should idle between 575-700 rpm in forward gear and the cam follower roller should not contact the throttle cam with engine in neutral.

Full throttle timing advance should be 17-19 degrees BTDC.

NOTE: Compare the above timing specification to the maximum advance specification on decal affixed to power head. Use specification on power head if it disagrees with above specification.

With timing light connected to number 1 cylinder spark plug lead, start engine and warm to normal operating temperature. Note timing at 4500-5000 rpm. Adjust screw (A—Fig. OM18-10 [typical]) as necessary to adjust.

COOLING SYSTEM

THERMOSTAT. A cooling system thermostat is used in each cylinder head to maintain water temperature of approximately 145° F (63° C). A relief valve adjacent to each thermostat opens at high engine speed when water pump impeller speed increases water pressure. On 200 and 225 hp models, the relief valve is located within each thermostat assembly.

Engine temperature can be checked using heat sensitive sticks such as Markal Thermomelt Stik. A 163° F (73° C) stick should not melt, but a 125° F (52° C) should melt, after engine reaches operating temperature. The remote control box is equipped with a overheat warning horn that is activated by temperature switches located in each cylinder head. Test temperature switches using a suitable continuity light or ohmmeter. Heat switches using a suitable oil bath with an accurate thermometer. On 1987 models, temperature switches should be open at 168°-182° F (75°-83° C) and should close at 205°-216° F (96°-102° C). On 1988 and 1989 models, temperature switch with tan wire should be open at 147°-177° F (64°-80° C) and close at 197°-205° F (92°-96° C). On 1988 and 1989 models, temperature switch with white/black wire should be open at 86°-92° F (30°-33° C) and close at 93°-99° F (34°-37° C).

WATER PUMP. The water pump is mounted on top of the gearcase. Rubber impeller is driven by the drive shaft. Separate gearcase from exhaust housing for access to water pump.

Apply OMC Adhesive M to "O" ring (7—Figs. OM18-26 or OM18-35) groove in impeller housing (4—Fig. OM18-26 or 3A—Fig. OM18-35) and OMC Gasket Sealing Compound to bottom of impeller plate (8). Lubricate impeller (6) and hold blades in while installing housing.

POWER HEAD

R&R AND DISASSEMBLE. Remove electric starter solenoid, electric starter, flywheel, stator and timer base. Remove air silencer, carburetors and fuel pumps or VRO pump. Disconnect and label interfering wires. Loosen bellcrank (30—Fig. OM18-20) screw on models prior to 1979 and disengage lower unit shift rod from bellcrank. Disconnect upper end of shift rod on models after 1978. On all models except 200 and 225 hp models, remove exhaust housing rear cover (six screws) and unbolt exhaust housing front cover and allow front cover to rest against exhaust housing. Remove two front rubber mount screws. Unscrew two engine-to-adapter stud nuts below exhaust cover. Unscrew nuts, two short screws and six long screws, shown in Fig. OM18-22, retaining engine to adapter and lift engine off drive unit. On 200 and 225 hp models, remove four screws and one nut from each side of upper end of drive shaft housing and two screws and one nut at rear of upper end of drive shaft housing. Lift power head from lower unit.

Transfer port covers should be marked before removal because all transfer port covers are not identical. Remove transfer port covers, exhaust covers and cylinder heads. Inlet manifold should be carefully removed by loosening screws evenly to prevent warping. Remove upper and lower crankcase head screws (2 and 11—Fig. OM18-21). Taper pin or pins (29—Fig. OM18-20) must be driven out toward the front. Loosen, but do not remove, center four screws in lower crankcase head (11—Fig. OM18-21), which hold retainer plate (7). Unscrew crankcase retaining screws and separate crankcase (28—Fig. OM18-20) from cylinder block (26).

Pistons, rods and crankshaft are now accessible for removal and overhaul as outlined in the appropriate following paragraphs.

ASSEMBLY. When assembling, the crankcase and inlet manifold must be completely sealed against both vacuum and pressure. Exhaust manifold and cylinder heads must be sealed against water leakage and pressure. Mating surfaces of water intake and exhaust areas between lower unit and power head must form a tight seal. It is recommended that all mating surfaces be carefully inspected for nicks, burrs, corrosion and warpage which might interfere with a tight seal. All of these surfaces may be lapped if necessary to provide a smooth, flat surface. DO NOT remove any more metal than is necessary. Mating surfaces of crankcase and cylinder block MUST NOT be lowered, but can be polished to remove imperfections.

Cylinder block and crankcase are positively located by a tapered dowel pin or pins. Dowel pin or pins must not be nicked, bent or distorted and dowel pin hole or holes must be clean and true. When installing dowel pin or pins, make sure that pin or pins are fully seated, but do not use excessive force.

Crankcase and cylinder block mating surfaces on models prior to 1979 are sealed by rubber sealing strips (27–Fig. OM18-20) which fit in grooves of crankcase mating surface. Make certain that grooves and mating surface are absolutely clean and free from old cement, nicks or foreign matter.

Refer to subsequent sections for assembly of piston, rod and crankshaft components. Install piston and rod assemblies in cylinder block with bearing in rod but do not install cap and bearing. Install lower head assembly (6 through 11–Fig. OM18-21) on crankshaft but do not tighten four bearing retainer plate (7) screws. Install top bearing head assembly (1, 2 and 3) and seal rings (4) on crankshaft. Install center main bearings (13 and 14) on crankshaft as outlined in CRANKSHAFT section.

Install crankshaft assembly in cylinder block making certain that holes in center main bearings align with dowel pins in cylinder block. Position connecting rods on crankshaft and install rod bearings (21 and 22) and rod caps (23).

When reassembling crankcase, make sure mating surfaces of crankcase halves are completely clean and free of old cement, nicks and burrs. On models prior to 1979, install sealing strips (27—Fig. OM18-20) and trim ends to extend approximately $^1/_{32}$ inch (0.79 mm) into bearing bores, then sparingly apply OMC Adhesive ''M'' to cylinder half of crankcase only. On models after 1978, apply OMC Gel-Seal II to one crankcase mating surface. Do not use sealers that will harden and prevent contact between crankcase mating surfaces. Immediately assemble crankcase halves after applying sealer and position halves by installing tapered locating dowel pin or pins, then install and tighten crankcase retaining screws to the torque listed in the CONDENSED SERVICE DATA table. When tightening the retaining screws, start in the center and work toward ends. Tighten the lower main bearing retainer plate screws (7—Fig. OM18-21) to the correct torque and check the crankshaft for binding.

On all models, except 200 and 225 hp models, note location of water deflectors shown at (D—Fig. OM18-23). Deteriorated water deflectors may result in overheating and hot spots. Deflectors are not as tall as water passages so water may drain from water jacket.

On all models, except 200 and 225 hp models, use a nonhardening sealant on all gasket surfaces and complete reassembly of cylinder head and covers. Threads of screws should be coated with nonhardening sealant to prevent water damage to threads, especially on motors operated in salt water. On 200 and 225 hp models, install cylinder head gaskets and intake manifold gaskets without sealant.

PISTONS, PINS, RINGS AND CYLINDERS. Before detaching connecting rods from crankshaft, mark piston, rod and cap for correct reassembly to each other and for installation into original cylinder. Pistons and rings are available in standard and 0.030 inch (0.76 mm) oversize. Refer to CONDENSED SERVICE DATA for service specifications. Maximum allowable cylinder bore out-of-round is 0.004 inch (0.10 mm). Maximum allowable cylinder bore taper is 0.002 inch (0.05 mm). Refer to CONDENSED SERVICE DATA for piston skirt-to-cylinder clearance on models prior to 1985. The manufacturer does not specify piston-to-cylinder clearance on models after 1984. If cyl-

inder and piston are within wear tolerance, clearance should be acceptable. If boring cylinder for oversize piston, add amount of piston oversize (0.030 in. [0.76 mm]) to standard cylinder bore diameter to determine correct cylinder oversize diameter.

Measure cylinder head flatness using a suitable straightedge and feeler gage. Resurface cylinder head if warped in excess of 0.004 inch (0.10 mm). Do not remove more than 0.010 inch (0.25 mm) of metal from head.

The piston pin is retained in piston by snap rings (18—Fig. OM18-21) in piston pin bosses. Snap rings should always be renewed once removed. Install snap rings with gap facing down.

On some models, one piston pin boss is press fit and the other is a loose fit. When removing or installing piston pin, always press pin from side marked ''L'' toward the tight side to prevent damage

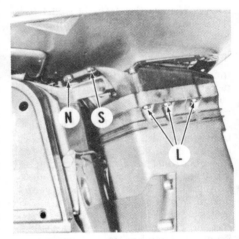

Fig. OM18-22—On all models except 200 and 225 hp models, remove nut (N), short screw (S) and long screws (L) from each side of outboard when removing power head.

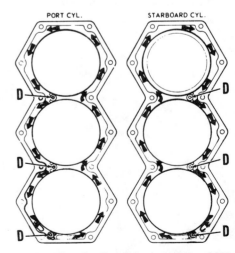

Fig. OM18-23—On all models except 200 and 225 hp models, water deflectors (D) must be installed in locations shown for proper water circulation in cylinder block.

to piston. The upper end of connecting rod is fitted with a caged needle roller bearing on 200 and 225 hp, and all other models prior to 1985. On 150 and 175 hp models after 1985, piston pin bearing consists of 28 loose needle bearing rollers and two thrust washers. Thrust washers should be installed with large diameter facing outward. On models with one loose pin boss and one press-fit pin boss, piston may be heated to ease pin installation.

The oil hole on small end of connecting rods should face flywheel. On all models, except 200 and 225 hp, pistons should be installed with long sloping side of crown facing exhaust ports (center of engine). On 200 and 225 hp models, pistons should be installed with stamped mark "EXHAUST" in crown facing exhaust ports. Thoroughly lubricate all friction and bearing surfaces during reassembly.

CONNECTING RODS, BEARINGS AND CRANKSHAFT. Individual connecting rod and piston assemblies may be removed after removing crankcase (28—Fig. OM18-20) and appropriate cylinder head (22). Before detaching connecting rods from crankshaft, mark rod, cap and bearings for reference during reassembly.

Crankpin bearings consist of a split retainer (cage) and 18 rollers on all models except 200 and 225 hp models. Sixteen roller bearings per crankpin bearing set are used on 200 and 225 hp models. Connecting rods are the "cracked cap" design. When rod cap and rod are correctly assembled, parting line between rod and cap should be nearly invisible. When reassembling, make certain that index marks (M—Fig. OM18-24) are aligned, oil hole (H) is toward top of motor and long sloping side or stamping "EXHAUST SIDE" of piston crown is to-

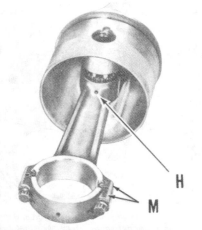

Fig. OM18-24 — Oil hole (H) should be toward top of motor and index marks (M) should be aligned.

ward center of engine (exhaust ports). On 1985 and later models equipped with precision ground rods, OMC Alignment Fixture 396749 is recommended to properly align connecting rod and rod cap when tightening rod cap screws.

NOTE: Precision ground rods are identified by grind marks running ACROSS corners on ears of connecting rod and rod cap.

On models prior to 1985, crankshaft seal rings (4—Fig. OM18-21) should have 0.0015-0.0025 inch (0.38-0.063 mm) side clearance in crankshaft groove. Seal rings are available in four thicknesses: 0.1565-0.1570 inch (3.3975-3.988 mm), 0.1575-0.1580 inch (4.000-4.013 mm), 0.1585-0.1590 inch (4.026-4.039 mm) and 0.1605-0.1610 inch (4.077-4.089 mm). On models after 1984, renew seal ring (4) if worn to less than 0.154 inch (3.91 mm). On all models, position seal ring gaps up (away from cylinders) when installing crankshaft assembly into cylinder block.

Bearing and head (2) must be serviced as a unit assembly. Lip of seal (1) should face inside of engine and should be pressed into head until flush with top surface of bearing head.

The center main bearings are split cage needle bearings. The two-piece outer race is held together with retaining ring (12) and is positioned in cylinder block by a dowel pin. Install bearing races (13) with ring groove facing toward bottom of engine. When reassembling, make certain that dowel pin in cylinder block bore engages hole in center bearing outer race.

The ball type lower main bearing (8) is located in lower bearing head (11). The bearing outer race is clamped to the bearing head with retainer plate (7). To disassemble lower bearing assembly, remove retainer plate screws and pull bearing head (11) from bearing (8). Remove snap ring (9), then remove bearing from crankshaft lower end using a suitable puller. The lower bearing should allow crankshaft end play within the limits specified in CONDENSED SERVICE DATA section. When assembling, position retainer (7) around crankshaft, then press bearing (8) onto journal and install snap ring (9). Seals (10) should be pressed into bearing head using OMC special tool 325453 on 200 and 225 hp models, and using OMC special tool 318619 or 326567 on all other models. Using special tools ensure that seals are installed at the correct depth in bearing head bore. Install new "O" ring(s) (6) in bearing head groove(s) and press bearing head onto outer race of bearing. Install screws into retainer (7), but do not tighten until crankcase is assembled.

Refer to CONDENSED SERVICE DATA section for service and torque specifications.

PROPELLER

An aluminum, three-blade propeller with built-in cushion clutch is standard on most motors. However, some motors are equipped with a stainless steel propeller. Optional propellers are available. Only propellers designed for use on these motors should be used. Refer to CONDENSED SERVICE DATA for desired engine speed at full throttle.

LOWER UNIT

Models Prior to 1979

REMOVE AND REINSTALL. To remove gearcase, disconnect upper end of shift rod from bellcrank (30—Fig. OM18-20), remove propeller and drain lubricant from gearcase. Mark location of trim tab (22—Fig. OM18-26) to aid during reassembly and remove trim tab. Remove two screws on each side of gearcase and two screws at rear.

NOTE: One rear screw is in trim tab cavity.

Separate gearcase from exhaust housing being careful not to bend shift rod.

To install gearcase, reverse removal procedure. Install a new "O" ring in end of drive shaft and coat splines with a suitable antiseize compound. Connector (24) bolt hole must be forward. Check length of gear shift rod (25). With shifter in neutral, distance from mating surface of gearcase (21) to center of hole in top of shift rod connector (24) should be $21^3/_8$-$21^7/_{16}$ inches (54.29-54.45 cm) on 1976 standard length models or $26^3/_8$-$26^7/_{16}$ inches (66.99-67.15 cm) on 1976 long leg models. Distance should be $21^9/_{16}$-$21^5/_8$ inches (54.77-54.93 cm) for 1977 and 1978 standard length models and $26^9/_{16}$-$26^5/_8$ inches (67.47-67.63 cm) for 1977 and 1978 long leg models. Distance for models after 1978 is $22^1/_{32}$-$22^3/_{32}$ inches (55.96-56.12 cm) for standard length models and $27^1/_{32}$-$27^3/_{32}$ inches (68.66-68.82 cm) for long leg models.

Apply OMC Adhesive "M" to gearcase and exhaust housing gasket surfaces. Be sure water tube is installed properly. Apply OMC Gasket Sealing Compound to threads of gearcase screws.

GEARCASE. To disassemble gearcase, separate gearcase from exhaust housing as outlined in previous section. Remove water pump housing (4—Fig. OM18-26), impeller (6), key and lower plate (8). Remove four screws holding propeller shaft bearing housing (69) and using a suitable puller, withdraw bearing housing from gearcase. Remove snap rings (66), thrust washer (64), thrust bearing (63), shift rod cover (28) and shift rod (25). Remove hydraulic shift and propeller shaft components by withdrawing push rod (37) and propeller shaft simultaneously. Hold drive shaft with OMC Tool 311875 or another suitable tool and unscrew pinion nut. Remove pinion (18), unscrew bearing housing (11) screws and withdraw drive shaft and components from gearcase. Bearing in housing (11) is not renewable but must be obtained as a unit assembly with housing. Remove forward gear (53) and oil pump (43). Do not lose 25 loose rollers in bearing (39) on models after 1977.

Inspect drive shaft splines, bearing surfaces and seal surfaces for wear or damage. Damaged splines may be caused by striking a submerged object and bending the exhaust housing. Check parallelism of top and bottom surfaces if questionable. If surfaces are not parallel, renew housing. Do not attempt to straighten it.

To remove bearing (17), pull bearing up and out using OMC Special Tool 385546 or other suitable puller. To install bearing, drive bearing down into gearcase with lettered end up using

OMC Special Tools 385546 and 321518 assembled as shown in Fig. OM18-27. Bearing is correctly positioned when plate of tool contacts gearcase. Apply Loctite to set screw (20).

Hydraulic shift components (30 through 37 – Fig. OM18-26) may be disassembled with OMC Tool 386112 by engaging pins on tool with holes in piston (34) and piston cap (30) and unscrewing cap from piston. Be careful not to bend or damage push rod (37). Remove pin (33) to separate valve (35), piston (34) and push rod. Cap (30) should be tightened to 12-15 ft.-lbs. (16.3-20.4 N·m).

Oil pump (43) is available as a unit assembly only. If necessary on models after 1977, remove and renew bearing (39). Bearing contains 25 loose rollers. Oil pump cover must be removed for access to pressure relief valve components (44 through 48) or to drive bearing cup (51) out of pump housing. Round sides of plug (47) and snap ring (48) must be together. Surfaces of rotors and housing must be flat.

Needle bearings (68 and 70) should not be removed from propeller shaft housing unless renewal is intended. Do not install used bearings. OMC Special Tool 321517 should be used to press aft bear-

ing into bearing housing (69) to ensure proper positioning. OMC Special Tool 314641 should be used to properly position forward bearing (68) in bore of housing. Seals (71) should be installed so that lip on aft seal is toward propeller and lip on forward seal is facing forward.

Install seals (9 and 10) with bottom seal (10) lip down and upper seal (9) lip up.

Thickness of shims (13) is varied to adjust mesh position of pinion gear (18) in forward and reverse gear. A shim gage, OMC Special Tool 321520, should be used to determine proper shimming.

Place pinion gear (18) on drive shaft and tighten retaining nut to 60-65 ft.-lbs. Install shims (13) that were removed during disassembly and leave thrust washer (14) and thrust bearing (15) off shaft. Hold shim gage firmly against shims and measure clearance between end of gage and pinion gear (Fig.

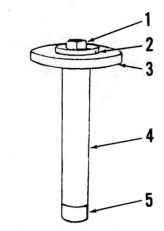

Fig. OM18-27 — View of pinion bearing installation tool.

1. Screw
2. Washer
3. Tool 385546 plate
4. Tool 321518
5. Bearing

Fig. OM18-26 — Exploded view of lower unit used on models prior to 1979. Components (39, 42, 57 and 58) are used on models after 1977 in place of components (51 and 52) used on 1976 and 1977 models.

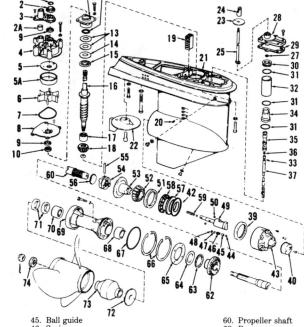

1. "O" ring
2. Grommet
2A. Grommet
3. Cover
4. Impeller housing
5. Plate
5A. Impeller liner
6. Impeller
7. "O" ring
8. Plate
9. Seal
10. Seal
11. Bearing & housing assy.
12. "O" ring
13. Shims
14. Thrust washer
15. Thrust bearing
16. Drive shaft
17. Needle bearing
18. Pinion gear
19. Water screen
20. Set screw
21. Gearcase
22. Trim tab
23. Seal
24. Shift rod connector
25. Shift rod
27. "O" ring
28. Cover
29. Gasket
30. Piston cap
31. "O" ring
32. Cylinder
33. Pin
34. Piston
35. Valve
36. Plug
37. Push rod
39. Bearing
40. Screen
42. Shim
43. Oil pump
44. Relief valve ball

45. Ball guide
46. Spring
47. Plug
48. Snap ring
49. Shift plunger
50. Detent balls
51. Bearing cup
52. Bearing cone
53. Forward gear
54. Clutch dog
55. Pin
56. Retaining spring
57. Thrust washer
58. Thrust bearing
59. Spring

60. Propeller shaft
62. Reverse gear
63. Thrust bearing
64. Thrust washer
65. Retainer plate
66. Snap rings
67. "O" rings
68. Needle bearing
69. Bearing housing
70. Needle bearing
71. Seals
72. Thrust bearing
73. Propeller bushing
74. Spacer

Fig. OM18-28 — View showing use of shim gage tool (G) as outlined in text.

OM18-28). There should be zero clearance between shims and gage.

NOTE: Make certain that enough shims are installed for an accurate check.

Shims are available in thicknesses of 0.002 inch and 0.005 inch and may be installed in any quantity to obtain proper clearance. Set the correct shims aside until drive shaft is installed.

To determine thickness of shims (42–Fig. OM18-26) on models after 1977, install thrust bearing (58) and washer (57) on face of gear housing (43). Place gear housing (43) on a surface plate with thrust bearing (58) against plate. Position OMC Tool 324797 over housing so step marked "1.862" is directly over outer edge of gear housing and measure gap between tool and housing as shown in Fig. OM18-29. Install shims (42–Fig. OM18-26) equal to measured gap.

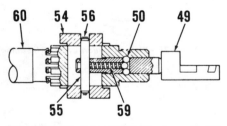

Fig. OM18-29 — Measure gap between OMC Tool 324797 and bearing housing as outlined in text to determine thickness of shims (42–Fig. OM18-26).

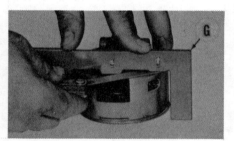

Fig. OM18-30 — Cross-sectional view of shift plunger (49) and dog clutch (54) components. Refer to Fig. OM18-26 for parts identification.

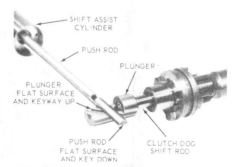

Fig. OM18-31 — View showing relative positions of shift assemblies when installed in gearcase. Refer to text for installation.

To assist in installing shift plunger components in propeller shaft, grind away the end of a 9/32 inch (7.14 mm) rod to form a long flat taper on one side. Rod should be approximately 4 inches (10.16 cm) long. Position clutch (54) on propeller shaft with pin hole in clutch and slot in shaft aligned. "PROP END" stamped on clutch must be towards propeller end of shaft. Place three shift balls (50) and spring (59) in plunger (49) as shown in Fig. OM18-30 and install plunger in propeller shaft so detent balls match grooves in propeller shaft. Align holes in clutch (54–Fig. OM18-26) and shift plunger (49) and insert tapered end of tool through holes to properly position detent spring. Carefully push tool out with retaining pin (55) and install pin retaining spring (56) in outer groove of clutch. Coils of spring must not overlap.

To reassemble gearcase, install oil pump (43), forward gear (53), thrust washer (57) and thrust bearing (58) on models after 1977. On models prior to 1978, install bearing (52) in place of thrust bearing and washer. Locating pin in oil pump (43) must align with pin hole in gearcase. Install drive shaft (16) and pinion gear (18) and tighten pinion nut to 60-65 ft.-lbs. (81.6-88.4 N·m). Lay gearcase on starboard side and install

propeller shaft with flat side of shift plunger (49) up until propeller shaft is bottomed. Install hydraulic shift assembly with flat on end of push rod (37) down. Insert shift assembly until flats on push rod (37) and shift plunger (49) are engaged (push rod will not turn). Place light pressure against shift cylinder (32) and slowly withdraw propeller shaft until key on end of push rod meshes with keyway in shift plunger as shown in Fig. OM18-31. When key and keyway are meshed, push shift assembly and propeller shaft in to complete engagement. Complete remainder of assembly noting the following points: Install snap rings (66–Fig. OM18-26) with flat side out. Install bearing housing (69) with "UP" mark toward water pump. Apply OMC Gasket Sealing Compound to threads of screws securing retainer plate (65) and bearing housing (69).

Models After 1978

REMOVE AND REINSTALL. To remove gearcase, disconnect upper end of shift rod then remove propeller and drain lubricant from gearcase. Mark location of trim tab (22—Fig. OM18-35) to aid during reassembly and remove trim

Fig. OM18-35 — Exploded view of typical lower unit used on models after 1978. Seal (4) is used on models prior to 1983.

1. "O" ring
2. Grommet
2A. Grommet
3. Water tube bracket
3A. Impeller housing
4. Seal
5. Impeller plate
5A. Impeller lining
6. Impeller
7. "O" ring
8. Plate
9. Seal
10. Seal
11. Bearing & housing assy.
12. "O" ring
13. Adjustment shims
14. Thrust washers
15. Thrust bearing
16. Drive shaft
17. Needle bearing
17A. Set screw
18. Pinion gear
19. Water screen
21. Gearcase
22. Trim tab
23. Shift rod seal
25. Shift rod
29. Shift rod cover
30. Gasket
31. Detent ball
32. Detent spring
34. Detent
36. Shift lever pin
37. Gear housing
38. Shift lever
39. Shift yoke
40. Shift shaft
41. Spring
50. Thrust washer
51. Thrust bearing
52. Forward gear
54. Dog clutch
55. Pin
56. Pin retaining spring
60. Propeller shaft
62. Reverse gear
63. Thrust bearing

64. Thrust washer
65. Retainer plate
66. Snap rings
67. "O" ring
68. Needle bearing

69. Bearing housing
70. Needle bearing
71. Seals
72. Thrust bushing
73. Propeller bushing

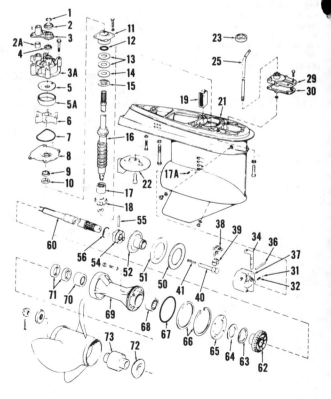

tab. Remove two screws on each side of gearcase and two screws at rear.

NOTE: One rear screw is in trim tab cavity.

Separate gearcase from exhaust housing being careful not to bend shift rod.

To install gearcase, reverse removal procedure. Install a new "O" ring in end of drive shaft and coat splines with a suitable water-resistant grease. Check adjustment of shift rod (25). With gearcase in neutral, measure distance from mating surface of gearcase (21) to center of hole in top of shift rod (25). Distance should be $21^{29}/_{32}$-$21^{31}/_{32}$ inches (556.4-558.0 mm) on 200 and 225 hp models. On 200 and 225 hp models equipped with extra long shaft, distance should be $26^{29}/_{32}$-$26^{31}/_{32}$ inches (683.4-685.0 mm). On all other models, distance should be $22^{1}/_{32}$-$22^{3}/_{32}$ inches (559.6-561.2 mm) on long shaft and $27^{1}/_{32}$-$27^{3}/_{32}$ inches (686.6-688.2 mm) on extra long shaft models. Screw shift rod up or down as necessary to adjust length. Top of shift rod should slant forward after adjustment. Apply OMC Adhesive M to gearcase and exhaust housing gasket surfaces. Be sure water tube guides and water tubes are installed properly. Apply OMC Gasket Sealing Compound to threads of gearcase.

GEARCASE. Gearcase may be disassembled in the following manner: Remove propeller, drain lubricant and remove gearcase as described in previous section. Remove screws securing shift rod cover (29–Fig. OM18-35), unscrew shift rod (25 and remove along with cover as an assembly. Remove water pump housing (3A), impeller (6), impeller key and lower plate (8). Remove four screws holding propeller shaft bearing housing (69) and using a suitable puller, remove bearing housing. Discard seals (71) and "O" ring (67). Remove snap rings (66), thrust washer assembly (64 and 63) and slide reverse gear (62) off propeller shaft. A special socket from OMC is available to hold drive shaft so nut securing pinion gear (18) can be removed. After pinion gear retaining nut is removed, unscrew the four screws securing upper drive shaft bearing housing (11). Pull drive shaft and associated parts out of gearcase. A puller may be necessary. Propeller shaft (60) may now be pulled from gearcase complete with forward gear (52), forward gear housing (37) and all associated parts.

Inspect drive shaft splines, bearing surfaces and seal surfaces for wear or damage. Damaged splines may be caused by striking a submerged object and bending the exhaust housing. Check parallelism of top and bottom surfaces if questionable. If surfaces are not parallel, renew housing. Do not attempt to straighten it.

Lower drive shaft bearing (17) should only be removed if renewal is intended. Do not reinstall a used bearing. Drive shaft bearing is held in position by a set screw (17A) as well as a press fit in gearcase. Set screw is located on starboard side in area of water intake. After removing set screw, install a suitable tool or OMC special tool with shouldered side of tool against bearing, and drive bearing down into propeller shaft cavity. New bearing is installed using a suitable tool or OMC special tool with lettered end of bearing down. Apply Loctite to set screw (17A) and install.

Forward gear (52) and propeller shaft (60) may be removed from propeller shaft gear housing (37) after dislodging pin retaining spring (56) and removing dog clutch assembly (55 and 54). Bearing housing and shifter mechanism assembly (38) may be disassembled by driving out shift lever pin (36).

Thickness of shims (13) is varied to adjust mesh position of pinion gear (18) in forward and reverse gear. A shim gage, OMC Special Tool 321520 or 315767, should be used to determine proper shimming.

Place pinion gear (18) on drive shaft and torque retaining nut to 60-65 ft.-lbs. (82-88 N·m). Install shims (13) that were removed during disassembly and leave thrust washer (14) and thrust bearing (15) off shaft. Hold shim gage firmly against shims and measure clearance between end of gage (G–Fig. OM18-28) and pinion gear. Install or remove shims to obtain zero clearance between gear and gage.

NOTE: Make certain that enough shims are installed for accurate check.

Shims are available in 0.002, 0.003, 0.004 and 0.005 inch sizes. Set the correct shims aside until drive shaft is installed.

Needle bearings (68 and 70–Fig. OM18-35) should not be removed from propeller shaft housing (69) unless renewal is intended. Do not reinstall used bearings. OMC special tools or suitable tools are used to install bearings in housing (69). Seals (71) should be installed so lip on aft seal is towards propeller and lip on forward seal is facing forward.

Assemble gearcase in the following manner: Renew all gaskets, seals and "O" rings. If lower drive shaft bearing (17) or propeller shaft bearings (68 and 70) have been removed, they too should be renewed. Install detent spring (32) and detent ball (31) in blind hole of housing (37). Hold spring and ball in position while installing detent (34). Assemble shift shaft (40), shift lever yoke (39), shift lever (38) and pin (36). Assemble forward gear (52) with thrust bearing (51 and 50) in gear housing. Place dog clutch (54) on propeller shaft (60) making sure hole in dog clutch is aligned with slot in propeller shaft and splined dogs are toward forward gear. Insert propeller shaft in forward gear and bearing housing assembly, then insert pin (55) through dog clutch propeller shaft and hole in shift shaft (40). Install pin retaining spring (56). Press shift detent (34) down and place propeller shaft, forward gear and gear housing assembly (37) into position in gearcase. Make sure locating pin (35) is seated in recess provided in gearcase.

Insert drive shaft (16). Install pinion gear retaining nut and tighten to 60-65 ft.-lbs. (82-88 N·m). Install shift rod (25) and shift rod cover (29) as an assembly. Thread shift rod fully into detent (34), back off two turns, pull rod to neutral (middle detent) and adjust for proper length. Refer to shift rod adjustment in REMOVE AND REINSTALL section for specifications.

Assemble thrust bearing (64 and 63) on reverse gear (62) and slide onto propeller shaft (60). Position bearing retainer plate (65) and install snap rings (66). Make sure that "O" ring (67) is fully seated in groove of bearing housing (69) and that seals (71) are properly installed. Lip of forward seal should be toward front and lip of aft seal should be toward propeller.

Installation of bearing housing (69) will be eased by using two guide pins, 10-inches long. Thread guide pin into bearing retainer plate (65) and slide bearing housing (69) into position. Coat bearing housing screws with sealing compound and install.

Install seals (9 and 10) in upper drive shaft bearing housing (11) with lip of lower seal (10) down and lip of upper seal (9) up. Place thrust bearing assembly (14 and 15) on drive shaft and install previously selected shim or shims (13). Coat screws that secure bearing housing (11) with sealing compound and install. Bottom edge of impeller plate (8) should be coated with OMC Adhesive "M" or equivalent and placed in position. Install impeller key, lubricate edges of impeller (6) and install on drive shaft. On models after 1984, impeller key is replaced with a drive cam. Install drive cam with flat side against drive shaft and sharp edge pointing in a clockwise direction when viewed from crankshaft end of drive shaft. Drive shaft should be turned clockwise while installing water pump housing (3A). Coat screws that secure water pump housing and water tube bracket with sealing compound and install.

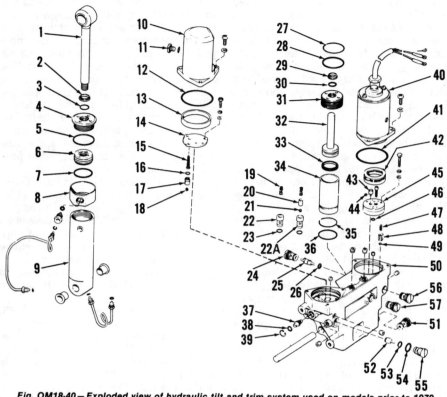

OPERATION. All models are equipped with a hydraulically actuated power tilt and trim system. Manifold (50 – Fig. OM18-40) contains valves, oil pump and trim cylinders. Oil pump motor, oil reservoir and tilt cylinder are attached to manifold. Electric oil pump motor is reversible and oil pump rotation is thereby changed to extend or retract trim and tilt cylinders. Note position of valves in Figs. OM18-40 and OM18-41. Turn manual release valve (37 – Fig. OM18-40) to manually raise or lower outboard.

Hydraulic system contains 25 ft. oz. (740 mL) of oil. Recommended oil is OMC Sea-Lube Power Trim/Tilt Fluid. Do not run pump without oil in reservoir. Oil level should reach fill plug (11) hole threads with outboard tilted in full up position. Hydraulic tilt should be recycled several times and oil level rechecked if system has been drained or lost a large amount of oil.

TROUBLE-SHOOTING. Be sure battery is fully charged, electrical connections are good, oil reservoir is full and air is not trapped in system before testing components.

OIL PUMP AND MOTOR. To check oil pump, unscrew plug (1 – Fig. OM18-42) and install a 2000 psi (13.8 MPa) pressure gage. Oil pressure should be 1300-1600 psi (9-11 MPa) with outboard tilted in full up position. Oil pressure less than specified may indicate leakage, faulty pressure relief valve (22A – Fig. OM18-40), directional valve (56), oil pump or pump motor. No-load current draw of pump motor should not exceed 18 amps. Motor must operate properly in both directions.

VALVES. Faulty valves will cause system malfunction. Note function of valves and carefully inspect valve components which may cause malfunction.

Fig. OM18-40 – Exploded view of hydraulic tilt and trim system used on models prior to 1979.

1. Shaft	16. "O" ring	30. "O" ring	43. Drive coupling
2. Wiper	17. Check valve	31. End cap	44. Ball
3. "O" ring	18. Valve ball	32. Piston	45. Oil pump
4. End cap	19. Springs	33. Piston ring	46. "O" ring
5. "O" ring	20. Spring seat	34. Trim cylinder	47. Spring
6. Piston	21. Ball	35. Retaining ring	48. Pump relief valve
7. "O" ring	22. Relief valve	36. "O" ring	49. Seal
8. Band	22A. Impact relief valve	37. Manual release	50. Manifold
9. Tilt cylinder	23. "O" ring	valve	51. Valve
10. Reservoir	24. Valve	38. "O" ring	52. Valve piston
11. Fill plug	25. Piston	39. Snap ring	53. "O" ring
12. "O" ring	26. "O" ring	40. Pump motor	54. "O" ring
13. Sleeve	27. Retaining ring	41. "O" ring	55. Valve
14. Plate	28. "O" ring	42. Oil pump filter	56. Valve
15. Screen	29. Wiper		57. Valve

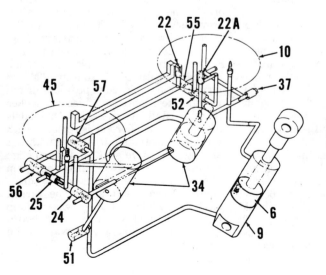

Fig. OM18-41 – Schematic of hydraulic tilt and trim system. Refer to Fig. OM18-40 for parts identification.

Fig. OM18-42 – View of oil pressure reading points.

Valves (24 and 56–Fig. OM18-40 or OM18-41) and valve piston (25) direct oil to tilt and trim cylinders from oil pump. Valve (57) directs oil to bottom of tilt cylinder when tilting outboard up and also directs oil to relief valve (22) which relieves system pressure at approximately 1500 psi (10.3 MPa). Valve (22A) relieves pressure during outboard impact and directs oil pressure to letdown valve piston (52) which allows oil to escape from bottom of tilt cylinder so top portion of tilt cylinder can be refilled after impact. Valves in tilt cylinder piston (6) allow oil to transfer from top to bottom of tilt cylinder during outboard impact. Valve (51) allows oil to flow from bottom of tilt cylinder during tilting down operation. Manual release valve (37) allows manual movement of outboard when valve is open.

TILT AND TRIM CYLINDERS. Tilt and trim system malfunction may be due to leaking "O" rings, seals and fittings in cylinders. Blocked oil lines may cause improper operation. Leaking valves in tilt cylinder piston (6–Fig. OM18-40) may allow unit to leakdown.

OVERHAUL. Filter valve seat (17–Fig. OM18-40) will be damaged if removed. Valves (24, 55, 56 and 57) are identical and may be interchanged. Valve (51) is taller than other valves and must not be interchanged. Motor must be serviced as a unit assembly. Apply OMC Nut Lock to piston shaft (1) threads and install piston (6) on shaft with small holes in piston up.

POWER TILT AND TRIM

Models After 1978

OPERATION. A hydraulically actuated power tilt and trim system is used. Manifold (50–Fig. OM18-45) contains valves, oil pump and trim cylinders. Oil pump motor, oil reservoir and tilt cylinder are attached to manifold. Electric oil pump motor is reversible and oil pump rotation is thereby changed to extend or retract trim and tilt cylinders. Note position of valves in Fig. OM18-45. Turn manual release valve counterclockwise to manually raise or lower outboard.

Hydraulic system contains approximately 25 fl. oz. (740 mL) of oil. Recommended oil is OMC Power Trim/Tilt Fluid or Dexron II automatic transmission fluid. Do not run pump without oil in reservoir. Oil level should reach fill plug (11) hole threads when tilt and trim pistons are fully extended. System should be cycled several times prior to checking oil level if system has been drained or lost a large amount of oil.

TROUBLE-SHOOTING. Be sure battery is fully charged, electrical connections are good, oil reservoir is full and air is not trapped in system before testing components.

To check oil pressure, first momentarily cycle system "UP" and "DOWN" a few times. Remove snap ring (39–Fig. OM18-45) and manual release valve (37), then install OMC gage "A" as shown in Fig. OM18-46. Operate system in the "UP" direction and observe gage after system stalls out at full extension. Gage reading should not drop below 100-200

psi (700-1400 kPa). Install OMC gage "B." Operate system in the "DOWN" direction and observe gage after system stalls out at fully retracted. Gage reading should not drop below 100-200 psi (700-1400 kPa).

To test check valves, screw each valve into OMC check valve tester 390063 (T–Fig. OM18-47). Use a suitable pressure tester (P) and apply 30 psi (207 kPa) of pressure to check valve. Check valve can be considered good if no pressure leakage is noted.

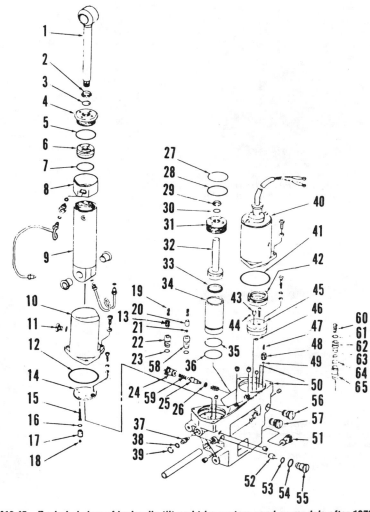

Fig. OM18-45 – Exploded view of hydraulic tilt and trim system used on models after 1978. A three-wire pump motor is used on 1979 and 1980 models.

1. Shaft	19. Spring	35. Retaining ring	51. Separation valve
2. Wiper	20. Spring seat	36. "O" ring	52. Valve piston
3. "O" ring	21. Ball	37. Manual release valve	53. "O" ring
4. End cap	22. Trim up relief valve	38. "O" ring	54. "O" ring
5. "O" ring	23. Piston	39. Snap ring	55. Impact Jetdown valve
6. Piston	24. Reverse lock check	40. Pump motor	56. Trim check valve
7. "O" ring	valve	41. "O" ring	57. Tilt check valve
8. Band	25. Piston	42. Oil pump filter	58. Impact sensor valve
9. Tilt cylinder	26. "O" ring	43. Drive coupling	59. Spring
10. Reservoir	27. Retaining ring	44. Ball	60. Spring
11. Fill plug	28. "O" ring	45. Oil pump	61. "O" ring
12. "O" ring	29. Wiper	46. "O" ring	62. Expansion relief valve
13. Needle	30. "O" ring	47. Spring	core
14. Plate	31. End cap	48. Trim down pump	63. "O" ring
15. Screen	32. Piston	relief valve	64. "O" ring
16. "O" ring	33. Piston ring	49. Seal	65. Expansion relief valve
17. Check valve	34. Trim cylinder	50. Manifold	seat
18. Valve ball			

Refer to the following for a list of symptoms and probable causes:

Symptoms	Probable Causes
Tilt Leakdown	1, 2, 3, 4, 5 or 6
Trim and Tilt Both Leak	7, 8 or 9
Reverse Lock Does Not Hold	2, 3, 6, 10, 11 or 12
Will Not Trim Out Under Load or Will Not Tilt	1, 2, 7 or 9
Will Not Trim or Tilt Down	2, 8, 10, 11 or 13

Key to Probable Causes
1. Trim Up Relief Valve
2. Manual Release Valve
3. Tilt Cylinder Valve or Seals
4. Tilt Check Valve
5. Impact Letdown Valve
6. Oil Line
7. Trim Cylinders Sleeve "O" Rings or Piston Seals
8. Trim Check Valve
9. Expansion Relief Valve or "O" Rings
10. Filter Valve Seat
11. Impact Sensor Valve
12. Reverse Lock Check Valve
13. Trim Down Pump Relief Valve

OVERHAUL. Oil pump must be serviced as a unit assembly. Motor is not serviceable with the exception of brushes. Refer to Fig. OM18-45 for exploded view of trim and tilt cylinders and manifold components. Keep all components separated during disassembly and identify each component, if needed, to assure correct position during reassembly.

POWER STEERING

200 And 225 Hp Models So Equipped

DRIVE BELT TENSION ADJUSTMENT. Loosen idler housing bolts (B – Fig. OM18-50) and rotate nuts (N) clockwise to reduce tension on drive belt and counterclockwise to increase tension on drive belt. Drive belt tension should be 25-30 pounds (111-133 N). Check belt tension using a suitable tension gage positioned midway between idler pulley (I) and flywheel pulley.

PRESSURE TEST. Remove plug (P – Fig. OM18-50) and install OMC Pressure Gage 983975 or a suitable 2000 psi (13.8 MPa) pressure gage. Remove fill plug (F) and install OMC Power Trim and Tilt fluid or Dexron II in reservoir until fluid level is even with groove around base of dipstick with plug end of dipstick resting on top of fill hole. Install plug (P) and tighten. Start engine and operate at 1000 rpm. Completely extend or retract cylinder rod and observe pressure gage. The pump relief pressure should be 850-1000 psi (5861-6895 kPa).

Fig. OM18-46 — Install OMC gage "A" or "B" into manual release valve (37 – Fig. OM18-46) port as shown to test system oil pressure. Refer to text.

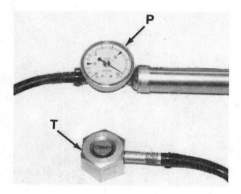

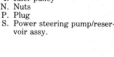

Fig. OM18-47 — Use OMC check valve tester 390063 (T) and a suitable pressure tester (P) to test check valves. Check valve can be considered good if no pressure leakage at approximately 30 psi (207 kPa) is noted.

Fig. OM18-50—View showing power steering pump/reservoir assembly used on 200 and 225 hp models so equipped. Refer to text.
  B. Bolts
  F. Fill plug
  I. Idler pulley
  N. Nuts
  P. Plug
  S. Power steering pump/reservoir assy.

EVINRUDE AND JOHNSON
8-CYLINDER MODELS

Year Produced	Evinrude Models	Johnson Models
1985	275TLCO, 275TXCO, 300TLCO	275TLCO, 275TXCO, 300TLCO
1986	275PTLCD, 275PTXCD, 300PTLCD	275PTLCD, 275PTXCD, 300PTLCD
1987	E275PLCU, E275PXCU	J275PLCU, J275PXCU
	E275CLCU, E275CXCU	J275CLCU, J275CXCU
	E300PLCU, E300PXCU	J300PLCU, J300PXCU
	E300CLCU, E300CXCU	J300CLCU, J300CXCU
1988	E275PLCC, E275PXCC	J275PLCC, J275PXCC
	E275CXCC, E300PLCC	J275CXCC, J300PLCC
	E300PXCC, E300CXCC	J300PXCC, J300CXCC
		J300PLCC, J300PXCC
		J300CXCC
1989	E300PLCE, E300PXCE	J300PLCE, J300PXCE
	E300CXCE	J300CXCE

CONDENSED SERVICE DATA

TUNE-UP

Hp/rpm	275/5500
	300/6000 (Prior to 1988)
	300/5500 (After 1987)
Bore:	
Prior to 1988	3.500 in.
	(88.90 mm)
After 1987	3.685 in.
	(93.600 mm)
Stroke	2.860 in.
	(72.64 mm)
Displacement:	
Prior to 1988	220 cu. in.
	(3605 cc)
After 1987	244 cu. in.
	(3998 cc)
Spark Plug—Champion	QL77JC4
Electrode Gap (Prior to 1989)	0.040 in.
	(1.0 mm)
Electrode Gap (After 1988)	0.030 in.
	(0.76 mm)
Sustained High Speeds	QL78V
Electrode Gap	Fixed
Ignition Type	CDI
Carburetor Make	Own
Idle Speed (in gear)	650 rpm
Fuel:Oil Ratio	VRO

SIZES—CLEARANCES

Piston Ring End Gap:	
Prior To 1987	0.005-0.018 in.
	(0.13-0.46 mm)
After 1986	0.019-0.031 in.
	(0.48-0.79 mm)
Lower Piston Ring Side Clearance	0.004 in. Max.
	(0.10 mm)
Standard Piston Diameter:	
Prior to 1988	3.4958-3.4968 in.
	(88.793-88.819 mm)
After 1987	3.6803-3.6823 in.
	(93.480-93.530 mm)

SIZES—CLEARANCES CONT.

Standard Cylinder Bore Diameter:	
Prior to 1988	3.4995-3.5005 in.
	(88.887-88.913 mm)
After 1987	3.6845-3.6855 in.
	(93.586-93.612 mm)
Maximum Allowable Cylinder Bore	
Out-of-Round	0.004 in.
	(0.10 mm)
Maximum Allowable Cylinder Bore	
Taper	0.002 in.
	(0.05 mm)
Crankshaft Diameters:	
Top Main	1.6199-1.6204 in.
	(41.15-41.16 mm)
Center Mains	2.1870-2.1875 in.
	(55.55-55.56 mm)
Bottom Main	1.5747-1.5752 in.
	(40.00-40.01 mm)
Crankpin	1.4995-1.5000 in.
	(38.09-38.10 mm)

TIGHTENING TORQUES

Connecting Rod	42-44 ft.-lbs.
	(57-60 N·m)
Crankcase Halves:	
Main Bearing Screws	26-30 ft.-lbs.
	(35-41 N·m)
Flange Screws	60-84 in.-lbs.
	(7-9 N·m)
Crankcase Head	72-96 in.-lbs.
	(8-11 N·m)
Cylinder Head	240-264 in.-lbs.
	(27-30 N·m)
Flywheel Nut	140-150 ft.-lbs.
	(190-204 N·m)
Lower Main Bearing Retainer Plate	
Screws	96-120 in.-lbs.
	(11-13 N·m)
Spark Plug	216-240 in.-lbs.
	(24-27 N·m)

TIGHTENING TORQUES CONT.

Standard Screws:

No. 6 .... 7-10 in.-lbs.
(0.8-1.2 N·m)
No. 8 .... 15-22 in.-lbs.
(1.6-2.4 N·m)
No. 10 .... 25-35 in.-lbs.
(2.8-4.0 N·m)
No. 12 .... 35-40 in.-lbs.
(4.0-4.5 N·m)

¼ Inch .... 60-80 in.-lbs.
(7-9 N·m)
5/16 Inch .... 120-140 in.-lbs.
(14-16 N·m)
⅜ Inch .... 220-240 in.-lbs.
(24-27 N·m)
7/16 Inch .... 340-360 in.-lbs.
(38-40 N·m)

LUBRICATION

The engine is lubricated by oil mixed with the fuel. Fuel should be regular leaded, unleaded or premium unleaded gasoline with a minimum pump octane rating of 87.

All models are equipped with variable ratio oiling (VRO). Two VRO pumps are used. The VRO system varies the fuel:oil ratio from approximately 150:1 at idle to approximately 50:1 at full throttle by sensing engine power output. Recommended oil is Evinrude or Johnson Outboard Lubricant, OMC 2-Cycle Motor Oil or a NMMA certified TC-WII motor oil. During engine break-in (first 10 hours of operation), a 100:1 fuel:oil mixture must be used in the fuel tank in combination with the VRO system. Oil level in VRO tank should be monitored to be sure VRO system is functioning. After break-in period, refill VRO tank and switch to straight gasoline in the fuel tank.

NOTE: On 3.6 GT and XP models when operated under high performance conditions, a premix of 50:1 must be used in fuel tank if VRO system is used and a premix of 25:1 must be used in fuel tank if VRO system is not used to ensure engine of proper lubrication.

On all recreational models when VRO system is not being used, the recommended fuel:oil ratio for normal operation and engine break-in is 50:1.

The lower unit gears and bearings are lubricated by oil contained in the gearcase. The recommended oil is OMC HI-VIS Gearcase Lube. The gearcase oil level should be checked after every 50 hours of operation and the gearcase should be drained and filled with new oil every 100 hours or once each season, whichever occurs first.

The gearcase is drained and filled through the same plug port. An oil level (vent) port is used to indicate the full oil level of the gearcase and to ease in oil drainage.

To drain the oil, place the outboard motor in a vertical position. Remove the drain plug and oil level plug and allow the lubricant to drain into a suitable container.

To fill the gearcase with oil, place the outboard motor in a vertical position. Add oil through the drain plug opening with an oil feeder until the oil begins to overflow from oil level plug port. Reinstall oil level plug with a new gasket, if needed, and tighten. Remove oil feeder, the reinstall drain plug with a new gasket, if needed, and tighten.

FUEL SYSTEM

CARBURETOR. Four two-barrel type carburetors are used. Each carburetor assembly has a common throttle body assembly (T—Fig. OM20-1) with separate main body assemblies (M). Idle mixture is controlled by idle air bleed jet (5), off idle mixture is controlled by intermediate air bleed jet (4) and high speed mixture is controlled by high speed fuel jet (9—Fig. OM20-2).

Fig. OM20-1—View showing two-barrel type carburetors. A common throttle body assembly (T) with separate main body assemblies (M) are used. View identifies position of intermediate air bleed jet (4) and low speed air bleed jet (5). Refer to text.

Fig. OM20-2—Exploded view of carburetor main body assembly.

1. Main body
2. Gasket
3. Plate
4. Intermediate air bleed jet
5. Low speed air bleed jet
6. Seal
7. Inlet needle & seat
8. Gasket
9. High speed jet
10. Gasket
11. Plug
12. Float bowl
13. Pin
14. Float

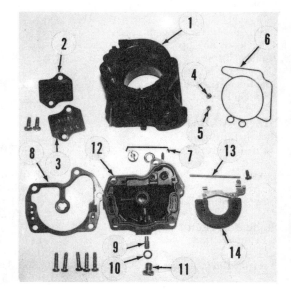

NOTE: Starboard carburetors supply fuel to port cylinders and port carburetors supply fuel to starboard cylinders.

The main body assemblies are constructed of a nonmetallic type material. Care must be used when working with the main body assembly. DO NOT overtighten any screws. Tighten each screw in small increments using a criss-cross tightening sequence.

If service is performed, note the following: Keep carburetor components for each carburetor separate from the others. The manufacturer does not recommend submerging the parts in carburetor or parts cleaning solutions. An aerosol type carburetor cleaner is recommended. The float and other components made of plastic and rubber should not be subjected to some cleaning solutions. Safety eyewear and solvent resistant gloves are recommended.

To determine the float level, invert float bowl (12—Fig. OM20-3) with the fuel inlet valve and float installed. The float should be flush with the float bowl gasket surface. Use a straightedge as

shown in Fig. OM20-3 to check float setting. Remove the float and carefully bend the float tang to adjust.

Recommended idle speed is 600-700 rpm with the engine running at normal operating temperature in forward gear. Loosen nut (N—Fig. OM20-4) and turn screw (I) to adjust idle speed.

SPEED CONTROL LINKAGE. The carburetor throttle valves are synchronized to open as the ignition is advanced. It is important that throttle valve opening and ignition timing synchronization be checked and adjusted if necessary.

The following procedure should be used to check and adjust synchronization of linkage. Move the speed control lever to the idle position and make sure follower roller (F—Fig. OM20-4) is not touching throttle cam (T). Loosen follower roller screw (C) and move roller away from throttle cam (T). On models prior to 1989, loosen screw (S) two complete turns, or on 1989 models screws, (S—Fig. OM20-5) ½ turn maximum. Make certain carburetor throttle valves

are completely closed, then retighten screw (S—Fig. OM20-4) or screws (S—Fig. OM20-5). Leave screw (C—Fig. OM20-4) loose on all models. Hold follower roller (F) against throttle cam (T) and adjust throttle cam stop screw (D) until alignment mark (M) is centered with follower roller (F). Withdraw roller (F) away from throttle cam (T) enough to allow throttle plates to close at idle and tighten screw (C). Adjust wide-open throttle (WOT) stop screw (W—Fig. OM20-6) so WOT mark (O—Fig. OM20-5) on follower roller bracket faces directly front-to-rear when the speed control lever is at WOT.

REED VALVES. Eight sets of leaf (reed) valves are used, one for each cylinder. The eight valves are positioned horizontally and are attached to the intake manifold with a gasket between each reed block and manifold. The leaf petals should seat very lightly against the valve block throughout their entire length with the least possible tension. The individual parts of the reed valve assembly are not available separately. Renew the reed valve assembly if petals are broken, cracked, warped or bent.

VRO TYPE FUEL PUMP. Two VRO fuel pumps are used. The VRO type fuel pump (1—Fig. OM20-8) meters the fuel:oil ratio from approximately 50:1 up to approximately 150:1 by sensing engine power output. During engine break-in or after any procedure that permitted air to enter VRO system, the fuel in the fuel tank must be mixed at a fuel:oil ratio of 50:1 to ensure the engine of proper lubrication. On 3.6 GT and XP

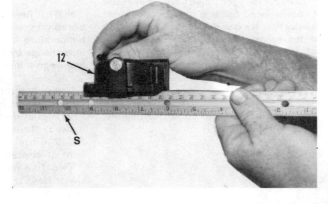

Fig. OM20-3 — With float bowl (12) inverted and fuel inlet valve and float installed, float should just touch straightedge (S). Refer to text.

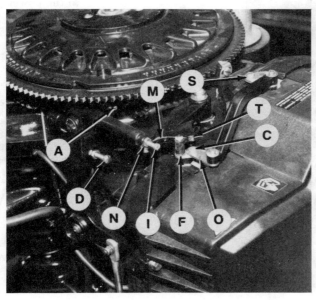

Fig. OM20-4—View of speed control linkage. Refer to text.

Fig. OM20-5—View of carburetor throttle shaft synchronization screws (S) on 1989 models. Refer to text.

models, a fuel:oil ratio of 25:1 must be used during testing of system if operated under high performance conditions.

To check the VRO system for proper operation, first fill the VRO oil tank with a recommended two-stroke motor oil and note oil level for future reference. Install the correct fuel:oil mixture in the fuel tank. After the recommended engine break-in period or after a suitable test period for other conditions, note the oil level in the VRO oil tank. If the oil level has dropped and the VRO system is operating properly, refill the VRO oil tank and switch to straight fuel or recommended fuel mixture.

NOTE: When the VRO system is not used, the inlet nozzle at the outboard motor connector must be capped and clamped to prevent dirt or moisture from entering the fuel system. The fuel in the fuel tank must be mixed at correct fuel:oil ratio. Refer to LUBRICATION section.

TESTING. Using a ''T'' fitting, connect a suitable vacuum gage and a length of clear plastic hose to fuel inlet fitting at lower engine cover. All connections should be clamped to prevent leakage. Start engine and allow to warm to normal operating temperature.

NOTE: When performing VRO system tests that require full throttle operation, install outboard motor into a suitable test tank with the correct test wheel installed.

Run motor at full throttle for two minutes minimum while observing clear hose and note vacuum reading. Vacuum reading should not exceed 4 inches Hg (13.5 kPa) and air bubbles should not be present in clear hose. Excessive vacuum indicates a restricted fuel line between fuel tank and motor. Air bubbles in clear hose indicates an air leak in fuel line between fuel tank and motor.

If vacuum reading is within 1-4 inches Hg (3.4-13.5 kPa) and no bubbles were noted in clear hose, proceed as follows: Remove clear hose and install a suitable 0-15 psi (0-103.4 kPa) pressure gage between VRO pump discharge port (5—Fig. OM20-8) and carburetors. Start engine and run at 800 rpm in forward gear. Pump output pressure should stabilize at not less than 3 psi (20.7 kPa).

If pressure is less than 3 psi (20.7 kPa), inspect pulse fitting for plugging or other damage. Pulse fitting is screwed in crankcase at end of hose attached to pulse nipple (4). Pulse fitting on models prior to 1988 is equipped with an integral flame arrestor and on 1988 and later models, pulse fitting is equipped with an integral check valve. Clean both type fittings by back-flushing with a suitable solvent.

NOTE: A plugged pulse fitting may result in power head damage due to inadequate lubrication. If excessive carbon deposits are noted, renew pulse fitting and repair cause of excessive carbon (backfiring) before returning outboard motor to service.

If pump pressure is low and pulse fitting is in acceptable condition, renew VRO pump assembly.

IGNITION SYSTEM

All models are equipped with a capacitor discharge ignition system which is triggered by sensor coils contained in timer base. To prevent damage to components, note the following list of precautions:

1. DO NOT disconnect any wires while motor is running or while ignition switch is ON.
2. DO NOT use any tachometer except those approved for use with this system.
3. DO NOT hold spark plug wires while checking for spark.
4. DO make certain that all wiring connections are clean and tightly joined.
5. DO make certain that wires do not bind moving parts or touch metal edges where they may chafe through insulation.

TROUBLE-SHOOTING. Trouble-shoot ignition system using an ohmmeter and a suitable peak reading voltmeter (PRV) such as Merc-O-Tronic Model 781 or Stevens Model CD-77.

NOTE: Resistance specifications are based on measurements taken at ambient temperature of 70° F (21° C). Resistance may change by approximately 10 ohms per one degree temperature variation.

Use only approved procedures to prevent damage to ignition components. The fuel system should be checked to make certain faulty running is not the result of fuel starvation, incorrect mixture or contaminated fuel.

Two five-pin connectors attach the timer base to the power packs. Two 2-pin connectors attach the charge coils to the power packs. Power coil orange

Fig. OM20-6 — Adjust wide-open throttle (WOT) stop screw (W) as outlined in text.

Fig. OM20-8 — View of VRO type fuel pump.
1. VRO fuel pump assy.
2. Oil inlet nipple
3. Fuel inlet nipple
4. Crankcase pulse nipple
5. Fuel mixture discharge nipple

and orange/black leads attach to power packs at the terminal board. Two single-pin connectors attach the stop circuit to the power packs. The shift interrupter switch is attached to the starboard power pack through an isolation diode and a single-pin connector.

INDEXING FLYWHEEL. Power packs with a defective isolation diode or other internal defect can result in erratic ignition system operation. To determine if each cylinder is firing at the proper time, proceed as follows: Remove all spark plugs. Rotate flywheel in clockwise direction until number 2 cylinder is at TDC. With number 2 cylinder at TDC, mark "2" on flywheel directly adjacent to timing pointer. Repeat procedure for all cylinders, placing each cylinder number on flywheel across from timing pointer. Place motor into a suitable test, start engine and run at rpm malfunction is evident. Connect a timing light alternately to each spark plug lead and verify cylinders are firing at their respective mark on flywheel. If not, be sure all wiring pins are properly located in connectors or renew power pack.

S.L.O.W. (Speed Limiting Overheat Warning). Models after 1987 are equipped with S.L.O.W. (speed limiting overheat warning) system. The S.L.O.W. function is activated when engine temperature exceeds 203° F (95° C). When activated, the S.L.O.W. system limits engine speed to approximately 2500 rpm. To resume normal operation, the engine must be stopped and cooled to 162° F (72° C). The S.L.O.W. system is activated by input from temperature switches located in port and starboard cylinder heads. A blocking diode located in the engine wiring harness is used to isolate the S.L.O.W. system from other warning signals.

To determine if the S.L.O.W. system is functioning properly, disconnect tan temperature switch leads from port and starboard temperature sensors. Place outboard motor into a suitable test tank with the correct test wheel installed. Start engine and run at 3500 rpm. Connect port side temperature switch lead (tan) to engine ground. Engine speed should slow to approximately 2500 rpm. Repeat test with starboard side temperature switch lead.

If S.L.O.W. system functions properly when tested at both temperature switch tan leads, refer to TEMPERATURE SWITCH section. If proper operation is noted at only one temperature switch lead, inspect condition of wiring harness and connectors and repair as necessary. If neither test indicates proper operation, proceed as follows: Loosen

power pack and remove orange and orange/black power coil leads from terminal board. Connect ohmmeter between engine ground and alternately to orange lead and orange/black lead. No resistance should be present between ground and either orange or orange/black leads. Connect ohmmeter between orange and orange/black leads. Renew power pack if resistance is within 86-106 ohms. If not, renew stator assembly.

NOTE: DO NOT start engine with power coil leads disconnected.

BLOCKING DIODE. If the S.L.O.W. function is activated by other warning horn systems, test blocking diode located in the wiring harness. Disconnect port and starboard temperature switch tan leads and wiring harness red connector. Connect an ohmmeter between either temperature switch tan lead and tan lead terminal inside harness red connector, then reverse ohmmeter leads. A high reading (infinity) should be indicated in one connection and a low reading (zero) in the other. If not, renew wiring harness assembly.

TEMPERATURE SWITCH. On models prior to 1988, temperature switches should be open at 168°-182° F (76°-83° C) and should close at 205°-216° F (96°-102° C). On 1988 and 1989 models, temperature switch with tan wire should be open at 147°-177° F (65°-79° C) and close at 197°-205° F (92°-96° C). On 1988 and 1989 models, temperature switch with white/black wire should be open at 86°-92° F (30°-34° C) and close at 93°-99° F (34°-38° C) Test switches using a suitable continuity light or ohmmeter. Heat switches using a suitable oil bath with an accurate thermometer.

QUICKSTART. Models after 1987 are equipped with the QuickStart function. The QuickStart circuit is activated each time the engine is started. QuickStart automatically advances ignition timing for approximately five seconds during starting (at all temperatures). QuickStart is also activated any time engine temperature is below 96° F (36° C). QuickStart is inoperative when engine speed exceeds 1100 rpm.

To determine if QuickStart is functioning properly, place outboard motor into a suitable test tank with the correct test wheel installed. Engine temperature must be above 96° F (36° C) before testing.

NOTE: Make sure speed control linkage, idle speed and ignition timing are properly adjusted before attempting to test Quick-Start system. Refer to SPEED CONTROL LINKAGE section.

Place marks on flywheel adjacent to timing pointer indicating TDC for all cylinders. Disconnect white/black lead between power pack and port side temperature switch. Connect a timing light to number 1 cylinder spark plug lead, start engine and run at idle speed in forward gear (not more than 900 rpm). The timing light should flash at the number 1 cylinder TDC mark on flywheel. Reconnect the white/black lead to the power pack. The number 1 cylinder TDC mark should shift to the right approximately 1 inch indicating ignition timing has returned to normal setting. Repeat test for each cylinder. Note that engine must be stopped before testing each remaining cylinder.

If one or more sensor coils do not operate properly, renew timer base assembly. If no sensor coils operate properly, disconnect white/black lead from power pack lead and connect ohmmeter between white/black lead and engine ground. Ohmmeter should indicate continuity with engine temperature below 89° F (32° C). If continuity is noted, test temperature switches. If not, connect ohmmeter between each power coil lead

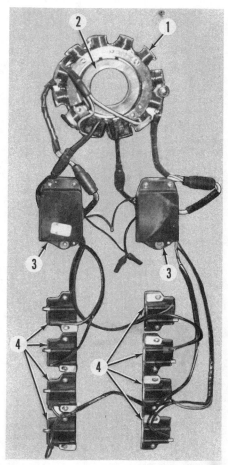

Fig. OM20-10 — View identifying stator assembly (1), timer base (2), power packs (3) and ignition coils (4) in CDI system.

(orange and orange/black) and engine ground. No continuity should be present between power coil leads and ground. Next, check resistance between orange and orange/black power coil leads. Renew power pack if resistance is within 86-106 ohms. If not, renew stator assembly.

If QuickStart system remains activated when engine speed exceeds 1100 rpm, renew power pack. If QuickStart system remains activated continuously, regardless of temperature, time activated and engine speed, test port side temperature switch, inspect power pack white/black lead and connector, test engine for undercooling condition or renew power pack.

TOTAL OUTPUT. On all models disconnect all spark plug leads from spark plugs and install a suitable spark tester to plug leads. Adjust tester spark gap to $^7/_{16}$ inch (11 mm). Refer to the appropriate following paragraphs:

On models prior to 1988, crank engine while observing spark tester. If normal spark is noted at all spark gaps, refer to RUNNING OUTPUT section. If no spark or weak spark is noted at all spark gaps, refer to STOP CIRCUIT section. If no spark is noted on cylinders 5 through 8, refer to SHIFT SWITCH section.

On models after 1987, loosen power pack and disconnect yellow/red lead one-pin connector. Ground power pack to engine using a suitable jumper lead. Disconnect white/black lead from port temperature switch and connect white/black lead to engine ground. Crank engine while observing spark tester. If normal spark output is noted at all spark gaps, refer to RUNNING OUTPUT section. If no spark output is noted at cylinders 1 through 5, refer to SHIFT SWITCH section. If normal spark output is noted at one or more cylinders,

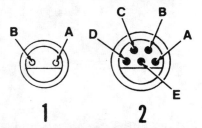

Fig. OM20-11 — View "1" identifies terminal ends in stator assembly connector and view "2" identifies terminal ends in timer base connector.

Fig. OM20-12 — View identifying shift interrupter switch (SI) located at base of intake manifold on engine's starboard side.

refer to CHARGE COIL section. If no spark output is noted at all spark gaps, refer to STOP CIRCUIT section.

SHIFT SWITCH. Shift interrupter switch (SI—Fig. OM20-12) is used to interrupt power supply to starboard power pack during gearcase shifting. Shift switch prevents starboard cylinders from firing, allowing easier engagement and disengagement of forward and reverse gears.

If during total output test, no spark output is present at cylinders 1 through 5, test shift switch as follows: Disconnect both yellow/black one-pin connectors between shift switch and power pack. Connect ohmmeter between engine ground and power pack side of shift switch wiring harness. No continuity should be indicated. Activate shift switch by depressing shift cable pin. Continuity should be indicated. Renew switch and harness if not as specified.

Next, connect ohmmeter between both switch harness one-pin connectors, note reading and reverse ohmmeter leads. A high (infinity) resistance reading should be noted with one connection and a low (zero) resistance reading should be noted with other connection. Renew switch and harness if not as specified.

STOP CIRCUIT. Disconnect one-pin connectors between power pack and key switch. Crank engine while observing spark tester. Normal spark output at all spark gaps indicate faulty key switch or stop circuit. Refer to CHARGE COIL section if no spark output is noted.

CHARGE COIL. Disconnect both (front and rear) two-pin stator connectors. Set PRV knobs to negative (−) and 500 on models prior to 1988, and positive (+) and 500 on models after 1987. Connect PRV between engine ground and terminal A of either stator two-pin connector. Crank engine while noting meter. Repeat test at remaining terminals of both two-pin connectors. If any voltage output is noted at any stator terminal, charge coil or wiring is shorted to ground.

Attach PRV black test lead to terminal A of forward stator two-pin connector and red test lead to terminal B. Crank engine while observing meter. Repeat test with PRV connected to rear two-pin connector. Charge coil cranking output should be 130 volts or more. If not, inspect condition of stator wiring and connectors. If wiring and connectors are acceptable, connect ohmmeter between terminals A and B of front two-pin connector, then repeat test on rear two-pin connector. Renew stator assembly if resistance is not within 955-985

ohms on models prior to 1988, 870-1070 ohms on 1988 models and 960-1010 ohms on 1989 models.

SENSOR COIL. Disconnect both five-pin connectors between timer base and power packs. Set PRV knobs to positive (+) and 5 if using Merc-O-Tronic Model 781, or S and 5 if using Stevens Model CD-77. Connect PRV between engine ground and alternately to each timer base terminal. Crank engine at each connection. Any output indicates sensor coil or wiring is shorted to ground. Repair wiring or renew timer base assembly.

Check sensor coil cranking output as follows on models prior to 1988. With PRV set to positive (+) and 5 (S and 5 on Stevens CD-77), connect black test lead to terminal E of port five-pin timer base connector. Connect red test lead alternately to terminals A, B, C and D of starboard timer base connector, then terminals A, B, C and D of port timer base connector. Crank engine at each test connection and note meter.

If output is 0.3 volt or more, refer to POWER PACK section. If output is less than 0.3 volt, inspect condition of timer base wiring and connectors. If wiring and connectors are acceptable, check sensor coil resistance as follows: Connect an ohmmeter between terminal E and alternately to the remaining terminals of five-pin connector. Repeat test on other five-pin connector. Renew timer base assembly if resistance is not within 35-45 ohms.

On models after 1987, check sensor coil output as follows: Set PRV knobs to Positive and 5 on Merc-O-Tronic Model 781 or S and 5 on Stevens Model CD-77. Connect PRV black test to terminal E of port five-pin connector. Connect red test lead alternately to terminals A, B, C, and D in starboard five-pin connector, then terminals A, B, C and D in port five-pin connector. If output is less than 0.2 volt, inspect condition of wiring and connectors. If wiring and connectors are acceptable, check sensor coil resistance. If output is 0.2 volt or more proceed as follows: Install a jumper lead from terminal E in power pack connector to terminal E of the timer base connector. Connect PRV black test lead to engine ground and alternately connect red test lead to terminals A, B, C and D of port five-pin timer base connector, then terminals A, B, C and D of starboard five-pin timer base connector. Crank engine at each test connection. If output is 1.2 volts or more, refer to POWER PACK section. If output is less than 1.2 volts, repair wiring, connectors or renew timer base.

To check sensor coil resistance on models after 1987, proceed as follows:

NOTE: Ohmmeter polarity must be determined before proceeding with sensor coil resistance test. Calibrate meter on Rx100 scale and connect leads to a known-good diode, then reverse leads. If first connection indicated very low resistance (zero ohm) and second connection indicated very high resistance (infinity), ohmmeter red lead is positive (+). If opposite result is noted, reverse ohmmeter leads so red lead is positive (+).

Connect ohmmeter red lead to terminal E in port timer base connector. Connect ohmmeter black lead alternately to terminals A, B, C and D in starboard timer base terminal, and terminals A, B, C and D in port timer base terminal.

NOTE: Timer base components may cause resistance readings to vary depending upon individual meter impedance. Readings may be higher or lower. If so, readings should be consistent.

If using Merc-O-Tronic Model M-700 ohmmeter, resistance should be 870-1070 ohms. If using Stevens Model AT-101 ohmmeter resistance should be 330-390 ohms.

Next, connect ohmmeter between E terminals of port and starboard timer base connectors. Ohmmeter should indicate 200-260 ohms. Connect ohmmeter between engine ground and each terminal in port and starboard timer base terminals. No continuity should be present between ground and any timer base terminal. If continuity is noted, repair grounded timer base wires or renew timer base assembly.

POWER PACK. Two power pack assemblies are used, one supplies cylinders 1 through 4 and one supplies cylinders 5 through 8.

To check power pack output on models prior to 1988, set PRV knobs to negative (−) and 500. Connect PRV black lead to engine ground. Connect red test lead alternately to each primary ignition coil terminal (primary lead connected to coil). Crank engine at each connection. Renew power pack if output is less than 100 volts. Repeat test at all ignition coils.

To check power pack output on models after 1987, remove primary leads from ignition coils. Connect primary lead of number 1 cylinder ignition coil (top starboard) to red lead of Stevens Load Adapter PL-88. Connect load adapter black lead to engine ground.

NOTE: If Stevens Load Adapter PL-88 is not available, fabricate adapter using Radio Shack 10 ohm, 10 watt resister, part 271-132, or equivalent.

Set peak reading voltmeter knobs to positive (+) and 500. Connect voltmeter red test lead to load adapter red lead and black test lead to engine ground. Crank engine while noting meter. Power pack output should be 100 volts or more. Repeat test at remaining ignition coils. If the specified voltage or more is present at all primary leads, refer to IGNITION COIL section. If low or no output is noted at any primary lead, renew power pack.

NOTE: Power packs marked "CDL" are equipped with integral speed limiting device, limiting engine speed to 6100 rpm on 275 hp models and 6700 rpm on 300 hp models.

IGNITION COILS. Ignition coils may be tested using a variety of testers available from various manufacturers. Follow tester manufacturer's instructions when testing coil.

Check ignition coil primary resistance by connecting ohmmeter between coil primary terminal and coil ground. Primary resistance should be 0.05-0.15 ohm. Check secondary resistance between primary terminal and high tension terminal. Secondary resistance should be 225-325 ohms. Renew coil if not as specified. Ignition coil high tension lead (spark plug lead) resistance should be near zero ohm.

RUNNING OUTPUT. To check running output, disconnect primary leads from ignition coils. Install terminal extenders (Stevens TS-77 or equivalent) on coil terminals, then reconnect coil primary leads to terminal extenders. Set voltmeter switches to positive (+) and 500. Connect tester black lead to engine ground.

NOTE: Outboard motor should be placed into a suitable test tank with the correct test wheel installed when checking running output.

Start engine and run at rpm that malfunction is evident. Alternately, connect red tester lead to terminal extender of each coil. USE CAUTION not to touch metal part of terminal extender or tester lead to prevent shock hazard. Power pack running output should be a continuous 230 volts or more on models prior to 1988 or 130 volts or more on models after 1987 at each ignition coil. If output is low at one or more coils, test charge coils as previously outlined in CHARGE COIL section. If NO output is noted at one or more coils, test sensor coils as previously outlined in SENSOR COIL section.

IGNITION TIMING. Connect a power timing light to number 1 cylinder (top starboard) spark plug lead. Place outboard motor into a suitable test tank with the correct test wheel installed. Start engine and run at 4500-5000 rpm in forward gear and note timing. Full throttle spark advance should be 17-19 degrees BTDC on 275 hp models and 15-17 degrees BTDC on 300 hp models. To adjust, stop engine and turn spark advance stop screw (A—Fig. OM20-4). Turning screw (A) clockwise one full turn will retard timing approximately one degree.

COOLING SYSTEM

THERMOSTAT. A cooling system thermostat is used in each cylinder head to maintain a water temperature of approximately 145° F (63° C). A relief valve within each thermostat opens at high engine speed when water pump impeller speed increases water pressure. Engine temperature can be checked using heat sensitive sticks, such as Markal Thermomelt Stik. A 163° F (73° C) stick should not melt, but a 125° F (52° C) stick should melt, after engine reaches operating temperature. The remote control box is equipped with a "hot horn" that is activated by either temperature sensing switch in each cylinder head.

On models prior to 1988, temperature switches should be open at 168°-182° F (75°-83° C) and should close at 205°-216° F (96°-102° C). On 1988 and 1989 models, temperature switch with tan wire should be open at 147°-177° F (64°-80° C) and close at 197°-205° F (92°-96° C). On 1988 and 1989 models, temperature switch with white/black wire should be open at 86°-92° F (30°-33° C) and close at 93°-99° F (34°-37° C) Test switches using a suitable continuity light or ohmmeter. Heat switches using a suitable oil bath with an accurate thermometer.

WATER PUMP. The water pump is mounted on top of the gearcase. Rubber impeller is driven by the drive shaft. Separate gearcase from exhaust housing for access to water pump.

Apply OMC Adhesive M to "O" ring (7—Fig. OM20-20) groove in impeller housing (3A) and OMC Gasket Sealing Compound to bottom of impeller plate (8). Lubricate impeller (6) and hold blades in while installing housing.

POWER HEAD

R&R AND DISASSEMBLE. Remove lower engine covers. Remove six screws attaching flywheel to power steering pump drive pulley. Remove flywheel nut, then withdraw flywheel. Remove stator assembly screws to allow access to three power steering pump/reservoir mounting screws. Remove screws then detach pump/reservoir from cylinder block and place to the side along with cooler and filter without disconnecting hoses. Disconnect and mark interfering wires. Disconnect upper end of shift rod. Remove five screws and one nut from each side of upper end of drive shaft housing and two screws and one nut at rear of upper end of drive shaft housing. Lift power head from lower unit.

Remove stator assembly, power steering drive pulley, timer base, power packs, tilt and trim junction box, rectifier/regulator assembly, electric starter and any wiring that will interfere with component removal. Remove air silencer, carburetors and VRO fuel pumps. Remove lower intake manifold, then remove upper intake manifold. Remove torsional damper at base of crankshaft. Remove upper and lower crankcase head (2 and 11 – Fig. OM20-15) screws. Cylinder block and crankcase aligning taper pin must be driven out towards front. Loosen but do not remove center four screws in lower

crankcase head (11) which hold retainer plate (7). Unscrew crankcase retaining screws and separate crankcase from cylinder block.

Pistons, rods and crankshaft are now accessible for removal and overhaul as outlined in the appropriate following paragraphs.

ASSEMBLY. When assembling, the crankcase and inlet manifold must be completely sealed against both vacuum and pressure. Cylinder heads must be sealed against water leakage and pressure. Mating surfaces of water intake and exhaust areas between lower unit and power head must form a tight seal. It is recommended that all mating surfaces be carefully inspected for nicks, burrs, corrosion and warpage which might interefere with a tight seal. All of these surfaces may be lapped if necessary to provide a smooth, flat surface. DO NOT remove any more metal than is necessary. Mating surfaces of crankcase and cylinder block MUST NOT be lowered, but can be polished to remove imperfections.

Cylinder block and crankcase are positively located by a tapered dowel pin. Dowel pin must not be nicked, bent or distorted and dowel pin hole must be clean and true. When installing dowel pin, make sure that pin is fully seated, but do not use excessive force.

Refer to subsequent sections for assembly of piston, rod and crankshaft components. Install piston and rod assemblies in cylinder block with bearing in rod but do not install cap and bearing. Install lower head assembly (6 through 11 – Fig. OM20-15) on crankshaft but do not tighten four bearing retainer plate (7) screws. Install top bearing head assembly (1, 2 and 3) and seal rings (4) on crankshaft. Face all seal ring gaps toward intake manifold side of crankshaft. Install center main bearings (13 and 14) on crankshaft as outlined in CONNECTING RODS, BEARINGS AND CRANKSHAFT section. Install crankshaft assembly in cylinder block making certain that holes in center main bearings align with dowel pins in cylinder block. Position connecting rods on crankshaft and install rod bearings (21 and 22) and rod caps (23).

When reassembling crankcase, make sure mating surfaces of crankcase halves are completely clean and free of old cement, nicks and burrs. Apply OMC Gel-Seal II to one crankcase mating surface. Do not use sealers which will harden and prevent contact between crankcase mating surfaces. Immediately assemble crankcase halves after applying sealer and position halves by installing tapered locating dowel pin. Then install and tighten crankcase retaining

screws to the torque listed in the CONDENSED SERVICE DATA table. When tightening the retaining screws, start in the center and work toward ends. Tighten the lower main bearing retainer plate (7) screws to the correct torque and check the crankshaft for binding.

Complete remainder of reassembly in reverse order of disassembly. Install cylinder head gaskets and intake manifold gaskets without a sealer. Install upper intake manifold first, then install lower intake manifold.

PISTONS, PINS, RINGS AND CYLINDERS. Before detaching connecting rods from crankshaft, mark piston, rod and cap for correct assembly to each other and for installation into the same cylinder from which they are removed. Separate bearing cages and rollers (21—Fig. OM20-15) for assembly into same location if they are to be reinstalled.

Pistons and rings are available in standard and 0.030 inch (0.76 mm) oversize. Top piston ring is semi-keystone design. Refer to CONDENSED SERVICE DATA section for service specifications. Rebore cylinder bores or renew cylinder block if cylinder bore taper exceeds 0.002 inch (0.05 mm) or if out-of-round more than 0.004 inch (0.10 mm). To determine cylinder bore diameter for oversize piston, add piston oversize amount (0.030 inch [0.76 mm]) to standard cylinder bore diameter.

The piston pin is retained in piston by snap rings in piston pin bosses. The upper end of connecting rod is fitted with a caged needle roller bearing. The piston pin and connecting rod bore are used as bearing races. Check bearing rollers, cage and bearing race surfaces for wear, scoring and overheating. When assembling, pistons can be heated slightly to facilitate installation of piston pins. The pistons on port side are installed to connecting rods differently than the starboard units. The stamping "Exhaust Side" on top of pistons must face cylinder bore exhaust ports. Connecting rod oil hole (H—Fig. OM20-16) must face flywheel end of crankshaft when connecting rod is assembled to crankshaft. Thoroughly lubricate all bearing surfaces before assembling.

CONNECTING RODS, BEARINGS AND CRANKSHAFT. Individual connecting rod and piston assemblies can be removed after removing crankcase and appropriate cylinder head. Before detaching connecting rods from crankshaft, mark rod and cap for correct assembly to each other and in original cylinder. Separate bearing cages and

Fig. OM20-15 – Exploded view of crankshaft and piston assemblies.

1. Seal	
2. Upper crankcase head & bearing	13. Main bearing outer race
3. "O" rings	14. Roller bearings & cages
4. Seal ring (12 used)	15. Piston rings
5. Crankshaft	16. Piston
6. "O" rings	17. Piston pin
7. Retainer plate	18. Snap ring
8. Ball bearing	19. Roller bearing
9. Snap ring	20. Connecting rod
10. Seals	21. Roller bearings & cages
11. Lower crankcase head	23. Rod cap
12. Retaining ring	

rollers for assembly to original crankpin if units are not renewed.

Connecting rods ride on roller bearings at both ends. The crankpin end of rod is drilled and finished, then carefully fractured to separate the cap from the rod. The parting line is not machined and when correctly assembled, the uneven parting line should be nearly invisible. When assembling, make certain that alignment dot on connecting rod and rod cap are aligned, oil hole (H – Fig. OM20-16) is toward top of motor and stamping "Exhaust Side" on piston head is toward cylinder bore exhaust ports. The machined sides of connecting rod and cap should be smooth when assembled. OMC Alignment Fixture 396749 is recommended to properly align connecting rod with rod cap during tightening of connecting rod screws.

Crankshaft seal rings (4 – Fig. OM20-15) should be renewed if thickness is less than 0.154 inch (3.91 mm).

Bearing and head (2) are a one-piece assembly and must be serviced as a unit. Lip of seal (1) should be toward inside and should be pressed in until flush with top surface of bearing head.

The center main bearings are split-cage roller bearings. The two-piece outer race is held together with retaining ring (12) and is positioned in cylinder block by a dowel pin. Install bearing races (13) with ring groove towards bottom of crankshaft. When assembling, make certain that dowel pin in cylinder block bore engages hole in center bearing outer race.

The ball type lower main bearing (8) is pressed onto crankshaft lower end. The bearing outer race is clamped to the bearing head with retainer plate (7). To disassemble lower bearing assembly, remove retainer plate screws and pull bearing head (11) from bearing (8). Remove snap ring (9), then remove bearing using a suitable puller. The lower bearing should be renewed whenever removed. Press a new bearing onto crankshaft until inner bearing race is

seated against crankshaft shoulder. Press seals (10) into bore in bearing head using OMC special tool 325453 to locate seals at correct depth in the bore. Install new "O" rings (6) in bearing head grooves, then slide bearing head onto outer race of bearing using guide pins. Install screws in to retainer (7) but do not tighten these screws until crankcase is assembled.

Refer to the CONDENSED SERVICE DATA table for dimensional data and recommended torque values. Refer to ASSEMBLY paragraphs for assembling the crankcase halves.

PROPELLER

Only stainless steel propellers can be used. Select a propeller that will allow the engine at full throttle to reach maximum operating rpm of 5000-6000 rpm on 275 hp models and 5500-6000 rpm on 300 hpm models.

REMOVE AND REINSTALL. To remove gearcase, disconnect upper end of shift rod then remove propeller and drain lubricant from gearcase. Mark location of trim tab (22 – Fig. OM20-20) to aid during reassembly and remove

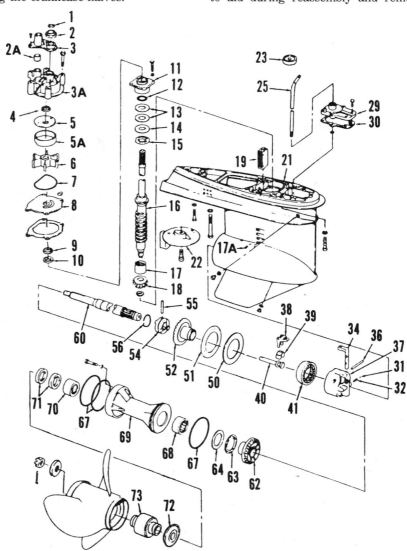

Fig. OM20-20 — Exploded view of typical lower unit.

1. "O" ring	29. Shift rod cover	54. Dog clutch
2. Grommet	30. Gasket	55. Pin
2A. Grommet	12. "O" ring	31. Detent ball	56. Pin retaining screw
3. Water tube bracket	13. Adjustment shims	32. Detent spring	60. Propeller shaft
3A. Impeller housing	14. Thrust washer	34. Detent	62. Reverse gear
4. "O" ring	15. Thrust bearing	36. Shift lever pin	63. Thrust bearing
5. Impeller plate	16. Drive shaft	37. Gear housing	64. Thrust washer
5A. Impeller lining	17. Needle bearing	38. Shift lever	67. "O" ring
6. Impeller	17A. Set screw	39. Shift yoke	68. Needle bearing
7. "O" ring	18. Pinion gear	40. Shift shaft	69. Bearing housing
8. Plate	19. Water screen	41. Bearing	70. Needle bearing
9. Seal	21. Gearcase	50. Thrust washer	71. Seals
10. Seal	22. Trim tab	51. Thrust bearing	72. Thrust bushing
11. Bearing & housing assy.	23. Shift rod seal	52. Forward gear	73. Propeller bushing
	25. Shift rod		

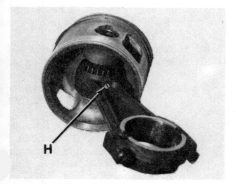

Fig. OM20-16 — Connecting rod oil hole (H) must face flywheel end of crankshaft when connecting rod is assembled to crankshaft.

trim tab. Remove two screws on each side of gearcase and two screws at rear.

NOTE: One rear screw is in trim tab cavity.

Separate gearcase from exhaust housing being careful not to bend shift rod.

To install gearcase, reverse removal procedure. Install a new "O" ring in end of drive shaft and coat splines with a suitable antiseize compound. Check length of gear shift rod (25). With shifter in neutral, distance from mating surface of gearcase (21) to center of hole in top of shift rod should be 22.41 inches (56.92 cm) on 20 inch (50.8 cm) transom models or 27.41 inches (69.62 cm) on 25 inch (63.5 cm) transom models. Top of shift rod should slant forward. Apply OMC Adhesive "M" to gearcase and exhaust housing gasket surfaces. Be sure water tube guides and water tube are installed properly. Apply OMC Gasket Sealing Compound to threads of gearcase screws.

GEARCASE. Gearcase may be disassembled in the following manner: Remove propeller, drain lubricant and remove gearcase as described in previous section. Remove screws securing shift rod cover (29 – Fig. OM20-20), unscrew shift rod (25) and remove shift rod and cover as an assembly. Remove water pump housing (5), impeller (6), impeller key and lower plate (8). Remove four screws holding propeller shaft bearing housing (69) and using a suitable puller, remove bearing housing. Discard seals (71) and "O" ring (67). Remove snap rings (66), thrust washer assembly (64 and 63) and slide reverse gear (62) off propeller shaft. A special socket from OMC is available to hold drive shaft so nut securing pinion gear (18) can be removed. After pinion gear retaining nut is removed, unscrew the four screws securing upper drive shaft bearing housing (11). Pull drive shaft and associated parts out of gearcase. A

puller may be necessary. Propeller shaft (60) may now be pulled from gearcase complete with forward gear (52), forward gear housing (37) and all associated parts.

Inspect drive shaft splines, bearing surfaces and seal surfaces for wear or damage. Damage splines may be caused by striking a submerged object and bending the exhaust housing. Check parallelism of top and bottom surfaces if questionable. If surfaces are not parallel, renew housing. Do not attempt to straighten it.

Lower drive shaft bearing (17) should only be removed if renewal is intended. Do not reinstall a used bearing. Drive shaft bearing is held in position by a set screw (17A) as well as a press fit in gearcase. Set screw is located on starboard side in area of water intake. After removing set screw, install a suitable tool or OMC special tool with shouldered side of tool against bearing, and drive bearing down into propeller shaft cavity. New bearing is installed using a suitable tool or OMC special tool with lettered end of bearing down. Apply Loctite to set screw (17A) and install.

Forward gear (52) and propeller shaft (60) may be removed from propeller shaft gear housing (37) after dislodging spring (56) and removing dog clutch assembly (55 and 54). Bearing housing and shifter mechanism assembly (38) may be disassembled by driving out shift lever pin (36).

Thickness of shims (13) is varied to adjust mesh position of pinion gear (18) in forward and reverse gear. A shim gage, OMC Special Tool 393185, should be used to determine proper shimming.

Place pinion gear (18) on drive shaft and torque retaining nut to 70-75 ft.-lbs. (95-102 N·m). Install bearing and housing assembly (11), thrust washer (14) and thrust bearing (15). Position drive shaft assembly in special tool as shown in Fig. OM20-21. Tighten preload screw (S – Fig. OM20-21) until groove around circumference of plunger (P) is even with end of preload screw (S), then tighten retaining nut (N). Position OMC Shim Gage 330224 (G) on guide pins of tool base and abut end with bearing and housing assembly (11 – Fig. OM20-20). Use a selection of feeler gages (F – Fig. OM20-21) and measure clearance between end of gage 330224 and pinion gear. Rotate bearing and housing assembly (11 – Fig. OM20-20) in ¼-turn increments and retake clearance measurement. Subtract the average clearance measurement from 0.030 inch (0.76 mm) to determine the correct shim (13) thickness. Shims (13) are available in 0.003, 0.004 and 0.005 inch thicknesses.

Needle bearings (68 and 70) should not

be removed from propeller shaft housing (69) unless renewal is intended. Do not reinstall used bearings. OMC special tools or suitable tools are used to install bearings in housing (69). Seals (71) should be installed so lip on aft seal is towards propeller and lip on forward seal is facing forward.

Assemble gearcase in the following manner: Renew all gaskets, seals and "O" rings. If lower drive shaft bearing (17) or propeller shaft bearings (68 and 70 have been removed, they too should be renewed. Install detent spring (32) and detent ball (31) in blind hole of housing (37). Hold spring and ball in position while installing detent (34). Assemble shift shaft (40), shift lever yoke (39), shift lever (38) and pin (36). Assemble forward gear (52) with thrust bearing (51 and 50) in gear housing. Place clutch (54) on propeller shaft (60) making sure hole in dog clutch is aligned with slot in propeller shaft and splined dogs are toward forward gear. Insert propeller shaft in forward gear and bearing housing assembly, then insert pin (55) through dog clutch propeller shaft and hole in shift shaft (40). Install pin retaining spring (56). Press shift detent (34) down and place propeller shaft, forward gear and gear housing assembly (37) into position in gearcase. Make sure locating pin (35) is seated in recess provided in gearcase.

Insert drive shaft (16). Install pinion gear retaining nut and tighten to 70-75 ft.-lbs. (90-102 N·m). Install shift rod (25) and shift rod cover (29) as an assembly. Thread shift rod fully into detent (34), back off two turns, pull rod to neutral (middle detent) and adjust for proper length. Refer to shift rod adjustment in REMOVE AND REINSTALL section for specifications.

Assemble thrust bearing (64 and 63) on reverse gear (62) and slide onto propeller shaft (60). Position bearing retainer plate (65) and install snap rings (66). Make sure that "O" ring (67) is fully seated in groove of bearing housing (69) and that seals (71) are properly installed. Lip of forward seal should be toward front and lip of aft seal should be toward propeller.

Install seals (9 and 10) in upper drive shaft bearing housing (11) with lip of lower seal (10) down and lip of upper seal (9) up. Place thrust bearing assembly (14 and 15) on drive shaft and install previously selected shim or shims (13). Coat screws that secure bearing housing (11) with sealing compound and install. Bottom edge of impeller plate (8) should be coated with OMC Gasket Sealing Compound or equivalent and placed in position. Install impeller drive cam with flat side against drive shaft and sharp

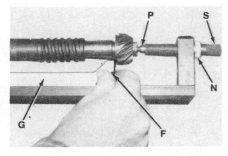

Fig. OM20-21 – View showing drive shaft positioned in OMC Shim Gage 393185. Refer to text for identification of components and procedure for measuring for correct thickness of shims (13 – Fig. OM20-20).

edge pointing in a clockwise direction when viewed from crankshaft end of drive shaft. Lubricate edges of impeller (6) and install on drive shaft. Drive shaft should be turned clockwise while installing water pump housing (5). Coat screws that secure water pump housing and water tube bracket with sealing compound and install.

POWER TILT AND TRIM

OPERATION. A hydraulically actuated power tilt and trim system is used. Manifold (50 – Fig. OM20-25) contains valves, oil pump and trim cylinders. Oil pump motor, oil reservoir and tilt cylinder are attached to manifold. Electric oil pump motor is reversible and oil pump rotation is thereby changed to extend or retract trim and tilt cylinders. Note postion of valves in Fig. OM20-25. Turn manual release valve counterclockwise to manually raise or lower outboard.

Hydraulic system contains approximately 25 fl. oz. (740 mL) of oil. Recommended oil is OMC Power Trim/Tilt Fluid or Dexron II automatic transmission fluid. Do not run pump without oil in reservoir. Oil level should reach fill plug (11) hole threads when tilt and trim pistons are fully extended. System should be cycled several times prior to checking oil level if system has been drained or lost a large amount of oil.

TROUBLE-SHOOTING. Be sure battery is fully charged, electrical connections are good, oil reservoir is full and air is not trapped in system before testing components.

To check oil pressure, first momentarily cycle system "UP" and "DOWN" a few times. Remove snap ring (39 – Fig. OM20-25) and manual release valve (37), then install OMC gage "A" as shown in Fig. OM20-26. Operate system in the "UP" direction and observe gage after system stalls out at full extension. Gage reading should not drop below 100-200 psi (700-1400 kPa). Install OMC gage "B." Operate system in the "DOWN" direction and observe gage after system stalls out at fully retracted. Gage reading should not drop below 100-200 psi (700-1400 kPa).

To check valves, screw each valve into OMC check valve tester 390063 (T – Fig. OM20-27). Use a suitable pressure tester (P) and apply 30 psi (207 kPa) of pressure to check valve. Check valve can be considered good if no pressure leakage is noted.

Refer to the following for a list of symptoms and probable causes:

Symptoms   **Probable Causes**
Tilt Leakdown . . . . 1, 2, 3, 4, 5 or 6

Trim and Tilt Both Leak . . . . . . 7, 8 or 9
Reverse Lock
    Does Not Hold . . . . 2, 3, 6, 10, 11 or 12
Will Not Trim Out Under
    Load or Will Not Tilt . . . . . . 1, 2, 7 or 9
Will Not Trim or
    Tilt Down . . . . 2, 8, 10, 11, or 13

Key To Probable Causes
1. Trim Up Relief Valve
2. Manual Release Valve
3. Tilt Cylinder Valve or Seals
4. Tilt Check Valve
5. Impact Letdown Valve
6. Oil Line
7. Trim Cylinders Sleeve "O" Rings or Piston Seals
8. Trim Check Valve
9. Expansion Relief Valve or "O" Rings
10. Filter Valve Seat
11. Impact Sensor Valve
12. Reverse Lock Check Valve
13. Trim Down Pump Relief Valve

OVERHAUL. Oil pump must be serviced as a unit assembly. Motor is not serviceable with the exception of brushes. Refer to Fig. OM20-25 for exploded view of trim and tilt cylinders

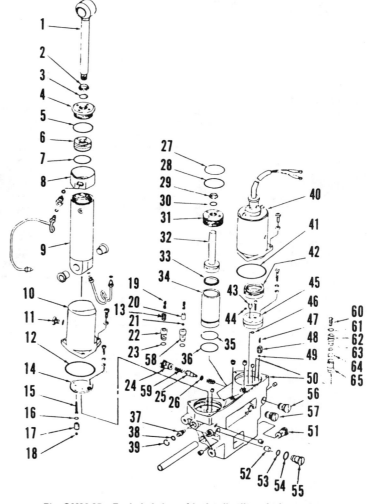

Fig. OM20-25 — Exploded view of hydraulic tilt and trim system.

1. Shaft	19. Spring	35. Retaining ring	51. Separation valve
2. Wiper	20. Spring seat	36. "O" ring	52. Valve piston
3. "O" ring	21. Ball	37. Manual release valve	53. "O" ring
4. End cap	22. Trim up relief valve	38. "O" ring	54. "O" ring
5. "O" ring	23. "O" ring	39. Snap ring	55. Impact letdown valve
6. Piston	24. Reverse lock check	40. Pump motor	56. Trim check valve
7. "O" ring	valve	41. "O" ring	57. Tilt check valve
8. Band	25. Piston	42. Oil pump filter	58. Impact sensor valve
9. Tilt cylinder	26. "O" ring	43. Drive coupling	59. Spring
10. Reservoir	27. Retaining ring	44. Ball	60. Spring
11. Fill plug	28. "O" ring	45. Oil pump	61. "O" ring
12. "O" ring	29. Wiper	46. "O" ring	62. Expansion relief valve
13. Needle	30. "O" ring	47. Spring	core
14. Plate	31. End cap	48. Trim down pump	63. "O" ring
15. Screen	32. Piston	relief valve	64. "O" ring
16. "O" ring	33. Piston ring	49. Seal	65. Expansion relief valve
17. Check valve	34. Trim cylinder	50. Manifold	seat
18. Valve ball			

Fig. OM20-26 — Install OMC gage "A" or "B" into manual release valve (37 — Fig. OM20-25) port as shown to test system oil pressure. Refer to text.

and manifold components. Keep all components separated during disassembly and identify each component, if needed, to ensure correct position during reassembly.

POWER STEERING

DRIVE BELT TENSION ADJUSTMENT. Loosen idler housing bolts (B – Fig. OM20-30) and rotate nuts (N) clockwise to reduce tension on drive belt and counterclockwise to increase tension on drive belt. Drive belt tension should be 25-30 pounds (111-113 N). Check belt tension using a suitable ten-sion gage positioned midway between idler pulley (I) and flywheel pulley.

PRESSURE TEST. Remove plug (P – Fig. OM20-30) and install OMC Pressure Gage 983975 or a suitable 2000 psi (13.8 MPa) pressure gage. Remove fill plug (F) and install OMC Power Trim and Tilt fluid or Dexron II in reservoir until fluid level is even with groove around base of dipstick with plug end of dipstick resting on top of fill hole. Install plug (P) and tighten. Start engine and operate at 1000 rpm. Completely extend or retract cylinder rod and observe pressure gage. The pump relief pressure should be 850-1000 psi (5861-6895 kPa).

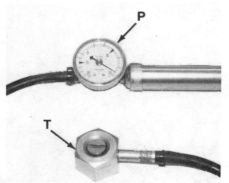

Fig. OM20-27 — Use OMC check valve tester 390063 (T) and a suitable pressure tester (P) to test check valves. Check valve can be considered good if no pressure leakage at approximately 30 psi (207 kPa) is noted.

Fig. OM20-30 — View showing power steering pump/ reservoir assembly. Refer to text.

B. Bolts
F. Fill plug
I. Idler pulley
N. Nuts
P. Plug
S. Power steering pump/ reservoir assy

SEA KING

MONTGOMERY WARD
619 West Chicago Avenue
Chicago, Illinois 60607

SEA KING 35, 45 & 55 HP

Year Produced	35 HP	45 HP	55 HP
1969	27935	27945	27955
	27936	27946	27956
1970	27035	.....	27055
1971	27035	.....	27055
	27036		27056
1972	27235	.....	27256
1973	27435	.....	27456
1974	52035	.....	52056
	52036		
1975	52035	.....	52056
	52036		
1976	52035	.....	52056
	52036		
1977	52035	.....	52056
	52036		
1979	52135	.....	.....
1980	52037	.....	.....

CONDENSED SERVICE DATA

TUNE-UP	35 HP	45 HP	55 HP
Hp/rpm	35/4750	45/4750	55/5250
Bore—Inches	3	3-1/8	3-3/16
Stroke—Inches	2.54	2.75	2.80
Number of Cylinders	2	2	2
Displacement—Cu. In.	35.9	42:18	44.7
Compression at Cranking Speed (Average)	95-105 psi	115-125 psi	145-155 psi
Spark Plug:			
Champion	L4J	L4J*	L4J*
Electrode Gap (Inch)	0.030	0.030*	0.030*
Ignition:			
Point Gap (Inch)	0.020§	0.020§	0.020§
Timing	See Text	See Text	See Text
Carburetor:			
Make	Tillotson	Tillotson	Tillotson
Model	OM or WB	OM or WB	WB
Fuel:Oil Ratio	**50:1	**50:1	**50:1

*A surface gap UL-18V Champion spark plug is used on models with capacitor discharge ignition.

**Use 24:1 fuel for first 10 hours and for severe service.

§Breaker point gap should be 0.015 on models with battery ignition.

SIZES—CLEARANCES (All Values In Inch)	35 HP	45 HP	55 HP
Piston Rings:			
End Gap	0.008-0.015	0.008-0.015	0.008-0.015
Side Clearance	0.002-0.003	0.002-0.003	0.002-0.003
Piston to Cylinder Clearance	0.005	0.005	0.005
Piston Pin Diameter	0.6875-0.68765	0.6875-0.68765	0.6875-0.68765
Crankshaft Bearing Clearance	Roller Bearing	Roller Bearing	Roller Bearing

TIGHTENING TORQUES	35 HP	45 HP	55 HP
(All Values In Inch-Pounds Unless Noted)			
Connecting Rod	150	150	150
Cylinder Head	270***	270***	270***
Flywheel Nut	75 Ft.-Lbs.	80 Ft.-Lbs.	70 Ft.-Lbs.
Main Bearing Bolts	270	270	270
Standard Screws:			
6-32	9	9	9
10-24	30	30	30
10-32	35	35	35
12-24	45	45	45
¼-20	70	70	70
5/16-18	160	160	160
3/8-16	270	270	270

***Refer to text for tightening cylinder head screws.

LUBRICATION

The power head is lubricated by oil mixed with the fuel. One-third pint of two-stroke Outboard Motor Oil should be mixed with each gallon of gasoline. The amount of oil in the fuel may be reduced after the first 10 hours of operation (motor is broken in), provided an NMMA certified TC-W II outboard motor oil is used and motor is subjected to normal service only. The minimum recommended fuel:oil ratio is 50:1.

Manufacturer recommends using no-lead automotive gasoline in motors with less than 55 hp although regular or premium gasoline with octane rating of 85 or greater may also be used. Regular or premium automotive gasoline with octane rating of 85 or greater must be used in motors with more than 54 hp.

The lower unit gears and bearings are lubricated by oil contained in the gearcase. A non-corrosive, leaded, Extreme Pressure SAE 90 Gear Oil, should be used. DO NOT use a hypoid type lubricant. The gearcase should be drained and refilled every 100 hours or once each year, and fluid maintained at the level of upper (vent) plug opening.

To fill the gearcase, have motor in an upright position and fill through lower plug hole on starboard side of gearcase until lubricant reaches level of upper vent plug opening. Reinstall and tighten both plugs, using new gaskets if necessary, to assure a water tight seal.

FUEL SYSTEM

CARBURETOR. Tillotson type WB carburetors are used. Refer to Fig. SK6-1). Normal initial setting is one turn open for idle mixture adjustment needle (12). Fixed jet (3) controls high speed mixture. The carburetor model number is stamped on the mounting flange. Float level is 13/32 inch from float to gasket surface. Care must be used in selecting the high speed fixed jet (3). A fixed jet which is too small will result in a lean mixture and possible damage to power head. Jet may be identified by the diameter (in thousandths of an inch) stamped on the visible end of installed jet. Optional jets are available which will improve performance when motor is used in high-altitude locations; optional jet sizes and recommended altitudes are as follows:

35 HP (WB-3A)

Altitude	Jet Size	Part Number
Standard	0.084	014302

35 HP (WB-3C)

Altitude	Jet Size	Part Number
Sea Level-1250 ft.	0.0785	014306
1250-3750 ft.	0.070	013430
3750-6250 ft.	0.068	013967
6250-8250 ft.	0.062	014187

35 HP (WB-12A)

Altitude	Jet Size	Part Number
Sea Level-1250 ft.	0.074	014303
1250-3750 ft.	0.072	015026
3750-6250 ft.	0.070	013430
6250-8250 ft.	0.068	013967

35 HP (WB-12B)

Altitude	Jet Size	Part Number
Sea Level-1250 ft.	0.074	014303
1250-3750 ft.	0.072	015026
3750-6250 ft.	0.070	013430
6250-8250 ft.	0.068	013967

35 HP (WB-17A)

Altitude	Jet Size	Part Number
Sea Level-1250 ft.	0.090	015406
1250-3750 ft.	0.088	013193
3750-6250 ft.	0.086	013949
6250-8250 ft.	0.084	014302

35 HP (WB-17A with "X" stamped on mount flange)

Altitude	Jet Size	Part Number
Standard	0.098	014152

35 HP (WB-17C)

Altitude	Jet Size	Part Number
Sea Level-1250 ft.	0.090	015406
1250-3750 ft.	0.088	013193
3750-6250 ft.	0.086	013949
6250-8250 ft.	0.084	014302

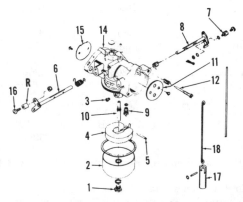

Fig. SK6-1—Exploded view of Tillotson WB type carburetor.

R. Roller
1. Bowl retaining screw
2. Fuel bowl
3. High speed jet
4. Float
5. Float pivot shaft
6. Throttle shaft
7. Connector
8. Choke shaft
9. Inlet needle & seat
10. Main nozzle
11. Choke plate
12. Idle mixture needle
13. Throttle body
14. Throttle body
15. Throttle plate
16. Eccentric screw
17. Choke solenoid plunger
18. Rod

45 HP (WB-4A)

Altitude	Jet Size	Part Number
Standard	0.096	012947

45 HP (WB-4C)

Altitude	Jet Size	Part Number
Sea Level-1250 ft.	0.086	013949
1250-3750 ft.	0.0785	014306
3750-6250 ft.	0.074	014303
6250-8250 ft.	0.068	013967

45 HP (WB-11A)

Altitude	Jet Size	Part Number
Sea Level-1250 ft.	0.082	014109
1250-3750 ft.	0.080	013194
3750-6250 ft.	0.0785	014306
6250-8250 ft.	0.076	013191

55 HP (WB-5A)

Altitude	Jet Size	Part Number
Standard	0.089	013367

55 HP (WB-5B)

Altitude	Jet Size	Part Number
Sea Level-1250 ft.	0.092	014152
1250-3750 ft.	0.084	014302
3750-6250 ft.	0.076	013191
6250-8250 ft.	0.074	014303

55 HP (WB-7A and WB-7B)

Altitude	Jet Size	Part Number
Sea Level-1250 ft.	0.086	013949
1250-3750 ft.	0.084	014302
3750-6250 ft.	0.082	014109
6250-8250 ft.	0.080	013194

55 HP (WB-15A)

Altitude	Jet Size	Part Number
Sea Level-1250 ft.	0.088	013193
1250-3750 ft.	0.086	013949
3750-6250 ft.	0.084	014302
6250-8250 ft.	0.082	014109

55 HP (WB-15A with "X" stamped on mount flange)

Altitude	Jet Size	Part Number
Standard	0.090	015406

55 HP (WB-15C)

Altitude	Jet Size	Part Number
Sea Level-1250 ft.	0.0937	014191
1250-3750 ft.	0.092	014190
3750-6250 ft.	0.090	015406
6250-8250 ft.	0.088	013193

55 HP (WB-27A)

Altitude	Jet Size	Part Number
Sea Level-1250 ft.	0.066	014188
1250-3750 ft.	0.064	014108
3750-6250 ft.	0.062	014187
6250-8250 ft.	0.060	014186

NOTE: Be sure that proper jet is installed before motor is used at a lower altitude.

The position of choke plunger rod (18) should be adjusted in connector (7) so that choke plate (11) is 0.010-0.040 inch open when choke is engaged and plunger (17) is bottomed in solenoid. Make certain that choke plate is free and returns to full open position.

SPEED CONTROL LINKAGE. On all models, ignition timing advance and throttle opening must be synchronized so that throttle is opened as timing is advanced.

To synchronize the linkage, first make certain that ignition timing is correctly set as outlined in IGNITION TIMING paragraph. Shift to forward gear and disconnect link (L—Fig. SK6-3) from tower shaft (T). With carburetor throttle closed, turn the eccentric screw (16) until roller (R) is exactly centered over the scribed line (S). Move the tower shaft (T) to full advance position and move the throttle cam until carburetor throttle is completely open. Vary the length of link (L) until the ball joint connector will just attach. Snap the ball joint connector onto ball stud and check maximum speed in neutral. If maximum rpm in neutral is not 1800-2500 rpm, it may be necessary to readjust speed control linkage.

Idle speed should be 700-800 rpm in forward gear (800-900 rpm in neutral) and is adjusted at idle screw (I).

REED VALVES. "Vee" type intake reed valves are used on all models. The reed plate is located between intake manifold and crankcase.

To remove the reed plate assembly after carburetor is removed, first remove the starter assembly and the screws retaining the intake manifold; then lift off manifold and the reed plate assembly. Refer to Fig. SK6-4.

Reed valve must be smooth and even with no sharp bends or broken reeds. Assembled reeds may stand open a maximum of 0.010 inch at tip end. Check seating visually.

Reed stop setting should be 9/32-inch when measured as shown in Fig. SK6-4. Renew reeds if petals are broken, cracked, warped or bent. Never attempt to bend a reed petal in an effort to improve performance; nor attempt to straighten a damaged reed. Never install a bent or damaged reed. Seating surface of reed plate should be smooth and flat. When installing reed petals and stops, proceed as follows: Install reed petals, stop, and the four retaining screws leaving screws loose. Slide the reed petals as far as possible toward mounting flange of reed plate and reed stops out toward tip of "Vee" as far as possible as indicated by arrows in Fig. SK6-6. Position reed petals and reed stops as outlined to provide maximum overlap; then, tighten the retaining screws.

PUDDLE DRAIN VALVES. All models are equipped with a puddle drain system designed to remove any liquid fuel or oil which might build up in the crankcase; thus providing smoother operation at all speeds and lessening the possibility of spark plug fouling during slow speed operation.

The puddle drain valve housing is located on the starboard side of power head, and can be removed as shown in Fig. SK6-5. The reed-type puddle drain valve petals must seat lightly and evenly against valve plate. Reed stops

Fig. SK6-3—Throttle link-age typcial of all 35-55 hp models. Refer to text for method of checking and adjusting.

A. High speed stop
I. Idle stop
L. Throttle link
N. Neutral stop
R. Roller
S. Scribed line
T. Tower shaft
16. Eccentric screw

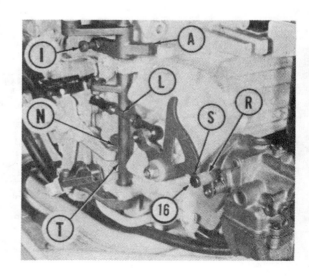

should be adjusted to 0.017-0.023 inch clearance at the tip. Blow out drain passages with compressed air while housing is off.

Later models are equipped with a recirculating puddle drain system. Fluid accumulated in puddle drain during slow speed operation is reintroduced to the cylinders once engine is returned to cruising speed. Inspect hoses and check valves when unit is disassembled.

FUEL PUMP. All models are equipped with a diaphragm type fuel pump which is actuated by pressure and vacuum pulsations from both crankcases as shown in Fig. SK6-6. The two stages operate alternately as shown.

NOTE: Either stage operating independently may permit the motor to run, but not at peak performance.

Most fuel pump service can be performed without removing the assembly from power head. Disconnect the pulse hoses and remove the retaining cap screws; then lift off the pump cover and diaphragm. Remove the sediment

Fig. SK6-4—Reed stop setting should be 9/32 inch when measured as shown. Holes in stops and petals are elongated and should be positioned as shown by arrows for maximum overlap.

Fig. SK6-5—View of puddle drain housing removed showing the two screens.

bowl and strainer. First stage inlet check valve can be driven out from below, using a ½-inch diameter drift. First stage outlet check valve can be lifted out after removing the retaining screws. The check valves must be installed to permit fuel to flow in the proper direction as shown. To renew the second stage outlet check valve, it is first necessary to remove pump body from power head, remove outlet fuel elbow and drive the check valve out from below. Check valve will be damaged, and a new unit must be installed. DO NOT remove the valve unless renewal is indicated. Install new valve carefully, using an 11/16-inch diameter punch.

Renew the diaphragm if cracked or torn, or badly distorted. Install check valves carefully to prevent damage, and reassemble by reversing the disassembly procedure.

IGNITION SYSTEM

Thirty-five horsepower models are equipped with either a battery or magneto ignition system. Forty-five hp models may be equipped with magneto ignition, battery ignition with a flywheel mounted alternator or capacitor discharge ignition. Fifty-five hp models may be equipped wtih magneto ignition, battery ignition or capacitor discharge ignition. Refer to the appropriate following paragraphs after determining type of ignition used.

All Models

R&R FLYWHEEL. A special puller (T-8931) is used to remove the flywheel on late model units. Pulling bosses are provided on the flywheel for puller installation.

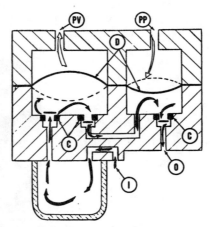

Fig. SK6-6—Cross-sectional view of the two stage fuel pump. Broken lines indicate position of diaphragm when pulse pressure and vacuum are reversed.

C. Check valves	O. Fuel outlet
D. Diaphragm	PP. Pulse pressure
I. Fuel inlet	PV. Pulse vacuum

NOTE: Models with alternators must have the three screws that secure the emergency starter collar removed, as well as the emergency starter collar. Make certain that aligning marks on flywheel and emergency starter collar are matched when reassembling.

Flywheel may be removed from models without puller bosses by using a special knockout nut (T-2910). Install the tool and apply upward pressure to rim of flywheel, then bump the tool sharply with a hammer to loosen flywheel from tapered portion of crankshaft.

The manufacturer recommends that mating surfaces of flywheel and crankshaft be lapped before flywheel is reinstalled. If evidence of working exists proceed as follows:

Remove flywheel key and apply a light coating of valve grinding or lapping compound to tapered portion of crankshaft. Install flywheel without key or crankshaft nut and rotate flywheel gently back and forth about ¼-turn. Move flywheel 90 degrees and repeat operation. Lift off flywheel, wipe off excess lapping compound and carefully examine crankshaft. A minimum of 90 percent surface contact should be indicated by the polished surface; continue lapping only if insufficient contact is evident. Thoroughly clean crankshaft and flywheel bore to remove all traces of lapping compound, then clean both surfaces with a non-oily solvent.

Reinstall crankshaft key and flywheel, then tighten flywheel nut to torque indicated in CONDENSED SERVICE DATA table.

POINT ADJUSTMENT. Breaker point gap should be 0.020 inch for models with magneto ignition and 0.015 inch for all other models. Both sets of points must be adjusted as nearly alike as possible.

NOTE: A variation of 0.0015-inch in point adjustment will change ignition timing one degree.

To adjust the points, first remove flywheel as previously outlined. Turn crankshaft clockwise until the rub block on one set of points is resting on high point of breaker cam approximately 10 degrees from first point of maximum opening. Mark the exact location of rub block contact for use in adjusting the other set of points. Loosen breaker point mounting screws and adjust point gap until a slight drag exists using a 0.020-inch feeler gage for models with magneto ignition and 0.015-inch feeler gage for all other models.

Turn crankshaft until the previously installed mark on breaker cam is aligned with the rub block on the other set of points and adjust the other set of points in the same manner.

NOTE: If mid-range of breaker plate movement is used, final positioning can be made by moving the speed control handle to correctly position the rub block at the same point of breaker cam.

Magneto Ignition

IGNITION TIMING. If ignition points are carefully adjusted as previously outlined and advance timing marks align when speed control linkage contacts the maximum advance stop, timing can be assumed to be correct. A punch mark on stator plate should align with the crankcase parting line on PORT side of power head at maximum ignition advance.

If maximum advance timing marks do not align, shorten or lenghten the timing advance link (L—Fig. SK6-7).

If advance timing marks are not present or if timing is in doubt, the manufacturer makes a special tool available for checking advance timing position. Refer to Fig. SK6-8 and the following paragraphs.

Two different timing tools are used. Special tool T-8938 is used to time 35 hp Manual Tiller models after Ser. No. 3001 and 45 hp Manual Tiller models after Ser. No. 3001. Special tool TA-2937-1 is used to time all other models.

To check the timing using the special tool, first make sure ignition points are properly adjusted as previously outlined. Remove upper spark plug and thread the tool body into spark plug opening. Turn crankshaft until upper piston is at TDC, then insert gage rod

into tool bore, 25 to 55 hp end out, until rod end contacts piston crown. With piston at extreme TDC, thread tool body in or out if necessary, until inner scribe line on gage rod is aligned with end of tool body; then turn crankshaft clockwise almost one complete revolution while applying pressure to end of gage rod, until outer scribe line aligns with tool body. Crankshaft should now be at correct position BTDC for maximum ignition advance.

NOTE: Crankshaft should not be rotated counterclockwise.

With crankshaft correctly positioned and breaker points properly adjusted, turn stator plate counterclockwise until points just open, and affix the maximum advance timing punch mark on stator plate.

Battery Ignition

IGNITION TIMING. If ignition breaker point gap is carefully adjusted as previously outlined and advance timing marks align when speed control linkage contacts maximum advance stop, timing can be assumed to be correct. A scribed line on breaker plate should align with a similar mark on starboard side of the upper bearing cage (TM—Fig. SK6-7) at maximum ignition advance.

If maximum advance timing marks do not align, shorten or lengthen the timing advance link (L).

If advance marks are not present or if timing is in doubt, the manufacturer makes a special tool available for checking ignition advance timing. Refer to Fig. SK6-8 and the following paragraph.

To check timing using the special timing tool, first make certain that ignition breaker point gap is correctly adjusted as previously outlined. Remove the upper spark plug and thread the tool body into spark plug opening. Turn crankshaft until upper piston is at TDC, then insert the gage rod with the 25 to 55 hp end out. With the piston at exactly TDC, thread the timing gage body in or out as necessary until the inner scribed line on gage rod is aligned with end of tool body. After gage body is correctly positioned, turn crankshaft clockwise almost one complete revolution while applying pressure to end of gage rod. Stop the crankshaft just as the first (outer) scribed line on rod aligns with tool body. The crankshaft should now be at correct position BTDC for maximum ignition advancement.

NOTE: Crankshaft should not be rotated counterclockwise.

With crankshaft correctly positioned and breaker point gap properly ad-

justed, turn the ignition breaker plate counterclockwise until the breaker points just open. Scribe the maximum advance timing marks on starboard side of breaker plate and upper bearing cage as shown at (TM—Fig. SK6-7).

Capacitor Discharge Ignition

IGNITION TIMING. To adjust ignition timing, remove the flywheel and carefully adjust breaker point gap for both breaker points as previously outlined. Remove both spark plugs and thread body of special timing gage TA-2937-1 into top spark plug opening. Insert the gage rod into tool body, rotate the crankshaft and carefully position top piston at exactly TDC.

NOTE: Gage rod should be installed with 25 to 55 hp end out.

With the top piston at TDC, thread timing tool body in or out as necessary until the inner scribed line on gage rod is aligned with end of tool body. After gage body is correctly positioned, turn the crankshaft clockwise almost one complete revolution while applying pressure to end of gage rod. Stop the crankshaft just as the first (outer) scribed line on rod aligns with tool body. The crankshaft should be at correct positon BTDC for maximum ignition advance timing.

NOTE: Crankshaft should not be rotated counterclockwise.

With the crankshaft correctly positioned and breaker point gap properly adjusted, connect one lead from timing test light (with battery) or ohmmeter to the breaker point terminal for white/brown wire and ground other test lead to motor. Move the speed control from slow toward fast (maximum advance) speed position and observe the test light or ohmmeter. The breaker points should just open (test light goes off or ohmmeter registers infinite resistance) when the speed control reaches maximum ignition advance. If the breaker points do not open, shorten link (L—Fig. SK6-7). If breaker points open too soon, lengthen link (L). If desired, the other set of breaker points can be synchronized using the timing gage (Fig. SK6-8) in the lower spark plug opening. Method of locating crankshaft for checking lower cylinder timing is similar. Timing test light or ohmmeter

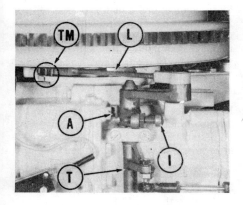

Fig. SK6-7—Timing advance linkage for motors equipped with battery ignition. Models equipped with magneto are similar except for location of timing marks (TM).

A. Advance stop
I. Idle stop
L. Link
T. Tower shaft
TM. Timing marks

Fig. SK6-8—Special tool is available for positioning piston at correct timing position. Refer to text for proper tool usage.

should be connected to breaker point terminal with brown wire. Synchronize the breaker points to open at correct time by varying the breaker point gap.

TROUBLESHOOTING. Use only approved procedures when testing to prevent damage to components. The fuel system should be checked to make certain that faulty running is not caused by incorrect fuel mixture or contaminated fuel.

CHECKING FOR SPARK. Remove the spark plugs and attach spark plug leads to a spark gap tester. With all wiring attached, attempt to start motor using the electric starter.

NOTE: Two conventional spark plugs (such as Champion L4J) with ground electrodes removed can be used to check for spark. Make certain that test plug shell is grounded against power head when checking.

If good regular spark occurs at tester (or test plugs), check fuel system and spark plugs. Also, make certain that wires from breaker points (1 and 2—Fig. SK6-9) to C-D unit (3), from C-D unit to ignition coils (4 and 5) and from coils to spark plugs are correct to provide spark to the proper cylinder.

If spark does not occur at tester (or test plugs), make certain that the small black wires on ignition coils (4 and 5) are attached to the negative (-) terminals and are securely grounded to the coil clamp screws. Also check continuity of the spark plug wires. If test plugs still do not spark, proceed with following checks.

WIRING. Engine missing, surging or failure to start can be caused by loose connections, corroded connections or short circuits. Electrical system components may also be damaged by faulty connections or short circuits.

Attach one lead of voltmeter to the terminal (10—Fig. SK6-9) where the blue wires are attached. Ground the other test lead to the metal case (housing) of the C-D unit (3). Turn the ignition switch ON and observe the test light or voltmeter. If the test light glows, current is available to the C-D unit. If checking with a voltmeter, voltage should be the same as available at the battery.

If test light does not glow or voltmeter indicates zero or low voltage, check the circuit breaker (6). If the circuit breaker is not faulty, check for broken wires, loose connections, faulty ignition switch or improper ground. Make certain that C-D unit (3) is properly grounded. Mounting surfaces on bracket and C-D unit must be free of all paint and the mounting bracket to motor ground wire must provide a good ground connection. Check the ground strap between power head and support plate. Before proceeding with remaining tests, make certain current is available to the C-D unit.

BREAKER POINTS. The breaker points are used to trigger the ignition system. Failure of breaker points to make contact (open circuit) or failure to break contact (short circuit) will prevent ignition just as in conventional magneto or battery ignition systems.

Remove the flywheel and check condition and gap of the breaker points as outlined in the preceding POINT ADJUSTMENT paragraphs. Check condition of all wires, making certain that ground wire from breaker plate to the alternator stator has good contact, especially at the stator end. Varnish should be scraped from stator before attaching ground wire. Check the BROWN and the WHITE/BROWN wires for short circuit to ground, for loose connections and for broken wire. Refer to IGNITION TIMING paragraphs and Fig. SK6-9. Make certain that breaker point wires and coil wires are properly connected to provide spark to the correct cylinder.

IGNITION COILS AND C-D UNIT. If the preceding checks do not indicate any malfunctions, the ignition coils can be tested using an ignition tester available from the following sources:

GRAHAM-LEE ELECTRONICS, INC.
4220 Central Ave. N.E.
Minneapolis, Minn. 55421

MERC-O-TRONIC INSTRUMENTS CORP.
215 Branch St.
Almont, Mich. 48003

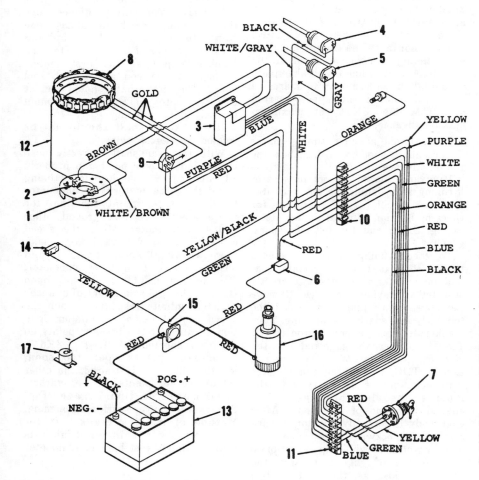

Fig. SK6-9—Wiring diagram for 55 hp motors with capacitor discharge ignition system. Yellow wires are for starting system, purple for charging, white for tachometer, green for choke, orange for heat indicator, red for battery positive, blue for ignition and black for ground.

1. Breaker points for top cylinder
2. Breaker points for bottom cylinder
3. Ignition capacitor discharge unit
4. Coil for top cylinder
5. Coil for bottom cylinder
6. Circuit breaker
7. Ignition and start switch
8. Alternator and stator
9. Rectifier
10. Terminal block at motor
11. Terminal block at dashboard
12. Alternator ground
13. Battery
14. Neutral interlock switch
15. Starter solenoid
16. Starter motor
17. Choke solenoid

An alternate method of checking is possible as follows:

Connect one lead of a 12 volt test light to each of the two primary terminals of one ignition coil. Turn ignition switch to the ON position, attempt to start motor with the electric starter and observe the test light.

NOTE: After checking one of the ignition coils, connect the 12 volt test light to the primary terminals of the other coil and check the coil.

If the 12 volt test light flashes but spark did not occur at the test plug as tested in the CHECKING FOR SPARK paragraphs, the coil or attaching wires are faulty.

NOTE: The test plug connected to the high tension spark plug wire will not fire with test light connected across the primary terminals. Inspect the black ground wire from negative (-) terminal of coil to the coil clamp screw and the high tension spark plug wire.

If the 12 volt test light does not flash, when connected to the coil primary terminals, make certain that current is available to the C-D unit as outlined in WIRING paragraphs. Make certain that breaker points and associated wires are not faulty as outlined in the BREAKER POINTS paragraphs in the TROUBLESHOOTING section. If current is still not available to the coil primary terminals, the C-D unit should be renewed.

COOLING SYSTEM

THERMOSTAT. The thermostat is located beneath a separate housing on top, rear face of cylinder head as shown in Fig. SK6-10. When installing the thermostat, position with "Vee" slot in visible end up as shown. Power head will overheat if run without thermostat installed.

WATER PUMP. All motors are equipped with a rubber impeller type water pump. Refer to Figs. SK6-11, SK6-18 and SK6-19. The water pump is mounted in the lower unit drive shaft housing (upper gearcase).

When cooling system problems are encountered, first check the thermostat to see that it is operating properly. Check the water inlet for plugging or partial stoppage, then if trouble is not corrected, remove the lower unit gearcase as outlined in LOWER UNIT section, and check the condition of water pump, water passages and sealing surfaces.

POWER HEAD

REMOVE AND DISASSEMBLE. To overhaul the power head, clamp the motor on a stand or support and remove the engine cover (shroud) and motor leg covers. Remove the starter, flywheel and magneto or alternator; fuel pump, carburetor and intake manifold. Disconnect all interfering wiring and linkage. Remove the cylinder head, and transfer port and exhaust covers if major repairs are required. Remove the power head attaching screws and lift off the cylinder block, crankshaft and associated parts as a unit.

NOTE: One of the power head attaching screws is located underneath the rear exhaust cover as shown in Fig. SK6-12. Cover must be removed for access to the screw.

To disassemble the power head, unbolt and remove the upper bearing cage; then unbolt and remove the crankcase front half. Pry slots are provided adjacent to retaining dowels for separating the crankcase; DO NOT pry on machined mating surfaces of cylinder block and crankcase front half.

Crankshaft, pistons and bearings are now accessible for removal and overhaul as outlined in the appropriate following paragraphs. Assemble as outlined in the ASSEMBLY paragraph.

ASSEMBLY. When reassembling, make sure all joint and gasket surfaces are clean, free from nicks and burrs, warped surfaces or hardenend cement or carbon. The crankcase and inlet manifolds must be completely sealed against both vacuum and pressure. Exhaust manifold and cylinder head must be sealed against water leakage and pressure. Mating surfaces of exhaust areas between power head and motor leg must form a tight seal.

Use a thin coating of Loctite, Grade "D" on upper and lower bearing bores of both halves of crankcase; and No. 1 Permatex on cap screw threads. The crankshaft upper seal should be installed with LOWER edge 0.150 inch from bearing counterbore as shown at (B—Fig. SK6-13).

Apply 3M-EC750 Sealer to mating surfaces of crankcase and to center main bearing bore; and install crankcase front half immediately. Tighten main bearing bolts to a torque of 270 inch-pounds. Make sure crankshaft turns freely before proceeding with assembly.

When installing cylinder head, coat the first ¾-inch of screw threads with "Permatex #2" or equivalent. Tighten the retaining screws progressively from the center outward. First to 100-125 inch-pounds torque, then to an even torque of 265-275 inch-pounds. After motor has been test run and cooled, retorque screws to 265-275 inch-pounds.

Fig. SK6-10—Removing thermostat from cylinder head. "Vee" slot should point up when thermostat is installed.

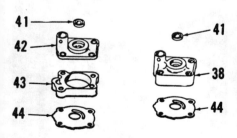

Fig. SK6-11—Variations of water pump bodies used on some models. Refer also to Figs. SK6-18 and SK6-19.

38. Water pump body
41. Seal
42. Cover
43. Pump housing
44. Back plate

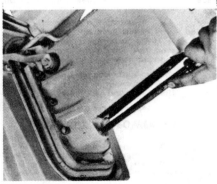

Fig. SK6-12—Rear exhaust cover must be removed from motor leg for access to power head rear attaching screw.

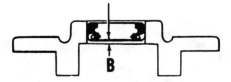

Fig. SK6-13—Cross-sectional view of crankshaft upper bearing cage showing correct seal location. Clearance (B) should be 0.150 inch.

PISTONS, PINS, RINGS & CYLINDERS. Piston on all models except late 55 hp models are fitted with three rings, while late 55 hp model pistons have two piston rings. Piston rings should be installed with the bevelled inner edge toward closed end of piston. Rings are pinned in place to prevent rotation in ring grooves.

The piston pin on early models is a tight press fit in connecting rod and a floating fit in piston bores. The special tool, Part No. T2990, should be used to install piston pin. Piston pin on later models rides in roller bearing in connecting rod. When assembling piston, pin and connecting rod, make sure long, tapering side of piston is assembled for installation toward exhaust side of cylinder and correlation marks (M—Fig. SK6-14) and lubrication hole (H) toward top (flywheel) end of crankshaft. Piston pin must be centered in connecting rod bore so that neither end of pin will extend through piston boss as rod is moved from side to side. All friction surfaces should be lubricated with new engine oil when assembling.

Pistons are available in standard sizes on all models and in oversizes on some models.

CONNECTING RODS, BEARINGS AND CRANKSHAFT. Before detaching connecting rods from crankshaft, make certain that rod and cap are properly marked for correct assembly to each other and in the correct cylinder. The needle rollers and cages at crankpin end of connecting rod should be kept with the assembly and not interchanged.

The bearing rollers and cages used in the two connecting rods and center main bearings are available only as a set which contains the rollers and cage halves for one bearing. The complete assembly should be installed whenever renewal is indicated. Bearing cages have bevelled match marks as shown by arrow, Fig. SK6-15. Match marks must be installed together and toward top (flywheel) end of crankshaft.

Upper main bearing is available only as an assembly with the crankshaft; bearing should not be removed from crankshaft when power head is being overhauled.

A non-fibrous grease can be used to hold loose needle bearing in position during assembly. All friction surfaces should be lubricated with new engine oil. Check frequently as power head is being assembled, for binding or locking of the moving parts. If binding occurs, remove the cause before proceeding with the assembly. When assembling, follow the procedures outlined in the ASSEMBLY paragraphs. Tightening torques are given in the CONDENSED SERVICE DATA tables.

Fig. SK6-15—When installing needle bearing cages, make sure bevelled ends (arrow) are together and to the top.

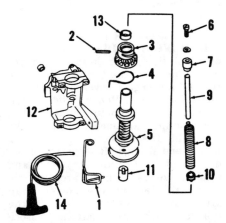

Fig. SK6-16—Exploded view of recoil starter assembly. Pinion (3) meshes with teeth on flywheel.

1. Rope guide	8. Recoil spring
2. Drive pin	9. Guide post
3. Pinion	10. Retainer
4. Pinion spring	11. Retainer extension
5. Starter spool	12. Mounting bracket
6. Lock screw	13. Interlock guide
7. Spring drive	14. Rope

MANUAL STARTER

Fig. SK6-16 shows an exploded view of the recoil starter assembly. Starter pinion (3) engages a starter ring gear on the flywheel.

To disassemble the starter, first remove the engine cover, then remove screw (6) in top of starter shaft.

NOTE: This screw locks pin (2) in place.

Thread the special tool (Part No. T-3139-1) in threaded hole from which screw (6) was removed. Tighten the tool until it bottoms; then turn tool handle slightly counterclockwise to relieve recoil spring tension, and push out pin (2). Allow the tool and spring drive (7) to turn clockwise to unwind the recoil spring (8). Pull up on tool to remove the recoil spring and components. Guide post (9) and spring retainer (10) can be lifted out after recoil spring is removed.

Recoil spring, pinion (3) or associated parts can be renewed at this time. To renew the starter rope, remove clamps (12) then remove the spool. Thread rope through hole in lower end of spool (5) and install the rope retainer approximately ½-inch from end of rope. Pull tight, then fully wind the rope onto spool and reinstall assembly. Make certain that retainer extension (11) is in place. With recoil spring and drive pinion (3) installed, use the special tool to wind the recoil spring counterclockwise eight turns. Align the holes in pinion (3), spool (5) and spring drive (7); then install the drive pin (2). Remove the tool and secure the pin with the locking screw (6). Recoil spring cavity should be partially filled with Lubriplate or similar grease when reassembling.

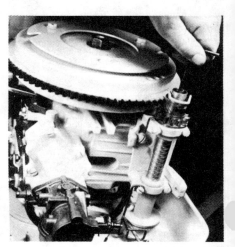

Fig. SK6-16A—View showing tool (T3139) used to pre-load the recoil spring.

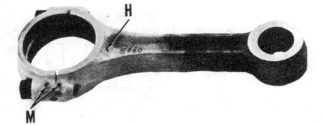

Fig. SK6-14—Correlation marks (M) and oil hole (H) should be toward the top when connecting rod is installed.

PROPELLER

The propellers for normal use have three blades and are protected by a cushioning-slip clutch. Various propellers are available and should be selected to provide full throttle operation within the recommended limits of 4500-5000 rpm for 1969 fifty-five hp motors; 5000-5500 rpm for 1970 and later fifty-five hp motors; 3000-4000 rpm for 35 hp and 45 hp Manual Tiller motors after serial number 3001; 4400-5100 rpm for all other 35 and 45 hp motors. Propellers other than those designed for the motor should not be used.

LOWER UNIT

R&R AND OVERHAUL. To remove the lower unit gearcase and drive shaft housing on early style lower unit shown in Fig. SK6-18, first remove the motor leg covers and disconnect the shift rod coupler as shown in Fig. SK6-17, remove the screws securing drive shaft housing to motor leg and remove the complete lower unit drive assembly.

To remove lower unit on later style lower unit shown in Fig. SK6-19, remove motor leg covers and unbolt lower unit from motor leg. Remove pin (43) connecting intermediate shift rod (1) and lower shift rod (10). Separate lower unit from motor leg.

Drain the gearcase and secure gearcase skeg in a vise. Disassemble and remove the drive shaft and water pump assembly (32 through 38—Fig. SK6-18 or SK6-19). Remove propeller nut, pin (30) and propeller (29). Carefully clean exposed end of propeller shaft and remove the two screws securing propeller shaft bearing cage (27) to gearcase. Rotate the bearing cage approximately ½-turn until tabs

are accessible from the sides; then using a soft hammer, gently tap the bearing cage rearward out of gearcase. Remove the gearcase rear retaining stud nut working through propeller shaft opening as shown in Fig. SK6-20.

Remove shift rod (1—Fig. SK6-18 or SK6-19), nut (2—Fig. SK6-18) and the gearcase front retaining stud nut, then lift off drive shaft housing.

Withdraw drive pinion (31) from top of gearcase and propeller shaft and

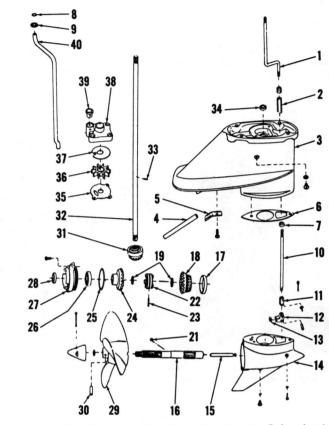

1. Shift rod
2. Nut
3. Drive shaft housing
4. Inlet water tube
5. Inlet plate
6. Gasket
7. Seal
8. Seal
9. Washer
10. Shift rod
11. Link
12. Shift arm
13. Yoke
14. Gearcase
15. Shift pin
16. Propeller shaft
17. Bearing cup
18. Front gear
19. Thrust washer
20. Ball
21. Ball
22. Clutch dog
23. Spring pin
24. Rear gear
25. Cage seal
26. Bearing
27. Bearing cage
28. Seal
29. Propeller
30. Propeller pin
31. Drive pinion
32. Drive shaft
33. Drive pin
34. Shaft seal
35. Back plate
36. Impeller
37. Top plate
38. Pump body
39. Grommet
40. Water tube

Fig. SK6-18—Exploded view of typical early lower unit and associated parts. Refer also to Fig. SK6-11 for other types of water pumps. Refer to Fig. SK6-19 for later type lower unit.

Fig. SK6-17—Disconnect the shift rod coupler before attempting to remove gearcase.

Fig. SK6-19—Exploded view of lower unit used on later models. Refer to Fig. SK6-18 for parts identification except for: 41. Drive shaft seal; 42. Upper drive shaft bearing; 43. Pin.

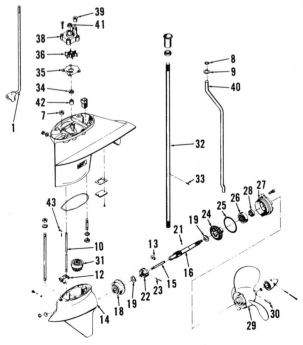

associated parts through rear opening. Withdraw front and rear gears from propeller shaft. Remove spring pin (23), clutch dog (22) and shift pin (15).

The drive shaft seal (34) should be installed with spring loaded lip toward top (power head). Propeller shaft seal (28) should be installed with spring loaded lip toward outside of bearing cage (27).

Drive gear backlash and bearing preload are fixed and not adjustable. Assemble by reversing the disassembly

procedure. Make sure that hole in clutch dog (22) is aligned with slot in propeller shaft (16) and hole in shift pin (15); then, insert spring pin (23).

When reinstalling shift rod (1—Fig. SK6-18) refer to Fig. SK6-21. Upper end of shift rod must point to rear, starboard, so that angle (A) from housing centerline is approximately 28 degrees; and bend of rod must clear pump housing (B) approximately 1/16 inch, when shifted to lowermost (forward detent) position.

After early stage lower unit is installed, refer to Fig. SK6-22 and adjust the shift linkage coupling as follows: Using the shift lever, move the linkage through "Forward," "Neutral" and "Reverse" detent positions and mark the intermediate shift link where it emerges from motor leg as shown at (F, N & R). If marks are not equally spaced (caused by interference in linkage), adjust by means of the turnbuckle connector (C) until interference is removed.

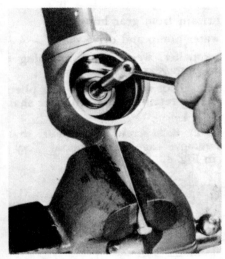

Fig. SK6-20—Gearcase rear nut is accessible through propeller shaft opening as shown.

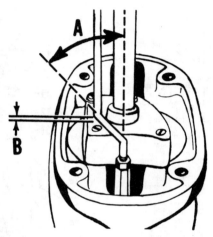

Fig. SK6-21—Before tightening shift rod locknut on early units, angle (A) should be 28° and minimum clearance (B) of 1/16-inch. Refer to text.

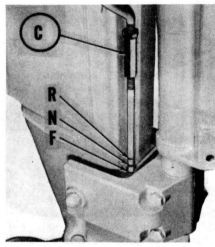

Fig. SK6-22—Check the shift linkage adjustment by marking detent positions as shown. Refer to text.

SUZUKI

SUZUKI AMERICA CORPORATION
3251 E. Imperial Highway
P.O. Box 1000
Brea, California 92621

SUZUKI DT30
(Prior To 1988)

CONDENSED SERVICE MANUAL

NOTE: Metric fasteners are used throughout outboard motor.

TUNE-UP

Hp/rpm	30/4800-5500
Bore	71 mm
	(2.80 in.)
Stroke	63 mm
	(2.48 in.)
Number of Cylinders	2
Displacement	499 cc
	(30.45 cu. in.)
Spark Plug:	
NGK	BR7HS
Electrode Gap	0.9-1.0 mm
	(0.035-0.039 in.)
Ignition Type	CDI
Carburetor Make	Mikuni
Idle Speed (in gear)	650-700 rpm
Fuel:Oil Ratio	50:1

SIZES—CLEARANCES

Piston Ring End Gap	0.2-0.4 mm
	(0.008-0.016 in.)
Piston-to-Cylinder Clearance:	
Prior To 1987	0.067-0.082 mm
	(0.0026-0.0032 in.)
After 1986	0.087-0.102 mm
	(0.0034-0.0040 in.)
Piston Pin Diameter	17.995-18.000 mm
	(0.7085-0.7087 in.)
Max. Crankshaft Runout at Main	
Bearing Journal	0.05 mm
	(0.002 in.)
Max. Connecting Rod Small End	
Side Shake	5.0 mm
	(0.020 in.)

TIGHTENING TORQUES

Power Head Mounting Screws	15-20 N·m
	(11-14 ft.-lbs.)
Crankcase:	
6 mm	8-12 N·m
	(6-8 ft.-lbs.)
8 mm	20-26 N·m
	(14-19 ft.-lbs.)

TIGHTENING TORQUES CONT.

Flywheel Nut	130-150 N·m
	(94-108 ft.-lbs.)
Cylinder Head Screws:	
6 mm	8-12 N·m
	(6-8 ft.-lbs.)
8 mm	20-26 N·m)
	(14-19 ft.-lbs.)
Gearcase Pinion Nut	18-22 N·m
	(13-16 ft.-lbs.)
Propeller Shaft Nut	27-30 N·m
	(19-21 ft.-lbs.)
Standard Screws:	
Unmarked or Marked "4"	
5 mm	2-4 N·m
	(2-3 ft.-lbs.)
6 mm	4-7 N·m
	(3-5 ft.-lbs.)
8 mm	10-16 N·m
	(7-12 ft.-lbs.)
10 mm	22-35 N·m
	(16-26 ft.-lbs.)
Stainless Steel	
5 mm	2-4 N·m
	(2-3 ft.-lbs.)
6 mm	6-10 N·m
	(5-7 ft.-lbs.)
8 mm	15-20 N·m
	(11-15 ft.-lbs.)
10 mm	34-41 N·m
	(25-30 ft.-lbs.)
Marked "7" or SAE Grade 5	
5 mm	3-6 N·m
	(2-5 ft.-lbs.)
6 mm	8-12 N·m
	(6-9 ft.-lbs.)
8 mm	18-28 N·m
	(13-20 ft.-lbs.)
10 mm	40-60 N·m
	(29-44 ft.-lbs.)

LUBRICATION

The power head is lubricated by oil mixed with the fuel. On models prior to 1987, fuel:oil ratio should be 30:1 during break-in (first five hours of operation) of a new or rebuilt engine and 50:1 for normal service. On models after 1986, fuel:oil ratio during engine break-in should be 25:1 and 100:1 for normal service. Recommended oil is Suzuki Outboard Motor Oil or a suitable equivalent NMMA (formerly BIA) certified TC-WII oil. Recommended fuel is regular or unleaded gasoline with a minimum pump octane rating of 85.

The lower unit gears and bearings are lubricated by approximately 230 mL (7.77 ozs.) of SAE 90 hypoid outboard gear oil. Reinstall vent and fill plugs securely using a new gasket, if necessary, to ensure a water-tight seal.

FUEL SYSTEM

CARBURETOR. A Mikuni B32-28 carburetor is used. Refer to Fig. SZ11-1 for exploded view. Initial setting of pilot air screw (6) from a lightly seated position should be $1\frac{1}{4}$ to $1\frac{3}{4}$ turns open on models prior to 1987 and $1\frac{1}{2}$ to 2 turns open on models after 1986. Final carburetor adjustment should be made with engine at normal operating temperature and running in forward gear. Adjust idle speed screw (2) so engine idles at approximately 650-700 rpm. Adjust pilot air screw so engine idles smoothly and will accelerate cleanly without hesitation. If necessary, readjust idle speed screw to obtain 650-700 rpm idle speed.

Main fuel metering is controlled by main jet (10). Standard main jet size for normal operation is #160. Standard pilot jet (4) size is #77.5 on models prior to 1987 and #85 on models after 1986.

To check float level, remove float bowl (14) and invert carburetor body (1). Distance (D—Fig. SZ11-2) between main jet and bottom of float should be 10-12 mm ($\frac{25}{64}$ to $\frac{15}{32}$ in.). Bend float tang to adjust float level.

FUEL FILTER. A fuel filter assembly is used to filter the fuel prior to entering the fuel pump assembly. Periodically unscrew cup (5—Fig.

SZ11-3) from base (1) and withdraw filter element (4). Clean cup (5) and filter element (4) in a suitable solvent and blow dry with clean compressed air. Inspect filter element (4). If excessive blockage or damage is noted, then the element must be renewed.

Reassembly is reverse order of disassembly. Renew "O" ring (3) and, if needed, seal (2) during reassembly.

FUEL PUMP. A diaphragm fuel pump (Fig. SZ11-4) is mounted on the side of power head cylinder block and is actuated by pressure and vacuum pulsations from the engine crankcase.

When servicing pump, scribe reference marks across pump body to aid in reassembly. Defective or questionable parts should be renewed. Diaphragm should be renewed if air leaks or cracks are found, or if deterioration is evident.

REED VALVES. The reed valves are located on a reed plate that is located behind the intake manifold. The intake manifold must be removed in order to remove reed plate and service reed valves.

Renew reed valves (2–Fig. SZ11-5) if petals are broken, cracked, warped, rusted or bent. Tip of reed petal must not stand open more than 0.2 mm (0.008 in.) from contact surface. Reed stop

Fig. SZ11-1—Exploded view of Mikuni B32-28 carburetor.

1. Body	
2. Idle speed screw	9. Main nozzle
3. Spring	10. Main jet
4. Pilot jet	11. Float
5. Spring	12. Pin
6. Pilot air screw	13. Gasket
7. Gasket	14. Float bowl
8. Needle & seat	15. Choke knob

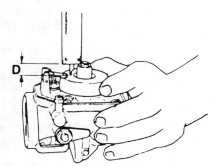

Fig. SZ11-2—Distance (D) for correct float level should be 10-12 mm (0.394-0.472 in.).

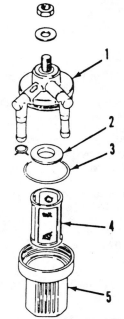

Fig. SZ11-3—Exploded view of fuel filter assembly.

1. Base		
2. Seal	4. Element	
3. "O" ring	5. Cup	

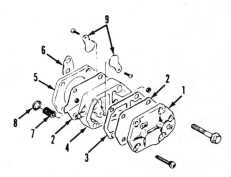

Fig. SZ11-4—Exploded view of diaphragm type fuel pump.

1. Cover		
2. Diaphragm		6. Gasket
3. Gasket		7. Spring
4. Valve body		8. Spring seat
5. Plate		9. Check valve

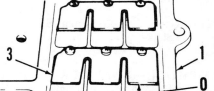

Fig. SZ11-5—View identifying reed plate (1), reed valves (2) and reed stops (3). Reed stop opening (0) should be 6.0-6.4 mm (0.24-0.25 in.).

opening (O) should be 6.0-6.4 mm (0.24-0.25 in.).

SPEED CONTROL LINKAGE. Place twist grip in the full closed position. Stator plate stopper (P – Fig. SZ11-8) should be in contact with cylinder block boss (D). Adjust rod (A – Fig. SZ11-6) length until mark (M) on throttle cam (C) is centered with roller (R). Rotate twist grip to the full throttle position. Stator plate stopper should be in contact with cylinder block boss. Adjust rod (B) length until throttle limiter (L) contacts stopper (S) on bottom engine cover.

IGNITION

A breakerless, capacitor discharge ignition system is used. Refer to Fig. SZ11-7 for wiring diagram.

Full throttle and full ignition advance should occur simultaneously. Ignition timing is mechanically advanced and must be synchronized with throttle opening.

To check ignition timing, first immerse lower unit of outboard motor in water. Connect a suitable tachometer to engine. Connect a power timing light to upper spark plug. Start engine and allow it to run until it reaches normal operating temperature. Shift into forward gear and note ignition timing. Timing pointer (T – Fig. SZ11-8) should be aligned with 2 degree ATDC mark (A) on flywheel. Loosen locknut and rotate screw (S) until idle speed timing is as recommended. Maximum advance timing should be 25 degrees BTDC (M) at 5000 rpm. Stop engine and loosen cap screws (C) and slide stator plate stopper (P) in slots to adjust maximum advance timing. Retighten cap screws (C) after recommended maximum advance tim-

ing is obtained. Reset idle speed timing as previously recommended.

If ignition malfunction occurs, check condition of spark plugs, and all wires and connections before trouble-shooting ignition circuit. Using Suzuki pocket tester 09900-25002 or a suitable ohmmeter, refer to the following test specifications and procedures to aid trouble-shooting.

To check secondary coil resistance of CDI unit, detach spark plug wires at spark plugs. Connect a tester lead to terminal end of each spark plug wire. Secondary coil resistance should be 2136-3204 ohms at 20°C (68°F).

Remove top cover of electrical parts holder for access to wire connectors. Remove top three-wire coupler and separate. To check charge coil (Fig. SZ11-7), connect a tester lead to black wire with red tracer and black wire of three-wire connector leading to stator plate. Charge coil can be considered satisfactory if resistance reading is within the limits of 102-154 ohms at 20°C (68°F).

To check pulser coil, connect a tester lead to red wire with white tracer and black wire of three-wire connector leading to stator plate. Pulser coil can be considered satisfactory if resistance reading is within the limits of 27.9-41.9 ohms at 20°C (68°F).

Check condition of battery lighting coil by separating connectors of yellow wire and red wire. Connect a tester lead to terminal end of wires leading to stator plate. Lighting coil can be considered satisfactory if resistance reading is within the limits of 0.24-0.36 ohms at 20°C (68°F).

If no component is found faulty in the previous tests, then the CDI unit must be renewed.

COOLING SYSTEM

WATER PUMP. A rubber impeller type water pump is mounted between the drive shaft housing and gearcase. A key in the drive shaft is used to turn the pump impeller. If cooling system problems are encountered, check water intakes for plugging or partial stoppage. If water intakes are clear, remove gearcase as outlined under LOWER UNIT and check condition of the water pump, water passages and sealing surfaces.

When water pump is disassembled, check condition of impeller (8 – Fig. SZ11-19) and plate (9) for excessive wear. Turn drive shaft clockwise (viewed from top) while placing pump housing over impeller. Avoid turning drive shaft in opposite direction when water pump is assembled.

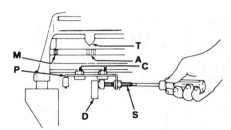

Fig. SZ11-8—Adjust idle speed timing and maximum advance timing as outlined in text.

A. 2° ATDC mark
C. Cap screws
D. Cylinder block boss
M. 25° BTDC mark
P. Stator plate stopper
S. Idle speed timing adjustment screw
T. Timing pointer

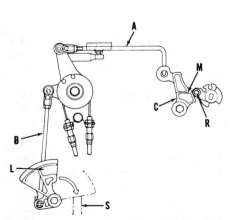

Fig. SZ11-6—View of speed control linkage. Adjust components as outlined in text.

A. Rod
B. Rod
C. Throttle cam
L. Throttle limiter
M. Mark
R. Roller
S. Stopper

Fig. SZ11-7—Wiring diagram of electrical system on models with electric starter.

B. Black
G. Green
R. Red
W. White
Y. Yellow
Bl. Blue
Br. Brown
B/R. Black with red tracer
Bl/R. Blue with red tracer
R/W. Red with white tracer
Y/G. Yellow with green tracer

THERMOSTAT. A thermostat (7—Fig. SZ11-14) is used to regulate operating temperature. Thermostat should start to open within the temperature

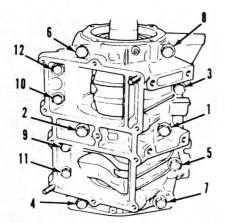

Fig. SZ11-9—Tighten crankcase screws in the sequence shown. Refer to CONDENSED SERVICE DATA for screw torques.

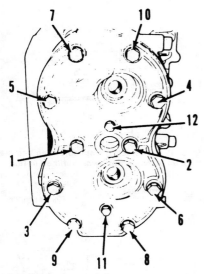

Fig. SZ11-10—Tighten cylinder head screws in sequence shown. Refer to CONDENSED SERVICE DATA for screw torques.

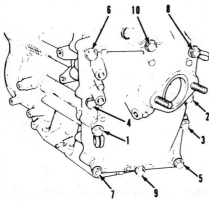

Fig. SZ11-11—Securely tighten intake manifold screws in sequence shown.

range of 48.5°-51.5° C (119°-125° F). Thermostat can be removed for inspection or renewal by removing cylinder head cover (6).

POWER HEAD

REMOVE AND REINSTALL. To remove the power head, first remove engine's top cover. Disconnect throttle cables, throttle limiting rod, fuel inlet hose at lower engine cover connector, choke knob and wires which will interfere with power head removal. Label wires, if needed, for later reference. Remove and carburetor's air intake cover, carburetor, rewind starter, starter motor relay and electric starter motor. Remove eight screws which secure power head assembly to drive shaft housing and lift off power head.

Before reinstalling power head, make certain drive shaft splines are clean then coat them with a light coating of water resistant grease. Install power head on drive shaft housing. Coat threads of retaining cap screws with silicone sealer and tighten screws to 15-20 N·m (11-14 ft.-lbs.). The remainder of installation is the reverse of removal procedure. Refer to SPEED CONTROL LINKAGE for synchronizing throttle opening with ignition advance.

DISASSEMBLY. Disassembly and inspection may be accomplished in the

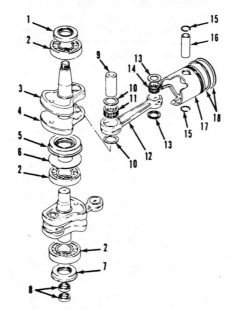

Fig. SZ11-12—Exploded view of piston and crankshaft assembly.

1. Seal	10. Thrust washers
2. Ball bearings	11. Roller bearing
3. Crank half	12. Connecting rod
4. Crank half	13. Thrust washers
5. Labyrinth seal	14. Roller bearing
6. Washer	15. Circlips
7. Seal	16. Piston pin
8. Seals	17. Piston
9. Crank pin	18. Piston rings

following manner. Remove electric starter bracket, exhaust tube, fuel filter and fuel pump. Remove flywheel and key, stator plate with pulser, charge and lighting coils. Remove electrical parts holder, speed control linkage, upper oil seal housing and stator retainer ring. Remove intake manifold, reed valve plate, exhaust cover and exhaust plate with gaskets. Remove cylinder head and cover with gaskets. Remove the twelve crankcase cap screws, then separate crankcase from cylinder block. Lift crankshaft assembly with pistons and connecting rod assemblies from cylinder block.

Engine components are now accessible for overhaul as outlined in the appropriate following paragraphs. Clean carbon from cylinder head and combustion chambers and remove any foreign material accumulation in water passages. Inspect components for damage and renew if needed. Refer to the following section for assembly procedure.

ASSEMBLY. Refer to specific service sections when assembling the crankshaft, connecting rods, pistons and reed valves. Make sure all joint and gasket surfaces are clean and free from nicks and burrs. Make sure all carbon, salt, dirt and sand are cleaned from the combustion chambers, exhaust ports and water passages.

Lubricate crankpin bearings and cylinder walls of cylinder block with Suzuki engine oil or a suitable NMMA certified two-stroke engine oil. Install crankshaft assembly in crankcase. Make sure flange of lower oil seal (7—Fig. SZ11-12) and middle labyrinth seal (5) fits properly in crankcase grooves. Make sure bearing pins engage notches in crankcase. Spread a coat of Suzuki Bond No. 1215 or a suitable equivalent on the mating surfaces of the crankcase and the cylinder block. Position crankcase half on cylinder block and tighten the crankcase screws in the sequence shown in Fig. SZ11-9 to torques shown in CONDENSED SERVICE DATA. Tighten the cylinder head screws in the sequence shown in Fig. SZ11-10 to torques shown in CONDENSED SERVICE DATA. Tighten the intake manifold screws in the sequence shown in Fig. SZ11-11.

PISTONS, PINS, RINGS AND CYLINDERS. Each piston is fitted with two piston rings. Piston ring end gap should be 0.2-0.4 mm (0.008-0.016 in.) with a maximum allowable ring end gap of 0.8 (0.031 in.). Piston rings are retained in position by locating pins. Standard piston pin diameter is 17.995-18.000 mm (0.7085-0.7087 in.). Install marked side of piston ring toward top of piston. Piston to cylinder wall clearance should be 0.067-0.082 mm (0.0026-0.0032 in.). Piston and rings are available in standard size as well as 0.25 mm (0.010 in.) and 0.50 mm (0.020 in.) oversizes. Cylinders should be bored to an oversize if either of the cylinders is out-of-round or taper exceeds 0.10 mm (0.004 in.). Install pistons on connecting rods so arrow on piston crown points toward exhaust port side of cylinder bore.

CONNECTING RODS, BEARINGS AND CRANKSHAFT. Connecting rods, bearings and crankshaft are a press together unit. Crankshaft should be disassembled ONLY by experienced service personnel and with suitable service equipment.

Caged roller bearings are used at both large and small ends of the connecting rods. Determine rod bearing wear from side to side as shown in Fig. SZ11-13. Normal side to side movement is 5.0 mm (0.20 in.) or less. Maximum limit of crankshaft runout is 0.05 mm (0.002 in.) measured at bearing surfaces with crankshaft ends supported.

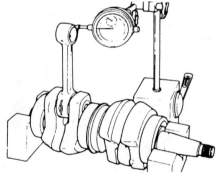

Fig. SZ11-13—Move connecting rod small end side to side to determine connecting rod, bearing and crank pin wear. Refer to text.

Apply Suzuki Super Grease "A" or a suitable high temperature grease to lip portion of lower crankshaft seal prior to installation.

MANUAL STARTER

Refer to Fig. SZ11-15 for an exploded view of manual starter assembly. Starter may be removed as a complete unit by detaching the neutral start cable and removing the three cap screws securing starter assembly to power head. To disassemble starter, proceed as follows: Remove starter handle (16—Fig. SZ11-15) and allow starter rope (14) to slowly wind onto pulley (4). Detach neutral start components. Invert starter housing (1) and remove cap screw (17). Withdraw plate (10) and spring (9).

Remove drive pawl (6) and return spring (5). Remove snap ring (8). Lift pulley (4) with starter rope (14) from starter housing. Use suitable hand and eye protection, and withdraw rewind spring (2) from starter housing (1). Be careful when removing rewind spring (2); a rapidly uncoiling starter spring could cause serious injury.

To reassemble, coat rewind spring area of starter housing (1) with a suitable water resistant grease. Install rewind spring (2) in starter housing. Rewind spring (2) must wind in a counterclockwise direction from the outer end. Wrap starter rope (14) in a clockwise direction 2½ turns onto pulley (4) when viewed from the flywheel side. Reassemble starter assembly by reversing disassembly procedure making certain rewind spring's hook properly engages groove in pulley (4). Apply water resistant grease to friction side of drive plate (10). Make sure slot (S—Fig. SZ11-16) in

drive plate properly engages tab (T) on starter housing boss and spring (9) fits into groove (G) in pulley (4).

To place tension on rewind spring (2—Fig. SZ11-15), pass starter rope (14) through rope outlet in housing (1),

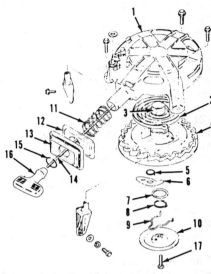

Fig. SZ11-15—Exploded view of manual starter assembly.

1. Housing	10. Plate
2. Rewind spring	11. Spring
3. Bushing	12. Rope guide
4. Pulley	13. Rubber plate
5. Return spring	14. Starter rope
6. Drive pawl	15. Clip
7. Spacer	16. Handle
8. Snap ring	17. Cap screw
9. Spring	

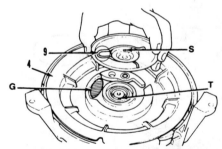

Fig. SZ11-16—During reassembly, slot (S) in drive plate must properly engage tab (T) on starter housing boss and spring (9) must fit into groove (G) in pulley (4).

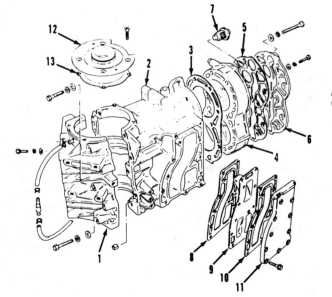

Fig. SZ11-14—Exploded view of cylinder block and crankcase assembly.

1. Crankcase
2. Cylinder block
3. Gasket
4. Cylinder head
5. Gasket
6. Cylinder head cover
7. Thermostat
8. Gasket
9. Exhaust plate
10. Gasket
11. Exhaust cover
12. Upper oil seal housing
13. Gasket

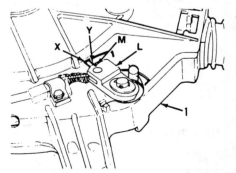

Fig. SZ11-17—For proper neutral start cable adjustment, mark (M) in lever (L) must be between marks (X and Y) on starter housing (1) when gear shift lever is in "Forward" or "Reverse" position.

spring (11), rope guide (12), rubber plate (13) and install rope handle (16). With starter rope (14) inserted in slot of pulley (4), rotate pulley 4 turns counterclockwise when viewed from the flywheel side. Secure pulley, then release starter rope (14) from slot in pulley and allow starter rope to slowly wind onto pulley. Do not place any more tension on rewind spring (2) than is necessary to draw rope handle up against housing.

Remount manual starter assembly and reassemble neutral start cable and associated components. With the gear shift lever in the "Forward" or "Reverse" position, mark (M–Fig. SZ11-17) in lever (L) must be between marks (X and Y) on starter housing (1). Adjust the length of the neutral start cable to obtain the correct adjustment.

ELECTRIC STARTER

Some models are equipped with electric starter shown in Fig. SZ11-18. Disassembly is evident after inspection of unit and reference to exploded view. Standard commutator outside diameter is 30 mm (1.18 in.) and should be renewed if worn to a diameter of 29 mm (1.14 in.) or less. Starter brushes have a standard length of 12.5 mm (0.492 in.) and should be renewed if worn to 9 mm (0.354 in.) or less. During reassembly, make sure upper and lower alignment marks on frame (6–Fig. SZ11-18) align with notches in frame head (5) and frame end (12). After reassembly, bench test starter before installing on power head.

LOWER UNIT

PROPELLER AND RUBBER DAMPER. A ratchet hub (50–Fig. SZ11-19) is used to provide shock protection for lower unit gears and shafts. Three-bladed propellers are used. Standard propeller has a 260.3 mm (10¼ in.) diameter and a 304.8 mm (12 in.)

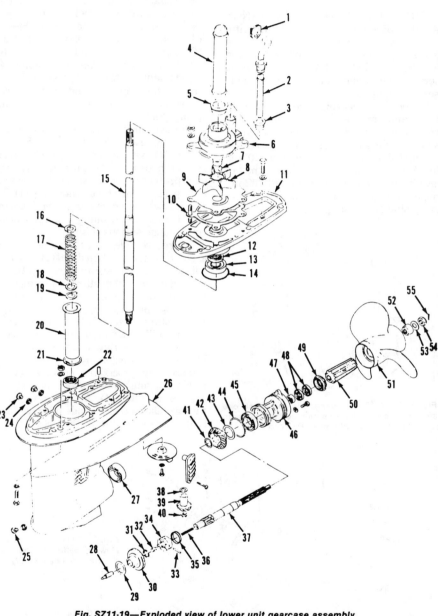

Fig. SZ11-19—Exploded view of lower unit gearcase assembly.

1. Grommet	15. Drive shaft		42. Reverse gear
2. Water tube	16. Washer	29. Shim	43. Shim
3. Grommet	17. Spring	30. Forward gear	44. "O" ring
4. Seal tube	18. Thrust washer	31. Shim	45. Bearing
5. Grommet	19. Washer	32. Spring guide	46. Bearing carrier
6. Water pump housing	20. Collar	33. Pin	47. Bearing
7. Key	21. Snap ring	34. Dog clutch	48. Seals
8. Impeller	22. Bearing	35. Retainer	49. Spacer
9. Plate	23. Level plug	36. Spring	50. Ratchet hub
10. Gasket	24. Gasket	37. Propeller shaft	51. Propeller
11. Upper bearing housing	25. Drain plug	38. Shim	52. Spacer
12. Seal	26. Housing	39. Pinion gear	53. Washer
13. Bearing	27. Bearing	40. Nut	54. Nut
14. "O" ring	28. Rod	41. Shim	55. Cotter pin

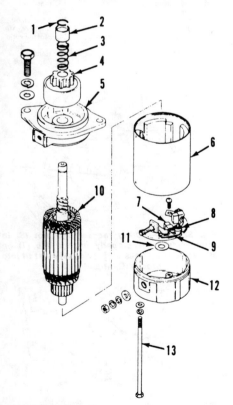

Fig. SZ11-18—Exploded view of electric start motor.

1. Retainer	
2. Stop	
3. Spring	8. Spring
4. Drive	9. Brush holder
5. Frame head	10. Armature
6. Frame	11. Thrust washer
7. Brush	12. Frame end
	13. Through-bolt

pitch on short shaft models and 279.4 mm (11 in.) pitch on long shaft models. Optional propellers are available from the manufacturer and should be selected to provide full throttle operation within the recommended limits of 4800-5500 rpm.

R&R AND OVERHAUL. Refer to Fig. SZ11-19 for exploded view of lower unit gearcase assembly. During disassembly, note the location of all shims and washers to aid in reassembly. To remove gearcase, first remove drain plug (25) and level (vent) plug (23) and drain gear lubricant. Loosen shift rod locknut (9 – Fig. SZ11-22 and turn adjustment nut (8) until upper and lower shift rods are separated. Remove cotter pin (55 – Fig. SZ11-19), nut (54), washer (53), spacer (52) and withdraw propeller (51) with ratchet hub (50). Withdraw spacer (49). Remove six lower unit cap screws. Withdraw lower unit assembly from drive shaft housing.

Remove bearing carrier (46) retaining screws. Being careful, use a suitable slide hammer and extract bearing carrier with propeller shaft assembly. Disassemble water pump assembly. Remove pinion nut (40) and withdraw pinion gear (39) and shim (38). Remove cap screws securing upper bearing hous-

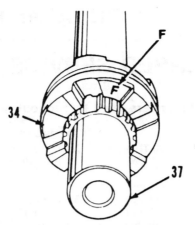

Fig. SZ11-21—Install dog clutch (34) on propeller shaft (37) so "F" mark is toward forward gear.

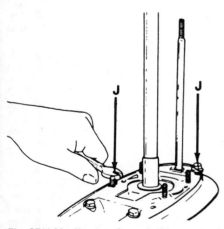

Fig. SZ11-20—Use two 6 mm jackscrews positioned as shown to withdraw upper bearing housing with drive shaft components.

ing, then use two 6mm cap screws positioned as shown in Fig. SZ11-20 and tighten screws in equal increments to withdraw upper bearing housing with drive shaft components. Remove forward gear (30 – Fig. SZ11-19) shim (29) and bearing (27). Remove screw from side of gearcase securing guide holder (13 – Fig. SZ11-22) and withdraw lower shift linkage components.

Inspect all components for excessive wear and damage. Apply a water resistant grease to lip portion of all seals. All seals and "O" rings should be renewed when unit is reassembled.

Reassemble lower unit by reversing disassembly procedure while noting the following: Install dog clutch (34 – Fig. SZ11-21) on propeller shaft (37) so "F" marked side is toward forward gear. Tighten pinion nut (40 – Fig. SZ11-19) to 18-22 N·m (13-16 ft.-lbs.). Tighten water pump housing (6) cap screws to 6-10 N·m (4-7 ft.-lbs.). Tighten bearing carrier (46) cap screws to 6-10 N·m (4-7 ft.-lbs.). Tighten propeller retaining nut to 27-30 N·m (19-21 ft.-lbs.). Assembled backlash between pinion gear (39) and forward gear (30) should be 0.1-0.2 mm (0.004-0.008 in.). Adjust thickness of shim (38) or shim (29) until recommended backlash is obtained. Recheck mesh

pattern between pinion gear and forward gear to determine if correct tooth contact is being made. Adjust pinion gear shim (38) or forward gear shim (29), if needed, to obtain correct mesh pattern. Assembled propeller shaft end play should be 0.2-0.4 mm (0.008-0.016 in.). Adjust thickness of shim (41) until recommended end play is obtained. Apply silicone sealer to lower unit and drive shaft housing mating surfaces. Tighten lower unit cap screws to 15-20 N·m (11-15 ft.-lbs.).

Adjust shift rod adjustment nut (8 – Fig. SZ11-22) until the proper engagement of "Forward," "Neutral" and "Reverse" is obtained. Tighten locknut (9) to secure adjustment nut (8) position. Fill gearcase with approximately 230 mL (7.77 ozs.) of SAE 90 hypoid outboard gear oil.

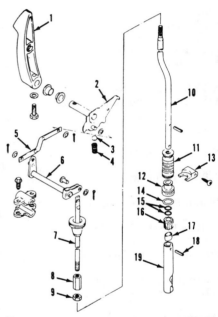

Fig. SZ11-22—Exploded view of shift control linkage components.

1. Shift lever
2. Cam
3. Detent ball
4. Detent spring
5. Rod
6. Shaft
7. Upper shift rod
8. Adustment nut
9. Locknut
10. Lower shift rod
11. Dust seal
12. Rod guide
13. Guide holder
14. "O" ring
15. "O" rings
16. Guide
17. Spacer
18. Pin
19. Shift cam

SUZUKI DT30C (After 1987)

CONDENSED SERVICE DATA

NOTE: Metric fasteners are used throughout outboard motor.

TUNE-UP

Hp/rpm	30/5000-5600 rpm
	(18.6 kW)
Number of Cylinders	3
Bore	62 mm
	(2.44 in.)
Stroke	60 mm
	(2.36 in.)
Displacement	543 cc
	(33.1 cu. in.)
Spark Plug	NGK B7HS-10
Electrode Gap	0.9-1.0 mm
	(0.035-0.039 in.)
Ignition	CDI
Carburetor:	
Make	Mikuni
Model	B26-20
Fuel:Oil Ratio	Automatic Metering

SIZES-CLEARANCES

Piston Ring End Gap	0.15-0.35 mm
	(0.006-0.014 in.)
Wear Limit	0.8 mm
	(0.030 in.)
Piston Pin Diameter	15.995-16.000 mm
	(0.6297-0.6299 in.)
Wear Limit	15.980 mm
	(0.6291 in.)
Piston Pin Bore Diameter	16.002-16.010 mm
	(0.6300-0.6303 in.)
Wear Limit	16.030 mm
	(0.6311 in.)
Standard Piston Diameter	61.920-61.935 mm
	(2.4378-2.4384 in.)
Standard Cylinder Bore	
Diameter	62.000-62.015 mm
	(2.4409-2.4415 in.)
Piston-to-Cylinder	
Clearance	0.072-0.087 mm
	(0.0028-0.0034 in.)
Wear Limit	0.167 mm
	(0.0066 in.)
Max. Crankshaft Runout	
at Main Journal	0.05 mm
	(0.002 in.)

SIZES—CLEARANCES CONT.

Max. Connecting Rod Small	
End Side Shake	5.0 mm
	(0.20 in.)

TIGHTENING TORQUES

Cylinder Head:	
6 mm	8-12 N·m
	(6-9 ft.-lbs.)
8 mm	21-25 N·m
	(15-18 ft.-lbs.)
Crankcase:	
6 mm	8-12 N·m
	(6-9 ft.-lbs.)
8 mm	20-26 N·m
	(15-19 ft.-lbs.)
Flywheel Nut	130-150 N·m
	(96-111 ft.-lbs.)
Standard Screws-	
Unmarked or Marked "4":	
5 mm	2-4 N·m
	(18-35 in.-lbs.)
6 mm	4-7 N·m
	(35-62 in.-lbs.)
8 mm	10-16 N·m
	(7-12 ft.-lbs.)
10 mm	22-35 N·m
	(16-26 ft.-lbs.)
Stainless Steel:	
5 mm	2-4 N·m
	(18-35 in.-lbs.)
6 mm	6-10 N·m
	(53-88 in.-lbs.)
8 mm	15-20 N·m
	(11-15 ft.-lbs.)
10 mm	34-41 N·m
	(25-30 ft.-lbs.)
Marked "7":	
5 mm	3-6 N·m
	(27-53 in.-lbs.)
6 mm	8-12 N·m
	(6-9 ft.-lbs.)
8 mm	18-28 N·m
	(13-21 ft.-lbs.)
10 mm	40-60 N·m
	(29-44 ft.-lbs.)

LUBRICATION

The power head is lubricated by oil mixed with the fuel. Model DT30C is equipped with automatic oil injection. Recommended oil is Suzuki Outboard Motor Oil or a good quality NMMA certified TC-WII engine oil. Recommended fuel is regular or unleaded gasoline having an 85 minimum octane rating. Manufacturer does not recommend using gasoline containing alcohol additives. However, unleaded gasoline containing ethanol (grain alcohol) may be used providing ethanol content does not exceed five percent and minimum octane rating is 85.

NOTE: Manufacturer recommends NOT using any gasoline containing methanol (wood alcohol).

During break-in (first 10 hours of operation) of a new or rebuilt engine, mix a recommended oil with the fuel at a 50:1 ratio in combination with the oil injection system to ensure adequate lubrication during break-in process. Be certain oil and fuel is thoroughly mixed in fuel tank. After initial 10 hours of operation, switch to straight gasoline in the fuel tank.

The lower unit gears and bearings are lubricated with oil contained in the gearcase. Recommended gearcase oil is Suzuki Outboard Motor Gear Oil or a suitable equivalent SAE 90 hypoid gear oil. Gearcase capacity is approximately 230 mL (7.8 ozs.). Lower unit oil should be changed after the first 10 hours of operation and after every 100 hours or seasonally thereafter. Reinstall drain and vent plugs securely, using a new gasket if necessary, to ensure watertight seal.

FUEL SYSTEM

CARBURETOR. Three Mikuni B26-20 carburetors are used. Refer to Fig. SZ11-35 for exploded view. Initial setting of pilot air screw (12) is 1½ to 2 turns out from a lightly seated position. Final adjustment should be made with engine at normal operating temperature and running in forward gear. Adjust idle speed with idle speed switch located on outside of lower cover so engine idles at approximately 650-700 rpm. Adjust pilot air screw so engine idles smoothly and will accelerate cleanly without hesitation. Readjust idle speed to 650-700 rpm is necessary.

Main fuel metering is controlled by main jet (5). Standard main jet for normal operation is #125. Standard pilot jet (11) for normal operation is #70 on 1988 models and #67.5 on 1989 models.

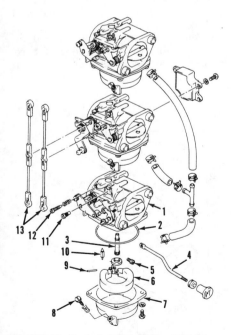

Fig. SZ11-35—Exploded view of Mikuni B26-20 carburetors used.

1. Body	8. Drain screw
2. Gasket	9. Float pin
3. High speed nozzle	10. Needle valve
4. Choke rod	11. Pilot jet
5. Main jet	12. Pilot screw
6. Float	13. Throttle control
7. Float bowl	rods

To check float level, remove float bowl (7) and invert carburetor body (1). Measure float level from float bowl mating surface to bottom of float at 180 degrees from needle valve as shown in Fig. SZ11-36. Float level should be 16.5-18.5 mm (0.65-0.73 in.). Bend tang on float to adjust float level.

FUEL FILTER. A fuel filter assembly is used to filter the fuel prior to entering the fuel pump. Periodically unscrew bowl (5—Fig. SZ11-37) and withdraw filter element (4). Clean bowl and filter element in a suitable solvent and blow dry with clean compressed air. Inspect filter element for excessive blockage or other damage and renew if necessary. Reassemble in reverse order of disassembly. Renew "O" ring (3) and seal (2) upon reassembly.

FUEL PUMP. A diaphragm-type fuel pump is used. Refer to Fig. SZ11-38 for exploded view. Fuel pump is mounted on the side of power head cylinder block and is actuated by crankcase pulsations.

When servicing pump, scribe reference marks on pump body to aid alignment during reassembly. Defective or questionable components should be renewed. Diaphragm should be renewed if air leaks or cracks are noted, or if deterioration is evident.

REED VALVES. The reed valves are located behind the intake manifold. The intake manifold must be removed to access reed block and valves assembly.

Renew reed valves (2—Fig. SZ11-39) if petals are broken, cracked, warped, rusted or bent, or if tip of petal stands open in excess of 0.2 mm (0.008 in.) from seat area. Do not attempt to bend or straighten a damaged reed petal. Reed stop opening (O) should be 3.8 mm (0.15 in.). When reassembling reed valve assembly, apply Suzuki Thread Lock 1342 or a suitable equivalent thread locking compound to threads of screws (4).

SPEED CONTROL LINKAGE. To adjust speed control linkage, loosen throttle lever adjusting screws (1—Fig. SZ11-40) on top and bottom carburetors and rotate throttle levers (2) counterclockwise to full closed position. Hold levers (2) closed and retighten screws (1). Adjust throttle link (4) so throttle arm (3) is against stopper (5) and clearance (C) is 0.5-1.5 mm (0.020-0.060 in.) with throttle in fully closed position. Make sure throttle plates are synchronized at full closed and full open positions.

If throttle cables require adjustment, loosen cable adjustment nuts and adjust cables so core wires are tight with no free movement in drum (6). Make sure arm (3) contacts stopper (5) when throt-

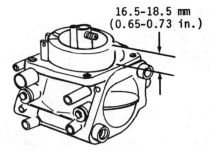

Fig. SZ11-36—Measure float level from float bowl mating surface to bottom of float 180 degrees from needle valve as shown. Bend tang on float to adjust float level.

16.5-18.5 mm (0.65-0.73 in.)

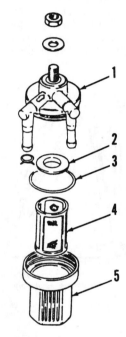

Fig. SZ11-37—Exploded view of fuel filter assembly.

1. Base	4. Filter
2. Seal	5. Bowl
3. "O" ring	

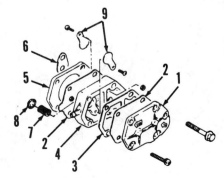

Fig. SZ11-38—Exploded view of fuel pump assembly.

1. Cover	
2. Diaphragm	6. Gasket
3. Gasket	7. Spring
4. Valve body	8. Spring seat
5. Plate	9. Check valve

tle is fully closed. Oil injection pump control linkage should be checked and/or adjusted after speed control linkage adjustment. Refer to OIL INJECTION section.

OIL INJECTION

CONTROL LINKAGE ADJUSTMENT. Make sure speed control linkage is properly adjusted. Initial length of pump control rod (5—Fig. SZ11-41) should be 77.5 mm (3.05 in.) as shown. With throttle in fully closed position, clearance (C) between lever stopper (6) and boss (7) on pump housing should be 1 mm (0.040 in.) or less, but stopper (6) should not contact boss (7). To adjust, loosen nuts (4) and adjust length of rod (5) as necessary. Make sure nuts (4) are securely tightened after adjustment. Af-

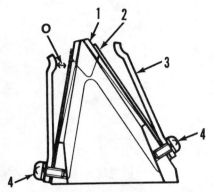

Fig. SZ11-39—Cross-sectional view of reed block and valves assembly.

1. Reed block
2. Reed petal
3. Reed stop
4. Screw
O. Reed stop opening

ter adjusting pump control linkage, recheck speed control linkage and readjust if necessary. Refer to SPEED CONTROL LINKAGE section.

OIL FLOW SENSOR. Inline filter contained in oil flow sensor should be periodically removed and cleaned in a suitable nonflammable solvent. Manufacturer recommends renewing filter if excessive plugging or contamination is noted.

To test oil flow sensor, remove sensor and connect a suitable ohmmeter between sensor red wire with blue tracer and black wire. Plug sensor inlet and connect a vacuum source to sensor outlet. With vacuum applied, ohmmeter should show continuity. Remove vacuum source and sensor should show infinity.

BLEEDING PUMP. To bleed trapped air from oil supply lines or pump, proceed as follows: Fill fuel tank with a 50:1 mixture of recommended gasoline and oil. Fill oil tank with a recommended oil. Loosen bleed screw (B—Figs. SZ11-41 or SZ11-42) two or three turns. Start engine and allow to idle at 650-700 rpm until no air bubbles are noted at bleed screw (B).

CHECKING OIL PUMP OUTPUT. Start engine and allow to warm-up for approximately five minutes. Stop engine, disconnect oil pump control rod from carburetor and remove oil tank. Connect oil gage 09900-20205 or a suitable equivalent to oil pump supply hose. Fill oil gage with a recommended oil un-

til oil is even with an upper reference mark. Bleed system as previously described. With oil pump control rod in fully closed position, start engine and allow to run at 1500 rpm for five minutes. Oil consumption should be 1.0-1.9 mL (0.035-0.065 oz.) in five minutes at 1500 rpm. Move oil pump control rod to fully open position, restart engine and allow to run at 1500 rpm for two minutes. Oil consumption should be 1.2-1.7 mL (0.04-0.06 oz.) in two minutes at 1500 rpm. Renew oil pump assembly (2—Fig. SZ11-42) if pump output is not as specified. After reinstalling oil tank, bleed air from oil injection system as previously described.

NOTE: Results of oil pump output test may vary according to weather conditions, testing error or other conditions. The manufacturer recommends repeating output test procedure two or three times to ensure the proper test results are obtained.

COOLING SYSTEM

WATER PUMP. A rubber impeller-type water pump is mounted between the drive shaft housing and gearcase. Key (7—Fig. SZ11-43) in the drive shaft is used to turn the impeller (6). If cooling system malfunction is encountered, check water intakes for plugging or partial restriction. If water intakes are clear, remove gearcase as outlined in LOWER UNIT section and check condition of water pump, water passages and sealing surfaces.

When water pump is disassembled, inspect impeller (6) and plate (8) for excessive wear or other damage. Turn

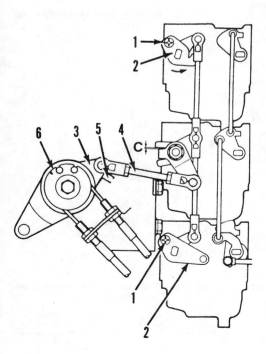

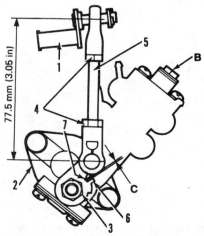

Fig. SZ11-40—View of speed control linkage. Adjust linkage as described in text.

1. Screw
2. Throttle lever
3. Throttle arm
4. Link rod
5. Stopper
6. Cable drum

Fig. SZ11-41—View of oil injection pump and control linkage. Refer to text for control linkage adjustment.

1. Throttle lever
2. Pump assy.
3. Pump lever
4. Adjustment nuts
5. Control rod
6. Stopper
7. Boss
B. Bleed screw

drive shaft clockwise (viewed from top) while placing pump housing (5) over impeller. Avoid turning drive shaft in opposite direction after water pump is reassembled.

THERMOSTAT. A thermostat is used to regulate operating temperature. Test thermostat by submersing in heated water with a suitable thermometer. Thermostat should start to open at 48°-52° C (118°-126° F). Thermostat can be removed for inspection or renewal after removing thermostat cover located in cylinder head.

ENGINE TEMPERATURE SENSOR. Engine temperature sensor is located at lower side of engine block. Sensor is normally open and changes to closed circuit when engine temperature reaches 32°-38° C (89.6°-100.4° F) on 1988 models and 36°-44° C (97°-111° F) on 1989 models. When sensor is open, ignition timing is automatically advanced approximately five degrees which increases idle speed and allows engine to warm-up quicker. When sensor closes, ignition timing and idle speed return to normal idle setting.

WATER FLOW SENSOR. Water flow sensor is located in cylinder head cover. Water flow sensor is designed to warn operator should cooling water flow to engine become insufficient. To test sensor, remove sensor from cylinder head cover and make sure sensor float moves freely. If not, remove pin securing float and carefully clean float and pin with water. Note that one side of pin hole in sensor is smaller than other side. Drive pin out toward larger hole. Connect a suitable ohmmeter between sensor wires and move float up and down. Ohmmeter reading should be zero ohm with float in down position and infinity with float in up position.

IGNITION

A breakerless, integrated circuit, capacitor discharge ignition system is used. Refer to Fig. SZ11-44 for wiring diagram. An integral ignition control module monitors throttle valve position (throttle valve sensor) and flywheel position (counter coil) and calculates and automatically adjusts ignition timing for optimum performance at all speeds above idle. Refer to Fig. SZ11-45. With throttle valves fully closed (idle speed), timing and idle speed are controlled by idle speed switch. Refer to IDLE SPEED SWITCH section.

TROUBLE-SHOOTING. If ignition malfunction occurs, check condition of spark plugs, and all wires and connections before trouble-shooting ignition system. Use only approved procedures to prevent damage to the components. The fuel system should be checked first to make certain that faulty operation is not the result of incorrect fuel mixture or contaminated fuel. Use Suzuki Pocket Tester 09900-25002 or a suitable ohmmeter to test ignition components and circuits. Refer to Figs. SZ11-44 and SZ11-46 when trouble-shooting ignition system.

CONDENSER CHARGING COIL. Flywheel must be removed for access to condenser charging coil. Make sure a suitable puller is used to remove flywheel. Disconnect condenser charging coil (5—Fig. SZ11-46) and connect tester between black wire with red tracer and green wire. Resistance should be 170-250 ohms. Renew condenser charging coil if resistance is not as specified.

PULSER COIL. Three pulser coils (2, 4 and 6—Fig. SZ11-46) are used, and if removed, must be reinstalled in original position on stator or engine will not start. Note color of pulser coil wires or mark coils for reference. Pulser coils-to-flywheel air gap should be 0.75 mm (0.03 in.) on 1988 models and 0.5 mm (0.020 in.) as shown in Fig. SZ11-47.

To test pulser coils, separate connectors leading from pulser coils. Attach one tester lead to a good engine ground and remaining tester lead to red wire with black tracer on number 1 coil, white wire with black tracer on number 2 coil and red wire with white tracer on number 3 coil. Renew pulser coil(s) if resistance is not within 170-250 ohms.

COUNTER COIL. Separate connector leading from counter coil (7—Fig. SZ11-46). Connect tester leads to orange wire with green tracer and black wire (1988 models) or black wire with green tracer (1989 models). Counter coil can be considered acceptable if resistance is within 160-240 ohms. Air gap between counter coil and flywheel ring gear teeth should be 0.5 mm (0.020 in.).

NOTE: Air gap between counter coil and flywheel ring gear teeth must be set to exactly 0.5 mm (0.020 in.) for proper operation of outboard motor. Make sure air gap is properly adjusted.

IGNITION COILS. Three ignition coils are used. Refer to Fig. SZ11-46. Separate wires at connectors leading from ignition coils and disconnect spark plug wires from coils. To test primary windings, connect tester between the following wires: Number 1 coil—orange wire and black wire; number 2 coil—blue wire and black wire; number 3 coil—gray wire and black wire. Primary winding resistance on all coils should be 0.1-0.4 ohm. Renew coil(s) if primary resistance is not as specified.

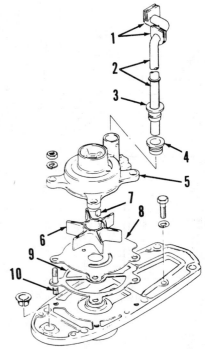

Fig. SZ11-43—Exploded view of water pump assembly.

1. Grommet		6. Impeller	
2. Water tube		7. Key	
3. Grommet		8. Plate	
4. Grommet		9. Gasket	
5. Housing		10. Stud	

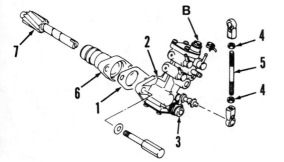

Fig. SZ11-42—Exploded view of oil injection pump assembly.

1. Gasket
2. Pump assy.
3. Pump lever
4. Adjusting nut
5. Control rod
6. Retainer
7. Driven gear

To test secondary windings, attach one tester lead to each spark plug wire terminal and remaining tester lead to orange wire on number 1 coil, blue wire on number 2 coil and gray wire on number 3 coil. Renew coil(s) if resistance is not within 1900-2700 ohms.

THROTTLE VALVE SENSOR. To test throttle valve sensor (5—Fig. SZ11-48), remove alignment pin attached to cover over throttle valve sensor and insert alignment pin (1) into hole in sensor and sensor cam (3). Align slot in cam (3) with throttle shaft. Disconnect throttle valve sensor connector (4). Connect test harness 09930-89530 or suitable jumper wires to a battery as shown in Fig. SZ11-48. Battery voltage must be nine volts or more. Connect positive (+) lead of a suitable digital voltmeter to test harness light green wire with red tracer and voltmeter negative (−) lead to battery

negative (−) terminal as shown. With throttle fully closed, voltmeter reading should be 0.45-0.55 volt. If not, remove rubber cap (2) and turn adjustment screw (under cap) as necessary to obtain the correct voltage reading. Note that turning adjustment screw clockwise will increase voltage and counterclockwise will decrease voltage.

NOTE: The manufacturer recommends using only a nonmetallic screwdriver to turn sensor adjusting screw or sensor voltmeter reading may not be valid. If metal screwdriver must be used, remove screwdriver from area of throttle valve sensor after adjustment to prevent erroneous voltmeter reading.

If sensor output voltage at closed throttle is below 0.45 volt, idle speed ignition timing will be fixed at 5 degrees BTDC and idle speed switch will be in-

operative. If sensor output voltage at closed throttle is above 0.55 volt, ignition timing at idle speed will not be correct. Refer to IDLE SPEED SWITCH section.

Once the specified voltage reading is obtained at closed throttle, remove alignment pin and open carburetor to wide-open throttle. Voltmeter reading should now be 2.7 volts or more. Do not attempt to adjust wide-open throttle sensor voltage. If wide-open throttle sensor voltage is not 2.7 volts or higher, renew sensor.

If throttle valve sensor is removed or renewed, install as follows: Insert alignment pin (1) as shown to align cam and sensor shaft. Align slot in sensor cam with carburetor throttle shaft and install sensor on carburetor. Lightly tighten mounting screws (7) to allow for adjustment of sensor position on carburetor. Connect test harness and

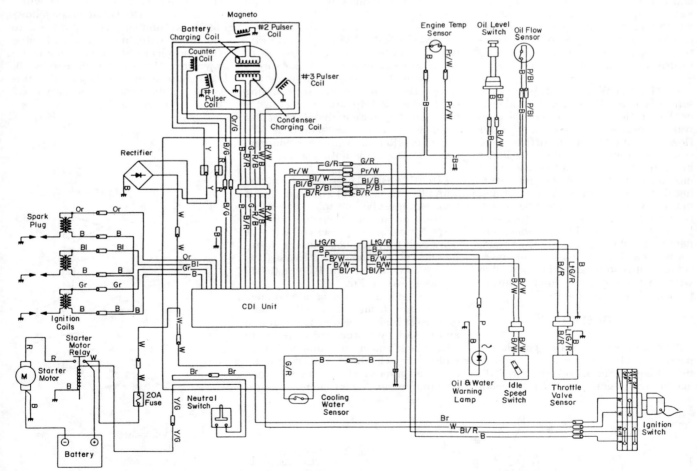

Fig. SZ11-44—Wiring diagram of electrical system on models equipped with electric starter.

B. Black					
G. Green	Pr. Purple				
P. Pink	B/G. Black with	R/B. Red with black	W/B. White with	Bl/B. Blue with black	Or/G. Orange with
R. Red	green tracer	tracer	black tracer	tracer	green tracer
Y. Yellow	B/R. Black with red	R/G. Red with green	W/R. White with red	Bl/P. Blue with pink	P/Bl. Pink with blue
W. White	tracer	tracer	tracer	tracer	tracer
Bl. Blue	B/W. Black with	R/W. Red with white	Y/B. Yellow with	Bl/R. Blue with red	Pr/W. Purple with
Br. Brown	white tracer	tracer	black tracer	tracer	white tracer
Gr. Gray	G/R. Green with red	R/Y. Red with yellow	Y/G. Yellow with	Bl/W. Blue with white	Lt G/R. Light green
Or. Orange	tracer	tracer	green tracer	tracer	with red tracer

Illustrations courtesy Suzuki

digital voltmeter as shown in Fig. SZ11-48. Make sure battery voltage is nine volts or more. Sensor output voltage at closed throttle should be 0.45-0.55 volt. If not, move position of sensor on carburetor to obtain specified voltage and securely tighten screws (7). Recheck voltage after tightening screws (7) and if necessary, remove cap (2) and turn adjustment screw to obtain 0.45-0.55 volt. Be sure to reinstall cap (2). After obtaining the correct voltage at closed throttle, remove alignment pin and check sensor output voltage at wide-open throttle. Voltage should be 2.7 volts or higher. Do not attempt to adjust wide-open throttle voltage.

IDLE SPEED SWITCH. Idle speed switch (8—Fig. SZ11-46) malfunction can be quickly verified by checking ignition timing and engine rpm while switching position of idle speed switch. Make sure engine is at idle speed when checking timing.

NOTE: A defective or maladjusted throttle valve sensor may cause idle speed switch to be inoperative or ignition timing at idle speed to be incorrect. Prior to testing idle speed switch, make sure throttle valve sensor is operating properly and correctly adjusted. Refer to THROTTLE VALVE SENSOR section.

Ignition timing at idle speed should be as shown in Fig. SZ11-49. Note that each position of switch should change engine idle speed approximately 50 rpm. If timing and engine rpm do not change with each switch position, idle speed switch is defective and must be renewed.

To test idle speed switch with Suzuki Pocket Tester 09900-25002 or a suitable ohmmeter, disconnect idle switch and connect tester between black wires with white tracer (Fig. SZ11-44). Switch resistance on 1988 models should be as follows: Position (A—Fig. SZ11-49)—zero ohm; position (B)—2200 ohms; position (C)—4700 ohms; position (D)—13,000 ohms; position (E)—infinity. Switch resistance on 1989 models should be as follows: Position (A—Fig. SZ11-49)—zero ohm; position B—11,000 ohms; position C—22,000 ohms; position D—68,000 ohms; position E—infinity. Renew idle speed switch if resistance values are not as specified.

If no components are found to be defective in the previous tests and ignition system malfunction is still suspected, install a known good CDI module and recheck engine operation.

CHARGING SYSTEM

BATTERY CHARGING COIL. Refer to Fig. SZ11-44. Flywheel must be re-

moved for access to battery charging coil. Be sure to use a suitable flywheel puller to remove flywheel. To test coil, separate wires at connectors leading from battery charging coil. On manual start models, connect one lead of Suzuki Pocket Tester 09900-25002 to terminal of yellow wire with red tracer and remaining tester lead to terminal of yellow wire. On models equipped with

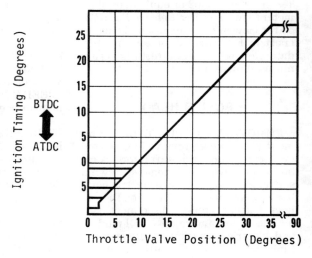

Fig. SZ11-45—Chart showing ignition timing in relation to throttle valve position.

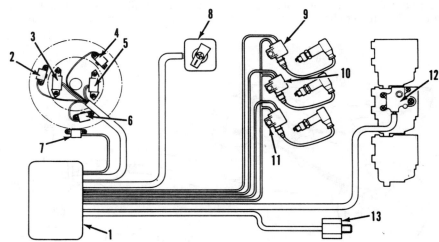

Fig. SZ11-46—Diagram of ignition system components.

1. CDI module
2. Number 2 pulser coil
3. Battery charging coil
4. Number 3 pulser coil
5. Condenser charging coil
6. Number 1 pulser coil
7. Counter coil
8. Idle speed switch
9. Number 1 ignition coil
10. Number 2 ignition coil
11. Number 3 ignition coil
12. Throttle valve sensor
13. Engine temperature sensor

Fig. SZ11-47—Air gap between pulser coils and flywheel should be 0.75 mm (0.029 in.) on 1988 models and 0.5 mm (0.020 in.) on 1989 models measured.

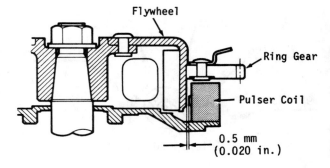

electric start, connect one tester lead to red wire and remaining tester lead to yellow wire. Battery charging coil can be considered acceptable if resistance is within 0.2-0.6 ohm.

RECTIFIER. Use Suzuki Pocket Tester 09900-25002 or equivalent ohmmeter to test rectifier. Refer to Fig. SZ11-50 for view of rectifier assembly and to chart in Fig. SZ11-51 for rectifier test data. Renew rectifier if test results are not as shown in chart.

POWER HEAD

REMOVE AND REINSTALL. To remove power head, remove engine cover, disconnect neutral start interlock cable from lever and remove rewind starter assembly. Remove electric parts holder cover and rectifier cover. Disconnect battery cables, disconnect CDI module wires, and remove CDI module and electric parts holder. Remove oil tank and disconnect throttle valve sensor, choke solenoid, warning lamp, idle speed switch and fuel hose. Disconnect ignition coil wires, remove silencer cover and disconnect choke lever. Remove

eight cap screws and separate power head from drive shaft housing.

Before reinstalling power head, make certain drive shaft splines are clean, then apply a light coat of water-resistant grease to shaft splines. Install power head on drive shaft housing while rotating propeller shaft to assist alignment of drive shaft and crankshaft splines. Apply a suitable silicone sealant to threads of retaining screws, then tighten screws to 15-20 N·m (11-15 ft.-lbs.). Remainder of installation is the reverse of removal procedure. Refer to SPEED CONTROL LINKAGE for adjustment procedure.

DISASSEMBLY. Disassemble power head as follows: Remove exhaust tube, carburetors, throttle control lever, rectifier, starter relay and starter motor. Remove fuel filter, fuel pump, oil pump, oil hoses, choke solenoid and intake manifold screws. Carefully pry off intake manifold using a screwdriver or suitable tool. Use caution not to damage mating surfaces. Remove rewind starter mounting brackets, ignition coils, engine temperature sensor, counter coil and starter pulley. Use a suitable puller and remove flywheel. Remove stator as-

sembly, cylinder head, exhaust cover, thermostat cover and thermostat. Remove 14 crankcase screws and carefully separate crankcase from cylinder block. Crankshaft assembly can now be removed from crankcase.

REASSEMBLY. Refer to specific service sections when reassembling the crankshaft, connecting rods, pistons and reed valves. Make sure all joint and gasket surfaces are clean and free from nicks and burrs. Cylinder head and block mating surfaces should not be warped in excess of 0.30 mm (0.012 in.). Cylinder head and block mating surfaces may be lapped using #400 or finer emery paper. Use caution when lapping to not remove any more material than necessary to true mating surfaces. Make sure all carbon, salt, dirt and sand are cleaned from the combustion chambers, exhaust ports and water passages. Lubricate crankpin bearings and cylinder walls with Suzuki Outboard Motor Oil or a suitable NMMA certified TC-WII engine oil. Coat crankcase-to-cylinder block mating surface with Suzuki Bond 1207B or suitable equivalent sealant. Tighten crankcase screws in sequence shown in Fig. SZ11-52. Tighten 6 mm screws to 8-12 N·m (6-9 ft.-lbs.) and 8 mm screws to 20-26 N·m (15-19 ft.-lbs.). Make sure two long clamps (L) are mounted on crankcase where shown. Rotate crankshaft after reassembling crankcase to check for locking or abnormal noise. If locking or abnormal noise is noted, crankcase must be disassembled to determine cause and repaired. Tighten cylinder head screws in sequence shown in Fig. SZ11-53. Tighten 6 mm screws to 8-12 N·m (6-9 ft.-lbs.) and 8 mm screws to 21-25 N·m (15-18 ft.-lbs.). Install clamps (C) where shown. Make sure mating surface of flywheel is clean prior to installation. Tighten flywheel nut to 130-150 N·m (96-111 ft.-lbs.) using appropriate tools. Refer to CONDENSED SERVICE DATA for other fastener tightening values.

PISTONS, PINS, RINGS AND CYLINDERS. Refer to CONDENSED SERVICE DATA for pistons, pins, rings

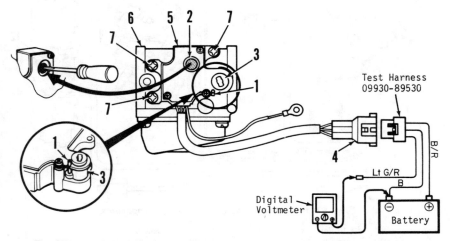

Fig. SZ11-48—Refer to text for throttle valve sensor testing and installation procedure.

1. Alignment pin	4. Connector	7. Mounting screw
2. Cap (adjustment screw)	5. Throttle valve sensor assy.	B. Black
3. Sensor cam	6. Carburetor	B/R. Black with red tracer
		LtG/R. Light green with red tracer

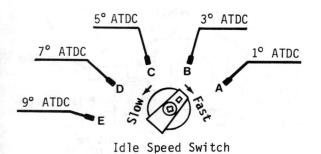

Idle Speed Switch

Fig. SZ11-49—Ignition timing at idle speed should be as shown at the corresponding idle speed switch positions.

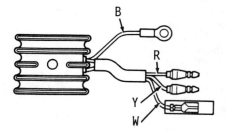

Fig. SZ11-50—View of rectifier assembly. Refer to chart in Fig. SZ11-51 to test rectifier.

and cylinder service specifications. Each piston is fitted with two piston rings. Pistons are equipped with locating pins in ring grooves to prevent piston ring rotation. Measure piston diameter 23 mm (0.9 in.) up from bottom of skirt at a right angle to piston pin bore. Pistons and rings are available in standard size and 0.25 mm (0.010 in.) and 0.50 mm (0.020 in.) oversize. Install pistons on connecting rods so arrow on piston crown will face exhaust ports upon reassembly. All cylinders should be bored to next oversize if any cylinder is out-of-round or tapered in excess of 0.10 mm (0.004 in.).

CRANKSHAFT, CONNECTING RODS AND BEARINGS. Connecting rods, bearings and crankshaft are a press together unit. Crankshaft should be disassembled ONLY by experienced service personnel using appropriate service equipment.

Determine connecting rod bearing wear from side-to-side movement as shown in Fig. SZ11-55. Normal side-to-side movement (A) is 5.0 mm (0.197 in.) or less. If movement exceeds 5.0 mm (0.197 in.), connecting rod, crankpin and crankpin needle bearing should be renewed. Maximum allowable crankshaft runout is 0.05 mm (0.002 in.) measured at bearing surfaces with ends of crankshaft supported in V-blocks.

Apply Suzuki Super Grease "A" or a suitable equivalent to seal lips. When installing crankshaft assembly into cylinder block, make sure seals properly engage grooves in block. Make sure bearing pins properly engage notches in cylinder block.

MANUAL STARTER

Refer to Fig. SZ11-56 for exploded view of manual rewind starter assembly. To remove starter assembly, remove screw (18) and clamp (19), detach neutral start cable (12) and remove three screws securing starter assembly to power head. To disassemble starter, remove cotter pin (13), washer (14), arm (15), spring (16) and lever (17). To relieve rewind spring tension, invert starter housing and grasp a section of rope, place rope into notch (N—Fig. SZ11-57) provided in rope pulley (7). Holding rope as shown, allow pulley (7) to rotate

clockwise relieving rewind spring tension. Remove screw (2—Fig. SZ11-56), plate (3) and friction spring (4). Remove pawl (5) and spring (6), then carefully lift out rope pulley (7) making sure rewind spring (8) remains in housing (11). Using suitable hand and eye protection, carefully remove rewind spring (8) from housing (11).

Inspect all components for excessive wear or other damage and renew as necessary. Reassemble starter in the reverse order of disassembly noting the following: Starting with inner coil, wind rewind spring into housing in clockwise direction. Apply a suitable water-resistant grease to rewind spring. Wind rope onto pulley (7) 2½ turns in counterclockwise direction (viewed from flywheel side) and install pulley (7) into housing. Make sure pulley properly engages hook on inner coil of rewind spring. Apply water resistant grease to both sides of plate (3). To preload rewind spring, place rope into notch of rope pulley as shown in Fig. SZ11-57 and rotate rope pulley four turns counterclockwise. Release rope and allow remaining rope to wind onto pulley. Install starter assembly on power head and connect neutral start cable. With clutch lever in neutral position, slot (S—Fig. SZ11-58) should align with mark (N) on housing (11). With clutch lever in for-

ward or reverse gear, slot (S) should be centered between marks (M). Loosen screw (18) and move cable (12) to adjust. Make sure starter will operate only in neutral position.

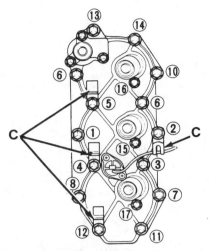

Fig. SZ11-53—Tighten cylinder head screws in sequence shown. Tighten 6 mm screws to 8-12 N·m (6-9 ft.-lbs.) and 8 mm screws to 21-25 N·m (15-18 ft.-lbs.). Note location of clamps (C).

Fig. SZ11-52—Tighten crankcase screws in sequence shown. Tighten 6 mm screws to 8-12 N·m (6-9 ft.-lbs.) and 8 mm screws to 20-26 N·m (15-19 ft.-lbs.). Make sure long clamps (L) are positioned as shown.

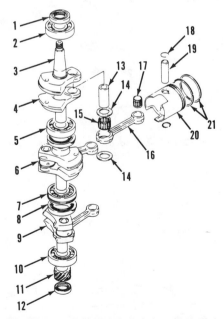

Fig. SZ11-54—Exploded view of piston and crankshaft assembly.

1. Seal	11. Oil pump drive gear
2. Main bearing	12. Seal
3. Crank half	13. Crank pin
4. Crank half	14. Thrust washer
5. Main bearing	15. Needle bearing
6. Center crankshaft assy.	16. Connecting rod
7. Main bearing	17. Needle bearing
8. Seal	18. Retainer
9. Lower crankshaft assy.	19. Piston pin
10. Main bearing	20. Piston
	21. Piston rings

Fig. SZ11-51—Refer to Fig. SZ11-50 and use chart shown to test rectifier assembly.

		(+) LEAD OF TESTER			
		Black	White	Yellow	Red
(–) LEAD OF TESTER	Black		5,500-8,500 Ω	2,200-3,200 Ω	2,200-3,200 Ω
	White	∞		∞	∞
	Yellow	∞	2,200-3,200 Ω		∞
	Red	∞	1,700-2,700 Ω	∞	

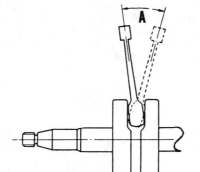

Fig. SZ11-55—Move connecting rod small end side-to-side to determine connecting rod, bearing and crankpin wear. Maximum allowable small end play (A) is 5.0 mm (0.197 in.).

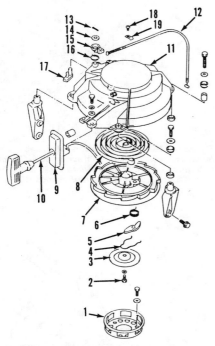

Fig. SZ11-56—Exploded view of manual starter assembly.

1. Cup	11. Housing
2. Screw	12. Neutral start cable
3. Plate	13. Cotter pin
4. Friction spring	14. Washer
5. Pawl	15. Arm
6. Spring	16. Spring
7. Rope pulley	17. Lever
8. Rewind spring	18. Screw
9. Rope guide	19. Clamp
10. Rope	

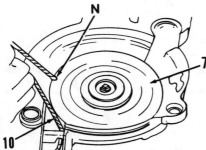

Fig. SZ11-57—To relieve rewind spring tension, grasp rope (10) as shown, place rope into notch (N) and allow pulley (7) to rotate clockwise.

ELECTRIC STARTER

Refer to Fig. SZ11-59 for exploded view of electric starter assembly used on models so equipped. Disassembly is evident after inspection of unit and referral to exploded view. Standard commutator outside diameter is 30 mm (1.18 in.). Renew armature (6) if commutator is worn to less than 29 mm (1.14 in.). Standard undercut between commutator segments is 0.5-0.8 mm (0.020-0.031 in.) with a minimum allowable undercut of 0.2 mm (0.008 in.). Renew brushes (8) if worn to 9 mm (0.354 in.) or less. During reassembly, make sure upper and lower alignment marks on frame (7) align with notches in end frames (5 and 10). Tighten through-bolts (11) to 15-20 N·m (11-15 ft.-lbs.). Bench test starter prior to installing on power head.

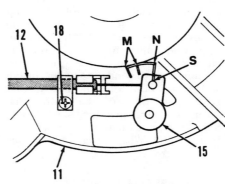

Fig. SZ11-58—With clutch lever in neutral position, slot (S) in arm (15) should align with mark (N) on housing (11). With clutch lever in forward or reverse gear, slot (S) should be in center of marks (M). Loosen screw (18) and move cable (12) to adjust.

LOWER UNIT

PROPELLER AND DRIVE CLUTCH. Protection for the motor is built into a special cushioning clutch in the propeller hub. No adjustment is possible on the propeller or clutch. Three-blade propellers are used. Propellers are available from the manufacturer in various diameters and pitches and should be selected to provide optimum performance at full throttle within the recommended limits of 5000-5600 rpm.

R&R AND OVERHAUL. Refer to Fig. SZ11-60 for exploded view of lower unit gearcase assembly. During disassembly, note the location of all shims and washers to aid in reassembly.

To remove gearcase, first remove drain plug (25) and level plugs (23) and drain gearcase lubricant. Loosen shift rod locknut (6—Fig. SZ11-61) and turn adjustment nut (5) until upper and lower shift rods are separated. Remove six screws and separate gearcase assembly from drive shaft housing. Remove propeller and two screws securing bearing carrier (36—Fig. SZ11-60) to gearcase (27). Using a suitable slide hammer type puller, carefully extract bearing carrier and propeller shaft assembly. Remove water pump housing (4), impeller (6), key (5), plate (7) and gasket (8). Install drive shaft holder 09921-29610 or equivalent on upper spline of drive shaft (14), then remove pinion gear nut (30) by turning drive shaft. Remove two remaining screws securing bearing housing (9) to gearcase. Use two 6 mm screws positioned as shown in Fig. SZ11-62 and tighten screws in equal increments to

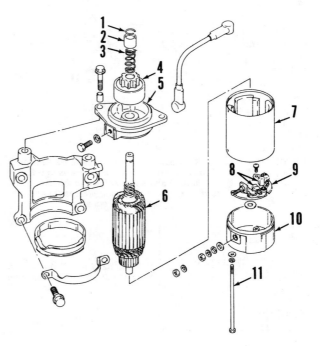

Fig. SZ11-59—Exploded view of electric starter assembly.

1. Retainer
2. Stop
3. Spring
4. Drive assy.
5. End frame
6. Armature
7. Frame
8. Brushes
9. Brush holder
10. End frame
11. Through-bolt

withdraw upper bearing housing and drive shaft components. Reach into gearcase and remove pinion gear (29—Fig. SZ11-60), shim (28), forward gear (54), shim (55) and bearing (57). Refer to Fig. SZ11-63 and remove screw securing shift rod guide holder (10—Fig. SZ11-61). Lift lower shift rod assembly out top of gearcase.

Inspect all components for excessive wear or other damage. Apply a suitable water-resistant grease to lip area of all seals. Renew all seals, gaskets and "O" rings upon reassembly.

Reassemble lower unit in reverse order of disassembly noting the following: Install dog clutch (51—Fig. SZ11-64) on propeller shaft (47) so side marked "F" is toward forward gear (54—Fig. SZ11-60). If removed, install pinion bearing (22) into gearcase using a suitable driver. Be sure lettered side of bearing (22) faces up. Apply Suzuki Thread Lock 1342 or a suitable equivalent to threads of pinion nut (30) and tighten nut to 27-30 N·m (20-22 ft.-lbs.). Forward gear-to-pinion gear backlash should be 0.1-0.2 mm (0.004-0.008 in.). Adjust thickness

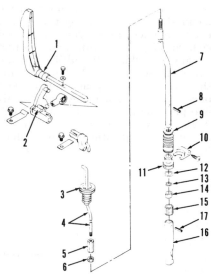

Fig. SZ11-61—Exploded view of shift control linkage components.

1. Shift lever		10. Guide holder	
2. Lever		11. Guide	
3. Boot		12. "O" ring	
4. Upper shift rod		13. "O" ring	
5. Adjustment nut		14. Spacer	
6. Locknut		15. Magnet	
7. Lower shift rod		16. Shift cam	
8. Pin		17. Pin	
9. Boot			

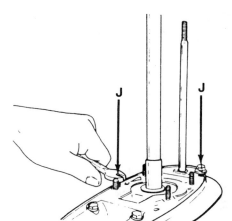

Fig. SZ11-62—Use two 6 mm jackscrews (J) to withdraw upper bearing housing with drive shaft components.

Fig. SZ11-60—Exploded view of lower unit gearcase assembly.

1. Grommet	15. Washer	30. Nut	44. Washer
2. Water tube	16. Spring	31. Shim	45. Nut
3. Grommet	17. Thrust washer	32. Reverse gear	46. Cotter pin
4. Water pump housing	18. Washer	33. Shim	47. Propeller shaft
5. Key	19. Collar	34. "O" ring	48. Spring
6. Impeller	20. Barrier	35. Bearing	49. Retainer
7. Plate	21. Snap ring	36. Bearing carrier	50. Pin
8. Gasket	22. Bearing	37. Bearing	51. Dog clutch
9. Bearing housing	23. Level plug	38. Seal	52. Pin
10. Seal	24. Gasket	39. Seal	53. Thrust washer
11. Bearing	25. Drain plug	40. Spacer	54. Forward gear
12. "O" ring	26. Gasket	41. Bushing	55. Shim
13. Bushing	27. Gearcase	42. Propeller	56. Push rod
14. Drive shaft	28. Shim	43. Spacer	57. Bearing
	29. Pinion gear		

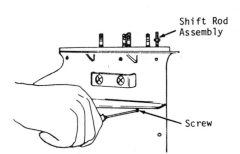

Fig. SZ11-63—To remove lower shift rod assembly, remove screw securing shift rod guide holder and pull shift rod out top of gearcase.

of shims (28 and 55) to obtain specified backlash. After obtaining the proper backlash, check pinion gear-to-forward gear mesh pattern. Add and subtract equally from shims (28 and 55) to obtain correct mesh pattern while maintaining the correct forward gear-to-pinion gear backlash. Assembled propeller shaft end play should be 0.2-0.4 mm (0.008-0.016 in.). Adjust thickness of shim (31) to obtain the specified propeller shaft

end play. Recheck pinion gear backlash. If necessary, adjust thickness of reverse gear shim (33) so backlash is the same as previously adjusted forward gear-to-

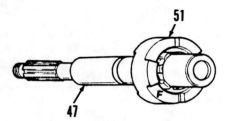

Fig. SZ11-64—Install dog clutch (51) on propeller shaft (47) so the "F" mark is facing forward.

pinion gear backlash setting. Tighten propeller shaft bearing carrier (36) screws to 15-20 N·m (11-15 ft.-lbs.).

Adjust shift rod adjustment nut (5 Fig. SZ11-61) until the proper engagement of "Forward," "Neutral" and "Reverse" is obtained. Tighten locknut (6) to secure adjustment nut. Refer to LUBRICATION section and fill gearcase with the appropriate type and amount of lubricant.

SUZUKI DT40
(Prior To 1984)

CONDENSED SERVICE DATA

NOTE: Metric fasteners are used throughout outboard motor.

TUNE-UP

	DT40
Hp	40
Bore	76 mm
Stroke	68 mm
Number of Cylinders	2
Displacement	617 cc
Spark Plug:	
NGK	B8HS
Electrode Gap	0.8-0.9 mm
Magneto:	
Breaker Point Gap	Breakerless
Carburetor:	
Make	Mikuni
Model	B401-32
Fuel:Oil Ratio	50:1

SIZES—CLEARANCES

Piston Ring End Gap	0.2-0.4 mm
Piston Pin Diameter	17.995-18.000 mm
Piston to Cylinder Wall	
Clearance	0.061-0.082 mm
Max. Crankshaft Runout at	
Main Bearing Journal	0.05 mm
Max. Con. Rod Small	
End Side Shake	5.0 mm

TIGHTENING TORQUES

Cylinder Head:	
6 mm	8-10 N·m
8 mm	20-23 N·m
Crankcase:	
6 mm	8-12 N·m
10 mm	40-60 N·m
Exhaust Cover	8-10 N·m
Flywheel Nut	200 N·m
Gearcase Pinion Nut	35 N·m
Propeller Shaft Nut	50 N·m
Standard Screws:	
Unmarked or Marked "4"	
5 mm	2-4 N·m
6 mm	4-7 N·m
8 mm	10-16 N·m
10 mm	22-35 N·m
Marked "7"	
5 mm	3-6 N·m
6 mm	8-12 N·m
8 mm	18-28 N·m
10 mm	40-60 N·m

LUBRICATION

The power head is lubricated by oil mixed with the fuel. Fuel:oil ratios should be 30:1 during break-in of a new or rebuilt engine and 50:1 for normal service when using an NMMA certified TC-WII, two-stroke engine oil or Suzuki "CCI" oil. If using any other type two-stroke engine oil, fuel:oil ratios should be 20:1 during break-in and 30:1 for normal service. Manufacturer recommends regular or no-lead automotive gasoline with octane of 85-95. Gasoline and oil should be thoroughly mixed.

The lower unit gears and bearings are lubricated by oil contained in the gearcase. SAE 90 hypoid outboard gear oil should be used. The gearcase should be drained and refilled after every 50 hours of use with 480 mL of gear oil. Reinstall vent and fill plugs securely, using a new gasket if necessary, to ensure a water tight seal.

FUEL SYSTEM

CARBURETOR. A Mikuni, type B401-32 carburetor is used. Refer to Fig. SZ12-1 for exploded view. Initial setting of pilot air screw (6) should be two turns out from a lightly seated position. Final carburetor adjustment should be made with engine at normal operating temperature and running in forward gear. Adjust throttle stop screw (4) so engine idles at approximately 650-700 rpm. Adjust pilot air screw so engine idles smoothly and will accelerate cleanly without hesitation. If necessary, readjust throttle stop screw to obtain 650-700 rpm idle speed.

Main fuel metering is controlled by main jet (10). Standard main jet size for normal operation is #200 on all models.

To check float level, remove float bowl and invert carburetor. Distance (A – Fig. SZ12-2) between main jet and bottom of float should be 16.7-18.7 mm. Adjust float level by bending float arm tang.

SPEED CONTROL LINKAGE. Ignition timing advance and throttle opening must be synchronized so that throttle is opened as timing is advanced.

To synchronize the linkage, first make certain that ignition timing is correctly set as outlined in IGNITION TIMING

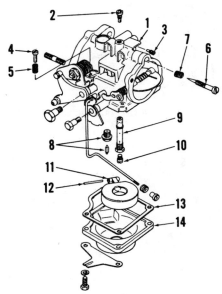

Fig. SZ12-1—Exploded view of Mikuni carburetor typical of all models.

1. Body	8. Inlet valve
2. Pilot jet	9. Main nozzle
3. Air jet	10. Main jet
4. Throttle stop screw	11. Float
5. Spring	12. Float pin
6. Pilot air screw	13. Gasket
7. Spring	14. Float bowl

section. Determine type of ignition system used, as noted in IGNITION section, then refer to Fig. SZ12-3 and adjust the length of stator link (S), carburetor link (C) and lower link (L) using values listed in the following table. Measure link rod lengths between adjusting nuts as shown on lower link (L).

Independent Ignition	Rod Length
Stator rod (S)	30 mm
Carburetor rod (C)	155.5 mm
Lower rod (L)	91 mm

Simultaneous Ignition	Rod Length
Stator rod (S)	37 mm
Carburetor rod (C)	155 mm
Lower rod (L)	92 mm

REED VALVES. The inlet reed valves are located on a reed plate between inlet manifold and crankcase. The reed petals should seat very lightly against the reed plate throughout their entire length with the least possible tension. Tip of reed petal must not stand open more than 0.2 mm from contact surface. Reed stop opening should be 9.9 mm.

Renew reeds if petals are broken, cracked, warped, rusted or bent. Never attempt to bend a reed petal or to straighten a damaged reed. Never install a bent or damaged reed. Seating surface of reed plate should be smooth and flat. When installing reeds or reed stop, make sure that petals are centered over the inlet holes in reed plate, and that the reed stops are centered over reed petals.

FUEL PUMP. A diaphragm type fuel pump is mounted on the side of power head cylinder block and is actuated by pressure and vacuum pulsations from the engine crankcases. Refer to Fig. SZ12-5 for exploded view of fuel pump assembly.

When servicing pump, scribe reference marks across pump body to aid in reassembly. Defective or questionable parts should be renewed. Diaphragm should be renewed if air leaks or cracks are found, or if deterioration is evident.

IGNITION

All models are equipped with either an independent or simultaneous, pointless electronic ignition system. One ignition coil is used on models with a simultaneous ignition system while two ignition coils are used on models with an independent ignition system. Refer to Fig. SZ12-6 for wiring diagram used on independent ignition models. Models with simultaneous ignition systems are similar.

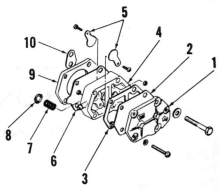

Fig. SZ12-5 — Exploded view of diaphragm type fuel pump assembly.

1. Cover	6. Diaphragm
2. Diaphragm	7. Spring
3. Gasket	8. Spring seat
4. Body	9. Base
5. Pump plates	10. Gasket

IGNITION TIMING. On independent ignition models, ignition timing should be 6° ATDC at 1000 rpm and 25° BTDC at 5000 rpm. On simultaneous ignition models, ignition timing should be 2° ATDC at 1000 rpm and 25° BTDC at 5000 rpm. On all models, initial setting of ignition timing may be accomplished by centering mark (M – Fig. SZ12-7) on stator plate with crankcase and cylinder block mating surfaces then adjust stator plate stop (S) so tab (T) just contacts boss on cylinder block.

Final ignition timing check can be made using a suitable power timing light. Immerse outboard in water and connect timing light to upper spark plug. Set engine throttle at full retard position and start engine. Refer to ignition timing specifications stated previously and check alignment of flywheel timing marks with index mark on flywheel cover. To check advance ignition timing, run engine at wide open throttle and note timing marks. Reposition stator plate stop to adjust ignition timing.

TROUBLE-SHOOTING. If ignition malfunction occurs, check and make sure malfunction is not due to spark plug, wiring or wiring connection failure. If spark is absent at both cylinders, first check neutral start interlock (NSI) operation. Check neutral switch adjustment; switch should depress at least 1 mm when shift linkage is in neutral position. Check condition of neutral switch (17 – Fig. SZ12-6) using Suzuki pocket tester number 09900-25002 or a suitable ohmmeter. Separate the wire connectors between switch (17) and NSI module (16) and attach a tester lead to each wire connected to switch. With shift linkage in neutral position, tester should read zero resistance. Moving shift linkage to "F" or "R" positions

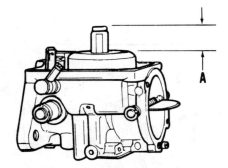

Fig. SZ12-2 — Float level (A) should be 16.7-18.7 mm.

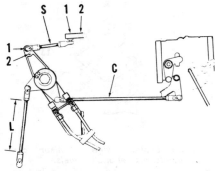

Fig. SZ12-3 — View of speed control linkage. Stator link (S) should be installed at position (1) for independent ignition and position (2) for simultaneous ignition. Refer to text for adjustment procedure.

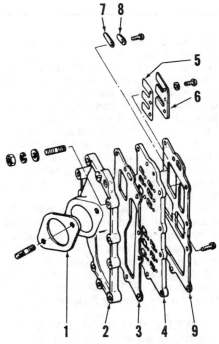

Fig. SZ12-4 — Exploded view of intake manifold and reed valve assembly.

1. Gasket	6. Reed stop
2. Manifold	7. Lubrication valve
3. Gasket	8. Valve stop
4. Reed plate	9. Gasket
5. Reed petals	

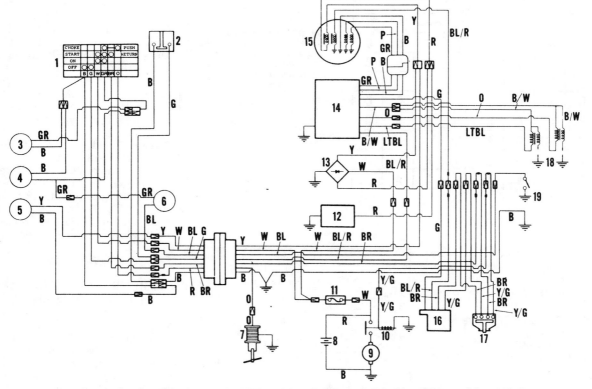

Fig. SZ12-6—Typical wiring diagram for DT40 models with independent ignition. Other models are similar.

1. Ignition switch	6. Overheat buzzer	11. 20 amp fuse	15. Stator	B. Black	Lt.Bl. Light blue
2. Emergency stop switch	7. Choke solenoid	12. Regulator	16. NSI module	BL. Blue	O. Orange
3. Hour meter	8. Battery	13. Rectifier	17. Neutral switch	BR. Brown	R. Red
4. Volt meter	9. Starter motor	14. CD ignition	18. Spark plugs	G. Green	W. White
5. Tachometer	10. Starter relay	module	19. Overheat sensor	GR. Gray	Y. Yellow

should cause tester to read infinite resistance. Renew neutral switch if required.

To check condition of NSI module, use tester or ohmmeter in conjunction with test chart shown in Fig. SZ12-8. Renew NSI module if required.

Trouble-shoot ignition circuit using Suzuki pocket tester number 09900-25002 or ohmmeter as follows:

Independent Ignition Models. On independent ignition models, check condition of capacitor charge coil (2 – Fig. SZ12-9) by separating the blue/red wire connector and black wire connector at stator and attach a tester lead to each

wire. Charge coil may be considered satisfactory if resistance reading is within the limits of 225-275 ohms.

Check condition of pulser coils (4) by separating the gray wire connector, pink wire connector and black wire connector at stator and attach tester positive lead to black wire. Attach negative lead to gray wire and note tester reading and then to pink wire and note tester reading. Resistance reading for each pulser coil should be within the limits of 180-220 ohms.

Check condition of each ignition coil as follows: Separate the orange wire connector and black/white wire connector at coil for top cylinder, then attach a tester lead to each wire and note tester reading. Separate light blue wire connector and black/white wire connector at coil for bottom cylinder, then attach a tester lead to each wire and note tester reading. Primary coil resistance reading should be within the limits of 0.87-1.17 ohms for each coil. Disconnect high tension wires from spark plugs. Attach

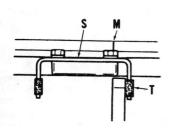

Fig. SZ12-7—Set ignition timing statically by centering mark (M) on stator plate with crankcase and cylinder block mating surface. Refer to text.

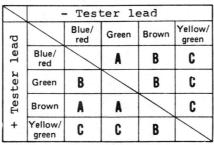

		– Tester lead			
		Blue/red	Green	Brown	Yellow/green
+ Tester lead	Blue/red		A	B	C
	Green	B		B	C
	Brown	A	A		C
	Yellow/green	C	C	B	

Fig. SZ12-8 – Use chart shown above and values listed below to test condition of NSI module.

A. 200k ohms or less
B. 200k ohms or more
C. Tester needle should show deflection then return toward infinite resistance

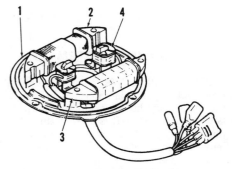

Fig. SZ12-9 – View of independent ignition stator plate components.

1. Stator plate
2. Capacitor charge coil
3. Lighting coil
4. Pulser coil

		\- Tester lead						
		Green	Grey	Pink	Black	Blue/red	Orange	Light blue	Black/white
Tester lead +	Green		A	A	A	B	C	C	C
	Grey	B		B	B	B	B	B	B
	Pink	B	B		B	B	B		
	Black	C	A	A		A	C	C	C
	Blue/red	B	B	B	B			B	B
	Orange	B	B	B	B	B		B	B
	Light blue	B	B	B	B	B	B		B
	Black/white	A	A	A	A		A	A	

Fig. SZ12-10—Use adjacent chart and values listed below to test condition of CD ignition module used on independent ignition systems.

A. 100k ohms or less
B. 100k ohms or more
C. Tester needle should show deflection then return toward infinite resistance

tester positive lead to high tension wire and negative lead to black/white wire. Secondary coil resistance reading should be within the limits of 5000-6800 ohms for each coil.

To check condition of CD ignition module, use tester or ohmmeter in conjunction with test chart shown in Fig. SZ12-10. Renew CD ignition module if required.

Simultaneous Ignition Models. On simultaneous ignition models, check condition of capacitor charge coil by separating the blue/red wire connector and gray wire connector at stator and attach a tester lead to each wire. Charge coil may be considered satisfactory if resistance reading is within the limits 135-165 ohms.

To check condition of ignition coil, separate the black/white wire connector at coil and remove high tension wires from spark plugs. Attach tester positive lead to black/white wire and negative lead to coil ground. Primary coil resistance reading should be within the limits of 0.08-0.10 ohms. Attach a tester lead to each high tension wire. Secondary coil resistance reading should be within the limits of 3000-4000 ohms.

To check condition of CD ignition module, use tester or ohmmeter in conjunction with test chart shown in Fig. SZ12-11. Renew CD ignition module if required.

COOLING SYSTEM

WATER PUMP. A rubber impeller type water pump is mounted between the drive shaft housing and gearcase. A key in the drive shaft is used to turn the pump impeller. If cooling system problems are encountered, check water intake for plugging or partial stoppage, then if not corrected, remove gearcase as outlined in LOWER UNIT section and check condition of the water pump, water passages and sealing surfaces.

		\- Tester lead				
		Green	Grey	Black/White	Blue/Red	Black
Tester lead +	Green		A	B	B	A
	Grey	C		A	B	A
	Black/White	C	C		B	C
	Blue/Red	A	B	B		B
	Black	C	A	A	B	

Fig. SZ12-11—Use chart shown above and values listed below to test condition of CD ignition module used on simultaneous ignition systems.

A. 100K ohms or less
B. 100K ohms or more
C. Tester needle should show deflection then return toward infinite resistance

When water pump is disassembled, check condition of impeller (4—Fig. SZ12-12) and plate (5) for excessive wear and damage. Reinstall plate (with side marked "UP" towards impeller. Turn drive shaft clockwise (viewed from top) while placing pump housing over impeller. Avoid turning drive shaft in opposite direction when water pump is assembled.

THERMOSTAT. A thermostat (3—Fig. SZ12-13) is used to regulate operating temperature. The thermostat is calibrated to control temperature within the range of 48.5°-51.5°C (119°-125°F). Thermostat can be removed for inspection or renewal by removing cylinder head cover.

POWER HEAD

REMOVE AND REINSTALL. To remove the power head, first remove upper cover and disconnect linkage, fuel lines and wires which interfere with power head removal. Remove carburetor, fuel filter, fuel pump, electric and/or recoil starter, ignition coil(s), ignition module, rectifier, neutral safety interlock switch, interlock rod, flywheel, and stator assembly before detaching power head from lower unit. Disconnect shift linkage at shift handle and at shi rod connector located below lower driv shaft housing mount (15—Fig. SZ12-15).

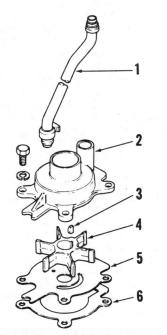

Fig. SZ12-12—Exploded view of water pump assembly.

1. Water tube
2. Pump housing
3. Key
4. Impeller
5. Plate
6. Gasket

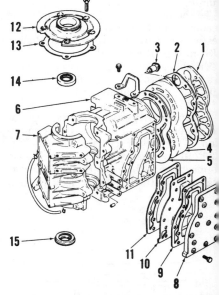

Fig. SZ12-13—Exploded view of crankcase assembly typical of all models.

1. Cylinder head cover
2. Gasket
3. Thermostat
4. Cylinder head
5. Head gasket
6. Cylinder block
7. Crankcase
8. Outer exhaust cover
9. Gasket
10. Inner exhaust cover
11. Gasket
12. Upper seal housing
13. Gasket
14. Upper crankshaft sea
15. Lower crankshaft sea

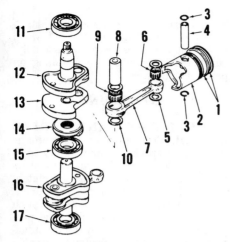

Fig. SZ12-14 — Exploded view of crankshaft assembly typical of all models.

1. Piston rings	10. Thrust washer
2. Piston	11. Ball bearing
3. Piston pin clip	12. Top crank half
4. Piston pin	13. Crank half
5. Thrust washer	14. Labyrinth seal
6. Needle bearing	15. Ball bearing
7. Connecting rod	16. Lower crankshaft
8. Crankpin	assembly
9. Needle bearing	17. Ball bearing

Remove screws securing power head assembly to lower unit and lift off power head.

Before reinstalling power head, check condition of drive shaft seal (1–Fig. SZ12-15). If seal renewal is required, apply a suitable high temperature grease to lip portion of seal and install into seal housing (3) with open side towards drive shaft housing (10). Make certain drive shaft splines are clean then coat them with a light coating of water resistant grease. Apply a suitable sealer to mating surfaces of power head and lower unit and install a new gasket. The remainder of installation is the reverse of removal procedure.

DISASSEMBLY. Disassembly and inspection may be accomplished in the following manner. Remove upper oil seal housing, exhaust cover, intake manifold and reed valves. Remove cylinder head and clean carbon from combustion chamber and any foreign material accumulation in water passages. Crankcase (7–Fig. SZ12-13) may be separated from cylinder block (6) and crankshaft and piston assembly removed after removal of crankcase retaining cap screws.

Engine components are now ready for overhaul as outlined in the appropriate following paragraphs. Refer to the following section for assembly procedure.

ASSEMBLY. Refer to specific service sections when assembling the crankshaft, connecting rod, piston and

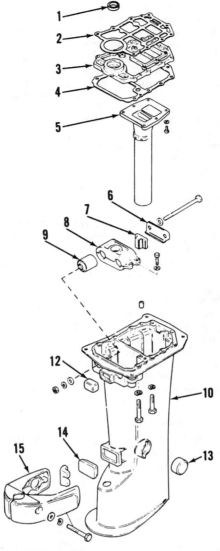

Fig. SZ12-15 — Exploded view of drive shaft housing and related components.

1. Drive shaft seal	8. Upper mount housing
2. Gasket	9. Rubber mount
3. Seal housing	10. Drive shaft housing
4. Gasket	12. Reverse thrust mount
5. Exhaust tube	13. Side mount
6. Plate	14. Lower thrust mount
7. Upper thrust mount	15. Lower mount cover

reed valves. Make sure all joint and gasket surfaces are clean, free from nicks and burrs and hardened cement or carbon.

Whenever the power head is disassembled, it is recommended that all gasket surfaces and mating surfaces without gaskets be carefully checked for nicks, burrs and warped surfaces which might interfere with a tight seal. Cylinder head, head end of cylinder block and some mating surfaces of manifold and crankcase should be checked on a surface plate and lapped if necessary to provide a smooth surface.

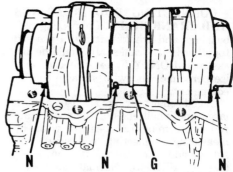

Fig. SZ12-16 — View of installed crankshaft assembly showing labyrinth seal locating groove (G) and main bearing locating notches (N).

Do not remove any more metal than is necessary.

When assembling power head, first lubricate all friction surfaces and bearings with engine oil. Install crankshaft assembly. Make certain labyrinth seal engages groove (G–Fig. SZ12-16) and main bearing locating pins engage notches (N) in cylinder block. Apply a coat of Suzuki Bond No. 4 or a suitable sealer to mating surfaces of cylinder block and crankcase and position crankcase on cylinder block. Using a crossing pattern, tighten the 10 mm crankcase screws to 40-60 N·m and the 6 mm crankcase screws to 8-12 N·m. Cylinder head gasket should be installed with gasket sealer. Position cylinder head and gasket on cylinder block and tighten head screws in sequence shown in Fig. SZ12-17 to 20-23 N·m. Cylinder head cover cap screws (C) should be tightened to 8-10 N·m.

Install crankshaft seal (14–Fig. SZ12-13) into upper seal housing (12) with open side towards cylinder block. Apply a suitable high temperature grease to lip portion of crankshaft seals (14 and 15), then install upper seal housing and lower crankshaft seal in cylinder block assembly.

RINGS, PISTONS AND CYLINDERS. The piston is fitted with two piston rings. Rings are interchangeable in grooves but must be installed with manufacturers marking toward closed end of piston. Piston ring end gap should be 0.2-0.4 mm with a maximum allowable ring end gap of 0.8 mm. Piston to cylinder wall clearance should be 0.061-0.082 mm. Pistons and rings are available in standard size as well as 0.25 mm and 0.50 mm oversizes. Cylinder should be bored to an oversize if cylinder is out-of-round or taper exceeds 0.10 mm. Install piston on connecting rod so arrow on piston crown will point towards exhaust port when piston is in cylinder.

CONNECTING ROD, BEARINGS AND CRANKSHAFT. Connecting rod, bearings and crankshaft are a pressed together unit. Crankshaft should be disassembled ONLY by experienced service personnel and with suitable service equipment.

Caged roller bearings are used at both large and small ends of the connecting rod. Determine rod bearing wear by measuring connecting rod small end side-to-side movement as shown at (A – Fig. SZ12-18). Normal side-to-side movement is 5 mm or less. Maximum allowable crankshaft runout is 0.5 mm measured at bearing surfaces with crankshaft ends supported.

When installing crankshaft, lubricate pistons, rings, cylinders and bearings with engine oil as outlined in ASSEMBLY section.

STARTERS

MANUAL STARTER. Refer to Fig. SZ12-20 for exploded view of overhead type manual starter assembly. Starter may be disassembled for overhaul or renewal of individual components as

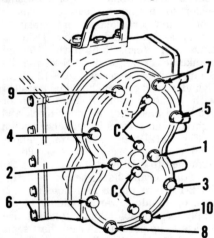

Fig. SZ12-17—Cylinder head cap screws should be tightened in the sequence shown above. Refer to text.

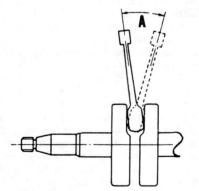

Fig. SZ12-18—Maximum side-to-side shake (A) at small end of connecting rod should be 5.0 mm or less.

follows: Remove engine top cowl and three cap screws securing starter assembly to power head. If starter spring remains under tension, pull starter rope and hold rope pulley (10 – Fig. SZ12-20) with notch in pulley adjacent to rope outlet. Pull rope back through outlet so that it engages notch in pulley and allow pulley to slowly unwind. Remove cap screw (17) and disassemble unit. Be careful when removing rewind spring (9); a rapidly uncoiling starter spring could cause serious injury.

Rewind spring is wound in a counterclockwise direction in starter housing. Rope is wound on rope pulley in a counterclockwise direction as viewed with pulley in housing. Reassemble starter assembly by reversing disassembly procedure. To place tension on rewind spring, pass rope through rope outlet in housing and install rope handle. Pull rope out and hold rope pulley so notch on pulley is adjacent to rope outlet. Pull rope back through outlet between notch in pulley and housing. Turn rope pulley counterclockwise four complete revolutions to place tension on spring. Do not place more tension on rewind spring than is necessary to draw rope handle up against housing.

ELECTRIC STARTER. Some models are equipped with electric starter shown in Fig. SZ12-21. Disassembly is evident after inspection of

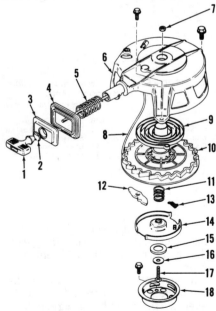

Fig. SZ12-20 — Exploded view of overhead starter assembly.

1. Rope handle	10.	Rope pulley
2. Retainer	11.	Spring
3. Rope guide	12.	Pawl
4. Grommet	13.	Spring
5. Spring	14.	Drive plate
6. Starter housing	15.	Spacer
7. Nut	16.	Washer
8. Rope	17.	Cap screw
9. Rewind spring	18.	Starter cup

unit and reference to exploded view. Starter brushes have a standard length of 14 mm and should be renewed if worn to 9.5 mm or less. After reassembly, bench test starter before installing on power head.

LOWER UNIT

PROPELLER AND DRIVE CLUTCH. Protection for the motor is built into a special cushioning clutch in the propeller hub. No adjustment is possible on the propeller or clutch. Three-bladed propellers are used. Standard propeller has a 330 mm pitch and a 292 mm diameter. Optional propellers are available from the manufacturer and should be selected to provide full throttle operation within the recommended limits of 4800-5500 rpm.

R&R AND OVERHAUL. Refer to Fig. SZ12-22 for exploded view of lower unit gearcase assembly used on all

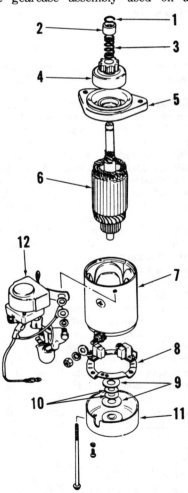

Fig. SZ12-21 — Exploded view of electric starter motor.

1. "C" ring	7.	Frame
2. Stop	8.	Brush assy.
3. Spring	9.	Thrust washers
4. Drive	10.	Shims
5. Frame head	11.	Brush cover
6. Armature	12.	Starter solenoid

models. During disassembly, note the location of all shims and thrust washers to aid in reassembly. To remove gearcase, first unscrew plug (30) and drain gear lubricant. Disconnect shift linkage at connector (2) located externally on the drive shaft housing. Remove the cap screws securing gearcase to drive shaft housing and separate gearcase assembly from drive shaft housing. Remove water pump assembly (Fig. SZ12-12). Remove propeller with related components from propeller shaft. Unscrew two bolts retaining gearcase end cap (50 – Fig. SZ12-22), then attach a suitable puller to propeller shaft (44) and withdraw propeller shaft assembly with gearcase end cap. Unscrew pinion nut (33) and remove pinion gear (32), then extract forward gear (36). Drive shaft (20) and related components may be withdrawn from gearcase after removal of bearing housing (13). Unscrew shift cam retaining screw (12) from gearcase to remove lower shift rod assembly.

Inspect gears for wear on teeth and on engagement dogs. Inspect clutch (40) for wear on engagement surfaces. Inspect shafts for wear on splines and on friction surfaces of gears and oil seals. Check shift cam (11) and shift pin (38) for excessive wear. Check condition of shift spring (43). Spring free length should be 69 mm with a minimum length of 67 mm. All seals and "O" rings should be renewed when unit is reassembled.

Backlash between pinion gear (32) and drive gears (36 and 46) should be 0.05-0.30 mm and is adjusted by varying thickness of shims (35) and thrust washer (47). Propeller shaft end play should be 0.05-0.30 mm and is adjusted by increasing or decreasing the thickness of thrust washers (37 and 45).

Reassemble gearcase by reversing disassembly procedure while noting the following: Install clutch (40) on propeller shaft (44) so "F" marked side (see Fig. SZ12-23) is towards forward gear (36 – Fig. SZ12-22). Tighten pinion nut (33) to 35 N·m. Apply water-resistant grease to mating surfaces of gearcase end cap (50) and gearcase. Apply silicone

sealer to gearcase and bearing housing (13) mating surfaces and to bearing housing and drive shaft housing mating surfaces.

With gearcase assembly installed, adjust shift linkage by first ensuring gearcase is in neutral. Adjust shift rod connector (2) so shift control handle is exactly between "F" and "R" positions, then tighten jam nut (1). Fill gearcase with outboard gear oil as outlined in LUBRICATION section.

Fig. SZ12-22 – Exploded view of lower unit gearcase assembly used on all models.

1. Nut
2. Connector
3. Dust seal
4. Rod guide
5. "O" ring
6. "O" ring
7. Lower shift rod
8. Magnet
9. Magnet holder
10. Pin
11. Shift cam
12. Cam retaining screw
13. Bearing housing
14. Seal
15. Needle bearing
16. Bearing race
17. Shim
18. Thrust bearing race
19. Thrust bearing
20. Drive shaft
21. Pin
22. Spring
23. Collar
24. Thrust washer
25. Washer
26. Needle bearings
27. Gearcase
28. Vent plug
29. Oil level plug
30. Drain plug
31. Strip seal
32. Pinion gear
33. Pinion nut
34. Taper bearing
35. Shim
36. Forward gear
37. Thrust washer
38. Shift pin
39. Spring guide
40. Clutch
41. Pin
42. Pin retainer
43. Shift spring
44. Propeller shaft
45. Thrust washer
46. Reverse gear
47. Thrust washer
48. "O" ring
49. Ball bearing
50. End cap
51. Needle bearings
52. Seal
53. Spacer
54. Washer
55. Propeller
56. Spacer
57. Lockwasher
58. Propeller nut

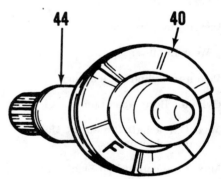

Fig. SZ12-23 – Install clutch (40) on propeller shaft (44) with "F" marked side towards forward gear.

SUZUKI DT35 (After 1986)
AND DT40 (After 1983)

CONDENSED SERVICE DATA

TUNE-UP

Hp/rpm	35/4800-5500
	40/4800-5500
Bore	79.0 mm
	(3.11 in.)
Stroke	71.0 mm
	(2.80 in.)
Number of Cylinders	2
Displacement	696 cc
	(42.47 cu. in.)
Spark Plug	NGK B8HS
Electrode Gap	0.8-0.9 mm
	(0.031-0.035 in.)
Ignition Type	Breakerless CDI
Carburetor Make	Mikuni
Carburetor Model	B40-32
Idle Speed	650-700 rpm

SIZES—CLEARANCES

Piston Ring End Gap	0.2-0.4 mm
	(0.008-0.016 in.)
Wear Limit	0.8 mm
	(0.031 in.)
Piston Pin Diameter	19.995-20.000 mm
	(0.7872-0.7874 in.)
Wear Limit	19.980 mm
	(0.7866 in.)
Piston Pin Bore Diameter	19.998-20.006 mm
	(0.7873-0.7876 in.)
Wear Limit	20.032 mm
	(0.7887 in.)
Piston-to-Cylinder Clearance	0.099-0.114 mm
	(0.0039-0.0045 in.)
Cylinder Bore Wear Limit	0.10 mm
	(0.0039 in.)
Max. Crankshaft Runout at Main Bearing Journal	0.05 mm
	(0.0020 in.)
Max. Connecting Rod Small End Side Shake	5.0 mm
	(0.20 in.)

TIGHTENING TORQUES

Cylinder Head Cover	8-12 N·m
	(6-9 ft.-lbs.)
Cylinder Head	20-26 N·m
	(15-19 ft.-lbs.)
Crankcase:	
6 mm	8-12 N·m
	(6-9 ft.-lbs.)
10 mm	46-54 N·m
	(34-40 ft.-lbs.)
Exhaust Cover	8-12 N·m
	(6-9 ft.-lbs.)
Flywheel Nut	200-210 N·m
	(147-155 ft.-lbs.)
Gearcase Pinion Nut	30-40 N·m
	(22-29 ft.-lbs.)
Propeller Shaft Nut	50-60 N·m
	(37-44 ft.-lbs.)
Standard Screws- Unmarked or Marked "4":	
5 mm	2-4 N·m
	(18-35 in.-lbs.)
6 mm	4-7 N·m
	(35-62 in.-lbs.)
8 mm	10-16 N·m
	(7-12 ft.-lbs.)
10 mm	22-35 N·m
	(16-26 ft.-lbs.)
Stainless Steel:	
5 mm	2-4 N·m
	(18-35 in.-lbs.)
6 mm	6-10 N·m
	(53-88 in.-lbs.)
8 mm	15-20 N·m
	(11-15 ft.-lbs.)
10 mm	34-41 N·m
	(25-30 ft.-lbs.)
Marked "7":	
5 mm	3-6 N·m
	(27-53 in.-lbs.)
6 mm	8-12 N·m
	(6-9 ft.-lbs.)
8 mm	18-28 N·m
	(13-21 ft.-lbs.)
10 mm	40-60 N·m
	(29-44 ft.-lbs.)

LUBRICATION

The power head is lubricated by oil mixed with the fuel. All models are equipped with automatic oil injection. The crankshaft driven oil pump varies the fuel:oil ratio depending upon carburetor throttle opening. Recommended oil is Suzuki Outboard Motor Oil or a good quality NMMA certified TC-WII en-

gine oil. Recommended fuel is regular or unleaded gasoline having an minimum octane rating of 85. Manufacturer does not recommend using gasoline containing alcohol additives. However, unleaded gasoline containing ethanol (grain alcohol) may be used providing ethanol content does not exceed five percent and minimum octane rating is 85.

NOTE: Manufacturer recommends NOT using any gasoline containing methanol (wood alcohol).

During break-in (first 10 hours of operation) of a new or rebuilt engine, mix a recommended oil with the fuel at a 50:1 ratio and use in the fuel tank in combination with the oil injection system to ensure adequate lubrication during break-in process. After initial 10 hours of operation, switch to straight gasoline in the fuel tank.

The lower unit gears and bearings are lubricated with oil contained in the gearcase. Recommended gearcase oil is Suzuki Outboard Motor Gear Oil or a suitable equivalent SAE 90 hypoid gear oil. Gearcase capacity is approximately 610 mL (20.6 fl. oz.). Lower unit oil should be changed after the first 10 hours of operation and after every 100 hours or seasonally thereafter. Reinstall drain and vent plugs securely, using a new gasket if necessary, to ensure water tight seal.

NOTE: Oil level in gearcase should be rechecked after running outboard motor a short time and topped off if necessary.

FUEL SYSTEM

CARBURETOR. Refer to Fig. SZ13-1 for an exploded view of the Mikuni B40-32 carburetor used on all models. Initial setting of pilot air screw (4) is 1½ to 2 turns out from a lightly seated position. Final adjustment should be made with engine at normal operating temperature and running in forward gear. Adjust pilot air screw so engine idles smoothly and will accelerate cleanly without hesitation. Adjust idle speed screw (15) so idle speed is 650-700 rpm at normal operating temperature in forward gear.

High speed fuel metering is controlled by main jet (9). Standard main jet for normal operation is #185 on models prior to 1987 and #190 on 1987 and later models. Standard pilot jet (2) for normal operation is #70 on models prior to 1987 and #77.5 on models after 1986.

To check float level, remove float bowl (14) and invert carburetor body (1). Measure float level (L—Fig. SZ13-2) from main jet (9) to float (11) as shown. Take measurement 180 degrees from inlet valve. Float level (L) should be 16.5-18.5 mm (0.65-0.73 in.) on models prior to 1987 and 17-19 mm (0.67-0.75 in.) on models after 1986. Bend tang on float to adjust float level.

FUEL FILTER. A fuel filter assembly is used to filter the fuel prior to entering the fuel pump. Periodically unscrew bowl (7—Fig. SZ13-3) and withdraw filter element (6). Clean bowl and filter element in a suitable solvent and blow dry with clean compressed air. Inspect filter element for excessive blockage or other damage and renew if necessary. Reassemble in reverse order of disassembly. Renew "O" ring (5) and seal (4) upon reassembly.

FUEL PUMP. A diaphragm-type fuel pump is used. Refer to Fig. SZ13-3 for exploded view. Fuel pump is mounted on the side of power head cylinder block

and is actuated by crankcase pulsations.

When servicing pump, scribe reference marks on pump body to aid alignment during reassembly. Defective or questionable components should be renewed. Diaphragm should be renewed if air leaks or cracks are noted, or if deterioration is evident.

REED VALVES. The reed valves are located behind the intake manifold (1—Fig. SZ13-6). The intake manifold must be removed to access reed valve assemblies.

Renew reed petals (3) if petals are broken, cracked, warped, rusted or bent, or if tip of petal stands open in excess

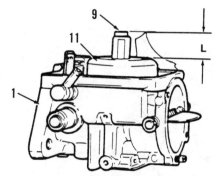

Fig. SZ13-2—Measure float level (L) from main jet (9) to float (11) as shown. Refer to text.

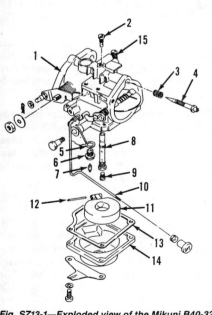

Fig. SZ13-1—Exploded view of the Mikuni B40-32 carburetor used.

1. Body	9. Main jet
2. Pilot jet	10. Choke rod
3. Spring	11. Float
4. Pilot air screw	12. Pin
5. Gasket	13. Gasket
6. Inlet valve seat	14. Float bowl
7. Inlet needle valve	15. Idle speed screw
8. Main nozzle	

Fig. SZ13-3—Exploded view of fuel filter and fuel pump assemblies.

1. Nut
2. Washer
3. Base
4. Seal
5. "O" ring
6. Filter element
7. Cup
8. Cover
9. Diaphragm
10. Gasket
11. Body
12. Diaphragm
13. Spring
14. Seat
15. Gasket
16. Valves

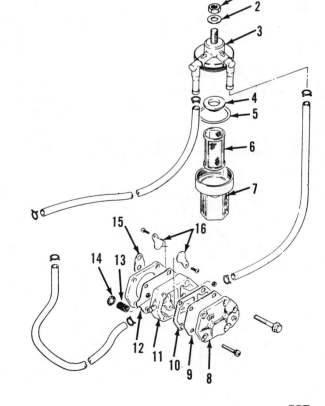

of 0.2 mm (0.008 in.) from seat area. Refer to Fig. SZ13-6. Do not attempt to bend or straighten a damaged reed. Opening between tip reed stop (4) and reed plate should be 7.6-8.0 mm (0.30-0.32 in.) on models prior to 1987 and 6.0-6.4 mm (0.24-0.25 in.) on models after 1986. When reassembling reed valve assembly, apply Suzuki Thread Lock 1342 or a suitable equivalent thread locking compound to threads of reed attaching screws (4).

SPEED CONTROL LINKAGE. Throttle opening and ignition timing advance must be synchronized for proper operation. To adjust speed control linkage and ignition timing, proceed as follows:

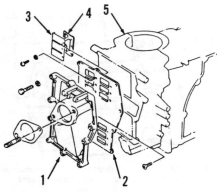

Fig. SZ13-5—Exploded view of reed valves and related components.

1. Intake manifold
2. Reed plate
3. Reed petals
4. Reed stop
5. Crankcase assy.

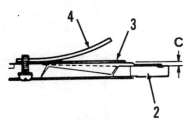

Fig. SZ13-6—Clearance (C) between reed petals (3) and reed plate (2) should not exceed 0.2 mm (0.008 in.).

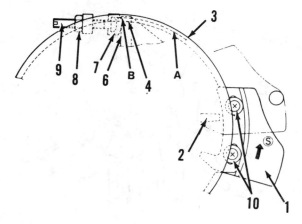

Fig. SZ13-8—Refer to text for speed control adjustment procedure.

1. Throttle cam
2. Crankcase stopper
3. Stator
4. Crankcase stopper
6. Crankcase-to-cylinder block mating surface
7. Cap
8. Nut
9. Idle timing screw
10. Screws
A. Stator mark
B. Stator mark

With engine not running, shift outboard into forward gear. Loosen throttle cam screws (10—Fig. SZ13-8) and open throttle until stator mark located at (A) is aligned with crankcase and cylinder block mating surfaces (6). Note that a hole is provided in flywheel to access screws (10). With mark (A) aligned with crankcase mating surfaces, slide throttle cam (1) against crankcase stopper (2) and retighten screws (10). Without disturbing position of stator (3), loosen screw (13—Fig. SZ13-9). Rotate carburetor throttle arm (14) so throttle valve is fully open, then hold cam roller (11) against throttle cam (1) and retighten screw (13).

Next, with engine not running, place outboard into forward gear. Rotate stator so mark (B—Fig. SZ13-8) is aligned with crankcase-to-cylinder block mating surface (6). Loosen nut (8) and turn screw (9) so cap (7) contacts stopper (4), then retighten nut (8). Rotate throttle limiter (17—Fig. SZ13-9) against stopper (18) and adjust the length of rod (16) so carburetor throttle valve is completely open, then retighten nut (15).

OIL INJECTION

The plunger-type oil pump is driven by a drive gear on the bottom of the crankshaft. Depending upon carburetor throttle valve opening, the oil pump varies the amount of oil delivered to the engine resulting in fuel:oil ratios from approximately 150:1 at idle to approximately 50:1 at full throttle. Oil is injected down stream from the incoming fuel and air mixture. An air/oil mixing valve located in the crankcase, mixes oil from injection pump with small amounts of air from crankcase pulsations to help emulsify the oil injected into the fuel and air stream. Refer to Fig. SZ13-10 for an exploded view of oil pump and related components.

BLEEDING PUMP. If oil pump, reservoir or oil lines have been removed, or if outboard motor has been in long term storage, air should be purged from oil injection system. To bleed air from injection system, first fill the oil reservoir. Open bleed screw (Fig. SZ13-12) until oil escapes. Allow oil to run out bleed screw for approximately five seconds, then retighten bleed screw.

CHECKING PUMP OUTPUT. Start engine and allow to warm-up for approximately five minutes. Stop engine and disconnect oil pump control rod (6—Fig. SZ13-10) from carburetor throttle lever. Disconnect the oil pump supply line from oil tank, plug tank outlet and remove tank. Connect Suzuki oil gage 09900-21602 or a suitable calibrated container to oil pump supply line. Fill oil gage with a recommended oil and bleed system as previously outlined. Refill oil gage, if necessary, to an upper reference mark. With oil pump control lever in the fully closed position (control rod pushed down), start engine and run at 1500 rpm for exactly five minutes. On models prior to 1986, oil pump output should be 2.2-2.8 mL (0.07-0.09 fl. oz.) in five minutes at 1500 rpm. On models after 1985, oil pump output should be 1.3-2.3 mL (0.044-0.08 fl. oz.) in five minutes at 1500 rpm. Next, move oil pump control lever to the fully open position (control rod pulled up). Start engine and run at 1500 rpm for exactly two minutes. Oil pump output should be 3.3-4.0 mL (0.11-0.14 fl. oz.) in two minutes at 1500 rpm on models prior to 1986, or 2.9-4.4 mL (0.098-0.149 fl. oz.) in two minutes at 1500 rpm on models after 1985. Renew oil pump assembly (1—Fig. SZ13-10) if output is not as specified. When installing pump (1) be certain driven gear (4) properly engages crankshaft drive gear and oil pump assembly. Bleed injection system as previously outlined.

NOTE: Results of oil pump output test may vary according to weather conditions, testing error or other conditions. The manufacturer recommends repeating output test procedure two or three times to ensure the proper results are obtained.

IGNITION

A capacitor discharge ignition (CDI) system is used. The primary ignition components are the flywheel, condenser charge coil (1—Fig. SZ13-13), pulser coil (2) stator (3) and CDI module. The ignition coils are contained in the CDI module. The CDI module is also equipped with an oil warning circuit and an rpm limiter to prevent engine speed from exceeding 5900 rpm.

Ignition timing is advanced electronically by the CDI module and mechanically by rotation of stator assembly (3). Ignition timing should be 1-3 degrees

ATDC at 1000 rpm and 24-26 degrees BTDC at 5000 rpm. Loosen screws (10—Fig. SZ13-8) and move throttle cam (1) to adjust full throttle timing advance. To adjust idle timing, loosen nut (8) and turn screw (9). Turning screw (9) clockwise advances timing.

TROUBLE-SHOOTING. Refer to Figs. SZ13-13, SZ13-15 and SZ13-16 for wiring diagrams typical of all models. Troubleshoot ignition system using Suzuki Pocket Tester 09900-25002 or a suitable equivalent ohmmeter.

NOTE: The resistance specifications for trouble-shooting ignition system are based on measurements taken at 20° C (68° F). Actual resistance values obtained while testing may vary depending upon ambient temperature, temperature of component and tester manufacturer.

CONDENSER CHARGE COIL. Disconnect charge coil connector and connect tester between green and black wires. Charge coil resistance should be 230-280 ohms on models prior to 1987 and 200-300 ohms on models after 1986. No continuity should be present between green charge coil wire and engine ground or charge coil core.

PULSER COIL. Disconnect wires at connector leading to pulser coil. Connect tester between white/red and black wires. Pulser coil resistance should be 175-210 ohms on models prior to 1987 and 160-230 ohms on models after 1986. No continuity should be present between pulser coil white/red wire and engine ground.

LIGHTING COIL. Disconnect lighting coil and connect tester between red and yellow wires. Lighting coil resistance should be 0.20-0.25 ohm on models prior to 1987 and 0.2-0.6 on models after 1986. No continuity should be present between lighting coil red wire and engine ground.

IGNITION COILS. Test ignition coil secondary winding resistance by connecting tester between spark plug high tension leads. Resistance should be 2300-3100 ohms on models prior to 1987 and 3100-3200 ohms on models after 1986. Renew CDI module if coil secondary resistance is not as specified.

CDI MODULE. Suzuki CDI Tester 09930-99810 or 09930-99830 and test harness 09930-89440 are available from the manufacturer to test the CDI module. Follow instructions provided with the tester.

COOLING SYSTEM

THERMOSTAT. A thermostat located in the cylinder head cover is used to regulate operating temperature. Test thermostat by immersing in heated water with an accurate thermometer. Thermostat should begin to open at 58.5°-61.5° C (137°-143° F). Renew thermostat if it fails to open within the specified temperature range. When installing thermostat, be certain bleed hole is facing direction shown in Fig. SZ13-17.

WATER PUMP. A rubber impeller type water pump is mounted between the drive shaft housing and gearcase. Drive key (6—Fig. SZ13-18) in the drive shaft turns impeller (5). When servicing water pump, inspect condition of water passages and sealing surfaces. Rotate drive shaft in clockwise direction when installing pump housing (4) over impeller. Avoid turning drive shaft in opposite direction after reassembling pump.

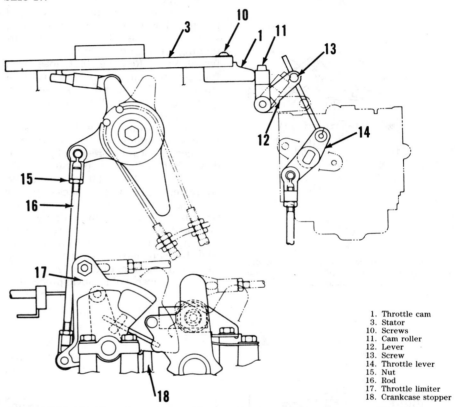

1. Throttle cam
3. Stator
10. Screws
11. Cam roller
12. Lever
13. Screw
14. Throttle lever
15. Nut
16. Rod
17. Throttle limiter
18. Crankcase stopper

Fig. SZ13-9—View of speed control linkage. Refer to text for adjustment procedure.

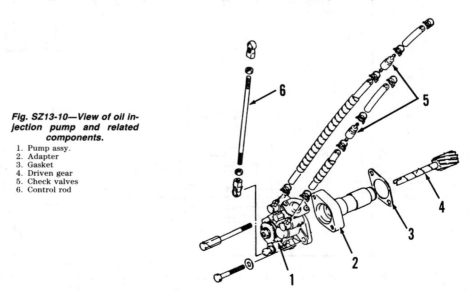

Fig. SZ13-10—View of oil injection pump and related components.
1. Pump assy.
2. Adapter
3. Gasket
4. Driven gear
5. Check valves
6. Control rod

POWER HEAD

REMOVE AND REINSTALL. Remove engine cover. Disconnect neutral start interlock cable from throttle limiter (17—Fig. SZ13-9). Disconnect and remove oil tank, remove the rewind starter and remove air box silencer. Disconnect oil pump control rod from carburetor and remove choke knob. Disconnect and remove carburetor. Remove throttle lever rod from throttle lever, disconnect battery cables from starter motor and remove two cables from starter relay. Disconnect brown and green/yellow wires from neutral start switch. Loosen electric parts holder attaching screw and disconnect all interfering wires. Remove inlet hose from fuel pump. Remove flywheel using a suitable puller. Remove power head mounting screws and lift power head off drive shaft housing.

Before installing power head, be sure drive shaft spines are clean. Apply a light coating of water-resistant grease to drive shaft splines. Apply Suzuki Silicone Seal 99000-31120 or a suitable equivalent to mating surfaces of power head and drive shaft housing and threads of power head mounting screws. Lower power head onto drive shaft housing while rotating power head slightly to engage crankshaft and drive shaft splines. Remainder of reinstallation is the reverse of removal procedure.

Be sure to properly route all wires and hoses to prevent interfering with moving parts.

DISASSEMBLY. Remove six screws and detach exhaust tube (23—Fig. SZ13-20). Remove starter motor and bracket, then disconnect wires inside the electric parts holder and CDI module holder. Remove stator assembly, upper oil seal housing (6) and stator retainer. Remove fuel pump and fuel filter, oil pump assembly, oil pump adapter and oil hoses. Remove 12 screws and detach intake manifold (1). Remove one screw securing reed plate, then detach reed plate assembly. Remove exhaust cover screws and carefully pry off exhaust cover (17), then exhaust plate (16). Remove lower oil seal housing, thermostat cover and thermostat. Remove 13 cylinder head screws.

NOTE: Cylinder head screws are stamped with numbers 1 through 13. When removing screws, remove in order starting with number 13.

Carefully separate cylinder head and cover by prying at the corners of head. Remove heat sensor from cylinder head. Remove two screws securing cylinder head cover to cylinder head and separate cover from head. Remove ten 14 mm and two 10 mm screws and carefully separate crankcase cover from cylin-

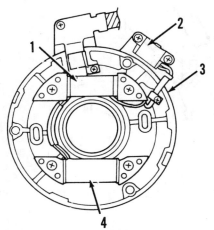

Fig. SZ13-12—View of injection pump bleed screw.

Fig. SZ13-13—View showing location of condenser charge coil (1), pulser coil (2) and lighting coil (4) on stator assembly (3).

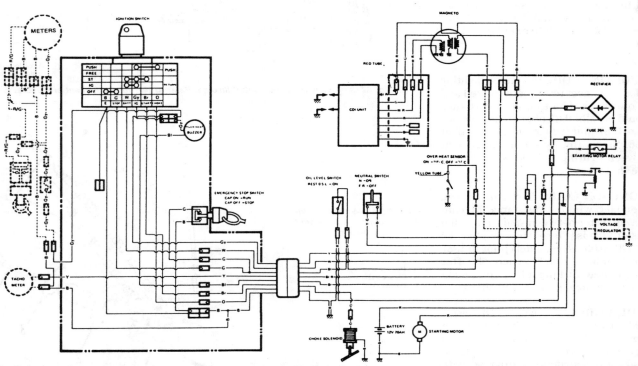

Fig. SZ13-15—Wiring diagram on models prior to 1987 equipped with electric start, remote control and optional voltage regulator. Refer to Fig. SZ13-16 for color code identification.

der block. Lift crankshaft, connecting rods and pistons assembly from cylinder block. Engine components are now accessible for inspection and overhaul as outlined in the appropriate service sections.

REASSEMBLY. Refer to specific service sections when reassembling crankshaft, connecting rods and pistons. Renew all gaskets and seals. Make sure all joint and gasket surfaces are clean and free of nicks or burrs and hardened sealer.

It is recommended that all gasket and mating surfaces be carefully checked for nicks, burrs and warped surfaces which might interfere with a tight seal. Cylinder head, cylinder block, exhaust cover, crankcase cover and intake manifold mating surfaces should be checked with a suitable straightedge and feeler gage. If surfaces are not flat to within 0.03 mm (0.0012 in.), surface should be lapped to provide a smooth surface. Do not remove more metal than necessary to true surface.

Lubricate all bearings and friction surfaces with a recommended engine oil. Lubricate lip of seals (1, 6, 12 and 13—

Fig. SZ13-21) with Suzuki Super Grease "A" (part 99000-25030) or a suitable equivalent water-resistant grease. Apply Suzuki Silicone Seal (part 99000-31120) or a suitable equivalent to both sides of lower bearing housing gasket.

NOTE: Seal (6) on models prior to 1989 is a labyrinth type seal. On models after 1988, a lip type seal is used. Lip type seal can be used on earlier models, however, labyrinth seal will not interchange with later models.

Place thrust ring (5) into groove in cylinder block, then install crankshaft assembly. Make certain main bearing locating pins engage notches in cylinder block. Flanges of seals (6 and 12) must fit securely in grooves in cylinder block. Apply a coat of Suzuki Bond No. 4 (part

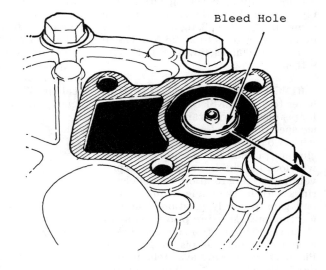

Fig. SZ13-17—Install thermostat with bleed hole facing direction shown.

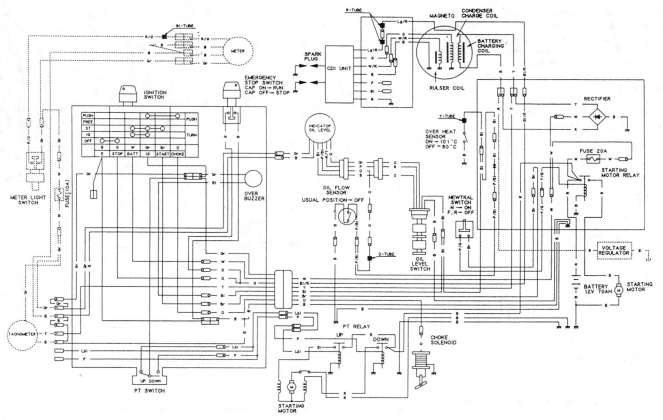

Fig. SZ13-16—Wiring diagram on models after 1986 equipped with electric start, remote control and power tilt.

B. Black	W. White	Gr. Gray	R/Y. Red with yellow tracer	Y/G. Yellow with green tracer	P/Bl. Pink with blue tracer
G. Green	Y. Yellow	Or. Orange	W/R. White with red tracer	Bl/R. Blue with red tracer	LtBl. Light blue
P. Pink	Bl. Blue	R/G. Red with green tracer			LtG/R. Light green with red tracer
R. Red	Br. Brown				

99000-31030) to mating surfaces of crankcase cover and cylinder block and position crankcase cover on cylinder block. Using the tightening sequence shown in Fig. SZ13-22, tighten the 10 mm screws to 46-54 N·m (34-40 ft.-lbs.) and the 6 mm screws to 8-12 N·m (6-9 ft.-lbs.). After assembling crankcase, check crankshaft rotation for binding or unusual noise. If binding or noise is noted, the reason must be determined and repaired before proceeding with assembly. Using the tightening sequence shown in Fig. SZ13-23, tighten 8 mm cylinder head screws to 20-26 N·m (15-19 ft.-lbs.) and 6 mm screws to 8-12 N·m (6-9 ft.-lbs.).

RINGS, PISTONS AND CYLINDER. Refer to CONDENSED SERVICE DATA for pistons, pins, rings and cylinder service specifications. Each piston is fitted with two piston rings. Top piston ring is chrome plated. Pistons are equipped with locating pins in ring grooves to prevent piston ring rotation. Install piston rings with marked side facing up and end gaps properly positioned around locating pins. Measure piston diameter 28 mm (1.10 in.) up from bottom of skirt at a right angle to piston pin bore. Pistons and rings are available in standard size, 0.25 mm (0.010 in.) and 0.50 mm (0.020 in.) oversize. Install pistons on connecting rods so arrow on piston crown will face exhaust ports upon reassembly. All cylinders should be bored to next oversize if any cylinder is worn, out-of-round or tapered in excess of 0.10 mm (0.004 in.).

CRANKSHAFT, CONNECTING RODS AND BEARINGS. Connecting

rods, bearings and crankshaft are a press together unit. Crankshaft should be disassembled ONLY by experienced service personnel using appropriate service equipment.

Determine connecting rod, crankpin and bearing wear from side-to-side as shown in Fig. SZ13-24. Normal side-to-side movement is 5.0 mm (0.197 in.) or less. If movement exceeds 5.0 mm (0.197 in.), connecting rod, crankpin and crankpin needle bearing should be renewed. Maximum allowable crankshaft runout is 0.05 mm (0.002 in.) measured at bearing surfaces with ends of crankshaft supported in V-blocks.

Apply Suzuki Super Grease "A" (part 99000-25030) or a suitable equivalent to seal lips. When installing crankshaft assembly into cylinder block, make sure

flanges of seals (6 and 12—Fig. SZ13-21) properly engage grooves in cylinder block. Make sure main bearing locating pins properly engage notches in cylinder block.

MANUAL STARTER

To remove manual starter assembly, disconnect neutral start cable (1—Fig. SZ13-26) and remove three screws securing housing (9) to power head. To disassemble starter, remove cotter pin securing arm (2), then remove arm (2), spring (3) and dog (6). Invert starter housing (9). Grasp rope and place rope into notch in outer diameter of pulley (14), then allow pulley to unwind in a clockwise direction until tension on rewind spring is relieved. Remove screw (21—

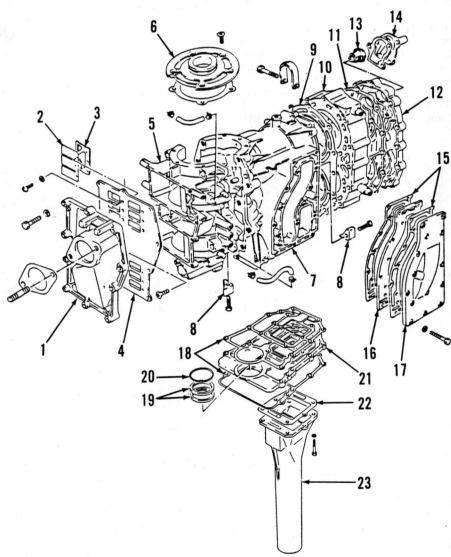

Fig. SZ13-20—Exploded view of crankcase, cylinder block and related components.

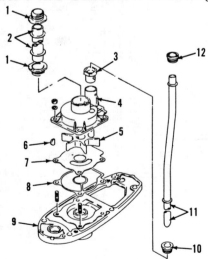

Fig. SZ13-18—Exploded view of water pump assembly.

1. Seal	7. Plate	
2. Seal tube	8. Gasket	
3. Grommet	9. Bearing retainer	
4. Housing	10. Grommet	
5. Impeller	11. Water tube	
6. Drive key	12. Grommet	

1. Intake manifold	7. Cylinder block	13. Thermostat	19. Seals
2. Reed petals	8. Anode	14. Cover	20. "O" ring
3. Reed stop	9. Gasket	15. Gasket	21. Lower oil seal
4. Reed plate	10. Cylinder head	16. Exhaust plate	housing
5. Crankcase cover	11. Gasket	17. Exhaust cover	22. Gasket
6. Oil seal housing	12. Cylinder head cover	18. Gaskets	23. Exhaust tube

Fig. SZ13-26) and drive plate (20), spring (16) and spring (19). Remove snap ring (18) and washer (17). Carefully lift rope pulley (14) with rope from housing, making sure rewind spring remains in housing. Using suitable hand and eye protection, remove rewind spring (13) from housing.

Reassembly is the reverse of disassembly procedure noting the following: Apply a suitable water-resistant grease to rewind spring (13), bushing (11) and washer (10). Starting with outer coil, wind rewind spring into housing in a counterclockwise direction. Use caution not to allow rewind spring to fly out of housing. Tie starter rope onto pulley (14) and thread through rope guide in housing (9). Install rope pulley by aligning slot in center hub with eye on inner coil of rewind spring, then place pulley into housing. Rotate pulley counterclockwise slightly to ensure pulley and rewind spring are properly engaged. Rotate pulley counterclockwise to wind rope onto pulley 2½ turns. Place rope into notch in pulley, then while holding rope in notch (N), rotate pulley four turns counterclockwise to preload rewind spring. Release rope and allow rewind spring to wind remainder of rope onto pulley. Install neutral start cable and adjust length of cable so mark (M—Fig. SZ13-27) is located between marks (X and Y) on starter housing (9) with shift lever in forward or reverse position. Starter should only be operable with outboard in neutral.

ELECTRIC STARTER

All models are equipped with the electric starter shown in Fig. SZ13-28. Disassembly is evident after inspection of unit and referral to exploded view. Frame (7) and end frames (5 and 9) are match marked for correct reassembly.

Standard commutator diameter is 30 mm (1.18 in.). Armature should be renewed if commutator diameter is less than 29 mm (1.14 in.). Mica between commutator segments should be undercut to 0.5-0.8 mm (0.020-0.031 in.) with a minimum undercut of 0.2 mm (0.008 in.). Standard brush length is 12.5 mm (0.49 in.) and should be renewed if worn to less than 9 mm (0.35 in.).

PROPELLER. Protection for lower unit and motor is provided by a cushioning rubber hub built into the propeller. Various propellers are available from the manufacturer. Select a propeller to allow outboard motor to operate within the specified speed range of 4800-5500 rpm at full throttle.

R&R AND OVERHAUL. Refer to Fig. SZ13-30 for exploded view of gearcase

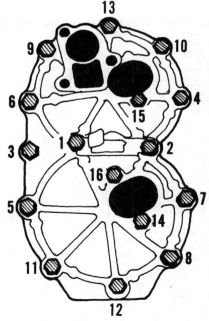

Fig. SZ13-21—Exploded view of crankshaft, connecting rods and pistons assembly.

1. Seal
2. Bearing
3. Crankshaft assy.
4. Bearing
5. Thrust ring
6. Seal
7. Bearing
8. Washer
9. Key
10. Oil pump drive gear
11. Washer
12. Seal
13. Seal
14. Crank pin
15. Washer
16. Bearing
17. Washer
18. Connecting rod
19. Snap ring
20. Piston pin
21. Piston
22. Piston rings

Fig. SZ13-22—Using the tightening sequence shown, tighten the 10 mm crankcase screws to 46-54 N·m (34-40 ft.-lbs.) and the 6 mm screws to 8-12 N·m (6-9 ft.-lbs.).

Fig. SZ13-23—Using the tightening sequence shown, tighten 8 mm cylinder head screws to 20-26 N·m (15-19 ft.-lbs.) and 6 mm screws to 8-12 N·m (6-9 ft.-lbs.).

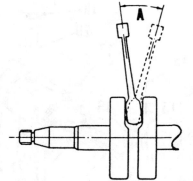

Fig. SZ13-24—Maximum allowable side-to-side shake (A) at small end of connecting rod is 5.0 mm (0.20 in.).

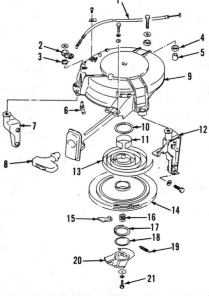

Fig. SZ13-26—Exploded view of manual rewind starter.

1. Neutral start interlock cable
2. Stopper arm
3. Spring
4. Bushing
5. Spacer
6. Pulley dog
7. Bracket
8. Rope handle
9. Housing
10. Washer
11. Bushing
12. Bracket
13. Rewind spring
14. Rope pulley
15. Pawl
16. Spring
17. Washer
18. Snap ring
19. Spring
20. Drive plate
21. Screw

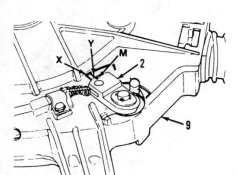

Fig. SZ13-27—For proper neutral start cable adjustment, mark (M) in arm (2) must be between marks X and Y on starter housing (9) when gear shift lever is in forward or reverse position.

assembly. During disassembly, note location of all shims and thrust washers for reference during reassembly.

To remove lower unit, first drain oil. Remove engine cover, loosen nut (7) and turn shift rod coupler (6) to separate upper and lower shift rods. Remove six screws securing gearcase to drive shaft housing, remove gearcase and place in a suitable holding fixture.

Remove the trim tab. Straighten tabs on lockwasher (62), remove propeller nut (63), propeller, thrust hub (61) and bushing (60). Remove two screws securing bearing carrier (55). Using Suzuki special tools (or equivalent) as shown in Fig. SZ13-31, pull propeller shaft assembly from gearcase. Slide water tube seal collar (2—Fig. SZ13-18) off drive shaft (31—Fig. SZ13-30) and remove water pump assembly (Fig. SZ13-18). To remove pinion gear (44—Fig. SZ13-30), fit Suzuki drive shaft holder (part 09921-29510) or equivalent splined tool, on top of drive shaft. Reach into gearcase and hold pinion nut (43) with the proper size wrench and rotate drive shaft to unscrew nut (43). After removing pinion gear (44), reach into gearcase and withdraw forward gear (39) along with shim

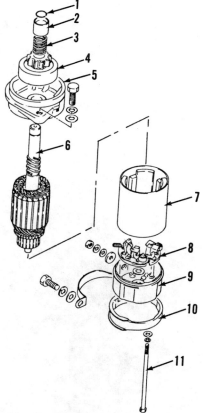

Fig. SZ13-28—Exploded view of electric starter.

1. Retainer
2. Stop
3. Spring
4. Drive gear assy.
5. End frame
6. Armature
7. Frame
8. Brushes & holder assy.
9. End frame
10. Damper
11. Through-bolt

(38) and bearing (37). Use two 6 mm jackscrews as shown in Fig. SZ13-32 to separate upper bearing housing (24—Fig. SZ13-30) from gearcase. When housing (24) is free, slide housing off drive shaft (31), then pull drive shaft assembly from gearcase. Remove collar (23) and washers (21 and 22).

Spring (20) can be removed from drive shaft (31) after removing pin (32). Dog clutch (45), shift pin (41) and guide (42) can be remove from propeller shaft (49) after removing retainer (46) and driving out pin (47).

Inspect gears for wear on teeth and on engagement dogs. Inspect dog clutch for wear on engagement surfaces. Inspect shafts for wear on splines and friction surfaces. Check shift cam (17) and shift pin (41) for excessive wear. Standard free length of shift spring (48) is 69 mm (2.72 in.). Renew spring (48) if free length is less than 67 mm (2.64 in.). Renew all seals and "O" rings during reassembly.

Backlash between pinion gear (44) and forward gear (39) should be 0.1-0.2 mm (0.004-0.008 in.) and is adjusted by varying thickness of pinion shim (28) and forward gear shim (38). To increase backlash, subtract equally from shims (28 and 38). To decrease backlash, add to shims (28 and 38) equally. Propeller shaft end play should be 0.2-0.4 mm (0.008-0.016 in.) and is adjusted by varying thickness of thrust washer (50). Check pinion gear-to-forward gear mesh pattern using a suitable gear marking compound. Vary thickness of shims (28 and 38) to obtain the optimum mesh between gears. After pinion and forward gear adjustment, and prior to installing propeller shaft and related components, check and record drive shaft end play. After installing propeller shaft assembly, recheck drive shaft end play. The second drive shaft end play measurement should not be less than when first checked. If so, subtract from shim (52) as necessary.

Reassemble gearcase by reversing disassembly procedure while noting the following: Thoroughly lubricate all friction and bearing surfaces. Install dog clutch (45) on propeller shaft (49) so mark (F—Fig. SZ13-33) is facing forward gear (39). Apply a suitable thread locking compound to threads of pinion nut (43) and tighten nut to 30-40 N·m (22-29 ft.-lbs.). Apply a suitable water-resistant grease to outer diameter of carrier (55—Fig. SZ13-30) and carrier "O" ring (53). Tighten carrier attaching screws to 15-20 N·m (11-14 ft.-lbs.). Tighten propeller nut (63) to 50-60 N·m (37-44 ft.-lbs.). Apply a light coat of water-resistant grease to drive shaft splines. Apply silicone sealer to mating surfaces of gearcase and drive shaft

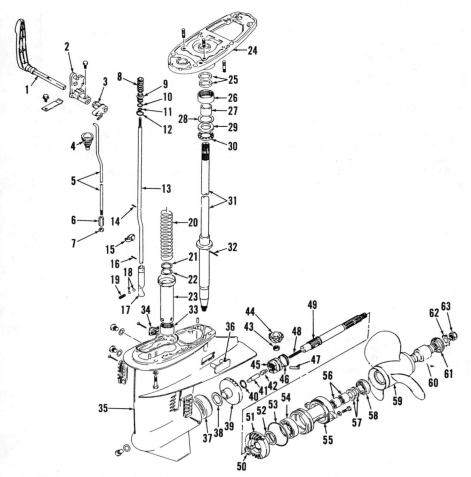

Fig. SZ13-30—Exploded view of lower unit gearcase assembly and shift linkage and components.

1. Shift lever	14. Pin	27. Bushing	40. Thrust washer	52. Shim
2. Plate	15. Magnet	28. Shim	41. Shift pin	53. "O" ring
3. Arm	16. Pin	29. Thrust washer	42. Spring guide	54. Bearing
4. Boot	17. Shift cam	30. Thrust bearing	43. Nut	55. Bearing carrier
5. Upper shift rod	18. Balls	31. Drive shaft	44. Pinion gear	56. Bearings
6. Coupler	19. Spring	32. Pin	45. Dog clutch	57. Seals
7. Jamb nut	20. Spring	33. Bearing	46. Retainer	58. Thrust hub
8. Seal	21. Thrust washer	34. Cover	47. Pin	59. Propeller
9. Guide	22. Washer	35. Gearcase	48. Spring	60. Bushing
10. "O" ring	23. Collar	36. Cover	49. Propeller shaft	61. Thrust hub
11. "O" ring	24. Bearing housing	37. Bearing	50. Thrust washer	62. Lockwasher
12. "O" ring	25. Seals	38. Shim	51. Reverse gear	63. Nut
13. Lower shift rod	26. Bearing	39. Forward gear		

housing and gearcase retaining screws. Tighten gearcase screws to 15-20 N·m (11-14 ft.-lbs.). Adjust coupler (6) so shift lever (1) travels equal distance from neutral to forward position as from neutral to reverse position.

POWER TILT

All models are equipped with power tilt system. An oil pump driven by a reversible electric motor provides oil pressure. A rocker control switch determines motor and pump rotation, thereby retracting or extending tilt cylinders.

NOTE: All models are equipped with power TILT only. Damage to the power tilt system may occur if attempt is made to use the system as power trim.

Power tilt pump assembly is equipped with manual release valve M—Fig. SZ13-36). Manual release valve (M) should in the closed position (clockwise) for normal operation. If power tilt malfunction occurs, outboard motor may be raised and lowered manually by opening the manual release valve (M) two turns maximum (counterclockwise).

Recommended oil is Dexron II or a suitable equivalent automatic transmission fluid. On early models (prior to serial number 613245), check oil level with the outboard motor in the fully down position. On later models (after serial number 613244), check oil level with the outboard motor tilted fully up. Refer to Fig. SZ13-35 to identify early and late pump assemblies. Oil level should be to bottom of fill plug hole on all models.

Bleed air from hydraulic system by tilting up and down through several cycles. Be sure to recheck oil level after several cycles and fill as necessary.

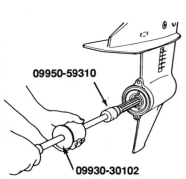

Fig. SZ13-31—Removing propeller shaft assembly using Suzuki propeller shaft remover 09950-59310 and slide hammer 09930-30102.

Fig. SZ13-32—Use two 6 mm jackscrews positioned where shown to withdraw upper bearing housing with drive shaft components.

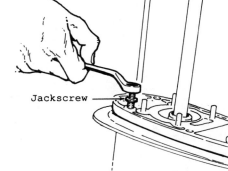

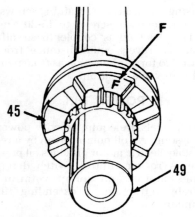

If power tilt malfunction occurs make sure malfunction is not due to wiring, connections or electric motor failure. To check down circuit pressure, disconnect down tube (D—Fig. SZ13-36) from pump and tilt cylinder. Connect a 34.5 MPa (5000 psi) pressure gage between pump and cylinder. Make sure manual release valve is fully closed (clockwise). Operate power tilt switch in the down direction until tilt cylinder rod is fully retracted. Down pressure should be 3000-7000 kPa (435-1015 psi). Remove test gage, reinstall down line (D) and

bleed air from hydraulic system making sure reservoir is full of oil. To test up pressure, remove up line (U) from pump and cylinder. Connect test gage between pump and cylinder in up circuit (U). Operate tilt switch in the up direction until cylinder rod is full extended. Up pressure should be 13,000-17,000 kPa (1885-2466 psi). Remove test gage and reinstall up line (U). Making sure reservoir is full of oil, bleed all air from hydraulic system. Renew pump and valve body assembly if hydraulic pressure is low or erratic.

Fig. SZ13-33—Install dog clutch (45) on propeller shaft (49) so mark (F) is facing forward gear (front).

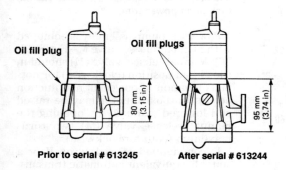

Fig. SZ13-35—View shows difference between early (prior to 1987) and late (after 1986) power tilt pump and motor assemblies.

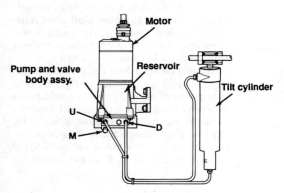

Fig. SZ13-36—View of pump assembly identifies manual release valve (M), up circuit (U) and down circuit (D).

SUZUKI DT50, DT60 AND DT65
(Prior to 1985)

CONDENSED SERVICE DATA

NOTE: Metric fasteners are used throughout outboard motor.

TUNE-UP
Hp/rpm:
DT50 ....50/4800-5500
DT60 ....60/4800-5500
DT65 ....65/4800-5500
Bore:
DT50 (Prior to 1984) ....80 mm
    (3.15 in.)
DT50 (1984), DT60 & DT65 ....84 mm
    (3.31 in.)
Stroke ....72 mm
    (2.83 in.)
Number of Cylinders 2
Displacement:
DT50 (Prior to 1984) ....723 cc
    (44.12 cu. in.)
DT50 (1984), DT60 & DT65 ....798 cc
    (48.69 cu. in.)
Spark Plug:
NGK B8HS*
Electrode Gap ....0.8-0.9 mm
    (0.031-0.035 in.)
Ignition Type ....Breakerless
Carburetor:
Make..Mikuni
Model B40-32
Fuel:Oil Ratio ....50:1†
*1984 DT50 models use NGK B8HS-10 spark plugs with an
  electrode gap of 1 mm (0.040 in.).
†1984 DT50 and 1983 and 1984 DT60 models are equipped
  with oil injection.

SIZES—CLEARANCES
Piston Ring End Gap ....0.2-0.4 mm
    (0.008-0.016 in.)
Piston Pin Diameter ....19.995-20.000 mm
    (0.7872-0.7874 in.)
Piston to Cylinder Wall Clearance:
DT50 (Prior to 1984)................0.097-0.112 mm
    (0.0038-0.0044 in.)
DT50 (1984), DT60 & DT65 ....0.112-0.127 mm
    (0.0044-0.0050 in.)
Max. Crankshaft Runout at Main
  Bearing Journal ....0.05 mm
    (0.002 in.)
Max. Connecting Rod Small End
  Side Shake ....5.0 mm
    (0.20 in.)

TIGHTENING TORQUES
Cylinder Head:
6 mm ....8-12 N·m
    (6-9 ft.-lbs.)
10 mm ....40-60 N·m†
    (29-44 ft.-lbs.)
Crankcase ....40-60 N·m†
    (29-44 ft.-lbs.)
Exhaust Cover ....8-12 N·m
    (6-9 ft.-lbs.)
Flywheel Nut ....200-210 N·m
    (145-152 ft.-lbs.)
Gearcase Pinion Nut ....30-40 N·m
    (22-29 ft.-lbs.)
Propeller Shaft Nut ....50-60 N·m
    (36-44 ft.-lbs.)
Standard Screws:
Unmarked or Marked "4"
5 mm ....2-4 N·m
    (2-3 ft.-lbs.)
6 mm ....4-7 N·m
    (3-5 ft.-lbs.)
8 mm ....10-16 N·m
    (7-12 ft.-lbs.)
10 mm ....22-35 N·m
    (16-26 ft.-lbs.)
Stainless Steel
5 mm ....2-4 N·m
    (2-3 ft.-lbs.)
6 mm ....6-10 N·m
    (5-7 ft.-lbs.)
8 mm ....15-20 N·m
    (11-15 ft.-lbs.)
10 mm ....34-41 N·m
    (25-30 ft.-lbs.)
Marked "7" or SAE Grade 5
5 mm ....3-6 N·m
    (2-5 ft.-lbs.)
6 mm ....8-12 N·m
    (6-9 ft.-lbs.)
8 mm ....18-28 N·m
    (13-20 ft.-lbs.)
10 mm ....40-60 N·m
    (29-44 ft.-lbs.)

†Torque values should be 46-54 N·m (34-39 ft.-lbs.) on DT50
(1984) and DT60 models.

LUBRICATION

The power head is lubricated by oil mixed with the fuel. On models without oil injection, fuel:oil ratios should be 30:1 during break-in of a new or rebuilt engine and 50:1 for normal service when using a NMMA certified TC-WII two-stroke engine oil or Suzuki "CCI" oil. When using any other type of two-stroke engine oil, fuel:oil ratios should be 20:1 during break-in and 30:1 for normal service. On models equipped with oil injection, for the first 5 hours of operation, mix fuel with oil in fuel tank at a ratio of 50:1 if Suzuki "CCI" oil or a NMMA certified TC-WII two-stroke oil is used. Mix fuel:oil at a ratio of 30:1 if any other type of two-stroke oil is used. Switch to straight fuel in fuel tank at the completion of the 5 hour break-in period. Manufacturer recommends regular or no-lead automotive gasoline having an 85-95 octane rating. Gasoline and oil should be thoroughly mixed in fuel tank when used on models without oil injection and when used during break-in period on models equipped with oil injection.

The lower unit gears and bearings are lubricated by oil contained in the gearcase. SAE 90 hypoid outboard gear oil

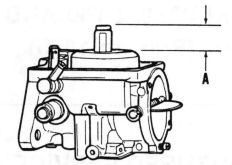

Fig. SZ14-2 — Refer to text for float level (A) specifications.

should be used. Gearcase capacity is approximately 650 mL (22 oz.) of gear oil and should be drained and refilled after the first 10 hours of use and then after every 50 hours of use. Reinstall vent and fill plugs securely, using a new gasket if needed, to ensure a watertight seal.

FUEL SYSTEM

CARBURETOR. Mikuni type B40-32 carburetors are used on all models. Refer to Fig. SZ14-1 for exploded view. Initial setting of pilot air screw (7) from a lightly seated position should be 1¾ to 2¼ turns on DT50 models prior to 1984 and DT65 models and 1⅝ to 2⅛ turns on 1984 DT50 models and DT60 models. Final carburetor adjustment should be made with engine at normal operating temperature and running in forward gear. Rotate timing adjustment screw (B – Fig. SZ14-11) in small increments until engine idles at approximately 650-700 rpm. Adjust pilot air screw so engine idles smoothly and will accelerate cleanly without hesitation. If necessary, readjust timing adjustment screw to obtain 650-700 rpm idle speed.

Main fuel metering is controlled by main jet (10). Standard main jet size for normal operation is number 165 on DT50 models prior to 1984, number 155 on 1984 DT50 models, number 160 on DT60 models and number 167.5 on DT65 models.

To check float level, remove float bowl and invert carburetor. Distance (A – Fig. SZ14-2) between main jet and bottom of float should be 16.5-18.5 mm (0.65-0.75 in.) on DT50 models prior to 1984 and DT65 models, 16.5-18 mm (0.65-0.71 in.) on 1984 DT50 models and 16-18 mm (0.63-0.71 in.) on DT60 models. Adjust float level by bending float tang.

To synchronize throttle plate opening of top carburetor with bottom carburetor, use Suzuki carburetor balancer 09913-13121 or equivalent and make adjustment at throttle shaft connector (5 – Fig. SZ14-1).

SPEED CONTROL LINKAGE. The carburetor throttle valves must be correctly synchronized to open as the ignition is advanced to obtain optimum performance. To adjust the speed control linkage, it is necessary to first check (and adjust if required) the ignition maximum advance as outlined in the IGNITION TIMING section. Disconnect carburetor link (C – Fig. SZ14-11) and rotate speed control lever (L) toward maximum speed position until it contacts maximum speed stop. Set carburetor throttle plates completely open then vary the length of carburetor link (C) until ball joint connector will just attach. Move speed control lever to full retard position. Clearance (A) at carburetor throttle shaft actuating levers should be 0.5-1.0 mm (0.020-0.040 in.).

REED VALVES. The inlet reed valves (Fig. SZ14-3) are located on a reed plate between inlet manifold and crankcase. The reed petals should seat very lightly against the reed plate throughout their entire length with the least possible tension. Tip of reed petal must not stand open more than 0.2 mm (0.008 in.)from contact surface. Reed stop opening should be 7.6-8.0 mm (0.30-0.31 in.) on DT50 models and 7.55-7.95 mm (0.30-0.31 in.) on DT60 and DT65 models.

Renew reeds if petals are broken, cracked, warped, rusted or bent. Never attempt to bend a reed petal or to straighten a damaged reed. Never install a bent or damaged reed. Seating surface of reed plate should be smooth

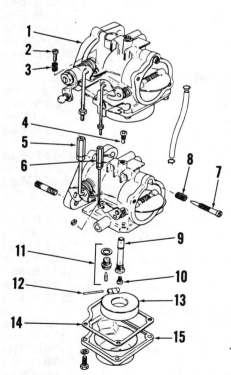

Fig. SZ14-1 — Exploded view of Mikuni carburetors typical of all models.

1. Body
2. Throttle stop screw
3. Spring
4. Pilot jet
5. Throttle shaft connector
6. Choke shaft connector
7. Pilot air screw
8. Spring
9. Main nozzle
10. Main jet
11. Inlet valve
12. Float pin
13. Float
14. Gasket
15. Float bowl

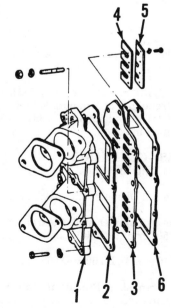

Fig. SZ14-3 — Exploded view of intake manifold and reed valve assembly.

1. Manifold
2. Gasket
3. Reed plate
4. Reed petals
5. Reed stop
6. Gasket

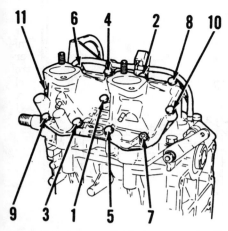

Fig. SZ14-4 — Inlet manifold cap screws should be tightened in the sequence shown above.

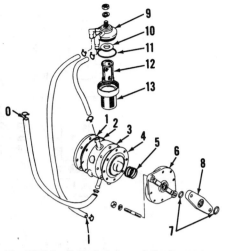

Fig. SZ14-5 — Exploded view of diaphragm type fuel pump and fuel filter assemblies.

1. Cover	
2. Diaphragm	9. Fuel filter body
3. Body	10. Packing
4. Diaphragm	11. "O" ring
5. Spring	12. Filter
6. Body	13. Bowl
7. "O" rings	I. Inlet
8. Insulator block	O. Outlet

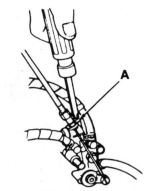

Fig. SZ14-6 — Use oil pump air bleed screw (A) to bleed trapped air from oil supply line or pump.

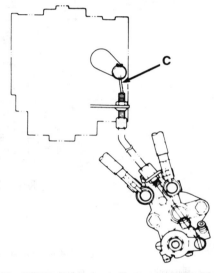

Fig. SZ14-7 — Disconnect oil pump control cable (C) at carburetor throttle lever and refer to text for checking oil pump output.

and flat. When installing reeds or reed stop, make sure that petals are centered over the inlet holes in reed plate, and that the reed stops are centered over reed petals. Apply a suitable high temperature grease to inlet manifold cap screw threads, then using sequence shown in Fig. SZ14-4 tighten cap screws.

FUEL PUMP. A diaphragm type fuel pump is mounted on the side of power head cylinder block and is actuated by pressure and vacuum pulsations from the engine crankcases. Refer to Fig. SZ14-5 for exploded view of fuel pump assembly.

When servicing pump, scribe reference marks across pump body to aid in reassembly. Defective or questionable parts should be renewed. Diaphragm should be renewed if air leaks or cracks are found, or if deterioration is evident.

FUEL FILTER. A fuel filter (9 through 13 – Fig. SZ14-5) is mounted on the side of power head cylinder block on all models. Filter should be disassembled and cleaned after every 50 hours of use. Renew "O" ring (11) if required.

OIL INJECTION

Models So Equipped

BLEEDING PUMP. To bleed trapped air from oil supply line or pump, first make sure outboard motor is in an upright position and oil tank is full. Open oil pump air bleed screw (A – Fig. SZ14-6) three or four turns to allow oil to seep out around screw threads. After five seconds or when no air bubbles are noticed, close air bleed screw (A).

CHECKING OIL PUMP OUTLET. Start engine and allow to warm-up for

approximately five minutes, then stop engine. Disconnect oil pump control cable (C – Fig. SZ14-7) at carburetor throttle lever. Detach oil supply line at oil tank outlet. Connect oil gage 09900-21602 to oil supply line. Fill oil gage with a recommended two-stroke oil unit even with an upper reference mark. With oil pump control cable (C) in released position, start engine and maintain engine speed at 1500 rpm. Allow engine to run for five minutes. After five minutes, stop the engine and observe oil gage. Recommended oil consumption is 2.7-3.5 mL (0.09-0.12 oz.) in five minutes at 1500 rpm.

To check oil pump at maximum output position, repeat previous procedure except use a suitable tool and hold oil pump control cable (C) in fully extended position. Recommended oil consumption is 4.6-5.6 mL (0.16-0.19 oz.) in five minutes at 1500 rpm.

If the obtained oil consumption measurements are not within the recommended limits, then oil pump must be renewed.

IGNITION

All models are equipped with either an independent or simultaneous pointless electronic ignition system. Simultaneous ignition system models are identified by the use of one ignition coil while two ignition coils are used on models with an independent ignition system. Simultaneous ignition models may have mechanical or electronic advance. Stator plate is movable on simultaneous ignition models with mechanical advance

while the stator plate is fixed on models with electronic advance. Refer to Fig. SZ14-8 for a typical wiring diagram of models with independent ignition. Models with simultaneous ignition systems are similar.

IGNITION TIMING. On independent ignition models, ignition timing should be 4° ATDC at 1000 rpm and 21° BTDC on DT60 models and 25° BTDC on all other models at 5000 rpm. On simultaneous ignition models with mechanical advance, ignition timing should be 3° ATDC at 1000 rpm and 25° BTDC at 5000 rpm. On simultaneous ignition models with electronic advance (fixed stator plate), ignition timing should be 8° BTDC at 1000 rpm and 25° BTDC at 5000 rpm.

Initial setting of ignition timing on all models with mechanical advance may be accomplished as follows: Set throttle at full advance position, then align mark

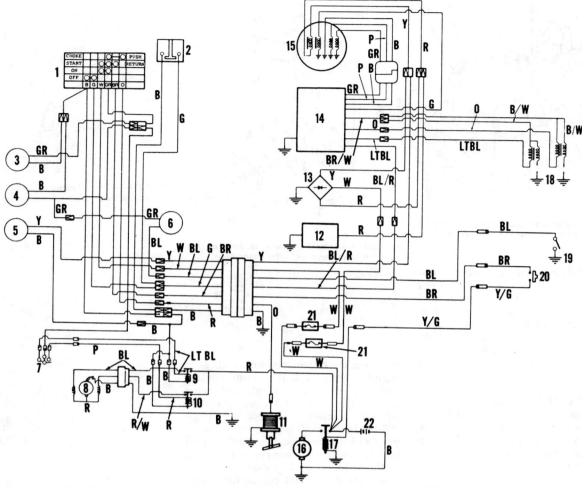

Fig. SZ14-8—Typical wiring diagram for models with independent ignition. Other models are similar.

1. Ignition switch	6. Overheat buzzer	10. "Down" solenoid	16. Starter motor
2. Emergency stop switch	7. Tilt and trim switch	11. Choke solenoid	17. Starter solenoid
3. Hour meter	8. Tilt and trim motor	12. Regulator	18. Spark plugs
4. Volt meter	9. "Up" solenoid	13. Rectifier	19. Overheat sensor
5. Tachometer		14. CD ignition module	20. Neutral switch
		15. Stator	21. 20 amp fuse

22. Battery
B. Black
BL. Blue
BR. Brown
G. Green

GR. Gray
LtBl. Light blue
O. Orange
P. Pink
R. Red
W. White
Y. Yellow

(M – Fig. SZ14-9) on stator plate with stationary mark (S) on upper seal housing. Loosen nut (N) on stator plate link to reposition stator plate.

Initial setting of ignition timing on all models with electronic advance may be accomplished by aligning mark (M – Fig. SZ14-10) on stator plate with center of stator plate retaining screw hole (H).

Final ignition timing check can be made using a suitable power timing light. Immerse lower unit of outboard motor in water and connect timing light to upper spark plug. Set engine throttle at full retard position and start engine. Refer to ignition timing specifications stated previously and check alignment of flywheel timing marks with index mark on electric starter cap on models with mechanical advance or with index mark on flywheel housing on models with electronic advance. To check ad-

vance ignition timing, run engine at wide open throttle and note timing marks.

On models with mechanical advance, full retard timing may be adjusted by turning bolt (B – Fig. SZ14-11) in or out as required and full advance timing may be adjusted by loosening nut (N) and

repositioning stator plate. On models with electronic advance, reposition stator plate to adjust ignition timing.

TROUBLE-SHOOTING. If ignition malfunction occurs, use only approved procedures to prevent damage to the

Fig. SZ14-9—On models with mechanical advance, set ignition timing statically by aligning mark (M) on stator plate with stationary mark (S) when throttle is in the full advance position.

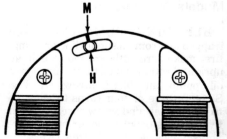

Fig. SZ14-10—On models with electronic advance, set ignition timing statically by aligning mark (M) on stator plate with center of screw hole (H).

components. The fuel system should be checked first to make certain that faulty running is not caused by incorrect mixture or contaminated fuel. Make sure malfunction is not due to spark plug, wiring or wiring connection failure. Trouble-shoot ignition circuit using Suzuki pocket tester number 09900-25002 or ohmmeter as follows:

Simultaneous Ignition Models. On simultaneous ignition models with electronic advance (fixed stator plate), check condition of low-speed capacitor charge coil by separating the red/black wire connector at stator and attach a tester lead. Attach the other tester lead to engine ground. Low-speed charge coil may be considered satisfactory if resistance reading is within the limits of 112-149 ohms. Check condition of high-speed charge coil by separating the red/black wire connector and blue/red wire connector at stator and attach a tester lead to each wire. High-speed

+Tester lead	-Tester lead	Charge	Pulser	Ground	Stop	Ignition
		Blue/Red	White/Red	Black	Blue/Red	Black/White
Charge	Blue/Red		A	A	A	A
Pulser	White/Red	B		B	B	B
Ground	Black	C	A		C	A
Stop	Blue/Red	A	A	A		A
Ignition	Black/White	C	C	C	C	

Fig. SZ14-13—Use chart shown above and values listed in Fig. SZ14-12 to test condition of CD ignition module used on simultaneous ignition models with mechanical advance.

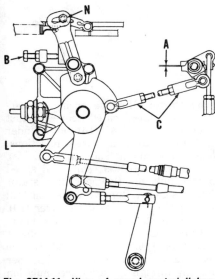

Fig. SZ14-11—View of speed control linkage used on models with mechanical advance. Models with electronic advance (fixed stator plate) are similar.

+Tester lead	-Tester lead	Charge &pulser	Charge	Ground	Ignition	Stop
		Blue/Red	Red/Black	Black	White/Black	Blue/Red
Charge &pulser	Blue/Red		B	A	A	A
Charge	Red/Black	C		A	A	A
Ground	Black	C	B		A	A
Ignition	White/Black	C	B	C		C
Stop	Blue/Red	A	B	A	A	

Fig. SZ14-12—Use chart shown above and values listed below to test condition of CD ignition module used on simultaneous ignition models with electronic advance.

A. 100k ohms or less
B. 100k ohms or more
C. Tester needle should show deflection then return toward infinite resistance

charge coil may be considered satisfactory if resistance reading is within the limits of 1.62-1.98 ohms.

To check condition of ignition coil, separate the white/black wire connector at coil and remove high tension wires from spark plugs. Attach tester positive lead to white/black wire and negative lead to coil ground. Primary coil resistance reading should be within the limits of 0.28-0.38 ohms. Attach a tester lead to each high tension wire. Secondary coil resistance reading should be within the limits of 2980-4030 ohms.

To check condition of CD ignition module, use tester or ohmmeter in conjunction with test chart shown in Fig. SZ14-12. Renew CD ignition module if required.

On simultaneous ignition models with mechanical advance, check condition of capacitor charge coil by separating the blue/red connector and black wire connector at stator and attach a tester lead to each wire. Charge coil may be considered satisfactory if resistance reading is within the limits of 135-165 ohms.

Check condition of pulser coil by separating the white/red wire connector and black wire connector at stator and attach a tester lead to each wire. Pulser coil may be considered satisfactory if resistance reading is within the limits of 7.29-8.91 ohms.

To check condition of ignition coil, separate the black/white wire connector at coil and remove high tension wires from spark plugs. Attach tester positive lead to black/white wire and negative lead to coil ground. Primary coil resistance reading should be within the limits of 0.076-0.104 ohms. Attach a tester lead to each high tension wire. Secondary coil resistance reading should be within the limits of 2980-4030 ohms.

To check condition of CD ignition module, use tester or ohmmeter in conjunction with test chart shown in Fig. SZ14-13. Renew CD ignition module if required.

Independent Ignition Models. On independent ignition models, check condition of capacitor charge coil by separating the green wire connector and black wire connector at stator and attach a tester lead to each wire. Charge coil may be considered satisfactory if resistance reading is within the limits of 225-275 ohms.

Check condition of pulser coils by separating the gray wire connector, pink wire connector and black wire connector at stator. Attach tester positive lead to black wire. Attach negative lead to gray wire and note tester reading, then attach negative lead to pink wire and note tester reading. Resistance reading for each pulser coil should be within the limits of 180-220 ohms.

Check condition of each ignition coil as follows: Separate the orange wire connector and black/white wire connector at coil for top cylinder, then attach a tester lead to each wire and note tester reading. Separate light blue wire connector and black/white wire connector at coil for bottom cylinder, then attach a tester lead to each wire and note tester reading. Primary coil resistance reading should be within the limits of 0.87-1.17 ohms for each coil. Disconnect high tension wires from spark plugs. Attach tester positive lead to high tension wire and negative lead to black/white wire.

Fig. SZ14-14—Use chart adjacent and values listed in Fig. SZ14-12 to test condition of CD ignition module used on independent ignition models.

+Tester lead	-Tester lead	Charge	Pulser		Ground	Stop	Ignition		
		Green	Gray	Pink	Black	Blue/Red	Orange	Light blue	Black/White
Charge	Green		A	A	A	B	C	C	C
Pulser	Gray	B		B	B	B	B	B	B
	Pink	B	B		B	B	B	B	B
Ground	Black	C	A	A		A	C	C	C
Stop	Blue/Red	B	B	B	B		B	B	B
Ignition	Orange	B	B	B	B	B		B	B
	Light blue	B	B	B	B	B	B		B
	Black/White	A	A	A	A	B	A	A	

Illustrations courtesy Suzuki

Secondary coil resistance reading should be within the limits of 5020-6790 ohms for each coil.

To check condition of CD ignition module, use tester or ohmmeter in conjunction with test chart shown in Fig. SZ14-14. Renew CD ignition module if required.

COOLING SYSTEM

WATER PUMP. A rubber impeller type water pump is mounted between the drive shaft housing and gearcase. A key in the drive shaft is used to turn the pump impeller. If cooling system problems are encountered, check water intake for plugging or partial stoppage, then if not corrected, remove gearcase as outlined in the appropriate section and check condition of the water pump, water passages and sealing surfaces.

When water pump is disassembled, check condition of impeller (4–Fig. SZ14-15) and plate (5) for excessive wear. Turn drive shaft clockwise (viewed from top) while placing pump housing over impeller. Avoid turning drive shaft in opposite direction when water pump is assembled.

THERMOSTAT. A thermostat (4–Fig. SZ14-16) is used to regulate operating temperature. The thermostat should start to open within the temperature range of 40°-44° C (104°-111° F). Thermostat can be removed for inspection or renewal by removing cylinder head cover.

POWER HEAD

REMOVE AND REINSTALL. To remove the power head, first remove up-

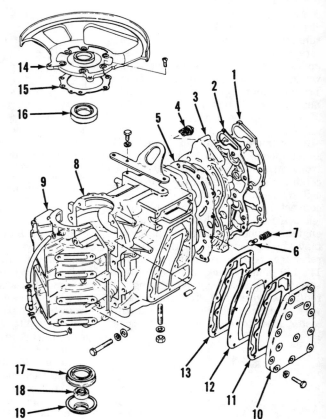

Fig. SZ14-16—Exploded view of crankcase assembly typical of all models.

1. Cylinder head cover
2. Gasket
3. Cylinder head
4. Thermostat
5. Head gasket
6. Valve
7. Spring
8. Cylinder block
9. Crankcase
10. Outer exhaust cover
11. Gasket
12. Inner exhaust cover
13. Gasket
14. Upper seal housing
15. Gasket
16. Upper crankshaft seal
17. Lower crankshaft seal
18. Drive shaft seal
19. Drive shaft seal housing

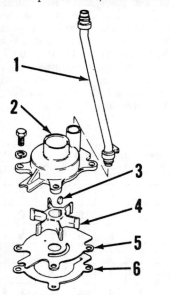

Fig. SZ14-15—Exploded view of water pump assembly.

1. Water tube
2. Pump housing
3. Key
4. Impeller
5. Plate
6. Gasket

per cover and disconnect linkage, fuel lines and wires which interfere with power head removal. Remove carburetors and electric choke solenoid. Remove plug from side of lower cover to obtain access to shift linkage. Unscrew nuts retaining shift arm (2–Fig. SZ14-25) to shaft (4), then disengage shaft (4) from shift rod (9). Remove screws securing power head assembly to lower unit and lift off power head.

Before reinstalling power head, check condition of drive shaft seal (18–Fig. SZ14-16). If seal renewal is required, it will be necessary to separate crankcase (9) and cylinder block (8) as outlined in the appropriate following paragraphs. Apply a suitable high temperature grease to lip portion of seal and install seal into seal housing (19) with open side towards lower unit. Make certain drive shaft splines are clean then coat them with a light coating of water resistant grease. Apply a suitable sealer to mating surfaces of power head and lower unit and install a new gasket. Coat power head to lower unit retaining cap screws adjacent to cap screw heads with silicone sealer. The remainder of installation is the reverse of removal procedure.

DISASSEMBLY. Disassembly and inspection may be accomplished in the following manner. Remove electric or

recoil starter. Remove wiring connection cover plate located above exhaust cover (10–Fig. SZ14-16) on cylinder block and separate all wire connections. Remove ignition module, ignition coil(s), fuel pump, fuel filter, shift and speed control linkage, flywheel and stator plate assembly. Remove upper oil seal housing (14), outer exhaust cover (10), inner exhaust cover (12), intake manifold and reed valves. Remove cylinder head cover (1) and cylinder head (3), then clean carbon from combustion chamber and any foreign material accumulation in water passages. Withdraw spring (7) and valve (6) from cylinder block. Unscrew crankcase retaining screws and separate crankcase (9) from cylinder block (8). Remove lower oil seal housing (19). Crankshaft and piston assembly may now be removed from cylinder block.

Engine components are now ready for overhaul as outlined in the appropriate following paragraphs. Refer to the following section for assembly procedure.

ASSEMBLY. Refer to specific service sections when assembling the crankshaft, connecting rod, piston and reed valves. Make sure all joint and gasket surfaces are clean, free from nicks and burrs and hardened cement or carbon. Whenever the power head is disassembled, it is recommended that all gasket

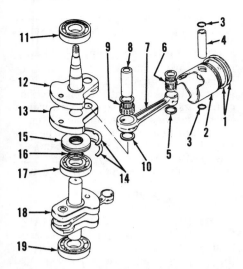

Fig. SZ14-17 — Exploded view of crankshaft assembly typical of all models.

1. Piston rings
2. Piston
3. Piston pin clip
4. Piston pin
5. Thrust washer
6. Needle bearing
7. Connecting rod
8. Crankpin
9. Needle bearing
10. Thrust washer
11. Ball bearing
12. Top crank half
13. Crank half
14. Thrust rings
15. Labyrinth seal
16. "O" ring
17. Ball bearing
18. Lower crankshaft assy.
19. Ball bearing

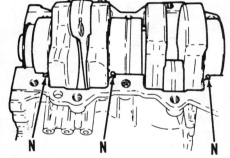

Fig. SZ14-18 — View of installed crankshaft assembly showing main bearing locating notches (N).

surfaces and mating surfaces without gaskets be carefully checked for nicks, burrs and warped surfaces which might interfere with a tight seal. Cylinder head, head end of cylinder block and some mating surfaces of manifold and crankcase should be checked on a surface plate and lapped if necessary to provide a smooth surface. Do not remove any more metal than is necessary.

When assembling power head, first lubricate all friction surfaces and bearings with engine oil. Place thrust rings (14 – Fig. SZ14-17) in cylinder block, then install crankshaft assembly. Make certain main bearing locating pins engage notches (N – Fig. SZ14-18) in cylinder block. Apply a suitable high temperature grease to lip portion of crankshaft and drive shaft seals, then install lower crankshaft seal (17 – Fig. SZ14-16) ensuring seal flange properly

engages groove in cylinder block. Install drive shaft seal (18) into seal housing (19) with open side towards lower unit. Apply a sufficient amount of water-resistant grease to seal housing (19) to fill area between lower crankshaft seal and drive shaft seal, then install seal housing to cylinder block. Apply a coat of Suzuki Bond No. 4 or a suitable sealer to mating surfaces of crankcase and cylinder block and position crankcase on cylinder block. Using tightening sequence shown in Fig. SZ14-19, tighten the crankcase screws to 46-54 N·m (34-39 ft.-lbs.) on DT50 (1984) and DT60 models and 40-60 N·m (29-44 ft.-lbs.) on all other models. Install upper crankshaft seal (16 – Fig. SZ14-16) into seal housing (14) with open side towards cylinder block, then install seal housing to cylinder block assembly.

Cylinder head gasket should be installed without the application of a gasket sealer. With valve (6) and spring (7) installed in cylinder block, position cylinder head, cylinder head cover and related gaskets on cylinder block then using tightening sequence shown in Fig. SZ14-20, tighten the 6 mm screws to 8-12 N·m (6-9 ft.-lbs.) and the 10 mm screws to 46-54 N·m (34-39 ft.-lbs.) on DT50 (1984) and DT60 models and 40-60 N·m (29-44 ft.-lbs.) on all other models.

RINGS, PISTONS AND CYLINDERS. The pistons are fitted with two piston rings. Piston rings are interchangeable in grooves but must be installed with manufacturers marking toward closed end of piston. Piston ring end gap should be 0.2-0.4 mm (0.008-0.016 in.) with a maximum allowable ring end gap of 0.8 mm (0.031 in.). Piston to cylinder wall clearance should be 0.097-0.112 mm (0.0038-0.0044 in.) on DT50 models prior to 1984 and 0.112-0.127 mm (0.0044-0.0050 in.) on all other models. Pistons and rings are available in standard size as well as 0.25

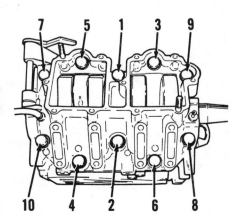

Fig. SZ14-19 — Crankcase cap screws should be tightened in the sequence shown above.

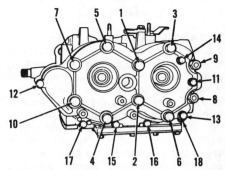

Fig. SZ14-20 — Cylinder head cap screws should be tightened in the sequence shown above. Refer to text for tightening torque specifications.

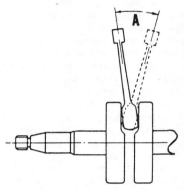

Fig. SZ14-21 — Maximum side-to-side shake (A) at small end of connecting rod should be 5 mm (0.20 in.) or less.

mm (0.010 in.) and 0.50 mm (0.020 in.) oversizes. Cylinder should be bored to an oversize if cylinder is out-of-round or taper exceeds 0.10 mm (0.004 in.). Install piston on connecting rod so arrow on piston crown will point towards exhaust port when piston is in cylinder.

CONNECTING RODS, BEARINGS AND CRANKSHAFT. Connecting rods, bearings and crankshaft are a pressed together unit. Crankshaft should be disassembled ONLY by experienced service personnel and with suitable service equipment.

Caged roller bearings are used at both large and small ends of the connecting rod. Determine rod bearing wear by measuring connecting rod small end side-to-side movement as shown at (A – Fig. SZ14-21). Normal side-to-side movement is 5 mm (0.20 in.) or less. Maximum allowable limit of crankshaft runout is 0.05 mm (0.002 in.) measured at bearing surfaces with crankshaft ends supported.

When installing crankshaft, lubricate pistons, rings, cylinders and bearings with engine oil as outlined in ASSEMBLY section.

STARTERS

MANUAL STARTER. Refer to Fig. SZ14-22 for exploded view of overhead type manual starter assembly used on some DT50 models. Starter may be disassembled for overhaul or renewal of individual components as follows: Remove engine top cowl and three cap screws securing starter assembly to power head. If starter spring remains under tension, pull starter rope and hold rope pulley (10) with notch in pulley adjacent to rope outlet. Pull rope back through outlet so that it engages notch in pulley and allow pulley to slowly unwind. Remove cap screw (21) and disassemble unit. Be careful when removing rewind spring (8); a rapidly uncoiling starter spring could cause serious injury.

Rewind spring is wound in a counterclockwise direction in starter housing. Rope is wound on rope pulley in a counterclockwise direction as viewed with pulley in housing. Reassemble starter assembly by reversing disassembly procedure. To place tension on rewind spring, pass rope through rope outlet in housing and install rope handle. Pull rope out and hold rope pulley so notch on pulley is adjacent to rope outlet. Pull rope back through outlet between notch in pulley and housing. Turn rope pulley counterclockwise four complete revolutions to place tension on spring. Do not place more ten-

sion on rewind spring than is necessary to draw rope handle up against housing.

ELECTRIC STARTER. Some models are equipped with electric starter shown in Fig. SZ14-23. Disassembly is evident after inspection of unit and reference to exploded view. Starter brushes have a standard length of 16 mm (0.63 in.) and should be renewed if worn to 9.5 mm (0.37 in.) or less. After reassembly, bench test starter before installing on power head.

LOWER UNIT

PROPELLER AND DRIVE CLUTCH. Protection for the motor is built into a special cushioning clutch in the propeller hub. No adjustment is possible on the propeller or clutch. Three-bladed propellers are used. Propellers are available from the manufacturer in various diameters and pitches and should be selected to provide optimum performance at full throttle within the recommended limits of 4800-5500 rpm.

R&R AND OVERHAUL. Refer to Fig. SZ14-24 for exploded view of lower unit gearcase assembly used on all models. During disassembly, note the location of all shims and thrust washers

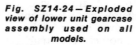

Fig. SZ14-23 — Exploded view of electric starter motor.

1. "C" ring	
2. Stop	
3. Spring	8. Brush assy.
4. Drive	9. Brush cover
5. Frame head	10. Thrust washer
6. Armature	11. "E" clip
7. Frame	12. End cap
	13. Starter solenoid

Fig. SZ14-24 — Exploded view of lower unit gearcase assembly used on all models.

1. Link
2. Shift arm
3. Bushings
4. Shift shaft
5. Dust seal
6. Rod guide
7. "O" ring
8. "O" ring
9. Shift rod
10. Pin
11. Magnet
12. Magnet holder
13. Pin
14. Shift cam
15. Bearing housing
16. Seal
17. Drive shaft
18. Bearing
19. Thrust washer
20. Spring
21. Washer
22. Collar
23. Snap ring
24. Shim
25. Needle bearings
26. Gearcase
27. Vent plug
28. Oil level plug
29. Drain plug
30. Strip seal
31. Pinion gear
32. Collar
33. Washer
34. Pinion nut
35. Taper bearing
36. Shim
37. Forward gear
38. Thrust washer
39. Shift pin
40. Spring guide
41. Clutch
42. Pin
43. Pin retainer
44. Shift spring
45. Propeller shaft
46. Shim

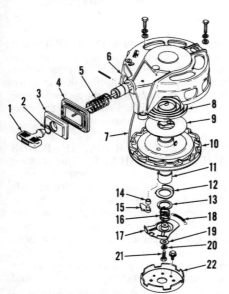

Fig. SZ14-22 — Exploded view of overhead starter assembly used on some models.

1. Rope handle	
2. Retainer	
3. Rope guide	13. Retainer
4. Grommet	14. Bushing
5. Spring	15. Pawl
6. Starter housing	16. Spring
7. Rope	17. Cover plate
8. Rewind spring	18. Spring
9. Plate	19. Washer
10. Rope pulley	20. Lockwasher
11. Bushing	21. Cap screw
12. Guide	22. Starter cup

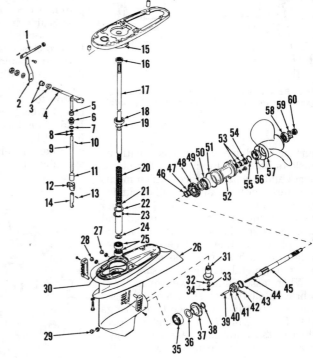

47. Thrust washer		54. Seal	
48. Reverse gear		55. Snap ring	
49. Shim		56. Spacer	
50. Bearing		57. Propeller	
51. "O" ring		58. Spacer	
52. End cap		59. Lockwasher	
53. Needle bearings		60. Propeller nut	

to aid in reassembly. To remove gearcase, first unscrew plug (29) and drain gear lubricant. Remove plug from side of lower engine cover to obtain access to shift linkage. Unscrew nuts retaining shift arm (2) to shaft (4), then disengage shaft (4) from shift rod (9). Remove the cap screws securing gearcase to drive shaft housing and separate gearcase assembly from drive shaft housing. Remove water pump assembly (Fig. SZ14-15). Remove propeller with related components from propeller shaft. Unscrew two screws retaining gearcase end cap (52–Fig. SZ14-24), then attach a suitable puller to propeller shaft (45) and withdraw propeller shaft assembly with gearcase end cap. Unscrew pinion nut (34) and remove pinion gear (31), then extract forward gear (37). Drive shaft (17) and related components may be withdrawn from gearcase after removal of bearing housing (15).

Inspect gears for wear on teeth and on engagement dogs. Inspect clutch (41) for wear on engagement surfaces. Inspect shafts for wear on splines and on friction surfaces of gears and oil seals. Check shift cam (14) and shift pin (39) for excessive wear. Check condition of shift

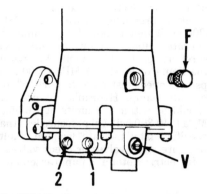

Fig. SZ14-27—View of pump assembly showing location of oil fill plug (F), release valve (V) and test ports (1 and 2).

spring (44). Spring free length should be 69 mm (2.72 in.) with a minimum length of 67 mm (2.64 in.). All seals and "O" rings should be renewed when unit is reassembled.

Backlash between pinion gear (31) and drive gears (37 and 48) should be 0.05-0.30 mm (0.002-0.012 in.) and is adjusted by varying thickness of shims (36 and 49). Propeller shaft end play should be 0.05-0.30 mm (0.002-0.012 in.) and is adjusted by increasing or decreasing the thickness of thrust washers (38 and 47) and shims (46).

Reassemble gearcase by reversing disassembly procedure while noting the following: Install clutch (41) on propeller shaft (45) so "F" marked side (see Fig. SZ14-25) is towards forward gear (37–Fig. SZ14-24). Tighten pinion nut (34) to 30-40 N·m (22-29 ft.-lbs.). Apply water-resistant grease to "O" ring (51). Apply silicone sealer to gearcase and bearing housing (15) mating surfaces and to bearing housing and drive shaft housing mating surfaces. Coat retaining cap screws adjacent to cap screw heads with silicone sealer.

With gearcase assembly installed, adjust shift linkage as follows: Set shift arm (2) exactly between "F" and "R" positions, then adjust link (1) so protrusion (P–Fig. SZ14-26) on shift lever (L) is centered over neutral safety interlock switch. Fill gearcase with outboard gear oil as outlined in LUBRICATION section.

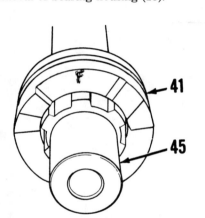

Fig. SZ14-25—Install clutch (41) on propeller shaft (45) with "F" marked side toward forward gear.

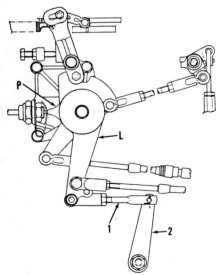

Fig. SZ14-26—Protrusion (P) on shift lever (L) should be centered on neutral safety switch when lower unit is in neutral.

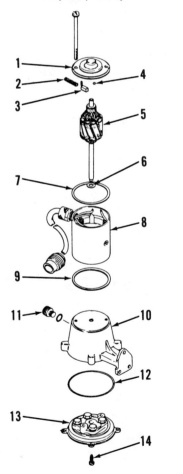

Fig. SZ14-28—Exploded view of power tilt and trim electric motor and pump assembly.

1. End cap	8. Frame
2. Spring	9. Gasket
3. Brush	10. Reservoir
4. Ball	11. Fill plug
5. Armature	12. "O" ring
6. Thrust washer	13. Pump assy.
7. Gasket	14. Cap screw

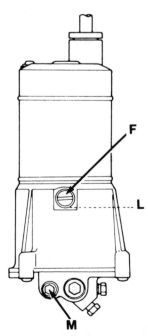

Fig. SZ14-29—View identifying manual release valve (M), fill plug (F) and recommended reservoir oil level (L) on power tilt and trim pump used on models DT50 (1984) and DT60 (1983-1984).

POWER TILT AND TRIM

Some models are equipped with a hydraulically actuated power tilt and trim system. An oil pump driven by a reversible electric motor provides oil pressure. A rocker control switch determines motor and pump rotation thereby retracting or extending tilt and trim cylinders. The pump is equipped with an automatic and manual release valve (V – Fig. SZ14-27) that when set in the manual position (vertical) enables movement of trim and tilt cylinders if the electric motor malfunctions.

Recommended oil is SAE 20W or SAE 30W motor oil or Dexron automatic transmission fluid. Do not run pump without oil in reservoir. Fill plug (F) is located in side of pump reservoir. Oil level should reach fill plug hole threads with outboard motor in a vertical position. Hydraulic tilt should be cycled several times and oil level rechecked if system has been drained or lost a large amount of oil.

If a malfunction occurs in tilt and trim system, first make sure malfunction is not due to wiring, wiring connection or electric motor failure. To check oil pressure, connect a 20.7 MPa (3000 psi) gage to port "1" on pump and operate pump. Hydraulic oil pressure at port "1" should be within the limits of 6.9-17.25 MPa (1000-2500 psi). Connect test gage to port "2" and operate pump. Hydraulic oil pressure should be within the limits of 1.66-5.52 MPa (240-800 psi). Oil pressure less than specified may indicate leakage, faulty pressure relief valves or check valves.

If electric motor and pump assembly is disassembled for repair or renewal of individual components, upon reassembly use Ingilis Company EP630548 flat black neobase or equivalent to provide a watertight seal.

NOTE: On Models DT50 (1984) and DT60 (1983-1984), the pump is equipped with a manual release valve (M—Fig. SZ14-29) that, when rotated two turns counterclockwise, enables movement of trim and tilt cylinders if the electric motor malfunctions.

Recommended oil is SAE 20W, SAE 10W30 or SAE 10W40 motor oil or Dexron automatic transmission fluid. Oil level (L) should reach fill plug (F) hole threads with outboard motor in a vertical position. Do not run pump without oil in reservoir.

SUZUKI DT55 AND DT65
(After 1984)

CONDENSED SERVICE DATA

NOTE: Metric fasteners are used throughout outboard motor.

TUNE-UP
Hp/rpm:
DT55 . . . . .55/4800-5500
DT65 . . . . .65/4800-5500
Bore . . . . .73 mm
(2.9 in.)
Stroke . . . . .71 mm
(2.8 in.)
Number of Cylinders 3
Displacement . . . . .891 cc
(54.4 cu. in.)
Spark Plug:
NGK B8HS
Electrode Gap:
Prior to 1986 . . . . .0.9-1.0 mm
(0.035-0.040 in.)
After 1985 . . . . . : . . . . .0.8-0.9 mm
(0.031-0.035 in.)
Ignition Type . . . . .Breakerless
Carburetor Make . . . . .Mikuni

SIZES—CLEARANCES
Piston Ring End Gap . . . . .0.2-0.4 mm
(0.008-0.016 in.)
Piston Pin Diameter . . . . .19.995-20.000 mm
(0.7872-0.7874 in.)
Piston Pin Bore Diameter. . . . . .19.998-20.006 mm
(0.7873-0.7876 in.)
Piston-to-Cylinder Clearance:
Prior to 1986 . . . . .0.112-0.127 mm
(0.0044-0.0050 in.)
After 1985 . . . . .0.099-0.114 mm
(0.0039-0.0045 in.)
Standard Piston Diameter . . . . .72.893-72.908 mm
(2.8698-2.8703 in.)
Cylinder Bore Diameter . . . . .73.000-73.015 mm
(2.8740-2.8746 in.)
Max. Cylinder Bore Wear . . . . .0.10 mm
(0.0039 in.)
Max. Crankshaft Runout at Main
Bearing Journal . . . . .0.05 mm
(0.002 in.)
Max. Connecting Rod Small End Side
Shake . . . . .5.0 mm
(0.20 in.)

TIGHTENING TORQUES
Cylinder Head Cover . . . . .8-12 N·m
(6-9 ft.-lbs.)
Cylinder Head. . . . . .20-26 N·m
(14-19 ft.-lbs.)
Crankcase:
6 mm . . . . .8-12 N·m
(6-9 ft.-lbs.)
10 mm . . . . .46-54 N·m
(34-39 ft.-lbs.)
Exhaust Cover . . . . .8-10 N·m
(6-7 ft.-lbs.)
Flywheel Nut . . . . .200-210 N·m
(145-152 ft.-lbs.)
Gearcase Pinion Nut . . . . .30-40 N·m
(22-29 ft.-lbs.)
Propeller Shaft Nut . . . . .50-60 N·m
(36-44 ft.-lbs.)
Standard Screws:
Unmarked or Marked "4"
5 mm . . . . .2-4 N·m
(2-3 ft.-lbs.)
6 mm . . . . .4-7 N·m
(3-5 ft.-lbs.)
8 mm . . . . .10-16 N·m
(7-12 ft.-lbs.)
10 mm . . . . .22-35 N·m
(16-26 ft.-lbs.)
Stainless Steel
5 mm . . . . .2-4 N·m
(2-3 ft.-lbs.)
6 mm . . . . .6-10 N·m
(5-7 ft.-lbs.)
8 mm . . . . .15-20 N·m
(11-15 ft.-lbs.)
10 mm . . . . .34-41 N·m
(25-30 ft.-lbs.)
Marked "7" or SAE Grade 5
5 mm . . . . .3-6 N·m
(2-5 ft.-lbs.)
6 mm . . . . .8-12 N·m
(6-9 ft.-lbs.)
8 mm . . . . .18-28 N·m
(13-20 ft.-lbs.)
10 mm . . . . .40-60 N·m
(29-44 ft.-lbs.)

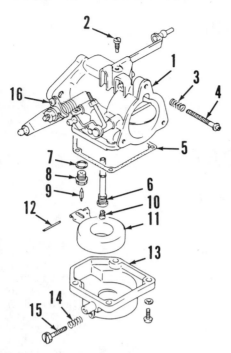

**Fig. SZ15-1—Exploded view of Mikuni car-
buretor typical of all models.**

1. Body
2. Pilot jet
3. Spring
4. Pilot air screw
5. Gasket
6. Main nozzle
7. Gasket
8. Seat
9. Needle
10. Main jet
11. Float
12. Pin
13. Float bowl
14. Spring
15. Drain plug
16. Screw

**Fig. SZ15-2—Adjust idle speed control knob (I) to
set engine idle speed. Note that on models after
1988, idle speed control switch is located on lower engine cover.**

**Fig. SZ15-3—Distance (D) for correct float level
should be 11-12 mm (0.43-0.47 in.) on DT55 models and 17-19 mm (0.67-0.75 in.) on DT65 models.
Bend tank (T) on float lever to adjust.**

LUBRICATION

The power head is lubricated by oil mixed with the fuel. All models are equipped with oil injection. The recommended oil is Suzuki Outboard Motor Oil or a suitable equivalent NMMA certified TC-WII engine oil. The recommended fuel is unleaded gasoline with a minimum pump octane rating of 85. During break-in period (first 15 hours of operation on models prior to 1987, or first 10 hours on later models), mix a recommended oil with fuel at a 50:1 ratio and use in combination with the normal oil injection system. Switch to straight gasoline in the fuel tank after break-in period.

The lower unit gears and bearings are lubricated by oil contained in the gearcase. The recommended oil is Suzuki Outboard Motor Gear Oil or a good quality SAE 90 hypoid gear oil. Gearcase capacity is approximately 650 mL (22 ozs.). Gear oil should be drained and refilled after the first 10 hours of operation and every 50 hours thereafter. Reinstall vent and fill plugs securely, using a new gasket if necessary. After operating for a short time, recheck oil level and refill if necessary.

FUEL SYSTEM

CARBURETOR. Mikuni type BV32-24 carburetors are used on DT55 models and Mikuni type BV-40-32 carburetors are used on DT65 models. Three carburetors are used. Refer to Fig. SZ15-1 for exploded view. Initial setting of pilot air screw (4) from a lightly seated position should be $1\frac{1}{8}$ to $1\frac{5}{8}$ turns on DT55 models prior to 1986, $1\frac{1}{2}$ to 2 turns on DT65 models prior to 1986 and $1\frac{1}{4}$ to $1\frac{3}{4}$ turns on all models after 1985. Final carburetor adjustment should be performed with engine at normal operating temperature and running in forward gear. Adjust idle speed control knob (I—Fig. SZ15-2) so engine idles at 650-700 rpm in forward gear. Note that idle speed control switch is located in the lower engine cover on late models. Each position of the idle speed switch changes idle speed approximately 50 rpm by changing ignition timing from eight degrees ATDC (slow) to TDC (fast). Adjust pilot air screw (4—Fig. SZ15-1) so engine idles smoothly and will accelerate cleanly without hesitation. If necessary, readjust idle speed switch so engine idles within 650-700 rpm.

Main fuel metering is controlled by main jet (10). Standard main jet size for normal operation is #117.5 on DT55 models prior to 1989, #120 on DT55 models after 1988, #147.5 on DT65 models prior to 1988, #150 on 1988 DT65 models and #155 on DT65 models after 1988.

Standard pilot jet (2) size for normal operation is #75 on DT55 models prior to 1989, #77.5 on DT55 models after 1988, #77.5 on DT65 models prior to 1989 and #80 on DT65 models after 1988.

To check float level, remove float bowl and invert carburetor. Distance (D—Fig. SZ15-3) between main jet and bottom of float should be 10-12 mm (0.39-0.47 in.) on DT55 models and 17-19 mm (0.67-0.75 in.) on DT65 models. Carefully bend tang (T) on float lever to adjust float level.

To synchronize carburetor throttle valves, first detach rod between throttle shaft lever on middle carburetor and throttle control lever. Loosen screw or screws (16—Fig. SZ15-1) on top and bottom carburetors. Throttle lever return spring pressure should cause respective throttle valve to close. Visually verify all throttle valves are closed, then retighten screw or screws (16) on top and bottom carburetors. Reconnect rod between throttle shaft lever on center carburetor and throttle control lever, then verify synchronization of throttle valves between all three carburetors.

SPEED CONTROL LINKAGE. The throttle valves of all three carburetors must be properly synchronized as outlined in the CARBURETOR section. On models prior to 1989, a throttle valve switch assembly is used to register middle carburetor throttle valve position. An idle switch and an acceleration switch make up throttle position switch assembly. Each switch has a roller mounted on a lever that contacts the throttle shaft cam mounted on the middle carburetor. As the cam is rotated, the lever on each switch activates a plunger, thus sending an electrical signal to the CDI module by which the ignition timing is altered to match throttle valve opening. When the throttle valve is fully closed, the idle switch is turned ON and the acceleration switch is turned OFF. When the throttle valve is opened, the idle switch is turned OFF and the acceleration switch is turned ON.

NOTE: Throttle shaft cam used on Model DT55 differs from throttle shaft cam used on Model DT65. Backside of throttle shaft cam is identified by a "B" on DT55 models and by an "A" on DT65 models. Make sure correct cam is used.

On models after 1988, a throttle valve sensor that varies output voltage according to throttle valve position is used in place of the on/off type switch used on earlier models. The throttle position sensor is mounted to the center carburetor and directly engages the carburetor throttle shaft. The CDI module uses information from the throttle valve sensor and the gear counter coil to determine the optimum ignition timing for all throttle openings. Refer to the IGNITION section for testing and adjusting procedures.

REED VALVES. The inlet reed valves (Fig. SZ15-4) are located on a reed plate between intake manifold and crankcase. Each cylinder is fitted with a reed plate that contains two reed valve assemblies. The reed petals should seat very lightly against the reed plate throughout their entire length with the least possible tension. Tip of reed petal must not stand open more than 0.2 mm (0.008 in.) from contact surface. Reed stop opening should be 7.6-8.0 mm (0.30-0.31 in.).

Renew reeds if petals are broken, cracked, warped, rusted or bent. Never attempt to bend a reed petal or to straighten a damaged reed. Never install a bent or damaged reed. Seating surface of reed plate should be smooth and flat. When installing reeds or reed stop, make sure that petals are centered over the inlet holes in reed plate, and that the reed stops are centered over reed petals. Apply Thread Lock "1342" or a suitable equivalent to threads of reed stop screws prior to installation.

FUEL PUMP. A diaphragm type fuel pump is mounted on the side of power head cylinder block and is actuated by pressure and vacuum pulsations from the engine crankcase. Refer to Fig. SZ15-5 for exploded view of fuel pump assembly.

Defective or questionable parts should be renewed. Diaphragm should be renewed if air leaks or cracks are found, or if deterioration is evident.

FUEL FILTER. Fuel filter (7 through 11 – Fig. SZ15-5) is mounted on the side of power head cylinder block. Filter should be disassembled and cleaned after every 50 hours of use. Renew "O" ring (9) if required.

OIL INJECTION

BLEEDING PUMP. To bleed trapped air from oil supply line or pump, first make sure outboard motor is in upright position. Detach supply line from oil tank and plug oil tank outlet. Open oil pump air bleed screw (A – Fig. SZ15-6) three or four turns. Hold oil filter level with outlet side on top. Pour oil through oil supply line until oil seeps out around screw threads. After five

seconds or when no air bubbles are noticed, close air bleed screw (A) and reconnect oil supply line to oil tank outlet.

CHECKING OIL PUMP OUTPUT. Start engine and allow to warm-up for approximately five minutes, then stop engine. Disconnect oil pump control rod (5—Fig. SZ15-6) from bottom carburetor throttle shaft lever. Detach oil supply line at oil tank outlet and plug oil tank outlet. Connect oil gage 09900-21602 to oil supply line. Fill oil gage with a recommended engine oil until even with an upper reference mark. Bleed air from system as previously outlined, then refill oil gage to an upper reference mark. With oil pump control rod (5) in released position, start engine and maintain engine speed at 1500 rpm. Allow engine to run for five minutes. After five minutes, stop engine and note oil gage. Oil consumption at 1500 rpm in five minutes should be 2.3-3.1 mL (0.078-0.105 fl. oz.) on DT55 models prior to 1986, 2.0-3.2 mL (0.068-0.108 fl. oz.) on DT65 models prior to 1986 and 1.9-3.2 mL (0.064-0.108 fl. oz.) on all models after 1985.

To check maximum oil pump output, repeat previous procedure except, hold oil pump control rod (5) in the fully open position. Start engine and maintain 1500 rpm for two minutes. Maximum oil pump output at 1500 rpm in two minutes should be 3.4-5.1 mL (0.115-0.172 fl. oz.) on DT55 models and 4.0-5.9 mL (0.135-0.199 fl. oz.) on DT65 models.

NOTE: Oil pump output may vary due to testing error and ambient temperature. Repeat test three or four times and determine average output.

If oil pump output is not within the specified limits, oil pump should be renewed.

NOTE: Oil pump used on DT55 models is identified by blue paint on top cover of pump assembly. Oil pump used on DT65 models is not painted.

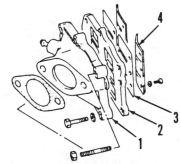

Fig. SZ15-4—Exploded view of intake manifold and reed valve assembly.

1. Intake manifold	3. Reed petals
2. Reed plate	4. Reed stop

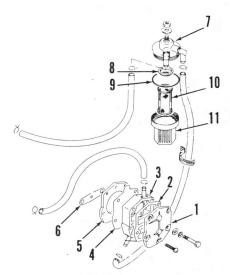

Fig. SZ15-5—Exploded view of diaphragm type fuel pump and fuel filter assemblies.

1. Cover	
2. Gasket	7. Filter base
3. Body	8. Gasket
4. Diaphragm	9. "O" ring
5. Inner plate	10. Filter element
6. Gasket	11. Cup

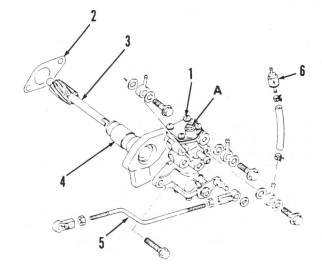

Fig. SZ15-6—Exploded view of oil injection pump and related components.

A. Air bleed screw
1. Pump assy.
2. Gasket
3. Driven gear
4. Retainer
5. Control rod
6. Check valve

IGNITION

A capacitor discharge ignition (CDI) system is used. If engine malfunction is noted and the ignition system is suspected, make sure the spark plugs and all electrical wiring are in good condition and all electrical connections are tight before trouble-shooting the CD ignition system.

The standard spark plug is NGK B8HS with an electrode gap of 0.9-1.0 mm (0.035-0.039 in.) on models prior to 1986 and 0.8-0.9 mm (0.031-0.035 in.) on models after 1985.

TESTING CDI SYSTEM AND BATTERY CHARGING COIL. Refer to Figs. SZ15-7, SZ15-8, SZ15-9 and SZ15-10, and the following sections for testing CDI components and battery charging coil. Use Suzuki Pocket Tester 09900-25002 or a suitable ohmmeter unless otherwise stated to test components. Renew the component or components if not within the specified limits.

CONDENSER CHARGING COIL. Unplug wires at connectors leading from condenser charging coil. Attach one tester lead to green wire connector and remaining tester lead to connector of black wire with red tracer. Tester should show 190-270 ohms. Leave tester lead connected to green wire connector and attach remaining tester lead to coil's core. Tester should show an infinite reading.

PULSER COIL. Three pulser coils are used. Unplug wires at connectors leading from pulser coils. Attach one tester lead to black ground wire and remaining tester lead to connector leading to pulser coil. Tester should show 170-250 ohms. Repeat test for each pulser coil. Disconnect tester leads and attach one tester lead to mounting ear on pulser coil and remaining tester lead to connector leading to pulser coil. Tester should show an infinite reading.

BATTERY CHARGING COIL. Unplug wires at connectors leading from battery charging coil. Attach one tester lead to red wire connector and remaining tester lead to connector of yellow wire. Tester should show 0.2-0.6 ohms. Leave tester lead connected to red wire connector and attach remaining tester lead to coil's core. Tester should show an infinite reading.

IGNITION COILS. Three ignition coils are used. Separate wires at connectors leading from ignition coils and discon-nect spark plug wires from coils. To test primary windings, connect tester between the following wires: Number 1 coil—orange wire and black wire; number 2 coil—blue wire and black wire; number 3 coil—gray wire and black wire. Primary winding resistance on all coils should be 0.5-0.8 ohm on models prior to 1988 and 0.1-0.3 ohm on models after 1987. Renew coil(s) if primary resistance is not as specified.

To test secondary windings, attach one tester lead to each spark plug wire terminal and remaining tester lead to orange wire on number 1 coil, blue wire on number 2 coil and gray wire on number 3 coil. Renew coil(s) if resistance is not within 4700-7000 ohms on models prior to 1988, 1700-2900 ohms on 1988 models and 6000-9000 ohms on 1989 models.

COUNTER COIL. On models after 1988, a gear counter coil is mounted along outer periphery of flywheel ring gear. The CDI module process information from the gear counter coil in combination with the throttle valve sensor to determine ignition timing. The gear counter coil can be identified by a "C" stamped in side of coil. To test counter coil, separate connector leading from counter coil. Connect tester leads to orange wire with green tracer and black wire with green tracer. Counter coil can be considered acceptable if resistance is within 170-250 ohms. Air gap between counter coil and flywheel ring gear teeth should be 0.5 mm (0.020 in.).

NOTE: Air gap between counter coil and flywheel ring gear teeth must be set to exactly 0.5 mm (0.020 in.) for proper operation of outboard motor. Make sure air gap is properly adjusted.

THROTTLE PLATE SWITCH (Models Prior to 1989). Unplug wires at connectors leading from throttle plate switch assembly. Attach one tester lead to black wire connector and remaining tester lead to connector of light green wire with red tracer. With lever on idle switch (I—Fig. SZ15-11) depressed, tester should show infinite resistance. With lever released, tester should show zero ohm. Leave the tester lead attached to the black wire connector and connect remaining tester lead to connector of brown wire with yellow tracer to test acceleration switch (A). Previous test procedure should be used and previous test results should be obtained.

THROTTLE VALVE SENSOR (Models after 1988). To test throttle valve sensor (5—Fig. SZ15-12), remove alignment pin attached to black cover over throt-

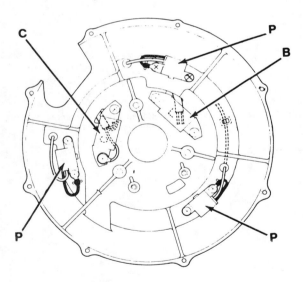

Fig. SZ15-7—View identifying location of pulser coils (P), condenser charge coil (C) and battery charge coil (B) on models prior to 1989. Refer to Fig. SZ15-8 for diagram of ignition system on models after 1988.

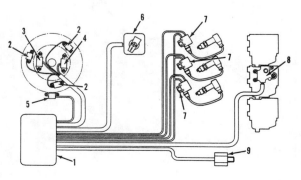

Fig. SZ15-8—Diagram of ignition system components on models after 1988.

1. CDI module
2. Pulser coils
3. Battery charging coil
4. Condenser charging coil
5. Gear counter coil
6. Idle speed switch
7. Ignition coils
8. Throttle position sensor
9. Coolant temperature switch

tle valve sensor and insert alignment pin (1) into hole in sensor and sensor cam (3). Align slot in cam (3) with throttle shaft. Disconnect throttle valve sensor connector (4). Connect test harness 09930-89530 or suitable jumper wires to a battery as shown in Fig. SZ15-12. Battery voltage must be nine volts or more. Connect positive (+) lead of a suitable DIGITAL voltmeter to test harness light green wire with red tracer and voltmeter negative (−) lead to battery negative (−) terminal as shown. With throttle fully closed, voltmeter reading should be 0.45-0.55 volt. If not, remove rubber cap (2) and turn adjustment screw (under cap) as necessary to obtain the correct voltage reading. Note that turning adjustment screw clockwise will increase voltage and counterclockwise will decrease voltage.

NOTE: The manufacturer recommends using only a nonmetallic screwdriver to turn sensor adjusting screw or sensor voltmeter reading may not be valid. If metal screwdriver must be used, remove screwdriver from area of throttle valve sensor after adjustment to prevent erroneous voltmeter reading.

If sensor output voltage at closed throttle is below 0.45 volt, idle speed ignition timing will be fixed at 5 degrees BTDC; idle speed switch will be inoperative. If sensor output voltage at closed throttle is above 0.55 volt, ignition timing at idle speed will be incorrect. Refer to IDLE SPEED SWITCH section.

Once the specified voltage reading is obtained at closed throttle, remove alignment pin and open carburetor to wide-open throttle. Voltmeter reading

should now be 2.6 volts or more. Do not attempt to adjust wide-open throttle sensor voltage. If wide-open throttle sensor voltage is not 2.6 volts or higher, renew sensor.

If throttle valve sensor is removed or renewed, install as follows: Insert alignment pin (1) as shown to align cam and sensor shaft. Align slot in sensor cam with carburetor throttle shaft and install sensor on carburetor. Lightly tighten mounting screws (7) to allow for adjustment of sensor position on carburetor. Connect test harness and digital voltmeter as shown in Fig. SZ15-12. Make sure battery voltage is nine volts or more. Sensor output voltage at closed throttle should be 0.45-0.55 volt. If not, move position of sensor on carburetor to obtain specified voltage and securely tighten screws (7). Recheck

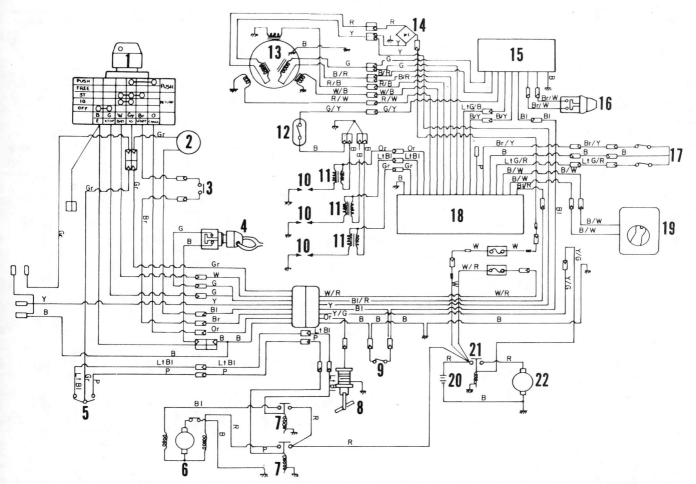

Fig. SZ15-9—Wiring diagram typical of all models prior to 1989. Model shown is equipped with power tilt and trim system. Refer to Fig. SZ15-10 for wiring diagram of 1989 models.

1. Ignition switch	8. Choke solenoid	17. Throttle plate switch assy.	G. Green	B/Y. Black with yellow tracer	Lg/R. Light green with red tracer
2. Overheat & oil warning buzzer	9. Oil level switch	18. CDI module	Gr. Gray	Bl/R. Blue with red tracer	R/B. Red with black tracer
3. Neutral switch	10. Spark plugs	19. Idle speed control switch	Lt.Bl. Light blue	Br/W. Brown with white tracer	R/W. Red with white tracer
4. Emergency stop switch	11. Ignition coils	20. Battery	O. Orange	Br/Y. Brown with yellow tracer	W/B. White with black tracer
5. Power tilt & trim switch	12. Cooling water sensor	21. Starter motor relay	P. Pink		
6. Power tilt & trim motor	13. Stator plate assy.	22. Starter motor	R. Red	G/Y. Green with yellow tracer	W/R. White with red tracer
7. Power tilt & trim motor relays	14. Rectifier		W. White		Y/G. Yellow with green tracer
	15. Low oil warning reset unit		Y. Yellow	Lg/B. Light green with black tracer	
	16. Oil warning reset switch		B. Black		
			Bl. Blue		
			Br. Brown	B/R. Black with red tracer	
				B/W. Black with white tracer	

voltage after tightening screws (7) and if necessary, remove cap (2) and turn adjustment screw to obtain 0.45-0.55 volt. Be sure to reinstall cap (2). After obtaining the correct voltage at closed throttle, remove alignment pin and check sensor output voltage at wide-open throttle. Voltage should be 2.6 volts or higher. Do not attempt to adjust wide-open throttle voltage.

IDLE SPEED SWITCH. Idle speed switch (6—Fig. SZ15-8) malfunction can be quickly verified by checking ignition timing and engine rpm while switching position of idle speed switch. Make sure engine is at idle speed when checking timing.

NOTE: A defective or maladjusted throttle valve sensor may cause idle speed switch to be inoperative or ignition timing at idle speed to be incorrect. Prior to testing idle speed switch, make sure throttle valve sen-

sor is operating properly and correctly ajusted. Refer to THROTTLE VALVE SENSOR section.

Note that each position of idle speed switch should change ignition timing two degrees and change engine idle speed approximately 50 rpm. If timing and engine rpm do not change with each switch position, idle speed switch may be defective.

CDI MODULE. Use Suzuki tool 09930-99810 or 09930-99830 with test harness 09930-89450 to test CDI module.

COOLING SYSTEM

WATER PUMP. A rubber impeller type water pump is mounted between the drive shaft housing and gearcase. A key in the drive shaft is used to turn the pump impeller. If cooling system problems are encountered, check water in-

take for plugging or partial restriction, then if not corrected, remove gearcase as outlined in the appropriate section and check condition of the water pump, water passages and sealing surfaces.

When water pump is disassembled, check condition of impeller (4—Fig. SZ15-13) and plate (5) for excessive wear. Turn drive shaft clockwise (viewed from top) while placing pump housing (2)

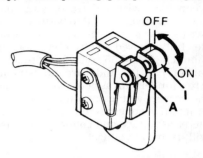

Fig. SZ15-11—Idle switch (I) and acceleration switch (A) used on models prior to 1989.

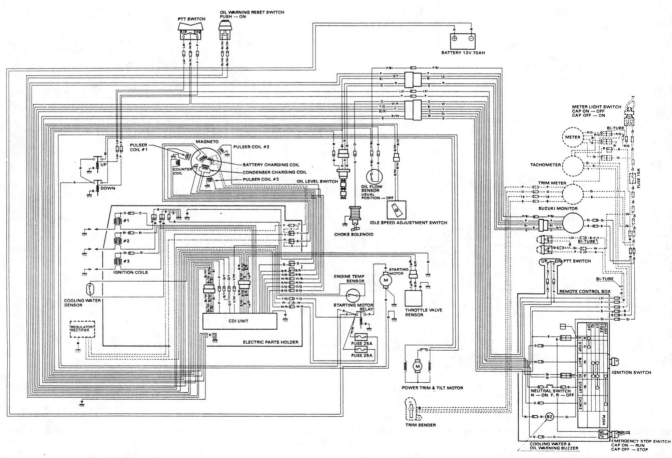

Fig. SZ15-10—Wiring diagram typical of models after 1988 equipped with remote control and power tilt and trim.

B. Black	Gr. Gray	G/Y. Green with yellow tracer	R/Y. Red with yellow tracer	Bl/R. Blue with red tracer	LtG. Light green
G. Green	Or. Orange	R/B. Red with black tracer	W/B. White with black tracer	Bl/W. Blue with white tracer	LtBl. Light blue
P. Pink	B/G. Black with green tracer	R/G. Red with green tracer	W/R. White with red tracer	Br/W. Brown with white tracer	P/Bl. Pink with blue tracer
R. Red	B/R. Black with red tracer	R/W. Red with white tracer	Y/G. Yellow with green tracer	Br/G. Orange with green tracer	Pr/W. Purple with white tracer
W. White	B/W. Black with white tracer				LtG/R. Light green with red tracer
Y. Yellow					
Bl. Blue					
Br. Brown					

over impeller. Avoid turning drive shaft in opposite direction after water pump is reassembled.

THERMOSTAT. A thermostat (7—Fig. SZ15-14) is used to regulate engine operating temperature. The thermostat should start to open within the temperature range of 40°-44° C (104°-111° F) on models prior to 1986 and 48°-52° C (118°-126° F) on models after 1985. Thermostat can be removed for inspection or renewal after removing thermostat housing (9).

POWER HEAD

REMOVE AND REINSTALL. To remove the power head, first remove engine cover. Disconnect wiring to oil tank. Remove oil supply line from oil tank outlet and plug outlet. Remove screws to withdraw oil tank. On models equipped with power tilt and trim, remove relays from side of cylinder head. Remove CDI module. Detach wiring from electric starter and starter relay that will interfere with power head removal. Remove engine flywheel. Dis-

connect fuel supply line from connector in bottom engine cover. Disconnect shift and throttle linkage. Remove pilot discharge water hose (11—Fig. SZ15-14) from fitting in bottom engine cover. Remove cover to expose power head retaining screws. Remove the nine screws and lift power head assembly with related engine components from lower unit assembly.

Before reinstalling power head, check condition of drive shaft seals (25—Fig. SZ15-15). If renewal of seals is required, it is necessary to separate crankcase (1—Fig. SZ15-14) from cylinder block (2) as outlined in the appropriate following paragraphs. Apply a suitable water-resistant grease to lip portion of seals and install seals into seal housing (26—Fig. SZ15-15) with open side of seals toward lower unit. Make certain drive shaft splines are clean, then coat splines with a light coat of water-resistant grease. Apply a suitable sealer to mating surfaces of power head and lower unit and install a new gasket. Coat area of power head retaining screws adjacent to screw heads with silicone sealer. Tighten the nine power head retaining screws to 18-28 N·m (13-20 ft.-lbs.). Remainder of reinstallation is the reverse of removal procedure.

DISASSEMBLY. Disassembly and inspection can be accomplished in the following manner. Remove ignition coils, electric starter and bracket, and idle speed adjusting switch and bracket. Remove throttle control arm and lever and

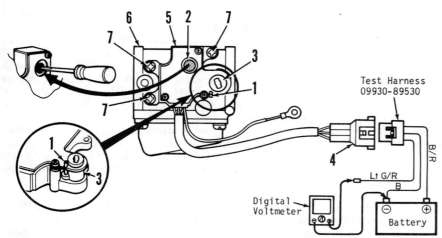

Fig. SZ15-12—Refer to test for throttle valve sensor testing and installation procedure.

1. Alignment pin
2. Cap (adjustment screw
3. Sensor cam
4. Connector
5. Throttle valve sensor assy.
6. Carburetor
7. Mounting screw
B. Black

B/R. Black with red tracer
LtG/R. Light green with red tracer

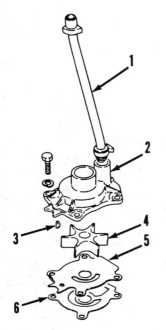

Fig. SZ15-13—Exploded view of water pump assembly.

1. Water tube
2. Pump housing
3. Key
4. Impeller
5. Plate
6. Gasket

Fig. SZ15-14—Exploded view of cylinder block and crankcase assembly.

1. Crankcase half
2. Cylinder block
3. Cylinder head gasket
4. Cylinder head
5. Cylinder head cover gasket
6. Cylinder head cover
7. Thermostat
8. Gasket
9. Thermostat housing
10. Cooling water sensor
11. Pilot discharge water hose

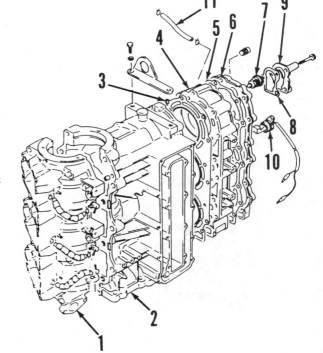

Suzuki DT55 & DT65 (After 1984)

OUTBOARD MOTOR

clutch control arm. Remove stator plate assembly. Remove oil injection pump (1—Fig. SZ15-6), retainer (4) and driven gear (3). Remove fuel pump and fuel filter assembly. Remove carburetors and electric choke solenoid. Remove intake manifolds and reed valve assemblies. Remove outer and inner exhaust covers. Remove cooling water sensor. Remove thermostat housing and withdraw ther-

mostat. Remove spark plugs, cylinder head cover and cylinder head, then clean carbon from combustion chamber and any foreign material accumulation in water passages. Unscrew crankcase retaining screws and separate crankcase (1—Fig. SZ15-14) from cylinder block (2). Crankshaft and piston assembly can now be removed from cylinder block.

Engine components are now accessible for overhaul as outlined in the appropriate following paragraphs. Refer to the following section for assembly procedures.

ASSEMBLY. Refer to specific service sections when assembling the crankshaft, connecting rod, piston and reed valves. Make sure all joint and gasket surfaces are clean, free from nicks and burrs and hardened cement or carbon.

Whenever the power head is disassembled, it is recommended that all gasket surfaces and mating surfaces without gaskets be carefully checked for nicks, burrs and warped surfaces that might interfere with a tight seal. Cylinder head, head end of cylinder block and some mating surfaces of manifold and crankcase should be checked on a surface plate and lapped if necessary to provide a smooth surface. Do not remove any more metal than is necessary.

When reassembling power head, lubricate all friction and bearing surfaces with a recommended engine oil. Apply a suitable high temperature grease to lip portion of crankshaft seal. Apply a suitable water-resistant grease to lip portion of drive shaft seals and install seals into seal housing (26—Fig. SZ15-15) with open side facing lower unit.

Place thrust rings (28) into cylinder block, then install crankshaft assembly. Make certain main bearing locating pins engage notches in cylinder block. Flanges of labyrinth seals (5 and 9), seal (24) and housing (26) must fit securely in grooves of cylinder block. Apply a coat of Suzuki Bond No. 4, or a suitable sealer to mating surfaces of crankcase and cylinder block and position crankcase on cylinder block. Using tightening

sequence shown in Fig. SZ15-16, tighten the 6 mm crankcase screws to 8-12 N·m (71-106 in.-lbs.) and the 10 mm screws to 46-54 N·m (34-39 ft.-lbs.). Tighten cylinder head screws in sequence shown in Fig. SZ15-17 to 20-26 N·m (14-19 ft.-lbs.).

RINGS, PISTONS AND CYLINDERS. The pistons are fitted with two piston rings. The top piston ring is chrome plated. Piston rings must be installed with manufacturer's marking facing top of piston. Rings are pinned in place to prevent ring rotation. Piston ring end gap should be 0.2-0.4 mm (0.008-0.016 in.) with a maximum allowable ring end gap of 0.8 mm (0.031 in.). Piston-to-cylinder clearance should be 0.112-0.127 mm (0.0044-0.0050 in.) on models prior to 1986 and 0.099-0.114 mm (0.0039-0.0045 in.) on models after 1985. Pistons and rings are available in standard size as well as 0.25 mm (0.010 in.) and 0.50 mm (0.020 in.) oversizes. Cylinder should be bored oversize if cylinder is out-of-round, tapered or worn in excess of 0.10 mm (0.004 in.). Install piston on connecting rod so arrow on piston crown will face toward exhaust port when piston is installed.

CONNECTING RODS, BEARINGS AND CRANKSHAFT. Connecting rods, bearings and crankshaft are a pressed-together unit. Crankshaft should be disassembled ONLY by experienced service personnel using the proper service equipment.

Caged roller bearing is used at top of crankshaft and caged ball bearings are used at the center and bottom of crankshaft. Determine rod bearing wear by measuring connecting rod small end

Fig. SZ15-15—Exploded view of crankshaft assembly

1. Seal
2. Roller bearing
3. Upper crankshaft assy.
4. Ball bearing
5. Labyrinth seal
6. Middle crankshaft upper half
7. Middle crankshaft lower half
8. Ball bearing
9. Labyrinth seal
10. Lower crankshaft assy.
11. Ball bearing
12. Thrust washers
13. Oil injection pump drive gear
14. Key
15. Thrust washers
16. Crank pin
17. Connecting rod
18. Needle bearing
19. Piston pin clips
20. Piston pin
21. Thrust washers
22. Needle bearing
23. Snap ring
24. Seal
25. Seals
26. Housing
27. Seal
28. Thrust rings

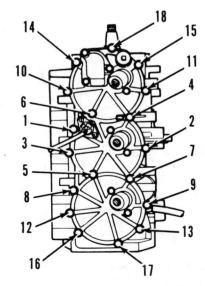

Fig. SZ15-16—Tighten crankcase screws in sequence shown. Tighten 6 mm screws to 8-12 N·m (71-106 in.-lbs.) and 10 mm screws to 46-54 N·m (34-39 ft.-lbs.).

Fig. SZ15-17—Tighten cylinder head screws in sequence shown to 20-26 N·m (14-19 ft.-lbs.).

584

Illustrations courtesy Suzuki

side-to-side movement as shown at (A—Fig. SZ15-18). Normal movement (A) is 5 mm (0.20 in.) or less. Maximum allowable crankshaft runout is 0.05 mm (0.002 in.) measured at bearing surfaces with crankshaft ends supported.

When installing crankshaft, lubricate pistons, rings, cylinders and bearings with engine oil as outlined in ASSEMBLY section.

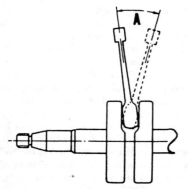

Fig. SZ15-18—Maximum allowable side-to-side shake (A) measured at connecting rod small end is 5.0 mm (0.20 in.) or less.

ELECTRIC STARTER

Models are equipped with the electric starter shown in Fig. SZ15-19. Disassembly is evident after inspection of unit and reference to exploded view. Starter brushes have a standard length of 16 mm (0.63 in.) and should be renewed if worn to 11.5 mm (0.45 in.) or less. After reassembly, bench test starter before installing on power head.

LOWER UNIT

PROPELLER AND DRIVE CLUTCH. Protection for the motor is built into a special cushioning clutch in the propeller hub. No adjustment is possible on the propeller or clutch. Three-blade

propellers are used. Various propellers are available from the manufacturer. Select a propeller to provide optimum performance at full throttle within the recommended speed range of 4800-5500 rpm.

R&R AND OVERHAUL. Refer to Fig. SZ15-20 for exploded view of lower unit gearcase assembly used on all models. During disassembly, note the location of all shims and thrust washers for reference during reassembly. To remove gearcase, first unscrew plug (59) and drain gear lubricant. Remove engine cover. Unscrew nut retaining shift arm (1) to shaft (2), then disengage shaft (2) from shift rod (3). Remove the screws securing gearcase to drive shaft housing and

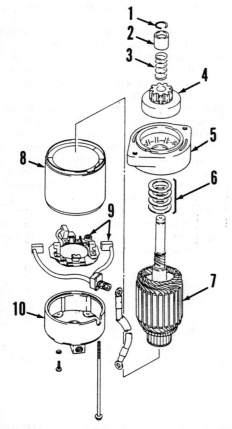

Fig. SZ15-19—Exploded view of electric starter motor.

1. "C" ring	6. Thrust washers
2. Stop	7. Armature
3. Spring	8. Frame
4. Drive	9. Brush assy.
5. Frame head	10. End housing

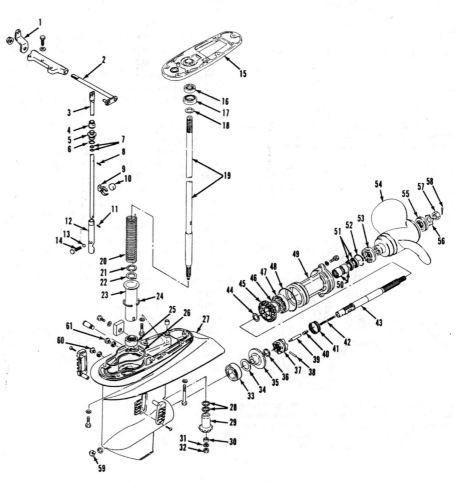

Fig. SZ15-20—Exploded view of lower unit gearcase assembly used on all models.

1. Shift arm	17. Bearing	32. Nut	47. Bearing
2. Shift shaft	18. Thrust washer	33. Bearing	48. "O" ring
3. Shift rod	19. Drive shaft	34. Shim	49. End cap
4. Dust seal	20. Spring	35. Forward gear	50. Needle bearings
5. Rod guide	21. Thrust washer	36. Thrust washer	51. Seals
6. "O" ring	22. Washer	37. Dog clutch	52. Snap ring
7. "O" rings	23. Collar	38. Pin	53. Spacer
8. Pin	24. Snap ring	39. Shift pin	54. Propeller
9. Magnet holder	25. Needle bearing	40. Spring guide	55. Spacer
10. Magnet	26. Seal	41. Pin retainer	56. Tab washer
11. Pin	27. Gearcase	42. Shift spring	57. Nut
12. Shift cam	28. Shims	43. Propeller shaft	58. Cotter pin
13. Detent ball	29. Pinion gear	44. Thrust washer	59. Drain plug
14. Spring	30. Collar	45. Reverse gear	60. Level plug
15. Bearing housing	31. Washer	46. Shim	61. Vent plug
16. Seal			

separate gearcase assembly from drive shaft housing. Remove water pump assembly (Fig. SZ15-13). Remove propeller with related components from propeller shaft. Unscrew two screws retaining gearcase end cap (49—Fig. SZ15-20), then attach a suitable puller to propeller shaft (43) and withdraw propeller shaft assembly with gearcase end cap (49). Unscrew pinion nut (32) and remove pinion gear (29), then extract forward gear (35). Drive shaft (19) and related components can be withdrawn from gearcase after removal of bearing housing (15).

Inspect gears for wear on teeth and on engagement dogs. Inspect dog clutch (37) for wear on engagement surfaces. Inspect shafts for wear on splines and on friction surfaces of gears and oil seals. Check shift cam (12) and shift pin (39) for excessive wear. Check condition of shift spring (42). Spring free length should be 73 mm (2.9 in.). All seals and "O" rings should be renewed when unit is reassembled.

Backlash between pinion gear (29) and drive gears (35 and 45) should be 0.1-0.2 mm (0.004-0.008 in.) and is adjusted by varying thickness of shims (34 and 46). Propeller shaft end play should be 0.2-0.4 mm (0.008-0.016 in.) and is adjusted by increasing or decreasing the thickness of thrust washer (44). Reassemble gearcase by reversing disassembly procedure while noting the following: Install dog clutch (37) on propeller shaft (43) so "REV" marked side is toward reverse gear (45). Tighten pinion nut (32) to 30-40 N·m (21-29 ft.-lbs.). Apply water-resistant grease to "O" ring (48). Apply silicone sealer to gearcase and bearing housing (15) mating surfaces and to bearing housing and drive shaft housing mating surfaces. Coat retaining cap screws adjacent to cap screw heads with silicone sealer.

Engage shift shaft (2) in shift rod (3) eyelet and attach shift arm (1). Secure with nut. Fill gearcase with outboard gear oil as outlined in LUBRICATION section.

POWER TILT AND TRIM

Some models are equipped with a hydraulically actuated power tilt and trim system. An oil pump driven by a reversible electric motor provides oil pressure. A rocker control switch determines motor and pump rotation, retracting or extending tilt and trim cylinders. The pump is equipped with a manual release valve (M—Fig. SZ15-22). Rotating manual release valve (M) two turns counterclockwise enables manual movement of trim and tilt cylinders if electric motor malfunctions.

Recommended power trim/tilt oil on models prior to 1987 is SAE 20, SAE 10W-30 or SAE 10W-40 motor oil, or Dexron automatic transmission fluid. Recommended oil on models after 1986 is Dexron II or equivalent. Do not run pump without oil in reservoir. Oil level should be even with bottom of fill plug hole. Power tilt system should be cycled several times and oil level rechecked if system has been drained or lost a large amount of oil.

NOTE: On models prior to 1987, outboard motor must be in full down position when checking oil level. On models after 1986, motor must be tilted fully up to check oil level.

If power trim/tilt malfunction occurs, make sure malfunction is not due to wiring, connections or electric motor failure. To check oil pressure, connect a 34.5 MPa (5000 psi) pressure gage to port (1—Fig. SZ15-22) on pump and operate pump in the UP direction. Hydraulic oil pressure at port (1) should be within 13,000-17,000 kPa (1885-2465 psi). Connect test gage to port (2) and operate pump in the DOWN direction. Hydraulic pressure should be within 2800-5600 kPa (406-812 psi). Oil pressure less than specified may indicate leakage, faulty pressure relief valves or check valves. The manufacturer recommends renewing pump and valve body assembly to service low pressure condition.

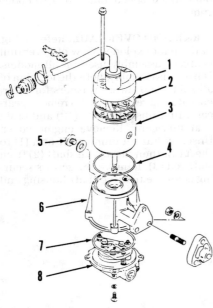

Fig. SZ15-21—Exploded view of power trim/tilt electric motor and pump assembly used on models prior to 1987. Later models are similar.

1. End cap
2. Gasket
3. Electric motor assy.
4. Gasket
5. Fill plug
6. Reservoir
7. "O" ring
8. Pump & valve body assy.

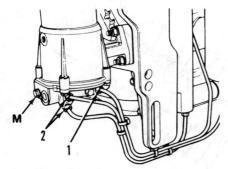

Fig. SZ15-22—View of pump assembly identifying test ports (1 and 2) and manual release valve (M) on models prior to 1987. Later models are similar. Refer to Fig. SZ15-23 to identify early and late models pump assemblies.

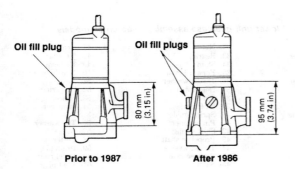

Oil fill plug

Oil fill plugs

80 mm (3.15 in.)

95 mm (3.74 in.)

Prior to 1987

After 1986

Fig. SZ15-23—View identifying early (prior to 1987) and later (after 1986) power trim/tilt pump assemblies.

SUZUKI DT75 AND DT85

CONDENSED SERVICE DATA

NOTE: Metric fasteners are used throughout outboard motor.

TUNE-UP
Hp/rpm:
DT75 . . . . 75/4800-5500
DT85 . . . . 85/4800-5500
Bore . . . . 84 mm
(3.31 in.)
Stroke . . . . 72 mm
(2.83 in.)
Number of Cylinders 3
Displacement . . . . 1197 cc
(73.04 cu. in.)
Spark Plug:
NGK B8HS
Electrode Gap . . . . 0.8-0.9 mm
(0.031-0.035 in.)
Ignition Type . . . . Breakerless
Carburetor Make . . . . Mikuni
Fuel:Oil Ratio 50:1*
*All models after 1985 and some earlier models are
equipped with oil injection.

SIZES—CLEARANCES
Piston Ring End Gap . . . . 0.2-0.4 mm
(0.008-0.016 in.)
Piston Pin Diameter . . . . 19.995-20.000 mm
(0.7872-0.7874 in.)
Piston-to-Cylinder Clearance:
DT75 (Prior to 1987) . . . . 0.077-0.093 mm
(0.0030-0.0037 in.)
DT85 (Prior to 1988) And DT75 (1987) . 0.112-0.127 mm
(0.0044-0.0050 in.)
All Models (1988) . . . . 0.135-0.165 mm
(0.0053-0.0065 in.)
All Models (1989) . . . . 0.12-0.15 mm
(0.0047-0.0059 in.)
Max. Crankshaft Runout at Main
Bearing Journal . . . . 0.05 mm
(0.002 in.)
Max. Connecting Rod Small End
Side Shake . . . . 5.0 mm
(0.20 in.)

TIGHTENING TORQUES
Cylinder Head (Prior to 1983):
6 mm . . . . 8-12 N·m
(6-9 ft.-lbs.)
10 mm . . . . 40-60 N·m
(29-44 ft.-lbs.)

TIGHTENING TORQUES CONT.
Cylinder Head (After 1982) . . . . 46-54 N·m
(34-39 ft.-lbs.)
Crankcase:
Prior to 1983 . . . . 40-60 N·m
(29-44 ft.-lbs.)
After 1982 . . . . 46-54 N·m
(34-39 ft.-lbs.)
Exhaust Cover . . . . 8-12 N·m
(6-9 ft.-lbs.)
Flywheel Nut . . . . 200-210 N·m
(145-152 ft.-lbs.)
Gearcase Pinion Nut:
Prior to 1983 . . . . 60-70 N·m
(43-50 ft.-lbs.)
After 1982 . . . . 70-80 N·m
(50-58 ft.-lbs.)
Propeller Shaft Nut . . . . 50-60 N·m
(36-44 ft.-lbs.)
Standard Screws:
Unmarked or Marked "4"
5 mm . . . . 2-4 N·m
(2-3 ft.-lbs.)
6 mm . . . . 4-7 N·m
(3-5 ft.-lbs.)
8 mm . . . . 10-16 N·m
(7-12 ft.-lbs.)
10 mm . . . . 22-35 N·m
(16-26 ft.-lbs.)
Stainless Steel
5 mm . . . . 2-4 N·m
(2-3 ft.-lbs.)
6 mm . . . . 6-10 N·m
(5-7 ft.-lbs.)
8 mm . . . . 15-20 N·m
(11-15 ft.-lbs.)
10mm . . . . 34-41 N·m
(25-30 ft.-lbs.)
Marked "7" or SAE Grade 5
5 mm . . . . 3-6 N·m
(2-5 ft.-lbs.)
6 mm . . . . 8-12 N·m
(6-9 ft.-lbs.)
8 mm . . . . 18-28 N·m
(13-20 ft.-lbs.)
10 mm . . . . 40-60 N·m
(29-44 ft.-lbs.)

LUBRICATION

The power head is lubricated by oil mixed with the fuel. On models without oil injection, fuel:oil ratio should be 30:1 during break-in (first 10 hours of operation) of a new or rebuilt engine and 50:1 for normal service.

During engine break-in (first 10 hours of operation) on models equipped with oil injection, a 50:1 fuel and oil mixture should be used in the fuel tank in combination with the oil injection system to ensure adequate power head lubrication. After break-in period, switch to straight gasoline in the fuel tank.

Recommended oil for all models is Suzuki Outboard Motor Oil or an equivalent NMMA certified TC-WII engine oil. Recommended fuel is regular or unleaded gasoline with a minimum pump octane rating of 85.

The lower unit gears and bearings are lubricated by oil contained in the gear-

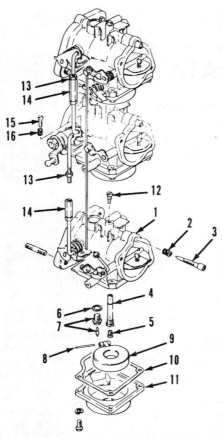

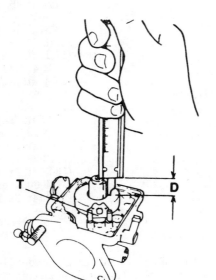

case. Suzuki Outboard Motor Gear Oil or a SAE 90 hypoid outboard gear oil should be used. Gearcase capacity is approximately 700 mL (23.7 oz.) of gear oil and should be drained and refilled after the first 10 hours of use and then after every 50 hours of use. Reinstall vent and fill plugs securely, using a new gasket if needed, to ensure a watertight seal.

FUEL SYSTEM

CARBURETOR. Mikuni Model B32-28 carburetor is used on DT75 models and Mikuni Model B40-32 carburetor is used on DT85 models. Refer to Fig. SZ16-1 for exploded view of carburetor. Initial setting of pilot air screw (3) from a lightly seated position should be 1 to $1\frac{1}{2}$ turns on DT75 models prior to 1987, $1\frac{3}{4}$ to $2\frac{1}{4}$ turns on DT75 models after 1986, $1\frac{3}{4}$ to $2\frac{1}{4}$ turns on DT85 models prior to 1988 and $1\frac{5}{8}$ to $2\frac{1}{8}$ turns on DT85 models after 1987. Final carburetor adjustment should be made with engine running in forward gear at normal operating temperature. On models prior to 1988, rotate timing adjust screw (B—Fig. SZ16-3) in small increments until engine idles at approximately 600-700 rpm in forward gear.

NOTE: On models after 1987, an idle speed adjustment switch located in the lower engine cover is used. Each position of the idle speed switch changes ignition timing two degrees resulting in approximately 50 rpm

idle speed change per each position of switch.

On all models, adjust pilot air screw so engine idles smoothly and accelerates cleanly without hesitation. If necessary, readjust timing screw (models prior to 1988) to obtain 600-700 rpm idle speed.

Main fuel metering is controlled by main jet (5). Standard main jet size for normal service is #140 on all DT75 models except 1987 models, #135 on 1987 DT75 models, #162.5 on DT85 models prior to 1987 and #157.5 on DT85 models after 1986.

Standard pilot jet (12) size for normal service is #80 on DT75 models prior to 1987, #87.5 on DT75 models after 1986, #75 on DT85 models prior to 1987 and #80 on DT85 models after 1986.

To check float level, remove float bowl and invert carburetor. Distance (D—Fig. SZ16-2) between main jet and bottom of float should be 12.5-14.5 mm (0.49-0.57 in.) on DT75 models prior to 1987, 10-12 mm (0.39-0.47 in.) on DT75 models after 1986, 17.5-19.5 mm (0.69-0.77 in.) on DT85 models prior to 1987 and 17-19 mm (0.67-0.75 in.) on DT85 models after 1986. Adjust float level by bending float tang (T).

To synchronize carburetor throttle valves on models prior to 1988, use Suzuki carburetor balancer 09913-13121 or equivalent and make adjustment at throttle shaft connectors (14—Fig. SZ16-1) with engine running at 1000 rpm. To synchronize throttle valves on models after 1987, loosen the throttle valve ad-

Fig. SZ16-1—Exploded view of Mikuni carburetors typical of all models.

1. Body	9. Float
2. Spring	10. Gasket
3. Pilot air screw	11. Float bowl
4. Main nozzle	12. Pilot jet
5. Main jet	13. Jam nut
6. Gasket	14. Connector
7. Needle & seat	15. Throttle stop screw
8. Pin	16. Spring

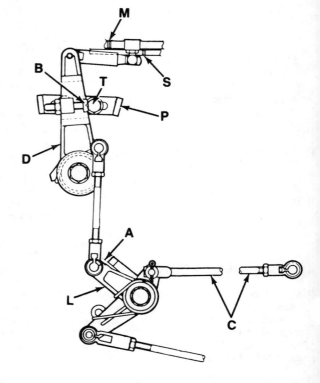

Fig. SZ16-3—View of speed control linkage typical of all models prior to 1988. Models after 1987 are similar. Refer to Fig. SZ16-4. Refer to text for identification of components and adjustment procedure.

Fig. SZ16-2—Distance (D) for correct float level should be 12.5-14.5 mm (0.49-0.57 in.) on DT75 models prior to 1987, 10-12 mm (0.39-0.47 in.) on DT75 models after 1986, 17.5-19.5 mm (0.69-0.77 in.) on DT85 models prior to 1987 and 17-19 mm (0.67-0.75 in.) on DT85 models after 1986.

justment screws (1—Fig. SZ16-4) located on throttle levers of top and bottom caburetors. Ensure that all throttle valves are completely closed, then retighten screws (1).

SPEED CONTROL LINKAGE. The carburetor throttle valves must be correctly synchronized to open as the ignition is advanced to obtain optimum performance. To adjust the speed control linkage, it is necessary to first check, and adjust if required, the ignition maximum advance (models prior to 1988) as outlined in the IGNITION TIMING section. Disconnect carburetor link (C—Figs. SZ16-3 or SZ16-4) and rotate speed control lever (L) toward maximum speed position until lever (L) contacts maximum speed stop on crankcase. Set carburetor throttle valves completely open, then vary the length of carburetor link (C) until ball joint connector will just attach. Move speed control lever to full retard position. Clearance (A—Fig. SZ16-3) at carburetor throttle shaft actuating levers should be 0-1 mm (0-0.39 in.).

REED VALVES. The intake reed valves are located on a reed plate between intake manifold and crankcase. The reed petals should seat very lightly against the reed plate throughout their entire length with the least possible tension. Tip of reed petal must not stand open more than 0.20 mm (0.008 in.) from contact surface. Reed stop opening should be 7.6-7.9 mm (0.30-0.31 in.).

Renew reeds if petals are broken, cracked, warped, rusted or bent. Never attempt to straighten or repair a damaged reed petal. Never install a bent or damaged reed petal. Seating surface of reed plate should be smooth and flat. When installing reeds or reed stop, make sure that petals are centered over the inlet holes in reed plate, and that the reed stops are centered over reed petals. Apply Suzuki Thread Lock 1342 or a suitable equivalent thread locking compound to threads of reed stop screws during reassembly.

FUEL PUMP. A diaphragm type fuel pump is mounted on the side of power head cylinder block and is actuated by pressure and vacuum pulsations from the engine crankcase. Refer to Fig. SZ16-5 for exploded view of fuel pump assembly.

When servicing pump, scribe reference marks across pump body to aid reassembly. Defective or questionable parts should be renewed. Diaphragm should be renewed if air leaks or cracks are found, or if deterioration is evident.

FUEL FILTER. A fuel filter (9 through 13—Fig. SZ16-5) is mounted on the side of power head cylinder block on all models. Filter should be disassembled and cleaned after every 50 hours of use. Renew ''O'' ring (11) if required.

OIL INJECTION

Models So Equipped

BLEEDING PUMP. To bleed trapped air from oil supply line or pump, first make sure outboard motor is in an up-

right position and oil tank is full. Open oil pump air bleed screw (A—Fig. SZ16-6) three or four turns to allow oil to seep out around screw threads. After five seconds, or when no air bubbles are noticed, close air bleed screw (A).

CHECKING OIL PUMP OUTPUT. Start engine and allow to warm-up for approximately five minutes, then stop engine. Disconnect oil pump control rod (5—Fig. SZ16-6) from bottom carburetor. Detach oil supply line at oil tank outlet and plug oil tank outlet. Connect Suzuki Oil Gage 09900-21602 to oil supply line. Fill oil gage with a recommended engine oil until even with an upper reference mark. If necessary, bleed system as previously outlined and refill oil gage.

With oil pump control lever in the released position (minimum output), start engine and run at 1500 rpm for exactly five minutes. After five minutes, stop engine and note oil gage. Oil consumption at 1500 rpm in five minutes should be 3.7-5.6 mL (0.12-0.19 fl. oz.) on models prior to 1986 and 2.2-3.7 mL (0.07-.12 fl. oz.) on models after 1985.

To check pump maximum output, repeat previous procedure except hold pump control lever in the fully open position and run engine at 1500 rpm for exactly two minutes. After two minutes, stop engine and note oil gage. Maximum oil pump output at 1500 rpm in two minutes should be 5.9-8.9 mL (0.20-0.30 fl. oz.) on DT75 models prior to 1986 and all DT85 models, and 5.0-7.5 mL (0.17-0.25 fl. oz.) on DT75 models after 1985.

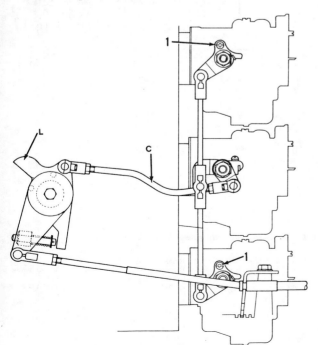

Fig. SZ16-4—View of throttle linkage used on all models after 1987. Refer to text for adjustment procedure.

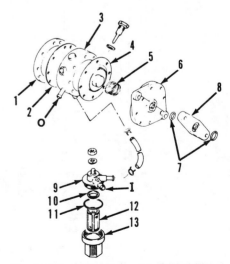

Fig. SZ16-5—Exploded view of diaphragm type fuel pump and fuel filter assemblies.

1. Cover	
2. Diaphragm	9. Fuel filter body
3. Body	10. Packing
4. Diaphragm	11. ''O'' ring
5. Spring	12. Filter
6. Body	13. Bowl
7. ''O'' rings	I. Inlet
8. Insulator block	O. Outlet

NOTE: Oil pump output will vary due to testing error and ambient temperature. Repeat test 2-3 times to ensure consistent results.

Renew oil pump assembly (1) if the specified output is not obtained.

NOTE: Full-open and full-closed marks on oil injection pump actuating lever should align with index mark on injection pump when lever is rotated to respective position.

IGNITION

All models prior to 1988 are equipped with Suzuki pointless electronic ignition System (PEI). Models after 1987 are equipped with Suzuki integrated circuit (IC) ignition system. On models equipped with IC ignition, the CDI module uses information provided by a gear counter coil mounted on the outer periphery of the flywheel and a throttle position sensor mounted on center carburetor to determine and electronically adjust ignition timing on speeds above idle. Refer to Fig. SZ16-7 for wiring diagram typical of models prior to 1988 and Fig. SZ16-8 for wiring diagram typical of later models.

IGNITION TIMING. Ignition timing on models prior to 1987 should be 7 degrees ATDC at 1000 rpm and 21.5 degrees BTDC at 5000 rpm. On 1987 models, ignition timing should be 3 degrees ATDC at 1000 rpm and 21.5 degrees BTDC at 5000 rpm. On models after 1987, slow speed timing is controlled by idle speed adjusting switch that varies timing from 1 degree BTDC to 7 degrees ATDC in 2 degree increments. Each position of idle speed switch changes idle speed approximately 50

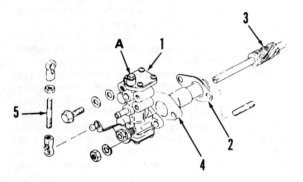

Fig. SZ16-6—Exploded view of oil injection pump and related components used on all models so equipped.

A. Air bleed screw
1. Pump assy.
2. Gasket
3. Driven gear
4. Retainer
5. Control rod

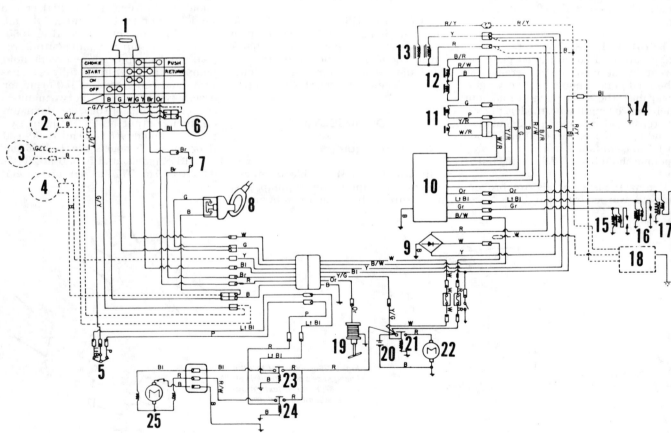

Fig. SZ16-7—Wiring diagram typical of all models prior to 1988 equipped with power trim/tilt.

1. Ignition switch
2. Volt meter
3. Hour meter
4. Tachometer
5. Power tilt & trim switch
6. Overheat & oil warning buzzer
7. Neutral switch
8. Emergency stop switch
9. Rectifier
10. CDI module
11. Pulser coils
12. Condenser charging coil
13. Battery charging coil
14. Overheat switch
15. Ignition coil (No. 3 cyl.)
16. Ignition coil (No. 2 cyl.)
17. Ignition coil (No. 1 cyl.)
18. Rectifier with voltage regulator
19. Choke solenoid
20. Battery
21. Starter motor relay
22. Starter motor
23. Power tilt & trim motor "UP" relay
24. Power tilt & trim motor "DOWN" relay
25. Power tilt & trim motor

Bl. Blue
Br. Brown
Gy. Gray
Lt Bl. Light blue
Or. Orange
B/R. Black with red tracer
B/W. Black with white tracer
G/Y. Green with yellow tracer

B. Black
G. Green
P. Pink
R. Red
W. White
Y. Yellow

R/W. Red with white tracer
R/Y. Red with yellow tracer
W/R. White with red tracer
Y/G. Yellow with green tracer
Y/R. Yellow with red tracer

rpm. The idle speed switch is the only provision for adjusting idle speed on models so equipped. Note that carburetor throttle valves must be fully closed for idle speed switch to function. Full advance timing on models after 1987 should be 18 degrees BTDC at full throttle and is controlled automatically by the IC ignition system.

On models prior to 1988, initial setting of ignition timing can be accomplished as follows: Set throttle at full advance position, then align mark (M—Fig. SZ16-3) on stator plate with stationary mark (S) on upper seal housing. Loosen two screws (T) on maximum advance stop plate (P) and position plate to lightly contact advance lever (D).

Maximum advance timing check can be made using a suitable timing light. Immerse lower unit of outboard motor in water and connect timing light to upper spark plug lead. Refer to ignition timing specifications previously stated and check alignment of flywheel timing marks with index mark on electric starter cap. To check advance timing, run engine at wide-open throttle and note timing marks.

Full retard timing can be adjusted by turning screw (B) as necessary. Adjust full retard timing so motor idles at 600-700 rpm in forward gear regardless of actual timing noted with timing light.

TROUBLE-SHOOTING. If ignition malfunction occurs, use only approved procedures to prevent damage to the components. The fuel system should be checked first to make sure that faulty running is not the result of incorrect fuel mixture or contaminated fuel. Make sure malfunction is not due to spark plugs, wiring or connections. Trouble-shoot ignition system using Suzuki Pocket Tester 09900-25002 or a suitable ohmmeter.

CONDENSER CHARGING COIL. On models prior to 1988, two condenser charge coils are used, low speed and high speed. Models after 1987 are equipped with one condenser charge coil. Disconnect wires at connectors leading from condenser charging coil(s). On models prior to 1988, attach tester between black wire with red tracer and red wire with white tracer (low speed charge coil). Resistance should be 680-831 ohms on 1986 and earlier models, and 600-900 ohms on 1987 models. Leave tester connected to red wire with white tracer and attach remaining tester lead to black wire (high-speed charge coil). Resistance should be 114-140 ohms on 1986 and earlier models and 100-150 ohms on 1987 models.

On models after 1987, attach tester between black and green charge coil wires. Resistance should be 170-250 ohms.

PULSER COIL. On models prior to 1987, two pulser coils are used. One pulser coil triggers cylinders 1 and 3 and the remaining coil triggers cylinder 2. On models after 1986, three pulser coils are used, one for each cylinder. To test pulser coils, disconnect wires between CDI module and pulser coils.

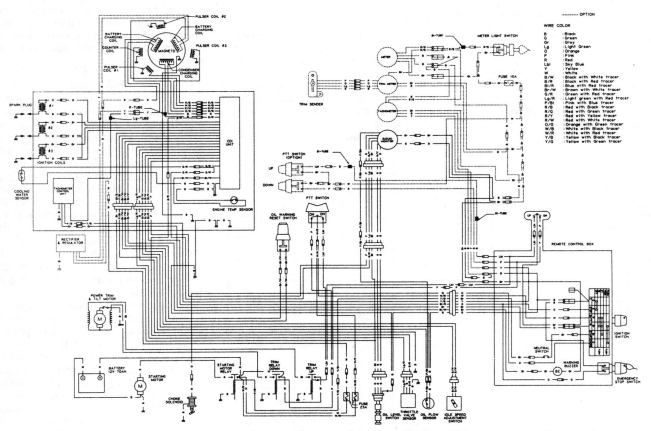

Fig. SZ16-8—Wiring diagram typical of models after 1987 equipped with power trim/tilt and battery charging coil.

B. Black	Or. Orange	LtG. Light green	R/Y. Red with yellow tracer	
G. Green	B/R. Black with red tracer	R/B. Red with black tracer	W/B. White with black tracer	Y/G. Yellow with green tracer	LtBl. Light blue
P. Pink				Or/G. Orange with green tracer
R. Red	B/W. Black with white tracer	R/G. Red with green tracer	W/R. White with red tracer	Bl/R. Blue with red tracer	P/Bl. Pink with blue tracer
W. White	G/R. Green with red tracer	R/W. Red with white tracer	Y/B. Yellow with black tracer	Br/W. Brown with white tracer	LtG/R. Light green with red tracer
Y. Yellow					
Gr. Gray					

On models prior to 1987, connect tester between green wire and yellow wire with red tracer. Note reading and connect tester between pink wire and white wire with red tracer. Resistance of both coils should be 320-391 ohms.

On 1987 models, connect tester between engine ground and alternately between green, pink and yellow wire with red tracer. Resistance should be 290-420 ohms at all test connections.

On models after 1987, connect tester between ground and alternately between red wire with black tracer, white wire with blue tracer and red wire with white tracer. Resistance at all test connections should be 160-240 ohms.

BATTERY CHARGING COIL. Disconnect wires leading from battery charging coil. On models prior to 1988, connect tester between red wire and yellow wire. Resistance should be 0.54-0.66 ohm on models prior to 1987 and 0.4-0.8 ohm on 1987 models. Next, connect tester between red wire and red wire with yellow tracer. Resistance should be 0.36-0.44 ohm on models prior to 1987 and 0.2-0.6 ohm on 1987 models.

On models after 1987, connect tester between red wire and yellow wire. Resistance should be 0.25-0.35 ohm.

IGNITION COILS. Three ignition coils are used on all models. Disconnect wires leading from ignition coils and secondary leads from spark plugs. Test coil primary winding resistance between coil primary terminal and engine ground. Primary resistance should be 0.21-0.29 ohm on models prior to 1987, 0.2-0.5 ohm on 1987 models and 0.2-0.3 ohm on models after 1987. Test coil secondary winding resistance between coil primary and secondary terminals. Secondary resistance should be 2130-2880 ohms on models prior to 1987, 4700-7000 ohms on 1987 models and 1800-2800 ohms on models after 1987.

NOTE: On models after 1987, ignition coil secondary leads are equipped with a resistance-type spark plug cap. Resistance of resistance spark plug cap should be 10,000 ohms. Be sure to add this value to coil secondary resistance if checking coil and secondary lead as a unit.

COUNTER COIL. On models after 1987, a gear counter coil is mounted along outer periphery of flywheel ring gear. The CDI module processes information from the gear counter coil in combination with the throttle valve sensor to determine ignition timing. To test counter coil, separate connector leading from counter coil. Connect tester leads between orange wire with green tracer and ground. Counter coil can be considered acceptable if resistance is within 160-240 ohms. Air gap between counter coil and flywheel ring gear teeth should be 0.5 mm (0.020 in.).

NOTE: Air gap between counter coil and flywheel ring gear teeth must be set to exactly 0.5 mm (0.020 in.) for proper operation of outboard motor. Make sure air gap is properly adjusted.

THROTTLE VALVE SENSOR (Models after 1987). To test throttle valve sensor (5—Fig. SZ16-10), remove alignment pin attached to black cover over throttle valve sensor and insert alignment pin (1) into hole in sensor and sensor cam (3). Align slot in cam (3) with throttle shaft. Disconnect throttle valve sensor connector (4). Connect test harness 09930-89530 or suitable jumper wires to a battery as shown in Fig. SZ16-10. Battery voltage must be nine volts or more. Connect positive (+) lead of a suitable DIGITAL voltmeter to test harness light green wire with red tracer and voltmeter negative (−) lead to battery negative (−) terminal as shown. With throttle fully closed, voltmeter reading should be 0.45-0.55 volt. If not, remove rubber cap (2) and turn adjustment screw (under cap) as necessary to obtain the correct voltage reading. Note that turning adjustment screw clockwise will increase voltage and counterclockwise will decrease voltage.

NOTE: The manufacturer recommends using only a nonmetallic screwdriver to turn sensor adjusting screw or sensor voltmeter reading may not be valid. If metal screwdriver must be used, remove screwdriver from area of throttle valve sensor after adjustment to prevent erroneous voltmeter reading.

If sensor output voltage at closed throttle is below 0.45 volt, idle speed ignition timing will be fixed at 5 degrees BTDC; idle speed switch will be inoperative. If sensor output voltage at closed throttle is above 0.55 volt, ignition timing at idle speed will be incorrect. Refer to IDLE SPEED SWITCH section.

Once the specified voltage reading is obtained at closed throttle, remove alignment pin and open carburetor to wide-open throttle. Voltmeter reading should now be 2.5 volts or more. Do not attempt to adjust wide-open throttle sensor voltage. If wide-open throttle sensor voltage is not 2.5 volts or higher, renew sensor.

If throttle valve sensor is removed or renewed, install as follows: Insert alignment pin (1) as shown to align cam and sensor shaft. Align slot in sensor cam with carburetor throttle shaft and install sensor on carburetor. Lightly tighten mounting screws (7) to allow for adjustment of sensor position on carburetor. Connect test harness and digital voltmeter as shown in Fig. SZ16-10. Make sure battery voltage is nine volts or more. Sensor output voltage at closed throttle should be 0.45-0.55 volt. If not, move position of sensor on carburetor to obtain specified voltage and securely tighten screws (7). Recheck voltage after tightening screws (7) and

⊖ TESTER LEAD / TESTER LEAD ⊕		CHARGE			PULSER				IGNITION			STOP
		Black/Red	Red/White	Black	Green	Pink	White/Red	Yellow/Red	Orange	Light Blue	Grey	Black/White
CHARGE	Black/Red		A	A	A	A	A	A	B	B	B	A
	Red/White	B		B	B	B	B	B	B	B	B	B
	Black	B	B		A	A	A	A	C	C	C	B
PULSER	Green	B	B	A		A	A	A	C	C	C	B
	Pink	B	B	B	B		B	B	B	B	B	B
	White/Red	B	B	A	A	A		A	C	C	C	B
	Yellow/Red	B	B	A	A	A	A		C	C	C	B
IGNITION	Orange	C	C	C	B	B	C	C		B	B	C
	Light Blue	C	C	C	B	B	C	C	B		B	C
	Grey	C	C	C	B	B	C	C	B	B		C
STOP	Black/White	A	A	A	A	A	A	A	C	C	C	

Fig. SZ16-9—Use above chart and values listed below to test condition of CDI module on models prior to 1987.

A. 100k ohms or less
B. 100k ohms or more

C. Tester needle should deflect, then return toward infinite resistance.

if necessary, remove cap (2) and turn adjustment screw to obtain 0.45-0.55 volt. Be sure to reinstall cap (2). After obtaining the correct voltage at closed throttle, remove alignment pin and check sensor output voltage at wide-open throttle. Voltage should be 2.5 volts or higher. Do not attempt to adjust wide-open throttle voltage.

IDLE SPEED SWITCH. Idle speed switch malfunction can be quickly verified by checking ignition timing and engine rpm while switching position of idle speed switch. Note that carburetor throttle valves must be fully closed for idle speed switch to function.

NOTE: A defective or maladjusted throttle valve sensor may cause idle speed switch to be inoperative or ignition timing at idle speed to be incorrect. Prior to testing idle speed switch, make sure throttle valve sensor is operating properly and correctly ajusted. Refer to THROTTLE VALVE SENSOR section.

Note that each position of idle speed switch should change ignition timing two degrees and change engine idle speed approximately 50 rpm. If timing and engine rpm do not change with each switch position, idle speed switch may be defective.

CDI MODULE. On models prior to 1987, use Suzuki Pock Tester 09900-25002 or a suitable ohmmeter and refer to chart in Fig. SZ16-9. On models after 1986, test CDI module using Stevens Model CD-77 peak reading voltmeter (PRV).

On 1987 models, set PRV to the negative (−) 500 range. Connect PRV black test lead to engine ground and red test lead alternately to each ignition coil primary terminal while running engine at 1000 rpm. CDI module output should be 160 volts or more at each test connection.

On models after 1987, set PRV to positive (+) 500 range. Connect PRV black test lead to engine ground. Disconnect ignition coil primary wires from coils. Connect red test lead alternately to each ignition coil primary wire. Crank engine at each connection. CDI module output should be 96 volts or more at each connection. If not renew CDI module.

COOLING SYSTEM

WATER PUMP. A rubber impeller-type water pump is mounted between the drive shaft housing and gearcase. A key in the drive shaft is used to turn the pump impeller. If cooling system problems are encountered, check water intake for plugging or partial stoppage, then if not corrected, remove gearcase as outlined in the appropriate section and check condition of the water pump, water passages and sealing surfaces.

When water pump is disassembled, check condition of impeller (4—Fig. SZ16-11) and plate (5) for excessive wear. Turn drive shaft clockwise (viewed from top) while placing pump housing (2) over impeller. Avoid turning drive shaft in opposite direction after water pump is reassembled.

THERMOSTAT. A thermostat (7—Fig. SZ16-12) is used to regulate engine operating temperature. The thermostat should start to open within the temperature range of 48°-52° C (118°-126° F) on 1987-1989 DT75 models and 40°-44° C (104°-111° F) on all other models.

Thermostat can be removed for inspection or renewal after removing thermostat housing (5).

POWER HEAD

REMOVE AND REINSTALL. To remove the power head, first remove engine cover. Detach battery cables. Remove fuel filter and disconnect fuel supply line from connector in lower engine cover. Disconnect shift and throttle linkage. Detach any wiring that will interfere with power head removal. Remove covers to expose power head retaining screws and nut. Remove the screws and nut, then lift power head assembly with related components from lower unit assembly.

Before reinstalling power head, check condition of drive shaft seal (15—Fig. SZ16-13). If seal renewal is required, it will be necessary to separate crankcase (1—Fig. SZ16-12) from cylinder block (2) as outlined in the appropriate following paragraphs. Apply a suitable water-resistant grease to lip area of seal and install seal into seal housing (16—Fig. SZ16-13). Make certain drive shaft splines are clean, then coat splines with a light coating of water-resistant grease. Apply a suitable sealer to mating surfaces of power head and lower unit and install a new gasket. Coat the area next to heads of power head to lower unit retaining screws with silicone sealer. Tighten the power head retaining screws and nut to 15-20 N·m (11-15 ft.-lbs.). The remainder of installation is the reverse of removal procedure.

DISASSEMBLY. Disassembly and inspection can be accomplished in the following manner. On models equipped with oil injection, disconnect wiring to

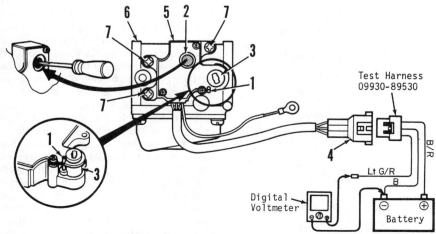

Fig. SZ16-10—Refer to text for throttle valve sensor testing and installation procedure.

1. Alignment pin	5. Throttle valve sensor assy.	B/R. Black with red tracer
2. Cap (adjustment screw)	6. Carburetor	LtG/R. Light green with red tracer
3. Sensor cam	7. Mounting screw	
4. Connector	B. Black	

Fig. SZ16-11—Exploded view of water pump assembly.

1. Water tube	4. Impeller
2. Pump housing	5. Plate
3. Key	6. Gasket

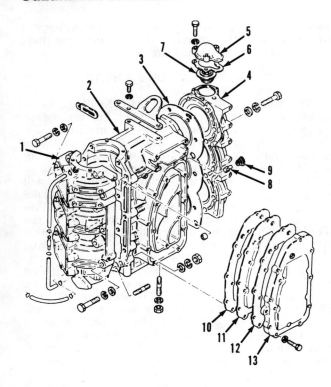

Fig. SZ16-12—Exploded view of cylinder block assembly typical of all models.

1. Crankcase half
2. Cylinder block
3. Gasket
4. Cylinder head
5. Thermostat housing
6. Gasket
7. Thermostat
8. Valve
9. Spring
10. Gasket
11. Inner exhaust cover
12. Gasket
13. Outer exhaust cover

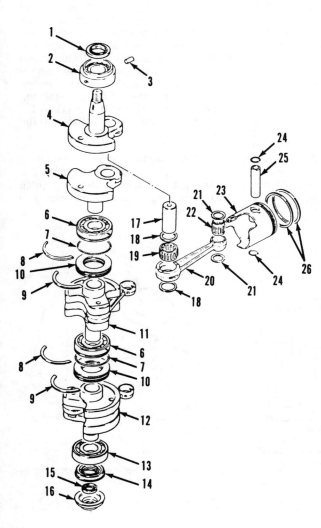

Fig. SZ16-13—Exploded view of crankshaft assembly typical of all models.

1. Seal
2. Roller bearing
3. Pin
4. Top crankshaft upper half
5. Top crankshaft lower half
6. Roller bearing
7. "O" ring
8. Bearing ring
9. Labyrinth seal ring
10. Labyrinth seal
11. Middle crankshaft half
12. Lower crankshaft half
13. Roller bearing
14. Seal
15. Seal
16. Seal housing
17. Crankpin
18. Thrust washer
19. Needle bearing
20. Connecting rod
21. Thrust washers
22. Needle bearing
23. Piston
24. Piston pin clips
25. Piston pin
26. Piston rings

oil tank. Remove oil supply line from oil tank outlet and plug. Remove cap screws to withdraw oil tank. On models equipped with power tilt and trim, remove relays from side of cylinder block. Remove carburetors and electric choke solenoid. Remove fuel pump assembly. Remove oil injection pump (1—Fig. SZ16-6), retainer (4) and driven gear (3). Remove ignition coils, electric starter, starter motor relay, rectifier and CDI module. Remove speed control linkage. Remove flywheel and stator plate assembly. Remove electric starter motor bracket and any remaining wiring that will interfere with cylinder block and crankcase separation. Remove intake manifolds and reed valve assemblies. Remove outer and inner exhaust covers. Remove thermostat housing and withdraw thermostat. Remove spark plugs, cylinder head, spring (9—Fig. SZ16-12) and valve (8), then clean carbon from combustion chamber and any foreign material accumulation in water passages. Unscrew crankcase retaining screws and separate crankcase (1) from cylinder block (2). Crankshaft and piston assembly can now be removed from cylinder block.

Engine components are now accessible for overhaul as outlined in the appropriate following paragraphs. Refer to the following section for assembly procedures.

ASSEMBLY. Refer to specific service sections when assembling the crankshaft, connecting rod, piston and reed valves. Make sure all joint and gasket surfaces are clean, free from nicks and burrs and hardened cement or carbon.

Whenever the power head is disassembled, it is recommended that all gasket surfaces and mating surfaces without gaskets be carefully checked for nicks, burrs and warped surfaces that might interfere with a tight seal. Cylinder head, head end of cylinder block and some mating surfaces of manifold and crankcase should be checked on a surface plate and lapped if necessary to provide a smooth surface. Do not remove any more metal than is necessary.

When assembling power head, first lubricate all friction surfaces and bearings with engine oil. Apply a suitable high temperature grease to lip area of crankshaft seal. Apply a suitable water-resistant grease to lip area of drive shaft seal and install seal into seal housing (16—Fig. SZ16-13). Place bearing retainers (8) and seal rings (9) into cylinder block, then install crankshaft assembly.

NOTE: Labyrinth seal (10) is not used on models after 1987. Later models are equipped with a metal slip-ring type seal.

Make certain main bearing locating pins engage notches in cylinder block. Apply a coat of Suzuki Bond No. 4 or a suitable equivalent sealer to mating surfaces of crankcase and cylinder block, then position crankcase on cylinder block. Tighten crankcase screws in sequence shown in Fig. SZ16-14. Refer to CONDENSED SERVICE DATA section for tightening specifications.

RINGS, PISTONS AND CYLINDERS. The piston are fitted with two piston rings. Piston rings must be installed with manufacturer's marking facing piston crown. Rings are pinned in place to prevent ring rotation. Piston ring end gap should be 0.2-0.4 mm (0.008-0.016 in.) with a maximum allowable gap of 0.8 mm (0.031 in.). Piston-to-cylinder clearance should be 0.077-0.093 mm (0.0030-0.0037 in.) on DT75 models prior to 1987, 0.112-0.127 mm (0.0044-0.0050 in.) on 1987 DT75 models and DT85 models prior to 1988, 0.135-0.165 mm (0.0053-0.0065 in.) on all 1988 models and 0.12-0.15 mm (0.0047-0.0059 in.) on all 1989 models. Piston and rings are available in standard size as well as 0.25 mm (0.010 in.) and 0.50 mm (0.020 in.) oversize. Cylinder should be bored to the next oversize if cylinder bore is tapered, out-of-round or worn in excess of 0.10 mm (0.004 in.). Install piston on connecting rod so arrow on piston crown will face exhaust port when piston is in cylinder.

CONNECTING RODS, BEARINGS AND CRANKSHAFT. Connecting rods, bearings and crankshaft are a pressed-together unit. Crankshaft should be disassembled ONLY by experienced service personnel using the proper service equipment.

The crankshaft is supported by a caged roller bearing at the top and caged ball bearings at the center and

bottom of crankshaft. Determine rod bearing, connecting rod and crankpin wear by measuring connecting rod small end side-to-side movement as shown at (A—Fig. SZ16-16). Normal movement (A) is 5 mm (0.20 in.) or less. Maximum allowable crankshaft runout is 0.05 mm (0.002 in.) measured at bearing surfaces with crankshaft ends supported.

When installing crankshaft, lubricate pistons, rings, cylinders and bearings with a recommended engine oil as outlined in ASSEMBLY section.

ELECTRIC STARTER

Models are equipped with electric starter shown in Fig. SZ16-17. Disassembly is evident after inspection of unit and reference to exploded view. Standard brush length is 16 mm (0.63 in.). Renew brushes if worn to 11.5 mm (0.45 in.) or less. After reassembly, bench test starter before installing on power head.

LOWER UNIT

PROPELLER. Protection for motor is provided by a special cushioning clutch built into the propeller hub. Three-blade propellers are used. Various propellers are available from the manufacturer. Select a propeller that will allow the outboard motor to run at the speed range of 4800-5500 rpm at full throttle.

R&R AND OVERHAUL. Refer to Fig. SZ16-18 for exploded view of lower unit gearcase assembly used on all models. During disassembly, note the location of all shims and thrust washers for reference during reassembly. To remove gearcase, first unscrew plug (34) and drain gear lubricant. Remove plug from side of lower engine cover to obtain access

to shift linkage. Unscrew nuts retaining shift arm (2) to shaft (4), then disengage shaft (4) from shift rod (5). Remove the screws securing gearcase to drive shaft housing and separate gearcase assembly from drive shaft housing. Remove water pump assembly (Fig. SZ16-11). Remove propeller with related components from propeller shaft. On models prior to 1983, remove seal ring (65—Fig. SZ16-18), washer (64) and snap ring (63) retaining gearcase end cap (58).

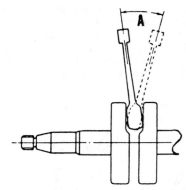

Fig. SZ16-16—Maximum side-to-side movement (A) at connecting rod small end should be 5 mm (0.20 in.) or less.

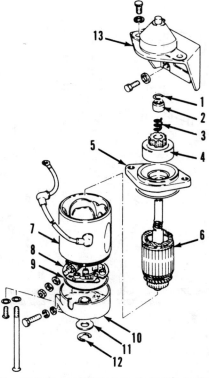

Fig. SZ16-17—Exploded view of electric starter motor.

1. "C" ring	8. Brush assy.
2. Stop	9. Gasket
3. Spring	10. End housing
4. Drive	11. Thrust washer
5. Frame head	12. "E" clip
6. Armature	13. Bracket
7. Frame	

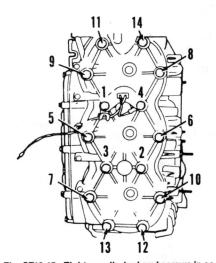

Fig. SZ16-14—Tighten crankcase screws in sequence shown. Refer to CONDENSED SERVICE DATA for torque values.

Fig. SZ16-15—Tighten cylinder head screws in sequence shown. Refer to CONDENSED SERVICE DATA for torque values.

NOTE: On models after 1982, gearcase end cap (58) is retained to gearcase by two screws.

Use a suitable puller and withdraw propeller shaft assembly with gearcase end cap. Unscrew pinion nut (50) and remove pinion gear (49), then extract forward gear (41). Drive shaft (20) and related components can be withdrawn from gearcase after removal of bearing housing (18).

Inspect gears for wear on teeth and on engagement dogs. Inspect dog clutch (45) for wear on engagement surfaces. Inspect shafts for wear on splines and on friction surfaces of gears and oil seals. Check shift cam (14) and shift pin (43) for excessive wear. Check condition of shift spring (48). All seals and "O"

rings should be renewed when unit is reassembled.

Backlash between pinion gear (49) and drive gears (41 and 53) should be 0.05-0.30 mm (0.002-0.012 in.) on models prior to 1983 and 0.1-0.2 mm (0.004-0.008 in.) on models after 1982. Backlash is adjusted by varying thickness of shims (40 and 54). Propeller shaft end play should be 0.05-0.30 mm (0.002-0.012 in.) on models prior to 1983 and 0.2-0.4 mm (0.008-0.016 in.) on models after 1982. Propeller shaft end play is adjusted by increasing or decreasing the thickness of shim (51).

Reassemble gearcase by reversing disassembly procedure while noting the following: Install dog clutch (45) on propeller shaft (56) so "F" mark (Fig. SZ16-19) is facing forward gear (41—Fig. SZ16-

18). Tighten pinion nut to 60-70 N·m (44-51 ft.-lbs.) on models prior to 1983 and 70-80 N·m (51-58 ft.-lbs.) on models after 1982. Apply water-resistant grease to "O" ring (57). Apply silicone sealer to gearcase and bearing housing (18) mating surfaces and to bearing housing and drive shaft housing mating surfaces. Coat retaining screws in area next to screw head with silicone sealer.

Engage shift shaft (4) in shift rod (5) eyelet and attach shift arm (2). Secure with nuts. Fill gearcase with outboard gear oil as outlined in LUBRICATION section.

POWER TILT AND TRIM

Some models are equipped with a hydraulically actuated power tilt and trim system. An oil pump driven by a reversible electric motor provides oil pressure. A rocker control switch determines motor and pump rotation thereby retracting or extending tilt and trim cylinders.

Early Type

The pump is equipped with an automatic and manual release valve (V—Fig. SZ16-20) that, when set in the manual

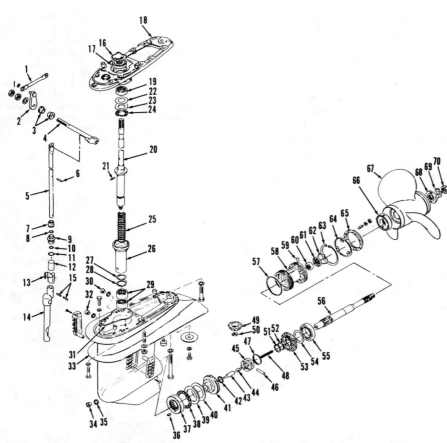

Fig. SZ16-18—Exploded view of typical lower unit gearcase assembly used on all models. On models after 1982, gearcase end cap (58) is retained to gearcase by two screws.

1. Link	19. Bearing	36. Pin	53. Reverse gear
2. Shift arm	20. Drive shaft	37. Bearing	54. Shim
3. Grommets	21. Pin	38. Thrust bearing	55. Bearing
4. Shift shaft	22. Shim	39. Thrust washer	56. Propeller shaft
5. Shift rod	23. Thrust washer	40. Shim	57. "O" ring
6. Pin	24. Thrust bearing	41. Forward gear	58. End cap
7. Dust seal	25. Spring	42. Thrust washer	59. Pin
8. "O" ring	26. Collar	43. Shift pin	60. Needle bearing
9. Rod guide	27. Thrust washer	44. Spring guide	61. Seal
10. "O" ring	28. Thrust washer	45. Dog clutch	62. Snap ring
11. "O" ring	29. Needle bearings	46. Pin	63. Snap ring
12. Magnet	30. Vent plug	47. Pin retainer	64. Washer
13. Magnet holder	31. Seal ring	48. Shift spring	65. Seal ring
14. Shift cam	32. Level plug	49. Pinion gear	66. Spacer
15. Pins	33. Gearcase housing	50. Nut	67. Propeller
16. Snap ring	34. Drain plug	51. Shim	68. Spacer
17. Seal	35. Gasket	52. Thrust washer	69. Tab washer
18. Bearing housing			70. Nut

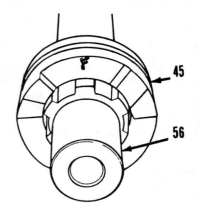

Fig. SZ16-19—Install dog clutch (45) on propeller shaft (56) with "F" marked side facing forward gear (41).

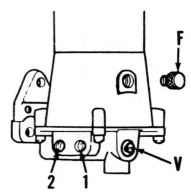

Fig. SZ16-20—View of early type pump assembly showing location of oil fill plug (F), release valve (V) and test ports (1 and 2).

Illustrations courtesy Suzuki

position (vertical), enables manual movement of trim and tilt cylinders if the electric motor malfunctions.

Recommended oil is SAE 20 or SAE 30 motor oil or Dexron automatic transmission fluid. Do not run pump without oil in reservoir. Fill plug (F) is located in side of pump reservoir. Oil level should reach fill plug hole threads with outboard motor in a vertical position. Hydraulic tilt should be cycled several times and oil level rechecked if system has been drained or lost a large amount of oil.

If malfunction occurs in tilt and trim system, first make sure malfunction is not due to wiring, wiring connection or electric motor failure. To check oil pressure, connect a 20.7 MPa (3000 psi) gage to port "1" on pump and operate pump. Hydraulic oil pressure at port "1" should be within the limits of 6.9-17.25 MPa (1000-2500 psi). Connect test gage to port "2" and operate pump. Hydraulic oil pressure should be within the limits of 1.66-5.52 MPa (240-800 psi). Oil pressure less than specified may indicate leakage, faulty pressure relief valves or check valves.

If electric motor and pump assembly are disassembled for repair or renewal of individual components, upon reassembly use Ingilis Company EP630548 flat black neobase or equivalent to provide a watertight seal.

Late Type

Two designs of late model pump are used. Refer to Fig. SZ16-24 to identify pump assembly prior to 1987 and after 1986. When checking or filling reservoir oil level on models prior to 1987, outboard motor must be trimmed fully down. When checking or filling reservoir on models after 1986, outboard motor must be tilted fully up.

Pump on all models is equipped with manual release valve (M—Fig. SZ16-23). If electric motor malfunction occurs, open manual release valve a maximum of two turns counterclockwise to enable manual movement of trim and tilt cylinders.

Recommended oil for models prior to 1987 is SAE 20, SAE 10W-30 or SAE 10W-40 motor oil, or Dexron automatic transmission fluid. Recommended oil for models after 1986 is Dexron automatic transmission fluid only. Do not run pump without oil in reservoir. Fill plug (5—Fig. SZ16-22) is located in side of reservoir. Oil level should reach fill plug hole. Hydraulic tilt should be cycled several times to bleed air and oil level rechecked if system has been drained or lost a large amount of oil.

If trim/tilt system malfunction occurs, make sure problem is not due to wiring, wiring connections or electric motor failure. To check oil pressure, connect a 34.5 MPa (5000 psi) gage to port (1— Fig. SZ16-23) on pump and operate pump in the UP direction. Hydraulic oil pressure at port (1) should be within 13-17 MPa (1885-2465 psi). To check down pressure, connect test gage to port (2) and operate pump in the DOWN direction. Hydraulic oil pressure should be within 28-56 MPa (406-812 psi). Oil pressure less than specified may indicate leakage, faulty pressure relief valves or check valves. The manufacturer recommends renewing pump and valve body assembly to service low pressure.

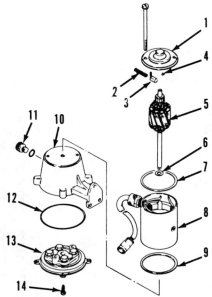

Fig. SZ16-21—Exploded view of early type power trim/tilt electric motor and pump assembly.

1. End cap	8. Frame
2. Spring	9. Gasket
3. Brush	10. Reservoir
4. Ball	11. Fill plug
5. Armature	12. "O" ring
6. Thrust washer	13. Pump assy.
7. Gasket	14. Cap screw

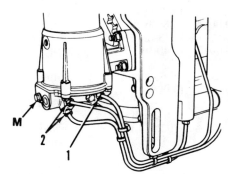

Fig. SZ16-23—View of late type pump assembly identifying test ports (1 and 2) and manual release valve (M). Refer to text.

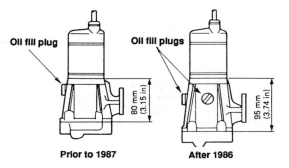

Oil fill plug   Oil fill plugs

80 mm (3.15 in)   95 mm (3.74 in)

Prior to 1987   **After 1986**

Fig. SZ16-22—Exploded view of late type power trim/tilt electric motor and pump assembly.

1. End cap	
2. Gasket	6. Reservoir
3. Electric motor assy.	7. "O" ring
4. Gasket	8. Pump & valve body
5. Fill plug	assy.

Fig. SZ16-24—View identifying later style power trim/tilt pump assemblies.

SUZUKI DT115 AND DT140
(Prior To 1986)

CONDENSED SERVICE DATA

NOTE: Metric fasteners are used throughout outboard motor.

TUNE-UP
Hp/rpm:
DT115 . . . . .115/4800-5500
DT140 . . . . .140/4800-5500
Bore . . . . .84 mm
　　　　　　　　　　　　　　　　　　　　(3.31 in.)
Stroke . . . . .80 mm
　　　　　　　　　　　　　　　　　　　　(3.15 in.)
Number of Cylinders 4
Displacement . . . . .1773 cc
　　　　　　　　　　　　　　　　　　　(108.20 cu. in.)
Spark Plug:
NGK B8HS
Electrode Gap . . . . .0.8-0.9 mm
　　　　　　　　　　　　　　　　　(0.031-0.035 in.)
Ignition Type . . . . .Breakerless
Carburetor Make . . . . .Mikuni

SIZES—CLEARANCES
Piston Ring End Gap . . . . .0.2-0.4 mm
　　　　　　　　　　　　　　　　　(0.008-0.016 in.)
Piston Pin Diameter . . . . .21.995-22.000 mm
　　　　　　　　　　　　　　　　　(0.8659-0.8661 in.)
Piston-to-Cylinder Clearance:
Prior to 1986 .112-0.127 mm
　　　　　　　　　　　　　　　　　(0.0044-0.0050 in.)
After 1985 . . . . .115-0.125 mm
　　　　　　　　　　　　　　　　　(0.0045-0.0049 in.)
Max. Crankshaft Runout at Main
Bearing Journal . . . . .0.05 mm
　　　　　　　　　　　　　　　　　　　(0.002 in.)
Max. Connecting Rod Small End
Side Shake . . . . .5.0 mm
　　　　　　　　　　　　　　　　　　　(0.20 in.)

TIGHTENING TORQUES
Cylinder Head:
6 mm . . . . .8-12 N·m
　　　　　　　　　　　　　　　　　(6-9 ft.-lbs.)
10 mm . . . . .40-60 N·m
　　　　　　　　　　　　　　　　(29-44 ft.-lbs.)

TIGHTENING TORQUES CONT.
Crankcase:
8 mm (Prior to 1986) . . . . .18-28 N·m
　　　　　　　　　　　　　　　　(13-20 ft.-lbs.)
8 mm (After 1985). . . . . .21-25 N·m
　　　　　　　　　　　　　　　　(16-18 ft.-lbs.)
10 mm (Prior to 1986). . . . . .40-60 N·m
　　　　　　　　　　　　　　　　(29-44 ft.-lbs.)
10 mm (After 1985) . . . . .46-54 N·m
　　　　　　　　　　　　　　　　(34-40 ft.-lbs.)
Connecting Rod. . . . . .30-35 N·m*
　　　　　　　　　　　　　　　　(22-26 ft.-lbs.)
Exhaust Cover . . . . .8-12 N·m
　　　　　　　　　　　　　　　　(6-9 ft.-lbs.)
Flywheel Nut . . . . .240-260 N·m
　　　　　　　　　　　　　　　　(177-191 ft.-lbs.)
Gearcase Pinion Nut:
Prior to 1986 .80-90 N·m
　　　　　　　　　　　　　　　　(58-65 ft.-lbs.)
After 1985 . . . . .100-110 N·m
　　　　　　　　　　　　　　　　(74-81 ft.-lbs.)
Propeller Shaft Nut .50-60 N·m
　　　　　　　　　　　　　　　　(36-44 ft.-lbs.)
Standard Screws:
Unmarked or Marked "4"
5 mm . . . . .2-4 N·m
　　　　　　　　　　　　　　　　(2-3 ft.-lbs.)
6 mm . . . . .4-7 N·m
　　　　　　　　　　　　　　　　(3-5 ft.-lbs.)
8 mm . . . . .10-16 N·m
　　　　　　　　　　　　　　　　(7-12 ft.-lbs.)
10 mm . . . . .22-35 N·m
　　　　　　　　　　　　　　　　(16-26 ft.-lbs.)
Marked "7" or SAE Grade 5
5 mm . . . . .3-6 N·m
　　　　　　　　　　　　　　　　(2-5 ft.-lbs.)
6 mm . . . . .8-12 N·m
　　　　　　　　　　　　　　　　(6-9 ft.-lbs.)
8 mm . . . . .18-28 N·m
　　　　　　　　　　　　　　　　(13-20 ft.-lbs.)
10 mm . . . . .40-60 N·m
　　　　　　　　　　　　　　　　(29-44 ft.-lbs.)

*Models after 1985 are equipped with a press-together crankshaft and connecting rod assembly.

LUBRICATION

The power head is lubricated by oil mixed with the fuel. All models are equipped with oil injection. The manufacturer recommends using Suzuki Outboard Motor Oil or a NMMA certified TC-WII engine oil. The recommended fuel is unleaded gasoline with a minimum pump octane rating of 85.

During break-in (first five hours of operation on models prior to 1986 or first 10 hours of operation on later models) of a new or rebuilt engine, a 50:1 fuel and oil mixture should be used in the fuel tank in combination with the oil injection system. After break-in period, switch to straight gasoline in the fuel tank.

FUEL SYSTEM

CARBURETOR. Mikuni Model B32-28 carburetors are used on DT115 models and Mikuni Model B40-32 carburetors are used on DT140 models. Refer to Fig. SZ17-1 for exploded view of carburetors. Initial setting of pilot air screw (3) from a lightly seated position is 1 to 1½ turns on DT115 models prior to 1986, 1⅛ to 1⅝ turns on DT140 models prior to 1986, 1¼ to 1¾ turns on 1986-1988 DT115 models, 1 to 1½ turns on 1986-1988 DT140 models, ⅞ to 1⅜ turns on 1989 DT115 models and 1⅛ to 1⅝ turns on 1989 DT140 models. Final adjustment should be made with engine at normal operating temperature and running in forward gear. On models prior to 1986, rotate timing adjustment screw (B—Fig. SZ17-3) in small increments until engine idles at approximately 600-700 rpm. On models after 1985, adjust idle timing switch to obtain 600-700 rpm. Note that idle timing is the only provision for adjusting idle speed on all models. Adjust pilot air screw so engine idles smoothly and will accelerate cleanly without hesitation. If necessary, readjust idle timing to obtain 600-700 rpm in forward gear.

Main fuel metering is controlled by main jet (5). Standard main jet size for normal operation on models prior to 1986 is #135 on DT115 models and #160 on DT140 models. On 1986-1988 DT115 models, standard main jet size is #132.5. On 1986-1988 DT140 models standard main jet size is #157.5 on top carburetor, #162.5 on third carburetor and #155 on second and fourth carburetors. Standard main jet size on 1989 models is #132.5 on DT115 models and #150 on DT140 models.

To check float level, remove float bowl and invert carburetor. Distance (D—Fig. SZ17-2) between main jet and bottom of float should be 10.4-12.4 mm (0.41-0.49 in.) on DT115 models prior to 1986, 10-12 mm (0.39-0.47 in.) on DT115 models after 1985 and 17-19 mm (0.67-0.75 in.) on all DT140 models. Adjust float by bending float tang (T).

On models prior to 1986, synchronize carburetor throttle valves by loosening throttle valve shaft nuts and throttle lever screws. Visually verify that all four throttle valves are completely closed, then retighten throttle lever screws and throttle shaft nuts.

On models after 1985, synchronize carburetor throttle valves by loosening throttle lever adjusting screws (S—Fig. SZ17-4) on top, second and third carburetors. Lightly rotate throttle lever on top carburetor clockwise, make sure all four throttle valves are completely closed, then retighten throttle lever screws.

NOTE: The manufacturer recommends applying Suzuki Thread Lock 1342 or equivalent thread locking compound to threads of throttle lever adjusting screws.

SPEED CONTROL LINKAGE. On models prior to 1986, the carburetor throttle valves must be correctly synchronized to open as the ignition is advanced to obtain optimum performance. To adjust the speed control linkage, it is necessary to first check, and adjust if required, the ignition maximum advance as outlined in the IGNITION TIMING section. Rotate speed control lever (L—Fig. SZ17-3) to align TDC mark (T) on stator plate with mark on upper end of cylinder block. With speed control lever (L) held in this position, mark (M) on throttle cam (C) should align with center of carburetor throttle lever roller (R). If not, loosen jam nuts (N) and rotate carburetor link (A) until correct setting is obtained then retighten jam nuts (N).

On models after 1985, ignition timing advance is accomplished electronically. To adjust throttle linkage, rotate throttle lever (3—Fig. SZ17-5) counterclockwise until throttle valves are fully open. With throttle valves completely open, throttle lever (3) should just contact stop (4) on crankcase. Loosen jam nuts (2) and adjust link rod (1) as necessary to adjust.

REED VALVES. The inlet reed valves are mounted on four reed plate assemblies located between intake manifold and crankcase. The reed petals should seat very lightly against the reed plate throughout their entire length with the least possible tension. Tip of reed petal must not stand open more than 0.2 mm (0.008 in.) from contact surface. Reed stop opening should be 7.9-8.3 mm (0.031-0.033 in.).

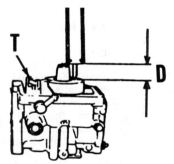

Fig. SZ17-2—Distance (D) for correct float level should be 10.4-12.4 mm (0.41-0.49 in.) on DT115 models prior to 1986, 10-12 mm (0.39-0.47 in.) on DT115 models after 1985 and 17-19 mm (0.67-0.75 in.) on all DT140 models.

Fig. SZ17-3—View of speed control linkage typical of all models prior to 1986. Refer to text for identification of components and servicing procedures.

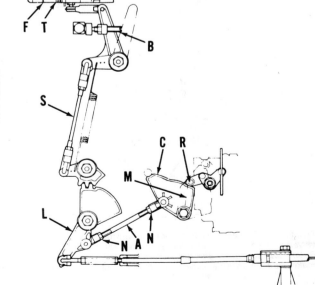

Fig. SZ17-1—Exploded view of typical carburetor setup used on all models. Mikuni type B40-32 carburetors are shown. Mikuni type B32-28 carburetors are similar.

1. Body
2. Spring
3. Pilot air screw
4. Main nozzle
5. Main jet
6. Gasket
7. Needle & seat
8. Pin
9. Float
10. Gasket
11. Float bowl
12. Pilot jet
13. Throttle lever synchronizing plate
14. Choke lever synchronizing plate
15. Clip

Illustrations courtesy Suzuki

Renew reeds if petals are broken, cracked, warped, rusted or bent. Never attempt to bend or straighten a damaged reed petal. Never install a bent or damaged petal. Seating surface of reed plate should be smooth and flat. Reed petals should be centered over inlet ports in reed plate and reed stops should be centered over reed petals. When reassembling reed valve assemblies, apply a suitable thread locking compound to screws securing reed petals and stops to reed plates.

FUEL PUMP. A diaphragm type fuel pump is mounted on the side of the power head and is actuated by crank-case pulsations. Refer to Fig. SZ17-6 for exploded view of fuel pump assembly.

When servicing pump, scribe reference marks across pump body to aid in reassembly. Defective or questionable parts should be renewed. Diaphragm should be renewed if air leaks or cracks are noted, or if deterioration is evident.

FUEL FILTER. A fuel filter (9—Fig. SZ17-6) is mounted on the side of the power head on all models. Filter should be disassembled and cleaned after every 50 hours of operation. Renew filter element (12) if excessive blockage is noted.

OIL INJECTION

BLEEDING PUMP. To bleed trapped air from pump or supply lines, fill oil reservoir with a recommended oil and add a 50:1 fuel and oil mixture to the fuel tank. Open bleed screw (A—Fig. SZ17-7) 2-3 turns, start engine and run at idle speed (600-700 rpm). Close bleed screw (A) after air bubbles are no longer noted at bleed screw.

CHECKING OIL PUMP OUTPUT. Start engine and allow to warm-up for approximately five minutes. Stop engine and disconnect oil pump control rod (5—Fig. SZ17-7) from bottom carburetor. Remove oil supply line at oil reservoir outlet and plug reservoir outlet. Connect Suzuki oil gage 09900-21602 or 09941-68710 to oil supply line and fill oil gage with a recommended oil. Bleed air from lines as previously outlined, then refill oil gage to an upper reference

mark. With oil pump control lever in the fully closed (idle) position, start engine and run at 1500 rpm for exactly five minutes. After five minutes, stop engine and note oil gage. Oil consumption in five minutes at 1500 rpm should be 6.0-7.3 mL (0.20-0.25 fl. oz.) on DT115 models prior to 1986, 8.0-9.8 mL (0.27-0.33 fl. oz.) on DT140 models prior to 1986 and 3.8-6.8 mL (0.13-0.23 fl. oz.) on all models after 1985.

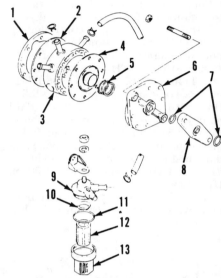

Fig. SZ17-6—Exploded view of diaphragm type fuel pump and fuel filter assemblies.

1. Cover	
2. Diaphragm	8. Insulator block
3. Body	9. Fuel filter body
4. Diaphragm	10. Packing
5. Spring	11. "O" ring
6. Body	12. Filter
7. "O" rings	13. Bowl

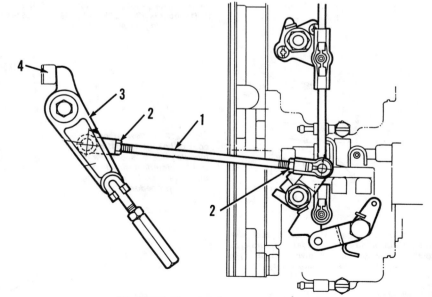

Fig. SZ17-5—Throttle linkage on models after 1985.

1. Link rod
2. Jam nuts
3. Throttle lever
4. Crankcase stop

Fig. SZ17-4—To synchronize carburetor throttle valves on models after 1985, loosen screws (S). Rotate top carburetor throttle lever clockwise, make sure all throttle valves are closed and retighten screws (S).

To check maximum oil pump output, repeat previous procedure except hold pump control lever in the fully open (full throttle) position and run engine for two minutes. Oil consumption in two minutes at 1500 rpm should be 10-12 mL (0.34-0.41 fl. oz.) on DT115 prior to 1986, 13.4-16.0 mL (0.45-0.54 fl. oz.) on DT140 models prior to 1986, 6.5-9.7 mL (0.22-0.33 fl. oz.) on DT 115 models after 1985 and 8.0-12.0 mL (0.27-0.41 fl. oz.) on DT140 models after 1985.

NOTE: Pump output test results may vary depending on testing error and ambient temperature. Repeat test 2-3 times to ensure consistent results.

Renew oil pump assembly (1) if output is not as specified.

NOTE: Index mark (I—Fig. SZ17-8) on oil injection pump must align with mark (M) on control lever when lever is in the released (closed) position. Loosen jam nuts and adjust control rod (5—Fig. SZ17-7) to adjust.

IGNITION

All models prior to 1986 are equipped with Suzuki pointless, electronic ignition (PEI). All models after 1985 are equipped with Suzuki integrated circuit (IC) ignition system. On models equipped with IC ignition, the CDI module uses information supplied by a gear counter coil mounted on the outer periphery of the flywheel and a throttle valve switch (throttle valve sensor on 1989 models) to determine and automatically set the optimum ignition timing. Refer to Fig. SZ17-9 for wiring diagram on models prior to 1986 and Fig. SZ17-10 for wiring diagram on later models.

IGNITION TIMING. On models prior to 1986, ignition timing should be 3 degrees ATDC at 1000 rpm and 23 degrees BTDC at 5000 rpm.

To adjust initial timing proceed as follows: Set throttle at full advance position, then note if mark (F—Fig. SZ17-3) on stator plate aligns with mark on upper end of cylinder block. If not, loosen jam nuts and adjust length of rod (S) until correct static ignition timing is obtained, then retighten jam nuts.

Final ignition timing check can be performed using a suitable timing light. Immerse lower unit of outboard motor in water and connect timing light to upper spark plug lead. Set engine throttle at full retard position and start engine. Refer to ignition timing specifications stated previously and check alignment of flywheel timing marks with timing pointer. To check advance timing, run engine at wide-open throttle and note timing marks.

Full retard timing can be adjusted by turning screw (B) as necessary to obtain 600-700 rpm in forward gear.

On models after 1985, slow speed timing is controlled by idle speed adjusting switch. Idle speed switch varies slow speed timing from 7 degrees ATDC to 1 degree BTDC on 1986-1988 models and 8 degrees ATDC to TDC on 1989 models. Each position of idle switch changes timing 2 degrees, which changes idle speed approximately 50 rpm per position. The idle speed switch is the only provision for adjusting idle speed on models so equipped. Note that carburetor throttle valves must be fully closed for idle speed switch to function. Full advance timing on models after 1985 should be 23 degrees BTDC at 5000 rpm on 1986-1988 models and 20 degrees BTDC at 5000 rpm on 1989 models. Full advance timing on all models after 1985 is controlled automatically by the IC ignition system.

TROUBLE-SHOOTING. If ignition malfunction occurs, use only approved procedures to prevent damage to the components. The fuel system should be checked first to make sure that faulty running is not the result of incorrect fuel mixture or contaminated fuel. Make sure malfunction is not due to spark plugs, wiring or connections. Trouble-shoot ignition system using Suzuki Pocket Tester 09900-25002 or a suitable ohmmeter. Refer to wiring diagrams in Figs. SZ17-9 and SZ17-10.

CONDENSER CHARGING COIL. All models are equipped with two condenser charge coils. Disconnect wires at connectors leading from condenser charging coil(s). On models prior to 1986, attach tester between black wire with red tracer and white wire with black tracer. Resistance should be 600-900 ohms. Connect tester between charge coil red wire with white tracer and brown wire. Resistance should be 100-150 ohms.

On 1986-1988 models, connect tester between green wire and black wire with red tracer. Note reading, then connect tester between brown wire and black wire with red tracer. Resistance at both test connections should be 170-250 ohms. On 1989 models, connect tester between green wire and black wire with red tracer. Note reading, then connect tester between the two black wires of remaining charge coil. Resistance should be 170-250 ohms at both test connections.

PULSER COIL. Two pulser coils are used on 1985 and earlier models; four pulser coils are used on 1986 and later models. To test pulser coils, disconnect wires between CDI module and pulser coils.

On models prior to 1986, connect tester between green wire and pink wire. Note reading and connect tester between yellow wire with red tracer and white wire with red tracer. Resistance of both coils should be 290-420 ohms.

On 1986 and later models, connect tester between engine ground and alternately between red wire with green tracer, white wire with black tracer, red wire with white tracer and white wire with green tracer. Resistance should be 170-250 ohms at all test connections.

When installing pulser coils on models after 1985, match number stamped on the coil with number embossed on the stator base. Air gap between flywheel and pulser coils should be 0.75 mm (0.003 in.). Suzuki pulser coil locating tool 09931-89420 should be used to properly locate pulser coils on stator plate.

BATTERY CHARGING COIL. Two battery charge coils are used on all models. Disconnect wires leading from battery charging coils. On models prior to 1986, connect tester between red wire and yellow wire. Resistance should be 0.4-

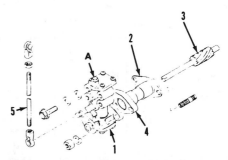

Fig. SZ17-7—Exploded view of oil injection pump and related components.

A. Air bleed screw
1. Pump assy.
2. Gasket
3. Driven gear
4. Retainer
5. Control rod

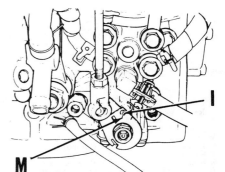

Fig. SZ17-8—Index mark (I) on oil injection pump must align with mark (M) on actuating lever when lever is in the released position.

0.8 ohm. Next, connect tester between red wire and red wire with yellow tracer. Resistance should be 0.2-0.6 ohm.

On 1986-1988 models, connect tester between the two yellow wires with red tracer, then between red wire and yellow wire. Resistance should be 0.1-0.3 ohm at both connections.

On 1989 models, connect tester between red wire and yellow wire. Note reading, then connect tester between the two yellow wires of remaining coil. Resistance should be 0.1-0.3 ohm at both connections.

IGNITION COILS. Four ignition coils are used on all models. Disconnect wires leading from ignition coils and secondary leads from spark plugs. Test coil primary winding resistance between coil primary terminal and engine ground, or coil black ground wire. Primary resistance should be 0.2-0.5 ohm

on models prior to 1986, 0.4-0.7 ohm on 1986-1988 models and 0.2-0.4 ohm on models after 1988. Test coil secondary winding resistance between coil primary and spark plug terminal. Secondary resistance should be 4700-7000 ohms on 1985 and earlier models, 5000-8000 ohms on 1986-1988 models and 6500-9500 ohms on 1989 models.

COUNTER COIL. On models after 1985, a gear counter coil is mounted along outer periphery of flywheel ring gear. The CDI module processes information from the gear counter coil in combination with the throttle valve switch or sensor to determine ignition timing. To test counter coil, separate connector leading from counter coil. Connect tester leads between orange wire with green tracer and black wire or engine ground. Counter coil can be considered acceptable if resistance is

within 170-250 ohms. Air gap between counter coil and flywheel ring gear teeth should be 0.5 mm (0.020 in.).

THROTTLE VALVE SWITCH (1986-1988 Models). To test throttle valve switch, disconnect wires at connectors leading from switch assembly. Connect an ohmmeter between light green wire with red tracer and black wire. With throttle valves fully closed, resistance should be zero ohm. With throttle valves opened slightly, infinite resistance should be noted. Next, connect ohmmeter between brown wire with yellow tracer and black wire. Infinite resistance should be noted with throttle valves closed and zero ohms should be noted with throttle valves open 15 degrees.

THROTTLE VALVE SENSOR (1989 Models). To test throttle valve sensor (5—Fig. SZ17-11), remove alignment pin

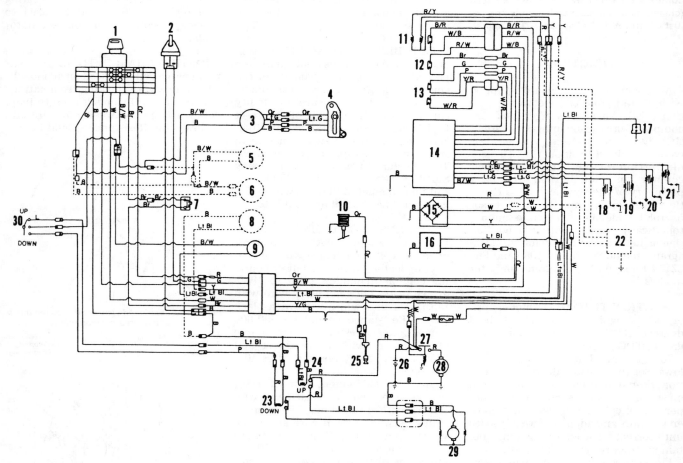

Fig. SZ17-9—Typical wiring diagram for all models prior to 1986.

1. Ignition switch	11. Battery charging coil	20. Ignition coil (No. 2 cyl.)	26. Battery	W. White	R/W. Red with white tracer
2. Emergency stop switch	12. Condenser charging coil	21. Ignition coil (No. 1 cyl.)	27. Starter motor relay	Y. Yellow	R/Y. Red with yellow tracer
3. Trim meter	13. Pulser coils	22. Rectifier with voltage regulator	28. Starter motor	Br. Brown	W/B. White with black tracer
4. Trim sender	14. CDI module	23. Power tilt & trim motor "DOWN" relay	29. Power tilt & trim motor	Gr. Gray	
5. Volt meter	15. Rectifier		30. Power tilt & trim switch	LtBl. Light blue	W/R. White with red tracer
6. Hour meter	16. Buzzer check unit	24. Power tilt & trim motor "UP" relay		LtG. Light green	
7. Neutral switch	17. Overheat sensor	25. Oil level switch		Or. Orange	Y/G. Yellow with green tracer
8. Tachometer	18. Ignition coil (No. 4 cyl.)			B. Black	
9. Overheat & oil warning buzzer	19. Ignition coil (No. 3 cyl.)			G. Green	Y/R. Yellow with red tracer
10. Choke solenoid				P. Pink	
				R. Red	

attached to black cover over throttle valve sensor and insert alignment pin (1) into hole in sensor and sensor cam (3). Align slot in cam (3) with throttle shaft. Disconnect throttle valve sensor connector (4). Connect test harness 09930-89530 or suitable jumper wires to a battery as shown in Fig. SZ17-11. Battery voltage must be nine volts or more. Connect positive (+) lead of a suitable DIGITAL voltmeter to test harness light green wire with red tracer and voltmeter negative (−) lead to battery negative (−) terminal as shown. With throttle fully closed, voltmeter reading should be 0.45-0.55 volt. If not, remove rubber cap (2) and turn adjustment screw (under cap) as necessary to obtain the correct voltage reading. Note that turning adjustment screw clockwise will increase voltage and counterclockwise will decrease voltage.

NOTE: The manufacturer recommends using only a nonmetallic screwdriver to turn sensor adjusting screw or sensor voltmeter reading may not be valid. If metal screw-

driver must be used, remove screwdriver from area of throttle valve sensor after adjustment to prevent erroneous voltmeter reading.

If sensor output voltage at closed throttle is below 0.45 volt, idle speed ignition timing will be fixed at 5 degrees BTDC and idle speed switch will be inoperative. If sensor output voltage at closed throttle is above 0.55 volt, ignition timing at idle speed will not be correct. Refer to IDLE SPEED SWITCH section.

Once the specified voltage reading is obtained at closed throttle, remove alignment pin and open carburetor to wide-open throttle. Voltmeter reading should now be 2.6 volts or more. Do not attempt to adjust wide-open throttle sensor voltage. If wide-open throttle sensor voltage is not 2.6 volts or higher, renew sensor.

If throttle valve sensor is removed or renewed, install as follows: Insert alignment pin (1) as shown to align cam and sensor shaft. Align slot in sensor cam with carburetor throttle shaft and in-

stall sensor on carburetor. Lightly tighten mounting screws (7) to allow for adjustment of sensor position on carburetor. Connect test harness and digital voltmeter as shown in Fig. SZ17-11. Make sure battery voltage is nine volts or more. Sensor output voltage at closed throttle should be 0.45-0.55 volt. If not, move position of sensor on carburetor to obtain specified voltage and securely tighten screws (7). Recheck voltage after tightening screws (7) and if necessary, remove cap (2) and turn adjustment screw to obtain 0.45-0.55 volt. Be sure to reinstall cap (2). After obtaining the correct voltage at closed throttle, remove alignment pin and check sensor output voltage at wide-open throttle. Voltage should be 2.6 volts or higher. Do not attempt to adjust wideopen throttle voltage.

IDLE SPEED SWITCH. Idle speed switch malfunction can be quickly verified by checking ignition timing and engine rpm while switching position of idle speed switch. Note that carburetor

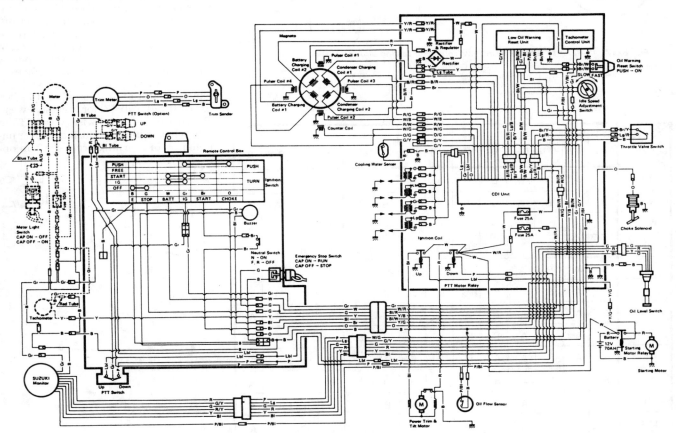

Fig. SZ17-10—Wiring diagram on 1986 and 1987 models. Later models are similar.

B. Black	Or. Orange	LtG. Light green	W/R. White with red tracer	Bl/R. Blue with red tracer	Or/G. Orange with green tracer
G. Green	B/R. Black with red tracer	R/G. Red with green tracer	Y/B. Yellow with black tracer	Bl/W. Blue with white tracer	P/Bl. Pink with blue tracer
P. Pink	B/W. Black with white tracer	R/W. Red with white tracer	Y/G. Yellow with green tracer	Br/Y. Brown with yellow tracer	LtG/B. Light green with black tracer
R. Red		W/B. White with black tracer			
W. White	B/Y. Black with yellow tracer		Y/R. Yellow with red tracer	LtBl. Light blue	LtG/R. Light green with red tracer
Y. Yellow		W/G. White with green tracer			
Bl. Blue	G/Y. Green with yellow tracer				
Br. Brown					
Gr. Gray					

throttle valves must be fully closed for idle speed switch to function.

NOTE: A defective or maladjusted throttle valve sensor may cause idle speed switch to be inoperative or ignition timing at idle speed to be incorrect. Prior to testing idle speed switch, make sure throttle valve sensor is operating properly and correctly adjusted. Refer to THROTTLE VALVE SENSOR section.

Note that each position of idle speed switch should change ignition timing two degrees and change engine idle speed approximately 50 rpm. If timing and engine rpm do not change with each switch position, idle speed switch may be defective.

CDI MODULE. On models prior to 1986, use Suzuki Pocket Tester 09900-25002 or a suitable ohmmeter and re-fer to chart in Fig. SZ17-12 to test CDI module.

On models after 1986, test CDI module using Stevens Model CD-77 peak reading voltmeter (PRV). To test module, remove spark plugs and make sure battery is fully charged and in good condition. Disconnect ignition coil primary leads from ignition coils. Set PRV control knobs to POSITIVE (+) and 500. Connect PRV black test lead to engine ground and red test lead to number 1 ignition coil primary wire (orange), crank engine and note meter. Repeat test at primary wires for each ignition coil. CDI module output should be 100 volts or more on 1986 and 1987 models and 160 volts or more on models after 1987. Renew CDI module if output is not as specified.

COOLING SYSTEM

WATER PUMP. A rubber impeller type water pump is mounted between the drive shaft housing and gearcase. A key in the drive shaft is used to turn the pump impeller. If cooling system problems are encountered, check water intake for plugging or partial restriction, then if not corrected, remove gearcase as outlined in the appropriate section and check condition of the water pump, water passages and sealing surfaces.

When water pump is disassembled, check condition of impeller (6—Fig. SZ17-13) and plate (7) for excessive wear. Turn drive shaft clockwise (viewed from top) when installing housing (1) over impeller. Avoid turning drive shaft in op-

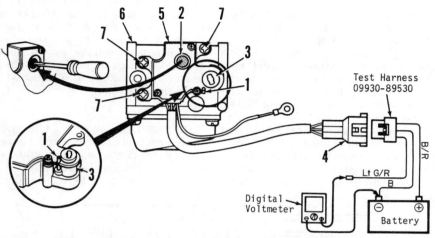

Fig. SZ17-11—Refer to text for throttle valve sensor testing and installation procedure.

1. Alignment pin
2. Cap (adjustment screw)
3. Sensor cam
4. Connector
5. Throttle valve sensor assy.
6. Carburetor
7. Mounting screw

B/R. Black with red tracer
LtG/R. Light green with red tracer
B. Black

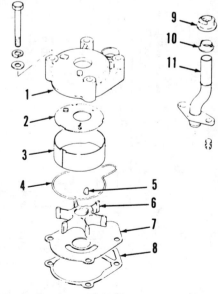

Fig. SZ17-13—Exploded view of water pump assembly.

1. Pump housing
2. Top plate
3. Liner
4. Seal ring
5. Key
6. Impeller
7. Plate
8. Gasket
9. Grommet
10. Tube guide
11. Water tube

Tester Lead (−) / Tester Lead (+)	B/R	R/W	W/B	Br	G	P	Y/R	W/R	Or	Lt Bl	Gr	Lt G	B/W	B
B/R		A	B	B	B	B	B	B	B	B	B	B	B	A
R/W	B		B	A	B	B	B	B	B	B	B	B	A	A
W/B	B	B		A	B	B	B	B	B	B	B	B	B	A
Br	B	A	B		B	B	B	B	B	B	B	B	A	A
G	B	A	B	A		B	B	B	B	B	B	B	A	A
P	B	A	B	A	B		B	B	B	B	B	B	A	A
Y/R	B	A	B	A	B	B		B	B	B	B	B	A	A
W/R	B	A	B	A	B	B	B		B	B	B	B	A	A
Or	B	A	B	A	A	B	B	B		B	B	B	A	A
Lt Bl	B	A	B	A	B	A	B	B	B		B	B	A	A
Gr	B	A	B	A	B	B	A	B	B	B		B	A	A
Lt G	B	A	B	A	B	B	A	B	B	B	B		A	A
B/W	B	B	B	B	A	A	A	A	A	B	B	B		A
B	B	A	B	A	A	A	A	A	B	B	B	A		

Fig. SZ17-12—Use above chart and values listed below to test condition of CDI module on models prior to 1986.

A. 100k ohms or less

B. More than 100k ohms

posite direction after pump is reassembled.

THERMOSTAT. A thermostat (7—Fig. SZ17-14) is used to regulate operating temperature. The thermostat should begin to open within 48°-52° C (118°-126° F) on models prior to 1986 and 40°-44° C (104°-111° F) on models after 1985.

POWER HEAD

REMOVE AND REINSTALL. To remove the power head, first remove engine cover. Detach battery cables. Disconnect wiring to oil tank. Remove oil supply line from oil tank outlet and plug tank outlet. Remove nut securing oil tank retaining band and withdraw oil tank. Remove rod used by oil tank retaining band to secure oil tank. Disconnect fuel supply line and water inspection hose from connectors in bottom engine cover. Disconnect shift and throttle linkage. Detach any wiring that will interfere with power head removal. Remove covers to expose power head retaining screws and nuts. Remove screws and nuts, then lift power head assembly with related engine components from lower unit assembly.

Before reinstalling power head, make certain drive shaft splines are clean, then coat splines with a light coating of water-resistant grease. Apply a suitable sealer to mating surfaces of power head and lower unit and install a new gasket. Apply Suzuki Thread Lock 1342 to power head retaining screws and nuts, then tighten to 34-41 N·m (25-30 ft.-lbs.). The remainder of installation is the reverse of removal procedure.

DISASSEMBLY. Disassemble power head for inspection and overhaul as follows: Remove electric starter. Remove junction box cover and four screws re-

taining electrical components holding plate to side of cylinder block. Unplug any connector that will interfere with holding plate removal, then remove holding plate. Remove electric choke solenoid. Remove fuel pump assembly. Remove oil injection pump (1—Fig. SZ17-7), retainer (4) and driven gear (3). Remove speed control linkage. Remove flywheel and stator plate assembly. Remove electric starter motor bracket and any remaining wiring that will interfere with cylinder block and crankcase separation. Remove intake manifold with carburetor assemblies. Remove reed valve assemblies. Remove outer and inner exhaust covers. Remove spark plugs, cylinder head cover, cylinder head and thermostat, then clean carbon from combustion chamber and any foreign material accumulation in water passages. Unscrew crankcase retaining screws and separate crankcase (1—Fig. SZ17-14) from cylinder block (2). On early models so equipped, remove connecting rod caps, then lift crankshaft from cylinder block. Push piston and connecting rod assemblies out cylinder head end of cylinder block. On later models, lift crankshaft, connecting rod and piston assembly from cylinder block as a unit.

Engine components are now accessible for inspection and overhaul as outlined in the appropriate following sections.

ASSEMBLY. Refer to specific service sections when reassembling the crankshaft, connecting rod, piston and reed valves. Make sure all joint and gasket surfaces are clean, free from nicks, burrs and hardened sealant or carbon. Whenever the power head is disassembled, it is recommended that all gasket and mating surfaces be checked carefully for nicks, burrs and warped

surfaces, which might interfere with a tight seal. Cylinder head, head end of cylinder block and some mating surfaces of manifold and crankcase should be checked on a surface plate and lapped if necessary to provide a smooth surface. Do not remove any more metal than necessary to true surface.

When assembling power head, first lubricate all friction surfaces and bearings with engine oil. Apply a suitable high temperature grease to lip area of crankshaft seal. Apply a suitable water-resistant grease to lip area of drive shaft seals and install seals into seal housing (15—Figs. SZ17-15 or SZ17-16). Place bearing ring (8) into cylinder block, then install crankshaft assembly. Make certain main bearing locating pins engage notches in cylinder block. Apply a coat of Suzuki Bond No. 4 or a suitable sealer to mating surfaces of crankcase and cylinder block and position crankcase on cylinder block. Tighten crankcase screws in sequence shown in Fig. SZ17-17. Tighten cylinder head screws in sequence shown in Fig. SZ17-18. Refer to CONDENSED SERVICE DATA for recommended tightening torques.

RINGS, PISTONS AND CYLINDERS. The pistons are fitted with two piston rings. Piston rings must be installed with manufacturer's marking toward top end

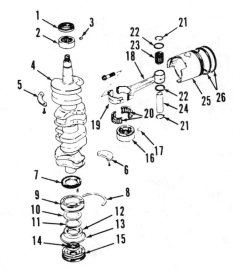

Fig. SZ17-15—Exploded view of crankshaft assembly typical of all models prior to 1986.

1. Seal
2. Roller bearing
3. Pin
4. Crankshaft
5. Upper balance weight
6. Lower balance weight
7. Oil injection pump drive gear
8. Bearing ring
9. Ball bearing
10. Washer
11. Snap ring
12. Seal
13. "O" ring
14. Seal
15. Seal housing
16. Bearing
17. Pin
18. Connecting rod
19. Rod cap
20. Needle bearing
21. Piston pin clips
22. Thrust washers
23. Needle bearing
24. Piston pin
25. Piston
26. Piston rings

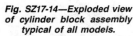

Fig. SZ17-14—Exploded view of cylinder block assembly typical of all models.

1. Crankcase half
2. Cylinder block
3. Gasket
4. Cylinder head
5. Gasket
6. Cylinder head cover
7. Thermostat
8. Gasket
9. Inner exhaust cover
10. Gasket
11. Outer exhaust cover
12. Cylinder head connector
13. Small crankcase plug (No. 1 cyl.)
14. Large crankcase plug (No. 2, 3 & 4 cyls.)

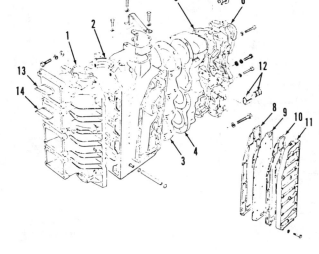

of piston. Rings are pinned in place to prevent ring rotation. Piston ring end gap should be 0.2-0.4 mm (0.008-0.016 in.) with a maximum allowable ring end gap of 0.8 mm (0.031 in.). Piston-to-cylinder clearance should be 0.112-0.127 mm (0.0044-0.0050 in.) on models prior to 1986 and 0.115-0.125 mm (0.0045-0.0049 in.) on models after 1985. Pistons and rings are available in standard size as well as 0.25 mm (0.010 in.) and 0.50 mm (0.020 in.) oversize. Cylinder should be bored to next oversize if cylinder is out-of-round, tapered or worn in excess of 0.10 mm (0.004 in.). Install piston on connecting rod so arrow on piston crown will face toward exhaust port when piston is in cylinder.

CONNECTING RODS, BEARINGS AND CRANKSHAFT. Before detaching connecting rods from crankshaft on ear-ly models, mark rod and cap for correct assembly to each other and in original cylinder. On models after 1985, crankshaft and connecting rods are a press-together unit (Fig. SZ17-16). Crankshaft should be disassembled ONLY by experienced personnel using the proper service equipment.

All wearing components should be reassembled in original location and direction. On models prior to 1986, connecting rod must be installed in cylinder with "UP" side on connecting rod and dot on rod cap ear facing toward flywheel end of crankshaft. Tighten connecting rod screws to 30-35 N·m (22-26 ft.-lbs.).

Determine crankpin, crankpin bearing and connecting rod wear by measuring connecting rod small end side-to-side movement as shown at (A—Fig. SZ17-19). Normal movement (A) is 5 mm

(0.20 in.) or less. Maximum allowable crankshaft runout is 0.05 mm (0.002 in.) measured at bearing surfaces with crankshaft ends supported.

When installing crankshaft, lubricate all friction and bearing surfaces with a recommended engine oil as outlined in ASSEMBLY section.

ELECTRIC STARTER

Models are equipped with electric starter shown in Fig. SZ17-20. Disassembly is evident after inspection of unit

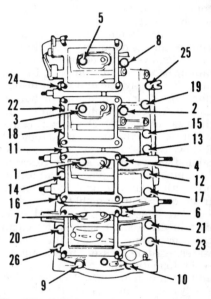

Fig. SZ17-17—Tighten crankcase screws in sequence shown. Refer to CONDENSED SERVICE DATA for torque values.

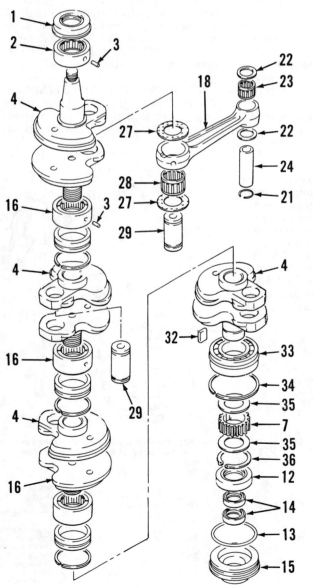

Fig. SZ17-16—Exploded view of crankshaft and connecting rod assembly used on models after 1985.

1. Seal
2. Bearing
3. Pin
4. Crankshaft
7. Oil pump drive gear
12. Seal
13. "O" ring
14. Seals
15. Seal housing
16. Bearing
21. Retainer
22. Thrust washer
23. Bearing
24. Piston pin
27. Thrust washer
28. Bearing
29. Crankpin
32. Key
33. Bearing
34. Snap ring
35. Washer
36. Snap ring

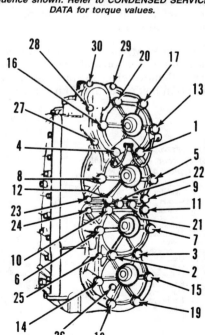

Fig. SZ17-18—Tighten cylinder head screws in sequence shown. Refer to CONDENSED SERVICE DATA for torque values.

Illustrations courtesy Suzuki

and reference to exploded view. Standard brush length is 16 mm (0.63 in.). Renew brushes if worn to 11.5 mm (0.45 in.) or less. After reassembly, bench test starter motor before reinstalling on power head.

LOWER UNIT

PROPELLER AND DRIVE CLUTCH. Protection for the motor is provided by a special cushioning clutch in the propeller hub. Three-blade propellers are used. Various propellers are available from the manufacturer. Select a propeller that will allow the outboard motor

to operate within the recommended limit of 4800-5500 rpm at full throttle.

R&R AND OVERHAUL. Refer to Fig. SZ17-21 for exploded view of lower unit gearcase assembly used on all models. During disassembly, note the location of all shims and thrust washers for reference during reassembly.

To remove gearcase, first unscrew plug (43) and drain gear lubricant. Remove drive shaft housing cover to obtain access to shift linkage. Pull out cotter pin, then withdraw pin (7) from connector (6). Remove the screws securing gearcase to drive shaft housing and separate

gearcase assembly from drive shaft housing. Remove water pump assembly (Fig. SZ17-13). Remove propeller with related components from propeller shaft. Unscrew two screws retaining gearcase end cap (67—Fig. SZ17-21), then attach a suitable puller to propeller shaft (61) and withdraw propeller shaft assembly with gearcase end cap. Unscrew pinion nut (53) and remove pinion gear (52), then extract forward gear (51). Drive shaft (34) and related components can be withdrawn from gearcase after removal of bearing housing (28).

Inspect gears for wear on teeth and on engagement dogs. Inspect dog clutch

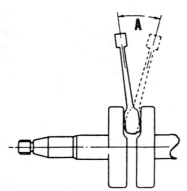

Fig. SZ17-19—Maximum allowable side-to-side shake (A) at small end of connecting rod should be 5 mm (0.20 in.) or less.

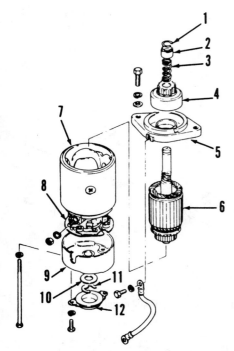

Fig. SZ17-20—Exploded view of electric starter motor.

1. "C" ring	7. Frame
2. Stop	8. Brush assy.
3. Spring	9. End housing
4. Drive	10. Thrust washer
5. Frame head	11. "E" clip
6. Armature	12. Bracket

Fig. SZ17-21—Exploded view typical of lower unit gearcase assembly used on all models.

1. Shift arm	28. Bearing housing	57. Dog clutch
2. Caps	29. "O" ring	58. Pin
3. Snap ring	30. Bearing	59. Pin retainer
4. Upper shift rod	31. Shim	60. Shift spring
5. Clip	32. Thrust washer	61. Propeller shaft
6. Connector	33. Thrust bearing	62. Thrust washers
7. Pin	34. Drive shaft	63. Reverse gear
8. Shift rod guide housing	35. Spring	64. Shim
9. Gasket	36. Thrust washer	65. Bearing
10. Seal	37. Thrust washer	66. "O" ring
11. Washer	38. Collar	67. End cap
12. "O" ring	39. Bearing	68. Bearings
13. Guide	40. Vent plug	69. Seal
14. "O" ring	41. Gasket	70. Snap ring
15. Snap ring	42. Level plug	71. Spacer
16. Lower shift rod	43. Drain plug	72. Propeller
17. Pin	44. Gearcase housing	73. Spacer
18. Spring	45. Trim tab	74. Tab washer
19. Collar	46. Forward gear bearing housing	75. Nut
20. Magnet holder	47. Bearing	
21. Magnet	48. Shim	
22. Pin	49. Thrust washer	
23. Pin	50. Thrust bearing	
24. Shift cam	51. Forward gear	
25. Ball	52. Pinion gear	
26. Spring	53. Nut	
27. Seal	54. Thrust washer	
	55. Shift pin	
	56. Spring guide	

(57) for wear on engagement surfaces. Inspect shafts for wear on splines and on friction surfaces of gears and oil seals. Check shift cam (24) and shift pin (55) for excessive wear. Check condition of shift spring (60). Renew all seals and "O" rings during reassembly.

No adjustment to forward gear shim (48) or reverse gear shim (64) is required unless forward gear or reverse gear is renewed. If a gear is renewed, shim adjustment should be made by comparing the values stamped on each gear. Thrust play of drive shaft (34) should be 0.25-0.40 mm (0.010-0.016 in.) and is adjusted by varying thickness of shim (31). Propeller shaft end play should be 0.2-0.4 mm (0.008-0.016 in.). Propeller shaft end play is adjusted by varying thickness of thrust washers (62).

Reassemble gearcase by reversing disassembly procedure while noting the following: Install dog clutch (57) on propeller shaft (61) so "F" marked side (Fig. SZ17-22) is facing forward gear (51—Fig. SZ17-21). Tighten pinion nut to 80-90

N·m (58-65 ft.-lbs.). Apply water-resistant grease to "O" ring (66). Apply silicone sealer to gearcase and bearing housing (28) mating surfaces. Coat threads of gearcase retaining screws with Suzuki Thread Lock 1342 or a suitable equivalent thread locking compound.

Install pin (7) through connector (6) and eyelet of lower shift rod (16), then retain with a new cotter pin. Fill gearcase with a recommended gear lubricant. Refer to LUBRICATION section.

POWER TRIM AND TILT

Models are equipped with a hydraulically actuated power trim and tilt system. An oil pump driven by a reversible electric motor provides oil pressure. A rocker control switch determines motor and pump rotation, thereby retracting or extending trim and tilt cylinders. The pump is equipped with an automatic and manual release valve (V—Fig.

SZ17-23). Turning manual release valve (V) counterclockwise will allow manual raising or lowering of outboard motor if the electric motor fails. Note that manual release valve should not be opened farther than 2-3 turns counterclockwise.

When checking or filling pump reservoir on models prior to 1987, outboard motor must be in the full down position. When checking or filling reservoir on models after 1986, tilt outboard motor to full up position. Refer to Fig. SZ17-25 to identify early (prior to 1987) and late model pump assemblies.

Recommended oil is SAE 20, SAE 30 or Dexron automatic transmission fluid on models prior to 1987 and Dexron II or equivalent automatic transmission fluid only on models after 1986. Do not run pump without oil in reservoir. Fill plug (F) is located on side of pump reservoir. Oil level should reach fill plug hole. Hydraulic tilt should be cycled several times and oil level rechecked if system

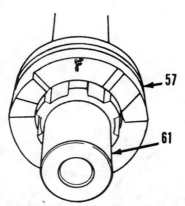

Fig. SZ17-22—Install dog clutch (57) on propeller shaft (61) with "F" mark facing forward gear.

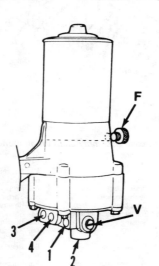

Fig. SZ17-23—View of pump assembly showing location of oil fill plug (F), release valve (V) and test ports (1, 2, 3 and 4).

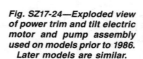

Fig. SZ17-24—Exploded view of power trim and tilt electric motor and pump assembly used on models prior to 1986. Later models are similar.

1. End cap
2. Spring
3. Brush
4. Ball
5. Armature
6. Thrust washer
7. Gasket
8. Frame
9. Gasket
10. Reservoir
11. Fill plug
12. "O" ring
13. Reservoir
14. Pump & valve body assy.

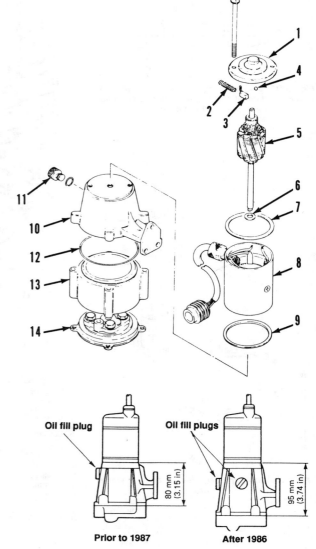

Fig. SZ17-25—Identify early and later model power trim/tilt pump assemblies by measuring reservoir as shown. Refer to text.

Oil fill plug

Oil fill plugs

80 mm (3.15 in)

95 mm (3.74 in)

Prior to 1987

After 1986

has been drained or lost a large amount of oil.

If malfunction occurs, first make sure malfunction is not due to wiring, connections or electric motor failure. To check oil pressure connect a 20.7 MPa (3000 psi) test gage to port (1) on pump and operate pump in the up direction. Hydraulic pressure in the up direction should be 13,000-17,000 kPa (1885-2465 psi). Repeat test at port (2). Next, connect test gage to port (3) and operate pump in the down direction. Hydraulic down pressure should be 2800-5600 kPa (406-812 psi). Repeat test at port (4). Low oil pressure may indicate leakage, faulty pressure relief valves or check valves. The manufacturer recommends renewing pump and valve body assembly to service low oil pressure.

If electric motor and pump assembly is disassembled for repair or renewal of components, use Ingilis Company EP630548 flat black neobase or equivalent to provide a watertight seal.

SUZUKI
DT90 AND DT100

CONDENSED SERVICE DATA

NOTE: Metric fasteners are used throughout outboard motor.

TUNE-UP
Hp/rpm:
DT90 . . . . .90/5000-5600
DT100 .100/5000-5600
Bore . . . . .84 mm
(3.31 in.)
Stroke . . . . .64 mm
(2.52 in.)
Number of Cylinders 4
Displacement . . . . .1419 cc
(86.6 cu. in.)
Spark Plug . . . . .NGK BR8HS-10
Electrode Gap . . . . .0.9-1.0 mm
(0.035-0.039 in.)
Ignition Type . . . . .Suzuki Microlink
Carburetor Make . . . . .Mikuni

SIZES—CLEARANCES
Piston Ring End Gap:
Standard . . . . .0.20-0.40 mm
(0.008-0.016 in.)
Wear Limit . . . . .0.80 mm
(0.031 in.)
Standard Piston Diameter . . . . .83.865-83.880 mm
(3.3018-3.3024 in.)
Standard Cylinder Diameter . . . . . . .84.000-84.015 mm
(3.3071-3.3077 in.)
Piston-to-Cylinder Clearance:
Standard . . . . .0.12-0.15 mm
(0.005-0.006 in.)
Wear Limit . . . . .0.22 mm
(0.0087 in.)
Piston Pin Diameter:
Standard . . . . .19.995-20.000 mm
(0.7872-0.7874 in.)
Wear Limit . . . . .19.980 mm
(0.7866 in.)
Piston Pin Bore Diameter:
Standard . . . . .20.002-20.010 mm
(0.7875-0.7878 in.)
Wear Limit . . . . .20.030 mm
(0.7886 in.)
Max. Allowable Crankshaft Runout at
Main Bearing Journal . . . . .0.05 mm
(0.002 in.)
Max. Allowable Connecting Rod Small
End Side Shake . . . . .5.0 mm
(0.20 in.)

TIGHTENING TORQUES
Cylinder Head Cover: . . . . .8-12 N·m
(71-106 in.-lbs.)
Cylinder Head .28-32 N·m
(21-24 ft.-lbs.)
Cylinders . . . . .46-54 N·m
(34-40 ft.-lbs.)
Exhaust Cover .8-12 N·m
(71-106 in.-lbs.)
Flywheel Nut .250-260 N·m
(184-192 ft.-lbs.)
Gearcase Pinion Nut . . . . .80-100 N·m
(59-73 ft.-lbs.)
Propeller Shaft Nut . . . . .50-62 N·m
(37-45 ft.-lbs.)
Water Pump Housing . . . . .15-20 N·m
(11-14 ft.-lbs.)
Standard Screws:
Unmarked or Marked ''4''
5 mm . . . . .2-4 N·m
(18-35 in.-lbs.)
6 mm . . . . .4-7 N·m
(35-62 in.-lbs.)
8 mm . . . . .10-16 N·m
(88-141 in.-lbs.)
10 mm . . . . .22-35 N·m
(16-25 ft.-lbs.)

Stainless Steel
5 mm . . . . .2-4 N·m
(18-35 in.-lbs.)
6 mm . . . . .6-10 N·m
(53-88 in.-lbs.)
8 mm . . . . .15-20 N·m
(11-14 ft.-lbs.)
10 mm . . . . .34-41 N·m
(25-30 ft.-lbs.)
Marked ''7'':
5 mm . . . . .3-6 N·m
(26-53 in.-lbs.)
6 mm . . . . .8-12 N·m
(71-106 in.-lbs.)
8 mm . . . . .18-20 N·m
(13-14 ft.-lbs.)
10 mm . . . . .40-60 N·m
(29-44 ft.-lbs.)

LUBRICATION

The power head is lubricated by oil mixed with the fuel. All models are equipped with oil injection. The recommended oil is Suzuki Outboard Motor Oil or a suitable equivalent NMMA certified TC-WII engine oil. The recommended fuel is unleaded gasoline with a minimum pump octane rating of 85.

During break-in (first five hours of operation), a 50:1 fuel and oil mixture should be used in the fuel tank in combination with the oil injection system to ensure adequate engine lubrication. After break-in period, switch to straight gasoline in the fuel tank.

The lower unit gears and bearings are lubricated by oil contained in the gearcase. The recommended oil is Suzuki Outboard Motor Gear Oil or a good quality SAE 90 hypoid gear lubricant. Gearcase capacity is 560 mL (18.9 fl. oz.). The gearcase oil should be changed after the first 10 hours of operation and every 100 hours thereafter.

FUEL SYSTEM

CARBURETOR. Mikuni BW36-24 carburetors are used on Model DT90 and Mikuni BW40-32 carburetors are used on Model DT100. Two carburetors are used on all models. Refer to Fig. SZ18-1 for exploded view.

Standard main jet (12) size for normal service is #132.5 on DT90 models and #165 on DT100 models. Standard pilot jet (6) size for normal service is #90 on DT90 models and #77.5 on DT100 models.

To check float level, remove float bowl and invert carburetor. Distance (D—Fig. SZ18-2) between bottom of float and float bowl mating surface on carburetor body should be 9.5-11.5 mm (0.37-0.45 in.). Carefully bend tang on float arm to adjust.

Initial setting of pilot air screw (3—Fig. SZ18-1) from a lightly seated position is $1\frac{1}{8}$ to $1\frac{5}{8}$ turns. Final adjustment should be performed with engine at normal operating temperature, running in forward gear. Adjust idle speed switch (on lower engine cover) to obtain 600-650 rpm in forward gear. Adjust pilot screw (3) so engine idles smoothly and will accelerate cleanly without hesitation.

NOTE: If unable to obtain 600-650 rpm in forward gear, adjust throttle stop screw on top carburetor as necessary or check adjustment of throttle valve sensor (2). Refer to IGNITION section.

FUEL PUMP. A diaphragm type fuel pump is used. Fuel pump is mounted on the power head and is actuated by crankcase pulsations. Refer to Fig. SZ18-4 for an exploded view of pump assembly.

Inspect diaphragms (2 and 4) for cracking, deterioration or other damage. Defective or questionable components should be renewed. Match marks are provided on cover (1) and body (3) for correct alignment during reassembly. Tighten cover screws evenly in a crossing pattern.

FUEL FILTER. A fuel filter (Fig. SZ18-4) is mounted on the power head. Filter should be disassembled to inspect element (12) every 50 hours of operation. Clean element in a suitable solvent. Renew element of excessive blockage is noted.

REED VALVES. The inlet reed valves are located on a V-shaped reed plate be-

tween intake manifold and crankcase. Refer to Fig. SZ18-6. The reed petals should seat very lightly against the reed plate throughout their entire length with the least possible tension. Renew reeds if tip of reed petal stands open more than 0.2 mm (0.008 in.) from contact surface. Reed stop opening should be 10.5 mm (0.413 in.) as shown in Fig. SZ18-7.

Renew reeds if petals are broken, cracked, warped, rusted or bent. Never attempt to bend a reed petal or straighten a damaged reed. Never install a bent or damaged reed. Seating surface of reed plate should be smooth and flat. When installing reeds or reed stop, make sure that petals are centered over the inlet ports in reed plate, and that reed stops are centered over reed petals. Apply Suzuki Thread Lock 1342 or a suitable equivalent thread locking compound to threads of reed stop screws during reassembly. Install reed valve assemblies to intake manifold with arrow embossed on inside of reed plate (on one end) facing toward outside of engine.

SPEED CONTROL LINKAGE. To synchronize carburetor throttle valves, loosen two screws (S—Fig. SZ18-8) on top carburetor throttle lever (L). Rotate lever (L) clockwise until throttle valves are completely closed, then retighten screws (S). Be sure throttle valves open and close at exactly the same time. With remote control in the neutral position, loosen jam nuts (N—Fig. SZ18-9) and adjust length of rod (1) so a clearance of

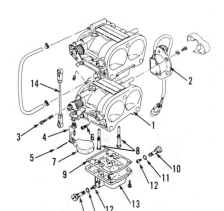

Fig. SZ18-1—Exploded view of carburetors used on all models.

1. Body	8. High speed nozzles
2. Throttle valve sensor	9. Gasket
3. Pilot screw	10. Main jet holder
4. Inlet valve & seat	11. Gasket
5. Pin	12. Main jets
6. Pilot jet	13. Float bowl
7. Float	14. Link rod

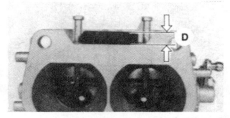

Fig. SZ18-2—Float height (D) should be 9.5-11.5 mm (0.37-0.45 in.). Bend tang on float arm to adjust.

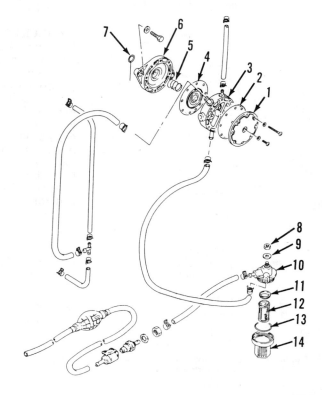

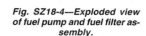

Fig. SZ18-4—Exploded view of fuel pump and fuel filter assembly.

1. Cover
2. Diaphragm
3. Body
4. Diaphragm
5. Spring
6. Inner plate
7. "O" ring
8. Nut
9. Washer
10. Filter base
11. Packing
12. Filter element
13. "O" ring
14. Cup

1 mm (0.04 in.) is present between throttle lever (4) and stopper (5) on carburetor. Refer to OIL INJECTION section for injection pump control linkage adjustment.

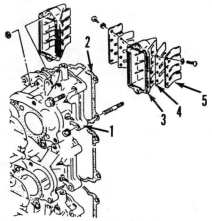

Fig. SZ18-6—Exploded view of intake manifold and reed valve assemblies.

1. Intake manifold
2. Gasket
3. Reed plate
4. Reed petals
5. Reed stop

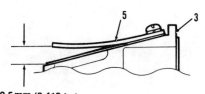

10.5 mm (0.413 in.)

Fig. SZ18-7—Distance between reed stop (5) and reed plate (3) should be 10.5 mm (0.413 in.) as shown. Clearance between reed petal (4) and reed plate (3) must not exceed 0.2 mm (0.008 in.).

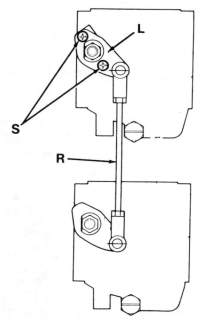

Fig. SZ18-8—Refer to text to synchronize carburetor throttle valves.

To ease engine starting, ignition timing is electronically advanced to 5 degrees BTDC. The starting ignition advance duration is 15 seconds when engine temperature is below 97°-110° C (36°-44° F) and 5 seconds when engine is warmed to 97°-110° C (36°-44° F) or above. After the initial timing advance period, idle speed timing is controlled by the idle speed adjustment switch. The idle speed adjustment switch varies timing from 7 degrees ATDC (slow) to TDC (fast), changing idle speed approximately 50 rpm per position.

Full throttle timing should be 23 degrees BTDC at 5000 rpm and is electronically controlled by the Micro Link processor. The processor uses information from the gear counter coil and the throttle valve sensor to determine the optimum ignition timing for all operating conditions. Refer to IGNITION section for throttle valve sensor adjustment procedure.

OIL INJECTION

BLEEDING PUMP. Air should be purged from injection system any time an injection system component has been removed or renewed, or if outboard motor has been in storage.

While bleeding the system, a 50:1 fuel and oil mixture must be used in the fuel tank to ensure proper engine lubrication during the bleeding procedure. Open the air bleed screw (B—Fig. SZ18-11) two or three turns. Start engine and run at 650-700 rpm until air is no longer noted at screw (B). Stop engine and tighten screw (B) securely.

CHECKING OIL PUMP OUTPUT. Start engine and warm-up for approximately five minutes. Stop engine, remove oil reservoir and disconnect oil pump control rod (2—Fig. SZ18-11) from carburetor. Connect Suzuki oil measuring cylinder 09941-68710 to oil pump inlet hose and fill with a recommended engine oil. Bleed air from system as previously outlined, then refill oil cylinder to an upper reference mark. Rotate oil pump control lever to the fully closed (clockwise) position, start engine and run at 1500 rpm for exactly five

minutes. After five minutes, stop engine and note oil measuring cylinder. Oil consumption in five minutes at 1500 rpm should be 2.5-4.5 mL (0.085-0.152 fl. oz.).

Next, refill oil cylinder, rotate oil pump control lever to the full-open (counterclockwise) position, start engine and run at 1500 rpm for exactly two minutes. Stop engine and note oil cylinder. Oil consumption in two minutes at 1500 rpm should be 6.0-9.0 mL (0.203-0.304 fl. oz.). After reconnecting oil pump control rod to carburetor, be sure carburetor throttle valves are properly synchronized (SPEED CONTROL LINKAGE) and check adjustment of oil pump control rod as outlined in PUMP CONTROL ROD ADJUSTMENT section.

NOTE: Oil pump output test results may vary depending on testing error and ambient temperature. To ensure accurate results, repeat test three times, or until results are consistent.

Renew oil pump assembly (1) if output is not as specified.

Be sure pump is properly engaged with driven gear (3) before tightening fasteners.

OIL FLOW SENSOR. Oil flow sensor (9—Fig. SZ18-11) is connected in-line between oil reservoir and oil pump. The oil flow sensor serves as an oil filter as well as a sensor to detect insufficient oil flow to pump. Should oil flow become restricted, the sensor circuit closes, signaling the microcomputer to decrease engine speed and activate the warning lamp and buzzer.

The sensor filter should be periodically removed and cleaned in a suitable solvent. Renew filter if excessive blockage is noted.

To test sensor, connect an ohmmeter between sensor pink/blue wire and black wire. No continuity should be present. Next, plug sensor inlet and apply a vacuum to the outlet port. Zero ohms should be noted with vacuum applied.

PUMP CONTROL ROD ADJUSTMENT. Make sure carburetor throttle

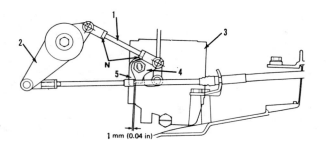

Fig. SZ18-9—View of throttle linkage on all models.

1. Link rod
2. Throttle arm
3. Carburetor
4. Throttle lever
5. Stopper
N. Nuts

1 mm (0.04 in)

valves are properly synchronized as described in SPEED CONTROL LINKAGE section. With throttle in the fully closed position, clearance (C—Fig. SZ18-12) between boss (4) and control lever (3) should be less than 1.0 mm (0.039 in.), but lever (3) should not be touching boss (4). Loosen nuts jam nuts (N) and vary length of rod (2) to adjust.

IGNITION

All models are equipped with Suzuki Micro Link ignition system. Micro Link is comprised of a capacitor discharge ignition system (CDI) and a microcomputer. The microcomputer processes information from various sensors and switches including throttle valve opening, engine rpm and shift lever position, then determines the optimum ignition timing. The Micro Link system also monitors oil level, oil flow, water flow and overspeed caution systems. If one or more caution systems indicate a malfunction, the microcomputer activates the appropriate warning buzzer and lamp, and reduces engine speed to a predetermined level.

TROUBLE-SHOOTING. Test ignition system using Stevens Model CD-77 or a suitable equivalent peak reading voltmeter (PRV) and Suzuki Pocket Tester 09900-25002 or a suitable equivalent ohmmeter. Refer to Figs. SZ18-14 and SZ18-15.

To check ignition system peak voltage, remove spark plugs, and refer to chart in Fig. SZ18-16. Output is measured at cranking speed only. Make sure battery is fully charged and in good condition. If peak voltage is less than specified in chart, renew component being tested.

If testing ignition components using Suzuki Pocket Tester 09900-25002, or an ohmmeter, refer to Figs. SZ18-14 and SZ18-15 and proceed as follows:

CONDENSER CHARGE COIL. Disconnect six-pin connector (Fig. SZ18-15) leading from stator plate. Connect ohmmeter between the black/red terminal and the green terminal. Resistance should be 180-270 ohms.

PULSER COILS. Disconnect the six-pin connector leading from stator plate. Connect tester between engine ground and alternately to the red/green, white/black, red/white and white/green terminals. Resistance at each terminal should be 160-230 ohms.

Air gap between pulser coils and the flywheel should be 0.75 mm (0.029 in.). The manufacturer recommends using Suzuki pulser coil locating tool (part 09931-88710) to properly position pulser coils.

GEAR COUNTER COIL. Unplug connectors leading from gear counter coil (8—Fig. SZ18-15). Connect tester between the orange/green and the black/green wire connectors. Resistance should be 160-230 ohms.

Air gap between counter coil and the flywheel ring gear teeth should be 0.5 mm (0.020 in.). Loosen counter coil mounting screws and slide coils as necessary to adjust.

BATTERY CHARGE COILS. Unplug the yellow and red wire connectors and connect tester between the two connectors. Resistance should be 0.4-0.6 ohm. Note that checking resistance between the yellow and red wires tests resistance of both battery charge coils.

IGNITION COILS. Ignition coil primary winding resistance should be 0.15-0.25 ohm. Connect tester between black and

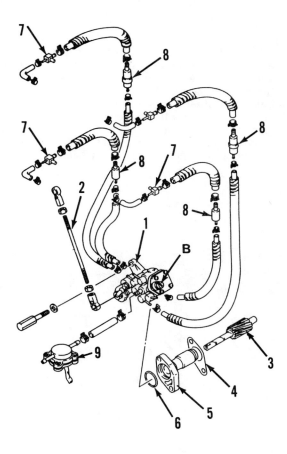

Fig. SZ18-11—Exploded view of oil injection pump and related components.
1. Pump assy.
2. Control rod
3. Driven gear
4. Gasket
5. Retainer
6. "O" ring
7. Air/oil mixing valve
8. Check valve
9. Oil flow sensor
B. Bleed screw

Fig. SZ18-12—Refer to text for oil pump control rod adjustment procedure.
1. Pump assy.
2. Control rod
3. Control lever
4. Boss
N. Jam nuts

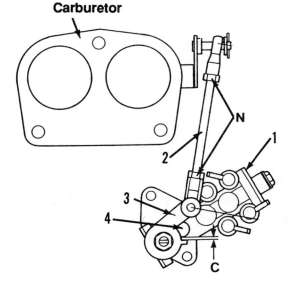

orange wires for number 1 coil, black and blue wires for number 2 coil, black and gray wires for number 3 coil and black and green wires for number 4 coil.

Secondary winding resistance should be 2600-3800 ohms, plus 10,000 ohms for the spark plug terminal cap. Test secondary resistance by connecting tester between the spark plug terminal and orange primary wire for number 1 coil, blue primary wire for number 2 coil, gray primary wire for number 3 coil and green primary wire for number 4 coil.

IDLE SPEED ADJUSTING SWITCH. Idle speed adjustment switch is used to adjust idle speed by changing ignition timing. Idle speed switch failure can be quickly verified by connecting a suitable timing light to the engine. Start engine and allow to idle. Note timing while changing position of idle speed switch. If timing does not change with each

switch position, idle speed switch is defective and should be renewed.

To test idle speed switch, disconnect wires and connect tester between the two black/white wires. Refer to Fig. SZ18-17. Resistance should be as follows: Position A—zero ohm; position B—1800-2600 ohms; position C—5600-8200 ohms; position D—16,000-23,000 ohms; position E—infinity.

THROTTLE VALVE SENSOR. The throttle valve sensor provides throttle position information to the Micro Link ignition system. The sensor is mounted on the port side of bottom carburetor. Drive gear (5—Fig. SZ18-18) engaged with carburetor throttle shaft (3) rotates driven gear (1) which turns the potentiometer shaft.

To test sensor, disconnect wires leading from sensor. Connect ohmmeter between light green/red wire and black wire. With throttle valves completely

closed, resistance should be 225-275 ohms. Open throttle valves slightly. Resistance should now be 4000-6000 ohms. Leave tester connected to the black wire. Connect remaining tester lead to the brown/yellow wire. With throttle valves completely closed, resistance should be 10,000 ohms. Open throttle valves slightly. Resistance should still be 10,000 ohms.

To install throttle valve sensor, remove sensor cover and remove alignment pin affixed to cover. Rotate sensor driven gear (1) to align holes in the driven gear and the sensor, then insert alignment pin in hole (2). Install sensor assembly on carburetor shaft and lightly tighten mounting screws in the center of adjusting slots. With carburetor throttle valves fully closed, install drive gear (5), aligning the timing marks on drive and driven gears (Fig. SZ18-19). Make sure throttle valves are fully closed, then install and tighten throttle shaft nut (4—Fig.

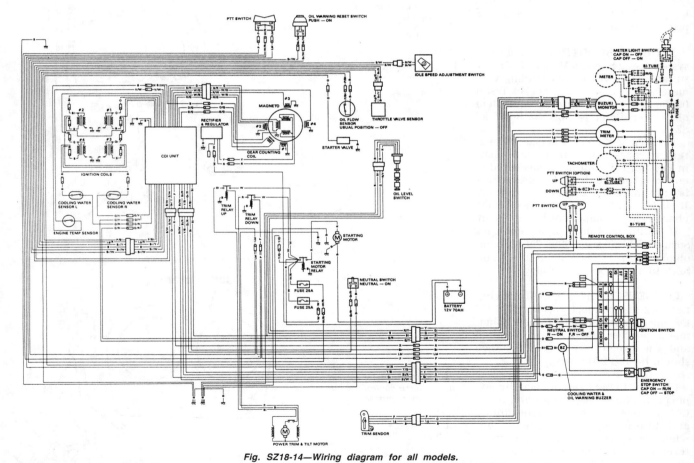

Fig. SZ18-14—Wiring diagram for all models.

B. Black	B/G. Black with green tracer	LtG. Light green	W/B. White with black tracer	Bl/R. Blue with red tracer	Gr/Y. Gray with yellow tracer
G. Green	B/R. Black with red tracer	R/G. Red with green tracer	W/G. White with green tracer	Bl/W. Blue with white tracer	LtBl. Light blue
P. Pink	B/W. Black with white tracer	R/W. Red with white tracer	W/R. White with red tracer	Br/W. Brown with white tracer	Or/G. Orange with green tracer
R. Red		R/Y. Red with yellow tracer	Y/B. Yellow with black tracer	Br/Y. Brown with yellow tracer	P/Bl. Pink with blue tracer
W. White	G/R. Green with red tracer				
Y. Yellow		V/W. Violet with white tracer	Y/G. Yellow with green tracer	Gr/R. Gray with red tracer	LtG/R. Light green with red tracer
Bl. Blue	G/Y. Green with yellow tracer				
Br. Brown					
Gr. Gray					
Or. Orange					

SZ18-18), tighten sensor mounting screws, remove alignment pin and affix to sensor cover and install sensor cover.

To adjust throttle valve sensor, remove oil pump control rod from pump lever and disconnect throttle valve sensor wires. Connect the red test lead of ohmmeter to the light green/red wire and black test lead to the black sensor wire. With throttle valves fully closed, resistance should be 225-275 ohms. If not, first make sure throttle valves are fully closed, then loosen sensor mounting screws and rotate sensor as necessary to obtain 250 ohms. Retighten sensor screws securely and reconnect oil pump control rod.

COOLING SYSTEM

WATER PUMP. A rubber impeller type water pump is mounted between the drive shaft housing and gearcase. A key in the drive shaft is used to turn the impeller. If cooling system malfunction is encountered, check water intake for plugging or partial restriction. If necessary, remove gearcase as outlined in the appropriate section and check condition of the water pump, water passages and sealing surfaces.

Inspect condition of impeller (1—Fig. SZ18-20) and plate (3) for excessive wear. Rotate drive shaft clockwise when placing water pump housing over im- peller. Avoid turning drive shaft in opposite direction after pump is reassembled.

THERMOSTAT. A thermostat located in each cylinder head is used to regulate operating temperature and function as a relief valve. The thermostat should begin to open within 40°-44° C (104°-111° F). Thermostat can be removed for inspection or renewal by removing thermostat housing.

WATER FLOW SENSOR. Water flow sensors are located in each cylinder head cover. Water flow around the sensor raises the float (Fig. SZ18-21) which opens the sensor switch. If water flow is interrupted, the float falls closing the switch and triggers the appropriate caution system.

Remove sensor by grasping the boss (Fig. SZ18-21) with pliers. Float should move freely. If not remove pin and thoroughly clean with water. Note that pin hole is smaller on one side. Remove and reinstall pin from the side of the larger hole.

To test sensor, connect on ohmmeter between sensor wires. With float in the up position (off), no continuity should be present. With float down (on), zero ohms should be noted.

POWER HEAD

REMOVE AND REINSTALL. To remove power head, first remove engine cover and disconnect battery. Disconnect cable from starter motor and starter relay, remove relay bracket, disconnect battery ground cable and power trim/tilt cable from engine. Remove flywheel cover. Remove power trim/tilt relays together with the relay holder. Remove electric parts holder cover, disconnect interfering wires, then remove electric parts holder assembly. Disconnect ground wires from each cylinder head. Remove oil reservoir. Disconnect and plug fuel supply hose at fuel filter. Disconnect throttle valve sen-

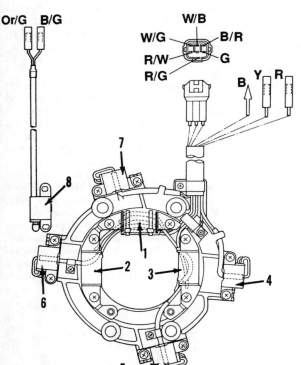

Or/G   B/G

W/B

W/G   B/R

R/W   G

R/G

B Y R

Fig. SZ18-15—View showing location of stator plate components.

1. Condenser charge coil
2. Battery charge coil (No. 1)
3. Battery charge coil (No. 2)
4. Pulser coil (No. 3)
5. Pulser coil (No. 4)
6. Pulser coil (No. 1)
7. Pulser coil (No. 2)
8. Gear counter coil
B. Black
G. Green
R. Red
Y. Yellow
B/G. Black with green tracer
B/R. Black with red tracer
R/G. Red with green tracer
R/W. Red with white tracer
W/B. White with black tracer
W/G. White with green tracer
Or/G. Orange with green tracer

Testing sequence		Test lead connection		Engine rpm (Cranking)	Peak voltage	Tester range
		Red lead	Black lead			
1	CDI output	No. 1 Orange	Ground	300	102V or over	POS 500
		No. 2 Blue	Ground			
		No. 3 Gray	Ground	300	121V or over	
		No. 4 Light green	Ground			
2	Condenser charging coil output	Black/Red	Green	300	108V or over	POS 500
				300	136V or over	
3	Pulser coil output	No. 1 Red/Green	Ground	300	3.0V or over	SEN 50
		No. 2 White/Black	Ground			
		No. 3 Red/White	Ground	300	4.9V or over	
		No. 4 White/Green	Ground			
	Counting coil output	Orange/Green	Black/Green	300	4.0V or over	SEN 50
				300	6.3V or over	
4	Battery charging coil output	Yellow	Red	300	4.8V or over	POS 50
				300	8.4V or over	

Fig. SZ18-16—Refer to text and chart shown when checking ignition system peak voltage.

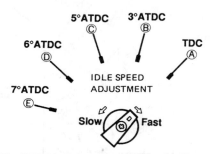

5°ATDC Ⓒ **3°ATDC** Ⓑ

6°ATDC Ⓓ   **TDC** Ⓐ

IDLE SPEED ADJUSTMENT

7°ATDC Ⓔ

Slow   **Fast**

Fig. SZ18-17—Refer to legend when checking resistance of idle speed adjustment switch.

A. Zero ohm
B. 1,800-2,600 ohms
C. 5,600-8,200 ohms
D. 16,000-23,000 ohms
E. Infinity

sor, oil sensor and starter valve wires. Remove front and rear lower engine covers. Remove 5 screws from power head side and 10 screws from lower unit side, securing power head lower unit. Remove cotter pin and push out clevis pin connecting upper shift rod to connector of lower shift assembly. Lift power head sufficiently to expose shift linkage. Detach clutch lever rod connector (R—Fig. SZ18-22) and upper shift rod (U) from clutch shaft (S). Lift power head assembly with related engine components from lower unit assembly.

Before installing power head, make certain drive shaft splines are clean, then coat splines with a light coating of water resistant grease. Reconnect clutch lever rod connector (R) and upper shift rod (U) to shift shaft (S) prior to fully lowering power head onto lower unit. Coat power head-to-lower unit screws with a suitable silicone sealant. Tighten 8 mm power head retaining screws to 15-20 N·m (11-15 ft.-lbs.) and 10 mm screws to 34-41 N·m (25-30 ft.-lbs.). Complete reinstallation by reversing order of removal procedure.

DISASSEMBLY. Using a suitable puller, remove flywheel. Remove stator assembly, gear counter coil, fuel pump and fuel filter. Remove starter valve. Remove starter motor and bracket. Disconnect the throttle control rod from carburetor and remove oil pump control rod. Remove throttle control lever and clutch lever. Disconnect and label oil hoses for reference during reassembly. Remove oil pump and oil flow sensor. Remove oil pump retainer with oil pump driven gear. Remove exhaust cover screws and carefully pry off cover at tabs provided for prying. Remove silencer cover. Remove cylinder head screws. Tap on the side of cylinder heads with a soft-face mallet to dislodge heads. Remove 11 screws and separate lower oil seal housing. Remove screws securing cylinders to crankcase, remove crankcase nuts and carefully separate cylinders from crankcase. Remove pistons from connecting rods. Remove carburetors, intake manifolds and reed valve assemblies. Remove clutch shaft. Remove 16 crankcase screws and remove crankcase from cylinder block.

Crankshaft assembly can now be removed from cylinder block.

Engine components are now accessible for inspection and overhaul as outlined in the appropriate service section.

REASSEMBLY. Refer to specific service sections when assembling the crankshaft, connecting rod, pistons and reed valves. Make sure all joint and gasket surfaces are clean, free from nicks, burrs and hardened gasket sealer.

Whenever the power head is disassembled, it is recommended that all gasket surfaces and mating surfaces be carefully checked for nicks, burrs and warped surfaces which might interfere with a tight seal. Cylinder heads, cylinders, head end of cylinder block and some mating surfaces of manifolds and crankcase should be checked on a surface plate and lapped if necessary to provide a smooth surface. Do not remove any more metal than necessary to true surface.

Thoroughly lubricate all friction surfaces and bearings with a recommended engine oil during reassembly. Apply a suitable high temperature grease to lip of upper crankshaft seal. Apply a suitable water-resistant grease to lip of drive shaft seal and install seal into lower oil seal housing. Place main bearing locating pins into crankcase side of cylinder block, then install crankshaft assembly. Make certain bearing locating pins engage main bearings and upper crankshaft seal fits in cylinder block groove. Make certain lower main bearing locating pin engages notch in cylinder block and "C" ring fits into cylinder block

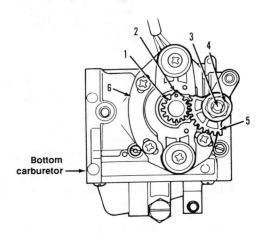

Bottom carburetor →

Fig. SZ18-18—View of throttle valve sensor.

1. Driven gear
2. Alignment pin hole
3. Carburetor throttle shaft
4. Throttle shaft nut
5. Drive gear

Timing marks

Alignment pin

Driven gear

Drive gear

Fig. SZ18-19—Install and adjust throttle valve sensor as outlined in the text.

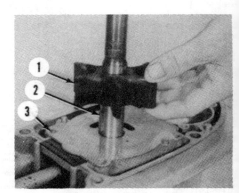

Fig. SZ18-20—View identifying water pump impeller (1), drive key (2) and plate (3).

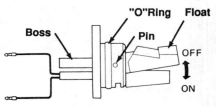

Boss · **"O"Ring** · **Pin** · **Float** · OFF · ON

Fig. SZ18-21—View of water flow sensor. Refer to text for testing procedure.

groove. End gaps on all crankshaft seal rings must face toward crankcase cover. Apply a coat of Suzuki Bond 1207B or a suitable sealer to mating surfaces of crankcase and cylinder block, then position crankcase on cylinder block. Tighten crankcase screws in sequence shown in Fig. SZ18-23.

Install cylinders on crankcase and tighten cylinder screws snug. Install Suzuki cylinder-to-crankcase alignment tool (part 09912-68720) and tighten alignment tool screws in sequence shown in Fig. SZ18-24, to 20-26 N·m (15-19 ft.-lbs.). Then, tighten cylinder screws and nuts using Suzuki tool 09911-78730, or a suitable 8 mm Allen wrench to 20-26 N·m (15-19 ft.-lbs.). Remove cylinder alignment tool 09912-68720 and retighten cylinder screws and nuts to 46-54 N·m (34-39 ft.-lbs.).

Install lower oil seal housing and tighten screws to 20-26 N·m (15-19 ft.-lbs.). Install cylinder heads and tighten screws to 28-32 N·m (21-23 ft.-lbs.) in sequence shown in Fig. SZ18-25.

RINGS, PISTONS, PINS AND CYLINDERS. Refer to CONDENSED SERVICE DATA for service specifications. The pistons are fitted with two keystone type piston rings. The top ring is chrome plated. Piston rings must be installed with the manufacturer's marking facing piston crown. Rings are pinned in place to prevent rotation in ring grooves. Pistons and rings are available in standard size and 0.25 mm (0.010 in.) and 0.50 mm (0.020 in.) oversizes.

Measure piston diameter 5 mm (0.20 in.) up from bottom of piston skirt at a right angle to the piston pin bore. Install pistons on connecting rods so arrows on piston crowns are facing toward exhaust ports. Always renew piston pin retainers (7—Fig. SZ18-27) once removed. Install retainers (7) with gap facing top of piston.

Cylinder should be bored to the next oversize if taper, out-of-round or wear exceeds 0.10 mm (0.004 in.).

Crankcase, cylinder, exhaust cover and cylinder head mating surfaces must be flat to within 0.030 mm (0.0012 in.).

If not, mating surface should be lapped on a surface plate. Do not remove more stock than necessary to true surface.

CONNECTING RODS, BEARINGS AND CRANKSHAFT. Connecting rods, rod bearings and crankshaft are a press-together unit. Crankshaft should be disassembled ONLY by experienced service personnel using the correct service equipment.

Crankshaft is supported by a caged roller bearing at top position, a split caged roller bearing at center position and a ball bearing at the bottom position. Determine connecting rod, rod bearing and crankpin wear by measuring connecting rod small end side-to-side movement as shown at (A—Fig. SZ18-28). Normal movement (A) is 5 mm (0.20 in.) or less. Maximum allowable crankshaft runout is 0.05 mm (0.002 in.) measured with crankshaft ends supported.

When installing crankshaft, lubricate all friction surfaces and bearings with a recommended engine oil.

ELECTRIC STARTER

All models are equipped with the electric starter motor shown in Fig. SZ18-30. Disassembly is evident after inspection of unit and referral to exploded view. Standard commutator diameter is 33 mm (1.30 in.) and minimum diameter is 32 mm (1.26 in.). Commutator segments should be under cut to 0.5-0.8 mm (0.020-0.031 in.) deep. Standard brush length is 16.0 mm (0.63 in.). Renew brushes if worn to 11.5 mm (0.45 in.). Match marks are provided on frame head (5), frame (6) and end frame (12) for correct alignment during reassembly. Tighten starter through-bolts to 15-20 N·m (11-14 ft.-lbs.).

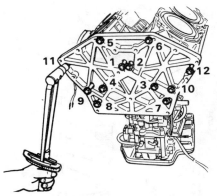

Fig. SZ18-24—To properly align cylinders to crankcase, install Suzuki cylinder/crankcase alignment tool 09912-68720, and tighten screws in sequence shown to 20-26 N·m (15-19 ft.-lbs.).

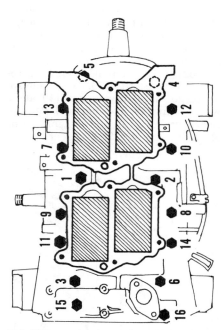

Fig. SZ18-23—Crankcase screw tightening sequence. Tighten 6 mm screws to 8-12 N·m (6-8 ft.-lbs.), 8 mm screws to 20-26 N·m (15-19 ft.-lbs.) and 10 mm screws to 46-54 N·m (34-39 ft.-lbs.).

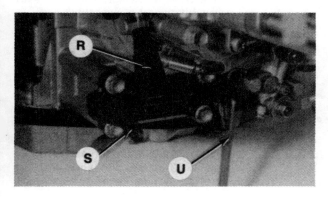

Fig. SZ18-22—Detach clutch lever rod connector (R) and upper shift rod (U) from clutch shaft (S) during power head removal. Refer to text.

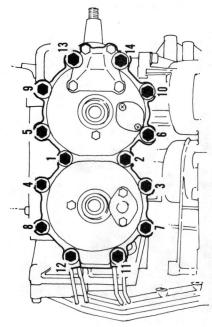

Fig. SZ18-25—Tighten cylinder head screws in sequence shown.

LOWER UNIT

PROPELLER AND SPLINED RUB-BER HUB. Protection for the outboard motor is provided by the splined rubber hub built into the propeller. Three-blade propellers are used. Various propellers are available from the manufacturer. Select a propeller that will provide optimum performance at full throttle within the recommended speed range of 5000-5600 rpm.

R&R AND OVERHAUL. Refer to Fig. SZ18-31 for exploded view of gearcase assembly. To remove gearcase, first drain lubricant then remove cotter pin and clevis pin connecting upper shift rod to connector (16). Remove trim tab. Remove seven screws securing gearcase to drive shaft housing, separate gearcase from drive shaft housing and place into a suitable holding fixture.

Note location of all shims and thrust washers for reference during reassembly. Shift gearcase into forward gear by pushing down on connector (16), then remove propeller and related components. Remove water pump assembly. Shift gearcase into neutral, remove three screws and remove lower shift assembly. Straighten tabs on washer (67) and remove ring nut (68). Using a suitable puller, pull propeller shaft bearing housing (65) along with propeller shaft (57) and related components from gearcase. Remove drive shaft bearing housing (32). Unscrew pinion nut (46), remove drive shaft (37), then remove pinion gear (45), forward gear (49) along with bearing (48) and shim (47). Remove thrust washers (39 and 40), protector (41) and collar (42). Slide spacer (50) off

propeller shaft, remove slider (51), remove retainer spring (53), push out pin (55), remove connector pin (52) and slide dog clutch (54) from propeller shaft. Remove pinion bearing (43) by driving bearing down into gear cavity.

Inspect gears for wear on teeth and on engagement dogs. Inspect dog clutch (54) for wear on engagement surfaces. Inspect shafts for wear on splines and on friction surfaces of gears and oil seals. Renew all "O" rings and seals during reassembly.

To disassemble shift assembly, remove pin (14) and yoke (15). Loosen nut (17) and remove connector (16) and nut (17) from shaft (18). Remove bolt (13), screws (11), springs (10) and balls (9), then pull shift rod assembly (18 through 29) from housing (7). Unscrew shaft (18). Unscrew vertical slider (29) and remove spring (28). Using two screwdrivers, remove forward plunger (19) and reverse plunger (27), and separate reverse sleeve (22) and forward sleeve (25) from lock sleeve (24).

NOTE: Do not remove pivot rod and shaft assembly (12) from housing (7). Pivot rod and shaft assembly is precisely set at the factory and should not be disassembled.

Reassemble shift assembly by reversing disassembly procedure while noting the following: Tighten reverse plunger (27) from forward sleeve (25) side to 3-6 N·m (27-53 in.-lbs.). Apply Suzuki Thread Lock 1342 or equivalent thread locking compound to threads on both ends of rod (20), threads of vertical slider (29), threads of shaft (18), threads of screws (11) and bolt (13). Coat balls (23 and 26) with a suitable water-resistant grease and install three balls into forward sleeve (25) and three balls into reverse sleeve (22). Renew all seals and "O" rings. Install nut (17) and connector (16) on shaft (18). Turn connector (16) as necessary to obtain a distance (D—Fig. SZ18-32) of 46 mm (1.81 in.) on long shaft models and 173 mm (6.81 in.) on extra long shaft models measured as shown. Note that shift assembly must be in the neutral position when measuring. After reassembly, make sure shift assembly operates smoothly.

Install pinion bearing (43—Fig. SZ18-31) with marked side facing up. Draw pinion bearing into gearcase using Suzuki special tools shown in Fig. SZ18-33, or suitable equivalent, until top of bearing (43) is 194 mm (7.6 in.) from mating surface of gearcase as shown.

If pinion gear (45) depth requires shim adjustment, proceed as follows: Assemble drive shaft as shown in Fig. SZ18-35 with orignial shim (35) and place into Suzuki Shim Gage 09951-08720 as shown. If no clearance is present at (S),

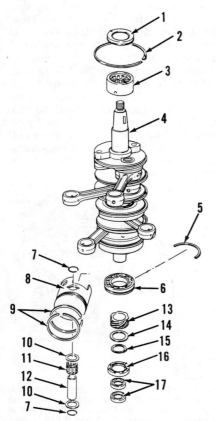

Fig. SZ18-27—Exploded view of crankshaft assembly and related components.

1. Seal	
2. Seal ring	
3. Bearing	10. Thrust washer
4. Crankshaft assy.	11. Bearing
5. "C" ring	12. Piston pin
6. Bearing	13. Oil pump drive gear
7. Retainer	14. Thrust washer
8. Piston	15. Snap ring
9. Piston rings	16. Seal
	17. Seals

Fig. SZ18-28—Maximum allowable side-to-side shake (A) at connecting rod small end is 5.0 mm (0.20 in.).

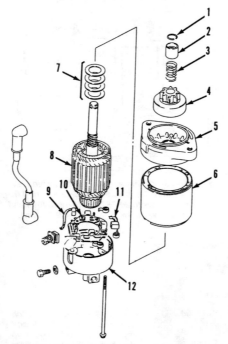

Fig. SZ18-30—Exploded view of electric starter motor.

1. "C" ring	7. Thrust washers
2. Stop	8. Armature
3. Spring	9. Brush (neg)
4. Drive gear assy.	10. Brush holder
5. Frame head	11. Brush (pos)
6. Frame	12. End frame

install a thinner shim (35). Tighten pinion nut (46) securely and tighten bearing housing screws to shim gage. Adjust shim gage support so drive shaft assembly is parallel to shim gage. Press drive shaft assembly against bearing housing (32) and measure clearance (S). Clearance (S) plus thickness of shim (35) is the required shim thickness for proper pinion gear depth.

NOTE: Shim (35) is available in sizes from 0.60 mm to 1.30 mm in 0.05 mm increments. Shim should be selected so only ONE shim is installed.

Backlash between forward gear (49—Fig. SZ18-31) and pinion gear (45) should be 0.5-0.65 mm (0.020-0.026 in.) and is adjusted by varying thickness of shim (47). Use only ONE shim (47). Backlash between reverse gear (59) and pinion gear (45) should be 0.7-0.85 mm (0.028-0.033 in.) and is adjusted by varying thickness of shim (60). Use only ONE shim (60).

Propeller shaft (57) end play should be 0.10-0.20 mm (0.004-0.008 in.). Adjust end play by varying thickness of thrust washer (58).

Remainder of reassembly is the reverse of disassembly noting the following: Apply Suzuki Thread Lock 1342 or a suitable thread locking compound to threads of pinion nut (46) and tighten to 80-100 N·m (59-73 ft.-lbs.). Install bearing housing (32) with the mark "F" facing forward. Install dog clutch (54) with the side with six dogs facing forward. Lubricate slider (51) and pin (52) with a suitable water-resistant grease. Apply a suitable water-resistant grease to lips of seals (63) and to "O" ring (66). When installing bearing housing (65) and propeller shaft assembly, position flat surface of slider (51) facing up, align slot in housing (65) with slot in gearcase housing and install key. Apply Suzuki Bond 1207B to threads of ring nut (68), install ring nut with the side marked "OFF" facing propeller and tighten to 150-175 N·m (111-129 ft.-lbs). Shift unit must be in the neutral position when installing. Tighten propeller nut to 50-62 N·m (37-45 ft.-lbs.). Apply water-resistant grease to drive shaft splines. Apply a suitable silicone sealant to gearcase-to-drive shaft housing mating surfaces and shank of gearcase mount-

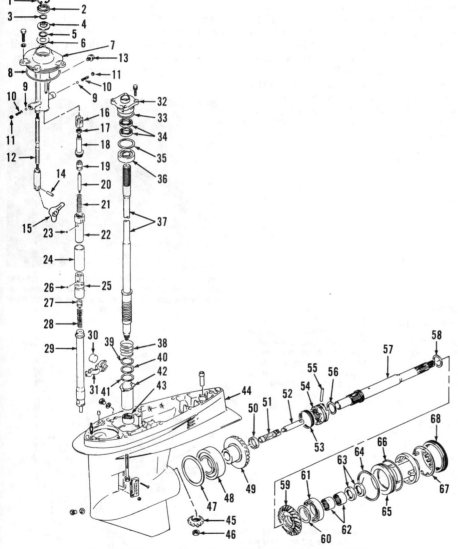

Fig. SZ18-31—Exploded view of lower unit gearcase assembly.

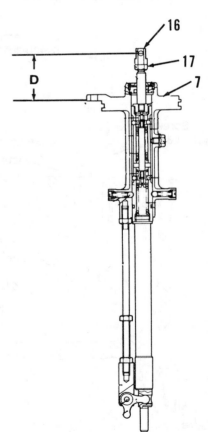

Fig. SZ18-32—Cross-sectional view of shift assembly. Distance (D) between housing (7) and center of hole in connector (16) with shift assembly in the neutral position, should be 46 mm (1.81 in.) on long shaft models and 173 mm (6.81 in.) on extra long shaft models. Tighten nut (17) securely.

1. Snap ring	14. Pin	28. Spring	42. Collar	56. Thrust washer
2. Seal	15. Pivot yoke	29. Vertical slider	43. Bearing	57. Propeller shaft
3. "O" ring	16. Connector	30. Magnet	44. Gearcase housing	58. Thrust washer
4. Guide	17. Nut	31. Magnet holder	45. Pinion gear	59. Reverse gear
5. "O" ring	18. Shaft	32. Bearing housing	46. Nut	60. Shim
6. Washer	19. Forward plunger	33. "O" ring	47. Shim	61. Bearing
7. Housing	20. Rod	34. Seals	48. Bearing	62. Bearings
8. "O" ring	21. Spring	35. Shim	49. Forward gear	63. Seals
9. Ball	22. Reverse sleeve	36. Bearing	50. Spacer	64. Spacer
10. Spring	23. Ball	37. Drive shaft	51. Slider	65. Propeller shaft
11. Screw	24. Lock sleeve	38. Spring	52. Connector pin	bearing housing
12. Pivot rod & shaft	25. Forward sleeve	39. Thrust washer	53. Retainer	66. "O" ring
assy.	26. Ball	40. Thrust washer	54. Dog clutch	67. Tab washer
13. Bolt	27. Reverse plunger	41. Protector	55. Pin	68. Ring nut

ing screws. Tighten gearcase screws to 50-60 N·m (37-44 ft.-lbs.). Fill gearcase with approximately 560 mL (18.9 oz.) of Suzuki Outboard Motor Gear Oil or a suitable equivalent SAE 90 hypoid gear lubricant. After operating outboard motor for several minutes, gearcase oil level should be checked and topped off if necessary.

POWER TRIM AND TILT

All models are equipped with a hydraulically actuated power trim and tilt system. Refer to Fig. SZ18-38 for an exploded view of the power trim/tilt pump, valve body and manifold assembly. An oil pump driven by a reversible electric motor provides oil pressure. A rocker switch determines motor and pump rotation thereby retracting or extending trim and tilt cylinders. The pump is equipped with manual release valve (M—Fig. SZ18-36). Rotating manual release valve two turns clockwise will allow manual movement of trim/tilt cylinders.

Recommended oil is Dexron automatic transmission fluid. Oil level should reach bottom of fill plug hole with outboard motor fully tilted up. Bleed air from system by tilting motor fully up and down through several cycles while maintaining reservoir oil level.

If power trim/tilt system malfunction occurs, first inspect wiring, wiring connections and electric motor. To test pressure, proceed as follows: Tilt outboard motor to full up position and engage tilt lock lever. Connect a 13.8 MPa (2000 psi) pressure gage between ports (X and Y—Fig. SZ18-37). Close valve (X) and open valve (Y). Operate power trim/tilt system in the UP direction. Up pressure at port (Y) should be 8.8-11.8 MPa (1280-1705 psi). Close valve (Y) and open valve (X). Operate system in the down direction. Down pressure at port (X) should be 2.7-5.5 MPa (398-796 psi). If pump pressure does not remain steady or does not reach specified specification, pump and valve body should be renewed.

To pressure-test tilt cylinder, connect test gage between ports (W and Y). Op-

erate tilt switch in the UP direction until tilt cylinder is fully extended. Close valve (Y) prior to releasing tilt switch. If gage reading does not remain steady, or if pressure does not reach pressure obtained in pump UP direction test, tilt cylinder should be disassembled and inspected for leakage. Connect test gage between ports (X and V). Operate tilt switch in the DOWN direction until tilt cylinder is fully retracted. Close valve (Y) before releasing tilt switch. If gage reading does not remain steady, or if pressure does not reach pressure obtained in pump DOWN pressure test, tilt cylinder should be disassembled and inspected for leakage.

Disassembly and reassembly of power trim/tilt motor is evident after inspection of unit. Match marks are provided on motor end cover and frame assembly for correct alignment during reas-

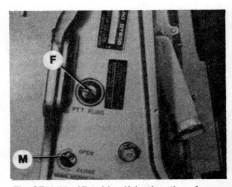

Fig. SZ18-36—View identifying location of power trim and tilt reservoir fill plug (F) and manual release valve (M). Manual release valve has left-hand threads.

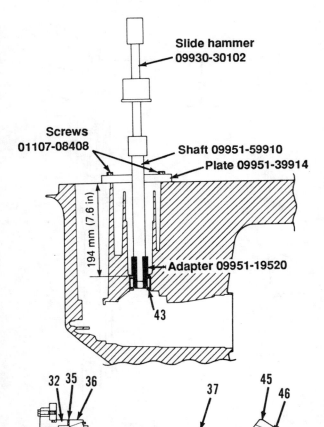

Fig. SZ18-33—Using Suzuki special tools shown, or suitable equivalent, draw pinion bearing (43) into gearcase until top of bearing (43) is 194 mm (7.6 in.) from mating surface of gearcase.

Fig. SZ18-35—To select the proper size pinion gear shim (35), assemble drive shaft as shown and place into Suzuki Shim Gage 09951-08720. Measure clearance (S) between shim gage and pinion gear (45). Clearance (S) is thickness of shim required for proper pinion gear depth.

32. Bearing housing
35. Shim
36. Bearing
37. Drive shaft
45. Pinion gear
46. Nut

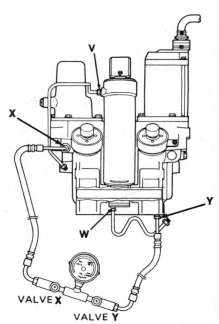

Fig. SZ18-37—Connect a 13.8 MPa (2000 psi) gage as shown to test hydraulic pump pressure. Refer to text.

sembly. Standard commutator diameter is 28 mm (1.102 in.). Renew armature if commutator diameter is less than 27 mm (1.062 in.). Standard brush length is 11.5 mm (0.45 in.). Renew brushes if worn to less than 5.5 mm (0.22 in.).

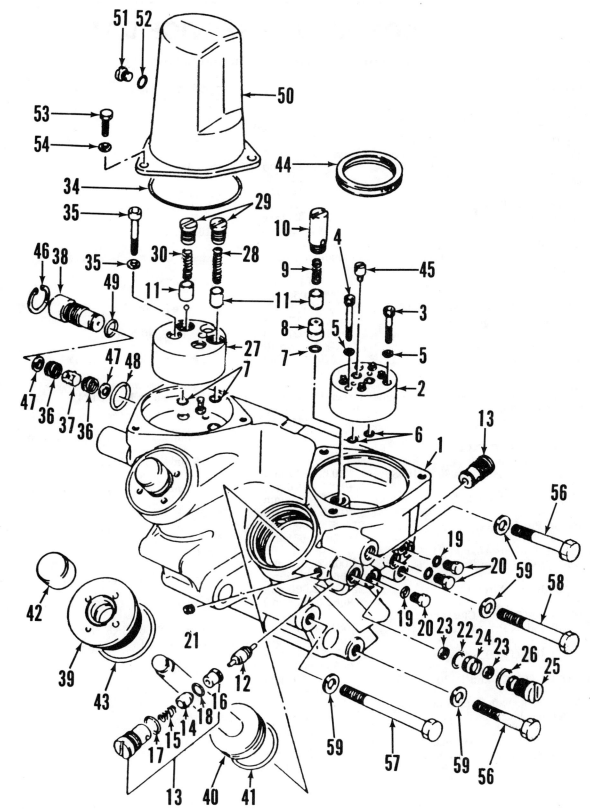

1. Manifold assy.
2. Pump assy.
3. Screw
4. Screw
5. Lockwasher
6. "O" ring
7. "O" ring
8. Bushing
9. Spring
10. Down pressure valve housing
11. Down pressure valve
12. Spool
13. Valve assy.
14. Check valve
15. Spring
16. Valve
17. "O" ring
18. "O" ring
19. "O" ring
20. Plug
21. Plug
22. "O" ring
23. Filter
24. Collar
25. Plug
26. "O" ring
27. Pressure valve housing
28. Spring
29. Pressure valve
30. Spring
31. Spring seat
32. Ball
33. Filter
34. Screw
35. Lockwasher
36. Spring
37. Valve
38. Manual valve plug
39. Nut
40. Piston assy
41. "O" ring
42. End cap
43. "O" ring
44. Filter
45. Drive coupler
46. Snap ring
47. Seal washer
48. "O" ring
49. "O" ring
50. Reservoir
51. Plug
52. "O" ring
53. Screw
54. Lockwasher
55. "O" ring
56. Screw
57. Screw
58. Screw
59. Lockwasher

Fig. SZ18-38—Exploded view of power trim/tilt pump, valve body and manifold assembly.

SUZUKI DT150, DT150SS, DT175 AND DT200

CONDENSED SERVICE DATA

NOTE: Metric fasteners are used throughout outboard motor.

TUNE-UP
Hp/rpm:
DT150 & DT150SS 150/5000-5600
DT175 . . . . .175/5000-5600
DT200 . . . . .200/5000-5600
Bore . . . . .84 mm
(3.31 in.)
Stroke . . . . .81 mm
(3.2 in.)
Number of Cylinders 6
Displacement . . . . .2693 cc
(164.3 cu. in.)
Spark Plug:
DT150, DT175 and DT200 (Except 1989 Models) . .NGK
B8HS-10
Electrode Gap .0.9-1.0 mm
(0.035-0.039 in.)
DT150SS (Except 1989 Models) . . . . .NGK B8HS
Electrode Gap .0.6-0.7 mm
(0.024-0.027 in.)
All 1989 Models . . . . .NGK BR8HS-10
Electrode Gap .0.9-1.0 mm
(0.035-0.039 in.)
Ignition Type:
Models Prior to 1989 . . . . . .Suzuki Integrated Circuit
Models After 1988 . . . . .Suzuki Micro Link
Carburetor Make . . . . .Mikuni

SIZES—CLEARANCES
Piston Ring End Gap:
All Models Except 1989 DT150SS . . . . . . .0.20-0.40 mm
(0.008-0.016 in.)
1989 Model DT150SS . . . . .0.40-0.60 mm
(0.016-0.024 in.)
Piston Pin Diameter . . . . .21.995-22.000 mm
(0.8659-0.8661 in.)
Piston Pin Bore Diameter:
All Models Prior To 1989 . . . . .22.002-22.010 mm
(0.8662-0.8665 in.)
All Models After 1988 . . . . .22.001-22.006 mm
(0.8662-0.8664 in.)
Piston-to-Cylinder Clearance:
All Models Prior to 1989 . . . . .0.130-0.140 mm
(0.005-0.0055 in.)
DT150SS (1989) . . . . .0.097-0.112 mm
(0.0038-0.0044 in.)
DT150, DT175 and DT200 (1989) . . . . . .0.155-0.165 mm
(0.006-0.0065 in.)
Max. Crankshaft Runout at Main
Bearing Journal . . . . .0.05 mm
(0.002 in.)
Max. Connecting Rod Small End
Side Shake . . . . .5.0 mm
(0.20 in.)

TIGHTENING TORQUES
Cylinder Head:
6 mm . . . . .8-12 N·m
(6-9 ft.-lbs.)
8 mm . . . . .28-32 N·m
(20-23 ft.-lbs.)
Cylinder . . . . .46-54 N·m
(34-40 ft.-lbs.)
Crankcase:
8 mm . . . . .21-25 N·m
(15-18 ft.-lbs.)
10 mm . . . . .46-54 N·m
(34-40 ft.-lbs.)
Exhaust Cover . . . . .8-12 N·m
(6-9 ft.-lbs.)
Flywheel Nut .250-260 N·m
(184-191 ft.-lbs.)
Gearcase Pinion Nut . . . . .140-150 N·m
(102-109 ft.-lbs.)
Propeller Shaft Nut . . . . .50-62 N·m
(36-45 ft.-lbs.)
Water Pump . . . . .15-20 N·m
(11-15 ft.-lbs.)
Standard Screws:
Unmarked or Marked "4"
5 mm . . . . .2.4 N·m
(2-3 ft.-lbs.)
6 mm . . . . .4-7 N·m
(3-5 ft.-lbs.)
8 mm . . . . .10-16 N·m
(7-12 ft.-lbs.)
10 mm . . . . .22-35 N·m
(16-26 ft.-lbs.)
Stainless Steel
5 mm . . . . .3-6 N·m
(2-3 ft.-lbs.)
6 mm . . . . .6-10 N·m
(5-7 ft.lbs.)
8 mm . . . . .15-20 N·m
(11-15 ft.-lbs.)
10 mm . . . . .34-41 N·m
(25-30 ft.-lbs.)
Marked "7" or SAE Grade 5
5 mm . . . . .3-6 N·m
(2-5 ft.-lbs.)
6 mm . . . . .8-12 N·m
(6-9 ft.-lbs.)
8 mm . . . . .18-28 N·m
(13-20 ft.-lbs.)
10 mm . . . . .40-60 N·m
(29-44 ft.-lbs.)

LUBRICATION

The power head is lubricated by oil mixed with the fuel. All models are equipped with oil injection. The manufacturer recommends using Suzuki Outboard Motor or an NMMA certified TC-WII engine oil. During break-in (first five hours of operation) of a new or rebuilt engine, mix fuel with oil in fuel tank at a ratio of 50:1. After completion of the five hour break-in period, switch to straight gasoline in the fuel tank. The recommended fuel is unleaded gasoline having a minimum octane rating of 85.

The lower unit gears and bearings are lubricated by oil contained in the gearcase. Suzuki Outboard Motor Gear Oil should be used. Gearcase capacity is approximately 1050 mL (35½ oz.) of gear oil and should be drained and refilled after the first 10 hours of use and then after every 100 hours of use. Reinstall drain and level plugs securely, using a new gasket if needed to ensure a watertight seal.

FUEL SYSTEM

CARBURETOR. Mikuni Model BW40-32 carburetors are used on all DT200 models, Mikuni Model BW40-28 carburetors are used on all DT175 models and

1986 DT150 and DT150SS models and Mikuni Model BW36-24 carburetors are used on DT150 and DT150SS models after 1986. Refer to Fig. SZ20-1 for exploded view of carburetors typical of all models.

Initial setting of pilot air screw (3) from a lightly seated position should be as follows: 1¼ to 1¾ turns on 1986 DT150 and DT150SS models, 1987 and 1988 DT150SS and DT200 models and 1989 DT150SS and DT175 models; 1½ to 2 turns on 1986 DT200 models, 1987 and 1988 DT175 models and 1989 DT150 and DT200 models; 1 to 1½ turns on 1987 and 1988 DT150 models.

Final carburetor adjustment should be performed with engine running at normal operating temperature in forward gear. Adjust idle speed switch (I—Fig. SZ20-2) so engine idles at 600-700 rpm in forward gear. Note that on models after 1988, idle speed switch is located at front of lower engine cowl. Adjust pilot air screws (3—Fig. SZ20-1) so engine idles smoothly and will accelerate cleanly without hesitation. If necessary, readjust idle speed switch to obtain 600-700 rpm in forward gear.

Main fuel metering is controlled by main jet (12). Standard main jet size for normal operation on 1986 models is #157.5 on DT150 models, #147.5 on DT150SS models and #167.5 on DT200 models; standard main jet size is #132.5 on 1987-1989 DT150 and DT150SS models; #142.5 on 1987-1989 DT175 models; #162.5 on 1987 and 1988 DT200 models and #165 on 1989 DT200 models.

To check float level, remove float bowl and invert carburetor. Distance (D—Fig. SZ20-3) between bottom of float and float bowl mating surface of carburetor body should be 9.5-11.5 mm (0.37-0.45 in.). Adjust float level by bending tang (T—Fig. SZ20-1) on float arm.

To synchronize throttle valve opening of all three carburetors, first detach rod (R—Fig. SZ20-4). Loosen screws (S) on top and center carburetors. Throttle lever return spring pressure should cause respective throttle valves to close. Visually verify all throttle valves are closed, then retighten screws (S) on top and middle carburetors. Reconnect rod (R), then verify that throttle valves are properly synchronized.

SPEED CONTROL LINKAGE. The throttle valves on all three carburetors must be properly synchronized as outlined in the CARBURETOR section.

On models prior to 1987, a throttle valve switch assembly is used to register bottom carburetor throttle valve position. With throttle valves fully closed, continuity between light green wire with red tracer and black wire on throttle valve switch should be noted. There

Fig. SZ20-2—Adjust idle speed control switch (I) to set engine idle speed. Note that on models after 1988, idle speed switch (I) is located on front of lower engine cover. View identifies electrical parts holder cover (C).

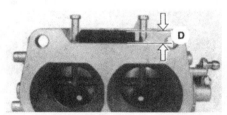

Fig. SZ20-3—Distance (D) for correct float level should be 9.5-11.5 mm (0.37-0.45 in.). Bend tang (T—Fig. SZ20-1) on float lever to adjust.

Fig. SZ20-4—Refer to text to synchronize throttle plate openings on all three carburetors. View identifies screws (S) and rod (R).

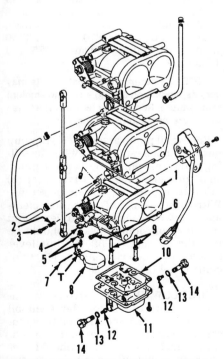

Fig. SZ20-1—Exploded view of Mikuni carburetors typical of all models.

1. Body
2. Spring
3. Pilot air screw
4. Gasket
5. Needle & seat
6. Pilot jet
7. Pin
8. Float
9. High speed nozzles
10. Gasket
11. Float bowl
12. Main jet
13. Gasket
14. Main jet holder
T. Tang

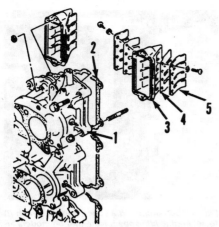

Fig. SZ20-5—Exploded view of intake manifold and reed valve assembly.

1. Intake manifold
2. Gasket
3. Reed plate
4. Reed petals
5. Reed stop

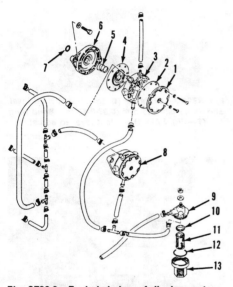

Fig. SZ20-6—Exploded view of diaphragm type fuel pump and fuel filter assemblies.

1. Cover
2. Diaphragm
3. Body
4. Diaphragm
5. Spring
6. Inner plate
7. "O" ring
8. Fuel pump assy.
9. Filter base
10. Packing
11. Filter element
12. "O" ring
13. Cup

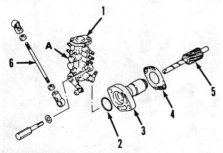

Fig. SZ20-7—Exploded view of oil injection pump and related components.

A. Air bleed screw
1. Pump assy.
2. "O" ring
3. Retainer
4. Gasket
5. Driven gear
6. Control rod

should be no continuity between brown wire with yellow tracer and black wire. When the throttle valves start to open, continuity between brown wire with yellow tracer and black wire should be noted.

On models after 1986, a throttle valve sensor is mounted to the center carburetor. Refer to IGNITION section for installation, adjustment and testing procedure.

REED VALVES. The inlet reed valves (Fig. SZ20-5) are located on a vee-shaped reed plate (3) between intake manifold (1) and crankcase. The reed petals should seat very lightly against the reed plate throughout their entire length with the least possible tension. Tip of reed petal must not stand open more than 0.20 mm (0.008 in.) from reed seat contact surface. Reed stop opening should be 7.4 mm (0.29 in.) on 1986 DT150 models, 1989 DT150 models, all DT175 and DT200 models and 1987 and 1988 DT150SS models. Reed stop opening should be 6.0 mm (0.24 in.) on 1987 and 1988 DT150 models and 1989 DT150SS models.

Renew reeds if petals are broken, cracked, warped, rusted or bent. Never attempt to bend a reed petal or to straighten a damaged reed. Never install a bent or damaged reed. Seating surface of reed plate should be smooth and flat. When installing reeds or reed stop, make sure petals are centered over the inlet holes in reed plate, and reed stops are centered over reed petals. Apply Thread Lock "1342" or a suitable equivalent to threads of reed stop screws prior to installation.

FUEL PUMP. Two diaphragm type fuel pumps are mounted on the side of power head cylinder block and are actuated by pressure and vacuum pulsations from the engine crankcase. Refer to Fig. SZ20-6 for exploded view of fuel pump assembly.

Defective or questionable parts should be renewed. Diaphragm should be renewed if air leaks or cracks are found, or if deterioration is evident.

FUEL FILTER. A fuel filter (9 through 13—Fig. SZ20-6) is mounted on the side of power head cylinder block. Filter should be disassembled and cleaned after every 50 hours of use. Renew "O" ring (12) if required.

OIL INJECTION

BLEEDING PUMP. To bleed trapped air from oil supply line or pump, first make sure outboard motor is in upright position and oil tank is full. Mix fuel in fuel tank with a recommended oil to a ratio of 50:1. Open oil pump air bleed screw (A—Fig. SZ20-7) three or four turns. Submerge lower unit of outboard motor in a suitable test tank. Start engine and allow to idle until all trapped air is expelled out around screw threads. When no air bubbles are noticed, stop engine and close air bleed screw (A).

CHECKING OIL PUMP OUTPUT. Start engine and allow to warm-up for approximately five minutes. Stop engine, remove oil reservoir and disconnect oil pump control rod (6—Fig. SZ20-7) from bottom carburetor. Connect Suzuki oil gage 09941-68710 to oil pump inlet hose. Fill oil gage with a recommended oil and bleed system as previously outlined. Refill oil gage to an upper reference mark with a recommended oil. With oil pump control rod (6) in the fully released (closed) position, start engine and run at 1500 rpm for exactly five minutes. After five minutes, stop engine and note oil gage. Oil consumption in five minutes at 1500 rpm should be 4.7-8.7 mL (0.159-0.294 oz.) on all models.

To check maximum pump output, repeat previous procedure except hold pump control rod (6) in the fully open position and run engine at 1500 rpm for exactly two minutes. Oil consumption at 1500 rpm in two minutes should be 11.5-17.2 mL (0.389-0.582 oz.) on all DT150SS models and DT150 models prior to 1989, 13.3-19.8 mL (0.450-0.670 oz.) on DT150 models after 1988 and all DT175 and DT200 models.

NOTE: Oil pump output test results may vary depending on testing error and ambient temperature. Repeat test two or three times to ensure consistent results.

Renew oil pump assembly (1) if pump output is not as specified. When installing pump assembly, be certain pump shaft properly engages driven gear (5) prior to tightening oil pump screws. With throttle valves fully closed, clearance between pump control lever and stop boss on pump housing should be less than 1 mm (0.039 in.) but lever should not touch stop. Adjust length of control rod (6) to adjust.

OIL FLOW SENSOR. An oil flow sensor is connected in-line between oil reservoir and oil pump. The oil flow sensor serves as an oil filter and as a sensor for inadequate oil flow. Should a restriction occur in the oil line to the pump, the sensor circuit will open (close on models after 1985), decreasing engine speed and activating the appropriate caution system.

The filter should be periodically cleaned in a suitable solvent. Renew filter if excessive blockage is noted.

IGNITION

A capacitor discharge ignition (CDI) is used. If engine malfunction is noted and the ignition system is suspected, make sure the spark plugs and all electrical wiring are in good condition and all electrical connections are clean and tight. Refer to CONDENSED SERVICE DATA section for recommended spark plugs and spark plug electrode gap.

Models after 1988 are equipped with Suzuki Micro Link ignition system. Micro Link is comprised of a capacitor discharge ignition system and a microcomputer. The microcomputer processes information from various sensors and switches including throttle valve opening, engine rpm and shift lever position, then determines the optimum ignition timing for all operating conditions. The Micro Link system also monitors oil level, oil flow, water flow and overspeed caution systems. Should one or more caution systems indicate a malfunction, the microcomputer will activate the appropriate warning buzzer and lamp, and reduce engine speed to a predetermined level.

TESTING CDI SYSTEM AND BATTERY CHARGING COILS. Refer to Figs. SZ20-8 and SZ20-9 and the following sections for testing CDI components and battery charging coils. Use Suzuki Pocket Tester 09900-25002 or a suitable ohmmeter to trouble-shoot ignition system.

CONDENSER CHARGE COIL. Unplug connector leading from condenser charge coil. Attach one tester lead to green wire terminal and remaining tester lead to terminal of black wire with red tracer. Condenser charge coil resistance should be 180-260 ohms on models prior to 1989 and 240-370 ohms on models after 1988.

PULSER COILS. Three pulser coils are used. Unplug connector leading from pulser coils. Attach tester leads between a suitable engine ground and terminal of red wire with black tracer for number one pulser coil, white wire with black tracer for number two coil and red wire with white tracer for number three coil. Each pulser coil resistance should be 160-240 ohms on all models.

When installing pulser coils, make sure air gap between coils and flywheel is 0.75 mm (0.029 in.). Suzuki pulser coil locating tool 09931-88710 may be used to ease coil adjustment.

GEAR COUNTER COIL. Unplug wires at connectors leading from counter coil. Connector tester between black wire and orange wire with green tracer. Gear counter coil resistance on all models

should be 160-240 ohms. When installing counter coil, make sure air gap between flywheel ring gear teeth and counter coil is 0.5 mm (0.020 in.) on models after 1988 and 0.75 mm (0.029 in.) on earlier models.

BATTERY CHARGE COILS. Three battery charge coils are used. Unplug wires at connectors leading from battery charging coils. Connect tester between red and yellow wires of number one coil, then red and yellow wires of coils two and three. On models prior to 1989, resistance should be 0.05-0.2 ohm on number one coil and 0.1-0.4 ohm on coils two and three. On models after 1988, battery charge coil resistance should be 0.2-0.4 ohm on all three coils.

IGNITION COILS. Six ignition coils are used. To check primary winding resistance, disconnect primary wires at coil and connect tester between primary terminal and black ground wire terminal at each coil. Primary resistance should be 0.05-0.15 ohm on all DT150SS models, 0.3-0.5 ohm on DT150, DT175 and DT200 models prior to 1988 and 0.1-0.3 ohm on DT150, DT175 and DT200 models after 1987.
To check secondary winding resistance, disconnect primary wires at coil and high tension leads at spark plugs. Connect tester between primary terminal and spark plug end of high tension leads. Secondary resistance should be 11,000-16,000 ohms on DT150SS models prior to 1988, 3300-4900 ohms on 1988 DT150SS models, 13,300-14,900 ohms on 1989 DT150SS models, 14,000-21,000 ohms on DT150, DT175 and DT200 models prior to 1988, 2600-3800 ohms on 1988 DT150, DT175 and DT200 models and 12,600-13,800 ohms on 1989 DT150, DT175 and DT200 models.

NOTE: Spark plug terminal cap is of the resistance-type on 1989 models. Resistance of spark plug terminal cap should be 10,000 ohms. Secondary winding resistance specifications previously listed include resistance of spark plug terminal cap.

IDLE SPEED ADJUSTING SWITCH. Idle speed adjustment switch is used to adjust idle speed by changing ignition timing. The switch changes timing from 6.5 degrees ATDC (slow) to 0.5 degree BTDC (fast). Idle speed switch failure can be quickly verified by connecting a suitable timing light to the engine. Start engine and allow to idle. Note timing while changing position of idle speed switch. If timing does not change with each switch position, idle speed switch is defective and should be renewed.

THROTTLE VALVE SWITCH ASSEMBLY (Models Prior to 1987). Unplug connector leading from throttle valve switch assembly. With throttle valves fully closed, continuity between light green wire with red tracer and black wire should be noted. There should be no continuity between brown wire with yellow tracer and black wire. When the throttle valves start opening, continuity between brown wire with yellow tracer and black wire should be noted.

THROTTLE VALVE SENSOR (Models After 1986). The throttle valve sensor provides throttle position information for determining the optimum ignition timing. The sensor is mounted on the port side of bottom carburetor. Drive gear (5—Fig. SZ20-10) engaged with carburetor throttle shaft (3) rotates driven gear (1) that turns the potentiometer shaft.

To test sensor, disconnect wires leading from sensor. Connect tester between light green/red wire and black wire. With throttle valves completely closed, resistance should be 200-250 ohms on models prior to 1989 and 225-275 ohms on models after 1988. Open throttle valves fully. Resistance should now be approximately 5000-5500 ohms on all models. Leave tester connected to the black wire. Connect remaining tester lead to the brown/yellow wire. With throttle valves completely closed, resistance should be 10,000 ohms. Open throttle valves slightly. Resistance should still be 10,000 ohms.

To install throttle valve sensor, remove sensor cover and remove alignment pin

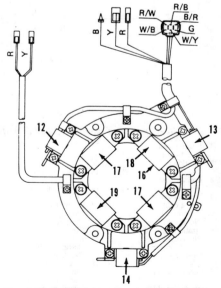

Fig. SZ20-8—View showing location of stator plate components.

12. Pulser coil (No. 1)	17. Battery charging coils
13. Pulser coil (No. 2)	(No. 2 & 3)
14. Pulser coil (No. 3)	18. IC power source cell
16. Battery charging coil	19. Condenser charging
(No. 1)	coil

affixed to cover. Rotate sensor driven gear (1) to align holes in the driven gear and the sensor, then insert alignment pin in hole (2). Install sensor assembly on carburetor shaft and lightly tighten mounting screws in the center of adjusting slots. With carburetor throttle valves fully closed, install drive gear (5), aligning the timing marks on drive and driven gears (Fig. SZ20-11). Make sure throttle valves are fully closed, then install and tighten throttle shaft nut (4—Fig. SZ20-10), tighten sensor mounting screws, remove alignment pin and affix to sensor cover and install sensor cover.

To adjust throttle valve sensor, remove oil pump control rod from pump lever and disconnect throttle valve sensor wires. Connect the red test lead of ohmmeter to the light green/red wire and black test lead to the black sensor wire. With throttle valves fully closed, resistance should be 200-250 ohms on models prior to 1989 and 225-275 on models after 1988. If not, first make sure throttle valves are fully closed, then loosen sensor mounting screws and rotate sensor as necessary to obtain 230 ohms on models prior to 1989 and 250 ohms on models after 1988. Retighten

sensor screws securely and reconnect oil pump control rod.

CDI MODULE. Test CDI module output using a Stevens Model CD-77 or a suitable equivalent peak reading voltmeter. Follow instructions included with tester.

COOLING SYSTEM

WATER PUMP. A rubber impeller type water pump is mounted between the drive shaft housing and gearcase. A key in the drive shaft is used to turn the

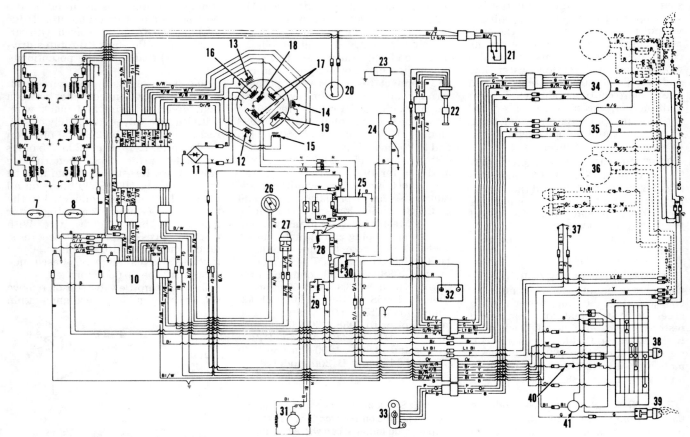

Fig. SZ20-9—Wiring diagram typical of early DT150 and DT200 models. Model DT150SS and later DT150, DT175 and DT200 models are similar.

1. Ignition coil (No. 1 cyl.)
2. Ignition coil (No. 2 cyl.)
3. Ignition coil (No. 3 cyl.)
4. Ignition coil (No. 4 cyl.)
5. Ignition coil (No. 5 cyl.)
6. Ignition coil (No. 6 cyl.)
7. Cooling water sensor (port side)
8. Cooling water sensor (starboard side)
9. CDI module
10. Low oil warning reset unit
11. Rectifier
12. Pulser coil (No. 1)

13. Pulser coil (No. 2)
14. Pulser coil (No. 3)
15. Counter coil
16. Battery charging coil (No. 1)
17. Battery charging coil (No. 2 & 3)
18. IC power source coil
19. Condenser charging coil
20. Oil flow sensor
21. Throttle plate sensor
22. Oil level switch
23. Starter valve
24. Starter motor

25. Rectifier with voltage regulator
26. Idle speed control knob
27. Oil warning reset switch
28. Power tilt & trim motor "UP" relay
29. Power tilt & trim motor "DOWN" relay
30. Starter motor relay
31. Power tilt & trim motor
32. Battery
33. Trim sender
34. Monitor
35. Trim meter
36. Tachometer

37. Power tilt & trim switch
38. Ignition switch
39. Emergency stop switch
40. Neutral switch
41. Overheat & oil warning buzzer

B. Black
G. Green
P. Pink
R. Red
W. White
Y. Yellow
Bl. Blue
Br. Brown
Gr. Gray
Lt Bl. Light blue
Lt G. Light green
Or. Orange
B/R. Black with red tracer

B/W. Black with white tracer
B/Y. Black with yellow tracer
Bl/R. Blue with red tracer
Bl/W. Blue with white tracer
Bl/Y. Blue with yellow tracer
Br/W. Brown with white tracer
Br/Y. Brown with yellow tracer
G/R. Green with red tracer
G/Y. Green with yellow tracer
Lt. G/B. Light green with black tracer
Lt. G/R. Light green with red tracer

Or/G. Orange with green tracer
R/B. Red with black tracer
R/G. Red with green tracer
R/W. Red with white tracer
R/Y. Red with yellow tracer
W/B. White with black tracer
W/G. White with green tracer
W/R. White with red tracer
W/Y. White with yellow tracer
Y/B. Yellow with black tracer
Y/G. Yellow with green tracer

pump impeller. If cooling system malfunction is noted, check water intake for plugging or partial restriction, then if necessary, remove the gearcase as outlined in the appropriate section and check condition of the water pump, water passages and sealing surfaces.

When water pump is disassembled, check condition of impeller (1—Fig. SZ20-12) and plate (3) for excessive wear. Rotate drive shaft clockwise (viewed from top) while placing pump housing over impeller. Avoid turning drive shaft in opposite direction after water pump is reassembled.

THERMOSTAT. A thermostat located at top of each cylinder head is used to regulate engine operating temperature. The thermostat should start to open within the range of 40°-44° C (104°-111° F). Thermostat can be removed for inspection or renewal by removing thermostat housing.

POWER HEAD

REMOVE AND REINSTALL. To remove the power head, first remove engine cover. Detach battery cables. Remove electrical parts holder cover (C—Fig. SZ20-2). Disconnect battery cables from starter motor and power tilt and trim motor relays. Remove fuel supply line from fuel filter inlet fitting. Remove electrical parts holder cover located between cylinder head covers. Disconnect any wiring that will interfere with power head removal. Remove the five screws located at base of removed electrical parts holder. Remove the two screws to withdraw front power head retaining screws cover. Remove the four screws from the engine side to withdraw rear power head retaining screws cover. Disconnect water inspection hose from connector in bottom engine cover. Remove cotter pin and clevis pin connecting upper shift rod to connector of lower shift assembly. Remove ten power head retaining screws, then lift power head high enough to expose shift linkage. Detach clutch lever rod connector (R—Fig. SZ20-13) and upper shift rod (U) from clutch shaft (S). Lift power head assembly with related engine components from lower unit assembly.

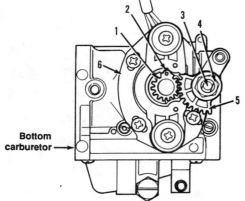

Bottom carburetor →

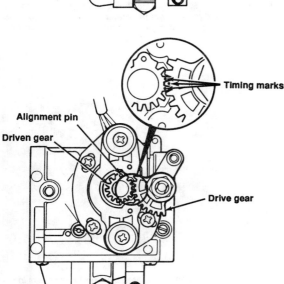

Timing marks

Alignment pin

Driven gear

Drive gear

Fig. SZ20-10—View of throttle valve sensor.

1. Driven gear
2. Alignment pin hole
3. Carburetor throttle shaft
4. Throttle shaft nut
5. Drive gear

Fig. SZ20-11—Refer to text to install and adjust throttle position sensor.

Before installing power head, make certain drive shaft splines are clean, then coat them with a light coating of water-resistant grease. Reconnect clutch lever rod connector (R) and upper shift rod (U) to shift shaft (S) prior to power head installation. Coat power head to lower unit retaining cap screws adjacent to cap screw heads with silicone sealer. Tighten 8 mm power head retaining screws to 15-20 N·m (11-15 ft.-lbs.) and 10 mm screws to 34-41 N·m (25-30 ft.-lbs.). The remainder of installation is the reverse of removal procedure.

DISASSEMBLY. Disassembly and inspection can be accomplished in the following manner. Disconnect wiring to oil tank. Remove oil supply line from oil tank outlet and plug tank outlet. Remove cap screws to withdraw oil tank. Remove flywheel, stator plate assembly and counter coil. Remove electrical parts holder beneath electric starter. Disconnect spark plug leads and remove electrical parts holder located between cylinder heads. Remove electric starter and bracket assembly. Remove fuel filter and fuel pump assemblies. Remove starter valve. Disconnect throttle control rod (R—Fig. SZ20-4) from bottom carburetor throttle lever, then remove carburetor assemblies. Remove oil injection pump, hoses (label for reassembly reference) and oil flow sensor. Remove speed control linkage. Remove outer and inner exhaust covers. Remove spark plugs, then remove cylinder heads with cylinder head covers. Remove the eleven cap screws and withdraw lower oil seal housing. Remove the eight cylinder retaining cap screws for each cylinder, then remove cylinders. Separate pistons from connecting rods. Remove intake manifolds and reed valve assemblies. Unscrew crankcase retaining screws and separate crankcase from cylinder block. Crankshaft assembly can now be removed from cylinder block.

Engine components are now accessible for overhaul as outlined in the appropriate following paragraphs. Refer to the following section for assembly procedures.

Fig. SZ20-12—View identifying water pump impeller (1), drive key (2) and plate (3).

ASSEMBLY. Refer to specific service sections when assembling the crankshaft, connecting rod, piston and reed valves. Make sure all joint and gasket surfaces are clean, free from nicks and burrs and hardened cement or carbon.

Whenever the power head is disassembled, it is recommended that all gasket surfaces and mating surfaces without gaskets be carefully checked for nicks, burrs and warped surfaces that might interfere with a tight seal. Cylinder heads, cylinders, head end of cylinder block and some mating surfaces of manifolds and crankcase should be checked on a surface plate and lapped if necessary to provide a smooth surface. Do not remove and more metal than is necessary.

When reassembling power head, first lubricate all friction surfaces and bearings with engine oil. Apply a suitable high-temperature grease to lip of upper crankshaft seal. Apply a suitable water-resistant grease to lip of drive shaft seal and install seal into lower oil seal housing. Place main bearing locating pins into crankcase portion of cylinder block, then install crankshaft assembly. Make certain bearing locating pins engage main bearings and upper crankshaft seal fits in cylinder block groove. Make certain lower main bearing locating pin engages notch in cylinder block and "C" ring fits into cylinder block groove. End gaps on all crankshaft seal rings must

face toward crankcase cover. Apply a coat of Suzuki Bond 1207B or a suitable sealer to mating surfaces of crankcase and cylinder block and position crankcase on cylinder block. Tighten crankcase screws in the sequence shown in Fig. SZ20-14. Refer to CONDENSED SERVICE DATA for torque values. Install cylinders and lightly tighten retaining screws. Using Suzuki alignment tool 09912-68710, attach tool to cylinders and cylinder block. Tighten screws in sequence shown in Fig. SZ20-15. Tighten 8 mm screws to 18-28 N·m (13-20 ft.-lbs.) and 10 mm screws to 40-60 N·m (29-44 ft.-lbs.). Tighten cylinder retaining screws to 46-54 N·m (34-40 ft.-lbs.). Remove Suzuki alignment tool 09912-68710 and install lower oil seal housing, tightening 8 mm screws to 18-28 N·m (13-20 ft.-lbs.) and 10 mm screws to 40-60 N·m (29-44 ft.-lbs.). Tighten cylinder head screws in sequence shown in Fig. SZ20-16. Refer to CONDENSED SERVICE DATA for cylinder head fastener torque values.

RINGS, PISTONS AND CYLINDER. Pistons on all DT150 models and DT150SS, DT175 and DT200 models prior to 1987 are fitted with two piston rings. Pistons on DT175 and DT200 models after 1986 are fitted with three piston rings. Pistons on 1987 and 1988 DT150SS are fitted with three piston rings while pistons on 1989 DT150SS

models equipped with SBC cylinder liners are fitted with two rings. Piston rings must be installed with manufacturer's marking facing crown of piston. Rings are pinned to prevent ring rotation in ring grooves.

NOTE: On late models, top and second piston rings are not interchangeable. Rings must be installed in the proper ring groove with the green mark on top ring and the blue mark on second ring facing piston crown. Rings may also be identified by the "RN" mark stamped in the top ring and "R" mark stamped in second ring. Stamped marks must face piston crown when installed.

Refer to CONDENSED SERVICE DATA for ring and piston service specifications. Pistons and rings are available in 0.25 mm and 0.50 mm oversizes. Cylinder should be bored to next oversize if cylinder bore taper, out-of-round or wear exceeds 0.10 mm (0.004 in.). Install piston on connecting rod so arrow on piston crown will face toward exhaust port when piston is installed. Install piston pin with closed end facing toward flywheel side of crankshaft.

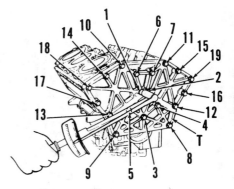

Fig. SZ20-15—Use Suzuki special tool (T) 09912-68710 and tighten screws in sequence shown to align cylinders and cylinder block. Refer to text for torque values.

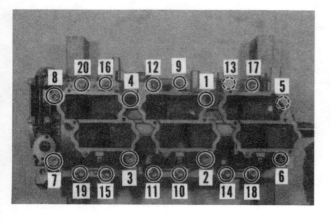

Fig. SZ20-13—Detach clutch lever rod connector (R) and upper shift rod (U) from clutch shaft (S) during power head removal. Refer to text.

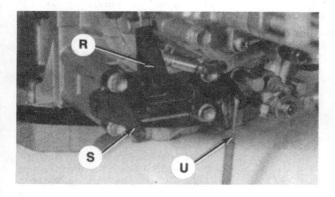

Fig. SZ20-14—Tighten crankcase screws in sequence shown. Refer to CONDENSED SERVICE DATA for torque values.

Fig. SZ20-16—Tighten cylinder head screws in sequence shown. Refer to CONDENSED SERVICE DATA for torque values.

CONNECTING RODS, BEARINGS AND CRANKSHAFT.

Connecting rods, bearings and crankshaft are a pressed-together unit. Crankshaft should be disassembled ONLY by experienced service personnel using the proper service equipment.

Caged roller bearings are used in middle and top of crankshaft. A caged ball bearing is used at bottom of crankshaft. Determine connecting rod, rod bearing and crankpin wear by measuring connecting rod small end side-to-side movement as shown at (A—Fig. SZ20-18). Normal movement (A) is 5 mm (0.20 in.) or less. Maximum allowable crankshaft runout is 0.05 mm (0.002 in.) measured at bearing journals with ends of crankshaft supported.

When installing crankshaft, lubricate pistons, rings, cylinders and bearings with a recommended engine oil as outlined in ASSEMBLY section.

ELECTRIC STARTER

Models are equipped with electric starter shown in Fig. SZ20-19. Disassembly is evident after inspection of unit and referral to exploded view. Starter brushes have a standard length of 16 mm (0.63 in.) and should be renewed if worn to 11.5 mm (0.45 in.) or less. After reassembly, bench test starter for proper operation prior to installing on power head.

LOWER UNIT

PROPELLER AND DRIVE CLUTCH.

Protection for the motor is built into a special cushioning clutch in the propeller hub. No adjustment is possible on the propeller or clutch. Three-bladed propellers are used. Propellers are available from the manufacturer in various diameters and pitches and should be selected to provide optimum performance at full throttle within the recommended limits of 5000-5600 rpm.

R&R AND OVERHAUL.

Refer to Fig. SZ20-20 for exploded view of lower unit gearcase assembly used on all models. During disassembly, note the location of all shims and thrust washers to aid in reassembly. To remove gearcase, first unscrew drain plug (48) and level plug (46) and drain gear lubricant. Remove cotter pin and clevis pin connecting upper shift rod to connector (16). Remove trim tab. Remove the screws securing gearcase to drive shaft housing and separate gearcase assembly from drive shaft housing. Remove water pump assembly and lower shift assembly. Remove propeller with related components from propeller shaft. Bend tabs of washer (73) away from ring nut (74),

then use special tool 09951-18710 to unscrew ring nut (74). Remove ring nut (74) and tab washer (73). Use a suitable puller and withdraw propeller shaft assembly with gearcase end cap (72). Unscrew pinion nut (50) and remove pinion gear (49), then extract forward gear (54). Drive shaft (37) and related components can be withdrawn from gearcase after removal of bearing housing (32).

Inspect gears for wear on teeth and on engagement dogs. Inspect dog clutch (59) for wear on engagement surfaces. Inspect shafts for wear on splines and on friction surfaces of gears and oil seals. All seals and ''O'' rings should be renewed when unit is reassembled.

Backlash between pinion gear (49) and forward drive gear (54) should be 0.50-0.65 mm (0.020-0.026 in.). Adjust by varying thickness of shim (51). Backlash between pinion gear (49) and reverse drive gear (64) should be 0.70-0.85 mm (0.028-0.033 in.). Adjust by varying

thickness of shim (65). Propeller shaft end play should be 0.05-0.20 mm (0.002-0.008 in.). Propeller shaft end play is adjusted by increasing or decreasing the thickness of thrust washer (63).

Reassemble gearcase by reversing disassembly procedure while noting the following: Install dog clutch (59) on propeller shaft (62) so side marked ''F'' (Fig. SZ20-21) is facing forward gear (54—Fig. SZ20-20). Tighten pinion nut (50) to 140-150 N·m (102-109 ft.-lbs.). Apply water-resistant grease to ''O'' ring (70) and end cap seals (68). Install ring

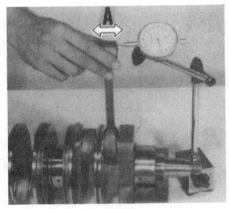

Fig. SZ20-18—Maximum side-to-side shake (A) at small end of connecting rod should not exceed 5.0 mm (0.20 in.).

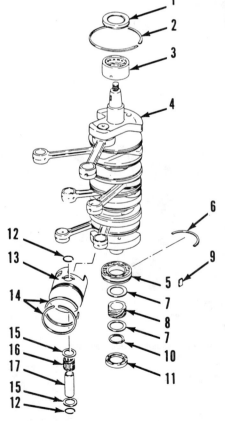

Fig. SZ20-17—Exploded view of crankshaft assembly typical of all models.

1. Seal
2. Snap ring
3. Roller bearing
4. Crankshaft assy.
5. Ball bearing
6. Bearing ring
7. Thrust washer
8. Oil injection pump drive gear
9. Key
10. Snap ring
11. Seal
12. Piston pin clips
13. Piston
14. Piston rings
15. Thrust washers
16. Needle bearing
17. Piston pin

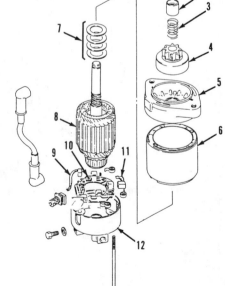

Fig. SZ20-19—Exploded view of electric starter motor.

1. "C" ring
2. Stop
3. Spring
4. Drive
5. Frame head
6. Frame
7. Thrust washers
8. Armature
9. Brush (+)
10. Brush holder
11. Brush (−)
12. End housing

nut (74) with side marked "OFF" facing out. Secure ring nut with tab washer (73). Apply silicone sealer to gearcase and drive shaft housing mating surfaces.

Coat shank area of gearcase retaining screws with silicone sealer and tighten to 50-60 N·m (36-44 ft.-lbs.). Apply water-resistant grease to propeller shaft splines. Install propeller and related components, then tighten propeller shaft nut to 50-62 N·m (36-45 ft.-lbs.) and secure nut with a new cotter pin.

Align connector (16) with upper shift rod. Install clevis pin and retain with a new cotter pin. Fill gearcase with outboard gear oil as outlined in LUBRICATION section.

POWER TRIM AND TILT

Models are equipped with a hydraulically actuated power trim and tilt system. An oil pump driven by a reversible electric motor provides oil pressure. A rocker control switch determines motor and pump rotation, thereby retracting or extending trim and tilt cylinders. The pump is equipped with a manual release valve (M—Fig. SZ20-22). Opening manual release valve (M) two turns clockwise allows manual movement of the tilt cylinders in the event of tilt system failure.

Recommended oil is Dexron automatic transmission fluid. Do not run pump without oil in reservoir. Fill plug (F) is located in side of pump reservoir. Oil level should reach fill plug hole threads with outboard motor in full tilt position. Hydraulic tilt should be cycled several times to bleed air if system has been

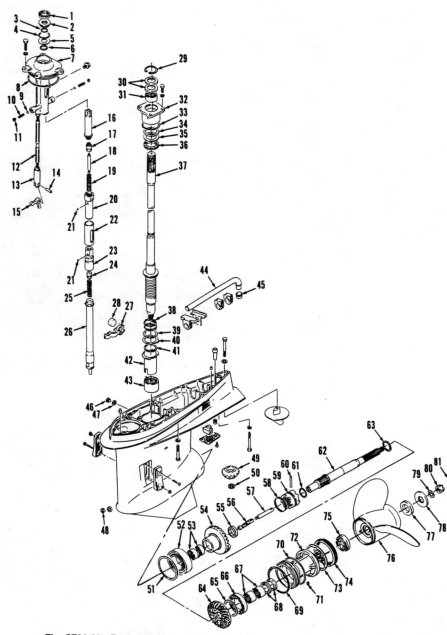

Fig. SZ20-20—Exploded view of lower unit gearcase assembly used on all models.

1. Seal	22. Lock sleeve	42. Collar	62. Propeller shaft
2. Guide	23. Forward sleeve	43. Bearing	63. Thrust washer
3. "O" ring	24. Forward plunger	44. Water tube	64. Reverse gear
4. "O" ring	25. Spring	45. Grommet	65. Shim
5. Washer	26. Vertical slider	46. Level plug	66. Bearing
6. Spacer	27. Magnet holder	47. Gasket	67. Bearings
7. Housing	28. Magnet	48. Drain plug	68. Seals
8. "O" ring	29. Snap ring	49. Pinion gear	69. Spacer
9. Ball	30. Seals	50. Nut	70. "O" ring
10. Spring	31. Bearing	51. Shim	71. Key
11. Screw	32. Bearing housing	52. Bearing	72. End cap
12. Pivot rod	33. "O" ring	53. Bearings	73. Tab washer
13. Pivot shaft	34. Shim	54. Forward gear	74. Ring nut
14. Pin	35. Thrust washer	55. Spacer	75. Spacer
15. Shifter yoke	36. Thrust bearing	56. Horizontal slider	76. Propeller
16. Connector	37. Drive shaft	57. Connector pin	77. Spacer
17. Reverse plunger	38. Spring	58. Pin retainer	78. Splined washer
18. Rod	39. Thrust washer	59. Dog clutch	79. Washer
19. Spring	40. Thrust washer	60. Pin	80. Nut
20. Reverse sleeve	41. Protector	61. Spacer	81. Cotter pin
21. Lock ball			

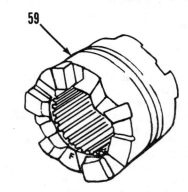

Fig. SZ20-21—Install dog clutch (59) on propeller shaft with side marked "F" facing forward gear.

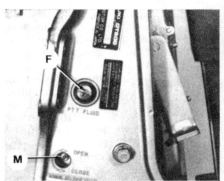

Fig. SZ20-22—View identifying location of power trim and tilt reservoir fill plug (F) and manual release valve (M). Manual release valve has left-hand threads.

drained or lost a large amount of oil. Be sure to maintain oil level during bleeding procedure.

If malfunction occurs in trim and tilt system, first make sure malfunction is not due to wiring, connections or electric motor failure. To test pump pressure, proceed as follows: Tilt outboard motor to full up position and lower tilt lock lever. Connect a 13.8 MPa (2000 psi) test gage between ports (X and Y—Fig. SZ20-21). Close valve (X) and open valve (Y). Operate rocker control switch in the UP direction. Oil pressure at port (Y) should be 8.83-11.7 MPa (1280-1700 psi). Close valve (Y) and open valve (X). Operate rocker switch in the DOWN direction. Oil pressure at port (X) should be 2.76-5.52 MPa (400-800 psi). Renew pump and valve body assembly if pressure readings are not within recommended limits.

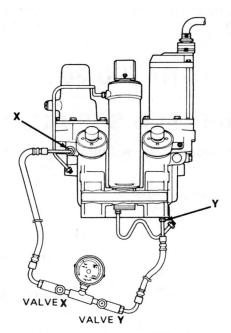

Fig. SZ20-23—Connect a 13.8 MPa (2000 psi) test gage as shown to test pump pressure. Refer to text.

TOHATSU

WESTERN ENGINE PRODUCTS INC.
984 North Lemon
Orange, CA 92667

NIMAC AMERICA INC.
500 Marathon Parkway
Lawrenceville, GA 30246

TOHATSU 30 HP

CONDENSED SERVICE DATA

NOTE: Metric fasters are used throughout outboard motor.

TUNE-UP

Hp/rpm 30/4800-5500
Bore . . . . .68 mm
(2.68 in.)
Stroke . . . . .59 mm
(2.32 in.)
Number of Cylinders 2
Displacement . . . . .430 cc
(26.2 cu. in.)

Spark Plug:
  Model M30A
    Champion L82
    NGK B7HS
      Electrode Gap . . . . .0.6-0.7 mm
(0.024-0.028 in.)
  Models M30A2 And M30A3
    Champion L82C10
    NGK B7HS-10
      Electrode Gap . . . . .0.9-1.0 mm
(0.035-0.040 in.)
Ignition Type . . . . .Breakerless CD
Ignition Timing . . . . .25° BTDC
Fuel:Oil Ratio 50:1

SIZES—CLEARANCES

Piston Ring End Gap .0.33-0.48 mm
(0.013-0.019 in.)
Piston Ring Side Clearance:
  Top . . . . .0.05-0.09 mm
(0.0020-0.0035 in.)
  Bottom . . . . .0.02-0.06 mm
(0.0008-0.0024 in.)
Piston Clearance . . . . .0.06-0.10 mm
(0.0024-0.0040 in.)
Piston Pin Clearance in Piston . . . . .0.001-0.013 mm
(0.00004-0.00051 in.)

SIZES—CLEARANCES CONT.

Connecting Rod Side Clearance:
  Standard . . . . .0.3-0.5 mm
(0.012-0.020 in.)
  Limit . . . . .0.7 mm
(0.027 in.)
Crankshaft Runout . . . . .0.05 mm
(0.002 in.)

TIGHTENING TORQUES

Crankcase . . . . .23.5-25.4 N·m
(208-225 in.-lbs.)
Cylinder Head:
  M30A . . . . .32.4-37.2 N·m
(287-329 in.-lbs.)
  M30A2 And M30A3 . . . . .23.5-25.4 N·m
(208-225 in.-lbs.)
Flywheel Nut . . . . .118-137 N·m
(87-101 ft.-lbs.)
Spark Plug . . . . .24.5 N·m
(217 in.-lbs.)
Standard Screws:
  No. 3 . . . . .0.6-0.8 N·m
(5-7 in.-lbs.)
  No. 4 . . . . .1.5-2 N·m
(13-17 in.-lbs.)
  No. 5 . . . . .2.4-3.4 N·m
(22-30 in.-lbs.)
  No. 6 . . . . .4.9-6.4 N·m
(43-56 in.-lbs.)
  No. 8 . . . . .11.3-15.2 N·m
(100-135 in.-lbs.)
  No. 10 . . . . .22.6-30.9 N·m
(200-273 in.-lbs.)

LUBRICATION

The power head is lubricated by oil mixed with the fuel. Recommended oil is Tohatsu outboard motor oil mixed at a fuel:oil ratio of 50:1. During engine break-in the fuel:oil ratio should be 20:1 for a period of 10 operating hours.

Lower unit gears and bearings are lubricated by oil contained in the gearcase. Recommended oil is Tohatsu gear oil or an SAE 80 gear oil. Gearcase oil capacity is 410 mL (13.8 oz) on M30A models and 250 mL (8.5 oz.) on M30A2 and M30A3 models. Change oil after initial 10 hours of operation and every 200 hours of operation thereafter.

FUEL SYSTEM

CARBURETOR. Refer to Fig. T8-1 for an exploded view of carburetor. Standard main jet (9) size is #175 on Model M30A2, #165 on Model M30A3 and #155 on Models M30A3 after serial number 21030. Initial setting of idle mixture screw (3) is approximately 1¼ turns open on Model M30A, ⅝ to 1⅛ turns on Model M30A2 and 1 to 1½ turns on Model M30A3. Adjust idle mixture and idle speed with engine running at normal operating temperature. Idle speed screw (1) should be adjusted so engine idles at 850-900 rpm with gearcase engaged in forward gear.

Adjust float level so float is parallel to

gasket surface with carburetor inverted and fuel bowl removed. Note clip (14) that secures inlet valve to float.

SPEED CONTROL LINKAGE. Carburetor throttle opening and ignition timing are synchronized by the speed control linkage so the carburetor throttle valve is opened as the ignition timing is advanced.

To adjust speed control linkage, disconnect lower link (7 – Fig. T8-2) and rotate bellcrank so "S" mark on throttle cam (4) is aligned with center of throttle lever roller (7 – Fig. T8-1). Rotate speed control grip to "START" position. Adjust length of lower link (7 – Fig. T8-2) by turning link ends so link can be attached to bellcrank and speed control rod (8) without disturbing position of bellcrank or speed control rod. Recheck adjustment and refer to IGNITION TIMING section and check ignition timing.

All models are equipped with a reverse speed limiting rod (24 – Fig. T8-12) and lever (21) which prevents excessive engine speed when motor is in reverse gear. With motor in reverse gear, adjust length of rod (24) by turning rod ends (15) so mark "R" on throttle cam (4 – Fig. T8-2) is aligned with center of throttle roller.

FUEL PUMP. A diaphragm type fuel pump is mounted on the starboard side of cylinder block. The pump is operated by crankcase pulsations. Refer to Fig. T8-3 for exploded view of fuel pump used on Model M30A and Fig. T8-4 for exploded view of fuel pump used on Models M30A2 and M30A3.

REED VALVES. The reed valves are attached to a plate which is located between the intake manifold and the crankcase as shown in Fig. T8-5. Inspect

reed valves and renew if cracked, bent or otherwise damaged. Do not attempt to straighten a reed valve petal. Reed valve seating surface of reed plate should be flat. Reed valve is available only as an assembly consisting of reed plate, reed petals and reed stops.

IGNITION

All models are equipped with a breakerless, capacitor discharge ignition system. The ignition exciter and trigger

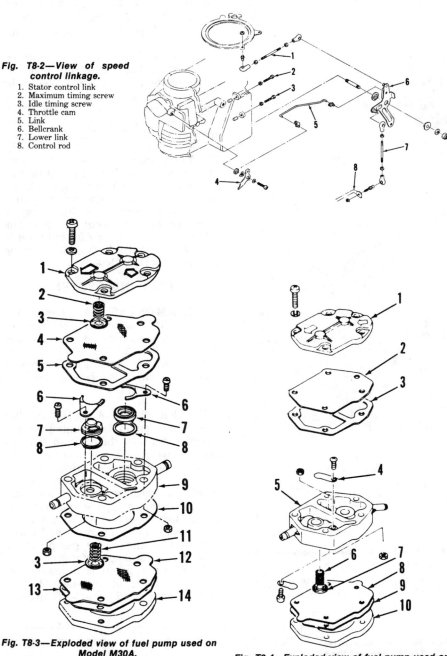

Fig. T8-2—View of speed control linkage.

1. Stator control link
2. Maximum timing screw
3. Idle timing screw
4. Throttle cam
5. Link
6. Bellcrank
7. Lower link
8. Control rod

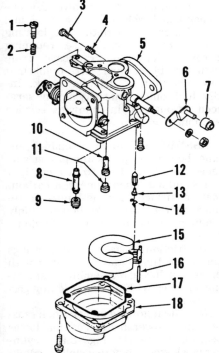

Fig. T8-1—Exploded view of carburetor.

1. Idle speed screw	10. Slow jet
2. Spring	11. Rubber cap
3. Idle mixture screw	12. Fuel inlet valve
4. Spring	13. Pin
5. Body	14. Clip
6. Lever	15. Float
7. Roller	16. Float pin
8. Main fuel nozzle	17. "O" ring
9. Main jet	18. Fuel bowl

Fig. T8-3—Exploded view of fuel pump used on Model M30A.

1. Cover	8. Gasket
2. Spring	9. Body
3. Spring seat	10. Gasket
4. Diaphragm	11. Spring
5. Gasket	12. Diaphragm
6. Retainer	13. Gasket
7. Check valve	14. Base

Fig. T8-4—Exploded view of fuel pump used on Models M30A2 and M30A3.

1. Cover	6. Spring
2. Diaphragm	7. Spring seat
3. Gasket	8. Diaphragm
4. Check valve	9. Gasket
5. Body	10. Base

coils as well as the lighting coil are located under the flywheel. The flywheel nut has left-hand threads. Tighten flywheel nut to 118-137 N·m (87-101 ft.-lbs.).

The following checks using an ohmmeter can be made to locate faulty ignition system components. Disconnect three-wire connector between stator plate and CD ignition module, then con-

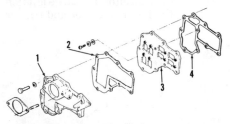

Fig. T8-5—View of reed valve assembly.

1. Intake manifold
2. Gasket
3. Reed valve assy.
4. Gasket

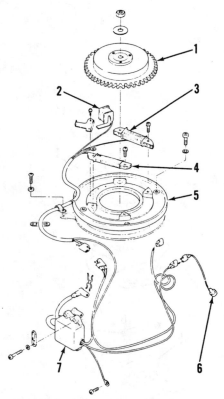

Fig. T8-6—Exploded view of ignition system.

1. Flywheel
2. Trigger coil
3. Lighting coil
4. Exciter coil
5. Stator plate
6. Ignition switch
7. Ignition module

nect one ohmmeter lead to stator plate. Connect remaining ohmmeter lead to red stator lead to check exciter coil. Ohmmeter reading should be 290 ohms. With ohmmeter leads connected to stator plate and blue stator lead to check trigger coil, ohmmeter reading should be 20 ohms. To check the CD ignition module, disconnect module leads and refer to chart in Fig. T8-7 for desired ohmmeter readings.

IGNITION TIMING. To adjust ignition timing, first refer to SPEED CONTROL LINKAGE section and check adjustment of speed control linkage, then proceed as follows:

Rotate speed control grip to full throttle position. The 25° BTDC mark on stator plate (5–Fig. T8-6) should be aligned with the mating surface line of the crankcase and cylinder block. If not, turn maximum ignition timing adjustment screw (2–Fig. T8-2). Rotate speed control grip to fully closed position. The 2° ATDC mark on the stator plate should be aligned with the mating surface line of the crankcase and cylinder block. If not, turn idle speed ignition timing adjustment screw (3). It may be necessary to adjust length of upper link (1) to set ignition timing for full throttle and idle speed. Recheck ignition timing if upper link (1) is detached.

COOLING SYSTEM

THERMOSTAT. A thermostat (25–Fig. T8-9) is located in the cylinder head. Thermostat should begin opening at 50°-54° C (122°-129° F) and be fully open at 65° C (149° F). Thermostat opening at maximum opening should be 3.0 mm (0.118 in.).

WATER PUMP. A rubber impeller type water pump is mounted on the gearcase between the drive shaft housing and gearcase. The impeller is driven by a Woodruff key in the drive shaft.

Whenever cooling problems are encountered, check water inlet for plugging or partial stoppage and the thermostat for proper operation, then if not corrected, remove gearcase and check condition of the water pump, water passages and sealing surfaces.

When water pump is disassembled, check condition of impeller (4–Fig. T8-16), liner (3) and plate (5). Turn drive

shaft clockwise (viewed from top) while placing pump housing over impeller. Avoid turning drive shaft in opposite direction when water pump is assembled. Tighten pump housing screws in a crossing pattern.

POWER HEAD

REMOVE AND REINSTALL. To remove power head, remove upper motor cover and disconnect ignition wires. Detach speed control lower link (7–Fig. T8-2). Detach starter lockout rod from shift shaft, disconnect fuel hoses and disengage choke control. Unscrew power head retaining screws and lift power head off drive shaft housing.

To install power head, reverse removal procedure. Apply water resistant grease to ends of crankshaft and drive shaft.

DISASSEMBLY. To disassemble power head, disconnect fuel lines and remove carburetor, fuel filter and fuel pump. Remove electric starter, if so equipped. Remove manual starter, disconnect ignition wires and remove ignition module. Detach speed control linkage. Remove flywheel, stator plate assembly, retainer (1–Fig. T8-9) and magneto ring (2). Remove exhaust cover (20) and cylinder head (22). Remove intake manifold and reed valve. Remove upper and lower seal housings (3 and 15). Unscrew labyrinth seal locating screw (8) and crankcase retaining screws. Separate crankcase from cylinder block and lift crankshaft assembly out of cylinder block. Individual components may now be serviced as outlined in following service sections.

ASSEMBLY. Before reassembling engine, be sure all joints and gasket surfaces are clean, free from nicks and burrs and hardened cement or carbon. Mating surfaces may be lapped to remove high spots or nicks, however, only a minimum amount of metal should be removed.

All friction surfaces and bearings should be thoroughly lubricated with engine oil during reassembly. Coat mating surfaces with a nonhardening gasket sealer.

Note the following points when reassembling power head: Position lower bearing retainer (11–Fig. T8-9) in cylinder block groove before installing crankshaft; position inner bearing retainer (10) in cylinder block groove after crankshaft has been installed. Be sure piston rings properly mate with piston ring groove pins and locating pins in bearings and labyrinth seal engage holes or notches in cylinder block when install-

Fig. T8-7—An ohmmeter should indicate the readings in the adjacent chart when testing the CD ignition module.

Connection of Tester Leads and Ident. of CD Module Leads	Tester (+) Lead			
	BROWN	RED	BLUE	BLACK
Tester (-) Lead — BROWN		Infinity	Infinity	Infinity
Tester (-) Lead — RED	Small deflection and soon returns			Zero
Tester (-) Lead — BLUE	300Ω - 1000Ω	Infinity		Infinity
Tester (-) Lead — BLACK	Small deflection and soon returns	Zero	Infinity	

ing crankshaft assembly in cylinder block. Tighten crankcase screws in steps to 23.5-25.4 N·m (208-255 in.-lbs.) using a crossing pattern; tighten the center screws first. Install seals (4 and 12) into seal housings so lips are facing engine. Install seal (13) into seal housing (15) so lip is facing away from engine. Tighten cylinder head retaining screws to 32.4-37.2 N·m (287-329 in.-lbs.) on M30A models and 23.5-25.4 N·m (208-225 in.-lbs.) on M30A2 and M30A3 models using the tightening sequence shown in Fig. T8-11.

PISTONS, PINS, RINGS AND CYLINDERS. The cylinders are equipped with an iron liner which may be bored to accept oversize pistons. Pistons and piston rings are available in standard size and 0.5 mm (0.020 in.) oversize. Each piston ring is located in the piston ring groove by a pin in each ring groove.

The piston pin is retained by circlips (37 – Fig. T8-10) which should be renewed if removed. The piston pin rides in a roller bearing in rod small end. Install piston on connecting rod so arrow on piston crown will point towards exhaust port.

CRANKSHAFT AND CONNECTING RODS. Crankshaft, connecting rods, crankpins and bearings are assembled as a pressed-together unit. Disassembly and reassembly of crankshaft unit should be performed ONLY by experienced personnel using the proper service equipment. Individual crankshaft components are available from the manufacturer. Refer to Fig. T8-12 for M30A models and Fig. T8-13 for M30A2 and M30A3 models for correct installation of crankshaft bearings and labyrinth seal so locating pins are on correct side.

MANUAL STARTER

Refer to Fig. T8-14 for an exploded view of manual starter. The starter may be disassembled after removing motor cover, detaching starter lock-out linkage and removing starter from power head. Remove rope handle and allow rope to wind into starter. Remove screw (16) and shaft (13), then carefully lift pulley (6) out of housing while being careful not to disturb rewind spring (5). If rewind spring must be removed care should be used not to allow spring to uncoil uncontrolled. Inspect pawl (10) for wear and freedom of movement. Renew and grease pawl if required.

When assembling starter, wind rewind spring in housing in a counterclockwise direction from outer end. Wind rope around rope pulley in a counterclockwise direction as viewed

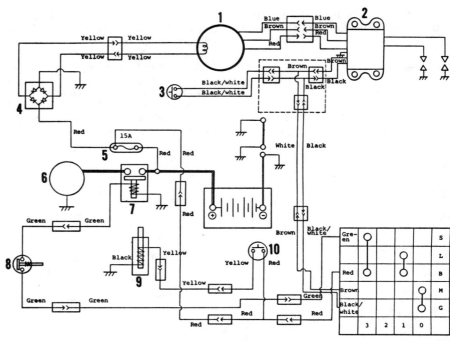

Fig. T8-8—Wiring diagram typical of electric start models. Other models are similar.

1. Stator plate
2. Ignition module
3. Starter safety switch
4. Rectifier
5. Fuse
6. Electric starter motor
7. Solenoid
8. Neutral switch
9. Choke solenoid
10. Choke solenoid switch

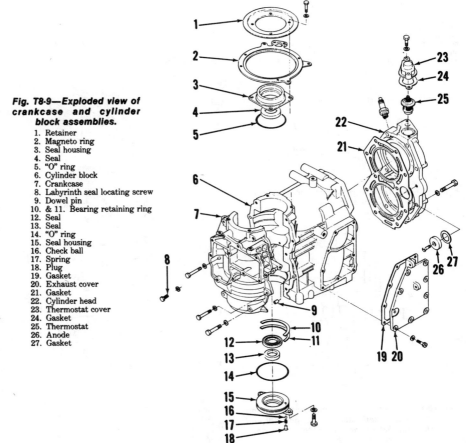

Fig. T8-9—Exploded view of crankcase and cylinder block assemblies.

1. Retainer
2. Magneto ring
3. Seal housing
4. Seal
5. "O" ring
6. Cylinder block
7. Crankcase
8. Labyrinth seal locating screw
9. Dowel pin
10. & 11. Bearing retaining ring
12. Seal
13. Seal
14. "O" ring
15. Seal housing
16. Check ball
17. Spring
18. Plug
19. Gasket
20. Exhaust cover
21. Gasket
22. Cylinder head
23. Thermostat cover
24. Gasket
25. Thermostat
26. Anode
27. Gasket

with pulley in housing. Pawl spring (8) must engage groove in shaft (13). Rotate

pulley three turns counterclockwise before passing rope through rope outlet to preload rewind spring.

A starter lockout mechanism (Fig. T8-15 is used to prevent starter usage when motor is in forward or reverse gear. Adjust length of lockout rod (13) by turning rod end so starter will operate with motor in neutral gear but not in forward or reverse gear.

ELECTRIC STARTER

Some models are equipped with an electric starter. Models equipped with an electric starter are also equipped with a battery charging system. Refer to Fig. T8-8 for a wiring diagram. Starter drive pinion and on some models, brush assembly, are only components serviceable on starter.

LOWER UNIT

PROPELLER AND SHEAR PIN. Lower unit protection is provided by a shear pin (32—Fig. T8-16) on M30A models. Be sure correct shear pin is installed for maximum protection to lower unit. Lower unit protection is provided by a clutch in propeller (55—Fig. T8-17) on M30A2 and M30A3 models.

The standard propeller has three blades and rotates clockwise. Various propellers are available to obtain best performance depending on outboard usage. Desired operating range at maximum engine speed is 4800-5500 rpm.

R&R AND OVERHAUL. To remove gearcase, disconnect shift rod coupler (44—Fig. T8-16) from lower shift rod (46) by driving out lower pin (45). Unscrew five cap screws securing gearcase

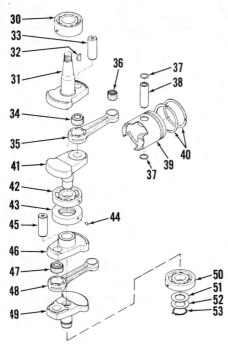

Fig. T8-10—Exploded view of crankshaft and piston assembly.

30.	Bearing	42.	Bearing
31.	Crankshaft half	43.	Labyrinth seal
32.	Key	44.	Pin
33.	Crankpin	45.	Crankpin
34.	Roller bearing	46.	Crankshaft half
35.	Connecting rod	47.	Roller bearing
36.	Roller bearing	48.	Connecting rod
37.	Circlip	49.	Crankshaft half
38.	Piston pin	50.	Bearing
39.	Piston	51.	Shim
40.	Piston rings	52.	Spacer
41.	Crankshaft half	53.	Snap ring

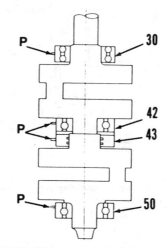

Fig. T8-13—When reassembling crankshaft on M30A2 and M30A3 models, install bearings (30, 42 and 50) and labyrinth seal (43) so locating pins (P) are positioned as shown.

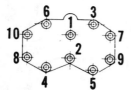

Fig. T8-11—Tighten cylinder head screws in sequence shown.

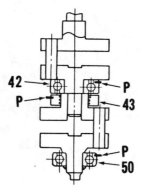

Fig. T8-12—When reassembling crankshaft on M30A models, install bearings (42 and 50) and labyrinth seal (43) so locating pins (P) are positioned as shown.

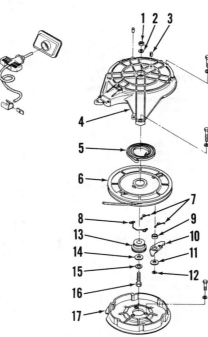

Fig. T8-14—Exploded view of manual starter.

1.	Nut		
2.	Washer		
3.	Pin	10.	Pawl
4.	Starter housing	11.	Washer
5.	Rewind spring	12.	"E" ring
6.	Rope pulley	13.	Shaft
7.	Spring links	14.	Washer
8.	Spring	15.	Lockwasher
9.	Bushing	16.	Screw
		17.	Starter cup

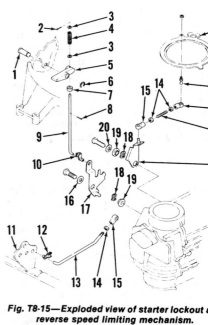

Fig. T8-15—Exploded view of starter lockout and reverse speed limiting mechanism.

1.	Pin		
2.	Cotter pin		
3.	Washer	14.	Locknut
4.	Spring	15.	Rod end
5.	Pawl	16.	Washer
6.	"E" ring	17.	Lever
7.	Collar	18.	Wave washer
8.	Cotter pin	19.	Bushing
9.	Rod	20.	Washer
10.	Rod end	21.	Pivot arm
11.	Shift shaft detent plate	22.	Magneto ring
12.	Rod end	23.	Pivot stud
13.	Rod	24.	Reverse speed limiting rod

to drive shaft housing and remove gearcase. Drain lubricant from gearcase and remove propeller. On Model M30A, remove shear pin. Remove water pump assembly. Remove bearing housing (38) and withdraw propeller shaft assembly. Drive out pin (29) to separate clutch (28) and spring (30) from propeller shaft. Unscrew pinion gear nut (22) and pull drive shaft (11) from gearcase. Pinion

gear (21) and forward gear (25) with bearing may now be removed. Use a suitable puller and remove roller bearing (13) by pulling towards gearcase top. Unscrew shift bushing retaining screw (17) and remove shift components (46 through 52) from gearcase.

Inspect components for excessive wear and damage. To reassemble gearcase, reverse disassembly procedure

while noting the following points: Lubricate all "O" rings and seals prior to assembly. Backlash between pinion gear and forward or reverse gear should be 0.08-0.13 mm (0.003-0.005 in.) and is adjusted by varying thickness of shim (9). Apply Loctite during final assembly and tighten pinion gear nut (22) to 23.5-25.4 N·m (208-225 in.-lbs.). Install clutch (28) on propeller shaft so grooved end is towards forward gear (25); see Fig. T8-18. When attaching gearcase to drive shaft housing, tighten fore and aft screws before tightening side screws.

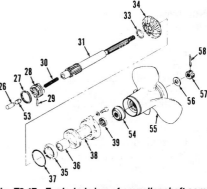

Fig. T8-17—Exploded view of propeller shaft components used on Models M30A2 and M30A3. A splined propeller shaft and propeller are used. Through-the-prop exhaust is used. Lower end of drive shaft (11—Fig. T8-16) is fitted with a collar and spring on later models. Water pump intakes are located on each side of gearcase housing below antiventilation plate. Refer to Fig. T8-16 for identification of components except for the following:

53. Spring holder		56. Washer
54. Thrust holder		57. Nut
55. Propeller		58. Cotter pin

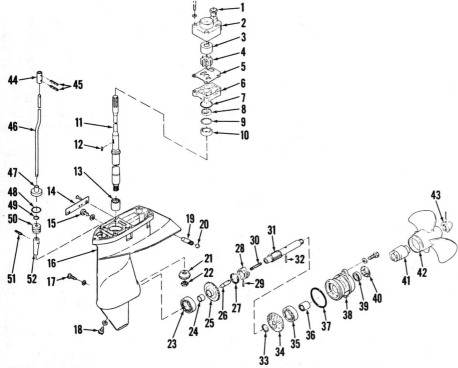

Fig. T8-16—Exploded view of lower unit assembly used on M30A models. Lower unit assembly used on Models M30A2 and M30A3 are similar except for components noted in Fig. T8-17.

1. Bushing		15. Vent plug		39. Seal	
2. Water pump housing		16. Gearcase		40. Spacer	
3. Liner		17. Shift bushing	27. Wire retainer	41. Hub	
4. Impeller		retaining screw	28. Clutch	42. Propeller	
5. Plate		18. Fill plug	29. Pin	43. Nut	
6. Pump base		19. Screen	30. Spring	44. Coupler	
7. "O" ring		20. Plug	31. Propeller shaft	45. Pin	
8. Seal		21. Pinion gear	32. Shear pin	46. Lower shift rod	
9. Shim		22. Nut	33. Thrust washer	47. Guide	
10. Bearing		23. Bearing	34. Reverse gear	48. "O" ring	
11. Drive shaft		24. Bushing	35. Bearing	49. "O" ring	
12. Key		25. Forward gear	36. Bearing	50. Bushing	
13. Bearing		26. Shift plunger	37. "O" ring	51. Pin	
14. Water inlet cover			38. Bearing housing	52. Shift cam	

Fig. T8-18—Install clutch so end with groove (G) is facing forward gear.

TOHATSU 35 AND 40 HP

CONDENSED SERVICE DATA

NOTE: Metric fasteners are used throughout outboard motor.

TUNE-UP
Hp/rpm 35/5700
40/5800
Bore . . . . .70 mm
(2.76 in.)
Stroke. . . . . .64 mm
(2.52 in.)
Number of Cylinders 2
Displacement . . . . .493 cc
(30.1 cu. in.)
Spark Plug:
  35 HP
    Champion L81Y
    NGK B7HS
      Electrode Gap . . . . .0.6-0.7 mm
      (0.024-0.028 in.)
  40 HP
    Champion L82YC
    NGK. B7HS-10
      Electrode Gap . . . . .0.9-1.0 mm
      (0.035-0.040 in.)
Ignition Type . . . . .Breakerless CD
Ignition Timing . . . . .25° BTDC
Fuel:Oil Ratio. 50:1

SIZES—CLEARANCES
Piston Ring End Gap:
  35 HP . . . . .0.2-0.4 mm
  (0.008-0.016 in.)
  40 HP. . . . . .0.25-0.4 mm
  (0.010-0.016 in.)
  Bottom Ring . . . . .0.2-0.4 mm
  (0.008-0.016 in.)
Piston Ring Side Clearance:
  35 HP
    Top Ring .0.05-0.09 mm
    (0.0020-0.0035 in.)
    Bottom Ring . . . . .0.02-0.06 mm
    (0.0008-0.0024 in.)
  40 HP
    Top Ring . . . . .Semi-Keystone
    Bottom Ring . . . . .0.02-0.06 mm
    (0.0008-0.0024 in.)
Piston Clearance:
  35 HP. . . . . .0.05-0.10 mm
  (0.0020-0.0040 in.)

SIZES—CLEARANCES CONT.
Piston Clearance:
  40 HP . . . . .0.08-0.13 mm
  (0.0031-0.0051 in.)
Piston Pin Clearance In Piston:
  35 HP . . . . .0.001-0.009 mm
  (0.00004-0.00035 in.)
  40 HP . . . . .0.007-0.010 mm
  (0.0003-0.0004 in.)
Connecting Rod Side Clearance . . . . .0.28-0.65 mm
(0.011-0.026 in.)
Connecting Rod Small End Shake:
  Standard . . . . .1.0 mm
  (0.040 in.)
  Limit . . . . .2.0 mm
  (0.079 in.)
Crankshaft Runout . . . . .0.05 mm
(0.002 in.)

TIGHTENING TORQUES
Crankcase . . . . .23.5-25.4 N·m
(208-225 in.-lbs.)
Cylinder Head. . . . . .32.4-37.2 N·m
(287-329 in.-lbs.)
Flywheel Nut . . . . .118-137 N·m
(87-101 ft.-lbs.)
Pinion Gear Screw .23.5-25.4 N·m
(208-225 in.-lbs.)
Propeller Nut . . . . .29.4-39.2 N·m
(260-347 in.-lbs.)
Spark Plug . . . . .24.5-29.4 N·m
(217-260 in.-lbs.)
Standard Screws:
  No. 3. . . . . .0.6-0.8 N·m
  (5-7 in.-lbs.)
  No. 4. . . . . .1.3-1.8 N·m
  (11-15 in.-lbs.)
  No. 5. . . . . .2.6-3.5 N·m
  (23-31 in.-lbs.)
  No. 6. . . . . .4.6-6.3 N·m
  (41-55 in.-lbs.)
  No. 8. . . . . .11.2-15.1 N·m
  (99-133 in.-lbs.)
  No. 10. . . . . .22.6-30.6 N·m
  (200-270 in.-lbs.)

LUBRICATION

The power head is lubricated by oil mixed with the fuel. Recommended oil is Tohatsu outboard motor oil mixed at a fuel:oil ratio of 50:1. During engine break-in the fuel:oil ratio should be 20:1 for a period of 10 operating hours.

Lower unit gears and bearings are lubricated by oil contained in the gearcase. Recommended oil is Tohatsu gear oil or a SAE 80 gear oil. Gearcase oil capacity is approximately 460 mL (15.5 oz.). Oil should be changed after initial 10 hours of operation and after every 200 hours of operation thereafter.

FUEL SYSTEM

CARBURETOR. Refer to Fig. T9-1 for an exploded view of carburetor. Initial setting of idle mixture screw (5) is 1¼ turns out from a lightly seated position. Adjust idle mixture and idle speed screws after motor temperature has normalized. Idle speed should be 900-950 rpm with motor engaged in forward gear.

To determine float height invert fuel bowl and measure float height as shown in Fig. T9-2. Float height should be 17-19 mm (0.67-0.75 in.) and is adjusted by bending float arm tang. Note clip (20) which secures fuel inlet valve to float arm.

Main jet (13 – Fig. T9-1) size for normal operation should be #220. Main air jet (10) size should be #120 and slow air jet (11) size should be #110.

SPEED CONTROL LINKAGE. Carburetor throttle opening and ignition timing are synchronized by the speed control linkage so the carburetor throttle valve is opened as the ignition timing is advanced.

(Model 35 HP). Prior to speed control linkage adjustment, refer to IGNITION TIMING section and check ignition timing. Detach lower link (7 – Fig. T9-3) and rotate bellcrank (4) so it is against advance speed stop screw (1). Throttle roller (9 – Fig. T9-1) should be against throttle cam stop (S – Fig. T9-4). Detach and adjust length of rod (5 – Fig. T9-3) by turning rod ends so throttle roller and cam are properly positioned. Adjust length of lower link (7) by turning ends so idle and full throttle markings on speed control grip are synchronized with idle and full throttle positions of bellcrank (4).

All models are equipped with a reverse speed stop (2 – Fig. T9-24) which prevents excessive engine speed when motor is in reverse gear. With motor in reverse gear, turn reverse speed adjusting screw (1) so mark (M – Fig. T9-4) on throttle cam is aligned with the center of throttle roller (9).

(Model 40 HP). To adjust speed control linkage, disconnect lower link (7 – Fig. 9-3) and rotate bellcrank so "S" mark on throttle cam (6) is aligned with center of throttle lever roller (9 – Fig. T9-1). Rotate speed control grip to "START" position. Adjust length of lower link (7 – Fig. T9-3) by turning link ends so link can be attached to bellcrank and speed control rod (8) without disturbing position of bellcrank or speed

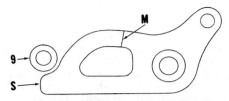

Fig. T9-4—On 35 hp models, throttle roller (9) should be against throttle cam stop (S) at maximum throttle. Throttle roller centerline should be aligned with throttle cam mark (M) when motor is in reverse gear. Refer to text for adjustment.

control rod. Recheck adjustment and refer to IGNITION TIMING section and check ignition timing.

All models are equipped with a reverse speed stop (2 – Fig. T9-24) which prevents excessive engine speed when motor is in reverse gear. With motor in reverse gear, turn reverse speed adjusting screw (1) so mark "R" on throttle cam (6 – Fig. T9-3) is aligned with the center of throttle roller (9 – Fig. T9-1).

FUEL PUMP. A diaphragm type fuel pump is mounted on the port side of the cylinder block. The pump is operated by crankcase pulsations. Refer to Fig. T9-5 for an exploded view of fuel pump used on 35 hp models and Fig. T9-6 for an exploded view of fuel pump used on 40 hp models.

REED VALVES. Two vee type reed valve assemblies (one for each cylinder) are located between the intake manifold and crankcase. Remove intake manifold and reed plate (4 – Fig. T9-7) for access to reed assemblies (6).

Renew reeds if petals are broken, cracked, warped or bent. Do not attempt to bend or straighten reeds. Reed seating surface on reed blocks should be smooth and flat. Reed stop setting should be 6.0-6.2 mm (0.236-0.244 in.) when measured as shown in Fig. T9-8.

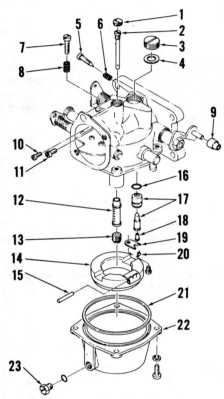

Fig. T9-1—Exploded view of carburetor.

1. Plug
2. Slow jet
3. Plug
4. Gasket
5. Idle mixture screw
6. Spring
7. Idle speed screw
8. Spring
9. Throttle roller
10. Main air jet
11. Slow air jet
12. Main nozzle
13. Main jet
14. Float
15. Float pin
16. Gasket
17. Fuel inlet valve
18. Pin
19. Retainer
20. Clip
21. "O" ring
22. Fuel bowl
23. Drain screw

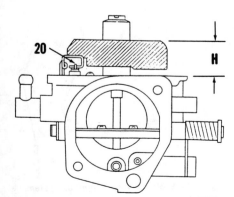

Fig. T9-2—Float height (H) should be 17-19 mm (0.67-0.75 in.). Clip (20) should secure float arm to fuel inlet valve.

Fig. T9-3—Exploded view of speed control linkage.

1. Maximum advance timing screw
2. Idle speed timing screw
3. Magneto control rod
4. Bellcrank
5. Throttle control rod
6. Throttle cam
7. Lower speed control link
8. Speed control rod

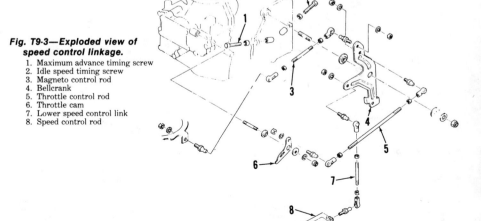

IGNITION

All models are equipped with a breakerless, capacitor discharge ignition system. The ignition exciter and trigger coils as well as the lighting coil are located under the flywheel. The flywheel nut has left-hand threads. Tighten flywheel nut to 118-137 N·m (87-101 ft.-lbs.).

The following checks using an ohmmeter may be made to locate faulty ignition system components. On 35 hp models, note if flywheel is equipped with two or four magnetic poles. Flywheel and stator plate using two poles are designated IIDA DENKI FS417114; flywheel and stator plate using four poles are designated IIDA DENKI FS412114. To check stator plate components, disconnect the three-wire connector between stator plate and ignition module, then connect one ohmmeter lead to stator plate. Connect remaining ohmmeter lead to red stator lead to check exciter coil. Ohmmeter reading should be 264-396 ohms on two-pole units, 240-360 ohms on four-pole units

and 232-348 ohms on 40 hp models. Disconnect ohmmeter lead from red stator lead and connect ohmmeter lead to blue stator lead to check trigger coil. Ohmmeter reading should be 16-24 ohms for either two- or four-pole ignitions and 40 hp models. Disconnect ohmmeter leads from blue stator lead and stator plate. Connect ohmmeter leads to yellow and white stator wires on 35 hp models and two yellow wires on 40 hp models to check lighting coil. Ohmmeter reading should be 0.56-0.84 ohms on two-pole ignitions, 0.8-1.2 ohms on four-pole ignitions and 0.27-0.41 ohms on 40 hp models. To check igntion module, disconnect module wire leads and using an ohmmeter refer to Fig. T9-12 for 35 hp models and Fig. T9-13 for 40 hp

models for a chart of desired ohmmeter readings. Use a tester which uses a testing voltage of three volts or less to prevent possible ignition module damage.

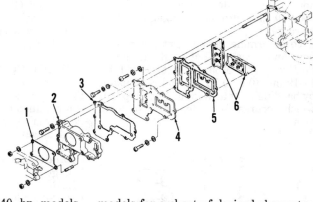

Fig. T9-7—Exploded view of reed valve and intake manifold assembly.
1. Gasket
2. Intake manifold
3. Gasket
4. Plate
5. Gasket
6. Reed valve assy.

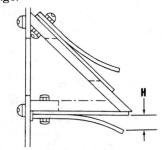

Fig. T9-8—Reed valve stop height (H) should be 6.0-6.2 mm (0.236-0.244 in.).

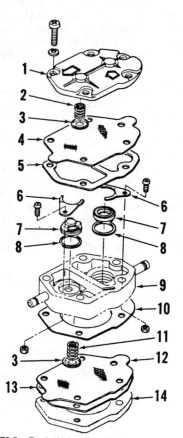

Fig. T9-5—Exploded view of fuel pump used on 35 hp models.

1. Cover	8. Gasket
2. Spring	9. Body
3. Spring seat	10. Gasket
4. Diaphragm	11. Spring
5. Gasket	12. Diaphragm
6. Retainer	13. Gasket
7. Check valve	14. Base

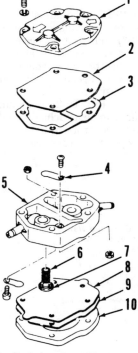

Fig. T9-6—Exploded view of fuel pump used on 40 hp models.

1. Cover	6. Spring
2. Diaphragm	7. Spring seat
3. Gasket	8. Diaphragm
4. Check valve	9. Gasket
5. Body	10. Base

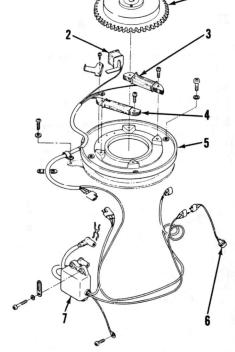

Fig. T9-9—Exploded view of ignition system.

1. Flywheel	
2. Trigger coil	5. Stator plate
3. Lighting coil	6. Ignition switch
4. Exciter coil	7. Ignition module

IGNITION TIMING. To adjust ignition timing, detach lower link (7 – Fig. T9-3) and rotate bellcrank (4) so it is against idle speed ignition timing screw (2). Ignition timing mark (B – Fig. T9-14) should be aligned with mating surface (S) of crankcase and cylinder block. Idle speed ignition timing should be 2° BTDC and is adjusted by turning adjusting screw (2 – Fig. T9-3). Rotate bellcrank so it is against maximum advance ignition timing screw (1). Ignition timing mark (A – Fig. T9-14) should be

Fig. T9-12 – The adjacent chart may be used when checking ignition module on 35 hp models. A low-voltage ohmmeter must be used.

Fig. T9-13 – The adjacent chart may be used when checking ignition module on 40 hp models. A low-voltage ohmmeter must be used.

Connection of Tester Leads and Ident. of CD Module Leads		Tester (+) Lead			
		BROWN	RED	BLUE	BLACK
Tester (-) Lead	BROWN		Infinity	Infinity	Infinity
	RED	Small deflection and soon returns			Zero
	BLUE	160 Ω	Infinity		Infinity
	BLACK	Small deflection and soon returns	Zero	Infinity	

Connection of Tester Leads and Ident. of CD Module Leads		Tester (+) Lead			
		BROWN	RED	BLUE	BLACK
Tester (-) Lead	BROWN		Infinity	Infinity	Infinity
	RED	Small deflection and soon returns			Zero
	BLUE	300 Ω - 1000 Ω	Infinity		Infinity
	BLACK	Small deflection and soon returns	Zero	Infinity	

aligned with mating surface (S) of crankcase and cylinder block. Maximum advance ignition timing should be 25° BTDC and is adjusted by turning adjusting screw (1 – Fig. T9-3). Adjust length of rod (3) if adjustment is not possible using screws (1 and 2). Reconnect lower link (7) and adjust speed control linkage if necessary.

COOLING SYSTEM

THERMOSTAT. A thermostat (27 – Fig. T9-17) is located in the cylinder head. Thermostat should begin opening at 50°-54° C (122°-129° F) and be fully open at 65° C (149° F). Thermostat opening at maximum opening should be 3.0 mm (0.118 in.).

WATER PUMP. A rubber impeller type water pump is mounted on the gearcase between the drive shaft housing and gearcase. The impeller is driven by a Woodruff key in the drive shaft.

Whenever cooling problems are encountered, check water inlet for plugging or partial stoppage and the thermostat for proper operation, then if not corrected, remove gearcase and check condition of the water pump, water passages and sealing surfaces. Note that water inlet covers on some models are marked "R" and "L" as shown in Fig. T9-16 and are interchangeable. Install water inlet cover on starboard side so "R" end is up and install water inlet cover on port side so "L" end is up.

When water pump is disassembled, check condition of impeller (8 – Fig. T9-15), liner (7) and plate (9). When installing liner in pump housing note that

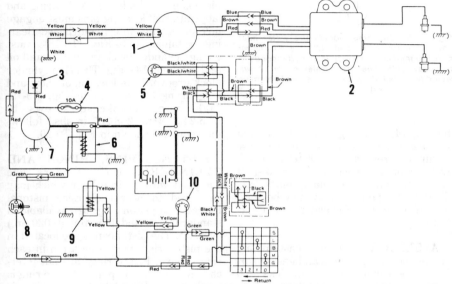

Fig. T9-10 – Typical wiring diagram for 35 hp models.

1. Stator plate
2. Ignition module
3. Rectifier
4. Fuse
5. Ignition switch
6. Starter solenoid
7. Starter motor
8. Neutral switch
9. Choke solenoid
10. Choke solenoid switch

Fig. T9-11 – Typical wiring diagram for 40 hp models.

1. Safety switch
2. Starter motor
3. Starter solenoid
4. Choke solenoid
5. Neutral switch
6. Stop switch
7. Battery
8. Rectifier
9. Flywheel magneto
10. CD module
11. Spark plugs
12. Tachometer
B. Black
G. Green
R. Red
W. White
Y. Yellow
Bl. Blue
Br. Brown
B/W. Black with white tracer

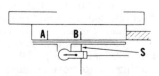

Fig. T9-14 – View showing location of full throttle timing mark (A) and idle speed timing mark (B). Refer to text for ignition timing adjustment.

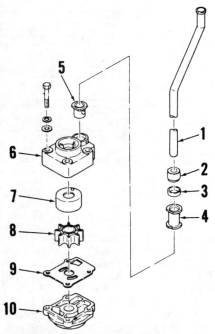

Fig. T9-15—Exploded view of water pump. Refer also to Fig. T9-25.

1. Water tube	6. Pump housing
2. Seal	7. Liner
3. Set ring	8. Impeller
4. Grommet	9. Plate
5. Grommet	10. Pump base

locating knob on upper end of liner must index with a corresponding indentation in housing. Turn drive shaft clockwise (viewed from top) while placing pump housing over impeller. Avoid turning drive shaft in opposite direction when water pump is assembled. Tighten pump housing screws in a crossing pattern.

POWER HEAD

REMOVE AND REINSTALL. To remove power head, remove upper motor cover and disconnect ignition wires and fuel hoses. Detach speed control link (7 – Fig. T9-3), starter interlock link (13 – Fig. T9-24) and choke rod. Unscrew engine mounting screws and lift power head off drive shaft housing.

To install power head, reverse removal procedure. Apply water resistant grease to ends of crankshaft and drive shaft.

DISASSEMBLY. To disassemble power head, disconnect fuel lines and remove carburetor, fuel filter and fuel pump. Remove electric starter, if so equipped. Remove manual starter, disconnect ignition wires and remove ignition module. Detach speed control linkage. Remove flywheel, stator plate assembly, retainer (1 – Fig. T9-17) and magneto ring (3). Remove exhaust cover (29) and cylinder head. Remove intake manifold and reed valve. Remove oil seal

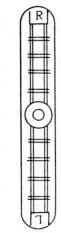

Fig. T9-16—On some models the water inlet cover is marked "R" and "L" at ends. Install cover so marked end which is up corresponds to gearcase side. The water inlet cover shown would be installed on starboard side of gearcase with "R" end up.

housing (4) retaining screws but do not remove seal housing. Remove crankcase retaining screws and separate crankcase from cylinder block. Lift crankshaft assembly out of cylinder block. Individual components may now be serviced as outlined in following service sections.

ASSEMBLY. Before reassembling engine, be sure all joints and gasket surfaces are clean, free from nicks and burrs and hardened cement or carbon.

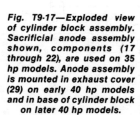

Fig. T9-17—Exploded view of cylinder block assembly. Sacrificial anode assembly shown, components (17 through 22), are used on 35 hp models. Anode assembly is mounted in exhaust cover (29) on early 40 hp models and in base of cylinder block on later 40 hp models.

1. Retainer
2. Seal ring
3. Magneto ring
4. Seal housing
5. Seal
6. "O" ring
7. Bleeder hose
8. Check valve
9. Fitting
10. Main bearing locating pin
11. Crankcase
12. Check valve
13. Dowel pin
14. Retainer
15. Seal
16. Cylinder block
17. Anode cover
18. Stud
19. "O" ring
20. Gasket
21. Anode
22. Nylon nut
23. Gasket
24. Cylinder head
25. Cover
26. Gasket
27. Thermostat
28. Gasket
29. Exhaust cover

Mating surfaces may be lapped to remove high spots or nicks, however, only a minimum amount of metal should be removed.

All friction surfaces and bearings should be thoroughly lubricated with engine oil during reassembly. Coat mating surfaces with a nonhardening gasket sealer.

Note the following points when assembling power head: Install seal housing (4 – Fig. T9-17) on crankshaft prior to installation of crankshaft assembly. Be sure piston rings properly mate with piston ring groove pins when inserting pistons into cylinder block. Bearing and labyrinth seal locating pins must engage hole or notches in cylinder block. Bearing retainer (34 – Fig. T9-18) must engage cylinder block groove. Install oil seal retainer (14 – Fig. T9-17) in cylinder block groove. Note location of short and long crankcase screws in Fig. T9-19. Tighten all crankcase screws to 23.5-24.5 N·m (208-225 in.-lbs.) following sequence shown in Fig. T9-20.

PISTONS, PINS, RINGS AND CYLINDERS. The cylinders are equipped with an iron liner which may be bored to accept oversize pistons. Pistons and piston rings are available in standard size and 0.5 mm (0.020 in.) oversize. The piston rings are located in the piston ring groove by a pin in each ring groove. Piston rings are not interchangeable. On 35 hp models, top ring is marked "T.TP" while bottom ring is

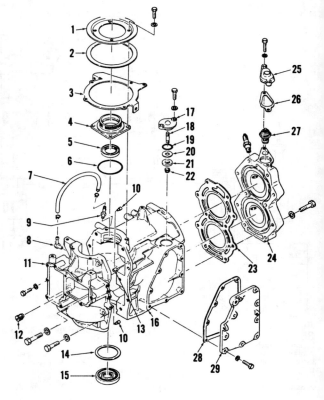

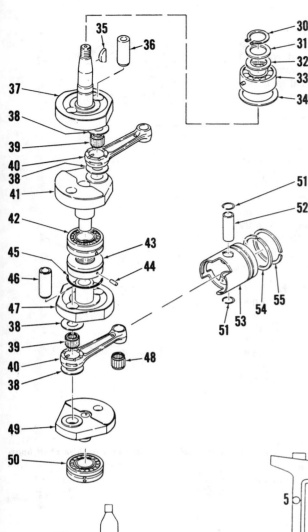

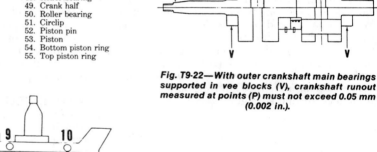

Fig. T9-18—Exploded view of crankshaft and piston assembly.

30. Snap ring
31. Washer
32. Shim
33. Ball bearing
34. Retainer
35. Woodruff key
36. Crankpin
37. Crank half
38. Thrust washer
39. Roller bearing
40. Connecting rod
41. Crank half
42. Roller bearing
43. Labyrinth seal
44. Locating pin
45. "O" ring
46. Crankpin
47. Crank half
48. Roller bearing
49. Crank half
50. Roller bearing
51. Circlip
52. Piston pin
53. Piston
54. Bottom piston ring
55. Top piston ring

Fig. T9-21—To determine connecting rod big end wear, move rod small end side to side as shown. Movement (A) should be 1.0 mm (0.040 in.) with a maximum allowable limit of 2.0 mm (0.079 in.).

Fig. T9-22—With outer crankshaft main bearings supported in vee blocks (V), crankshaft runout measured at points (P) must not exceed 0.05 mm (0.002 in.).

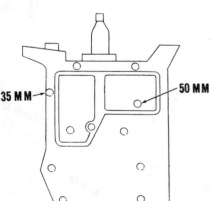

Fig. T9-19—View showing location of short (35 mm) and long (50 mm) crankcase screws.

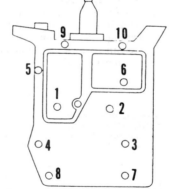

Fig. T9-20—Tighten crankcase screws to 23.5-24.5 N·m (208-225 in.-lbs.) following sequence shown.

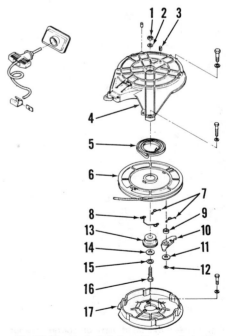

Fig. T9-23—Exploded view of manual starter.

1. Nut
2. Washer
3. Pin
4. Starter housing
5. Rewind spring
6. Rope pulley
7. Spring links
8. Spring
9. Bushing
10. Pawl
11. Washer
12. "E" ring
13. Shaft
14. Washer
15. Lockwasher
16. Screw
17. Starter cup

marked "T." Install piston ring so mark is towards piston crown. On 40 hp models, top piston ring is semi-keystone shaped.

The piston pin is retained by circlips (51 – Fig. T9-18) which should be renewed if removed. The piston pin rides in a roller bearing in rod small end. On 35 hp models, install piston so arrow on piston crown will point towards exhaust port. On 40 hp models, install piston so "UP" stamped on piston crown will face towards flywheel end of crankshaft.

CRANKSHAFT AND CONNECTING RODS. Crankshaft, connecting rods, crankpins and bearings are assembled as a pressed-together unit. Disassembly and assembly of crankshaft should be performed by a shop experienced in repair of this type crankshaft. Individual crankshaft components are available.

Determine rod bearing wear by moving small rod end from side-to-side as shown in Fig. T9-21. Normal side to side movement is 1.0 mm (0.040 in.) while maximum allowable limit is 2.0 mm (0.079 in.). Connecting rod side clearance should be 0.28-0.65 mm (0.011-0.026 in.).

Check crankshaft runout by supporting outer main bearings in vee blocks. Maximum allowable crankshaft runout measured at points (P – Fig. T9-22) is 0.05 mm (0.002 in.).

MANUAL STARTER

Refer to Fig. T9-23 for an exploded view of manual starter. The starter may be disassembled after removing motor cover, detaching starter lockout linkage and removing starter from power head. Remove rope handle and allow rope to wind into starter. Remove screw (16) and shaft (13), then carefully lift pulley (6) out of housing while being careful not to disturb rewind spring (5). If rewind spring must be removed care should be used not to allow spring to uncoil uncontrolled. Inspect pawl (10) for wear and freedom of movement. Renew and grease pawl if required.

When assembling starter, wind rewind spring in housing in a counterclockwise direction from outer end. Wind rope around rope pulley in a counterclockwise direction as viewed with pulley in housing. Pawl spring (8) must engage groove in shaft (13). Rotate pulley three turns counterclockwise before passing rope through rope outlet to preload rewind spring.

A starter lockout mechanism (Fig. T9-24) is used to prevent starter usage when motor is in forward or reverse gear. Adjust length of lockout rod (13) by turning rod end so starter will operate with motor in neutral gear but not in forward or reverse gear.

ELECTRIC STARTER

Some models are equipped with an electric starter. Models equipped with an electric starter are also equipped with a battery charging system. Refer to Fig. T9-10 or T9-11) for a wiring diagram. Starter drive pinion and on some models, brush assembly, are only components serviceable on starter.

LOWER UNIT

PROPELLER AND DRIVE HUB. The propeller is equipped with a splined cushion type hub to protect the lower unit. Propeller hub is not serviceable. Rotation of the three-blade propeller is clockwise. Various propellers are available to obtain best performance depending on outboard usage. Desired operating range at maximum engine speed is 5200-5900 rpm.

R&R AND OVERHAUL. To remove gearcase, disconnect shift rod coupler (20 – Fig. T9-25) from lower shift rod (21) by driving out lower pin (19). Unscrew six cap screws securing gearcase to drive shaft housing and remove

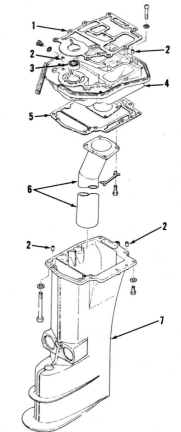

Fig. T9-26—Exploded view of drive shaft housing.

1. Gasket
2. Dowel pin
3. Seal
4. Base
5. Gasket
6. Exhaust tube
7. Drive shaft housing

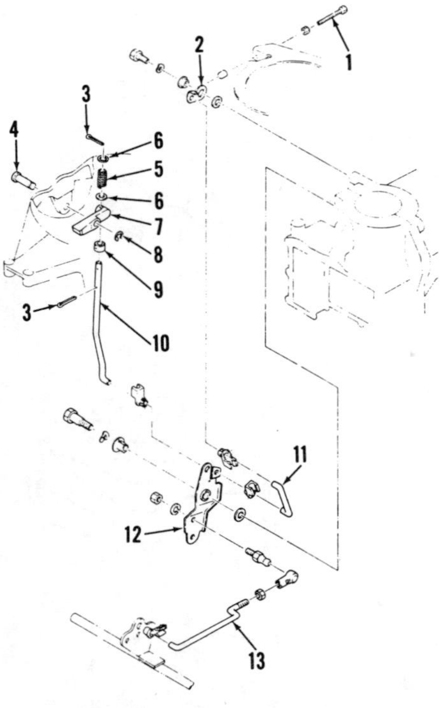

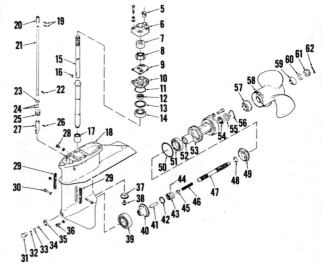

Fig. T9-25—Exploded view of gearcase. Components (31 through 35) are not used on 40 hp models.

5. Grommet
6. Water pump housing
7. Liner
8. Impeller
9. Plate
10. Pump base
11. "O" ring
12. Seal
13. Shim
14. Bearing
15. Drive shaft
16. Woodruff key
17. Bearing
18. Gearcase
19. Pin
20. Coupler
21. Lower shift rod
22. Pin
23. "O" ring
24. "O" ring
25. Bushing
26. Pin
27. Shift cam
28. Vent plug
29. Water inlet
30. Shift bushing retainer screw
31. Detent plug
32. Spring
33. Spacer
34. Detent ball
35. Seal
36. Fill plug
37. Pinion gear
38. Screw
39. Bearing
40. Forward gear
41. Shift plunger
42. Retainer

43. Clutch
44. Pin
45. Spring guide
46. Spring
47. Propeller shaft
48. Thrust washer
49. Reverse gear
50. "O" ring
51. Bearing
52. Bearing

53. Bearing housing
54. Seal
55. Washer
56. Clip
57. Spacer
58. Propeller
59. Spacer
60. Washer
61. Nut
62. Cotter pin

Fig. T9-24— Exploded view of starter lockout linkage. A cap nut is used in place of cotter pin (3) on later 40 hp models.

1. Reverse speed screw
2. Stop
3. Cotter pin
4. Pin
5. Spring
6. Washer
7. Pawl
8. "E" ring
9. Collar
10. Rod
11. Link
12. Bellcrank
13. Rod

gearcase. Remove propeller then drain gearcase lubricant. Remove water pump assembly. Remove bearing housing (53) and withdraw propeller shaft assembly. Drive out pin (44) to separate clutch (43), spring guide (45) and spring (46) from propeller shaft. Unscrew pinion gear retaining screw (38) and pull drive shaft (15) from gearcase. Pinion gear (37) and forward gear (40) with bearing may now be removed. Use a suitable puller and remove roller bearing (17) by pulling towards gearcase top. Unscrew shift bushing retaining screw (30) and detent assembly (31 through 34), on models so equipped, and remove shift components (21 through 27) from gearcase.

Inspect components for excessive wear and damage. Inner roller bearings in forward and reverse gears (40 and 49) are available only as a unit with gear. Clutch spring (46) length should be 90 mm (3.54 in.); renew spring if length is less than 88 mm (3.46 in.). Clutch spring pressure should be 48.02 newtons (10.79 lbs.) at 71.5 mm (2.81 in.) on 35 hp models and 51 newtons (11.46 lbs.) at 71.5 mm (2.81 in.) on 40 hp models. Propeller shaft diameter at forward gear bearing contact surfaces should be 19.987-20.000 mm (0.7868-0.7874 in.) with a wear limit of 19.975 mm (0.7864 in.). Propeller shaft diameter at contact surface for bearing housing roller bearing (52) should be 21.987-22.000 mm (0.8656-0.8661 in.) with a wear limit of 21.975 mm (0.8651 in.). Propeller shaft runout must be less than 0.2 mm (0.0079 in.). Drive shaft diameter at contact surface for roller bearing (17) should be 21.987-22.000 mm (0.8656-0.8661 in.) with a wear limit of 21.975 mm (0.8651 in.). Drive shaft runout must be less than 0.5 mm (0.0197 in.).

To reassemble gearcase, reverse disassembly procedure while noting the following points: Lubricate all "O" rings and seals prior to installation. Backlash between pinion gear and forward or reverse gear should be 0.15-0.25 mm (0.006-0.010 in.) and is adjusted by varying thickness of shim (13). Apply Loctite during final assembly and tighten pinion gear retaining screw (38) to 23.5-25.4 N·m (208-225 in.-lbs.). Install clutch (43) so end closest to pin (44) groove is towards forward gear (40).

TOHATSU 50, 55, 60 AND 70 HP

CONDENSED SERVICE DATA

NOTE: Metric fasteners are used throughout outboard motor.

TUNE-UP

Hp/rpm	50/4500-5500
	55/4500-5500
	60/4500-5500
	70/5000-5500

Bore:
50 and 55 HP	81 mm
	(3.19 in.)
60 and 70 Hp	86 mm
	(3.38 in.)
Stroke	72.7 mm
	(2.86 in.)
Number of Cylinders	2

Displacement:
50 and 55 Hp	749 cc
	(45.7 cu. in.)
60 and 70 Hp	845 cc
	(51.6 cu. in.)
Spark Plug	NGK B8HS-10
Electrode Gap	1.0 mm
	(0.039 in.)
Ignition Type	Breakerless CD
Ignition Timing	See Text
Fuel:Oil Ratio	50:1

SIZES—CLEARANCES

Piston Ring End Gap	0.25-0.4 mm
	(0.010-0.016 in.)

Piston Ring Side Clearance:
Top Ring	Semi-Keystone

Piston Ring Side Clearance:
Bottom Ring	0.04-0.08 mm
	(0.0015-0.0031 in.)

SIZES—CLEARANCES CONT.

Piston Clearance	0.08-0.13 mm
	(0.0031-0.0051 in.)
Piston Pin Clearance In Piston	Interference-0.010 mm
	(Interference-0.0004 in.)
Crankshaft Runout	0.05 mm
	(0.002 in.)

TIGHTENING TORQUES

Crankcase	23.5-25.4 N·m
	(208-225 in.-lbs.)
Cylinder Head	32.4-37.2 N·m
	(287-329 in.-lbs.)
Flywheel Nut	137-157 N·m
	(101-116 ft.-lbs.)
Pinion Gear Nut	59 N·m
	(43 ft.-lbs.)
Spark Plug	24.5-29.4 N·m
	(217-260 in.-lbs.)

Standard Screws:
No. 3	0.6-0.8 N·m
	(5-7 in.-lbs.)
No. 4	1.3-1.8 N·m
	(11-15 in.-lbs.)
No. 5	2.6-3.5 N·m
	(23-31 in.-lbs.)
No. 6	4.6-6.3 N·m
	(41-55 in.-lbs.)
No. 8	11.2-15.1 N·m
	(99-133 in.-lbs.)
No. 10	22.6-30.6 N·m
	(200-270 in.-lbs.)

LUBRICATION

The power head is lubricated by oil mixed with the fuel. Recommended oil is Tohatsu outboard motor oil mixed at a fuel:oil ratio of 50:1. During engine break-in, the fuel:oil ratio should be 20:1 for a period of 10 operating hours.

Lower unit gears and bearings are lubricated by oil contained in the gearcase. Recommended oil is Tohatsu gear oil or an SAE 80 gear oil. Oil should be changed after initial 10 hours of operation and every 200 hours of operation thereafter. Gearcase oil capacity is approximately 920 mL (31.1 oz.).

FUEL SYSTEM

CARBURETOR. The power head is equipped with two carburetors that are not interchangeable. Refer to Fig. T10-1 for an exploded view of carburetor. Before adjusting idle speed, back out idle speed screw (1) and note if throttle plates for both carburetors are closed. If not, adjust throttle link between carburetors. Check choke plate movement of both carburetors and if not synchronized, adjust length of link between choke levers of carburetors. Adjust idle mixture and idle speed screws after motor temperature has normalized.

Adjust float level so float is parallel to gasket surface with carburetor inverted and fuel bowl removed. Note clip (11) that secures inlet valve to float.

Slow speed fuel mixture is metered by slow speed jet (7). High speed fuel mixture is metered by main jet (6).

SPEED CONTROL LINKAGE. Carburetor throttle opening and ignition timing are synchronized by the speed control linkage so the carburetors are opened as the ignition timing is advanced.

Before adjusting carburetor throttle link, refer to IGNITION TIMING section and be sure ignition timing is set correctly. Adjust length of throttle link (5 – Fig. T10-2) by turning ends so carburetors are fully open when bellcrank (8) contacts maximum advance screw (7), and when throttle roller just con-

tacts throttle cam (4) as bellcrank contacts idle speed timing screw (6).

FUEL PUMP. A diaphragm type fuel pump is mounted on the port side of the power head. The fuel pump is actuated by crankcase pulsations. Refer to Fig. T10-3 for an exploded view of fuel pump used on early models and Fig. T10-4 for an exploded view of fuel pump used on later models.

REED VALVES. Two vee-type reed valve assemblies (one per cylinder) are located between the intake manifold and crankcase. Remove intake manifold for access to reed valve assemblies. Refer to Fig. T10-5 for an exploded view of reed valves and related components.

Renew reeds if petals are broken, cracked, warped or bent. Do not attempt to bend or straighten reed petals. Reed seating surface on reed blocks should be smooth and flat. Reed stop opening (A—Fig. T10-6) should be 9 mm (0.35 in.) on early 55 hp models and 10.0-10.2 mm (0.39-0.40 in.) on late 55 hp and all other models.

IGNITION

All models are equipped with a breakerless, capacitor discharge ignition system. The ignition exciter and trigger coils as well as the battery charging coil

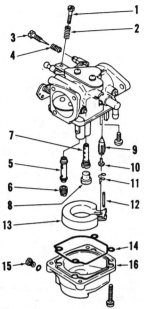

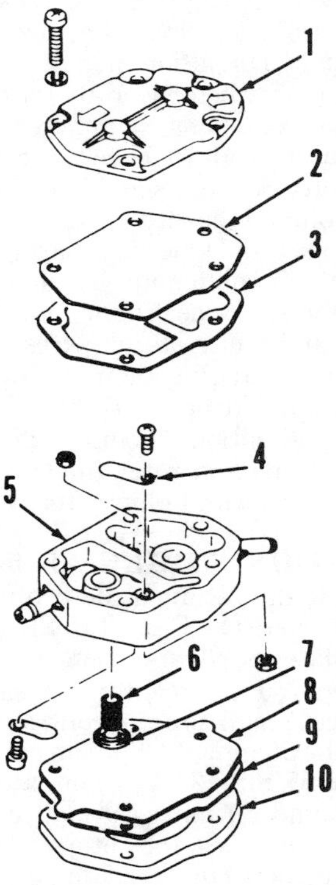

Fig. T10-1—Exploded view of carburetor.

1. Idle speed screw
2. Spring
3. Idle mixture screw
4. Spring
5. Main nozzle
6. Main jet
7. Slow jet
8. Rubber cap
9. Fuel inlet valve
10. Pin
11. Clip
12. Float pin
13. Float
14. Gasket
15. Drain plug
16. Fuel bowl

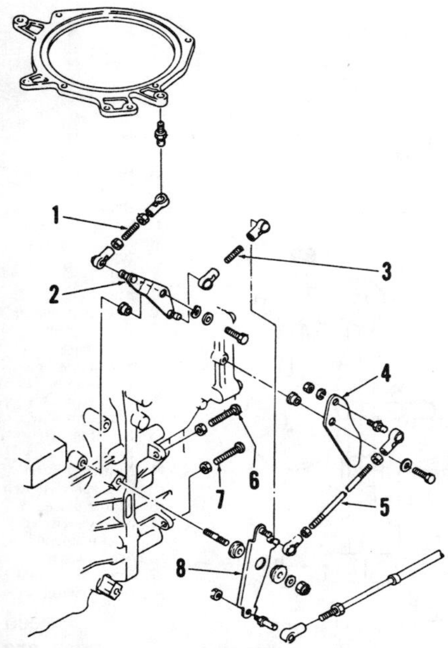

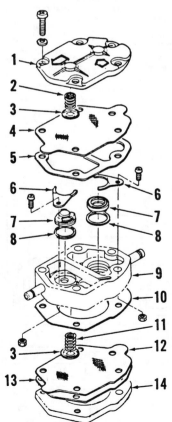

Fig. T10-3—Exploded view of fuel pump.

1. Cover
2. Spring
3. Spring seat
4. Diaphragm
5. Gasket
6. Retainer
7. Check valve
8. Gasket
9. Body
10. Gasket
11. Spring
12. Diaphragm
13. Gasket
14. Base

Fig. T10-2—View of speed control linkage.

1. Magneto control rod
2. Lever
3. Intermediate rod
4. Throttle cam
5. Throttle link
6. Idle speed timing screw
7. Maximum advance ignition timing screw
8. Bellcrank

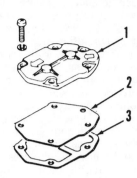

Fig. T10-4—Exploded view of fuel pump used on late models.

1. Cover
2. Diaphragm
3. Gasket
4. Check valve
5. Body
6. Spring
7. Spring seat
8. Diaphragm
9. Gasket
10. Base

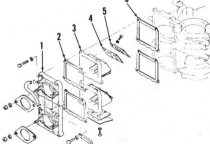

Fig. T10-5—Exploded view of intake manifold and reed valve assembly.

1. Intake manifold
2. Gasket
3. Reed body
4. Reed petals
5. Reed stop
6. Gasket

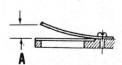

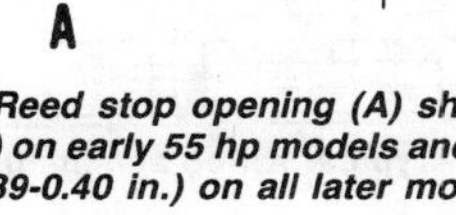

Fig. T10-6—Reed stop opening (A) should be 9 mm (0.35 in.) on early 55 hp models and 10.0-10.2 mm (0.39-0.40 in.) on all later models.

are located under the flywheel. An ignition cutout switch (9 – Fig. T10-9) is used to prevent engine overspeeding. Tighten flywheel nut to 137-157 N·m (101-116 ft.-lbs.).

The following checks using an ohmmeter can be made to locate faulty ignition system components. Disconnect three-wire connector between stator plate and CD ignition module, then connect one ohmmeter lead to stator plate. Connect remaining ohmmeter lead to red stator lead to check exciter coil. Ohmmeter reading should be 290 ohms. With ohmmeter leads connected to stator plate and blue stator lead to check trigger coil, ohmmeter reading should be 20 ohms. Connect ohmmeter leads to yellow and white stator wires to check battery charging coil. Ohmmeter reading should be 0.34 ohm. To check the CD ignition module, disconnect module leads and refer to chart in Fig. T10-10 for desired ohmmeter readings.

IGNITION TIMING. Before adjusting ignition timing, detach magneto control rod (1 – Fig. T10-2) and intermediate rod (3) and measure distance between rod end centers of each rod. Distance for magneto control rod (1) should be 55 mm (2.16 in.) on early 55 hp models, 57 mm (2.24 in.) on later 55 hp models and 50 mm (1.97 in.) on 70 hp models. Distance for intermediate rod (3) should be 40 mm (1.57 in.) on early 55 hp models, 43 mm (1.69 in.) on later 55

hp models and 45 mm (1.77 in.) on 70 hp models. Adjust length by turning rod ends, then reattach both rods.

To adjust ignition timing, rotate bellcrank (8) so it contacts idle speed igni-

tion timing screw (6). Ignition timing should be 10 degrees ATDC on early 55 hp models, TDC on later 55 and early 70 hp models, 6 degrees ATDC on 50 and 60 and late 70 hp models as indicated

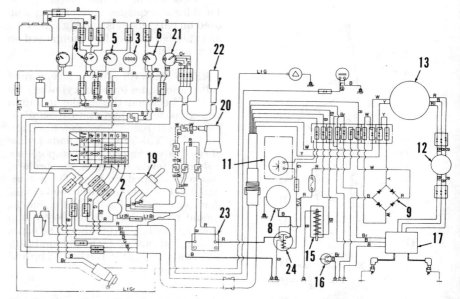

Fig. T10-8—Typical wiring schematic for 55 hp models with serial number 11804 and later, and 70 hp models with serial number 10911 and later. Models 50 and 60 hp are similar.

B. Black	Lt. G. Light green	6. Tachometer	17. CDI module
G. Green	Lt. Bl. Light blue	8. Starter motor	19. Power tilt & trim switch
P. Pink	Y/G. Yellow with green tracer	9. Rectifier	20. Power tilt & trim motor
R. Red		11. Neutral switch	
W. White	2. Overheat buzzer	12. Overspeed switch	21. Trimmeter
Y. Yellow	3. Hour meter	13. Stator plate	22. Trim sensor
Bl. Blue	4. Fuel gage	15. Choke solenoid	23. Battery
Br. Brown	5. Speedometer	16. Stop switch	24. Starter solenoid
Or. Orange			

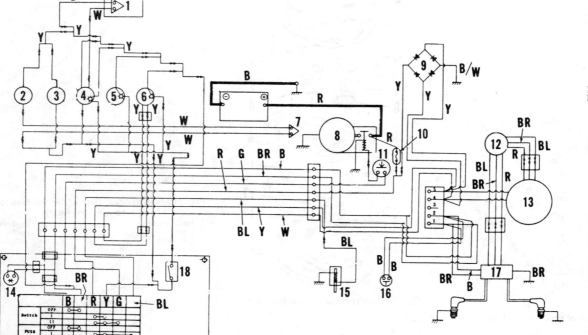

Fig. T10-7—Typical wiring schematic for 55 hp models prior to engine number 11804 and 70 hp models prior to engine number 10911.

B. Black
BL. Blue
BR. Brown
G. Green
R. Red
W. White
Y. Yellow
1. Fuel Sensor
2. Overheat buzzer
3. Hour meter
4. Fuel gage
5. Speedometer
6. Tachometer
7. Starter sensor
8. Starter motor
9. Rectifier
10. Fuse
11. Neutral switch
12. Overspeed switch
13. Stator plate
14. Safety switch
15. Choke solenoid
16. Stop switch
17. Ignition module
18. Lamp switch

by timing mark on stator plate aligned with crankcase and cylinder block mating surface. Turn idle ignition timing screw (6) to adjust idle speed timing. Rotate bellcrank so it contacts maximum advance timing screw (7). Ignition timing should be 25 degrees BTDC on 50 and 55 hp models and 22.5 degrees BTDC on 60 and 70 hp models.

COOLING SYSTEM

THERMOSTAT. A thermostat (3–Fig. T10-13) is located in the cylinder head. Thermostat should begin opening at 60° C (140° F).

WATER PUMP. A rubber impeller type water pump is mounted on the upper surface of the gearcase. The impeller is driven by a Woodruff key in the drive shaft.

Whenever cooling problems are encountered, check water inlet for plugging or partial stoppage and the thermostat for proper operation, then if not corrected, remove gearcase and check condition of the water pump, water passages and sealing surfaces. Note that water inlet covers on some models are marked "R" and "L" as shown in Fig. T10-11 and are interchangeable. Install water inlet cover on starboard side so "R" end is up and install water inlet cover on port side so "L" end is up.

When water pump is disassembled, check condition of impeller (8–Fig. T10-12), liner (7) and plate (9). When installing liner in pump housing note that locating knob on upper end of liner must index with a corresponding indentation in housing. Turn drive shaft clockwise (viewed from top) while placing pump housing over impeller. Avoid turning drive shaft in opposite direction after pump is assembled. Tighten pump housing screws in a crossing pattern.

POWER HEAD

REMOVE AND REINSTALL. To remove power head, remove upper motor cover and disconnect fuel hose and interfering wires. Detach remote control wires. Unscrew engine mounting screws and lift power head off drive shaft housing.

To install power head, reverse removal procedure. Apply water resistant grease to ends of crankshaft and drive shaft. Apply sealer to engine base gasket except in shaded area shown in Fig. T10-15.

DISASSEMBLY. To disassemble power head, disconnect fuel hoses and remove air cleaner, carburetors, fuel filter and fuel pump. Disconnect wire leads then remove electric starter and electrical components. Remove flywheel and stator plate (6–Fig. T10-9). Detach speed control linkage. Remove retainer (7) and magneto ring (8). Remove exhaust cover (16–Fig. T10-13), cylinder head cover (14) and cylinder head (12). Remove intake manifold and reed valve assembly. Remove oil seal housing (24) retaining screws but do not remove housing. Unscrew crankcase retaining screws and separate crankcase from cylinder block. Lift crankshaft assembly out of cylinder block. Individual components are now accessible for service as outlined in following service sections.

ASSEMBLY. Before reassembling engine, be sure all joints and gasket surfaces are clean, free from nicks and burrs and hardened cement or carbon. Mating surfaces may be lapped to remove high spots or nicks, however, only

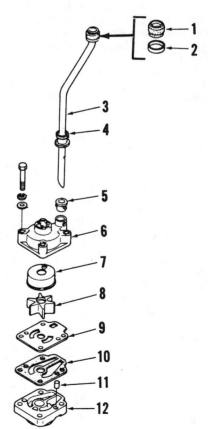

Fig. T10-12—Exploded view of water pump. Refer also to Fig. T10-19.

1. Grommet	7. Liner
2. Retainer	8. Impeller
3. Water tube	9. Plate
4. Grommet	10. Gasket
5. Seal	11. Dowel pin
6. Pump housing	12. Pump base

Fig. T10-9—Exploded view of ignition components.

1. Rope pulley	8. Magneto control ring
2. Flywheel	9. Overspeed switch
3. Exciter coil	10. Cover
4. Trigger coil	11. Terminal block
5. Battery charging coil	12. Ignition module
6. Stator plate	13. Rectifier
7. Retainer	

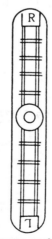

Fig. T10-11—On some models, the water inlet cover is marked "R" and "L" at ends. Install cover so marked end which is up corresponds to gearcase side. The water inlet cover shown would be installed on starboard side of gearcase with "R" end up.

Fig. T10-10—An ohmmeter should indicate the readings in the adjacent chart when testing the CD ignition module.

Connection of Tester Leads and Ident. of CD Module Leads		Tester (+) Lead			
		BROWN	RED	BLUE	BLACK
Tester (-) Lead	BROWN		Infinity	Infinity	Infinity
	RED	Small deflection and soon returns			Zero
	BLUE	300Ω - 1000Ω	Infinity		Infinity
	BLACK	Small deflection and soon returns	Zero	Infinity	

a minimum amount of metal should be removed.

All friction surfaces and bearings should be thoroughly lubricated with engine oil during reassembly. Coat mating surfaces with a nonhardening gasket sealer.

Note the following points when assembling power head: Be sure piston rings properly mate with piston ring groove pins when inserting pistons into cylinder block. Labyrinth seal and bearings must engage locating pins in cylinder block. Bearing retaining rings (40 – Fig. T10-14) must engage grooves in cylinder block and crankcase. Install seal (22 – Fig. T10-13) in seal housing (24) so lip will point away from engine and install seal (21) so lip will point towards engine. Tighten crankcase screws to 23.5-25.4 N·m (208-225 in.-lbs.) following sequence shown in Fig. T10-16.

PISTON, PIN, RINGS AND CYLINDER. The cylinders are equipped with an iron liner which may be bored to accept oversize pistons. Piston and piston rings are available in standard size and 0.5 mm (0.020 in.) oversize.

Piston rings are located in the piston ring groove by a pin in each ring groove. Piston rings are not interchangeable. The top piston ring is a semi-keystone type and must be installed as shown in Fig. T10-17.

The piston pin is retained by circlips (47 – Fig. T10-14) which should be renewed if removed. The piston pin rides in a roller bearing in rod small end. Install piston so "UP" mark is towards flywheel.

CRANKSHAFT AND CONNECTING ROD. Crankshaft, connecting rods, crankpins and bearings are assembled as a pressed-together unit. Disassembly and assembly of crankshaft should be performed by a shop experienced in repair of this type crankshaft. Individual crankshaft components are available. Refer to Fig. T10-14 for an exploded view of crankshaft assembly.

BREATHER VALVES. Each cylinder is equipped with a breather valve (5 – Fig. T10-13) to scavenge liquid fuel/oil and transfer it to the opposite cylinder. The breather valve for the upper cylinder is connected by a hose to a fitting for the lower cylinder, and vice versa. When installing flapper valve, install valve so flap is pointing down as shown in Fig. T10-18.

ELECTRIC STARTER

All models are equipped with an electric starter. Starter brushes, drive and relay are available. Refer to Fig. T10-7 or Fig. T10-8 for a wiring diagram.

LOWER UNIT

PROPELLER AND DRIVE HUB. The propeller is equipped with a cushion type hub to protect the lower unit. Pro-

peller hub is not available separately from propeller. Rotation of the three-blade propeller is clockwise. Various propellers are available to obtain best performance depending on outboard usage. Desired operating range at maximum engine speed is 4500-5500 rpm for 55 hp models and 5000-5500 rpm for 70 hp models.

R&R AND OVERHAUL. To remove gearcase, disconnect shift rod coupler (54 – Fig. T10-19) from lower shift rod (61) by driving out lower pin (55). Unscrew six cap screws securing gearcase to drive shaft housing and remove gearcase. Remove propeller then drain gearcase lubricant. Remove water pump

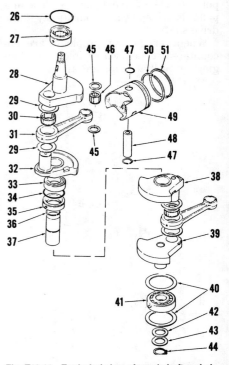

Fig. T10-14—Exploded view of crankshaft and piston assembly. Later models are equipped with three piston rings.

27. Roller bearing	39. Crank half
28. Crank half	40. Retainer
29. Thrust washer	41. Ball bearing
30. Roller bearing	42. Shim
31. Connecting rod	43. Washer
32. Crank half	44. Snap ring
33. Roller bearing	45. Thrust washer
34. "O" ring	46. Roller bearing
35. Labyrinth seal	47. Circlip
36. Circlip	48. Piston pin
37. Center crankshaft journal	49. Piston
	50. Piston ring
38. Crank half	51. Piston ring

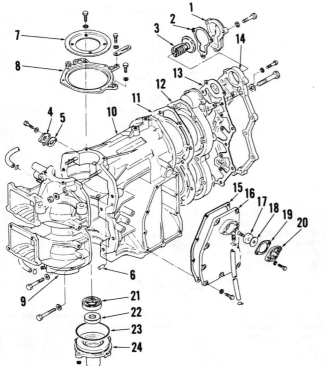

Fig. T10-13—Exploded view of crankcase.

1. Thermostat cover
2. Gasket
3. Thermostat
4. Fitting
5. Breather valve
6. Dowel pin
7. Retainer
8. Magneto control ring
9. Crankcase
10. Cylinder block
11. Gasket
12. Cylinder head
13. Gasket
14. Cover
15. Gasket
16. Exhaust cover
17. Anode
18. Gasket
19. Gasket
20. Cover
21. Seal
22. Seal
23. "O" ring
24. Seal housing

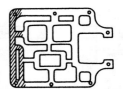

Fig. T10-15 — Do not apply sealer to shaded area of engine base gasket.

assembly. Unscrew and remove cap (46). Remove snap ring (45) then use a suitable puller to remove bearing housing (40). Withdraw propeller shaft assembly. Remove retainer spring (33) and drive out pin (31) to separate shift plunger (29), spring (30) and clutch (32) from propeller shaft. Unscrew pinion gear retaining nut (24) and pull drive shaft (17) from gearcase. Pinion gear (23) and forward gear (28) with bearing may now be removed from gearcase. If necessary, use a suitable puller to extract bearing (26) cup from gearcase while being careful not to lose or damage shims (25). Use a suitable puller and remove roller bearing (20). Remove retainer (56) and remove shift components (57 through 63).

Inspect components for excessive wear and damage. To reassemble gearcase, reverse disassembly procedure while noting the following points: Lubricate all "O" rings and seals prior to installation. Install spring (19) with large end towards bearing (20). Adjust gear mesh position using shims (15). Tohatsu tool number 353-72250-0 is available to determine gear mesh position. When installing pinion gear nut for final assembly, apply Three Bond 1303B or an equivalent to threads and tighten nut to 59 N·m (43 ft.-lbs.). Backlash between pinion gear and forward or reverse gear should be 0.08-0.26 mm (0.003-0.010 in.) and is adjusted by varying thickness of shims (25 and 37). Tohatsu tool number 353-72255-0 is available to determine gear backlash. Install clutch (32) so grooved end is nearer forward gear. Install seal (42) so open side is towards bearing housing (40). Install seal (14) so open side is away from pump base (12).

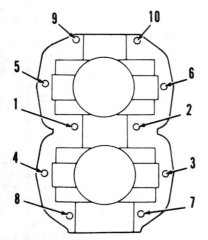

Fig. T10-16-Tighten crankcase screws to 23.5-25.4 N·m (208-225 in.-lbs.) following sequence shown.

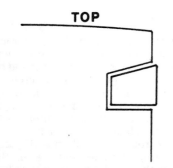

Fig. T10-17—Install top piston ring so beveled side is toward top of piston.

Fig. T10-18—Install breather valve (5—Fig. T10-13) so flap (F) points down.

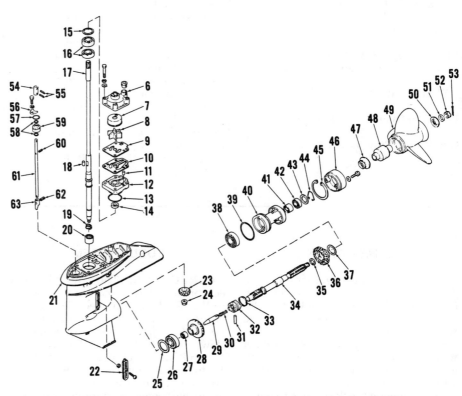

Fig. T10-19—Exploded view of gearcase. On later models, components (43 and 44) are not used. A clutch ball and spring holder are located between shift plunger (29) and spring (30).

6. Water pump housing	21. Gearcase	36. Reverse gear	
7. Liner	22. Water inlet cover	37. Shim	
8. Impeller	23. Pinion gear	38. Ball bearing	51. Washer
9. Plate	24. Nut	39. "O" ring	52. Nut
10. Gasket	25. Shim	40. Bearing housing	53. Cotter pin
11. Dowel pin	26. Taper roller bearing	41. Roller bearing	54. Coupler
12. Pump base	27. Roller bearing	42. Seal	55. Pin
13. "O" ring	28. Forward gear	43. Washer	56. Retainer
14. Seal	29. Shift plunger	44. Retainer	57. "O" ring
15. Shim	30. Spring	45. Snap ring	58. "O" ring
16. Ball bearings	31. Pin	46. Cap	59. Bushing
17. Drive shaft	32. Clutch	47. Thrust piece	60. Pin
18. Impeller drive key	33. Spring retainer	48. Hub	61. Shift rod
19. Spring	34. Propeller shaft	49. Propeller	62. Pin
20. Roller bearing	35. Thrust washer	50. Thrust washer	63. Shift cam

TOHATSU 90 HP

CONDENSED SERVICE DATA

NOTE: Metric fasteners are used throughout outboard motor.

TUNE-UP

Hp/rpm 90/5250
Bore . . . . .86 mm
(3.38 in.)
Stroke . . . . .72.7 mm
(2.86 in.)
Number of Cylinders 3
Displacement . . . . .1267 cc
(77.3 cu. in.)
Spark Plug. . . . . .NGK B8HS-10
Champion L78C10
Electrode Gap. . . . . .1.0 mm
(0.039 in.)
Idle Speed (In Forward Gear) . . . . .550-750 rpm
Ignition Type . . . . .CDI
Ignition Timing:
Slow Speed . . . . .5 Degrees ATDC
Maximum Advance . . . . .20 Degrees BTDC
Fuel:Oil Ratio . . . . .See Text

SIZES—CLEARANCES

Piston Ring End Gap . . . . .0.25-0.40 mm
(0.010-0.016 in.)
Wear Limit . . . . .0.8 mm
(0.031 in.)
Piston-to-Cylinder Clearance . . . . .0.08-0.13 mm
(0.003-0.005 in.)
Crankshaft Runout . . . . .0.05 mm Max.
(0.0020 in.)

TIGHTENING TORQUES

Crankcase:
8 mm . . . . .23.5-25.5 N·m
(17-19 ft.-lbs.)
10 mm . . . . .37.3-41.2 N·m
(27-30 ft.-lbs.)
Cylinder Head .29.4-34.3 N·m
(22-25 ft.-lbs.)
Exhaust Cover .12.7-14.7 N·m
(9-11 ft.-lbs.)
Flywheel Nut . . . . .137-157 N·m
(101-116 ft.-lbs.)
Gearcase-to-Drive Shaft Housing:
8 mm . . . . .23.5-25.5 N·m
(17-19 ft.-lbs.)
10 mm . . . . .37.3-41.2 N·m
(27-30 ft.-lbs.)
Spark Plug . . . . .24.5-29.4 N·m
(18-22 ft.-lbs.)
Standard Screws:
4 mm . . . . .1.3-1.8 N·m
(12-16 in.-lbs.)
5 mm . . . . .2.6-3.5 N·m
(23-31 in.-lbs.)
6 mm . . . . .4.6-6.3 N·m
(41-56 in.-lbs.)
8 mm . . . . .11.2-15.1 N·m
(99-133 in.-lbs.)
10 mm . . . . .22.6-30.6 N·m
(17-23 ft.-lbs.)

LUBRICATION

The power head is lubricated by oil mixed with the fuel. Recommended oil is Tohatsu Genuine 2-Cycle Engine Oil. Recommended fuel is unleaded gasoline with a minimum octane rating of 88. Fuel:oil ratio on models not equipped with oil injection is 50:1 for normal service and 25:1 during engine break-in (first 10 hours of operation).

During engine break-in (first 10 hours of operation) on models equipped with oil injection, a 25:1 fuel and oil mixture should be used in the fuel tank to ensure sufficient power head lubrication. Switch to straight gasoline in the fuel tank after break-in period.

Lower unit gears and bearings are lubricated by oil contained in the gearcase. Recommended oil is Tohatsu Genuine Gear Oil. Gearcase capacity is approximately 830 mL (28 fl. oz.).

FUEL SYSTEM

CARBURETOR. The power head is equipped with three carburetors. Refer to Fig. T11-1 for exploded view of carburetor used. Standard main jet (6) size for normal operation is #150. Standard slow jet (7) size for normal operation is #75. Initial setting of pilot screw (3) is 1¼ to 1¾ turns out from a lightly seated position. Final adjustment should be made with engine running at normal operating temperature. Adjust pilot screw (3) to obtain highest engine speed, then adjust idle speed screw to obtain 550-750 rpm in forward gear.

Float level should be 18-21 mm (0.71-0.83 in.) from float bowl gasket surface to bottom of float with carburetor inverted and float bowl removed. Note clip (11) that secures inlet valve to float.

Carburetor throttle valves must be synchronized to open and close at ex-

actly the same time. To synchronize throttle valves, loosen throttle lever screws (S—Fig. T11-2) on center and bottom carburetors. Note that screws (S) have left-hand threads. Back-out idle speed screw (11) on top carburetor until throttle valve of top carburetor is fully closed. Make sure throttle valve of center carburetor is fully closed by lightly rotating throttle shaft lever, then tighten throttle lever screw (left-hand threads). Repeat procedure on bottom carburetor. After adjustment, make sure all throttle valves are synchronized.

SPEED CONTROL LINKAGE. Carburetor throttle valve opening and ignition timing advance should be synchronized by the speed control linkage to obtain optimum performance.

Length of advance rod (1—Fig. T11-2) should be 124 mm (4.9 in.) measured between center of each connector as shown. Disconnect rod (1), loosen jam nut and turn connector as necessary to adjust. Loosen nut and adjust length of high speed stopper (5) to 22 mm (0.87 in.) measured as shown. Move bellcrank (4) to full speed position. With bellcrank (4) contacting high speed stopper (5), carburetor throttle valves should be fully open. If not, adjust length of throttle rod (3) as necessary to adjust. Distance between center of carburetor linkage connectors should be 110 mm (4.33 in.) measured as shown. Disconnect linkage and vary length of linkage as necessary to adjust.

To adjust ignition timing, rotate bellcrank (4) to the idle position. Timing at idle speed should be 5 degrees ATDC and is adjusted at idle speed timing screw (2). Rotate bellcrank (4) to the full throttle position. Adjust screw (7) so maximum timing advance is 20 degrees BTDC.

Oil pump control rod should be adjusted after adjusting carburetor, speed control linkage or ignition timing. Refer to OIL INJECTION section.

FUEL PUMP. A diaphragm type fuel pump is mounted to the power head and is actuated by crankcase pulsations. Refer to Fig. T11-3 for an exploded view of fuel pump.

REED VALVES. Three reed valve assemblies (one per cylinder) are located between intake manifold and crankcase. Remove intake manifold (1—Fig. T11-4) for access to reed valves.

Renew reeds if petals are broken, cracked, warped or bent. Never attempt to bend or straighten reeds. Reed seating surface on reed blocks should be smooth and flat. Reeds should seat lightly against reed block along their entire length with the least possible tension. Reed stop opening (O—Fig. T11-5) should be 10-12 mm (0.39-0.47 in.). Carefully bend reed stop to adjust opening (O).

OIL INJECTION

BLEEDING PUMP. To bleed air trapped between oil reservoir and pump, fill reservoir with a recommended oil, loosen bleed screw (B—Fig. T11-7) and allow oil and air to flow from bleed screw opening. After all air is purged, securely retighten bleed screw.

To bleed air trapped between pump and intake manifold, start engine and allow to idle until no air bubbles are noted in transparent oil line.

NOTE: If outboard motor is new, or excessive air is present in oil injection system, it is recommended that a 50:1 fuel and oil mixture be used in the fuel to ensure adequate power head lubrication during the bleeding process.

ADJUST PUMP CONTROL ROD. With speed control in the full throttle position, angled side of cutout (C) should be aligned with mark (M) on pump housing. Disconnect and adjust length of pump control rod as necessary to align mark and cutout.

IGNITION

Models are equipped with a breakerless, capacitor discharge ignition (CDI) system. The ignition exciter, trigger and battery charging coils are located under the flywheel. Refer to SPEED CONTROL LINKAGE section for ignition timing procedure and specifications.

Trouble-shoot ignition system using Tohatsu Tester Hioki Model 3000, or a

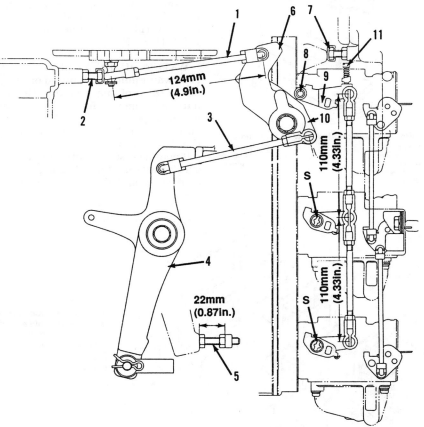

Fig. T11-1—Exploded view of carburetor. Three carburetors are used. Top carburetor is shown.

1. Idle speed screw	9. Inlet valve
2. Spring	10. Pin
3. Pilot screw	11. Clip
4. Spring	12. Pin
5. Main nozzle	13. Float
6. Main jet	14. Gasket
7. Slow jet	15. Drain plug
8. Rubber cap	16. Float bowl

Fig. T11-2—View of speed control linkage.

1. Timing advance rod	5. High speed stopper	9. Cam follower
2. Idle speed timing screw	6. Advance lever	10. Throttle cam
3. Throttle rod	7. Maximum advance timing screw	11. Idle speed screw
4. Advance arm	8. Cam follower roller	S. Screws

suitable equivalent ohmmeter. Refer to Figs. T11-8 and T11-9 when trouble-shooting ignition system.

To test exciter coil, disconnect white/yellow and white green wires leading from stator plate. Connect tester leads between disconnected wires. Resistance should be 174-236 ohms.

Disconnect trigger coil wires and connect tester alternately between black wire and white/red, white/black and

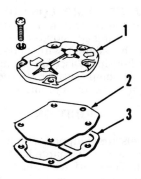

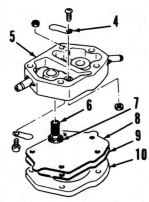

Fig. T11-3—Exploded view of fuel pump.

1. Cover	6. Spring
2. Diaphragm	7. Spring seat
3. Gasket	8. Diaphragm
4. Check valve	9. Gasket
5. Body	10. Base

white/blue wires. Resistance at all three connections should be 167-225 ohms.

Ignition coil primary winding resistance should be 0.19-0.25 ohm. Connect tester between black/white primary wire and black ground wire. Coil secondary winding resistance should be 3600-4800 ohms. Check secondary resistance by connecting tester between spark plug end of high tension lead and black ground wire.

To test battery charge coil, disconnect yellow and white wires leading from charge coil and connect tester between wires. Resistance should be 0.19-0.29 ohm. To test rectifier assembly, disconnect rectifier wires and refer to Fig. T11-10.

Use a process of elimination to trouble-shoot CDI module. If all other ignition components are in acceptable condition, substitute a known-good CDI module and run engine.

COOLING SYSTEM

THERMOSTAT. A thermostat located in the cylinder head cover is used to regulate engine operating temperature. Thermostat may be removed for inspection or renewal after removing thermostat cover at top of cylinder head cover. Thermostat should begin to open at 60° C (140° F) and be fully open at 70° C (158° F).

WATER PUMP. A rubber impeller type water pump is mounted on the upper surface of the gearcase. Gearcase must be removed for access to water pump. Impeller (8—Fig. T11-12) is driven by Woodruff key (14) that engages the drive shaft.

If cooling system malfunction occurs, check water inlet for plugging or partial restriction and thermostat for proper

operation. If necessary, remove lower unit gearcase and inspect condition of water pump, water passages and sealing surfaces.

When water pump is disassembled, inspect condition of impeller (8), liner (7) and plate (10). When installing liner (7) in housing (6), note that locating knob on top of liner must index with notch in housing. Turn drive shaft clockwise (viewed from top) when installing housing over impeller. Avoid turning drive shaft in opposite direction after housing is installed. Tighten housing screws securely in a crossing pattern.

POWER HEAD

REMOVE AND REINSTALL. To remove power head, remove upper motor cover and disconnect fuel hose and interfering wires. Disconnect power trim/tilt wires. Disconnect shift assist mechanism. Unscrew eight drive shaft housing-to-power head screws and lift power head off drive shaft housing.

To install power head, reverse removal procedure. Apply water-resistant grease to splines of crankshaft and drive shaft. Apply a suitable sealer to both sides of gasket between power head and drive shaft housing.

DISASSEMBLY. Mark all wearing components for location and direction for reference during reassembly. To disassemble power head, disconnect fuel

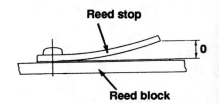

Fig. T11-5—Reed stop opening (O) should be 10-12 mm (0.39-0.47 in.) measured as shown. Carefully bend reed stop to adjust.

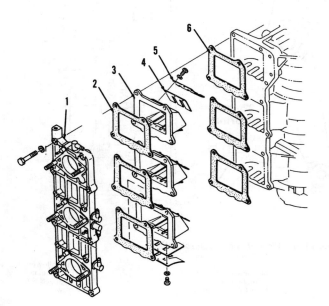

Fig. T11-4—Exploded view of reed valve assemblies and intake manifold.

1. Intake manifold
2. Gasket
3. Reed block
4. Reed petals
5. Reed stop
6. Gasket

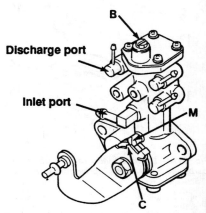

Fig. T11-7—View of oil injection pump assembly. Refer to text for bleeding and control lever adjustment.

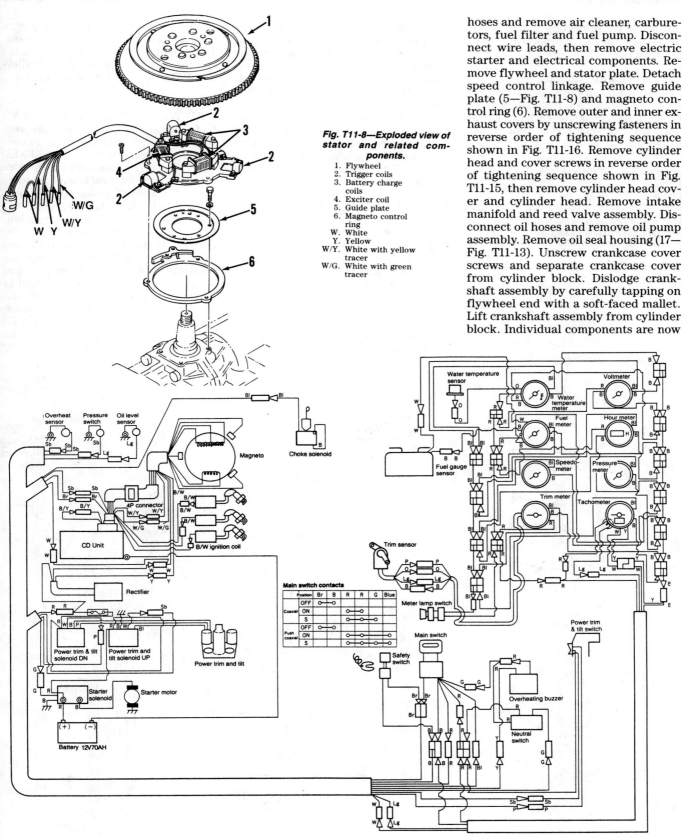

hoses and remove air cleaner, carburetors, fuel filter and fuel pump. Disconnect wire leads, then remove electric starter and electrical components. Remove flywheel and stator plate. Detach speed control linkage. Remove guide plate (5—Fig. T11-8) and magneto control ring (6). Remove outer and inner exhaust covers by unscrewing fasteners in reverse order of tightening sequence shown in Fig. T11-16. Remove cylinder head and cover screws in reverse order of tightening sequence shown in Fig. T11-15, then remove cylinder head cover and cylinder head. Remove intake manifold and reed valve assembly. Disconnect oil hoses and remove oil pump assembly. Remove oil seal housing (17—Fig. T11-13). Unscrew crankcase cover screws and separate crankcase cover from cylinder block. Dislodge crankshaft assembly by carefully tapping on flywheel end with a soft-faced mallet. Lift crankshaft assembly from cylinder block. Individual components are now

Fig. T11-8—Exploded view of stator and related components.

1. Flywheel
2. Trigger coils
3. Battery charge coils
4. Exciter coil
5. Guide plate
6. Magneto control ring
W. White
Y. Yellow
W/Y. White with yellow tracer
W/G. White with green tracer

Main switch contacts

	Position	Br	B	R	R	G	Blue
Coaxial	OFF	o—o					
	ON			o—o—o			
	S			o—o—o			
Push coaxial	OFF	o—o					
	ON			o—o—o			
	S			o—o—o			

Fig. T11-9—Wiring diagram on models equipped with oil injection and power trim/tilt.

B. Black
G. Green
P. Pink
R. Red
W. White
Y. Yellow

Bl. Blue
Br. Brown
Or. Orange
B/W. Black with white tracer

B/Y. Black with yellow tracer
LtG. Light green
W/B. White with black tracer

W/G. White with green tracer
W/R. White with red tracer

W/Y. White with yellow tracer
LtBl. Light blue

accessible for inspection and overhaul as outlined in the appropriate service sections.

REASSEMBLY. Before reassembling engine, be sure all joints and gaskets surfaces are clean, free from nicks, burrs or hardened sealer or carbon. Mating surfaces may be lapped to remove high

		Tester (+) Lead			
Rectifier Wires		Black	Red	White	Yellow
Tester (−) Lead	Black		Continuity	Continuity	Continuity
	Red	Infinity		Infinity	Infinity
	White	Infinity	Continuity		
	Yellow	Infinity	Continuity	Infinity	

Fig. T11-10—Chart showing tester lead connections and desired results for testing rectifier. Renew rectifier if results differ from those shown.

spots or nicks, however, only a minimum amount of metal should be removed.

All friction and bearing surfaces should be thoroughly lubricated with engine oil during reassembly. Coat mating surfaces with a nonhardening gasket sealer.

Note the following points when reassembling power head: Be sure piston rings properly mate with locating pins in ring grooves when inserting pistons into cylinder block. Be sure locating pins in main bearings properly engage notches in cylinder block and crankcase when installing crankshaft. Install seal (15—Fig. T11-13) into seal housing (17) with lip facing down and seal (14) with lip facing up. Lower seal housing (17) is marked for the correct installation direction. Tighten cylinder head and cover screws in sequence shown in Fig. T11-15 in two steps to final tightness indicated in CONDENSED SERVICE DATA. Tighten exhaust cover screws in sequence shown in Fig. T11-16. When installing crankcase cover screws, tighten

10 mm screws first. Start with screws nearest center and work outward. Then, tighten 8 mm screws using same method. Refer to CONDENSED SERVICE DATA section for torque values.

PISTONS, PINS, RINGS AND CYLINDERS. Two piston rings are used on early models and three rings are used on later models. Refer to CONDENSED SERVICE DATA section for ring service specifications. Top ring is semi-keystone design. Standard piston diameter is 85.92-85.94 mm (3.3827-3.3835 in.) measured 10 mm (0.4 in.) up from bottom of piston skirt. Piston-to-cylinder clearance should be 0.08-0.13 mm (0.003-0.005 in.). Pistons and rings are available in standard size and 0.5 mm (0.020 in.) oversize. Cylinder should be bored oversize if worn, tapered or out-of-round 0.06 mm (0.0024 in.) or more. Piston pin retainers (8—Fig. T11-17) should be renewed once removed. Install pistons on connecting rods so "UP"

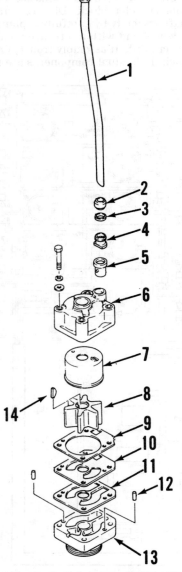

Fig. T11-12—Exploded view of water pump.

1. Water tube	8. Impeller
2. Grommet	9. Gasket
3. Collar	10. Plate
4. Grommet	11. Gasket
5. Seal	12. Dowel
6. Housing	13. Base
7. Liner	14. Woodruff key

Fig. T11-13—Exploded view of crankcase and cylinder block assembly.

1. Crankcase cover	7. Cover	13. Gasket	18. Breather valve
2. Cylinder block	8. Cylinder head cover	14. Seal	19. Breather valve
3. Gasket	9. Gasket	15. Seal	cover
4. Cylinder head	10. Outer exhaust cover	16. "O" ring	20. Gasket
5. Thermostat	11. Gasket	17. Seal housing	21. Cover
6. Gasket	12. Inner exhaust cover		

mark on piston crown is toward flywheel.

CRANKSHAFT, BEARINGS AND CONNECTING RODS. Crankshaft, bearings, crankpins and connecting rods are assembled as a pressed-together unit. Individual crankshaft components are not available. Renew crankshaft assembly if connecting rod small end side-to-side play (A—Fig. T11-19) is 2 mm (0.079 in.) or more. Renew crankshaft assembly if crankshaft runout is 0.05 mm (0.002 in.) or more measured at bearing journals with ends of crankshaft supported.

BREATHER VALVES. Each cylinder is equipped with a breather valve (18—Fig. T11-13) to scavenge liquid fuel/oil and transfer it to the opposite cylinder. Install breather valves with flap (F—Fig. T11-18) facing down.

ELECTRIC STARTER

All models are equipped with an electric starter. Standard brush length is 14-15 mm (0.55-0.59 in.) and should be renewed at 12 mm (0.47 in.) or less. Insulation between commutator segments should be undercut to 0.5-0.8 mm (0.020-0.031 in.).

LOWER UNIT

PROPELLER AND DRIVE HUB. The propeller is equipped with a cushion type hub to protect the lower unit. Three-blade propellers are used. Standard propeller is 11 inch diameter with 21 inch pitch. Make sure propeller will allow full throttle operation within the recommended range of 5000-5500 rpm.

R&R AND OVERHAUL. To remove gearcase, disconnect shift rod coupler (13—Fig. T11-21) from lower shift rod (18) by driving out lower pin (14). Remove cover (23) and plug (24), then screw under cover (23). Remove remain-

Fig. T11-18—Install crankcase breather valves (18—Fig. T11-13) so flap (F) points down.

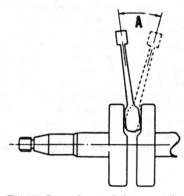

Fig. T11-19—Determine crankpin, connecting rod and bearing wear by measuring connecting rod small end side-to-side play (A) as shown. Renew crankshaft assembly if play (A) is 2 mm (0.079 in.) or more.

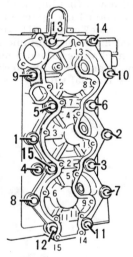

Fig. T11-15—Tighten cylinder head and cover screws in sequence shown.

Fig. T11-17—Exploded view of crankshaft, connecting rods and pistons assembly.

1. "O" ring
2. Upper main bearing and seal assy.
3. Woodruff key
4. Crankshaft assy.
5. Thrust washer
6. Bearing
7. Piston
8. Piston pin retainer
9. Piston rings
10. Piston pin
11. Spacer
12. Washer
13. Bearing
14. Oil pump drive gear
15. Shim
16. Snap ring
17. Washer

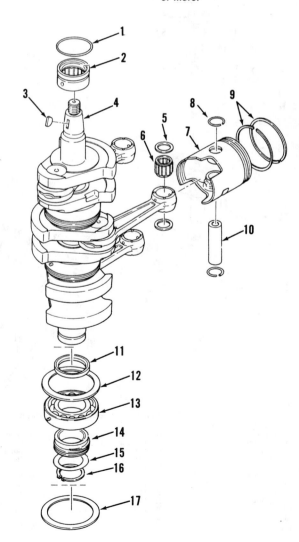

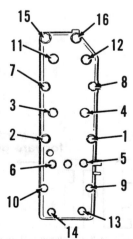

Fig. T11-16—Tighten exhaust cover screws in sequence shown.

ing gearcase screws, separate gearcase from drive shaft housing and place into a suitable holding fixture.

Remove propeller and related components, drain lubricant and remove water pump assembly. Detach water pump base (1) from gearcase by carefully prying on both sides of base (1). Remove screw securing bearing carrier (45), pull carrier using a suitable internal expanding puller, then withdraw propeller shaft assembly from gearcase. Remove retainer spring (36) and push out pin (34) to separate plunger (30), ball (31), spring holder (32), spring (33) and dog clutch (35) from propeller shaft (37). Unscrew pinion gear retaining nut (39) and pull drive shaft (7) from gearcase. Pinion gear (38) and forward gear (29) along with bearing (26) can now be withdrawn from gearcase. If necessary, use

a suitable puller to extract bearing cup (25) from gearcase. Use a suitable puller to pull roller bearing (11) out top of gearcase. Remove clamp (12) and lower shift components (13 through 21).

Inspect all components for excessive wear or other damage. To reassemble gearcase, reverse disassembly procedure while noting the following points: Lubricate all "O" rings and seals prior to installation. Install spring (9) with end with coils closer together facing down. Tohatsu shim gage 3B7-72250-0 is available to set pinion gear (39) depth. Pinion gear depth is adjusted with shims (4). Backlash between pinion gear and forward and reverse gear should be 0.08-0.16 mm (0.003-0.006 in.). Adjust forward gear backlash with shim (27) and reverse gear backlash with shim (42). Propeller shaft end play should be 0.2-

0.4 mm (0.008-0.016 in.) and is adjusted by varying thickness of thrust washer (40). When installing pinion gear nut (39) for final assembly, apply Three Bond 1303B or an equivalent thread locking compound to threads and tighten to 98-118 N·m (73-87 ft.-lbs.). Install clutch (35) so thin end is facing forward gear as shown in Fig. T11-22.

POWER TRIM AND TILT

Some models are equipped with a hydraulically actuated power trim and tilt system. An oil pump driven by a reversible electric motor provides oil pressure. The pump is equipped with a manual release valve (35—Fig. T11-23) that will allow manual up and down tilting of motor when opened (counterclockwise). Close manual valve for normal service.

Recommended oil is Dexron automatic transmission fluid. Do not run pump without oil in reservoir. Oil level should reach bottom of fill plug (48) hole. Tilt outboard motor fully up (cylinders extended) to check or add oil to reservoir.

To bleed air from hydraulic system, open manual valve (35) and manually tilt motor up and down five to six times, then close manual valve.

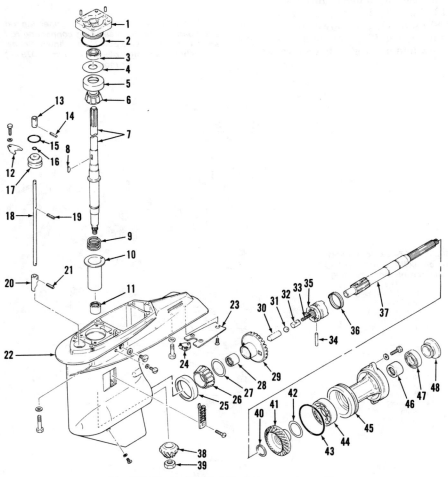

Fig. T11-21—Exploded view of gearcase assembly.

1. Water pump base & seal carrier assy.
2. "O" ring
3. Seal
4. Shim
5. Bearing cup
6. Bearing cone
7. Drive shaft
8. Key
9. Spring
10. Spring guide
11. Bearing
12. Clamp
13. Coupler
14. Roll pin
15. "O" ring
16. "O" ring
17. Bushing
18. Lower shift rod
19. Roll pin
20. Shift cam
21. Roll pin
22. Gearcase housing
23. Cover
24. Plug
25. Bearing cup
26. Bearing cone
27. Shim
28. Bearing
29. Forward gear
30. Shift plunger
31. Ball
32. Spring holder
33. Spring
34. Pin
35. Dog clutch
36. Retaining spring
37. Propeller shaft
38. Pinion gear
39. Pinion nut
40. Thrust washer
41. Reverse gear
42. Shim
43. "O" ring
44. Bearing
45. Bearing carrier
46. Bearing
47. Seal
48. Thrust hub

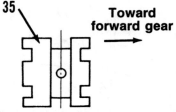

Fig. T11-22—Install dog clutch (35) on propeller shaft (37—Fig. T11-21) with thin end facing forward gear.

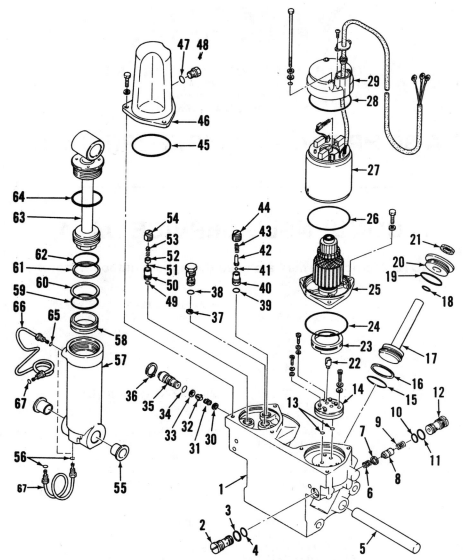

Fig. T11-23—Exploded view of power trim/tilt system.

1. Manifold assy.	18. "O" ring	35. Manual valve
2. Valve seat	19. "O" ring	36. Snap ring
3. "O" ring	20. Nut	37. Filter
4. "O" ring	21. Seal	38. "O" ring
5. Pin	22. Coupler	39. "O" ring
6. Spring	23. Filter	40. DOWN relief valve
7. Spring seat	24. "O" ring	41. Ball
8. Spool valve	25. Armature assy.	42. Plunger
9. Spring	26. "O" ring	43. Spring
10. "O" ring	27. Frame assy.	44. Plug
11. "O" ring	28. "O" ring	45. "O" ring
12. Valve seat	29. End frame assy.	46. Reservoir
13. "O" rings	30. Seal	47. "O" ring
14. Pump assy.	31. Spring	48. Fill plug
15. "O" ring	32. Collar	49. "O" ring
16. Backup ring	33. Seal	50. UP relief valve
17. Piston	34. "O" ring	51. Ball

52. Plunger
53. Spring
54. Plug
55. Bushing
56. "O" rings
57. Cylinder
58. Piston
59. "O" ring
60. Backup ring
61. Backup ring
62. "O" ring
63. Piston
64. "O" ring
65. "O" ring
66. Oil line
67. Oil line

YAMAHA

YAMAHA MOTOR CORPORATION U.S.A.
Marine Division
6555 Katella Avenue
Cypress, CA 90630

YAMAHA 30 HP TWO-CYLINDER (PRIOR TO 1987)

CONDENSED SERVICE DATA

NOTE: Metric fasteners are used throughout outboard motor.

TUNE-UP

Hp/rpm	30/4500-5500
Bore	72 mm
	(2.84 in.)
Stroke	61 mm
	(2.40 in.)
Number of Cylinders	2
Displacement	496 cc
	(30.3 cu. in.)
Spark Plug – NGK	B7HS
Electrode Gap	0.5-0.6 mm
	(0.020-0.024 in.)
Ignition	CDI
Idle Speed (in gear)	750-850 rpm
Fuel:Oil Ratio	100:1

SIZES – CLEARANCES

Piston Ring End Gap	0.2-0.4 mm
	(0.008-0.016 in.)
Lower Piston Ring Side Clearance	0.04-0.08 mm
	(0.0016-0.0032 in.)
Piston Skirt Clearance	0.060-0.065 mm
	(0.0024-0.0026 in.)
Crankshaft Runout – Max.	0.03 mm
	(0.0012 in.)

SIZES – CLEARANCES CONT.

Connecting Rod Small End Shake:	
Standard	0.8 mm
	(0.03 in.)
Limit	2.0 mm
	(0.08 in.)

TIGHTENING TORQUES

Crankcase	27 N·m
	(19 ft.-lbs.)
Cylinder Head	27 N·m
	(19 ft.-lbs.)
Flywheel	160 N·m
	(115 ft.-lbs.)
Standard Screws:	
5 mm	5 N·m
	(44 in.-lbs.)
6 mm	8 N·m
	(71 in.-lbs.)
8 mm	18 N·m
	(13 ft.-lbs.)
10 mm	36 N·m
	(25 ft.-lbs.)
12 mm	43 N·m
	(31 ft.-lbs.)

LUBRICATION

The power head is lubricated by oil mixed with the fuel. Fuel should be regular leaded, low lead or unleaded gasoline with a minimum pump octane rating of 84. Recommended oil is YAMALUBE 100/1 Two-Cycle Lubricant. Normal fuel:oil ratio is 100:1. During the first 10 hours of operation, the fuel:oil ratio should be increased to 25:1.

Lower unit gears and bearings are lubricated by oil contained in the gearcase. Recommended oil is YAMALUBE Gearcase Lube. Lubricant is drained by removing vent and drain plugs in the gearcase. Refill through drain plug hole until oil has reached level of vent plug hole.

FUEL SYSTEM

CARBURETOR. Refer to Fig. Y16-1 for an exploded view of carburetor. Recommended standard main jet (15 – Fig. Y16-1) size is #135 and recommended standard pilot jet (6) size is #54. Main jet (15) size should be reduced from standard recommendation by one size for altitudes of 2500 to 5000 feet (750 to 1500 m), two sizes for altitudes of 5000 to 7500 feet (1500 to 2250 m) and three sizes for altitudes of 7500 feet (2250 m) and up. Initial adjustment of idle mixture screw (21) is 1¼ to 1¾ turns out from a lightly seated position. Recommended idle speed is 750-850 rpm (in gear) with the engine at normal operating temperature.

To determine the float level, remove the carburetor and float bowl)14). Invert carburetor body (1) and slowly raise float (11). Note whether float (11) is parallel with surface of carburetor body when needle of fuel inlet valve (10) just breaks contact with float (11) tang. If not, adjust float (11) tang until proper float level is obtained.

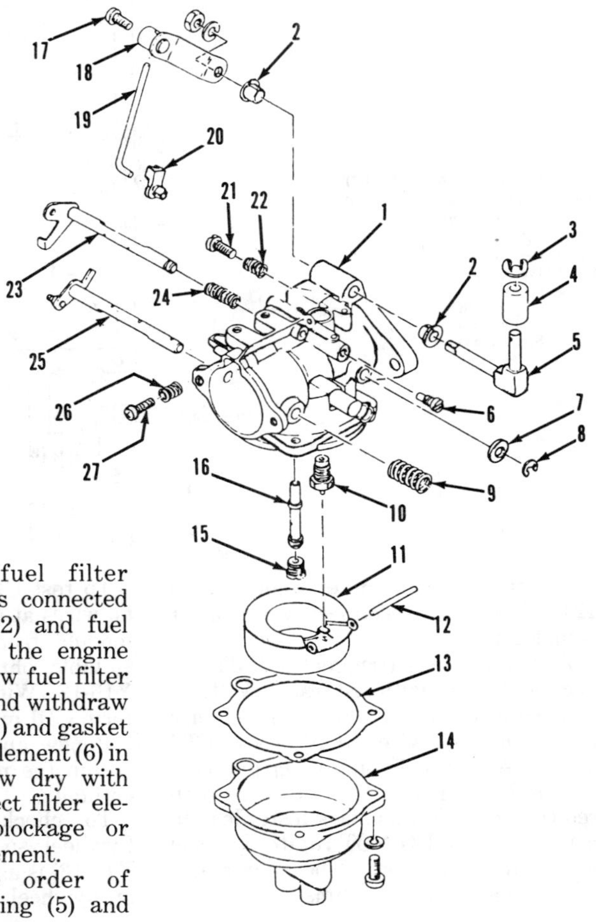

Fig. Y16-1 — Exploded view of carburetor.

1. Body
2. Bushing
3. Clip
4. Cam follower roller
5. Cam follower
6. Pilot jet
7. Washer
8. Clip
9. Spring
10. Fuel inlet valve
11. Float
12. Pin
13. Gasket
14. Float bowl
15. Main jet
16. Main nozzle
17. Screw
18. Throttle arm
19. Link
20. Link keeper
21. Idle mixture screw
22. Spring
23. Throttle shaft
24. Spring
25. Choke shaft
26. Spring
27. Idle speed screw

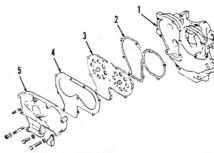

Fig. Y16-6 — Exploded view of reed valve and intake manifold assembly.

1. Crankcase half
2. Gasket
3. Reed valve assy.
4. Gasket
5. Intake manifold

FUEL FILTER. A fuel filter assembly (1 – Fig. Y16-3) is connected between fuel supply line (2) and fuel pump inlet line (3). With the engine stopped, periodically unscrew fuel filter cup (7) from filter base (4) and withdraw filter element (6), "O" ring (5) and gasket (8). Clean cup (7) and filter element (6) in a suitable solvent and blow dry with clean compressed air. Inspect filter element (6). If excessive blockage or damage is noted, rewew element.

Reassembly is reverse order of disassembly. Renew "O" ring (5) and gasket (8) during reassembly.

FUEL PUMP. The diaphragm type fuel pump is located on the port side of the engine. Refer to Fig. Y16-4 for an exploded view of fuel pump. Alternating pressure and vacuum pulsations in the crankcase actuates the diaphragm and

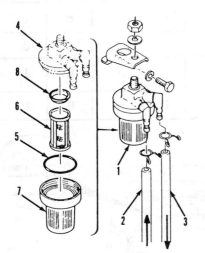

Fig. Y16-3 — Exploded view of fuel filter assembly, fuel hoses and mounting brackets.

1. Fuel filter assy.
2. Fuel supply line
3. Fuel pump inlet line
4. Filter base
5. "O" ring
6. Filter element
7. Cup
8. Gasket

check valves in the pump. Fuel pump assembly uses reed valve type check valves.

Make certain that all gaskets, diaphragms and check valves are in good condition when reassembling unit. Coat fuel pump mounting with a non-hardening type gasket sealer making certain that passage in center is not blocked with gasket sealer.

REED VALVE. The reed valve assembly is located between the intake manifold and crankcase. Refer to Fig. Y16-6 for a view of reed valve assembly.

Cracked, warped, chipped or bent reed petals will impair operation and should be renewed. Do not attempt to

straighten or repair bent or damaged reed petals. Reed petals should seat smoothly against reed plate along their entire length. Make sure reed petals are centered over reed plate passages. Height of reed stop should be 5.4 mm (0.21 in.). Renew reed stop if height adjustment is 0.3 mm (0.012 in.) more or less than specified, or damage is noted.

SPEED CONTROL LINKAGE. To synchronize ignition and throttle control linkage, first make sure the ignition timing has been correctly adjusted. Detach magneto base plate control rod (3 – Fig. Y16-9) from throttle control lever. Place magneto base plate in full advanced position. Rotate twist grip to full throttle position. Adjust length of control rod (3) until rod end slides onto throttle lever ball socket without disturbing position of throttle lever.

With the twist grip held in full throttle position, blockout lever (2) should contact bottom cowling stopper. If not, readjust blockout lever control rod (1) until the proper adjustment is obtained.

With wide-open mark on throttle cam centered on carburetor throttle cam roller (4 – Fig. Y16-1), make sure carburetor throttle plate is in wide-open position. If not, loosen screw (17) and adjust rod (19) to alter throttle plate opening.

Fig. Y16-4 — Exploded view of fuel pump assembly.

1. Base
2. Gasket
3. Diaphragm
4. Check valves
5. Spring plate
6. Spring
7. Body
8. Gasket
9. Diaphragm
10. Cover

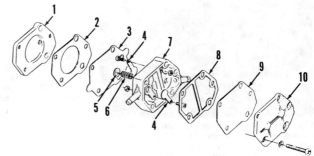

IGNITION

All models are equipped with a capacitor discharge ignition (CDI) system. If engine malfunction is noted and the ignition system is suspected, make sure the spark plugs and all electrical connections are tight before proceeding to trouble-shooting the CD ignition system.

Proceed as follows to test CDI system components: Refer to Fig. Y16-11. To test ignition coil, disconnect black wire (B) and orange wire (O) at connectors and spark plug boots from spark plugs. Use a suitable ohmmeter and connect red tester lead to orange wire (O) and black tester lead to black wire (B). The primary winding resistance reading should be 0.08-0.10 ohms. Connect red tester lead to terminal end in one spark plug boot and black tester lead to terminal end in remaining spark plug boot. The secondary winding resistance reading should be 2,975-4,025 ohms. Use a suitable coil tester or Yamaha tester YU-33261 to perform a power test. Connect tester leads as outlined in tester's handbook. On Yamaha tester YU-33261, a steady spark should jump a 8 mm (0.31 in.) gap with voltage selector switch in "CDI" position. A surface insulation test can be performed using a suitable coil tester or Yamaha tester YU-33261 and following tester's handbook.

To check source (charge) coil, disconnect black wire (B) and brown wire (Br) at connectors leading from magneto base plate. Use a suitable ohmmeter and connect red tester lead to brown wire (Br) and black tester lead to black wire (B). DO NOT rotate flywheel while mak-

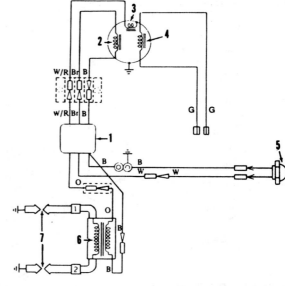

Fig. Y16-11 – View identifying CDI system components.
1. CDI module
2. Charge coil
3. Pulser coil
4. Lighting coil
5. Stop switch
6. Ignition coil
7. Spark plugs

ing test. The ohmmeter should read 121-147 ohms. Reconnect wires after completing test.

To check pulser (trigger) coil, disconnect white wire with red tracer (W/R) at connector leading from magneto base plate and black wire (B) at back of CDI unit. Use a suitable ohmmeter and connect red tester lead to white wire with red tracer (W/R) and black tester lead to black wire (B). DO NOT rotate flywheel while making test. The ohmmeter should read 12.6-15.4 ohms.

To test CDI module, first disconnect all wires at connectors and remove CDI module from outboard motor. Use a suitable ohmmeter and refer to Fig. Y16-12. With reference to chart, perform CDI module resistance tests.

Renew any components that are not within the manufacturer's recommended limits.

To check ignition timing, rotate flywheel so timing pointer (TP-Fig. Y16-13) is aligned with 25° BTDC mark on flywheel. Rotate magneto base plate

Fig. Y16-9 – View of blockout lever control rod (1), blockout lever (2) and stator base plate control rod (3). Locknuts (N) and adjuster (A) are used to adjust cable slack. Refer to text.

Fig. Y16-12 – Use adjacent chart and values listed below to test condition of CD ignition module. Before making test (J), connect CDI module's orange wire and black wire together. Then disconnect wires and perform test.

A. Zero
B. Infinity
C. 9,000-19,000 ohms
D. 2,000-6,000 ohms
E. 80,000-160,000 ohms
F. 70,000-150,000 ohms
G. 33,000-63,000 ohms
H. 7,000-17,000 ohms
I. 15,000-35,000 ohms
J. Tester needle should show deflection then return toward infinite resistance.

Red Test Lead \ Black Test Lead	CDI UNIT LEADS				
CDI UNIT LEADS	White	Black	Brown	White w/Red	Orange
White	A	B	B	B	B
Black	C	A	D	B	J
Brown	E	F	A	B	J
White w/Red	G	H	I	A	J
Orange	B	B	B	B	A

Fig. Y16-13 – Full advance occurs when stop bracket tab (T) contacts timing pointer (TP). Refer to text for ignition timing adjustment.

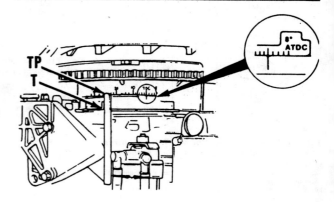

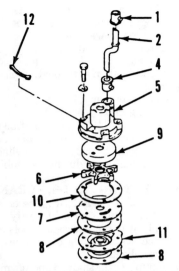

Fig. Y16-15 — Exploded view of water pump assembly.

1. Seal
2. Water tube
4. Seal
5. Pump housing
6. Impeller
7. Plate
8. Gasket
9. Liner
10. Gasket
11. Base
12. Spacer

so stop bracket tab (T) is against timing pointer. The stamped mark on the magneto base plate should be aligned with 0° (TDC) mark on flywheel. Adjust timing by loosening stop bracket retaining screws and relocating bracket.

COOLING SYSTEM

WATER PUMP. A rubber impeller type water pump is mounted between the drive shaft housing and gearcase. Water pump impeller (6 – Fig. Y16-15) is driven by a key in the drive shaft.

When cooling system problems are encountered, first check water inlet for plugging or partial stoppage. Be sure thermostat located in cylinder head operates properly. If the water pump is suspected defective, separate gearcase from drive shaft housing and inspect

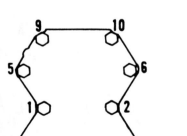

Fig. Y16-17 — Tighten crankcase screws in sequence shown above.

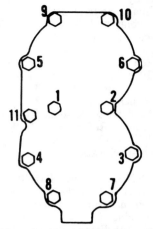

Fig. Y16-18 — Tighten cylinder head screws in sequence shown above.

pump. Make sure all seals and mating surfaces are in good condition and water passages are unobstructed. Check impeller (6) and plate (7) for excessive wear. When reassembling, coat gasket surfaces with a thin coating of Yamaha Bond No. 4.

POWER HEAD

R&R AND OVERHAUL. The power head can be removed for disassembly and overhaul as follows: Clamp outboard motor to a suitable stand and remove engine cowl and starter assembly. Disconnect speed control cables, fuel line and any wiring that will interfere with power head removal. Remove or

disconnect any component that will interfere with power head removal. Remove six screws securing power head to drive shaft housing and lift power head free. Remove flywheel, ignition components, carburetor, intake manifold and reed valve assembly. Remove screws retaining exhaust cover (18 – Fig. Y16-20) and withdraw. Crankcase halves can be separated after removal of ten screws securing crankcase half (1) to cylinder block. Crankshaft and pistons are now accessible for removal and overhaul as outlined in the appropriate following paragraphs.

ASSEMBLY. Two-stroke engine design dictates that intake manifold and crankcase are completely sealed against both vacuum and pressure. Exhaust manifold and cylinder head must be sealed against water leakage and pressure. Mating surfaces of water intake and exhaust areas between power head and drive shaft housing must form a tight seal.

Whenever the power head is disassembled, it is recommended that all gasket surfaces of crankcase halves be carefully checked for nicks, burrs or warped surfaces which might interfere with a tight seal. The cylinder head, head end of cylinder block, and the mating · surfaces of manifolds and crankcase may be checked and lapped, if necessary, to provide a smooth surface.

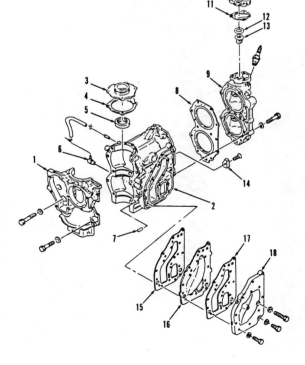

Fig. Y16-20 — Exploded view of cylinder block assembly.

1. Crankcase
2. Cylinder block
3. Oil seal housing
4. Gasket
5. Oil seal
6. Check valve
7. Dowel pin
8. Gasket
9. Cylinder head
10. Thermostat cover
11. Gasket
12. Spacer
13. Thermostat
14. Anode
15. Gasket
16. Inner exhaust plate
17. Gasket
18. Exhaust cover

Do not remove any more metal than is necessary to obtain a smooth finish. Thoroughly clean the parts with new oil on a clean, soft rag, then wash with soapsuds and clean rags.

Mating surface of crankcase halves may be checked on the lapping block, and high spots or nicks removed, but surfaces must not be lowered. If extreme care is used, a slightly damaged crankcase can be salvaged in this manner. In case of doubt, renew the crankcase assembly.

The crankcase halves are positively located during assembly by the use of two dowel pins. Check to make sure that dowel pins are not bent, nicked or distorted and that dowel holes are clean and true. When installing pins, make certain they are fully seated, but do not use excessive force.

The mating surfaces of the crankcase halves must be sealed during reassembly using a Yamaha Bond No. 4 or a nonhardening type of gasket sealer. Make certain that surfaces are thoroughly cleaned of oil and old sealer before making a fresh application. Apply sealer evenly and use sparingly, so excess does not squeeze into crankcase cavity.

Tighten the crankcase screws to 27 N·m (19 ft.-lbs.) following the sequence shown in Fig. Y16-17. Tighten the cylinder head screws to 27 N·m (19 ft.-lbs.) following the sequence shown in Fig. Y16-18. Refer to CONDENSED SERVICE DATA section for general torquing specifications.

PISTONS, PINS, RINGS AND CYLINDERS. Cylinder bore should be measured in several different locations to determine if an out-of-round or tapered condition exists. Inspect cylinder wall for scoring. If minor scoring is noted, cylinders should be honed to smooth out cylinder wall.

Recommended piston skirt to cylinder clearance is 0.060-0.065 mm (0.0024-0.0026 in.). Recommended piston ring end gap is 0.2-0.04 mm

(0.008-0.016 in.) for both rings. The top piston ring is semi-keystone shaped. The recommended lower piston ring side clearance is 0.04-0.08 mm (0.0016-0.0032 in.). Make sure piston rings properly align with locating pins in ring grooves.

When reassembling, install new piston pin retaining clips (4–Fig. Y16-22) and make sure that "UP" on dome of piston is towards flywheel end of engine. Coat bearings, pistons, rings and cylinder bores with engine oil during assembly.

CONNECTING RODS, CRANK-SHAFT AND BEARINGS. The crankshaft assembly should only be disassembled if the necessary tools and experience are available to service this type of crankshaft.

Maximum crankshaft runout measured at bearing outer races with crankshaft ends supported in lathe centers is 0.03 mm (0.0012 in.). Maximum connecting rod big end side clearance should be less than 0.3 mm (0.012 in.). Side-to-side shake of connecting rod small end measured as shown in Fig. Y16-23 should be a maximum of 2.0 mm (0.08 in.).

Crankshaft, connecting rods and center section components are available only as a unit assembly. Outer main bearings (17 and 24–Fig. Y16-22) are available individually.

Thirty-four needle bearings (7) are used in each connecting rod small end. Rollers can be held in place with petroleum jelly while installing piston.

Lubricate bearings, pistons, rings and cylinders with engine oil prior to installation. Tighten crankcase and cylinder head screws as outlined in ASSEMBLY section.

STARTER

MANUAL STARTER. When starter rope (5–Fig. Y16-25) is pulled, pulley (7) will rotate. As pulley (7) rotates, drive

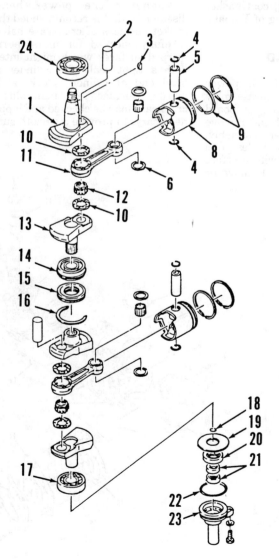

Fig. Y16-22 – Exploded view of crankshaft assembly.

1. Crank half
2. Crankpin
3. Key
4. Clip
5. Piston pin
6. Washer
7. Needle bearings
8. Piston
9. Piston rings
10. Thrust washers
11. Connecting rod
12. Roller bearing
13. Crank half
14. Bearing & snap ring
15. Labyrinth seal
16. Snap ring
17. Bearing
18. "O" ring
19. Washer
20. Oil seal
21. Oil seals
22. "O" ring
23. Lower oil seal housing

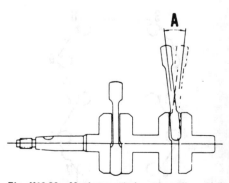

Fig. Y16-23 – Maximum shake at small end of connecting rod (A) should be less than 2.0 mm (0.08 in.).

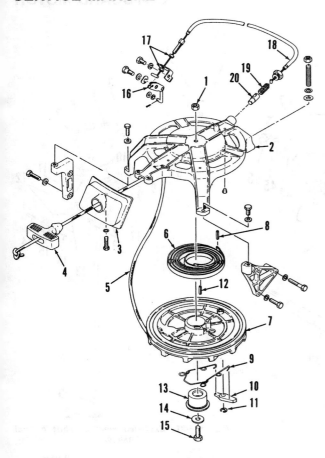

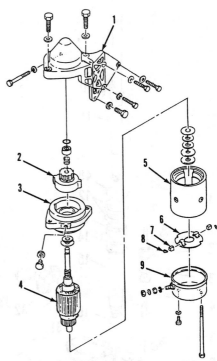

Fig. Y16-25—Exploded view of manual starter assembly.

1. Nut
2. Housing
3. Rope guide
4. Handle
5. Starter rope
6. Rewind spring
7. Pulley
8. Pin
9. Pawl spring
10. Pawl
11. Clip
12. Pin
13. Shaft
14. Washer
15. Bolt
16. Lever & link
17. Adjusting nuts
18. Starter lockout cable
19. Spring
20. Plunger

Fig. Y16-28—Exploded view of electric starter assembly.

1. End frame
2. Drive assy.
3. Frame cover
4. Armature
5. Frame
6. Brush plate
7. Brush
8. Brush spring
9. End cover

pawl (10) moves to engage with the flywheel thus cranking the engine.

When starter rope (5) is released, pulley (7) is rotated in the reverse direction by force from rewind spring (6). As pulley (7) rotates, the starter rope is rewound and drive pawl (10) is disengaged from the flywheel.

Safety plunger (20) engages lugs on pulley (7) to prevent starter engagement when the gear shift lever is in the forward or reverse position.

To overhaul the manual starter, proceed as follows: Remove the engine top cover. Remove the screws retaining the manual starter to the engine. Remove starter lockout cable (18) at starter housing (2). Note plunger (20) and spring (19) located at cable end; care should be used not to lose components should they fall free. Withdraw the starter assembly.

Check pawl (10) for freedom of movement and excessive wear of engagement area or any other damage. Renew or lubricate pawl (10) with a suitable water-resistant grease and return starter to service if no other damage is noted.

To disassemble, remove clip (11) and withdraw pawl (10) and pawl spring (9). Untie starter rope (5) at handle (4) and allow the rope to wind into the starter. Remove bolt (15), washer (14) and shaft (13), then place a suitable screwdriver

blade through hole (H–FIg. Y16-26) to hold rewind spring (6–Fig. Y16-25) securely in housing (2). Carefully lift pulley (7) with starter rope (5) from housing (2). BE CAREFUL when removing pulley (7) to prevent possible injury from rewind spring. Untie starter rope (5) and remove rope from pulley (7) if renewal is required. To remove rewind spring (6) from housing (2), invert housing so it sits upright on a flat surface, then tap the housing top until rewind spring (6) falls free and uncoils.

Inspect all components for damage and excessive wear and renew if needed.

Fig. Y16-26—View showing proper installation of pawl spring (9), pawl (10) and clip (11). Pulley hole (H) is used during pulley withdrawal. Refer to text.

To reassemble, first apply a coating of a suitable water-resistant grease to rewind spring area of housing (2). Install rewind spring (6) in housing (2) so spring coils wind in a counterclockwise direction from the outer end. Make sure the spring outer hook is properly secured around starter housing pin (8). Wind starter rope (5) onto pulley (7) approximately 2½ turns counterclockwise when viewed from the flywheel side. Direct remaining starter rope (5) length through notch in pulley (7).

NOTE: Lubricate all friction surfaces with a suitable water-resistant grease during reassembly.

Assemble pulley (7) to starter housing making sure that pin (12) engages hook end in rewind spring (6). Install shaft (13), washer (14) and bolt (15). Apply Loctite 271 or 290 or an equivalent thread fastening solution, on bolt (15) threads, then install nut (1) and securely tighten.

Thread starter rope (5) through starter housing (2), rope guide (3) and handle (4) and secure with a knot. Turn pulley (7) 2 to 3 turns counterclockwise when viewed from the flywheel side, then release starter rope (5) from pulley notch and allow rope to slowly wind onto pulley.

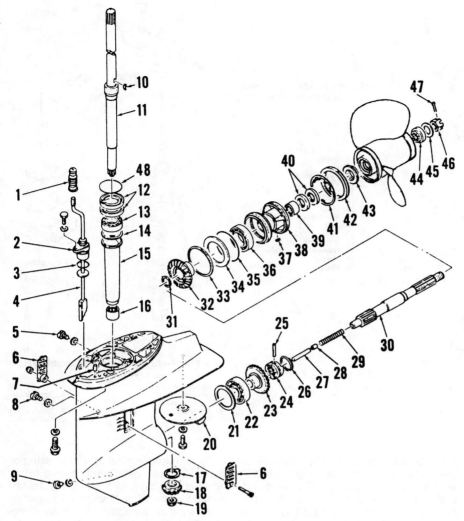

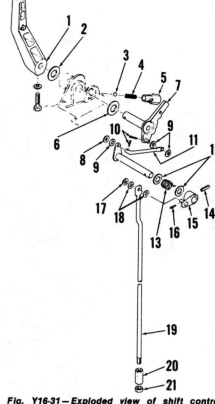

Fig. Y16-30 — Exploded view of gearcase assembly.

Fig. Y16-31 — Exploded view of shift control linkage.

1. Boot	13. Bearing	25. Pin	37. Key
2. Retainer	14. Shim	26. Spring clip	38. Bearing housing
3. "O" ring	15. Drive shaft tube	27. Shift plunger	39. Needle bearing
4. Lower shift rod	16. Needle bearing	28. Spring guide	40. Oil seals
5. Vent plug	17. Thrust washer	29. Spring	41. Tab washer
6. Water inlet cover	18. Pinion gear	30. Propeller shaft	42. Nut
7. Dowel	19. Nut	31. Thrust washer	43. Spacer
8. Oil level plug	20. Trim tab	32. Reverse gear	44. Spacer
9. Drain plug	21. Shim	33. Shim	45. Washer
10. Key	22. Taper roller bearing	34. Thrust washer	46. Nut
11. Drive shaft	23. Forward gear	35. "O" ring	47. Cotter pin
12. Oil seals	24. Dog clutch	36. Ball bearing	48. "O" ring

1. Shift control handle	
2. Washer	12. Washers
3. Detent ball	13. Spring
4. Spring	14. Pin
5. Guide	15. Arm
6. Washer	16. Cotter pin
7. Cam	17. Washer
8. Washer	18. Washers
9. Washer	19. Upper shift rod
10. Pins	20. Coupler nut
11. Link	21. Locknut

NOTE: Do not apply any more tension on rewind spring (6) than is required to draw starter handle (4) back into the proper released position.

Install spring (9), pawl (10) and clip (11) as shown in Fig. Y16-26. Remount manual starter assembly.

Adjust starter lockout assembly by turning adjusting nuts (17 – Fig. Y16-25) at cable (18) end so starter will engage when gear shift lever is in neutral position, but will not engage when gear shift lever is in forward or reverse position. Plunger (20) end should recess in starter housing (2) 1 mm (0.04 in.) when gear shift lever is in neutral position.

ELECTRIC STARTER. Some models are equipped with an electric starter motor. Refer to Fig. Y16-28 for an exploded view of the starter motor. Commutator undercut should be 0.5-0.8 mm (0.02-0.03 in.) with a minimum limit of 0.2 mm (0.008 in.). Minimum brush length is 10 mm (0.394 in.).

During reassembly, adjust shims so armature end play is 1.5-2.0 mm (0.06-0.08 in.).

LOWER UNIT

PROPELLER AND DRIVE HUB. Lower unit protection is provided by a cushion type hub in the propeller. Stand-

ard propeller that will allow the engine at full throttle to reach maximum operating range or 4500-5500 rpm.

R&R AND OVERHAUL. Most service on lower unit can be performed after detaching gearcase from drive shaft housing. To remove gearcase, attach outboard motor to a suitable stand and remove vent and drain plugs in gearcase to allow lubricant to drain. Loosen locknut (21 – Fig. Y16-31) and remove coupler nut (20). Remove four bolts securing gearcase to drive shaft housing and carefully separate gearcase from drive shaft housing. Remove water pump being careful not to lose impeller key (10 – Fig. Y16-30). Remove propeller.

Disassemble gearcase by bending back locking tab of lockwasher (41), then remove nut (42) and lockwasher (41). Using a suitable puller attached to propeller shaft, extract components (24

Fig. Y16-32 — Install clutch so (F) mark is towards forward gear.

through 40) from gearcase. Disassemble propeller shaft assembly as required being careful not to lose shims (33). Detach spring clip (26) and pin (25) to remove dog clutch (24), spring guide (28) and spring (29). Use a suitable puller to separate ball bearing (36) from reverse gear (32).

To remove drive shaft, unscrew pinion gear nut (19) and withdraw shaft (11). Forward gear (23) and bearing (22) cone may now be removed. Use a suitable puller to extract bearing cup; do not lose shims (21). Pull oil seals (12) and bearing (13) out of gearcase being careful not to lose shims (14). Remove drive shaft tube (15) then drive bearing (16) down into gear cavity. Lower shift rod (4) may be removed after unscrewing retainer (2).

Inspect gears for wear on teeth and in engagement dogs. Inspect dog clutch (24) for wear on engagement surfaces. Inspect shafts for wear on splines and on friction surfaces of gears and oil seals. Check shift cam for excessive wear on shift ramps. All seals and "O" rings should be renewed during reassembly.

Assemble gearcase by reversing disassembly procedure. Install oil seals (12) with lips away from bearing (13). Install thrust washer (17) with grooved side facing pinion gear (18). Tighten pinion gear nut (19) to 34-38 N·m (25-28 ft.-lbs.). Forward gear backlash should be 0.2-0.5 mm (0.008-0.020 in.) and reverse gear backlash should be 0.7-1.0 mm (0.028-0.039 in.).

Install dog clutch (24) so "F" marked side (see Fig. Y16-32) is towards forward gear (23 – Fig. Y16-30). Shift plunger (27) is installed with round end towards cam on lower shift rod (4). Apply Yamaha Grease A or a water resistant grease to drive shaft upper splines.

With gearcase assembled and installed, synchronize gear engagement with gear selector handle by turning shift rod adjusting coupler nut (20 – Fig. Y16-31), then tighten locknut (21).

YAMAHA

30, 40 AND 50 HP THREE-CYLINDER MODELS

CONDENSED SERVICE DATA

NOTE: Metric fasteners are used throughout outboard motor.

TUNE-UP

Hp/rpm	30/4500-5500
	40/4500-5500
	50/4500-5500
Bore:	
30 Hp	59.44 mm
	(2.34 in.)
40 and 50 Hp	67.06 mm
	2.64 in.)
Stroke:	
30 Hp	59.44 mm
	(2.34 in.)
40 and 50 Hp	66 mm
	2.60 in.)
Number of Cylinders	3
Displacement:	
30 Hp	496 cc
	(30.27 cu. in.)
40 and 50 Hp	698 cc
	(42.6 cu. in.)
Spark Plug:	
30 and 40 Hp	NGK B7HS-10
Electrode Gap	0.9-1.0 mm
	(0.035-0.039 in.)
40 Hp	NGK B8HS-10
Electrode Gap	0.9-1.0 mm
	(0.035-0.039 in.)
Ignition Type	CDI
Idle Speed (in gear):	
30 Hp	600-700 rpm
40 and 50 hp	550-650 rpm
Fuel:Oil Ratio	See Text

SIZES—CLEARANCES

Piston Ring End Gap:	
30 Hp	0.15-0.30 mm
	(0.006-0.012 in.)
40 and 50 Hp	0.4-0.6 mm
	(0.016-0.024 in.)
Piston Ring Side Clearance	See Text

SIZES—CLEARANCES CONT.

Piston Clearance:	
30 Hp	0.035-0.040 mm
	(0.0014-0.0016 in.)
40 and 50 Hp	0.060-0.065 mm
	(0.0024-0.0026 in.)
Maximum Crankshaft Runout	0.05 mm
	(0.002 in.)

TIGHTENING TORQUES

Crankcase:	
6 mm	11 N·m
	(8 ft.-lbs.)
8 mm	28 N·m
	(21 ft.-lbs.)
Cylinder Head	30 N·m
	(22 ft.-lbs.)
Exhaust Cover:	
30 Hp	8 N·m
	(71 in.-lbs.)
40 and 50 Hp	28 N·m
	(21 ft.-lbs.)
Flywheel:	
30 Hp	100 N·m
	(74 ft.-lbs.)
40 and 50 Hp	140 N·m
	(103 ft.-lbs.)
Spark Plug	25 N·m
	(18 ft.-lbs.)
Standard Screws	
5 mm	5 N·m
	(44 in.-lbs.)
6 mm	8 N·m
	(71 in.-lbs.)
8 mm	18 N·m
	(13 ft.-lbs.)
10 mm	36 N·m
	(25 ft.-lbs.)
12 mm	43 N·m
	(32 ft.-lbs.)

LUBRICATION

The power head is lubricated by oil mixed with the fuel. Fuel should be unleaded gasoline with a minimum pump octane rating of 84. The manufacturer does not recommend using alcohol extended gasoline, however, if gasoline with alcohol additives must be used, inspect condition of fuel lines and related components each six months minimum and take extra precautions to prevent fuel from being contaminated with water. The recommended oil is YAMA-LUBE Two-Cycle Lubricant or equivalent NMMA certified TC-WII engine oil.

All models are equipped with Yamaha Precision Blend oil injection system. The oil injection system varies fuel:oil ratio from approximately 200:1 at idle to approximately 50:1 at full throttle by sensing throttle opening and engine rpm. During engine break-in period (first 10 hours of operation), a 50:1 fuel and oil mixture should be used in the fuel tank in combination with the oil injection system to ensure adequate power head lubrication. After break-in period, switch to straight gasoline in the fuel tank. Make sure oil injection system is functioning (oil level dropping in reservoir) prior to switching to straight gasoline.

The lower unit gears and bearings are lubricated by oil contained in the gearcase. Recommended oil is YAMALUBE Gearcase Lube or a suitable SAE 90 hypoid gear lubricant. Gearcase capacity is 200 mL (6.8 fl. oz.) on 30 hp models and 350 mL (11.8 fl. oz.) on 40 and 50 hp models. Lubricant is drained by removing vent and drain plugs in the gearcase. Refill gearcase through drain plug hole until oil reaches level of vent plug hole to prevent air pockets.

FUEL SYSTEM

CARBURETOR. Refer to Fig. Y17-1 for carburetor used on 30 hp models. Note that center carburetor with integral fuel pump is shown. Refer to Fig. Y17-2 for exploded view of carburetor used on 40 and 50 hp models.

On 30 hp models, standard main jet (6) size for normal operation is #102. Initial setting of pilot screw (3—Fig. Y17-1) is $\frac{5}{8}$ to $1\frac{1}{8}$ turns out on top carburetor, $1\frac{1}{4}$ to $1\frac{3}{4}$ turns out on center carburetor and 1 to $1\frac{1}{2}$ turns out on bottom carburetor.

On 40 hp models, standard main jet (6) size is as follows:

1984 Models:
  Top and Bottom Carburetors . . #130
  Center Carburetor . . . . #135
1985 and 1986 Models:
  Top and Bottom Carburetors . . #125
  Center Carburetor . . . .#130
1987 and 1988 Models and 1989 Models With Carburetor Stamped 6H407:
  Top and Bottom Carburetors . . #115
  Center Carburetor . . . . #120
1989 Models With Carburetor Stamped 6H410:
  Top and Bottom Carburetors . . #120
  Center Carburetor . . . . #125

On 40 hp models, initial setting of pilot screw (3—Fig. Y17-2) from a lightly seated position is $1\frac{3}{8}$ to $1\frac{7}{8}$ turns on 1984 models, $1\frac{1}{8}$ to $1\frac{5}{8}$ turns on 1985 and 1986 models, $1\frac{1}{4}$ to $1\frac{3}{4}$ turns on 1987 and 1988 models and 1 turn on 1989 models.

On 50 hp models, standard main jet size (6) is #140 on 1984 models, #135 on 1985 and 1986 models, #130 on 1987 and 1988 models and #135 on 1989 models. Initial setting of pilot screw (3) is $1\frac{1}{2}$ to 2 turns on 1984 models, $1\frac{1}{4}$ to $1\frac{3}{4}$ turns on 1985 and 1986 models, $1\frac{5}{8}$ to $2\frac{1}{8}$ turns on 1987 and 1988 models and $1\frac{3}{4}$ turns on 1989 models.

To determine float level on all models, remove float bowl (13) and invert carburetor. Float level (L—Fig. Y17-3) should be 17-18 mm (0.67-0.71 in.) on 30

hp models and 12-16 mm (0.47-0.63 in.) on 40 and 50 hp models measured as shown. If float level is not as specified, inspect condition of inlet valve assembly, and if acceptable, bend float arm to obtain specified float level.

FUEL FILTER. A fuel filter assembly is connected between fuel supply line and fuel pump inlet. Periodically unscrew fuel filter cup from filter base and withdraw filter element, ''O'' ring and gasket. Clean cup and filter element in a suitable solvent and dry with compressed air. Renew filter element if excessive blockage or damage is noted.

Renew ''O'' ring and gasket and reassemble fuel filter by reversing disassembly procedure.

FUEL PUMP. A diaphragm-type fuel pump is mounted to the power head on 40 and 50 hp models (Fig. Y17-4). The

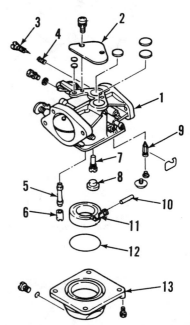

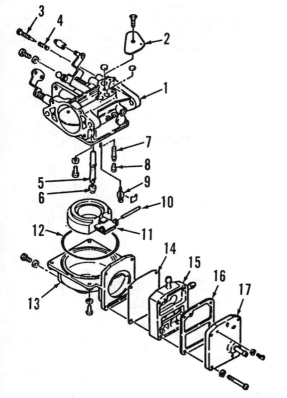

Fig. Y17-1—Exploded view of center carburetor with integral fuel pump used on 30 hp models. Top and bottom carburetors are not equipped with fuel pump.

1. Body
2. Cover
3. Pilot screw
4. Spring
5. Main nozzle
6. Main jet
7. Pilot jet
8. Cap
9. Inlet needle
10. Pin
11. Float
12. Gasket
13. Float bowl
14. Diaphragm
15. Pump body
16. Gasket
17. Cover

Fig. Y17-2—Exploded view of carburetor used on 40 and 50 hp models. Refer to Fig. Y17-1 for component identification.

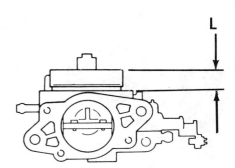

Fig. Y17-3—Float level (L) should be 17-18 mm (0.67-0.71 in.) on 30 hp models and 12-16 mm (0.47-0.63 in.) on 40 and 50 hp models measured as shown.

fuel pump is an integral part of center carburetor on 30 hp models (Fig. Y17-1). Fuel pump is actuated by crankcase pulsations.

Inspect all diaphragms and gaskets for cracking, deterioration or other damage and renew as necessary. Inspect check valves for warpage and proper spring tension. Renew check valve if warped, cracked or other damage is noted.

REED VALVES. The reed valves are located between the intake manifold and the crankcase. Refer to Fig. Y17-6 for exploded view of valve assemblies. Reed valves may be removed for inspection or renewal after removal of intake manifold (1).

Renew reed petals if cracked, warped, chipped or bent. Renew reed petals if tip of petal stands open more than 0.9 mm (0.035 in.). Never attempt to bend or straighten reeds. Never turn a reed over for reuse. Reed petals should seat smoothly against reed plate along their entire length with the least possible tension. Make sure reed petals are centered over intake ports. Apply a suitable thread locking compound to threads of reed stop mounting screws during assembly.

Reed stop opening (O—Fig. Y17-7) should be 2.5-2.8 mm (0.098-0.110 in.) on 30 hp models, 1.7 mm (0.07 in.) on 40 and 50 hp models prior to 1987 and 6 mm (0.24 in.) on 40 and 50 hp models

after 1986. Carefully bend reed stop to adjust opening (O).

30 Hp Models

SPEED CONTROL LINKAGE. To synchronize ignition and throttle control linkage, first make sure ignition timing has been properly adjusted. Before adjusting timing, be sure timing pointer is properly adjusted. Remove spark plugs and install a suitable dial indicator in number 1 spark plug hole. Rotate engine CLOCKWISE and position number 1 piston at TDC. With number 1 piston at TDC, timing pointer should be aligned with TDC mark on flywheel. If not, loosen timing pointer screw and move pointer as necessary to align with TDC mark.

Maximum timing advance should be 24-26 degrees BTDC. To adjust maximum timing advance, rotate flywheel CLOCKWISE to align timing pointer with 25 degree BTDC mark on flywheel. Move magneto control lever (2—Fig. Y17-8) to the full advance position. Timing marks on stator plate and flywheel should be aligned as shown in Fig. Y17-

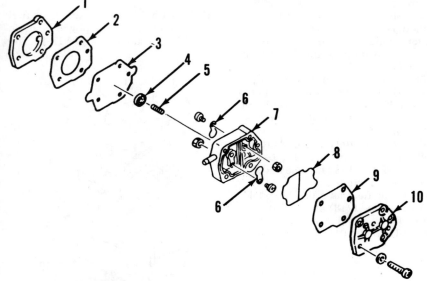

Fig. Y17-4—Exploded view of fuel pump used on 40 and 50 hp models.

1. Inner body	6. Check valve
2. Gasket	7. Outer body
3. Diaphragm	8. Packing
4. Spring seat	9. Diaphragm
5. Spring	10. Cover

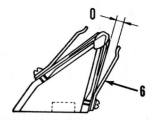

Fig. Y17-7—Reed stop opening (O) between tip of closed reed petal and reed stop (6) should be 2.5-2.8 mm (0.098-0.110 in.) on 30 hp models, 1.7 mm (0.07 in.) on 40 and 50 hp models prior to 1987 and 6 mm (0.24 in.) on 40 and 50 hp models after 1986.

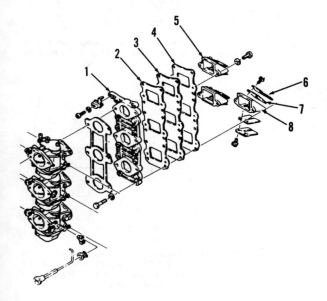

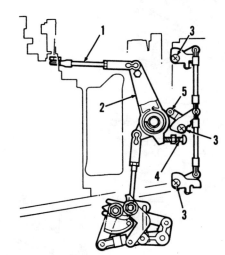

Fig. Y17-6—Exploded view of reed valves and related components. Plate (3) is not used on 30 hp models.

1. Intake manifold
2. Gasket
3. Plate
4. Gasket
5. Reed valve assy.
6. Reed stop
7. Reed petal
8. Reed block

Fig. Y17-8—Speed control linkage on 30 hp models.

1. Magneto control rod	
2. Magneto control lever	4. Idle speed timing screw
3. Screws	5. Throttle roller

9. Adjust length of magneto control rod (1—Fig. Y17-8) as necessary to adjust. If checking maximum timing advance with a timing light, connect timing light to number 1 spark plug lead (top). Engine speed should be over 4500 rpm when check maximum timing. Stop engine to adjust timing.

Idle speed timing should be 4-6 degrees ATDC. To adjust, rotate flywheel CLOCKWISE and align 5 degrees ATDC mark on flywheel with timing pointer. Move magneto control lever (2—Fig. Y17-8) to the fully retarded position. Adjust idle speed timing screw (4) to align timing marks on stator and flywheel as shown in Fig. Y17-9.

To synchronize carburetor throttle valves, back-off idle speed screw on top carburetor so throttle valve is fully closed. Loosen throttle lever screws (3—Fig. Y17-8) on top and bottom carburetors. Note that screws (3) have left-hand threads. Lightly rotate throttle roller (5) toward closed position and retighten screws (3).

To adjust pick-up timing, start engine and position magneto control lever (2)

so timing is 2 degrees ATDC using a timing light. Loosen screw (3) on center carburetor (left-hand threads), push throttle roller (5) into contact with throttle cam and retighten screw (3).

Oil injection pump control linkage should be adjusted after adjusting speed control linkage. Proceed as follows: Disconnect oil pump control rod (1—Fig. Y17-10) from lever (2). Set carburetor lever (4) to the fully open position, rotate oil pump lever (5) to the fully open (rich) position, then adjust length of rod (1) so rod will attach to lever (2) without disturbing position of levers (4) or (5).

40 And 50 Hp Models

Models 40 and 50 hp after 1988 are equipped with an electronic ignition advance system in place of earlier mechanical advance system used on 1984-1988 models. Idle speed timing should be 5 degrees ATDC and is adjusted by varying length of rod (1—Fig. Y17-12). Adjust wide-open throttle stop with screw (2).

To adjust timing on models prior to 1989, place outboard motor into a suitable test tank and connect a timing light and a suitable shop tachometer to the engine. Start engine, move the magneto control lever (3—Fig. Y17-13) to the closed throttle position and note timing.

Adjust idle timing screw (1) to obtain 5 degrees ATDC. Next, move the magneto control lever (3) to the full throttle position. Turn maximum advance screw (2) as necessary to obtain 25 degrees BTDC.

After adjusting timing, adjust idle speed screw (1—Fig. Y17-14) to obtain 750-850 rpm with gearcase in neutral, then stop engine. With magneto control lever in the closed throttle position, cam follower roller (4) should be touching throttle cam (2). If not disconnect throttle cam control rod (6) and adjust length of rod so roller (4) contacts throttle cam (2).

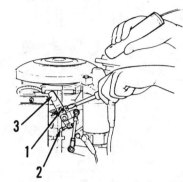

Fig. Y17-13—Refer to text to adjust ignition timing on 40 and 50 hp models prior to 1989.
1. Idle timing screw
2. Maximum advance screw
3. Magneto control lever

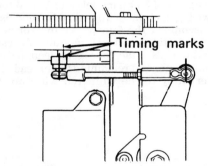

Fig. Y17-9—View of timing marks on stator and flywheel. Refer to text when adjusting ignition timing.

Timing marks

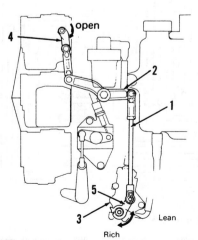

Fig. Y17-10—Adjust oil injection pump control linkage as outlined in text.
1. Control rod
2. Control lever
3. Oil pump assy.
4. Carburetor lever
5. Oil pump lever

open
Rich
Lean

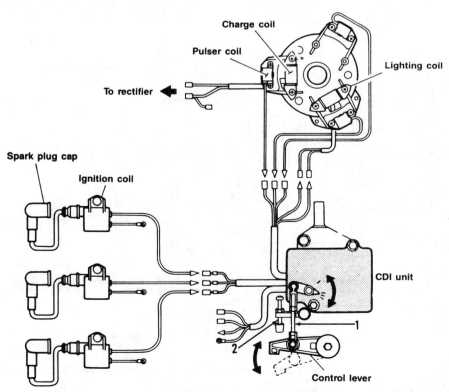

Fig. Y17-12—Diagram of ignition system used on 40 and 50 hp models after 1988. Refer to text.
1. Idle speed control rod
2. Wide-open throttle stop adjusting screw

Charge coil
Pulser coil
Lighting coil
To rectifier
Spark plug cap
Ignition coil
CDI unit
Control lever

To synchronize throttle valves, loosen throttle lever screws (3) on top and center carburetors. Note that screws (3) have left-hand threads. Making sure all throttle valves are fully closed, lightly press down on cam follower (5) and retighten screws (3).

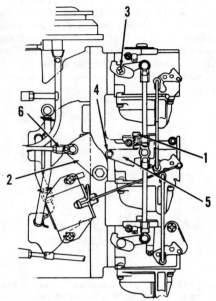

Fig. Y17-14—Refer to text to adjust speed control linkage on 40 and 50 hp models prior to 1989.

1. Idle speed screw
2. Throttle cam
3. Throttle valve adjusting screw
4. Cam follower roller
5. Cam follower
6. Throttle cam control rod

To adjust oil injection pump control rod, disconnect control rod and set throttle control and oil pump lever to the fully open position. Adjust length of control rod so rod will reattach without disturbing position of throttle and oil pump lever.

OIL INJECTION

BLEEDING PUMP. Oil injection system is self bleeding on 30 hp models. If a large amount of air is present in injection system, disconnect oil pump control rod from pump and advance pump lever to the fully open position.

NOTE: A 50:1 fuel:oil mixture must be used in the fuel tank during bleeding procedure.

Start engine and run at idle speed. Alternately, disconnect each oil delivery hose at intake manifold and allow oil to flow from line until air is purged. Be sure to reconnect oil pump control rod.

On 40 and 50 hp models, oil injection system is gravity bled as follows: Make sure outboard motor is in upright position. Remove oil reservoir vent valve or fill cap. Open bleed screw on pump 3-4 turns. After several seconds, make sure oil is flowing from bleed screw hole, then retighten screw.

CHECKING OIL PUMP OUTPUT. Start engine and run at idle for approx-imately five minutes to warm engine. Remove engine cover and install a suitable tachometer. Disconnect one oil line from the intake manifold and insert line into a suitable graduated container. Disconnect oil pump control rod from pump lever and rotate lever to full-open position. Start engine and run at 1500 rpm for three minutes. The pump should discharge 0.76 mL (0.026 fl. oz.) in three minutes.

IGNITION

All Models

All models are equipped with capacitor discharge ignition (CDI) system. If engine malfunction is noted and ignition system is suspected, make sure spark plugs and wiring are in acceptable condition. Make all electrical connections are clean and tight. Make sure malfunction is not the result of fuel delivery or other fuel system malfunction or failure.

The manufacturer recommends using Yamaha Pocket Tester YU-3112-A or multimeter YU-33263 to test ignition components. Proceed as follows to test CDI system: Refer to Figs. Y17-15 for wiring diagram of 30 hp models and Y17-16 for wiring diagram of 40 and 50 hp models. Disconnect the four-pin connector between stator and CDI module. To test pulser coils, attach one tester lead to the black wire and remaining tester lead alternately to the white/red wire (no. 1

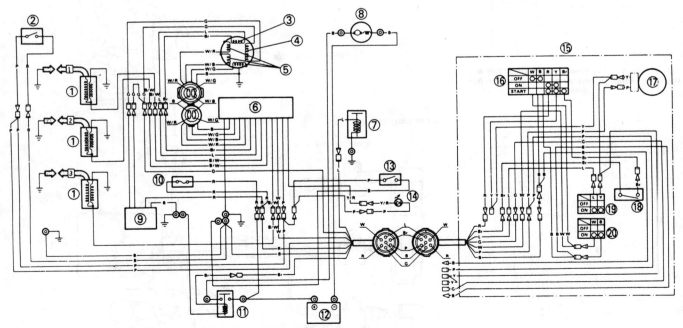

Fig. Y17-15—Wiring diagram on 30 hp models equipped with electric starter and remote control.

1. Ignition coils	8. Starter motor	15. Remote control assy.	B. Black
2. Thermo switch	9. Rectifier	16. Main switch	G. Green
3. Charge coil	10. Fuse (10 amp)	17. Buzzer	L. Blue
4. Lighting coil	11. Starter relay	18. Neutral switch	P. Pink
5. Pulser coil	12. Battery	19. Choke switch	R. Red
6. CDI module	13. Oil level gage	20. Stop switch	W. White
7. Choke solenoid	14. Warning light		

Y. Yellow	W/G. White with green tracer
Br. Brown	W/R. White with red tracer
B/W. Black with white tracer	Y/R. Yellow with red tracer
W/B. White with black tracer	

pulser) white/black wire (no. 2 pulser) and white/green wire (no. 3 pulser). Resistance at all three connections should be 311-380 ohms.

To test condenser charge coil, disconnect blue and brown wires between stator and CDI module. Connect tester leads between blue and brown wires. Resistance should be 185-225 ohms.

To test lighting coil, disconnect the two green wires between stator and rectifier. Connect tester between the green wires. Resistance should be 0.24-0.36 ohm on 30 hp models, 0.23-0.34 ohm on 40 and 50 hp models equipped with the standard 80 watt alternator and 0.22-0.32 on 40 and 50 hp models equipped with optional 120 watt alternator.

NOTE: Charge coil and lighting coil are a unit assembly. If either coil fails, the charge coil and lighting coil assembly must be renewed.

Check ignition coil primary winding resistance between black wire terminal and black/white wire primary terminal. Primary resistance should be 0.46-0.62 ohm. Check coil secondary winding re-

sistance between black/white primary terminal and spark plug end of high tension lead. Secondary resistance should be 5355-7245 ohms. If ignition coil resistance is only slightly out of specification, check spark intensity using a spark tester before failing ignition coil.

Use a suitable coil tester or Yamaha YU-33261-A to perform a coil power test. Connect tester as described in instructions provided with tester. Using Yamaha coil tester YU-33261-A, a steady spark should jump an 8 mm (0.31 in.) gap with voltage selector switch in the "CDI" position.

NOTE: Do not crank or start engine without providing a spark gap or grounding secondary high tension leads. Cranking or starting engine with an open high tension lead will damage CDI module.

Test the CDI module using Electro-Specialties tester Model 1-Y (Yamaha part YU-91022). Follow instructions provided with tester. Isolate main switch, emergency stop switch and all wiring by disconnecting white lead on CDI module prior to testing.

COOLING SYSTEM

THERMOSTAT. A thermostat located in top of the cylinder block is used to regulate engine operating temperature. Thermostat can be removed for inspection or renewal after removing thermostat cover. Thermostat should be closed at 48° C (118° F) and should be open a minimum of 3 mm (0.12 in.) at temperatures above 52° C (126° F).

WATER PUMP. A rubber impeller type water pump is mounted between the drive shaft housing and gearcase. Water pump impeller (3—Fig. Y17-18) is driven by key (12) that engages drive shaft.

If cooling system malfunction occurs, first check water inlet for plugging or partial restriction. Be sure thermostat is operating properly. If necessary, separate gearcase from drive shaft housing and inspect water pump. Make sure all seals and mating surfaces are in acceptable condition and that water passages are unobstructed. Check impeller (3) and wear plate (5) for excessive wear.

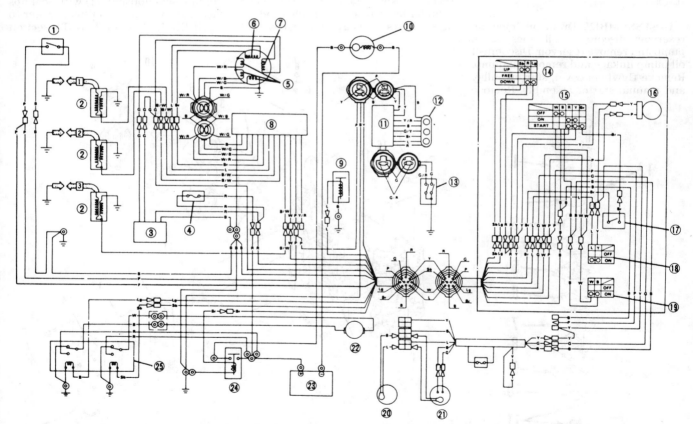

Fig. Y17-16—Wiring diagram on 40 and 50 hp models equipped with electric start, remote control and power trim/tilt.

1. Thermo switch	10. Starter motor	17. Neutral switch	25. Power trim/tilt relay	Y. Yellow
2. Ignition coils	11. Control unit assy.	18. Choke switch		Br. Brown
3. Rectifier	12. Oil level warning	19. Stop switch	B. Black	Lg. Light green
4. Fuse (10 amp)	lamps	20. Trim meter	G. Green	Sb. Light blue
5. Pulser coil	13. Oil level sensor	21. Tachometer	L. Blue	B/W. Black with white
6. Charge coil	14. Power trim/tilt	22. Power trim/tilt	P. Pink	tracer
7. Lighting coil	switch	motor	R. Red	G/Y. Green with yellow
8. CDI module	15. Main switch	23. Battery	W. White	tracer
9. Choke solenoid	16. Buzzer	24. Starter relay		

W/B. White with black tracer
W/G. White with green tracer
W/R. White with red tracer
Y/R. Yellow with red tracer

Press seals (11) into base (8) with seal lips facing toward impeller. Coat seal lips with a suitable water-resistant grease. Rotate drive shaft clockwise when installing housing (1) over impeller. Avoid turning drive shaft in opposite direction after housing is installed.

POWER HEAD

REMOVE AND REINSTALL. To remove power head, remove engine cowl and starter. Disconnect speed control and shift cables, fuel delivery hose and any wiring that will interfere with power head removal. Remove or disconnect any component that will interfere with power head removal. Remove six screws securing power head to drive shaft housing and lift power head free.

Reverse removal procedure to reinstall power head. Make sure drive shaft and crankshaft splines are clean. Apply a light coat of water-resistant grease to drive shaft splines. Avoid excess application. Rotate flywheel slightly to align splines while lowering power head onto drive shaft housing. Tighten six power head mounting screws to 21 N·m (15 ft.-lbs.).

DISASSEMBLY. Drain oil injection reservoir, disconnect oil lines at oil pump and remove reservoir. Disconnect oil pump linkage and remove oil pump. Remove flywheel cover, starter pulley and manual starter assembly. Remove flywheel using a suitable bolt-type puller. Be sure to retrieve flywheel key. Remove choke solenoid, ignition coils, disconnect and remove CDI module, then disconnect magneto and throttle control linkage. Remove lighting coil, magneto base retainer and stator assembly. Remove carburetor air cover and carburetors. Disconnect oil delivery lines at intake manifold, then remove intake manifold and reed valve assemblies. Remove exhaust covers being careful not to damage mating surfaces. Remove cylinder head cover and cylinder head. Dislodge cylinder head by tapping on end with a suitable soft-face mallet. DO NOT attempt to separate cylinder head by prying. Remove thermostat and lower oil seal housing. Remove crankcase cover screws and separate cylinder block and crankcase cover. Note that tabs are provided on each side of cylinder block for prying. Crankshaft assembly and pistons are now accessible for removal, inspection and overhaul as outlined in the appropriate service sections.

REASSEMBLY. It is recommended that all gasket surfaces of crankcase and cylinder block be carefully checked for nicks, burrs or warped surfaces that might interfere with a tight seal. The cylinder head, mating surfaces of manifolds and crankcase may be checked and lapped, if necessary, to provide a smooth surface. Do not remove any more metal than is necessary to true mating surface. Mating surface of crankcase cover and cylinder block may be checked on the lapping block, and high spots or nicks removed, but surfaces MUST NOT be lowered. If extreme care is used, a slightly damaged crankcase can be salvaged in this manner. In case of doubt, renew the crankcase assembly. Cylinder head must be resurfaced if warped in excess of 0.1 mm (0.004 in.). Do not remove any more material than necessary to true mating surface.

Renew all seals, gaskets and ''O'' rings. All bearing and friction surfaces should be thoroughly lubricated during assembly using a recommended engine oil. Apply Yamabond #4 or a suitable equivalent sealer to mating surfaces of cylinder block and lower oil seal housing. Apply Yamaha Quick Gasket to threads of cylinder head and exhaust cover screws. Install seals (9—Fig. Y17-20) into seal housing (11) with seal lips facing away from power head. Refer to CONDENSED SERVICE DATA section

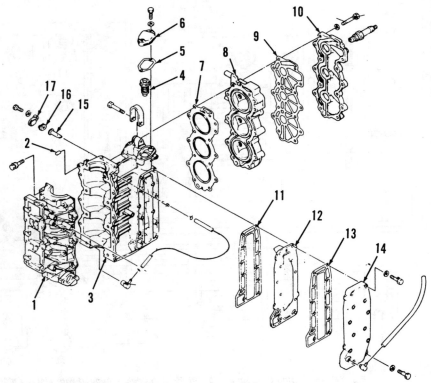

Fig. Y17-18—Exploded view of water pump assembly.

1. Housing	7. Dowel pin
2. Liner	8. Base
3. Impeller	9. Gasket
4. Gasket	10. ''O'' ring
5. Plate	11. Seals
6. Gasket	12. Key

Fig. Y17-19—Exploded view of cylinder block and crankcase assembly on 30 hp models. Models 40 and 50 hp are similar.

1. Crankcase cover	7. Gasket	13. Gasket
2. Dowel pin	8. Cylinder head	14. Outer exhaust cover
3. Cylinder block	9. Gasket	15. Anode
4. Thermostat	10. Cylinder head cover	16. Grommet
5. Gasket	11. Gasket	17. Cover
6. Cover	12. Inner exhaust cover	

for torque specifications. Tighten crankcase cover screws in two steps in sequence shown in Fig. Y17-22. Tighten cylinder head screws in sequence shown in Fig. Y17-23 and exhaust cover screws in sequence shown in Fig. Y17-24.

PISTONS, PINS, RINGS AND CYLINDERS. Early models are equipped with three piston rings. Top ring is semi-keystone shape and second and third are standard square shape. As a running change on 1989 models, the bottom ring is eliminated and the top and bottom rings are semi-keystone shape. Locating pins are present in piston ring grooves. Be certain ring end gaps are properly positioned around locating pins when installing piston in cylinder. Install square rings with manufacturer's marking facing crown of piston. On 30 hp models, piston ring side clearance for semi-keystone rings is 0.07-0.11 mm (0.003-0.004 in.) and 0.05-0.09 mm (0.002-0.0035 in.) on square rings. On 40 and 50 hp models, piston ring side clearance on semi-keystone rings is 0.03-0.05 mm (0.0012-0.002 in.) and 0.03-0.07 mm (0.0012-0.003 in.) on square rings.

Standard cylinder bore diameter is 59.50 mm (2.3425 in.) on 30 hp models

and 67.00-67.02 mm (2.6377-2.6385 in.) on 40 and 50 hp models. Maximum allowable cylinder taper is 0.08 mm (0.0031 in.). Maximum allowable cylinder out-of-round is 0.05 mm (0.0020 in.). Refer to CONDENSED SERVICE DATA section for piston-to-cylinder clearance. Pistons and rings are available in 0.25 mm (0.010 in.) and 0.50 mm (0.020 in.) oversizes. Connecting rod small end bearing consists of 28 loose bearing rollers on 30 hp models and 31 loose bearing rollers on 40 and 50 hp models. Piston pin is a slip fit in piston. No play should be noted between pin and pin bore in piston. Install thrust washers (12—Fig. Y17-20) with convex side facing out. Install pistons on rods so "UP" mark on piston crown faces toward top of engine. Always renew piston pin retainers during reassembly.

CRANKSHAFT, CONNECTING RODS AND BEARINGS. Crankshaft, connecting rods, rod bearings and crankpins are a pressed-together unit assembly. Maximum crankshaft runout is 0.05 mm (0.020 in.) measured at main bearings with ends of crankshaft supported in V-blocks. Connecting rod small end bearing consists of 28 loose needle bearing rollers on 30 hp models and 31 loose bearing rollers on 40 and 50 hp models. Thoroughly lubricate all bearing and friction surfaces during reassembly. Locating pins located in cylinder block must properly engage main bearings and labyrinth seal. Rotate crankshaft assembly during reassembly to check for binding or unusual noise and repair as necessary.

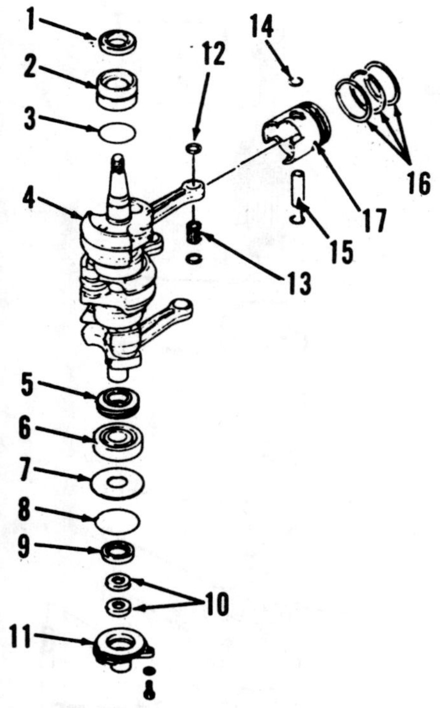

STARTER

MANUAL REWIND STARTER. Disconnect neutral interlock cable from starter housing. Remove three screws securing starter assembly to power head and lift off starter. Invert starter and remove "E" ring (10—Fig. Y17-26), pawl (9) and spring (8). Remove rope guide (18), roller (5) and bushing (4). Grasp rope and place into notch in outer periphery of rope pulley (7), then allow pulley to unwind in clockwise direction to relieve tension on rewind spring (6). Remove nut (1) and screw (13). Remove shaft (11) and carefully lift rope pulley (7) along with rope out of housing. Do not allow rewind spring (6) to fly out of housing (2).

NOTE: A hole is provided in rope pulley to insert a screwdriver or similar tool to hold

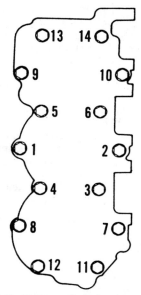

Fig. Y17-23—Tighten cylinder head screws in sequence shown.

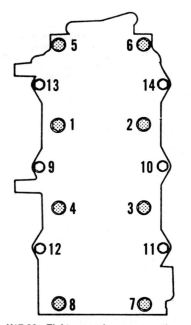

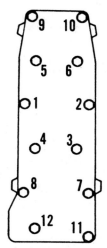

Fig. Y17-20—Exploded view of crankshaft assembly used on 30 hp models. Models 40 and 50 hp are similar. Models after 1988 are equipped with two piston rings (17).

1. Seal	
2. Bearing	10. Seals
3. "O" ring	11. Seal housing
4. Crankshaft assy.	12. Thrust washer
5. Oil pump drive gear	13. Bearing rollers
6. Bearing	14. Piston pin retainer
7. Washer	15. Piston pin
8. "O" ring	16. Piston rings
9. Seal	17. Piston

Fig. Y17-22—Tighten crankcase cover screws in sequence shown.

Fig. Y17-24—Tighten exhaust cover screws in sequence shown.

rewind spring (6) in place while removing rope pulley (7).

If necessary, carefully remove rewind spring (6) from housing after removing rope pulley to complete disassembly.

Inspect all components for excessive wear or damage. Inspect pawl (9) for cracks, excessive wear or other damage. Make sure rope pulley (7) is not cracked, chipped or worn.

New starter rope should be 209.5 cm (82.5 in.) long. Wind rewind spring into housing in counterclockwise direction, starting with outer coil. Wind rope onto pulley (7) three turns in clockwise direction, place rope into notch in outer periphery of pulley and install pulley into housing. Make sure pulley properly engages rewind spring. Lubricate outer diameter of shaft (11) with a suitable water-resistant grease and install shaft (11), screw (13) and nut (1). Holding rope in notch of pulley, rotate pulley two turns counterclockwise to preload rewind spring, then allow remainder of rope to wind onto pulley. Complete reassembly by reversing disassembly procedure.

With gearcase in neutral, adjust nuts (16) so end of interlock plunger is aligned with hole in underside of housing (Fig. Y17-27) on 30 hp models or aligned with inner surface of housing on 40 and 50 hp models. Check interlock cable adjustment by cranking engine with manual starter. Manual starter should only operable with gearcase in neutral.

ELECTRIC STARTER. All models are equipped with the electric starter motor shown in Fig. Y17-28. Disassembly is evident after inspection of unit and referral to exploded view. Standard commutator diameter is 30 mm (1.18 in.). Renew armature if commutator diameter is less than 29 mm (1.14 in.). True commutator in a suitable lathe if out-of-round or tapered 0.2 mm (0.008 in.) or more. Renew brushes if worn to less than 9 mm (0.35 in.). Insulation between commutator segments should be undercut to 0.5-0.8 mm (0.020-0.031 in.).

LOWER UNIT

PROPELLER AND DRIVE HUB. Lower unit protection is provided by a cushion type hub in the propeller. Various propellers are available from the manufacturer. Select a propeller that will allow full throttle operation within the engine speed of 4500-5500 rpm.

R&R AND OVERHAUL. Note location of all shims and thrust washers for reference during reassembly. To remove lower unit, shift into reverse gear, loosen jam nut (Fig. Y17-31) and unscrew coupler to separate upper shift from lower shift shaft (51—Figs. Y17-29 and Y17-30). Remove trim tab, remove gearcase screws and separate gearcase from drive shaft housing. Place gearcase into a suitable holding fixture, remove drain and vent plugs and drain oil. Remove water pump assembly (1 through 8), being sure to retrieve impeller drive key

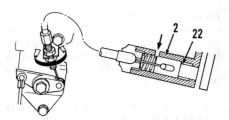

Fig. Y17-27—On 30 hp models, adjusting nuts (16—Fig. Y17-26) should be positioned so end of plunger (22) is aligned with hole in underside of housing as shown with gearcase in neutral. On 40 and 50 hp models, end of plunger should be aligned with inside surface of housing with gearcase in neutral.

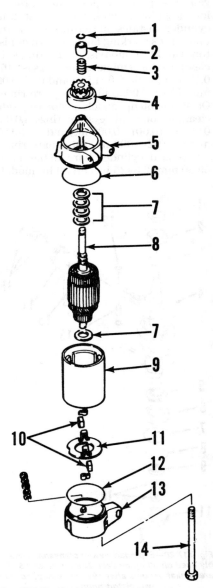

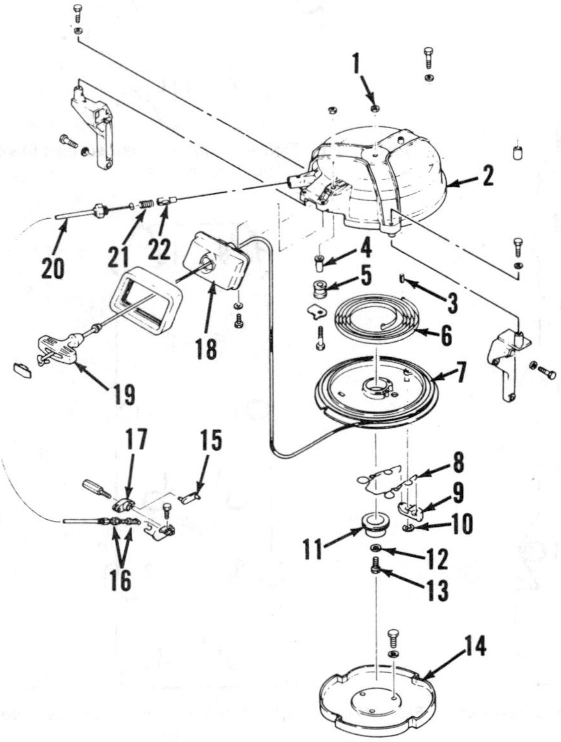

Fig. Y17-26—Exploded view of manual rewind starter used on 40 and 50 hp models. Starter used on 30 hp models is similar.

1. Nut
2. Housing
3. Pin
4. Bushing
5. Roller
6. Rewind spring
7. Rope pulley
8. Pawl spring
9. Pawl
10. "E" ring
11. Shaft
12. Washer
13. Screw
14. Cup
15. Lever
16. Adjusting nuts
17. Arm
18. Rope guide
19. Rope handle
20. Neutral interlock cable assy.
21. Spring
22. Plunger

Fig. Y17-28—Exploded view of electric starter motor.

1. Retaining ring
2. Stopper
3. Spring
4. Drive gear assy.
5. End frame
6. "O" ring
7. Washers
8. Armature
9. Frame assy.
10. Brushes
11. Brush plate
12. "O" ring
13. End frame
14. Through-bolt

(13). Remove water pump base (8) and extract seals (11) from base (8) using a suitable puller. Remove shift components (51 through 53) from gearcase. Remove propeller. Straighten locking tab on tab washer (43) and remove ring nut using Yamaha special tool YB-6075 on 30 hp models or YB-6048 on 40 and 50 hp models. Using a suitable puller, withdraw bearing carrier (39), being careful not to loose key (40). Remove seals (42) from carrier (39). Remove bearing (41) from carrier (39) only if renewal is necessary. Remove propeller shaft assembly. Disassemble propeller shaft by removing cross pin retainer (31) and pushing out cross pin (29). Slide dog clutch (30) off propeller shaft and remove related shift components (22 through 25). Rotate drive shaft (12) while holding pinion nut (19) to unscrew nut (19), then remove nut (19), pinion gear (20) and thrust washer (21), if used. Remove forward gear (28), bearing (27) and shim (26). Lift drive shaft (12) out top of gearcase, along with bearing (14). Use a suitable internal expanding puller to remove bearing (14) race and shim (15). If renewal is necessary, remove bearing (17) by driving down into gear cavity. If necessary, remove bearing (38) from reverse gear (34) using a bearing splitter and a suitable press.

Inspect all components for excessive wear or other damage. Inspect gears for wear on teeth and engagement dogs. Note that forward gear (28), reverse gear (34) and pinion gear (20) should be renewed as a set. Inspect dog clutch for wear on engagement surfaces. Inspect shafts for wear on splines and on friction surfaces of gears and oil seals. Renew propeller shaft shaft (32) if shaft runout exceeds 0.02 mm (0.0008 in.). Renew drive shaft (12) if shaft runout exceeds 0.5 mm (0.020 in.). Do not attempt to straighten shafts. Check shift cam for excessive wear on shift ramps.

Renew all seals and "O" rings. Thoroughly lubricate all bearing and friction surfaces during reassembly. Lubricate seal lips with a suitable water-resistant grease. Press or drive bearings from side of bearing with manufacturer's marking.

Pinion gear depth should be adjusted to provide the optimum mesh with forward gear. The entire length of the gear teeth should be in contact with minimum drive shaft end play. Adjust pinion gear depth by adding or subtracting thickness of shim (15).

Forward gear backlash should be 0.2-0.5 mm (0.008-0.020 in.) on 30 hp models and 0.09-0.26 mm (0.0004-0.010 in.) on 40 and 50 hp models. Adjust forward gear backlash by adjusting thickness of shim (26). Pinion gear depth may require readjustment after changing for-

ward gear backlash. Reverse gear backlash should be 0.7-1.0 mm 0.028-0.039 in.) on 30 hp models and 0.75-0.88 mm (0.030-0.035 in.) on 40 and 50 hp models. Adjust reverse gear backlash by adjusting thickness of shim (35).

Reassemble gearcase by reversing disassembly procedure noting the following: On 30 hp models, install dog clutch (30) on propeller shaft (32) with "F" mark facing forward (Fig. Y17-32). On 40 and 50 hp models, install dog clutch (30—Fig. Y17-30) on propeller shaft (32) with thinner side facing forward as shown in Fig. Y17-33. Install seals (42—Figs. Y17-29 and Y17-30) with seal lips facing propeller. Tighten pinion nut (19) to 50 N·m (37 ft.-lbs.) on 30 hp models and 75 N·m (55 ft.-lbs.) on 40 and 50 hp models. Be sure key (40) is properly positioned when installing carrier (39) into gearcase. Tighten ring nut (44) to 90 N·m (66 ft.-lbs.) on 30 hp models and 130 N·m (96 ft.-lbs.) on 40 and 50 hp models. Apply a light coat of water-resistant grease to drive shaft splines. Avoid excess application. Tighten propeller nut to 35 N·m (26 ft.-lbs.). Tighten 10 mm gearcase-to-drive shaft housing screws to 40 N·m (29 ft.-lbs.) and 8 mm screws to 21 N·m (15 ft.-lbs.).

To adjust shift linkage, place shift lever and lower shift rod into reverse position. Screw coupler (Fig. Y17-31) onto lower shift shaft (51) 8-9 mm (0.31-0.035 in.), then secure with jam nut.

POWER TILT

Some 40 hp models are equipped with a power tilt system. An oil pump driven by a reversible electric motor provides oil pressure. A rocker control switch determines motor and pump rotation, thereby extending or retracting tilt cylinder. The pump is equipped with a manual release valve (9—Fig. Y17-34). Opening manual valve (9) will allow manual movement of tilt cylinder if power tilt malfunction occurs.

The recommended oil is Yamaha Power Trim/Tilt Fluid. Fill plug is located on side of pump reservoir (Fig. Y17-35). Oil level should be checked and filled with tilt cylinder fully retracted. Reservoir capacity is 170 mL (5.7 fl. oz.) and is full when oil level is at bottom of fill plug hole.

To bleed trapped air from hydraulic system, first make sure reservoir is full. Turn manual valve fully clockwise. Slowly, pull upward on tilt rod until fully extended. Recheck oil level, then turn manual valve fully counterclockwise. Slowly push tilt rod down until fully retracted. Repeat procedure as necessary until all trapped air is purged from system.

If tilt malfunction occurs, make sure malfunction is not due to wiring, connections, relays, switch or motor. To test pump pressure, remove drain plugs and connect a suitable hydraulic test gage as

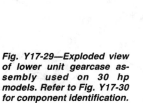

Fig. Y17-29—Exploded view of lower unit gearcase assembly used on 30 hp models. Refer to Fig. Y17-30 for component identification.

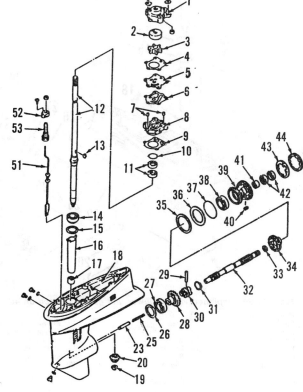

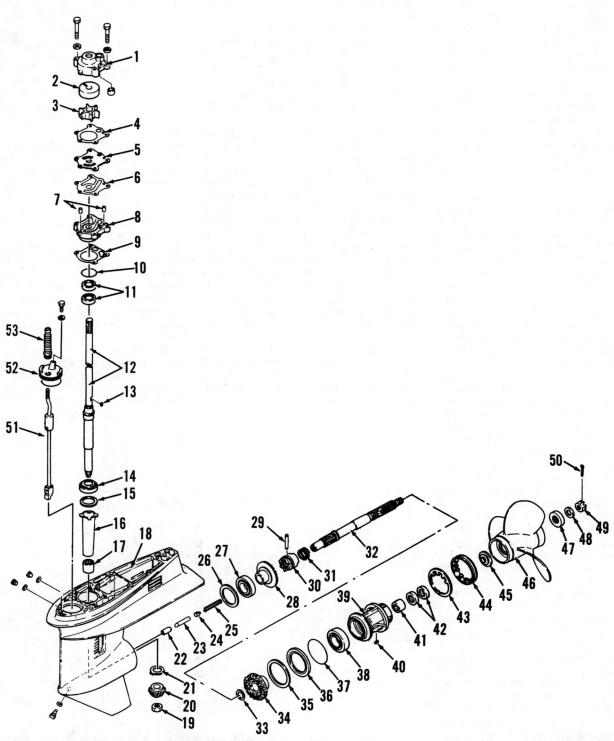

Fig. Y17-30—Exploded view of lower unit gearcase used on 40 and 50 hp models. Some late models do not use pinion gear thrust washer (21).

1. Pump housing	10. "O" ring	19. Nut	28. Forward gear	37. "O" ring	46. Propeller
2. Liner	11. Seals	20. Pinion gear	29. Cross pin	38. Bearing	47. Thrust hub
3. Impeller	12. Drive shaft	21. Thrust washer	30. Dog clutch	39. Bearing carrier	48. Washer
4. Gasket	13. Key	22. Follower	31. Cross pin retainer	40. Key	49. Nut
5. Plate	14. Bearing	23. Shift plunger	32. Propeller shaft	41. Bearing	50. Cotter pin
6. Gasket	15. Shim	24. Shift slide	33. Thrust washer	42. Seals	51. Lower shift shaft &
7. Dowel pin	16. Sleeve	25. Spring	34. Reverse gear	43. Tab washer	cam assy.
8. Base	17. Bearing	26. Shim	35. Shim	44. Ring nut	52. Bracket
9. Gasket	18. Gearcase housing	27. Bearing	36. Thrust washer	45. Thrust hub	53. Boot

shown in Fig. Y17-36. Make sure pump reservoir is full. Move tilt switch to the UP direction until cylinder is fully extended and note pressure gage. Up pressure should be 3400-3900 kPa (493-566 psi). Next, operate tilt switch in the DOWN direction until cylinder is fully retracted, then note pressure gage. Down pressure should be 2900-3400 kPa (421-493 psi).

POWER TRIM AND TILT

PRO 50 models are equipped with power trim and tilt system. An oil pump driven by a reversible electric motor provides oil pressure. A rocker control switch determines motor and pump rotation, thereby extending or retracting cylinders. The pump is equipped with a manual release valve (39—Fig. Y17-38). Opening (counterclockwise) manual valve (39) will allow manual movement of cylinders if power trim/tilt malfunction occurs.

The recommended oil is Yamaha Power Trim/Tilt Fluid. Fill plug (50) is located on side of pump reservoir. Oil level should be checked and filled with cylinders fully retracted. Reservoir is full when oil level is at bottom of fill plug hole.

To bleed trapped air from hydraulic system, tilt outboard motor fully up, then open manual release valve and allow outboard motor to return to the down position by its own weight. Repeat as necessary until all air is purged.

If trim/tilt system malfunction occurs, first make sure malfunction is not due to faulty wiring, wiring connections, relays, switch or electric motor. Make sure oil leakage is not present at cylinders or hydraulic lines, and that reservoir is full.

To test pump output pressure, disconnect hydraulic lines at bottom of reservoir and upper chamber of tilt cylinder (53). Connect test gage (Yamaha YB-

6181) to the tilt cylinder and reservoir as shown at (A—Fig. Y17-39). Close manual release valve (clockwise) and tilt outboard motor up, then down, then open manual release valve to bleed any air in system. Return manual release valve to the closed position. Operate trim/tilt switch in the up direction, noting pressure gage while traveling up. Continue operating in the up direction for three seconds after full up is reached, and note test gage. During upward movement, pressure should be 0-490 kPa (0-71 psi). After full up is reached, pressure should be zero. Next, tilt outboard motor down, continue for three seconds after full down, then note pressure gage. Down pressure should be 4018-5390 kPa (583-782 psi).

Repeat procedure with test gage connected as shown at (B). Pressure while tilting up should be 0-490 kPa (0-71 psi), and after reaching full up, pressure should be 9310-11,270 kPa (1350-1635 psi). Down pressure should be 588-1078 kPa (85-156 psi).

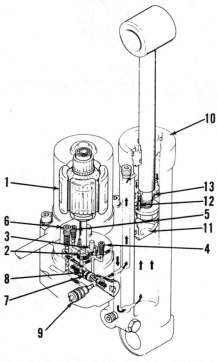

Fig. Y17-34—Sectional view of power tilt system used on early 50 hp models.

1. Electric motor	8. Main valve
2. Drive gear	9. Manual valve
3. Driven gear	10. Tilt cylinder
4. Down relief valve	11. Free piston
5. Up relief valve	12. Shock absorber
6. Up relief valve	valve
7. Shuttle piston	13. Check valve

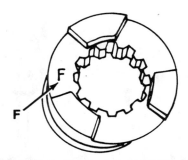

Fig. Y17-32—On 30 hp models, install dog clutch on propeller shaft with "F" mark facing forward.

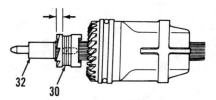

Fig. Y17-33—On 40 and 50 hp models, install dog clutch (30) on propeller shaft (32) with thin side facing forward as shown.

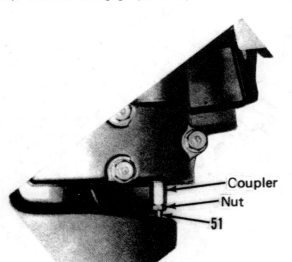

Coupler

Nut

51

Fig. Y17-31—View showing lower shift rod (51), coupler and jam nut.

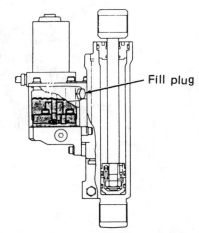

Fill plug

Fig. Y17-35—Oil level on power tilt system should be at bottom of fill plug hole.

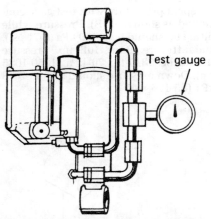

Fig. Y17-36—To test pump hydraulic pressure on tilt system, connect test gage as shown. Refer to text.

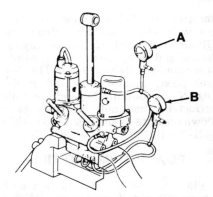

Fig. Y17-39—View showing test gage connection for checking tilt pressure (A) and trim pressure (B).

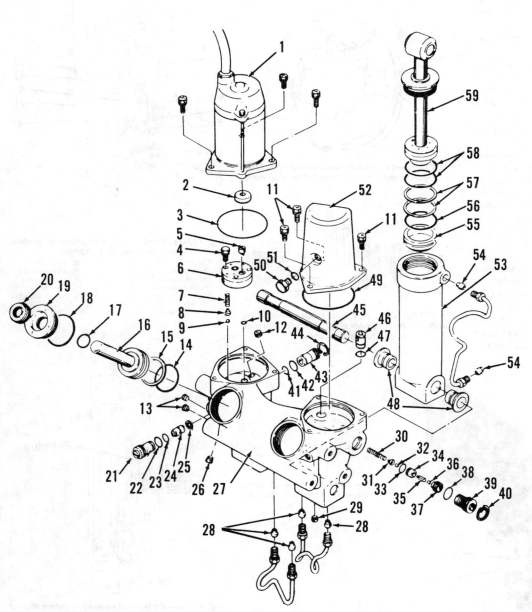

1. Motor assy.
2. Seal
3. "O" ring
4. Screw
5. Coupler shaft
6. Pump assy.
7. Spring
8. Valve support pin
9. Ball
10. "O" ring
11. Screws
12. Plug
13. Plugs
14. "O" ring
15. Backup ring
16. Piston & rod assy.
17. "O" ring
18. "O" ring
19. End cap
20. Seal
21. Main valve
22. "O" ring
23. "O" ring
24. Shuttle piston
25. Backup ring
26. Plug
27. Housing assy.
28. Seats
29. Plug
30. Spring
31. Manual release pin
32. Ball
33. "O" ring
34. Valve seat
35. Manual release rod
36. Ball
37. Seat screw
38. "O" ring
39. Manual release screw
40. Snap ring
41. "O" ring
42. "O" ring
43. Main valve
44. Snap ring
45. Shaft
46. Up release valve
47. "O" ring
48. Bushing
49. "O" ring
50. Fill plug
51. "O" ring
52. Reservoir
53. Tilt cylinder
54. Seat
55. Free piston
56. "O" ring
57. Backup rings
58. "O" rings
59. Piston & rod assy.

Fig. Y17-38—Exploded view of power trim/tilt assembly used on PRO 50 models.

YAMAHA 70 AND 90 HP MODELS

CONDENSED SERVICE DATA

NOTE: Metric fasteners are used throughout outboard motor.

TUNE-UP

Hp/rpm 70/4500-5500
                    90/4500-5500

Bore:
  70 Hp . . . . .72.0 mm
                (2.83 in.)
  90 Hp . . . . .82.0 mm
                (3.23 in.)

Stroke:
  70 Hp . . . . .69.5 mm
                (2.74 in.)
  90 Hp . . . . .72 mm
                (2.83 in.)

Number of Cylinders 3

Displacement:
  70 Hp . . . . .849 cc
                (51.8 cu. in.)
  90 Hp . . . . .1140 cc
                (69.6 cu. in.)

Spark Plug. . . . . .NGK B8HS-10
  Electrode Gap . . . . .0.9-1.0 mm
                (0.035-0.039 in.)

Ignition Type . . . . .CDI

Idle speed:
  In Neutral . . . . .750-850 rpm
  In Forward Gear . . . . .550-650 rpm

Fuel:Oil Ratio. . . . . .See Text

SIZES—CLEARANCES

Piston Ring End Gap:
  70 Hp . . . . .0.3-0.5 mm
                (0.012-0.020 in.)
  90 Hp . . . . .0.4-0.6 mm
                (0.016-0.024 in.)

Piston Ring Side Clearance—
Semi-Keystone Ring:
  70 Hp . . . . .0.02-0.06 mm
                (0.0008-0.0024 in.)
  90 Hp . . . . .0.03-0.065 mm
                (0.012-0.0026 in.)

Plain Ring:
  All Models . . . . .0.03-0.07 mm
                (0.012-0.0028 in.)

Piston Clearance:
  70 Hp . . . . .0.050-0.055 mm
                (0.0020-0.0022 in.)

  90 Hp . . . . .0.060-0.065 mm
                (0.0024-0.0026 in.)

Maximum Crankshaft Runout:
  70 Hp . . . . .0.05 mm
                (0.002 in.)
  90 Hp . . . . .0.02 mm
                (0.0008 in.)

Connecting Rod Big End Side Play . . . . . . .0.20-0.33 mm
                (0.008-0.013 in.)

TIGHTENING TORQUES

Connecting Rod:
  90 Hp . . . . .35 N·m
                (26 ft.-lbs.)

Crankcase:
  6 mm (90 Hp) . . . . .12 N·m
                (9 ft.-lbs.)
  8 mm (70 Hp) . . . . .12 N·m
                (9 ft.-lbs.)
  10 mm (All Models) . . . . .40 N·m
                (29 ft.-lbs.)

Cylinder Head . . . . .30 N·m
                (22 ft.-lbs.)

Cylinder Head Cover . . . . .8 N·m
                (71 in.-lbs.)

Exhaust Cover:
  70 Hp . . . . .8 N·m
                (71 in.-lbs.)
  90 Hp . . . . .18 N·m
                (13 ft.-lbs.)

Flywheel: . . . . .160 N·m
                (118 ft.-lbs.)

Lower Seal Housing. . . . . .8 N·m
                (71 in.-lbs.)

Spark Plug . . . . .25 N·m
                (18 ft.-lbs.)

Standard Screws
  5 mm . . . . .4.0 N·m
                (35 in.-lbs.)
  6 mm . . . . .8.0 N·m
                (71 in.-lbs.)
  8 mm . . . . .18 N·m
                (13 ft.-lbs.)
  10 mm . . . . .36 N·m
                (25 ft.-lbs.)
  12 mm . . . . .42 N·m
                (31 ft.-lbs.)

LUBRICATION

The power head is lubricated by oil mixed with the fuel. Fuel should be unleaded gasoline with a minimum pump octane rating of 86. The manufacturer does not recommend using alcohol extended gasoline; however, if gasoline with alcohol additives must be used, inspect condition of fuel lines and related components at a minimum of each six months operation and take extra precautions to prevent fuel from being contaminated with water. The recommended oil is Yamaha Two-Stroke Oil or equivalent NMMA certified TC-WII engine oil. All models are equipped with Yamaha Precision Blend oil injection system. The oil injection system varies fuel:oil ratio from approximately 200:1 at idle to approximately 50:1 at full throttle by sensing throttle opening and engine rpm. During engine break-in period (first 10 hours of operation), a 50:1 fuel and oil mixture should be used in the fuel tank in combination with the oil injection system to ensure adequate power head lubrication. After break-in period, switch to straight gasoline in the fuel tank. Make sure oil injection system is functioning (oil level dropping in reservoir) prior to switching to straight gasoline.

The lower unit gears and bearings are lubricated by oil contained in the gearcase. Recommended oil is YAMALUBE Gearcase Lube or a suitable SAE 90 hypoid gear lubricant. Gearcase capacity is 610 mL (20.6 fl. oz.). Gearcase oil should be checked after the first 10 hours of operation, then every 100 hours thereafter. Lubricant is drained by removing vent and drain plugs in the gearcase. Refill gearcase through drain plug hole until oil reaches level of vent plug hole to prevent air pockets.

FUEL SYSTEM

CARBURETOR. Three one-barrel carburetors are used. Refer to Fig. Y18-1 for carburetor used on all models. Standard main jet (6) size for normal operation is #150 on 70 hp models and #165 on 90 hp models. Standard pilot jet (7) size for normal operation is #78 on 70 hp models prior to 1989, #72 on 70 hp models after 1988, #80 on 90 hp models prior to 1989 and #78 on 90 hp models after 1988. Initial setting of pilot screw (3) from a lightly seated position is $1\frac{5}{8}$ to $2\frac{1}{8}$ turns on 1984 70 and 90 hp models, $1\frac{1}{8}$ to $1\frac{5}{8}$ turns on 1985-1989 70 hp models, $1\frac{1}{4}$ to $1\frac{3}{4}$ turns on 1985 to 1988 90 hp models and $1\frac{1}{8}$ to $1\frac{5}{8}$ turns on 1989 90 hp models.

To determine float level on all models, remove float bowl (13) and invert carburetor. Float level (L—Fig. Y18-2) should be 12-16 mm (0.47-0.63 in.) on 70 hp models and 16.5-22.5 mm (0.65-0.88 in.) on 90 hp models. If float level is not as specified, inspect condition of inlet valve needle and seat assembly. If inlet valve assembly is in acceptable condition, carefully bend float arm to obtain the specified float level.

FUEL FILTER. A fuel filter assembly is connected between fuel supply line and fuel pump inlet. Periodically unscrew fuel filter cup from filter base and withdraw filter element and "O" ring.

Clean cup and filter element in a suitable solvent and dry with compressed air. Renew filter element if excessive blockage or damage is noted. Renew "O" ring if necessary, and reassemble fuel filter by reversing disassembly procedure.

FUEL PUMP. A diaphragm-type fuel pump is used. Refer to Fig. Y18-3. The fuel pump is mounted to the power head and is actuated by crankcase pulsations.

Inspect all diaphragms and gaskets for cracking, deterioration or other damage and renew as necessary. Renew check valves if warped, cracked or other damage is noted. Note that pump cover is marked "IN" and "OUT" for reference during reassembly.

REED VALVES. The reed valves are located between the intake manifold and the crankcase. Refer to Fig. Y18-5 for exploded view of valve assemblies. Reed valves may be removed for inspection or renewal after removal of intake manifold (1). Note location of beveled corner on reed petals and reed stops for reference during reassembly.

Renew reed petals if cracked, warped, chipped or bent. Renew reed petals if tip of petal stands open more than 0.2 mm (0.0.008 in.). Never attempt to bend or straighten reeds. Never turn a reed over for reuse. Reed petals should seat smoothly against reed plate along their entire length with the least possible tension. Make sure reed petals are centered over intake ports. Apply a suitable thread locking compound to threads of reed stop mounting screws during assembly.

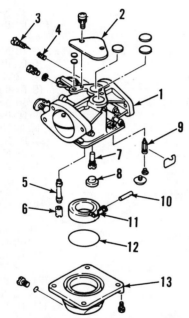

Fig. Y18-1—Exploded view of carburetor used on all models.

1. Body	8. Cap
2. Cover	9. Inlet needle
3. Pilot screw	10. Pin
4. Spring	11. Float
5. Main nozzle	12. Gasket
6. Main jet	13. Float bowl
7. Pilot jet	

Fig. Y18-2—Float level (L) should be 12-16 mm (0.47-0.63 in.) on 70 hp models and 16.5-22.5 mm (0.65-0.88 in.) on 90 hp models.

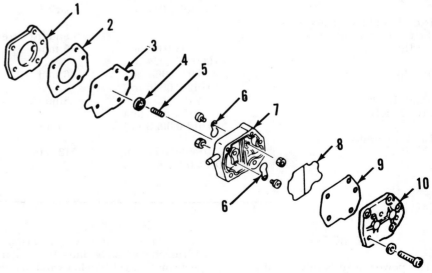

Fig. Y18-3—Exploded view of fuel pump typical of all models.

1. Inner body		
2. Gasket	5. Spring	8. Packing
3. Diaphragm	6. Check valve	9. Diaphragm
4. Spring seat	7. Outer body	10. Cover

Reed stop opening (O—Fig. Y18-6) should be 9.8-10.0 mm (0.386-0.393 in.). Renew reed stop (6) if opening (O) is not as specified.

All Models

SPEED CONTROL LINKAGE. To synchronize ignition and throttle control linkage, first make sure timing pointer and ignition timing have been properly adjusted. To check timing pointer adjustment, remove spark plugs and install a suitable dial indicator into number 1 spark plug hole. Rotate engine CLOCKWISE and position number 1 piston at TDC. With number 1 piston at TDC, timing pointer should be aligned with TDC mark on flywheel. If not, loosen timing pointer screw and move pointer as necessary to align with TDC mark.

WARNING: Be very careful while working near rotating flywheel while performing timing adjustments.

Remove propeller, install the correct test wheel (Yamaha part YB-1620) and place outboard motor into a suitable test tank when checking ignition timing. Connect timing light to number 1 (top) spark plug lead. Engine should be at normal operating temperature when checking and adjusting timing.

70 Hp Models

Start engine, move magneto control lever (1—Fig. Y18-7) to the fully closed-throttle position and note timing. Idle timing should be 3-5 degrees ATDC on 1984 models and 6-8 degrees ATDC on 1985-1989 models. Loosen locknut and turn idle timing screw (2) to adjust. Next, manually move magneto control lever (1) to the full-throttle position, loosen locknut and turn maximum advance screw (3) to obtain 19-20 degrees BTDC.

NOTE: Engine must be running at more than 4500 rpm when checking maximum advance timing.

To check and adjust pickup timing, move magneto control lever (1) to fully closed-throttle position, start engine and adjust idle speed screw (on center carburetor) to obtain 750-850 rpm in neutral. With magneto control lever (1) in the closed throttle position, throttle roller (7) should lightly contact throttle cam (6) and throttle valves should be fully closed. If not, disconnect throttle link (5) and adjust length of link (5) as necessary.

To synchronize carburetor throttle valves, back-off idle speed screw (I—Fig. Y18-8) until center carburetor throttle valve is fully closed. Loosen throttle lever screws (S) on upper and center carburetors (left-hand threads). Lightly push down on cam follower (8) closing throttle valves, then retighten screws (S). Readjust idle speed screw (I) to obtain 750-850 rpm in neutral, or 550-650 rpm in forward gear.

Oil injection pump control linkage adjustment should be checked after adjusting speed control linkage. Back-off idle speed screw until throttle valves are closed. With throttle valves closed, marks (M—Fig. Y18-9) on pump lever and pump body should be aligned. Disconnect control rod and adjust length of rod to adjust. Be sure to readjust idle speed screw to specified rpm (CONDENSED SERVICE DATA).

90 Hp Models

Start engine, move magneto control lever (1—Fig. Y18-11) to the fully closed-

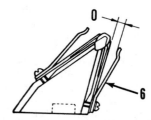

Fig. Y18-6—Reed stop (6) opening (O) measured between tip of closed reed and tip of reed stop should be 9.8-10.0 mm (0.386-0.393 in.). Renew reed stop (6) if opening (O) is not as specified.

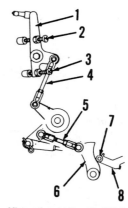

Fig. Y18-7—View of speed control linkage used on 70 hp models.

1. Magneto control lever
2. Idle timing screw
3. Maximum advance timing screw
4. Link
5. Throttle link
6. Throttle cam
7. Cam follower roller
8. Cam follower

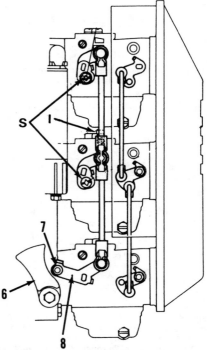

Fig. Y18-8—Refer to text to synchronize carburetor throttle valves on 70 hp models.

S. Throttle lever screws
6. Throttle cam
7. Throttle roller
8. Cam follower

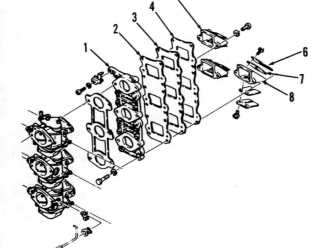

Fig. Y18-5—Exploded view of reed valves, intake manifold and related components.

1. Intake manifold
2. Gasket
3. Plate
4. Gasket
5. Reed valve assy.
6. Reed stop
7. Reed petals
8. Reed block

throttle position and note timing. Loosen locknut and turn idle timing screw (2) as necessary to obtain 4-6 degrees ATDC on 1984 models and 9-11 degrees ATDC on all models after 1984. Move control lever (1) the fully advanced position and note timing. Loosen locknut and turn maximum advance screw (3) to obtain 21-23 degrees BTDC.

NOTE: Engine must be running at more than 4500 rpm when checking or adjusting maximum advance timing.

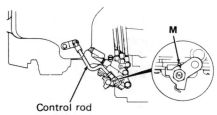

Fig. Y18-9—With carburetor throttle valves fully closed, marks on oil pump lever and pump body should be aligned. Adjust length of pump control rod to adjust.

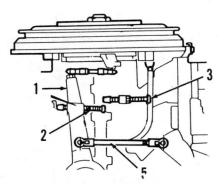

Fig. Y18-11—View of speed control linkage used on 90 hp models.

1. Magneto control lever
2. Idle timing screw
3. Maximum advance timing screw
5. Throttle link

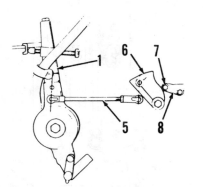

Fig. Y18-12—To adjust pickup timing on 90 hp models, move magneto control lever (1) to the closed throttle position and adjust idle speed to 750-850 rpm. Throttle roller (7) should just contact throttle cam (6) and throttle valves should be closed. Adjust length of link (5) to adjust.

1. Magneto control lever
5. Throttle link
6. Throttle cam
7. Throttle roller
8. Cam follower

To adjust pickup timing, move magneto control rod (1) to the closed-throttle position. Start engine and adjust idle speed to 750-850 rpm in neutral, then stop engine. Throttle roller (7—Fig. Y18-12) should lightly contact throttle cam (6) and throttle valves should be closed. If not, adjust length of throttle link (5) as necessary.

To synchronize carburetor throttle valves, back-off idle speed screw (I—Fig. Y18-13) until throttle valve of center carburetor is fully closed. Loosen throttle lever screws (S) on top and bottom carburetors (left-hand threads). Lightly push down on cam follower (8) closing all throttle valves, then retighten screws (S). Be sure to adjust idle speed to screw (I) to specified rpm (CONDENSED SERVICE DATA).

To adjust oil pump control linkage, back-off idle speed screw (8) until throttle valves are closed. Marks (M—Fig. Y18-9) on pump lever and pump body should be aligned. If not, adjust length of control rod as necessary. Be sure to readjust idle speed screw (I—Fig. Y18-13) to specified rpm (CONDENSED SERVICE DATA).

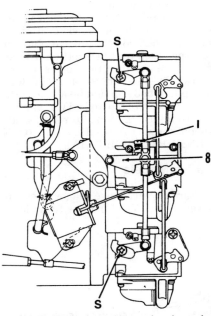

Fig. Y18-13—Refer to text to synchronize carburetor throttle valves.

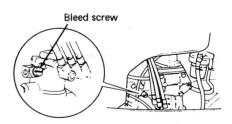

Fig. Y18-15—Loosen bleed screw to purge air from injection system. Refer to text.

OIL INJECTION

BLEEDING OIL PUMP. To bleed trapped air from oil injection system, place outboard motor in an upright position and remove oil reservoir fill cap. Loosen pump bleed screw (Fig. Y18-15) and allow air to escape from around bleed screw. Once air-free oil begins to flow, securely retighten bleed screw. If a large amount of air is present, oil lines should be disconnected and filled with oil prior to performing bleeding procedure.

CHECKING OIL PUMP OUTPUT. Pump output test must be performed with a 50:1 fuel:oil mixture in the fuel tank. Oil temperature should be within 10°-30° C (58°-86° F) for accurate output test results. Start engine and warm to normal operating temperature. Disconnect number 1 cylinder oil injection line from intake manifold and insert oil line into a suitable graduated container. Disconnect oil pump control rod (Fig. Y18-9) from oil pump and move pump lever to the full-throttle position. Start engine and run at 1500 rpm for exactly three minutes. Oil pump output at 1500 rpm in three minutes should be 1.97-2.77 mL (0.067-0.094 fl. oz.) on 70 hp models and 2.7-3.73 mL (0.091-0.126 fl. oz.) on 90 hp models. Repeat test on each remaining oil line. Reconnect pump control rod and bleed injection system as previously described after performing output test.

NOTE: Pump output test data is compiled using Yamaha Two-Stroke Oil. Actual test results may vary depending on brand of oil used, ambient temperature, oil temperature and testing error. Repeat test as necessary to ensure consistent results.

If pump output is low, inspect oil delivery and discharge lines for restrictions or leakage. If no restrictions or leakage is noted, renew oil pump assembly.

IGNITION

All Models

All models are equipped with capacitor discharge ignition (CDI) system. Model 70 hp is equipped with an independent ignition system using a single charge coil and three pulser (trigger) coils. Model 90 hp is equipped with two charge coils and two pulser (trigger) coils. One pulser coil controls cylinders 1 and 3, while remaining pulser coil controls cylinder number 2. Refer to Fig. Y18-16 for wiring diagram on 70 hp models and Fig. Y18-17 for wiring diagram on 90 hp models.

If engine malfunction is noted and ignition system is suspected, make sure spark plugs and wiring are in acceptable condition. Make all electrical connections are clean and tight. Make sure malfunction is not the result of fuel delivery or other fuel system malfunction or failure.

The manufacturer recommends using Yamaha Pocket Tester YU-3112 to test ignition components. Proceed as follows to test ignition system: Disconnect the pulser coil leads from the CDI module. On 70 hp models, attach one tester lead to the black wire and remaining tester lead alternately to the white/red wire, white/black wire and white/green wire. Resistance at all three connections should be 117-143 ohms. On 90 hp models connect tester between the white/black and white/green wires, then between the white/red and white/yellow wires. Pulser coil resistance should be 342-418 ohms at both connections.

To test charge coil on 70 hp models, disconnect charge coil wires from CDI module and connect tester between black and brown wires. Charge coil resistance should be 148.5-181.5 ohms. To test charge coils on 90 hp models, disconnect charge coil wires from CDI module. Connect one tester lead to the brown wire and remaining tester lead to the blue wire. Resistance should be 765-935 ohms. Leave test lead connected to blue wire and switch remaining lead to the red lead. Resistance should again be 765-935 ohms.

To test lighting coil, disconnect lighting coil wires from the rectifier. Connect tester between the two green wires. Lighting coil resistance should be 0.36-0.54 ohm on 70 hp models and 0.54-0.66 ohm on 90 hp models.

To test rectifier/regulator assembly, disconnect wires, refer to Fig. Y18-18 and connect tester as shown in chart. Renew rectifier/regulator assembly if results are not as specified in chart.

Test ignition coil primary winding resistance between coil primary terminal and coil ground wire. Primary resistance should be 0.20-0.24 ohm on 70 hp models and 0.23-0.27 ohm on 90 hp models. To test ignition coil secondary winding resistance, remove spark plug terminal and boot and connect tester between primary terminal and end of high tension lead. Secondary resistance should be 4320-5280 ohms on 70 hp models and 2250-2750 ohms on 90 hp models. If ignition coil resistance is only slightly out of specification, check spark intensity using a spark tester before failing ignition coil.

Use a suitable coil tester or Yamaha YU-33261 to perform a coil power test. Connect tester as described in instructions provided with tester. Using Yamaha coil tester YU-33261, a steady spark should jump an 8 mm (0.31 in.) gap with voltage selector switch in the "CDI" position.

NOTE: Do not crank or start engine without providing a spark gap or grounding secondary high tension leads. Cranking or

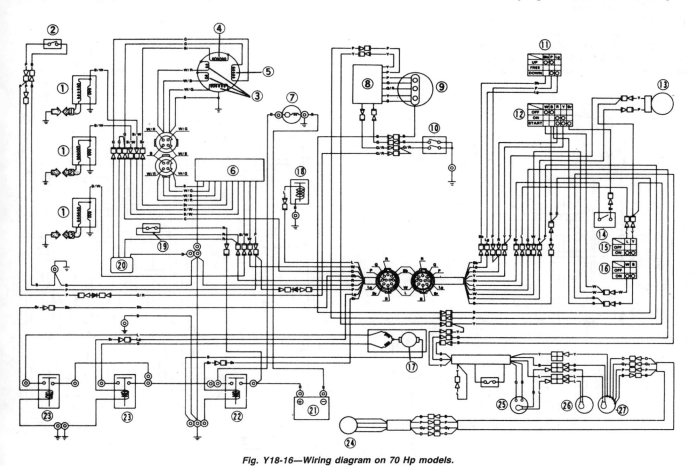

Fig. Y18-16—Wiring diagram on 70 Hp models.

1. Ignition coils	17. Power trim/tilt motor	25. Tachometer		G/Y. Green with yellow tracer
2. Thermo switch	18. Choke solenoid	26. Speedometer	Y. Yellow	W/B. White with black tracer
3. Pulser coils	19. Fuse	27. Trim meter	Br. Brown	
4. Charge coil	20. Rectifier		Lg. Light green	W/G. White with green tracer
5. Lighting coil	21. Battery		Gy. Gray	
6. CDI module	22. Starter relay	B. Black	Sb. Light blue	W/R. White with red tracer
7. Starter motor	23. Power trim/tilt relay	G. Green	B/W. Black with white tracer	
8. Control module	24. Trim sensor	L. Blue		W/Y. White with yellow tracer
9. Oil level warning lamps		O. Orange	G/R. Green with red tracer	
10. Oil level sensor		P. Pink		
11. Power trim/tilt switch		R. Red		
12. Main switch		W. White		
13. Caution buzzer				
14. Neutral switch				
15. Choke switch				
16. Emergency stop switch				

POWER HEAD

starting engine with an open high tension lead will damage CDI module.

Test the CDI module using Electro-Specialties tester Model 1-Y (Yamaha part YU-91022). Follow instructions provided with tester. Isolate main switch, emergency stop switch and all wiring by disconnecting white lead from CDI module prior to testing.

COOLING SYSTEM

THERMOSTAT. A thermostat located in top of the cylinder block on 70 hp models and top of cylinder head on 90 hp models is used to regulate engine operating temperature. Thermostat can be removed for inspection or renewal after removing thermostat cover.

WATER PUMP. A rubber impeller type water pump is mounted between the drive shaft housing and gearcase. Water pump impeller (8—Fig. Y18-20) is driven by a key that engages drive shaft.

If cooling system malfunction occurs, first check water inlet for plugging or partial restriction. Be sure thermostat is operating properly. If necessary, separate gearcase from drive shaft housing and inspect water pump. Make sure all

seals and mating surfaces are in acceptable condition and that water passages are unobstructed. Check impeller (8) and wear plate (11) for excessive wear.

Press seals (16) into base (13) with seal lips facing toward impeller. Coat seal lips with a suitable water-resistant grease. Rotate drive shaft clockwise when installing housing (6) over impeller. Avoid turning drive shaft in opposite direction after housing is installed.

REMOVE AND REINSTALL. Remove engine cowl and disconnect battery cables. Disconnect leads from power trim/tilt motor and relays, then remove relays. On 70 hp models, remove CDI module cover, disconnect starter relay and fuse lead, then remove starter relay from lower engine cowl. On 90 hp models, disconnect ground lead from

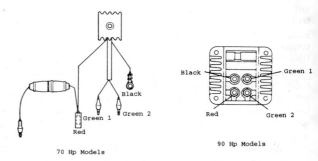

Fig. Y18-18—Refer to chart for test connections and desired results when testing rectifier/regulator assembly.

⊖ Tester ⊕ Tester	Green 1	Green 2	Red	Black
Green 1		Infinity	Continuity	Infinity
Green 2	Infinity		Continuity	Infinity
Red	Infinity	Infinity		Infinity
Black	Continuity	Continuity	Continuity	

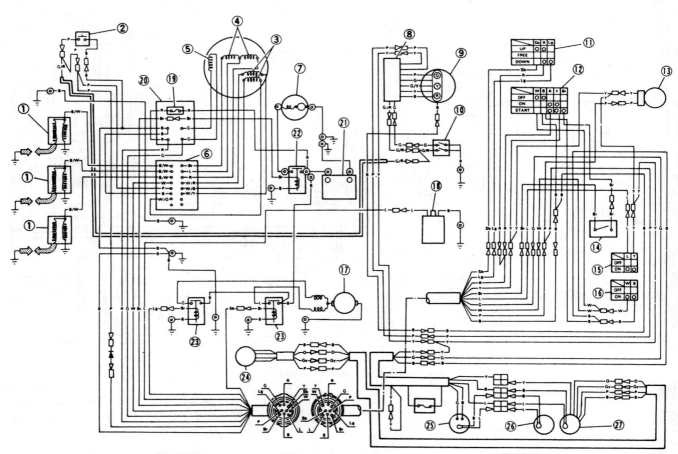

Fig. Y18-17—Wiring diagram on 90 hp models. Refer to Fig. Y18-16 for component and color code identification.

cylinder head cover and remove oil reservoir. On all models, disconnect fuel supply hose at fuel filter. Remove cooling water pilot hose from exhaust cover. Remove shift and throttle cables and disconnect choke link. Remove front and rear lower engine cowls. Remove 11 power head mounting screws, lift power head off drive shaft housing and place into a suitable holding fixture.

NOTE: Two dowel pins are used to properly align power head and drive shaft housing. Dowel pins may stick in bottom of power head during removal. If so, be sure to retrieve pins to prevent loss. Refer to Fig. Y18-26 for correct location of dowel pins.

When reinstalling power head, make sure dowel pins are driven into drive shaft housing at locations shown in Fig. Y18-26. Place a new gasket between power head and drive shaft housing. Make sure drive shaft and crankshaft splines are clean and apply a light coat of water-resistant grease to splines. Avoid excess application. Place power head onto drive shaft housing and tighten power head screws to 21 N·m (15 ft.-lbs.). Complete remainder of reinstallation by reversing removal procedure.

DISASSEMBLY. All wearing components should be marked for location and direction for reference during reassembly. Remove flywheel using a suitable puller. Be sure to retrieve flywheel key. Remove carburetors, fuel filter and fuel pump.

On 70 hp models, disconnect and remove choke solenoid. Remove ignition coils, disconnect and remove wiring harness, remove CDI module and starter motor. Disconnect and remove magneto control lever and speed control linkage. Remove lighting coil, pulser assembly and retainer. Disconnect and remove any wires or linkage that will interfere with power head disassembly.

On 90 hp models, remove CDI module cover and disconnect wires from module. Disconnect wires from rectifier/regulator assembly. Remove magneto control lever and speed control linkage. Remove stator assembly, pulser assembly and retainer. Remove choke solenoid, ignition coils, then disconnect and remove wiring harness. Remove rectifier, starter relay, CDI module and module bracket. Remove starter motor. Disconnect any wires or linkage that will interfere with power head disassembly.

On all models, disconnect oil injection hoses at intake manifold and remove oil injection pump with hoses. Extract oil pump driven gear from crankcase. Remove intake manifold and reed valve assemblies. On 90 hp models, remove ther-

mostat cover, thermostat and pressure relief valve. On all models, remove cylinder head cover and cylinder head. Dislodge cylinder head by tapping on one end with a suitable soft-face mallet. Do not attempt to pry off head. Remove exhaust covers. Note that tabs are provided on inner exhaust cover for prying covers from cylinder block. Remove screws securing lower oil seal housing, then remove crankcase screws. Separate crankcase cover from cylinder block by carefully prying at tabs located on both sides of crankcase cover. DO NOT pry between mating surfaces of cylinder block and crankcase cover. Remove lower oil seal housing. Crankshaft, connecting rods, bearings and piston assemblies are now accessible for inspection and overhaul as outlined in the appropriate service sections.

REASSEMBLY. It is recommended that all gasket surfaces of crankcase and cylinder block be carefully checked for nicks, burrs or warped surfaces that might interfere with a tight seal. The cylinder head, mating surfaces of manifolds and crankcase may be checked and lapped, if necessary, to provide a smooth surface. Cylinder head should be resurfaced if warped in excess of 0.1 mm (0.004 in). Do not remove any more metal than is necessary to true mating surface. Mating surface of crankcase cover and cylinder block may be checked on the lapping block, and high spots or nicks removed, but surfaces MUST NOT be lowered. If extreme care is used, a slightly damaged crankcase can be salvaged in this manner. In case of doubt, renew the crankcase assembly.

Reassemble power head by reversing disassembly procedure. Renew all seals, gaskets and "O" rings. All bearing and friction surfaces should be thoroughly lubricated during assembly using a recommended engine oil. Apply Yamabond #4 or a suitable equivalent sealer to mating surfaces of cylinder block and lower oil seal housing. Install seals (17 and 18 Figs. Y18-24 or Y18-25) into seal housing (20) with seal lips facing away from power head. Rotate crankshaft frequently during reassembly to check for binding or abnormal noise; any noise or binding must be repaired before proceeding with assembly. Refer to CONDENSED SERVICE DATA section for torque specifications. Tighten crankcase cover, cylinder head and exhaust cover screws in two steps. Refer to Figs. Y18-28 through Y18-32 for the recommended fastener tightening sequences.

PISTONS, PINS, RINGS AND CYLINDERS. Early models are equipped with three piston rings. Top ring is semi-keystone shape and second and third are standard square shape. As

a running change on 1989 models, the bottom ring is eliminated and the top and bottom rings are both semi-keystone shape. Locating pins are present in piston ring grooves. Be certain ring end gaps are properly positioned around locating pins when installing piston in cylinder. Install square rings with manufacturer's marking facing crown of piston. Refer to CONDENSED SERVICE DATA section for piston ring service specifications.

Standard cylinder bore diameter is 72.00-72.02 mm (2.8346-2.8354 in.) on 70 hp models and 82.00-82.02 mm (3.2283-3.2291 in.) on 90 hp models. Maximum allowable cylinder taper is 0.08 mm (0.0031 in.). Maximum allowable cylinder out-of-round is 0.05 mm (0.0020 in.). Refer to CONDENSED SERVICE DATA section for piston-to-cylinder clearance. Pistons and rings are available in 0.25 mm (0.010 in.) and 0.50 mm (0.020 in.) oversizes. Connecting rod small end bearing consists of 28 loose bearing rollers. Yamaha special tools YB-6287 (70

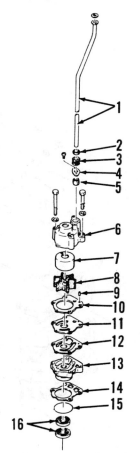

Fig. Y18-20—Exploded view of water pump assembly.

1. Water tube	
2. Seal	10. Gasket
3. Grommet	11. Plate
4. Retainer	12. Gasket
5. Grommet	13. Pump base & seal
6. Housing	housing assy.
7. Liner	14. Gasket
8. Impeller	15. "O" ring
9. Dowel	16. Seals

hp) or YB-6107 (90 hp) are available to ease bearing rollers and piston pin installation. Piston pin is a slip fit in piston. No play should be noted between pin and pin bore in piston. Install thrust washers (6—Figs. Y18-24 or Y18-25) with convex side facing out. Install pistons on rods so ''UP'' mark on piston crown faces toward top of engine. Always renew piston pin retainers during reassembly.

70 Hp Models

CRANKSHAFT, CONNECTING RODS AND BEARINGS. On 70 hp models crankshaft, connecting rods, rod bearings and crankpins are a pressed-together unit assembly. Refer to Fig. Y18-24. Maximum crankshaft runout is 0.05 mm (0.020 in.) measured at main bearings with ends of crankshaft supported in V-blocks. Connecting rod small

end bearing consists of 28 loose needle bearing rollers. Thoroughly lubricate all bearing and friction surfaces during reassembly. Locating pins located in cylinder block must properly engage main bearings and labyrinth seal.

90 Hp Models

CRANKSHAFT, CONNECTING RODS AND BEARINGS. Match mark connecting rod cap and rod prior to removing rod cap. Connecting rods and bearings are available separately from crankshaft on 90 hp models. Refer to Fig. Y18-25. Maximum allowable crankshaft runout is 0.02 mm (0.0008 in.) measured at each main bearing journal with ends of crankshaft supported in V-blocks. Measure connecting rod big end side play as shown at (B—Fig. Y18-34). If side play (B) in not within 0.20-0.33 mm (0.008-0.013 in.), remove connect-

ing rod and inspect connecting rod and crankshaft. If connecting rod small end side-to-side play (A) exceeds 2 mm (0.079 in.), inspect condition of connecting rod, crankpin and bearing. Locating pin holes on upper and center main bearings should face toward top of engine when installed. Install oil pump drive gear (15) with recessed side facing snap ring (16). Install connecting rods so the ''YAMAHA'' cast in the rod is facing top of engine.

NOTE: The manufacturer recommends renewing connecting rod screws upon reassembly.

Use the following procedure to align rod and rod cap during reassembly: Install bearings (12) and caps (21). Finger tighten screws making sure rod cap and rod are perfectly aligned. Tighten screws to 17 N·m (12 ft.-lbs.), then to 35

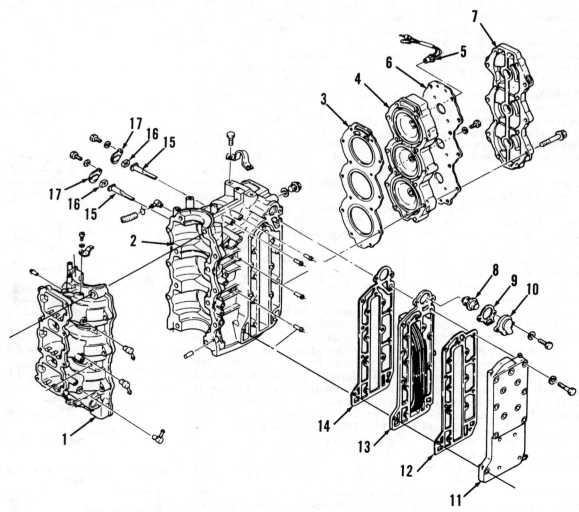

Fig. Y18-22—Exploded view of crankcase and cylinder block assembly on 70 hp models.

1. Crankcase cover
2. Cylinder block
3. Gasket
4. Cylinder head
5. Thermo switch
6. Gasket
7. Cylinder head cover
8. Thermostat
9. Gasket
10. Cover
11. Outer exhaust cover
12. Gasket
13. Inner exhaust cover
14. Gasket
15. Anode
16. Grommet
17. Covers

N·m (26 ft.-lbs.). Recheck rod and cap for proper alignment. If perfect alignment is not obtained, loosen rod screws and repeat above procedure. If rod and cap are aligned, loosen screws one half turn, retighten to 17 N·m (12 ft.-lbs.), then to 35 N·m (26 ft.-lbs.).

STARTER

ELECTRIC STARTER. Refer to Figs. Y18-35 or Y18-36 for exploded view of starter motors used. Disassembly and reassembly is evident after inspection of unit and referral to exploded view. True commutator by turning on a suitable lathe if commutator runout exceeds 0.2 mm (0.008 in.). Armature should be renewed if commutator diameter is less than 29 mm (1.14 in.) on 70 hp models and 31 mm (1.22 in.) on 90 hp models. Minimum brush length is 9 mm (0.35 in.) on 70 hp models and 12 mm (0.47 in.) on 90 hp models. Insulation between commutator segments should be undercut to 0.5-0.8 mm (0.020-0.031 in.) with a minimum of 0.2 mm (0.008 in.). On 90 hp models apply a suitable sealing compound to mating surfaces of end frame

(15—Fig. Y18-36) and frame (10). On all models, lubricate bushings and friction surfaces with a suitable water-resistant grease.

LOWER UNIT

PROPELLER AND DRIVE HUB. Lower unit protection is provided by a cushion type hub in the propeller. Various propellers are available from the manufacturer. Select a propeller that will allow full throttle operation within the recommended speed range of 4500-5500 rpm.

R&R AND OVERHAUL. To remove gearcase, place shift lever into neutral position, tilt outboard motor fully up and engage tilt lock lever. Remove trim tab and five gearcase mounting screws. Separate gearcase from drive shaft housing and place into a suitable holding fixture.

Note location and thickness of all shims for reference during reassembly. Drain gearcase oil. Remove water pump assembly (1 through 10—Fig. Y18-38) Remove propeller and thrust hub (49).

Straighten tabs of tab washer (47) and remove ring nut (48) using Yamaha special tool YB-34447 or equivalent. Pull bearing carrier (43) from gearcase. Be sure to retrieve key (44). Remove retainer plate (18) and pull lower shift rod out of gearcase, then pull propeller shaft assembly (27 through 30 and 34 through 37) from gearcase. Remove pinion nut (25) by holding nut (25) and turning drive shaft (11), then remove drive shaft (11), pinion gear (26) and forward gear and bearing from gearcase. If necessary, remove bearing (32) race and bearing (13) race from gearcase using a suitable slide-hammer puller with internal expanding jaws. Remove shim (14) and sleeve (15). To remove bearing (16), drive bearing down into gear cavity using a suitable driver.

To disassemble propeller shaft, remove shift cam (27) from cam follower (28), remove crosspin retainer (36), push out crosspin and slide dog clutch (35) off propeller shaft. Using a thin blade screwdriver, remove shift balls (29) from the neutral position, then remove follower (28) and plunger and spring assembly (30). Remove seals (46) and bear-

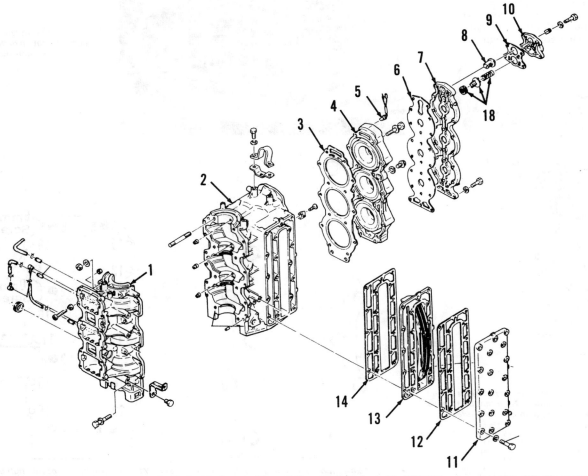

Fig. Y18-23—Exploded view of crankcase and cylinder block assembly on 90 hp models. Refer to Fig. Y18-22 for component identification except pressure relief valve assembly (18).

ing (45) from carrier (43). If necessary, remove bearing (13) from drive shaft (11), bearing (32) from forward gear (33) and bearing (41) from reverse gear (38) using a bearing splitter and a suitable press.

NOTE: Do not remove bearings (13, 32 and 41) unless renewal is necessary.

Inspect all components for excessive wear or other damage. Inspect gears for wear on teeth and engagement dogs. Note that forward gear (33), reverse gear (38) and pinion gear (26) should be renewed as a complete set. Inspect dog clutch for wear on engagement surfaces. Inspect shafts for wear on splines and on friction surfaces of gears and oil seals. Renew propeller shaft if runout exceeds 0.02 mm (0.0008 in.). Renew drive shaft (11) if runout exceeds 0.5 mm (0.020 in.) measured at point (A—Fig. Y18-39) or 0.02 mm (0.0008 in.) measured at points (B or C).

Renew all seals, gaskets and "O" rings during reassembly. Install seals (46) into carrier (43) with lips facing propeller. Install seals (10) into water pump base (7) with lips facing up. Lubricate all seal lips with a suitable water-resistant grease. Apply a suitable corrosion-resistant sealer to outer diameter of carrier (43) where carrier contacts gear cavity.

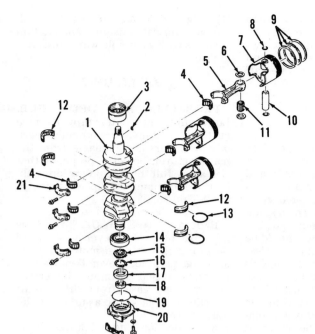

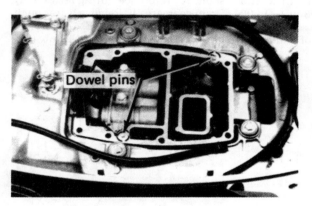

Fig. Y18-25—Exploded view of crankshaft assembly used on 90 hp models. Note that bottom piston ring is eliminated on late models.

1. Crankshaft
2. Woodruff key
3. Bearing
4. Bearing
5. Connecting rod
6. Thrust washer
7. Piston
8. Retainer
9. Piston rings
10. Piston pin
11. Bearing rollers
12. Bearing half
13. Retainer
14. Bearing
15. Oil pump drive gear
16. Snap ring
17. Seal
18. Seal
19. "O" ring
20. Seal housing
21. Connecting rod cap

Fig. Y18-26—View showing correct location of dowel pins in drive shaft housing.

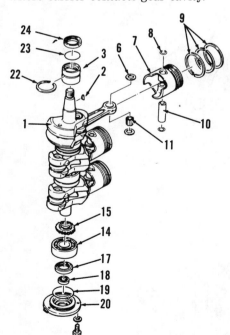

Fig. Y18-24—Exploded view of crankshaft assembly used on 70 hp models. Note that bottom piston ring is eliminated on late models.

1. Crankshaft assy.
2. Woodruff key
3. Bearing
6. Thrust washer
7. Piston
8. Retainer
9. Piston rings
10. Piston pin
11. Bearing rollers
14. Bearing
15. Oil pump drive gear
17. Seal
18. Seal
19. "O" ring
20. Seal housing
22. Retainer
23. "O" ring
24. Seal

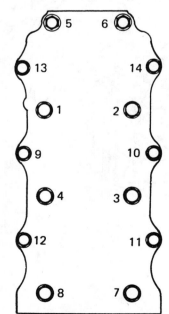

Fig. Y18-28—Crankcase cover tightening sequence on 70 hp models. Tighten screws in two steps.

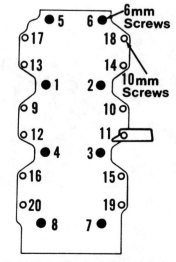

Fig. Y18-29—Crankcase cover tightening sequence on 90 hp models. Tighten screws in two steps.

Illustrations courtesy Yamaha

Reassemble gearcase by reversing disassembly procedure while noting the following: Shim (14) should be adjusted to obtain the best possible mesh between pinion gear and forward gear. Install original shim (31), bearing race (32) and forward gear (33) into gearcase. Install drive shaft assembly into gearcase, install pinion gear (26) and tighten pinion nut (25) to 95 N·m (70 ft.-lbs.). Using a suitable gear marking compound, adjust thickness of shim (14) so teeth of gears (26 and 33) are engaged along their entire length.

Forward gear backlash should be 0.09-0.28 mm (0.004-0.011 in.) and is adjusted

by varying thickness of shim (31). Reverse gear backlash should be 0.75-1.13 mm (0.030-0.044 in.) and is adjusted by varying thickness of shim (39).

When reassembling propeller shaft, position shift cam follower (28) so balls (29) are located in the neutral detent. Dog clutch should be installed on propeller shaft with the "F" mark facing forward. Place shift cam (27) into cam follower (28) with the "F" mark facing forward. When installing shift rod (21), make sure shift rod properly engages shift cam. Tighten ring nut (48) to 145 N·m (107 ft.-lbs.), then make sure ring nut is secured by tab washer (47).

Make sure gearcase will correctly shift into forward, neutral and reverse positions by rotating lower shift rod (21). Gearcase must be in neutral when installing on drive shaft housing. Drive shaft splines should be lightly lubricated with water-resistant grease. Tighten gearcase-to-drive shaft housing screws to 40 N·m (29 ft.-lbs.).

POWER TRIM AND TILT

All models are equipped with power trim and tilt system. An oil pump driven by a reversible electric motor provides oil pressure. A rocker control switch determines motor and pump rotation, thereby extending or retracting cylinders. The pump is equipped with a manual release valve (39—Fig. Y18-40). Opening (counterclockwise) manual valve (39) will allow manual movement of cylinders if power trim/tilt malfunction occurs.

The recommended oil is Yamaha Power Trim/Tilt Fluid. Fill plug (50) is lo-

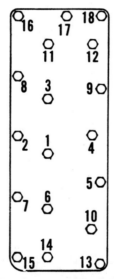

Fig. Y18-30—Tighten cylinder head screws in sequence shown on all models.

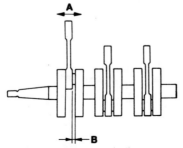

Fig. Y18-32—On 90 hp models, tighten exhaust cover screws in sequence shown.

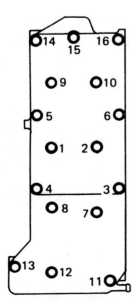

Fig. Y18-31—On 70 hp models, tighten exhaust cover screws in sequence shown.

Fig. Y18-34—On 90 hp models, connecting rod big end side play (B) should be within 0.20-0.33 mm (0.008-0.013 in.). Connecting rod small end side-to-side play (A) should not exceed 2 mm (0.079 in.). Refer to text.

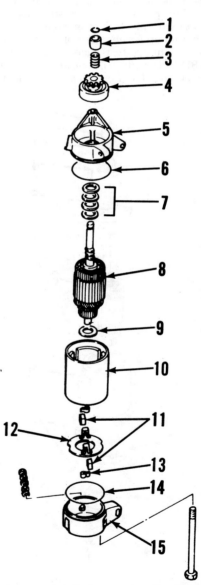

Fig. Y18-35—Exploded view of the Hitachi Model S108-97 starter motor used on 70 hp models.

1. Clip
2. Stopper
3. Spring
4. Drive assy.
5. End frame
6. "O" ring
7. Washers
8. Armature
9. Washer
10. Frame assy.
11. Brush
12. Brush plate
13. Brush spring
14. "O" ring
15. End frame

cated on side of pump reservoir. Oil level should be checked and filled with cylinders fully retracted. Reservoir is full when oil level is at bottom of fill plug hole.

To bleed trapped air from hydraulic system, tilt outboard motor fully up, then open manual release valve and allow outboard motor to return to the down position by its own weight. Repeat as necessary until all air is purged.

If trim/tilt system malfunction occurs, first make sure malfunction is not due to faulty wiring, wiring connections, relays, switch or electric motor. Make sure oil leakage is not present at cylinders or hydraulic lines, and that reservoir is full.

To test pump output pressure, disconnect hydraulic lines at bottom of reservoir and upper chamber of tilt cylinder (53). Connect test gage (Yamaha YB-6181) to the tilt cylinder and reservoir as shown at (A—Fig. Y18-41). Close manual release valve (clockwise) and tilt outboard motor up, then down, then open manual release valve to bleed any air in system. Return manual release valve to the closed position. Operate trim/tilt switch in the up direction, noting pressure gage while traveling up. Continue operating in the up direction for three seconds after full up is reached, and note test gage. During upward movement, pressure should be 0-490 kPa (0-71 psi). After full up is reached pressure should be zero. Next, tilt outboard motor down, continue for three seconds after full down, then note pressure gage. Down pressure should be 4018-5390 kPa (583-782 psi).

Repeat procedure with test gage connected as shown at (B). Pressure while tilting up should be 0-490 kPa (0-71 psi), and after reaching full up, pressure should be 9310-11,270 kPa (1350-1635 psi). Down pressure should be 588-1078 kPa (85-156 psi).

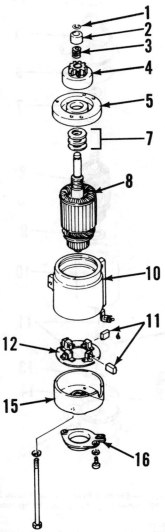

Fig. Y18-36—Exploded view of the Hitachi Model S114-263 starter motor used on 90 hp models. Refer to Fig. Y18-35 for component identification except cover (16).

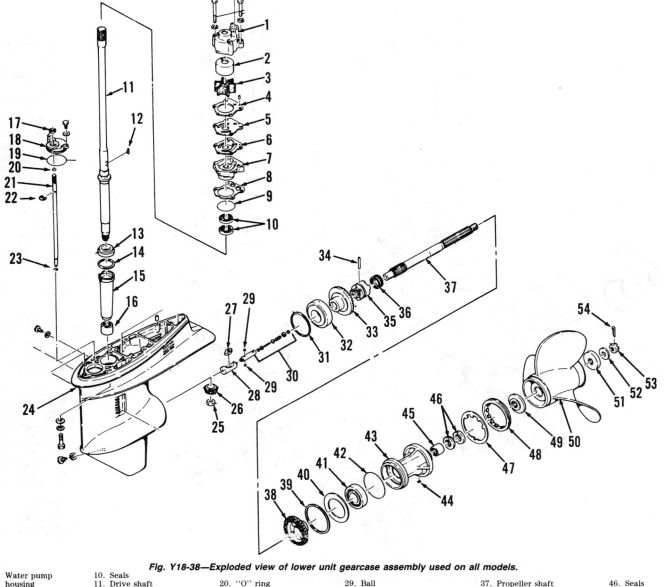

Fig. Y18-38—Exploded view of lower unit gearcase assembly used on all models.

1. Water pump housing	10. Seals	20. "O" ring	29. Ball	37. Propeller shaft	46. Seals
2. Liner	11. Drive shaft	21. Lower shift shaft	30. Shift plunger & spring assy.	38. Reverse gear	47. Tab washer
3. Impeller	12. Impeller drive key	22. "E" ring		39. Shim	48. Ring nut
4. Gasket	13. Bearing & race assy.	23. Clip	31. Shim	40. Thrust washer	49. Thrust hub
5. Plate	14. Shim	24. Gearcase housing	32. Bearing & race assy.	41. Bearing & race assy.	50. Propeller
6. Gasket	15. Sleeve	25. Pinion nut	33. Forward gear	42. "O" ring	51. Spacer
7. Base	16. Bearing	26. Pinion gear	34. Crosspin	43. Bearing carrier	52. Washer
8. Gasket	17. Seal	27. Shift cam	35. Dog clutch	44. Key	53. Nut
9. "O" ring	18. Retainer plate	28. Shift cam follower	36. Crosspin retainer	45. Bearing	54. Cotter pin
	19. "O" ring				

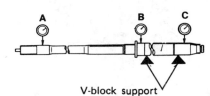

Fig. Y18-39—Renew drive shaft if runout exceeds 0.5 mm 0.020 in.) measured at point A, or 0.02 mm (0.0008 in.) measured at points B or C.

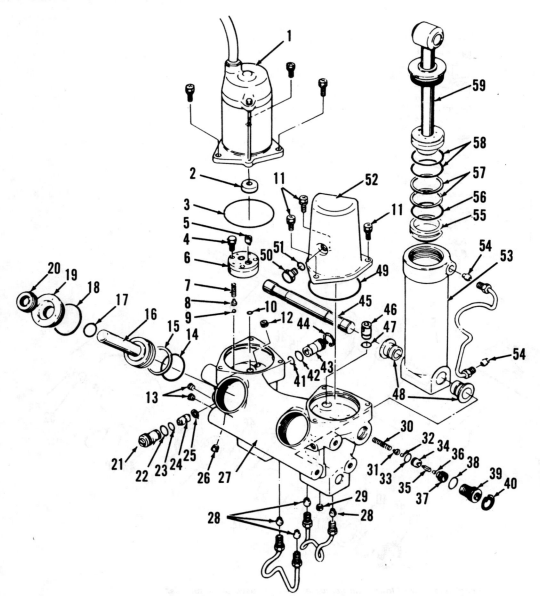

1. Motor assy.
2. Seal
3. "O" ring
4. Screw
5. Coupler shaft
6. Pump assy.
7. Spring
8. Valve support pin
9. Ball
10. "O" ring
11. Screws
12. Plug
13. Plugs
14. "O" ring
15. Backup ring
16. Piston & rod assy.
17. "O" ring
18. "O" ring
19. End cap
20. Seal
21. Main valve
22. "O" ring
23. "O" ring
24. Shuttle piston
25. Backup ring
26. Plug
27. Housing assy.
28. Seats
29. Plug
30. Spring
31. Manual release pin
32. Ball
33. "O" ring
34. Valve seat
35. Manual release rod
36. Ball
37. Seat screw
38. "O" ring
39. Manual release screw
40. Snap ring
41. "O" ring
42. "O" ring
43. Main valve
44. Snap ring
45. Shaft
46. Up release valve
47. "O" ring
48. Bushing
49. "O" ring
50. Fill plug
51. "O" ring
52. Reservoir
53. Tilt cylinder
54. Seat
55. Free piston
56. "O" ring
57. Backup rings
58. "O" rings
59. Piston & rod assy.

Fig. Y18-40—Exploded view of power trim/tilt assembly.

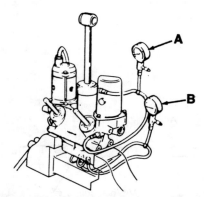

Fig. Y18-41—View showing test gage connection for checking tilt pressure (A) and trim pressure (B).

YAMAHA V-4 AND V-6 MODELS

CONDENSED SERVICE DATA

NOTE: Metric fasteners are used throughout outboard motor.

TUNE-UP

Hp/rpm 115/5000
130/5800
150/5000
175/5500
200/5500
220/5800
225/5800

Bore . . . . .90 mm
(3.542 in.)

Stroke . . . . .68 mm
(2.677 in.)

Displacement
V-4 Models . . . . .1730 cc
(105.6 cu. in.)
V-6 Models . . . . .2596 cc
(158.4 cu. in.)

Spark Plug:
115 Hp . . . . .NGK B8HS-10
150 (After 1985),
Pro V 150, 175 and 200 Hp . . . . .NGK B8HS-10
150 Hp (Prior to 1986) . . . . .NGK B7HS-10
220 Hp (V-6 Special) . . . . .NGK BR8HS-10
225 Hp (V-6 Excel) . . . . .NGK BR9HS-10
Electrode Gap (All Models) . . . . .0.9-1.0 mm
(0.035-0.039 in.)
Ignition Type . . . . .CDI
Idle Speed (in forward gear):
115 and 130 Hp . . . . .600-700 rpm
150, 175, 200 and 220 Hp . . . . .600-650 rpm
Pro V 150 and 225 Hp . . . . .550-600 rpm
Fuel:Oil Ratio . . . . .See Text

SIZES—CLEARANCES

Piston Ring End Gap .0.3-0.5 mm
(0.012-0.020 in.)

Piston Ring Side Clearance:
Semi-Keystone Ring . . . . .0.030-0.065 mm
(0.0012-0.0026 in.)
Plain Ring . . . . .0.040-0.075 mm
(0.0016-0.0029 in.)

Piston Clearance:
V-6 Excel (225 Hp) . . . . .0.050-0.055 mm
(0.0020-0.0022 in.)
All Other Models Prior to 1989 . . . . . .0.085-0.090 mm
(0.0033-0.0035 in.)

All Other Models After 1988 . . . . . . .0.080-0.085 mm
(0.0031-0.0033 in.)
Maximum Allowable Crankshaft Runout . . . . . .0.02 mm
(0.0008 in.)
Standard Cylinder Bore Diameter . . . . . .90.00-90.02 mm
(3.5433-3.5440 in.)
Maximum Allowable Taper . . . . .0.08 mm
(0.0031 in.)
Maximum Allowable Out-of-Round . . . . .0.05 mm
(0.0020 in.)

TIGHTENING TORQUES

Connecting Rod Cap . . . . .37 N·m
(27 ft.-lbs.)
Crankcase:
8 mm . . . . .18 N·m
(13 ft.-lbs.)
10 mm . . . . .40 N·m
(29 ft.-lbs.)
Cylinder Head . . . . .30 N·m
(22 ft.-lbs.)
Cylinder Head Cover .8 N·m
(71 in.-lbs.)
Exhaust Cover . . . . .8 N·m
(71 in.-lbs.)
Intake Manifold . . . . .8 N·m
(71 in.-lbs.)
Flywheel . . . . .160 N·m
(118 ft.-lbs.)
Lower Oil Seal Housing . . . . .8 N·m
(71 in.-lbs.)
Spark Plug . . . . .25 N·m
(18 ft.-lbs.)
Upper Bearing Housing . . . . .8 N·m
(71 in.-lbs.)
Standard Screws:
5 mm . . . . .5 N·m
(44 in.-lbs.)
6 mm . . . . .8 N·m
(71 in.-lbs.)
8 mm . . . . .18 N·m
(13 ft.-lbs.)
10 mm . . . . .36 N·m
(26 ft.-lbs.)
12 mm . . . . .43 N·m
(32 ft.-lbs.)

LUBRICATION

The power head is lubricated by oil mixed with the fuel. Fuel should be unleaded gasoline with a minimum pump octane rating of 89 on V-6 Special (220 hp) and V-6 Excel (225 hp) models and 86 on all other models. The manufacturer does not recommend using alcohol extended gasoline; however, if gasoline with alcohol additives must be used, inspect condition of fuel lines and related components at a minimum of each six months operation and take extra precautions to prevent fuel from being contaminated with water. The recommended oil is Yamaha Two-Stroke Oil or equivalent NMMA certified TC-WII engine oil. All models are equipped with Yamaha Precision Blend oil injection system. The oil injection system varies fuel:oil ratio from approximately 200:1 at idle to approximately 50:1 at full throttle by sensing throttle opening and engine rpm. During engine break-in period (first 10 hours of operation), a 50:1 fuel and oil mixture should be used in the fuel tank in combination with the oil injection system to ensure adequate power head lubrication. After break-in period, switch to straight gasoline in the fuel tank. Make sure oil injection system is functioning (oil level dropping in reservoir) prior to switching to straight gasoline.

The lower unit gears and bearings are lubricated by oil contained in the gearcase. Recommended oil is YAMALUBE Gearcase·Lube or a suitable SAE 90 hypoid gear lubricant. Gearcase capacity is 790 mL (26.7 fl. oz.) on 115 and 130 hp models, 900 mL (30.4 fl. oz.) on 220 hp models, 910 mL (30.8 fl. oz.) on 150, 175 and 200 hp models and 980 mL (33.1 fl. oz.) on Pro V 150 and 225 hp models. Gearcase oil should be checked after the first 10 hours of operation, then every 100 hours thereafter. To drain lubricant, tilt outboard motor fully up, then remove drain and vent plugs. Refill gearcase through drain plug hole until oil reaches level of vent plug hole.

FUEL SYSTEM

CARBURETOR. Refer to Fig. Y20-1 for an exploded view of the Teikei carburetor used on early models and Fig. Y20-2 for an exploded view of the Nikki carburetor used on mid 1986 and later models. V-4 models are equipped with two carburetors. V-6 models are equipped with three carburetors. Position of carburetors is not interchangeable. Early model carburetors are two-barrel design with one common float. Later model carburetors (mid 1986 and later) are two-barrel design with two separate floats.

Pilot screw (4) adjustment is set at the factory and may vary from engine-to-engine. If pilot screw adjustment is required, each pilot screw should be adjusted equally. When removing pilot screw during carburetor service, record the number of turns required to lightly seat the pilot screw for reference during reassembly. If setting of pilot screw is unknown, initial setting from a light-

ly seated position should be as outlined in the following chart:

115 Hp—
1984 (Carb No. 6E502) . . . $1\frac{7}{8}$ to $2\frac{3}{8}$
1985 (Carb No. 6E503) . . . $1\frac{1}{4}$ to $1\frac{3}{4}$
Early 1986 (Carb No. 6E510):
Starboard . . . . $1\frac{7}{8}$ to $2\frac{3}{8}$
Port. . . . . $1\frac{5}{8}$ to $2\frac{5}{8}$
Late 1986 and 1987-1989
(Carb No. 6E511) . . . . $\frac{3}{8}$ to $\frac{7}{8}$

130 Hp (Carb No. 6L100) . . . . $\frac{5}{8}$ to $2\frac{1}{8}$

150 Hp—
1984 (Carb No. 6G400) . . . $2\frac{1}{8}$ to $2\frac{5}{8}$
1985 and Early 1986
(Carb No. 6G402) . . . . $\frac{7}{8}$ to $1\frac{3}{8}$
Late 1986 and 1987-1989
(Carb No. 6G403) . . . . 1 to $1\frac{1}{2}$

Pro V 150—
1986 and 1987 (Carb No. 6J900):
Starboard . . . . $\frac{3}{4}$ to $1\frac{1}{4}$
Port. . . . . $1\frac{1}{4}$ to $1\frac{3}{4}$
1988 and 1989 (Carb

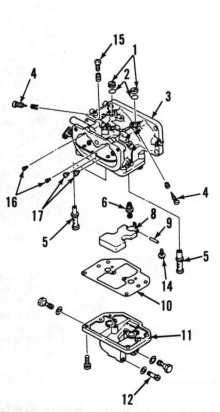

Fig. Y20-1—Exploded view of the Teikei two-barrel carburetors used on early models.

1. Bypass plugs
2. Gaskets
3. Body
4. Pilot screws
5. Main nozzles
6. Inlet valve assy.
8. Float
9. Pin
10. Gasket
11. Float bowl
12. Main jets
14. Set screw
15. Idle speed screw
16. Pilot air jets
17. Main air jets

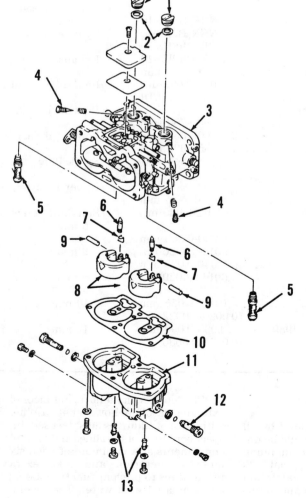

Fig. Y20-2—Exploded view of Nikki two-barrel carburetors used on mid 1986 and later models.

1. Bypass plugs
2. Gaskets
3. Body
4. Pilot screws
5. Main nozzles
6. Inlet valves
7. Clips
8. Floats
9. Pins
10. Gasket
11. Float bowl
12. Main jets
13. Pilot jets

696

No. 6J902): Starboard . . . ¹/₂ to 1¹/₄
Port . . . . 1 to 1¹/₂

175 Hp—
1984 (Carb No. 6G500) . . . 1⁷/₈ to 2³/₈
1985 and Early 1986 (Carb
No. 6G502): Starboard . . . ⁷/₈ to 1³/₈
Port . . . . 1¹/₂ to 2
Late 1986, 1987 and 1988
(Carb No. 6G5031 . . . . . . ¹/₈ to 1⁵/₈
1989 (Carb No. 6G505): . . 1¹/₄ to 1³/₄

200 Hp—
1984 (Carb No. 6G600) . . . 1⁷/₈ to 2³/₈
1985 and Early 1986 (Carb
No. 6G602): Starboard . . 1⁷/₈ to 2³/₈
Port . . . . 1¹/₄ to 1³/₄
Late 1986 and 1987 (Carb
No. 6G603): Starboard . . . ⁵/₈ to 1¹/₈
Port . . . . 1³/₈ to 1⁷/₈
1988 (Carb No. 6G603):
Starboard . . . . ⁵/₈ to 1¹/₈
Port . . . . 1 to 1¹/₂
1989 (Carb No. 6G606):
Starboard . . . . ¹/₂ to 1
Port . . . . 1 to 1¹/₂

220 Hp (V-6 Special)—
1985 and Early 1986
(Carb No. 6G701) . . . . . . 1¹/₄ to 1³/₄
Late 1986 (Carb No. 6G702):
Starboard . . . . ¹/₂ to 1
Port . . . . 1³/₈ to 1⁷/₈

225 Hp (V-6 Excel)—
1987 and 1988
(Carb No. 6K700) . . . . ³/₄ to 1¹/₄
1989 (Carb No. 6K700) 1¹/₂

Final pilot screw adjustment should be made with engine running at normal operating temperature. Adjust pilot screws so engine idles smoothly and does not hesitate during acceleration.

Refer to chart in Fig. Y20-3 for standard jet sizes for normal operation. To check float level, remove float bowl and invert carburetor. Measure from float bowl mating surface to bottom of float as shown in Fig. Y20-4. Float level (L) should be 12-13 mm (0.47-0.51 in.) on the early Teikei carburetors (one float) and 16 mm (0.63 in.) on later Nikki carbure-

tors (two floats). Note that view in Fig. Y20-4 shows early 1986 and prior carburetor. Measure float level on later carburetors with two floats using the same method. Adjust float level by carefully bending tang on float arm.

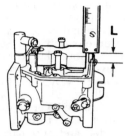

Fig. Y20-4—Float level (L) measured from float bowl mating surface to float as shown should be 12-13 mm (0.47-0.51 in.) on the early Teikei carburetors and 16 mm (0.63 in.) on mid 1986 and later models equipped with Nikki carburetors. View shows Teikei carburetor. Float level is measured the same on Nikki carburetors except two floats require adjustment. Bend tang on float arm(s) to adjust float level.

Model	Carburetor stamped mark	Main jet	Main air jet	Pilot jet	Pilot air jet
115 hp					
1984	6E502	#175	#160	#94	#50
1985	6E503	#175	#250	#84	#60
1986	6E510	#170	2.5 mm	#88	0.5 mm
1986-on	6E511	#180	2.5 mm	#78	#60
130 hp	6L100	#180	#220	#82	#60
150 hp					
1984	6G400	#125	#130	#94	#50
1985-1986	6G402	#130	#190	#90	#50
1987	6G403	#124	#210	#74	#60
1988-on	6G403	#124	#210	#80	#60
150 hp Pro V					
1986 and 1987	6J900	#124	#210	#80	#60
1988-on	6J902	#124	#210	#82	#60
175 hp					
1984	6G500	#125	0.9 mm	#94	#50
1985-1986	6G502	#130	#180	#90	#50
Late 1986 and 1987	6G503	#124	#200	#72	#60
1988	6G503	#124	#200	#76	#60
1989	6G506	#126	#200	#76	#60
200 hp					
1984	6G600	#155	#160	#94	#60
1985-1986	6G602	#160	#210	#88	#50
Late 1986 and 1987	6G603	#146	#210	#82	#60
1988	6G603	#124	#270	#84	#60
1989	6G606	#146	#296	#84	#60
220-225 hp					
1984	6G700	#165	#170	#100	#60
1985-1986	6G701	#170	#230	#90	#50
Late 1986 and 1987-on	6G702	*	#270	#76	#60
	6K700	#160	#270	#76	#60

Fig. Y20-3—Chart depicting the recommended jet sizes for normal operation.

* Top carburetor #160, center and bottom carburetors #156.

Synchronize carburetor throttle valves by backing off idle speed screw until screw is not touching stop. Idle speed screw is located on the top carburetor on 1984 V-4 and V-6 models, bottom carburetor on 1985 and later V-4 models and center carburetor on 1985 and later V-6 models. Disconnect oil pump control rod from bottom carburetor. Loosen throttle lever screw (S—Fig. Y20-6) on top and bottom carburetors, or top carburetor only on 1985 and later V-4 models. Note that throttle lever screws have left-hand threads. Make sure all throttle valves are fully closed by manually moving linkage, then retighten throttle lever screws (S). On models after 1984, throttle levers are spring loaded and automatically synchronize when throttle lever screws are loosened. Check adjustment by opening and closing carburetors; throttle valves on all carburetors must open and close simultaneously. Check oil pump control rod adjustment as outlined in SPEED CONTROL LINKAGE section. Start engine and readjust idle speed screw to specified rpm (CONDENSED SERVICE DATA).

FUEL PUMP. Diaphragm type fuel pumps are used. Refer to Fig. Y20-8 for exploded view. V-6 models are equipped with two fuel pumps. Fuel pump(s) are mounted to power head and actuated by crankcase pulsations.

Minimum fuel pump output pressure is 39.3 kPa (5.7 psi). Inspect all diaphragms and gaskets for cracking, deterioration or other damage and renew as necessary. Renew check valves if warped, cracked or other damage is noted. Note that pump cover is marked "IN" and "OUT" for reference during reassembly.

FUEL FILTER. A fuel filter assembly is connected between fuel supply line and fuel pump inlet. Periodically unscrew fuel filter cup from filter base and withdraw filter element and "O" ring. Clean cup and filter element in a suitable solvent and dry with compressed air. Renew filter element if excessive blockage or damage is noted. Renew "O" ring if necessary, and reassemble fuel filter by reversing disassembly procedure.

REED VALVES. The reed valves are located between the intake manifold and the crankcase. Refer to Fig. Y20-9 for exploded view of valve assemblies used on V-6 models. Reed valve assemblies used on V-4 models are the same except four valve assemblies are used instead of six. Reed valves may be removed for inspection or renewal after removal of intake manifold (1). Note location of beveled corner on reed petals and reed stops for reference during reassembly.

Renew reed petals if cracked, warped, chipped or bent. Renew reed petals if tip of petal stands open more than 0.2 mm (0.0.008 in.) on V-4 models or 0.9 mm (0.035 in.) on V-6 models. Never attempt to bend or straighten reeds. Never turn a reed over for reuse. Reed petals should seat smoothly against reed plate along their entire length with the least possible tension. Make sure reed petals are centered over intake ports. Apply a suitable thread locking compound to threads of reed stop mounting screws during assembly.

Reed stop opening (O—Fig. Y20-10) should be 6.2-6.8 mm (0.24-0.27 in.) on 115, 130, 220 and 225 hp models and 6.3-6.7 mm (0.25-0.26 in.) on all other

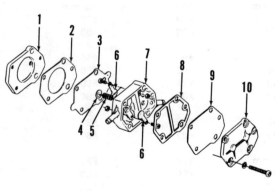

Fig. Y20-6—View of throttle lever adjusting screw (S). Refer to text when synchronizing throttle valves.

Fig. Y20-8—Exploded view of fuel pump assembly.

1. Inner cover
2. Gasket
3. Diaphragm
4. Spring seat
5. Spring
6. Check valve
7. Body
8. Gasket
9. Diaphragm
10. Outer cover

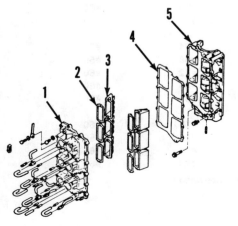

Fig. Y20-9—Exploded view of reed valves and related components on V-6 models.

1. Intake manifold
2. Gasket
3. Reed valve assy.
4. Gasket
5. Crankcase cover

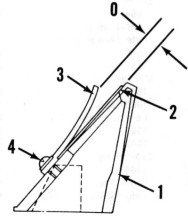

Fig. Y20-10—Measure reed stop opening (O) between tip of reed stop (3) and closed reed petal (2) as shown. Refer to text.

1. Reed block	3. Reed stop
2. Reed petal	4. Screw

models. Renew reed stop (3) if opening (O) is not as specified.

All Models Except 220 and 225 hp

SPEED CONTROL LINKAGE. Synchronize carburetor throttle valves as outlined in CARBURETOR section. Make sure timing pointer is aligned with TDC mark on flywheel when number 1 piston is positioned at TDC. If necessary, install a suitable dial indicator into number 1 spark plug hole and adjust timing pointer as necessary.

Prior to adjusting timing, place outboard motor into a suitable test tank, start engine and allow to warm to normal operating temperature. Connect a suitable timing light to number 1 spark plug lead.

CAUTION: Use extreme caution while working near rotating flywheel or other moving engine parts. Avoid touching ignition system high tension components while engine is running.

Start engine, move magneto control lever (2—Fig. Y20-11 or Y20-12) to the idle position and note timing. Make sure idle timing screw (3) is touching stop. Idle timing should be 6-8 degrees ATDC on Pro V 150 models and 4-6 degrees ATDC on all other models. Adjust idle timing screw (3) as necessary to obtain specified full-retarded timing. Next, move magneto control lever (2) to full-advance position and note timing. Make sure lever (2) is touching screw (4) and that engine is running at 4500 rpm or more. Adjust screw (4) so timing is 21-23 degrees BTDC on 130, 175 and 200

hp models, 22-24 degrees BTDC on 115 hp models, 23-25 degrees BTDC on 150 hp models and 27-29 degees BTDC on Pro V 150 models. After ignition timing is properly adjusted, set idle speed to specified rpm (CONDENSED SERVICE DATA).

To adjust pickup timing, first disconnect throttle link (5—Fig. Y20-13). Adjust length (L) of link to 53.5 mm (2.11 in.) on 115 hp models, 53.0 mm (2.09 in.) on 130 hp models and 42 mm (1.65 in.) on all other models. Reconnect throttle link (5) and start engine. Slowly move magneto control lever (2—Fig. Y20-13) until pickup timing is 6 degrees ATDC on Pro V 150 models or 4 degrees ATDC on all other models (using timing light). Without moving magneto control lever (2), move throttle roller (7) and cam (6) together until lightly touching. Center of roller (7) should be aligned with mark (M) on cam (6). If not, loosen screw (S) and adjust position of roller (7) as necessary to align mark (M) with center of roller (7). Note that screw (S) has left-hand threads.

Models 220 Hp (V-6 Special) and 225 Hp (V-6 Excel)

The 220 and 225 hp models are equipped with Yamaha Micro-Computer Ignition System (YMIS). Ignition advance is controlled by the computer and does not require adjustment. The computer determines the optimum timing advance based on information input from various sensors, primarily the throttle position and crankshaft position (rpm) sensors. Refer to IGNITION section for adjustment and testing of sensors. Ignition timing may be checked to

verify proper operation of the YMIS system.

Make sure timing pointer is aligned with TDC mark on flywheel when number 1 piston is at TDC. If necessary, install a suitable dial indicator into number 1 spark plug hole and adjust timing pointer as necessary. Connect timing light to number 1 spark plug lead and place outboard motor into a suitable test tank. Idle timing should be 4-9 degrees ATDC on 220 hp models and 3-7 degrees ATDC on 225 hp models. Maximum timing advance should be 20-25 degrees BTDC on 220 hp models and 24-28 degrees BTDC on 225 hp models.

NOTE: When checking maximum timing advance on YMIS equipped models, carburetors must be wide-open throttle and engine running at 5500 rpm or more.

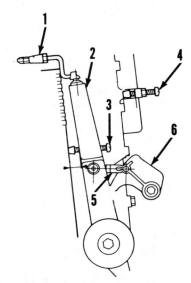

Fig. Y20-12—Speed control linkage used on V-6 models except 220 (V-6 Special) and 225 (V-6 Excel) hp models. Refer to Fig. Y20-11 for component identification.

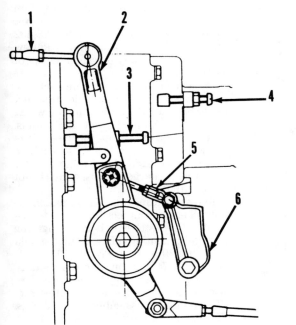

Fig. Y20-11—Speed control linkage used on V-4 models.
1. Magneto control link
2. Magneto control lever
3. Idle timing screw
4. Maximum advance timing screw
5. Throttle link
6. Throttle cam

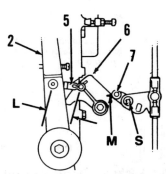

Fig. Y20-13—Refer to text to adjust pickup timing on V-4 and V-6 models except 220 and 225 hp models.

2. Magneto control lever
5. Throttle link
6. Throttle cam
7. Throttle roller
M. Mark
S. Screw

To adjust pickup point on 220 and 225 hp models, first remove throttle link (5—Fig. Y20-15) and adjust length of link (5) to 72 mm (2.83 in.) on 220 hp models and 42 mm (1.65 in.) on 225 hp models. Slowly advance lever (2) until throttle cam (6) and roller (7) just contact (throttle valves closed). Center of roller (7) should be aligned with arrow (220 hp) or stamped mark (225 hp) on throttle cam (6). If not, loosen screw (S) and adjust roller as necessary. Note that screw (S) has left-hand threads.

All Models

Oil pump control rod should be adjusted after speed control linkage adjustment. Back-off idle speed screw until throttle valves are fully closed. Disconnect oil pump control rod from oil pump and move pump control lever to the fully closed position. Adjust length of control rod so rod will connect to oil pump without disturbing position of pump lever or carburetor throttle valves.

OIL INJECTION

BLEEDING PUMP. To bleed air from oil pump, make sure oil reservoir has sufficient oil, outboard motor is in upright position, then remove reservoir

vent valve or fill cap. Loosen pump bleed screw (Fig. Y20-16) and allow air to gravity bleed from bleed screw hole. Once air-free oil is flowing from bleed screw hole, retighten bleed screw. If a large amount of air is present in pump and lines, fill oil lines with oil, then bleed as previously outlined. Air may be purged from injection system with engine running if a 50:1 fuel:oil mixture is used in fuel tank.

CHECKING PUMP OUTPUT. Pump output test must be performed with a 50:1 fuel:oil mixture in the fuel tank. Oil temperature should be within 10°-30° C (58°-86° F) for accurate output test results. Start engine and warm to normal operating temperature. Disconnect number 1 cylinder oil injection line from intake manifold and insert oil line into a suitable graduated container. Disconnect oil pump control rod from oil pump and move pump lever to the full-throttle position. Start engine and run at 1500 rpm for exactly three minutes. Oil pump output at 1500 rpm in three minutes should be 2.6-4.0 mL (0.088-0.135 fl. oz.) on all models. Repeat test on each remaining oil line. Reconnect pump control rod and bleed injection system as previously described after performing output test.

NOTE: Pump output test data is compiled using Yamaha Two-Stroke Oil. Actual test results may vary depending on brand of oil used, ambient temperature, oil temperature

and testing error. Repeat test as necessary to ensure consistent results.

If pump output is low, inspect oil delivery and discharge lines for restrictions or leakage. If no restrictions or leakage is noted, renew oil pump assembly. It is recommended to label oil discharge lines during removal from pump for reference upon reassembly.

IGNITION

All models are equipped with capacitor discharge ignition (CDI). Prior to trouble-shooting ignition system, first make sure engine malfunction is not the result of fuel delivery or other fuel system malfunction or failure. Make sure spark plugs and ignition system wiring are in acceptable condition. Make sure all electrical connections are clean and tight. The manufacturer recommends testing ignition system components using Yamaha Pocket Tester YU-3112.

On all models, stator assembly (3—Fig. Y20-17) contains two charge coils and eight battery charging (lighting) coils. On V-4 models, timer base (4) contains two pulser (trigger) coils, one for cylinders 1 and 2 and one for cylinders 3 and 4. On V-6 models, timer base contains three pulser coils, one for cylinders 1 and 2, one for cylinders 3 and 4 and one for remaining cylinders 5 and 6. On all models, each cylinder is provided with a separate ignition coil.

To test pulser coils, disconnect pulser coil leads from CDI module. On V-4 models, connect tester between white/red and white/yellow wires, then white/black and white/green wires. On V-6 models, connect tester between white/red and white/green wires, then white/black and white/blue wires, then white/yellow and white/brown wires. Pulser coil resistance should be 288-432 ohms at all test connections. Renew pulser coil assembly if resistance is not as specified.

To test charge coils, disconnect charge coil leads from CDI module. Connect tester between the brown and red wires. Resistance should be 840-1260 ohms. Next, connect tester between the black/red and blue wires. Resistance should be 102-152 ohms. Renew stator assembly if charge coil resistance is not as specified.

To test lighting coil, disconnect lighting coil leads from rectifier/regulator assembly. Connect tester between lighting coil leads. Lighting coil resistance should be 0.19-0.29 ohm on Pro V 150 models and 0.50-0.74 ohm on all other models. Renew stator assembly if lighting coil resistance is not as specified. To test rectifier/regulator assembly, refer to Figs. Y20-22, Y20-23 and Y20-24.

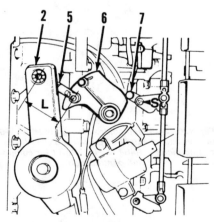

Fig. Y20-15—View of speed control linkage used on 220 and 225 hp models. Refer to text to adjust pickup point.

2. Lever
5. Throttle link
6. Throttle cam
7. Throttle roller
S. Screw

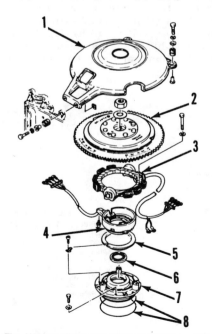

Fig. Y20-17—Exploded view of ignition system and upper seal housing typical of all models.

1. Flywheel cover
2. Flywheel
3. Stator assy.
4. Timer base
5. Retainer
6. Seal
7. Upper oil seal housing
8. "O" rings

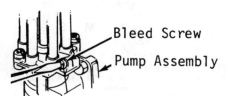

Fig. Y20-16—Loosen bleed screw to purge air from oil injection system. Refer to text.

NOTE: Rectifier/regulator test data shown in Figs. Y20-22, Y20-23 and Y20-24 is compiled using Yamaha Pocket Tester YU-3112. Test results in the field may be the exact opposite from what shown, depending on individual ohmmeter polarity. If exact opposite occurs, rectifier/regulator can be considered acceptable.

Ignition coil primary winding resistance should be 0.2-0.3 ohm on all models. Coil secondary winding resistance should be 2000-3000 ohms on all models. When testing secondary resistance, remove spark plug terminal boot and connect tester between primary terminal and high tension lead. If ignition coil resistance is only slightly out of specification, check spark intensity using a suitable coil tester before failing coil. Connect tester as described in instructions provided with tester. Using Yamaha coil tester (part YU-33261), or

equivalent, a steady spark should jump an 8 mm (0.31 in.) gap with voltage selector switch in the "CDI" position.

NOTE: Do not crank or start engine without providing a spark gap or grounding secondary high tension leads. Cranking or starting engine with an open high tension lead will damage CDI module.

Test the CDI module using Electro-Specialties tester Model 1-Y (Yamaha part YU-91022). Follow instructions provided with tester. Isolate main switch, emergency stop switch and related wiring by disconnecting white lead from CDI module prior to testing.

YMIS Equipped Models

V-6 Special (220 hp) and V-6 Excel (225 hp) models are equipped with the Yamaha Micro-Computer Ignition Sys-

tem (YMIS). Models equipped with YMIS use a thermo sensor, crankshaft position sensor, throttle position sensor and knock sensor not found on other models. Test YMIS components using Yamaha pocket tester YU-3112. If another ohmmeter is used, readings obtained may not agree with those specified due to ohmmeter internal resistance.

The throttle position sensor is mounted to the top carburetor and is engaged with the carburetor throttle shaft to read throttle valve opening. To test sensor, disconnect sensor from YMIS control unit. Connect tester between black and white sensor wires. Resistance should be 16-24 with sensor at idle position. Connect tester between sensor red and white wires. Resistance should be 800-1200 ohms with sensor at idle position. Next, connect tester between sensor red and black wires. Resistance should be 800-1200 ohms. Re-

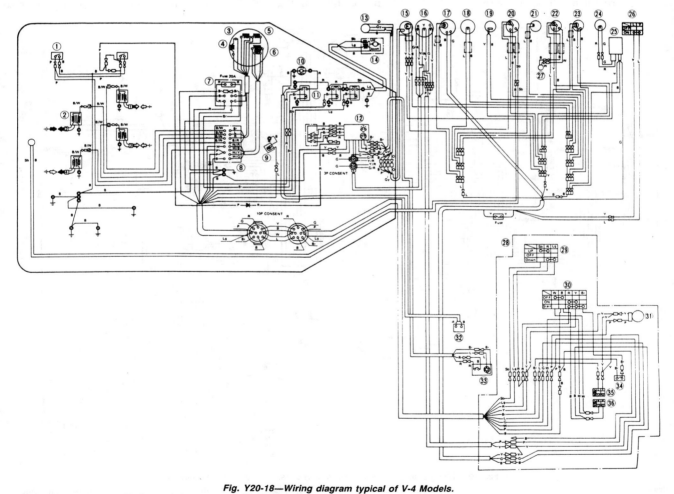

Fig. Y20-18—Wiring diagram typical of V-4 Models.

1. Thermo switch	12. Control unit	21. Water pressure meter	29. Trim/tilt switch
2. Ignition coil	13. Trim sensor	22. Fuel gage	30. Main switch
3. Magneto assy.	14. Trim/tilt motor	23. Voltmeter	31. Buzzer
4. Lighting coil	15. Trim gage	24. Charge lamp	32. Battery
5. Charge coil	16. Oil level warning lamps	25. Charge warning unit	33. Oil level gage
6. Pulser coil	17. Tachometer	26. Lamp switch	34. Neutral switch
7. Rectifier/regulator	18. Speedometer	27. Fuel sensor	35. Choke switch
8. CDI module	19. Hour meter	28. Remote control assy.	36. Emergency stop switch
9. Choke solenoid	20. Water temperature gage		
10. Starter motor			
11. Starter relay			

G. Green	B/W. Black with white tracer
L. Blue	
O. Orange	W/B. White with black tracer
P. Pink	
R. Red	W/G. White with green tracer
W. White	
Y. Yellow	W/R. White with red tracer
Gy. Gray	
Lg. Light green	W/Y. White with yellow tracer
Sb. Light blue	
B. Black	

new throttle position sensor if resistance is not as specified. If removing sensor, match mark sensor and bracket so sensor can be installed in original position. Apply a suitable thread locking compound to threads of sensor mounting screws.

Yamaha test harness YU-6283 and digital multimeter YU-33262 are required to adjust throttle position sensor. Connect test harness and multimeter between sensor and YMIS module as shown in Fig. Y20-26. Back-off idle speed screw so throttle valves are fully closed. Turn on main switch and rotate sensor as necessary to obtain 0.40-0.42 volt with throttle fully closed, then tighten sensor screws. Note that a suitable thread locking compound should be applied to sensor screws prior to tightening. Open and close throttle several times to be sure sensor voltage returns to 0.40-0.42 volt when throttle is closed. Be sure to readjust idle speed screw.

The knock sensor is mounted in the cylinder head at the number 6 cylinder (port) on models prior to 1987 and at the number 5 cylinder (starboard) on models after 1986. The knock sensor detects detonation and signals YMIS module to retard ignition timing. To test knock sensor, connect tester between the sensor terminal and the sensor body (ground). Renew sensor if continuity is noted between terminal and ground.

The crankshaft position sensor provides engine speed information and crankshaft angle (position) to the YMIS module by counting flywheel ring gear teeth that pass a specific point during a specific time. Crankshaft position sensor is mounted on top of the power head adjacent to the flywheel. To test sensor, unplug sensor connector and attach tester between the sensor blue wires. Air gap between crankshaft sensor and ring gear teeth should be 0.5-1.5 mm (0.020-0.059 in.) as shown in Fig. Y20-27.

The thermo sensor provides engine temperature information to the YMIS module. To test thermo sensor, disconnect sensor and connect tester between sensor leads.

NOTE: Do not confuse thermo sensor with the thermo switch. The thermo sensor is connected to the YMIS module; the thermo switches are connected to the CDI module.

With ambient temperature at 4°-6° C (39.2°-42.8° F) sensor resistance should be 20,600-26,400 ohms; at 24°-26° C (75.2°-78.8° F) resistance should be 76,500-93,700 ohms; at 49°-51° C (90.2°-123.8° F) resistance should be 25,200-30,800 ohms. Renew thermo sensor if resistance is not as specified.

COOLING SYSTEM

THERMOSTAT. A thermostat is located in each cylinder head cover to

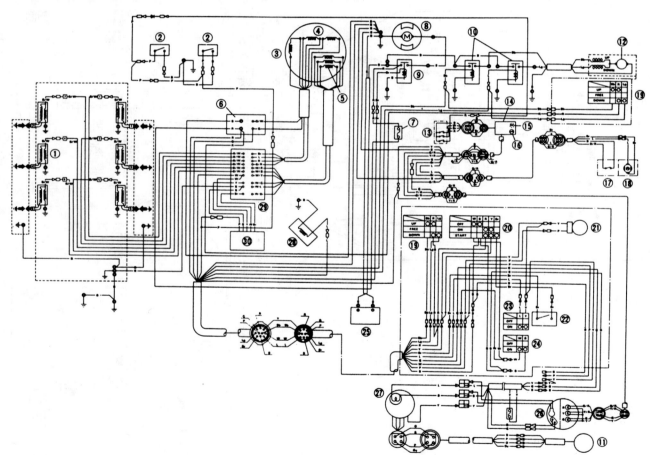

Fig. Y20-19—Wiring diagram typical of 150, Pro V 150, 175 and 200 hp models.

1. Ignition coil	11. Trim sensor	19. Power trim/tilt switch	27. Trim meter
2. Thermo switch	12. Power trim/tilt motor	20. Main switch	28. Choke solenoid
3. Lighting coil	13. Oil level sensor (main reservoir)	21. Buzzer	29. CDI module
4. Charge coil	14. Control unit	22. Neutral switch	30. Control unit
5. Pulser coil	15. Tilt switch	23. Choke switch	
6. Rectifier/regulator	16. Emergency switch	24. Emergency stop switch	
7. Fuse (20 amp)	18. Oil feed pump motor	25. Battery	
8. Starter motor		26. Tachometer & oil level warning lamps	
9. Starter relay			
10. Power trim/tilt relay			

Br. Brown	W/Br. White with brown tracer
Gy. Gray	W/R. White with red tracer
Lg. Light green	W/L. White with blue tracer
Sb. Light blue	W/R. White with red tracer
B/R. Black with red tracer	W/Y. White with yellow tracer
B/W. Black with white tracer	Y/R. Yellow with red tracer
G/R. Green with red tracer	
B. Black	
G. Green	
L. Blue	
O. Orange	
P. Pink	
R. Red	
W. White	
Y. Yellow	
G/W. Green with white tracer	

regulate engine operating temperature. Thermostats can be removed for inspection or renewal after removal of thermostat covers. Models are equipped with either a 48° C (118° F) or a 52° C (126° F) thermostat. Thermostat rating is marked on thermostat flange. Thermostat should be renewed with one of the same temperature rating. Minimum thermostat opening at rated temperature is 3 mm (0.12 in.).

All models are equipped with a pressure relief valve to regulate cooling system operating pressure. On V-4 models, a pressure relief valve is located under each thermostat cover. On V-6 models, pressure relief valve and cover is located in outer exhaust cover.

WATER PUMP. A rubber impeller type water pump is mounted between the drive shaft housing and gearcase. Water pump impeller (11—Fig. Y20-29) is driven by a key that engages drive shaft.

If cooling system malfunction occurs, first check water inlet for plugging or partial restriction. Be sure thermostats

are operating properly. If necessary, separate gearcase from drive shaft housing and inspect water pump. Make sure all seals and mating surfaces are in acceptable condition and that water passages are unobstructed. Check impeller (11), housing liner (10) and wear plate (12) for excessive wear.

Apply a suitable water-resistant grease to grommets (3 and 4), seals (1 and 5) and tips of impeller vanes. If liner (10) is renewed, apply Yamabond No. 4 or a suitable equivalent sealant to outer diameter of liner prior to installation into housing. Rotate drive shaft clockwise when installing housing (6) over impeller. Avoid turning drive shaft in opposite direction after housing is installed. Apply a suitable thread locking compound to threads of housing screws during reassembly.

POWER HEAD

REMOVE AND REINSTALL. Remove engine cover and disconnect battery. Disconnect battery wires from starter

relay and starter motor. Disconnect red lead between starter relay and fuse. Disconnect wires from power trim/tilt relays. Remove plate from bottom engine cowl and remove wire harness. Disconnect ground wires from cylinder block or exhaust cover. Disconnect and remove cooling system pilot hose from

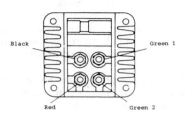

$\ominus$ Tester Tester $\oplus$	Green 1	Green 2	Red	Black
Green 1		Infinity	Continuity	Infinity
Green 2	Infinity		Continuity	Infinity
Red	Infinity	Infinity		Infinity
Black	Continuity	Continuity	Continuity	

Fig. Y20-22—View showing ohmmeter connections when testing rectifier/regulator assembly on V-4 models, and 150, 175 and 200 hp models. Renew rectifier/regulator if test results differ from chart. Refer to text.

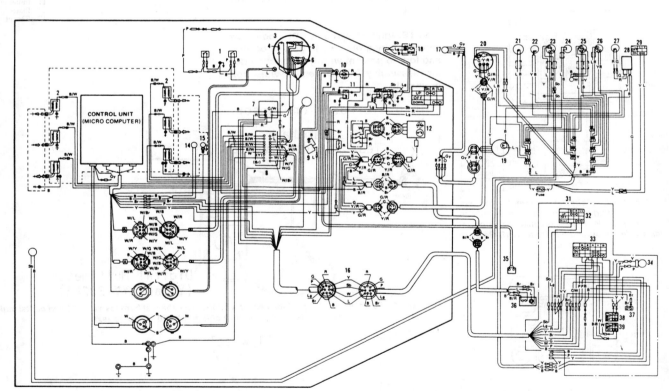

Fig. Y20-20—Wiring diagram typical of 220 and 225 hp models.

1. Thermo switch	14. Thermo sensor	25. Fuel gage	36. Oil level gage	Y. Yellow	W/Br. White with
2. Ignition coil	15. Knock sensor	26. Voltmeter	37. Neutral switch	Gy. Gray	brown tracer
3. Magneto assy.	16. Ten-pin	27. Charge lamp	38. Choke switch	Lg. Light green	W/G. White with green
4. Lighting coil	connector	28. Charge warning	39. Emergency stop	Sb. Light blue	tracer
5. Charge coil	17. Trim sensor	unit	switch	B/R. Black with red	W/L. White with blue
6. Pulser coil	18. Trim/tilt motor	29. Lamp switch		tracer	tracer
7. Rectifier/regulat-	19. Trim gage	30. Fuel sensor		B/W. Black with white	W/R. White with red
or	20. Tachometer	31. Remote control		tracer	tracer
8. CDI module	21. Speedometer	assy.		G/R. Green with red	W/Y. White with
9. Choke solenoid	22. Hour meter	32. Trim/tilt switch		tracer	yellow tracer
10. Starter motor	23. Water	33. Main switch		W/B. White with black	Y/R. Yellow with red
11. Starter relay	temperature gage	34. Buzzer		tracer	tracer
12. Control unit	24. Water pressure	35. Battery		B. Black	
13. Throttle sensor	meter			G. Green	
				L. Blue	
				O. Orange	
				P. Pink	
				R. Red	
				W. White	

bottom of exhaust cover. Remove hairpin clips securing shift rod lever, then remove shift rod lever by pushing down on rod. Remove shift rod bracket from power head. Disconnect fuel supply hose at the fuel filter and disconnect choke rod link at the carburetor. Disconnect oil supply line at bottom cowl. Remove flywheel cover. Remove front and rear lower engine aprons. Remove ten 8 mm screws and two 8 mm nuts securing power head to drive shaft housing. Remove flywheel nut and screw a suitable lifting eye onto crankshaft.

NOTE: At this point, there should be no hoses, wires or linkage that will interfere with power head removal.

Using a suitable hoist, lift power head from drive shaft housing while carefully prying between exhaust cover and lower engine cowling with a wooden pry bar. The power head must be lifted straight up or crankshaft and drive shaft splines may be damaged. Be sure to support cylinder side of power head while lifting. Once free, check power head for

locating pins. If locating pins came off with power head, remove and install them into drive shaft housing. Secure power head to a suitable holding fixture.

Make sure two locating pins are securely installed in drive shaft housing. Gasket between power head and drive shaft housing should be renewed. Do not use sealant on gasket. Lightly lubricate drive shaft splines with a suitable water-resistant grease and carefully lower power head onto drive shaft housing. Tighten the ten screws and two nuts securing power head to 18 N·m (13 ft.-lbs.). Complete reinstallation by reversing removal procedure.

DISASSEMBLY. Refer to Fig. Y20-30 for an exploded view of crankcase and cylinder block assembly used on V-6 models (V-4 models are similar). Disconnect and plug oil line at the oil pump, disconnect oil level sensor and remove oil reservoir. Disconnect oil pump control module. Remove flywheel using a suitable bolt-type puller. Be sure to retrieve flywheel key. Remove covers from CDI module and rectifier/regulator. Disconnect all wires from CDI module and rectifier.

NOTE: Ignition wires at CDI module are separated by grommets in groups of three and four to prevent wrong connection during reassembly. DO NOT remove wires from grommets.

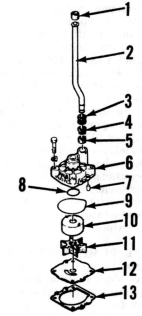

Fig. Y20-29—Exploded view of water pump.

1. Seal		8. "O" ring	
2. Water tube		9. "O" ring	
3. Grommet		10. Liner	
4. Grommet		11. Impeller	
5. Seal		12. Plate	
6. Housing		13. Gasket	
7. Dowel pin			

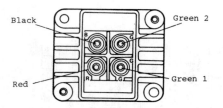

Fig. Y20-23—View showing ohmmeter connections when testing rectifier/regulator assembly on Pro V 150 models. Renew rectifier/regulator assembly if test results differ from chart. Refer to text.

Tester ⊖ / Tester ⊕	Green 1	Green 2	Red	Black
Green 1		Infinity	Continuity	Continuity
Green 2	Infinity		Continuity	Infinity
Red	Infinity	Infinity		Infinity
Black	Continuity	Continuity	Continuity	

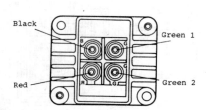

Fig. Y20-24—View showing ohmmeter connections when testing rectifier/regulator on 220 and 225 hp models. Renew rectifier/regulator if test results differ from chart. Refer to text.

Tester ⊖ / Tester ⊕	Green 1	Green 2	Red	Black
Green 1		3,000-300,000 Ω	50-5,000 Ω	100-100,000 Ω
Green 2	Infinity		50-5,000 Ω	Infinity
Red	Infinity	Infinity		Infinity
Black	50-5,000 Ω	50-5,000 Ω	200-20,000 Ω	

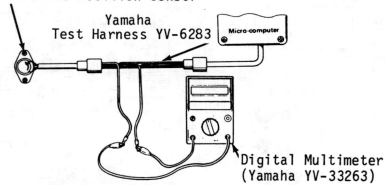

Fig. Y20-26—To adjust throttle position sensor, connect Yamaha test harness YU-6283 and digital multimeter YU-33263 (or equivalent) as shown. Refer to text.

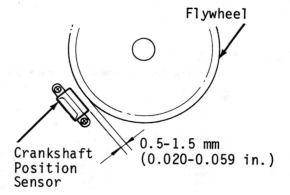

Fig. Y20-27—Adjust crankshaft position sensor so 0.5-1.5 mm (0.020-0.059 in.) air gap is present between sensor and flywheel ring gear teeth.

Remove rectifier/regulator and CDI module from the bracket. Remove three screws securing stator assembly and remove stator. Disconnect magneto control rod from timer base, remove four timer base retainers, then remove timer base assembly. Disconnect wires from choke solenoid, ignition coils and thermo sensor. Remove starter relay, ignition coils, spark plugs, starter motor and CDI

module mounting bracket. Remove choke solenoid. Remove intake silencer, carburetors, fuel pump(s), fuel filter and related fuel system components. Disconnect oil injection lines at intake manifold and remove oil pump. Oil injection lines should be labeled for reference during reassembly. Remove throttle cam, magneto control lever and throttle control arm and spring assem-

bly. Remove shift slide bracket. Disconnect crankcase drain hoses from connectors on cylinder block and remove intake manifold and reed valve assemblies. Remove screws securing upper and lower seal housings, then remove crankcase cover screws. Separate crankcase cover from cylinder block by carefully prying on each side of crankcase. DO NOT pry between crankcase mating

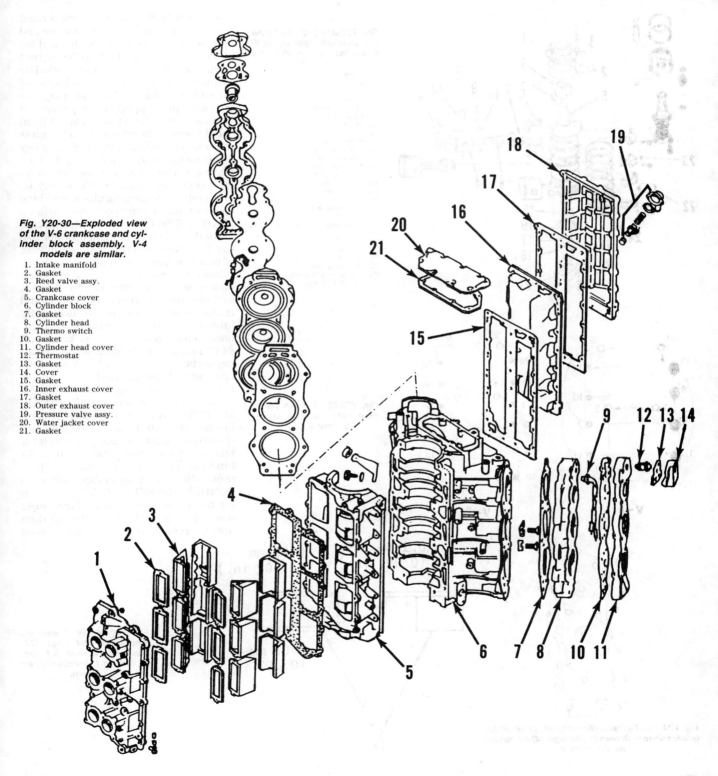

Fig. Y20-30—Exploded view of the V-6 crankcase and cylinder block assembly. V-4 models are similar.

1. Intake manifold
2. Gasket
3. Reed valve assy.
4. Gasket
5. Crankcase cover
6. Cylinder block
7. Gasket
8. Cylinder head
9. Thermo switch
10. Gasket
11. Cylinder head cover
12. Thermostat
13. Gasket
14. Cover
15. Gasket
16. Inner exhaust cover
17. Gasket
18. Outer exhaust cover
19. Pressure valve assy.
20. Water jacket cover
21. Gasket

surfaces. Once crankcase cover is dislodged, lift cover straight away from cylinder block to prevent crankshaft seal rings from catching on crankcase cover. Remove upper and lower seal housings. Remove thermostat covers, thermostats and cylinder head covers. Tabs are provided on cylinder head covers for prying. On models so equipped, remove

thermo sensors from each cylinder head by pulling straight out of cylinder head. Loosen ALL cylinder head screws, then remove screws, and pry head loose from cylinder block by prying at tabs provided. Do not pry between head and cylinder block mating surfaces. On V-6 models, remove pressure valve cover from exhaust cover. Note that cover is

under spring pressure. Hold cover securely while removing pressure valve cover screws. Remove exhaust cover screws and carefully separate outer and inner exhaust covers from cylinder block by prying at tabs located on covers. Internal engine components are now accessible for inspection and overhaul as outlined in the appropriate service sections.

REASSEMBLY. It is recommended that all gasket surfaces of crankcase and cylinder block be carefully checked for nicks, burrs or warped surfaces that might interfere with a tight seal. The cylinder head, mating surfaces of manifolds and crankcase may be checked and lapped, if necessary, to provide a smooth surface. Cylinder head should be resurfaced if warped in excess of 0.1 mm (0.004 in). Do not remove any more metal than is necessary to true mating surface. Mating surface of crankcase cover and cylinder block may be checked on the lapping block, and high spots or nicks removed, but surfaces MUST NOT be lowered. If extreme care is used, a slightly damaged crankcase can be salvaged in this manner. In case of doubt, renew the crankcase assembly.

Reassemble power head by reversing disassembly procedure. Renew all seals, gaskets and "O" rings. All bearing and friction surfaces should be thoroughly lubricated during assembly using a recommended engine oil. Apply Yamabond #4 or a suitable equivalent sealer to mating surfaces of cylinder block and lower oil seal housing. Install seal into upper bearing housing (1—Fig. Y20-31) with lip facing down. Install seals (18 and 19) into lower seal housing (21) with lips facing down. Rotate crankshaft frequently during reassembly to check for binding or abnormal noise; any noise or binding must be repaired before proceeding with assembly. Refer to CONDENSED SERVICE DATA section for torque specifications. Place upper bearing housing (1) on crankshaft then install crankshaft into cylinder block

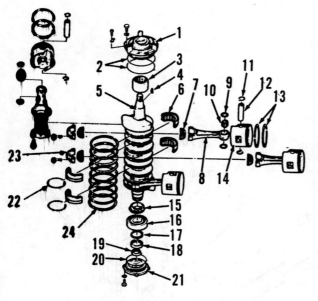

Fig. Y20-31—Exploded view of crankshaft assembly on V-6 models. V-4 models are similar.

1. Upper bearing housing
2. "O" rings
3. Bearing
4. Woodruff key
5. Crankshaft
6. Main bearing half
7. Connecting rod bearing half
8. Connecting rod
9. Thrust washer
10. Bearing rollers
11. Retaining ring
12. Piston pin
13. Piston rings
14. Piston
15. Oil pump drive gear
16. Bearing
17. Snap ring
18. Seal
19. Seal
20. "O" ring
21. Lower seal housing
22. Retaining ring
23. Connecting rod cap
24. Crankshaft seal rings

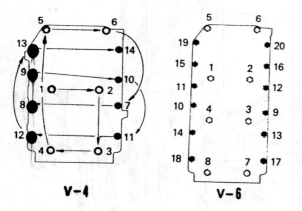

V-4   **V-6**

Fig. Y20-32—Tighten crankcase cover screws in sequence shown.

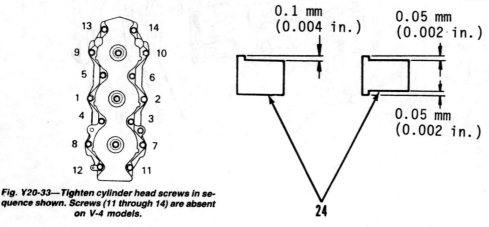

Fig. Y20-33—Tighten cylinder head screws in sequence shown. Screws (11 through 14) are absent on V-4 models.

0.1 mm (0.004 in.)

0.05 mm (0.002 in.)

0.05 mm (0.002 in.)

24

Fig. Y20-34—Total wear on crankshaft seal rings (24) must not exceed 0.1 mm (0.004 in.) measured as shown.

making sure main bearing locating pins in cylinder block properly engage holes in bearings. Install lower seal housing (21), then install crankcase cover. Tighten crankcase cover screws in sequence shown in Fig. Y20-32. Tighten cylinder head screws in sequence shown in Fig. Y20-33. Tighten intake manifold and exhaust cover screws in a rotating pattern starting with center screws.

PISTONS, PINS, RINGS AND CYLINDERS. Pistons, connecting rods and rod caps should be marked for cylinder location and direction prior to removal.

On models prior to 1989, bottom piston ring is square shape and should be installed with manufacturer's marking facing crown of piston. On models after 1988, both piston rings are semikeystone shape. Pistons with two semikeystone rings can be identified by the "W" stamped in piston crown. Locating pins are present in piston ring grooves to prevent ring rotation. Be certain ring end gaps are properly positioned around locating pins when installing pistons. Refer to CONDENSED SERVICE DATA section for piston ring service specifications. Pistons located in port cylinders are marked "P" on piston crown and starboard pistons are marked "S." Pistons must be installed in original cylinders with "UP" mark in crown facing flywheel. Standard cylinder bore is 90.00-90.02 mm (3.5433-3.5440 in.). Maximum allowable cylinder bore taper is 0.08 mm (0.003 in.). Maximum allowable cylinder out-of-round is 0.05 mm (0.002 in.). Pistons and rings are available in 0.25 mm and 0.50 mm oversizes. Piston diameter should be measured 10 mm (0.39 in.) up from bottom of skirt at right angle to piston pin. Refer to CONDENSED SERVICE DATA for piston-to-cylinder clearance. Connecting rod small end bearing (10—Fig. Y20-31) consists of 30 loose bearing rollers. Yamaha special tool YB-6240 is available to ease bearing roller installation. Thrust washers (9) must be installed with convex side facing outward. No noticeable play should be present between piston pin and connecting rod (with bearing [10] installed) or bore in piston. Always renew piston pin retainers (11) upon reassembly.

CRANKSHAFT, CONNECTING RODS AND BEARINGS. Match mark connecting rod and cap prior to removing rod cap. Maximum allowable crankshaft runout is 0.02 mm (0.0008 in.) measured at each main bearing journal with ends of crankshaft supported in V-blocks. Install center main bearing (6—Fig. Y20-31) outer races so locating pin hole is facing away from flywheel end

of engine. Renew seal rings (24) if total wear exceeds 0.1 mm (0.004 in.) measured as shown in Fig. Y20-34. When installing crankshaft into cylinder block, position seal ring (24—Fig. Y20-31) end gaps toward crankcase cover. Install oil pump drive gear (15) with marked side facing bearing (16). Install connecting rods on crankshaft so the "YAMAHA" cast in the rod is facing top of engine.

NOTE: The manufacturer recommends renewing connecting rod screws upon reassembly.

Use the following procedure to align rod and rod cap during reassembly: Install bearings (7) and caps (23). Finger tighten screws making sure rod cap and rod are perfectly aligned. Tighten screws to 18 N·m (13 ft.-lbs.), then to 37 N·m (27 ft.-lbs.). Recheck rod and cap for proper alignment. If perfect alignment is not obtained, loosen rod screws and repeat above procedure. If rod and cap are aligned, loosen screws one half turn, retighten to 18 N·m (13 ft.-lbs.), then to 37 N·m (27 ft.-lbs.).

ELECTRIC STARTER

Refer to Fig. Y20-36 for an exploded view of starter motor. Disassembly and reassembly of starter is evident after referral to exploded view and inspection of unit.

Standard commutator diameter is 33 mm 1.30 in.). Commutator should be trued by turning on a suitable lathe if commutator runout exceeds 0.2 mm (0.008 in.). Armature should be renewed if commutator diameter is less than 31 mm (1.22 in.). Renew brushes if worn to less than 12 mm (0.47 in.). Insulation between commutator segments should be undercut to 0.5-0.8 mm (0.02-0.03 in.).

LOWER UNIT

PROPELLER. Lower unit protection is provided by a cushion type hub in the propeller. Various propellers are available from the manufacturer. Select a propeller that will allow full throttle operation within the recommended speed range of 4,800-5,800 rpm on 130, 220 and 225 hp models and 4,500-5,500 rpm on all other models.

R&R AND OVERHAUL. To remove gearcase, place shift lever into neutral position, tilt outboard motor fully up and engage tilt lock lever. Pry out cap at rear of drive shaft housing, directly above trim tab to expose trim tab screw. Remove screw and trim tab. Unclip pitot tube from swivel bracket. Remove sev-

en screws securing lower unit and separate lower unit from drive shaft housing. Place lower unit into a suitable holding fixture and drain gearcase oil.

Note location and thickness of all shims for reference during reassembly. Remove water pump assembly (17 through 23—Fig. Y20-37). Remove propeller and related components. Straighten tabs on tab washer (51) and remove

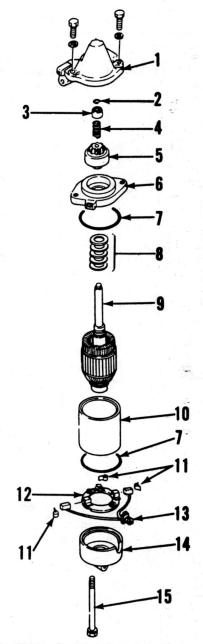

Fig. Y20-36—Exploded view of electric starter motor.

1. Cover	9. Armature
2. Retainer ring	10. Frame assy.
3. Collar	11. Brush springs
4. Spring	12. Brush plate
5. Drive gear assy.	13. Brushes
6. Drive end cover	14. Commutator end
7. "O" ring	frame
8. Shims	15. Through-bolt

ring nut (52) using Yamaha special tool YB-34447 or equivalent. Pull bearing carrier (48) from gearcase. Be sure to retrieve key (47). Remove retainer plate (4) and pull lower shift rod (7) out of gearcase. Note that gearcase must be in neutral to remove lower shift rod. Extract propeller shaft assembly from gearcase. Loosen pinion nut (54) by holding nut (54) with a 22 mm socket and turning drive shaft (13). Remove housing (26), shim pack (10), thrust bearing (11), drive shaft (13), sleeve (14), pinion gear (53) and forward gear (31) from gearcase. If necessary, remove forward gear bearing race and shim (28) from gearcase using a suitable slide-hammer puller with internal expanding jaws. Jaws of puller must be positioned

parallel to antiventilation plate to properly engage bearing race. To remove bearing (16), drive bearing down into gear cavity using a suitable driver. Make sure all bearing rollers are present in bearing (16) to prevent bearing outer race from collapsing during removal.

To disassemble propeller shaft, remove crosspin retainer (39) and push out crosspin (38). Slide dog clutch (37) off propeller shaft, then slowly extract shifter (32) and shift slider (33). Do not allow steel balls to spring out of shift mechanism. Note that three different diameter balls are used. Note location of each size ball.

Inspect all components for excessive wear or other damage. Inspect gears for wear on teeth and engagement dogs.

Note that forward gear (31), reverse gear (42) and pinion gear (53) should be renewed as a complete set. Inspect dog clutch for wear on engagement surfaces. Inspect shafts for wear on splines and on friction surfaces of gears and oil seals. Renew propeller shaft (40) if runout exceeds 0.02 mm (0.0008 in.). Renew drive shaft (13) if runout exceeds 0.5 mm (0.020 in.).

Renew all seals, gaskets and "O" rings during reassembly. Install seals (50) into carrier (48) with lips facing propeller. Install seals (25) into housing (26) with lips facing up. Lubricate all seal lips with a suitable water-resistant grease. Apply a suitable corrosion-resistant sealer to outer diameter of carrier (48) where carrier contacts gear cavity.

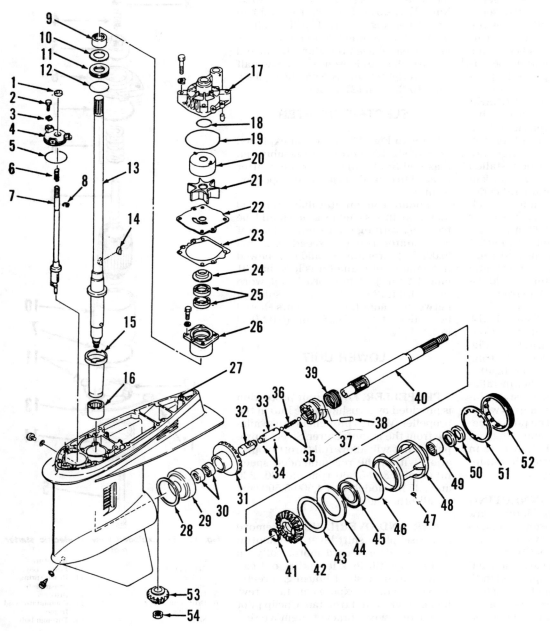

Fig. Y20-37—Exploded view of lower unit gearcase assembly.

1. Seal
2. Screw
3. Washer
4. Plate
5. "O" ring
6. Spring
7. Lower shift rod
8. Clip
9. Bearing
10. Shim
11. Thrust bearing
12. "O" ring
13. Drive shaft
14. Key
15. Sleeve
16. Bearing
17. Water pump housing
18. "O" ring
19. "O" ring
20. Liner
21. Impeller
22. Plate
23. Gasket
24. Seal cover
25. Seals
26. Bearing housing
27. Gearcase housing
28. Shim
29. Bearing & race assy
30. Bearings
31. Forward gear
32. Shifter
33. Shift slider
34. Balls
35. Balls
36. Spring
37. Dog clutch
38. Crosspin
39. Crosspin retainer
40. Propeller shaft
41. Thrust washer
42. Reverse gear
43. Shim
44. Thrust washer
45. Bearing
46. "O" ring
47. Key
48. Bearing carrier
49. Bearing
50. Seals
51. Tab washer
52. Ring nut
53. Pinion gear
54. Pinion nut

Reassemble gearcase by reversing disassembly procedure while noting the following: Shim (10) should be adjusted to obtain the best possible mesh between pinion gear (53) and forward gear (31). Tighten pinion nut (54) to 96 N·m (71 ft.-lbs.). Bearing (16) must be drawn into gearcase using Yamaha special tools YB-6029, YB-6169 and YB-6246 or equivalent. Refer to Fig. Y20-38 when reassembling propeller shaft assembly to ensure correct placement of steel balls. Dog clutch (37) may be installed on propeller shaft (40) in either direction. Tighten ring nut (52) to 190 N·m (140 ft.-lbs.). Gearcase must be in neutral to install lower shift rod (7).

Forward gear backlash measured at the drive shaft should be 0.27-0.38 mm (0.011-0.015 in.) and is adjusted by varying thickness of shim (28). Invert gearcase assembly when checking forward gear backlash to properly load drive shaft (13). Propeller shaft should be locked by installing carrier (48) puller and tightening puller screw against propeller shaft.

Reverse gear backlash measured at the drive shaft should be 0.95-1.22 mm (0.037-0.048 in.) and is adjusted by varying thickness of shim (43). Check reverse gear backlash with gearcase assembly inverted. Install propeller on propeller shaft backward and tighten

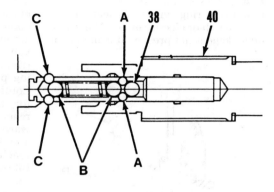

Fig. Y20-38—Sectional view of propeller shaft and shift mechanism.

38. Crosspin
40. Propeller shaft
A. Steel balls 4.8 mm (0.189 in.) diameter
B. Steel balls 8.7 mm (0.342 in.) diameter
C. Steel balls 5.6 mm (0.220 in.) diameter

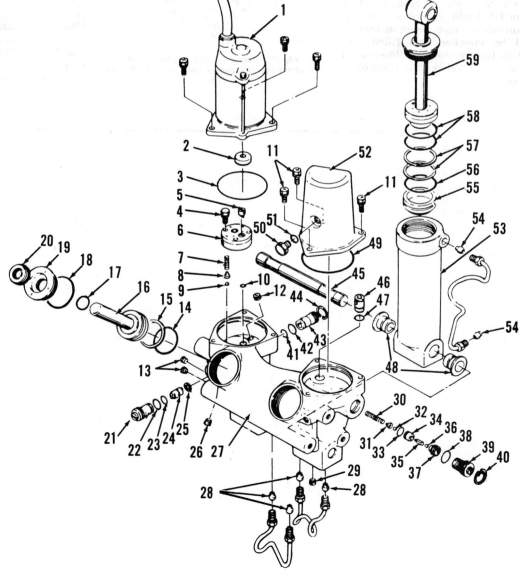

Fig. Y20-40—Exploded view of power trim/tilt assembly used on all models except Pro V 150. Power trim/tilt assembly on Pro V models is similar.

1. Motor assy.
2. Seal
3. "O" ring
4. Screw
5. Coupler shaft
6. Pump assy.
7. Spring
8. Valve support pin
9. Ball
10. "O" ring
11. Screws
12. Plug
13. Plugs
14. "O" ring
15. Backup ring
16. Piston & rod assy.
17. "O" ring
18. "O" ring
19. End cap
20. Seal
21. Main valve
22. "O" ring
23. "O" ring
24. Shuttle piston
25. Backup ring
26. Plug
27. Housing assy.
28. Seats
29. Plug
30. Spring
31. Manual release pin
32. Ball
33. "O" ring
34. Valve seat
35. Manual release rod
36. Ball
37. Seat screw
38. "O" ring
39. Manual release screw
40. Snap ring
41. "O" ring
42. "O" ring
43. Main valve
44. Snap ring
45. Shaft
46. Up release valve
47. "O" ring
48. Bushing
49. "O" ring
50. Fill plug
51. "O" ring
52. Reservoir
53. Tilt cylinder
54. Seat
55. Free piston
56. "O" ring
57. Backup rings
58. "O" rings
59. Piston & rod assy.

propeller shaft nut to lock propeller shaft.

Make sure water tube properly engages water tube seal when installing lower unit on drive shaft housing. Tighten seven gearcase-to-drive shaft housing screws to 40 N·m (29 ft.-lbs.). Refer to LUBRICATION section for gearcase lubricant capacity.

POWER TRIM AND TILT

All models are equipped with power trim and tilt system. An oil pump driven by a reversible electric motor provides oil pressure. A rocker control switch determines motor and pump rotation, thereby extending or retracting cylinders. The pump is equipped with a manual release valve (39—Fig. Y20-40). Opening (counterclockwise) manual valve (39) will allow manual movement of cylinders if power trim/tilt malfunction occurs.

The recommended oil is Yamaha Power Trim/Tilt Fluid. Fill plug (50) is located on side of pump reservoir. Oil level should be checked and filled with cylinders fully retracted. Reservoir is full when oil level is at bottom of fill plug hole.

To bleed trapped air from hydraulic system, tilt outboard motor fully up, then open manual release valve and allow outboard motor to return to the down position by its own weight. Repeat as necessary until all air is purged.

If trim/tilt system malfunction occurs, first make sure malfunction is not due to faulty wiring, wiring connections, relays, switch or electric motor. Make sure oil leakage is not present at cylinders or

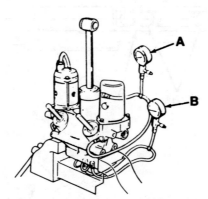

Fig. Y20-41—View showing test gage connection for checking tilt pressure (A) and trim pressure (B).

hydraulic lines, and that reservoir is full.

To test pump output pressure, disconnect hydraulic lines at bottom of reservoir and upper chamber of tilt cylinder (53). Connect test gage (Yamaha YB-6181) to the tilt cylinder and reservoir as shown at (A—Fig. Y20-41). Close manual release valve (clockwise) and tilt outboard motor up, then down, then open manual release valve to bleed any air in system. Return manual release valve to the closed position. Operate trim/tilt switch in the up direction, noting pressure gage while traveling up. Continue operating in the up direction for three seconds after full up is reached, and note test gage. During upward movement, pressure should be 0-490 kPa (0-71 psi). After full up is reached pressure should be zero. Next, tilt outboard motor down, continue for three seconds after full down, then note pressure gage. Down pressure should be 4018-5390 kPa (583-782 psi).

Repeat procedure with test gage connected as shown at (B). Pressure while tilting up should be 0-490 kPa (0-71 psi), and after reaching full up, pressure should be 9310-11,270 kPa (1350-1635 psi). Down pressure should be 588-1078 kPa (85-156 psi).

NOTES

NOTES

NOTES

NOTES

NOTES

NOTES